The Oxford History of the Ancient Near East

The Oxford History of the Ancient Near East
Editors: Karen Radner, Nadine Moeller, and D. T. Potts

This groundbreaking, five-volume series offers a comprehensive, fully illustrated history of Egypt and Western Asia (the Levant, Anatolia, Mesopotamia, and Iran), from the emergence of complex states to the conquest of Alexander the Great. Written by a highly diverse, international team of leading scholars, whose expertise brings to life the people, places, and times of the remote past, the volumes in this series focus firmly on the political and social histories of the states and communities of the ancient Near East. Individual chapters present the key textual and material sources underpinning the historical reconstruction, paying particular attention to the most recent archaeological finds and their impact on our historical understanding of the periods surveyed.

Volume 1: From the Beginnings to Old Kingdom Egypt and the Dynasty of Akkad

Volume 2: From the End of the Third Millennium BC to the Fall of Babylon

Volume 3: From the Hyksos to the Late Second Millennium BC

The Oxford History of the Ancient Near East

Volume III: From the Hyksos to the Late Second Millennium BC

Edited by

KAREN RADNER
NADINE MOELLER
D. T. POTTS

OXFORD
UNIVERSITY PRESS

OXFORD
UNIVERSITY PRESS

Oxford University Press is a department of the University of Oxford. It furthers
the University's objective of excellence in research, scholarship, and education
by publishing worldwide. Oxford is a registered trade mark of Oxford University
Press in the UK and certain other countries.

Published in the United States of America by Oxford University Press
198 Madison Avenue, New York, NY 10016, United States of America.

Library of Congress Cataloging-in-Publication Data
Names: Radner, Karen, editor, author. | Moeller, Nadine, editor, author. |
Potts, Daniel T., editor, author.
Title: The Oxford history of the ancient Near East /
edited by Karen Radner, Nadine Moeller, and Daniel T. Potts.
Description: New York : Oxford University Press, 2022. |
Includes bibliographical references and index. |
Contents: Volume 3. From the Hyksos to the late second millennium BC
Identifiers: LCCN 2020002854 | ISBN 9780190687601 (v. 3: hardback) |
ISBN 9780190687625 (v. 3: epub) | ISBN 9780197601204 (v. 3: online)
Subjects: LCSH: Egypt—Civilization. | Egypt—Antiquities. |
Egypt—History—Sources. | Middle East—Civilization. |
Middle East—Antiquities. | Middle East—History—Sources.
Classification: LCC DT60 .O97 2020 | DDC 939.4—dc23
LC record available at https://lccn.loc.gov/2020002854

DOI: 10.1093/oso/9780190687601.001.0001

1 3 5 7 9 8 6 4 2

Printed by Sheridan Books, Inc., United States of America

Contents

Preface

THIS IS THE third volume of the *Oxford History of the Ancient Near East*, which is devoted to Egypt and Nubia, Anatolia, the Levant and the Aegean, and Mesopotamia and Iran during the second half of the second millennium BC, broadly corresponding to the Late Bronze Age. The book's cover depicts a colorless, chalcedony cylinder seal of Middle Assyrian date, together with its modern impression on a strip of clay. Acquired between 1885 and 1908 by Pierpont Morgan, the seal is today housed in the collection of the Morgan Library & Museum, New York (accession number 0595) and shows a griffin-demon, down on one knee, grasping the tail of a bull. The name of the seal's owner, one Aššur-kimuya, appears beneath the demon's wings. This is the third specimen in our collection of five beautiful cylinder seals from different parts of the Near East that grace the individual covers of the *Oxford History of the Ancient Near East*, highlighting the region's cultural commonalities and differences, its endlessly fascinating iconography, and the high level of craftsmanship found across the region.

In contrast to the essentially regional narratives that characterize the first and second volumes of the *Oxford History of the Ancient Near East*, the histories of the vast geographical horizon stretching from the Nile to Iran in the period dealt with here were closely connected and often intimately entangled. With the Late Bronze Age, we largely leave behind the problems that impeded correlation and synchronization of local chronologies in the preceding periods, as the absolute chronology of Western Asia at this era is on much more solid, if not yet absolutely certain, ground. If regnal dates are known, the uncertainty margins are generally relatively narrow, no more than a decade; the individual chapters discuss the available source materials and the resultant possibilities and challenges for establishing relative and absolute chronologies.

The following Time Chart on pp. xiii-xv presents a concise overview of the chronological coverage of this volume; for more details, we refer the reader to the tables provided in Chapters 23 and 24 (for the Egyptian rulers of the Second Intermediate Period), in Chapter 29 (for the rulers of Mittani and the synchronisms with contemporary monarchs), and in Chapter 32 (for the Assyrian royal house and its contemporaries), which underpin and deepen the information given in our chart. Although many Elamite rulers of the Late Bronze Age are known by name, we only include Kidin-Hutran (late thirteenth century BC) and his successors in our chart, as both the sequencing and dating of the earlier kings—including Untaš-Napiriša, the famous founder of Chogha Zanbil—are still very tentative, with little agreement among specialists; the reader is referred to the in-depth discussions in Chapter 34. Absolute dates are given for the New Kingdom rulers of Egypt and for the Assyrian kings, but not for the monarchs of Hatti, Mittani, Babylonia, and Elam, as these regional chronologies are dependent on those of Egypt and especially Assyria. The earlier parts of our chart should be consulted together with the time chart given in the second volume of the *Oxford History of the Ancient Near East*, as there is some chronological overlap. The dates given for the last rulers of the First Dynasty of Babylon are those of the Middle Chronology (see chapter 11 in volume 2 for details).

The second volume of the *Oxford History of the Ancient Near East* closed with the decline of the Middle Kingdom in Egypt and the collapse of the kingdom of Babylon in Mesopotamia, and the present volume picks up the regional strands of history in Lower and Upper Egypt, where new regional states arose at Avaris and Thebes, and in Anatolia and northern and southern Mesopotamia, where relatively recently arrived warrior elites established the Hittite state and the kingdoms of Mittani and Karaduniaš (Kassite Babylonia). Eventually reunited under Theban leadership, Egypt under the Eighteenth Dynasty and later the Ramessides was the superpower of the age, whose influence deeply shaped the culture and society of its neighbors, especially Nubia and the Levant, which were integrated to different degrees into the Egyptian state administration. Egypt's only serious political rival was the Hittite Empire, with its center deep in the mountains of central Anatolia. It was in the coastal cities of the northern Levant, with their hugely important ports of trade, that the political and commercial interests of the two powers first collided, leading to close engagement both on the battlefield and at the negotiating table. Eventually, Hittite ambitions in the Levant stalled not because of Egypt, but because of the growing power of the northern Mesopotamian kingdom of Assyria, first at the expense of its former overlord Mittani and increasingly also of the Hittite state. Compared to the nuanced and detailed reconstructions that are possible for these polities, political developments in Nubia, Iran, and the Aegean, where the available sources are more limited in scope, are far less clear. There is no doubt, however, that states in these regions were integral participants in the long-distance commerce, power politics, and exchange of ideas and cultural practices that defined the ancient Near East in the Late Bronze Age.

Like the two previous volumes of the *Oxford History of the Ancient Near East*, this book brings together the expertise, perspectives, and talent of an exciting mix of distinguished scholars from across the globe, each an established expert in their subject area. We are honored that they have agreed to contribute the twelve chapters that constitute the present volume, covering the time "from the Hyksos to the late second millennium BC." Their work showcases a wide range of approaches to history-writing that the very different bodies of available sources enable and necessitate, from the analysis of monumental, domestic, and funerary architecture and the study of diverse expressions of material culture (e.g., pottery, seals, and coffins) to the consideration of the region's geographical and climatic characteristics and the interpretation of a great many different text genres recorded on stone, clay, and papyrus. Draft manuscripts for the chapters were received between November 2018 and September 2020.

Our editorial work on the *Oxford History of the Ancient Near East* was supported by the Center for Advanced Studies of LMU Munich (CAS[LMU]), which awarded fellowships to Nadine Moeller and Dan

Potts in July 2016, 2017, and 2018. In these three weeks spent together in Munich, the groundwork that underpins this volume was laid, while much of the joint editorial work on the chapters of the third volume was accomplished during our 2019 meetings in Chicago, Penjwin (Kurdish Autonomous Region of Iraq), and Pouillon (Chalosse region, France). When the global COVID-19 (Sars-CoV-2) pandemic made it impossible for us to meet in 2020 due to travel restrictions, we were able to continue our close collaboration across continents and time zones. While we certainly missed our time together, our joint GoogleDrive folders ensured that work on the volume progressed relatively smoothly, and our long-established WhatsApp group "OHANE Editors" turned into our most important mode of communication.

In transcribing Egyptian proper nouns, we follow the conventions of *The Oxford History of Ancient Egypt*, edited by Ian Shaw (OUP 2004, rev. ed.). We do not use hyphenation to separate the components of Hittite personal names, or the Indo-European names of the Mittani rulers (e.g., Tudhaliya, Parattarna), but we follow normal practice in marking the individual words within Akkadian proper nouns (e.g., Aššur-uballiṭ, Kar-Tukulti-Ninurta), and also within Elamite, Hurrian, and Kassite names (e.g., Šutruk-Nahhunte, Urhi-Teššub, Burna-Buriaš). In accordance with Hittite phonology, the sibilants in Hittite names are realized as /s/ rather than /š/ (e.g., Hattusa instead of Hattuša; Mursili instead of Muršili). Whenever a person or place is widely known by a conventional spelling, we use that (e.g., Tiglath-pileser instead of Tukulti-apil-Ešarra, Cutha instead of Kutiu). We do not use any long vowels in proper nouns, including modern Arabic and Farsi place names.

We are very grateful that the Alexander von Humboldt Foundation, via the International Award for Research in Germany 2015 to Karen Radner, allowed us to engage the help of several individuals whose expertise and attention to detail smoothed the editorial process very considerably. At LMU Munich, we thank Denise Bolton for language-editing several chapters; Thomas Seidler for consolidating and checking the chapter bibliographies, and Dr Andrea Squitieri for creating the individual chapter maps. We are also grateful to Philipp Seyr (Liège) for his diligent efforts in harmonizing the Egyptian names and spellings across the volume. The index was prepared by Luiza Osorio Guimarães da Silva (Chicago), who was also instrumental in harmonizing proper nouns across chapters and volumes. As ever, we are indebted to our friend and editor at Oxford University Press, Stefan Vranka, who initiated the *Oxford History of the Ancient Near East* and greatly aided our work at every step, on this volume and on all others. To all of these individuals and also and especially to our authors, we owe a debt of gratitude in making the timely publication of this book possible, despite the challenging times many of us experienced in 2020 and 2021.

Time Chart

	Egypt	Anatolia	Mesopotamia		Iran
			Syria	Iraq	Babylonia
1750 BC	**Second Intermediate Period** (1750–1550)				
	Fourteenth Dynasty (selected) *Eastern Nile Delta* Yaʿammu Yakbim Qareh ʿAmmu Sheshi Yaʿqub-Her			**First Dynasty of Babylon** … Samsu-iluna (1749–1712) Abi-ešuh (1711–1684) Ammi-ditana (1683–1647) Ammi-ṣaduqa (1646–1626) Samsu-ditana (1625–1595)	
	Last kings of Thirteenth Dynasty				
1650 BC	**Fifteenth Dynasty** *"Hyksos"* Salitis (Skhr) Bnon Khyan Yanassi	*Hatti* … Hattusili I Mursili I			
	Sixteenth Dynasty (selected) *Thebes* Djehuty Mentuhotepi (Sankhenra) Nebiryraw I (Sewadjenra) Bebiankh (Seuserenra)				
1580 BC		…		**Kassite Dynasty** … … …	
	Seventeenth Dynasty *Thebes* Rahotep (Sekhemra Wahkhau) Sobekemsaf I (Sekhemra Wadjkhau) Sobekemsaf II (Sekhemra Shedtawy) Intef V (Sekhemra Wepmaat) Intef VI (Nubkheperra) Intef VII (Sekhemra Heruhermaat) Ahmose I (Senakhtenra) Taa (Seqenenra) Kamose (Wadjkheperra)				
	Apepi Khamudi				

BC	New Kingdom (1550–1069)	Ḫatti	Mittani	Assyria	Babylonia	Elam
1550 BC	**Eighteenth Dynasty (1550–1292)**	Telipinu			...	...
	Ahmose II (1550–1525)				Agum II	
	Amenhotep I (1525–1504)		...		Burna-Buriaš I	
	Thutmose I (1504–1492)		Šuttarna I	...		
	Thutmose II (1492–1479)		...	Puzur-Aššur III		...
	♀ Hatshepsut (1479–1458) | Thutmose III (1479–1425)			...		
				Aššur-nadin-aḫḫe I (?–1431)		
				Enlil-naṣir II (1430–1425)		
		Tudhaliya I	Sauštatar	Aššur-nerari II (1424–1418)	Kara-indaš	
	Amenhotep II (1425–1397)			Aššur-bel-nišešu (1417–1409)	Kadašman-Harbe I	
				Aššur-rem-nišešu (1408–1401)	Kurigalzu I	
	Thutmose IV (1397–1388)	...	...	Aššur-nadin-aḫḫe II (1400–1391)	Kadašman-Enlil I	
	Amenhotep III (1388–1350)	Suppiluliuma I	Artatama	Eriba-Adad I (1390–1364)	Burna-Buriaš II	
	Amenhotep IV = Akhenaten (1350–1334)		Šuttarna II	Aššur-uballiṭ I (1363–1328)		
			Tušratta		Kara-ḫardaš	
	Smenkhkara/Neferneferuaten (?)				Nazi-Bugaš	...
	Tutankhaten = Tutankhamun (1333–1321)	Arnuwanda II	Šattiwaza	Enlil-nerari (1327–1318)	Kurigalzu II	
	Ay (1323–1319)	Mursili II				
	Horemheb (1319–1292)	Muwatalli II	Šattuara I	Arik-den-ili (1317–1306)		...
1295 BC	**Nineteenth Dynasty (1292–1185)**		Wasašatta	Adad-nerari I (1305–1274)	Nazi-Maruttaš	
	Rameses I (1292–1290)	Mursili III = Urḫi-Teššub			Kadašman-Turgu	
	Sety I (1290–1279)					
			Šattuara II	Shalmaneser I (1273–1244)	Kadašman-Enlil II	...
	Rameses II (1279–1213)	Hattusili III			Kudur-Enlil	
				Tukulti-Ninurta I (1243–1207)	Šagarakti-Šuriaš	
		Tudhaliya IV			Kaštiliaš IV	
					Enlil-nadin-šumi	Kidin-Hutran

Merenptah (1213–1203)		Aššur-nadin-apli (1206–1203)	Kadašman-Harbe II	Šutruk-Nahhunte I
Amenmessu (1203–1199)		Aššur-nerari III (1202–1197)	Adad-šuma-iddina	
Sety II (1199–1193)		Enlil-kudurri-uṣur (1196–1192)	Adad-šuma-uṣur	
Saptah/Q Tausret (1193–1185)		Ninurta-apil-Ekur (1191–1179)		
20th Dynasty (1185–1069)				
Sethnakht (1185–1181)	Suppiluliuma II	Aššur-dan I (1178–1133)	Meli-Šipak	Kutir-Nahhunte
Rameses III (1181–1150)			Marduk-apla-iddina I	
			Zababa-šuma-iddina	
Rameses IV		Ninurta-tukulti-Aššur (1133)	Enlil-nadin-ahi	Šilhak-Inšušinak
Rameses V		Mutakkil-Nusku (1132)		
Rameses VI		Aššur-reša-iši (1132–1115)	**Second Dynasty of Isin**	
Rameses VII		Tiglath-pileser I (1114–1076)	…	Hutelutuš-Inšušinak
Rameses VIII		Ašared-apil-Ekur (1075–1074)	Nebuchadnezzar I	
Rameses IX		Aššur-bel-kala (1073–1056)	…	
Rameses X		Eriba-Adad II (1055–1054)		
Rameses XI (1099–1069)		…		

The Contributors

Kathlyn M. (Kara) Cooney (PhD, Johns Hopkins University) is a professor of Egyptian Art and Architecture and Chair of the Department of Near Eastern Languages and Cultures at UCLA. Cooney's research in coffin reuse, primarily focusing on the Twenty-first Dynasty, is ongoing. Her research investigates the socioeconomic and political turmoil that have plagued the period, ultimately affecting funerary and burial practices in ancient Egypt. This project has taken her around the world over the span of ten years to study and document more than 300 coffins in collections around the world, including Cairo, London, Paris, Berlin, and Vatican City.

Geoff Emberling (PhD, University of Michigan) is associate research scientist at the Kelsey Museum of Archaeology, University of Michigan. He has directed archaeological projects at Tell Brak, Syria, and more recently in Sudan, first a salvage project in the Fourth Cataract, then the later Kushite royal cemetery at el-Kurru. His current project is at Gebel Barkal, the temple center and capital city of Kush in the first millennium BC. His recent work includes *Graffiti as Devotion along the Nile and Beyond* (Kelsey Museum, 2019), co-edited with Suzanne Davis, a volume published in conjunction with an exhibit at the Kelsey Museum.

Irene Forstner-Müller is the head of the Cairo Branch of the Austrian Archaeological Institute. A leading specialist in Middle Kingdom and Second Intermediate Period Egypt, her research has a special focus on the archaeology of Egyptian settlements. She has directed the excavations at Tell el-Dabʻa, the capital of the Hyksos, in the eastern Nile delta, for many years and more recently also the Joint Egyptian-Austrian mission to Kom Ombo.

Pierre Grandet (PhD and Habilitation, Université Paris-Sorbonne) teaches Egyptian language, history, and civilization at the Kheops Institute in Paris. His current research focuses on the publication of the Hieratic ostraca from Deir el-Medina kept in the collections of the Institut Français d'Égypte (Cairo) and of the Louvre (Paris).

Elizabeth Minor (PhD, University of California, Berkeley) is a visiting assistant professor of Anthropology at Wellesley College. She co-directs the Es-Selim R4 Archaeology Project in Sudan, a Kerma Period settlement site within the Northern Dongola Reach, and directs the Wellesley College Hall Archaeology Project in Massachusetts, at the site of a historical dormitory fire. Both projects are community-based participatory excavations. Her publications focus on Nubian archaeology and deal with issues such as funerary culture, sacrifice, and commemoration.

Nadine Moeller (PhD, University of Cambridge) is professor of Egyptian Archaeology at Yale University. Her research focuses on ancient Egyptian urbanism, on which she has recently published a book: *The Archaeology of Urbanism in Ancient Egypt* (Cambridge University Press, 2016). She has participated in numerous fieldwork projects in Egypt and since 2001, she has been directing excavations at Tell Edfu in southern Egypt.

Behzad Mofidi-Nasrabadi (PhD, Eberhard Karls Universität Tübingen 1997, Habilitation, Johannes Gutenberg-Universität Mainz 2013) is Außerplanmäßiger Professor for Near Eastern archaeology at Mainz University. He has directed archaeological excavations at Chogha Zanbil and Haft Tappeh in Iran since 1999. His publications include several monographs and articles on Mesopotamian funerary rituals as well as the history and archaeology of Elam, with his most recent books focusing on the urban structure and socioeconomic characteristics of Chogha Zanbil.

Dimitri Nakassis (PhD, the University of Texas at Austin) is professor of Classics at the University of Colorado Boulder. His research interests focus on landscape archaeology, economic history, and the administration of Late Bronze Age states in the Aegean. He is co-director of the

Western Argolid Regional Project, an archaeological survey in Greece, and the Pylos Tablets Digital Project, a comprehensive program to document the administrative documents from the Mycenaean palace at Pylos.

Nicky Nielsen (PhD, University of Liverpool) is a senior lecturer in Egyptology at the University of Manchester. He has excavated and published on the site of Tell Nabasha in the eastern Nile delta. His publications deal with New Kingdom material culture and settlement archaeology as well as inscribed material of the Middle Kingdom and Late Period.

Susanne Paulus (PhD, University of Münster) is an associate professor of Assyriology at the Oriental Institute of the University of Chicago. Her research focuses on the socioeconomic and legal history of Babylonia, especially during the Kassite period. Her monograph *Die babylonischen Kudurru-Inschriften von der kassitischen bis zur frühneubabylonischen Zeit* (Ugarit-Verlag, 2014) is a comprehensive edition and discussion of all inscriptions on a characteristic type of Babylonian monument known as *kudurru*.

Daniel Polz studied Egyptology, prehistory, and linguistics at the University of Heidelberg. After positions as a research associate at the Cairo branch of the German Archaeological Institute (1991–1994) and as assistant and then associate professor at the Department of Near Eastern Languages and Cultures at the University of California, Los Angeles (1993–1998), he returned to Cairo in 1999 as the local German Archaeological Institute's Associate Director. Since 1991, he has directed the excavations at Dra Abu el-Naga (Western Thebes/Luxor). His books include *Der Beginn des Neuen Reiches: zur Vorgeschichte einer Zeitenwende* (De Gruyter, 2007).

D. T. Potts (PhD, Harvard University) is professor of Ancient Near Eastern Archaeology and History at the Institute for the Study of the Ancient World, New York University. A corresponding member of the German Archaeological Institute, he has worked in Iran, the United Arab Emirates, Saudi Arabia, Turkey, Armenia, and the Kurdish Autonomous Region of Iraq. His numerous books include *The Archaeology of Elam: Formation and Transformation of an Ancient Iranian State* (Cambridge University Press, 2nd ed., 2015) and *Nomadism in Iran: From Antiquity to the Modern Era* (Oxford University Press, 2014).

Karen Radner (PhD, University of Vienna) holds the Alexander von Humboldt Chair of the Ancient History of the Near and Middle East at LMU Munich. A member of the German Archaeological Institute and the Bavarian Academy of Sciences and Humanities, her numerous books include *A Short History of Babylon* (Bloomsbury, 2020) and *Ancient Assyria: A Very Short Introduction* (Oxford University Press, 2015), as well as editions of cuneiform archives from Iraq, Syria, and Turkey.

Hervé Reculeau (PhD, École Pratique des Hautes Études, Paris) is associate professor of Assyriology at the Oriental Institute, the Department of Near Eastern Languages and Civilizations, and the College of the University of Chicago. His research focuses on the interactions between technology, environment, and socioeconomic structures in ancient Mesopotamia. His books include *Climate, Environment and Agriculture in Assyria in the 2nd half of the 2nd millennium BCE* (Harrassowitz, 2011); *Mittelassyrische Urkunden aus dem Archiv Assur 14446* (with Barbara Feller; Harrassowitz, 2012); and *L'agriculture irriguée à Mari: essai d'histoire des techniques* (Société pour l'Étude du Proche-Orient Ancien, 2018).

Eva von Dassow teaches the history, languages, and literature of the ancient Near East at the University of Minnesota. Her publications include *State and Society in the Late Bronze Age: Alalah under the Mittani Empire* (2008). Her recent scholarship includes studies on the Hurro-Hittite "Song of Liberation"; writing as an interface between language and reader; and citizenship in Late Bronze Age polities. Currently she is working on a new history of the ancient Near East, and a book on freedom and governance in ancient Near Eastern societies.

Mark Weeden (PhD, SOAS University of London) concentrates his research on the ancient written cultures of northern Syria and Anatolia, particularly cuneiform and Anatolian Hieroglyphic. He is Associate Professor in Ancient Middle Eastern Languages at the Department of Greek and Latin at University College London. The editor-in-chief of the Ancient Near East section of Brill's Handbook of Oriental Studies series and co-editor of the journal *Iraq*, his books include *Hittite Logograms* *and Hittite Scholarship* (Harrassowitz, 2011) and, edited together with Lee Ullmann, *Hittite Landscape and Geography* (Brill, 2017). He is an epigrapher for various archaeological projects, including the Japanese Institute of Anatolian Archaeology excavations at Kaman-Kalehöyük, Büklükale, and Yassıhöyük and the University of Toronto excavations at Tell Tayınat.

Abbreviations

AfO	Archiv für Orientforschung
AJA	American Journal of Archaeology
ÄL	Ägypten & Levante
AMIT	Archäologische Mitteilungen aus Iran und Turan
AnSt	Anatolian Studies
AoF	Altorientalische Forschungen
APA	Acta Praehistorica et Archaeologica
ArchAnz	Archäologischer Anzeiger
ASAE	Annales du Service des Antiquités de l'Égypt
BaM	Baghdader Mitteilungen
BASOR	Bulletin of the American Schools of Oriental Research
BIFAO	Bulletin de l'Institut Français d'Archéologie Orientale
BiOr	Bibliotheca Orientalis
BMSAES	British Museum Studies in Ancient Egypt and Sudan
CAD	The Assyrian Dictionary of the Oriental Institute of the University of Chicago
CdE	Chronique d'Égypte
CDLB	Cuneiform Digital Library Bulletin
CRIPEL	Cahiers de Recherches de l'Institut de Papyrologie et d'Égyptologie de Lille
DAFI	Cahiers de la délégation archéologique française en Iran
EA	Egyptian Archaeology
GM	Göttinger Miszellen
IEJ	Israel Exploration Journal
IrAnt	Iranica Antiqua
IstMit	Istanbuler Mitteilungen

JAEI	*Journal of Ancient Egyptian Interconnections*
JANEH	*Journal of Ancient Near Eastern History*
JANER	*Journal of Ancient Near Eastern Religions*
JAOS	*Journal of the American Oriental Society*
JARCE	*Journal of the American Research Center in Egypt*
JCS	*Journal of Cuneiform Studies*
JCSMS	*Journal of the Canadian Society for Mesopotamian Studies*
JEA	*Journal of Egyptian Archaeology*
JEH	*Journal of Egyptian History*
JMA	*Journal of Mediterranean Archaeology*
JNES	*Journal of Near Eastern Studies*
MDAIK	*Mitteilungen des Deutschen Archäologischen Instituts Abteilung Kairo*
MDOG	*Mitteilungen der Deutschen Orient-Gesellschaft*
MIO	*Mitteilungen des Instituts für Orientforschung*
NABU	*Nouvelles Assyriologiques Brèves et Utilitaires*
NEA	*Near Eastern Archaeology*
OJA	*Oxford Journal of Archaeology*
OLZ	*Orientalistische Literaturzeitung*
RA	*Revue d'Assyriologie et d'archéologie orientale*
RdE	*Revue d'Égyptologie*
RlA	*Reallexikon der Assyriologie und Vorderasiatischen Archäologie*
SAAB	*State Archives of Assyria Bulletin*
SAK	*Studien zur altägyptischen Kultur*
SMEA	*Studi Micenei ed Egeo-Anatolici*
UF	*Ugarit-Forschungen*
WdO	*Die Welt des Orients*
ZA	*Zeitschrift für Assyriologie und Vorderasiatische Archäologie*
ZÄS	*Zeitschrift für ägyptische Sprache und Altertumskunde*
ZOrA	*Zeitschrift für Orient-Archäologie*

23

The Hyksos State

Irene Forstner-Müller

23.1. Introduction

In its most narrow sense, the term "Hyksos" refers to a group of six rulers who ruled the northern part of Egypt as the Fifteenth Dynasty during the Second Intermediate Period.[1] Writing much later in the third century BC during the Ptolemaic period, the priest Manetho (as even later quoted by Flavius Josephus) explains the term as "*Hykussos*: shepherd kings. *Hyk* means in their priests' language 'king,' *usos* 'shepherd' in the people's language, put together it means *Hykussos*."[2] In fact, this expression is derived from the Egyptian term *heka khasut*, "ruler of the foreign lands," which is also attested in original sources from the time of the Fifteenth Dynasty (see section 23.3). Manetho records furthermore:

> . . . unexpectedly, from the regions of the East, invaders of obscure race marched in confidence of victory against our land. By main force they easily seized it without striking a blow and having overpowered the rulers of the land, they then burned our

---

1. The author is indebted to Pamela Rose for correcting the language and to Astrid Hassler for preparing the illustrations.

2. Flavius Josephus, *Contra Apionem* 1: 82.

Irene Forstner-Müller, *The Hyksos State* In: *The Oxford History of the Ancient Near East*. Edited by: Karen Radner, Nadine Moeller, and D. T. Potts, Oxford University Press. © Oxford University Press 2022. DOI: 10.1093/oso/9780190687601.003.0023

cities ruthlessly, razed to the ground the temples of the gods, and treated all the natives with a cruel hostility, massacring some and leading into slavery the wives and children of others.[3]

Until relatively recently, researchers have followed uncritically Manetho's statement that the Hyksos were invaders from the Near East. While a more unorthodox view saw a link to the Hurrians of northern Mesopotamia,[4] more commonly their origin was connected with the Israelites.[5] A widely held view sees the ancestors of the "Hyksos" as coming to Egypt from the eastern Mediterranean coast/Syro-Palestine as the result of several waves of immigration.[6] However, none of these assumptions represents an accurate or complete assessment of the reasons for the emergence of the Hyksos state.

The present chapter first surveys the situation at Middle Kingdom–period Tell el-Dab'a and provides the background for the presence of the "Hyksos" in the eastern Nile delta (figure 23.1). We then turn to the reconstructed sequence of the Fifteenth Dynasty, the Hyksos rulers, before focusing on the territory of the Hyksos state. It then summarizes the relevant results of the excavations at this site, ancient Avaris, the capital of the Hyksos state, followed by a discussion of its administration and its contacts outside Egypt. The chapter closes with an assessment of the end of the Hyksos state and its aftermath.

23.2. "Hyksos prehistory" in Middle Kingdom Tell el-Dab'a

The settlement of population groups originating from regions in the Near East in the eastern Nile delta of Egypt is a well-known phenomenon

---

3. Flavius Josephus, *Contra Apionem* 1: 73. Translation after Waddell 1964: 79.

4. Helck 1971: 102–103.

5. For a recent overview, see Schneider 2018a.

6. So still argued recently in Wilkinson 2010: 184. For the difficulties of understanding the Hyksos as a population group or even "race," see Candelora 2018.

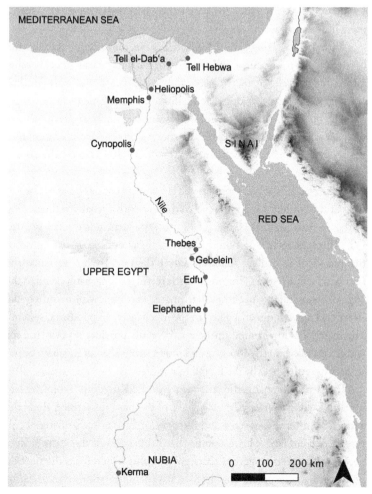

FIGURE 23.1. Map of sites mentioned in this chapter. Prepared by Andrea Squitieri (LMU Munich).

in antiquity. As early as the fourth millennium BC, there is evidence for intensive cultural contact attested by elements of material culture (cf. chapter 2 in volume 1). Therefore, the appearance of "Hyksos culture" is not a unique event occurring suddenly in the Second Intermediate Period, but is the result of a long tradition of cultural contacts between Egypt and its eastern neighbors. Manetho's narrative of a conquest of

Egypt by an enemy from the east—the Hyksos—is therefore likely a mere literary topos.

With the beginning of the Middle Kingdom, the eastern Nile delta, the border region to the Sinai and the eastern Mediterranean coast, became a focus of interest for the rulers of the late Eleventh and early Twelfth Dynasties. The Egyptian kings habitually founded settlements at the fringes of their country in order to urbanize areas that had not been previously settled. A well-known example of this practice was in the Fayum, and another was the establishment of a settlement at modern Tell el-Dabʿa in the eastern Nile delta.

The first traces of habitation at Tell el-Dabʿa go back as far as the beginning of the Middle Kingdom (end of the Eleventh Dynasty or beginning of the Twelfth Dynasty) when a planned settlement was created in Area F/I.[7] This settlement was soon abandoned, and after a hiatus, two consecutive phases of settlement followed during the mid-Twelfth Dynasty, the later of which, attested in the north of the town, most probably dated to the reign of Senusret III.[8] All of these settlements were built with an orthogonal street grid in what one may liken to the much later "Hippodamic system." The material culture found in these settlements provides no evidence for any discernible eastern influence, and thus it seems that an Egyptian population was settled here by the Egyptian state.

The situation changed in the later Middle Kingdom. From the late Twelfth Dynasty onward, traits typical of populations settling along the eastern Mediterranean coast and further east appear in the material culture of Tell el-Dabʿa.[9] If we assume that the carriers of this culture were people with an Asiatic ethnic background, this would form the starting point for a development that later led to the foundation of the Hyksos state in the Fifteenth Dynasty with its capital Avaris.[10] For the time being, the question of whether these new arrivals migrated to the eastern

---

7. Czerny 1999.

8. Czerny 2015; Forstner-Müller et al. 2005.

9. Bietak 1991; 2010b: 149.

10. For the mixing of Egyptian and "Hyksos" material culture, see the case study by Bader 2013: 276–279.

Nile delta of their own accord or were settled there by the Egyptian state must remain open.

These groups and/or individuals did not arrive as separate waves of immigration, but their presence at Tell el-Dab'a resulted from a continuous process of interaction and exchange between the delta and the neighboring regions to the east.[11] Due to the highly centralized organization of the Egyptian state in the Middle Kingdom, the first immigrants may have been specialists brought there by state authority in order to take on roles in seafaring, the military, and the expeditionary forces.[12] We may assume that Egypt's wealth and security—as proverbial (albeit at a much later time) in the Bible (e.g., the "flesh pots of Egypt" in Exodus 16:3)— provided incentives to boost immigration.

The population of Avaris was certainly not a closed community in the anthropological sense that could be compared with other populations in the Levant. Terms borrowed from the Bible, such as "Canaanites,"[13] are therefore not appropriate for describing the people of Avaris (and the eastern delta), as this would imply far too close a relationship with eastern Mediterranean population groups.

In Avaris, fully acculturated, partly acculturated, and authentically Egyptian populations lived side by side, and archaeologically, no ethnically defined town quarters can be discerned.[14] The town quarters and cemeteries of Avaris were probably not grouped according to ethnicity but according to the functional relationships between the inhabitants of the houses and those buried in the associated graves.[15]

At the end of the Middle Kingdom, during the Thirteenth Dynasty, the weakness of central state power resulted in the emergence of a

---

11. Bietak 2010b: 149.

12. Bietak 2010b: 141–142.

13. This biblical term is also problematic with regard to its relationship to the Hebrews, whom the Bible portrays as coming out of Egypt and conquering Canaan; cf. Assmann 1998.

14. Against Bietak 2016; 2018.

15. For the analysis and interpretation of town quarter R/III in Avaris, see Forstner-Müller, Jeuthe, Michel, and Prell 2015: 21; against Bietak 2016: 269–272.

"Hyksos culture"—or at least a "Hyksos consciousness"—from this mixed population and eventually in the secession of the northern part of Egypt from the rest of the country, under the rule of the Fifteenth Dynasty.

With the exception of King Apepi, the rulers of the Fifteenth Dynasty did not have Egyptian but northwest Semitic names.[16] This of course need not to be seen as an argument in favor of the hypothesis that the Hyksos were invaders from the east. However, the preference for northwest Semitic names certainly indicates that the mixed population group living in Egypt since the Middle Kingdom had managed to retain elements of their original background over time. In any case, the rise to prominence of a population element distinct from the Egyptian majority raises questions about the modalities of settlement and acculturation in Middle Kingdom Egypt[17] and how this group (and others) interacted with the Egyptian state.

Without doubt, the extent of the fusion between Egyptian and foreign elements in the Hyksos culture is without precedent in Egypt's earlier history.[18] The fact that this process of acculturation and assimilation started already in the late Middle Kingdom[19] highlights the fact that historical traditions and the archaeological record are often not congruent.[20] The emergence of the Hyksos state in the eastern Nile delta manifests itself primarily in a material culture[21] that is distinct from that of the rest of contemporary Egypt.[22] Its "foreignness" manifests itself most

16. For these names, see the detailed discussion by Schneider 1998: 34, 39–49.

17. Recently discussed in detail by Bietak 2010b: 159–156.

18. See also Bietak in Hein 1994: 39.

19. For evidence of the phenomenon of a distinctive visualization of a "Hyksos culture" within the material culture in the Egyptian eastern delta on the basis of ceramics, see Bietak et al. 2001; Aston 2004: 53; Kopetzky 2010: 272–273.

20. For this topic and its complicating factors, see Schneider 2003: 339.

21. Bietak et al. 2001.

22. Forstner-Müller and Müller 2006: 99.

clearly in funerary culture, some of whose characteristics are alien to traditional Egyptian practices.[23]

23.3. Sequence and chronology of the Hyksos rulers

The reconstruction of the Fifteenth Dynasty period is difficult due to the paucity and fragmentary state of the available sources. The political landscape therefore remains largely obscure, and even the chronology and sequence of the kings of the Fifteenth Dynasty are debated. Among the few sources on this subject, the most important are the Turin King List and the sequence provided by the Ptolemaic priest Manetho, transmitted by authors such as Josephus.[24] Only two fragmentary lines in the Turin King List can be safely assigned to the Fifteenth Dynasty,[25] and only one royal name, Khamudi, survives, mentioned as the last king of the Fifteenth Dynasty: this is the only attestation of this ruler. If we assume that the comparatively well-attested King Apepi was the only Hyksos king who ruled for a long period of time (at least thirty-three years), we may identify him with the king listed on a third fragment of the Turin King List as Khamudi's immediate predecessor.[26] In addition to the problematic source situation, another difficulty is the identification of the Hyksos names known from the Greek versions given by Manetho with the names rendered in hieroglyphics on the contemporary sources such as the sealings.

Over the course of the Fifteenth Dynasty, the titulary used by the Hyksos rulers underwent changes. The first kings of the dynasty used the epithet "Hyksos," as a royal inscription from a monumental limestone lintel found in Tell el-Dabʿa shows. The inscription mentions the otherwise unknown ruler *Skrhr* (generally interpreted as corresponding

---

23. Summarized in Forstner-Müller 2010a, with further literature.

24. Schneider 2018b: 278.

25. Ryholt 1997: 118.

26. Ryholt 1997: 118.

to Sikru-Haddu) who bears the traditional Nebty and Golden Horus names of the Egyptian royal titulary together with the title "Hyksos," which replaces the "Son of Ra" title in the traditional sequence, followed by his name written in the cartouche.[27]

During the reign of Khyan, a change took place that happened in three steps.[28] In the first phase, "Hyksos Khyan" is used as the only designation, i.e., "Khyan, Ruler of the Foreign Lands" (cf. section 23.1); in the second phase, the titles "Son of Ra" and "Hyksos Khyan" appear together; and in the third and final phase, the Hyksos title is omitted and only "Son of Ra, Khyan" and "Good God, Seuserenra" remain in use. This remarkable development may not only provide information about the position of Khyan in the overall chronological sequence, but also sheds light on the evolving self-conception and representation of the Fifteenth Dynasty rulers.

The titles of any Egyptian king were an important means of contact and communication between the ruler, his subjects, and the gods. They can be interpreted as part of a ruler's official state program.[29] Thus it appears that during the earlier period of the Fifteenth Dynasty, the title Hyksos was part of the royal program and the kings wanted to represent themselves consciously and publicly as "Rulers of the Foreign Lands." During the reign of Khyan, however, the royal titles evolved into a purely Egyptian titulary following the existing tradition, and the Hyksos titles were used side by side in this period of transition.

The best sources available to us for reconstructing the Second Intermediate Period and for establishing the relative chronologies of Egypt and the eastern Mediterranean are seal impressions bearing royal names. King Khyan is currently the only Fifteenth Dynasty ruler to be attested on seal impressions from Avaris. These sealings were found in two parts of the town: in the domestic town quarter of Area R/

---

27. Bietak 1994: 150–152.

28. Following Ryholt 2018: 268–269.

29. Gundlach 1998: 17–20.

0   2cm

FIGURE 23.2. Seal impression of the Hyksos ruler Khyan from Avaris. Photo by Axel Krause, © ÖAI/ÖAW, with kind permission.

III and in the palace of Area F/II (figure 23.2).[30] The earliest evidence for a sealing bearing this king's name comes from Area R/III in a context dating to the beginning of the Fifteenth Dynasty.[31] Unlike earlier assumptions, Khyan's reign can therefore not be placed in the later Fifteenth Dynasty but must be slotted into the early Fifteenth Dynasty, as also confirmed by the recently found sealings bearing his name from Edfu.[32] This adjustment in the relative chronology has important

30. Sartori 2009: 285–287, figs. 6–11.

31. Forstner-Müller and Rose 2013: 64; 69–71, figs. 4–9; Forstner-Müller and Reali 2018.

32. Moeller and Forstner-Müller 2018a: 13.

implications not only for Egypt, but also for the chronology of the wider Mediterranean world.[33]

The change in the royal titles under Khyan provides hints that can aid in the reconstruction of the chronological sequence of the Fifteenth Dynasty. As we have already discussed, King Khamudi has to be placed at the very end of the sequence of rulers, according to Manetho and the Turin King List; moreover, there are arguments to see King Apepi as Khamudi's predecessor, while King Khyan certainly is a ruler of the earlier Fifteenth Dynasty.[34] Khyan's successor may have been Yanassi, assuming that this person is the same as the one known from a stele found in Tell el-Dab'a[35] on which Yanassi is mentioned as the king's (that is, Khyan's) eldest son. Sikru-Haddu, who bears only the title "Hyksos" and not "Son of Ra" in the lintel inscription, and Bnon, who is only known from Manetho's sequence, are likely predecessors of Khyan. Table 23.1 presents, with due caution, a suggested sequence of the kings of the Fifteenth Dynasty.

Converting this tentative relative sequence into absolute chronology is impossible, as the length of the period under the rule of the Fifteenth Dynasty kings is uncertain: the traditional total sum of regnal years of this dynasty is 108, but this has recently been subjected to critical scrutiny.[36] Kim Ryholt[37] reads the total as 140–149 years, and Thomas Schneider[38] suggests either 160–169 years or 180–189 years.

Then there is the issue of the chronological overlap between the Fourteenth and Fifteenth Dynasties at the beginning of the "Hyksos Period," and the overlap between the Fifteenth, Seventeenth, and

---

33. Moeller and Forstner-Müller 2018a: 9–13; Höflmayer 2018.

34. Forstner-Müller and Reali 2018; Moeller and Marouard 2018.

35. Bietak 1981b: 63–71; Ryholt 2018: 279.

36. For this discussion, see recently Schneider 2018b: 282–284.

37. Kim Ryholt, personal communication (April 2019). Cf. also Schneider 2018b: 282 n. 37.

38. Schneider 2018b: 283.

Table 23.1. The reconstructed sequence of the kings of the Fifteenth Dynasty

Kings of the Fifteenth Dynasty	Copyists of Manetho[a]	Hieroglyphic Evidence[b]
1. Sikru-Haddu	Salitis	Sikru-Haddu (Demotic Saker)
2. ?	Bnon	*Not attested*
3. Khyan	Apakhnan	('Apaq-)Ḥayrān
4. Yanassi	Iannas Yannas	Yinaśśi'-Ad
5. Apepi	Apophis	Apapi
6. Khamudi	*Not attested*	Ḫālmu'di

[a] The writing of the names follows Schneider 2018b: 278.
[b] Following Schneider 2018b: 278.

Eighteenth Dynasties at its end.[39] Such an overlap clearly existed between the last years of the Fifteenth Dynasty, the last years of the Seventeenth Dynasty, and the beginning of the Eighteenth Dynasty. The Seventeenth Dynasty Theban ruler Kamose was a contemporary of the Hyksos ruler Apepi.[40] The reign of the last Hyksos king Khamudi fell entirely into the reign of Ahmose, the first king of the Eighteenth Dynasty and the founder of the New Kingdom, while the final regnal years of Apepi overlap with the beginning of Ahmose's reign, as shown by the relief fragments from Ahmose's pyramid temple in Abydos.[41]A further overlap between the regnal years of the Fifteenth and Eighteenth Dynasties can be deduced from the famous passage on the verso of Papyrus Rhind that mentions that in the eleventh regnal year of the ruling king (most probably Khamudi), the city of Heliopolis was conquered and "he of the

39. For a summary of this problematic topic, see V. Müller 2018: 199–206, with further literature.

40. Gardiner 1916: 95–110; Habachi 1972.

41. Harvey 1994.

South" (most probably Ahmose) captured Tjaru (Greek Sile, modern Tell Hebwa) in the Sinai.[42]

The beginnings of the Fifteenth Dynasty remain equally obscure.[43] The sealings from Avaris seem to indicate an overlap between the Thirteenth, Fourteenth, and Fifteenth Dynasties,[44] but this cannot be verified as there is no discernible overlap in other aspects of the material culture of the eastern delta region.[45]

23.4. The territory of the Hyksos state

Despite the paucity of sources, much has been written on the nature of the Hyksos state.[46] Oren, who uses the term "Hyksos kingdom," implied that the Hyksos kings ruled over an extensive territory with close allies or vassals in Palestine (kingdom of Sharuhen).[47] Bietak assumed that the Hyksos ruled over a territory that was not limited to the eastern delta but reached as far south as Gebelein in Upper Egypt, controlled in the form of a vassal state.[48]

Most research has focused on the extent of territory, while sidelining the question of the means by which this territory would have been controlled. To what extent did the very elaborate ideas and practices of state and government, as developed and maintained in Egypt during the Middle Kingdom, survive into the Second Intermediate Period,

---

42. Peet 1923: col. 2 and 3. For further discussion of this passage, see sections 23.4 and 23.8.

43. Bietak et al. 2001.

44. For the recently discovered seal impressions of Khyan and a king of the Thirteenth Dynasty, see Moeller and Marouard 2011; 2018; Moeller and Forstner-Müller 2018a: 13.

45. Only the material culture of the Thirteenth and Fifteenth Dynasties can be distinguished from each other, while the Fourteenth Dynasty remains obscure.

46. See also Forstner-Müller and Müller 2006.

47. Oren 1997.

48. Bietak 1994: 26. This interpretation was recently challenged by Polz 2006.

and specifically in the Hyksos state? Only a better understanding of the administrative and hierarchical structure of Hyksos rule will allow answers to this question and will elucidate to what extent new concepts were applied by the new rulers.

Due to the scarcity of reliable textual sources, research on this subject must rely largely on archaeological evidence. It has been demonstrated that the Fifteenth Dynasty period saw a significant change in material culture,[49] as attested in the eastern delta as far south as Heliopolis[50] and further eastward into the Sinai.[51] If one accepts the general idea of a congruence of material culture and its carriers, one may therefore assume that the Hyksos (sometimes) ruled over these regions. That the region of the Sinai was at least for some time part of the territory under Hyksos control finds support in the already-discussed Papyrus Rhind, which mentions a Hyksos stronghold in Tjaru (Greek Sile, modern Tell Hebwa) that was besieged for three years and finally conquered by Ahmose.[52] Typically for an "Intermediate Period," multiple parties will have attempted to control as large a part of Egypt as possible, and significant fluctuation in the territory under the control of the different Hyksos kings is therefore likely. As already discussed, the development of the royal titulary from openly using the title Hyksos, "Ruler of the Foreign Lands," to employing only traditional Egyptian titles (see section 23.3) may reflect changing political needs.

According to Manetho, the first king of the Fifteenth Dynasty, Salitis, ruled over both Lower and Upper Egypt,[53] and in his monumental building inscription from Tell el-Dabʿa, King *Skrḥr* used the traditional Nebty title,[54] which means that he at least was in a position to claim publicly to

---

49. Bietak et al. 2001; Aston 2004: 53.

50. Schiestl 2008.

51. Bietak and Kopetzky 2012: 105–128; also M. Abdel Maksoud, personal communication (April 2019).

52. Ryholt 1997: 187.

53. As quoted by Flavius Josephus, *Contra Apionem* I: 77.

54. Bietak 1994.

hold power over Upper Egypt. The question of whether Hyksos control in Egypt ever reached beyond the eastern Nile delta to include Heliopolis and, at least temporarily, Memphis,[55] is hugely significant. Objects showing affinities to the Hyksos material culture were found in Gebelein in Upper Egypt,[56] and the already discussed seal impressions of King Khyan were recently unearthed in Edfu.[57] They are not necessarily evidence of Hyksos occupation or control of these regions, but still point toward the existence of lines of communication and exchange, be it between overlord and client or between trading partners.[58]

However, there is clearly a lack of certain goods from within Egypt at Avaris. On the one hand, the ceramic imports from Upper Egypt, which were never very common in the late Middle Kingdom, now disappeared completely.[59] On the other hand, high-quality raw material for silex tools from Upper Egypt was replaced with inferior local materials.[60] Thus it would seem that the Hyksos state had restricted access to regions in Egypt beyond the eastern delta.

23.5. Avaris, the capital of the Hyksos state

The town of Avaris, the capital of the Hyksos state and later the southern part of Piramesses, the delta residence of the Ramesside kings,[61] is

---

55. According to Manetho, as quoted by Flavius Josephus, I: 77, the first Hyksos ruler, Salitis, established the capital in Memphis and reigned from there.

56. Polz 2006; 2018: 231.

57. Moeller and Marouard 2011; 2018.

58. According to Manetho, as quoted by Flavius Josephus, I: 77: "He [Salitis] . . . received tributes from both Upper and Lower Egypt."

59. Kopetzky 2009: 275.

60. Tilmann 2007: 85, 91. However, Jeuthe 2015: 69 recently cast doubt on the presumed link between the changes in the use of silex raw material and political events.

61. Bietak and Forstner-Müller 2011: 23 n. 1, with earlier literature.

today partly covered by the modern village of Tell el-Dab'a in the modern province of Sharqeya (figure 23.3). The identification of Avaris with Tell el-Dab'a was first suggested by Labib Habachi[62] and later supported by Manfred Bietak.[63]

In its heyday, Avaris was the capital of the rulers of the Fifteenth Dynasty. With an area of ca. 260 hectares, it was among the most important cities of the second millennium BC in the ancient Near East. Like other major settlements in the Nile delta after the Prehistoric period, Avaris lies on one of the main branches of the Nile. In the case of Avaris, this is the Pelusiac branch, the Nile's easternmost main branch during the second millennium BC. At the time, this was the most important Nile branch, but only insignificant remains of this branch are still visible today west of the village of Khata'na. The long-term excavations of the Austrian Archaeological Institute at Tell el-Dab'a have brought to light a huge amount of information, shedding new light on the history and nature of the site.[64]

From the beginning of the Middle Kingdom to the end of the Second Intermediate Period, the town underwent a significant change in size, demography, and ethnic composition, as well as other sociopolitical patterns such as urban layout.[65]

As already stated, the earliest known settlement located in Area F/I goes back to the end of the Eleventh Dynasty or the beginning of the Twelfth Dynasty.[66] After a hiatus in occupation which can be seen throughout the excavated parts of Tell el-Dab'a, the settlement shifted

---

62. Habachi 2001.

63. Bietak 1981a.

64. For an overview of the current state of research, see Bietak 2010a: 11; Forstner-Müller 2014. Detailed information about the site and the research conducted there can be found on the webpage of the Austrian Archaeological Institute (www.oeai.at) and on the webpage of the excavation at Tell el-Dab'a (www.auaris.at).

65. For the development of Avaris, see also Bietak 2010a with alternative conclusions.

66. See Bietak in Hein 1994: 39 and Czerny 1999.

FIGURE 23.3. Map of Tell el-Dabʿa, ancient Avaris. Plan by Astrid Hassler, © ÖAI/ÖAW, with kind permission.

to the north, to Area R/I south of the modern village Ezbet Rushdi el-Sughayar, where a planned settlement[67] and possibly also a temple[68] were built during the mid-Twelfth Dynasty. Later in the Twelfth Dynasty, perhaps during the reign of Senusret III, these structures were partly overbuilt by a new settlement and temple.[69] During the later Twelfth Dynasty, this area formed the nucleus from which the town expanded, mainly to the south,[70] where areas that had not been occupied previously were now settled. The expansion of the settlement is related to the city's growth in population during the late Middle Kingdom, when "Asiatic" immigrants are attested for the first time in Avaris.[71] From this point onward, the characteristic mixture of Egyptian and Near Eastern elements can be found within the material culture of Tell el-Dab'a, eventually culminating in the "Hyksos culture" of the Fifteenth Dynasty, which can be found throughout the eastern delta.[72] At this time, parts of southern Tell el-Dab'a, namely areas A/II[73], A/IV[74] and F/I,[75] were settled.[76] During the Thirteenth Dynasty, new parts of the town were developed to the south of Ezbet Rushdi in Areas R/II[77] and R/IV.[78] The latter is of special interest, as it was part of the late Middle Kingdom harbor district. The southern limit of Area R/IV was defined by a massive wall,

67. For the older planned settlement, see also Czerny 2015: 31–72.

68. Forstner-Müller et al. 2005.

69. Czerny 2015: 73–74, 151–159.

70. Against Bietak 2010a: 18, who sees the "nucleus" of Avaris in Area F/I.

71. Bietak 2010b: 139–140, 153.

72. Aston 2004: 53; Kopetzky 2010: 272–273.

73. Forstner-Müller 2007.

74. See the preliminary discussion by Irmgard Hein on www.auaris.at (last accessed September 20, 2020).

75. Schiestl 2009: 24–25, 31–32, 219–319.

76. In general, see Bietak 2010a: 17, fig. 9a.

77. Sa. Müller 2013: 110–111, fig. 1.

78. Forstner-Müller, Hassler, Matić and Rose 2015: 75, fig. 60; Forstner-Müller 2021.

which most probably constitutes the harbor wall of this period. It is during that period, in the mid-Thirteenth Dynasty, that the name of Avaris (*hut-waret*) is attested for the first time, on a papyrus seal impression bearing the name of a mayor of Avaris called Ameny-Seneb-Nefer.[79] As this seal impression was found in a secondary context,[80] it is possible that the name for the town was already in use before this date.

During the earlier Thirteenth Dynasty, an impressive elite house with an attached garden and cemetery was erected in Area F/I.[81] In the later Thirteenth Dynasty, this building was abandoned and overbuilt by large houses[82] and tombs.[83] During this same period, a sacred precinct with temples,[84] priests' houses, and cemeteries[85] came into existence in Area A/II. The temple of god Seth/Baʿal Zephon, one of the main deities of Avaris, was located here.[86] This area continued to be the religious center of the town until the end of the New Kingdom.[87]

With the collapse of the centralized Egyptian state during the Thirteenth Dynasty, Avaris became one of the provincial capitals of the Fourteenth Dynasty, and eventually, in the Fifteenth Dynasty, it became the capital of the Hyksos realm. By now the town had reached its greatest extent.[88] It expanded in all directions: to the north as far as the modern village of Ezbet Machali, to the south to the now-disappeared southern

---

79. Czerny 2015: 21–22, 382–383.

80. Czerny 2015: 21–22.

81. Schiestl 2009, with further literature.

82. M. Müller 2015: 339–370.

83. For the tombs of the later phases in Area F/I, see Kopetzky 1993.

84. See Bietak 2010b: 139, 143–144, 154–156, figs. 4, 10.

85. For the cemeteries of the late Middle Kingdom in Area A/II, see Forstner-Müller 2008; 2010a.

86. Forstner-Müller 2010b: 111; for the cult of this god in Avaris, see Bietak 2010b: 157, fig. 14, with further literature.

87. Bietak and Forstner-Müller 2011.

88. Forstner-Müller 2010b: 103–123, 109.

feeder channel of the main harbor at Ezzawin, to the east to the modern village of Sama'na, and to the west it was limited by the Pelusiac branch of the Nile. Precincts of cemeteries, temples, and palaces were spatially separated from the rest of the town by enclosure walls, and this spatial organization remained intact until the beginning of the New Kingdom.[89]

The town thus underwent a change in function from a frontier settlement founded and planned by the centralized Egyptian state at the beginning and middle of the Twelfth Dynasty to a provincial capital during the Fourteenth Dynasty and finally to the political center of a realm that controlled at least northern Egypt under the "Hyksos" rulers of the Fifteenth Dynasty.

In the following, we first survey funerary practices as attested at Avaris during the Fifteenth Dynasty, then detail the relatively limited evidence for temples and religious beliefs, and finally discuss the palace(s) occupied by the Hyksos rulers.

23.5.1. Funerary practices at Avaris

Of the numerous peculiarities of Avaris that distinguish it from a traditional Egyptian settlement, the fusion of funerary and domestic spheres is perhaps the most remarkable. From the late Middle Kingdom onward, houses with associated tombs[90] are attested at Tell el-Dab'a, as well as dedicated cemeteries, such as the cemetery connected to the elite complex of the late Twelfth Dynasty and the Thirteenth Dynasty in Area F/I.[91]

From the beginning, the funerary culture of the inhabitants of Avaris combines Egyptian and Syro-Palestinian elements, providing parallels to typical features of the Middle Bronze Age culture in the Near East, such as weaponry (exclusively in association with male burials), certain types of ceramics, and donkey burials. Metal pins, found usually on the

89. Forstner-Müller 2008: 119–120.

90. Kopetzky 1993.

91. Schiestl 2009.

left shoulder of the deceased, may suggest that the woolen wrap-around garments, popular throughout the Near East, were worn instead of Egyptian linen attire. Whether this is a fashion choice or should be seen as a marker of ethnicity[92] must remain unclear.

Strikingly, Middle Bronze Age elements with parallels in the Near East are more frequent in the funerary culture than Egyptian ones; the opposite is true for the everyday material culture of the living, in which the Egyptian elements clearly dominate. The earliest evidence of Near Eastern characteristics in the funerary culture of Avaris derives from the cemetery in Area F/I and dates to the late Twelfth Dynasty.[93] High officials in the service of the king of Egypt were buried in the richly decorated tombs at this cemetery and expressed their social standing through the Egyptian value system, without denying their links to Syro-Palestinian culture (figure 23.4). The Egyptian-style funerary chapels of their tombs exhibit a high degree of acculturation.

During the Fifteenth Dynasty, we can observe an increasing consolidation and standardization within the funerary material culture of the eastern Nile delta region, especially in relation to burial inventories and architectural details of the tombs.[94] Typically, there is a separation between the above-ground structures, such as the funerary chapels that suggest traditional Egyptian cult activity, and the subterranean burial with pronounced Syro-Palestinian characteristics. The key characteristics of funerary culture here, most importantly the combination of Egyptian-style superstructures and Syro-Palestinian-style underground burials, as well as the basic arrangement of the burial and the offerings within the tombs, continued until the end of Hyksos rule.

Evidence for the conduct of differentiated rituals at the burial places after the funeral points to social stratification among the communities, as well as to the lasting effect of the acculturation process that survived

92. Thus Bietak 2016; 2018.

93. Schiestl 2009: 217–317.

94. Forstner-Müller and Müller 2006: 97–98.

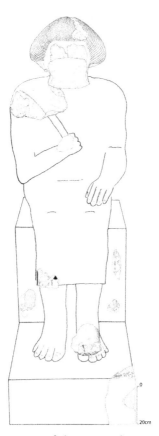

FIGURE 23.4. Reconstruction of the statue of an Asiatic dignitary. From Avaris, cemetery in Area F/I. Drawing by Robert Schiestl, © ÖAI/ÖAW, with kind permission.

or even increased in subsequent generations.[95] The cemeteries document hierarchies of sacrificial acts and feasts, characterized by varying degrees of intimacy or exclusivity: there are individual offering pits directly at or very near the burial, while less exclusive offerings were deposited all over

95. Forstner-Müller 2008: 113–117; for the offering deposits, see V. Müller 2008.

the cemetery, and further offering pits were found in the vicinity of the mortuary chapels at the center of cemeteries.[96]

We can observe certain changes in funerary culture. At first, whenever there were multiple burials in one tomb, there was a clear tendency toward gender distinction, i.e., men and women were buried separately, and this custom is attested all over Egypt, for example also in the far south at Elephantine.[97] During the later Fifteenth Dynasty, however, large mudbrick tombs with a built shaft were constructed, usually directly integrated into the residential architecture or else located in the courtyard of private houses. These tombs, too, contained multiple burials, but now the genders were mixed, suggesting that the tombs served entire families, regardless of an individual's gender. The emergence of this type of shaft tomb as part of a private house is clearly linked to the expansion of the town and the greater density of its occupation.

In this later period, the evidence for warrior tombs (figure 23.5) and donkey burials ends, too. At Avaris, warrior tombs disappear in the mid-Fifteenth Dynasty,[98] but this is a wider phenomenon because by the beginning of the Late Bronze Age, the custom of burying a man as a warrior with his weapons had fallen out of use throughout Syro-Palestine and the wider Near East.[99]

The abandonment of the practice of warrior burials has been linked to changes in the perception of social hierarchies[100] that preferred to showcase the status of the deceased differently. The elevated social standing formerly expressed through personal weapons was now channeled into the political order and command structure of the late Hyksos state as the individual was absorbed into this larger unit, which quite possibly considered the burial of valuable military equipment a waste. Seen in

96. Forstner-Müller 2008: 115–117; V. Müller 2008: 279–314.

97. Stefan Seidlmayer, personal communication (April 2019).

98. The latest warrior burial at Avaris is dated to the mid-Fifteenth Dynasty; Forstner-Müller 2008: 49.

99. Philip 1995: 153.

100. Philip 1995: 140–154.

(a)

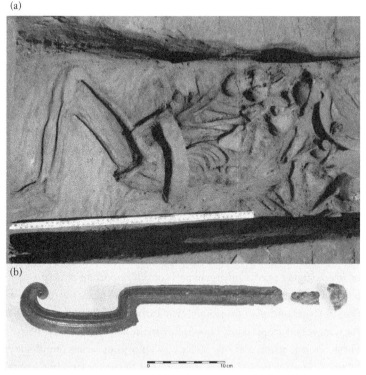

(b)

FIGURE 23.5. A warrior burial (a) and the scimitar (b) found therein. From Avaris. Photos by Irene Forstner-Müller (tomb) and Niki Gail (scimitar), © ÖAI/ÖAW, with kind permission.

this light, the disappearance of weapons from funerary contexts may also indicate an increasingly close connection between state administration and the military.[101] In any case, the fact that the custom of warrior burials was abandoned in Avaris while the Fifteenth Dynasty was still in power shows that this change was not related to the emergence of a supposedly more cosmopolitan lifestyle in the time of the Eighteenth Dynasty,[102]

101. Cf. Forstner-Müller and Müller 2005: 200; Forstner-Müller 2008: 49, 124.

102. Philip 1995: 154.

nor to developments in Syro-Palestine during the Late Bronze Age, but was the result of local factors.

23.5.2. The temples of Avaris

Before the later Middle Kingdom, we do not know of any deity connected with the area of Tell el-Dab'a. The only cult that is possibly attested is an ancestor cult for King Amenemhat I in Ezbet Rushdi.[103]

One of the main deities worshipped in Avaris was the Egyptian god Seth in his syncretic form merged with Ba'al Zephon (Ba'al Ṣapunu). The cult of this northern Syrian storm god was already locally attested in the late Middle Kingdom on a cylinder seal.[104] This god became the "Lord of Avaris" and was still venerated as an ancestor god ("Father of the Fathers") in the Ramesside period (Nineteenth Dynasty).[105] His temple was the main sanctuary of the town and was located in the eastern part of Avaris (figure 23.6). Only small parts of this important structure could be excavated, and only magnetometry surveys have made the reconstruction of its ground plan possible.[106] The earliest architectural remains of the temple that are presently known date to the later Fifteenth Dynasty.[107] However, it is attested as one of the city's most important temples even by the Ramesside period, when it was one of the major landmarks of the cultic topography of the new residence called Piramesses.[108]

The "Syro-Palestinian Temple District" is located in the vicinity of the Seth temple. Founded at the beginning of the Thirteenth Dynasty, it was in use until the early Eighteenth Dynasty.[109] The compound

---

103. See Arnold 2010: 185–186 and cf. section 23.5.

104. Bietak 2010b: 157–158.

105. Bietak 1990.

106. Forstner-Müller 2010b: 111, fig. 5.

107. Bietak 1990.

108. Bietak and Forstner-Müller 2011: 34, fig. 6.

109. Bietak 2010b: 154–156.

FIGURE 23.6. Temple of Seth at Avaris, combining the results of mapping, geophysical prospecting, and excavation. Image prepared by Irene Forstner-Müller, © ÖAI/ÖAW, with kind permission.

comprised a group of larger temples with ground plans that are not Egyptian in style, as well as cemeteries that contain smaller shrines. These shrines especially manifest the new political power in Avaris and highlight the city's distinct polycultural and religious traditions during the Second Intermediate Period, where elements of Egyptian and Near Eastern architecture, lifestyles, and belief systems coexisted. Beyond this main sacred district, small temples were encountered in excavation areas throughout the town, in Area F/I[110] and possibly Area R/III.[111]

110. Forstner-Müller 2010b: 111–112, fig. 7.

111. This material is still unpublished.

23.5.3. The palace(s) of Avaris

The main palace of the Fifteenth Dynasty was located in the southern part of Avaris in Area F/II, just to the north of the modern village Khata'na (figure 23.7). It was discovered in the course of a magnetometer survey[112] and subsequently was investigated by archaeological excavation.[113]

This palace was certainly the seat of the government of the kings of the Fifteenth Dynasty, having replaced an earlier palace of the late Middle Kingdom. Both palaces show the same orientation, and this also corresponds to the orientation of the later Eighteenth Dynasty palace district in Ezbet Helmi.[114]

The layout of the Fifteenth Dynasty palace in Area F/II can be almost completely reconstructed by combining the results of the magnetometer survey and the archaeological excavations. It exhibits features belonging to both Egyptian and Near Eastern architectural traditions.[115] The building is a large complex with groups of rooms, courtyards, storage rooms, staircases, and towers. It was accessible from the north via a kind of vestibule. The southern part of the palace was almost completely destroyed by later activities.

Of special interest is a foundation deposit that was discovered at one of the corners of the palace,[116] following the tradition of Egyptian foundation pits. The objects recovered from this deposit include an inscribed faience plaque (its inscription is unfortunately no longer visible) and further faience objects, as well as a piece of copper. Before depositing the objects, pale yellow sand was poured into the pit, which shows that traditional Egyptian ritual practices were known and applied in the construction of the Fifteenth Dynasty palace.

---

112. Bietak, Forstner-Müller, and Herbich 2006.

113. Bietak and Forstner-Müller 2006; 2009; Bietak et al. 2012–2013.

114. Forstner-Müller 2012: 683.

115. Against Bietak et al. 2012–2013: 19, 26.

116. Forstner-Müller 2011: 2–3; 2015.

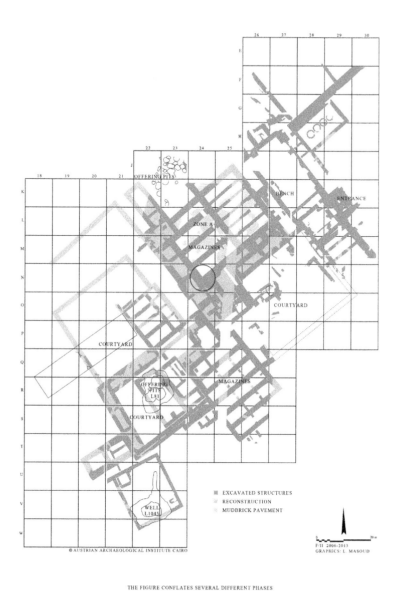

THE FIGURE CONFLATES SEVERAL DIFFERENT PHASES

FIGURE 23.7. Plan of the Fifteenth Dynasty palace in Area F/II of Avaris. Plan by Leila Masoud, © ÖAI/ÖAW, with kind permission.

At least two phases of construction can be identified.[117] The original dating of the early phase to the reign of King Khyan[118] must now be revised.[119] The exact date of its abandonment could also not be determined, but a connection with the expulsion of the last Hyksos ruler from Avaris at the beginning of the Eighteenth Dynasty is conceivable.[120]

Another possible palace, but with a different orientation, was discovered to the west. The massive building was partly excavated,[121] but it is covered today largely by the modern Didamun Canal and a major road connecting Faqus and Tanis.

23.6. The administration of the Hyksos state

Among the elements of material culture associated with the Hyksos rule, the most significant group of finds consists of the already mentioned seals and sealings with scarab impressions, and these provide some insights into mechanisms of state control and communication, internally and externally.

The traditional view was that the Hyksos state knew no centralized administration and that this consequently led to its collapse. However, the by now over one thousand sealings found at Tell el-Dab'a in recent years clearly demonstrate the existence of a Hyksos administration. This enormous number of seal impressions has resulted in a significant improvement of the understanding of the administrative organization of Avaris during the late Middle Kingdom and the Second Intermediate Period (Thirteenth to Fifteenth Dynasties), but our knowledge of the

---

117. Bietak et al. 2012–2013: 19–32.

118. Bietak et al. 2012–2013: 25.

119. Forstner-Müller and Rose 2012: 184.

120. The dating of this palace is disputed. The present author here follows the dating of Karin Kopetzky, who puts the abandonment of the palace at the end of the Fifteenth Dynasty (Tell el-Dab'a Stratum D/2). Cf. Forstner-Müller and Rose 2012: 184.

121. Forstner-Müller 2010b: 114.

details of the administration under the Fifteenth Dynasty nevertheless remains very limited. It should be noted that in addition to the large number of Egyptian-style stamp sealings, the excavations at Tell el-Dabʻa also brought to light several sealings from cylinder seals from Syria and Mesopotamia,[122] as well as a small fragment of a clay tablet inscribed in cuneiform script and the Akkadian language.[123]

Some of the Egyptian-style stamp seal impressions bear the names of Egyptian officials.[124] Although these were found in layers dating to the Thirteenth and Fifteenth Dynasties, due to the characteristic spelling of names and titles they can be dated without exception to the Thirteenth Dynasty and therefore the later Middle Kingdom. This evidence shows that at that time, there was a lively exchange between Avaris and the Egyptian central government at the then capital city of Itj-tawy, and also provides information on specific administrative processes.

During the Fifteenth Dynasty, however, most of the titles of officials that were clearly present in the Thirteenth Dynasty material from Avaris are no longer attested.[125] Since titles such as the previously ubiquitous "vizier" disappear from the material record, we could argue that the elaborate administrative system of the Middle Kingdom was no longer in existence at Avaris, although the practice of sealing was still very popular.

The general absence of officials' names and titles on these sealings is the clearest sign that the administrative system of the Middle Kingdom did not continue at Avaris in all aspects. We can assume that with the separation of the Hyksos state from the rest of Egypt, the administration of the Fifteenth Dynasty would have generally undergone changes. However, as demonstrated by the writing equipment inscribed with

---

122. Collon and Lehmann 2011; Collon et al. 2011; van Koppen and Lehmann 2012–2013.

123. van Koppen and Radner 2009: 115–118.

124. The seal impressions bearing titles of Egyptian officials are currently being studied by Marcel Marée.

125. Marcel Marée, personal communication (April 2019); and see also Quirke 2004.

the name of Fifteenth Dynasty ruler Apepi[126] and the verso text of the mathematical Papyrus Rhind (the only papyrus attested from this king's reign),[127] certain Egyptian administrative traditions continued to be practiced at least during that reign. Yet despite the clear continuities, most obviously in the practice of sealing for authentication and security (as also conducted all over the contemporary Near East), there is much that is new: even the sealing practices under the Fifteenth Dynasty rulers differed in detail from those used in earlier periods.[128] Sealing objects was—as with the rest of Middle Bronze Age culture—a popular activity. However, the known administrative structure of the Thirteenth Dynasty was no longer in use, as is shown by the lack of officials' names and titles on the sealings.[129]

When and how did the administration of the Fifteenth Dynasty disassociate itself from the residence at Itj-tawy? To what extent, if any, did the seemingly marginalized central administration survive in Lower Egypt in parallel to the newly established state centered on Avaris? What changes (if any) took place in Avaris and in the eastern Nile delta after the foundation of the Hyksos state, both "horizontally" in regard to each individual's function within the workings of the state and "vertically" along the lines of the state hierarchy? Is it even possible to describe the characteristics of the administration of the Hyksos state? There are many open questions and very few certain answers.[130] Fundamentally, this is due to the fact that the chronological relationship between the Thirteenth, Fourteenth, and Fifteenth Dynasties is not well established. What is clear is that despite Manetho's sequencing, they were not consecutive; as we have discussed earlier (section 23.3), overlaps are not only possible, but even likely: one can assume that the Fifteenth Dynasty

126. Wildung 1994: 152.

127. Peet 1923; discussed by Quirke 1994: 156–158.

128. Marcel Marée, personal communication (April 2019).

129. Marcel Marée, personal communication (April 2019).

130. For an overview of the administrative restructuring processes at the time, see Shirley 2013: 523–570.

was coeval with the late Thirteenth Dynasty and that the Fourteenth Dynasty was coeval at least with the earlier Thirteenth Dynasty.

This lack of clarity makes the overall interpretation of the evidence from the Avaris sealings difficult. The sealings may hint at administrative and commercial exchange between the still-existing government of the Thirteenth Dynasty at Itj-tawy and the rulers of the Fourteenth and early Fifteenth Dynasties at Avaris. Compared to those of the Thirteenth Dynasty, the attested Fourteenth Dynasty sealings show a much reduced range of official titles: only "Treasurer" and "Elder King's Son" are attested,[131] although the number of seal impressions known per official is much larger than before.[132] Finally, the Fifteenth Dynasty sealings show royal, figurative, and pseudo-inscriptional designs and only feature very few titles,[133] and this is largely comparable to the contemporary situation at Thebes[134] and Elephantine[135] in Upper Egypt.

23.7. Contacts with the regions beyond Egypt: Near East, Cyprus, and Nubia

With the beginning of the Fifteenth Dynasty, contacts between Avaris and Egypt's traditional partners of the Middle Kingdom declined significantly.[136] However, finds from southern Palestine, the Aegean, Anatolia, and even southern Mesopotamia bear the name of King Khyan,[137] and this seems to indicate that the Hyksos state was still integrated into a far-reaching network of exchange during his reign. Based on the testimony

---

131. Ryholt 2018: 238, 260–263.

132. Marcel Marée, personal communication (April 2019).

133. Marcel Marée, personal communication (April 2019); see also Ben-Tor 2007: 185–186.

134. Polz 2007: 13–14.

135. von Pilgrim 1996: 253.

136. See also Kopetzky 2009: 275; 2015: 157.

137. Höflmayer 2018: 145–146.

of material culture, the contacts between Avaris and the Near East reached their peak during the late Middle Kingdom. It seems surprising that the rise to power of the Hyksos and the establishment of their capital at Avaris did not result in an increase in trade and importation; instead, the town lost its previous role as a major node in the interregional trade networks.[138]

If one considers the ancient world as a market economy with complex networks governing supply and demand, it becomes evident that the dissolution of the Egyptian territorial state had marked consequences for the wider region. The emergence of the new political structure in Lower Egypt destroyed the established mechanisms of distribution inside Egypt, and the significance of the Egyptian market as a partner in long-distance trade shrank dramatically to a fraction of the size it had been during the Middle Kingdom. As a result, trade between the Hyksos-ruled area and outside is likely to have been gradually reduced.

Imported pottery and cylinder sealings are crucial for our understanding of the nature of relations between Avaris and the Near East. With regard to ceramic imports, in particular storage jars from Syro-Palestine, the Fifteenth Dynasty certainly saw changes, as both the amount and range of this pottery decreased significantly.[139] It took until the late Second Intermediate Period for the trading volume with the Near East to increase again.[140]

So far, the impressions of cylinder seals from Syro-Palestine and Mesopotamia that provide evidence for goods imported to the town are usually found in Thirteenth Dynasty contexts.[141] A fragment of a clay tablet inscribed in cuneiform script using the Akkadian language (figure 23.8) was found in a secondary archaeological context in the infill of a Ramesside well near the Hyksos-period palace in Area F/II at Avaris.[142] It can be identified as a letter and perhaps provides evidence for a direct

---

138. Kopetzky 2009: 275; 2015.

139. Kopetzky 2009: 275; 2015: 157.

140. Kopetzky 2009: 275.

141. Collon and Lehmann 2011; Collon et al. 2013; van Koppen and Lehmann 2012–2013; Forstner-Müller, Hassler, Matić, and Rose 2015.

142. Bietak and Forstner-Müller 2009: 96.

0   1cm

FIGURE 23.8. Cuneiform tablet from Avaris. Photo by Axel Krause, © ÖAI/ ÖAW, with kind permission.

correspondence between a ruler of Avaris and a king of Babylon.[143] It is equally possible, though, that the letter was written in the late Middle Kingdom[144] during the time of the most intensive contact between Avaris and the Near East. In any case, this isolated find is not sufficient to enable us to form an understanding of the nature, frequency, and intensity of these communications.

The reduced contacts with the Near East are perhaps most clearly noticeable in the composition of the metal of the Middle Bronze Age

143. van Koppen and Radner 2009.

144. The earlier hypothesis that the dating of this find is linked to the Hyksos palace (Bietak and Forstner-Müller 2009: 106–108, figs. 19–20) can no longer be upheld.

weapons at Avaris. During the Middle Kingdom, weapons were made of bronze, that is, an alloy of copper and tin; the predominant material used during the Fifteenth Dynasty was copper alone, which points to the fact that access to tin was limited or blocked as a result of the interruption of the traditional trade routes from the Near East into Egypt. The copper was most likely imported from Cyprus, together with the Cypriot pottery that is now attested, for the first time and in large quantities, in the corresponding archaeological record.[145] With the beginning of the Fifteenth Dynasty, Cyprus clearly emerged as a new partner in trade for Avaris.

In contrast to the reduced links with the Near East, contacts with Nubia were intensified during the Fifteenth Dynasty. In the later Second Intermediate Period, contacts between the Nubian kingdom of Kush and the Hyksos rulers seem to have been frequent and intensive.[146] That Nubians played an important role in southern Egypt and even invaded the region is well known.[147] At some point, the ruler of Kush probably had control over the southernmost part of Egypt, including Elephantine.[148] At least sometimes, the rulers in the south and the Hyksos rulers were allies,[149] and as the Kamose Stele emphasizes,[150] an important route linked Avaris to the southern regions through the oases

---

145. For the Cypriot pottery from Tell el-Dabʿa and its distribution, see Bietak and Maguire 2009; for Cyprus as a new trading partner, see Bietak 1994: 48–49; for Cypriot pottery in funerary contexts, see Forstner-Müller 2008: 58, 82.

146. For the "Kamose Steles," see Gardiner 1916: 95–110; Habachi 1972. For the implications on the archaeology of this period, see Bourriau 1999: 43–48; also Gratien 1978; 2004; Polz 1998: 225, 229.

147. For the complex situation, see also the autobiography of Sobeknakht: Davies 2003: 52–54.

148. Polz 2018. It is presumably not a coincidence that a seal bearing the title "Ruler of Kush" was found in Elephantine in contemporaneous layers: von Pilgrim 2015.

149. The extension to the south is not clear; cf. Polz 2006; 2018: 231.

150. Gardiner 1916: 95–110; Habachi 1972.

of the Western Desert.[151] This route was especially important when the traditional Nile route was blocked, as may have been done by the rulers of Thebes on occasion during the Second Intermediate Period.

The Nubian component within the material culture of Avaris mostly consists of pottery, with Nubian ceramics appearing at the beginning of the Fifteenth Dynasty.[152] Even outside the socially and religiously highly charged funerary contexts, ceramics that were not used for transport can be much valued as precious, "fashionable" commodities, such as the high-quality, visually distinctive Nubian bowls found in domestic contexts at Avaris. Less obviously conspicuous commodities such as Nubian cooking pots may have been highly valued, resulting in import and imitation.[153] However, it is unclear whether the pottery was made in Nubia and brought to Avaris through trade or gift exchange, or whether it was made by Nubians who lived in Avaris.[154]

Whether the Nubian pottery found in Avaris is evidence for Nubian populations living there cannot be answered conclusively.[155] While we have seen that various elements of material culture at Avaris clearly demonstrate that actual "Asiatics" lived there, it is equally clear because of its fabric that the Cypriot pottery found at Avaris was imported to the town, and not produced by Cypriots settled there. The situation is more complex for Nubian pottery which is made of Nile clay: it is not currently possible to differentiate between Nile clay pottery produced in different parts of Egypt and Nubia.

It is worth pointing out that no Nubian burials or funerary elements have ever been identified at Avaris. If we want to entertain the idea that Nubians actually lived at the town, then the question arises as

---

151. Colin 2005: 35–47; D. Darnell 2002: 147; J.C. Darnell 2002: 170, fig. 9.

152. Forstner-Müller and Rose 2012: 181.

153. Forstner-Müller and Rose 2012: 200.

154. Forstner-Müller and Rose 2012: 200. On the topic of the Nubian pottery and Egypt, see also De Souza 2020.

155. Forstner-Müller and Rose 2012: 200; Matić 2016.

to what their role within the general population of Avaris would have been;[156] most likely, we would expect them among specialist groups such as military personnel, which typically have high proportions of foreigners.[157]

23.8. The end of the Hyksos state

The decline and end of Hyksos rule is closely connected with the rise of the Seventeenth and Eighteenth Dynasties. At the end of the Seventeenth Dynasty, the political reality of a more or less peaceful coexistence between Upper and Lower Egypt changed when the Theban ruler Seqenenra Taa started military operations against the Hyksos.[158] He was probably killed in battle: his mummy features a mortal head wound, which was very likely caused by a Middle Bronze Age weapon type as we can easily imagine the Hyksos troops to have used.[159]

His successor and son Kamose continued the incursions against the Hyksos king Apepi and started a campaign to expel the Hyksos in order to reunify Egypt under Theban rule.[160] We can only speculate to what extent the account of the events that led to his eventual success, as described in the Kamose Steles, was based on fact. Kamose probably never came farther north than the nome of Cynopolis in Middle Egypt, and thus would not have reached Memphis or the Nile delta, nor would he have attacked Avaris.[161] The detail in the first Kamose Stele that the

---

156. Cf. also Forstner-Müller and Rose 2012: 200; Matić 2016.

157. Schneider 2003: 339.

158. Whether the tale in Papyrus Sallier I, in which the Hyksos king Apepi demands that the Theban ruler silence his hippopotami as he was not able to sleep in faraway Avaris, reflects actual contact between Apepi and Seqenenra Taa is disputed: Schneider 1998: 76–98, 163. It remains possible that both reigned at the same time.

159. Bietak 1994: 28, fig. 10.

160. Gardiner 1916: 95–110; Habachi 1972.

161. Ryholt 1997: 172–175.

Theban king managed to intercept a message from Apepi to his ally, the ruler of Kush, shows that the Hyksos state and the kingdom of Kush were political allies.

Ahmose, the brother of Kamose, the first king of the Eighteenth Dynasty and the founder of the New Kingdom, was able to reunify Egypt by conquering the area ruled by the Hyksos. However, the circumstances surrounding the capture of Avaris are obscure. An entry in a diary copied on the back of Papyrus Rhind reads:

Regnal Year 11, second month of Shemu, Heliopolis was entered. First month of Akhet, day 23, he of the South broke into Tjaru [Greek Sile, modern Tell Hebwa].[162]

There is little doubt that the regnal year referred to here is that of the Hyksos king Khamudi, whereas "he of the South" is Ahmose.[163]

Further information on Ahmose's war against the Hyksos is provided by the royal navy officer Ahmose, son of Ibana, in his tomb at Elkab.[164] According to his autobiography, the Theban forces conducted four attacks on Avaris. The fourth (and last) was successful and resulted in the expulsion of the Hyksos. In the final campaign, Ahmose conquered Tjaru (Greek Sile), the last Hyksos stronghold, after a siege of three years.[165] The victory over the Hyksos is also shown on limestone relief fragments found in Ahmose's mortuary temple at Abydos that depict battle scenes between the Thebans and the Hyksos.[166]

However, the archaeological record unearthed at Avaris does not reflect Ahmose's conquest, as no signs of destruction have been

---

162. Peet 1923: Papyrus Rhind, col. 2 and 3.

163. Schneider 2006: 195.

164. Sethe 1914: 1–6.

165. Sethe 1914: 3–5.

166. Harvey 1994.

found that could be associated with this event.[167] The material culture in Avaris shows a slow, almost invisible transition from the pottery types characterizing the very late Fifteenth Dynasty into those of the early Eighteenth Dynasty.[168] Perhaps this indicates that while the Hyksos rulers were expelled, the population of Avaris was allowed to stay.

In the Eighteenth Dynasty, however, settlement activity was restricted to certain parts of the town.[169] This shrinking of the town's size[170] does not necessarily mean that its inhabitants were evicted. Rather, Avaris, no longer a capital city and administrative center, may have been less attractive to potential settlers. At the temple of Seth/Ba'al Zephon, the cult continued and even rose to new prominence as the ancestral cult of the Ramesside Nineteenth Dynasty, which probably originated in this part of Egypt.[171]

23.9. Aftermath

The kings of the Ramesside Nineteenth Dynasty who originated from the eastern Nile delta founded a new residence at the site of ancient Avaris, Piramesses, the glorious "City of Rameses," and emphasized their

---

167. Bietak 2010b: 164. Some bodies unearthed at Ezbet Helmi, exhibiting injuries that can be interpreted as combat wounds, may provide evidence for the war between the Hyksos and the Theban state at Avaris. The excavator of these bodies originally associated them with the conquest of Avaris, but they were later dated to the early Eighteenth Dynasty. The ongoing re-evaluation of the dating of the archaeological phases of Ezbet Helmi now dates the bodies to the period of transition between the very late Second Intermediate Period and the beginning of the Eighteenth Dynasty (David Aston and Irmgard Hein, personal communication, April 2019), and this again makes a connection with the conquest of Avaris possible.

168. Bietak 2010b: 169–170.

169. Bietak 2010b: 164.

170. Bietak 2010b: 165.

171. Bietak 2010b: 164; Bietak and Forstner-Müller 2011: 36, fig. 7 (Four Hundred Years Stele).

close link to Seth/Ba'al Zephon, their dynastic god and traditionally Avaris's main deity.

However, the Hyksos period under the Fifteenth Dynasty was considered a dark epoch of illegitimate foreign rule in Egyptian history.[172] Already the Eighteenth Dynasty queen Hatshepsut passed a negative judgment on it when she claimed in her famous Speos Artemidos inscription that she

> ... raised up what was dismembered beginning when the Asiatics were in the midst of the delta, (in) Avaris, with vagrants in their midst, toppling what had been made. They ruled without the Sun.[173]

Nevertheless, it is evident that essential aspects of the New Kingdom state had their roots in the Hyksos state and the Second Intermediate Period more generally. Apart from the transfer of technological innovations in weaponry and chariotry, the new performance-related concept of kingship of the Eighteenth Dynasty, with its war-specific profile, may be traced back to Near Eastern ideals.[174] The expansionism of the New Kingdom, which is closely linked to its much-admired "cosmopolitanism," can be seen as a direct legacy of the connections already present in the Second Intermediate Period.

REFERENCES

Arnold, D. 2010. Image and identity: Egypt's eastern neighbours, East delta people and the Hyksos. In Marée, M. (ed.) 2010: 183–221.

Allen, J.P. 2002. The Speos Artemidos inscription of Hatshepsut. *Bulletin of the Egyptological Seminar* 16: 1–17.

Assmann, J. 1998. *Moses der Ägypter: Entzifferung einer Gedächtnisspur.* Munich: Hanser.

---

172. For a recent summary, with further literature, see Schneider 2018a.

173. Allen 2002.

174. Forstner-Müller and Müller 2006: 99.

Aston, D.A. 2004. *Tell el-Dab'a XII: a corpus of the late Middle Kingdom and Second Intermediate Period pottery*. In collaboration with M. Bietak and with the assistance of B. Bader, I. Forstner-Müller, and R. Schiestl. Vienna: Verlag der Österreichischen Akademie der Wissenschaften.

Bader, B. 2013. Cultural mixing in Egyptian archaeology: the "Hyksos" as a case study. *Archaeological Review from Cambridge* 28: 257–286.

Ben-Tor, D. 2007. *Scarabs, chronology and interconnections: Egypt and Palestine in the Second Intermediate Period*. Fribourg: Fribourg Academic Press; Göttingen: Vandenhoeck & Ruprecht.

Bietak, M. 1981a. *Avaris and Piramesse: archaeological exploration in the eastern Nile delta*. Oxford: Oxford University Press.

Bietak, M. 1981b. Eine Stele des ältesten Königssohnes des Hyksos Chajan. *MDAIK* 37: 63–73.

Bietak, M. 1990. Zur Herkunft des Seth von Avaris. *ÄL* 1: 9–16.

Bietak, M. 1991. Egypt and Canaan during the Middle Bronze Age. *BASOR* 281: 28–72.

Bietak, M. 1994. Historische und archäologische Einführung. In Bietak, M., and Hein, I. (eds.) 1994: 17–57.

Bietak, M. 2010a. Houses, palaces and development of social structure in Avaris. In Bietak, M., Czerny E., and Forstner-Müller, I. (eds.), *Cities and urbanism in ancient Egypt*. Vienna: Verlag der Österreichischen Akademie der Wissenschaften, 11–68.

Bietak, M. 2010b. From where came the Hyksos and where did they go? In Marée, M. (ed.) 2010: 139–182.

Bietak, M. 2016. The Egyptian community in Avaris during the Hyksos Period. *ÄL* 26: 263–274.

Bietak, M. 2018. The many ethnicities of Avaris: evidence from the northern borderland of Egypt. In Budka, J., and Auenmüller, J. (eds.), *From microcosm to macrocosm: individual households and cities in ancient Egypt and Nubia*. Leiden: Sidestone, 73–92.

Bietak, M., and Forstner-Müller, I. 2006. Eine palatiale Anlage der frühen Hyksoszeit (Areal F/II): vorläufige Ergebnisse der Grabungskampagne 2006 in Tell el-Dab'a. *ÄL* 16: 63–78.

Bietak, M., and Forstner-Müller, I. 2009. Der Hyksos-Palast bei Tell el-Dab'a: zweite und dritte Grabungskampagne (Frühling 2008 und Frühling 2009). *ÄL* 19: 92–119.

Bietak, M., and Forstner-Müller, I. 2011. The topography of New Kingdom Avaris and Per Ramesses. In Collier, M., and Snape, S. (eds.), *Ramesside studies in honour of Kenneth A. Kitchen*. Bolton: Rutherford Press, 23–50.

Bietak, M., Forstner-Müller, I., and Herbich, T. 2007. Geophysical survey and its archaeological verification: discovery of a new palatial complex in Tell el-Dabʻa. In Hawass, Z.A., and Richards, J. (eds.), *The archaeology and art of ancient Egypt: essays in honor of David B. O'Connor, vol. 1*. Cairo: Supreme Council of Antiquities, 119–125.

Bietak, M., Forstner-Müller, I., and Mlinar, C. 2001. The beginning of the Hyksos Period at Tell el-Dabʻa: a subtle change in material culture. In Fischer, P. (ed.), *Contributions to the archaeology and history of the Bronze and Iron Ages in the Eastern Mediterranean: studies in honour of Paul Aström*. Vienna: Holzhausen, 171–181.

Bietak, M., and Kopetzky, K. 2012. The Egyptian pottery of the Second Intermediate Period from northern Sinai and its chronological significance. In Ahituv, S., Mayer, I., Gruber, M.I., Lehmann, G., and Talshir, Z. (eds.), *All the wisdom of the East: studies in Near Eastern archaeology and history in honor of Eliezer D. Oren*. Fribourg: Fribourg Academic Press; Göttingen: Vandenhoeck & Ruprecht, 105–128.

Bietak, M., and Maguire, L. 2009. *Tell el-Dabʻa, XXI: the Cypriot pottery and its circulation in the Levant*. Vienna: Verlag der Österreichischen Akademie der Wissenschaften.

Bietak, M., Math, N., Müller, V., and Jurman, C. 2012–2013. Report on the excavations of a Hyksos palace at Tell el-Dabʻa/Avaris (23rd August–15th November 2011). *ÄL* 22/23: 17–53.

Bourriau, J. 1999. Some archaeological notes on the Kamose texts. In Leahy, A., and Tait, J. (eds.), *Studies on ancient Egypt in honour of H.S. Smith*. London: Egypt Exploration Society, 43–48.

Candelora, D. 2018. Entangled in orientalism: how the Hyksos became a race. *JEH* 11: 45–72.

Colin, F. 2005. Kamose et les Hyksos dans l'oasis de Djesdes. *BIFAO* 105: 35–47.

Collon, D., and Lehmann, M. 2011. Report on the sealings found in the 2009 excavations at Tell el- Dabʻa. *ÄL* 20: 67–70.

Collon, D., Lehmann, M., and Müller, S. 2012/13. Tell el-Dabʻa sealings, 2009–2011. *ÄL* 22/23: 95–104.

Czerny, E. 1999. *Tell el-Dab'a, IX: eine Plansiedlung des frühen Mittleren Reiches.* Vienna: Verlag der Österreichischen Akademie der Wissenschaften.

Czerny, E. 2015. *Tell el-Dab'a, XXII: der Mund der beiden Wege. Die Siedlung und der Tempelbezirk des Mittleren Reiches von 'Ezbet Ruschdi.* Vienna: Verlag der Österreichischen Akademie der Wissenschaften.

Darnell, D. 2002. Gravel of the desert and broken pots in the road: ceramic evidence from the routes between the Nile and Kharga Oasis. In Friedman, R. (ed.), *Egypt and Nubia: gifts of the desert.* London: British Museum Press, 156–177.

Darnell, J.C. 2002. Opening the narrow doors of the desert: discoveries of the Theban desert road survey. In Friedman, R. (ed.), *Egypt and Nubia: gifts of the desert.* London: British Museum Press, 132–155.

Davies, V.W. 2003. Kush in Egypt: a new historical inscription. *Sudan & Nubia* 7: 52–54.

De Souza, A. 2020. Melting pots: entanglement, appropriation, hybridity, and assertive objects between the Pan-Grave and Egyptian ceramic traditions. *JAEI* 27: 1–23.

Forstner-Müller, I. 2007. The colonization/urbanization of the tell area A/II at Tell el- Dab'a and its chronological implications. *ÄL* 17: 83–95.

Forstner-Müller, I. 2008. *Tell el-Dab'a, XVI: die Gräber des Areals A/II von Tell el-Dab'a.* Vienna: Verlag der Österreichischen Akademie der Wissenschaften.

Forstner-Müller, I. 2010a. Tombs and burial customs at Tell el-Dab'a during the late Middle Kingdom and Second Intermediate Period. In Marée, M. (ed.) 2010: 127–138.

Forstner-Müller, I. 2010b. Settlement patterns at Avaris: a study on two cases. In Bietak, M., Czerny, E., and Forstner-Müller, I. (eds.), *Cities and urbanism in ancient Egypt.* Vienna: Verlag der Österreichischen Akademie der Wissenschaften, 103–123.

Forstner-Müller, I. 2011. Ritual activity in a Hyksos palace of the 15th Dynasty (Hyksos) at Avaris. In Gundlach, R., and Spence, K. (eds.), *Palace and temple.* Wiesbaden: Harrassowitz, 1–22.

Forstner-Müller, I. 2012. The urban landscape of Avaris in the Second Intermediate Period. In Matthews, R., and Curtis, J. (eds.), *Proceedings of the 7th international congress on the archaeology of the ancient Near East, vol. 1.* Wiesbaden: Harrassowitz, 681–693.

Forstner-Müller, I. 2014. Neueste Forschungen in Tell el-Dab'a, dem antiken Avaris. *Sokar* 29: 30–45.

Forstner-Müller, I. 2015. A foundation deposit in a Hyksos palace at Avaris. In Maïla-Afeiche, A.M. (ed.), *Cult and ritual on the Levantine coast and its impact on the Eastern Mediterranean realm*. Beirut: Ministère de la Culture, Direction Générale des Antiquités, 529–538.

Forstner-Müller, I. 2021. Some remarks on the main harbour of Avaris. In Tenu, A., and Yoyotte, M. (eds.), *Le roi et le fleuve: exemples d'usages pluriels de l'espace*. Paris: Éditions Khéops, 109–123.

Forstner-Müller, I., Hassler, A., Matić, U., and Rose, P. 2015. Grabungen des Österreichischen Archäologischen Instituts Kairo in Tell el-Dab'a/Avaris, B: der Hafen von Avaris: das Areal R/IV, erster Vorbericht. *ÄL* 25: 72–88.

Forstner-Müller, I., Jeuthe, C., Michel, V., and Prell, S. 2015. Grabungen des Österreichischen Archäologischen Instituts Kairo in Tell el-Dab'a/Avaris, A: das Areal R/III, zweiter Vorbericht. *ÄL* 25: 17–71.

Forstner-Müller, I., and Moeller, N. (eds.) 2018. *The Hyksos ruler Khyan and the early Second Intermediate Period in Egypt: problems and priorities of current research*. Vienna: Holzhausen.

Forstner-Müller, I., and Müller, W. 2005. Das Phänomen der Waffengräber am Fallbeispiel von Ägypten und Rom: zur Appropriation militärischer Ausrüstung in Gesellschaften unterschiedlicher Komplexität. In Ladstätter, S., Brandt, B., and Gassner, V. (eds.), *Synergia: Festschrift für Friedrich Krinzinger*, vol. 2. Vienna: Phoibos, 199–206.

Forstner-Müller, I., and Müller, W. 2006. Die Entstehung des Hyksosstaates: Versuch einer sozioarchäologischen Modellbildung anhand der materiellen Kultur Tell el-Dab'as. In Czerny, E., Hein, I., Hunger, H., Melman, D., and Schwab, A. (eds.), *Timelines: Festschrift in honour of Manfred Bietak*. Leuven: Peeters, 93–102.

Forstner-Müller, I., Müller, W., Herbich, T., Schweitzer C., and Weißl, M. 2005. Preliminary report on the geophysical survey at 'Ezbet Rushdi/Tell el-Dab'a in spring 2004. *ÄL* 14: 101–109.

Forstner-Müller, I., and Reali, C. 2018. King Khyan and Avaris: some considerations concerning Khyan seal impressions from Area R/III at Tell el-Dab'a. In Forstner-Müller, I., and Moeller, N. (eds.) 2018: 91–124.

Forstner-Müller, I., and Rose, P. 2012. Nubian pottery at Avaris in the Second Intermediate Period and the New Kingdom: some remarks. In Forstner-Müller, I., and Rose, P. (eds.), *Nubian pottery from Egyptian cultural contexts of the Middle Kingdom and Early New Kingdom.* Vienna: Holzhausen, 181–212.

Gardiner, A.H. 1916. The defeat of the Hyksos by Kamose: the Carnarvon Tablet, no. 1. *JEA* 3: 95-110.

Gratien, B. 1978. *Les cultures Kerma: essai de classification.* Lille: Presses Universitaires du Septentrion.

Gratien, B. 2004. From Egypt to Kush: administrative practices and movements of goods during the Middle Kingdom and the Second Intermediate Period. In Kendall, T. (ed.), *Nubian Studies 1998.* Boston: Department of African-American Studies, Northeastern University, 74–82.

Gundlach, R. 1998. *Der Pharao und sein Staat: die Grundlegung der ägyptischen Königsideologie im 4. und 3. Jahrtausend.* Darmstadt: Wissenschaftliche Buchgesellschaft.

Habachi, L. 1972. *The second stela of Kamose and his struggle against the Hyksos ruler and his capital.* Glückstadt: Augustin.

Habachi, L. 2001. *Tell el‑ Dab'a, I: Tell el-Dab'a and Qantir: the site and its connection with Avaris and Piramesse.* Vienna: Verlag der Österreichischen Akademie der Wissenschaften.

Harvey, S. 1994. Monuments of Ahmose at Abydos. *EA* 4: 3–5.

Hein, I. (ed.) 1994. *Pharaonen und Fremde: Dynastien im Dunkel.* Vienna: Eigenverlag der Museen der Stadt Wien.

Helck, W. 1971. *Die Beziehungen Ägyptens zu Vorderasien im 3. und 2. Jahrtausend v. Chr.* Wiesbaden: Harrassowitz. 2nd rev. ed.

Höflmayer, F. 2018. An early date for Khyan and its implications for Eastern Mediterranean chronologies. In Forstner-Müller, I., and Moeller, N. (eds.) 2018: 91–124.

Jeuthe, C. 2015. Die Silexartefakte der Zweiten Zwischenzeit. In Forstner-Müller, I., Jeuthe, C., Michel, V., and Prell, S. 2015: 48–69.

Kopetzky, K. 1993. *Datierung der Gräber der Grabungsfläche F/I von Tell el-Dab'a anhand der Keramik.* MA thesis, University of Vienna.

Kopetzky, K. 2010. *Tell el-Dab'a, XX: die Chronologie der Siedlungskeramik der Zweiten Zwischenzeit aus Tell el-Dab'a.* Vienna: Verlag der Österreichischen Akademie der Wissenschaften.

Kopetzky, K. 2015. Some remarks on the relation between Egypt and the Levant during the late Middle Kingdom and Second Intermediate Period. In Miniaci, L., and Grajetzki, W. (eds.), *The world of Middle Kingdom Egypt (2000–1550 BC), vol. II.* London: Golden House, 143–160.

Mahmud, N.A., Faris, G., Schiestl, R., and Raue, D. 2008. Pottery of the Middle Kingdom and the Second Intermediate Period from Heliopolis. *MDAIK* 64: 189–205.

Marée, M. (ed.) 2010. *The Second Intermediate Period (Thirteenth–Seventeenth Dynasties): current research, future prospects.* Leuven: Peeters.

Matić, U. 2016. "Nubian" archers in Avaris: a study of culture historical reasoning in archaeology of Egypt. *Issues in Ethnology and Anthropology* 9: 697–721.

Moeller, N., and Forstner-Müller, I. 2018. Introduction. In Forstner-Müller, I., and Moeller, N. (eds.) 2018: 7–14.

Moeller, N., and Marouard, G. 2011. Khayan sealings from Tell Edfu. *ÄL* 21: 87–121.

Moeller, N., and Marouard, G. 2018. The context of the Khyan sealings from Tell Edfu and further implications for the Second Intermediate Period in Upper Egypt. In Forstner-Müller, I., and Moeller, N. (eds.) 2018: 173–198.

Müller, M. 2015. Late Middle Kingdom society in a neighborhood of Tell el-Dab'a /Avaris. In Müller, M. (ed.), *Household studies in complex societies: (micro) archaeological and textual approaches.* Chicago: The Oriental Institute of the University of Chicago, 339–370.

Müller, S. 2013. Rettungsgrabung 'Ezbet Rushdi/Tell el-Dab'a (Areal R/II): Vorbericht über die Grabungskampagnen 2008/2009. *ÄL* 22/23: 109–117.

Müller, V. 2008. Tell el-Dab'a, XVII: *Opferdeponierungen in der Hyksoshauptstadt Auaris (Tell el-Dab'a) vom späteren Mittleren Reich bis zum frühen Neuen Reich, I: Auswertung und Deutung der Befunde und Funde.* Vienna: Verlag der Österreichischen Akademie der Wissenschaften.

Müller, V. 2018. Chronological concepts for the Second Intermediate Period and their implication for the interpretation of its material culture. In Forstner-Müller, I., and Moeller, N. (eds.) 2018: 199–216.

Oren, E. 1997. The "Kingdom of Sharuhen" and the Hyksos kingdom. In Oren, E. (ed.), *The Hyksos: new and archaeological perspectives.* Philadelphia: University of Pennsylvania Museum of Archaeology and Anthropology, 335–367.

Peet, T.E. 1923. *The Rhind Mathematical Papyrus BM 10.057 and 10.058.* London: Hodder & Stoughton.

Philip, G. 1995. Warrior burials in the ancient Near Eastern Bronze Age: the evidence from Mesopotamia, western Iran and Syria-Palestine. In Campell,

S., and Green, A. (eds.), *The archaeology of death in the ancient Near East*. Oxford: Oxbow, 140–154.

Polz, D. 1998. Theben und Auaris. In Guksch, H., and Polz, D. (eds.), *Stationen: Beiträge zur Kulturgeschichte Ägyptens, Rainer Stadelmann gewidmet*. Mainz: Zabern, 219–231.

Polz, D. 2006. Die Hyksos-Blöcke aus Gebelên: zur Präsenz der Hyksos in Oberägypten. In Czerny, E., Hein, I., Hunger, H., Melman, D., and Schwab, A. (eds.), *Timelines: Festschrift in honour of Manfred Bietak*. Leuven: Peeters, 239–247.

Polz, D. 2007. *Der Beginn des Neuen Reiches: zur Vorgeschichte einer Zeitenwende*. Berlin: De Gruyter.

Polz, D. 2018. The territorial claim and the political role of the Theban state at the end of the Second Intermediate Period. A case study. In Forstner-Müller, I., and Moeller, N. (eds.) 2018: 217–234.

Quirke, S. 1994. Kat. Nr. 134: Mathematischer Papyrus, Rhind II. In Bietak, M., and Hein, I. (eds.) 1994: 152.

Quirke, S. 2004. Identifying officials of the fifteenth dynasty. In Bietak, M. (ed.), *Scarabs of the second millennium BC from Egypt, Nubia, Crete and the Levant: chronological and historical implications*. Vienna: Verlag der österreichischen Akademie der Wissenschaften, 171–193.

Reali, C. 2013. The seal impressions from ʿEzbet Rushdi, Area R/III of Tell el-Dabʿa: preliminary report. *ÄL* 22/23: 67–73.

Ryholt, K. 1997. *The political situation in Egypt during the Second Intermediate Period, c. 1800–1550 BC*. Copenhagen: Museum Tusculanum Press.

Ryholt, K. 2018. Seals and history of the 14th and 15th Dynasties. In Forstner-Müller, I., and Moeller, N. (eds.) 2018: 235–276.

Sartori, N. 2009. Die Siegel aus Areal F/II in Tell el-Dabʿa, erster Vorbericht. *ÄL* 19: 281–292.

Schiestl, R. 2008. Die Keramik aus der Nekropole in der Sharia Balsam und die Keramik aus dem Areal 200, Schnitt in Quadrat K 21. In Mahmud, N.A., et al. 2008: 191–205.

Schiestl, R. 2009. *Die Palastnekropole von Tell el-Dabʿa: die Gräber des Areals F/I der Straten d/2 und d/1*. Vienna: Verlag der Österreichischen Akademie der Wissenschaften.

Schneider, T. 1998. *Ausländer in Ägypten während des Mittleren Reiches und der Hyksoszeit, Teil 1: die ausländischen Könige*. Wiesbaden: Harrassowitz.

Schneider, T. 2003. *Ausländer in Ägypten während des Mittleren Reiches und der Hyksoszeit, Teil 2: die ausländische Bevölkerung*. Wiesbaden: Harrassowitz.

Schneider, T. 2006. The relative chronology of the Middle Kingdom and the Hyksos Period (Dyns. 12–17). In Hornung, E., Krauss, R., and Warburton, D. (eds.), *Ancient Egyptian chronology*. Leiden: Brill, 168–196.

Schneider, T. 2018a. Hyksos research in Egyptology and Egypt's public imagination: a brief assessment of fifty years of assessments. *JEH* 11: 73–86.

Schneider, T. 2018b. Khyan's place in history: a new look at the chronographic tradition. In Forstner-Müller, I., and Moeller, N. (eds.) 2018: 277–286.

Sethe, K. 1914. Die Lebensgeschichte des Admirals Iꜥḥmś (Amosis). In Steindorff, G. (ed.), *Urkunden der 18. Dynastie, vol. IV/1*. Leipzig: Hinrichs, 1–6.

Shirley, J.J. 2013. Crisis and restructuring of the state: from the Second Intermediate Period to the advent of the Ramesses. In Moreno García, J.C. (ed.), *Ancient Egyptian administration*. Leiden: Brill, 521–606.

Tilmann, A. 2007. *Neolithikum in der Späten Bronzezeit: Steingeräte des 2. Jahrtausends aus Auaris/Piramesse*. Mainz: Zabern.

van Koppen, F., and Lehmann, M. 2012–2013. A cuneiform sealing from Tell el-Dabʿa and its historical context. *ÄL* 22/23: 91–94.

van Koppen, F., and Radner, K. 2009. Ein Tontafelfragment aus der diplomatischen Korrespondenz der Hyksosherrscher mit Babylonien. In Bietak, M., and Forstner-Müller, I. 2009: 115–118.

von Pilgrim, C. 1996. *Elephantine, XVIII: Untersuchungen in der Stadt des Mittleren Reiches und der Zweiten Zwischenzeit*. Mainz: Zabern.

von Pilgrim, C. 2015. An authentication sealing of the "Ruler of Kush" from Elephantine.In Jiménez-Serrano, A., and von Pilgrim, C. (eds.), *From the delta to the cataract: studies dedicated to Mohamed el-Bialy*. Leiden: Brill, 218–226.

Waddell, W.G. 1964. *Manetho* (Loeb Classical Library 350). Cambridge, MA: Harvard University Press.

Wildung, D. 1994. Kat. Nr. 127: Schreibzeug, ꜥAaweserreꜥ Apophis. In Hein, I. (ed.) 1994: 152.

Wilkinson, T. 2013. *The rise and fall of ancient Egypt*. New York: Random House.

24

Upper Egypt before the
New Kingdom

Daniel Polz

24.1. Introduction and sources

In accordance with ancient Egyptian tradition and sources, the classical
mainland of Egypt (figure 24.1), extending from the First Nile Cataract
in the south to the Mediterranean Sea, is generally divided into two main
parts: Lower and Upper Egypt.[1] Each of these parts is itself subdivided
into major administrative units that vary in number over time and are
referred to as "nomes" (provinces). Upper Egypt extends from the First
Cataract (the 1st Upper Egyptian nome) to the area south of Memphis
(the 22nd Upper Egyptian nome). Lower Egypt stretches from Memphis
to the Mediterranean coast (the 1st–16th Lower Egyptian nomes).[2]
Thus, theoretically, the geographical area examined in this chapter covers the larger part of the country, the region spanning from south of
Memphis to slightly beyond modern-day Aswan. Practically, however,

---

1. The author is indebted to Cara K. Smith for correcting the English of this chapter.

2. These numbers refer to the Twelfth Dynasty list of nomes in the Karnak kiosk of
Senusret I, the so-called *Chapelle Blanche* (Lacau and Chevrier 1969: pl. 3; 42); on
the historical development of the nomes, see Helck 1974; cf. Gomaà 1986; 1987.

Daniel Polz, *Upper Egypt before the New Kingdom* In: *The Oxford History of the Ancient Near East.* Edited
by: Karen Radner, Nadine Moeller, and D. T. Potts, Oxford University Press. © Oxford University Press 2022.
DOI: 10.1093/oso/9780190687601.003.0024

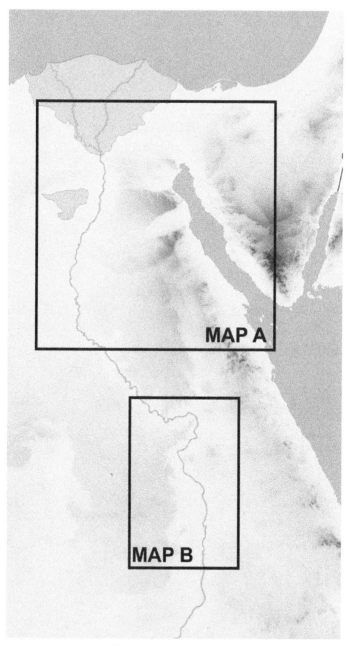

FIGURE 24.1A. Maps of sites mentioned in this chapter. Prepared by Andrea
Squitieri (LMU Munich).

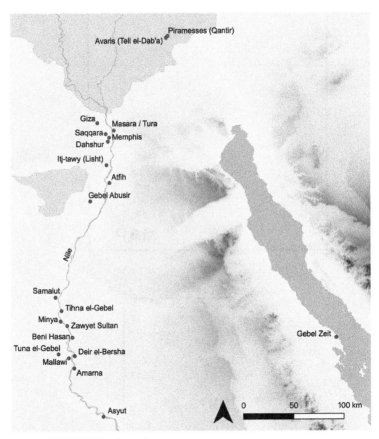

FIGURE 24.1B. Detail map A.

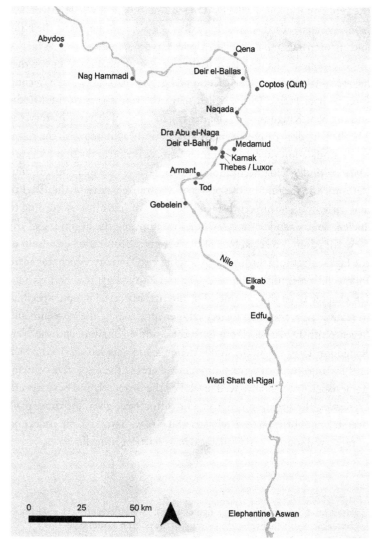

FIGURE 24.1C. Detail map B.

the geographical focus will be on the southern part of Upper Egypt, i.e., from Aswan to Abydos, covering a distance of ca. 383 km along the Nile[3] and encompassing the 1st to 8th Upper Egyptian nomes.[4]

The present chapter deals with a period of pharaonic Egypt that has occasionally been labeled one of Egypt's "dark ages,"[5] the Second Intermediate Period (SIP), which spans the time between the Middle and the New Kingdoms (cf. chapter 12). In terms of dynastic history, the Middle Kingdom can be defined as the period beginning with the country's reunification after the First Intermediate Period in the mid-Eleventh Dynasty under King Mentuhotep II (ca. 2055–2004 BC) and continuing until the decline of the powerful centralized state of the Twelfth and early to mid-Thirteenth Dynasties after ca. 1700 BC. According to ancient sources and common scholarly definition, the beginning of the New Kingdom is marked by a military event, the so-called expulsion of the Hyksos by the first rulers of the Eighteenth Dynasty, which was again followed by a reunification of Upper and Lower Egypt around 1550 BC (cf. chapter 26 in this volume). For internal historical reasons specified in section 24.2, the main focus of this chapter will be the Sixteenth and Seventeenth Dynasties. From both the Middle Kingdom and the New Kingdom, a vast corpus of source material and data has survived which enables us to reconstruct the different spheres of the respective contemporary society to an advanced level. For the Sixteenth and Seventeenth Dynasties, the situation is not so straightforward; given the time span's overall length of approximately 100 years (1650–1550 BC), the collection of preserved sources and available data is startlingly small.

---

3. Based on a summation of the figures given in Baedeker's travel guidebooks (Baedeker 1891: 78–295) for the journey up the Nile on a steamboat.

4. The occasionally applied term "Middle Egypt" does not follow an ancient geographical perception but is the modern Egyptological definition of the larger region of Minya and Asyut.

5. Cf. Shaw 2003: 11–13; on the inherent although unjustified negative connotation of the term "intermediate period" as opposed to the "kingdoms" of earlier and later times, see Franke 1988: 245–248. Cf., however, Ryholt 1997: 311–312, who sees a justification in the usage of the term "intermediate."

The main body of SIP sources consists of (a) contemporary monuments, burials, objects, and texts, such as the usually short inscriptions on funerary and (rarely) historical steles, or in decorated tombs; and (b) non-contemporary textual references to the period that can be found in documents such as the Turin King List, the king list in the temple of Karnak, an administrative text on a papyrus of late Ramesside times,[6] and in the decoration of a few non-royal tombs in the Theban necropolis.[7] In addition, Manetho's seminal (though lost) historical work *Aegyptiaca* of third century BC Ptolemaic times, and still later excerpts thereof, refer to certain aspects of the SIP.[8]

The overall small number of contemporary sources are not evenly spread over the entire period. A large portion of them consist almost exclusively of short inscriptions on scarabs or scarab-shaped seals that mention the names of royal and non-royal individuals and sometimes one or two titles of the latter group. Due to the absence of other sources, these small objects have frequently been utilized for the reconstruction of historical and chronological aspects of the period.[9]

Given the existing source material, our picture of the cultural history of the SIP is rather fragmentary. Therefore, new archaeological data can substantially alter our reconstruction of this epoch. During the past decade, the monuments of two kings who seem to have ruled over a certain part of Upper Egypt during this period have newly come to light. The first, a hitherto unknown ruler, the "King of Upper and Lower Egypt, Useribra, Son of Ra, Senebkay," had a small, decorated tomb

---

6. The Abbott Papyrus (British Museum, BM EA 10221), one of the so-called Tomb Robbery Papyri; Peet 1930: 28–45; cf. Winlock 1924; Polz and Seiler 2003: 5–10.

7. Cf. Redford 1986: 45–55.

8. Helck 1956; for Manetho's work in general and the Greek and Latin texts of its excerpts, see Waddell 1948. For a thorough contribution on Manetho and his works, see Gundaker 2018.

9. Stock 1942; von Beckerath 1964; Ryholt 1997: 34–65; Bietak and Czerny 2004. For the most recent discussion of the possible historical impact of seals and seal impressions, see the studies of Ben-Tor 2018; Forstner-Müller and Reali 2018; Moeller and Marouard 2018; Ryholt 2018: 235 (where two forthcoming contributions on the topic were announced).

erected in one of the necropolises of Abydos. According to the excavator Josef Wegner, Senebkay (and seven more unnamed royal individuals who had their tombs nearby) may be dated to the Sixteenth Dynasty or to a separate local and contemporaneous one known as the "Abydos Dynasty."[10]

The second newly identified king is, historiographically, an equally interesting case: within the precinct of the temple of Ptah at Karnak, two inscribed blocks of a monumental limestone gate were uncovered (figure 24.2) that once formed the entrance to a temple-owned granary (*shenut*).[11] The blocks show the prenomen and nomen of a Theban ruler of whom until now—with one exception[12]—only the prenomen, Senakhtenra, was known.[13] His newly discovered nomen, Ahmose (now Ahmose I), and its hieroglyphic spelling leave little doubt that he was the grandfather of the two presumed brother-kings[14] Wadjkheperra Kamose and Nebpehtyra Ahmose (now Ahmose II), whose subsequent reigns mark the classical end of the Seventeenth Dynasty and the beginning of the Eighteenth.

---

10. Wegner 2015: 71–73; 2018: 301–302. This dynasty was originally introduced into scholarly discussion by Ryholt on the basis of three royal funerary steles from Abydos (Ryholt 1997: 163–166, 264–265, 392; cf. Franke 2013: 10–11). It is under dispute whether or not this "Abydos Dynasty" really existed. The assumption would presuppose the existence of an independent local or regional center of power in the Abydos area. Given the fact that the cemeteries at Abydos have always been one of ancient Egypt's most important religious and funerary cult places (the mythical tomb of the god Osiris was located here), local rulers of the Sixteenth Dynasty with no cemetery tradition of their own may well have chosen the place for their royal interments. Recently, Wegner 2018 put forward new arguments in favor of a regional "Abydos Dynasty" that had only limited access to resources.

11. Biston-Moulin 2012; Biston-Moulin, Thiers, and Zignani 2012.

12. His name appears on a small stamp seal allegedly found in the necropolis of Dra Abu el-Naga in Western Thebes: Mariette 1872: pl. 52c; Mariette and Maspero 1889: 17.

13. Ryholt 1997: 278–280; 396–397.

14. It is still uncertain if the two kings were in fact brothers. They may have had a different family relation; see Ryholt 1997: 272–280.

FIGURE 24.2. Left door jamb of a limestone gate built by Senakhtenra Ahmose I in the precinct of the Ptah temple at Karnak (CFEETK 136053). © CNRS-CFEETK/Sébastien Biston-Moulin; photo by L. Moulié.

Clearly, these new results from archaeological enterprises do not merely add two more kings to the existing lists, but are also enlarging our historical picture of the time. They broaden our knowledge of temple-building and hence cult activities (through evidence of Ahmose I installing or reinstalling a granary for the temple of Ptah at Karnak), as well as funerary architecture and burial customs (such as Senebkay and further contemporary kings founding a local cemetery at Abydos with tombs of an unusual architectural layout).

24.2. *Chronology and dynastic history*

In light of the aforementioned scarcity of sources, the chronological scope of this chapter covers the period from the end of the Thirteenth Dynasty to the end of the Seventeenth Dynasty, with the Fourteenth and Fifteenth Dynasties being omitted here, as they refer to local rulers and the so-called Hyksos in the northern part of Egypt, respectively (cf. chapter 23 in this volume). Following Kim Ryholt's and Detlef Franke's subdivision of the long-lasting Thirteenth Dynasty into four periods of uneven length,[15] the mid-Thirteenth Dynasty marks a time when the well-organized state of the Middle Kingdom had finally collapsed. It appears that until that point, the administrative and political structure of the centralized state of the Twelfth Dynasty had not essentially changed, even in the distant Twelfth Dynasty fortresses in Nubia,[16] although a shift in the organization may be observable for some.[17] By the middle of the Thirteenth Dynasty, however, the court was no longer able to govern the entire country. Over the next 100 years or so, the Egyptian territory became parceled into smaller, partially contemporaneous entities, which were governed by regional or even local rulers. Many of these petty rulers still assumed full royal names and titles,

---

15. Franke 1988: 272–273; slightly modified in Franke 2008: 270–275, following Ryholt 1997: 296–299.

16. E.g., Raue 2019: 574–580.

17. Knoblauch 2019: 380–383.

even though their area of influence and political power may have been rather limited.

The internal dynastic chronology of the Second Intermediate Period in Upper Egypt used here largely follows Ryholt's approach.[18] Older scholarly approaches define a long Seventeenth Dynasty immediately following the Thirteenth Dynasty, the Sixteenth Dynasty completely omitted as being purely Lower Egyptian, or "Asian vassals" of the Hyksos,[19] or left unspecified.[20] In Ryholt's scheme, a first Upper Egyptian Theban Sixteenth Dynasty (with its beginning perhaps partially overlapping with the late Thirteenth Dynasty) was followed by a short second Theban Seventeenth Dynasty, more or less contemporaneous with the Fifteenth Hyksos Dynasty in Lower Egypt (cf. chapter 23).

The following paragraphs outline the key historical data on the Thirteenth, Sixteenth, and Seventeenth Dynasties. It must be emphasized that the basis for almost all considerations of the rulers of these dynasties is the (in places extremely fragmented) papyrus containing the Turin King List—a once-comprehensive list of the rulers of ancient Egypt created during the New Kingdom. It is also important to note that all recent historical interpretations of the papyrus rely on Ryholt's reassembly of certain fragments and the resulting reconstruction of the list.[21]

24.2.1. The Thirteenth Dynasty

According to Ryholt and Franke,[22] the first part of the Thirteenth Dynasty lasted from approximately 1795 to 1750 BC, with the court

---

18. Ryholt 1997.

19. von Beckerath 1997: 136.

20. E.g., von Beckerath 1964: 165–203; Hayes 1973; Franke 1988: 262–272; Dodson 1991; Helck 1992; von Beckerath 1999.

21. Cf. Ryholt 2004.

22. Ryholt 1997: 296–299; Franke 2008: 270–275; 285–287 (chronological table of the Eleventh to early Eighteenth Dynasties).

still residing at Memphis or at Itj-tawy (modern Lisht, ca. 35 km south of Memphis), and the major burial grounds being located at Saqqara and Dahshur. The second part of the dynasty (ca. 1750–1720 BC) includes some major royal players, such as the kings Sobekhotep III and IV and Neferhotep I. Interestingly, some of the more important rulers of the period emphasized their non-royal descent in short texts inscribed on scarabs. Already at this stage, the Upper Egyptian city of Elkab began to play a major political role through the family of the royal wife and queen Nubkhaes. The court still seems to have been situated in the northern part of the country, and at least some of the royals were buried there. The third part of the dynasty (ca. 1720–1680 BC) shows a strong decline in building activities and textual sources. At least one ruler was buried in the Saqqara necropolis during this time. However, this does not necessarily mean that the court still resided in the north. In Franke's opinion, "king Aya's reign . . . introduced the finale of this period and, perhaps, the beginning of the 'so-called Second Intermediate Period.'"[23]

Lastly, the fourth part of the Thirteenth Dynasty (ca. 1680–1645 BC) may have partially overlapped with the Sixteenth Dynasty in Upper Egypt. It is by no means clear where the rulers of this last part of the Thirteenth Dynasty had their main residence (if they had one at all), which part of the country they controlled, and where they were buried. The prevailing scholarly assessment of the political and cultural-historical situation at this point in time is again best illustrated in a statement by Franke:

The Dynasty ended in obscurity and with the conquest of Memphis by the Hyksos army. At least from now on, Egyptian kingship was restricted to Upper Egypt.[24]

---

23. Franke 2008: 272; cf. Davies 2010: 225 with n. 16 (with extensive bibliography).

24. Franke 2008: 273.

24.2.2. The Sixteenth Dynasty

In Upper Egypt, the Thirteenth Dynasty is followed by the first Theban, that is, the Sixteenth Dynasty (ca. 1650–1580 BC[25]), perhaps with a short overlap of unknown length. Based on Ryholt's reconstruction of column 11 of the Turin King List,[26] the dynasty comprised at least fifteen rulers who may have governed a southern Upper Egyptian rump state from the Theban area.[27] The evidence for Thebes playing a central role during this dynasty is twofold:[28]

(1) In contrast to the kings of the late Thirteenth Dynasty after Sobekhotep VII, some of the Sixteenth Dynasty rulers or contemporary non-royal persons have left monuments at Karnak (Sobekhotep VIII, Neferhotep III, Mentuhotepi, and Nebiryraw I).

(2) A number of the rulers of the Sixteenth Dynasty are listed in the Karnak King List (Djehuty, Sobekhotep VIII, Mentuhotepi, Nebiryraw I, and Bebiankh), while none of the kings of the Thirteenth Dynasty after Sobekhotep VII are listed therein.

However, contrary to their successors in the following Seventeenth Dynasty, no tombs of these Sixteenth Dynasty rulers have been found in the Theban necropolis,[29] and it seems possible that they were buried elsewhere, perhaps in their respective families' hometowns.[30] The list of

---

25. The absolute dates for the Sixteenth and Seventeenth Dynasties here and in the following are based on Shaw 2003: 484.

26. Ryholt 1997: 152–156, fig. 14 (illustration of the reconstructed column 11).

27. However, only in Eusebius's version of the Manethonian epitome, the Sixteenth Dynasty is called "Theban"; see Waddell 1948: 93; Ryholt 1997: 151.

28. Ryholt 1997: 159–162; 332–410 ("Catalogue of Attestations").

29. With one possible exception: A canopic chest inscribed with King Djehuty's name was found with the burial of his royal wife, Queen Mentuhotep, at Dra Abu el-Naga; see Ryholt 1997: 259–260; 388 (with further references).

30. E.g., in the Edfu/Elkab area or at Abydos. This may explain why in the Turin King List the Sixteenth Dynasty is separated from the Seventeenth Dynasty by one line in which a summation of regnal years is given (col. 11,15, cf. Ryholt

the rulers of the Sixteenth Dynasty includes kings with longer reigns, such as Nebiryraw I (ca. twenty-six years) and Seuserenra Bebiankh (ca. twelve years). Some rulers from outside the Theban area are also attested at Coptos, Gebelein, Elkab, and Edfu, but also as far as Gebel Zeit on the Red Sea shore.[31] This fact may indicate that their scope of political power or influence was not restricted to a mere local level. However, at a certain point after the reign of King Nebiryraw, some allied Nubian forces seem to have attempted a conquest or at least conducted a raid into southern Upper Egypt as far north as the Elkab/Edfu area.[32]

24.2.3. The Seventeenth Dynasty

According to Ryholt's reconstruction of column 11 of the Turin King List, only two lines of the kings of the Seventeenth Dynasty are preserved after the summation of the regnal years of the Sixteenth Dynasty (11,16–11,17).[33] Both lines are in a highly fragmentary state, and it seems difficult to assign specific names to the few existent hieratic signs. Since the rest of column 11 is lost, none of the rulers of the Seventeenth Dynasty are known from the Turin King List. Most of them appear, however, in the Karnak King List (see table 24.1). The dynasty lasted from ca. 1580 until 1550 BC and comprised at least nine rulers, whose relative positions have been a matter of discussion.[34]

1997: 153, fig. 14). The *Vorlage* for the Turin King List may have listed the two dynasties according to different royal capitals, with the Seventeenth Dynasty perhaps marked as "Theban." Ryholt assumes that a *"Fifteenth Dynasty conquest of Thebes"* marks the turning point between the Sixteenth and Seventeenth Dynasties (Ryholt 1997: 5, n. 8; cf. 304–309). Since there is no evidence of a Hyksos conquest of Upper Egypt (see Schneider 2006: 183; Polz 2007: 8–11; Franke 2008: 279; Allen 2010: 5), the reason for a differentiation of the two dynasties must be sought elsewhere.

31. Ryholt 1997: 159–162 with fig. 15.

32. Davies 2003a: 6; 2003b; Franke 2008: 276; cf. Polz 2018: 231 with n. 66.

33. Ryholt 1997: 153, fig. 14.

34. For an overview of the different scholarly views regarding the position of the rulers of the dynasty over the past fifty years, see Polz 2007: 7, Table 1; cf. Schneider 2006: 181–192.

Table 24.1. Sequence of rulers of the Sixteenth and
Seventeenth Dynasties and their attestations in the
Turin King List and Karnak King List

Turin King List (column, line; after Ryholt 1997; 2004)	Karnak King List (numbers after Lepsius 1842)	Royal Prenomen and **Nomen**	Approximate Dates BC (after Shaw 2003: 484)
Sixteenth Dynasty			
[10, last line(s)]		[perhaps one or more names lost]	
11,1	1	Sekhemra Sementawy **Djehuty**	1650–
11,2	44	Sekhemra Seusertawy **Sobekhotep** VIII	
11,3	—	Sekhemra Seankhtawy **Neferhotep** III	
11,4	—	Sankhenra **Mentuhotepi**	
11,5	59ᵃ	Sewadjenra **Nebiryraw** I	
11,6	—	— **Nebiryraw** II	
11,7	—	Semenenra —	
11,8	28	Seuserenra **Bebiankh**	
11,9	—	Sekhemra **Shedwaset** —	
11,10	—	—ra— (?)	
[11,11–14]		[four names lost]	–1580
[11,15]		[summation: 15(?) kings]	
Seventeenth Dynasty			
11,16		—userra (?)	
11,17		—user— (?)	
[rest of the column lost]	54	Sekhemra Wahkhau **Rahotep**	1580–

(continued)

Table 24.1. Continued

Turin King List (column, line; after Ryholt 1997; 2004)	Karnak King List (numbers after Lepsius 1842)	Royal Prenomen and Nomen	Approximate Dates BC (after Shaw 2003: 484)
—	58	Sekhemra Wadjkhau **Sobekemsaf** I	
—	48	Sekhemra Shedtawy **Sobekemsaf** II	
—	17 (?)[b]	Sekhemra Wepmaat **Intef** V	
—	27	Nubkheperra **Intef** VI	
—	—	Sekhemra Heruhermaat **Intef** VII	
—	29	Senakhtenra **Ahmose** I	
—	30	Seqenenra **Taa**	
—	—	Wadjkheperra **Kamose**	−1550
Eighteenth Dynasty			
	—	Nebpehtyra **Ahmose** II	1550−1525
	—	Djeserkara **Amenhotep** I	1525−1504

[a] Since there are two entries in the Karnak list naming the prenomen of a King Sewadjenra (nos. 33 and 59), Ryholt (1997: 389) was uncertain which one referred to Nebiryraw I. A recently published stele from Gebel Zeit (Régen and Soukiassian 2008: 56–58) leaves no doubt that no. 33 must be assigned to King Sehetepibra of the Thirteenth Dynasty, while no. 59 should pertain to Nebiryraw I (Marée 2009: col. 151–155).

[b] A King Intef at this position in the Karnak List is remarkable. In the positions 14, 15, and possibly 16, three more kings with this name are mentioned, Intef II–IV; no. 12 is a "count" Intef (= Intef I) and no. 13 a King Mentuhotep (I). All these names certainly refer to the Intef kings of the Eleventh Dynasty and their ancestors. King Intef VI of the Seventeenth Dynasty shows up under no. 27 with his name Nubkheperra. Since the third Intef king of the Seventeenth Dynasty, Intef VII, was only ephemeral and unlikely to show up in any list, the Intef of no. 17 may well refer to either Intef V of the Seventeenth Dynasty or to yet another, earlier king with the name Intef of the Thirteenth Dynasty (Ryholt 1997: 342).

The lengths of the reigns of single rulers, a subject that is heavily debated in the attempt to arrive at absolute chronological dates for the period immediately preceding the Eighteenth Dynasty, will not be dealt with here. The reconstruction of the sequence of the SIP rulers appears to be more beneficial to the historical study of this time because it is a necessary prerequisite for any further consideration of the political and historical developments. For example, it is of little relevance whether the three regnal years of King Nubkheperra Intef attested by his own monuments were indeed sufficient time to realize a somewhat extended building program, or whether one should, on the basis of his building activities, consider his reign to span additional years. A much more essential question is his exact position within the dynastic scheme of the SIP: Did he reign at the beginning of the "long" Seventeenth Dynasty, as has been proposed by a number of scholars,[35] or should he rather be placed some eighty or ninety years later, at the end of this dynasty, as suggested by others?[36]

Over the past decades, several attempts have been put forward to reconstruct the sequence of SIP rulers in Upper Egypt. The present author created a reconstruction in 2007[37] based on Ryholt's conclusions and other available data, which is, with several adaptations, reproduced here (table 24.1).[38]

Naturally, the aforementioned scarceness of sources leads to a number of uncertainties, especially regarding the dynastic relations between the group of Intef kings (Intef V–VII) and the "Ahmosides" (Ahmose I, Taa, Kamose, and Ahmose II). Before this time, no direct family ties can be established between these two groups. A number of observations,

---

35. von Beckerath 1964; Franke 1988; von Beckerath 1999.

36. Hayes 1973; Dodson 1991: 37; Helck 1992; Ryholt 1997: 265–272; for a synopsis of the quoted differing views, see Polz 2007: 5–11 with Table 1; for a comparison of the views of Franke 1988 and Ryholt 1997, see Schneider 2006: 185, fig II.7.2.

37. Polz 2007: 7, Table 1. The sequence of kings of the Sixteenth Dynasty follows mostly the reconstruction of Ryholt 1997: 151–159; 259–264.

38. The table is a compilation of the respective lists of Ryholt 1997: 153, 410; Polz 2007: 7, Table 1; and Franke 2008: 287.

however, seem to suggest rather close ties, though not necessarily through family. The four or five decades during which these Theban rulers reigned over a larger part of southern Upper Egypt also mark a period of transition from the regional kingdom of the Seventeenth Dynasty to the centralized state of the Eighteenth Dynasty. During this half century or so, all major foundations were laid for one of ancient Egypt's most dynamic and innovative eras, the New Kingdom. Therefore, a closer look at the known sources of information on the protagonists of this transitional phase and their relations to each other seems appropriate.

First, the two gilded wooden coffins of Intef V and Intef VI are so similar in style, workmanship, and decoration that one has to assume that they were manufactured at the same time and by the same workshop.[39] In addition, a short inscription on Intef V's coffin explicitly notes that his coffin was given to him by his brother Intef (that is, Intef VI). The same striking similarity can be observed in the two *pyramidia* (top stones) of the two brothers' pyramids in the necropolis of Dra Abu el-Naga in Western Thebes.[40]

The two royal coffins in turn are very similar to the coffins of Seqenenra Taa and his presumed mother and wife of Ahmose I, Queen Ahhotep (I)[41]—a fact that has been noticed previously.[42] Thus the four coffins cannot be chronologically separated from each other, all the more so considering that this group of coffins is distinctly different in style and decoration from those of the succeeding royals Ahmose II, Ahhotep II, and Ahmose Nefertari.[43]

---

39. Polz 2007: 22–34 with pls. 2–4 and 6–7; cf. Miniaci 2011b: 118–119.

40. Polz 2007: 133–138; 2010: 345–350.

41. Daressy 1909: 1–2, pls. I–II; Winlock 1924: pl. XVI.

42. Steindorff 1895: 91–95; Winlock 1924: 274–275; Hayes 1973: 70. The non-gilded wooden coffins of Heruhermaat Intef VII and Kamose are not considered here since both were originally prefabricated coffins for non-royal individuals; on the development of coffins of the time, see Miniaci 2011b: 115–127.

43. Daressy 1909: 3–4, pls. III–IV; 8–9, pls. VIII–IX.

Another somewhat oblique form of evidence may also point to the close ties between the last rulers of the Seventeenth Dynasty and those of the early Eighteenth Dynasty. At a certain point during the Seventeenth Dynasty, a change occurred in the orientation of a single hieroglyphic sign, the crescent, which was throughout pharaonic history almost invariably written in this form: ⌒. For only a short time at the end of the SIP, the sign was reversed, with the points facing up: ◡.[44] The orientation of the sign was reverted again between the eighteenth and the twenty-second year of Ahmose II's reign.[45] The sign is part of the name of the moon god *Iah* ("Ah"), and as such it is one component of both royal and non-royal Egyptian personal names of the period (e.g., Ahmose, Ahhotep, Ahnefer, etc.). The earliest currently known attestation of the up-pointing form can be found on a stele of the high military official Ahnefer from the Osiris temple area at Abydos. Ahnefer is depicted together with his king, Intef VI. The aforementioned recently discovered door frame from the Ptah temple area at Karnak is inscribed with the cartouches of Senakhtenra Ahmose I, the latter name also written with the up-pointing crescent (figure 24.2). Furthermore, the same form of the *iah*-sign also occurs on a stele of King Seqenenra Taa and a stele fragment from Karnak.[46] In short, although later sporadic examples of the reverted ◡ form are known,[47] it seems highly significant that this form occurred consistently only throughout the subsequent reigns

---

44. In Gardiner's list of the hieroglyphic signs, the former variant of the sign is labeled "crescent moon," with the latter as an "alternative form" used during the Eighteenth Dynasty; see Gardiner 1973: 486.

45. The obscure reversion of the *iah*-sign at the end of the Second Intermediate Period was already noticed by Vandersleyen 1971: 205–228, who did not have access to all of the material that is available today. With new material at hand, the time span of the reverted sign can be defined more precisely; see Polz 2007: 14–20.

46. Jacquet-Gordon 1999: 179–184 with figs. 17.2–3.

47. Seidlmayer 1991: 325–327. Almost one millennium after the beginning of the Eighteenth Dynasty, during the Twenty-sixth Dynasty, King Ahmose III (570–526 BC) had his name spelled in both forms; see von Beckerath 1999: 218–219.

of the last four rulers[48] of the Seventeenth Dynasty and the first ruler of the Eighteenth Dynasty.

Finally, a funerary stele of a non-royal individual named Iuf from a cemetery at Edfu[49] may also indicate the closer dynastic, if not genealogical relations, of the Intef and Ahmoside families at the end of the Seventeenth and the beginning of the Eighteenth Dynasties: from the inscriptions on this stele, it is obvious that the wife of King Intef VI, Queen Sobekemsaf, had her royal tomb in a cemetery at Edfu. The priest Iuf was ordered by Queen Ahhotep, the mother of King Ahmose II, to restore this tomb after it had begun to decay. Both queens are depicted sitting on a stool, with Queen Sobekemsaf embracing Queen Ahhotep beside her, indicating a close relation of the two royal women.[50]

Returning to the first part of the Seventeenth Dynasty, through a number of more recent discoveries and new interpretations of long known objects, it seems possible to establish with a fair amount of plausibility genealogical ties between the group of Intef kings and their predecessors Sobekemsaf I and II.[51] A pivotal point was the discovery in 1992 of several decorated and inscribed sandstone blocks in the mountainous region west of the Theban necropolis.[52] These blocks seem to

---

48. Heruhermaat Intef VII must be disregarded in this discussion since the only known object that can be ascribed to him is his coffin, in whose short inscription the word *iah* does not appear.

49. Cairo Museum, CG 34009: Lacau 1909: 16–17, pl. VI (right).

50. Polz 2007: 38–42. Queen Sobekemsaf is also named and depicted on another stele fragment from Edfu (Polz 2018: 229–230 with figs. 14–15). The masculine instead of the feminine form of the queen's name (Sobekemsa*f* instead of Sobekemsa*s*) may also be indicative of her relation to the two Sobekemsaf kings, with one of them supposedly being her father; in the stele's inscriptions, Queen Sobekemsaf bears the titles of "king's wife, king's sister, and king's daughter"; see Lacau 1909: 16–17.

51. Polz 2007: 45–50.

52. Darnell and Darnell 1993: 49–52, fig. 4 (left door jamb); Polz 2018: 226, fig. 11 (left and right door jambs).

have been part of a small sanctuary which was constructed by Intef VI. Two of them are fragments of this building's door frame. The inscription on the left door jamb mentions King [Nubkheperra] Intef, son of a King Sobekem[saf]. The much destroyed text on the right door jamb can be read as "born of the king's mother and [king's] wife." Without doubt, Intef VI is of royal descent, and son of one of the two known kings of the dynasty with the name Sobekemsaf. For a number of reasons detailed elsewhere, this king can only be Sobekemsaf II.[53] Since he himself is most likely the son of Sobekemsaf I, a close genealogical relation of the two Sobekemsaf kings and the two Intef kings can be established; as mentioned earlier, Intef V's coffin was prepared for him by his brother, Intef VI.

On the basis of these reconstructed genealogical ties and with regard to the question of dynastic continuity or discontinuity, it is obvious that there are clear indications for an uninterrupted sequence of rulers belonging to one family spanning from the time of Ahmose I to Amenhotep I (table 24.2). Therefore, the dynastic break between the Seventeenth and the Eighteenth Dynasties, as indicated in the Manethonian epitome, is not caused by an interrupted family line. This hiatus owes its existence to a new political situation: the aforementioned expulsion of the Hyksos and the subsequent reunification of the country, which is discussed in more detail in section 24.6.

24.3. Territory

Any attempt to establish the geographical sphere of influence, that is, the territorial claim of a ruler or a group of rulers during the SIP, meets with a number of obstacles, and the scarcity of available data may lead to an overinterpretation of the data that is available. For example, one ruler of the Sixteenth Dynasty, Seuserenra Bebiankh, seems to be mentioned in the Karnak King List (no. 28) and in the Turin King List (11,8), both

---

53. Polz 2007: 34–38.

Table 24.2. Reconstructed genealogical relations of the kings of the
Seventeenth Dynasty

King	Genealogical Relation to Predecessor	Genealogical Relation to Successor
Seventeenth Dynasty		
—userra (?)	—	—
—user— (?)	—	—
Sekhemra Wahkhau Rahotep	unknown	father?
Sekhemra Wadjkhau Sobekemsaf I	son?	father
Sekhemra Shedtawy Sobekemsaf II	son	father
Sekhemra Wepmaat Intef V	son	brother
Nubkheperra Intef VI	brother	unknown
Sekhemra Heruhermaat Intef VII	unknown	unknown
Senakhtenra Ahmose I	unknown	father
Seqenenra Taa	son	father
Wadjkheperra Kamose	son	brother?
Eighteenth Dynasty		
Nebpehtyra Ahmose II *	brother?	father
Djeserkara Amenhotep I	son	—

* Ahmose II was either the brother or nephew of Kamose; his grandmother, Tetisheri,
was the wife of either Senakhtenra or Seqenenra.

being non-contemporaneous sources. Currently, Bebiankh is known
from only two contemporaneous objects: a stele found in the galena
mines at Gebel Zeit on the Red Sea,[54] and an inscribed bronze dagger,

---

54. Polz 2007: 93–94; Régen and Soukiassian 2008: 18–20, 57, 62; Marée 2009: 157–
159 with fig. 6.

allegedly from a tomb at Naqada.[55] The stele, being per se an immobile or stationary object tied to a certain place, provides evidence for activities at Gebel Zeit during his reign. The dagger, being a mobile and valuable object meant to be carried and perhaps passed on over generations, could have arrived at Naqada at a later date; therefore, it must be disregarded as a means to define the scope of Bebiankh's sphere of influence. The range of the king's activities and influence as attested so far is thus limited to Thebes and the Red Sea shore, including, of course, the caravan routes to and from Gebel Zeit through the Wadi Qena and/or the Wadi Hammamat.

Our archaeological knowledge of ancient Egypt does not evenly encompass all periods and regions. While certain parts of the country have experienced thorough and long-lasting archaeological examinations (e.g., the larger Giza and Saqqara areas, Minya, Amarna, Abydos, Luxor, etc.), other parts have been investigated only randomly or even neglected (e.g., parts of the delta, the Western and Eastern Deserts, larger areas of Middle and Upper Egypt outside the central temples, settlements, cemeteries, etc.). This uneven pattern of examination has led to a large number of archaeological white spots dispersed over the country for which insufficient data are available. With respect to the SIP, this situation is illustrated by the results of two extended systematic surveys conducted during the mid-1970s to early 1980s, when a larger portion of Middle Egypt was investigated by a team from Tübingen University.[56] The aim of this historical-topographical investigation was the location of larger settlements on the basis of ancient Egyptian lists of toponyms (the onomasticon of Amenemope and the Wilbour Papyrus).[57] The overall survey area stretches approximately 170 km along the Nile between the (modern) towns of Mallawi and Samalut in the south and between Samalut and Gebel Abusir (at the entrance to the Fayum) in the north. The surveyed area comprises the sites of major ancient settlements and

---

55. British Museum, BM EA 66062: Budge 1892: 93; Ryholt 1997: 390.

56. Kessler 1981.

57. Gardiner 1947; Gardiner and Faulkner 1941–1952.

necropolises such as Deir el-Bersha, Tuna el-Gebel, Beni Hasan, Zawyet
Sultan, Minya, Tihna el-Gebel, etc.

According to its published results,[58] the Tübingen survey yielded
material from practically every period of pharaonic Egypt from the late
Old Kingdom through Ptolemaic times except for the SIP, which appears
to be almost nonexistent in the region's material culture. During the survey, no substantial objects or installations were identified which could be
ascribed with certainty to the time of a SIP ruler known from the king
lists or from the monuments of other sites in Egypt. This remarkable
absence of finds persists in the regions to the south and the north of the
Tübingen survey's coverage area. As Ryholt's meticulous catalogue of the
attestations of SIP rulers shows, only very few kings of the Thirteenth,
Sixteenth, and Seventeenth Dynasties are known to have left monuments in the area spanning from south of Lisht in the north to Abydos
in the south,[59] covering approximately 521 km of length along the Nile.[60]

The impression given by this absence of SIP monuments, of course,
can hardly be correct, as it is not conceivable that a region of this size
was unsettled for such a long period of time. It can be presumed that in
many settlement sites, heavy strata of New Kingdom and later occupation times superimpose those dating to the SIP, making the latter almost
untraceable by surface survey. Only through extended settlement excavations would it be possible to gain a clearer picture of both the occupational situation in Middle Egypt during the SIP and the respective areas
of influence of its local or regional potentates. Until such excavations
are carried out, however, one has to live with the notion that the SIP
rulers of the Thirteenth, Sixteenth, and Seventeenth Dynasties were not

---

58. Kessler 1981; Gomaá 1986; 1987; Gomaá et al. 1991. Note also the maps B II 1–4
    of the *Tübinger Atlas des Vorderen Orients* (*TAVO*); for the Second Intermediate
    Period, see especially map B II 4.

59. E.g., Sobekhotep IV in Atfih (22nd, northernmost Upper Egyptian
    nome): Ryholt 1997: 349, 352 ("it is notable that his reign is the best attested of
    the entire SIP"—perhaps not a surprise).

60. Calculated from the distances on a steamboat or a sailing boat (*dahabiyya*) given
    by Baedeker 1891: 17, 51.

actively engaged in the region to the extent that would have resulted in attributable sacral, funerary, or administrative buildings.

24.4. *Official building work and other activities*

In general, the presence or absence of official building activities during the time under review here is regarded as indicative of the court's access to manpower, resources, and means of transportation and logistics; hence, it is an indicator for the availability of economic resources in the broadest sense. These building activities comprise sacral constructions (temples, chapels, sanctuaries, but also the endowment of steles and statues, etc.) and profane constructions (palaces, fortifications, storehouses, granaries, food-producing facilities, etc.). Throughout ancient Egypt, the former are predominantly built with stone,[61] whereas the latter are constructed with unfired mudbricks. Since stone-built structures are likely to be decorated and/or inscribed, their remains in the archaeological record are often easier to attribute to a certain period or ruler than mudbrick buildings.

Admittedly, the interpretation of the remains of official building activities is strongly dependent on archaeological chance. This may be exemplified by the following case. On the basis of the number and quality of the objects and built legacy of the Seventeenth Dynasty ruler Sobekemsaf II, one would conclude that he did not have sufficient means or opportunity to carry out substantial building activities. However, an administrative document of much later times, the already mentioned Abbott Papyrus, relates that Sobekemsaf II had left "*ten important works/ monuments (weput denesut/menu)*" in the temple of Karnak that were still present some 450 years after the king had commissioned them.[62]

In spite of the uncertainty of the archaeological record, a closer look at the known architectural elements and other remains seems to indicate

---

61. Arnold 1991: 3–5.

62. Peet 1930: 41 with n. 19; pl. III, 6, line 4.

only very modest building activities during the Sixteenth Dynasty. A number of rulers are known to have erected steles in Karnak (Djehuty, Sobekhotep VIII, Neferhotep III, Mentuhotepi, and a non-royal person contemporary with Nebiryraw I), but these were presumably set up within the long-existing temple complex of the Middle Kingdom. Architectural blocks attested to this dynasty are found at various places in southern Upper Egypt (at Deir el-Ballas,[63] Edfu, Elkab).[64] They are mostly of unknown context and purpose, although some may have been parts of stone gates.[65]

During the course of the following (Seventeenth) Dynasty, the picture becomes clearer.[66] At the beginning of the dynasty, King Rahotep ordered restorations to be made in the Osiris temple at Abydos ("renewal work on the enclosure wall"[67]) and the temple of Min at Coptos. At this point, it must be emphasized that this and all other "restorations" of sacred buildings in ancient Egypt were not carried out with the modern sense of "historic monument preservation" in mind. Instead, they primarily aimed at reinstalling the technical, architectural, and economic basis for the cult of the gods and goddesses in the temples, shrines, and sanctuaries.[68]

Rahotep's successor, Sobekemsaf I, endowed an almost life-size granite statue to the Osiris temple at Abydos, and restored and enlarged the temples of the god Montu at Medamud and Tod. Presumably, he erected a small building at Karnak to which he also endowed a statue and a pair

---

63. A small limestone block with the prenomen and nomen of King Djehuty seems to have originally come from this site and may point to an occupation of Deir el-Ballas as early as the early Sixteenth Dynasty (cf. Eder 2002: 139; Polz 2007: 76).

64. Ryholt 1997: 388–391.

65. The blocks of Djehuty in Edfu could have belonged to a small chapel, see Falk et al. 1985: 15–23; Dodson 1994: 32 (photograph).

66. For specific evidence of the activities of the Seventeenth Dynasty rulers listed in the following, see Ryholt 1997: 392–400; Polz 2007: 61–95 (both with further references).

67. Polz 2007: 62–63, 315, fig. 88.

68. On pharaonic dedication and restoration texts in general, see Grallert 2001.

of miniature obelisks. He also appears to have been active in the temple of the Eleventh Dynasty ruler Mentuhotep II at Deir el-Bahri. In addition, he commissioned an expedition to the quarries in the Wadi Hammamat to procure stone, along with perhaps another expedition to the region of Wadi Shatt el-Rigal, where a graffito of the royal name Sobekemsaf is preserved.[69] Moreover, a small shrine or *naos* found at Gebelein, as well as the lower part of a double statue on the island of Elephantine (with doubtful provenience), are inscribed with his name. The case of his presumed son and successor Sobekemsaf II has already been mentioned. His successor Intef V is known only from objects connected with his pyramid and burial at Dra Abu el-Naga on the Theban West Bank.

During the reign of Intef V's brother and successor Intef VI, a distinct increase in building and other activities is observable.[70] Small stone-built and decorated chapels were erected in the old Osiris temple at Abydos and the Min temple at Coptos (figure 24.3); a small sanctuary was built on the Theban end of the Farshut Road, a montane track on the plateau of the Western Desert leading from Luxor to the Nag Hammadi area and cutting short the Nile bend between Armant and Nag Hammadi. Intef VI endowed several steles to the temple of Karnak and a statue to the Mentuhotep temple at Deir el-Bahri. Additionally, he had an elaborate burial for himself constructed in the necropolis of Dra Abu el-Naga in Western Thebes, including a small mudbrick pyramid with an inscribed limestone capstone (*pyramidion*) and two mid-size obelisks. A pyramidion of the same size and executed in the same style bearing the names of Intef V housed at the British Museum in London indicates that Intef VI had also organized a similarly shaped burial for his elder brother and predecessor. A number of contemporary high officials are known to have erected steles in the Osiris temple at Abydos (Ahnefer and Nakht) and in Edfu (Hornakht), as well as at a small funerary chapel close to the king's pyramid at Dra Abu el-Naga (Teti). All of these monuments display

---

69. Since the graffito only gives the nomen of a King Sobekemsaf and no prenomen, the inscription could theoretically also refer to his successor, Sobekemsaf II; see Polz 2007: 91–92.

70. The following is based on the more detailed discussion in Polz 2018.

FIGURE 24.3. Limestone block showing the god Min with King Intef VI behind him; from Intef VI's sanctuary in the temple of Min at Coptos (UC 14780). Courtesy of the Petrie Museum of Egyptian Archaeology, University College London; photo by Mary Hinkley.

the king's name. From the aforementioned chapel on the Farshut Road, from a royal decree on a wall of the Middle Kingdom temple of Min at Coptos, and from a stele found in the galena mines at Gebel Zeit on the Red Sea shore, one can infer that the routes leading through the Western and Eastern Deserts in Upper Egypt had once again come under the control of the Theban court during the reign of Intef VI.

For the first time during the SIP, the name of a temple or chapel connected with a contemporaneous ruler seems to be preserved. On the stele of Nakht from the Osiris temple at Abydos mentioned earlier, the high official is depicted together with his king, Intef VI.[71] In the stele's

---

71. Polz 2018: 225–226, fig. 10.

inscriptions, a "temple of Intef in Abydos" (*hut Ini-itef em abedju*) is mentioned, presumably referring to the chapel that Intef VI had erected there and in whose vicinity the stele was found. This chapel may also be mentioned in a literary text (the so-called harper's song), probably dating to the same period.[72] In addition, another mention of the same building with a slightly different name might occur on a hitherto unpublished stele of an individual called Iuy, whose father held the position of a "great funerary priest in the House of Intef" (*hem-ka aa en per Ini-itef*; figure 24.4).

Intef VI's successor, Intef VII, seems to have been an ephemeral ruler of whom only his wooden, non-royal coffin is known. The next king in line, Ahmose I, is now known from two architectural blocks, which were discovered recently in the area of the Ptah temple at Karnak.[73] These limestone blocks are parts of a gate, newly erected by the king for the granary of Karnak's main god, Amun-Ra (figure 24.2). Ahmose's successor, Seqenenra Taa, endowed a number of steles to the Karnak temple, and he may have erected or decorated a limestone gate at the Northern Palace at Deir el-Ballas (cf. section 24.5).[74]

The last king of the Seventeenth Dynasty, Kamose, set up his famous three steles, known as the "Kamose Steles," at Karnak (one of them being a reused limestone pillar of a chapel of the Twelfth Dynasty King Senusret I[75]) and endowed a *naos* to the temple. Two rock inscriptions at the Nubian sites of Toshka East and Arminna East that mention his name together with the name of his successor Ahmose II have been interpreted as proof of military activities in the region by the time of Kamose, but the historicity of this campaign has been questioned.[76]

At an undetermined point in time during the SIP, two large-scale non-sacral mudbrick buildings were erected near the modern site of Deir

72. Polz 2003: 84–86.

73. Biston-Moulin 2012.

74. Lacovara 1997: 14–15; Eder 2002: 139; Polz 2007: 76–77, 347–348.

75. Habachi 1972: 28–30.

76. Krauss 1993: 19–25.

FIGURE 24.4. Stele of the official Iuy mentioning his father Amunaa, a priest in the temple of King Intef (VI?). Modern cast of the now lost stele, formerly in the Museum of Tallinn (Helsinki NM 14560:26). © The Finnish Heritage Agency, Archaeological Collections; photo by Ilari Järvinen.

el-Ballas (on the West Bank of the Nile, ca. 6 km northwest of Coptos, i.e., modern Quft, on the East Bank). Both were called "palaces" by the original excavator George Reisner, but only the Northern Palace displays the architecture of a royal building of this type.[77] The Southern Palace

77. Lacovara 1997: 2–3.

was constructed as a massive platform, which has been interpreted as some kind of watchtower where the activities on the Nile and in the nearby harbor of Coptos could be observed.[78] The presence of a large royal palace, an extended settlement or even city surrounding it, and the solid observation point indicates, at the end of the Second Intermediate Period, in the words of Peter Lacovara, "the strategic importance of the site at the crossroads of the Wadi Hammamat and Western Desert routes and neighboring Coptos."[79]

However, there seems to be no trace thus far of a larger temple or sanctuary at Deir el-Ballas, as one would expect at a site of such importance. Deir el-Ballas must be viewed in connection with the larger city of Coptos on the opposite side of the Nile (as discussed in section 24.5), and it has been suggested that the two cities may well have functioned as a temporary capital that was military in character, at least for the last rulers of the Seventeenth Dynasty.[80]

24.5. On the organization of the state

Over the past twenty years, a number of publications have discussed several aspects of the organization and administration of the ancient Egyptian state at various periods and places,[81] including some with a special focus on the SIP in Upper Egypt (i.e., the Sixteenth and Seventeenth Dynasties).[82] As with the topics dealt with so far, the data that would be required for an attempt to reconstruct the organization of the state during this time are shown to be neither homogeneous nor plentiful when compared to those of the Twelfth and Eighteenth Dynasties. However,

---

78. Lacovara 2018: 283–284 with figs. 4–5.

79. Lacovara 2018: 288.

80. Polz 1998: 225–226, 229.

81. E.g., Grajetzki 2003; 2009; Moreno García (ed.) 2013; Moreno García 2019; cf. also Gundlach and Taylor (eds.) 2009; Gundlach and Spence (eds.) 2011.

82. Ryholt 1997; Polz 2007; Marée 2010; Miniaci 2011a; Shirley 2013; Ilin-Tomich 2014; Polz 2018.

the crucial points of development can be outlined as follows. In the heyday of the Middle Kingdom during the Twelfth Dynasty, the country—
including the Nubian territories in the south—was organized as a
centralized state, which was governed from the capital Itj-tawy in a very
efficient and well-structured fashion (cf. chapter 19 in volume 2). Below
the king and the royal sphere, the highest-ranking administrative entity
was the office of the vizier, the head of the country's civil administration.[83]
According to an early Eighteenth Dynasty meticulous textual description
of the vizier's duties,[84] the three most important of his manifold responsibilities being the (1) "managing director of the *per nesut*" (i.e., the "royal
palace"), (2) "head of the civil administration," and (3) "king's deputy."[85]
Further high-ranking officials with state-wide duties and responsibilities
on the level below the vizier include, among others, the "royal sealer"
(*khetemeti biti*), the "treasurer" (*imi-ra khetemet*), the "overseer of troops"
(*imi-ra mesha*), and the "overseer of sealers" (*imi-ra khetemetiu*).[86]

From a structural point of view, this well-established and fully functional administrative system survived the end of the Twelfth Dynasty and
continued to exist until well into the Thirteenth Dynasty, and even into
the Sixteenth Upper Egyptian Dynasty. For example, the last attested
vizier before the New Kingdom in Upper Egypt held this office during
the reign of Nebiryraw I.[87] A remarkable parallel development can be

---

83. At times, the vizier's office seems to have been split in two, with a southern vizier
and a northern vizier in charge concurrently and responsible for Lower Egypt
and Upper Egypt, respectively: van den Boorn 1988: 335; Grajetzki 2009: 22–23.

84. The most completely preserved version of the text was found in the tomb of
Rekhmira at Thebes (TT 100); it has been proposed by van den Boorn 1988: 375
to view these "Duties of the Vizier" as a genuine work of the "second half of the
reign of Ahmose [II]," and not, as previously assumed, a text of Middle Kingdom
times; see van den Boorn 1988: 333–374. But this has not been universally
accepted, and more recently the text's origin has again been dated back to the
Middle Kingdom: e.g., Pardey 2003; Grajetzki 2009: 16; 2013: 228–232; Quirke
2004: 18–24.

85. van den Boorn 1988: 310–324.

86. Grajetzki 2000: 43–78, 116–129, 146–157; 2010: 305.

87. Grajetzki 2000: 30 (I.34); 2009: 41; Shirley 2013: 549–552.

detected in the utilization of a fundamental technical and economic tool of ancient Egyptian administration, i.e., the stamp seal. During the preceding periods of the Middle Kingdom, and the Thirteenth, Fourteenth, and Fifteenth Dynasties, these often scarab-shaped seals were produced and used abundantly.[88] The last attested and securely dated royal seals currently known were produced during the reign of King Merneferra Ay of the mid-Thirteenth Dynasty,[89] who was also the last monarch of the Thirteenth Dynasty known to have left monuments in both Upper and Lower Egypt.[90]

During the later Sixteenth Dynasty and throughout the Seventeenth, no more viziers are attested, and seals seem to have been no longer used in Upper Egypt's administration.[91] The reasons for these noticeable changes were presumably manifold; one obvious reason may have been the geopolitical fact that the overall size of the parceled Upper Egyptian state's area both during the later Thirteenth Dynasty and the Sixteenth to Seventeenth Dynasties was drastically reduced; thus, the institution of the vizier's office and his responsibilities may have become superfluous.[92]

However, many if not most of the other crucial administrative offices below the vizier's level must have been functional even in the fragmented rump state of the later SIP. This is evidenced by the fact that quite a few of the aforementioned officials' titles remained in use throughout the Sixteenth and Seventeenth Dynasties. But the comparatively few known sources also seem to indicate a shift in the weighting of functions and, accordingly, of titles. Evidently, the military component of the royal

---

88. Ryholt 1997: 34–65; Ben-Tor 2004; Shirley 2013: 526–536 (with Table 1). Cf. the recent seriation of seals and seal impressions by Ryholt 2018.

89. Ryholt 1997: 354–356; cf. Grajetzki 2010: 305.

90. Ben-Tor 2004: 28.

91. von Pilgrim 1996: 252–254; Polz 2007: 307; Shirley 2013: 546–556.

92. Cf. Shirley 2013: 537. The first known vizier after the Second Intermediate Period is attested only after the reunification of the country during the reign of Ahmose II was completed: Imhotep held this office under the reign of Thutmose I: Helck 1958: 285; 433; cf. Leblanc 1989: 89 (index *s.v.* Imhotep).

administration gained importance, and an age-old title, "king's son" (*sa nesut*), begins to appear more frequently.[93] Throughout the majority of the SIP, this title was certainly not referring to the royal descent of the official on whom the king had bestowed it; instead, the title was indicative of a very intimate relationship to the ruler who entrusted his "royal sons" with special duties and essential responsibilities[94] that in some cases may have included those entrusted to the vizier at earlier times.

Regarding the civil administration of the Upper Egyptian state, it appears that the presumed highest officials' titles similarly reflect "old" Middle Kingdom customs. On the decorated walls of a small mud-brick funerary chapel in the immediate vicinity of the pyramid of King Nubkheperra Intef of the Seventeenth Dynasty (figure 24.5),[95] its owner Teti lists his main titles, which do not include any military capacities: "hereditary prince, count, royal sealer, sole companion, treasurer" (*iri-pat, hati-a, khetemeti-biti, semer wati, imi-ra khetemet*). Given the uniquely privileged position of his chapel beside the pyramid of his king in the necropolis of Dra Abu el-Naga in Western Thebes, one is inclined to assume that Teti held one of the most prominent, if not the highest, positions in the civil administration of his ruler's court at the time.[96]

A regularly recurring question aims to determine the physical structure(s) and the place(s) from which Upper Egypt was ruled by the kings of the Sixteenth and Seventeenth Dynasties or, in other words, the king's residence.[97] As has been stated earlier, during the Twelfth and at least the first half of the Thirteenth Dynasties, the country was ruled from the royal residence at Lisht or, more generally, the Memphite area. There are indications that this location was indeed used as a residence

---

93. On the history of the title, see Schmitz 1976; cf. Spalinger 2013: 423.

94. Occasionally, this title appears with specific complements pointing to a particular relation with the king, e.g., "king's son of the ruler Intef" (Polz 2018: 225, fig. 9) and "king's son of the victorious [ruler]" (Polz 2018: 227).

95. Polz and Seiler 2003: 10–14; Polz 2018: 227–229.

96. Polz 2018: 227–229.

97. As discussed by Ryholt 1997: 69–183 and, more recently, Hagen 2016: 155–158 (with further references).

FIGURE 24.5. Decorated wall of the chapel of the treasurer Teti beside the pyramid of King Intef VI in the necropolis of Dra Abu el-Naga/Western Thebes. © German Archaeological Institute Cairo; *Structure from Motion* image by Christine Ruppert.

for the later part of the Thirteenth Dynasty as well,[98] although the kings may not have reigned over the entire country at that time.[99] In spite of

---

98. Ryholt 1997: 79–80.

99. Cf. the interesting stele of the priest Horemkhawef from Hierakonpolis, in whose text he reports how he received two new statues at Lisht (Itj-tawy) in the presence of the king himself. The king's name is not given, but a dating of Horemkhawef's stele to the very end of the Thirteenth Dynasty can be established with a fair amount of plausibility; see Ryholt 1997: 79–80; Davies 2010: 225 with n. 16–17.

the statements in some versions of the Manethonian epitome that the Sixteenth and the Seventeenth Dynasties were of Theban origin[100] and of modern scholars' tendencies to follow this assertion, there are no clear textual or archaeological signs in the contemporary sources of a permanent royal residence in the Theban area.

One should, perhaps, consider the question of a "residence" at the time from a different angle.[101] Earlier, in section 24.4, there was given a list of the main places in Upper Egypt where the activities of rulers of the Sixteenth and Seventeenth Dynasties are attested (e.g., Abydos, Deir el-Ballas/Coptos, Thebes, Gebelein, Esna/Edfu). Each of these places was of more than merely local or temporary importance, but held importance both before and after this period as well. In the immediate vicinity of some of these places (e.g., Edfu South, Hierakonpolis North, Ombos/Naqada, Abydos South), King Huni or Sneferu of the Fourth Dynasty had small and solid stone pyramids erected, evidently as signs of the royal claim to power and territory.[102] Additionally, it is interesting to note that some of these places were also used for royal burials during the Sixteenth and Seventeenth Dynasties. Queen Mentuhotep, wife of the Sixteenth Dynasty ruler Djehuty, was buried in the Theban necropolis, although no ruler of this dynasty is known to have been buried there; their burial places remain unknown. The wife of King Intef VI, Queen Sobekemsaf, was buried in the necropolis of Edfu, whereas his own burial and that of his brother and predecessor Intef V—both including small pyramids—were located in the Theban necropolis. The grandmother of King Ahmose II, Queen Tetisheri, also seems to have had her tomb there; however, a chapel in the shape of a pyramid was

---

100. According to Eusebius's version, the Sixteenth Dynasty comes from Thebes, and following Africanus' version, the Seventeenth Dynasty likewise consists of Theban rulers; see Waddell 1948: 93–95; Ryholt 1997: 5; 323–325; cf. Redford 1986: 240.

101. Cf. Raven 2009: especially 153–155, who generally questions the existence of just one royal residence or capital at New Kingdom times.

102. Polz 2019: 67–68 (with further references).

built for her at Abydos,[103] and quite a number of rulers of the Sixteenth Dynasty were interred at Abydos as well.[104]

The wide geographical spread of these building activities and royal burial places in Upper Egypt during the Sixteenth and Seventeenth Dynasties may have been the result of two different but closely connected developments:

(1) On a local or limited regional level, the places mentioned were administered and controlled by members of certain families or groups, in some cases continuously over several generations (as evidenced in the *stèle juridique* and in several tombs in Elkab).[105]

(2) The Theban rulers of these dynasties, whose origins are in most cases unknown, must ultimately have come from one or more of these families or groups, and naturally did not have an established permanent royal residence at their disposal. Following routine local or regional administrative needs (jurisdiction, irrigation matters, building projects, religious and cult issues, etc.), the rulers would have had to move from one of these centers to the next within their territory,[106] together with their presumably voluminous administrative entourage.[107]

This, in turn, would have made it necessary for the court to have permanent and/or temporary but sufficiently large installations in which to reside. Archaeologically, there currently seems to be no clearly

---

103. Polz 2007: 100 (with further references); 2019: 65–66 with fig. 33.

104. For the rulers of the so-called Abydos Dynasty, see Wegner 2015; 2018.

105. The prosopographical data from the Elkab tombs of Renseneb and Sobeknakht are a vivid example of long-lasting local "dynasties" of high officials with marriage connections to the ruling royal family; see the recent meticulous reconstruction of their family trees over several generations by Davies 2010: 234–235 with fig. 10.

106. Bietak 2018: 23–24.

107. For a different point of view concerning the size of the traveling entourage, see Raven 2004: 154.

identified remains of such installations except for one: the already mentioned North Palace at Deir el-Ballas, opposite the old city and temple of Coptos. Here, it seems that we are looking at a relatively short-lived but elaborately constructed royal building complex that was erected and used during the SIP, featuring a number of non-royal houses of different sizes, including "villas," and supposedly, therefore, belonging to members of higher social levels.[108] The so-called South Palace, some 1,000 meters south of this complex and featuring a huge platform constructed of mud-bricks in the same casemate technique as the North Palace, may well have functioned as a location for the execution of some of the aforementioned administrative needs. These installations, together, could have served as a temporary seat of the Upper Egyptian government.[109]

The system of a traveling kingdom (German *Reisekönigtum*)[110] displays close parallels to a similar way of ruling a territory that was newly established in Central Europe during the time of the Carolingian dynasty (eighth–tenth century AD) and remained in place until late medieval times. Here, the so-called *Königspfalzen* ("royal palaces," from Latin "palatium") were dispersed across the emperors' territories and regularly visited by them and their large entourages.[111] Among others, the *Königspfalzen* have served a number of basic purposes that closely mirror the purposes of those parallel structures from the Second Intermediate Period described earlier; in the words of Egon Wamers, "In spite of all the variations . . . , a constant triad of worldly representation, religious

---

108. Lacovara 2018: 283–284 (as opposed to the houses in the workmen's village further south, see plan in fig. 2); 1990: 3–4 with figs. 1.2, 1.10; plans 3 and 5.

109. The South Palace has been interpreted as a platform from which ship movements on the Nile were observed during quarrels with the Hyksos; this may have been an additional purpose, but the huge construction with its "broad flight of stairs" appears to be too elaborate to have served solely as an observation post (Lacovara 1990: 5 with fig. 1.14, plan 4; pl. VIIa–b; 2018: 283–286 with figs. 4–5).

110. Köpp-Junk 2015: 231–232, 307; Hagen 2016: 156–158 (both with further references to the traveling kingdom in medieval Europe).

111. E.g., Blaich 2013: 117–120; Ehlers 2016.

cult practice and economical power is always discernible," and they also "served a function within the court offices."[112]

The titles of some of the high officials present when the king resided in the *Pfalzen* indicate that they were responsible for the basic functions of the medieval court; these strongly resemble the titles of the key positions in the Middle Kingdom court and the SIP rump state's administration mentioned earlier.[113]

In a recent contribution, Fredrik Hagen has argued that the installation of the "traveling kingdom" continued to be in use to a certain extent through the following New Kingdom's Eighteenth to Twentieth Dynasties, in spite of the existence of certain centers in Egypt which, in their basic character, could be labeled "residences" (e.g., at Thebes, Memphis, and Qantir/Piramesses).[114] The traveling kingdom, therefore, seems to have been an integral part of the organization of the state in ancient Egypt: it was more the rule than the exception, especially in times of a decentralized state. It might well be that this part of the state's organization traces back to the early Old Kingdom times, when the previously mentioned small and solid stone pyramids were erected as regional markers of royal power. It is certainly not a mere coincidence that at later times these centers often seem to have become the "capitals" of the nomes.[115] These administrative entities would originally have been organized from the regional palaces, the *Pfalzen*. One might even speculate if this situation is reflected in an old high-ranking, but obscure court title from the Old and Middle Kingdoms, the "Great One of the Upper Egyptian Ten" (*wer medju shemaw*),[116] where the "Ten" would stand for the ten southernmost regional palaces—the heartland of Upper Egypt.

---

112. Wamers 2017: 149.

113. Wamers 2017: 152 with fig. 3.

114. Köpp-Junk 2015: 231–232; Hagen 2016: 157–158; cf. Lacovara 2009: especially 107–110.

115. Köpp-Junk 2015: 307; Polz 2019: 67–68.

116. On this title, see Franke 2003: 76–78; Quirke 2004: 87; Franke 2013: 86–87.

It is interesting to note that the title was still in use during the SIP,[117] and that the number of attestations to title holders seem to have increased after the mid-Thirteenth Dynasty.[118]

24.6. The Theban state's conflict with the Hyksos and Kerma states and the beginning of the New Kingdom

The historical and political developments at the end of the Seventeenth Dynasty and the very early Eighteenth, which eventually led to the expulsion of the Hyksos and the powerful reunified state of the New Kingdom, have long been a matter of research and discussion in Egyptology. Over the decades, the focus was placed on the relation of the Hyksos state in the northern part of the country with its counterpart, the Theban rump state in southern Egypt. It is only in recent years that this focus has slightly shifted. Since the British Museum's project in the necropolis of Elkab discovered a hitherto unknown historical inscription in the decorated rock-tomb of a local potentate, Sobeknakht, several other historically relevant sources have had to be re-evaluated.[119] The new inscription clearly mentions some sort of a military invasion of southern Upper Egypt carried out by an obviously allied force of Egypt's southern neighbors. All unspecified contemporary and later mentions of the "enemies" of the Theban rump state should, therefore, be considered to be referring to either the Hyksos state, the Kerma state, or both.

---

117. E.g., Polz 2007: 62–63; 314–316 with fig. 88; Franke 2013: 121–122 (EA 245), 153–158 (EA 428). Officials bearing this title are also mentioned in the early Eighteenth Dynasty text "Duties of the Vizier": van den Boorn 1988: 33; 336; Quirke 2004: 18.

118. Quirke 2004: 87.

119. Davies 2003a; 2003b; 2010. For the respective passages of the biographical text in the tomb of the governor of Elkab, Sobeknakht, see Davies 2003a: 6. For the last phase of the Classic Kerma period at the end of the Egyptian Second Intermediate Period, see Bonnet and Valbelle 2010; Raue 2019; and see also chapter 25 in this volume.

In addition to the new historical inscription, among the most important sources for the reconstruction of the events leading to the expulsion of the Hyksos are the three "Kamose Steles," erected in the temple of Karnak,[120] and the "Carnarvon Tablet," a writing board roughly contemporary with the steles.[121] The much later "Tale of Apepi and Seqenenra," a literary text of early Ramesside date, has also frequently been utilized to reconstruct the later reception of the events which preceded Egypt's reunification, partially including its underlying psychology and ideology.[122] The unique historical texts of the steles not only describe Kamose's campaigns against his adversaries, but also detail his justification for initiating the campaigns. The Theban ruler complains that his rulership and territory are being threatened by the Hyksos ruler in the north and the Kerma ruler in the south, "each man having his (own) portion of this Egypt, sharing the land with me."[123]

On the basis of the discovery of new material and recent studies on the topic, an attempt can be made at a prosaic assessment of the political situation at the end of the Second Intermediate Period in Upper Egypt.[124] At least from the reigns of the last rulers of the Seventeenth Dynasty onwards there are clear indications of a fully functional state on the political, economic, and administrative levels, including provisions and logistics. A partly reorganized military force (the "king's sons," the

---

120. The first complete publication of the second stele was by Habachi 1972; for an important study of parts of the text prior to Habachi's publication, see Stadelmann 1965. Note the comprehensive treatment by Smith and Smith 1976, who postulated the existence of a third stele, "a hypothetical twin" of the second stele (Smith and Smith 1976: 49). Potential fragments of this third stele have been discovered in the temple of Karnak as early as in 1901 AD, but were tentatively identified as such only recently; see Gabolde 2005; cf. Van Siclen 2010.

121. For English translations of the second stele and the tablet, see Simpson 2003.

122. For an English translation, see Wente 2003. For a recent evaluation of the texts of both the steles and the tale, see Spalinger 2010 with references.

123. Simpson 2003: 346; cf. Smith and Smith 1976: 59.

124. Similar in Polz 2018: 230–231.

"entire army of Coptos"[125]) secured the routes necessary for the development and utilization of resources and presumably also long-distance trade (the oases, the Western and Eastern Desert routes, and the Red Sea coast). The Upper Egyptian rump state at that time was a regional player. Its territory was limited in size, and its means and claims are certainly not to be compared with the advanced and complex forms of state seen in the Middle or New Kingdom time periods. On the other hand, the size of this political entity should not be underestimated, stretching at least from Edfu in the south to Abydos in the north and including vital areas in the Eastern Desert and along the Red Sea shore, as well as certain territories of the Western Desert—an area covering almost a third of the country's mainland. The foundations of such a rump state could not have been developed during the reigns of just one or two rulers. There must have been preceding phases during which the structural foundations were laid; these would have been developed during the reigns of Intef VI's predecessor and brother Intef V and the two Sobekemsaf kings, whose activities are well attested.[126]

By this time, the two other regional political centers of power had developed: the Hyksos state in the northern and northeastern parts of Egypt (chapter 23 in this volume) and the Kerma state in the south.[127] In earlier treatises on the question of how far the political influence of the Hyksos rulers extended into the Upper Egyptian territories, a Hyksos "domination" over middle and southern Egypt has been suggested, which at one point led to a military strike by a Hyksos army and the eventual destruction of Thebes.[128] In view of recent archaeological findings, however, the assumption that southern Upper Egypt was controlled or dominated by the Hyksos rulers at the end of the SIP seems extremely

---

125. The term could point to a "standing army" being garrisoned permanently in Coptos; Spalinger 2013: 434–435.

126. Polz 2007: 61–95.

127. See now Raue 2018: 208–262; 2019; and cf. chapter 25 in this volume.

128. Ryholt 1997: 143–148; for opposing views, see Schneider 2006: 183; Polz 2007: 8–11; cf. Allen 2010: 5.

difficult to maintain. This does not exclude a Hyksos presence of some kind at that time, be it through trade or other economic relations.[129] The evidence of the objects inscribed with titles and names of Hyksos rulers found in Upper Egypt (at Luxor and Gebelein) does not weigh heavily enough to change this picture.[130]

On the southern side, in light of the recently recovered tomb inscriptions from Elkab, among other evidence, the Kerma state may have controlled the area from the First Cataract to somewhere south of Edfu.[131] As demonstrated elsewhere, there are no indications in the archaeological and epigraphical material that the area south of Edfu was part of the territory claimed during the reign of Intef VI, and no such evidence appears until the end of the Seventeenth Dynasty.[132] The discovery on Elephantine Island of an inscribed scarab-shaped seal of a late SIP to early Eighteenth Dynasty date with the name of a Nubian ruler written in a classical royal Egyptian cartouche ("ruler of Kush," *heqa en Keshi*) seems to support this interpretation.[133] A number of Egyptian officials seem to have been employed in the administration of the Nubian rulers: there is a noticeable presence of Egyptians, including military personnel, at Buhen during the very end of the Second Intermediate Period, some of whom served the "ruler of Kush."[134]

Based on the relevant available Egyptian sources, including the new inscription from Elkab and other evidence, the historical events

---

129. As the Khyan seal impressions from Edfu suggest: Moeller and Marouard 2018; Forstner-Müller and Reali 2018; Ben-Tor 2018.

130. Polz 2006.

131. On the development of the Kerma state during the Second Intermediate Period, see Raue 2018: 213–220.

132. Polz 2018: 230.

133. Fitzenreiter 2014; von Pilgrim 2015; cf. Polz 2018: 230.

134. Kubisch 2007: 86–88; 166–178. On paleographic grounds (the inverted *iah*-sign; see section 24.2 and Polz 2007: 14–20), at least three steles of these officials from Buhen can be dated to the period between the reigns of Intef VI and Ahmose II (steles "Buhen 1," "Buhen 2," and "Buhen 5").

surrounding the end of the SIP and the beginning of the New Kingdom can be summarized as follows:[135]

(1) During the Sixteenth Dynasty, at least one but presumably several more military campaigns were carried out against the regional rulers of southern Upper Egypt by Nubian forces. According to the inscriptions on the steles erected in the temple of Karnak, two rulers of the Sixteenth Dynasty (Neferhotep III and Mentuhotepi) may have successfully repelled the attacks of "foreigners" against Thebes. It has been argued that these "foreigners" must have been the Hyksos,[136] but the term might well refer to a southern enemy.

(2) During the later part of the Sixteenth and the first half of the Seventeenth Dynasties, the Upper Egyptian rulers restored temples and temple institutions, reinstalled and secured important trade routes to the Western and Eastern Deserts and the Red Sea, and reorganized the state's administration.

(3) In the late Seventeenth Dynasty, a possible military conflict caused the violent death of the Upper Egyptian ruler Seqenenra. At least two of the five different injuries on the skull of his well-preserved body have been interpreted as originating from the strokes of a weapon of non-Egyptian style.[137] The detailed circumstances, including the exact date and place as well as the outcome of this conflict, however, are not known; the forensic interpretation that the king may have been killed while fighting from a chariot, which is based on various examinations of his skull, is not convincing.

---

135. Cf. Polz 2007: 303–311 (German summary), 374–380 (English summary), 381–392 (Arabic summary).

136. Vernus 1982; 1989; Ryholt 1997: 304–306. In view of the new biographical inscription from Elkab and genuine Egyptian objects from Upper Egyptian sites found in the tombs of cemeteries in Kerma, the Hyksos association does not seem compelling.

137. A Syro-Palestinian Middle Bronze Age–type battle axe: Bietak and Strouhal 1974: 45–51; Bietak 1994: 27–28, fig. 10; 186–187 (catalogue numbers 205, 206, 208).

(4) Early in the reign of Seqenenra's presumed successor Kamose, military campaigns were launched against the Theban rulers' rival, the Hyksos ruler Apepi, who resided in his capital Avaris in the northeastern Nile delta. These campaigns seem to have been a success for the Theban forces, but they obviously did not achieve their initial goal, which was the expulsion of the northern rival.

(5) This goal was finally achieved during the reign of Kamose's successor Ahmose II, whose forces expelled the Hyksos ruler and took Avaris— although probably not through total destruction as Kamose's earlier text would suggest: in the archaeological record at Avaris (Tell el-Dab'a), there is no evidence of a destruction layer at this point in time (cf. chapter 23 in this volume).

(6) Within the time span of the reigns of Kamose and Ahmose II (and probably also mentioned on one or even two of the "Kamose Steles"),[138] one or more military campaigns were mounted against the Kerma ruler in the south.

(7) During his long reign of ca. twenty-five years, Ahmose II consolidated the Egyptian state through large-scale building and other activities all over the country, including areas in Middle and Lower Egypt to which his predecessors had no direct access.[139]

The preceding historical scenario finally leads to the question of what the motives were behind Kamose's and Ahmose's military strikes against the Hyksos ruler in the north and the Kerma ruler in the south. For now, it is by no means clear whether the aforementioned contemporary and later textual sources (including Manetho's *Aegyptiaca* and its later excerpts) do indeed reflect the Upper Egyptian rulers' "traumatic

---

138. Smith and Smith 1976: 66–69; Gabolde 2005: 37–38.

139. E.g., a recently and accidentally discovered lintel of a temple building for the god Nemty, erected and decorated by Ahmose II before his twenty-second year of reign near the modern city of Asyut (Abdel-Raziq 2017); or the resumption of work to procure fine limestone blocks in the quarries of Tura/Masara south of Cairo, dated to his twenty-second year of reign (Lepsius 1849–1859; cf. Harvey 2003: 23).

experience" of being oppressed by foreign rulers,[140] indicating that their campaigns against the Hyksos were consequently "wars of liberation,"[141] or whether they should be interpreted as a narrative that was used to justify the vigorous expansion and violent military actions of the Theban side undertaken for the sake of regaining power, influence, and access to resources over the entire country and beyond—albeit through actions partially directed against their own people.[142] After all, both interpretive approaches reflect an ideological point of view on the side of modern scholarship, and the former approach may well have its roots in an unhesitating "adoption of the negative Theban/Manethonian discourse."[143]

REFERENCES

Abdel-Raziq, A. 2017. An unpublished lintel of Ahmose-Nebpehtyre from El-Atâwla. *JARCE* 53: 1–9.

Allen, J.P. 2010. The Second Intermediate Period in the Turin King List. In Marée, M. (ed.) 2010: 1–10.

Arnold, D. 1991. *Building in Egypt: pharaonic stone masonry*. Oxford: Oxford University Press.

Baedeker, K. 1891. *Ägypten: Handbuch für Reisende, zweiter Theil: Ober-Ägypten und Nubien bis zum zweiten Katarakt*. Leipzig: Baedeker.

Ben-Tor, D. 2004. Second Intermediate Period scarabs from Egypt and Palestine: historical and chronological implications. In Bietak, M., and Czerny, E. (eds.) 2004: 27–42.

Ben-Tor, D. 2018. The sealings from the administrative unit at Tell Edfu: chronological and historical implications. In Forstner-Müller, I., and Moeller, N. (eds.) 2018: 83–90.

---

140. Spalinger 2010.

141. E.g., Grimal 1988: 238–240; Redford 1993: 98–122. For similar examples of this rather Egypto-centric scholarly view, see Schneider's recent assessment of five decades of Hyksos research (Schneider 2018).

142. Cf. Polz 1998: 230.

143. Schneider 2018: 82. The validity of this adoption, both contemporaneously and later, of a "Theban interpretation" of the campaigns against the Hyksos was already questioned in Polz 1998.

Bietak, M. 2018. Introduction to palaces in Egypt: what they tell us about the ruler, administration and culture. In Bietak, M., and Prell, S. (eds.), *Palaces in ancient Egypt and the ancient Near East, vol. I: Egypt.* Vienna: Verlag der Österreichischen Akademie der Wissenschaften, 23–38.

Bietak, M., and Czerny, E. (eds.) 2004. *Scarabs of the second millennium BC from Egypt, Nubia, Crete and the Levant: chronological and historical implications.* Vienna: Verlag der Österreichischen Akademie der Wissenschaften.

Bietak, M., and Strouhal, E. 1974. Die Todesumstände des Pharaos Seqenenre' (17. Dynastie): Vorbericht. *Annalen des Naturhistorischen Museums Wien* 78: 29–52.

Biston-Moulin, S. 2012. Le roi Sénakht-en-Rê Ahmès de la XVIIe dynastie. *Égypte Nilotique et Méditerranéenne* 5: 61–71.

Biston-Moulin, S., Thiers, C., and Zigniani, P. 2012. Erster archäologischer Nachweis für Pharao Senachtenre Ahmose. *Antike Welt* 2012, no. 3: 4.

Blaich, M.C. 2013. Überlegungen zur Herrscherrepräsentation in ostsächsischen Pfalzen und Domburgen des 10./11. Jahrhunderts. *Mitteilungen der Deutschen Gesellschaft für Archäologie des Mittelalters und der Neuzeit* 25: 117–126.

Bonnet, C., and Valbelle, D. 2010. The Classic Kerma period and the beginning of the New Kingdom. In Marée, M. (ed.) 2010: 359–365.

Budge, E.A.W. 1892. On some Egyptian bronze weapons in the collection of John Evans, Esq., and the British Museum. *Archaeologia* 53: 83–94.

Daressy, G. 1909. *Cercueils des cachettes royales.* Cairo: Institut français d'archéologie orientale.

Darnell, D., and Darnell, J.C. 1993. The Luxor-Farshût desert road survey. *The Oriental Institute Annual Report* 1992–1993: 48–55.

Davies, W.V. 2003a. Sobeknakht of Elkab and the coming of Kush. *EA* 23: 3–6.

Davies, W.V. 2003b. Kush in Egypt: a new historical inscription. *Sudan & Nubia* 7: 52–54.

Davies, W.V. 2010. Renseneb and Sobeknakht of Elkab: the genealogical data. In Marée, M. (ed.) 2010: 223–240.

Dodson, A. 1991. On the internal chronology of the Seventeenth Dynasty. *GM* 120: 33–38.

Dodson, A. 1994. From Dahshur to Dra Abu el Naga: the decline & fall of the royal pyramid. *KMT: a Modern Journal of Ancient Egypt* 5, no. 3: 25–39.

Eder, C. 2002. *Die Barkenkapelle des Königs Sobekhotep III. in Elkab: Beiträge zur Bautätigkeit der 13. und 17. Dynastie an den Göttertempeln Ägyptens.* Turnhout: Brepols.

Ehlers, C. 2016. Königspfalzen. *Handwörterbuch zur deutschen Rechtsgeschichte, vol. III.* Berlin: Erich Schmidt Verlag: 60–71. 2nd rev. ed.

Falk, M., Klie, S., and Schulz, A. 1985. Neufunde ergänzen Königsnamen eines Herrschers der 2. Zwischenzeit. *GM* 87: 15–23.

Fitzenreiter, M. 2014. Ein Siegelstempel aus Elephantine. *MDAIK* 68: 43–54.

Forstner-Müller, I., and Moeller, N. (eds.) 2018. *The Hyksos ruler Khyan and the early Second Intermediate Period in Egypt: problems and priorities of current research.* Vienna: Holzhausen.

Forstner-Müller, I., and Reali, C. 2018. King Khyan and Avaris: some considerations concerning Khyan seal impressions from Area R/III at Tell el-Dabʿa. In Forstner-Müller, I., and Moeller, N. (eds.) 2018: 91–123.

Franke, D. 1988. Zur Chronologie des Mittleren Reiches, Teil II: die sogenannte 'Zweite Zwischenzeit' Altägyptens. *Orientalia* 57: 245–274.

Franke, D. 2003. Die Stele des Jayseneb aus der Schachtanlage K01.12. In Polz, D., and Seiler, A. (eds.), *Die Pyramidenanlage des Königs Nub-Cheper-Re Intef in Draʿ Abu el-Naga.* Mainz: Zabern, 73–83.

Franke, D. 2008. The late Middle Kingdom (Thirteenth to Seventeenth Dynasties): the chronological framework. *JEH* 1: 267–287.

Franke, D. 2013. *Egyptian stelae in the British Museum from the 13th to 17th Dynasties.* London: British Museum Press.

Gabolde, L. 2005. Une troisième stèle de Kamosis? *Kyphi: Bulletin du Cercle Lyonnais d'Égyptologie Victor Loret* 4: 35–42.

Gardiner, A.H. 1947. *Ancient Egyptian onomastica.* Oxford: Oxford University Press.

Gardiner, A.H. 1973. *Egyptian grammar, being an introduction to the study of hieroglyphs.* Oxford: Oxford University Press. 3rd rev. ed.

Gardiner, A.H., and Faulkner, R.O. 1941–52. *The Wilbour Papyrus, vols. I–IV.* Oxford: Oxford University Press.

Gomaà, F. 1986. *Die Besiedelung Ägyptens während des Mittleren Reiches, I: Oberägypten und das Fayyūm.* Wiesbaden: Reichert.

Gomaà, F. 1987. *Die Besiedelung Ägyptens während des Mittleren Reiches, II: Unterägypten und die angrenzenden Gebiete.* Wiesbaden: Reichert.

Gomaà, F., Müller-Wollermann, R., and Schenkel, W. 1991. *Mittelägypten zwischen Samalūṭ und dem Gabal Abū Ṣīr: Beiträge zur historischen Topographie der pharaonischen Zeit.* Wiesbaden: Reichert.

Grajetzki, W. 2000. *Die höchsten Beamten der ägyptischen Zentralverwaltung zur Zeit des Mittleren Reiches: Prosopographie, Titel und Titelreihen.* Berlin: Achet Verlag.

Grajetzki, W. 2009. *Court officials of the Egyptian Middle Kingdom.* London: Duckworth.

Grajetzki, W. 2010. Notes on administration in the Second Intermediate Period. In Marée, M. (ed.) 2010: 305–312.

Grajetzki, W. 2013. Setting a state anew: the central administration from the end of the Old Kingdom to the end of the Middle Kingdom. In Moreno García, J.C. (ed.) 2013: 215–258.

Grallert, S. 2001. *Bauen – Stiften – Weihen.* Berlin: Achet Verlag.

Grimal, N. 1988. *Histoire de l'Égypte ancienne.* Paris: Fayard.

Gundaker, R. 2018. Manetho. *Das wissenschaftliche Bibellexikon im Internet.* Retrieved from http://www.bibelwissenschaft.de/stichwort/25466/ (last accessed October 2019).

Gundlach, R., and Spence, K. (eds.) 2011. *Palace and temple: 5th symposium on Egyptian royal ideology.* Wiesbaden: Harrassowitz.

Gundlach, R., and Taylor, J.H. (eds.) 2009. *Egyptian royal residences: 4th symposium on Egyptian royal ideology.* Wiesbaden: Harrassowitz.

Habachi, L. 1972. *The second stela of Kamose and his struggle against the Hyksos ruler and his capital.* Glückstadt: Augustin.

Hagen, F. 2016. On some movements of the royal court in New Kingdom Egypt. In van Dijk, J.J. (ed.), *Another mouthful of dust: Egyptological studies in honour of Geoffrey Thorndike Martin.* Leuven: Peeters, 155–181.

Harvey, S.P. 2003. Abydos. *The Oriental Institute Annual Report 2002–2003*: 15–25.

Hayes, W.C. 1973. Egypt: from the death of Ammenemes III to Seqenenre II. In Edwards, I.E.S., Gadd, C.J., Hammond, N.G.L., and Sollberger, E. (eds.), *The Cambridge ancient History, vol. II, part 1: history of the Middle East and the Aegean region c. 1800–1380 B.C.* Cambridge: Cambridge University Press, 42–76. 3rd ed.

Hein, I. (ed.) 1994. *Pharaonen und Fremde: Dynastien im Dunkel.* Vienna: Eigenverlag der Museen der Stadt Wien.

Helck, W. 1956. *Untersuchungen zu Manetho und den ägyptischen Königslisten*. Berlin: Akademie-Verlag.

Helck, W. 1958. *Zur Verwaltung des Mittleren und Neuen Reiches*. Leiden: Brill.

Helck, W. 1974. *Die altägyptischen Gaue*. Wiesbaden: Reichert.

Helck, W. 1992. Anmerkungen zum Turiner Königspapyrus. *SAK* 19: 150–216.

Ilin-Tomich, A. 2014. The Theban kingdom of Dynasty 16: its rise, administration and politics. *JEH* 7: 143–193.

Jacquet-Gordon, H. 1999. Two stelae of king Seqenenre' Djehuty-Aa of the Seventeenth Dynasty. In Teeter, E., and Larson, J.A. (eds.), *Gold of praise: studies on ancient Egypt in honor of Edward F. Wente*. Chicago: The Oriental Institute of the University of Chicago, 179–184.

Kessler, D. 1981. *Historische Topographie der Region zwischen Mallawi und Samalut*. Wiesbaden: Reichert.

Knoblauch, C. 2019. Middle Kingdom fortresses. In Raue, D. (ed.), *Handbook of ancient Nubia, vol. 1*. Berlin: De Gruyter, 367–391.

Köpp-Junk, H. 2015. *Reisen im Alten Ägypten: Reisekultur, Fortbewegungs- und Transportmittel in pharaonischer Zeit*. Wiesbaden: Harrassowitz.

Krauss, R. 1993. Zur Problematik der Nubienpolitik Kamoses sowie der Hyksosherrschaft in Oberägypten. *Orientalia* 62: 17–29.

Kubisch, S. 2007. *Lebensbilder der 2. Zwischenzeit: Biographische Inschriften der 13.–17. Dynastie*. Berlin: De Gruyter.

Lacau, P. 1909. *Stèles du nouvel empire: catalogue général des antiquités égyptiennes du Musée du Caire, 34001–34189, vol. 1*. Cairo: Institut français d'archéologie orientale.

Lacau, P., and Chevrier, H. 1969. *Une chapelle de Sésostris Ier à Karnak: planches*. Cairo: Institute français d'archéologie orientale.

Lacovara, P. 1990. *Deir el-Ballas: preliminary report on the Deir el-Ballas expedition, 1980–1986*. Winona Lake, IN: Eisenbrauns.

Lacovara, P. 1997. *The New Kingdom royal city*. London: Kegan Paul International.

Lacovara, P. 2009. The development of the New Kingdom royal palace. In Gundlach, R., and Taylor, J.H. (eds.) 2009: 83–110.

Lacovara, P. 2018. Deir el-Ballas. In Bietak, M., and Prell, S. (eds.), *Palaces in ancient Egypt and the ancient Near East, vol. I: Egypt*. Vienna: Verlag der Österreichischen Akademie der Wissenschaften, 283–291.

Lepsius, K.R. 1842. Die Königsreihen von Karnak. In Lepsius, K.R., *Auswahl der wichtigsten Urkunden des aegyptischen Alterthums*. Leipzig: Wigand, pl. I.

Lepsius, K.R. 1849–1859. *Denkmaeler aus Aegypten und Aethiopien V, Abtheilung III, Blatt 3a-b*. Berlin: Nicolaische Buchhandlung.

Marée, M. 2009. The 12th–17th Dynasties at Gebel el-Zeit: a closer look at the inscribed royal material. *BiOr* 66: 147–162.

Marée, M. (ed.) 2010. *The Second Intermediate Period (Thirteenth-Seventeenth Dynasties): current research, future prospects*. Leuven: Peeters.

Mariette, A. 1872. *Monuments divers recueillis en Égypt et en Nubie*. Paris: Vieweg.

Mariette, A., and Maspero, G. 1889. *Monuments divers recueillis en Égypte et en Nubie. Texte par G. Maspero*. Paris: Vieweg.

Miniaci, G. 2011a. Through change and tradition: the rise of Thebes during the Second Intermediate Period. In Buzi, P., Picchi, D., and Tecchi, M. (eds.), *Aegyptiaca et Coptica: studi in onore di Sergio Pernigotti*. Oxford: Archaeopress, 235–249.

Miniaci, G. 2011b. *Rishi coffins and the funerary culture of Second Intermediate Period Egypt*. London: Golden House.

Moeller, N., and Marouard, G. 2018. The context of the Khyan sealings from Tell Edfu and further implications for the Second Intermediate Period in Upper Egypt. In Forstner-Müller, I., and Moeller, N. (eds.) 2018: 173–197.

Moreno García, J.C. (ed.) 2013. *Ancient Egyptian administration*. Leiden: Brill.

Pardey, E. 2003. Die Datierung der "Dienstanweisung für den Wesir" und die Problematik von *Tp rsj* im Neuen Reich. In Kloth, N., Martin, K., and Pardey, E. (eds.), *Es werde niedergelegt als Schriftstück: Festschrift für Hartwig Altenmüller zum 65. Geburtstag*. Hamburg: Buske, 323–334.

Parkinson, R., and Quirke, S. 1992. The coffin of prince Herunefer and the early history of the Book of the Dead. In Lloyd, A.B. (ed.), *Studies in pharaonic religion and society in honour of J. Gwyn Griffiths*. London: Egypt Exploration Society, 37–51.

Peet, T.E. 1930. *The great tomb-robberies of the Twentieth Egyptian Dynasty, being a critical study, with translations and commentaries, of the papyri in which these are recorded*. Oxford: Clarendon Press.

Polz, D. 1998. Theben und Avaris: zur "Vertreibung" der Hyksos. In Guksch, H., and Polz, D. (eds.), *Stationen: Beiträge zur Kulturgeschichte Ägyptens, Rainer Stadelmann gewidmet*. Mainz: Zabern, 219–231.

Polz, D. 2003. "Ihre Mauern sind verfallen . . . , ihre Stätte ist nicht mehr": der Aufwand für den Toten im Theben der Zweiten Zwischenzeit. In Guksch, H., Hofmann, E., and Bommas, M. (eds.), *Grab und Totenkult im Alten Ägypten*. München: Beck, 75–87.

Polz, D. 2006. Die Hyksos-Blöcke aus Gebelên: zur Präsenz der Hyksos in Oberägypten. In Czerny, E., Hein, I., Hunger, H., Melman, D., and Schwab, A. (eds.), *Timelines: studies in honour of Manfred Bietak.* Leuven: Peeters, 239–247.

Polz, D. 2007. *Der Beginn des Neuen Reiches: zur Vorgeschichte einer Zeitenwende.* Berlin: De Gruyter.

Polz, D. 2010. New archaeological data from Dra' Abu el-Naga and their historical implications. In Marée, M. (ed.) 2010: 343–353.

Polz, D. 2018. The territorial claim and the political role of the Theban state at the end of the Second Intermediate Period. A case study. In Forstner-Müller, I., and Moeller, N. (eds.) 2018: 217–233.

Polz, D. 2019. *Die sogenannte Hundestele des Königs Wah-Anch Intef aus el-Târif. Eine Forschungsgeschichte.* Wiesbaden: Harrassowitz.

Polz, D., and Seiler, A. 2003. *Die Pyramidenanlage des Königs Nub-Cheper-Re Intef in Dra' Abu el-Naga: ein Vorbericht.* Mainz: Zabern.

Quirke, S. 2004. *Titles and bureaux of Egypt, 1850–1700 BC.* London: Golden House.

Raue, D. 2018. *Elephantine und Nubien vom 4.–2. Jahrtausend v. Chr.* Berlin: De Gruyter.

Raue, D. 2019. Nubians in Egypt in the 3rd and 2nd millennium BC. In Raue, D. (ed.), *Handbook of ancient Nubia, vol. 1.* Berlin: De Gruyter, 567–588.

Raven, M.J. 2009. Aspects of the Memphite residence as illustrated by the Saqqara New Kingdom necropolis. In Gundlach, R., and Taylor, J.H. (eds.) 2009: 153–164.

Redford, D.B. 1986. *Pharaonic king-lists, annals and day books: a contribution to the study of the Egyptian sense of history.* Mississauga: Benben Publications.

Redford, D.B. 1993. *Egypt, Canaan, and Israel in ancient times.* Cairo: American University in Cairo Press.

Régen, I., and Soukiassian, G. 2008. *Gebel el-Zeit II: le matériel inscrit, Moyen Empire—Nouvel Empire.* Cairo: Institut français d'archéologie orientale.

Ryholt, K.S.B. 1997. *The political situation during the Second Intermediate Period, ca. 1800–1550 B.C.* Copenhagen: Museum Tusculanum Press.

Ryholt, K.S.B. 2004. The Turin King List. *ÄL* 14: 135–155.

Ryholt, K.S.B. 2018. Seals and history of the 14th and 15th Dynasties. In Forstner-Müller, I., and Moeller, N. (eds.) 2018: 235–276.

Schmitz, B. 1976. *Untersuchungen zum Titel S3-NJSWT "Königssohn."* Bonn: Habelt.

Schneider, T. 2006. The relative chronology of the Middle Kingdom and the Hyksos period (Dyns. 12–17). In Hornung, E., Krauss, R., and Warburton, D. (eds.), *Ancient Egyptian chronology.* Leiden: Brill, 168–196.

Schneider, T. 2018. Hyksos research in Egyptology and Egypt's public imagination: a brief assessment of fifty years of assessments. *JEH* 11: 73–86.

Seidlmayer, S.J. 1991. Eine Schreiberpalette mit änigmatischer Aufschrift. *MDAIK* 47: 319–330.

Shaw, I. 2003. Introduction: chronologies and cultural change in Egypt. In Shaw, I. (ed.), *The Oxford history of ancient Egypt.* Oxford: Oxford University Press, 1–15. New ed.

Shirley, J.J. 2013. Crisis and restructuring of the state: from the Second Intermediate Period to the advent of the Ramesses. In Moreno García, J.C. (ed.) 2013: 521–606.

Simpson, W.K. 2003. The Kamose texts. In Simpson, W.K. (ed.), *The literature of ancient Egypt: an anthology of stories, instructions, stelae, autobiographies, and poetry.* Cairo: American University in Cairo Press, 345–350.

Smith, H.S., and Smith, A. 1976. A reconsideration of the Kamose texts. *ZÄS* 103: 48–76.

Spalinger, A. 2010. Two screen plays: "Kamose" and "Apophis and Seqenenre." *JEH* 3: 115–135.

Spalinger, A. 2013. The organisation of the Pharaonic army (Old to New Kingdom). In Moreno García, J.C. (ed.) 2013: 393–478.

Stadelmann, R. 1965. Ein Beitrag zum Brief des Hyksos Apophis. *MDAIK* 20: 62–69.

Steindorff, G. 1895. Die Könige Mentuhotep und Antef: zur Geschichte der 11. Dynastie. *ZÄS* 33: 77–96.

Stock, H. 1942. *Studien zur Geschichte und Archäologie der 13. bis 17. Dynastie Ägyptens, unter besonderer Berücksichtigung der Skarabäen dieser Zwischenzeit.* Glückstadt: Augustin.

van den Boorn, G.P.F. 1988. *The duties of the vizier: civil administration in the early New Kingdom.* London: Kegan Paul.

Vandersleyen, C. 1971. *Les guerres d'Amosis, fondateur de la XVIII dynastie.* Brussels: Fondation Égyptologique Reine Élisabeth.

Van Siclen, C.C., III. 2010. The third stela of Kamose. In Marée, M. (ed.) 2010: 355–358.

Vernus, P. 1982. La stèle du roi Sekhemsankhtaouyrê Neferhotep Iykhernofret et la domination Hyksôs (stèle Caire JE 59635). *ASAE* 68: 129–135.

Vernus, P. 1989. La stèle du pharaon *Mntw-htpj* à Karnak: un nouveau témoignage sur la situation politique et militaire au début de la D.P.I. *RdE* 40: 145–161.

von Beckerath, J. 1964. *Untersuchungen zur politischen Geschichte der zweiten Zwischenzeit in Ägypten*. Glückstadt: Augustin.

von Beckerath, J. 1997. *Chronologie des pharaonischen Ägypten. Die Zeitbestimmung der ägyptischen Geschichte von der Vorzeit bis 332 v. Chr.* Mainz: Zabern.

von Beckerath, J. 1999. Theban Seventeenth Dynasty. In Teeter, E., and Larson, J.A. (eds.), *Gold of praise: studies on ancient Egypt in honor of Edward F. Wente*. Chicago: The Oriental Institute of the University of Chicago, 21–25.

von Pilgrim, C. 1996. *Untersuchungen in der Stadt des Mittleren Reiches und der Zweiten Zwischenzeit*. Mainz: Zabern.

von Pilgrim, C. 2015. An authentication sealing of the "Ruler of Kush" from Elephantine. In Jiménez-Serrano, A., and von Pilgrim, C. (eds.), *From the delta to the cataract: studies dedicated to Mohamed el-Bialy*. Leiden: Brill, 218–226.

Waddell, W.G. 1948. *Manetho*. London: Heinemann.

Wamers, E. 2017. Carolingian *Pfalzen* and law. *Danish Journal of Archaeology* 6: 149–163.

Wegner, J. 2015. A royal necropolis at South Abydos: new light on Egypt's Second Intermediate Period. *NEA* 78: 68–78.

Wegner, J. 2018. Woseribre Seneb-Kay: a newly identified Upper Egyptian king of the Second Intermediate Period. In Forstner-Müller, I., and Moeller, N. (eds.) 2018: 286–305.

Wente, E.F. 2003. The quarrel of Apophis and Seknenre. In Simpson, W.K. (ed.), *The literature of ancient Egypt: an anthology of stories, instructions, stelae, autobiographies, and poetry*. Cairo: American University in Cairo Press, 69–71.

Wildung, D. 1974. Aufbau und Zweckbestimmung der Königsliste von Karnak. *GM* 9: 41–48.

Winlock, H.E. 1924. The tombs of the kings of the Seventeenth Dynasty at Thebes. *JEA* 10: 217–277.

25

Early Kush

THE KINGDOM OF KERMA

Geoff Emberling and Elizabeth Minor

25.1. Introduction

The kingdom of Kerma was an African state located along the Nile
river south of Egypt, on the edge of the ancient Middle Eastern world-
system.[1] It had complex and well-documented relations with Egypt—
trade partner, military adversary, source of immigrants—from the late
Old Kingdom (ca. 2300 BC) until its conquest by Egyptian armies at the
beginning of the New Kingdom (ca. 1500 BC). The kingdom of Kerma
also developed trade relations with regions further to the south and
west, although these are much less well documented, and it mediated
the exchange of products from inner Africa to Egypt and the broader
Mediterranean and Middle East.

---

1. The region as a whole is often termed "Nubia." It is anachronistic for the period
discussed here, but can be useful as a broad geographic designation. A more
neutral modern term is "Middle Nile region." "Nubian" also refers to languages
spoken in the region today. For Kush as part of the ancient world system, see
Hafsaas-Tsakos 2009.

Geoff Emberling and Elizabeth Minor, *Early Kush* In: *The Oxford History of the Ancient Near East*. Edited
by: Karen Radner, Nadine Moeller, and D. T. Potts, Oxford University Press. © Oxford University Press 2022.
DOI: 10.1093/oso/9780190687601.003.0025

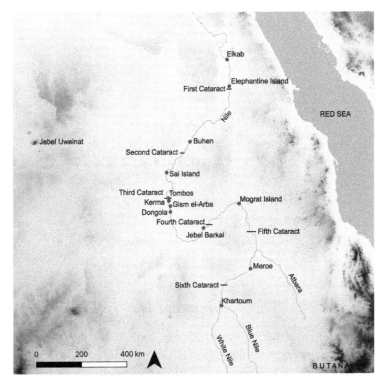

FIGURE 25.1. Sites mentioned in this chapter. Prepared by Andrea Squitieri (LMU Munich).

The settlement at Kerma[2] itself is located immediately upstream of the Third Cataract, at the downstream end of an extensive fertile stretch of the Middle Nile known as the Dongola Reach (figure 25.1). Kerma grew from a small, newly founded fortified village in Kerma *ancien* (2500–2000 BC), to a fortified settlement of 3 hectares in Kerma *moyen* (2000–1750 BC), to a fully urban settlement of about

---

2. Although the ancient name of Kerma is not known with certainty, Rilly 2017: 80 has recently suggested that it could have been *Shaka* or *Saka*.

25 hectares in Kerma *classique* (1750–1500 BC).[3] In its last phase, Kerma was centered around a monumental mudbrick temple known as the "Deffufa" (a Nubian-language term for fortified structures), but the settlement also included a palace, public audience hall, chapels, houses of varying size, and abundant evidence for production of ceramics, faience, and glazed quartz, objects in copper alloy, as well as bread. An enormous cemetery for the city was constructed some 3.5 km to the east, along an earlier channel of the Nile, and by the end of the Kerma period as many as 40,000 burials had been placed there,[4] including large tumulus burials for the last kings of Kerma, which contained up to 400 sacrificial victims, as well as elite subsidiary burials. Distinctive Kerma ceramics are also found along the Nile over a distance of more than 1,000 km, extending from the First Cataract in the north to the Fifth Cataract in the south, suggesting regional connections if not direct control.

For scholars, Kerma poses a number of challenges. To begin with, its ancient name in its earlier phases remains uncertain—some have identified it with ancient *Yam* (known in Egyptian texts of the later Old Kingdom), while it was certainly the center of ancient Kush from 2000 BC onward. Furthermore, it does not conform readily to archaeological models of states, empires, and cities, like other African polities.[5] This is one reason the less precise term "kingdom" is often used, but as a relatively small settlement Kerma challenges us to rethink our evaluations of complexity. Moreover, the fact that Kerma was a non-literate city poses challenges in evaluating its history, political ideology, and religious beliefs that appear nonetheless to have been distinctly different from Egyptian practices.

---

3. We retain the phase names given by the Swiss excavators of the site to avoid confusion in abbreviation that would result between "Middle Kerma" and "Middle Kingdom."

4. Bonnet and Honegger 2021.

5. E.g., Southall 1956; 1999; Edwards 1998; S. McIntosh 1999; R. McIntosh 2015.

25.2. History of exploration
and interpretation

Kerma was first noted by the European explorers following the invasion of Sudan by an army of Mohammed Ali, pasha of Egypt, in 1820–1821. These early Europeans focused on two monumental mudbrick structures both known as Deffufas—one in the settlement and one in the cemetery—which they interpreted variously as fortresses or pyramids. The Royal Prussian expedition of Richard Lepsius in 1844 was the first to recognize the site as an important early settlement: "Without doubt, this is the oldest and most important locality in all of Dongola [province]."[6]

The first excavations at Kerma, however, were not carried out until 1913, when George Reisner began work at the site. Between 1913 and 1916, he investigated structures of the settlement around the Western Deffufa and excavated hundreds of burials in the cemetery around the Eastern Deffufa, including four tumuli up to 90 m in diameter that included up to 400 sacrificial burials.[7] Despite looting in the central burial chambers of the tumuli, the abundance of pottery, funerary equipment, and personal adornments recovered from the cemetery displayed the luxury materials and skilled artisanry available to the Kerman elite.

Reisner's cultural bias in interpreting the remains has been widely discussed. His racial theory of cultural development and cultural change led him to suppose that the city, its monumental architecture, and its imposing burials could not have been the products of a local African culture, but must have been the work of Egyptian governors.[8] This view also led him to propose that smaller burials with fewer Egyptian objects in them must have been a later degeneration.[9]

Reisner's views were very quickly challenged and were never widely accepted. Hermann Junker had questioned Reisner's assumption that

---

6. Lepsius 1913: 245 (authors' translation).

7. Reisner 1923a; 1923b; Dunham et al. 1982.

8. Reisner 1923a: 76–79.

9. Reisner 1923a: 488.

Kerma was an Egyptian settlement.[10] Torgny Säve-Söderbergh demonstrated that Tumulus KIII, which Reisner had suggested was the burial of the Twelfth Dynasty Egyptian official Djefaihapy, included fragments of statues, seals, and scarabs that dated to the Thirteenth Dynasty, up to two centuries later than Djefaihapy's known death.[11] Fritz Hintze argued that the material evidence at Kerma corroborated Egyptian texts describing conflict between Kush and Egyptian rulers in Thebes, as well as an alliance between the Hyksos rulers of Lower Egypt and Kush. Therefore, Kerma was the capital of Kush, the large tumuli were royal burials, and the wealth at the site demonstrated the power of the Kushite civilization at its zenith.[12] Brigitte Gratien analyzed Kerma pottery in comparison with regional centers, and argued that Reisner's chronology of the site must be reversed.[13] Instead of a degenerating Egyptian culture descending into more Nubian forms, the long sequence of development and social stratification of the Kerma culture culminated in the Kerma *classique*, during which a significant quantity of Egyptian goods were imported.

Kerma, however, was still seen by many scholars as a weaker and less developed neighbor of Egypt. In a magisterial summary of ancient Nubia written after the conclusion of the Aswan Dam salvage project between the First and Second Cataracts by one of its most active participants, William Y. Adams commented on the lack of knowledge about Upper Nubia, broadly speaking. He maintained, however, that "the power of the Nubians grew in proportion to the weakness and division within Egypt"; that "Egyptian officials oversaw the manufactures and the export trade of Kerma on behalf of the native ruler"; and that overall, Kerma was to be located "between the Tribal and Dynastic stages of Nubian cultural development."[14]

---

10. Junker 1920: 19–26.

11. Säve-Söderbergh 1941: 103–116.

12. Hintze 1964: 83.

13. Gratien 1978; 2011.

14. Adams 1977: 216.

Continuing reappraisals of the size, power, and relative independence of Kerma began in 1973, when Charles Bonnet inaugurated a Swiss project at Kerma, and the team has since recovered extensive information about the settlement and cemetery. Several points about this impressive and careful excavation are important for understanding its results. With some exceptions, Bonnet and his team made a decision to focus on clearing the entire surface of the site rather than excavating deeply. They did this largely to avoid destroying the surface architecture and in fact have now reconstructed the uppermost architecture over much of the surface of the site. This has resulted in a remarkable knowledge of the entire urban plan, but with gaps in our knowledge of the earlier settlement. Publication of the settlement excavation to date has included regular substantive preliminary reports, regular synthetic studies, a final report on soundings around the Deffufa,[15] and a recent report on the architecture of the city as a whole.[16] Study of the artifacts recovered in these excavations is ongoing, but they have not yet been published in detail.

A broader regional picture of the upstream agricultural hinterland of Kerma was provided by the archaeological survey of Derek Welsby in the 1990s.[17] David O'Connor had proposed, based on his reanalysis of Egyptian texts, that Nubian polities of the later third and early second millennium BC were much larger than previously thought.[18] His analysis was later supported by the recovery of Kerma material throughout the Fourth Cataract region during salvage excavations during the early 2000s[19] and indeed by reports of Kerma material further upstream and in the Bayuda desert.[20] A further reappraisal of the threat to Egypt posed by Kerma's military came from examination of the Egyptian tomb inscription of Sobeknakht at Elkab, dating from the Second Intermediate

---

15. Bonnet 2004.

16. Bonnet 2014; see also Bonnet 2019.

17. Welsby 2001.

18. O'Connor 1986; 1993.

19. E.g., Paner 2014; Emberling et al. 2014.

20. Paner 2018.

Period (ca. 1600 BC), which documented a raid by an alliance of African partners—Kush, Wawat, *Khenthennefer*, Punt, and *Medjay*—deep into Egypt.[21] The result of this research was increasingly to suggest that Kerma was a more powerful polity than previously suspected and that its dependence on Egypt had previously been overstated.

25.3. Ancient names and historical geography

The ancient name for the polity of which Kerma was the capital remains uncertain for its earlier period, and depends on matching Egyptian textual references to the archaeological record of the Middle Nile region. During the Sixth Dynasty of Egypt (ca. 2345–2181 BC), two categories of texts provide indications of the historical geography of Nubia. One category is the execration texts that curse foreign people and lands, and the other is autobiographical texts of Egyptian trader-agents who traveled into Nubia, particularly Harkhuf. Of particular interest for Kerma is the land of *Yam*, to which Harkhuf made four journeys to "open the route" for trade.[22] The location of *Yam* has been widely debated,[23] with some supporting an identification of *Yam* with Kerma,[24] but the discussion has recently been reopened with the discovery of a rock inscription in the Gebel Uweinat in the far southwestern corner of Egypt that mentions *Yam*, suggesting that it could be located to the west of the Nile.[25]

Beginning in the Twelfth Dynasty of Egypt (ca. 1985–1773 BC), Egyptian execration texts no longer refer to *Yam*, but begin to refer to Kush, which is undoubtedly the indigenous name for Kerma during the Kerma *moyen* and Kerma *classique* periods. Whether the name of the Kerma polity changed because of a dynastic or cultural change, or

---

21. Davies 2003.

22. See Török 2009: 59–60.

23. O'Connor 1986.

24. E.g., Rilly 2017: 72.

25. Discussion in Cooper 2012; Williams 2021.

whether *Yam* is to be located elsewhere and Kush was simply not mentioned earlier, is not yet clear.

It should be noted that Egyptian texts contain a range of terms for the people living in the Middle Nile that correspond to some degree with archaeological material in the region, although the meaning of the Egyptian terms changed with context and through time. A general term for the region was Ta-Seti, meaning "Land of the Bow." Farmers living in the Nile valley were called *Nehesy*, while nomadic people living in the Eastern Desert were called *Medjay*. To some extent, *Nehesy* refers to the archaeological culture known as the C-Group,[26] while *Medjay* refers to people whose material culture is designated Pan-Grave,[27] although particularly in the latter case the material culture is considerably more varied than the single Egyptian term would suggest. For understanding of the kingdom of Kerma, these terms are a reminder that the Middle Nile region was not culturally uniform during these centuries.

25.4. *Geographical and environmental setting*

Kerma today is located about 1.5 km to the east of the modern Nile channel, with its cemetery being a further 3.5 km to the east of the settlement itself. Geomorphology[28] and archaeological survey upstream[29] make it clear not only that the course of the Nile has changed since antiquity, but also that it changed during the Kerma period.

A settlement of the Pre-Kerma period[30] dating to around 3000 BC was located in what would later become the cemetery of Kerma. At that time, at least one channel of the Nile ran through the cemetery. By 2500 BC, however, that channel had largely dried up and the new settlement

---

26. Hafsaas-Tsakos 2006.

27. Liszka and De Souza 2021.

28. Marconologo and Surian 1997.

29. Welsby 2001.

30. Honegger 2021.

was built on an island in the Nile to the west. While the site today is not on the Nile bank, excavations suggest that a seasonal channel also ran through the site.

Climate change played a significant role in shifts in the Nile course from a braided set of channels in earlier periods to a concentration of Nile flow into a single channel by the end of the Kerma *classique*. Recent regional and more local environmental studies suggest a drier period in the area during 2700–2250 BC[31] that would correspond to the foundation of the new settlement. A worldwide drought around 2200 BC (the 4.2 kya event) appears not to have disrupted settlement at Kerma,[32] although it more or less coincides with the end of the Old Kingdom state in Egypt, even if the causal relationship has recently been doubted.[33] A further drying of one of these Nile branches has been dated by geomorphology to ca. 2000 BC.[34]

25.5. The Kerma trajectory

The long history of occupation at Kerma, both in settlement and cemetery areas, illustrates the trajectory of its development.

25.5.1. Pre-Kerma settlement (3000 BC)

The earliest settlement in the area of Kerma is dated to about 3000 BC, in what is termed the "Pre-Kerma" period. Located under the Kerma period cemetery, the Pre-Kerma occupation was documented over an area of about 1.5 hectares but may originally have extended over an area as large as 10 hectares.[35] The settlement was composed of wooden structures, delineated by postholes, including palisades, cattle pens, two

31. Macklin et al. 2015.

32. Macklin et al. 2013.

33. Moreno García 2015.

34. Macklin et al. 2013.

35. Honegger 2005: 242.

rectangular buildings, and fifty round huts. The dwelling huts average 4 m in diameter, and several larger huts that may have served as elite residences, meeting places, or workshops reached 7 m in diameter. Over 250 round storage pits are clustered in the inner area of the settlement, likely for communal food storage. The settlement walls were rebuilt over time, with a triple palisade built around the perimeter that restricted entrance to one or two gates.[36] Pre-Kerma pottery shares formal elements with A-Group ceramics known mainly from Lower Nubia, such as rippled and painted surface treatments, while also including black-topped red ware types that appear to be precursors to Kerma *ancien* vessels.[37] The Pre-Kerma settlement demonstrates the early importance of cattle to local economies,[38] as well as shared pottery traditions between Lower and Upper Nubia. No Egyptian pottery has been found in any Pre-Kerma contexts at Kerma, suggesting that significant contact had not yet occurred.[39]

Pre-Kerma settlement in the landscape around Kerma is relatively sparse,[40] although a number of storage pits have been found in association with Pre-Kerma ceramics on Sai Island, about 100 km north of Kerma. These pits contained the earliest domesticated wheat and barley known from the Middle Nile,[41] significant in part because they must have been introduced from the north via contacts with Egypt.

25.5.2. Kerma *ancien* (2600–2000 BC)

There appears to be a gap of up to five centuries between the end of the Pre-Kerma settlement at Kerma and the known beginning of the Kerma

---

36. Honegger 2004a; 2004b.

37. Honegger 2004a: 87.

38. Honegger 2004b.

39. Honegger 2004a: 87.

40. Honegger 2005.

41. Garcea and Hildebrand 2009.

ancien,[42] although recent excavation in the Kerma cemetery has recovered evidence of an earlier phase of Kerma *ancien* dating to as early as 2600 BC,[43] and it is possible that this gap would be filled by deeper excavation in the Kerma settlement itself.

On current evidence, the settlement at Kerma was first established during Kerma *ancien* II (2400–2300 BC) on what was at that time one or two islands. It appears to have consisted of three small fortified areas (figure 25.2).

The central settlement, perhaps 0.7 hectares in area, was defended by fortifications made of *jalous* (packed mud) that included gates, large bastions, and an exterior ditch or moat.[44] The fortifications enclosed an early version of the Western Deffufa, the religious center of the settlement,[45] although little is known about its early form. Other structures in the central settlement were either round huts, of which only postholes survive, or rectangular mudbrick structures. Numerous pits interpreted as being for storage of grain were found, as were a significant number of firing areas for ceramics within and immediately outside the fortifications. Some Kerma *ancien* burials were also found near the settlement, although the majority of burials were in the Eastern Cemetery.[46]

To the southwest, an area termed the *agglomération sécondaire* was built across a seasonal Nile channel. Covering an area of perhaps just

---

42. Each of the major Kerma phases has been subdivided, but there appear to be different systems in use by members of the Swiss team, and it is not simple to distinguish them from publications. Privati 1999 proposed four subphases for Kerma *ancien*, eight for Kerma *moyen*, and two for Kerma *classique*, all based on analysis of ceramics excavated from the cemetery, but did not assign them absolute dates. Bonnet 2014 provided maps of the city, but marks buildings as belonging to one of the three main phases or to two phases that overlap (KA-KM and KM-KC). Most recently, Honegger 2018: 22 proposed a revision of the KA sequence in four phases (but labeled 0–3 rather than 1–4), with a number of ^{14}C dates that provide a clear absolute chronology.

43. Honegger 2018.

44. Bonnet 2014: 216–224.

45. Bonnet 2004: 12; Bonnet 2014: 250.

46. Bonnet 2014: 238.

FIGURE 25.2. Plan of the city of Kerma during the Kerma *ancien* period (2400–2000 BC). Courtesy of Charles Bonnet.

0.1 hectare, this area was also surrounded by walls that seem to have protected a structure with associated workshops that Bonnet interprets as a shrine relating to a cult of ancestral rulers.[47]

To the northeast of the central settlement, another building interpreted as a small chapel was built within fortification walls, covering a still smaller area. This structure was built of mudbrick and wood.[48]

Bonnet's identification of these structures as shrines or chapels depends largely on their later histories, in particular the fact that in some form these buildings persisted for the next 900 years, having similar architectural plans and (in the case of the *agglomération sécondaire*) associated craft workshops. Bonnet interprets even this small early settlement as having included a palace of a powerful ruler, depending in part on his interpretation on the identification of this early settlement as *Yam* that was the focus of the Egyptian official Harkhuf's repeated embassies during this period.[49]

It is difficult to evaluate these interpretations, in large part because Kerma remains without parallel in the archaeology of sub-Saharan Africa. It may be noted, however, that two aspects of this interpretation are anomalous in the context of reconstructions of early cities—the fact that most of the built settlement is oriented around structures interpreted as shrines, and the notion that the community was at the same time organized around the figure of a powerful ruler. We have scarcely begun to consider what kinds of social networks might have structured this early settlement and provided support to the ruler of the kingdom, however powerful he may have been.

Kerma *ancien* burials are located in the northern section of the cemetery and take the form of steep tumuli about 2 m high with flexed burials generally oriented east-west. The deceased were often laid on a cowhide in a round pit with hands under their face as if sleeping. An unusually well-preserved burial of a man and his bow shows the continuing importance of archery, although the skeletal remains at Kerma

---

47. Bonnet 2014: 243–247.

48. Bonnet 2014: 248–249.

49. Bonnet 2014: 250.

in general do not show a high rate of violent injuries.[50] Even in the earliest burials, there are indications of elite status that include bed burials and some burials with a single human sacrificial burial. A tradition of burying sheep with the dead began in this period, and some of the sheep were buried with ostrich feather discs and horn ornaments.[51] Bonnet has argued that these burials represent a form of Kushite divinity that would later be syncretized into the ram-headed form of Amun.[52] Further animal symbolism included deposits of cattle horns in the grave or bucrania outside the burial.[53]

These burial practices show some similarities to contemporary C-Group burials in Lower Nubia, including the occasional presence of stone steles as grave monuments and ceramic bowls placed outside the tombs that were probably left after graveside feasts.[54]

Trade contacts with Egypt may have begun as early as Kerma *ancien*. Two Old Kingdom Egyptian boat captains are named in a hieratic inscription on a sandstone stele that was reused in a Middle Kerma chapel foundation.[55] Hundreds of fragmentary stone vessels with Egyptian hieroglyphic inscriptions that name Sixth Dynasty pharaohs are found in a deposit next to the Western Deffufa.[56] Unless these vessels came from later Kerman raids of a Sixth Dynasty regional *ka*-chapel (as fragments naming Twelfth Dynasty kings are also found in the same context), the deposit suggests an instance of trade contact or gift exchange with Egypt, perhaps in the context of expeditions like that described by Harkhuf.

50. Judd 2002.

51. Bonnet 1992.

52. Bonnet 1984: 15–17.

53. Chaix et al. 2012.

54. Honegger 2011; Welsby 2018.

55. Bonnet 1990.

56. Reisner 1923a: 30–31; Lacovara 1991.

In the broader Middle Nile region, a large Kerma *ancien* cemetery on Sai Island to the north of Kerma has been sampled,[57] and both cemeteries and settlement sites are found in the Northern Dongola Reach.[58] There are also a few Kerma *ancien* cemeteries in the Fourth Cataract region that represent settlement of people from Kerma in the region.[59] How these settlements related to Kerma itself is not clear, but it seems unlikely given the small size of Kerma itself that they could have been politically controlled directly from Kerma.

At the end of Kerma *ancien*, the fortified settlement of Kerma expanded to a size of 3 hectares and the fortifications were rebuilt to protect this area, consisting as before of a ditch and wall made of packed mud that included both bastions and gateways. A rectangular mudbrick structure with a rounded enclosure wall about 30 m long is significantly larger than other buildings of this time and is proposed by Bonnet to be the royal residence during this period.[60] A large round building designated as the "Great Hut" was also built next to the possible palace, at the intersection of the two main routes through the town and close to the main entrance to the Deffufa complex. Rebuilt at least eight times,[61] usually after fires, this structure was important enough to be in use for nearly 600 years. The structure may have been built entirely of wood in its earlier phases, but the clearly visible structure was built of mudbrick, about 12 m in diameter, with interior columns and a portico also supported by columns. The Great Hut likely served as an audience hall, as its form is similar to historically known sub-Saharan audience halls.

57. Gratien 1986.

58. Welsby 2001.

59. Emberling 2012.

60. Bonnet 2014: 57–58.

61. Bonnet 2014: 170.

25.5.3. Egypt and Kush

Beginning in about 1950 BC (during the Twelfth Dynasty), Egypt expanded its control of the Nile valley south of Aswan, building a series of imposing fortresses to below the Second Cataract and controlling movement of *Nehesy* and *Medjay*. This expansion was intended to control access to the gold sources in the Wadi Allaqi east of the Nile, and the scale of the forts shows the seriousness of the military threats posed by Kerma.[62]

The name "Kush" first appeared in Egyptian texts of this time, both royal steles and execration texts, and it is from these latter texts that we have the names of some rulers of Kush: Teriahi, Awawi (son of Kawi and his wife Kuni), and Nedjeh.[63] Egyptian texts also began to use the fixed phrase "Wretched Kush" as part of a designation of Kush as one of the primary enemies of the Egyptian state.

At the same time, people from the Middle Nile region clearly moved to Egypt, burying their dead in cemeteries there (like the tombs of Nubian mercenaries at Gebelein[64] or the C-Group cemetery at Hierakonpolis[65]). Some Nubian archers also served as mercenaries in the employ of an official in Upper Egypt.[66]

25.5.4. Kerma *moyen* (2000–1750 BC)

During the Kerma *moyen* period (2000–1750 BC), the Deffufa was enlarged and a complex for religious rituals and production of ceramics and bread was added to its east and west sides (figure 25.3). The settlement of Dokki Gel, a site about 1 km to the north, may have been

---

62. Emberling 2014: 135.

63. Rilly 2017: 71–72.

64. Fischer 1961.

65. See recently Schröder 2018.

66. Lacovara 2011.

FIGURE 25.3. Plan of the city of Kerma during the Kerma *moyen* period (2000–1750 BC). Courtesy of Charles Bonnet.

founded during this period,[67] although its earlier phases are not known in detail. Inside the northern gate in the fortification walls was a large open space that Bonnet interprets as a holding area for royal herds.[68]

Kerma *moyen* burials show a marked increase in social stratification. Bed burials continue, and funerary chapels are constructed for some burials. Human sacrifices increase in number to as many as seven individuals. Some elite burials contain Egyptian trade goods such as mirrors and kohl pots, and also large jars.[69] Locally made bronze daggers are in an Egyptian style with a lunate pommel.[70] A limited number of burials were interred in large tumuli with up to a hundred cattle bucrania, while one burial was surrounded by a ring of nearly 5,000.[71] These bucrania were not likely the result of a single feast given the quantity of meat that would have been involved. Isotope analysis[72] suggests that the cattle had been raised in varied environments and may have been sent as gifts in honor of the deceased from a wide area.

Middle Kerma sites are found from the Second Cataract to the upstream end of the Fourth Cataract, seemingly not including the southern bend of the Nile—about 600 km in total length. The density of settlements and cemeteries in the Northern Dongola Reach survey increased as much as 400 percent, and cemeteries of this date were also significantly more common than previously.[73]

The only rural settlements of this period that have been excavated are two small sites at Gism el-Arba, about 30 km south of Kerma. These were agricultural villages, including houses and rectangular structures with interior rows of stones that have been interpreted as storage structures

---

67. Rilly 2017: 81.

68. Bonnet 2014: 95–97.

69. Bourriau 1991.

70. Vercoutter 1960.

71. Chaix et al. 2012.

72. Iacumin et al. 2001.

73. Welsby 2003; Paner and Borcowski 2005; Paner et al. 2010; Emberling 2014.

or granaries.[74] Similar structures were found on sites in the Northern Dongola Reach survey,[75] although interestingly none have been reported from Kerma itself.

25.5.5. Kerma *classique* (1750–1500 BC)

During the Kerma *classique* period, Kerma grew to its largest size (figure 25.4). The excavated area is approximately 20 hectares, but the ancient city extends under the modern settlement. The fortifications were rebuilt with stone foundations to encompass this larger area. At the center of the town was the Deffufa at the scale we see it today. It was a mudbrick structure originally about 24 m high.[76] Access into the structure was by a staircase on its western side. The staircase led to an altar and a chapel that were deep in the center of the Deffufa, and stairs then continued to the top of the building. Additional chapels were built into the mudbrick massif on the north and south sides, and other buildings with dolomitic marble column bases on the north, west, and east sides were also interpreted as chapels.

We cannot be certain of the cosmological significance of the Deffufa, but it seems possible that it represented an artificial mountain in which deities were thought to reside. It is notable that Egyptian temples in Nubia during the New Kingdom included a number of rock-cut temples (including the temples of Rameses II at Abu Simbel), although this was not a common Egyptian practice prior to their conquest of Kush. Also notable in this regard are the later Kushite rock-cut temples at Gebel Barkal, of which the best preserved is the Mut temple,[77] which were part of a theology that held that Amun in his Kushite form was born in, and also resided in, the mountain itself.

---

74. Gratien et al. 2003–2008.

75. Welsby 2001.

76. Bonnet 2004: 46.

77. Kendall and Mohamed 2016: 12–22.

FIGURE 25.4. Plan of the city of Kerma during the Kerma *classique* period (1750–1500 BC). Courtesy of Charles Bonnet.

The Deffufa and its surrounding structures were clearly ritual in nature, but like temples in Egypt it also served economic functions. Copper-smelting ovens were found in close proximity to the Deffufa,[78] as were remains of faience production.[79]

Specialized craft production, including copper smelting as well as manufacture of the highly specialized Kerma *classique* burnished eggshell ware, was also found in the *agglomération secondaire* to the southwest.

The Great Hut continued in use during Kerma *classique*, and a new structure interpreted as a palace was built as well.[80] The palace walls enclosed a relatively modest area of 55 × 30 m, not much larger than some other houses in the city, and shared with them architectural features including courtyards and round granaries. The palace was distinguished from those houses, however, by an "archive room" that contained over 5,000 seal blanks, and a large rectangular building to the south that appears to have been used for storage.[81]

While it is sometimes said that the city was inhabited only by the elite, houses in Kerma *classique* in fact display a wide range of construction techniques and sizes, from large structures made of mudbrick to smaller round huts made of posts set into postholes (which were not as comprehensively excavated[82]).

In addition to the existing parts of the city, a river port was in use during Kerma *classique*.[83] It is in the area of the modern town of Kerma and has not been comprehensively excavated, but its presence suggests an increasing volume of trade, likely including grain shipments, during Kerma *classique*.

This is also the time when Kush reached its largest extent. Large Kerma *classique* burial mounds on Sai Island to the north[84] and Mograt

---

78. Bonnet 2004: 33–38.

79. Reisner 1923b: 135.

80. Bonnet 2014: 165–167.

81. Bonnet 2014: 125–126.

82. Bonnet 2014: 180.

83. Bonnet 2014: 212.

84. Gratien 1986: 337.

Island at the upstream end of the Fourth Cataract[85] suggest the development of regional elites within Kush, and settlement on Sai Island has been documented but not extensively excavated.[86] Occupation at the rural agricultural site of Gism el-Arba continued.[87] Settlement in the Northern Dongola Reach survey area reached its peak, as did occupation of the Fourth Cataract region, where gold mining seems to have begun.[88]

The Egyptian centralized state of the Middle Kingdom began to disintegrate after 1750 BC, and some scholars have assumed that the growth of Kerma was only possible because of this collapse of Egyptian control. However, the growth in population around Kerma during Kerma *moyen*, noted earlier, shows that Kerma grew despite the presence of Egyptian fortresses. With the end of the Middle Kingdom, the forts in Lower Nubia were no longer occupied by rotating garrisons of Egyptian soldiers, but were occupied by Kush. In one case, the Egyptian commander of a fort expressed allegiance to Nedjeh, king of Kush.[89]

A stele from Buhen depicting a figure wearing the white crown of Upper Egypt, carrying a bow and mace, is often suggested to be a depiction of a king of Kush,[90] perhaps the only such representation. The negative evidence for visual representations of Kerman kings poses a strong distinction of Nubian conceptions of rulership in comparison with pharaonic Egypt. Rather than arguing against the sociopolitical power of Kerman kings, this demonstrates an essential difference in conceptions of kingship between the neighboring regions. Egypt had a long tradition of pharaonic power, codified into a distinctive visual set of royal representations and motifs. Kerma *classique* kings drew upon long-standing traditions to implement performances of power, basing their legitimacy within Nubian conceptions of death, afterlife, and mythology. For

85. Weschenfelder 2014.

86. Gratien and Olive 1981; Hesse 1981; D'Ercole 2017.

87. Gratien 1999; 2003.

88. Emberling et al. 2014.

89. Kendall 1997: 29.

90. H. Smith 1976: 84; cf. Knoblauch 2012.

example, they depicted their status through types of iconography that held local, indigenously Nubian significance, such as lions, scorpions, and hippopotami. In conjunction with this program of legitimization, Kerma *classique* kings paired their control of imported Egyptian sculpture, which stood as material evidence of their ascending interregional political power, with internal power systems that manifested as mass inhumations.[91] Therefore, Kerma *classique* kingship was constructed through reference to long-standing indigenous Kerman modes of power, as well as newly developing interregional power structures.

The agricultural economy of Kerma during Kerma *classique* was still based on wheat and barley[92]—the transition to the African complex of millet and sorghum seems on present evidence to have taken place later and further south.[93] Study of faunal remains suggests that people in agricultural villages ate more fish and those in Kerma itself ate more cattle— a higher status food.[94]

Kerma *classique* (KC) tumuli follow established Kerman funerary traditions in a magnified form and scale. The southern section of the Eastern Cemetery at Kerma (figure 25.5) contains the largest funerary monuments at the site: four successively larger royal tumuli and funerary chapels are arranged in a line that runs northeast to southwest— Tumulus KXVI (KC Generation 1); Tumulus KX and Funerary Chapel KXI (KC Generation 2); Tumulus KIV (KC Generation 3); and Tumulus KIII and Funerary Chapel KII (KC Generation 4). The major tumuli have complex internal mudbrick supporting structures, as well as separate subsidiary elite burials which were constructed directly into the earthen disk of the tumulus (figures 25.6 and 25.7).[95] Two funerary chapels share the massive mudbrick architectural construction technique found in the Western Deffufa, while their straight axes and

91. Minor 2012.

92. Vila 1987.

93. Fuller and Lucas 2021.

94. Chaix 2006.

95. Reisner 1923a: 95–96, 135, 190, 272.

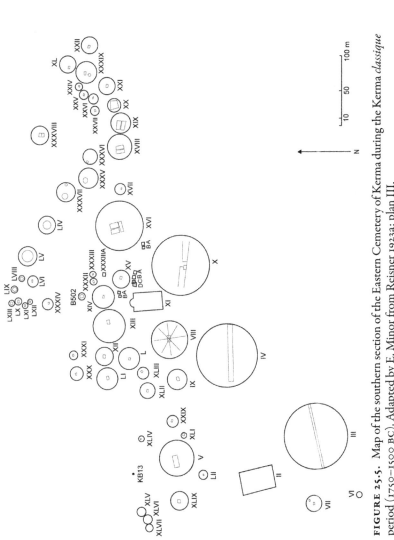

FIGURE 25.5. Map of the southern section of the Eastern Cemetery of Kerma during the Kerma *classique* period (1750–1500 BC). Adapted by E. Minor from Reisner 1923a: plan III.

FIGURE 25.6. View of Royal Tumulus KIII looking north toward Funerary Chapel KII. © Museum of Fine Arts, Boston.

interior wall decoration demonstrate mortuary ritual traditions.[96] To the southwest, a group of unassociated burials (designated KB by Reisner) are also poorly preserved but contain fragmentary funerary equipment equivalent to that found in the elite subsidiary graves.[97] These multiple sectors and burial types attest to the increasing social complexity and shifting hierarchies among the Kerma *classique* community.[98]

Two royal Kerma *classique* funerary complexes include funerary chapels set to the northwest of the massive tumuli. Funerary Chapel KXI was built in combination with Tumulus KX and may have been altered for reuse by the king interred in the subsequent Tumulus KIV.[99] The

---

96. Bonnet 2000.

97. Reisner 1923a: 507–522.

98. Minor 2012.

99. O'Connor 1984; Bonnet 2000: 65.

FIGURE 25.7. Subsidiary grave from Tumulus KIV with deceased individuals on *angareeb* funerary beds, sacrificed individuals, and funerary feast. © Museum of Fine Arts, Boston.

axial plan of Funerary Chapel KXI leads from an entrance corridor at the south to a room with a central line of five columns, steps lead to a second corridor that opens to a longer room with nine columns, a painted altar base, and a thin stairway accessed on the eastern side.[100] The original plan consisted of a single room with mudbrick walls 8–9 m in thickness and a rounded apse protruding on the northern end, which was then expanded by the addition of the front room and an additional thickness of 2–3 m on the walls, which were finally capped in sandstone, and the final dimensions of the chapel are 50 × 27 m.[101] The ceiling was made of stone blocks inlaid with large faience rosettes (perhaps a Kerman manner of depicting stars), made from reshaped and recycled faience

---

100. Reisner 1923a: 255–259; Bonnet 2000.

101. Reisner 1923a: 258; Bonnet 2000.

vessels.[102] Although only the lower section of the walls are preserved, polychrome wall paintings lead from the entrance to the altar base. The entrance corridor includes a sailboat and nilotic fishing scene, rows of red hippopotami, a pair of bulls fighting across a well, a woman in rowboat with an attendant, a phyle of cattle, elephants, and other animals. The first room includes rows of giraffes on the west side and registers of rowboats (possibly depicting different Nubian and/or Egyptian groups in conflict) on the east. Rows of giraffes lead from the second corridor to the second room and continue along the western wall, while the eastern wall has a set of scenes of a brown bull fighting with a white and black spotted bull. The preserved altar base depicts two figures, one female and the other climbing a ladder to whatever ritual focus is no longer present. This upward movement may be connected to the religious rituals that would have used the side staircase in this room, as well as the city-based religious rituals that wound through the vertical path in the Eastern Deffufa to its roof.[103] Overall, the themes of rows of indigenous animals and boats fit within the long existing Nubian artistic tradition of rock art,[104] and the focus on movement and confrontation along a north–south axis may reflect political conflict with Egypt during this period.[105]

Funerary Chapel KII was built in combination with Tumulus KIII, the last of the royal Kerma *classique* burials in the Eastern Cemetery. This monumental mudbrick chapel is also referred to as the Eastern Deffufa and reaches 51 m in length and 31 m in width, and with walls preserved to a height of 10 m and a thickness of 15–16 m.[106] The axial plan follows the model set by the final form of Funerary Chapel KXI, with an entrance corridor, first room with four central pillars and stairwell on the eastern side, a second corridor, and second room with four central pillars. As in Funerary Chapel KXI, the first room contained wall paintings

---

102. Reisner 1923a: 266–267; Lacovara 1998.

103. Bonnet 2000.

104. Kleinitz and Koenitz 2006.

105. Minor 2012.

106. Bonnet 2000.

of animals on the western side and sailboats on the eastern side,[107] but these were no longer visible upon re-excavation.[108] The front façade and the second room were decorated with modeled faience tiles that are a distinctly Kerman artistic tradition. Two monumental lions flanked the front entrance to the chapel, pacing toward each other.[109] Other tile elements formed a cavetto cornice, plant buds or shoots, and the majority are trapezoids with "rills" or modeled parallel lines that would have formed a complex geometric pattern.[110] A large granite plinth carved with a winged sun disc spanned the entrance to Funerary Chapel KII, and this Egyptian religious motif was mirrored on the imported stele of Intef, which had been obtained from the Heqaib complex on Elephantine and was found along the east side of the chapel entrance.[111] The incorporation of faience and lion decorations in Funerary Chapel KII fit within the larger decorative program of this last Kerma *classique* king, while the form of the chapel demonstrates continuity in the ritual practices associated with the royal funerary cult.[112]

The four royal Kerma *classique* tumuli reach up to 100 m in diameter and have interior architectural features built in mudbrick.[113] The later three royal tumuli have two walls that run across the diameter of the earthen mound to create a transverse corridor. A series of thinner walls extend perpendicularly from the transverse corridor and act to reinforce the large earthen mound. The royal burial chamber is a set of two mudbrick rooms, sometimes with barrel vaulting, at the direct center of the transverse corridor. The central location of the royal burial chamber was easily discovered by grave robbers, and the only remnants of royal

---

107. Reisner 1923a: 124; Lacovara 1986.

108. Bonnet and Valbelle 2000.

109. Reisner 1923a: 129.

110. Minor 2012.

111. Reisner 1923a: 126–127; Minor 2014.

112. Minor 2012.

113. Reisner 1923a: 95.

funerary equipment are fragmentary. Royal burial goods were partially recovered, scattered out from the center of the tumulus, including funerary beds, animal sculptures, and funerary boat models in wood, stone, glazed quartz, and faience.[114]

Several hundred fragments of imported Egyptian stone sculpture, representing at least ninety individual statues, were interred in the Kerma *classique* royal tumuli.[115] The majority of the sculptures are figural and fall into Middle Kingdom and Second Intermediate Period types. Several inscribed fragments contain names and titles of individuals with known cenotaphs at the Heqaib and Satet temple complexes at Elephantine, suggesting that the First Cataract was a major point of contact between Kermans and Egyptians.[116] The collection and subsequent interment of these Egyptian sculptures provides material evidence of the military incursions and/or political influence of each generation of Kerma *classique* kings. The king of the first generation (KXVI) was able to obtain only four Egyptian sculptures. By the second generation (KX), the king included at least twenty-five Egyptian sculptures, incorporating examples originally installed in the Satet temple in Elephantine. The third generation (KIV) continued to forcibly collect material from Elephantine but in a lesser volume, with only fourteen individual statues. The fourth and final Kerma *classique* king (KIII) undertook a resurgence of collecting in Elephantine and further north to Elkab, and interred at least thirty-seven sculptures that include the sole complete statue, that of lady Sennuwy.[117] Sennuwy and her husband Djefaihapy, whose fragmented sculpture is also present in KIII, are known to have been buried in Asyut and therefore their statues may represent a diplomatic gift from the Hyksos.[118] Alternately, based on Djefaihapy's official capacity as the "Great Headsman of the South," and stylistic similarities between

114. Reisner 1923a: 138–140, 192–194, 276–279, 391–394.

115. Reisner 1923b: 22–48.

116. Valbelle 2004.

117. Minor 2012.

118. O'Connor 1974; Wenig 1978.

the couple's statues and the Elephantine workshop, their sculptures may have originated from an otherwise unattested cenotaph in the First Cataract area.[119]

The later three royal Kerma *classique* tumuli have mass interments of human sacrifices arranged along the length of the transverse corridor, set alongside the imported Egyptian sculpture. The practice peaked in the second generation (Tumulus KX), with at least 322 sacrificed individuals,[120] and declined to 100 sacrificed individuals by the fourth generation (Tumulus KIII).[121] The inclusion of sacrifices speaks to the power of the Kerman king to dictate his subjects' deaths on a massive scale,[122] and Egyptian loot emphasizes his success in military raids in foreign territory.[123] The manner of death was most likely poisoning, as it left no physical evidence on the skeletons or naturally preserved soft tissue, and suffocation, strangulation, or throat cutting would leave at least a few accidental visible marks in such a large sample group.[124] Bioarchaeological evidence shows that sacrificed individuals in the royal tumuli corridors had lived in the Kerma area, did not have significantly increased signs of physiological stress, and therefore were not prisoners of war nor servants who had lived lives of hard manual labor.[125] The range of personal adornments among sacrifices includes highly decorated individuals who may have been selected by the king as they held key religious, political, or economic roles in the community, who then brought along their own contingent of sacrifices, which led to the notably large mass interments.[126]

---

119. Minor 2012; Moreno García 2017.

120. Reisner 1923a: 312.

121. Reisner 1923a: 81.

122. Parker Pearson 1999: 18, 166.

123. Bonnet 1997; Davies 2003; Valbelle 2004: 182.

124. Buzon and Judd 2008; Judd and Irish 2009; *contra* Reisner 1923a: 65–79, who assumed that they were buried alive.

125. Buzon and Judd 2008.

126. Minor 2012.

25.5.6. Elite burials of the Kerma *classique* period

Elite Kermans constructed their own rectangular graves into the royal tumuli and brought along their own sacrificed individuals on a significantly smaller scale (figure 25.5). These subsidiary graves allow for an understanding of the social hierarchy of the Kerman community, as these private individuals had a real or desired relationship to the deceased king,[127] and may have gained access through merit of office or family associations. Although restricted, a cross section of the Kerman community is represented in the private subsidiary burials, as there is a range in size, complexity, and wealth of burial goods within them.[128] The primary deceased individuals were set on wooden funerary beds in a flexed position, with their heads to the east and laid on their right sides to face north. The elaborateness of funerary beds is an index of status, as burials with ivory-inlaid beds have the highest average wealth of accompanying funerary goods.[129] The ivory inlays of local and fantastical animals may represent a codification of the Kerman worldview, as lines of flying animals are set above ground-dwelling ones, as well as delineating family or group affiliations.[130] The same corpus of decorative animals are found on iridescent mica hat appliques in some elite burials.[131] Several graves of elite women buried in decorated leather skirts, including one wearing a silver headdress, suggest an important female religious role in the community.[132]

Kerma *classique* funerary equipment included small Egyptian imports and objects made locally to replicate them. The use of imported and replicated Egyptian material culture in private KC graves increased over time, with a rapid rise in the fourth generation, and these foreign-marked

---

127. Adams 1977: 211.

128. Minor 2012.

129. Minor 2012.

130. Minor 2012.

131. Reisner 1923b: 274.

132. Minor 2018b.

objects were concentrated in the highest status graves (inlaid bed burials). Cosmetic implements, mirrors, and kohl makeup containers are among the most common Egyptian imports. The use of replicas, such as modified bronze mirrors or uninscribed scarabs, was more prevalent in lower status graves (non-inlaid bed or hide-wrapped burials). Other Egyptian imports or replicas were used in ways outside of their original intentions. For example, wooden headrests were often placed at the feet of the deceased, scarabs were sewn into garments as decorative elements, faience vessels were formed into lids for imported alabaster vessels, and one ivory magic/apotropaic wand was reworked into a distinctively Kerman dagger handle. As imported and replicated Egyptian material culture increased in use over the Kerma *classique* period, indigenous Nubian funerary equipment did not decrease in use, demonstrating that this case of cultural entanglement was an additive process, rather than appropriation or acculturation.[133]

The social relationships between the primary deceased individual and the sacrificed individuals in private graves may be based on networks of indebtedness created during life. Sacrifices in elite graves also demonstrate a range of personal adornment and were arranged around a communal funerary feast and set of serving and drinking vessels. In a few graves, large vessels contain barley beer or porridge residue and woven giraffe hair beer filter straws set beside them may have been used for communal consumption during feasting.[134] Rather than a strict master–servant relationship, the grouped arrangement of elite Kerma *classique* graves suggests that the primary and sacrificed individuals had a mutable relationship built during life.

25.6. Egyptian conquest

At the end of the Second Intermediate Period, the Kerma kingdom fell under a series of Egyptian campaigns, part of the reunification of Egypt

---

133. Minor 2012.

134. Minor 2018b.

and the beginning of the New Kingdom colonial control of Nubia. In the texts of kings Kamose and Ahmose there is evidence of violent military campaigns reaching Kerman settlements. The role of the creation of these texts was not an impartial record, but was instead an integral practice in the symbolic propaganda of the pharaoh as the vanquisher of chaotic elements.[135]

The three steles of Kamose address conflict with rulers of Kush at the end of the Second Intermediate Period. In regnal Year 3, the First Kamose Stele records Kamose arguing with his court that the current loss of Egyptian territory is unacceptable: "I should like to know what purpose serves my strength, when one prince is in Avaris and another is in Kush, and I sit united with [an Asiatic] and a [Nubian], each man holding his slice of Egypt, who share the land with me."[136] Prior Egyptian campaigns against Nubia are referenced in the second stele of Kamose, as part of a letter from the Hyksos ruler to the new ruler of Kush.[137] This letter was purportedly carried by a Hyksos agent, who was captured by Kamose's soldiers in the desert, and was used as evidence for a Hyksos-Kerma alliance. The Hyksos ruler Apepi invites the Kerman king to coordinate dual northern and southern military campaigns against Upper Egypt.[138] Fragments of a third stele from Karnak contain several references to Nubians (*nehesyu*), originally likely including further information on his Nubian campaigns.[139]

Ahmose, Kamose's successor, continued military campaigns against Kerma, in tandem with ongoing attacks against the Hyksos. These campaigns reached the Second Cataract forts, using them as a base to continue south. Details are contained in the biographies of the soldiers Ahmose, son of Ibana, and Ahmose Pennekhbet. King Ahmose's troops went to the region of *Khenthennefer* first, which may refer to the

---

135. Baines 1996.

136. Gardiner 1916: 99.

137. Habachi 1972; Bonnet and Valbelle 2010: 363.

138. Habachi 1972; Smith 1976: 61; Morris 2005: 68.

139. Van Siclen 2010.

region directly south of the Second Cataract, or perhaps Sai Island.[140] The subsequent campaign of Amenhotep I reached "the Upper Well," perhaps referring to Selima oasis.[141] The settlement of Kerma may not have been breached until the reign of Thutmose I, as recorded in the Tombos Stele.[142]

Kerma was destroyed by the Egyptians, confirmed by destruction levels found in the city and religious areas of Kerma.[143] The date of the destruction levels have been suggested to be from the close of the "Hyksos Period,"[144] to as late as the reign of Thutmose II.[145] Politically, the Kerma kingdom was effectively neutralized by the reign of Thutmose I. He was the first pharaoh to ensure colonial control of the Third Cataract region by enlisting the loyalty of several local Nubian leaders, who would function to control the region under his pharaonic authority.[146]

25.7. Post-Kerma

The end of the Kerma Kingdom was not sudden, and religious and daily life practices continued under Egyptian colonial control. A final large tumulus, perhaps the burial of a terminal Kerman king, is located nearer to the Nile under modern habitation.[147] Kermans continued to live and practice their cultural traditions in nearby areas. Excavations at Tombos, close to Kerma, demonstrate that Nubian and Egyptian residents

---

140. Goedicke 1965; Vandersleyen 1971; O'Connor 1987: 115; Morris 2005: 70–71.

141. Berg 1987: 7; Morris 2005: 71.

142. Sethe 1906 (*Urk.* IV 83.17–84.5); Bradbury 1986; Morris 2005: 72.

143. Bonnet and Valbelle 2004: 68–73.

144. Bonnet 1979: 8; Morris 2005: 68.

145. Bonnet 2001: 228; Morris 2005: 69.

146. Morris 2005: 92–93.

147. Bonnet 1990: nos. 305–306; 2000: 144–152, fig. 110.

intermarried during the New Kingdom occupation, and that Kerman funerary traditions and foodways persisted to a degree.[148]

The conclusion of military conflict between Egyptians and Kermans was a decisive Egyptian foray into the south, evidenced by burned destruction levels at the city and necropolis of Kerma.[149] Ahmose bragged of summarily executing Nubian rebels and defeating all his southern rivals.[150] Archaeological finds, however, offer other evidence for Kermans living and producing material culture throughout Egypt in the period directly after the destruction of their Nubian capital. Kerma pottery found in late Second Intermediate Period–early New Kingdom contexts in Avaris demonstrates that a contingent of Kermans played a role at the Hyksos capital, perhaps as mercenaries.[151] Janine Bourriau presents significant evidence of Kermans living and dying in Egypt, with distinctive Kerma beakers and other pottery found in early Eighteenth Dynasty funerary contexts at Thebes, as well as domestic contexts at Kahun, Hierakonpolis, Edfu, and Memphis.[152] At Saqqara, an early Eighteenth Dynasty grave contained two faience vessels in the forms of a Kerma beaker and a rhyton. As the other burial goods in this grave included a mix of Egyptian and Nubian funerary goods, including Kerma *classique* ceramic beakers, Bourriau suggested that the deceased was an Egyptianized Kerman, and that the faience vessels with distinctive bubbled glaze were manufactured at Kerma by Nubian artisans.[153] At Deir el-Ballas, excavations have uncovered a significant amount of Nubian cookware sherds, fragments of leather kilts, and bone awls like those found at Kerma.[154] Faience tile fragments from the early Eighteenth Dynasty palace area at

---

148. Smith 2003a; Smith and Buzon 2014.

149. Morris 2005: 68; Bonnet and Valbelle 2010: 360.

150. Morris 2005: 71.

151. Dirminti 2014; Aston and Bietak 2017.

152. Bourriau 1991.

153. Bourriau 1991: 139–140.

154. Lacovara 1990: 4, 7, 16–18.

Deir el-Ballas have nearly identical decorative shapes and manufacturing processes as tiles found at Funerary Chapel KII at Kerma.[155] This evidence shows that Kermans were actively engaged with Egyptians during the Kerma *récent* period or early Eighteenth Dynasty, continuing aspects of their own cultural practices despite the Egyptian conquest of their capital and the dissolution of their independent Nubian kingdom.

There remain questions, especially regarding the connections and experiences of provincial areas within the Kerma kingdom, which are currently understood through partial evidence, as new regional Kerman settlements and cemeteries are identified. Evidence from the long occupation of the Sai Island settlement includes the development of distinctive cooking and storage vessels,[156] as well as lithic industries.[157] The settlement site of Gism el-Arba demonstrates the move from mud and timber to rectangular mudbrick architecture.[158] Many Kerma settlement sites that have been identified through large-scale regional surveys have not yet been excavated in depth.[159]

25.8. Conclusions

This review of the state of knowledge about early Kush suggests that excavation, survey, and archaeological analysis over the past forty years have very significantly increased our knowledge of the kingdom of Kerma. While disciplinary histories and proximity to Egypt have sometimes led to underestimates of its complexity, it is now best seen as an early African empire. It controlled a large area of the Middle Nile

---

155. Elizabeth Minor, personal observation, on the basis of unpublished museum records and unpublished excavation records held at the Phoebe A. Hearst Museum of Anthropology, Berkeley.

156. D'Ercole et al. 2017.

157. Gratien and Olive 1981; Hesse 1981.

158. Gratien 1999; 2003.

159. Welsby 2001; Smith 2003b; Smith and Herbst 2005; Osman and Edwards 2012; Nordström 2014.

and encompassed a range of local cultures visible in archaeological and historical records. It was a neighbor of Egypt whose development proceeded along its own trajectory that was affected by but not entirely determined by Egypt.

In comparative terms, early Kush is distinctive in many ways, and we expect that ongoing research will continue to elucidate them. Its representation of political power was carried out in the mortuary realm rather than through textual or iconographic representations of kings, or in palaces that were on an entirely different scale of magnitude than the houses of nobles. Subsistence was agricultural but also pastoral, and urban concentrations were small relative to the size of the territory controlled by Kush.

Some outstanding questions include the nature of the economy of Kush. Was trade managed entirely by the king and palace, or were there independent artisans and merchants who worked outside royal control? Conceptions of the gods and human relationship to the divine realm remain difficult to elucidate, although hints of worship of royal ancestors at Kerma, the idea that the dead are sleeping, and the notion of gods in the earth or in mountains provide some basis for further investigation. As for all periods of history along the Middle Nile, we still know nothing about contacts with regions to the west and south, and further archaeological investigation in those regions remains a priority.

REFERENCES

Adams, W.Y. 1977. *Nubia: corridor to Africa.* Princeton, NJ: Princeton University Press.

Aston, D., and Bietak, M. 2017. Nubians in the Nile delta: à propos Avaris and Peru-nefer. In Spencer, N., Stevens, A., and Binder, M. (eds.), *Nubia in the New Kingdom: lived experience, pharaonic control and indigenous traditions.* Leuven: Peeters, 491–524.

Baines, J. 1996. Contextualizing Egyptian representations of society and ethnicity. In Cooper, J., and Schwartz, G. (eds.), *The study of the ancient Near East in the twenty-first century: the William Foxwell Albright centennial conference.* Winona Lake, IN: Eisenbrauns, 339–384.

Berg, D.A. 1987. Early 18th Dynasty expansion into Nubia. *Journal of the Society for the Study of Egyptian Antiquities* 17: 1–14.

Bonnet, C. 1979. Remarques sur la ville de Kerma. In Vercoutter, J. (ed.), *Hommages à la mémoire de Serge Sauneron, vol. 1.* Cairo: Institut français d'archéologie orientale, 1–10.

Bonnet, C. 1984. Les fouilles archéologiques de Kerma (Soudan): rapport préliminaire sur les Campagnes de 1982–1983 et 1983–1984. *Genava: Revue des Musées d'Art et d'Histoire de Genève* 32: 5–20.

Bonnet, C. 1990. *Kerma, royaume de Nubie: l'antiquité africaine au temps des pharaons.* Geneva: Mission archéologique de l'Université de Genève au Soudan.

Bonnet, C. 1992. Excavations at the Nubian royal town of Kerma: 1975–91. *Antiquity* 66: 611–625.

Bonnet, C. 1997. The kingdom of Kerma. In Wildung, D. (ed.), *Sudan: ancient kingdoms of the Nile.* Paris: Institute du Monde Arabe, 89–95.

Bonnet, C. 2000. *Édifices et rites funéraires à Kerma.* Paris: Errance.

Bonnet, C. 2004. *Le temple principal de la ville de Kerma et son quartier religieux.* Paris: Errance.

Bonnet, C. 2014. *La ville de Kerma: une capitale nubienne au sud de l'Égypte.* Lausanne: Favre.

Bonnet, C. 2019. *The black kingdom of the Nile.* Cambridge, MA: Harvard University Press.

Bonnet, C., and Honegger, M. 2021. The eastern cemetery of Kerma. In Emberling, G., and Williams, B.B. (eds.), *The Oxford handbook of ancient Nubia.* Oxford: Oxford University Press, 213–226.

Bonnet, C., and Valbelle, D. 2010. The Classic Kerma period and the beginning of the New Kingdom. In Marée, M. (ed.), *The Second Intermediate Period (Thirteenth-Seventeenth Dynasties): current research, future prospects.* Leuven: Peeters, 359–366.

Bourriau, J. 1991. Relations between Egypt and Kerma during the Middle and New Kingdoms. In Davies, W.V. (ed.), *Egypt and Africa: Nubia from prehistory to Islam.* London: British Museum Press, 129–144.

Buzon, M., and Judd, M. 2008. Investigating health at Kerma: Sacrificial versus nonsacrificial individuals. *American Journal of Physical Anthropology* 136: 93–99.

Chaix, L. 2006. New data about rural economy in the Kerma culture: the site of Gism el-Arba (Sudan). In Kroeper, K., Chłodnicki, M., and

Kobusiewicz, M. (eds.), *Archaeology of early northeastern Africa in memory of Lech Krzyżaniak*. Poznań: Poznań Archeological Museum, 25–38.

Chaix, L., Dubosson, J., and Honegger, M. 2012. Bucrania from the eastern cemetery at Kerma (Sudan) and the practice of cattle horn deformation. In Kabaciński, J., Chłodnicki, M., and Kobusiewicz, M. (eds.), *Prehistory of northeastern Africa: new ideas and discoveries*. Poznań: Poznań Archaeological Museum, 189–212.

Cooper, J. 2012. Reconsidering the location of Yam. *JARCE* 48: 1–21.

Davies, V. 2003. Kush in Egypt: a new historical inscription. *Sudan & Nubia* 7: 52–54.

D'Ercole, G., Budka, J., Sterba, J.H., Garcea, E.A., and Mader, D. 2017. The successful "recipe" for a long-lasting tradition: Nubian ceramic assemblages from Sai Island (northern Sudan) from prehistory to the New Kingdom. *Antiquity* 91: 24–42.

Dirminti, E. 2014. Between Kerma and Avaris: the first kingdom of Kush and Egypt during the Second Intermediate Period. In Anderson, J.R., and Welsby, D.A. (eds.), *The Fourth Cataract and beyond*. Leuven: Peeters, 337–345.

Dunham, D., D'Auria, S., and Reisner, G.A. 1982. *Excavations at Kerma, part VI: subsidiary Nubian graves*. Boston: Department of Egyptian and Ancient Near Eastern Art, Museum of Fine Arts.

Edwards, D. 1998. Meroe and the Sudanic kingdoms. *Journal of African History* 39: 175–193.

Emberling, G. 2012. Archaeological salvage in the Fourth Cataract, northern Sudan (1991–2008). In Fisher, M., Lacovara, P., D'Auria, S., and Ikram, S. (eds.), *Ancient Nubia: African kingdoms on the Nile*. Cairo: American University in Cairo Press, 71–77.

Emberling, G. 2014. Pastoral states: toward a comparative archaeology of early Kush. *Origini* 36: 125–156.

Emberling, G., Williams, B., Ingvoldstad, M., and James, T.R. 2014. Peripheral vision: identity at the margins of the early kingdom of Kush. In Anderson, J.R., and Welsby, D.A. (eds.), *The Fourth Cataract and beyond*. Leuven: Peeters, 329–336.

Fisher, H. 1961. The Nubian mercenaries of Gebelein during the First Intermediate Period. *Kush* 9: 44–80.

Fuller, D.Q., and Lucas, L. 2021. Savanna on the Nile: long-term agricultural diversification and intensification in Nubia. In Emberling,

G., and Williams, B.B. (eds.), *The Oxford handbook of ancient Nubia.* Oxford: Oxford University Press, 927–954.

Garcea, E.A.A., and Hildebrand, E.A. 2009. Shifting social networks along the Nile: Middle Holocene ceramic assemblages from Sai Island, Sudan. *Journal of Anthropological Archaeology* 28: 304–322.

Gardiner, A.H. 1916. The defeat of the Hyksos by Kamose: the Carnarvon Tablet, no. 1. *JEA* 3: 95–110.

Goedicke, H. 1965. The location of Ḥnt-ḥn-nfr. *Kush* 13: 102–111.

Gratien, B. 1978. *Les cultures Kerma: essai de classification.* Lille: Presses Universitaires du Septentrion.

Gratien, B. 1986. *Saï I: la nécropole Kerma.* Paris: Éditions du Centre National de la Recherche Scientifique.

Gratien, B. 2003. L'habitat 2 de Gism el-Arba: rapport préliminaire sur un centre de stockage Kerma. *CRIPEL* 23: 29–43.

Gratien, B. 2011. Les cultures Kerma: essai de classification, trente ans après. In Rondot, V., Alpi, F., and Villeneuve, F. (eds.), *La pioche et la plume: autour du Soudan, du Liban et de la Jordanie. Hommages archéologiques à Patrice Lenoble.* Paris: Presse de l'Université Paris-Sorbonne, 225–236.

Gratien, B., and Olive, M. 1981. Fouilles à Saï, 1977–1979. *CRIPEL* 6: 69–169.

Gratien, B., Marchi, S., Sys, D., and Dissaux, R.-P. 2003–2008. Gism el-Arba habitat 2: campagne 2005–2006. *Kush* 19: 21–35.

Habachi, L. 1972. *The second stela of Kamose and his struggle against the Hyksos ruler and his capital.* Glückstadt: Augustin.

Hafsaas-Tsakos, H. 2006. *Cattle pastoralists in a multicultural setting: the C-Group people in Lower Nubia 2500–1500 BCE.* Bergen: Center for Development Studies.

Hafsaas-Tsakos, H. 2009. The kingdom of Kush: an African centre on the periphery of the Bronze Age world system. *Norwegian Archaeological Review* 42: 50–70.

Hesse, A. 1981. L'enclos SAV2 de l'île de Saï (Soudan) in Etudes sur l'Egypte et le Soudan anciens. *CRIPEL* 6: 7–67.

Hintze, F. 1964. Das Kerma-Problem. *ZÄS* 91: 79–86.

Honegger, M. 2004a. The Pre-Kerma: a cultural group from Upper Nubia prior to the Kerma civilisation. *Sudan & Nubia* 8: 38–46.

Honegger, M. 2004b. The Pre-Kerma settlement at Kerma: new elements throw light on the rise of the first Nubian kingdom. In Kendall, T. (ed.),

Nubian studies, 1998. Boston: Department of African-American Studies, Northeastern University, 83–94.

Honegger, M. 2005. Kerma et les débuts du néolithique africain. *Genava: Revue des Musées d'Art et d'Histoire de Genève* 53: 239–249.

Honegger, M. 2011. The beginning of the Kerma civilisation in the eastern cemetery. In Honegger, M., Bonnet, C., Valbelle, D., Ruffieux, P., Fallet, C., Bundi, M., and Dubosson, J. (eds.), *Archaeological excavations at Kerma (Sudan): preliminary report to the 2010–2011 season*. Neuchâtel: Université de Neuchâtel, 9–14.

Honegger, M. 2018. New data on the origins of Kerma. In Honegger, M. (ed.), *Nubian archaeology in the XXIst century*. Leuven: Peeters, 19–34.

Honegger, M. 2021. The Pre-Kerma culture and the beginning of the Kerma kingdom. In Emberling, G., and Williams, B.B. (eds.), *The Oxford handbook of ancient Nubia*. Oxford: Oxford University Press, 143–156.

Iacumin, P., Bocherens, H., and Chaix, L. 2001. Keratin C and N stable isotope ratios of fossil cattle horn from Kerma (Sudan): a record of dietary changes. *Il quaternario* 14: 41–46.

Judd, M. 2002. Ancient injury recidivism: an example from the Kerma period of ancient Nubia. *International Journal of Osteoarchaeology* 12: 89–106.

Judd, M., and Irish, J. 2009. Dying to serve: the mass burials at Kerma. *Antiquity* 83: 709–722.

Junker, H. 1920. *Bericht über die Grabungen der Akademie der Wissenschaften in Wien auf den Friedhöfen von El-Kubanieh-Nord, Winter 1910–1911*. Vienna: Alfred Hölder.

Kendall, T. 1997. *Kerma and the kingdom of Kush, 2500–1500 BC: the archaeological discovery of an ancient Nubian empire*. Washington, DC: National Museum of African Art, Smithsonian Institution.

Kendall, T., and El-Hassan, A.M. 2016. *A visitor's guide to the Jebel Barkal temples*. Retrieved from http://www.jebelbarkal.org/frames/VisGuide.pdf (last accessed July 15, 2019).

Kleinitz, C., and Koenitz, R. 2006. Fourth Nile Cataract petroglyphs in context: the ed-Doma and Dirbi rock-art survey. *Sudan & Nubia* 10: 34–42.

Knoblauch, C. 2012. The ruler of Kush (Kerma) at Buhen during the Second Intermediate Period: a reinterpretation of Buhen Stela 691 and related objects. In Knoblauch, C., and Gill, J.C. (eds.), *Egyptology in Australia and New Zealand, 2009*. Oxford: Archaeopress, 85–96.

Lacovara, P. 1986. The funerary chapels at Kerma. *CRIPEL* 8: 49–58.

Lacovara, P. 1990. *Deir el-Ballas: preliminary report on the Deir el-Ballas expedition, 1980–1986*. Winona Lake, IN: Eisenbrauns.

Lacovara, P. 1991. The stone vase deposit at Kerma. In Davies, W.V. (ed.), *Egypt and Africa: Nubia from prehistory to Islam*. London: British Museum Press, 118–128.

Lacovara, P. 1998. Nubian faience. In Friedman, F.D. (ed.), *Gifts of the Nile: ancient Egyptian faience*. London: Thames & Hudson, 46–49.

Lacovara, P. 2011. A Nubian model soldier and the costume of a Kerma warrior. In Aston, D., Bader, B., Gallorini, C., Nicholson, P., and Buckingham, S. (eds.), *Under the potter's tree: studies on ancient Egypt presented to Janine Bourriau*. Leuven: Peeters, 541–546.

Lepsius, K.R. 1913. *Denkmäler aus Aegypten und Aethiopien: Text, vol. 5*. Leipzig: Hinrichs.

Liszka, K., and De Souza, A. 2021. Pan-Grave and Medjay: at the intersection of archaeology and history. In Emberling, G., and Williams, B.B. (eds.), *The Oxford handbook of ancient Nubia*. Oxford: Oxford University Press, 227–250.

Macklin, M.G., Toonen, W.H.J., Woodward, J.C., Williams, M.A.J., Flaux, C., Marriner, N., Nicoll, K., Verstraeten, G., Spencer, N., and Welsby, D. 2015. A new model of river dynamics, hydroclimatic change and human settlement in the Nile Valley derived from meta-analysis of the Holocene fluvial archive. *Quaternary Science Reviews* 130: 109–123.

Macklin, M.G., Woodward, J.C., Welsby, D.A., Duller, G.A.T., Williams, F.M., and Williams, M.A.J. 2013. Reach-scale river dynamics moderate the impact of rapid Holocene climate change on floodwater farming in the Desert Nile. *Geology* 41: 695–698.

Marconlogo, B., and Surian, N. 1997. Kerma: les sites archéologiques de Kerma et de Kadruka dans leur contexte géomorphologique. *Genava: Revue des Musées d'Art et d'Histoire de Genève* 45: 119–123.

McIntosh, R.J. 2015. Different cities: Jenne-jeno and African urbanism. In Yoffee, N. (ed.), *Early cities in comparative perspective, 4000 BCE–1200 CE*. Cambridge: Cambridge University Press, 364–380.

McIntosh, S.K. 1999. Pathways to complexity: an African perspective. In McIntosh, S.K. (ed.), *Beyond chiefdoms: pathways to complexity in Africa*. Cambridge: Cambridge University Press, 1–30.

Minor, E. 2012. *The use of Egyptian and Egyptianizing material culture in Nubian burials of the Classic Kerma period*. PhD thesis, University of

California, Berkeley. Retrieved from https://escholarship.org/uc/item/onnomofv (last accessed September 18, 2020).

Minor, E. 2014. The use of Egyptian and Egyptianizing material culture in Classic Kerma burials: winged sun discs. In Feldman, M., and Casanova, M. (eds.), *Luxury goods: production, exchange, and heritage in the Near East during the Bronze and Iron Ages*. Paris: De Boccard, 225–234.

Minor, E. 2018a. Decolonizing Reisner: the case study of a Classic Kerma female burial for reinterpreting early Nubian archaeological collections through digital archival resources. In Honegger, M. (ed.), *Nubian archaeology in the XXIst century*. Leuven: Peeters, 251–262.

Minor, E. 2018b. One more for the road: beer, sacrifice and commemoration in ancient Nubian burials of the Classic Kerma period. In Incordino, I., Mainieri, S., D'Itria, E., Pubblico, M.D., Rega, F.M., and Salsano, A. (eds.), *Current research in Egyptology 2017*. Oxford: Archaeopress, 126–138.

Moreno García, J.C. 2015. Climatic change or sociopolitical transformation? Reassessing the late 3rd millennium BC in Egypt. In Meller, H., Risch, R., Jung, R., and Arz, H.W. (eds.), *2200 BC: a climatic breakdown as a cause for the collapse of the Old World?* Halle: Landesamt für Denkmalpflege und Archäologie, 1–16.

Moreno García, J.C. 2017. Trade and power in ancient Egypt: Middle Egypt in the late third/early second millennium BC. *Journal of Archaeological Research* 25: 87–132.

Morris, E.F. 2005. *The architecture of imperialism: military bases and the evolution of foreign policy in Egypt's New Kingdom*. Leiden: Brill.

Nordström, H.Å. 2014. *The West Bank survey from Faras to Gemai: sites of Early Nubian, Middle Nubian and Pharaonic age*. Oxford: Archaeopress.

O'Connor, D. 1974. Political systems and archaeological data in Egypt, 2600–1780 BC. *World Archaeology* 6: 15–38.

O'Connor, D. 1984. The significance of the monumental buildings Kerma I, II, and XI. *JARCE* 21: 65–108.

O'Connor, D. 1986. The locations of Yam and Kush and their historical implications. *JARCE* 23: 27–50.

O'Connor, D. 1987. The location of Irem. *JEA* 73: 99–136.

O'Connor, D. 1993. *Ancient Nubia: Egypt's rival in Africa*. Philadelphia: University of Pennsylvania Museum of Archaeology and Anthropology.

Osman, A., and Edwards, D. 2012. *The archaeology of a Nubian frontier: survey on the Nile Third Cataract, Sudan*. Leicester: Mauhaus.

Paner, H. 2014. Kerma culture in the Fourth Cataract of the Nile. In Anderson, J.R., and Welsby, D.A. (eds.), *The Fourth Cataract and beyond*. Leuven: Peeters, 53–79.

Paner, H. 2018. The western Bayuda desert at the end of the 3rd and during the 2nd millennium BC: archaeological heritage. In Lohwasser, A., Karberg, T., and Auenmüller, J. (eds.), *Bayuda studies*. Wiesbaden: Harrassowitz, 285–308.

Paner, H., and Borcowski, Z. 2005. Gdańsk archaeological museum expedition: a summary of eight seasons' work at the Fourth Cataract. *Gdánsk Archaeological Museum and Heritage Protection Fund: African Reports* 4: 89–115.

Paner, H., Pudło, A., and Borcowski, Z. 2010. Funerary customs in the GAME Fourth Cataract concession in the light of radiocarbon analysis. In Godlewski, W., and Łajtar, A. (eds.), *Between the cataracts: proceedings of the 11th conference for Nubian studies, part 2, fasc. 2: session papers*. Warsaw: Warsaw University Press, 61–76.

Parker Pearson, M. 1999. *The archaeology of death and burial*. College Station: Texas A&M University Press.

Privati, B. 1999. La céramique de la nécropole orientale de Kerma (Soudan): essai de classification. *CRIPEL* 20: 41–69.

Reisner, G.A. 1923a. *Excavations at Kerma, parts I–III*. Cambridge, MA: Peabody Museum of Harvard University.

Reisner, G.A. 1923b. *Excavations at Kerma, parts IV–V*. Cambridge, MA: Peabody Museum of Harvard University.

Rilly, C. 2017. Histoire du Soudan des origines à la chute du sultanat Fung. In Cabon, O. (ed.), *Histoire et civilisations du Soudan*. Paris: Soleb, 26–445.

Säve-Söderbergh, T. 1941. *Ägypten und Nubien: ein Beitrag zur Geschichte altägyptischer Aussenpolitik*. Lund: Håkan Ohlssons Boktryckeri.

Schröder, M.-K. 2018. Nubian pottery assemblage from the C-Group cemetery HK27C at Hierakonpolis. In Honegger, M. (ed.), *Nubian archaeology in the XXIst century*. Leuven: Peeters, 243–250.

Sethe, K. 1906. *Urkunden der 18. Dynastie, 1. Band, 4. Abteilung*. Leipzig: Hinrichs.

Smith, H.S. 1976. *The fortress of Buhen: the inscriptions*. London: Egypt Exploration Society.

Smith, S.T. 2003a. *Wretched Kush: ethnic identities and boundaries in Egypt's Nubian empire*. London and New York: Routledge.

Smith, S.T. 2003b. The University of California Dongola Reach expedition, West Bank reconnaissance survey, 1997–1998. *Kush* 18: 157–172.

Smith, S.T., and Buzon, M.R. 2014. Identity, commemoration and remembrance in colonial encounters: burials at Tombos during the Egyptian New Kingdom empire and its aftermath. In Porter, B.W., and Boutin, A.T. (eds.), *Remembering and commemorating the dead: recent contributions in bioarchaeology and mortuary analysis from the ancient Near East*. Boulder: University of Colorado Press, 323–365.

Smith, S.T., and Herbst, G. 2005. The UCSB West (left) Bank archaeological survey from el-Kab to Mograt. *Gdánsk Archaeological Museum and Heritage Protection Fund: African Reports* 4: 133–144.

Southall, A. 1956. *Alur society: a study in processes and types of domination*. Cambridge: Heffer.

Southall, A. 1999. The segmentary state and the ritual phase in political economy. In McIntosh, S.K. (ed.), *Beyond chiefdoms: pathways to complexity in Africa*. Cambridge: Cambridge University Press, 31–38.

Török, L. 2009. *Between two worlds: the frontier region between ancient Nubia and Egypt, 3700 BC–AD 500*. Leiden: Brill.

Valbelle, D. 2004. The cultural significance of iconographic and epigraphic data found in the Kingdom of Kerma. In Kendall, T. (ed.), *Nubian studies, 1998*. Boston: Department of African-American Studies, Northeastern University, 176–185.

Vandersleyen, C. 1971. *Les guerres d'Amosis, fondateur de la XVIIIe dynastie*. Brussels: Fondation Égyptologique Reine Élisabeth.

Van Siclen, C.C., III. 2010. The third stela of Kamose. In Marée, M. (ed.), *The Second Intermediate Period (Thirteenth-Seventeenth Dynasties): current research, future prospects*. Leuven: Peeters, 355–358.

Vercoutter, J. 1960. A dagger from Kerma. *Kush* 8: 265.

Vila, A. 1987. *La cimetière Kermaïque d'Ukma ouest*. Paris: CNRS Éditions.

Welsby, D.A. 2001. *Life on the desert edge: seven thousand years of settlement in the northern Dongola Reach, Sudan*. Oxford: Archaeopress.

Welsby, D.A. 2003. *Survey above the Fourth Nile Cataract*. Oxford: Archaeopress.

Welsby, D.A. 2018. Kerma ancient cemeteries: from the Batn el-Hajar to the Fourth Cataract. In Honegger, M. (ed.), *Nubian archaeology in the XXIst century*. Leuven: Peeters, 35–63.

Wenig, Steffen. 1978. *Africa in antiquity: the arts of ancient Nubia and the Sudan, vol. 1: the essays.* Brooklyn, NY: The Brooklyn Museum.

Weschenfelder, J. 2014. Preliminary report of the first field season of the Kerma cemetery MOG034 on Mograt Island, Sudan. *Der Antike Sudan: Mitteilungen der Sudanarchäologischen Gesellschaft zu Berlin* 25: 145–154.

Williams, B.B. 2021. Kush in the wider world during the Kerma period. In Emberling, G., and Williams, B.B. (eds.), *The Oxford handbook of ancient Nubia.* Oxford: Oxford University Press, 179–200.

26

The New Kingdom of Egypt under the Eighteenth Dynasty

Nicky Nielsen

26.1. Forged in fire: the trauma of the Hyksos and the emergence of the heroic king

Egypt's New Kingdom (figure 26.1) was founded as a result of civil strife and war.[1] However, unlike the civil conflict that led to the foundation of the Middle Kingdom (chapters 12 and 13 in volume 2), the early rulers of the Eighteenth Dynasty had a convenient foreign enemy: the Hyksos (chapter 23 in this volume). The expulsion of the Hyksos from the Egyptian Nile delta permitted a patrician family from Thebes to assume an unprecedented level of control and dominance both within Egyptian society and outside of Egypt's borders. The Eighteenth Dynasty represented in many ways a series of unparalleled highs—in empire-building, art, economy, and construction—and a series of crushing lows of pharaonic history; a period of rulers who appear at times almost manically

---

1. The following bibliographical abbreviations are used in this chapter: *Urk.* I = Sethe 1933; *Urk.* IV = Sethe 1906–1909; Helck 1955–1958. KV stands for a tomb in the Valley of the Kings, while TT stands for "Theban Tomb," a tomb on the western Nile bank of Thebes. The dates follow Beckerath 1997.

Nicky Nielsen, *The New Kingdom of Egypt under the Eighteenth Dynasty* In: *The Oxford History of the Ancient Near East*. Edited by: Karen Radner, Nadine Moeller, and D. T. Potts, Oxford University Press. © Oxford University Press 2022. DOI: 10.1093/oso/9780190687601.003.0026

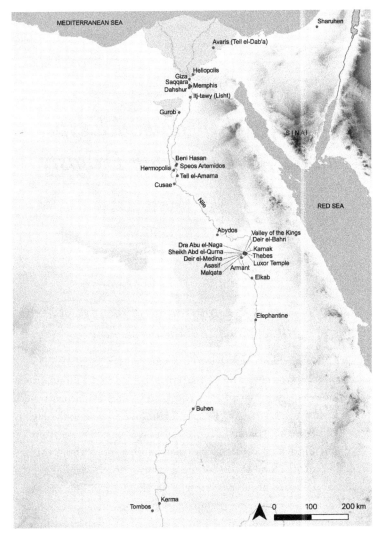

FIGURE 26.1. Sites mentioned in this chapter. Prepared by Andrea Squitieri (LMU Munich).

efficient; a time of legendary leaders, both male and female, some of whom were idolized within Egypt during later years, others who achieved less in life—notably Tutankhamun (1333–1323 BC), who has been raised by our modern society to the level of an A-list celebrity because of his burial goods, his tomb, and the circumstances surrounding its discovery.

The national trauma caused by the Hyksos occupation of northern Egypt during the Second Intermediate Period remains a palpable factor within the royal family of the early to mid-Eighteenth Dynasty. The Hyksos appear as villains in the dedicatory inscriptions carved during the reign of Hatshepsut (1479–1458 BC) at Speos Artemidos more than a century after the last Hyksos warrior had been expelled from the delta's loamy soil:

> I have restored what was ruined, and have raised up what was neglected previously (at the time) when Aamu [i.e., Hyksos] were in the midst of Avaris of the Northland, and strangers in the midst of them overturned what had been made. They ruled with Ra, no one acting according to the divine command [...].[2]

The Hyksos became a justification for an aggressive foreign policy pursued by the first ruler of the Eighteenth Dynasty, Ahmose (1550–1525 BC), and his immediate successor, attempting to establish a "buffer zone" of vassal territories and city-states to prevent easy incursion into Egypt proper, but as Hatshepsut's inscription shows, they also functioned well as a foil, a juxtaposition to the re-established Theban dynasty of monarchs ruling with the approval of Amun-Ra, rebuilding and reorganizing what had been lost and destroyed.

Rebuilding what had been lost also applied to the authority of the king. But whereas the Middle Kingdom rulers had striven to portray themselves as wise and responsible statesmen, physically expressed by the alarmingly large ears and deeply furrowed brows found on many pieces of Twelfth Dynasty royal statuary, in particular that of Senusret III,[3] the

---

2. Gunn and Gardiner 1918: 55; see also Fairman and Grdseloff 1947.

3. Freed 2010: 900–901.

martial origins of the Eighteenth Dynasty required a different sort of ruler: a hero. The battered remains of Seqenenra Taa (figure 26.2), in many ways the spiritual founder of the Theban royal line and certainly the instigator of the war between the Theban forces and the Hyksos, presents a different type of ruler: a military commander leading from the front. Whether the image of the king trampling enemies in his chariot

FIGURE 26.2. Copper-alloy battle axe inscribed with the names of King Seqenenra Taa. Los Angeles County Museum of Art (accession number M.80.203.43). Photograph courtesy Los Angeles County Museum of Art. CC0 1.0 Universal (CC0 1.0) Public Domain Dedication.

followed by his loyal troops is entirely fictitious or not is debatable. But the image reflects a fundamental shift in what was expected of the king during the New Kingdom. The king could not merely govern from the capital and occasionally dispatch raids or invasions to Nubia and the Levant. The king had to be present. The king had to be a campaigner.

Nowhere is this evolving role of the king more apparent than in the literary genre known as the *Königsnovelle*. While this type of text is attested from the Middle Kingdom onward,[4] its episodes become increasingly focused on the king's martial prowess as opposed to the king's role as a builder, emphasized for instance in the Twelfth Dynasty *Königsnovellen* of Senusret I,[5] or the king as a participant in religious ceremonies, as in the Neferhotep Stele dating to the Second Intermediate Period.[6] The Kamose texts dating to the very end of the Seventeenth Dynasty and the war between the Thebans and the Hyksos very well reflects the structure of this textual corpus. In the beginning of the text the king is introduced sitting at rest in the palace. Then he is either approached by a messenger, or he simply begins speaking directly to his council. It is the king's first-person speech which drives the narrative, in combination with the dialogue that emerges when the council members provide their opinion. Often the advice provided by the king's councilors represents the "easy way out" of a specific situation, thereby allowing the king to assume a heroic mantle by dismissing his lily-livered courtiers and setting out a bolder strategy.

In the Kamose Stele, the king's oration focuses on his role as a supposed supreme ruler who is still forced to share part of what he considers Egyptian territory with two "foreign" rulers—the Hyksos in the North and the king of Kush in the South:

His Majesty spoke in his palace to the council of officials which was in his following: To what effect do I perceive it, my might,

---

4. Spalinger 2011: 366.

5. Hirsch 2009: 76.

6. Hofmann 2004: 85–99.

while a ruler is in Avaris and another in Kush, I sitting joined with
an Asiatic and a Nubian each man having his (own) portion of
this Egypt, sharing the land with me?[7]

After some further rhetorical questions, Kamose's courtiers reply to
their king:

> And [then] they drew their tongues in unison: "We are content
> with our [part of] Egypt. Elephantine is firmly in our control, and
> the middle section is with us as far as Cusae [. . .]. Should one who
> acts against us come, then we shall act against him.[8]

In essence, the courtiers rebuff the king to a certain extent, arguing for a
continuation of the status quo. Unsurprisingly, Kamose is unhappy with
this advice: "They [these words] were disturbing in the heart of his Majesty."
Kamose proceeds to lay out a plan for launching his fleet northward to push
the Hyksos out from Egyptian territory. The heroic king, of course, over-
came his cowardly counsel.

In addition to martial prowess and bravery, the Eighteenth Dynasty
king also relied on a "sportier" image than his Middle Kingdom predecessors. Amenhotep II (1425–1397 BC), the seventh pharaoh of the Eighteenth
Dynasty, emphasized this to an unprecedented degree. He ordered himself
depicted engaging in physical exercise, for instance firing arrows at a bronze
target, and a similar scene is described in great detail on the Karnak Stele:

> Submission was made to his majesty by Unqi. His majesty
> reached Kadesh. Its prince came out in peace to his majesty. They
> were made to take the oath of fealty, and all their children as well.
> Thereupon his majesty shot at two targets of copper in hammered
> work, in their presence, on the south side of this town.[9]

---

7. Simpson 2003: 346–349.

8. Simpson 2003: 346–349.

9. Pritchard 1969: 246.

The extent of Amenhotep's martial prowess and "sportiness" is emphasized to an even greater extent in a stele found in the temple of
Amenhotep II at Giza in the 1930s by Selim Hasan:[10]

> Now further, his majesty appeared as king as a goodly youth.
> When he had matured and completed eighteen years on his
> thighs in valor, he was one who knew every task of Montu: there
> was no one like him on the field of battle. He was one who knew
> horses: there was not his like in this numerous army. There
> was not one therein who could draw his bow. He could not be
> approached in running.

Later in the same text, the king further proves his archery skills by shooting four copper targets from his chariot with such precision and power
that the arrows not only penetrate the targets, but come out the other
side and drop to the ground: "It was really a deed which had never been
done nor heard of by report [...],"[11] as the text concludes.

And as the role of the king changed, so did the role of his entourage.
The early to mid-Eighteenth Dynasty court was full of officials whose
positions and wealth were either secured by, or depended on, prowess
on the field of battle. Ahmose, son of Ibana, Ahmose Pennekhbet, and
Amenemhab are among the best known, and while their tomb biographies, which frequently focus on their military exploits and the rewards
they received for their bravery, can be traced back to some Twelfth
Dynasty biographies, most famously the one belonging to Khusobek
now held in the Manchester Museum,[12] they nevertheless represent
somewhat of a novelty in terms of detail and structure. The physical
prowess and "lead-from-the-front" attitude of the king is mirrored in the
behavior of these officials. Perhaps the most graphic of these accounts
that highlight the tomb owner's bravery, strength, and endurance is

---

10. Hasan 1937: 40; 1949: 40.

11. Pritchard 1969: 244.

12. Peet 1914.

the description of the clever trick of dispatching a mare in heat against the front line of Egyptian chariots by the prince of Qadesh during the reign of Thutmose III (1479–1425 BC) found in the tomb biography of Amenemhab:

> The prince of Qadesh sent forth a mare before the army in order to disrupt them. She entered among the army [. . .] I pursued after her on foot, with my sword, and I ripped open her belly; I cut off her tail, I set it before the king while there was thanksgiving to god for it![13]

The focus on the king as a valiant warrior served multiple purposes. Fundamentally, it was a reflection of Egypt's foreign policy priorities which were increasingly geared toward building and maintaining a "buffer zone" of vassal states on its eastern borders. But the king's role as a conquering hero also had a clearly defined religious element. The king, by conquering foreign lands, was spreading *maat*—order, the correct way of the world—and defeating chaos, *isfet*. In doing so, the king and his armies secured vast quantities of loot—the Annals of Thutmose III, for instance, list over 2,000 horses and more than 800 chariots taken during a single campaign alongside a plethora of gold, prisoners, and other commodities.[14] This loot was brought back to Egypt and gifted to Egypt's many temples as a reflection of pharaoh's gratitude to the gods for his victory. And no deity benefited more during the Eighteenth Dynasty from this largess than the Hidden One, the supreme god of the Theban Dynasty: Amun-Ra at Karnak.

26.2. The rise of the Hidden One

The origins of Amun are obscure. A few references to the deity and his female counterpart, Amunet, survive from the Old Kingdom funerary

---

13. Gabriel 2009: 179.

14. Lichtheim 1976: 33.

corpus known collectively as the Pyramid Texts, namely in Spell 206 from the pyramid of Unas at Saqqara which states: "You have your bread-loaf, Amun and Amunet, you pair of the gods, who joined the gods with their shadows,"[15] and Spell 521 from the pyramid of Pepy I, which specifically associated Amun with the imagery of thrones and power:[16] "Your envoys have gone, your runners have run, your announcers have bustled, and they will say to the Sun that you have come, Pepi, as Geb's son, the one on Amun's throne."[17]

The actual foundation of the Karnak temple in Thebes and its association with Amun is difficult to define. Montu, the Warrior God whose name was incorporated into the names of the early rulers of the Eleventh Dynasty, was the preeminent deity of the settlement. Clear evidence of the worship of Amun is found from the late First Intermediate Period onward and comes from a column dating to the reign of Wahankh Intef II found at Karnak which specifically mentions the deity Amun.[18] More solid evidence for the functioning of a temple or shrine dedicated to Amun at Karnak comes from the later Eleventh Dynasty on private and royal monumental architecture, such as a highly fragmentary stele currently held in the Manchester Museum, which reads:

> I was one who provided [a group of] 20 individuals. I was the sealer of the great fields, besides the portions of my father's property. I made provisions for the temple of Amun in the years of scarcity. I was the sealer of the sacred oxen, at each festival of the opening of a season, and I paid attention to the altar tables as far as the opening of the year festival. I acted as herdsman in charge

15. Allen 2015: 55.

16. For a further discussion of the association of Amun with power already in these early sources, see Warburton 2012: 122.

17. Allen 2015: 184.

18. Blyth 2006: 7.

of the donkeys, and as herdsman in charge of the goats, and as herdsman in charge of […].[19]

Unfortunately, in the case of this stele, both the full titulary and name of the officiant have been deliberately chiseled out, perhaps in an act of *damnatio memoriae*.

Far from being the focal point of Egypt's official religious life as it was during the Eighteenth Dynasty, Karnak during the Middle Kingdom was a much more provincial structure. The temple and its deity were no doubt important; its association with the Theban Twelfth Dynasty would have ensured that, and similarly there is clear evidence of the temple being favored with donations from the state.[20] But Amun's and Karnak's role on the national stage did not begin until the advent of the Theban Eighteenth Dynasty. An account by Ahmose (1550–1525 BC), the first ruler of a unified Egypt following the expulsion of the Hyksos, describes how he restored the Karnak temple after a natural disaster—possibly a combination of an earthquake and a series of torrential rainstorms.[21] The focus of the early Eighteenth Dynasty royal family on Karnak and Amun also led to the appearance of a novel religious role associated with this deity, that of "God's Wife of Amun" (*hemet netjer net Imen*). The title "God's Wife" (*hemet netjer*) appeared during the First Intermediate Period and several non-royal elite women held it during the Middle Kingdom.[22]

---

19. Manchester Museum, accession number 5052; found by Flinders Petrie during his work in Thebes and published in Petrie 1909: 17, pl. 10.

20. E.g., the Mit Rahina Annals of Amenemhat II record the donation of a cult statue and various equipment such as an incense burner and vessels to the temple of Amun at Karnak; see Altenmüller and Moussa 1991: 20–21.

21. This account is known from the "Tempest Stele," first published by Vandersleyen 1967. See also Polinger Foster and Ritner 1996; Allen and Wiener 1998; Ritner and Moeller 2014.

22. See, e.g., the wooden statuette dating to the Twelfth Dynasty (Rijksmuseum van Oudheden Leiden, accession number A.H.113) belonging to the non-royal woman Imertnebes who held the title "God's Wife" (*hemet netjer*) and "Hand of the God" (*djeret netjer*). Given the statuette's Theban origin, it is likely that the god in question, even though it is not clearly spelled out, was Amun. See further information in Millard 1976: 280–281.

However, Ahmose Nefertari, the principal wife of the dynasty founder Ahmose, began the tradition of the God's Wife of Amun title being held only by Egyptian queens and princesses. After her death, the title passed to her daughter, and from her to arguably the most famous holder of this office: Hatshepsut (see section 26.7.2).

The financial income from this position is laid out clearly in the Donation Stele of Ahmose.[23] In this text, Ahmose—in front of his court—bestows the office of Second Prophet of Amun on his Great Royal Wife, Ahmose Nefertari, who holds this in addition to her title of God's Wife. A long list of royal donations to the office include gold, grain, clothing, wigs, ointments of various types, and a cadre of servants with an income of 600 *shenau*.[24]

With the increasing national prominence came also change for the deity of Amun himself. Due to his preeminence he became identified with another deity commonly associated with rule and kingship, the sun god Ra, transforming into Amun-Ra. Later Amun would become identified with other deities as well, for instance the fertility god Min becoming Amun-Min. Such was the flexibility of the Egyptian pantheon that the association of Amun with Ra did not diminish the separate worship of Ra himself, and Eighteenth Dynasty rulers continued to patronize the temple of Ra at Heliopolis.

The attention which the early Eighteenth Dynasty rulers lavished on the sacred landscape at Thebes did not limit itself to donations of royal offices. It manifested in a spree of monumental constructions at Karnak and elsewhere in Thebes, molding and changing the sacred landscape of the entire city. It also heralded the birth of new religious festivities to add to the existing Theban festival calendar. The Beautiful Festival of the Valley during which inhabitants of the city flocked to the tombs of their ancestors to feast and give offerings had developed since the Middle

---

23. Gitton 1976.

24. Also translated as *seniu* (*shenatj*), a weight-value specifically for silver, equivalent to 7.5 g, meaning that the total amount in the Donation Stele would be roughly 4.5 kg of silver.

Kingdom, but it was now joined by the Opet Festival[25]—arguably the most noted and long-lived of the Theban religious traditions.[26] During this festival, first attested in the reign of Hatshepsut, the statue of Amun-Ra of Karnak (*ipet isut*, "The Most Select of Places"), along with his consort Mut and son Khonsu, would be carried on a sacred barque, stopping at multiple smaller shrines en route, to the Luxor temple (*ipet resyt*, "The Southern Sanctuary") where Amun-Ra of Karnak and Amun of Luxor would come face to face.

This festival was linked not only to rebirth and regeneration, but also to the divine foundations of pharaoh's power, as the ruler was often either coronated or re-coronated at the height of this particular celebration, thereby further emphasizing the connection between Amun-Ra and the ruling monarch. The role of Amun-Ra as the theological guarantor of pharaoh's right to rule is also spelled out clearly in royal monumental inscriptions dating to the early New Kingdom, such as the Karnak Stele of Ahmose:

> The king of Upper and Lower Egypt, Lord of the Two Lands, Nebpehtyra, son of Ra, his beloved: Ahmose, may he live forever, son of Amun-Ra, of his body, his beloved, his heir, to whom his throne was given, a truly good god, mighty of arms, there are no lies within him.[27]

With festivals came donations of vast amounts of material wealth from the rulers of the early to mid-Eighteenth Dynasty to the Amun priesthood and temple. A sadly fragmentary but nonetheless revealing set of inscribed blocks found in the Karnak temple dating to the reign of

---

25. Darnell 2010.

26. The Opet Festival continued from the New Kingdom in some form at least until the Roman Period, and is reflected in several modern religious festivals and traditions in present-day Luxor, in particular the processions held annually in honor of the holy man Yusuf al-Haggag during which boats are carried through the streets in an echo of the Sacred Barque of Amun being transported overland from Karnak to the Luxor temple.

27. Transcription following *Urk.* I: 14–24, translation by the present author.

Thutmose III (1479–1425 BC) encapsulates the kinds of offerings and donations given by the royal family to their patron deity and includes not just foodstuffs such as bread, beer, hundreds of cakes of various kinds, meats, and poultry, but also incense, myrrh, and even stranger items such as livestock and "golden pails" into which their milk could be poured before being presented to the god.[28] But the donations of Thutmose III to the Karnak temple and its priesthood did not limit itself to exotica from his many campaigns or food for the conduct of offerings. According to the Annals of his campaigns, he donated during his reign more than 152,000 *deben* (or 14 tons) of gold to the Karnak temple.[29] This figure may of course be inflated—it would certainly be in the interest of the king and his architects to exaggerate the donations he had gifted to the temple. But even a tenth of the quantity stated represents an enormous amount of wealth and, combined with other donations—including prisoners of war and land for them to farm—such royal attention clearly raised both the profile and the economic (and arguably, political) power of the temple and its priesthood.

By far the most obvious demonstration of the new Theban dynasty's loyalty to Amun-Ra of Karnak was the extensive building activity carried out at the temple starting from the very beginning of the period. The reconstruction works of Ahmose at Karnak detailed on the "Tempest Stele" have already been discussed. His successors followed in his footsteps. Amenhotep I ordered the construction of an exquisite alabaster barque shrine as well as a limestone gateway. Thutmose I drastically enlarged the sacred landscape at Karnak, adding two stone pylons (the Fourth and Fifth Pylons) as well as a hypostyle (columned) hall and granite obelisks. Obelisks were also added to the temple during the reign of Hatshepsut along with the *chapelle rouge* ("Red Chapel") built as a barque shrine to house the "Userhat-Amun," the gold-leaf covered barque which transported Amun-Ra, hidden from the eyes of the world inside a gilded shrine on the deck, during festivals. Hatshepsut's successor

---

28. Gardiner 1952.

29. Janssen 1975: 154.

Thutmose III further enlarged the temple, adding the Sixth and Seventh Pylons, demolishing the *chapelle rouge* and also rebuilding a small temple dedicated to the god Ptah found within the Amun complex:

> My majesty found this temple built of mudbrick, its columns and its doors in wood, which went to ruin. My majesty ordered to stretch the line for the temple again, edifying it in perfect white sandstone, the walls protecting it being made of bricks in durable work for eternity.[30]

Our knowledge of the construction programs of the early Eighteenth Dynasty rulers at Karnak has been immensely augmented by a singular private biography. This biography belonged to Ineni, a high-ranking official, mayor of Thebes, and—crucially—royal architect.[31] The full list of Ineni's titles is rather extensive, as he served at the court of no less than five rulers: Amenhotep I (1525–1504 BC), Thutmose I (1504–1492 BC), Thutmose II (1492–1479 BC), and the joint rule of Thutmose III and Hatshepsut (1479–1458 BC); but during this lengthy career, Ineni was at various times placed in charge of all craftsmen working at Karnak, in charge of royal works, overseer of storehouses, and responsible for administrating divine offerings.

Ineni's biography, found preserved on the walls of his Theban tomb (TT 81), describes not only the various construction programs undertaken by the rulers Ineni served, but also provides some details concerning the organizational aspects of the building works:

> I saw the great monuments which he built at Karnak, erecting a splendid columned hall, erecting great pylons beside it from beautiful white limestone, erecting the magnificent flagpoles in

---

30. Charloux and Thiers 2017: 11.

31. Dziobek 1992.

front of the temple from cut timber from the top of the terrace (Lebanon), its tips from electrum. I saw the erection of [. . .] with electrum. I saw the erection of the great gate "Magnificent is the Power of Amun," its great door from copper from Setjet, the sacred image upon it fashioned from gold. I saw the building of the two great obelisks in front of the temple from granite. I saw the building of a magnificent ship of 120 cubits in length and 40 cubits in width, to ship these obelisks. They came in peace, safe and sound, and landed at Karnak. I saw the digging of a lake, His Majesty made for himself on the west side of the city. Its banks were planted with all kinds of sweet trees.[32]

The clear link between the new Theban royal house and the god Amun-Ra of Karnak led to one of the most significant religious reimaginings of the pharaonic period. In the span of a few centuries, Thebes went from being a regional capital, home to an ambitious family of nobles with their eyes on the throne of Egypt and plans to topple and expel the Hyksos rulers in the north, to become the single most important religious and cultural center in Egypt. The role of Amun, his rebirth as Amun-Ra, a god of kingship and victories, no doubt contributed hugely to this change. And not only did the Eighteenth Dynasty rulers lavish their wealth and attention on Karnak temple itself; rather, they drastically altered the sacred landscape of the entire settlement and its environs by expanding upon existing traditions and founding entirely novel ones as well. Perhaps the most crucial development of the mortuary and religious landscape was, very much like the expansion of the Karnak temple under the early Thutmosid rulers, overseen by that long-lived architect Ineni: the decision to hide royal burials within two large wadis on the western bank of the Nile, overlooked by a pyramidal mountain peak today named el-Qurn: the Valley of the Kings.

---

32. Translation following *Urk.* I: 53–62.

26.3.   Unseen and unheard: a new royal burial ground

The Theban rulers of the late First Intermediate Period had chosen to construct their tombs, not in the form of mastabas or pyramids, but rather as rock-cut chambers on the west bank of the Nile. The ascendant Seventeenth Dynasty rulers maintained this tradition, choosing the necropolis of Dra Abu el-Naga as their final resting place. While the tombs of this protoroyalty were mostly looted in antiquity, some material remained to be obtained by early archaeologists and collectors. A notable artifact discovered at this cemetery is the wooden coffin of King Nubkheperra Intef now on display in the British Museum.[33] This ruler reigned during the latter part of the Seventeenth Dynasty,[34] a member of a royal house that would later be led by King Seqenenra Taa, who died in battle against the Hyksos, as well as his sons Kamose and Ahmose, the founder of the Eighteenth Dynasty.

After his death, Nubkheperra Intef was buried in a sycamore wood coffin, wrapped in a shroud inscribed with funerary literature intended to ease his passage to the afterlife. In the early nineteenth century AD, the grave was discovered and emptied of its contents. The coffin was sold to Henry Salt, the British consul general of Egypt and an ardent collector of Egyptian antiquities. After his death in 1827, a portion of Salt's vast collection was sold to the British Museum in 1835, including the coffin of Nubkheperra Intef.

It is likely that the most famous descendants of Nubkheperra Intef, Seqenenra Taa, Kamose, and Ahmose were all buried at Dra Abu el-Naga as well.[35] But their tombs as well were opened in antiquity, during the Third Intermediate Period, and their coffins moved by priests from Karnak to a cache at Deir el-Bahri, which over time came to house nearly

---

33. British Museum, BM EA 6652; for further information, see Taylor 2001: 78, fig. 45. See also chapter 24 in this volume.

34. Schneider 2006: 187; Franke 2008.

35. Polz 2005.

FIGURE 26.3. Fragment of a limestone relief most likely depicting Amenhotep I. Metropolitan Museum of Art (accession number 45.2.7). Photograph courtesy Metropolitan Museum of Art. CC0 1.0 Universal (CC0 1.0) Public Domain Dedication.

fifty royal mummies and their coffins.[36] In the late nineteenth century AD, this cache was opened by the archaeologist Emile Brugsch after pieces of royal funerary equipment had begun circulating on the antiquities market, and the royal mummies were shipped to the Cairo Museum.

Amenhotep I (1525–1504 BC; figure 26.3), the son of Ahmose, most likely followed in the footsteps of his father and he too was buried at Dra

---

36. Maspero 1889; Graefe 2003.

Abu el-Naga, although some debate remains about the precise location of his burial.[37] Amenhotep I's successor Thutmose I, however, evidently felt that a break with this burial tradition was needed. Rather than order his tomb to be constructed at Dra Abu el-Naga, Thutmose I (1504–1492 BC) set his sights on a spot in a nondescript valley behind the mortuary temple of the founder of Egypt's Middle Kingdom, Mentuhotep II (see chapter 22 in volume 2). The biography of Ineni provides us with a fascinating eyewitness account about the construction of this first royal tomb in what would become perhaps the most famous royal necropolis on the planet:

> I saw the digging of the rock tomb of His Majesty in private, with no one seeing, with no one hearing. I investigated what could be useful for this [. . .] in excellent work. My mind was vigilant seeking what would be useful. I established fields of clay to block their tombs in the necropolis. These were works that had not been done before.[38]

The reference to clay fields could perhaps be an allusion to setting up and triggering landslides of loose rocks and gravel to cover the entrances to the royal tombs.

The shift toward hidden royal burials, as opposed to earlier structures such as the royal pyramids of the Old and Middle Kingdoms which rather broadcasted their contents, also led to a change in the spatial layout of the architectural components of the royal mortuary cult. Fundamental to the perpetuation of the royal *ka* was the mortuary temple, a location where offerings could be continuously given to the king, a memorial structure intended to guarantee the king's successful arrival in the afterlife. With the tombs hidden in the Valley of the Kings, these mortuary structures could not be built directly in front of, or physically connected to, the royal tomb. Instead, the mortuary

---

37. Grimal 1988: 202; Shaw and Nicholson 1995: 28.

38. Translation following *Urk.* I: 53–62.

temples were constructed separate from the tomb on the west bank of the Nile river (figure 26.4). Thutmose I's mortuary temple has not survived, but that of his daughter Hatshepsut has. Her mortuary temple at Deir el-Bahri is perhaps one of the most recognizable monuments in the Theban necropolis, and it highlights very well the various purposes these grand constructions played.

The *Djeser-Djeseru* ("Holy of Holies") of Hatshepsut employs a combination of terraced gardens inspired in part by the nearby mortuary temple of Mentuhotep II, as well as the "classic" components of a New Kingdom temple—pylons, colonnades, hypostyle halls, and smaller chapels and sanctuaries. A sanctuary to Amun and another dedicated to Hatshepsut and her stepson Thutmose III (1479–1425 BC) served as a spiritual portal between the world of the living and the king's eternal spirit through which offerings could be brought to guarantee the royal afterlife. A barque shrine provided a terminus point to the Opet Festival

FIGURE 26.4. Hatshepsut's mortuary temples on the Theban West Bank at Deir el-Bahri. Photograph by Steven Snape.

procession, reinforcing the links between eastern and western Thebes, between the temple of Amun-Ra at Karnak and Hatshepsut's royal personage.[39] The walls of her mortuary temple were decorated with scenes celebrating triumphant moments of her reign, such as the successful return of a vast trading expedition to the distant land of Punt.[40] Another set of reliefs also explores her divine birth and serves to legitimize her claim to the throne. The kings of the later Eighteenth Dynasty followed suit and constructed their own grand mortuary temples on the processional route between Karnak and Hatshepsut's mortuary temple at Deir el-Bahri, although many of these have since been mostly or wholly destroyed by encroaching agriculture.

Along with changes to the wider configuration of the mortuary cult came also changes to the decorative program of the royal tomb. From the early Eighteenth Dynasty and the joint tomb of Thutmose I and Hatshepsut (KV 20) onward, a new funerary liturgy was placed on the walls of the royal burial chambers: the *Amduat* (*imy-duati*, meaning "That which is in the Underworld").[41] This text was composed for similar reasons as the Old Kingdom Pyramid Texts and the Middle Kingdom private funerary literature such as the Coffin Texts, namely to provide a mythological road map for the deceased's successful journey to the afterlife. The *Amduat* differs from the Pyramid Texts in that it relies to a greater extent on illustrations accompanying the various spells and textual descriptions, with the most complete example of the *Amduat* being found on the walls of the burial chamber in the tomb of Thutmose III (KV 34).[42] Written, rather than carved, using light-stroke almost calligraphic cursive hieroglyphs and illustrated with rather simplistic stick-figures, the artists who painted the *Amduat* used a restrained palette of black and red primarily, mimicking the style and appearance of a text written on a papyrus scroll.

---

39. Dodson 1988.

40. Creasman 2014.

41. Hornung 1999: 27–45.

42. Richter 2008.

The *Amduat* describes the journey of the sun god Ra through the underworld during the hours of darkness. The aim of this journey is for the aged god to "go backward in time," to be rejuvenated in the Waters of Nun, to be merged with the corpse of Osiris and to re-emerge youthful and radiant as Khepri, an aspect of Ra as the morning sun after his journeyings. The journey of Ra (and the deceased pharaoh whom he represents) was conducted on the solar barque and involved a whole crew of deities, allies of the sun god whom the text names and enumerates. Those enemies faced by Ra, such as the serpent Apophis, are also named. By providing names of both allies and enemies, the text equips the deceased pharaoh with the power both to call upon allies to aid in the struggles which take place in the *duat*, and also to name and therefore control and harm enemies in the same realm.

Thutmose III's tomb (KV 34) typifies the shape of a royal tomb in the Valley of the Kings during this period. From the entrance, located some 30 m above ground-level in a narrow gorge within the Valley, a series of stairways and passages lead downward to a ritual shaft before continuing in a 90-degree "dog leg" bend toward a vestibule and the burial chamber itself, complete with four annexes radiating off it. This shape was maintained until the post-Amarna Period burial of Horemheb (1319–1292 BC), which was entirely linear, dispensing with the 90-degree turn, a design which continued in use through the Ramesside period. The tomb of Horemheb in the Valley of the Kings also employed relief carved decoration, rather than painted decoration as had been the case in the royal burials of the early to mid-Eighteenth Dynasty.[43]

Due to the extensive looting of the royal necropolis in antiquity, the actual contents of these royal tombs were largely dispersed either by the looters themselves, or—during the Third Intermediate Period—by priests from Karnak temple, who opened many royal tombs and moved the royal mummies and much of their burial equipment to the Deir el-Bahri Royal Cache.[44] As such, the most useful sources to inform about

---

43. Brack and Brack 1980.

44. Belova 2003.

the content of royal tombs[45] during this period are, somewhat ironically, the accounts of the looters themselves. These accounts, known collectively as the Tomb Robbery Papyri,[46] are a series of sanitized legal documents dating to several official state investigations conducted during the Late Ramesside period in an attempt to curb the widespread looting of tombs in the Theban necropolis. These accounts provide a snapshot of what met the thieves as they broke into otherwise unopened royal burials in the Theban necropolis, in this case the tomb of the Seventeenth Dynasty Theban ruler Sobekemsaf II at Dra Abu el-Naga:

> We found this noble mummy of this king equipped like a warrior. A large number of sacred-eye amulets and ornaments of gold was at his neck, and his headpiece of gold was on him. The noble mummy of this king was all covered with gold, and his inner coffins were bedizened with gold and silver inside and outside with inlays of all kinds of precious stones. We appropriated the gold which we found on this noble mummy of this god and on his eye amulets and his ornaments which were at his neck and on the inner coffins in which he lay.[47]

When all the loot had been melted down, the thieves were left with nearly 15 kg of gold as a reward for the night's work. They would not, however, live to enjoy their ill-gotten gains. They were captured and interrogated following a royal investigation into the looting of the Theban necropolis during the reign of Rameses IX (see chapter 28 in this volume) and were most likely put to death for their crime.

Comparing the treasures of King Sobekemsaf II of the Seventeenth Dynasty—a time of civil strife with the Egyptian state reduced to near-vassal status by the Hyksos rulers in the north—and those of Tutankhamun (1333–1323 BC), who died toward the end of the

---

45. S.T. Smith 1992; Kawai 2000.

46. Peet 1930.

47. Papyrus Amherst; translation after Peet 1930: 48.

Eighteenth Dynasty, underlines how much the royal treasuries grew during the golden years of the mid-Eighteenth Dynasty. Tutankhamun's famous gold mask alone weighs more than 10 kg, and this mask was only a single golden artifact among many hundreds found by Howard Carter inside the boy-king's tomb in 1922 and 1923 AD.[48] The wealth of the state during the Eighteenth Dynasty, a wealth built upon the success of its conquests, foreign raids, diplomacy, and trading missions, manifested itself in increasingly elaborate tombs, burial assemblages, and mortuary temples for its royals. But such extensive tomb construction required specialized personnel, and in addition the secrecy which surrounded the location of the royal tomb in the Valley of the Kings could not function with rapidly shifting groups of workers coming and going in and out of the valley. The rulers of the early Eighteenth Dynasty addressed these problems effectively by constructing and maintaining a settlement of craft specialists who worked on the royal tomb: the village of Deir el-Medina.

26.4. Artists and the state

Much of our information regarding the community of artisans and builders living at the village of Deir el-Medina (known alternatively as the "Great Place" or the "Place of Truth" in Egyptian textual sources) comes from the Nineteenth and Twentieth Dynasties.[49] This evidence includes both archaeological material in the form of the dwellings and tombs built by the workers at or near the village, as well as a wealth of administrative documentation in the form of hieratic ostraca, many of them found in a large pit north of the village, with further evidence coming from various areas of the Valley of the Kings.[50] Attempting to reconstruct the function and daily routine of the Eighteenth Dynasty village at Deir el-Medina on the basis of Ramesside evidence would, however, be a

---

48. Carter 1933.

49. Démarrée 2016: 75–77.

50. Černý and Gardiner 1957.

fallacy. Eighteenth Dynasty Deir el-Medina and Nineteenth–Twentieth Dynasty Deir el-Medina were not one continuous, unchanging settlement. To the contrary, evidence suggests a wholesale reorganization of the village following the Amarna Period, in particular during the reign of Horemheb (1319–1292 BC).[51] Not only was the village expanded markedly, its entire bureaucratic system most likely also changed. As such, aside from certain common denominators, Ramesside Deir el-Medina was most likely a significantly different place from its Eighteenth Dynasty antecedent village.

Without this evidence available to us, what can be meaningfully said about the Eighteenth Dynasty community of workmen at Deir el-Medina? First, while much of the earlier village was built over during the Ramesside phase of remodeling, some fragments remain and allow tentative reconstruction. The Eighteenth Dynasty village was much smaller, covering around 50 percent of the area taken up by the village during its Ramesside heyday.[52] Unlike the Ramesside village, the Eighteenth Dynasty settlement contained a large open space, most likely for stabling pack donkeys and other animals.[53] More fundamentally, there is no evidence of religious structures of the types built at the site during the Nineteenth Dynasty. In addition, it seems likely that some craft specialists did not live in the village permanently with their families for generations, as many did during later periods, but were rather brought from ateliers and workshops throughout Egypt in order to aid in the construction of the royal tombs in the Valley of the Kings.[54]

Most problematic in the reconstruction of life at Deir el-Medina during the Eighteenth Dynasty is, however, the lack of administrative accounts. The thousands of hieratic ostraca covering almost all aspects of village life during the Ramesside period (see chapter 27 in this volume) provide an immense level of personal information, allowing scholars to

---

51. Uphill 2000: 326.

52. Bruyère 1939: pl. V–VII; Bonnet and Valbelle 1975; 1976.

53. Müller 2014.

54. Zivie 2013: 97–110.

reconstruct the legal feuds, economic transactions, work rhythms, and personal relationships of the Ramesside villagers. In place of these, the Eighteenth Dynasty occupants left only somewhat puzzling ostraca covered, not with hieratic symbols, but with so-called workmen's marks found in the Valley of the Kings.[55] These marks bear no direct resemblance to hieratic or hieroglyphic signs, but were most likely identity markers of organizations, institutions, individual people, or work gangs, used as a basis for recording their presence and serving perhaps as a rough draft of more complex administrative documentation written on papyrus.

What can then be deduced about the organization of those who worked to construct the new royal tombs in the Valley of the Kings given the state of the evidence? If the biography of Ineni discussed earlier is taken at face value, it seems that he—who aside from being scribe, a count, an overseer of storehouses, was also overseer of all works—directly commanded and directed the workers who dug the first tomb in the Valley, that of Thutmose I (1504–1492 BC). Another high-ranking member of the community was Kha, buried in Theban Tomb 8 (TT 8) with his wife Merit. Kha held the title "overseer of construction in the Great Place," with the Great Place (*set aat*) denoting Deir el-Medina during the Eighteenth Dynasty.[56] Although he was buried very near the village, there is no convincing evidence that the village was his permanent residence in life. It is entirely possible that he lived in the Theban settlement on the eastern bank of the Nile and simply oversaw, in the same way that Ineni did, the work undertaken in the Valley of the Kings through regular inspections. Even though other Eighteenth Dynasty tombs have been found in the environs of Deir el-Medina, very few

---

55. Haring 2014; Soliman 2015.

56. The more familiar term "Place of Truth" (*set maat*), along with the traditional title held by the workmen "servant in the Place of Truth" (*sedjem ash em set maat*), only came into usage during the later part of the Eighteenth Dynasty and in particular during the Ramesside period; see Demarée 2016: 76.

inscribed artifacts were found associated with these,[57] and many were reused during the Nineteenth and Twentieth Dynasties, leaving only scatterings of Eighteenth Dynasty ceramics evidencing the presence of their former occupants.

If the community itself was much smaller during the early and mid-Eighteenth Dynasty, is it then perhaps possible that the settlement was either occupied only temporarily, or alternatively housed only a core of artisans supplemented when required by specialists from elsewhere in Egypt? The latter interpretation seems likely, and evidence from elsewhere in Egypt certainly emphasizes the essentially transient nature of the draftsmen and artists who decorated tombs, both royal and private, in the Theban necropolis during the Eighteenth Dynasty. Perhaps the most convincing example was discovered at Saqqara in 1996: the tomb of Thutmose and Kenna.[58] Both held the title "overseer of painters in the Place of Truth" and date to the immediate post-Amarna era (see section 26.7.6). Both these men then must have worked and overseen work in the Valley of the Kings, but they chose to be buried not in Thebes, but far north in Memphis, possibly indicating that they were not Theban by birth, but had simply worked in the Theban necropolis for a portion of their lives. From the texts found in the tomb, it also appears that both their fathers held similar titles, suggesting that they belonged to a family of artists and painters who had worked at multiple sites in Egypt.

Another example of such artistic families is a stele belonging to the painter Dedia,[59] who lists no less than seven generations of ancestors, all working as artisans and painters (some of whom may even have been of non-Egyptian origin).[60] Certainly such high-skilled and experienced painters would have been popular guests both on royal construction projects and in private settings, such as for the decoration of private

---

57. Aside from smatterings of, for instance, funerary cones bearing basic information such as names and family, such as several examples belonging to Amenwahsu and his wife Meryra; see Bruyère 1929: 17.

58. Zivie 2013.

59. Lowle 1976.

60. Vivas Sainz 2017: 109–110.

tombs. While later than the Eighteenth Dynasty, an inscription found in the Twentieth Dynasty tomb of Setau encapsulates the standing of such craft specialists, in this case a "scribe of the Divine Books" by the name of Meryra, whose talent for creating beautiful texts and paintings in tombs was evidently sought after:

> With his own hands did he make the inscriptions when he came to decorate the tomb of Setau [. . .] As for the Scribe of the Divine Books, Meryra, he is no [mere] copyist. His inspiration comes from his heart. No master gives him a model to copy, for he is a scribe of dexterous fingers and of good understanding in all things.[61]

The status of certain artists is displayed in full at the late-Eighteenth Dynasty settlement of Akhetaten (modern Tell el-Amarna). Constructed rapidly during the early reign of Akhenaten (1350–1334 BC), excavations of the city have yielded vast quantities of royal sculpture—almost all of it fragmented and deliberately broken following a sustained period of *damnatio memoriae* in the immediate post-Amarna Period following the city's abandonment. During work at the site in 1912 AD, the German archaeologist Ludwig Borchardt uncovered a large villa which served as the home of the sculptor Thutmose and also as his artistic atelier. Within this workshop, Borchardt uncovered the famous "Berlin Bust" of Akhenaten's principal wife, Nefertiti. Studies of the other royal and non-royal sculptural material found in the workshop, in particular a large collection of plaster heads and "trial pieces," suggests that Thutmose and his apprentices worked for both royal and non-royal clients.[62] They produced their models in clay and plaster, presumably so the final appearance could be agreed with their patrons before the final stone copies were manufactured. It is likely that the royal image was carefully crafted and then disseminated throughout Egypt to other sculptors in other

---

61. Montet 1958: 160.

62. See e.g., Laboury 2005.

workshops, thus ensuring consistency of the royal depictions throughout the kingdom. Given the essentially transitory nature of many artists at this time, it is also entirely possible that a sculptor like Thutmose would have made trips to other settlements around Egypt, supervising and consulting on other royal construction projects.[63]

Artists such as sculptors and painters had, if not an actual agency over the royal image, then certainly a responsibility for it and for guaranteeing its consistency across multiple royal construction projects in many different locations within and without Egypt's borders. However, unlike modern artists, Egyptian artists did not sign their work. As such, it is almost always impossible during any period of pharaonic history to definitely attribute specific works of art—pieces of sculpture or decorated tombs—to a specific named artist. There are, though, some exceptions to this general rule[64] and perhaps the most informative of these[65] is the painter Userhat who was employed by the Karnak temple during the reign of Thutmose IV (1397–1388 BC). Unusually, Userhat is represented twice in the tomb of the second high priest of Amun, Amenhotep Sise (TT 75),[66] and marked out not just by his title "painter of Amun" (*sesh qedut en Imen*, literally "scribe of the outlines of Amun")[67] but also by a painter's palette held in the hand—one of the tools of his trade. This self-representation in the tomb of a patron can be considered somewhat akin to the artistic concept of *in assistenza*, used widely during the Italian Renaissance where an artist would represent himself somewhere in a

---

63. For an extensive discussion of the work practices and remits of the sculptors working at Tell el-Amarna, see Ashton 2016.

64. An example of this practice is the Middle Kingdom painter Horime-Niankhu who is depicted in the tomb of Djehutihotep at Deir el-Bersha; see Newberry 1895: pls. 12 and 15.

65. Sometimes artists depicted themselves in private tombs to highlight their association with the creation of the tomb paintings, but mostly these artists are distinguished only by the title rather than by the names; see Laboury 2015.

66. Davies 1923b.

67. The title *sesh qedut* was used extensively from the Middle Kingdom onward; see, e.g., Stefanović 2012.

painting ordered by their patron, usually unobtrusively, blending in with the background.[68] It seems inconceivable that Userhat would have been permitted to place himself in not one, but two of the most important scenes in the tomb of his superior without Amenhotep Sise's full knowledge and indeed his approval. Given that Userhat most likely worked at the Amun temple, in the same location as Amenhotep Sise, it seems likely that he was specifically chosen to decorate Amenhotep Sise's tomb from among the many artists and artisans working at the temple, possibly on the basis of his skills, by this high-ranking priest. It is unlikely that Userhat himself would ever have been able to gather sufficient resources to build a tomb as grand as his superior's and as such his inclusion in Amenhotep Sise's tomb not only represented a recognition for his work, but possibly as importantly a chance to be represented by name and rank in a grander tomb than Userhat himself would ever have.

Artistic expression underwent several radical changes during the Eighteenth Dynasty, most notably perhaps the change to Amarna-style depictions of the human form, more fluid, elongated, and in some ways expressive than the more stylized depictions of the earlier Eighteenth Dynasty. But while the artistic canon evolved and changed, and while much ink has been spilled charting these developments, far less information is available about the artists who created these images, in temples, in royal and private tombs and even in private homes. What can, however, be gleaned from the evidence is that, as today, some artists achieved important positions through their abilities, taking responsibility for the creation and "mass-production" of the approved royal image, as well as decorating the eternal resting places both of royalty and members of the private elite. The mobility of certain artists seems likely, although no texts clearly lay out this process.[69] This itinerance may support the

---

68. A prime example of this practice is the *Procession of the Magi* in the Palazzo Medici-Riccardi in Florence, a multi-wall fresco wherein the artist Benozzo Gozzoli (1421–1487 AD) chose to represent himself twice, in one scene as a youngster and in another as an old man. In one depiction, Gozzoli even made his identification obvious by painting his name on the hat worn by his self-portrait.

69. Vivas Sainz 2017: 118.

notion by extension that the royal tombs in the Valley of the Kings—as well as perhaps private tombs in Thebes and elsewhere in Egypt—not only relied on a local talent pool, but could bring in specialists from other temple workshops throughout the Nile valley.

Perhaps the smaller scale of Deir el-Medina during this period, as well as the lack of documentary evidence of the sort generated by the established Ramesside community living permanently in the village, can be explained by working with the assumption that only a small group of workers were housed in the village, maybe even on a temporary basis when the construction work in the Valley of the Kings required it, a group supplemented by specialists brought in to work on specific aspects of the royal tomb, supervised by highly skilled master artists and craftsmen like the overseer of the Great Place Thutmose, or earlier, the architect Ineni.

This arrangement underwent a drastic change following the re-establishment of royal authority in Thebes, and the wholesale abandonment of Tell el-Amarna and its associated royal necropolis during the reign of Horemheb (1319–1292 BC). The changes to royal funerary architecture and the much grander scale of the tomb desired by Horemheb and his Ramesside successors would have required a larger permanent workforce of various specialists and by extension the expansion of both the physical village of Deir el-Medina as well as its entire subsistence and administrative network. And alongside changes to royal funerary architecture from the Second Intermediate Period, through the Eighteenth Dynasty and into the post-Amarna Period and the early Nineteenth Dynasty, came also changes to private burial customs in Thebes and elsewhere in Egypt.

26.5. Innovation and tradition: private mortuary customs during the Eighteenth Dynasty

Throughout pharaonic history, private high-ranking individuals would seek to associate their own burials with those of the monarch. This is particularly noticeable during the Old Kingdom at sites such as Giza and

Saqqara (see chapters 5 and 7 in volume 1) or the Middle Kingdom cemeteries at Dahshur and Lisht (see chapter 19 in volume 2) where private mastaba tombs cluster around royal pyramids, their deceased inhabitants continuing their service to the monarch in their afterlife. With the move of royal burials to a secluded valley on the Theban West Bank during the early Eighteenth Dynasty, private tomb architecture had to adapt. While it was no longer possible to arrange a burial immediately next to a royal tomb, it instead became imperative for high officials and courtiers of the early to mid-Eighteenth Dynasty to be buried within the "Domain of Amun," meaning in association with the cult of Amun-Ra at Karnak and the wider festival and sacred landscape at Thebes. As a result, private cemeteries on the Theban West Bank at locations such as Sheikh Abd el-Qurna and the Asasif became hives of funerary activity.

Rock-cut tombs had been the norm at Thebes for centuries, going back to the impressive *saff* tombs of the late Eleventh Dynasty.[70] One of these, the tomb of Henenu (TT 313),[71] a high steward of Mentuhotep II, consists of a 40-m-long shaft cut horizontally into the cliffs at Deir el-Bahri within sight of the mortuary temple of the king himself. While much of the tomb's decoration was entirely destroyed in antiquity, enough material remained for the excavators to determine that the tomb's walls would have been decorated with delicate carvings in raised relief. This is in contrast to the later rock-cut tombs of the Eighteenth Dynasty, which favored painted decoration on plastered surfaces.[72] With the shift of royal attention from Thebes to Itj-tawy during the Twelfth Dynasty, the private burials of the officials and courtiers too shifted away from the southern city only to return during the Seventeenth and Eighteenth Dynasties as Thebes again rose in national prominence.

The blueprint of a "typical" Eighteenth Dynasty private Theban tomb was constructed, not wholly unsurprisingly, on the orders of the

---

70. Snape 2011: 167.

71. Zamacona 2019.

72. Bryan 2010: 1000–1007.

prolific architect Ineni.[73] Ineni's tomb may have originally been a Middle Kingdom *saff*-type construction, usurped and adapted to suit the architect's vision. The tomb is visually striking due to the six columns which support a shallow portico at the tomb's entrance. A central doorway leads through a narrow corridor to a smaller rear hall and the shaft to the burial chamber where Ineni's coffin would be laid to rest. The plan of Ineni's tomb resembles an inverted T, and this design would become standard during the Eighteenth Dynasty, albeit without the six columns that give Ineni's tomb its distinctive appearance.

Another example of this type of tomb construction dating to the mid-Eighteenth Dynasty is TT 181, a tomb belonging to two sculptors who were most likely associated with the nascent workforce at Deir el-Medina, Nebamun, and Ipuky.[74] The tomb is cut into the cliffs at Deir el-Bahri and is fronted by a small square courtyard cut into the bedrock and shared with another tomb (TT 337). The tomb's entrance structure has been wholly destroyed, but a painting inside the tomb itself details its overall appearance, and there are also the rows of ceramic funerary cones stamped with the names and titles of the tomb owner,[75] which became another common decorative element of Eighteenth Dynasty tombs at Thebes. While adhering to the typical Theban T-shaped design, the tomb of Nebamun and Ipuky is of course much smaller than those of Ineni and other Eighteenth Dynasty high officials, as should be expected given the comparative lower status of the sculptors Nebamun and Ipuky. The tomb's decorative program includes scenes showing offerings given to the deceased, a banquet, and the funerary cortege.

The decorative program in Eighteenth Dynasty private Theban tombs falls into two overall stages.[76] During the pre-Amarna Period, tomb scenes included not only depictions of "daily life," such as the

---

73. Dziobek 1992.

74. Davies 1925.

75. Snape 2011: 187.

76. For an extensive discussion of the problematic modern distinction between scenes of "daily life" and scenes of "ritual activity" in Theban tombs, see Hartwig 2004: 49–50.

tomb owner and their families fishing and fowling, hunting, banqueting, overseeing agricultural or industrial activity (such as copper smelters depicted in the tomb of Hepu, TT 66),[77] but also some depictions of the funeral and funerary processions, as well as the deceased giving or being presented with offerings.[78] Along with these were also depictions of the king and scenes highlighting the role played by the tomb owner in the state administration. The latter include, for instance, the extravagant scenes of foreign tribute bearers, most famously those found in the tomb of the vizier Rekhmira,[79] which served to highlight both the extent of Rekhmira's responsibilities as well as his contribution to the successful management and enrichment of the ancient Egyptian state. The religious revolution of the Amarna period and its aftermath gave rise to a new corpus of tomb scenes, more focused on religion and ritual, which would be carried through to the Ramesside period, coinciding with a general change in the perception of the function of tombs and their architecture.[80]

The extensive reuse and looting of the private cemeteries in the Theban area has rendered meaningful analysis of the actual contents of burials problematic. With only a handful of tombs in the Theban necropolis being found largely intact by archaeologists (out of thousands), only very general observations can be made with regard to the types of material required in a burial assemblage. S.T. Smith divides these objects into two overarching categories: (1) material produced specifically for the tomb, and (2) objects of daily life reused for the purpose of the burial.[81] Within the first category the undoubtedly most important object was the coffin, typically during the Eighteenth Dynasty being a wooden anthropoid type with the decoration varying, depending on the

77. Graziadio 2014: fig. 3.

78. Snape 2011: 190–194; for an extensive catalogue of Theban tomb scenes, see Kampp 1996.

79. Davies 1943; Anthony 2016.

80. Manniche 2003; Lemos et al. 2017: 179.

81. S.T. Smith 1992.

status of the deceased, from plain painted wood to much more elaborate inlaid and gilded examples.[82] Along with the coffin were other material purposely produced for inclusion in the burial, such as funerary masks,[83] shabtis,[84] canopic vessels and chests,[85] amulets and jewelry,[86] and also inscribed materials such as funerary papyri,[87] as well as more delicate items such as garlands and bouquets of flowers.[88] In the second category of materials, those relating to daily life, are primarily found containers such as woven baskets,[89] and ceramic storage vessels such as amphorae.[90]

---

82. For a representation of the social hierarchy apparent in choice of coffins even among the Theban "elite," contrast the painted wooden coffin of Tamyt (British Museum, BM EA 6661), which appears to have not been made specifically for this owner, with the far more elaborate gilded coffins of Queen Tiye's parents Yuya and Tuya from KV 46, now in the Cairo Museum.

83. An example of a gilded funerary mask from the early Eighteenth Dynasty can be found in the Metropolitan Museum of Art, New York (accession number 36.3.1), belonging to Hatnefer, the mother of the high official Senenmut, who was prominent during the reign of Hatshepsut.

84. For an overview of the typically Theban "stick shabtis" of the Seventeenth and Eighteenth Dynasties, see Whelan 2011.

85. The example in the Art Institute of Chicago (accession number 1892.38a–b) belongs to Amenhotep, the overseer of the builders of Amun.

86. Andrews 1994.

87. Books of the Dead inscribed on papyrus became a more common feature in private burials from the reign of Hatshepsut onward, continuing in some form until the Roman period. Examples from the Eighteenth Dynasty include several held in the Petrie Museum of Archaeology (University College London), belonging to Hepres (UC 71000), Hor (UC 71004), and Nebettawy (UC 71005), as well as a more complete and beautifully decorated example belonging to the Royal Scribe Nakht, held in the British Museum (BM EA 10471).

88. For an extensive discussion of these artifacts, see Tomashevska 2019.

89. See, e.g., a decorated storage basket found in the tomb of Hatnefer and Ramose (TT 71) at Sheikh Abd el-Qurna (Metropolitan Museum of Art, New York, accession number 36.3.57a–b).

90. Such as a sealed storage amphora containing oil found in the tomb of Hatnefer and Ramose (TT 71) at Sheikh Abd el-Qurna (Metropolitan Museum of Art, New York, accession number 36.3.83).

When considering funerary practices and tomb assemblages of the Eighteenth Dynasty it is not, however, sufficient to simply study and discuss the elite burials in the Theban necropolis. Cemeteries were associated with provincial settlements as well, and these can often provide a more nuanced picture preserving the burials of far humbler individuals than the courtiers buried in Thebes. An illustrative example of such modest burials dating to the Eighteenth Dynasty can be found at Gurob in the Fayum, the site of a settlement and palace dating to the reign of Thutmose III (1479–1425 BC). During excavations at the site during the early twentieth century, W.L.S. Loat discovered several interments dating to the Eighteenth Dynasty which included no wooden coffin,[91] but rather a simple woven reed mat wrapped around the body.[92] The burial goods found were also far simpler than those found in more well-appointed burials and included pottery vessels as well as some items of personal hygiene and adornment, such as a mirror and kohl tube.[93] A contemporary burial of two infants[94] also yielded some blue beads. Another contemporary burial found by Loat did include a coffin, although this was manufactured from clay and painted with yellow bands and a depiction of the goddess Nut.[95]

---

91. Loat 1905.

92. Loat 1905: 2: "In one case the body had been placed in a roughly-made trench, dimensions 7 ft. × 1 ft. 9 in. × 3 ft., lying approximately N.-E. and S.-W., on the top of a large 'kom' or eminence. Covering the body was a closely woven mat of grass, which was wonderfully well preserved considering that it dated from the XVIIIth Dynasty. Resting on the mat, and leaning against the end of the tomb at the right hand side of the head, was a large red earthenware pot (pl. VII, i). When the upper mat was removed, the body was found lying wrapped in another mat, composed of sticks made from the ribs of the date palm, round which a rope had been bound to prevent its coming undone (pl. VII, 2), beneath the head was a small two-handled vase (pl. Ill, 99)."

93. Loat 1905: 2.

94. One of the simple reed coffins from this burial (along with the infant inside) is now held in the Manchester Museum (accession no. 3496); see David and Tapp 1984: 16.

95. Loat 1905: 3. This coffin is now in the Manchester Museum (accession no. 3508).

The political changes of the early Eighteenth Dynasty did not only manifest themselves in Thebes. In northern Egypt royal attention became increasingly focused on the old capital city at Memphis and, as a result, the Old Kingdom cemetery of Saqqara, almost abandoned during the Middle Kingdom aside from a scattering of tombs, became yet again a choice burial ground for members of the state's administrative elite, in particular during the post-Amarna era and the reigns of Tutankhamun (1333–1323 BC), Ay (1323–1319 BC), and Horemheb (1319–1292 BC). Early to mid-Eighteenth Dynasty tombs of high officials have been discovered at Saqqara, notably those of Hatshepsut's treasurer Nehsy and his successor Meryra, located on the eastern escarpment of the Saqqara plateau,[96] as well as the Tomb of the vizier Aperel, dating to the time of Amenhotep III (1388–1350 BC).[97] These tombs take the shape of rock-cut shafts, not dissimilar to their Theban counterparts rather than the mastaba-style tombs favored at Saqqara during the Old Kingdom. It is curious, given the importance of Memphis as a royal administrative center, that more tombs from this period have not been located. One explanation could be a desire among the elite—even those working and living in Memphis—to be buried closer to the king and within the domain of Amun. Another possibility is that these early Eighteenth Dynasty tombs at Saqqara were looted and usurped by later burials and have therefore not been recognized in the archaeological record.

Following the end of the Atenist socio-religious experiment conducted by Akhenaten (1351–1334 BC) and the restoration of Egypt's traditional pantheon, new elite tombs began to be constructed on the Saqqara plateau. These differ radically in their architecture from their contemporary Theban counterparts, with most taking the shape of a traditional New Kingdom temple as their inspiration. These tombs, in particular those of Maya,[98] the overseer of the treasury and overseer of

96. Zivie 1984.

97. Zivie 1988.

98. Raven 2001.

works, and that of the generalissimo (and later pharaoh) Horemheb,[99] both dating to the reign of Tutankhamun, are distinguished by their superstructures which comprise first a pylon, followed by an outer courtyard, storerooms, an inner courtyard, and several offering chapels. The substructures take the form of tomb shafts which can be accessed from the inner courtyard. Branching off from the shaft are subterranean tomb chambers, decorated with carved limestone reliefs, where the coffins and other burial goods of the deceased would have been placed.

The decorative program in the Saqqara tomb of Horemheb comprises predominantly scenes of military life as befitted a general: troops marching and setting up camp, transporting prisoners, and Horemheb himself being honored by Tutankhamun and given the "gold of valor." Unlike the painted decoration typical of Eighteenth Dynasty Theban tombs, the decorative program in the tomb of Horemheb (as well as those of other late-Eighteenth Dynasty notables buried in the necropolis) is carved, mimicking the decorative techniques used in the much earlier Old Kingdom mastabas at the site which would have been visible during the New Kingdom. Some scenes make it clear that the artists who decorated the late-Eighteenth Dynasty tombs at Saqqara certainly visited the nearby Old Kingdom mastabas and drew inspiration from the depictions they found there. Scenes showing the procession of statues of the tomb owner, as found, e.g., in the tomb of Maya,[100] are evidently inspired by Old Kingdom tomb scenes showing the same event, such as those from the Fifth Dynasty tomb of Hetepherakhty, which originally stood west of Djoser's Step Pyramid at Saqqara but is now located in the Rijksmuseum van Oudheden in Leiden.[101] In this way, innovation and tradition were merged as the necropolis of Saqqara

---

99. Martin 1989.

100. Graefe 1975: figs. 6a–b, pl. 58.

101. Eaton-Kraus 1984: 148–149, pl. X.

continued to expand through the late-Eighteenth Dynasty and into the Ramesside period.

Private tomb architecture and construction underwent significant changes during the Eighteenth Dynasty, changes that reflect the broader social and economic developments. The early Theban tombs looked back toward, and were inspired by, early Middle Kingdom tombs, while the Theban tombs of the mid-Eighteenth Dynasty, decorated with flowing and multicolored reliefs, exude a sensuous opulence that came with Egypt's increasing wealth and power derived from its growing empire in the Near East and Nubia. Elite tombs at Saqqara following the tumultuous Amarna period incorporate clear elements of traditional temple architecture into their tombs, a fashion which would continue at the site during the Ramesside period. But in the same manner as the Theban tombs of the early Eighteenth Dynasty, the Saqqara tombs constructed later in the dynasty incorporate traditional or archaizing elements into their innovative designs—for instance by taking inspiration for specific scenes and motifs from the wealth of decorated Old Kingdom mastabas found at the site.

But in this discussion, it can be easy to lose sight of a simple yet crucial fact: the fashions and trends of tomb architecture, of painting techniques and tomb equipment in elite tombs on the Theban West Bank would not have mattered much to the vast majority of the population living along the banks of the Nile. As the simple reed and clay coffins at Gurob and other sites throughout Egypt testify, this vast but far quieter majority were buried in much the same way as they had been for thousands of years, in simple coffins made of easily accessible materials, with few burial goods, mostly in the form of objects of daily use repurposed for burials. As always when we study a civilization like pharaonic Egypt, where the balance of data is so heavily skewed in favor of the elite sphere, where far more chapels and temples have been excavated and published than farming villages, it is vital to bear this discrepancy in mind, and to remember that for the vast majority of the ancient Egyptian population, the political, social, cultural, and economic changes discussed in these pages would most likely have been far more unremarkable than they might seem to us.

26.6. Economy and industry

The construction of elaborate tombs, decorated with painting utilizing a wealth of pigments and minerals, filled with objects made from a variety of precious materials, some native but many imported from Nubia and the Near East, naturally presupposed a functional economy supported by extensive production of certain goods and materials valued outside of Egypt's borders and therefore valuable trade commodities. Scenes of weapons production, smelting, and casting found in many Theban tombs certainly give the impression of an extensive and well-organized industrial program supported and sponsored by state institutions.[102] And while the scenes of tribute bearers give the impression that the Egyptian state did not have to actually engage in trade with foreign cultures, but rather could simply sit back and let the tribute roll in,[103] the reality, as revealed by both archaeology and texts of the period, presents a far more varied picture—a picture where Egypt, using a mixture of military power, imperial politics, and carefully controlled trade with precious commodities, garnered an enormous amount of wealth and influence which were channeled into both royal and private construction projects and temple endowments.

The economic wealth garnered through royal military exploits did not solely come into the ownership of cult and royal institutions. Some went to private ownership through a series of rewards given to soldiers who participated in royal campaigns. Ahmose, son of Ibana, from Elkab, who served in the armies of the dynasty founder Ahmose (1550–1525 BC) and of Amenhotep I (1525–1504 BC), records receiving a large tract of

---

102. See, e.g., scenes of bronze smelting and the manufacture of various weapons of war, including shields, arrows, and chariot components depicted in the tomb of Hepu (TT 66; Davies 1963: pl. 8) and the tomb of Puyemra (TT 39; Davies 1923a: pl. 23) from Thebes, along with the Saqqara tomb of Kyiri (Quibell 1912: 75) and also the early Ramesside tomb of Ipuy (Quibell and Hayter 1927: pl. 13) which continues the theme.

103. See, e.g., the Nubian tribute bearers depicted in the tomb of Tutankhamun's Viceroy Huy at Thebes, a copy of which is held in the Metropolitan Museum of Art, New York (accession no. 30.4.21).

land as well as dozens of slaves—many of them named in the biography in his tomb as a reward for his long and loyal service.[104] The biography of Amenemhab dating to the mid-Eighteenth Dynasty explains how Amenemhab captured both prisoners of war and also looted various precious items which he then brought to the king, where they were counted.[105] A reward was then given to Amenemhab, taking the form of either slaves (presumably to work land owned by the official in Egypt) or precious objects such as weapons and gold jewelry. The contemporary soldier Ahmose Pennekhbet, for instance, records receiving a wealth of different materials as rewards from the monarch, such as bracelets, necklaces, daggers, axes, and even headdresses and a fan.[106]

The transference of this property within families also underwent changes during the Second Intermediate Period and early New Kingdom, continuing into the Ramesside period. During the Old Kingdom, inheritance rights were related solely to the first-born son, who inherited the full estate as his personal property.[107] By the early New Kingdom, a more nuanced system had been implemented whereby property, including land, was inherited by all descendants but held in trust by a specific individual, usually the first-born, who acted as a *rudju*,[108] a caretaker of sorts who in theory should share out the profits of an estate equally among the other inheritors. In reality, of course, this system was open to abuse, as is evidenced on the stele of Mes,[109] an early Ramesside inscription, which details a complex legal dispute stretching back several generations within a family. The tort revolves around a plot of land originally granted

---

104. *Urk.* I: 14–24; for a complete translation of Ahmose's biography, see Lichtheim 1976: 11–15.

105. Redford 2003: 170, see also Breasted 1906: 227–235.

106. Breasted 1906: 9–12, 18, 35, 143–144.

107. See, e.g., this system resulting in a dispute between two brothers in Papyrus Berlin P 9010: Sethe 1926.

108. The term *rudju* refers to a generic administrator who was, in the context of private property and inheritance, often—though not always—a family member, for instance the eldest-born son.

109. Eyre 2015: 173.

to the family during the reign of Horemheb (1319–1292 BC) and then held in trust by various *rudju*-caretakers who shared the profits equally among the other owners. However, by the time of the inscription, the relationships between the *rudju* and his family members had evidently soured to the extent that a court divided the land into individual parcels, distributing these among the other claimants and taking away the overall management responsibilities from the *rudju*.

If an individual wished to bequeath items, ownership, or even titles to specific family members, they could, as in earlier times, draw up an *imyt-per*,[110] a transfer deed or testament, of which some examples are known from the Eighteenth Dynasty, although as can be seen from the stele of Senimose from the reign of Thutmose III (1479–1425 BC), which records an extensive legal battle between various family members, the contents of an *imyt-per* could be challenged in court.[111]

Through standard inheritance and *imyt-per* testaments, the private wealth garnered by officers on campaigns remained within their families and allowed them to expand their holdings, perhaps by purchasing more farmland and employing others to work the land alongside the prisoners of war and their descendants. The grain and other profits generated from this production would, it might be suspected, have further enriched these families, leading to an increasing militarization of the elite and the eventual emergence of military families so powerful that individual members such as Horemheb and Paramessu (who later became Rameses I) could take royal power for themselves.

The Egyptian economy was based around the concept of barter,[112] exchanging items of like value in kind, rather than through the medium of coinage. In order to standardize the bartering system to a certain extent, a complex system of weights and measures were used based around the *deben*, a weight of copper used to express the perceived value of an item during a trade—whether an object or an animal. Any village,

---

110. Logan 2000.

111. Logan 2000: 64–65.

112. Kemp 1991: 248–260.

any town would have been filled with a complex pattern of trades, bartering, and exchanges between households, although sadly much of our evidence for such low-level transactions comes from the Ramesside period and the unique settlement of Deir el-Medina.[113] To reconstruct the mercantile environment in an Eighteenth Dynasty village, by contrast, we are largely reliant on artistic depictions such as those found in the tombs of Qenamun (TT 62)[114] and Khaemhat (TT 57),[115] both dating to the Eighteenth Dynasty, as well as some early Ramesside examples, such as the tomb of Huy and Kenro (TT 54).[116]

A relief in the tomb of Qenamun, the mayor of Thebes, shows foreign merchants, most likely Syrians, disembarking from their ships and meeting Egyptian traders sitting under awnings, at what appears to be temporary booths on the river bank.[117] Two Egyptian men and one woman sit in the three booths displaying their wares, which include cloth, sandals, and foodstuffs. The trader in the middle register is holding a pair of scales, possibly weighing a metal against a known set of stone weights as part of a transaction. The Syrian merchants disembarking from their ship are carrying sealed amphorae, perhaps containing oils and wine, which they are evidently intending to barter for the Egyptian goods on offer. An interesting reversal of this scene is depicted in the tomb of Khaemhat (TT 57), where a fleet of Egyptian ships are shown arriving at an Egyptian outpost in Nubia.[118] They depict Egyptians transporting grain, which they are bartering with Nubian merchants, arranged in similar fashion along the banks of the river offering not only foodstuffs,

---

113. See, e.g., the seminal studies of Ramesside economy utilizing a wealth of sources from Deir el-Medina by Černý 1954 and Janssen 1975.

114. Davies and Faulkner 1947.

115. Pino 2005.

116. Originally this tomb was constructed for the sculptor Huy during the reign of Thutmose IV, although the market scene in question was most likely commissioned when the tomb was usurped by the priest Kenro during the early Nineteenth Dynasty.

117. Davies and Faulkner 1947: pl. VIII.

118. Pino 2005: fig. 2.

but also Nubian luxury products such as unguents and incense, and even wine and honey. The scenes are highly detailed and even show animated individuals, their arms raised, either bartering fiercely or—as one scholar has hypothesized—possibly having a hard time understanding each other's languages. By contrast, the market scene in the tomb of Huy and Kenro does not show any foreign merchants, but focuses on what seems to be a local market with primarily women selling simple wares—foodstuffs such as fish and eggs—to other members of local farming communities.[119]

That these market scenes are depicted on the riverbank is unsurprising. It is likely that most markets were placed either temporarily or permanently along the banks of the river, thus taking full advantage of the Nile as a transport artery. The closest Egyptian term which from context seems to mean "marketplace" (*meryt*) is in fact also the term for "riverbank," further emphasizing this geographical location. While most markets probably involved mainly members of the local community and perhaps visitors from villages nearby upstream or downstream, a class of individuals, known as *shutiu*, a term commonly translated as "merchant,"[120] seem to have lived a somewhat nomadic existence, traveling from the state institutions such as temples and harem palaces to which they were frequently attached, throughout the country trading the surplus products produced at their institutions along, perhaps, with materials given as royal donations following military campaigns. The Ramesside-period Papyrus Lansing describes these merchants in action: "The merchants travel downstream and upstream. They are as busy as can be, carrying goods from one town to another. They supply him who has wants."[121]

At a state level, large-scale trading expeditions represented vast investments of labor and resources, and their successful completion was often celebrated in the same manner as one would celebrate a victorious

---

119. Pino 2005: 96.

120. Allam 1998.

121. Lichtheim 1976: 170.

army returning from campaign. Perhaps the most exalted Eighteenth Dynasty trading expedition was the one dispatched during the reign of Hatshepsut (1479–1458 BC) to the distant land of Punt.[122] The expedition is described in reliefs at Hatshepsut's mortuary temple at Deir el-Bahri, and while the rulers of Punt are described as giving the wealth to the Egyptians as a tribute, it is far more likely that the Egyptians traded for it, with the text referring to the Egyptian expedition receiving the nobles of Punt and giving them gifts from Egypt and even treating them to a banquet. Hatshepsut's expedition brought back large quantities of myrrh and even myrrh-trees, along with various precious minerals, ivory, ebony, and even animals such as baboons, back to Egypt. Some of these materials would be donated to the Karnak temple, others still used in Hatshepsut's own mortuary temple.

The framing of what was essentially trade as tribute-giving is typical in Egyptian royal monumental texts of the period. Similarly, the Amarna Letters—a corpus of diplomatic correspondence in the cuneiform script and (mostly) the Akkadian language dating to the later part of the Eighteenth Dynasty[123]—talk of diplomatic gift-giving and tributes, language that somewhat simplifies what was most likely a far more complex international system of trade and barter. The quantities of material shipped from Egypt on behalf of the Egyptian ruler to his allies in Assyria, Babylon, and Mittani (and probably also, although the letters do not mention them, the Mycenaean city-states), and the material received by the Egyptian state in exchange certainly seem too excessive to be simple diplomatic gifts and should most likely be interpreted instead as formal state-level trade.[124]

Archaeologically, international trade in the eastern Mediterranean has left few clear traces, aside from the traded materials themselves. An exception is the shipwreck of Uluburun discovered off the southern

---

122. Creasman 2004.

123. For an accessible translation, see Moran 1992.

124. Liverani 1999: 326; Cappellini and Caramello 2009.

coast of Turkey in 1982 AD.[125] The ship, which sank toward the end of the Amarna Period, contained a wealth of trade goods, some Egyptian and some originating from other cultures in the eastern Mediterranean and even further afield.[126] The raw materials included copper ingots, tin, and raw blue glass of Egyptian manufacture, and also ivory and hippopotamus tusks. Worked materials included weapons, extensive assemblages of gold jewelry, as well as amphorae of oils and resins. The contents of the ship closely match the kinds of diplomatic gifts discussed in the Amarna Letters, and it was perhaps a transport vessel carrying these artifacts to one of the large Mycenaean palaces on the Greek mainland.

As such, even though the ship was most likely not Egyptian in origin, the contents of the trading vessel found at Uluburun give us a clear indication of the kinds of goods which made their way to and from Egypt and Egyptian territories during the Eighteenth Dynasty. The most notable portion of the cargo from an Egyptian perspective is perhaps the sheer quantity of glass, in particular blue glass, beads as well as ingots of blue glass which could be melted and reworked into desired shapes on arrival at their destination. Blue glass was a significant Egyptian export during this period, and more widely the color blue seems intrinsically linked to Egypt's Eighteenth Dynasty, from the blue perfume bottles and faience tiles at Tell el-Amarna to the ubiquitous blue-painted pottery found at almost every major Eighteenth Dynasty settlement, temple, and mortuary site.[127] While earlier scholars believed that glass was an Egyptian invention, later research has shown that the technology originated in

---

125. Bass 1991; Pulak 2001; 2008.

126. Among the cargo found on the Uluburun shipwreck were, for instance, beads manufactured from Baltic amber, and while this of course does not evidence direct trade links between northern Europe and the Mediterranean during the Late Bronze Age, it certainly underlines the diversity of materials traded in the Eastern Mediterranean at this time; see Ingram 2014.

127. For a discussion of cobalt-blue pigments in New Kingdom Egypt, see Abe et al. 2012; for the use of cobalt as a pigment in blue-painted pottery from the Eighteenth Dynasty, see Shortland, Tite, and Hope 2006; and for a general overview of blue-painted pottery from the later part of the Eighteenth Dynasty, see Aston 2011.

Asia and the Near East. It is likely that the Egyptian campaigns in the area during the early Eighteenth Dynasty resulted in the capture of glass-makers who were brought back to Egypt to practice and teach the technology.[128] The blue glass so favored by the Egyptians, most likely because of its visual similarity to lapis lazuli, was produced in vast quantities at Eighteenth Dynasty sites, with evidence in particular coming from the capital of Akhetaten (Tell el-Amarna).[129]

The presence of blue glass products on the Uluburun shipwreck shows its importance as an international export, although glass was also imported into Egypt during this time.[130] The process of glass manufacture involved the heating of silica, natron, and lime and coloring the mixture with cobalt.[131] This process is similar to the manufacture of Egyptian faience and it is likely that these vitreous productions were carried out closely together. While it is clear that some glass production, in particular at Tell el-Amarna, was conducted in large (and most likely royal) workshops, more recent evidence has suggested that the production of glass beads was more widespread, even taking place in private houses in the city.[132] In this we can perhaps glimpse an intersection between the smaller local trade along the riverbank and the larger-scale state-supported international trade networks across the eastern Mediterranean.

The Eighteenth Dynasty represented a time of technological innovation and change within Egypt. From a military perspective, the war against the Hyksos and the early forays into the Near East saw the inclusion of chariots and compound bows to the Egyptian arsenal. The

128. Nicholson, Jackson, and Trott 1997.

129. Shortland 2000; Nicholson 2007.

130. See, for instance, a reference in a letter of the Amarna correspondence (EA 323) wherein Yidya, the mayor of Ashkelon, notes sending thirty pieces of glass to the Egyptian court as a tribute.

131. Hodgkinson, Röhrs, Müller, and Reiche 2019.

132. For an extensive discussion on the topic of the manufacture of luxury goods in suburban settings at Tell el-Amarna, see Hodgkinson 2016: 53–186.

military campaigns themselves then led to further technological innovations, such as the introduction of industrial glass-making to Egypt.
The wealth gathered by the kings of the Eighteenth Dynasty through
warfare, tribute, and as a result of mining and quarrying expeditions dispatched to Egypt's periphery to mine for gold and precious gemstones
was used in a complex game of diplomatic trade with the great powers of
the ancient Near East. The wealth of Egypt, in particular its widespread
access to gold, is a constant theme in the Amarna Letters,[133] although it is
clear that from the point of view of the other "great kings" of the ancient
Near East, the Egyptian king did not always distribute this wealth of
gold fairly among them: "Gold is as plentiful as dust [in your country],"
complains the king of Assyria, adding rather harshly: "Why are you so
sparing of it?"[134]

Gold was certainly more difficult to obtain than dust, even for the
Egyptians.[135] But the phrasing, and the seemingly endless lists of diplomatic gifts, along with the archaeological remains of industrial production centers and heavily laden shipwrecks carrying, among other items,
precious cargo from Egypt, underline the impression that Egypt during the height of the Eighteenth Dynasty was a state enjoying immense
wealth and the international power and prestige that came from it. For a
dynasty which had begun its rise to power by fighting a rear-guard action
against a superior enemy, it was an astounding reversal of fortunes, a
reversal made possible not just by a series of competent rulers along with
their advisers, but more widely by the labor of the population, by warfare
and diplomacy, by trade and industry.

---

133. See, e.g., the extensive list of gold and other valuables dispatched by the
Egyptians to the king of Babylon in a letter from the Amarna correspondence
(EA 14): "These are the objects which Akhenaten, the great king, King of
Egypt, sent to his brother Burna-Buriaš, the great king, king of Babylon: Total
of all the gold: 1200 minas. Total of all the silver: 292 minas. Total of all the
bronze: 860 minas. Total of the linen-cloth: 1092 [individual pieces of cloth-
ing]." Translation after Moran 1992: 27–37.

134. Westbrook 2000: 378–379.

135. For a thorough overview of gold-mining in ancient Egypt, see Klemm 2013.

26.7. A historical survey of the Eighteenth Dynasty
26.7.1. After the expulsion of the Hyksos

The expulsion of the Hyksos was not a singular cataclysmic event, but rather a series of campaigns, losses and gains, launched from Thebes with the aim of dislodging the Hyksos from their main power base in the eastern Nile delta: the city of Avaris.[136] Several frontal assaults on the city, both during the reign of the Theban ruler Kamose of the Seventeenth Dynasty, failed with the Thebans taking control of the city's hinterland rather than the settlement itself, resulting in an effective blockade of the city of Avaris—at least along its southern limits, as hinted in the Kamose Stele:

> I placed the brave guard-flotilla to patrol as far as the desert-edge with the remainder (of the fleet) behind it, as if a kite were preying upon the territory of Avaris.[137]

But the Hyksos still maintained control of their supply lines east of the city, the route leading across the Sinai Peninsula past their fortress at Sharuhen[138] and into Canaan. Without shutting off this potential route of reinforcement and supply, Avaris could not be effectively starved into submission.

It was Kamose's successor, his brother Ahmose (1550–1525 BC), who would eventually take the city of Avaris. However, on Kamose's death, Ahmose was still a young boy, and power seems to have passed temporarily to his mother Ahhotep,[139] who ruled as regent in his name and

---

136. For a current overview of the excavations of Avaris (Tell el-Dabʻa) conducted by the Austrian mission under Manfred Bietak and Irene Forstner-Müller, see, e.g., Bietak 1996; Bietak, Math, Müller, and Jurman 2012–2013; Forstner-Müller 2014. See also chapter 23 in this volume.

137. Translation adapted from Ryholt 1997: 173.

138. Shea 1979; Oren 1997.

139. Schmitz 1978.

may even have led Theban troops in battle,[140] setting an example for a long line of powerful royal women throughout the Eighteenth Dynasty. Ahmose's ascension may have given fresh impetus to the Theban attack on their Hyksos rivals, although Ahmose altered the Egyptian strategy significantly: rather than attempt further frontal assaults on Avaris, he led his armies east of the city and took control of the Sinai forts along the Ways of Horus, including the massive structure at Tjaru. In doing so, he effectively cut the Hyksos supply line and left Avaris wholly isolated.[141]

Ahmose exploited the weakened position of the city and launched three attacks on Avaris. After the third try, the city fell, although the accounts of the final series of battles are only known from Egyptian sources, and mainly from tomb biographies such as the biography of Ahmose, son of Ibana, who led a Theban detachment during the assaults on the city: "Then Avaris was despoiled, and I brought spoil from there: one man, three women; total, four persons. His majesty gave them to me as slaves."[142]

These accounts are somewhat light on strategic detail and as tomb biographies they cannot be considered objective historical sources. The lack of any Hyksos counterpoint to the Egyptian narrative furthermore creates a significant bias in the available records. Some events recorded by Ahmose, son of Ibana, have however been supported by archaeological discoveries at the site of Avaris, the modern-day village of Tell el-Dab'a

---

140. A stele raised in the Karnak temple by King Ahmose honoring his mother Ahhotep specifically refers to her having military command: "She has looked after her soldiers, she has guarded her, she has brought back her fugitives and collected together her deserters, she has pacified Upper Egypt and expelled her rebels," see Hawass 2009: 47.

141. The Rhind Mathematical Papyrus (most likely written by a scribe in Memphis working under Hyksos direction, given the refusal to refer to Ahmose by the title "King") records the Egyptian capture of the fortress: "Regnal Year 11, second month of Shomu – Heliopolis was entered. First month of Akhet, day 23 – this southern prince broke into Tjaru. Day 25 – it was heard tell that Tjaru had been entered. Regnal Year 11, first month of Akhet, the birthday of Seth – a roar was emitted by the Majesty of this god. The birthday of Isis – the sky poured rain." Translation after Redford 1993: 128.

142. Lichtheim 1976: 13.

in the northeastern Nile delta. The biography of Ahmose, son of Ibana, makes frequent references to Ahmose capturing or seizing "hands," by which is meant that he, after killing an enemy, cut off the fallen soldier's right hand and brought it to the royal herald as evidence of his bravery and skill:

> Then there was fighting on the water in *Pa-djedku* of Avaris. I made a seizure and carried off a hand. When it was reported to the royal herald the gold of valor was given to me. Then they fought again in this place; I again made a seizure there and carried off a hand.[143]

Recent excavations at the Eighteenth Dynasty palace built by King Ahmose atop the ruins of the Hyksos citadel following his conquest of Avaris have revealed a deposit of human hands, buried in the palace foundations.[144] Perhaps these hands belonged to Hyksos nobles, or even members of the Hyksos royal line who did not escape the city in time.

After his conquests of Avaris, with the Hyksos on the run, Ahmose pursued his fleeing enemies across the Sinai Peninsula and out of Egypt. On the way he reached the Hyksos fortress of Sharuhen and besieged it for three years before it finally fell and the last Hyksos stronghold within Egyptian territory was brought back under Egyptian control.[145]

The latter part of Ahmose's reign was dedicated to two overarching concerns: re-establishing control of Egypt, primarily through a series of monumental construction projects throughout the Nile valley and in the Nile delta, and a series of foreign conquests—primarily in Nubia—aimed at returning control of the Middle Kingdom fortifications below

---

143. Lichtheim 1976: 12.

144. Bietak, Dorner, and Jánosi 2001: 60, 64, fig. 21.

145. Biography of Ahmose, son of Ibana: "Then Sharuhen was besieged for three years. His majesty despoiled it and I brought spoil from it: two women and a hand. Then the gold of valor was given to me, and my captives were given to me as slaves." Translation after Lichtheim 1973: 13.

the First and Second Cataracts to Egyptian control.[146] The great fortress of Buhen, which had switched its allegiance to the kingdom of Kush and their ruler based at Kerma during the Second Intermediate Period (see chapter 25 in this volume), seemingly passed back under Egyptian control without bloodshed and Ahmose installed a new commander, Turi,[147] who also served as his viceroy of Nubia, tasked with relaunching expeditions for gold and other minerals from the dormant quarries and mines in the Nubian desert.

Ahmose began large-scale royal constructions at several of Egypt's most important traditional cult sites, in particular his native Thebes. His donations to Karnak temple and his claim to have restored the temple following its destruction in a series of cataclysmic storms has already been described, but in addition to his building projects at Karnak, he also constructed a monumental cult temple at Abydos,[148] and in addition may also have undertaken construction activity in the eastern Nile delta, possibly as a way of marking the return of Egyptian authority in an area which had been dominated by the Hyksos for a century.[149]

At Avaris, Ahmose built a large royal palace, decorated with a series of Minoan-style friezes showing traditional Cretan motifs such as bulls, acrobats, and labyrinths.[150] The precise purpose of these reliefs remains somewhat mysterious. No contemporary Minoan material has been found associated with these depictions, and they predate the depictions

---

146. Trigger 1976: 107, 118–119; Arnold 2003: 39.

147. H. Smith 1976: pl. LXXX.

148. Crucially, Ahmose constructed a vast pyramidical cult complex at the site and later he was further memorialized at the site in a smaller chapel constructed by his son Amenhotep I; see extensive discussions and descriptions of these structures in Harvey 1998.

149. The evidence for this is slight, although a fragment of a scarab inscribed with the titular and name of Ahmose Nefertari (British Museum, BM EA 18468) was found by Flinders Petrie while excavating the site of Tell Nebesha near Avaris (Tell el-Dab'a).

150. Bietak, Marinatos, and Palivou 2007. See also chapter 31 in this volume.

of Minoan envoys in Theban tombs by nearly a century.[151] Nor is it clear
whether they are the work of Minoan artists brought to Egypt specifically for the purposes of executing these decorations, or whether they
are imitations made by Egyptian artists, possibly under the direction of
Minoan masters. One possible explanation for their presence could be
an alliance between Ahmose and one or more Minoan rulers, an alliance
which may even have been sealed by Ahmose's marriage to a Minoan
princess. However, while tempting, this theory lacks clear evidence and
so a comprehensive explanation for the presence of these Minoan scenes
at Tell el-Dab'a remains elusive.

Ahmose's control of Egypt did not occur unopposed, however. At
least two instances of direct military threats against his rule are known.
The first came from Aata,[152] possibly a Nubian who may have been in
the pay of the kingdom of Kush. This Nubian incursion into Egyptian
territory was, however, dealt with rapidly if we believe the biography
of Ahmose, son of Ibana, and Aata and several of his officers were captured alive. A more pressing threat came soon after from Tetian, an
Egyptian who rallied a group of "malcontents," possibly Egyptians who
had either been allied to the Hyksos or perhaps simply opposed the new
Theban royal family. Tetian's rebellion was dealt with harshly by King
Ahmose: "Then came that foe named Tetian. He had gathered the malcontents to himself. His majesty slew him; his troop was wiped out."[153]

In taking Ahmose Nefertari as his Great Royal Wife, Ahmose continued the tradition begun by his father Seqenenra Taa, of consanguineous
marriages.[154] The same pattern continued through much of the dynasty,
and Ahmose's and Ahmose Nefertari's son and successor Amenhotep

---

151. E.g., in the tomb of Rekhmira, see Davies 1943.

152. From the biography of Ahmose, son of Ibana: "Then Aata came to the South.
His fate brought on his doom. The gods of Upper Egypt grasped him. He was
found by his majesty at Tent-taa. His majesty carried him off as a living captive,
and all his people as booty. I brought two young warriors as captives from the
ship of Aata." Translation after Lichtheim 1976: 13.

153. Lichtheim 1976: 13.

154. Middleton 1962.

I (1525–1504 BC) also took his sister, Ahmose Meritamun, as his chief consort. In doing so, power was maintained within a very small circle, all directly related to one another.

Amenhotep I's reign and policies were in many ways direct continuations of his father's. Many building projects begun by Ahmose had remained unfinished at his death and were now completed by Amenhotep.[155] Amenhotep also continued his father's foreign policy priorities of exerting greater influence and control of both Upper and Lower Nubia, chipping away at the power of the kingdom of Kush, securing control of caravan routes in Egypt's Western Desert, as well as gathering resources and booty to help fund the increased building activity, in particular at Karnak where Amenhotep ordered the construction of the White Chapel,[156] a barque shrine which copied the design of an earlier structure built during the reign of Senusret I. In addition, he constructed temples in Nubia on the new Egyptian frontier at Sai Island.[157] Even though the community at Deir el-Medina were most likely initially brought together during the reign of his successor Thutmose I, it was Amenhotep I whom the villagers deified and later worshipped during the Ramesside period, including by carrying statues of this king in procession through the village[158] and employing the statue of the king as an oracle to pass legal judgments on the community.[159]

Amenhotep and his consort Ahmose Meritamun had only a single child, a boy, but the young prince died young, leaving the new dynasty with its first major succession problem. It was solved seemingly without the need for bloodshed or civil war (at least no record of one has survived in the textual record) when Thutmose I (1504–1492 BC) ascended to the throne. His mother, Senseneb, was almost certainly a commoner and

155. Bryan 2000: 214–215.

156. Blyth 2006: 36.

157. Lindblad 1984: 27–28; Minault-Gout 2007: 282, fig. lc.

158. Černý 1927; Lesko 1994: 127.

159. Sweeney 2008.

it is unclear who his father was.[160] His sister and chief consort, Queen Ahmose, may have been related to the Theban Dynasty, although this is also uncertain. She may simply have been Thutmose I's sister, whom he married to mirror the consanguineous traditions of the Theban line.

Thutmose I's policies, both foreign and domestic, represented very much a continuity of the priorities of his royal predeccesors Ahmose and Amenhotep. Thutmose campaigned extensively in Nubia and delivered the final crushing blow to the Kingdom of Kush when he conquered their capital at Kerma, an event commemorated on the Tombos Stele set up north of the destroyed settlement:

> After he tied the moving campaign to the landing posts, the superiors and their villages belong to him in veneration, and the skin-garbed are (either) dancing for His Majesty or are in respect for his uraeus: After he overthrew the chief of the Nubians, the despoiled Nubian belongs to his grip. After he had gathered the border markers of both sides, no escape existed among the evil-of-character; those who had come to support him, not one thereof remained. As the Nubian have fallen to terror and are laid aside throughout their lands, their stench, it floods their wadis, their blood is like a rainstorm. The carrion-eating birds over it are numerous, those birds were picking and carrying the flesh to another (desert) place.[161]

Despite the relative brevity of his reign, lasting little more than a decade, Thutmose's reign had a marked impact on the sacred landscape of Thebes. He drastically extended the Karnak temple complex by adding the First Pylon gateway (also known as the fifth pylon), as well as large obelisks and flagpoles, as detailed in the biography of his chief architect Ineni.[162] In addition, he undertook major construction projects at other

---

160. Naville 1897.

161. Goedicke 1996.

162. Dziobek 1992.

important Egyptian sites, notably the old capital of Memphis,[163] and also began the construction of the royal necropolis in the Valley of the Kings (see section 26.3).

Thutmose's line of succession was in theory guaranteed by the fact that he had several sons, in addition to his two daughters Nefertubity and Hatshepsut, although two of these—Amenmose and Wadjmose—predeceased their father. So it was his third son, Thutmose II (1492–1479 BC), who took the throne after his father's death. Thutmose II took his sister Hatshepsut as his consort, although his heir in turn, Thutmose III, was born to a lesser royal wife, Iset. Thutmose II's grandmother, the wife of Amenhotep I, Ahmose Meritamun, had inherited the crucial political, economic, and religious title God's Wife of Amun from Ahmose Nefertari, and she now passed it to Thutmose II's principal wife Hatshepsut, who would later go on to hold far more exalted positions, those of queen regent and eventually pharaoh.

26.7.2. King Hatshepsut (1479–1458 BC)

The reign of Thutmose II (1492–1479 BC) was both short and rather unremarkable. Aside from some minor building activity at Karnak temple, his reign is primarily defined by two military campaigns: one to Nubia (which was not led by the young king in person),[164] and the other one to Sinai.[165] It is possible that he suffered from an unknown disease which eventually claimed his life before he reached the age of thirty.

163. Bryan 2000: 222.

164. This revolt, possibly orchestrated to take advantage of the fragile position of the Egyptian state in the immediate transition following the death of Thutmose I, resulted initially in an Egyptian withdrawal to one or more Egyptian fortifications: *Urk.* IV: 139.12–16: "[...] Wretched Kush was rising in rebellion, those who were subjects of the Lord of the Two Lands planning a plot [...] to steal the cattle from behind the fort [...]"; see also Lorton 1990: 671.

165. Both the campaign against *Shasu* bedouin on the Sinai Peninsula and a possible campaign in Syria are recorded in the biography of Ahmose Pennekhbet from Elkab, although the latter is poorly preserved; see Breasted 1906: 51.

For a second time, the Theban Dynasty faced a possible crisis of succession. With the pharaoh dead and his heir, Thutmose III, barely more than a baby, Thutmose II's sister-wife Hatshepsut took control of the state as a regent of Thutmose III. The elderly architect and statesman Ineni describes this transfer of power in some detail:

> His son stood in his place as king of the Two Lands, having become ruler upon the throne of the one who begat him. His sister, Divine Consort, Hatshepsut, settled the [affairs] of the Two Lands by reason of her plans. Egypt was made to labor with bowed head for her, the excellent seed of the god, which came forth from him. The bow-rope of the South, the mooring-stake of the Southerners; the excellent stem-rope of the Northland is she; the mistress of command, whose plans are excellent, who satisfies the Two Regions, when she speaks.[166]

In governing on behalf of an underaged monarch, Hatshepsut (1479–1458 BC) was copying the actions of earlier royal women of the Theban dynasty, including Ahhotep, who had taken control of Thebes and the Theban armies during the war with the Hyksos until her son Ahmose, the eventual father of the New Kingdom, came of age.

Hatshepsut diverged from Ahhotep in a crucial way, however. She did not remain a regent, but eventually took on royal titles and was depicted in royal regalia as pharaoh. In doing so, she emulated the late Middle Kingdom ruler Sobekneferu,[167] the daughter of Amenemhat III, who had assumed the throne of Egypt and ruled as king as the only child of the former pharaoh. Hatshepsut already had extensive experience in state administration and economy when her brother-husband died, having held the powerful office of God's Wife of Amun. And even though she took on royal attributes, her relationship with her ward, Thutmose III, does not seem to have been fractious. For a significant portion of her

---

166. Breasted 1906: 142–143.

167. Bryan 2000: 228–229.

reign, the young king played a secondary role to his co-ruler but remained in charge of the powerful Egyptian army. It seems inconceivable that this joint rule was not amicable given that Thutmose, through the army, had enough power to challenge his stepmother if he had wished to do so.

Hatshepsut legitimized her reign through a series of mythological narratives at the innovative mortuary temple she ordered to be constructed at Deir el-Bahri. One of these narratives centers around Hatshepsut's conception and birth.[168] The text claims that her mother, Ahmose, was impregnated not by Thutmose I (1504–1492 BC), but rather by Amun-Ra of Karnak, taking the form of the king:

He made his form like the majesty of this husband, the king Thutmose I. He found her (Queen Ahmose) sleeping in the beauty of her palace. She waked at the fragrance of the god, which she smelled in the presence of his majesty.[169]

After consummation, Amun-Ra speaks to Ahmose and prophecies about the future of the child now growing inside the queen:

Khnemet-Amun-Hatshepsut shall be the name of this my daughter whom I have placed in thy body, this saying which comes out of thy mouth. She shall exercise the excellent kingship in this whole land. My soul is hers, my bounty is hers, my crown is hers, that she may rule the Two Lands that she may lead all the living.[170]

In a nearby section of inscriptions and reliefs, the new pharaoh Hatshepsut is shown during her coronation being crowned by her actual father, Thutmose I. A speech to the court is placed in the mouth of the deceased Thutmose, in which he assures the assembled courtiers (as well

---

168. For depictions and discussions of these scenes, see Roehrig et al. 2005: 86–87; also Breasted 1906: 75–87.

169. Breasted 1906: 80.

170. Breasted 1906: 80.

as the gods) that Hatshepsut is indeed his chosen successor: "She is my successor upon my throne, she assuredly is who shall sit upon my wonderful seat."[171]

But even though Hatshepsut's rule could be in this way religiously justified, from a purely political point of view, it is clear that Hatshepsut maintained order at the court through a series of shrewd decisions, one of which seems to have been to continue taking advice from many of the older statesmen who had served her father, and some of whom were old enough to have served Ahmose (1550–1525 BC) and Amenhotep I (1525–1504 BC) as well. These old generals and courtiers included figures such as the architect Ineni and also the military officer and nobleman Ahmose Pennekhbet.[172] In his biography Ahmose Pennekhbet, who had cut his teeth fighting in the armies of Ahmose nearly half a century before, recognizes Hatshepsut's kingship by using her chosen throne name Maatkara and remarks how he was trusted enough to serve as a tutor to Hatshepsut's daughter by Thutmose II (1492–1479 BC), the princess Neferura.[173] Aside from the elder courtiers like Ineni and Ahmose Pennekhbet, Hatshepsut also utilized the talents of the steward Senenmut,[174] a commoner hailing from the city of Armant, south of Thebes. Senenmut rose to an exalted position during Hatshepsut's reign, being chiefly responsible for some of her most impressive construction projects, including the quarrying, transport, and decoration of two vast obelisks in front of Karnak temple.[175] In return, Senenmut was rewarded with an unusually large number of private statues, given "as favors" to him by the monarch.[176] Several of these show him holding princess Neferura

---

171. Breasted 1906: 97.

172. Breasted 1906: 9–12, 35, 50–51, 143–144.

173. Forbes 1994.

174. There has been extensive research and speculation about the origin and precise role of Senenmut at the court of Hatshepsut; for general overviews of this individual and the associated monuments, see in particular Meyer 1982; Dorman 1988.

175. Stanton 2020.

176. For overviews of some of these statues, see Meyer 1982; Dorman 1988.

on his lap, signifying perhaps that he too, like Ahmose Pennekhbet, had served as the young girl's tutor at some stage in her life.[177]

It seems that for part of her reign Hatshepsut was grooming Neferura to hold the same kind of responsibility and role that Hatshepsut herself did. She conferred the title of God's Wife of Amun upon her daughter, although tragically Neferura most likely died before the end of her mother's reign from unknown causes, and while a possible location of her grave was uncovered by Howard Carter, the grave did not contain her body or other burial goods.[178]

Hatshepsut's reign represented in many ways a period of stability and development for the Egyptian state. While there is some limited evidence of foreign campaigns undertaken during her reign, the most significant foreign mission was the trade mission she launched to the distant land of Punt. She sponsored extensive construction projects throughout Egypt, primarily of course in Thebes, but also at Hermopolis, at Cusae, and at Beni Hasan, where she built the Speos Artemidos temple,[179] whose inscriptions have been discussed earlier in this section. When she was laid to rest in her tomb in the Valley of the Kings (KV 20), the courtiers and nobles in Thebes could do so reflecting back on two decades of relative peace and prosperity for themselves and the state. Hatshepsut's successor, her stepson Thutmose, was anything but peace-loving, however. During his lengthy solo-reign, Egypt's armies would march across the Near East, conquering and forging an empire which spanned from the banks of the Euphrates to the Third Cataract in Nubia.

During the later parts of Thutmose III's solo-reign, a series of destructive campaigns were launched against Hatshepsut's legacy. During this *damnatio memoriae*, her names, titles, and depictions were methodically chiseled out of multiple temples throughout Egypt. Many of her statues were also removed from their original locations to be smashed or otherwise disfigured. This destructive campaign

---

177. E.g., British Museum, BM EA 174, and Cairo Museum, CG 42114.

178. Dodson and Hilton 2004: 130–141.

179. Bryan 2000: 229–232.

naturally fired the imaginations of generations of Egyptologists. Some
have hypothesized that Thutmose engaged in this campaign of destruction to avenge himself on a woman he viewed as a usurper; others lay
the blame for the campaign at the foot of Thutmose III's son and
successor Amenhotep II (1425–1397 BC), a young ruler eager to disassociate himself from Hatshepsut and her reign. The former theory
is deeply problematic. First, given the power and status Thutmose III
held during Hatshepsut's reign, it seems unlikely that he resented her
while she was alive. Surely this resentment would have resulted in a
civil war or a palace coup given his command of the Egyptian army.
And furthermore, the campaign of destruction did not take place until
several decades after Hatshepsut's death. It seems inconceivable that
Thutmose, after Hatshepsut's death, would spend decades brooding
over his stepmother and her reign before finally deciding to attack
her legacy. If there had really been resentment between the two, such
a campaign of destruction would have been expected to begin at the
moment of her death.

In truth, the *damnatio memoriae* against Hatshepsut was somewhat half-hearted. Her vast temple at Deir el-Bahri was allowed to
remain standing, and while she was expunged from later Ramesside
king lists,[180] her reign was not entirely erased and many of her statues
and monuments remain to this day with limited or no destruction at
all. Perhaps she simply represented a derivation from the norm and as
such had the potential to undermine Thutmose III's own legitimacy and
the legitimacy of his son Amenhotep II.[181] In that case, the erasure of
Hatshepsut's legacy may have been an act inspired not by emotions but
by political calculation. This interpretation might in turn explain why
the campaign was not as virulent or as far-reaching as might otherwise
be expected.

---

180. E.g., the Abydos King List of Sety I (see chapter 27 in this volume), which
    excludes not only Hatshepsut but also other "controversial" Eighteenth
    Dynasty rulers such as Akhenaten.

181. Tyldesley 1998a: 225.

26.7.3. The warrior kings: Thutmose III
(1479–1425 BC), Amenhotep II (1425–1397 BC),
and Thutmose IV (1397–1388 BC)

The reign of Thutmose III (1479–1425 BC) was certainly one of the most spectacular high-points of the Eighteenth Dynasty from the Egyptian perspective. His memory, and no doubt his reputation as an extraordinarily capable military leader, even caused the early Ramesside ruler Sety I to incorporate Thutmose III's throne name—along with that of Amenhotep III—into his own, thus signifying his intention to fill the very large shoes left by these two rulers.[182] During the very early reign of Thutmose III, his stepmother fulfilled purely the role of a regent, retaining her title God's Wife of Amun. However, at least by Year 7,[183] Hatshepsut's regency changed; rather than a temporary regent, she began utilizing royal titulary, turning her into a co-regent of Thutmose III, an equal, rather than merely a placeholder. This shift in the power balance led to a curious intermediary stage with Hatshepsut frequently represented with "kingly" royal names, but more feminine "queenly" costumes.[184] Gradually, these depictions evolved until she appeared in the traditional masculine form of a king on some of her most notable monuments, including in her mortuary temple at Deir el-Bahri.[185] We

---

182. For a discussion of Sety's royal names and his decision to incorporate the royal names of Thutmose III and Amenhotep III into his own, see Nielsen 2018: 78–81.

183. Dorman 2006: 45–46.

184. A good example of this hybrid representation is the famous statue of Hatshepsut from Deir el-Bahri, part of which is in the collections of the Metropolitan Museum of Art in New York (accession number 29.3.3) and part in the Rijksmuseum van Oudheden in Leiden (accession number F1928/9.2); see Roehrig et al. 2005: 170–171. This statue shows Hatshepsut seated and wearing a dress but also the *nemes* headdress usually only worn by (male) kings, thus combining feminine attire with a typical symbol of royal authority.

185. Hatshepsut appears, for instance, depicted as a traditional male pharaoh, wearing a short kilt and the blue war crown typical of Eighteenth Dynasty pharaohs, alongside Thutmose III, dressed similarly and wearing the White Crown of Upper Egypt, in a stele now held in the collections of the Vatican Museum (accession number 22780).

can only guess at the precise relationship between her and the, presumably teenaged, Thutmose III. He is by no means absent from the royal monumental record during this co-regency, nor was he or his royal status excluded from private biographies.[186]

Indeed, any notion that Hatshepsut had moved to usurp Thutmose, gathering more and more power which her child-co-ruler could not oppose, is simply not confirmed by the evidence. Rather, the evolving nature of her representations may simply be attempts to depict—in a diplomatic fashion—a concept unusual to the Egyptian state, rather than a gradual assumption of increasing levels of power. Hatshepsut may in fact have done more than anyone to ensure the succession of Thutmose III by ruling effectively and enriching the country through her trade expeditions and building works. Certainly, the country had benefited greatly from Hatshepsut's conscientious and effective reign before Thutmose III took sole control of at some point prior to Year 22 of his reign.[187] With solid state finances, an extensive ongoing program of royal building works, and a highly effective army which Thutmose III himself may at this point have been leading for years, the young king was ready to flex his muscles on the international scene and to begin pushing back Egypt's boundaries abroad.

Thutmose's first major hurdle came from the king of Qadesh. This ruler rebelled against Egyptian rule, joined in his revolt by the king of Megiddo and no doubt backed by Egypt's hereditary rivals in the Levant, the kingdom of Mittani (see chapter 29 in this volume).[188] Thutmose reacted with impressive swiftness, bringing a massive army across

---

186. Except from the biography of Ineni where, as noted by Dorman 2006: 41, any royal titulary of Thutmose III is excluded from the description of the death of Thutmose II and the rise to power of Hatshepsut. This section of the biography instead mentions only Hatshepsut herself and her role. Thutmose III himself is described simply as the son of Thutmose II, without any of the lengthy royal names and titles one would usually expect in such an inscription.

187. It is still unclear whether Hatshepsut died at this time or whether she simply handed over power to her stepson, stepped back from the levers of power, and so was no longer represented in the royal monumental record.

188. Redford 2003: 202–209.

the Sinai Peninsula to take the city of Megiddo and crush the revolt. Through a series of quick decisions and gambles, including leading the bulk of his force through a narrow pass in the Jezreel Valley, he surprised the Canaanite armies waiting for him in front of the city, prompting them to break ranks and flee back toward Megiddo. At this point, the young king lost control of his own troops, however, and the Egyptian soldiers—rather than pursuing their enemies and pressing home their advantage—began looting the abandoned Canaanite encampments in front of Megiddo's near-impregnable walls. This lapse allowed the kings of Qadesh and Megiddo to escape the battlefield safely with the majority of their host intact and withdraw into the safety of Megiddo itself. Thutmose, no doubt furious at the behavior of his men, was forced into a prolonged siege, but when Megiddo finally capitulated, his patience was rewarded with an uncommonly large amount of booty, paid as tribute to the victorious Egyptians and brought back to be donated to the temple of Amun-Ra at Karnak.[189]

The details surrounding Thutmose III's multiple military exploits in the Levant have survived primarily because of a series of lengthy and, in some cases, relatively detailed lists engraved upon the walls of one of the inner sanctuaries of the temple of Amun-Ra at Karnak, intended—not for the eyes of curious historians and Egyptologists—but rather for the eyes of the god himself. While the structure was largely destroyed in antiquity, the inscriptions (known collectively as the Annals of Thutmose III)[190] have survived largely intact, although they are spread across several locations and museum collections. The earlier campaigns, in particular the Year 23 campaign which ended in the capture of Megiddo, are far more detailed than later campaigns, which often record little more than lists of booty and captives taken back to Egypt. Altogether, the annals suggest

189. Several fragments, including descriptions of the booty brought back from the siege of Megiddo, are now held in the Louvre; see Andreu, Rutschowscaya, and Ziegler 1997: 109–110.

190. For a critical analysis of the Annals with particular attention paid to the differences between the descriptions of the early campaign against Megiddo and later campaigns, which tend to be far briefer and lighter on detail, see Spalinger 1977.

that Thutmose undertook at least seventeen campaigns in the Near East, capturing hundreds of cities and settlements.[191] From the point of view of historicity, the annals are of course potentially problematic documents: they were never intended to be unbiased historical records, quite the opposite. They were meant as self-congratulatory descriptions of the victories which the Egyptian king had won on behalf of his patron deity Amun-Ra. As such, their content should always be open to question and inquiry, including the impressive lists of booty, which may have been exaggerated to further underline the king's successes.

In addition to the Annals, literary sources from later periods also provide some information about Thutmose's foreign policy. For instance, a literary tale of the Ramesside period, known as "The Siege of Djoppa,"[192] tells the story of one of Thutmose's generals, Djehuti—a real general of Thutmose and not a literary creation—who allegedly ended an Egyptian siege against the Canaanite settlement of Djoppa by hiding his soldiers in reed baskets, tying them to a caravan of donkeys and tricking the city's defenders to open their gates for these "supplies." The narrative, and in particular Djehuti's trick, can be seen as a precursor to both the story of the Trojan Horse as told in Homer's *Illiad* and the tale of Ali Baba and the Forty Thieves.[193]

Other aspects of Thutmose's foreign policy became apparent with the discovery of a small rock-cut tomb at Wadi Gabbanat el-Qurud[194] near Thebes in 1916. Inside the tomb were the burials of three of Thutmose's minor wives, Menhet, Menwi, and Merti. Their names suggest a Canaanite origin, and it is likely that they were married to the Egyptian pharaoh either as physical tokens of submission by minor Canaanite princes or to seal diplomatic agreements or treatises. The role of diplomatic marriages in the government of the growing Egyptian empire in

191. Redford 2003.

192. For an extensive discussion and analysis of this text, see Davies 2003.

193. Manassa 2010.

194. Lilyquist 2004.

the Near East continued to become increasingly important, with the practice reaching perhaps its zenith during the reign of Amenhotep III.

The wealth secured from Thutmose's campaigns across the Near East was invested into a super-charged royal construction program. Karnak, of course, received the lion's share of royal attention with Thutmose ordering the construction of two further pylon gateways (Pylon VI and Pylon VIII), several new shrines, and barque stations for use during the Opet Festival and the Beautiful Festival of the Valley. In addition, he made alterations to existing parts of the temple, reconstructed a hypostyle hall built by his grandfather Thutmose I, and also removed the beautiful quartzite chapel built by Hatshepsut known as *chapelle rouge*.[195] His capture of Canaanite and Hurrian craft specialists led to new industrial innovations within Egypt, including the spread of glass-making technology.[196] The state administration continued initially largely unchanged from the co-regency to Thutmose's sole rule, with many high officials retaining the positions they had held during the co-rule with Hatshepsut.[197]

Gradually, as Thutmose III's sole reign progressed, younger officials joined the ranks of the royal bureaucracy, many of them drawn from the officer class who had served with the king on campaigns and many of them serving in positions of trust close to the king.[198] One such trusted companion to Thutmose was his barber, Sibastet,[199] who had been a successful officer and captured a slave during a campaign in the Near East.

195. Burgos and Larché 2006.

196. Nicholson, Jackson, and Trott 1997.

197. The group of officials who maintained their positions from the time of the co-rule of Hatshepsut and Thutmose III to that of the sole rule of Thutmose III included, e.g., the vizier Useramun who is buried in TT 61; for a discussion of Useramun, his family, and his tomb, see Shirley 2010.

198. The division between military and civilian roles was not always clear-cut and it seems likely that some individuals with "civilian" titles performed their roles occasionally in military settings; see Shirley 2011.

199. Linage 1939.

Another was the "overseer of royal works" and tax collector Minmose,[200] who similarly served in Thutmose's armies and in the armies of his successor Amenhotep II. This tendency to promote and reward military individuals—and also require "civilian" officials to participate in military campaigns—no doubt led to the increasing militarization of the elite within Egyptian society to the point that, by the end of the Eighteenth Dynasty, these high-ranking and wealthy military officers could form an effective power block and seize control of the country under Horemheb and later Rameses I.[201]

Thutmose's reign ended with his death during his fifty-fourth year on the throne. The succession was guaranteed by his son, Amenhotep II (1425–1397 BC), who—like Thutmose III—was born to one of the lesser royal wives. Like Thutmose III, Amenhotep II too had been given command of the army some years prior to Thutmose's death, and the two seemingly shared power during this period in a co-regency similar to the one which had existed between Hatshepsut and Thutmose III.[202] Very much a ruler in the mold of his father, Amenhotep's reign is characterized by a continuation of the aggressive pursuit of military victories in the Near East, in particular repeated clashes with the kingdom of Mittani. Less is known about the structure and administration of Mittani than about other kingdoms of the Late Bronze Age due to a dearth of written evidence from Mittani itself (cf. chapter 28 in this volume). Instead, the Mittanians and their rulers are frequently known primarily from Egyptian and Hittite source material, which is often biased by its very nature. Mittani appears at times more a confederation of powerful cities under a single ruler than a unified kingdom in the sense of pharaonic Egypt.[203] Its territory straddled large sections of both the Tigris and Euphrates river valleys, giving it control of multiple trade

---

200. Redford 2003: 173.

201. Gnirs 1996.

202. On the co-regency between Thutmose III and Amenhotep II, see in particular Redford 1965.

203. Cf. Jarol 1986.

routes as well as good agricultural land. The population was Hurrian and was ruled by a warrior elite known as *maryannu*.[204] These warrior-nobles were in particular associated with chariots and archery, and several were encountered and captured both during the reigns of Thutmose III and Amenhotep II.

Amenhotep II spent much of his early reign putting down rebellions and reinforcing Egyptian dominance across the Levant, rebellions which in some cases had evidently been instigated by Mittani as a way of waging proxy-war against the Egyptians. Eventually, in Year 9 of Amenhotep II's reign, it seems likely that Mittani sought peace,[205] a peace that was further strengthened by the marriage of Amenhotep II's son, Thutmose IV, to a Mittanian princess during the latter's reign.[206] The reason for Mittani's decision to conclude a peace with Egypt may have been the growing power of the Hittite Empire based in modern-day central and southern Turkey. Alongside the Assyrian Empire to the south, the Hittites represented an existential threat to Mittani, who found themselves caught between two potential enemies. Indeed, during the later part of the Eighteenth Dynasty and the early Nineteenth Dynasty, Mittani would suffer repeated Assyrian and Hittite invasions before finally collapsing, their territory divided up among the victors.

Amenhotep II died after more than three decades on the throne, but his son Thutmose IV (1397–1388 BC) had a far shorter reign and is primarily remembered for the unique Dream Stele set up between the feet of the sphinx at Giza.[207] The stele commemorates a specific event during which Thutmose IV—while still a prince—slept in front of the

---

204. Albright 1930; Reviv 1972.

205. Redford 1993: 1992.

206. This marriage is alluded to in a letter from the Amarna correspondence (EA 29) written during the reign of Akhenaten: "When [Menkheperura], the father of Nimmureya wrote to Artamana my grandfather, he asked for the daughter of my grandfather, the sister of my father. He wrote 5, 6 times, but he did not give her. When he wrote my grandfather 7 times, then only under such pressure, did he give her." Translation after Moran 1992: 93.

207. Bryan 1991: 38–43.

half-buried statue. The sphinx spoke to him and commanded that he clear it from the drifts of sand which had obscured its body:

> Now the statue of the very great Khepri [the Great Sphinx] rested in this place, great of fame, sacred of respect, the shade of Ra resting on him [. . .] One of these days it happened that prince Thutmose came traveling at the time of midday. He rested in the shadow of this great god. [Sleep and] dream [took possession of him] at the moment the sun was at zenith. Then he found the majesty of this noble god speaking from his own mouth like a father speaks to his son, and saying: "Look at me, observe me, my son Thutmose. I am your father Horemakhet-Khepri-Ra-Atum. I shall give to you the kingship [upon the land before the living [. . .] The sand of the desert, upon which I used to be, [now] confronts me; and it is in order to cause that you do what is in my heart that I have waited."[208]

Given that Thutmose IV was not Amenhotep II's eldest son, and given that his rise to power may have been at the expense of his older brother Amenhotep who had held the title of high priest of Ptah during the last years of Amenhotep II's reign,[209] it is very tempting to view the Dream Stele, and in particular the Sphinx's promise to give Thutmose IV kingship, as a rather obvious attempt to justify his rule.

Like most of the rulers of the Eighteenth Dynasty, Thutmose IV's chosen successor—his son Amenhotep III (1388–1350 BC)—was born not to his principal wife Nefertari but rather to a lesser wife, Mutemwiya. Upon Thutmose's (possibly premature) death, Amenhotep III rose to the throne while still a young man, a fact confirmed by his rather impressively long reign of nearly four decades. His reign would mark a turning point in the history of the Eighteenth Dynasty—it would in many ways represent the absolute pinnacle of Egyptian achievement in industry,

---

208. Translation adapted from Bryan 2000: 247.

209. For an in-depth discussion of this prince and other royal sons of Amenhotep II, see Bryan 1991: 38–92.

artistry, and indeed the art of diplomacy. It would also see the resurgence of a powerful royal wife, far more present in the royal monumental record and in statecraft than the wives of Thutmose III, Amenhotep II, and Thutmose IV. But simultaneously, religious developments during the reign of Amenhotep III would also lead directly to one of the most confusing and controversial periods of the Eighteenth Dynasty: the reign of the so-called heretic pharaoh, Akhenaten.

26.7.4. The sun king: Amenhotep III (1388–1350 BC)

Amenhotep III (1388–1350 BC) was in many ways the *roi soleil* of ancient Egypt. He took the throne at a time of peace and general prosperity. Egypt's long-standing proxy war with the kingdom of Mittani had ended and the peace had been sealed by the marriage of a Mittanian princess to Amenhotep III's father Thutmose IV (1397–1388 BC). The Hittite state did not yet pose a direct threat to Egypt, nor did the more distant kingdoms of Assyria and Babylonia. Egypt's vassal states were seemingly content with the political situation and there are no records of major revolts or uprisings against Egyptian rule in the Near East during Amenhotep III's reign. Nubia too remained largely peaceful during his reign, aside from a single rebellion,[210] which began during the early part of Amenhotep's reign and was swiftly dealt with.

Amenhotep rose to the throne at a relatively young age and some kind of regency similar to that employed during the early reign of Thutmose III (1479–1425 BC) cannot be excluded,[211] although unlike Hatshepsut, Amenhotep's regent remained invisible in the royal monumental record. Among the first political decisions made by the young king (or perhaps by his advisers) was his marriage to Tiye, the daughter of two nobles, Yuya and Tuya, hailing from the city of Akhmim.[212] It is possible that

---

210. Kozloff 2012: 70–81.

211. Bryan 2000: 253.

212. Berman 2001: 5–7.

Tiye's mother Tuya was a descendant of King Ahmose and thus had blood-links to the early Theban dynasty. The marriage may then have functioned to cement Amenhotep III's claim to the throne, although it may also have been arranged to ensure the loyalty of a powerful faction of nobles in the immediate aftermath of Thutmose IV's death and the transfer of power to Amenhotep III. The marriage of Amenhotep III and Tiye was recorded on several commemorative scarabs as occurring in Year 2 of the young king's reign,[213] although it may in fact have taken place earlier, during the first year of Amenhotep's reign. Throughout Amenhotep's reign, commemorative faience and stone scarabs were used to communicate important events. Several hundred of these have been found and they can be grouped into at least five categories based on the events they record:[214]

(1) Marriage scarabs: commemorating the marriage between Amenhotep III and Queen Tiye; usually dated to Year 2 of his reign.

(2) Wild bull hunt scarabs: this smaller group commemorates a royal bull hunt wherein the king personally killed ninety-six bulls. These too are dated to the second year of his reign.

(3) Lion-hunt scarabs: a larger group commemorating the amount of lions killed by Amenhotep III during a series of hunts conducted throughout his first ten years on the throne.

(4) Kelu-Heba scarabs:[215] these commemorate a diplomatic marriage between Amenhotep III and Kelu-Heba, princess of Mittani, during Amenhotep's tenth regnal year.

(5) Irrigation/lake scarabs: this series commemorates the construction of an artificial lake in Queen Tiye's native town of Akhmim during the eleventh year of Amenhotep's reign.

---

213. Blankenberg-Van Delden 1969; 1976.

214. The list given here is adapted from Brandl, Bunimovitz, and Lederman 2013: 72.

215. These scarabs also describe the impressively large entourage which accompanied the princess: "Marvel brought to His Majesty, life, prosperity and health: the daughter of the prince of Naharina Šuttarna, Kelu-Heba and 317 women of her harem."

These large scarabs provide an interesting overview of royal affairs during Amenhotep's reign and have perhaps emphasized the rather peaceful and tranquil nature of his reign by comparison to the yearly campaigns of his predecessors Thutmose III (1479–1425 BC) and Amenhotep II (1425–1397 BC). The scarabs convey an image of a king at ease, participating in hunts and engaging in diplomacy. These hunts, while no doubt pleasurable diversions for any monarch, nevertheless served a political purpose. The hunting of lions and bulls, two animals heavily associated with kingship, are acts of political propaganda, and it is unclear whether the careful and detailed tallies of animals successfully hunted by the king can be taken at face value.

Diplomacy, in lieu of warfare, was perhaps the single most defining characteristic of Egypt's relationship with the wider world during Amenhotep's reign. The Amarna Letters provide us with a wealth of diplomatic correspondence between Amenhotep III and various foreign rulers (although by and large the assemblage preserves only the letters sent *to* the Egyptian court and not the replies sent back, leaving the corpus incomplete).[216] Amenhotep's confidence and Egypt's strong position on the international stage are particularly noticeable in a lengthy correspondence between Amenhotep III and Kadašman-Enlil I of Babylon (see chapter 33 in this volume), wherein Amenhotep refuses to send an Egyptian princess to marry the king of Babylon, despite the fact that the latter had sent a princess to Egypt to marry Amenhotep. In the letter, the clearly aggrieved Kadašman-Enlil accepted Amenhotep's refusal and asked him instead to send any Egyptian noblewoman whom the king of Babylon would then present at his court as a princess of Egypt:

> Moreover, you my brother when I wrote to you about marrying your daughter in accordance with your practice of not giving a daughter, wrote to me saying, "From time immemorial no daughter of the king of Egypt is ever given to anyone." Why not? You are king, you do as you please. Were you to give a daughter who

216. For an accessible English translation of the Amarna correspondence, see Moran 1992.

would say anything? Since I was told of this message I wrote as follows to my brother saying "Someone's grown daughters beautiful women must be available. Send me a beautiful woman as if she were your daughter. Who is going to say she is no daughter of the king?"[217]

Kadašman-Enlil also reminded Amenhotep III that his own daughters were available for the Egyptian king to marry.

Due to the nature of the available evidence which mostly pertains to the Egyptian elite, it is not possible to gauge how well the wider population of the country fared during Amenhotep's reign, although some indications may suggest that the increasing wealth of the country, combined with a series of very bountiful harvests,[218] resulted in a period of relative prosperity throughout the Egyptian hierarchy from farmers to members of the elite. Amenhotep, like his predecessors before him, channeled a good deal of the state's wealth into vast construction projects, arguably one of the most wide-ranging and complex construction projects of any king of the New Kingdom, possibly bar Rameses II (1279–1213 BC), who himself usurped a great number of Amenhotep's buildings by having his royal names chiseled out and replaced with Rameses' own. Amenhotep naturally lavished a great deal of attention on the Karnak temple,[219] redesigning the temple's main entrance, but also contributed to other important Theban landmarks such as the Luxor temple.[220] In addition, he also undertook large-scale construction outside Egypt's borders, building several so-called temple towns in Nubian territory.[221] His own mortuary temple

---

217. Translation after Moran 1992: 9.

218. Bryan 2000: 253.

219. Blyth 2006: 104–118.

220. For an extensive discussion of Amenhotep III's (and other ruler's) building work at Luxor temple, see Bell 1985.

221. E.g., at Soleb; see Morkot 1987: 34–35.

is now entirely destroyed, with above ground only the two so-called Memnon Colossi surviving.[222]

In addition to the worship of Egypt's traditional pantheon, Amenhotep III also favored the god Aten,[223] a solar deity depicted as a falcon-headed man. Increasingly and in particular during the final years of his reign, Amenhotep's focus shifted increasingly toward the solar aspects of ancient Egyptian religion, although construction continued at temples dedicated to other deities throughout Egypt. This increasing focus on the Aten would continue throughout the reign of Amenhotep's successor Amenhotep IV (later Akhenaten; 1351–1334 BC), and the sun disk would eventually supplant all other Egyptian deities and be given primacy among the Egyptian pantheon for a short period.

Due to Amenhotep's long and stable reign, and due to the increased wealth of the elite population, a great deal of evidence for the administration of Amenhotep's Egypt has survived, including statues and tombs belonging to some of the king's chief advisors and ministers. Among these were famously Amenhotep, son of Hapu,[224] a chief of all works who is attested on no less than nine different cult statues. This is an impressive amount of statuary for a single official which may evidence— as with the many statues of Senenmut—Amenhotep's popularity at the court. Born most likely during the reign of Amenhotep II (1425–1397 BC) or alternatively Thutmose IV (1397–1388 BC), Amenhotep, son of Hapu, died during the final years of Amenhotep III's reign. Many of the inscriptions appearing on his statues provide a great deal of evidence for his career development, serving as an illustration of how officials could rise through the ranks during the mid-Eighteenth Dynasty:

I was appointed to be inferior king's-scribe; I was introduced into the divine book, I beheld the excellent things of Thoth; I was equipped with their secrets; I opened all their [passages (?)];

222. Sourouzian et al. 2006.

223. Johnson 1996; Bryan 2000: 254; Johnson 2001: 88–93.

224. Teeter 1995.

one took counsel with me on all their matters [. . .] My lord
again showed favor to me; the King of Upper and Lower Egypt,
Nibmare, he put all the people subject to me, and the listing of
their number under my control, as superior king's-scribe over
recruits [. . .] My lord a third time showed favor to me; Son
of Ra, Amenhotep (III), Ruler of Thebes, the sun-god is he, to
whom hath been given an eternity of his jubilees without end. My
lord made me chief of all works.[225]

From royal scribe to chief of all works via a stint holding a title related
to the military ("scribe of the recruits"), Amenhotep was permitted
to construct a small funerary temple next to Amenhotep III's, further
evidence of his high standing at court. After his death, like the famous
royal architect Imhotep of the Third Dynasty, Amenhotep, son of Hapu,
was partly deified and worshipped as a god of healing, a tradition which
persisted into the Late Period. Other high officials of Amenhotep III's
reign included the viziers Amenhotep Huy[226] and Ramose, whose tomb
at Thebes (TT 55) includes several famous depictions and a large and
well-preserved relief showing a funerary procession.[227]

In addition to works on temples and shrines throughout Egypt,
Amenhotep III also oversaw the construction of a new royal palace.
Known today as Malqata (and during the Eighteenth Dynasty as *per-hay*,
"the House of Joy"), this vast palatial estate was built at Thebes on the
western bank of the Nile.[228] It was constructed largely from plastered mudbrick decorated with paintings in bright, primary colors, and included
royal apartments, quarters for servants, kitchens, and storerooms, as well
as a harbor connected to the river Nile via an artificial canal.

The end of Amenhotep's reign, following the celebration of his *heb
sed*—the jubilee celebration in honor of his thirtieth regnal year—was

---

225. Breasted 1906: 374–376.

226. Eigner 1983.

227. Davies 1941.

228. O'Connor 1978.

seemingly tainted by a serious disease. In the tomb of Kheruef (TT 92),[229] a steward of Amenhotep's wife Queen Tiye, Amenhotep III is depicted unusually as a frail and elderly man, evidently ill and showing his advanced years. In addition, the king ordered the manufacture of large numbers of black granite statues of the goddess Sekhmet, a deity associated both with disease and with healing. These statues were buried in caches in particular in Thebes, and it is possible that they were intended as offerings given to the goddess by a king desperately seeking to be alleviated of whatever symptoms ailed him. Whatever ailment the king may have had, it seemingly claimed him during his thirty-eighth regnal year.[230] He left behind his great royal wife Tiye, a large number of other wives whom he had married as part of diplomatic negotiations with Egypt's international allies and competitors, along with a host of children. With Tiye he had fathered at least a half-dozen children, including the heir presumptive, Prince Thutmose, who predeceased his father. In his place, Amenhotep III was succeeded by his second son, who ruled initially as Amenhotep IV before changing his name to better suit his religious predilections: Akhenaten.

26.7.5. The "heretic" king: Akhenaten (1350–1334 BC)

The relative brevity of Akhenaten's reign (1350–1334 BC) and the socio-religious experimentations and upheavals it caused stand in almost direct contrast to the sheer quantity of scholarly ink that has been spilled on what is colloquially known as the Amarna period.[231] The drastic changes to Egyptian artistic style this reign occasioned has fascinated and continues to fascinate both scholars and pseudo scholars. In reality, Akhenaten's reign was in some ways a continuation of developments already set in motion by his father. Amenhotep III's increasing focus on the solar aspects of Egyptian religion, the attention he paid to the relatively minor

---

229. Epigraphic Survey 1980.

230. Kozloff and Bryan 1992: 39.

231. See in particular Kemp 2012.

solar deity Aten, was continued into the reign of his son, but Akhenaten advanced this attention to uncommon heights, eventually excluding all other Egyptian deities from the royal pantheon and focusing solely on the worship of the Aten to the detriment of Egypt's traditional temple structures.

While Akhenaten initially was crowned and held the traditional five names associated with Egyptian royalty, including his birth-name Imenhetep Netjer Heqawaset (meaning "Amenhotep, God and Ruler of Thebes") as well as his throne name: Neferkheperura Waenra (meaning "The Beautiful One of the Manifestations of Ra, the Unique One of Ra"),[232] it is clear that from the very beginning of his reign he intended to alter the hierarchy of the Egyptian pantheon as well as the manner in which pharaoh interacted with the gods. During the early years of his reign, this desire for change is manifestly apparent in the king's building program.[233] As his predecessors before him, he devoted a great deal of resources to construction work in Thebes, but rather than adding to the Karnak temple, he instead constructed a new grouping of temples which lay to the east of the Karnak enclosure.

Within this enclosure at eastern Karnak, the solar deity known as "The Living One, Ra-Horus of the Horizon who Rejoices in the Horizon in his Identity of Light which is in the Sun-Disc"[234] took prominence. The name itself is more commonly given as "The Living Aten" or simply "The Aten," a deity who had been worshipped as a standard anthropomorphized falcon-headed man wearing a sun-disk on his head during the reign of Amenhotep III. This iconography changed and the Aten became represented simply as a sun disk from which rays ending in hands emanated. These hands of the sun disk were usually depicted touching the king and the king's family, underlining the connection between Akhenaten, his Great Royal Wife Nefertiti, and the Aten. The religious role of the Great Royal Wife also changed during Akhenaten's

---

232. Leprohon 2013.

233. Davies 1923c; Redford 1973; 1975.

234. van Dijk 2000: 267–268.

reign, with one of the temples built by Akhenaten at Thebes devoted entirely to Nefertiti, wherein the queen conducted a number of religious rituals usually reserved only for the king.[235]

Our knowledge of Akhenaten's complex of temples at Thebes, possibly known by the overall title *hery em akhet en Iten*, "Rejoicing in the Horizon of the Aten," is generally poor.[236] After Akhenaten's reign ended, a concerted drive in particular by Horemheb was launched to destroy these temple structures and recycle their building materials in Horemheb's own construction work at Karnak. As such, aside from some limited archaeological evidence and a certain amount of the so-called *talatat* blocks from which the temples were constructed, we are largely reliant on textual references to these structures. It seems likely that Akhenaten built at least four individual temples within the domain of *hery em akhet en Iten*, the most famous of these undoubtedly being the *gem pa Iten*, a phrase whose reading is subject to some debate but may mean "The Aten Is Discovered." It was within this structure that the young king, possibly during his third year, celebrated his *heb sed*, a jubilee festival usually held to mark thirty years on the throne. Akhenaten's choice to have his *heb sed* festival at this early stage and in the particular settings of his new Aten complex are somewhat enigmatic, but it may be that he used this event to change his throne names, removing references to the god Amun in his birth name, which became *Akheniten* (meaning "Living Spirit of the Aten").[237] His throne name, *Neferkheperura Waenra* (meaning "The Beautiful One of the Manifestations of Ra, the Unique One of Ra") remained unchanged, possibly because of the reference to the solar deity Ra-Horakhty. However, references to Thebes, both in his Nebty name and Golden Horus name, were altered and replaced by references to the Aten and also to the new capital Akhetaten, which the king was constructing north of Thebes at a place known today as Tell el-Amarna.

---

235. van Dijk 2000: 268–269.

236. Hoffmeier 2015: 97–108.

237. Leprohon 2013: 104–105.

For his new capital, Akhenaten chose a plain on the desert edge some 250 km north of Luxor. The construction of the city was most likely ordered at least by Year 5 of his reign and construction evidently moved fast. By Year 6, several of the boundary stele carved at the edges of the settlement to delineate its limits record a visit by the king to his new city:

> On that day one was in Akhetaten in the carpeted tent made for his majesty in Akhetaten, the name of which is "The Aten is Content." The king appeared mounted on the great chariot of fine gold like Aten when he dawns in the lightland and fills the Two Lands with his love. Setting out on the good road to Akhetaten on the first anniversary of visiting it which his majesty had done so as to found it as a monument to the Aten, according to the command of his father "Ra-Horakhty who rejoices in lightland in his name Shu who is Aten" who gives life forever, to make for him a monument in its midst.[238]

Following his inspection, Akhenaten provides offerings of foodstuffs and luxury items to the nascent cult of the Aten at the city, and the inscription ends with an oath wherein the king swears to ensure that the new city remains forever in the ownership of the Aten.

It is likely that Akhenaten took up permanent residence in the new city shortly after the events detailed in the Year 6 boundary steles. He was certainly present in the city during Year 8,[239] when an addendum was added to the stele noting that the king had reaffirmed his oath to the Aten. The settlement constructed by Akhenaten at Tell el-Amarna has been the subject of archaeological exploration for well over a century.[240] Its rapid construction (and rapid abandonment) has left it as somewhat of a time capsule, allowing archaeologists a glimpse into the daily life and bureaucratic organization of a capital city during the Eighteenth Dynasty. No

---

238. Translation after Lichtheim 1976: 49.

239. Lichtheim 1976: 51.

240. Kemp and Garfi 1993.

significant occupation postdates the Amarna period and no large-scale modern cities have been constructed on top of the archaeological site unlike, for instance, at Thebes and Memphis where the modern cities of Luxor and Cairo have obscured much of the urban archaeology from the pharaonic era. The city itself comprised several residential quarters (known as the North Suburb, the Main City, and the South Suburbs) as well as large religious and administrative structures (figure 26.5).[241] Most impressive perhaps was the Great Aten Temple which dominated the northern part of the Central City.

The Great Aten Temple provides a window into the mind of Akhenaten himself and the ways in which he viewed his god.[242] The architecture differs radically from the cult temple of Amun-Ra at Karnak and other more traditional Egyptian temples of the New Kingdom. These structures relied to a greater extent on shadows and darkness, with the inner sanctums lit only by braziers and torches, the cult statues hidden away and visible only to the high priest. But the Aten, by its very nature, was visible to everyone, although this of course did not mean that everyone had access to the Great Aten Temple or could take part in the worship of the Aten on equal footing with the king. The Great Aten Temple comprises a vast enclosure, inside of which is a large rectangular structure known as the Long Temple. But within and around this temple are hundreds of small mudbrick platforms, possibly intended to hold offerings given to the Aten by being placed under the open sky. At the back of the enclosure is a separate, smaller structure, also complete with offering platforms, which may represent the holy of holies, perhaps the private chapel for the king and the royal family. The idea of public participation in the worship of the Aten remains a subject of speculation, but it is certainly possible that crowds, either of hand-picked courtiers or more widely composed of inhabitants of the city,

241. For the results of the modern excavation of various sections of the city, see Kemp and Stevens 2010a; 2010b; Stevens 2006; Spence 2012; 2015; Weatherhead 2007.

242. For a detailed discussion of this structure in light of recent excavations, see Kemp 2012: 86–94.

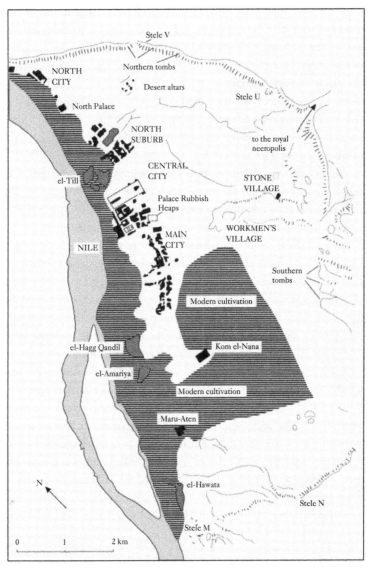

FIGURE 26.5. Plan of the city of Tell el-Amarna. Prepared by the author.

could access the large open spaces inside the enclosure and observe the royal family at prayer.

Public spectacle was certainly an important feature at Amarna, and the city's official structures were constructed to a great extent to facilitate royal processions and festivals.[243] A long path known today as the Royal Road defines the axis of the city, connecting the Great Aten Temple, the Great Palace, the North Riverside Palace, and other state structures, allowing the king and his family to process with their entourage through the city from their living quarters. This spectacle is represented in several tombs of state officials which were constructed during the city's brief occupation. Scenes of the king leaning out from a window of appearances in one of the royal palaces and handing out golden chains to his ministers also testify to the public life of the royal family.[244]

The fundamental role of Akhenaten himself and his family in the worship of the Aten became even more pronounced following Year 9 of his reign. The traditional Egyptian pantheon was essentially banned and replaced by the Aten as the sole deity to be worshipped within Egypt. Egypt's traditional cults and temples came to a standstill, and a royal campaign to erase the names of other deities—a completely impossible task given the sheer amount of religious inscriptions and depictions throughout Egypt—was launched. To worship the Aten, private individuals needed to worship the royal family as conduits to the god, and steles and cult statues of Akhenaten and Nefertiti have been found in household shrines at several large villas at Tell el-Amarna.[245] Akhenaten's motives for these changes have long been the subject of debate. Was the king truly a religious fanatic? Or were his moves against Amun-Ra at Karnak and the other traditional Egyptian cults inspired more by politics than by devotion to the Aten? In attacking Karnak and other major temple foundations, Akhenaten was attacking immensely rich and powerful institutions.

---

243. Kemp 2004.

244. Kemp 1976.

245. For an extensive discussion of private religion at Tell el-Amarna, see Stevens 2006.

The Karnak temple and its priests and bureaucracy had come to control vast tracts of land, thousands of people, and immense quantities of wealth donated to the god following the successful military campaigns of the early and mid-Eighteenth Dynasty. In later times, the high priest of Karnak would rival the king in terms of power and wealth, a situation which led to the effective disintegration of the centralized Egyptian state during the Third Intermediate Period (see chapter 35 in volume 4). Were Akhenaten's attacks on Karnak an attempt to clip the wings of the Theban priesthood and in the same stroke make the worship of Egypt's new chief deity conditional on what was in effect the worship of himself and his family?

The role and representation of the royal family, in particular the Great Royal Wife Nefertiti,[246] also changed dramatically during Akhenaten's reign. His mother, Queen Tiye, retained a powerful position at court during her son's early reign, so powerful that foreign kings even sought to communicate with her directly.[247] The days of Thutmose III and Amenhotep II, where royal wives remained very much in the background, were well and truly over. Both Tiye and in particular Akhenaten's own Great Royal Wife, Nefertiti, were frequently represented in the royal monumental record. The representations of Akhenaten and Nefertiti, along with their daughters, highlight the monumental changes to the Egyptian artistic canon undertaken during Akhenaten's reign. Frequently the king and queen are shown embracing, holding hands, and sitting with their children on their laps, a far more familial and intimate set of scenes than anything depicted during the earlier parts of the Eighteenth Dynasty (figure 26.6).

This more expressionistic royal imagery would not last long beyond the Amarna Period itself, but it remains, alongside the unusual depictions of Akhenaten with broad hips, a narrow face, and a "pear-shaped" body, one of the most unusual features of his reign.[248]

---

246. Tyldesley 1998b.

247. E.g., in a letter of the Amarna correspondence (EA 26) where Tušratta, the king of Mittani, contacts Queen Tiye directly to discuss the succession from Amenhotep III to Akhenaten and expresses his desire to continue peaceful and good relations with the Egyptians; for a translation, see Moran 1992: 84–86.

248. van Dijk 2000: 272–276.

FIGURE 26.6. Nefertiti depicted kissing one of her daughters; a ray of the sun-disk Aten holding an *ankh*-key symbolizing life can also be seen. Brooklyn Museum, Charles Edwin Wilbour Fund (accession number 60.197.8). Photograph courtesy Brooklyn Museum. CC0 1.0 Universal (CC0 1.0) Public Domain Dedication.

The precise end of Akhenaten's reign, along with its immediate aftermath, remains, as so many aspects of this period, a subject of intense debate in scholarly circles. The highest regnal year discovered from Akhenaten's year is Year 16,[249] and it is unlikely that the king ruled for long beyond this point, dying perhaps in his seventeenth year of reign. The immediate succession is murky at best. Akhenaten and Nefertiti had six daughters, and Akhenaten had a male successor, the young Prince Tutankhaten, most likely a son by his lesser wife Kiya. The prince was probably very young upon Akhenaten's death and the immediate succession seemingly involved two individuals, Smenkhkara and Neferneferuaten. The former may have formed a brief co-regency with Akhenaten, but the evidence

---

249. Van der Perre 2012: 195–197.

for this is extremely scant.[250] So is any useful information about the background of this ruler, who is evidenced on only a handful of inscriptions. Similarly, the precise identity of Neferneferuaten remains a subject of debate, with some scholars suggesting that she was in fact Nefertiti,[251] governing for a short period either in a co-regency with Smenkhkara or by herself.

The immediate confusion following Akhenaten's death was not resolved until Tutankhaten was crowned king when he was around the age of eight. It is likely that the actual governing was conducted not by the boy king, but rather by a number of officials who had held posts at court during the reign of Akhenaten. Chief among these were the courtier Ay,[252] who had held a number of high-ranking military and civil posts during the reign of Akhenaten and who may have been tangentially related to Akhenaten's mother Tiye. During the young king's reign, another powerful military officer rose to prominence, the commoner Horemheb, who rose to the post of commander-in-chief of Tutankhamun's armies and hereditary prince, a title usually reserved for the designated successor of pharaoh. Between them, these three men—Tutankhamun (1333–1323 BC), Ay (1323–1319 BC), and Horemheb (1319–1292 BC)—would shape the closing act of the Eighteenth Dynasty and lay the seeds for a new dynasty, a dynasty of soldiers, to take the throne of Egypt.

26.7.6. The post-Amarna era

While some occupation continued at Tell el-Amarna even after Tutankhaten's coronation, the court relatively quickly returned to Memphis and Thebes, perhaps as early as the first year of Tutankhaten's reign (1333–1323 BC). To demonstrate his intention—or perhaps the intention of his courtiers—to definitively break with his father's religious

---

250. Murnane 1977: 213–215.

251. See, e.g., Dodson and Hilton 2004: 285.

252. On Tutankhamun's court and the main courtiers evidenced in the textual and archaeological record, see in particular van Dijk 1996.

reforms, the new king changed his name from Tutankhaten (meaning "Living Image of Aten") to Tutankhamun (meaning "Living Image of Amun"). In addition, a number of inscriptions heralding Tutankhamun's reign as a period of restoration and return to normality were commissioned, inscriptions which present the results of Akhenaten's reign in a distinctly negative light:

> He [Tutankhamun] has restored what was ruined, as monuments of eternity. He has dispelled chaos throughout the Two Lands, and order was established [. . .] Now, when his Majesty arose as ruler, the temples of the gods and goddesses from Elephantine to the delta marshes were in ruin [. . .] the land was in distress, the gods were turning away from this land.[253]

Tutankhamun's abrupt departure from Amarna and abandonment of his father's policies may have been occasioned by the increasingly powerful standing army.[254] It seems inconceivable that Akhenaten could have accomplished the widespread socio-religious reforms he desired in the face of solid opposition from the army, and indeed the presence of Ay, a high-ranking military general and master of horse, as one of his closest advisors may evidence the army's tacit support for Akhenaten. However, upon his death and following the confusing interim before Tutankhamun was crowned, it seems likely that the army decided against continuing the Amarna experiment. In a later inscription, the general Horemheb claims that he had been summoned before Tutankhamun and that he advised the young king to return the court to Memphis after "[. . .] the palace [had] fallen into rage [. . .],"[255] possibly an allusion to an attempted coup or simply the chaotic conditions during the immediate post-Amarna succession.

---

253. *Urk.* IV: 2025–32; translation by the present author.

254. For a discussion of the role of the military in the reign of Akhenaten, see van Dijk 2000: 270–271.

255. Dodson 2009: 111.

Horemheb and the army's support of the young boy king was, however, seemingly conditional. Horemheb functioned in many ways as a regent for the young Tutankhamun, but a regent who was given titles to suggest that he would succeed to the throne in case Tutankhamun died without an heir. This insurance policy may have been intended to prevent a civil war from breaking out should the king die childless, but in reality, when Tutankhamun's death, young and childless, did in fact come to pass, this insurance policy did not work. Horemheb did not succeed the boy king; rather, it was Akhenaten's advisor Ay who ascended to the throne. Most of Tutankhamun's reign was seemingly dedicated to restoration and attempts to return the machinery of state and the Egyptian religious cults to normal. In terms of foreign policy, major changes to the international landscape had occurred during Akhenaten's reign, the chief being that Egypt's rival-turned-ally Mittani had been comprehensively defeated by the Hittite Empire based in Anatolia. The Hittites were fast becoming the dominant power in the Near East, a shifting power balance which led to conflict between Egypt and the Hittites (see chapters 27, 28, and 30 in this volume), a conflict which would continue until the reign of Rameses II (1279–1213 BC).

Tutankhamun's death occurred unexpectedly. The king was still in his teens when he died, most likely from a combination of frail health and some kind of accident.[256] The hypothesis that he was murdered to make way for a new ruler is certainly tempting, but it lacks solid evidence. It is likely that when the young king died, his chief advisor Horemheb was not in Egypt but was abroad, possibly leading a campaign against the Hittites. With the heir presumptive absent, a power vacuum opened up but was rapidly filled by Akhenaten's advisor Ay.[257] Scenes in the tomb of Tutankhamun show Ay conducting the funeral rights for the young

256. A number of scholars have speculated that the death of Tutankhamun may have been murder; see, e.g., Doherty 2002; King, Cooper, and DeNevi 2006; Brier 2010. However, the general consensus is now that his death was most likely the result of an existing illness in combination with another disease, possibly malaria; see, e.g., Timmann and Meyer 2010.

257. For a detailed discussion of the struggle of succession following the death of Tutankhamun and the various players involved, see in particular van Dijk 1996.

king, taking the place of Horus to the king's Osiris, thereby placing himself in the position of heir apparent. Seemingly to bolster his claim, Ay married Tutankhamun's widow, his half-sister Ankhesenamun. The transfer of power from Tutankhamun to Ay may not have gone entirely smoothly, however. There is some limited evidence to suggest that the widowed queen attempted to resist Ay's advancement and his plan to marry her. According to Hittite sources, she sent a letter to the Hittite king Suppiluliuma requesting that he send her one of his sons:

> My husband has died, and I have no son. But they say, you have many sons. If you would send me one of your sons, then he would become my husband. I do not want to take a servant of mine and make him my husband. I am afraid.[258]

Suppiluliuma after some hesitation sent one of his sons, Zannanza, to Egypt, but the prince apparently died en route, possibly as a result of direct intervention from Egyptian courtiers unwilling to see a Hittite on the Egyptian throne. It is also possible that the approach to the Hittites was instigated by Ay himself as an attempt to create peace between Egypt and the Hittite Empire and to undermine Horemheb, who was at the time leading Egypt's troops in a series of major confrontations with the Hittites. The death of Zannanza ended any chance of a peaceful reconciliation of Egypt and the Hittites, however. Ankhesenamun herself seemingly died shortly after marrying Ay and helping legitimize his claim to the throne.

Ay's reign (1323–1319 BC) was short and characterized by an attempt to conclude a peace with the Hittites,[259] and by attempts to prevent Horemheb from ascending the throne upon Ay's own death. Ay appointed a new commander-in-chief of the army, possibly one of his own family members, clearly intending to found his own dynasty and relying on the powerful military faction to back his successor over

---

258. Dodson 2009: 60. See also chapter 30 in this volume.

259. van Dijk 2000: 284.

Horemheb. However, this plan seemingly failed. When Ay died, his chosen successor, Nakhtmin, also vanished from the Egyptian records,[260] and Horemheb, so long denied the crown, finally ascended the throne, in what may have amounted to an actual military coup.

The policies and priorities of Horemheb (1319–1292 BC) are known from the *Great Edict of Horemheb*,[261] an impressively detailed document wherein the king presents various strategies to fight what he viewed as widespread corruption and lack of centralized control in the country. The *Edict* addresses a series of situations, such as corrupt military officials or other state bureaucrats collecting illegal taxes or confiscating produce destined for the royal storerooms, and prescribes a series of harsh punishments, including physical mutilation and banishment to the Egyptian border fortresses to live and serve as regular soldiers.

In addition to his attempts to restore the country's political structures, Horemheb devoted himself to a reinvigorated building program, helped by a reorganization of the workmen at Deir el-Medina. Horemheb also abandoned the tomb he had constructed in the Saqqara necropolis while still only a private official in favor of a royal burial in the Valley of the Kings (KV 57).[262] This tomb broke with the previous Eighteenth Dynasty tradition; rather than the common L-shaped form, it employs a straight shaft broken by a series of chambers and annexes and decorated with carved and painted reliefs rather than the painted plaster of the earlier Eighteenth Dynasty.

Horemheb's arguably major failing, certainly from his perspective, was his inability to father children. His first marriage to a woman named Amenia is known only from a single statue in the British Museum (BM EA 36), and it seemingly did not result in any children, male or female. His second marriage to Mutnedjmet (who was herself possibly a minor royal related to the Amarna dynasty and whose marriage to Horemheb

---

260. Schulman 1964.

261. Kruchten 1982.

262. Davis 1912.

served to legitimate his reign)[263] was also childless, with the younger queen possibly dying in childbirth.[264] As he grew older, the issue of succession no doubt troubled Horemheb, having lived through the chaotic interim following the death of Akhenaten. In order to secure a succession, he turned to his military power base and selected an old comrade, Paramessu,[265] a military commander whom Horemheb had named his vizier. On a later Ramesside inscription, Paramessu is described as the "Hereditary Prince of the Whole Land," the same title Horemheb was granted by Tutankhamun. This title effectively identified Paramessu as Horemheb's heir presumptive and so guaranteed the succession, even if Horemheb died without a child.

26.8. Paving the way for the Ramesside Dynasty

Like Horemheb himself, his choice of successor, Paramessu, came from a relatively common background and had no blood-links to the Theban dynasty. Paramessu had been a high-ranking military officer before he became vizier and it is entirely plausible that the two men campaigned together. But unlike Horemheb, Paramessu had a son, Sety, and may even have already had a grandson, the future Rameses II. By pronouncing Paramessu his successor, Horemheb was guaranteeing not just the immediate succession, he was in many ways laying the foundations of a new dynasty, a dynasty which would to a large degree be built not by Paramessu—who ruled as Rameses I (1319–1292 BC)—but by his son, Sety I (1290–1279 BC) and his grandson Rameses II (1279–1213 BC).

In many ways, while Horemheb is counted as the last king of the Eighteenth Dynasty, the dynasty had in a truer sense ended prior to his

---

263. Although this notion, as discussed by Martin 1991: 96, is highly unlikely given that Mutnedjmet herself, even if she was Nefertiti's sister, would not have been born royal and so it is difficult to argue that her marriage to Horemheb would have earned any specific legitimacy to his rule.

264. Martin 1982: 275–278.

265. On the succession of the early Ramesside rulers, see Nielsen 2018: 38–46.

accession. Ay may have had some relation to the Theban royal family through Queen Tiye, but Tutankhamun was the last in the line stretching back at least to the reign of Thutmose I. Horemheb represented a new type of ruler, a ruler who came from a military background and whose power base was squarely in the military sphere. This tendency would repeat itself with Horemheb's successor, Paramessu, who most likely had no blood-ties to the Theban royal family but rather was a military commander from northern Egypt. The Eighteenth Dynasty began officially with King Ahmose, but in reality had its antecedents in an old Theban family of nobles rising to power during the confusion of the Second Intermediate Period. Its rulers figure as some of the most recognizable names from ancient Egypt within the broader public: Hatshepsut, the female pharaoh; the general Thutmose III; the builder Amenhotep III; the "heretic" Akhenaten; and—most famously despite the brevity of his reign—the boy king Tutankhamun. Other powerful Egyptian royal dynasties would follow, and other long and prosperous reigns (in particular that of Rameses II). But the international order in the Late Bronze Age eastern Mediterranean, a political game which rulers such as Amenhotep III had played so well, would soon come under sustained threat, and Egypt's place in the world, as well as the composition of its state and rulership, would be radically changed.

REFERENCES

Abe, Y., Harimoto, R., Kikugawa, T., Yazawa, K., Nishisaka, A., Kawai, N., Yoshimura, S., and Nakai, I. 2012. Transition in the use of cobalt-blue colorant in the New Kingdom of Egypt. *Journal of Archaeological Science* 39: 1793–1808.

Albright, W.F. 1930. Mitannian *maryannu*, "chariot-warrior," and the Canaanite and Egyptian equivalents. *AfO* 6: 217–221.

Allam, S. 1998. Affaires et opérations commerciales. In Grimal, N., and Menu, B. (eds.), *Le commerce en Égypte ancienne*. Cairo: Institut français d'archéologie orientale, 133–156.

Allen, J.P. 2015. *The ancient Egyptian pyramid texts*. Atlanta, GA: Society of Biblical Literature.

Altenmüller, H., and Moussa, A.M. 1991. Die Inschrift Amenemhets II. aus dem Ptah-Tempel von Memphis: ein Vorbericht. *SAK* 18: 1–48.

Andreu, M., Rutschowscaya, H., and Ziegler, C. 1997. *L'Égypte au Louvre*. Paris: Hachette.

Andrews, C. 1994. *Amulets of ancient Egypt*. London: British Museum Press.

Anthony, F.B. 2016. *Foreigners in ancient Egypt: Theban tomb paintings from the early Eighteenth Dynasty*. London: Bloomsbury.

Arnold, D. 2003. *Encyclopedia of ancient Egyptian architecture*. London: I.B. Tauris.

Ashton, S. 2016. Egyptian sculptors' models: functions and fashions in the 18th Dynasty. In Bourriau, J., and Phillips, J. (eds.), *Invention and innovation: the social context of technological change, 2: Egypt, the Aegean and the Near East, 1650–1150 B.C.* Oxford: Oxbow, 176–199.

Aston, D.A. 2011. Blue-painted pottery of the late Eighteenth Dynasty: the material from the tomb of Maya and Merit at Saqqara. *Cahiers de la Céramique Égyptienne* 9: 1–36.

Bass, G.F. 1991. Evidence of trade from Bronze Age shipwrecks. In Gale, N.H. (ed.), *Bronze Age trade in the Mediterranean*. Gothenburg: Paul Åströms, 69–81.

von Beckerath, J. 1997. *Chronologie des pharaonischen Ägypten: die Zeitbestimmung der ägyptischen Geschichte von der Vorzeit bis 332 v. Chr.* Mainz: Zabern.

Bell, L. 1985. Luxor Temple and the cult of the royal *ka*. *JNES* 44: 251–294.

Belova, G.A. 2003. TT 320 and the history of the royal cache during the Twenty-First Dynasty. In Hawass, Z. (ed.), *Egyptology at the dawn of the twenty-first century. Cairo*. Cairo: American University in Cairo Press, 73–80.

Berman, L.M. 2001. Overview of Amenhotep III and his reign. In O'Connor, D., and Cline, E.H. (eds.), *Amenhotep III: perspectives on his reign*. Ann Arbor: University of Michigan Press, 1–25.

Bietak, M. 1996. *Avaris: the capital of the Hyksos: recent excavations at Tell el-Dab'a*. London: British Museum Press.

Bietak, M., Dorner, J., and Janosi., P. 2001. Ausgrabungen in dem Palastbezirk von Avaris: Vorbericht Tell el-Dab'a/'Ezbet Helmi 1993–2000. *ÄL* 11: 27–119.

Bietak, M., Marinatos, N., and Palivou, C. 2007. *Taureador scenes in Tell El-Dab'a (Avaris) and Knossos*. Vienna: Verlag der Österreichischen Akademie der Wissenschaften.

Bietak, M., Math, N., Müller, V., and Jurman, C. 2012–2013. Report on the excavations of a Hyksos palace at Tell el-Dab'a/Avaris. *ÄL* 22/23: 17–53.

Blankenberg-Van Delden, C. 1969. *The large commemorative scarabs of Amenophis III*. Leiden: Brill.

Blankenberg-Van Delden, C. 1976. More large commemorative scarabs of Amenophis III. *JEA* 62: 74–80.

Blyth, E. 2006. *Karnak: evolution of a temple*. London and New York: Routledge.

Bonnet, C., and Valbelle, D. 1975. Le village de Deir el-Médineh: reprise de l'étude archéologique. *BIFAO* 75: 317–342.

Bonnet, C., and Valbelle, D. 1976. Le village de Deir el-Médineh: étude archéologique (suite). *BIFAO* 76: 429–446.

Brack, A., and Brack, A. 1980. *Das Grab des Haremheb, Theben Nr. 78*. Mainz: Zabern.

Brandl, B., Bunimovitz, S., and Lederman, Z. 2013. Beth-Shemesh and Sellopoulo: two commemorative scarabs of Amenhotep III and their contribution to Aegean chronology. *The Annual of the British School at Athens* 108: 67–95.

Breasted, J.H. 1906. *Ancient records of Egypt, vol. II: the Eighteenth Dynasty*. Chicago: University of Chicago Press.

Brier, B. 2010. *The murder of Tutankhamen: a true story*. New York: Berkley Trade.

Bruyère, B. 1929. *Rapport sur les fouilles de Deir El Médineh, 1928*. Cairo: Institut français d'archéologie orientale.

Bruyère, B. 1939. *Rapport sur les fouilles de Deir El Médineh, 1934–35*. Cairo: Institut français d'archéologie orientale.

Bryan, B.M. 1991. *The Reign of Thutmose IV*. Baltimore, MD: John Hopkins Press.

Bryan, B.M. 2000. The 18th Dynasty before the Amarna period. In Shaw, I. (ed.), *The Oxford history of ancient Egypt*. Oxford: Oxford University Press, 207–264.

Bryan, B.M. 2010. Pharaonic painting through the New Kingdom. In Lloyd, A.B. (ed.), *A companion to ancient Egypt, vol. I*. Malden, MA: Wiley-Blackwell, 990–1007.

Burgos, F., and Larché, F. 2006. *La Chapelle Rouge: le sanctuaire de barque d'Hatshepsout I: fac-similés et photographies des scènes.* Paris: Éditions Recherche sur les Civilisations.

Cappellini, A., and Caramello, S. 2009. An economic perspective on relationships between Near Eastern kingdoms during the Late Bronze Age. In Hudecz, A., and Petrik, M. (eds.), *Commerce and economy in ancient Egypt: proceedings of the third international congress for young egyptologists.* Oxford: Archaeopress, 27–34.

Carter, H. 1933. *The tomb of Tut-Ankh-Amen: discovered by the late earl of Carnarvon and Howard Carter.* London: Cassell.

Černý, J. 1927. Le culte d'Aménophis Ier chez les ouvriers de la nécropole Thébaine. *BIFAO* 27: 159–203.

Černý, J. 1954. *Prices and wages in Egypt in the Ramesside period.* Paris: Librairie des Méridiens.

Černý, J., and Gardiner, A.H. 1957. *Hieratic ostraca.* Oxford: Oxford University Press.

Charloux, G., and Thiers, C. 2017. The early temple of Ptah at Karnak. *EA* 50: 11–15.

Creasman, P.P. 2014. Hatshepsut and the politics of Punt. *African Archaeological Review* 31: 395–405.

Darnell, J.C. 2010. Opet festival. In Wendrich, W. (ed.), *UCLA Encyclopedia of Egyptology.* Los Angeles: University of California, Los Angeles. Retrieved from http://digital2.library.ucla.edu/viewItem.do?ark=21198/zz0025n765 (last accessed September 11, 2020).

Davies, D.P. 2003. *The taking of Joppa.* MPhil thesis: Durham University. Retrieved from https://core.ac.uk/download/pdf/9347516.pdf (last accessed September 11, 2020).

Davies, N. deG. 1923a. *The tomb of Puyemre at Thebes.* New York: Metropolitan Museum of Art.

Davies, N. deG. 1923b. *Tombs of two officials of Thutmosis the Fourth (nos. 75 and 90).* London: Egypt Exploration Society.

Davies, N. deG. 1923c. Akhenaten at Thebes. *JEA* 9: 132–152.

Davies, N. deG. 1925. *The tomb of two sculptors at Thebes.* New York: Metropolitan Museum of Art.

Davies, N. deG. 1941. *The tomb of the vizier Ramose based on preliminary work by the late T.E. Peet.* London: Egypt Exploration Society.

Davies, N. deG. 1943. *The tomb of Rekh-Mi-Re at Thebes, vol. I.* New York: Metropolitan Museum of Art.

Davies, N. deG., and Faulkner, R.O. 1947. A Syrian trading venture to Egypt. *JEA* 33: 40–46.

Davies, N.M. 1963. *Scenes from some Theban tombs: nos. 38, 66, 162 with excerpts from 81.* Oxford: Oxford University Press.

Davis, T.M. 1912. *The tombs of Harmhabi and Touatânkhamanou.* London: Archibald Constable.

de Linage, J. 1939. L'acte d'établissement et le contrat du mariage d'un esclave sous Thoutmès III. *BIFAO* 38: 217–234.

Demarée, R.J. 2016. The workmen who created the royal tombs. In Wilkinson, R.H., and Weeks, K.R. (eds.), *The Oxford handbook of the Valley of the Kings.* Oxford: Oxford University Press, 75–86.

Dodson, A. 1988. Two royal reliefs from the temple of Deir el-Bahari. *JEA* 74: 212–214.

Dodson, A. 2009. *Amarna sunset: Nefertiti, Tutankhamun, Ay, Horemheb and the Egyptian counter-reformation.* Cairo: American University in Cairo Press.

Dodson, A., and Hilton, D. 2004. *The complete royal families of ancient Egypt.* London: Thames & Hudson.

Doherty, P.C. 2002. *The mysterious death of Tutankhamun.* New York: Carroll & Graf.

Dorman, P.F. 1988. *The monuments of Senenmut: problems in historical methodology.* London and New York: Kegan Paul International.

Dorman, P.F. 2006. Early reign of Thutmose III: an unorthodox mantle of coregency. In Cline, E.H., and O'Connor, D. (eds.), *Thutmose III: a new biography.* Ann Arbor: University of Michigan Press, 39–68.

Dziobek, E. 1992. *Das Grab des Ineni: Theben Nr. 81.* Mainz: Zabern.

Eaton-Kraus, M. 1984. *The representation of statuary in private tombs of the Old Kingdom.* Wiesbaden: Harrassowitz.

Eigner, D. 1983. Das thebanische Grab des Amenhotep, Wesir von Unterägypten: die Architektur. *MDAIK* 39: 39–50.

Epigraphic Survey. 1980. *The tomb of Kheruef: Theban Tomb 192.* Chicago: The Oriental Institute of the University of Chicago.

Eyre, C. 2015. *The use of documents in pharaonic Egypt.* Oxford: Oxford University Press.

Fairman, H.W., and Grdseloff, B. 1947. Texts of Hatshepsut and Sethos I inside Speos Artemidos. *JEA* 33: 12–33.

Forbes, D.C. 1994. Princess Neferure: Hatshepsut's intended successor. *KMT: A Modern Journal of Ancient Egypt* 5, no. 4: 36–43.

Forstner-Müller, I. 2014. Neueste Forschungen in Tell el-Dabʿa, dem antiken Avaris. *Sokar* 29: 30–45.

Franke, D. 2008. The late Middle Kingdom (Thirteenth to Seventeenth Dynasties): the chronological framework. *JEH* 1: 267–287.

Freed, R. 2010. Sculpture of the Middle Kingdom. In Lloyd, A.B. (ed.), *A companion to ancient Egypt, vol. I*. Malden, MA: Wiley-Blackwell, 882–912.

Gabriel, R.A. 2009. *Thutmose III: the military biography of Egypt's greatest warrior king*. Washington, DC: Potomac Books.

Gardiner, A.H. 1952. Thutmosis III returns thanks to Amun. *JEA* 38: 6–23.

Gitton, M. 1976. La résiliation d'une fonction religieuse: nouvelle interprétation de la stèle de donation d'Ahmès Néfertary. *BIFAO* 76: 65–89.

Gnirs, A.M.1996. *Militär und Gesellschaft: ein Beitrag zur Sozialgeschichte des Neuen Reiches*. Heidelberg: Heidelberger Orientverlag.

Goedicke H. 1996. The Thutmosis I inscription near Tomâs. *JNES* 55: 161–176.

Graefe, E. 1975. Das Grab des Schatzmeisters und Bauleiters Maya in Saqqara. *MDAIK* 31: 187–222.

Graefe, E. 2003. The royal cache and the tomb robberies. In Strudwick, N., and Taylor, J.H. (eds.), *The Theban necropolis: past, present and future*. London: British Museum Press, 75–82.

Graziadio, G. 2014. The oxhide ingots production in the Eastern Mediterranean. *Egitto e Vicino Oriente* 37: 5–25.

Grimal, N. 1988. *A history of ancient Egypt*. Oxford: Blackwell.

Gunn, B., and Gardiner, A.H. 1918. New renderings of Egyptian texts, II: the expulsion of the Hyksos. *JEA* 5: 36–67.

Haring, B. 2014. Workmen's marks and the early history of the Theban royal necropolis. In Toivari-Viitala, J., Vartianinen, T., and Uvanto, S. (eds.), *Deir el-Medina studies*. Helsinki: Finnish Egyptological Society, 87–100.

Hartwig, M. 2004. *Tomb painting and identity in ancient Thebes, 1419–1372 BCE*. Brussels: Fondation Égyptologique Reine Élisabeth.

Harvey, S.P. 1998. *The cults of king Ahmose at Abydos*. PhD thesis, University of Pennsylvania. Retrieved from https://repository.upenn.edu/dissertations/AAI9829912/ (last accessed September 11, 2020).

Hasan, S. 1937. The great limestone stela of Amenhotep II. *ASAE* 37: 129–134.

Hasan, S. 1949. *The Sphinx: its history in the light of recent excavations*. Cairo: Government Press.

Hawass, Z. 2009. *Silent images: women in pharaonic Egypt*. Cairo: American University in Cairo Press.

Helck, W. 1955–1958. *Urkunden der 18. Dynastie, Abteilung IV, Heft 17–22.* Berlin: Akademie Verlag.

Hirsch, E. 2009. Residences in texts of Senwosret I. In Gundlach, R., and Taylor, J.H. (eds.), *Egyptian royal residences.* Wiesbaden: Harrassowitz, 69–82.

Hodgkinson, A.K. 2018. *Technology and urbanism in Late Bronze Age Egypt.* Oxford: Oxford University Press.

Hodgkinson, A.K., Röhrs, S., Müller, K., and Reiche, I. 2019. The use of cobalt in 18th Dynasty blue glass from Amarna: the results from an on-site analysis using portable XRF technology. *Science & Technology of Archaeological Research* 5. Retrieved from https://doi.org/10.1080/20548923.2019.1649083 (last accessed September 11, 2020).

Hoffmeier, J.K. 2015. *Akhenaten and the origins of monotheism.* Oxford: Oxford University Press.

Hofmann, B. 2004. *Die Königsnovelle: Strukturanalyse am Einzelwerk.* Wiesbaden: Harrassowitz.

Hornung, E. 1999. *The ancient Egyptian books of the afterlife.* Ithaca, NY: Cornell University Press.

Ingram, R. 2014. Vitreous beads from the Uluburun shipwreck. *Polish Archaeology in the Mediterranean* 23: 225–245.

Janssen, J.J. 1975. *Commodity prices from the Ramessid period: an economic study of the village of necropolis workmen at Thebes.* Leiden: Brill.

Jarol, R.E. 1986. *A reconstruction of the contributions of Mitanni to the ancient Near East.* Unpublished MA thesis, Wilfrid Laurier University, Waterloo, ON. Retrieved from https://scholars.wlu.ca/cgi/viewcontent.cgi?article=2424 (last accessed September 11, 2020).

Johnson, W.R. 1996. Amenhotep III and Amarna: some new considerations. *JEA* 82: 65–82.

Johnson, W.R. 2001. Monuments and monumental art under Amenhotep III: evolution and meaning. In O'Connor, D., and Cline E.H. (eds.), *Amenhotep III: perspectives on his reign.* Ann Arbor: University of Michigan Press, 63–94.

Kampp, F. 1996. *Die thebanische Nekropole: zum Wandel des Grabgedankens von der XVIII. bis zur XX. Dynastie.* Mainz: Zabern.

Kawai, N. 2000. Development of the burial assemblage of the Eighteenth Dynasty royal tombs. *Orient* 35: 35–59.

Kemp, B.J. 1976. The window of appearance at El-Amarna and the basic structure of the city. *JEA* 62: 81–99.

Kemp, B.J. 1991. *Ancient Egypt: anatomy of a civilization*. London and New York: Routledge.

Kemp, B.J. 2004. *Ancient Egypt: anatomy of a civilization*. London and New York: Routledge. 2nd rev. ed.

Kemp, B.J. 2012. *The city of Akhenaten and Nefertiti: Amarna and its people*. London: Thames & Hudson.

Kemp, B.J., and Garfi, S. 1993. *A survey of the ancient city of El-'Amarna*. London: Egypt Exploration Society.

Kemp, B.J., and Stevens, A. 2010a. *Busy lives at Amarna: excavations in the main city (grid 12 and the house of Ranefer, N49.18), vol. I: the excavations, architecture and environmental remains*. London: Egypt Exploration Society.

Kemp, B.J., and Stevens, A. 2010b. *Busy lives at Amarna: excavations in the main city (grid 12 and the house of Ranefer, N49.18), vol. II: the objects*. London: Egypt Exploration Society.

King, M.R., Cooper, G.M., and DeNevi, D. 2006. *Who killed king Tut? Using modern forensics to solve a 3,300-year-old mystery: with new data on the Egyptian CT scan*. Amherst, NY: Prometheus.

Klemm, R. 2013. *Gold and gold mining in ancient Egypt and Nubia: geoarchaeology of the ancient gold mining sites in the Egyptian and Sudanese desserts*. Berlin: Springer.

Kozloff, A., and Bryan, B.M. 1992. *Royal and divine statuary in Egypt's dazzling sun: Amenhotep III and his world*. Bloomington: Indiana University Press; Cleveland, OH: Cleveland Museum of Art.

Kozloff, A.P. 2012. *Amenhotep III: Egypt's radiant pharaoh*. Cambridge: Cambridge University Press.

Kruchten, J.-M. 1982. *Le decret d'Horemheb: traduction, commentaire épigraphique, philologique et institutionnel*. Brussels: Université de Bruxelles.

Laboury, D. 2005. Dans l'atelier du sculpteur Thoutmose. In Cannuyer, C. (ed.), *La langue dans tous ses états: Michel Malaise in honorem*. Brussels: Société belge d'études orientales, 289–300.

Laboury, D. 2015. On the master painter of the tomb of Amenhotep Sise, second high priest of Amun under the reign of Thutmose IV (TT 75). In Jasnow, R., and Cooney, K. (eds.), *Joyful in Thebes: egyptological studies in honour of Betsy M. Bryan*. Atlanta, GA: Lockwood Press, 327–337.

Lemos, R., von Seehausen, P.L., di Giovanni, M., Giobbe, M., Menozzi, O., and Brancaglion Jr., A. 2017. Entangled temporalities in the Theban necropolis: a materiality and heritage approach to the excavation of Theban Tomb 187. *Journal of Eastern Mediterranean Archaeology & Heritage Studies* 5: 178–197.

Leprohon, R.J. 2013. *The great name: ancient Egyptian royal titulary*. Atlanta, GA: Society of Biblical Literature.

Lesko, L.H. (ed.) 1994. *Pharaoh's workers: the village of Deir el-Medina*. Ithaca, NY: Cornell University Press.

Lichtheim, M. 1976. *Ancient Egyptian literature: the New Kingdom*. Berkeley and Los Angeles: University of California Press.

Lilyquist, C. 2004. *The tomb of Thutmosis III's foreign wives*. New York: Metropolitan Museum of Art.

Lindblad, I. 1984. *Royal sculpture of the early Eighteenth Dynasty in Egypt*. Stockholm: Medelhavsmuseet.

Liverani, M. (ed.) 1999. *Le lettere di el-Amarna, vol. 2: le lettere dei 'grandi re'*. Brescia: Paideia.

Loat, W.L.S. 1905. *Gurob*. London: Quaritch.

Logan, T. 2000. The *Jmyt-pr* document: form, function and significance. *JARCE* 37: 49–73.

Lorton, D. 1990. The Aswan/Philae inscription of Thutmosis II. In Israelit-Groll, S. (ed.), *Studies in egyptology presented to Miriam Lichtheim*. Jerusalem: Magnes Press, 668–679.

Lowle, D.A. 1976. A remarkable family of draughtsmen-painters from early Nineteenth-Dynasty Thebes. *Oriens Antiquus* 15: 91–106.

Manassa, C. 2010. Defining historical fiction in New Kingdom Egypt. In Melville, S.C., and Slotsky, A.L. (eds.), *Opening the tablet box: Near Eastern studies in honor of Benjamin R. Foster*. Leiden: Brill, 245–269.

Manniche, L. 2003. The so-called scenes of daily life in the private tombs of the Eighteenth Dynasty: an overview. In Strudwick, N., and Taylor, J. (eds.), *The Theban necropolis: past, present and future*. London: British Museum Press, 42–45.

Martin, G.T. 1982. Queen Mutnodjmet at Memphis and el-Amarna. In Centre national de la recherche scientifique (ed.), *L'Égyptologie en 1979: axes prioritaires de recherches, vol. II*. Paris: Presses du Centre national de la recherche scientifique, 275–278.

Martin, G.T. 1989. *The Memphite tomb of Horemheb, commander-in-chief of Tutankhamun*. London: Egypt Exploration Society.

Martin, G.T. 1991. *The hidden tombs of Memphis*. London: Thames & Hudson.

Maspero, G. 1889. *Les momies royales de Deir el-Bahari*. Paris: E. Leroux.

Meyer, C. 1982. *Senenmut: eine prosopographische Untersuchung*. Hamburg: Borg.

Middleton, R. 1962. Brother-sister and father-daughter marriage in ancient Egypt. *American Sociological Review* 27: 603–611.

Millard, A. 1976. *The position of women in the family and in society in ancient Egypt, with special reference to the Middle Kingdom*. PhD thesis, University of London. Retrieved from https://discovery.ucl.ac.uk/id/eprint/1349381/ (last accessed September 11, 2020).

Minault-Gout, A. 2007. Les installations du début du Nouvel Empire à Sai. In Gratien, B., and Geus, F. (eds.), *Mélanges offerts à Francis Geus*. Villeneuve-d'Ascq: Université Charles-de-Gaulle - Lille III, 275–293.

Montet, P. 1958. *Everyday life in Egypt in the days of Ramesses the Great*. London: Arnold.

Moran, W.L. 1992. *The Amarna Letters*. Baltimore, MD: Johns Hopkins University Press.

Morkot, R.G. 1987. Studies in New Kingdom Nubia, 1: politics, economics and ideology—Egyptian imperialism in Nubia. *Wepwawet: Research Papers in Egyptology* 3: 29–49.

Müller, M. 2014. Deir el-Medina in the dark: the Amarna period in the history of the village. In Toivari-Viitala, J., Vartiainen, T., and Uvanto, S. (eds.), *Deir el-Medina studies*. Helsinki: Finnish Egyptological Society, 154–167.

Murnane, W. 1977. *Ancient Egyptian coregencies*. Chicago: The Oriental Institute of the University of Chicago, 213–215.

Naville, E. 1897. La succession des Thoutmès d'après un mémoire récent. *ZÄS* 35: 30–67.

Newberry, P.E. 1895. *El-Bersheh, 1: the tomb of Tehuti-hetep*. London: Egypt Exploration Fund.

Nicholson, P. 2007. *Brilliant things for Akhenaten: the production of glass, vitreous materials and pottery at Amarna site O45.1*. London: Egypt Exploration Society.

Nicholson, P., Jackson, C.M., and Trott, K.M. 1997. The Ulu Burun glass ingots, cylindrical vessels and Egyptian glass. *JEA* 83: 143–153.

Nielsen, N. 2018. *Pharaoh Seti I*. Barnsley: Pen & Sword.

O'Connor, D.B. 1978. *Excavations at Malkata and the Birket Habu, 1971–1974, under the direction of David B. O'Connor and Barry J. Kemp*. Warminster: Aris & Phillips.

Oren, E.D. 1997. The "Kingdom of Sharuhen" and the Hyksos kingdom. In Oren, E.D. (ed.), *The Hyksos: new historical and archaeological perspectives.* Philadelphia: University of Pennsylvania Museum of Archaeology and Anthropology, 253–283.

Peet, T.E. 1914. *The stela of Sebek-khu: the earliest record of an Egyptian campaign in Asia.* Manchester: Manchester University Press.

Peet, T.E. 1930. *The great tomb robberies of the Twentieth Egyptian Dynasty.* Oxford: Clarendon Press.

Petrie, W.M.F. 1909. *Qurneh.* London: Quaritch.

Pino, C. 2005. The market scene in the tomb of Khaemhat (TT 57). *JEA* 91: 95–105.

Polinger Foster, K., and Ritner, R.K. 1996. Texts, storms and the Thera eruption. *JNES* 55: 1–14.

Polz, D. 2005. The royal and private necropolis of the Seventeenth and early Eighteenth Dynasties at Dra' Abu el-Naga. In Daoud, K., Bedier, S., and Abd el-Fatah, S. (eds.), *Studies in honor of Ali Radwan.* Cairo: Supreme Council of Antiquities, 233–245.

Pritchard, J.B. (ed.) 1969. *Ancient Near Eastern texts relating to the Old Testament.* Princeton, NJ: Princeton University Press. 3rd rev. ed.

Pulak, C. 2001. The cargo of the Uluburun ship and evidence for trade with the Aegean and beyond. In Bonfante, L., and Karageorghis, V. (eds.), *Italy and Cyprus in antiquity: 1500–450 BC.* Nicosia: Costakis and Leto Severis Foundation, 13–60.

Pulak, C. 2008. The Uluburun shipwreck and Late Bronze Age trade. In Aruz, J., Benzel, K., and Evans, J.M. (eds.), *Beyond Babylon: art, trade and diplomacy in the second millennium BC.* New York: Metropolitan Museum of Art; New Haven, CT: Yale University Press, 289–310.

Quibell, J.E. 1912. *Excavations at Saqqara (1908–9, 1909–10): the monastery of Apa Jeremias.* Cairo: Institut français d'archéologie orientale.

Quibell, J.E., and Hayter, A.G.K. 1927. *Excavations at Saqqara: Teti pyramid north side.* Cairo: Cairo: Institut français d'archéologie orientale.

Raven, M.J. 2001. *The tomb of Maya and Meryt.* London: Egypt Exploration Society.

Redford, D.B. 1965. The coregency of Thutmosis III and Amenophis II. *JEA* 51: 107–122.

Redford, D.B. 1973. Studies on Akhenaten at Thebes, I: a report on the work of the Akhenaten Temple Project of the University Museum, University of Pennsylvania. *JARCE* 10: 77–94.

Redford, D.B. 1975. Studies on Akhenaten at Thebes, II: a report on the work of the Akhenaten Temple Project of the University Museum, The University of Pennsylvania, for the Year 1973–4. *JARCE* 12: 9–14.

Redford, D.B. 1993. *Egypt, Canaan and Israel in ancient times.* Princeton, NJ: Princeton University Press.

Redford, D.B. 2003. *The wars in Syria and Palestine of Tuthmosis III.* Leiden: Brill.

Reviv, H. 1972. Some comments on the Maryannu. *IEJ* 22: 218–228.

Richter, B.A. 2008. The *Amduat* and its relationship to the architecture of the early 18th Dynasty royal burial chambers. *JARCE* 44: 73–104.

Ritner, R.K., and Moeller, N. 2014. The Ahmose "Tempest Stela": Thera and comparative chronology. *JNES* 73: 1–19.

Roehrig, C.H., Dreyfus, R., and Keller, C.A. (eds.) 2005. *Hatshepsut, from queen to pharaoh.* New York: Metropolitan Museum of Art; New Haven, CT: Yale University Press.

Ryholt, K.S.B. 1997. *The political situation in Egypt during the Second Intermediate Period, c. 1800–1550 BC.* Copenhagen: Museum Tusculanum Press.

Schmitz, B. 1978. Untersuchungen zu zwei Königinnen der frühen 18. Dynastie, Ahhotep und Ahmose. *CdE* 53: 207–221.

Schneider, T. 2006. The relative chronology of the Middle Kingdom and the Hyksos period (Dyns. 12–17). In Hornung, E., Krauss, R., and Warburton, D. (ed.), *Ancient Egyptian chronology.* Leiden: Brill, 168–196.

Schulman, A.R. 1964. Excursus on the "military officer" Nakhtmin. *JARCE* 3: 124–126.

Sethe, K. 1906–1909. *Urkunden der 18. Dynastie, Abteilung IV, Heft 1–16.* Leipzig: Hinrichs.

Sethe, K. 1926. Ein Prozessurteil aus dem Alten Reich. *ZÄS* 61: 67–79.

Sethe, K. 1927. *Urkunden der 18. Dynastie, vol. I.* Leipzig: Hinrichs.

Sethe, K. 1933. *Urkunden des ägyptischen Altertums, I: Urkunden des Alten Reichs.* Leipzig: Hinrichs. 2nd rev. ed.

Shaw, I., and Nicholson, P. 1995. *The dictionary of ancient Egypt.* London: British Museum Press.

Shea, W.H. 1979. The conquest of Sharuhen and Megiddo reconsidered. *IEJ* 29: 1–5.

Shirley, J.J. 2010. One tomb, two owners: Theban tomb 122—re-use or planned family tomb? In Hawass, Z., and Wegner, J.H. (eds.), *Millions of jubilees: studies in honor of David P. Silverman*. Cairo: Supreme Council of Antiquities, 271–301.

Shirley, J.J. 2011. What's in a title? Military and civil officials in the Egyptian 18th Dynasty military sphere. In Bar, S., Kahn, D., and Shirley, J. J. (eds.), *Egypt, Canaan and Israel: history, imperialism, ideology and literature.* Leiden: Brill, 291–319.

Shortland, A.J. 2000. *Vitreous materials at Amarna: the production of glass and faience in 18th Dynasty Egypt.* Oxford: British Archaeological Reports.

Shortland, A.J., Tite, M.S., and Hope, C. 2006. Cobalt blue painted pottery from 18th Dynasty Egypt. In Maggetti, M., and Messiga, B. (eds.), *Geomaterials in cultural heritage.* London: The Geological Society, 91–99.

Simpson, W.K. (ed.) 2003. *The literature of ancient Egypt: an anthology of stories, instructions, stelae, autobiographies, and poetry.* New Haven, CT: Yale University Press.

Smith, H. 1976. *The fortress of Buhen: the inscriptions.* London: Egypt Exploration Society.

Smith, S.T. 1992. Intact tombs of the Seventeenth and Eighteenth Dynasties from Thebes and the New Kingdom burial system. *MDAIK* 48: 193–231.

Snape, S. 2011. *Ancient Egyptian tombs: the culture of life and death.* Malden, MA: Wiley-Blackwell.

Soliman, D. 2015. Workmen's marks in pre-Amarna tombs at Deir el-Medina. In Budka, J., Kammerzell, F., and Rzepka, S. (eds.), *Non-textual marking systems in ancient Egypt (and elsewhere).* Hamburg: Widmaier, 109–132.

Sourouzian, H., Stadelmann, R., Madden, B., and Gayer-Anderson, T. 2006. Three seasons of work at the temple of Amenhotep III at Kom el Hettan, part I: work at the Colossi of Memnon. *ASAE* 80: 323–366.

Spalinger, A. 1977. A critical analysis of the "Annals" of Thutmose III (Stücke V–VI). *JARCE* 14: 41–54.

Spalinger, A.J. 2011. Königsnovelle and performance. In Callender, V.G., Bareš, L., Bárta, M., Janák, J., and Krejčí, J. (eds.), *Times, signs and pyramids: studies in honour of Miroslav Verner.* Prague: Charles University, 351–375.

Spence, K. 2012. Amarna: palaces, houses and outlying settlements. In Seyfried, F. (ed.), *In the light of Amarna: 100 years of the discovery of Amarna.* Petersberg: Michael Imhof Verlag, 50–55.

Spence, K. 2015. Ancient Egyptian houses: architecture, conceptualization and interpretation. In Müller, M. (ed.), *Household studies in complex societies: (micro) archaeological and textual approaches.* Chicago: The Oriental Institute of the University of Chicago, 83–99.

Stanton, P. 2020. Hatshepsut's obelisks at Karnak: commemorating a *sed*-festival. *Teaching History* 54: 21–25.

Stefanović, D. 2012. *sš ḳdwt*: the attestations from the Middle Kingdom and the Second Intermediate Period. In Kóthay, K.A. (ed.), *Art and society: ancient and modern contexts of Egyptian art.* Budapest: Museum of Fine Arts, 185–198.

Stevens, A. 2006. *Private religion at Amarna: the material evidence.* Oxford: Archaeopress.

Stiebing, W.H. 1993. *Uncovering the past: a history of archaeology.* Oxford: Oxford University Press.

Sweeney, D. 2008. Gender and oracular practices in Deir el-Medina. *ZÄS* 135: 154–164.

Taylor, J.H. 2001. *Death and the afterlife in ancient Egypt.* London: British Museum Press.

Teeter, E. 1995. Amenhotep son of Hapu at Medinet Habu. *JEA* 81: 232–236.

Timmann, C., and Meyer, C.G. 2010. Malaria, mummies, mutations: Tutankhamun's archaeological autopsy. *Tropical Medicine & International Health* 15: 1278–1280.

Tomashevska, M. 2019. *Sacred floral garlands and collars from the New Kingdom period and early Third Intermediate Period in ancient Egypt.* MA thesis, Leiden University. Retrieved from https://openaccess.leidenuniv. nl/handle/1887/77994 (last accessed September 11, 2020).

Trigger, B. 1976. *Nubia under the pharaohs.* London: Thames & Hudson.

Tyldesley, J. 1998a. *Hatchepsut: the female pharaoh.* London: Penguin.

Tyldesley, J. 1998b. *Nefertiti: Egypt's sun queen.* London: Viking.

Uphill, E.P. 2000. Some matters relating to the growth and walls of Deir el-Medina. In Demarée, R.J., and Egberts, A. (eds.), *Deir el-Medina in the third millennium AD.* Leiden: NINO, 325–330.

Van der Perre, A. 2012. Nefertiti's last documented reference (for now). In Seyfried, F. (ed.), *In the light of Amarna: 100 years of the discovery of Amarna.* Petersberg: Michael Imhof Verlag, 195–197.

Vandersleyen, C. 1967. Une tempête sous le règne d'Amosis. *RdE* 19: 123–125.

van Dijk, J. 1996. Horemheb and the struggle for the throne of Tutankhamun. *The Bulletin of the Australian Centre of Egyptology* 7: 29–42.

van Dijk, J. 2000. The Amarna period and later New Kingdom. In Shaw, I. (ed.), *The Oxford history of ancient Egypt*. Oxford: Oxford University Press, 263–307.

Vivas Sainz, I. 2017. Egyptian artists in the New Kingdom: travelling artists and travelling ideas? In Chyla, J.M., Dębowska-Ludwin, J., Rosińska-Balik, K., and Walsh, C. (eds.), *Current research in Egyptology 2016*. Oxford: Oxbow, 107–120.

Warburton, D.A. 2012. *Architecture, power and religion: Hatshepsut, Amun and Karnak in context*. Münster: LIT Verlag.

Weatherhead, F.J., and Kemp, B.J. 2007. *The main chapel at the Amarna workmen's village and its wall paintings*. London: Egypt Exploration Society.

Westbrook, R. 2000. Babylonian diplomacy in the Amarna Letters. *JAOS* 120: 377–382.

Whelan, P. 2011. Small yet perfectly formed: some observations on Theban stick shabti coffins of the 17th and early 18th Dynasty. *Egitto e Vicino Oriente* 34: 9–22.

Wiener, M.H., and Allen, J.P. 1998. Separate lives: the Ahmose Tempest Stela and the Theran eruption. *JNES* 57: 1–28.

Zamacona, C.G. 2019. Imagining Henenu. *NEA* 82: 75–81.

Zivie, A. 1984. Un chancelier nommé Nehesy. In Daumas, F. (ed.), *Mélanges Adolphe Gutbub*. Montpellier: Université de Montpellier, 245–252.

Zivie, A. 1988. 'Aper-el et ses voisins: considérations sur les tombes rupestres de la XVIIIᵉ dynastie à Saqqarah. In Zivie, A. (ed.), *Memphis et ses nécropoles au Nouvel Empire: nouvelles données, nouvelles questions*. Paris: Centre national de la Recherche scientifique, 103–112.

Zivie, A. 2013. *La tombe de Thoutmes: directeur des peintres dans la place de Maât* (Les Tombes du Bubasteion à Saqqara 2). Toulouse: Caracara.

27

The New Kingdom of Egypt under the Ramesside Dynasty

Kathlyn M. Cooney

27.1. Perceptions and misperceptions about the Ramesside period

There are some uncontested facts about the Ramesside period, and these can be built into a historical narrative. The basics are: the Ramesside period (1292–1069 BC) began with a king Rameses of the Nineteenth Dynasty and ended with a king Rameses of the Twentieth Dynasty.[1] The two dynasties lasted about 225 years. The base of power for both dynasties was the city of Piramesses in the eastern Nile delta (figure 27.1).[2] The Ramesside period had a decidedly northern, even Levantine, direction, in comparison to the Seventeenth and Eighteenth Dynasties, both belonging to Theban kings of Upper Egypt. Despite the fact that most of the action was to be found in Egypt's north, our textual and even

---

1. The dates generally follow von Beckerath 1997, but correcting Sethnakht's reign to 4 years (1185–1181 BC) because of a new stele found in Luxor in 2006 (published by Boraik 2007), which mentions Sethnakht's Year 4. Consequently, the reign of Rameses III is dated to 1181–1150 BC.

2. For the latest literature on Piramesses, see Forstner-Müller 2018.

Kathlyn M. Cooney, *The New Kingdom of Egypt under the Ramesside Dynasty* In: *The Oxford History of the Ancient Near East*. Edited by: Karen Radner, Nadine Moeller, and D. T. Potts, Oxford University Press.
© Oxford University Press 2022. DOI: 10.1093/oso/9780190687601.003.0027

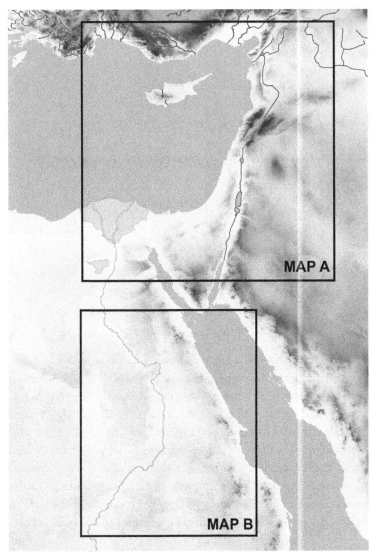

MAP A

MAP B

FIGURE 27.1A. Map of sites mentioned in this chapter. Prepared by Andrea Squitieri (LMU Munich).

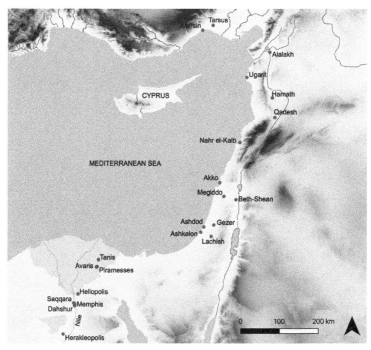

FIGURE 27.1B. Detail map A.

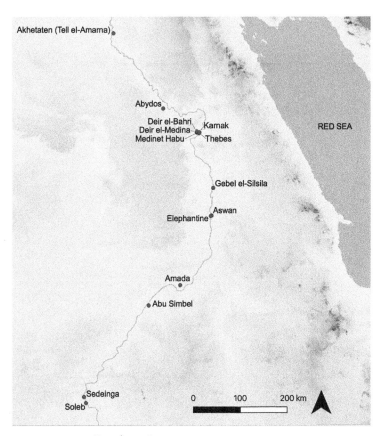

FIGURE 27.1C. Detail map B.

architectural evidence for the Ramesside period is nonetheless southern, producing a skewed, confusing, and even contested, history.

From a collection of names, places, relative dates, archaeological sites, as well as economic, ideological, military, and political evidence, historians have constructed a historical narrative of degeneracy, a sad imitation of greater times long gone, a poor copy of Egypt's political and cultural heights during the Eighteenth Dynasty. How much of this story is accurate? While it is true that the Ramesside period saw the contraction of Egypt's hegemony in Syria, the Levant, Kush, and Nubia,[3] extraordinary economic contraction and lessening monumental production, especially in its later years, and generations of mass migrations, destabilizing the land, it seems that the Ramesside period's worst failing, from the perspective of the Egyptological historian, is usually that it followed Egypt's Eighteenth Dynasty (see chapter 26 in this volume), an apex of steady growth, consistent wealth, and high-quality artistic production under able and well-known rulers like Hatshepsut (1479–1458 BC), Thutmose III (1479–1425 BC), and Amenhotep III (1388–1350 BC), to whom the Ramesside period kings are always compared to their detriment. Even the fact that the Eighteenth Dynasty ended in Akhenaten's self-created social trauma does little to limit Egyptologists' laudatory opinion of this earlier dynasty in comparison to the Nineteenth and Twentieth Dynasties.

Should we see the Ramesside period in a different way? It is indeed documentable that most Ramesside kings witnessed a steady decline of authority, experiencing palace infighting so intense that it resulted in not one, but two, civil wars, one at the end of the Nineteenth Dynasty and another at the end of the Twentieth Dynasty, punctuated by palace discord so competitive that it resulted in the murder of King Rameses III (1181–1150 BC) himself in the middle of the Twentieth Dynasty.[4] Not to downplay any of the rulers' weaknesses or deficiencies in ruling strategy, the Ramesside period was also punctuated by one of the most devastating

---

3. Van de Mieroop 2007.

4. Vernus 1993; Kitchen 2008: 350–363.

social and global apocalypses the Mediterranean and ancient Near East had ever known—the Bronze Age Collapse—evidence of which is visible in destruction layers from dozens of archaeological sites in the northern and eastern Mediterranean and documented in visual and textual monuments within Egypt.[5] If we take a broader perspective, the eventual fall of the Twentieth Dynasty was part of a larger crisis in economic, political, and climatic systems, not a miscalculation of one or two dynastic families. Egypt held on the longest during the Bronze Age Collapse, after all; political systems in southeastern Europe, Anatolia, Syria, and the Levant had expired first and with the most devastating effects. By contrast, the demise of the New Kingdom in Egypt still allowed extraordinary continuity of earlier political, economic, and ideological systems as it moved into the so-called Third Intermediate Period. Nonetheless, when the Ramesside kings did finally fall from power, historians tend to draw a stark line between the Nineteenth and Twentieth Dynasties, on the one hand, and the Twenty-first Dynasty on the other, even though decentralized and competitive ruling strategies remained largely unchanged from one period to the next. In many ways, the historical creation of a crisp division between the New Kingdom and the Third Intermediate Period can be understood as the chief reason why Egyptologists do not see the Ramesside period for what it was, a runway that paved the way to the ensuing Iron Age.

As we separate the Bronze Age (prosperity!) from the Iron Age (collapse and decentralization!), many historians highlight the reign of Rameses II (1279–1213 BC) of the Nineteenth Dynasty, ignoring the rest of the kings of the Ramesside period. In so focusing on Rameses "the Great," we are seemingly trying to save face by looking at the entire period through this king's eyes, all the while knowing that despite (his) claims to the contrary, this same monarch lost his Syrian territories in battles with the Hittites, was forced to sign a peace treaty with the same sworn enemy to create a regional defense, and although his building campaign shouts excess, he may have reused more statuary of ancestor kings

---

5. Cline 2014; Knapp and Manning 2016: 99–149.

than he made from scratch.[6] Under closer perusal, Rameses the Great does little to rescue the Ramesside period from its own poor reputation.[7]

And yet, if historians turn their attention solely to the discord and political loss of the Ramesside period, we find ourselves looking for someone to blame for the downturn, like Merenptah (1213–1203 BC) of the Nineteenth Dynasty or Rameses VI of the Twentieth Dynasty, the assumption being that political problems derive solely from individual leaders and their strategies, rather than from the complex social contexts in which they ruled. And thus we are back to square one, viewing the Ramesside period as sorely lacking in comparison to the Eighteenth Dynasty with its kings of brilliant military and economic strategy (Thutmose III and Amenhotep III), but far superior to the following Twenty-first Dynasty (with no strong king who could even unite the whole of Egypt).

If the Ramesside period does indeed represent an extraordinary downward slide,[8] how do we analyze the reasons for Egypt's slow tumble down the hill? Despite cautions against it, comparisons to the Eighteenth and Twenty-first Dynasties are still necessary to see the profound and continuous social changes underway during the Ramesside period; however, those same comparisons are not always useful in terms of understanding the Ramesside social system on its own terms. Eighteenth Dynasty assumptions have colored our view of the Ramesside period so much that we cannot understand, or even recognize, clear and visible adaptations because we insist on seeing Ramesside institutions as ruled by the same social conditions and systems as those of the Eighteenth Dynasty. This methodology will not work, any more than we can understand the Twelfth Dynasty through a system of the Fourth Dynasty. A key warning from the trenches of Ramesside period historiography could be: one cannot and should not study systems of decentralization through the rubrics of the centralized.

---

6. Magen 2011.

7. *Contra* Kitchen 1985; Tyldesley 2000; Schlögl 2017.

8. Cooney 2018.

27.2. Egypt's empire

Monumental displays of power have led many historians to uncritically conclude that the Ramessides possessed a growing empire in the Levant and Kush, when, in reality, Egypt could sustain its grandeur in regional agricultural and mineral wealth quite well with limited geographic hegemony over the southern Levant and Nubia with no growth beyond.[9] Nineteenth Dynasty campaigning extended up into northern Syria to the Orontes river, or down into Kush as far as the Fourth or Fifth Cataracts—only when Egyptian kings really wanted to make a statement, when the crown wanted to grow palace incomes with systematic extraction within hegemonic systems in foreign territories—but Egypt's power never expanded imperially beyond these areas because it was not in Egypt's economic or social need.[10] The bare fact that we have the best written, architectural, and archaeological evidence for Egypt's "empire" during the Ramesside period is not because any true empire existed specifically at this time, but because there were social demands for the documentation of control over these foreign areas, that is, more need for the recording of quotas and deliveries, more letters and more outreach, not because Egypt possessed a strong empire under firm administration, but because Ramesside Egypt had so many more activated political agents who needed to prove their power within an increasingly decentralized context.

Egypt's system of foreign control in the Levant, Nubia, and Kush was hegemonic, not imperial, in the Ramesside period and even before that; in other words, it did not demand inclusion of the sustained differences of multiple ethnic groups or languages, diverse territories, different religious systems, or cultures. Nilotic Egypt, at its most centralized, allowed foreigners into its hegemonic systems if they "Egyptianized."[11] Egyptian

---

9. *Contra* Redford 1992; Morris 2005; 2018. For a comparison of Egyptian political systems with West Asian political systems and a similar conclusion that Egypt was not imperially bent, see Warburton 2003a; 2003b.

10. E.g., Rameses II's First, Second, and Third Syrian campaigns; see Kitchen 1985.

11. Schneider 2010b: 143–163; van Pelt 2013: 523–550; Lakomy 2016.

culture was not imperially flexible, but instead culturally dominant. It demanded (and in many ways, still demands) cultural cohesion and agreement, even within the increasing decentralization of the Ramesside period. In general, Egyptian culture and politics did not encourage diversity beyond what was already considered "Egyptian" within its various regions of the Nile valley and delta—though the desert, oases, and seashore were a different story—unless that otherness brought wealth or prestige to its Egyptian stakeholders—for example, the Eastern Desert trader marked by his colorful garments, hair style, and weapons, or the warrior driving a horse-drawn chariot originally from Western Asia, broadcasting culturally specific, and coveted, skills, knowledge, and their resulting products.[12] Egypt did not need to continually expand its territory beyond those easily exploited regions of mineral and trade wealth because they existed on its very doorsteps—in Nubia and the southern Levant. Fortresses were built, to be sure, during the Ramesside period, replete with towers and gateways and fortification walls, but within a hegemonic system of control, not within an imperial system based on territorial expansion and steady economic growth.[13]

Rameses II (1279–1213 BC), Merenptah (1213–1203 BC), and Rameses III (1181–1150 BC) published their forays abroad in intricate detail, including battle tactics, locations, and strategy, all of which leads us to, uncritically, see the Ramesside period as a system of imperialism.[14] But foreign campaigns, whether successful or not, do not necessarily imply imperialism in function and form. Any claims by Ramesside kings to control all foreign lands are constructions of state identity, not actual facts of a legitimate imperial system.[15] Canaano-Akkadian script was used to transmit

---

12. For a discussion of the "International Style," see Feldman 2006.

13. On fortresses, see, e.g., Török 2009; Burke and Lords 2010; Burke, Pielstöcker, and Karoll 2017.

14. E.g., the Qadesh inscriptions of Rameses II (Lichtheim 2006: 57), as well as the "Sea Peoples" inscriptions of Rameses III from Medinet Habu (Breasted 1906: 35–114) and the Papyrus Harris I (Grandet 1994).

15. Indeed, the ancient Egyptians had no hope when true imperial forces invaded their lands in the ensuing Iron Age. They were no match for the Assyrian Empire of the seventh century BC, the Babylonian Empire of the sixth century BC, the

diplomatic and economic information between rulers of the Eighteenth and Nineteenth Dynasties,[16] and it may have been used to directly administer foreign territories in Nubia and Canaan.[17] Beyond that, Egypt traded with the Levant, Cyprus, Anatolia, and even with Punt; but it did not invade them, incorporate them, administer them, and rule them like imperial territory. Egypt's leaders, including the Ramessides, did not think like emperors, choosing not to style themselves as rulers over the entire world, but instead as god-kings over Egypt and the Egyptians, however we are to understand those concepts. The rest of the world was nothing compared to Egypt's god-given bounty, to be sure, as expressed in countless royal hymns and campaign steles, and its rulers were god-kings of their own special and largely self-sufficient divine realm.[18]

27.3. The truth behind the untruths

As with so many Egyptian documents, most Ramesside records about territories and military exploits are to be found on monuments for public or temple display, demanding that we scrutinize whether the Ramesside kings achieved what they said they achieved and for the stated reasons. For instance, after perusing carefully commissioned accounts of particular battles—such as Rameses II's Battle of Qadesh, Merenptah's

---

Persian Empire of the fifth and fourth centuries BC, or Alexander's empire of the fourth century BC. Egypt would also be no match for the Roman Empire that successfully took it into its grasp before the turn of the millennium, any more than it could repel the Ottoman Empire or the British, or now, the economic empires of the United States and the Arabian Peninsula—because it is self-sufficient in food and resources and internally oriented geographically. See Kuhrt 1995.

16. Mandell 2015.

17. In the Amarna Letters of the Eighteenth Dynasty, there are a few examples of Akkadian texts from the Levant exchanged between local rulers and Egyptian garrison officials, e.g., an Egyptian official ordering the ruler of Taanach to send troops to the Egyptian garrison; the Egyptian officials are designated as *šakin mati* (Akkadian "governor"); see Morris 2005: 141.

18. Assmann 1970; Lichtheim 2006.

campaigns into the Levant, and Rameses III's rout of the Libyans or the Sea Peoples (see chapter 28 in this volume)—scholars often read the given narratives uncritically, focusing instead on the names of mercenaries or tribes, campaign details, battle tactics, place names, forgetting that we are reading documentation produced by an authoritarian regime displayed monumentally for political and ideological agendas. Countless research articles analyze battle sites, crunch numbers of soldiers of opposing armies, ascertain where exactly a particular battle occurred, and too few of us question the reason so many facts were recorded for public consumption by the literate elite.[19]

Having said all of that, there is no reason to throw out the baby with the bath water. The power brokers of the Ramesside period excelled at manipulating and displaying facts and story for political ends, yes, but not all of the information contained therein consists, therefore, of lies and spin. Battle narratives as well as royal hymns can indeed be grounded in human reality, but only if we grapple with the political agendas for writing such accounts or the potential audiences meant to be swayed by them. If we rise above the weeds—critically examining the narratives and the veracity thereof—we can ask how these different and detailed[20] accounts served a new Ramesside social system, one in which there were more stakeholders, more kingmakers if you will, more elites who needed to be convinced of the king's great power. In other words, if we know the Ramesside kings for their bombastic displays of power or overwrought narratives about prowess in battle, it is not because they were "greater"

---

19. For examples of such positivist scholarship, see Murnane 1990; Goedicke 1966; Manassa 2003; Spalinger 2005. On narrative and how we need to read between the lines, see also Eyre 2018. For examination of the Egyptian elite as "invisible actors" with a massive impact on the Egyptian state, see Moreno García 2020: 87–107.

20. This is not to say that Thutmose III did not go into detail about his invasion of Megiddo and the strategy of moving through a narrow pass against the wishes of his generals in his own historical annals, but this account was not displayed prominently or monumentally by Thutmose III, rather only in text form in the inner chambers of Karnak temple, where his annals were located, implying a more closed and limited agenda in comparison to Rameses II and other kings of the Ramesside period. Cf. Sternberg-el Hotabi 2005.

than anything that had come before, but because they needed to convince more people of that greatness than ever before. The Ramesside king had to create political spin as never before, indicative of his expanded reliance on elites who were, en masse, key decision makers.

27.4. The release of state secrets during the Ramesside period

Indeed, how and where texts were produced can tell us a great deal about a quickly changing society. For instance, the Ramesside period is known to be a time when underworld text creation explodes, when narratives and rituals heretofore unseen were carved into tomb and temple walls for the first time.[21] On the surface, such production seems indicative of great innovation, but a critical gaze reveals that this is not necessarily the case, that instead we are dealing with a mass release of data previously kept top secret. The Ramesside period was not necessarily the time of these texts' creation, but rather when many secret texts and images were *published* in stone or papyrus for the first time. It was during the Ramesside period when elite society demanded and allowed the Book of Gates or Caverns to be carved into a given royal tomb, and when scenes of the Royal Harem were chiseled into the inner rooms of a gateway at a king's mortuary temple. They put so much out there, these Ramesside kings, that their greatness seems assured in our eyes, but the very act of publication—of letting previously controlled and secret information known only to an initiated few out into larger society—was indicative of deep and unsettling social change,[22] and even a more vulnerable king who had to demonstrate his grandeur to his elites in a way he had not needed to before.

---

21. Hornung 1999; Werning 2011; Teeter 2012: 27–65; Roberson 2012; 2013; 2016.

22. One could make the same argument for a variety of "publications" of secret texts through time in Egyptian culture, beginning with the "Pyramid Texts" inscribed onto royal burial chamber walls for the first time by King Unas at the end of the Fifth Dynasty and only increasingly in the Sixth Dynasty, just before the fall of the Old Kingdom.

In the Eighteenth Dynasty, the secret book "What Is in the Underworld" (otherwise known as the *Amduat*) was copied directly onto the burial chamber walls of Thutmose III or Amenhotep II from pattern books by one or two scribes, quickly and with no artistic preparation or embellishment, not to mention polychromy, keeping the design to line drawings and hieratic-like hieroglyphs precisely because such a speedy transfer limited human access to the tightly controlled document.[23] The Ramesside kings, however, treated that same *Amduat* text very differently, insisting on putting it on their own tomb walls with careful carving of full figures and complex painting in bright colors, thus openly publishing previously exclusive religious material and information—to the craftsmen who would need many pattern books circulating around the worksite to lay out each hour onto the limestone, to the priests who were in charge of such texts, and to the elites and priests who visited the tomb while it was under construction for years.[24] These Ramesside kings did not or could not have themselves buried in the Eighteenth Dynasty way, the secret way, precisely because they needed a larger social statement.

To put it simply, the Ramesside kings needed to prove their greatness more than those Eighteenth Dynasty kings who could keep their cards close to the vest. Ramesside kings, arguably starting with Horemheb, needed buy-in from more social actors than Egypt had ever previously allowed. And so, the Nineteenth Dynasty kings opened up many previously secret aspects of their burial preparations, widening the tomb, expanding and embellishing the entrance, making what was previously tightly controlled and inaccessible now readable and available, even creating tombs with monumental entrance ways by the end of the Ramesside period. No longer were kings interred in the Valley of the Kings in hidden

---

23. Roehrig 2006: 238–259 (especially 246–248); Richter 2008: 73–104.

24. There is no direct evidence for pattern books, just the assumption that such multi-step artistic creation in the Ramesside Valley of the Kings tombs would have demanded them. And although there is no evidence that Deir el-Medina artisans ever included these underworld texts in their own tombs, there is evidence that they included iconography from them, particularly in the so-called monochrome tombs. See Bruyère 1952.

cliff-side chambers with "no one seeing; no one hearing."[25] Ramesside royal tombs were splashy and conspicuous affairs. We Egyptologists are drawn in, too, thinking of these tombs as more fabulous, more colorful, more expensive, more powerful, like their rulers, but such elements are not markers of exclusive power, but rather illustrative of a new social system in which kings needed their elite people to be impressed by novel avenues of display. The Ramesside kings understood that monumental production worked on human minds to create the impression of power; indeed, it continues to work on ours.

The explosion of underworld books in the Ramesside period— the "Book of the Night and Day," the "Book of Gates," the "Book of Earth," the "Book of Caverns," the "Book of the Heavenly Cow," all expansions and glosses of profound theological thinking about death and the afterlife[26]—are thus indicative not of growing social power or material wealth of the king, but of a new and striking neediness of the monarch.[27] All of this religious information, previously under lock and key, was now open to elite Theban society and beyond, in a way that Eighteenth Dynasty monarchs and officials had not allowed or did not need to show. While many Egyptologists assume a kind of teleology of afterlife evolution, or another step in the "democratization of the afterlife," or, most commonly, a significant increase in religious intellectual production because of a growth in personal piety, there are other social reasons to explain such a massive data dump of previously exclusive texts.

The Ramesside kings required legitimate and visible proof of their kingship (in Thebes for these tomb publications, but elsewhere in Egypt for the publication of previously secret religious texts in temples), and such production only grew more visible and accessible in the Twentieth Dynasty. Even scenes from the king's harem are published for the first time during the reign of Rameses III at his mortuary temple at Medinet

---

25. For this comment from the tomb of Ineni, see Breasted 1906: II 43.

26. Hornung 2002.

27. *Contra* Assmann 1995a.

Habu—intimate and ritualized details, representations of naked young women, information about the king's private life that heretofore was left completely unmentioned.[28] This amount of access into an ideological world that was previously so secret makes us feel that we know these kings better and that they were indeed "Making Egypt Great Again," but there are other explanations for why the Ramesside kings let these birds fly out of their hands.

For it was not just the kings who had access to what was previously secret. Egyptian elites now seem to have had greater access to texts and imagery that were previously exclusive.[29] It's from the Ramesside period that we learn so much about underworld beliefs, creation theology, ritual details, with the assumption by many scholars that these texts, now published, have earlier origins.[30] Indeed, the skilled and literate nature of the Ramesside Deir el-Medina craftsmen[31] is a result of the publication of so many underworld books; the Ramesside kings needed artisans of agency and knowledge to systematize such complex decorations, certainly more so than in the Eighteenth Dynasty, when only a few skilled men were needed to quickly copy the secret *Amduat* onto the king's burial chamber walls.

27.5. Can religion drive change in a society?

The social landscape of display was changing, and quickly. Much ink has been spilled on John Baines' notion of decorum in ancient Egypt—what

---

28. Epigraphic Survey 1970.

29. Indeed that dichotomy between "daily life" scenes of Eighteenth Dynasty tombs and ritual-religious scenes of Nineteenth Dynasty tombs have been interpreted as a choice in what was culturally appropriate to represent, when really, the shift was likely representative of social competition to display ideological knowledge and proximity to religious structures by showing what had previously not been socially acceptable for display in a social space. For the notion of the tomb as a social space, see Assmann 2003.

30. Assmann 1970; Hornung 1999.

31. Davies 2018.

was appropriate to show, when and where, a kind of Egyptological understanding of Bourdieu's habitus.[32] Ramesside period decorum shows profound change, one might even say destabilization, as a wider variety of people were able to publish all sorts of things never allowed out of temple or palace hands before. The expectations for decoration programs of a typical elite tomb of the Ramesside period in Thebes or Saqqara witness considerable change, including fewer craft and so-called daily life scenes and more religious imagery, including more images of the gods themselves.[33] Why were elites of the Ramesside period allowed to show themselves in the company of the gods so often when this was, seemingly, tightly controlled in the Eighteenth Dynasty? We talk of personal piety or *Gottesnähe* (German, literally "proximity to god")—a new and more personal connection to divinity—driving such changes in subject matter,[34] but with such religiously driven explanations for change we again might overlook the real social and economic drivers.[35] New Ramesside tomb innovation is less indicative of piety and more evocative of elites jockeying to show their special access to the temple and its institutional system of social protection. By showing images of gods and sacred spells, elites were broadcasting access to and membership in the temple institutions of Egypt, and each new style or break in decorum betrayed a new arena of political competition of elites, one in which patronage of the temple was rising in importance.

The so-called religious changes of the Ramesside period were likely more about money and institutions than they were about any new religious fervor in elite or craft communities, as people looked less to

32. Baines 1995, drawing on Bourdieu and Nice 1977; Bourdieu 1984.

33. Erman 1911; Morenz 1973: 101–106; Assmann 1984; Teeter 2012: 34. For a discussion of traditional assumptions, see Teeter 2012. For a recent examination in which the tomb is seen to function as a kind of temple space in the Ramesside period, see Hofmann 2018.

34. Assmann 1995b: Baines and Frood 2011; Luiselli 2014.

35. The subject of personal piety is a tricky one and has been much criticized of late. For a discussion on how most of the traditions cited as evidence for personal piety actually started in the Eighteenth Dynasty, see Teeter 2012: 36.

kingship, and the official positions one could get through proximity to the king, and turned instead to temples—institutions that could now be relied on to create jobs and wealth and that increasingly organized society better than the crown or vizierate.[36] The reason so much of elite society published religious scenes and texts so visibly was because there were social rewards for cleaving close to the temple, its gods, its priests, its power brokers within an arena of social competition in which veiled religious knowledge and access were now overtly displayed. When so often we see the Ramesside period as a time when religion was pushing social change, it would be better to see profound social and economic change as pushing shifts in religious thinking and behavior.

The Ramesside period is often seen through a religious lens, as a cultural break in reaction to Amarna religious excesses. Indeed, the Ramesside period's place in Egyptian history is colored by the Eighteenth Dynasty's most complicated king, Akhenaten (1350–1334 BC), whose self-created religious upheavals defined what came after,[37] fomenting a reaction to the religious turbulence of the Amarna period, as people clung to the old gods in anxiety and fear after Akhenaten tore so many wounds across Egypt.[38] This is not to say that such trauma did not occur, but it might be better to view the changes of this period not as shifts in religious sentiment but as shifts in social patronage, from palace to temple, from king to institution. No social change is driven purely by religious sentiment or spiritual anxiety.

Indeed, the Ramesside period is arguably an outgrowth of Amarna period social innovations, not a reaction against them.[39] Akhenaten

---

36. The amount of administrative texts produced by temples in the Ramesside period are likely evidence of exactly this increasing importance of temple institutions; Gardiner 1948; Haring 1997. For a Ramesside period onomasticon that describes crown, vizier, and army administration, see Grandet 2018.

37. Assmann 1995a: 195. See also Assmann 2001: 222, stating "But its [the Amarna period's] consequences were so deep and so wide that they cannot be underestimated."

38. Breasted 1912; Brand 2000: 382; van Dijk 2000: 287; Teeter 2012.

39. *Contra* Manassa Darnell 2015.

relied heavily on the army to implement his social changes and political shifts.[40] He empowered a new military professionalism and elite class. The Ramesside period thus inherited a more institutionalized military system increasingly able to act independently from the king—either in support or in opposition. The last king of the Eighteenth Dynasty—Horemheb (1319–1292 BC)—likely found his origin in Egypt's hierarchically organized yet socially decentralized and flexible military ranks.[41] The family of Rameses I (1292–1290 BC) also found its origins in this newly professionalized military system.[42] Although this military institution began with the religious zealotry of Akhenaten, who needed the army to enact quick social and physical change, it was the Ramesside period that witnessed the logical conclusion of this social trajectory of a king empowering Egypt's military system, with the important caveat that now each Ramesside king had to prove himself to that self-same military system.[43]

27.6. An explosion of documentation

The Ramesside period is notable for new artistic content and styles, but it is also known for its production of more documentation of all kinds. A variety of new information found its way into publication at this time. On limestone and pottery ostraca we see notes about workshops or financial exchanges, even innovative sketches;[44] on papyri we see legal proceedings, including interrogations or trials.[45] We see medical texts[46]

---

40. Redford 1984: 72, 175; Kemp 1995; 2013.

41. Martin et al. 1989; Dodson 2009; Booth 2009; 2013; Bryson 2018.

42. Helck 1939; Cruz-Uribe 1978; Brand 2000: 336–341.

43. Eyre 2012: 138 states: "The Ramesside period is characterized by a militarization of society and government." See also Moreno García 2020: 172–185.

44. Cooney 2012.

45. Eyre 2012; 2018. For more on administrative papyri, see Gardiner 1948; Haring 1997.

46. Leitz 1999.

and dream texts,[47] each allowing its bearer to diagnose disease in body and mind. Even temples commit their financial holdings to papyrus, noting the amounts of land in their control.[48] It's not that people did not have economic lives in the Eighteenth Dynasty, but they did not have the same need to record those economic lives. This explosion of social, economic, and administrative documentation is indicative of social change in which there were more players with more agency who now had to rely on record keeping to manufacture their social power in institutional contexts. In the Eighteenth Dynasty, the right connections, the right wink and a smile, it seems, got you what you wanted. In the Nineteenth Dynasty, society now demanded proof in triplicate.

Social systems of the Nineteenth and Twentieth Dynasties were different from those of the Eighteenth Dynasty, demanding more data creation and collection by more people within society. The possible reasons are many, but the act of documentation itself stems from personal agency within a competitive arena, particularly the need to physically prove your social power. The mass of new documentation suggests that the Ramesside period was characterized by less centralized palace and vizierate control, and instead by more decentralized temple and army institutional control, creating less ad hoc decision-making by independent agents who had amassed great power, resulting in more bureaucracy at every level of society.[49] People now needed to document more about their lives—their transactions, their legal proceedings, their disputes, their work, their family members, their ancestors, their prayers, their ritual activity, their skill sets, their social places in the world, everything. It is important to remember that even in today's society, people only write things down when they need to—either when they are directly compelled by a patron, boss, or institution, or when social systems encourage such recording. Such social documentation implied the existence of more social agency at more levels of society. Indeed, institutionalization itself

47. Szpakowska 2010; 2011a; 2011b.

48. Haring 1997; 2003; Donker van Heel and Haring 2003.

49. Raedler 2006.

allowed more social agents than ever before, and every Egyptian who could read and write was now engaged in self-documentation. During the Ramesside period, more people not only had the ability to write and rewrite their social stories, but they now felt they had to communicate in written and visual form to manufacture power. Even though there is little direct evidence in its favor—how would we measure it, except in the production of documents in higher numbers—we can expect that literacy spiked within Egyptian society during the Ramesside period.[50] The amount of data itself is indicative of this social change.

27.7. The rise of a new Levantine kingship?

Thus far, we have discussed evidence from the Valley of the Kings, Deir el-Medina, Karnak temple—all of them Theban locales, where low population and aridity created better preservation. Indeed, the location of our surviving evidence about the Ramesside period drives much of our thinking about the period. Because so much of our evidence comes from Egypt's Nile valley in the south, particularly from the Theban region, many Egyptologists also assume a continuance of the Eighteenth Dynasty's (not to mention the Eleventh, Twelfth, or Seventeenth Dynasties') southern kingship—in cultural, political, and religious terms. Egyptology's bias in favor of southern kings creates a lopsided and unfair assessment of Ramesside original production and cultural orientation. Our understanding of histories and tales come from our southern bias, a provincial and even conservative (Theban) point of view, rather than from the cosmopolitan and boundary-crossing perspective of the Ramesside kings of the eastern delta.[51]

Indeed, we may have completely missed the point of the *Tale of Apepi and Seqenenra*, a story about the Seventeenth Dynasty created in the Ramesside period. We see it as a put-down of the hated Hyksos invaders (see chapter 23 in this volume), stupid and foolish men who deserve

---

50. Baines and Eyre 1983: 86–91.

51. Bács 2017.

ridicule, but recent re-examination suggests that this Ramesside text was instead complementary to Apepi, who is depicted as sophisticated and clever, while it was the southern king Seqenenra (see chapter 24 in this volume) who is depicted as a provincial and dim king.[52] Just because the Eighteenth Dynasty kings found power in criticizing the Hyksos does not mean the Nineteenth Dynasty held them with the same contempt. The Ramesside kings were not men of Thebes, to say the least, but northern military men with delta homelands. They felt the need to build their Temples of Millions of Years on Thebes' West Bank and to dig their final resting places into its western hills, to be sure, but these were men of Seth, of the delta, and their family organization and social contexts were quite different from any Thebans. Their Valley of the Kings tombs were a purposeful display of their inheritance of the old kingships of the Seventeenth and Eighteenth Dynasties, kind of like marrying into the old family, but the Ramesside kings were decidedly different in political and religious methodology.

27.8. A decentralized and competitive society

Many things had changed since the extraordinary highs and deep lows of the Eighteenth Dynasty. Indeed, the entire Ramesside period can be understood as a rebalancing of power after the audacious stunts of kings like Akhenaten (or even his father Amenhotep III; 1388–1350 BC). For one thing, no longer would the Egyptian elites give unfettered and unbridled power to their king, not even to a king like Rameses II. From now on, every king would have to work with a stronger and more vocal elite, men who now expected recognition for their own work, who felt entitled to hand down their own positions to their eldest sons,[53] who would not kowtow to their king and would not follow him in ridiculous schemes that laid Egypt low. The balance of power had shifted, and not in the king's favor. His was a power now bridled, as was the power of his queen.

---

52. For this new assessment, see Candelora 2019b.

53. Raedler 2006.

Ramesside royal strategies of procreation and family were also decidedly different from those of the Eighteenth Dynasty. Incestuous couplings between royal brother and sister were no longer as commonplace or expected in the Nineteenth and Twentieth Dynasties, as they had been previously in the Eighteenth Dynasty.[54] Such incestuous unions maintained power among a select few within a closed society, excluding everyone else. But the new balance of power in the Ramesside period between king and elite would not allow elites to be cut out of the administration of Egypt. Egyptologists know of few openly expressed unions between royal son and royal daughter, thus limiting the kind of internal power such relationships could produce. Indeed, there is no evidence that Nefertari was a sister to Rameses II (1279–1213 BC), or that Tausret was a sister of Sety II (1199–1193 BC), or that Rameses III (1181–1150 BC) married his sisters and elevated any of them to Great Royal Wife. The Ramesside kings did not rely on the placement of their daughters or sisters in the position of the God's Wife of Amun position either, as had been so common in the earlier part of the Eighteenth Dynasty.[55]

We do not see evidence of any biological issue from such unions rising to power, either, as we had in the Eighteenth Dynasty.[56] The royal

---

54. Although marriage to half-sisters did occur, there seems to be less reliance on the offspring of those unions; see Dodson and Hilton 2004.

55. Queen Tausret may be an exception, given how powerful she was, but she was neither a king's daughter nor a king's sister and seems to have been used as a political tool by the chancellor Bay. The fact that she was named God's Wife of Amun is indicative of the great political power that came with this priestly position, but the fact remains that Tausret was not descended from royalty; see Callender 2004. In the Eighteenth Dynasty, there are many examples of royal women using offices like the God's Wife of Amun for political advancement. In the Nineteenth and Twentieth Dynasties, the office of God's Wife of Amun seems deficient in comparison as a tool of power. For more on the office of God's Wife of Amun, see Robins 1983; Bryan 2005; Ayad 2007; 2009; 2016.

56. Amenhotep I was the product of two generations of full brother-sister procreation, and we should not be surprised he had no offspring, thus inviting Thutmose I into a kingship to which he had not been born. We can examine Tutankhamun as a product of incest, now genetically proven, perhaps one possible reason for his untimely death; see Hawass et al. 2010.

family was undoubtedly genetically healthier for avoiding the incest of previous royal generations, but eschewing this royal prerogative also systematically removed royal women from positions of power, taking what had been a closed, protectionist system that named only few, genetically connected people to power, instead splaying it wide open, into a raging infection of dozens of competitive elements. Ironically, this new adaptation toward more broadly construed power did not mean that members of the royal family were not interrelated. Indeed, members of the Ramesside royal family were all probably connected to one another more closely than would be considered healthy today for legally married couples, as first, second, and third cousins.

There was a new political pressure in the Ramesside period to publicly identify royal offspring, whether they were crown prince or not, whether they were male or female, as the line-ups of royal children in the temples of Rameses II and Rameses III prove.[57] In the Eighteenth Dynasty, although it was never explicitly stated, the mention of a prince in public displays was exceedingly rare, and generally only done, we assume, when said son was named as the next heir to his father, the king. Otherwise, Eighteenth Dynasty royal sons were absent from the temple spaces viewed by Egyptian elites, melting into normal elite society after one of their brothers was chosen to be king. This practice of making king's sons invisible must have kept the competition down at the time of succession, when a choice had to be made over who would become king next. But in the Ramesside period, king's sons were publicly identified, and with abandon.[58] Decorum had changed. It seems members of the Ramesside royal family were free to advertise their connection to the king, to fly their power like a banner to other elites, and presumably to their own brothers, of whom there were many because the harem of the Nineteenth and Twentieth Dynasties seems to have exploded in size and

---

57. Weeks 1995; Haring 1997; Fisher 2001; Leblanc 2016.

58. Indeed, this may have been a Levantine or delta-style strategy. Cf. Candelora 2019b, who links Hyksos kinship structure to the title King's Son in the Ramesside period, arguing that both systems of rule follow an openly displayed kinship structure.

complexity, too.[59] Everyone wanted a shout-out, and the new decentralized system of power demanded that these king's children, the highest of Egypt's elites, be identified to everyone as such.

In Ramesside Egypt, the running of the ever more complex Egyptian state demanded broader political coverage, social expertise, deal making, alliance building, and family connection. Sons were useful. Now that a different kind of social complexity had set in, the king's extended family members were formally placed with their own hereditary positions in the temple, treasury, military, and so on, like a general placing lieutenants in strategic offices and locations. The Ramesside king could no longer keep all the control in centralized fashion. He had to contend with an established mass of decentralized and connected family power that needed to be appeased—with honors and recognition, with titles and income—in exchange for their cooperation. No matter that he was perceived as divine incarnate, the king needed his sons to make himself strong.

27.9. Patronage and personal agency

Ramesside systems were rife with shifts in patronage and upheavals of the social norms.[60] What was previously "state funded," or sourced from a state monopoly, through personal intervention of the king and personal connection to his vizier, was now often institutionalized in complex army and/or temple systems with visible bureaucracies.[61] The Ramesside period should be seen as a construct of changing social systems—from

---

59. Redford 2002; Shaw 2011; Roth 2012. For idealized scenes of the harem of Rameses III, see Epigraphic Survey 1970.

60. Eyre 2011. For a different understanding of Ramesside society organized around "favor" of the king, see Guksch 1994; Raedler 2009; Binder 2012. Such an outlook uncritically views the king as having all the power in the center of the circle of power, because this is what is explicitly stated in most available sources. Raedler 2012 takes a more critical view, seeing the growing numbers of named elites and family members as endemic of significant patronage shifts from the Eighteenth to Nineteenth Dynasties and the concomitant loss of the king's power to a more powerful and competitive group of elites.

61. Haring 2007: 165; Cooney 2007.

one ruled by personal connection to the king to one ruled by the increasingly professionalized institutions of army and temple. Instead of the tightly organized and impenetrable old patrician units of family power of the Seventeenth and Eighteenth Dynasties, the Nineteenth and Twentieth Dynasties would sort themselves out through military and temple hierarchies and competition, allowing even men from mercenary families to rise up to the top of the social pyramid.[62]

These two institutions—temple and army—were the power brokers of the Ramesside period, and they would remain so throughout the Third Intermediate Period to follow (see chapter 25 in this volume and chapter 36 in volume 4). They seem to have remained largely separate in income and personnel from the king's treasuries and from each other throughout the Nineteenth Dynasty, but by the end of the Twentieth Dynasty, temple and army started to merge out of defensive and creative adaptation, with the High Priest of Amun eventually holding the highest military authority in the south.[63] The concomitant privatization of these patronage shifts—from king and his vizierate to high priest and general—is visible too. Mercenaries were necessary elements of army recruitment; professionalized priests could pass down their lineages within their own families.[64]

27.10.   *Writing a history of the Ramesside period*

There are many ways to write a history of the Ramesside period, and perhaps focusing on the mass of society would be the most helpful way to go

---

62. Wilkinson 2010: 282–368.

63. That is not to say there was no interchange of personnel between the two institutions, just that few men show leadership in *both* institutions at the same time until late in the Twentieth Dynasty. For example, the high priest of Amun under Rameses II, Bakenkhonsu, began his career as an archer in Sety I's army, then entered the Amun priesthood. Later his two sons, Paser and Amenmesses, would become governors of Thebes; see Jansen-Winkeln 1993.

64. For a discussion of the continuity of positions within families, see Raedler 2016.

about it—on the agricultural laborers, soldiers, local priests, craftsmen, housewives, and householders. But such an approach would miss the real power brokers at the top of the system and lose sight of how much the system itself was changing. Keeping all the many assumptions about the Ramesside period in mind, perhaps it is best to use a traditional narrative path that tracks power from king to king, reign to reign, so that we can identify changing patterns in the manufacture of that power, as well as the rise of conflicts and shifting patrons. The following is organized into five different periods within the Ramesside period, each of which is representative of its own power players and patterns:

(1) its beginnings with Horemheb (1319–1292 BC) at the end of the Eighteenth Dynasty and then on to Rameses I (1292–1290 BC) and Sety I (1290–1279 BC) of early Nineteenth Dynasty;

(2) the reign of Rameses II (1279–1213 BC) and his son Merenptah (1213–1203 BC);

(3) the later Nineteenth Dynasty, including the civil war between Sety II and Amenmessu and the female king Tausret;

(4) the reign of Rameses III (1181–1150 BC), including the palace competition that resulted in his murder; and finally,

(5) the end of the Ramesside kings, including civil war and the eventual failure of kingship in Bronze Age Egypt.

27.10.1. The beginnings of the Ramesside period

If the Eighteenth Dynasty was a time of expanding power led by a small circle of royals at court, supported by exclusive, patrician families, then the Ramesside period was a time of diminishing political returns in which power was wielded more broadly by leadership of and membership in complex, and sometimes unwieldy, institutions. How did this new social reality come to be? One could argue that it was the reliance of Akhenaten (1350–1334 BC) on military yes-men that moved Egypt inexorably in this direction. From this perspective, the Ramesside period could be said to have begun with the death of Tutankhamun (1333–1323 BC), the last king of the Eighteenth Dynasty family lineage. When his chief royal wife Ankhesenamun was denied rule as a female king (as had happened at the end of the Twelfth Dynasty and which we might expect in the Eighteenth Dynasty closed royal system, too), a non-royal, Ay, seized power instead, and the age of the divine dynastic succession in Egypt was over. When Ankhesenamun was forced to "marry her servant" (if the letter from the Hittite king about Queen Tahamunzu did indeed refer to Ankhesenamun), such a partnership would have justified Ay's kingship through marriage to the last member standing of the royal lineage.[65] Egypt would never be the same again.

The king list of Sety I at Abydos skips to Horemheb (1319–1292 BC) after Amenhotep III (1388–1350 BC), essentially cutting out all Amarna kings, including Ay (1323–1319 BC), himself not of royal blood, proving that, for the Ramessides, Horemheb's reign marked their new beginning.[66] Horemheb's power grab can be seen as a coup against the Eighteenth Dynasty royal family that created new power bases within military systems.[67] Horemheb may have accompanied Akhenaten on his schemes of religious excess to Middle Egypt, but if he did, he now erased that part of his past. Horemheb was from Herakleopolis Magna at the entrance to the Fayum.[68] The tomb he had prepared before his kingship was placed at the necropolis of Saqqara.[69] Horemheb found his base of power in Memphis and Heliopolis, not in the southern Nile valley. Still, he knew that Thebes was the homeland of the Eighteenth Dynasty kings. He thus started a campaign to ideologize his reign with a great edict set up at Karnak temple, alongside some significant new temple structures, including a great pylon quickly made with old blocks from Akhenaten's kingship on a filled-in quay, embellished with no less than eight massive

---

65. Known as the "Zannanza Affair" and recorded in the "Deeds of Suppululiuma"; see Theis 2011 and chapters 28 and 30 in this volume.

66. Gundlach 2003.

67. Kitchen 1975: I 176–179; Redford 1986.

68. For the life of Horemheb, see Hari 1965; Philips 1977; Dodson 2009; Kawai 2010; Booth 2013.

69. Martin et al. 1989.

Lebanese cedar trunks, each over ten stories tall, plated in bronze and electrum, inlaid with lapis lazuli.[70] He ensured that his allegiance to the ancestor kings of Thebes was on display; his Son of Ra name ended in "beloved of Amun, Divine Ruler of Thebes." And, like the kings of the Eighteenth Dynasty, he was buried in the Valley of the Kings on Thebes' West Bank.[71] Every Tutankhamun statue on view was claimed by him, the previous name erased, Horemheb's incised upon it instead.[72]

But make no mistake, Horemheb's new kingship was not based on old family power from conservative and stodgy Thebes, but on a New Man's northern military connections.[73] It seems that connections to military power were needed now more than ever. The years of opportunistic campaigning by warrior kings like Ahmose (1550–1525 BC), Thutmose I (1504–1492 BC) and III (1479–1425 BC), or Amenhotep II (1425–1397 BC), were long gone. Egypt's hegemony in the Levant still held,[74] but the Hittites were extending their power south, eating away territory that had once been Egypt's (see chapter 30 in this volume). We should likely assume that Egypt's elite—northern and southern—was in favor of this takeover by a military man with aspirations, rather than pushing for some candidate three degrees removed from a failed dynasty.

------

70. His building program was quickly realized, and not built to last. According to Blyth 2006, the pylon in question was falling apart by the time the Ptolemies were ruling Egypt.

71. Davis and Crane 1912; Roehrig 2016: 183.

72. E.g., the statue in the Oriental Institute Museum of the University of Chicago (accession number D.15824): Green, Evans, and Teeter 2017: 52–54.

73. Particularly if Horemheb was the same man as Paatenemheb, scribe of the King and general during the reign of Akhenaten. During the reign of Tutankhamun, we see a man with a similar name, Horemheb, appear as general of generals. Cf. Wilkinson 2010, stressing the military institutional might as the foundation of the Ramesside period.

74. There was no clear reduction of Egypt's presence in the Southern Levant during Horemheb's reign, and indeed there might have been an expansion after Akhenaten's reign. But the Ramesside period as a whole was a time of sustaining and then reducing territory, as it went forward, in comparison to the trends of expansion and growth during most of the Eighteenth Dynasty; see Weinstein 1981.

Horemheb may have even had mercenary roots himself, though there is no direct evidence for this. It seems he was so worried about the perception of his own past that he created a theological justification for his royal power grab, a story claiming the Horus of his hometown Herakleopolis had known that he would someday become king, keeping him safe, because he was destined for the throne.[75] His (new?) name Horemheb, "Horus is in festival," assuming he had to change a name previously used during the Amarna period, worked perfectly for such a claim. His first kingly steps included a thorough destruction of Akhenaten's heresy and a dismantling of the sacred city of Akhetaten (modern Tell el-Amarna), setting Egypt back onto a path of religious orthodoxy. Like King Amenhotep I, whose (incestuously determined?) lack of heir caused him to choose Thutmose I as his successor, Horemheb's lack of an heir steered him toward another military man, this one named Paramessu, a general of the chariotry, with origins in the eastern delta.

Horemheb named Paramessu as his adopted heir to the throne by titling him "King's Son."[76] Statues of this man were found at Karnak's Tenth Pylon, seated in a scribal position and wearing a long wig.[77] At some point, Paramessu changed his name to Rameses Meryamun, "Ra is born, beloved of Amun," which he now wrote in a single cartouche, as a king's chosen heir and crown prince would do.

In the coming generations, the attention of Egypt's elites would soon shift north to a new capital city, Piramesses, "the House of Rameses," in the eastern delta.[78] Egypt's nascent royal power so often came from its south; its first royal dynasty was from Abydos; subsequent reorganizations of royal power came from Thebes in the Eleventh and Seventeenth Dynasties. This new reorganization, however, was decidedly different,

---

75. See the Coronation Edict on the back of his dyad statue and the Karnak Edict of Horemheb, inscribed at the base of his Tenth Pylon at Karnak (Turin 1379); see Gardiner 1953; Gabolde 1987.

76. Aldred 1968: 100–102; Miller 1986: 9–11; Polz 1986: 161–164; Murnane 1995: 192–196.

77. Blyth 2006.

78. The city was likely started by Sety I; see Bietak and Forstner-Müller 2011.

probably because the base of Egypt's military hegemony was situated in the north, and the north was now the source of its kingly power, too.[79] For many conservative Egyptians and probably for many patricians along the Nile valley, this new Ramesside dynasty may have been perceived as an "outsider" family. Like the Hyksos kings before them, these were men from the eastern delta, probably with Levantine origins. Their family names included Seth, an Egyptian god of the Red Lands associated with foreign storm gods like Ba'al. These men were of military, mercenary stock. They were "Egyptianized", to be sure, but the maintenance of the very name Seth suggests they still clung to many northern or even Levantine traditions, nonetheless.[80]

The Nineteenth Dynasty thus found its start when a military leader became king as Rameses I (1292–1290 BC). His eastern delta roots became ever more apparent when a son with the name of Seth— Sety I (1290–1279 BC) to modern Egyptologists—took the throne.[81] For some Egyptians, having an upstart named Seth on the throne of Osiris must have seemed religious treason, but no dissatisfaction about the new Ramesside dynasty is ever recorded, just circumstantial indications that it was a sensitive issue.[82] For instance, Sety I was always careful in how his name was written in places of Osirian significance, particularly at his limestone temple to Osiris at Abydos where he usually used the *tit*-knot of protection instead of the Seth animal to spell out his name.[83]

79. Indeed, the early Eighteenth Dynasty kings set up military campaigns launching from the city of Tell el-Dab'a, which is arguably what made this site of Qantir so useful as a major military installation: see Bietak and Forstner-Müller 2011; Bietak 2017; Bietak and von Rüden 2018.

80. Candelora 2017: 201–208 (especially n. 50, n. 53); 2019a.

81. Masquelier-Loorius 2013.

82. For a discussion on how the "Quarrel of Apepi and Seqenenra" and its focus on the Seth cult might be a subtle rebellion by Theban scribal priests against Ramesside rule, see Di Biase-Dyson 2013: 229, n. 182. For arguments against this view, see Candelora 2020.

83. Brand 2000: 192–219.

The origins and identity of the Ramesside family need to be problematized in this northern light. Ethnicity of the Ramesside kings does not need to be discussed as a reason for conflict or a driver for particular types of rule, nor does the available evidence really allow such analysis of ethnic identity. Perhaps the family of Rameses I considered itself Levantine in origin, as had the Hyksos centuries earlier (their Sethian names suggest it), but we can nonetheless discuss the geographic and potential mercenary origins of this royal family within a military institution of growing complexity and importance within the eastern delta, a cosmopolitan and culturally hybrid part of Egypt with deep ties to the Levant going back millennia.[84]

Egyptologists talk of the Hyksos kings of the Fifteenth Dynasty (chapter 23 in this volume) or the Libyan kings of the Twenty-first through Twenty-fourth Dynasties (chapters 35 and 36 in volume 4) or the Kushite kings of the Twenty-fifth Dynasty (chapter 37 in volume 4) as having foreign identities, but we generally do not analyze the Ramesside kings in such terms, even though their roots are likely just as foreign, possibly stemming back to Levantine families and Levantine social structures.[85] Both Rameses I of the Nineteenth Dynasty and Sethnakht (1185–1181 BC) of the Twentieth Dynasty probably found their military beginnings in the mercenary past of their fathers and grandfathers. How far back in the past, we can never know, but we cannot expect such problematic family histories to have been proudly expressed.

These Ramesside men were quite different from what had come before, and everyone must have perceived it. The Egyptian priest-historian Manetho of the third century BC created the break between the Eighteenth and Nineteenth Dynasties for a reason, and it probably had something to do with the northern origins of this military family, perhaps even their perceived Levantine ethnic background.[86] Horemheb had established his own link with the Eighteenth Dynasty family

---

84. Candelora 2019a.

85. Cruz-Uribe 1978: 237–244.

86. Waddell 1940.

through marriage, as well as having taken over Tutankhamun's statuary, thus linking himself to Thebes. But these Ramesside men did not even try to marry into the old family—as Thutmose I (1504–1492 BC) likely had with the Eighteenth Dynasty family of Amenhotep I (1525–1504 BC), or as Ay (1323–1319 BC) had likely married a daughter of Akhenaten (1350–1334 BC). Either way, perhaps there was no royal female left to marry, or it was decided that there should be no more attempts to placate any elites of the Nile valley or to link this northern lineage with the older, more venerable, divine one of the south. Instead we see a fresh start, genetically, socially, and regionally.

From all we can see, the transition from the Eighteenth to the Nineteenth Dynasty was bloodless, implying a lack of force and outright agreement by all the power players involved, certainly even the blessing of the previous king Horemheb, himself a military man, who must have known, as his longish reign was coming to an end, that he had no (appropriate?) offspring to rule after him. In typical Egyptian fashion, actions of militarism were avoided in the same moment that overt military rule was embraced. Indeed, one could argue that just as Mohammed Morsi was pushed aside for General Abdel Fattah el-Sisi in 2013 AD, the ancient Egyptian army drove Akhenaten's religious extremism out in favor of Horemheb's new military order in which another military man, Paramessu, was chosen as heir.[87] Paramessu's other title, "Lieutenant of His Majesty in Upper and Lower Egypt,"[88] was an unusual and special title indicating he was somehow handpicked by Horemheb and groomed for the kingship. This Paramessu would have had time to prepare himself before the death of Horemheb, to turn away from his old life on the march and move into the palaces. Eventually, as King Rameses I, he would have found himself closeted away with priests and seers to create his initiations and investiture, learning new and complicated rituals as Egypt's chief priest, empowering himself to take on a harem of his own. And the family of Rameses I would have had time to prepare their

---

87. For Rameses I and his origins, see Polz 1986.

88. Grandet 2016: 16–19.

own strategies as well; we can imagine brothers and nephews, sisters and nieces, sons and daughters, cousins and distant relations all jockeying for their place in this new royal game.

Maybe because he was a delta man, or maybe because he knew that his rule was setting Egypt off into a new direction after the great chaos of Akhenaten (who by now was openly called a heretic), Rameses I styled his new throne names off those of the founder of the Eighteenth Dynasty, Ahmose (1550–1525 BC), proudly responsible for "expelling" the Hyksos. Instead of Nebpehtyra, "Lord of the Strength of Ra," as Ahmose was called, Rameses I's new throne name was Menpehtyra "The Strength of Ra Endures."[89] Some Egyptians may have found irony in a king himself descended from Levantine invaders naming himself after the monarch responsible for expelling just such interlopers. Perhaps Rameses I was only following the most astute politicians—taking the most obvious weakness and turning it into a positive by openly acknowledging his family's past membership in a problematic and marginalized group and then stating that that membership was now defunct.

The Four Hundred Year Stele found at Tanis suggests that Rameses I already had a son and grandson when he took the throne,[90] an aberrant admission according to the old, Eighteenth Dynasty, rules of kingship. Another stele in the Oriental Institute Museum in Chicago tells us that Rameses I's father was also called Sety and had been a military commander, too:[91] all strangely personal and overtly human things to point out for a god-king—certainly in the eyes of the most conservative Egyptians and something completely inappropriate in any Eighteenth Dynasty court context (one wonders if any patrician families rolled their eyes at such upstart revelations of family background or the vagaries of mortal existence pre-divinity?). Thutmose I (1504–1492 BC) of the Eighteenth Dynasty had never mentioned his father or wife or children prior to his kingship, as there seem to have been strong cultural

---

89. Leprohon 2013: 108.

90. Murnane 1995: 185–217. See also Kitchen 1979: 287–288.

91. Cruz-Uribe 1978: 237–244.

strictures at knowing such earthly details about the new divine Horus. But the Ramessides were not shy about claiming a strong and vigorous family of sons; indeed, it seems to have constituted a foundation of their political power. This, as much as the family's military heritage, tells us that Egyptian politics had changed significantly since the Eighteenth Dynasty. What had been a close-to-the-vest circle of royal family members and court intimates about which little was divulged to the outside world was now a well-publicized and well-known set of New Men with ambitions and past lives they not only did not try to hide, but openly displayed on monumental steles. Perhaps these Ramessides did not have to pretend divinity prior to investiture specifically because they were not trying to marry into the Theban royal family of old.

The Four Hundred Year Stele even states that Rameses I's family came from ancestors with titles like "vizier", "royal scribe", "master of horse", and "fan-bearer of the king's right", personal details that perhaps eased anxious minds ruminating about a messy succession when Rameses I would meet his end. The same stele celebrates the re-establishment of the cult of Seth at Avaris, the Hyksos stronghold of old where—fittingly or shockingly, depending on your perspective—the city of Piramesses and the base of Ramesside power would be located.[92] Cultural norms were being broken.

Choosing an accomplished general as its next king came with a price. If he had proven himself on the battlefield, then he was already an adult male, and adult males died easily in ancient Egypt. Rameses I flew to heaven after only a year and a half on the throne. The son and chosen successor, Sety I (1290–1279 BC), was cognizant of his place as restorer of kingship and order after the great harm caused by a megalomaniacal and ideologically obsessed Akhenaten (1350–1334 BC) of the Eighteenth Dynasty. But Sety I must also have been aware of the fact that he was named for a storm god of the desert, Seth, a divinity associated with Ba'al of the Levant, but, for whatever reason, he chose not to change his name. He just added the epithet "beloved of Ptah," a shout-out to his main capital city of Memphis before the re-establishment of Qantir in

---

92. Candelora 2017: 207, n. 50.

the eastern delta. Sety's new throne name was Menmaatra, "The Justice of Ra Is Established," a clear link to the throne name Nebmaatra, "Lord of the Justice of Ra" of Amenhotep III (1425–1397 BC).[93]

It was thus of strategic political and ideological importance that Sety I focused building operations at the site of Abydos, burial place of Osiris and ground zero of strong Upper Egyptian kingship.[94] Like Rameses I's mimicking of Eighteenth Dynasty Theban founder Ahmose's throne name, Sety I was interested in connecting his kingship to the southern land from which kingship arose at the very beginning of Egypt's state formation. His Abydos temple dedicated to Osiris was the ultimate pious display to southern models of Osirian kingship, and its building must have been accompanied by multiple pilgrimages to broadcast his orthodoxy. At this temple, he visibly placed his kingship at the center of a cosmic unity of the gods of Memphis, Heliopolis, Abydos, and Thebes.

Sety I seems to have been aware that he was infiltrating an archaic club that likely would not previously have had him as a member, and so within his Abydos temple, he depicted himself and his son Rameses, his chosen heir, in front of the cartouche names of sixty-seven previous kings, going all the way back to the first king of Egypt who found his origins within Egypt's south, if not at Abydos itself, then nearby.[95] Not included were those kings who were perceived to have caused Egypt harm: the female king Hatshepsut (1479–1458 BC) and any ruler connected to Akhenaten's heresy (see chapter 26 in this volume), including the Aten follower Akhenaten himself, but also Smenkhkara, Tutankhamun, and Ay. Horemheb (1319–1292 BC) remained; that old military man was the reason for the Ramesside family's dynasty in the first place. A statue of Sety I, showing the kneeling king with a smiling mouth set into a broad face, probably once displayed at his Osiris temple at Abydos, is now in the Metropolitan Museum of Art (figure 27.2).

---

93. Gundlach 2003; Masquelier-Loorius 2013: 31–35.

94. Brand 2000.

95. Kitchen 1975: I 176–179; Redford 1986.

FIGURE 27.2. Statue of Sety I, made of granodiorite. The Metropolitan Museum of Art, New York. Rogers Fund, 1922 (accession number 22.2.21). CCo 1.0 Universal (CCo 1.0) Public Domain Dedication.

Sety I may have had an insecure streak as the son of an old general, not born into the palace. Indeed, with every stone that was cut for his temples or for his tomb, he ordered his artisans to take the time to create works of not only great quality and care, but ingenuity. He seems to have modeled his monumental production on that of Amenhotep III, his namesake. His limestone temple at Abydos is thus filled with scenes of extraordinary creativity, cut with masterful lines and expertly filled with color. His tomb (KV 17), cut into the Theban Valley of the Kings, was the most extensively and painstakingly decorated of the entire royal necropolis.[96] His tomb was also the longest of its kind at 136 m, with passages

---

96. Hornung, Burton, and Hill 1991.

extending even beyond the burial chamber holding his sarcophagus. He ordered the workmen to cut an unprecedented tunnel from the burial chamber deeper into the western hillside, the reasons for which remain mysterious. His memorial "Qurna" temple on Thebes' West Bank and his Abydos temple each included chapels for his father Rameses I. Sety I also likely began the transformation of an open courtyard between Pylons 2 and 3 at Karnak into the extraordinary hypostyle hall later finished by his son Rameses II.[97] His monumental reliefs are still visible on the hall's western side. Indeed, many of Sety's other artistic works—like colossal statuary or obelisks, are now believed to have been taken over by his son Rameses II (1279–1213 BC).[98]

This was a dynasty founded on military might, and during his ten- or eleven-year reign,[99] Sety I kept his guns blazing. Frequent campaigning, particularly against his Hittite enemies of Anatolia, was documented in temple scenes throughout Egypt, but is particularly well-preserved at Karnak temple at Thebes on the northern wall of the hypostyle hall.[100] His foreign campaigns focused on the northeast, especially the southern Levant, where he regained the fortified cities of Beth-Shean and Yenoam, and in the northern Levant, where he demanded better trading deals with local kings for cedar and resins. He also moved into Syria, taking back hegemony over the stronghold city of Qadesh on the Orontes river from the Hittites.[101] He documented all of these victories in reliefs at temples throughout Egypt, but they survive best at the temple of Amun-Ra at Karnak in Thebes.[102] Taking Qadesh meant picking a fight with a powerful Hittite enemy that the Egyptians were not fully prepared to take on, at least in the long run. Although many Egyptologists claim it was Sety I who restored Egypt's "empire," it seems Egypt could not keep

---

97. Vandersleyen 1995; Brand 2000: 228–249.

98. Revez and Brand 2015: 308.

99. Beckerath 1997: 190.

100. Revez and Brand 2015.

101. Murnane 1990: 51–65; Spalinger 2005: 195–197. See also chapter 28 in this volume.

102. Epigraphic Survey 1986.

Qadesh even during his reign. It would fall back into Hittite hands, a secondary state polity with functional imperial systems and strategies, leaving a problem for the young Rameses in the early years of his kingship.[103]

Sety I was likely forty-something years of age when he died, lining up with his ten- to eleven-year reign length from documentary evidence. Sety I's mummy was found in Theban Tomb (TT) 320, the so-called royal cache at Deir el-Bahri by Émile Brugsch,[104] and examination of that mummy corroborates a death around that age.[105] His alabaster coffin is now housed in the Sir John Soane Collection in London.[106]

Although much ink has been spilled about whether or not Sety I and Rameses II had a co-regency, the evidence suggests instead that it was Ramesside policy to name (and depend upon) the crown prince before the death of the king.[107] Sety was, after all, named during the reign of his own father Rameses I. And Rameses II was named and pictured in the Abydos temple of his father. No formal concept of co-regency is needed, if we understand the Ramesside transfer of kingly power as more transparent and openly declared than what we saw earlier in the Eighteenth Dynasty.

27.10.2. Rameses II and Merenptah

When Rameses II (1279–1213 BC) came to the throne, he was already the second Rameses of that name in his family dynasty. We should likely assume a name change—to Rameses—for the boy at some point, since his grandfather had been renamed as Rameses himself, at least according to

---

103. Warburton 2003b.

104. For the royal cache discovered at Deir el-Bahri, see Maspero 1882; Brugsch 1889; Daressy 1909; Belova 2003; Niwiński 2007; Graefe and Belova 2010.

105. Smith 1912.

106. Anonymous 1844; Budge 1908; Taylor and Dorey 2017.

107. See Brand 2000: chapter 4. Kitchen 1985: 27–30 thus rejects the term co-regency and instead prefers the term "prince regency."

the Four Hundred Year Stele. The choice of name is telling; this family already understood kinship, lineage and marketing. The name Seth was not as helpful to them and was thus rarely used by this family, with only two kings of that name; but there were to be eleven kings named Rameses.

Rameses II himself likely understood the need to broadcast his membership to this tribe. Even his throne name, Usermaatra Setepenra, "The Justice of Ra is Powerful, Chosen of Ra," was a shout-out to the founder of Ramesside militaristic power, Horemheb, who was the first to include the epithet Setepenra with his name.[108] Indeed, there may have been some reason for Rameses II to be insecure about his place on the throne, at least initially. It is possible that there were other plans for succession within a certain fan bearer (and royal son?) named Mehy, singled out in his father Sety I's Karnak reliefs, as his names and images were carefully removed and replaced with Rameses II's form and cartouche.[109] If this redecoration indicates some kind of disagreement about the chosen heir, we will never know. The extraordinary sixty-seven-year reign of Rameses II, however, does indicate that the king was a very young man at his accession, maybe barely in his teens, perhaps suggesting that some older son(s) were passed over.

Unlike his father, Rameses II would not have remembered much time when he was not the king's son. He may not have been the crown prince for all of his father's reign, but palace life was his normal state. He would have seen his father go on campaign, maybe even accompanied him on some of them, and his own kingship would experience the repercussions of these campaigns, particularly in the Levant and Syria. It was to the northeast that Rameses II cast his eye during the first five years of his reign. This new king was young and, we can presume, interested in creating his legacy in the manner of Thutmose III of the Eighteenth Dynasty. In Rameses' Year 2, he faced a group of so-called *Shardana* (*Sherden*) people of the north, one of the first mentions of such Sea

---

108. For full titulary, see von Beckerath 1999; Gundlach 2003.

109. But see the debate in Murnane 1977: 60–61; 1990: 107–114; 1995: 199; Epigraphic Survey 1986: pls. 6, 10, 12, 23 and 29; Brand 2011: 51–84.

Peoples, attacking Egyptian cargo vessels in the Mediterranean.[110] The origins of these *Shardana* people are disputed, but their name may be connected to the now-named island of Sardinia.

The Eighteenth Dynasty warlord kings before him had expanded their influence all the way into northern Syria, and now Rameses II wanted to repeat their glories, like later Marc Antony wanting to mimic Alexander the Great's exploits in Asia. In other words, Rameses II's military agenda started with what his father could not finish, much like George W. Bush re-invading Iraq after George H. W. Bush's visible failure. In Year 4, Rameses started those Syrian campaigns, resulting in an inscription carved into the rocks at the Nahr el-Kalb in Lebanon, just north of Beirut.

But now the Hittites called. The Syrian city of Qadesh was already back in Hittite hands, and the city's leaders refused to pay tribute to nonexistent Egyptian overlords. In his fifth year, Rameses moved his forces north.[111] He took on the Hittites under the leadership of King Muwatalli at the city of Qadesh on the Orontes river. According to some who have reconstructed the battle tactics, this was the largest chariot battle ever known, including some 5,000 charioteers.[112] Spies were captured and interrogated. Mercenaries fought on each side. The details of the battle are many and the scholarly literature beyond extensive.[113] Suffice it to say that Rameses II and the divisions of his army—named after the gods Ra, Ptah, Amun, and Seth—were outnumbered. The accounts tell us that were it not for the strategic brilliance and bravery of Rameses, all alone and undefended ("No officer was with

---

110. For more on the *Shardana* (*Sherden*) people, see Giacomo 2015: 631–638; Dayton 1984: 353–371, and cf. chapter 28 in this volume.

111. The Battle of Qadesh occurred in Rameses' Second Syrian Campaign (Year 5), whereas the stele was not carved until later campaigns in Year 8 or 9; see Kitchen 1979: 223–224.

112. Spalinger 2005.

113. To highlight but a few: Goedicke 1966; Goedicke 1985; Murnane 1990; Spalinger 2002; Hasel 2011.

me, no charioteer, no soldier of the army, no shield-bearer"[114]), all would have been lost.

Two detailed documents—one called by Egyptologists the Poem and the other the Bulletin—record the fated meeting between Egypt and Hatti.[115] These accounts are represented in many places where Rameses II commissioned monumental construction, including Karnak and Luxor temples, Abu Simbel, his mortuary complex at the Ramesseum, and his temple at Abydos. When images are preserved, the king is shown at superhuman scale in his chariot, charging forward to save the day. It is a heroic tale reminiscent of Thutmose III (1479–1425 BC) leading the charge at Megiddo, or of Ahmose (1550–1525 BC) expelling the "vile and foreign" Hyksos out of Egypt and sieging their cities in the southern Levant. If Rameses II's geographic background gave pause to any of his elites, this was a perfect method to dispel any doubt that he would combat the forces of chaos and keep Egypt safe. This was Rameses' moment, par excellence.

And yet, Hittite documentation from their capital city of Hattusa (modern Boğazköy) suggests a different account in which Rameses slunk from the battle in defeat, Qadesh not taken, empire not re-won.[116] Spin, it seems, was everything. The Qadesh battle of Year 5 was recounted by Rameses II again and again, even though, significantly, Qadesh itself did not seem to return to paying Egypt any tribute. Perhaps the siege of Qadesh's high walls proved too difficult, or other logistical problems prevailed, but Rameses would rewrite the outcome nonetheless. From their perspective, Egypt returned from Syria having proven a point. In his eighth and ninth years, Rameses II continued campaigns in the Levant, focusing on sites where Thutmose III had previously been, and building multiple fortresses in Canaan especially, suggesting some

---

114. Lichtheim 1976: 65.

115. Breasted 1904; Gardiner 1960; Lichtheim 1976: 57; Ockinga 1987; Spalinger 2002.

116. Ockinga 1987; Bryce 2006. For a Ramesside letter to the Hittites referencing complaints about the veracity of the Egyptian account, see Kitchen 1979: 13.

attempt at administrative control over the southern Levant, though not the north.[117]

Things got complicated for the Hittites at this point, as there was a succession crisis at Hattusa. A deposed Hittite king fled to Egypt, and the new king Hattušili III demanded his return.[118] In Year 21 of Rameses II, a treaty was struck, the first written treaty preserved to human history.[119] It is recorded in both Hittite cuneiform and Egyptian hieroglyphs, with detailed descriptions about terms and whose territory was whose. Essentially, we see a mutual nonaggression pact by two regional states, sealed with the marriage of Rameses II to the Hittite princess Maathorneferura.[120] Over the *longue durée*, we might understand this alliance as the last gasp of two kings leading regional states to create a united force against the growing empires in the east that would find their true strength with the Iron Age. But for now, it was just a treaty, the details of which we have preserved at Karnak temple.[121] It was likely at this point, around his twenty-first regnal year, that Rameses II would decorate his temples in earnest with scenes of his imperial conquest in Syria in Year 5.

The new capital city of Piramesses was now strong and functional, described more as an industrial compound of weapons manufacture than anything else, as texts mention the construction of thousands of chariots in the weeks leading up to the campaign.[122] Rameses' father Sety I had

117. Burke et al. 2017.

118. Bryce 1998: xii–xiv; Hoffner 2009.

119. Langdon and Gardiner 1920; Allam 2010.

120. According to the Marriage Stele; see Kitchen 1975–1990: 257. A papyrus with her name (Petrie Museum, University College London, P.32795) provides evidence that Maathorneferura was living in Rameses II's harem at Gurob; see Gardiner 1948: x–xi, 22–24; Kitchen 1979: 857; Roth 2003; Fisher 2013.

121. Langdon and Gardiner 1920; Blyth 2006.

122. Drawing mainly on the results of the excavations led by Edgar Pusch, Wilkinson 2010: 314 states about Piramesses that it was "less pleasure dome and more military-industrial complex," as "the city's very foundation had been prompted by an upsurge in military activity in the Near East." For the excavations, see Pusch 1991; 1999; Dorner 1999; Bietak 2010.

already built a royal palace here near the Fifteenth Dynasty Hyksos forti-fied city of Avaris (*hut waret*) where the Four Hundred Year Stele was ostensibly first set up before it was moved to Tanis.[123] It was Rameses II who turned this palace into his new capital city, calling it Piramesses, "The House of Rameses," naming it after himself, to be sure, but also after the entire Ramesside clan that began with his grandfather Rameses I. Rameses II even retained the old Seth temple to the south of the city.[124]

His father Sety I had likely built a palace here because of his fam-ily's deep roots in the northeast delta region. This was their homeland. Rameses II's new capital of Piramesses was quite close to the strongholds of the Levantine-Hyksos warlords who had taken Egypt before, as well as to the Ways of Horus that led to Canaan and on to Syria. Ongoing excavations have uncovered a variety of new finds, including vast indus-trial areas and weapons installations, but also horse stables and, of course, sumptuous palaces, all set upon the raised *gezira*s where habitation would not be submerged by the yearly Nile floods.[125] Although there is no explicit documentation to this effect (and we should not expect it), the creation of this new capital city likely pulled Egypt even further apart into two opposing camps, marking the Ramesside kings as north-erners through and through, widening the ever-present divide between north and south, an unhealed Egyptian wound that would be opened again after the reign of Rameses II's son Merenptah.

Rameses II's building campaign is often remarked upon by Egyptologists as one of quantity rather than quality, of taking rather than creating.[126] He is most well-known for putting up temples as quickly and extensively as possible, often choosing sunken relief in sand-stone because it saved time and allowed massive structures bridging long divides simultaneously (Karnak's Hypostyle Hall could not have been

---

123. Bietak and Forstner-Müller 2011.

124. Habachi 1974.

125. Bietak and Forstner-Müller 2011; Franzmeier and Moje 2018.

126. Already Edwards 1888 commented on the abundant statues of Rameses II, but also on his reuse of other kings' statues. See also Sourouzian 1988; Bryan 2007; Brand 2010a; 2010b; Lorand 2011; Magen 2011; Connor 2017.

built without sandstone or sunk relief). Rameses II is also known as a
reuser of kings' temples and images before him. He took so many statues of Amenhotep III (1388–1350 BC) that his own portrait had to be
reshaped and reformed through that reuse, giving him two visages, one
a long and slender face, with thin lips and a long, aquiline nose, as seen
in his statue now in Turin's Museo Egizio, and another based on his constant reuse of Amenhotep III, with a broad and square face, full lips, and
wide nose, as seen even in non-reused monumental statuary throughout
Egypt, from his Temple to the Hearing Ear built at Karnak, to his Abu
Simbel temple hewn out of the live rock in the hills above the Second
Cataract of the Nile far to Egypt's south. Indeed, his choice of portrait
carved from the living rock at Abu Simbel was modeled on his mentor
Amenhotep III likely because it was that king who had previously built
so extensively in Nubia, at nearby Soleb and Sedeinga.

In other ways, Rameses II was only following his namesake Horemheb
in his wholesale reuse of previous kings' statuary. Horemheb had gone
on a re-inscription and usurpation spree where the Amarna kings
Smenkhkara, Tutankhamun, and Ay were concerned.[127] Now Rameses II
did the same, but using the production of earlier monarchs, particularly
Amenhotep III. Indeed, royal ownership of monuments, as we define
it, was broken by the time history reached Rameses II, for Rameses did
not just replace the royal names; he also modified the appearance of the
sculpture. And after him, his own son Merenptah would take this legacy
and run with it, creating statuary and structures largely reused from previous kings.[128]

Comparison of the relief work commissioned by father Sety I and
son Rameses II—at Abydos or at the Karnak Hypostyle Hall—shows
that the younger king did not demand the quality or artistry of his father,
but instead asked for steady, efficient, expansive, and above all, highly
visible work produced in large quantity. His goal, as the surviving evidence shows, was to blanket Egypt with his name and images in the

127. Brand 1999.

128. Royal ownership, as defined by Bryson 2018.

most monumental way possible. His hypostyle hall at Karnak continues to marvel with its massive scale, the broadest and tallest such columned hall preserved in Egypt.[129] His great pylon at Luxor temple showed him in bright, carved polychromy, defeating Hittite forces at Qadesh almost single-handedly.[130] He fronted it with two monumental seated statues of himself, four more standing statues, and two monolithic obelisks. Behind the pylon, he created a new solar court, filling the space with so many recut and reused standing statues that it is hard for the Egyptologist to sort out which were reused from Amenhotep III and which were made by him.[131] The solar court he built at Luxor temple shows none of the elegance or symmetry of the court built by Amenhotep III just beyond it in the same complex, but Rameses' demand to realign the axis with already existing Theban festival processional ways is apparent, as it created a trapezoidal shaped court when seen in bird's-eye view from above, betraying what must have been painstaking mathematical calculations to literally slant the court to the east. Rameses II was a man not concerned with qualitative details, but with the big picture. He added architecture and monumental statuary to Luxor temple in order to highlight his kingship within the larger Theban festival landscape, and he found engineers who could link his extension of this temple with already existing processional routes, moving half a dozen colossal statues of Amenhotep III from the West Bank of Thebes, to boot.

In contrast to most Eighteenth Dynasty monarchs, Rameses II showed little interest in adding to the secret shrines and back spaces into which earlier kings had felt the need to insert their names and figures. This Nineteenth Dynasty monarch was investing in big, open splashes of architecture and color, communicating to larger masses of people in the most public and visible places, not focusing his monuments on the holy-of-holies where only a few high elites could assemble. There are social conclusions to draw from such building patterns: Rameses II's building

129. Blyth 2006.

130. Abd el-Razik 1974; 1975.

131. Sourouzian 1988; Magen 2011.

program suggests that he felt the need to prove himself to a larger collection of elites, soldiers, craftsmen, and priests, in contrast to rulers like Amenhotep I or Hatshepsut, or even Amenhotep III, who concentrated their efforts on those most sacred and exclusive temple locations in Karnak and Luxor and thus to a more closed society of policymakers.

Rameses II's memorial temple, called today the Ramesseum, but "Rameses United with Thebes" by the ancient Egyptians, was situated where we would expect, on the West Bank of Thebes.[132] It had dozens of mudbrick granaries surrounding the stone temple. If almost 400 boatloads of wheat and barley were needed to fill such a granary, then the wealth displayed by Rameses II to his Theban people was truly extraordinary.[133] This economic wealth seemed in the control of the crown, but in just a few years, it would become apparent that treasuries and agricultural wealth connected to mortuary temples only empowered the institution of the Amun priesthood, rather than the king and his palaces. What seems to have been commissioned and owned outright by the king, to our eyes, would soon be in the hands of temple institutions who could channel wealth away from the king's own palace storerooms. From this perspective, the shift in patronage from king to temple was already underway.

One of Egypt's longest-lived rulers, Rameses II celebrated an unprecedented number of *sed* festivals to renew his kingship, the first one after the traditional thirty years of rule, and then a festival every two years or so thereafter.[134] His tomb in the Valley of the Kings (KV 7) is a testament to how the king displayed his power to his people.[135] He was not interested in lasting work, it seems, but in the present need to display grandeur. He chose a site, one must assume against the wishes of Theban engineers who knew the potential for flooding of the area, presumably

---

132. For the Ramesseum, see Griffith et al. 1898; Leblanc, Lecuyot, and Maher-Taha 2003; Leblanc 2016.

133. Wilkinson 2000: 311.

134. Erman 1891; Habachi 1971.

135. Leblanc 1997; 2009.

because it was better suited for ostentatious display. He eschewed laborious work to dig secret tunnels into the mountain, as his father Sety I had, preferring instead to maximize the visibility of his wealth.

The unique and grand tomb of his many sons (KV 5) was also placed in the same visible location in the King's Valley, easily found from the path by an elite ostensibly allowed to visit the sacred valley.[136] In the end, both tombs would be devastated by millennia of floods, their reliefs and colorful decoration long since destroyed. In the Valley of the Queens, Rameses established a new necropolis for his highly ranked wives, particularly for his Great Royal Wife Nefertari. Her tomb remains a testament to the skills of the Deir el-Medina workmen, whose artistic expression is just as fresh in the necropolis of the workmen's village within the polychrome tomb of Sennedjem (TT 1), as well as the so-called monochrome tombs of the same time period, known for their unusual iconography and creative expression.[137]

Toward the end of Rameses II's reign, there were harbingers of hard times to come. Incursions from the northwest were starting to become a problem, and Rameses started a line of fortresses along the northwest delta, each 50 miles from the other, a giant western wall to match the Ways of Horus along the northeast delta.[138] Egypt was bracing its borders against incursions by migrants who now seemed to come with greater frequency and in greater numbers.

As the king approached his eightieth year of life, crown princes must have been named and then died in succession, each time causing a mini upheaval of anxiety, as all the hierarchies and successions had to be rethought, until finally, the title of crown prince landed on the thirteenth son—a certain Merenptah—who got the position in Year 55 of his father. Everyone in Ramesside elite circles was likely related, and those connections were almost certainly carefully documented within

---

136. Aston and Weeks 1992; Weeks 2006.

137. Bruyère 1952.

138. For overviews, see Habachi 1955; 1980; Thomas 2000; Snape 2003; Morris 2005; Snape and Wilson 2007; Forstner-Müller 2018.

the family, albeit verbally, as far as we can tell. Within each new administration, each family would have looked to its own connection to the king, whether direct or circuitous, to its own nearest patriarch, its own king's son. The extended Ramesside family would likely have been one of ever forming and splintering alliances, some short lived, others seemingly unbreakable. And all the while, Rameses II continued to live on, while his sons died.

Even Prince Merenptah would wait for twelve years as heir to the throne before the kingship finally came to him. It is amazing Merenptah had any life left to give his country, considering the normal ancient Egyptian life span. He must have been at least fifty years old, with a wife and grown sons of his own, each with his own household and bastions of power, when he ascended the throne (1213–1203 BC). He probably had dozens of children, grandchildren, and even great-grandchildren already, all of whom now expected a slice of the pie. Although the appearances of a strong and centralized kingship were kept up with Merenptah's accession and although decorum was maintained by distinguished elites, the slices were getting increasingly thin, and the fighting for each morsel fiercer.

Perhaps we can blame some of this new competition on Rameses II's longevity. Even though most Egyptologists have long since dismissed a long reign, and the ostensible senility of an aged king, as a prime mover for collapse as too simplistic, it is worth asking again what the repercussions of Rameses' near seven decades in power were. In a normal reign of ten or twenty years, power moved seamlessly to the next generation. This generational hand-off of power was destabilized by Rameses' long life. Not only did Rameses II skip two generations, but he skipped three, not only seeing many of his own sons, and probably many of his grandsons, predecease him, but also effectively multiplying the number of candidates to vie for power and thus increasing social competition overall within the elite status group. In other words, if Rameses II had fifty named sons, and if only thirty or so were still living at his death, then there was still the competition from all the offspring of those sons, 500 or more young men, looking for their shot in the army, priesthood, or at court. Rameses II's longevity meant an expansion of competition among more stakeholders, not a decrease of it.

Thus, a long reign can manufacture a kind of generational crisis, effectively pitting the few older men left against the hungry younger set tired of waiting for their chance. Indeed, in Egypt, there is some slight evidence that the later Nineteenth Dynasty civil war was a battle of the older generation (Sety II) against the younger (Amenmessu), the proverbial uncle Seth versus the nephew Horus struggle, but with actual warlords, each with entourages and families of their own.[139] The long reign of Rameses II had not left Egyptian society on firm footing, as just ten to twelve years after his death, the land was plunged into a civil war between north and south, old and young.

Add to this the compounding social problems of the later Nineteenth Dynasty and we can see that the brightest years of the Ramesside period were already over. Merenptah's Year 5 brought with it a double whammy of revolt in Nubia plus invasions from a coalition of Libyans and so-called Sea Peoples.[140] These Sea Peoples seem to have come from southeastern Europe in mass migrations as their lands were devastated by drought, famine, and environmental collapse. Many had been pirates on the move already in the earlier Nineteenth Dynasty. Others had sold their services as mercenaries. Indeed, Merenptah's own army had Sea People mercenaries in it, in the same way that the United States Army employs many Central American non-citizens (hoping to become naturalized citizens) at its southern border to capture Central American migrants. Boundaries of who and what counted as Egyptian became fuzzy as need drove privatization of the armed forces. These new Sea Peoples brought extraordinary new protective gear and weaponry with them, allowing them to work as highly defensible, heavy infantry, difficult to bring down, even developing speedy chariots. The Libyan–Sea Peoples coalition apparently invaded from the west, entering the Nile valley near the necropolis of Dahshur, crossing Middle Egypt to infiltrate the eastern delta from

139. Janssen 1997: 99–109; Dodson 2016: 131.

140. Bakry 1973; Kitchen 1982: 2–12; 2004; Schulman 1987.

the south. This was the beginning of the Bronze Age collapse, character-ized by massive movements of peoples whom the Egyptians attempted to name—"Ekwesh, Teresh, Lukka, Sherden, Shekelesh, Northerners coming from all lands"[141]—and whose weapons and markings they tried to depict—horned helmet for the *Shardana* (*Sherden*), plumed head-dress for the *Pulasti* (*Peleset*), and so on.[142]

According to Merenptah, the coalition was defeated in a great battle at the site of *Perira* in the western delta; 6,000 were killed and almost 10,000 imprisoned.[143] What happened to such prisoners of war is not clear, but we can assume that many settled somewhere in Egypt, put to work in agriculture, building, and war.[144] Another group of Libyans invaded in Year 8. They kept coming. Whatever these invaders were called and wherever they came from, their advance was relentless and although the Egyptians tell us they were able to beat them again and again, there was no way to expel all of these people. Mass migrations are most uncontrollable in the vast humanity that comes with them. Scores of these migrants stayed in Egypt. Many invaders brought their women, children, and livestock. This was a desperate attempt for many to find new livable homes; the military invasion itself was a secondary result of a larger, unwieldy population movement. And thus, migrants settled in Egypt in large numbers, most often in the delta, Middle Egypt, and the Fayum, creating new livelihoods for themselves, and reorganizing (or destabilizing) Egyptian society with scores of newly created or enlarged villages and towns. Meanwhile, the Egyptian army readied itself for the next series of assaults, increasingly dependent on mercenaries from the same social groups they were fighting. Egypt's day in the sun, as ruler of the Mediterranean, African, and Near Eastern worlds, was over. From

---

141. According to the inscription on the Sixth Pylon of the Karnak temple: Breasted 1906: 243. Cf. chapter 28 in this volume.

142. See Cline and O'Connor 2003: 107–138; 2012.

143. Kitchen 1982: 38–39.

144. For more on this idea, see the various discussions of the Wilbour Papyrus in Gardiner and Wilbour 1941; Wachsmann 2013: 225–238; Antoine 2014.

here on out in its history, Egypt would always be looking for the next external attack.

Indeed, the aged King Merenptah was forced to campaign in Canaan too, racing all over the Levant according to the famous (and reused) stele in the Egyptian Museum (Cairo) in a scrambled attempt to maintain Egyptian hegemony over the region. He recorded the various cities and polities vanquished during this great military expedition on a victory stele that he would set up at his Temple of Millions of Years in Thebes.[145] The stele mentions strongholds like Gezer and Ashkelon, taken into Egyptian hegemony. Even a tribal people of Israel (written *yeserir*) are mentioned as having submitted to Egypt's control, and the text also documents that many live captives were brought back to Egypt, probably to act as slaves and servants in Egypt's fine houses, estates, and urban spaces, including their growing capital city of Piramesses, indeed the same Pithom of the biblical narrative, and maybe also in mines and quarries. It was a triumph, and elite Egyptians would have seen the evidence of success and even economic growth all around them; perhaps many wealthy Egyptians even received some of these Canaanite servants into their homes and villas, while they saw production from the gold mines and stone quarries increase.

Egypt was now unavoidably globalized, replete with foreign peoples and decision-makers. West Asian, Libyan, and the Sea Peoples' influences were growing in Egyptian spheres of power.[146] Even the extended family of the Ramesside kings may have considered themselves related to Canaanites, even though they were certainly "Egyptianized" now. Many of the people at court would have come from elsewhere. Some of the king's own royal butlers and serving men may have had Levantine origins.[147]

---

145. Kitchen 1982; Ahlström and Edelman 1985; Nibbi 1996; Goedicke 2004. For the place of this stele in the broader context of discussions of the biblical Exodus, see Frerichs and Lesko 1997.

146. See Leahy 1990; Snape 2012.

147. Note, e.g., the butler named Yemen or Yanini in the employ of the royal court, accused of working with a number of Thebans to murder King Rameses III, according to the "Harem Conspiracy Papyri"; see Vernus 1993: 112–114; Snape 2012: 426. But note Schneider 2010b: 155 who explicitly argues against

Egypt has always had connections with the Levant, but there were more back-and-forth interactions at this point than any other. If we are to pick any one time for the biblical stories preserved in the Exodus, this would be it. If Jewish cultural memory has preserved any kernels of historical truth within its fantastical tales of hardened hearts, parted seas, and Egyptian army destruction, it could be found in Merenptah's Egypt when tens of thousands of Levantine people were brought as live captives, many ultimately sent into slavery in Egypt's urban spaces, where more established Egyptianized Levantines already acted as scribes and officials for the Egyptian crown.

Egypt's elites of the early Ramesside period showed every sign of living well. Increased professionalism in the ranks of army, temple, and palace now employed legions of royal family members. The king's many sons were his best and most loyal lieutenants. Khaemwaset, for example, had the luxury to act as chief agent for his father Rameses II, marking millennia-old structures of archaic kings with his father's name, thus pulling in the blessings of the wise royal ancestors with the embellishment of ancient pyramid sites.[148] Funerary production by elites in the north and south, at places like Saqqara and Thebes, was extensive and expensive. The Theban woman Henutmehyt, for example, was buried with a fully gilded and partially cedar nested coffin set.[149] Kings' sons and statesmen had stone sarcophagi of hard granodiorite or red granite commissioned. Officials set up statues of themselves seated in the archaic scribal pose or kneeling, holding statuettes of their divinities, displaying their piety in temples throughout the land.[150] They covered these statues with inscriptions broadcasting their knowledge of literature, the scribal arts, and secret religious rites.[151]

Helck's claim that there would be a wealth of relevant evidence; see also Higginbotham 2012.

148. Fisher 2001; Charron and Barbotin (eds.) 2016.

149. Taylor 1999.

150. Baines and Frood 2011: 1–17.

151. Frood 2007; 2016; Baines and Frood 2011: 1–17.

To many Egyptians' eyes, we can imagine, everything seemed to be working just fine. Rebellions abroad had been put down; invasions had been repelled; allies were fed; oaths were upheld; mercenaries were hired; temples were built; monumental statuary was raised. Egypt was strong and wealthy; the economy was growing; there were reminders of all of this daily. Merenptah even respected the peace treaty originally set up by his father Rameses II by shipping masses of grain to the kings of Hatti in Anatolia as famine had settled upon their lands.[152] The Hittites were an old rival, but the Sea Peoples seem to have united even bitter enemies into protective alliances. And it seems Egypt still had plenty of grain to send to their suffering new allies, certainly more than other polities in the ancient Near East. Egypt was the lucky one of the Mediterranean and Near Eastern region, not dependent on rain from the sky but from their upside-down river and its water from the monsoons of the Asian subcontinent via the Ethiopian highlands. Another source of Egypt's continued wealth and stability came from its hegemony over Nubia and Kush and concomitant ownership of the mineral wealth that came with it, most particularly, gold. And so, the Egyptians were able to send grain and supplies with Egyptian armed forces to Anatolia. By the time they arrived, however, it was too late. Hatti had already been burned. The years to come would see the fall of great dynasties all around the Mediterranean to famine, mass migration and war.

In many ways, Egypt's strength was all just a façade, and there are clues that the foundation of Rameses II's sons and grandsons had deep cracks. Merenptah's own Temple of Millions of Years was largely quarried from another great king's temple, relying on Amenhotep III's masonry, rather than finding the stone in Egyptian and Nubian quarries himself and doing the work from scratch.[153] Economic contraction was visible in the lack of building at Egypt's great temples after Rameses II. And with the death of King Merenptah, son of Rameses, King of Kings, signs of political rivalry were now apparent at the very top of society.

---

152. In the Great Karnak Inscription, reference is made to the sending of grain to Hatti; see Kitchen 1982: 23–24; Beckman 2000.

153. Sourouzian 1989.

27.10.3. The end of the Nineteenth Dynasty and civil war

Merenptah (1213–1203 BC) had named a crown prince on his public monuments, a son named Sety Merenptah, becoming the Sety II in our modern Egyptological king lists and chronologies. When Merenptah died after only a decade or so of rule, the destabilizing effects of the long reign of Rameses II were still making themselves felt. His chosen successor Sety II was contested.[154] There was, it seems, a southern claimant to the throne. A man named Amenmessu, of unclear parentage but likely somehow related to Rameses II and Merenptah, stepped forward.[155] This southern king Amenmessu seems to have had southern military connections as well. He may have even been the same individual as a certain Messuy, the old viceroy of Kush under Merenptah, the official in charge of Nubia and its vast riches and in the perfect position, politically and economically, from which to launch a power grab from the south.[156] Amenmessu ruled for four years (1203–1199 BC) and built more than one would expect, at least in Thebes, but eventually he lost his bid for the throne. Sety II won his crown back (1199–1193 BC). But the damage was real: two rival kings fighting for domination of Egypt, one with a foundation of power in the north, the other in the south, one with access to northern mercenaries, the other to all the gold in the world. And this was only the first in a series of such north-south rivalries as Egypt readied itself to enter the Iron Age. Since the Seventeenth Dynasty, Egypt had not been a land with internal warlording and military competition among rival claimants to the throne. These were the ways of Canaan, Syria, and Mesopotamia, but not Egypt. But if the Ramesside period was characterized by professionalized military and decentralized family power with multiple, competing stakeholders, then this discord had a source.

---

154. Dodson 1999.

155. Schneider 2011: 445–451.

156. Schneider 2011: 445–451; Dodson 2016: 31–46. See also Krauss 1976; Dodson 1986: 196–198; 1987: 224–229; 1990: 153–155; 1995: 115–128; 1997: 41–48; 1999.

The exact reason for the family rift and royal rivalry is unclear, as we should expect in an authoritarian regime that perfected and idealized, hiding their *Realpolitik*, rather than publishing rifts and discord. The problems may have started when a woman named Tausret was named Great Royal Wife, pushing another high-born woman aside. Or, it may have begun when a chancellor of potential Syrian origin by the name of Bay was able to claim more power.[157] For whatever reason, Amenmessu saw that he and his kin had been cut out of power and succession, and he made his move, using all his access from his years as viceroy of Kush to the military, riches, manpower, not to mention political connections, to take the kingship in Egypt's southern Nile valley. His handiwork is all over Thebes, where he left a significant amount of monumental statuary, steles, and temples for one whose reign was so short and contested.[158]

According to scattered and broken evidence, Amenmessu declared his rival kingship within Sety II's first year from his stronghold in Nubia.[159] Fighting continued until Amenmessu took Thebes and the surrounding territories a year and a half later. People used to continuity and centrality of rule, who had faith in their government institutions, found that faith shattered. The royal names that Amenmessu took upon his accession to the throne were all Theban, including "Great of Might Who Makes Thebes Great for The One who Created Him" and "Amenmessu, Ruler of Thebes."[160] Amenmessu was not a man to tell half-truths, apparently; he only claimed what he had won. He likely planned his assault of the north, ready to change his throne names later to reflect his expanding rule over all of Egypt when he took the delta too.

Sety II, meanwhile, must have been ensconced in Piramesses, with various officials and generals, trying to determine the best course of action against this powerful rival. What do we know? Amenmessu's

---

157. For Tausret, see von Beckerath 1962; Altenmüller 2001: 222–231; 2003; Callender 2004; Gilmour and Kitchen 2012; Creasman 2013; Johnson and Brand 2013.

158. Yurco 1979; Dodson 1985.

159. Cardon 1979; Dodson 2016.

160. Hardwick 2006.

gambit was paying off in Thebes. He had the luxury of constructing grand statuary and adding on to Egypt's stately temples—a sure sign that there was income flowing into Thebes to secure raw materials and to pay craftsmen. Egyptologists always use material production to measure political power. In other words, if statues were being built in good numbers, then this king's Theban foundation of power was strong. Amenmessu started his Temple of Millions of Years and his tomb in the Valley of the Kings (KV 10).

Ostensibly any work on the tomb of Sety II in this royal valley had been halted by the usurper Amenmessu.[161] The texts from Deir el-Medina named their current Theban king "Mese" or "Mose," probably a shortened version of Amenmessu.[162] Why this familiarity and lack of formality was used is unclear. Indeed, the similarity to the name Moses of the biblical narrative has been enough to elicit scholarly attention to other similar details, such as disputes about rule,[163] but Amenmessu's base of support was southern, Nubian, not, at least as far as we can tell, Canaanite. It would be Sety II and Tausret who would connect themselves to Canaanite mercenary forces and administrative aid, not Amenmessu.

After a few years of playing king in Thebes, Amenmessu was defeated by Sety II with his greater military resources. The details of his defeat are not given in any of our surviving texts, but after his fourth year of rule, Amenmessu was replaced by Sety II at Thebes. If there was a public execution, texts do not record it. If Amenmessu went into exile, we do not see it documented. We should assume, however, that all the top players in the game lost people close to them; it was their extended family embroiled in this affair, after all. But we do not know the painful details of this civil war. We only know that Nineteenth Dynasty Egypt had all too easily split into warring factions of north and south.

---

161. Dodson 1999.

162. Papyrus Salt 124; see Janssen 1997: 99–109.

163. Georg 2000; Krauss 2000; 2001.

It was around this time that Sety II began his campaign of erasure and re-inscription, essentially putting his name into all the cartouches on all of the statues and steles and reliefs that Amenmessu had carved during his short reign.[164] What the Thebans thought of all this, we will never know, but it must have been bewildering for those on the bottom rungs of society. Theban craftsmen seem to have been ordered to cut out Amenmessu's name wherever they found it. Even Amenmessu's tomb was ordered to be ritually destroyed, hieroglyphs shaved and cut, names excised. Work began again on the Valley of Kings tomb of Sety II and, it seems, his Great Royal Wife, Tausret, was buried in the same valley, an unusual honor given to a royal woman, no matter how highly ranked.[165]

At this point, a new and mysterious player appeared on the scene: the Great Overseer of the Seal of the Entire Land, a man named Bay.[166] Bay was a chancellor, a money man, a kind of CEO who doled out wealth and thus influence. It seems he was sent to Thebes to consolidate the king's power there. It may have been he who ordered the building of a triple barque shrine at Karnak temple, dedicated in Sety II's name to the gods Amun, Mut, and Khonsu, because he also ordered the removal of Sety II's crown prince on that same structure, in favor of his own image.[167] To remove a crown prince and replace that image with a non-royal official was unprecedented. That this official may have actually been of foreign origin—Syrian or Levantine, perhaps relocated to the northeast delta of Egypt—makes the narrative that much more extraordinary.[168] Sety II seems to have been relying on a foreign mercenary contingent to see his plans fulfilled in Thebes and elsewhere, using an outside bureaucrat perhaps because there was no one else he could trust among his extended

---

164. Krauss 1977; Habachi 1978; Schaden 1993.

165. KV 15 and KV 14, respectively.

166. Černý 1966; Dodson 2011.

167. Johnson and Brand 2013.

168. For discussions on Bay's foreign origins and his career, see Bierbrier 2011: 19–21; Dodson 2011: 145–158.

Ramesside family, many of whom had already flouted his authority, beset by their fluctuating alliances and complicated hierarchies and loyalties. Bay's re-inscription on Sety II's triple barque shrine was a public power grab in a place potentially hostile to the rule of Sety II. The shrine was located at the front of Karnak temple itself, on the most public processional way there. Bay was making sure that every Theban witnessed his power and influence over the crown.

Mercenary behavior seems to have been everywhere in Egypt, even in the royal court. Bay seems to have remained loyal to the king, maybe even helping Sety II take the Theban area again. Indeed, Sety II seems to have owed him something—and something big—because Bay was given free rein to implement his control over the south after the reconsolidation of power and to show his social place in unprecedented ways. Not only did he display himself along the Theban processional ways in the company of the king himself, but he had the audacity to represent himself the same size as the king, something no man had ever done before in Egyptian reliefs.[169] It had not taken Egypt long to go from the days of kowtowing to Akhenaten to rivaling the king's authority. And there were to be more unprecedented actions by the chancellor Bay: he ordered a tomb for himself in the sacred Valley of the Kings itself, just next to that of the king and queen—with a straight axis, dozens of meters in length, just like a king's tomb. This was strange. Sety II seems not to have had the power or will to stop him.

Sety II would not live much longer. Evidence in his tomb in the Valley of the Kings suggests an order had been given to speed up the work because the king was dead in his sixth year.[170] Most of his time on the throne had been spent fighting for control of Egypt, rather than ruling it. There is even evidence that Deir el-Medina workmen disrespected the tomb and the king buried in it, as the chief workman Paneb was accused of taking food provisions deposited in the sepulcher for himself

169. Johnson and Brand 2013.

170. Dodson 1999.

and was even said to have lounged on top of the king's sarcophagus with the monarch inside.[171]

It seems that Bay (and maybe Tausret) were left in control, and Egypt was plunged into uncertainty. The next king—Saptah—was not only a mere child, but also disabled with a club foot probably originating from cerebral palsy.[172] Queen Tausret, it seems, would act as regent for the boy king. It was also at this time that Tausret found new authority, as she was named God's Wife of Amun at Thebes, ostensibly moving her from the palaces of Qantir in the north down to her own new bastion of power in the south.[173] Tausret would share the same priestly position once held by Hatshepsut herself (see chapter 26 in this volume), and like her, she would utilize it to gain further authority as time went on. The office of God's Wife of Amun had not been used as an arm of political power for quite some time. Indeed, the post seems to have been manipulated to justify Tausret acting as regent to a boy who was not her own son.

Even if Tausret was seen as decision-maker for Saptah by the Egyptians, since she did hold the title "The Great Noblewoman of Every Land," seemingly representative of her regency, it seems to have been Bay calling all the shots, maybe even moving her south and thus out of sight. Just as he had done with the short-lived Sety II's kingship, Bay made sure to mark Saptah's kingship with his own presence, and in every published image of the young king, the chancellor haunted his steps, appearing right behind him in numerous scenes—in carvings at Aswan, Abu Simbel, Amada, at Gebel el-Silsila.[174] At the latter location, Bay even includes the unique inscription that he was the one "who established the king on the seat of his father whom he loved,"[175] another unprecedented claim of Bay's, that he himself was kingmaker. No commoner had ever

171. Papyrus Salt 124; see Kitchen 2003: 409; Dodson 2016: 80. Such behavior would make sense if many Thebans still felt loyalty to Amenmessu, not Sety II.

172. von Beckerath 1962; Aldred 1963.

173. Callender 2004.

174. Dodson 2011.

175. Porter and Moss 1937: 211; Dodson 2011; 2016: 86.

taken such public and visible liberty vis à vis Egyptian kingship before, not even Senenmut for Hatshepsut.

We will probably never know to whom the young king Saptah was related, if he was Sety II's son or not,[176] and it really does not matter. The material point is: this boy seems to have been tailor-made for the chancellor Bay to step into informal power and make himself the puppet master. It was a canny move, to choose a child king, a boy for whom decisions had to be made by a female regent, who, in turn, could be controlled or kept out of the way by chancellor Bay, working, almost certainly, with other elites. It gave the appearance of keeping to traditional ways of ancient Egyptian rule, while simultaneously allowing the exercise of that power by someone wholly unconnected to the royal family.

Thus, all of these political machinations could have been engineered by the Egyptian elite bureaucracy. There was a new young king—a ten-year-old at accession, according to the possible age of his mummy—whom they could control; they likely had authority over the boy's regent as well. Tausret was not brought up for a position of power within the royal family; indeed, she stemmed from an elite Ramesside society that largely frowned upon giving women such political authority, that did not give royal women priestly titles, estates, and power, as had been the norm in the Eighteenth Dynasty.

The boy-king in question was likely not even the son of the previous king, Tausret's dead husband, but potentially of her dead husband's son. The mere fact that we do not know the identity of the boy-king's father indicates he was disconnected and weak. Everyone would have seen the new king's disabilities. Saptah would never pivot to a position of strength.[177] Later king lists would not even include Saptah, even though Sety II was listed, certainly unexpected if Saptah had the backing of his

176. For more on Saptah, Bay, and the end of the Nineteenth Dynasty, see also von Beckerath 1962; Lesko 1966; Schneider 2003.

177. There is even possible evidence (discussed by Dodson 2016: 83–85) that there were two rulers called Saptah: one who left the scene in the first year, only to be replaced by another Saptah with radically different titulary, although most Egyptologists contend that the references apply to one and the same king.

people as Sety's heir. Saptah was likely nothing more than a pawn of Bay's (and other men), and Tausret may have been the same thing. Some scholars see Bay and Tausret paired, as they were in reliefs at Amada temple, suggesting a sexual relationship between the two to some commentators.[178]

The evidence of Bay's hold on Egypt's political power are everywhere; right next to Tausret's tomb in the King's Valley, his own sepulcher was growing, resembling that of a king's. Bay even set himself up as the powerbroker in diplomatic relations. A cuneiform text found at the northern Syrian harbor city of Ugarit called him the "Chief of the Bodyguards of the Great King of the Land of Egypt, Baya."[179] In texts he had inscribed in Egypt, he tells us that he "casts out falsehood and promotes truth"—in other words, he was a man who got people in line.[180] In another text, Bay tells King Saptah that he "put my eye on you when you were alone,"[181] implying an unusual claim of responsibility for the king's personal safety and even that there was danger to the young king. Bay made sure to put his visible presence front and center on already existing monuments everywhere he could, but he ordered nothing new built. If the construction of new monuments is indicative of Egyptian power, then it is a striking fact that there was almost no temple building during Saptah's reign. Perhaps Bay felt the need to spend the money elsewhere and in other ways, likely funneling ample funds to elites in return for their support.

---

178. Dodson 2016: 100 says, "The nature of the relationship between Tausret and Bay cannot be other than a matter of speculation, but the parallelism seen at Amada and implicitly in the Valley of the Kings, clearly echoes that of royal consorts. There is, of course, a temptation to declare the two lovers, or even spouses, given that the queen was a widow, and Bay without a known wife: it can only be emphasized that such conclusions cannot be any more than speculation or even historical fiction."

179. On the cuneiform text RS.86.2230, see Dodson 2016: 102–103.

180. A depiction at Old Shellac Road at Aswan shows Bay standing behind Saptah (bearing the titles "Chancellor, Sole Companion, Great Chief Treasurer of the Whole Land") with Sety, King's Son of Kush: see de Morgan et al. 1894: 28 (6); Dodson 2011: 148; 2016: 86.

181. For the relief at Deir el-Bahri at the podium of the Eleventh Dynasty funerary complex of Mentuhotep II, see Gardiner 1958: 17–18; Dodson 2011: 148; 2016: 88.

There were no single actors in this Ramesside Egypt; the *Realpolitik* of consensus building is largely invisible in perfected temples, statues, and tombs, but it is during a weak king's reign that decentralized rule by many is most circumstantially visible.

The evidence for a big political move comes from Deir el-Medina. From there, we have a record dated to Year 5 of Saptah that "[t]he scribe of the Tomb Paser said: Pharaoh, life, prosperity and health, has killed the great enemy, Bay."[182] As usual, the Egyptians were vague about their *Realpolitik*. No reasons or details were given. The text was not found by archaeologists in the palace or great temple, but at a workmen's village, just a simple ink drawn memo on a limestone chip, a note preserved by the men who had been building tombs belonging to all of the interested parties—Saptah, Tausret, and Bay. We can be sure that they stopped work on Bay's tomb immediately, because the Syrian chancellor had been taken out of power, although the method of removal is veiled. All the glory for the act was given to King Saptah, the "pharaoh" mentioned in the text, a boy who was at that point perhaps approaching fifteen years of age. We could suspect it was Tausret herself, again in company with interested elites, who dispatched this interloper from the Egyptian halls of power with the backing of the High Priesthood of Amun.

Later Egyptian posterity would not remember Bay well, if he is to be identified with the Irsu (or: "the one who made himself") mentioned in the Great Harris Papyrus, written in the reign of Rameses IV, a few generations after all of this messy history:

Then another time came with empty years when Irsu, a Syrian, was among them as a chief, having put the entire land into subjugation before him; each joined with his companion in plundering their goods, and they treated the gods as they did men, and no offerings were made in the temples.[183]

---

182. On the ostracon O. IFAO 1254, see Janssen 1984; Grandet 2000.

183. Grandet 1994: I 335, II 217–224; Dodson 2011.

If we see Bay as Irsu, the Syrian,[184] we can understand after the fact that some Egyptians saw this time as empty years, i.e., a time when no legitimate king ruled, a time when Egypt's morality, norms, and virtues were abandoned for the ambitions of non-consecrated power holders. As soon as Bay was gone, the orders likely went out to have him erased from temples throughout Egypt. Indeed, the triple barque shrine at Karnak built by Sety II still bears the scars of his removal (although careful scrutiny still shows traces of his name). Bay's names and images were chiseled away from statuary and temples—at Deir el-Bahri, at Amada, at Karnak. His tomb in the Valley of the Kings was defaced and ritually deactivated.

Less than two years later, Saptah was dead too, not yet into his sixth year of kingship, maybe not even sixteen years of age.[185] There were no explanations given in the formal textual record. Orders were given to remove all of the young king's names from not only Tausret's tomb, where they were replaced with those of her dead husband Sety II, but in Saptah's own tomb as well. Saptah's coffins, sarcophagi, and canopic chest were found by archaeologists, smashed and washed into adjacent areas in the Valley of the Kings, indicating that while he was buried in state, some of his funerary objects were purposefully destroyed.[186]

Around this time, Tausret publicly claimed her status as Great Royal Wife of the dead king Sety II on monuments throughout Egypt. It seems she wanted to create a new royal lineage—one that completely removed King Saptah and went straight from Sety II to herself as female king. Tausret was crowned king with a series of new names ostensibly granted in temple rituals throughout Egypt. Her names connected her to Heliopolis in the north (Horus name: "Strong Bull Beloved of Maat, Beautiful as King like Atum") and Thebes in the south (Prenomen: "Daughter of Ra,

---

184. There is considerable disagreement about the identity of this "Irsu"; see Dodson 2011: 157. It is also debated whether Saptah, through his mother, may have been of Syrian or otherwise foreign ancestry; see Drenkhahn 1980.

185. According to the ostracon O. Cairo CG 25792; see Cerný 1935: 89–90, 112, pl. 8; Altenmüller 1992: fig. 19; Johnson 1998. Cf. also Altenmüller 1984: 37–38; 1994: 19–28.

186. Davis 1908; Dodson 2016: 108–111.

Beloved of Amun"). She even changed her given name at her ascension, becoming "Tausret, Beloved of Mut"—a shout-out to Amun's protective and often violent consort resident at Thebes.

Indeed, by connecting her kingly person to the lioness goddess Mut, Tausret may have been effectively communicating her modus operandi to her elites; Mut was capable of brutal acts, to be sure, but only on behalf of what was right and true, only on behalf of her husband-father, the sun god. When she took the kingship, Tausret also enlarged her Valley of the Kings tomb, cutting it deeper into the mountainside, adding the *Amduat* and the "Book of Gates," both texts reserved only for monarchs, not meant for queens and not previously inscribed in her sepulcher.[187] She had her images in the tomb modified, ordering the king's blue crown carved onto her head.[188]

Tausret ordered a Temple of Millions of Years for herself at the edge of the flood plain in western Thebes, distributing many foundation depositions to sanctify the space, putting up a mudbrick pylon to add monumentality and majesty to the temple where she would be worshipped and offered to as a god.[189] She commissioned new statuary of herself as king, one of which survives, a piece showing her as a woman with breasts, tight waist, full hips, and narrow shoulders, but dressed in the masculine long pleated kilt, shirt, and apron favored by kings like Rameses II (1279–1213 BC). She was visually claiming descent from this great King of Kings. Her new royal names are preserved on the surface of this one remaining statue, found by archaeologists near Heliopolis in the vicinity of modern-day Cairo.[190]

Tausret ruled only two to four years after the death of the young Saptah.[191] The fact that Tausret was able to take the throne for herself at

187. McCarthy 2008: 83–113.

188. Altenmüller 1984; 1994.

189. Wilkinson 2011: 166; Creasman 2013: 15.

190. For more on this statue, see Roehrig 2012: 55–58.

191. The timing is debated; compare the different historical conclusions in Dodson 2016: 116–117 with those of Callender 2012: 42.

all is a testament to ancient Egypt's deference to dynasty and the status quo, to the habit of giving the power to the one who was already exercising it. The fact that she was likely removed from power fits the context of competition for late Nineteenth Dynasty politics. Tausret's eventual death is not explained to us, but we can suspect that her rule was seen as illegitimate and that she was eliminated. A stele from Elephantine tells us, in oblique terms, how the next king was chosen amidst all the chaos:

> The land had been in confusion . . . [the great god] stretched out his arm and selected his majesty in life, prosperity, health from among the millions. . . . Fear of him seized the hearts of combatants before him; they fled like sparrows with a falcon after them. They left silver and gold . . . which they had given to these Asiatics in order for them to bring soldiers. . . . Their plans failed and the plans were futile, as every god and goddess performed wonders for the good god, proclaiming the onset of a slaughter under him. . . . In Year 2 . . . there were no opponents [left] of his majesty, life, prosperity, health, in any lands.[192]

It seems that a warlord arose from among the strongmen left in Rameses II's extended family, took down Tausret and her supporters, and had himself installed in her place. This warlord's name was Sethnakht (1185–1181 BC), meaning "Seth is strong," and he was the founder of the Twentieth Dynasty. For once, the Egyptians are not shy about telling us that he took the throne by force; they just do not say from whom he took power.[193] A later text, the same Great Harris Papyrus that mentioned Irsu the Syrian, tells us that after those "empty years,"

> the gods then inclined themselves to peace, so as to put the land in its proper state in accordance with its normal condition, and they established their son, who came forth from their flesh, as ruler

192. Kaiser et al. 1972: 192, pl. 49; also see Kitchen 1983a: 111; Wente and Peden 1996: 164–766.

193. Kitchen 2012: 2–3.

of every land, upon their great throne, Userkhaura Setepenra
Meryamun, son of Ra, Sethnakht Meryra Meryamun.[194] He was
Khepri Seth when he was enraged; he set in order the entire land
that had been rebellious; he killed the rebels who were in the land
of Egypt. He cleansed the great throne of Egypt, being the ruler
of the Two Lands on the throne of Atum.[195]

Tausret herself is most likely to have been the rebel whom Sethnakht
killed. Sethnakht may have even been a royal insider, a courtier and/or
lieutenant of Tausret.

When Sethnakht took the throne, his own newly granted king's
names broadcast his achievements and his own justification for power.
He was "The One Powerful of Arm Who Drives out His Rebels" and
"The One Who Smites the Nine Bows Who Oppose Kingship."[196] We
will see no censure for his ambitions or outright claims to have committed violence because he did it against the "rebel" in support of divine
kingship itself. When he died after just a few years of rule, Sethnakht
was buried in KV 14, Tausret's hastily redone tomb, by order of his son
Rameses III, further proof of her dismissal from the throne.[197]

27.10.4. Rameses III and the Twentieth Dynasty

After the short but eventful reign of his warlord father Sethnakht,
Rameses III (1181–1150 BC; figure 27.3) would continue as king of a new
Egyptian Dynasty, the Twentieth. To shore up a nascent and vulner-
able kingship, he needed ideological models. He looked directly to the
Nineteenth Dynasty and the long reign of Rameses II (1279–1213 BC).
Rameses III copied both of Rameses II's kingly names and switched up
the epithets: Rameses III was Usermaatra Meryamun, following Rameses

---

194. Grandet 1994.

195. Grandet 1994.

196. von Beckerath 1997.

197. Schneider 2010a: 386–387.

FIGURE 27.3. Rameses III proceeding from his palace to participate in the Feast of Min ceremonies. Medinet Habu, second court, north wall. Photograph by Marissa Stevens.

II's Usermaatra Setepenra.[198] Rameses III's birth name was Rameses Hekaiunu, following Rameses II's name Rameses Meryamun. He would follow Rameses II in many other endeavors: his memorial temple architecture, which followed the previous Rameses' plan and scale almost exactly, though situated further to the south; his expeditions to the Sinai, including Edom's copper mines, and to the mysterious land of Punt; the population of his harem including the daughters of Egypt's wealthy families and the production of dozens of children whom he depicted on his temple walls; even his portrait.[199] Although nowhere close to the near seventy years of Rameses II, Rameses III had a long-lived reign of about thirty years and he, too, wanted to become King of Kings.

But Rameses III had problems of which Rameses II could not have dreamed; while the earlier Rameses was opportunistically picking fights,

198. von Beckerath 1999.

199. Grandet 1993; O'Connor 2012.

Rameses III was attempting to save Egypt from oblivion in a world that seemed to be falling to pieces. In many ways, we talk about Rameses III as a copyist, not an innovator, as a minimalist, not a hoarder, but the demands on his energies were defensive, not offensive. His architectural and artistic production, while respectable, was nothing compared to his mentor and hero.[200] Rameses III was not able to make the same cultural mark as his predecessor, but he did not have the cultural context in which to do it. As the son of a military man and likely a military man himself before his father's kingship, Rameses III knew what he needed to do to prove his royal divinity, and he kept to the script. He followed the expectations of kingly requirements. Rameses III was not raised a royal; he cut his teeth on the battlefield with his father Sethnakht. If anyone was prepared for the repeated and brutal onslaught of migratory invasions Egypt suffered at this point in time, it was this king. But his military acumen came at a steep price, because Rameses would walk into a minefield of a different sort, of palace politics, intrigue, and regional competitions for which he would prove sorely unprepared and even naïve. He would pay with his life.

Rameses III inherited a failing Egypt within a world in turmoil, holding on to the appearance of great power in the middle of a collapse of massive proportions. In Year 5, he fought off invasions of Libyans in the Western Desert.[201] Pirates roamed the Mediterranean. The Sea Peoples were combining their forces into coalitions to create new concerted and organized attacks.[202] The great Syrian city of Ugarit had fallen, as had Hatti (see chapter 30 in this volume). The Hittites had written diplomatic letters on cuneiform tablets asking for aid, all disconcertingly found still in their kilns by archaeologists.[203] Hattusa had been burned, its destruction layer matching the same material culture and circumstantial evidence as dozens of other archaeological sites up and down the

---

200. O'Connor 2012; Mojsov 2012.

201. Kahn 2018.

202. Cline and O'Connor 2012; Haider 2012; Sternberg-el Hotabi 2012.

203. Cline and O'Connor 2012: 13–14.

eastern Mediterranean coast: towns on the island of Cyprus, as well as Miletos, Troy, Mersin, Tarsus, Alalakh, Hamath, Qatna, Qadesh, Akko, Lachish, Ashdod, Ashkelon. All had been destroyed.

In Year 8 of his reign, a Sea Peoples coalition including the *Pulasti* (*Peleset*), *Danuna* (*Denyen*), *Shardana* (*Sherden*), *Meshwesh*, and *Ṣikala* (*Tjeker*) attacked (cf. figure 28.6).[204] According to the detailed textual and pictorial accounts depicted on the exterior walls of his memorial temple at Medinet Habu, Rameses III led extensive land and sea battles, culminating in a storied defense of archers who shot volleys against the approaching ships as they were about to land on the coast and breach the mouth of the Nile.[205] Rameses III made his mark fighting the tides of migration, like King Merenptah before him. Unlike Rameses II's Qadesh inscription, the veracity of which is so often doubted by historians, there is actually less reason to doubt the truth of Rameses III's military leadership as depicted on his temple walls— because even with no allies left to help him, he maintained Egypt's continued existence long beyond his reign.[206] Indeed, the most amazing part of Rameses III's reign is that Egypt survived at all, when every other Mediterranean state, save the well-defended northern Levantine city-states, had fallen to the migratory onslaughts. The defeated prisoners of war were settled in the Nile delta and southern Canaan, many of them used as soldiers.[207] There was little rest for this king. In the later part of his reign, he had to deal with more wars against Libyans in the Western Desert and delta.[208]

---

204. Cline and O'Connor 2012.

205. Sweeney and Yasur-Landau 1999; Drews 2000; O'Connor 2000; Cline and O'Connor 2003; Kahn 2010.

206. Egyptologists, however, have not been so uncritical, arguing that Rameses III simply copied much of his war reliefs from Rameses II: see in particular Helck 1962. For an analysis of historicity and reassessment thereof, see Kahn 2018; also Cifola 1988; 1994: 1–23.

207. Harris Papyrus of Rameses IV: see Grandet 1994.

208. Snape 2012: 422–423.

Military threats were one thing, but economic plights were not as easy to repel. There is little information from Egypt's north,[209] but in the south, where material culture was better preserved, the signs of scarcity increased as the Ramesside period marched on. In Year 28, Theban texts indicate that the skilled craftsmen of Deir el-Medina went on their first strike over unpaid grain rations.[210] The reason for the lack of payment is unclear, but what is visible in the documentation is a palace and vizier on the back foot. The craftsmen went to the mortuary temple of Horemheb demanding grain and were paid, it seems, only a portion of it. The affair calmed down for a bit, but then in Year 29, the artisans struck again over lack of payment. This strike was more drawn out and contentious. This time the workers headed to the funerary temple of Rameses III at Medinet Habu, presumably still under construction, and then to the temple of Thutmose III for a sit-in, a display of dissatisfaction almost certainly punctuated by lots of yelling and noise, and then on to the Ramesseum, the temple of Rameses II, all the while loudly demanding payment of grain rations and their dues of meat, oil, and vegetables. When they threatened to call the vizier through their own personal channels, the craftsmen finally received payment, but in just a few weeks, rations went unpaid again. In Year 30, the jubilee year of Rameses III, there was again a period of non-payment to the craftsmen.

Were the palace treasuries depleted? Why was the vizier—the king's chief deputy—not paying his men? There is evidence of grain inflation during this period, causing many historians to suspect a series of failed or diminished harvests, impeding the ability of the crown to pay its extensive staff throughout Egypt.[211] With many people on the payroll and with a hierarchy of (often corrupt) officials paid first, we can imagine the grain meant for the local artisans was already gone by the time it reached the area. During earlier Ramesside times, institutions of palace

---

209. Hirsch 2003.

210. Grandet 2006; cf. also Edgerton 1951; Demarée, Mathieu, and Černý 2001; Müller 2004.

211. Janssen 2004; Eyre 2012.

and army had become bloated, creating many CEO-type men at the top, likely directly related to the royal family, who were given funds to distribute to their ranks below. This worked when prosperity ruled, but when bad harvests and scarcity set in, much income had likely already been promised or skimmed away by those top men determined to keep their share. A great deal of wealth must have been redirected to unexpected, high-needs projects like mercenaries and defense, not to mention jubilee preparations for the king, leaving nothing for the common priests, soldiers, bureaucrats, and craftsmen toward the bottom of the system.

The Deir el-Medina strikes mark a key feature of the Ramesside period—the failure of long-established patrons to pay and protect their employees.[212] Such failures in patronage are long and drawn-out affairs, accompanied by all the pain that goes with such transitions (US readers, for example, may find themselves reminded of the loss of well-paying industrial jobs in cities like Detroit or the closure of coal mines in West Virginia). The strikes by the Deir el-Medina workers at Thebes highlight a larger truth, namely the increased weakness of the palace institution, led by the vizier, in particular. The palace demonstrated little ability to cover its regional responsibilities throughout Egypt, leaving so many unpaid workers that they looked to local institutions to fill the vacuum. For their part, the Deir el-Medina artisans found new patrons in the mayor of western Thebes and the high priest of Amun, both with access to rich storerooms in Karnak and the West Bank that had not yet been depleted. The vizier and palace had failed them.

A word about our sources is needed here. Almost everything we know about the later Ramesside period comes from Egypt's south. Thebes's aridity preserves material in a way that the delta does not, true, but there may be more to the story than just the lack of preservation of northern evidence. Some researchers have noted a shocking lack of elite coffins from the north for the Twentieth and Twenty-first Dynasties, for example, linking it to the decimation of Egypt's northern elite and

---

212. Eyre 2011.

governmental institutions.[213] If patronage systems in Egypt's south were failing—far from the mass migrations of Sea Peoples and disturbances of Libyans in delta regions—then how functional were the cities of Memphis or Heliopolis or Piramesses, so much closer to the onslaught? Funerary production is reflective of larger patterns of personal wealth and social stability in Egypt. There is evidence of Twentieth Dynasty Theban coffins of high quality and cost, but few, if any, from necropolis locations like Saqqara or Dahshur. The necropolis of Piramesses has still not been investigated, however, potentially removing a significant portion of evidence from our data sets.[214]

As palace institutions failed, people looked to the local temples to keep things running. As the wealthy temple complex of Amun at Thebes became owner of Upper Egypt's purse strings, people increasingly demonstrated their close connection to that temple.[215] Membership in this powerful, professionalized priesthood was everything for a Theban family, and people marked their connections in any way they could. No surprise that so many royal and non-royal monuments betray increased piety, access to complicated religious iconography and ritual, or complicated religious intellectualism. Even Rameses III was trying to show his priestly abilities. His new temple, placed perpendicular to Karnak's front pylon, was a tour de force of religious intellectualism, pulling in all the available strands of Osirian-solar thought.[216]

There is even evidence from western Thebes that people were losing faith in the traditional legal court system, composed of elders and statesmen, including the great *kenbet* supervised by the vizier himself. Instead, people began to solve their disputes with a variety of Amun

---

213. Raven 2017. For the significant impact of Libyan invasions and incursions on northern Egypt, see also Snape 2012: 425.

214. Although the evidence is limited, it appears that few elite burials are to be found at Piramesses; see Franzmeier and Moje 2018.

215. Kubisch 2018.

216. For recent work on Rameses III's temple at Medinet Habu, see McClain 2015: 14–16; McClain and Johnson 2013: 177–186; Simon 2016. Note that Brett McClain is preparing a study on Rameses' Karnak temple (Chubb et al. 1936).

oracles—statues of the god in covered shrines brought into a public area, held aloft by priests whose movements reflected divine thought and will.[217] If someone had stolen your goat and you wanted to get to the bottom of it, it was better to take the matter directly to the god (and thus the temple institution), rather than the village or the crown, waiting until the next festival day and presenting your question to the statue when it was brought out. The priests' organic and public movements— toward written documents placed in the court, or even toward particular persons assembled there—seemed more trusted, more effective socially, more reflective of communal agreement, less prone to self-dealing and corruption, and more transparent. Whatever the actual mechanism of these "oracular" decisions—whether the priests agreed ahead of time what decision to make or whether they allowed drunken or drugged states to lead them—it was now perceived that the community at large was making the call, publicly, rather than a single corrupt official in a back room of a palace outlet or a huddled group of court elders who had already been paid off. More and more legal cases were heard by a variety of oracles as the Ramesside period continued, some provincial and local, others state supported and connected to the biggest temples, and it was all reflective of the same massive patron shift visible throughout the Theban region, and almost certainly, though we do not have the documentation to prove it, all over Egypt.[218]

Rameses III followed Rameses II in one particular way that did not necessarily work in Egypt's favor. A thirty-year reign seems a thing of legends, something to strive for, perhaps, the method of keeping Egypt on strong footing. And yet any reign over twenty years skipped a generation, multiplying the competitors for all sorts of jobs and resources, increasing the number of young elite men without employment waiting in the wings. Indeed, there is strong textual and physical evidence that the competition among Rameses III's sons and grandsons reached a fever pitch.

---

217. Note, e.g., an example in the British Museum (BM EA 10335); see Dawson 1925.

218. Eyre 2012.

FIGURE 27.4. Head of the mummy of Rameses III. Reproduced from Smith
1912: pl. LI.

After his jubilee in Year 30 and during his thirty-third year of rule,
King Rameses III was killed in a conspiracy hatched within his own
Theban harem.[219] Indeed, recent examinations of his mummy (figure
27.4) have revealed a slash in his throat, certainly deep enough to have
killed him.[220] And archaeologists have uncovered reams of papyrus documenting a series of trials held to accuse Egyptian women, male officials,
and royal sons of the harem of collusion, sorcery, and violence against
the king.[221] The charges are never explicitly clarified. Word of the grisly

219. Turin Judicial Papyrus: Buck 1937. For overviews, see Vernus 1993: 109–120;
        Redford 2002; Snape 2012.

220. Hawass et al. 2012.

221. Goedicke 1963.

deed had likely already spread to all who needed to know; no reason to put such shameful acts against the king into writing, giving it any more power than it already had. The harem conspiracy documentation is indicative of Egyptian methods of veiling *Realpolitik* within administrative writing. Egyptologists could not say from the documentation alone whether Rameses III was actually killed or not; only examination of his mummy proved that. This caveat haunts the entire enterprise of Egyptology—because, if this court documentation was kept so vague in purpose and yet so detailed in methodology, how much truth can we expect to be hidden behind other records of the period? It seems when we read such intricate recordings that the Egyptians were telling us all we need to know—in the so-called Harem Conspiracy court cases, in the Tomb Robbery Papyri, in the Strike Papyri—and yet so very much is purposefully obfuscated. Of this fact the historian must be ever cognizant, demanding the use of circumstantial evidence and hypothetical conclusions based on normal human behavior within certain social systems.

Piecing together the documentation and filling in the unwritten gaps of this conspiracy, it seems a queen named Tiy worked assiduously and secretly to hatch a plot to get her son onto the throne. Her son's name is Pentaweret in the texts, "He of the Great (Female) One," maybe his real name, but more likely a pseudonym so as not to give this particular prince any power among entourages or regional factions.[222] The plan was likely to kill the king and to find a way to move the throne to this prince. There were many people accused of involvement, which makes sense. Killing the king—in this case during a ritual at the temple, or during a harem visit at the same temple palace—was likely the easiest part of the plot; the more difficult part would have been the strategy of placing the chosen son past his brothers onto the Egyptian throne itself. We can also suspect that elder sons of Rameses III were also targeted by the conspirators—picked out with violence or collusion. The people involved were accused of using sorcery, dark magic if you like, to enchant those they needed to influence, to

---

222. Snape 2012: 412–413.

confuse them.[223] They made figures out of wax, voodoo dolls, to control their victims. The trial included interrogations to get the full story out of all those involved, to make sure that people named names. That questioning was almost certainly accompanied by torture. The end result for most of those accused was death—either suicide by one's own hand, or death as the Egyptians chose to dispatch it, perhaps even by slow impalement on a sharpened spike put through the upper abdomen, a slow, cruel, and public death, the Egyptian version of crucifixion. The court documents tell us that some of the judges were accused of corruption and payoffs, and perhaps even of receiving sexual favors by women of the harem to hand out a better verdict. Trying to influence the judges did not work, or so we are told. In the end, there were three hearings, all long and involved, and thirty-eight people were sentenced to death.

All of this implies that the royal succession had become more politically competitive and complicated than at any other time in the New Kingdom. It is also indicative of long felt regional differences between Egypt's north and south. These Theban men and women would not have tried to position their young candidate for the throne if they did not think they could pull it off, after all. Royal succession had become messy, so messy that all kinds of unimaginable things were now possible within a shifting game played by the craftiest of political minds. This unstable reality at the top of the social pyramid had already allowed many non-normative political moves, including Horemheb's coup d'état, Amenmessu's claim of the throne in Thebes, Bay's placement of Saptah as king, the installment of Tausret as God's Wife of Amun and then possibly as king thereafter, and Sethnakht's coup d'état. All of these political moves would have been aberrant in an Eighteenth or even an early Nineteenth Dynasty reality. Now they were par for the course.

Ironically, it was also during the reign of Rameses III that scenes from a royal harem were depicted for the first time.[224] The representations find themselves on the upper floors of the gateway in front of the king's

223. Ritner 1993: 192–200. The Turin Judicial Papyrus discusses how these individuals were punished; see Buck 1937.

224. Epigraphic Survey 1970.

Temple of Millions of Years at Medinet Habu, a gateway shaped like a defensive tower. In the depictions, Rameses III seems quite pleased with his situation, a bland smile on his face as he fondles and caresses his beauties, holding mandrake fruits, reaching for his harem girls. Scene after scene show naked women in the company of the king. Some are playing *senet* naked. Some are playing instruments naked. Others are offering food or other luxuries, always naked or with their garments opened. All have fabulously baroque head coverings. Each young lady is shown as prepubescent and fresh. The king is shown seated on his throne, never standing, and while his own state of dress is uncertain, he often holds a mandrake or flower above his lap, at his pubic area. In some scenes, he might "chuck" one of the ladies under the chin. In other scenes, he fondles their nether regions (these images have been vandalized by later Christians, seemingly offended by the subject matter). To our eyes, the depictions are staid; no orgies are shown. No sexual intercourse is depicted. But everywhere there are the subtle markers of the sexuality that the harem provided to the king: women shaking vaginally shaped sistra or holding vaginally shaped flowers. The sexual congress was ordained by the gods. Their king was the Bull of Egypt, able and meant to populate the royal nurseries with thousands of his offspring.

This harem, or whatever one chooses to call this collection of women for the express purpose of kingly procreation, was a place of beauty and divinely inspired sexual congress, but these idealized scenes leave out the dangers that a collection of partially enfranchised royal family members and harem women with conflicting agendas and diverse family loyalties could inflict upon the king, who, lured by sex, was dispatched with a cut to his throat likely before he even knew what had happened to him. This regicide did not happen because of the "true" nature of women, their resentments and plots, as so many have claimed.[225] No, this conspiracy involved the court, male and female. And it happened at Thebes.

---

225. E.g., Wilkinson 2010: 338, reasoning that the harem institution itself was to blame: "There was something about the claustrophobic atmosphere that fed the bitter jealousies and personal rivalries of the king's many wives. With little to occupy their minds besides weaving and idle pleasures, the more ambitious concubines nurtured resentments, angry at the lowly status of their offspring

It may even highlight that constant tension between north and south, Piramesses versus Thebes.[226] This is the kind of decentralized political power the Ramesside period was now engaged in at the highest levels—underhanded methods of changing one's fate, making one's own luck. To kill a king reflected the ultimate crisis of patronage. The subterfuge was reflective of a fragmented and overly large extended family of inside players, all with competing agendas, all with some small bit of power in an increasingly deregulated system, all vying for the same prize—the kingship itself, or at least some kind of better access to it. Despite the ongoing patronage shifts of the Ramesside period, such problems would not end anytime soon for Egypt. Rameses III had been a long-lived monarch himself, regicide or not, and there were more than enough established adult sons to vie with one another for power, pulling Egypt into yet more palace discord and more civil upheavals after his death.

27.10.5. Crisis and the end of the Twentieth Dynasty

The Twentieth Dynasty seems to have conceived of itself as a forever Egypt by necessity. Every king after Sethnakht bore the same birth name (although we can imagine that it would have been highly improbable for all of these kings to have been born Rameses; their names must have been changed when they ascended the throne). Their throne names mimicked what had come before, too, homaging Amenhotep III (1388–1350 BC), Rameses II (1279–1213 BC), and Rameses III (1181–1150 BC) with new

---

and wondering how they might improve their own and their children's fortunes."

226. Cooney 2021 suggests that the high priesthood of Amun of the late Twentieth Dynasty and into the Twenty-first Dynasty would cleave to the Theban kings of the Seventeenth and early Eighteenth Dynasty, highlighting their connections to divinized patron-kings like Amenhotep I or Thutmose III. This is even visible in their treatment of the New Kingdom monarch's bodies and body containers, in which Twentieth Dynasty Ramesside kings were put into substandard coffins, while earlier kings of the Theban Eighteenth Dynasty were treated with much more respect. On Ramesside evidence for this cultural and political separation between north and south, see the "Tale of Apepi and Seqenenra" and the new reading suggested by Candelora 2020.

combinations of the same thing. The Twentieth Dynasty was one big idea, one big reign, one high concept, as its kings kept trying to replicate the good parts of the past. These kings were based at the palace of Piramesses in the northeastern delta, far from Thebes, from which all of our documentation comes. It goes without saying that textual silence from the north is the biggest problem for historians writing about this period.

If the regicide of Rameses III was indicative of conflict between northern and southern patrician families, then perhaps we should not be surprised to see crown funding for Thebes cut back to the bone in the following reigns. Temple building from Rameses IV to XI is almost nonexistent. None of these kings had their own Temple of Millions of Years. All these Twentieth Dynasty kings added to, claimed, and celebrated already existing temple structures. Indeed, might we see lack of buildings by Rameses IV as a refusal to grant his patronage to the south, instead of automatically assuming it means economic weakness of the king and crown? We could assume that few royal visits were made to Thebes in the latter part of the Twentieth Dynasty, as this era was characterized by the retreat of the king from the Nile valley, the withholding of his patronage from Thebes and the surrounding areas. But the later Twentieth Dynasty is also about the loss of Egyptian hegemony in West Asia. The power of the Egyptian king was shrinking. The south responded by cleaving to powerful temple institutions, particularly the Amun temple at Thebes, and working with the King's Son of Kush, channeling viceroy gold and wealth directly to the temple hierarchy, perhaps bypassing the king entirely. Everyone was betraying their patron and being betrayed in turn. Late Ramesside Egypt was a time of breakups and new romances. And it was complicated.

Rameses IV seems to have been the chosen heir of Rameses III, and as such he must have been an old man by the time he took the throne, certainly in his forties and probably older. Even though his rule was rather short, only about six years, king's sons, grandsons, and great-grandsons must have been vying for positions of power at a time when there was less and less to go around (figure 27.5).

FIGURE 27.5. Inscription of Rameses III reinscribed for Rameses IV and usurped by Rameses VI, Eastern High Gate of Medinet Habu. Photograph by Marissa Stevens.

Evidence from Thebes suggests that in the absence of a strong crown, the high priesthood of Amun was looking to create new sources of revenue. They got creative in their staffing of certain ventures. One expedition to the Wadi Hammamat—the long valley known for its greywacke stone and gold leading to the Red Sea from the city of Coptos in the Nile valley—took place in Year 3 of Rameses IV.[227] The vizier is mentioned, but how involved he was, we cannot really know. The main players seem to have been the high priest of Amun, Ramesesnakht and the mayor of Thebes. They drafted a number of Deir el-Medina artisans into service as well (which is the only reason historians have the papyrus documenting the work at all, because it was purportedly found at this village), and so the men normally in charge of carving and painting royal tombs with sacred underworld books were somehow meant to find gold out in a

---

227. On the so-called Goldmine Papyrus (Museo Egizio di Torino, C. 1879, C. 1969, C. 1899), see Harrell and Brown 1992; Lull and Requena 2004.

desert wadi they had never visited, doing work in which they were not specialists.[228] It seems the Amun high priest had to make do with the human assets he had at his disposal, rather than running this expedition the way it would have been done in a time of centrality. The numbers are staggering: around 10,000 men went into the wadi; 900 died, giving us a 10% mortality rate.[229] As so often in ancient Egypt, people were cheaper than material wealth.

As for Rameses IV, we must be mindful that he was the son of a murdered monarch.[230] Like Senusret I of the Twelfth Dynasty, son of Amenemhat I, also killed in a palace setting by people he had trusted (see chapter 19 in volume 2), Rameses IV would have been careful to only liaise with close colleagues and family members. From this moment on, we see little information about the Egyptian kings, little evidence they ever visited their southern harems or took part in Theban rituals for Amun. They built few temples, except what the High Priesthood of Amun was willing to support (and probably even fund) at the Khonsu temple in Karnak.[231] They had no superpowers with which to contend— no Mittani or Hittites (chapters 29 and 30 in this volume)—just decentralized and scrappy incursions of Libyans who continued to engage in desert raids or other descendants of the Sea Peoples, many now melted into society, having entered the military ranks as soldiers for hire.[232] But now that the kings had lost their influence over the south, they had

---

228. Romer 1984: 129–130. Note, however, Burger Robin 2019, who argues that the exploitation of the Wadi Hammamat was only for greywacke stone, not for gold. The search for gold, however, would explain why there are few to no greywacke statues of late Ramesside kings, despite their documented activity in the area.

229. This loss of life is highlighted by Wilkinson 2010: 344.

230. For the collected evidence on Rameses IV, see Peden 1994.

231. Blyth 2006. An exception would be the beginnings of a mortuary temple of Rameses IV, but it remained unfinished: see Snape 2012: 415.

232. See Eyre 2012: 109–110, stating, "By the reign of Ramesses III, it seems clear that the important political power base lay with the military, in which immigrants—both individually and as 'tribal' groups—played a major part." Cf. also Snape 2012.

also relinquished their access to its gold and mineral wealth. Their only sources of real wealth were delta wheat and barley, and from what late Theban records we have, price inflation for grain was still an issue, suggesting scarcity here too.[233] The only thing Rameses IV did not neglect was his afterlife. Because it was ideologically demanded that his tomb be placed in the belly of the Theban beast, we should not be surprised that he doubled the Deir el-Medina crew from 60 to 120—a massive number of workers, to build a royal tomb in a scant amount of time, yes, but perhaps also because Rameses IV needed to stack the Valley of Kings with loyalists from the north who would protect his tomb goods and his body. He also seems to have required more men for non-funerary work—like that expedition to the Wadi Hammamat. There is also some evidence that he paid these artisans with silver, not with grain, unprecedented and, when we look at the larger picture, sinister in its meaning.[234]

With the death of Rameses IV, Egypt moved on to the reign of Rameses V, probably not the son of Rameses IV, but yet another son of Rameses III, who ruled for such a short period of time he had barely started his tomb in the Valley of the Kings before he succumbed to death.[235] His four-year reign shows almost complete inattention to the south, beyond a crackdown on corruption among priests at the temple in Elephantine.[236] All our evidence shows that the priestly powerbrokers of Thebes had fully and inexorably moved into the breach left by

---

233. Janssen 1975.

234. Sinister because an influx of metal probably means an increase in tomb recommodification and state-driven looting of the necropolis; on the ostracon O. DeM 435, see Helck 1975: 262–263; Cooney 2007: 15. In this situation, the chiefs received 10 *deben* each, the 30 workers received 5 *deben* each, and an additional 21 workers received 2 *deben* each; Helck also suggests that metal vessels entered the Deir el-Medina community as "gifts" when the crew built tombs and funerary furniture for high officials, such as the vizier. For the idea that this was a more common form of payment toward the end of the Twentieth Dynasty, see Valbelle 1985: 152. Cf. also Haring 1997: 252, 263–268, noting: "It is not always easy to distinguish between the collection and redistribution of tools, and the distribution of copper as wages" (264).

235. Snape 2012: 413.

236. Vernus 1993: chapter 4.

the crown.[237] The high priest of Amun, the mayor of eastern Thebes, the mayor of western Thebes, even the Deir el-Medina leadership, all of them were getting in on the game of finding new revenue sources, trying out new patrons. And it was around this time that the Wilbour Papyrus was commissioned, analyzing the agricultural resources belonging to the Amun priesthood along a 100-mile stretch of land in Middle Egypt.[238] The temple institution was, apparently, trying to figure out every last means of accounting financial income, estimating tax revenue anew, marking their territory, either with the support of the king, or precisely because of the absence of the king and the crown's finances. Why create a document for tax purposes unless the crown tax collector had abandoned his post? Or to use another analogy, when one mafia boss is bumped off, another one will step in, sending out his lieutenants to all the clients in the area, letting them know the identity of their new protector. Even Libyan raiders were trying to source new income, and their raids increased in frequency into the southern Nile valley and into the Theban region itself. The temple at Medinet Habu, surrounded by its thick and high mudbrick walls, became a safe haven for many in western Thebes, and even the villagers of Deir el-Medina retreated here time and again.[239] The deserts were no longer safe, particularly with so many commodities hidden in them over the generations. Security systems everywhere, including in the necropolis, had broken down.

And there may have been pestilence, too. Mummy evidence suggests that Rameses V himself died of smallpox, or some other epidemic.[240] The next king, yet another son of Rameses III, Rameses VI, took that last

---

237. Ockinga 2012.

238. Gardiner 1948; also Eyre 2012.

239. Haring 1997.

240. New studies have questioned the existence of smallpox in antiquity. Recently, the virus' DNA was sequenced, and was shown to have had a common ancestor only dating back to the 1500s of the Common Era; however, this does not mean that a smallpox-type epidemic did not exist, merely that smallpox in the form of the virus that we know today may not yet have existed; see Anderson 2016.

unfinished Theban tomb for himself.[241] The news kept getting worse. Grain prices were still high and even increasing. With low harvests, the tax revenues, whether collected by crown or temple, were obviously lower than necessary. We get word that the Deir el-Medina crew was cut down to sixty, causing consternation in the village and, we must assume, extensive bribery to job bosses to stay on the payroll. No new buildings were added to the Theban temple complex. The reigns of Rameses VII and VIII were the shortest yet. Both were perhaps even sons of Rameses III, although scholars disagree. But no matter, the overly long reign of that old warrior king was still making itself felt.[242]

Thebes was now ruled by patrician families connected to the Amun priesthood. The king was gone in all but name and tomb. Patterns of rule were now decentralized, and people were learning which patrons they could trust. In some ways it was a creative time for the Amun priesthood, which now had to turn generations of ideology about kingship and his saving grace back toward Amun as King of the Gods. For generations, Egyptian powerbrokers had been placing their sons in positions of power after them when they could; now nepotism was the order of the day. Self-dealing and skimming off the top were expected and part of the system; corruption was thus more a question of whom you were working for rather than if you were doing it. Militarism was also the norm, and the Amun priesthood was quickly coming into competition with military powerbrokers, especially the King's Son of Kush, viceroy of the South.[243]

We now need to follow the reigns of high priests of Amun, alongside the kings, to write our history.[244] Ramesesnakht passed the high office on to his son Nesamun, who passed it on to his son Amenhotep. The kings were still commissioning tombs in their sacred Valley, but perhaps, by the time the cash reached Thebes from Piramesses, it was all depleted,

---

241. Rameses VI is also the last pharaoh of this period for whom we have inscriptional evidence of Egypt's presence in the Levant and Sinai; see Mumford 2006.

242. Eyre 1980: 168–170.

243. Eyre 2012.

244. For the late Ramesside period, see Barwik 2011.

everyone having taken their cut. The tombs of these later kings were not cut deeply into the rock, and the will to protect what was inside seems to have diminished. It is a wonder that the Ramesside kings continued to have themselves buried here at Thebes at all. These monarchs were not Theban in origin, of course. There is no evidence that they spent any of their time here. This was their Abydos, to be sure, their ground zero for justifying the sacred nature of their kingship by depositing their bodies among the company of divine ancestors, but it would not be long before the Egyptian kings of the Twenty-first Dynasty would choose their own new capital city of Tanis and its safe and secure temple confines for their royal tombs instead.[245] In many ways, these Valley of the Kings tombs did the opposite of what they are supposed to do, their entrances becoming wider and grander, big enough to fit a barque of the god Amun even, tomb-temple spaces more fit for ritual display than hidden secret chambers of eternal safety. We might suspect that some of the latest Ramesside kings were not deposited in the Valley of the Kings at all, their retainers waiting it out for necropolis security to return. Just because a tomb was cut there for a given king does not mean that king was actually interred therein, especially for a northern king in a southern town potentially hostile to their mostly absent leadership.

Indeed, the entire necropolis of Thebes was being pillaged. There is every indication that, by this point, the Theban high priests of Amun were using the Valley of the Kings as their own personal bank vault, a new revenue source to fund their regimes in the absence of crown money or tax income. Papyri documentation, particularly from the reign of Rameses IX, records a series of court proceedings in which interrogations and testimony are recorded about infiltration into royal and non-royal tombs in the Theban necropolis, the so-called Tomb Robbery Papyri.[246] The tombs of the Seventeenth Dynasty royal family had been pillaged, according to court documentation, an affront to those Theban originators of kingly power. Even the recently sealed tomb of Rameses

---

245. Montet 1947; 1951; 1960.

246. Most notably, the Papyri Abbott and Mayer: Maspero 1871; Peet 1915a; 1915b; 1930; Ridealgh 2014; Niwiński 2017.

VI had been broken into, according to papyri and graffiti.[247] Nothing on the West Bank was safe; even the mortuary temples of Rameses II (1279–1213 BC) and Rameses III (1181–1150 BC) were pillaged, precious metals stripped from doors and floors, imported wooden planks taken to make coffins. The formal investigation of all of this robbery was led by high officials, including the high priest of Amun—which does not necessarily absolve them of tomb robbery. The high priesthood was probably cracking down on illicit pillaging that was bypassing their own careful and systematic clearing of the Valley and West Bank of Thebes. The fact that the bodies of the high priests and their families were all found cached together with the kings of the New Kingdom (in Theban Tomb 320 at Deir el-Bahri) indicates that the Amun priesthood had indeed opened up each and every royal tomb, stripped each royal mummy of its pectorals, masks, arm bands, finger and toes stalls, all of it, and rewrapped them with new linens, minus their treasures.[248] There is a complicated story told by hieratic inscriptions on dockets, mummy braces, and reused wooden coffins,[249] but suffice it to say that by the first part of the Twenty-first Dynasty, all of the known wealth was removed from the Valley. Only the aberrant and seemingly forgotten Amarna tombs were left uncollected, waiting for archaeologists to find them in the twentieth century.

The shifting patronage system of Thebes is visible in the Tomb Robbery Papyri. Turf wars between the mayors of eastern Thebes (Paser) and western Thebes (Paweraa) seem to have started much of the disagreement. Evidence from Deir el-Medina indicates a variety of disputes about tomb spaces and evidence of break-ins and theft within private tombs. Guards who were paid to protect tomb spaces stole from the ancestors whose families employed them, turning over wealth to shady characters who sold and reprocessed all the goods found in the tomb; and thus, we see actual evidence of old patrons being discarded while

247. Vinson 2001; Peden 2001.

248. Peet 1930; Aston 2009: 220; Strudwick 2013. For an examination of the royal cache at Deir el-Bahri 320 and KV 35, see Cooney 2021.

249. Reeves 1990; Aston 2009; Cooney 2011: 3–44; 2017: 87–98; 2021; Reeves 2015; 2016: 117–134.

new ones were taken on. Other documents from Deir el-Medina record all the fungible goods found in unclaimed tombs in their village necropolis, recording tomb goods (metals, linens, sandals, funerary equipment, furniture, everything but the mummy, which could not be bought or sold), ostensibly so that the men witnessing the inventory could split the goods among themselves.[250]

In the end, the tomb robbery prosecutions seem to have been overruled by the vizier Khaemwaset—perhaps because he was getting a cut of the proceeds from those being indicted. Indeed, the main culprit, the mayor of western Thebes, Paweraa, survived accusations of corruption and theft, and from later evidence, historians can see that the robberies continued unabated. The mayor of western Thebes seems to have come up victorious, at least temporarily, probably because of his access to such golden riches in the elite cemeteries to pay off vizier, guards, and middlemen. There was a second tomb robbery investigation dated to the reign of Rameses XI (1099–1069 BC), this time led by the vizier himself, the last vestige of the crown's power in Thebes.[251] During this trial, the artisans of Deir el-Medina were implicated—no surprise given their line of work within the Valleys of the Kings and Queens, the institutional memory they commanded, and the company they kept. This was a battle between crown representatives and local Theban institutions. There were more interrogations. More beatings were ordered to extract information. There was even a theft from Karnak temple itself, and it seems the chief guard of that god's house was implicated.

We should not misunderstand these investigations as some noble and ethical intent on the part of vizier or high priest of Amun to keep the necropolis secure and protected. These are merely competitions between rivals for the same turf and treasures, not to mention the signs of a society that was shifting its allegiances and morals, creating a new cultural agreement to reuse all of the commodities that surplus and plenty had allowed their ancestors to squirrel away in their hidden burial chambers.

---

250. Cooney 2014: 16–28.

251. Papyri Mayer A and B; see Peet 1915a; 1915b; Ridealgh 2014.

People even negotiated their own funerary practices by burying their dead in reused coffins, and there is circumstantial evidence that some only inhabited a given coffin for a short time, before it was reused again. Indeed, recent research has proven that most, if not all, coffins of this time period were reused. Very few Twentieth Dynasty coffins have survived into the archaeological record, and that is likely because they were all remade and updated with Twenty-first Dynasty decoration.[252]

In many ways, the south was the safer place to be during the Late Bronze Age collapse. The Nile valley was more easily unified geographically and more protectable from invasion via the desert. It was arguably more conservative and culturally stable, less prone geographically to incursions of migrants in large numbers. But now, even the south was breaking down into increased decentralization. It probably did not help that a giant bank vault of wealth was now fair game for whoever had the strategy, political protection, and military might to claim it. The vultures were descending to feast upon the riches left behind. In many ways, what was most provincial—Thebes and its leaders, the high priesthood of Amun—was now holding all the cards. It was likely the high priesthood that funded and commissioned new buildings at Karnak, because it is here that we see the high priest Amenhotep depicting himself on the same scale as the king. The satellite Khonsu temple was now ground zero for all rituals and festivals of visible importance.[253]

Things came to a head in Years 17–19 of Rameses XI when, for unclear reasons, the high priest of Amun, Amenhotep, came into conflict with the viceroy, King's Son of Kush, Panehsy who launched an attack on Medinet Habu itself. Panehsy then overreached, it seems, when he named himself general and overseer of the Amun granaries, a move which put him in direct competition with Rameses XI himself, in addition to the high priest. Rameses XI then sent the general Piankh, who drove the viceroy Panehsy into Nubia. During this time, the situation in Thebes was bad. Temples and tombs were openly looted; everyone was taking

---

252. Cooney 2011: 3–44; 2017: 87–98; 2018: 63–87.

253. Blyth 2006.

sides, some with the viceroy, some with the crown and high priest, and everyone probably remaining as flexible as possible, knowing that this was a battlefield of shifting alliances and allegiances. Eventually, something unprecedented happened. Rameses XI declared a kind of "rebirth" or "renaissance," called a *wehem mesut*, "Repeating of Births," probably indicating that some kind of truce had been reached.[254] Piankh, that general sent by the king, was named the new high priest of Amun, general, and viceroy, an extraordinary and unprecedented confluence of powers. Theban years were now measured by this *wehem mesut*, not by the reign years of Rameses XI. Southern rule was checked, but now unified under one man. Army and temple institutions that had been separate were now united, and funded by new sources of Theban revenue.

The new general and high priest of Amun, Piankh, got busy, heading south to destroy Panehsy. When he did so, he left his wife Nodjmet in charge of Thebes, a clear sign that in the absence of formal power systems, informal family structures could work well enough. There is evidence in the Late Ramesside Letters that these new powerbrokers—Piankh and Nodjmet—were willing to eliminate those who tried to go around them, including the purposeful disappearance of a few policemen who were going to rat out some vaguely referenced activity (in the necropolis or in the Valley of the Kings?) that no one wanted revealed. The letter even mentions securing the dispatched men in baskets and throwing them into the Nile, certainly a mafia-like way to avoid transparency, with more payoffs of more agents.[255]

With Piankh, we see Thebes crawl out of some of the worst turmoil it had ever known. Piankh then handed off his power to his chosen successor, a general named Herihor,[256] perhaps as Horemheb had handed off his power to his general Rameses I so many hundreds of years before. Herihor may have even taken on Piankh's wife Nodjmet, in a kind of

---

254. Snape 2012: 427–428.

255. Late Ramesside Letter 21: Wente 1990: 183; also Eyre 2012: 133–134.

256. The order of Piankh and Herihor is hotly disputed; see Jansen-Winkeln 1992; Thijs 1998; 2005; Broekman 2002; Snape 2012: 428.

informal dynastic succession, if she was the same woman—kind of like Thutmose I (1504–1492 BC) marrying into the family of Amenhotep I (1525–1504 BC), some five hundred years earlier. And this new high priest Herihor also took a bold step forward; he took on royal cartouche names, naming himself king when Rameses XI died in the north.[257]

We learn many things from this civil war. First, military power was paramount, only now it was connected to religious institutions and what was left of Egypt's hegemony of Nubian gold mines and mineral stores. Second, there was still cooperation between the Amun high priesthood and the crown at this point, so much so that the king sent aid if it served him. Third, the king still, apparently, had resources—enough to send men south to protect what was a very important investment to Piramesses in getting a share of Thebes's new income stream. The most important thing to conclude from this civil war is that once political and military authority had been reimposed on the region, the looting of the King's and Queen's Valleys could continue on a scale not seen before and with impunity. What had occurred before Rameses XI must have amounted to nothing more than small-scale incursions and opportunistic revenue creation. Now, however, was likely the time when the massive sarcophagi of god-kings like Sety I (1290–1279 BC) and Rameses II (1279–1213 BC) were opened and their solid gold coffins removed, to be repurposed, funding both north and south, perhaps a material manifestation of that brokered truce that the *wehem mesut* represented. The graffiti of Thutmose and his son Butehamun, knowledgeable artisans from Deir el-Medina, likely date to this period, showing the systematic marking and exploitation of every known space in necropolis wadis that had protected royal treasures for so long.[258] No surprise, then, that Psusennes I of the Egyptian Twenty-first Dynasty (see chapter 35 in volume 4) was found buried in a reused sarcophagus of Merenptah (1213–1203 BC).[259]

---

257. Snape 2012: 432–437.

258. Sadek 1974: no. 3651; Kitchen 1983b: 879.

259. Montet 1951.

In some ways, the Twentieth Dynasty went out with a bang. Rameses XI ruled for an astounding thirty years. He had created new revenue streams. He had helped broker a peace after civil war, returning centralization to Thebes. But he still could not save a united Egypt. He had empowered a high priesthood of Amun so much that Thebes would finalize its shift in patronage from crown to temple and, ultimately, claim a part of the kingship for itself. For whatever reason, despite the long reign of Rameses XI, we see no evidence of any sons following in the footsteps of their father. If they existed, they were pushed out or predeceased the old king, certainly a likelihood with a thirty-year rule. In the end, the crown passed to a man named Nesubanebdjed (called Smendes in many Greek texts), almost certainly of Libyan (and thus, at this time, Sea Peoples) extraction, who married one of the king's daughters to secure his divine spot. He did not have the power, it seems, to shut down Herihor's presumptions to the same throne in Thebes. Piramesses's harbors had already been silting up for some time, and so the great capital city was moved, block by block, colossal by colossal, obelisks and all, to a new location further north in the Nile delta, to the site of Tanis, where the vulnerable Egyptian kings of the Twenty-first and Twenty-second Dynasties would be based instead.

27.11. Coming full circle

And so we come full circle: the same mechanisms that had allowed Rameses I (1292–1290 BC) and Sethnakht (1185–1181 BC), men of the eastern delta and of probable Levantine ancestry, to claim the throne of Egypt now paved the way for Nesubanebdjed, a Libyan of likely Sea Peoples ancestry, to start Egypt's Twenty-first Dynasty. It was the social mobility of a growing mercenary military institution that rewarded the strategy and wiles of such operators. Indeed, even the generals Piankh and Herihor were of Libyan extraction, having risen through the ranks of a professionalized military. The entire Ramesside period is defined and organized by mercenary-military institutions, and, it seems, mercenaries would rule Egypt still, for many years to come.

REFERENCES

Abd El-Razik, M. 1974. The dedicatory and building texts of Ramesses II in Luxor Temple, I: the texts. *JEA* 60: 142–160.

Abd El-Razik, M. 1975. The dedicatory and building texts of Ramesses II in Luxor Temple, II: interpretation. *JEA* 61: 125–136.

Ahlström, G.W., and Edelman, D. 1985. Merneptah's Israel. *JNES* 44: 59–61.

Aldred, C. 1963. The parentage of King Siptah. *JEA* 49: 41–48.

Aldred, C. 1968. Two monuments of the reign of Horemheb. *JEA* 54: 100–106.

Allam, S. 2010. Der Vertrag Ramses' II. mit dem Hethiterkönig Hattušili III. (nach der hieroglyphischen Inschrift im Karnak-Tempel). In Barta, H., Rollinger, R., and Lang, M. (eds.), *Staatsverträge, Völkerrecht und Diplomatie im alten Orient und in der griechisch-römischen Antike.* Wiesbaden: Harrassowitz, 81–115.

Altenmüller, H. 1984. Der Begräbnistag Sethos' II. *SAK* 11: 37–47.

Altenmüller, H. 1992. Bemerkungen zu den neu gefundenen Daten im Grab der Königin Twosre (KV 14) im Tal der Könige von Theben. In Reeves, C.N. (ed.), *After Tut'ankhamūn: research and excavation in the royal necropolis at Thebes.* London and New York: Kegan Paul International, 141–164.

Altenmüller, H. 1994. Das Graffito 551 aus der thebanischen Nekropole. *SAK* 21: 19–28.

Altenmüller, H. 2001. The tomb of Tausert and Setnakht. In Weeks, K.R. (ed.), *The Treasures of the Valley of the Kings: tombs and temples of the Theban West Bank in Luxor.* Cairo: American University in Cairo Press, 222–231.

Altenmüller, H. 2003. Tausrets Weg zum Königtum: Metamorphosen einer Königin. In Gundlach, R., and Rößler-Köhler, U. (eds.), *Das Königtum der Ramessidenzeit: Voraussetzungen — Verwirklichung — Vermächtnis.* Wiesbaden: Harrassowitz, 109–128.

Anderson, A. 2016. *Smallpox evolution, history explored with genome sequence from ancient remains.* Retrieved from https://www.genomeweb.com/ sequencing/smallpox-evolution-history-explored-genome-sequence-ancient-remains (last accessed September 10, 2019).

Anonymous (ed.) 1844. *A general description of Sir John Soane's museum, with brief notices of some of the more interesting works of art therein.* London: Shaw.

Antoine, J.-C. 2014. Social position and the organisation of landholding in Ramesside Egypt: an analysis of the Wilbour Papyrus. *SAK* 43: 17–46.

Assmann, J. 1970. *Der König als Sonnenpriester: ein kosmographischer Begleittext zur kultischen Sonnenhymnik in thebanischen Tempeln und Gräbern.* Glückstadt: Augustin.

Assmann, J. 1984. Das Grab mit gewundenem Abstieg: zum Typenwandel des Privat-Felsgrabes im Neuen Reich. *MDAIK* 40: 277–290.

Assmann, J. 1995a. *Egyptian solar religion in the New Kingdom: Re, Amun and the crisis of polytheism.* London and New York: Kegan Paul International.

Assmann, J. 1995b. Geheimnis, Gedächtnis und Gottesnähe: zum Strukturwandel der Grabsemantik und der Diesseits-Jenseitsbeziehungen im Neuen Reich. In Assmann, J., Dziobek, E., Guksch, H., and Kampp, F. (eds.), *Thebanische Beamtennekropolen: neue Perspektiven archäologischer Forschung.* Heidelberg: Heidelberger Orientverlag, 281–293.

Assmann, J. 2001. *The search for god in ancient Egypt.* Ithaca, NY: Cornell University Press.

Assmann, J. 2003. The Ramesside tomb and the construction of sacred space. In Strudwick, N., and Taylor, J.H. (eds.), *The Theban necropolis: past, present, and future.* London: British Museum Press, 46–52.

Aston, B.G., and Weeks, K.R. 1992. The Theban Mapping Project and work in KV 5. In Reeves, C.N. (ed.), *After Tut'ankhamūn: research and excavation in the royal necropolis at Thebes.* London and New York: Kegan Paul International, 99–121.

Aston, D.A. 2009. *Burial assemblages of Dynasty 21–25: chronology — typology — developments.* Vienna: Verlag der Österreichischen Akademie der Wissenschaften.

Ayad, M.F. 2007. On the identity and role of the god's wife of Amun in rites of royal and divine dominion. *Journal of the Society for the Study of Egyptian Antiquities* 34: 1–13.

Ayad, M.F. 2009. *God's wife, god's servant: the god's wife of Amun.* London and New York: Routledge.

Ayad, M.F. 2016. Gender, ritual, and manipulation of power: the god's wife of Amun (Dynasty 23–26). In Blöbaum, A.I., Lohwasser, A., and Becker, M. (eds.), *"Prayer and power": proceedings of the conference on the god's wives of Amun in Egypt during the first millennium BC.* Münster: Ugarit-Verlag, 89–106.

Bács, T.A. 2017. Traditions old and new: artistic production of the late Ramesside period. In Gillen, T. (ed.), *(Re)productive traditions in ancient Egypt*. Liège: Université de Liège, 305–332.

Baines, J. 1995. Egyptian art and aesthetics. In Baines, J., Beckman, G., Sasson, J.M., and Rubinson, K.S. (eds.), *Civilizations of the ancient Near East.* New York: Charles Scribner, 2581–2582.

Baines, J., and Eyre, C.J. 1983. Four notes on literacy. *GM* 61: 65–96.

Baines, J., and Frood, E. 2011. Piety, change and display in the New Kingdom. In Collier, M., and Snape, S. (eds.), *Ramesside studies in honour of K.A. Kitchen.* Bolton: Rutherford Press, 1–17.

Bakry, H.S.K. 1973. The discovery of a temple of Merenptaḥ at On: Merenptaḥ commemorates his victory over the Libyans. *Aegyptus* 53: 3–21.

Barwik, M. 2011. *The twilight of Ramesside Egypt: studies on the history of Egypt at the end of the Ramesside period.* Warsaw: Agade.

Beckman, G. 2000. Hittite chronology. *Akkadica* 119–120: 19–32.

Belova, G.A. 2003. TT320 and the history of the royal cache during the Twenty-First Dynasty. In Hawass, Z. (ed.), *Egyptology at the dawn of the twenty-first century: proceedings of the eighth international congress of egyptologists, Cairo.* Cairo: American University in Cairo Press, 73–80.

Bierbrier, M. 2011. Bye-bye Bay. In Collier, M., and Snape, S. (eds.), *Ramesside studies in honour of K.A. Kitchen.* Bolton: Rutherford Press, 19–21.

Bietak, M. 2010. Houses, palaces and development of social structure in Avaris. In Bietak, M., Czerny, E., and Forstner-Müller, I. (eds.), *Cities and urbanism in ancient Egypt.* Vienna: Verlag der Österreichischen Akademie der Wissenschaften, 11–68.

Bietak, M. 2017. Harbours and coastal military bases in Egypt in the second millennium B.C.: Avaris, Peru-Nefer, Pi-Ramesse. In Willems, H., and Dahms, J.-M. (eds.), *The Nile: natural and cultural landscape in Egypt.* Bielefeld: transcript, 53–70.

Bietak, M., and Forstner-Müller, I. 2011. The topography of New Kingdom Avaris and Per-Ramesses. In Collier, M., and Snape, S. (eds.), *Ramesside studies in honour of K.A. Kitchen.* Bolton: Rutherford Press, 23–50.

Bietak, M., and von Rüden, C. 2018. Contact points: Avaris and Pi-Ramesse. In Spier, J., Potts, T., and Cole, S.E. (eds.), *Beyond the Nile: Egypt and the classical world.* Los Angeles, CA: J. Paul Getty Museum, 18–23.

Binder, S. 2012. Das Ehrengold als Machtinstrument des Königs. In Beinlich, H. (ed.). *"Die Männer hinter dem König."* Wiesbaden: Harrassowitz, 1–16.

Blyth, E. 2006. *Karnak: evolution of a temple.* London and New York: Routledge.

Booth, C. 2009. *Horemheb: the forgotten pharaoh.* Stroud: Amberley.

Booth, C. 2013. Horemheb: founder of the Nineteenth Dynasty. *Ancient Egypt: the History, People and Culture of the Nile Valley* 78: 10–17.

Boraik, M. 2007. Stela of Bakenkhonsu, high-priest of Amun-Re. *Memnonia* 18: 119–126.

Bourdieu, P. 1984. *Distinction: a social critique of the judgement of taste.* Cambridge: Cambridge University Press.

Bourdieu, P., and Nice, R. 1977. *Outline of a theory of practice.* Cambridge: Cambridge University Press.

Brand, P.J. 1999. Secondary restorations in the post-Amarna period. *JARCE* 36: 113–134.

Brand, P.J. 2000. *The monuments of Seti I: epigraphic, historical, and art historical analysis.* Leiden: Brill.

Brand, P.J. 2010a. Reuse and restoration. In Wendrich, W. (ed.), *UCLA Encyclopedia of Egyptology.* Los Angeles: University of California, Los Angeles. Retrieved from https://escholarship.org/uc/item/2vp6065d (last accessed November 29, 2019).

Brand, P.J. 2010b. Usurpation of monuments. In Wendrich, W. (ed.), *UCLA Encyclopedia of Egyptology.* Los Angeles: University of California, Los Angeles. Retrieved from https://escholarship.org/uc/item/5gj996k5 (last accessed November 29, 2019).

Brand, P.J. 2011. The date of the war scenes on the south wall of the great hypostyle hall and the west wall of the *cour de la cachette* at Karnak and the history of the late Nineteenth Dynasty. In Collier, M., and Snape, S. (eds.), *Ramesside studies in honour of K.A. Kitchen.* Bolton: Rutherford Press.

Breasted, J.H. 1904. The battle of Kadesh: a study in the earliest known military strategy. In Breasted, J.H. (ed.), *Investigations representing the departments: Semitic languages and literatures, Biblical and Patristic Greek.* Chicago: University of Chicago Press, 81–126.

Breasted, J.H. 1906. *Ancient records of Egypt: historical documents from the earliest times to the Persian conquest.* Chicago: University of Chicago Press.

Breasted, J.H. 1912. *Development of religion and thought in ancient Egypt: lectures delivered on the Morse Foundation at Union Theological Seminary.* London: Hodder & Stoughton.

Broekman, G.P.F. 2002. The founders of the Twenty-first Dynasty and their family relationships. *GM* 191: 11–18.

Brugsch, É. 1889. *La tente funéraire de la princesse Isimkheb provenant de la trouvaille de Déir el-Baharî*. Vienna: Holzhausen.

Bruyère, B. 1952. *Tombes thébaines de Deir el Médineh à décoration monochrome*. Cairo: Institut français d'archéologie orientale.

Bryan, B.M. 2005. Property and the god's wives of Amun. In Lyons, D., and Westbrook, R. (eds.), *Women and property in ancient Near Eastern and Mediterranean societies*. Washington, DC: Center for Hellenic Studies, 1–15.

Bryan, B.M. 2007. A "new" statue of Amenhotep III and the meaning of the *khepresh* crown. In Hawass, Z.A., and Richards, J. (eds.), *The archaeology and art of ancient Egypt: essays in honor of David B. O'Connor, vol. 1*. Cairo: Supreme Council of Antiquities, 151–167.

Bryce, T. 1998. *The kingdom of the Hittites*. Oxford: Oxford University Press.

Bryce, T. 2006. The "eternal treaty" from the Hittite perspective. *BMSAES* 6: 1–11.

Bryson, K.M. 2018. *The reign of Horemheb: history, historiography, and the dawn of the Ramesside era*. PhD thesis, Johns Hopkins University, Baltimore, MD. Retrieved from https://jscholarship.library.jhu.edu/handle/1774.2/61052 (last accessed September 15, 2020).

Buck, A.D. 1937. The judicial papyrus of Turin. *JEA* 23: 152–164.

Budge, E.A.W. 1908. *An account of the sarcophagus of Seti I, king of Egypt, BC 1370*. London: British Museum.

Burger Robin, S. 2019. *Late Ramesside royal statuary*. Wallasey: Abercromby Press.

Burke, A.A., and Lords, K.V. 2010. Egyptians in Jaffa: a portrait of Egyptian presence in Jaffa during the Late Bronze Age. *NEA* 73: 2–30.

Burke, A.A., Peilstöcker, M., Karoll, A., Pierce, G.A., Kowalski, K., Ben-Marzouk, N., Damm, J.C., Danielson, A.J., Fessler, H.D., Kaufman, B., Pierce, K.V.L., Höflmayer, F., Damiata, B.N., and Dee, M. 2017. Excavations of the New Kingdom fortress in Jaffa, 2011–2014: traces of resistance to Egyptian rule in Canaan. *AJA* 121: 85–133.

Callender, V.G. 2004. Queen Tausret and the end of Dynasty 19. *SAK* 32: 81–104.

Callender, V.G. 2012. Female Horus: the life and reign of Tausret. In Wilkinson, R.H. (ed.), *Tausret: forgotten queen and pharaoh of Egypt*. Oxford: Oxford University Press, 25–47.

Candelora, D. 2017. Defining the Hyksos: a reevaluation of the title *ḥḳꜣ ḫꜣswt* and its implications for Hyksos identity. *JARCE* 53: 203–221.

Candelora, D. 2019a. Hybrid military communities of practice: the integration of immigrants as the catalyst for Egyptian social transformation in the 2nd millennium. In Mynářová, J., Kilani, M., and Alivernini, S. (eds.), *A stranger in the house: the crossroads III*. Prague: Charles University, 25–47.

Candelora, D. 2019b. Hyksos identity negotiation in an eastern delta middle ground. *MDAIK* 75: 77–94.

Candelora, D. 2020. *Redefining the Hyksos: immigration and identity negotiation in the Second Intermediate Period*. PhD thesis, University of California, Los Angeles. Retrieved from https://escholarship.org/uc/item/01d9d70t (last accessed September 15, 2020).

Cardon, P.D. 1979. Amenmesse: an Egyptian royal head of the Nineteenth Dynasty in the Metropolitan Museum. *Metropolitan Museum Journal* 14: 5–14.

Černý, J. 1935. *Ostraca hiératiques, nos. 25501–25832*. Cairo: Institut français d'archéologie orientale.

Černý, J. 1966. A note on the chancellor Bay. *ZÄS* 93: 35–39.

Charron, A., and Barbotin, C. (eds.) 2016. *Khâemouaset, le prince archéologue: savoir et pouvoir à l'époque de Ramsès II*. Ghent: Snoeck.

Chubb, J.A., Greener, L., Nelson, H.H., Schott, S., Seele, K.C., Wilber, D.N., Bollacher, A., Canziani, V., Leichter, H., and Martindale, R.C. 1936. *Reliefs and inscriptions at Karnak, vol. 1: Ramses III's temple within the great enclosure of Amon, part 1*. Chicago: The Oriental Institute of the University of Chicago.

Cifola, B. 1988. Ramses III and the Sea Peoples: a structural analysis of the Medinet Habu inscriptions. *Orientalia* 57: 275–306.

Cifola, B. 1994. *The role of the Sea Peoples at the end of the Late Bronze Age: a reassessment of textual and archaeological evidence*. Rome: Istituto per l'Oriente.

Cline, E.H. 2014. *1177 BC: the year civilization collapsed*. Princeton, NJ: Princeton University Press.

Cline, E.H., and O'Connor, D. 2003. The mystery of the Sea Peoples. In O'Connor, D., and Quirke, S. (eds.), *Mysterious lands*. London: UCL Press, 107–138.

Cline, E.H., and O'Connor, D. 2012. The Sea Peoples. In Cline, E.H., and O'Connor, D. (eds.), *Ramesses III: the life and times of Egypt's last hero*. Ann Arbor: University of Michigan Press, 180–208.

Connor, S. 2017. Le torse de Ramsès, le pied de Mérenptah et le nez d'Amenhotep: observations sur quelques statues royales des collections turinoises (cat. 1381, 1382 et 3148). *Rivista del Museo Egizio* 1. Retrieved from https://doi.org/10.29353/rime.2017.507 (last accessed November 28, 2019).

Cooney, K.M. 2007. *The cost of death: the social and economic value of ancient Egyptian funerary art in the Ramesside period.* Leiden: NINO.

Cooney, K.M. 2011. Changing burial practices at the end of the New Kingdom: defensive adaptations in tomb commissions, coffin commissions, coffin decoration, and mummification. *JARCE* 47: 3–44.

Cooney, K.M. 2012. Apprenticeship and figured ostraca from the ancient Egyptian village of Deir el-Medina. In Wendrich, W. (ed.), *Archaeology and apprenticeship: body knowledge, identity, and communities of practice.* Tucson: University of Arizona Press, 145–170.

Cooney, K.M. 2014. Private sector tomb robbery and funerary arts reuse according to West Theban documentation. In Toivari-Viitala, J., Vartiainen, T., and Uvanto, S. (eds.), *Deir el-Medina studies.* Helsinki: Finnish Egyptological Society, 16–28.

Cooney, K.M. 2017. Reuse of Egyptian coffins in the 21st Dynasty: ritual materialism in the context of scarcity. In Amenta, A., and Guichard, H. (eds.), *Proceedings: first Vatican coffins conference.* Vatican: Edizioni Musei Vaticani, 87–98.

Cooney, K.M. 2018. The end of New Kingdom Egypt: how ancient Egyptian funerary materials can help us understand society in crisis. In Kubisch, S., and Rummel, U. (eds.), *The Ramesside period in Egypt: studies into cultural and historical processes of the 19th and 20th Dynasties.* Berlin: De Gruyter, 63–87.

Cooney, K.M. 2021. You're in or you're out: the inclusion or exclusion of sacred royal bodies in the tomb of the 21st Dynasty High Priests of Amun. In Laneri, N. (ed.), *The sacred body: materializing the divine through human remains in antiquity.* Oxford: Oxbow, 59–81.

Creasman, P.P. 2013. Excavations at pharaoh-queen Tausret's temple of millions of years: 2012 season. *Journal of the Society for the Study of Egyptian Antiquities* 39: 5–21.

Cruz-Uribe, E. 1978. The father of Ramses I: OI 11456. *JNES* 37: 237–244.

Daressy, G. 1909. *Catalogue général des antiquités égyptiennes du Musée du Caire, no. 61001–61044, cercueils des cachettes royales.* Cairo: Institut français d'archéologie orientale.

Davies, B.G. 2018. *Life within the five walls: a handbook to Deir el-Medina.* Wallasey: Abercromby Press.

Davis, T.M., and Crane, L. (eds.) 1912. *The tombs of Harmhabi and Touatânkhamanou.* London: Archibald Constable.

Dawson, W.R. 1925. An oracle papyrus: BM 10335. *JEA* 11: 247–248.

Dayton, J.E. 1984. Sardinia, the Sherden and Bronze Age trade routes. *Annali dell'Istituto universitario orientale* 44: 353–371.

De Morgan, J., Bouriant, U., Legrain, G., Jéquier, G., and Barsanti, A. 1894. *Catalogue des monuments et inscriptions de l'Égypt antique.* Vienna: Holzhausen.

Demarée, R.J., Mathieu, B., and Černý, J. 2001. *A community of workmen at Thebes in the Ramesside period.* Cairo: Institut français d'archéologie orientale.

Di Biase-Dyson, C. 2013. *Foreigners and Egyptians in the late Egyptian stories: linguistic, literary and historical perspectives.* Leiden: Brill.

Dodson, A. 1985. The tomb of king Amenmesse: some observations. *Discussions in Egyptology* 2: 7–11.

Dodson, A. 1986. Was the sarcophagus of Ramesses III begun for Sethos II? *JEA* 72: 196–198.

Dodson, A. 1987. The Takhats and some other royal ladies of the Ramesside period. *JEA* 73: 224–229.

Dodson, A. 1990. King Amenmesse at Riqqa. *GM* 117–118: 153–155.

Dodson, A. 1995. Amenmesse in Kent, Liverpool, and Thebes. *JEA* 81: 115–128.

Dodson, A. 1997. Messuy, Amada, and Amenmesse. *JARCE* 34: 41–48.

Dodson, A. 1999. The decorative phases of the tomb of Sethos II and their historical implications. *JEA* 85: 131–142.

Dodson, A. 2009. *Amarna sunset: Nefertiti, Tutankhamun, Ay, Horemheb, and the Egyptian counter-reformation.* Cairo: American University in Cairo Press.

Dodson, A. 2011. Fade to grey: the chancellor Bay, éminence grise of the late Nineteenth Dynasty. In Collier, M., and Snape, S. (eds.), *Ramesside studies in honour of K.A. Kitchen.* Bolton: Rutherford Press, 145–158.

Dodson, A. 2016. *Poisoned legacy: the fall of the Nineteenth Egyptian Dynasty.* Cairo: American University in Cairo Press.

Dodson, A., and Hilton, D. 2004. *The complete royal families of ancient Egypt*. London: Thames & Hudson.

Donker van Heel, K., and Haring, B.J.J. 2003. *Writing in a workmen's village: scribal practice in Ramesside Deir el-Medina*. Leuven: Peeters.

Dorner, J. 1999. Die Topographie von Piramesse: Vorbericht. *ÄL* 9: 77–83.

Drenkhahn, R. 1980. *Die Elephantine-Stele des Sethnacht und ihr historischer Hintergrund*. Wiesbaden: Harrassowitz.

Drews, R. 2000. Medinet Habu: oxcarts, ships, and migration theories. *JNES* 59: 161–190.

Edgerton, W.F. 1951. The strikes in Ramses III's twenty-ninth year. *JNES* 10: 137–145.

Edwards, A.B. 1888. *A thousand miles up the Nile*. London and New York: Routledge.

Epigraphic Survey. 1930. *Medinet Habu I: earlier historical records of Ramses III*. Chicago: The Oriental Institute of the University of Chicago.

Epigraphic Survey. 1970. *Medinet Habu: the eastern high gate*. Chicago: The Oriental Institute of the University of Chicago.

Epigraphic Survey. 1986. *Reliefs and inscriptions at Karnak, vol. 4: the battle reliefs of King Sety I*. Chicago: The Oriental Institute of the University of Chicago.

Erman, A. 1891. Das achte Jubiläum Ramses' II. *ZÄS* 29: 128.

Erman, A. 1911. Denksteine aus der thebanischen Gräberstadt. *Sitzungsberichte der Preußischen Akademie der Wissenschaften zu Berlin* 1911: 1086–1110.

Eyre, C.J. 1980. An accounts papyrus from Thebes. *JEA* 66: 108–119.

Eyre, C.J. 2011. Patronage, power, and corruption in pharaonic Egypt. *Journal of Public Administration* 34: 701–711.

Eyre, C.J. 2012. Society, economy, and administrative process in late Ramesside Egypt. In Cline, E.H., and O'Connor, D. (eds.), *Ramesses III: the life and times of Egypt's last hero*. Ann Arbor: University of Michigan Press, 101–150.

Eyre, C.J. 2018. The accessibility of Ramesside narrative. In Kubisch, S., and Rummel, U. (eds.), *The Ramesside period in Egypt: studies into cultural and historical processes of the 19th and 20th Dynasties*. Berlin: De Gruyter, 89–102.

Feldman, M. 2006. *Diplomacy by design: luxury arts and an "international style" in the ancient Near East, 1400–1300 BCE*. Chicago: University of Chicago Press.

Fisher, M. 2013. A diplomatic marriage in the Ramesside period: Maathorneferure, daughter of the great ruler of Hatti. In Collins, B.J., and Michalowski, P. (eds.), *Beyond Hatti: a tribute to Gary Beckman*. Atlanta, GA: Lockwood Press, 75–119.

Fisher, M.M. 2001. *The sons of Ramses II*. Wiesbaden: Harrassowitz.

Forstner-Müller, I. 2018. Center and periphery: some remarks on the delta and its borders during the Ramesside period. In Kubisch, S., and Rummel, U. (eds.), *The Ramesside period in Egypt: studies into cultural and historical processes of the 19th and 20th Dynasties*. Berlin: De Gruyter, 103–112.

Franzmeier, H., and Moje, J. 2018. The missing dead? On the question of the burial grounds of Pi-Ramesse. In Kubisch, S., and Rummel, U. (eds.), *The Ramesside period in Egypt: studies into cultural and historical processes of the 19th and 20th Dynasties*. Berlin: De Gruyter, 113–126.

Frerichs, E.S., and Lesko, L.H. (eds.) 1997. *Exodus: the Egyptian evidence*. Winona Lake, IN: Eisenbrauns.

Frood, E. 2007. *Biographical texts from Ramesside Egypt*. Leiden: Brill.

Frood, E. 2016. Temple lives: devotion, piety, and the divine. In Giovetti, P., and Picchi, D. (eds.), *Egypt, millenary splendour: the Leiden collection in Bologna*. Milan: Skira, 316–323.

Gabolde, M. 1987. Ay, Toutankhamon et les martelages de la stèle de la restauration de Karnak (CG 34183). *Bulletin de la Société d'Égyptologie de Genève* 11: 37–61.

Gardiner, A.H. 1948. *Ramesside administrative documents*. Oxford: Oxford University Press.

Gardiner, A.H. 1953. The coronation of king Haremḥab. *JEA* 39: 13–31.

Gardiner, A.H. 1958. Only one king Siptaḥ and Twosre not his wife. *JEA* 44: 12–22.

Gardiner, A.H., and Wilbour, C.E. 1941. *The Wilbour Papyrus*. Oxford: Oxford University Press.

Gardiner, S.A. 1960. *The Kadesh inscriptions of Ramesses II*. Oxford: Oxford University Press.

Georg, M. 2000. Mose - Name und Namensträger: Versuch einer historischen Annäherung. In Otto, E. (ed.), *Mose: Ägypten und das Alte Testament*. Stuttgart: Verlag Katholisches Bibelwerk, 17–42.

Giacomo, C. 2015. From the Mediterranean Sea to the Nile: new perspectives and researches on the Sherden in Egypt. In Kousoulis, P., and Lazaridis,

N. (eds.), *Proceedings of the tenth international congress of Egyptologists.* Leuven: Peeters, 631–638.

Gilmour, G., and Kitchen, K.A. 2012. Pharaoh Sety II and Egyptian political relations with Canaan at the end of the Later Bronze Age. *IEJ* 62: 1–21.

Goedicke, H. 1963. Was magic used in the harem conspiracy against Ramesses III? (P. Rollin and P. Lee). *JEA* 49: 71–92.

Goedicke, H. 1966. Considerations on the battle of Kadesh. *JEA* 52: 71–80.

Goedicke, H. (ed.) 1985. *Perspectives on the battle of Kadesh.* Baltimore, MD: Halgo.

Goedicke, H. 2004. Remarks on the "Israel Stela." *Wiener Zeitschrift für die Kunde des Morgenlandes* 94: 53–72.

Graefe, E., and Belova, G. (eds.) 2010. *The royal cache TT 320: a re-examination.* Cairo: Supreme Council of Antiquities.

Grandet, P. 1993. *Ramsès III: histoire d'un règne.* Paris: Pygmalion.

Grandet, P. 1994. *Le papyrus Harris I (BM 9999).* Cairo: Institut français d'archéologie orientale.

Grandet, P. 2000. L'execution du chancellor Bay: O. IFAO 1864. *BIFAO* 100: 339–356.

Grandet, P. 2006. Les grèves de Deîr el-Médînéh. In Molin, M. (ed.), *Les régulations sociales dans l'antiquité.* Rennes: Presses Universitaires de Rennes, 87–96.

Grandet, P. 2016. L'avènement de la XIXe dynastie. In Charron, A., and Barbotin, C. (eds.), *Khâemouaset, le prince archéologue: savoir et pouvoir à l'époque de Ramsès II.* Ghent: Snoeck, 16–19.

Grandet, P. 2018. The "chapter on hierarchy" in Amenope's onomasticon (# 67–125). In Kubisch, S., and Rummel, U. (eds.), *The Ramesside period in Egypt: studies into cultural and historical processes of the 19th and 20th Dynasties.* Berlin: De Gruyter, 127–137.

Green, J., Evans, J.M., and Teeter, E. (eds.) 2017. *Highlights of the collections of the Oriental Institute Museum.* Chicago: The Oriental Institute of the University of Chicago.

Griffith, F.L., Spiegelberg, W., Quibell, J.E., Paget, R.F.E., and Pirie, A.A. 1898. *The Ramesseum: the tomb of Ptah-hetep.* London: Quaritch.

Guksch, H. 1994. *Königsdienst: zur Selbstdarstellung der Beamten in der 18. Dynastie.* Heidelberg: Heidelberger Orientverlag.

Gundlach, R. 2003. Sethos I. und Ramses II.: Tradition und Entwicklungsbruch in der frühramessidischen Königsideologie.

In Gundlach, R., and Rößler-Köhler, U. (eds.), *Das Königtum der Ramessidenzeit: Voraussetzungen — Verwirklichung — Vermächtnis.* Wiesbaden: Harrassowitz, 17–53.

Habachi, L. 1955. Découverte d'un temple-forteresse de Ramsès II. *La Revue du Caire* 33: 62–65.

Habachi, L. 1971. The jubilees of Ramesses II and Amenophis III with reference to certain aspects of their celebration. *ZÄS* 97: 64–72.

Habachi, L. 1974. Sethos I's devotion to Seth and Avaris. *ZÄS* 100: 95–102.

Habachi, L. 1978. King Amenmesse and viziers Amenmose and Kha'emtore: their monuments and place in history. *MDAIK* 34: 57–67.

Habachi, L. 1980. The military posts of Ramesses II: on the coastal road and the western part of the delta. *BIFAO* 80: 13–30.

Haider, P.W. 2012. The Aegean and Anatolia. In Cline, E.H., and O'Connor, D. (eds.), *Ramesses III: the life and times of Egypt's last hero.* Ann Arbor: University of Michigan Press, 151–160.

Hardwick, T. 2006. The golden Horus name of Amenmesse? *JEA* 92: 255–260.

Hari, R. 1965. *Horemheb et la reine Moutnedjemet ou la fin d'une dynastie.* Geneva: La Sirène.

Haring, B.J.J. 1997. *Divine households: administratie and economic aspects of the New Kingdom royal memorial temples in Western Thebes.* Leiden: NINO.

Haring, B.J.J. 2003. From oral practice to written record in Ramesside Deir el-Medina. *Journal of the Economic and Social History of the Orient* 46: 249–272.

Haring, B.J.J. 2007. Ramesside temples and the economic interests of the state: crossroads of the sacred and the profane. In Fitzenreiter, M. (ed.), *Das Heilige und die Ware: Eigentum, Austausch und Kapitalisierung im Spannungsfeld von Ökonomie und Religion.* London: Golden House, 165–170.

Harrell, J.A., and Brown, V.M. 1992. The oldest surviving topographical map from ancient Egypt (Turin papyri 1879, 1899, 1969). *JARCE* 29: 81–105.

Hasel, M.G. 2011. The battle of Kadesh: identifying New Kingdom polities, places, and peoples in Canaan and Syria. In Kahn, D., Shirley, J.J., and Bar, S. (eds.), *Egypt, Canaan and Israel: history, imperialism, ideology and literature.* Leiden: Brill, 65–86.

Hawass, Z., Gad, Y.Z., Ismail, S., Khairat, R., Fathalla, D., Hasan, N., Ahmed, A., Elleithy, H., Ball, M., Gaballah, F., Wasef, S., Fateen, M., Amer, H.,

Gostner, P., Selim, A., Zink, A., and Pusch, C.M. 2010. Ancestry and pathology in King Tutankhamun's family. *Journal of the American Medical Association* 303: 638–647.

Hawass, Z., Ismail, S., Selim, A., Saleem, S.N., Fathalla, D., Wasef, S., Gad, A.Z., Saad, R., Fares, S., Amer, H., Gostner, P., Gad, Y.Z., Pusch, C.M., and Zink, A.R. 2012. Revisiting the harem conspiracy and death of Ramesses III: anthropological, forensic, radiological, and genetic study. *British Medical Journal* 345. Retrieved from https://doi.org/10.1136/bmj.e8268 (last accessed November 28, 2019).

Helck, H.-W. 1939. *Der Einfluss der Militärführer in der 18. ägyptischen Dynastie*. Leipzig: Hinrichs.

Helck, W. 1962. *Die Beziehungen Ägyptens zu Vorderasien im 3. und 2. Jahrtausend v. Chr*, Wiesbaden: Harrassowitz.

Helck, W. 1975. *Wirtschaftsgeschichte des alten Ägypten im 3. und 2. Jahrtausend vor Chr.* Leiden: Brill.

Higginbotham, C.R. 2012. The administrative structure under Ramesses III. In Cline, E.H., and O'Connor, D. (eds.), *Ramesses III: the life and times of Egypt's last hero*. Ann Arbor: University of Michigan Press, 66–100.

Hirsch, E.N. 2003. Ramses III. und sein Verhältnis zur Levante. In Gundlach, R., and Rößler-Köhler, U. (eds.), *Das Königtum der Ramessidenzeit: Voraussetzungen — Verwirklichung — Vermächtnis*. Wiesbaden: Harrassowitz, 197–238.

Hoffner, H.A. 2009. *Letters from the Hittite kingdom*. Atlanta, GA: Society of Biblical Literature.

Hofmann, E. 2018. Der Vorhof der Privatgräber—nur ein sakraler Ort? Die Anlagen von TT 157 des Nebwenenef und TT 183 des Nebsumenu. In Kubisch, S., and Rummel, U. (eds.), *The Ramesside period in Egypt: studies into cultural and historical processes of the 19th and 20th Dynasties*. Berlin: De Gruyter, 149–174.

Hornung, E. 1999. *The ancient Egyptian books of the afterlife*. Ithaca, NY: Cornell University Press.

Hornung, E. 2002. Exploring the beyond. In Bryan, B.M., and Hornung, E. (eds.), *The quest for immortality: treasures of ancient Egypt*. Washington, DC: National Gallery of Art, 24–51.

Hornung, E., Burton, H., and Hill, M. 1991. *The tomb of Pharaoh Seti I*. Zürich: Artemis & Winkler.

Jansen-Winkeln, K. 1992. Das Ende des Neuen Reiches. *ZÄS* 119: 22–37.

Jansen-Winkeln, K. 1993. The career of the Egyptian high priest Bakenkhons. *JNES* 52: 221–225.

Janssen, J.J. 1975. *Commodity prices from the Ramesside period.* Leiden: Brill.

Janssen, J.J. 1984. A curious error (O. IFAO 1254). *BIFAO* 84: 303–306.

Janssen, J.J. 1997. *Village varia: ten studies on the history and administration of Deir el-Medina.* Leiden: NINO.

Janssen, J.J. 2004. *Grain transport in the Ramesside period: Papyrus Baldwin (BM EA 10061) and Papyrus Amiens.* London: British Museum Press.

Johnson, G.B. 1998. A great find revisited, no. 9: KV 47, the Theban tomb of Siptah. *KMT: A Modern Journal of Ancient Egypt* 9: 46–64.

Johnson, K.L., and Brand, P.J. 2013. Prince Seti-Merenptah, chancellor Bay, and the bark shrine of Seti II at Karnak. *JEH* 6: 19–45.

Kahn, D. 2010. Who is meddling in Egypt's affairs? The identity of the Asiatics in the Elephantine stele of Sethnakhte and the historicity of the Medinet Habu Asiatic war reliefs. *JAEI* 2: 14–23.

Kahn, D. 2018. Ramesses III and the northern Levant: a reassessment of the sources. In Kubisch, S., and Rummel, U. (eds.), *The Ramesside period in Egypt: studies into cultural and historical processes of the 19th and 20th Dynasties.* Berlin: De Gruyter, 175–188.

Kaiser, W., Bidoli, D., Grossmann, P., Haeny, G., Jaritz, H., and Stadelmann, R. 1972. Stadt und Tempel von Elephantine: dritter Grabungsbericht. *MDAIK* 28: 157–200.

Kawai, N. 2010. Ay versus Horemheb: the political situation in the late Eighteenth Dynasty revisited. *JEH* 3: 261–292.

Kemp, B.J. 1995. Unification and urbanization of ancient Egypt. In Baines, J., Beckman, G., Sasson, J.M., and Rubinson, K.S. (eds.) *Civilizations of the ancient Near East.* New York: Charles Scribner, 679–690.

Kemp, B.J. 2012. *The city of Akhenaten and Nefertiti: Amarna and its people.* London: Thames & Hudson.

Kitchen, K.A. 1975. *Ramesside inscriptions, historical and biographical, I.* Oxford: Blackwell.

Kitchen, K.A. 1979. *Ramesside inscriptions, historical and biographical, II.* Oxford: Blackwell.

Kitchen, K.A. 1982. *Ramesside inscriptions, historical and biographical, IV.* Oxford: Blackwell.

Kitchen, K.A. 1983a. *Ramesside inscriptions, historical and biographical, V.* Oxford: Blackwell.

Kitchen, K.A. 1983b. *Ramesside inscriptions, historical and biographical, VI.* Oxford: Blackwell.

Kitchen, K.A. 1985. *Pharaoh triumphant: the life and times of Ramesses II, king of Egypt.* Warminster: Aris & Phillips.

Kitchen, K.A. 2003. *Ramesside inscriptions, translated & annotated: translations, IV: Merenptah & the late Nineteenth Dynasty.* Malden, MA: Wiley-Blackwell.

Kitchen, K.A. 2004. The victories of Merenptah, and the nature of their record. *Journal for the Study of the Old Testament* 28: 259–272.

Kitchen, K.A. 2008. *Ramesside inscriptions, translated & annotated: translations, V: Setnakht, Ramesses III, and contemporaries.* Malden, MA: Wiley-Blackwell.

Kitchen, K.A. 2012. Ramesses III and the Ramesside period. In Cline, E.H., and O'Connor, D. (eds.), *Ramesses III: the life and times of Egypt's last hero.* Ann Arbor: University of Michigan Press, 1–26.

Knapp, A.B., and Manning, S.W. 2016. Crisis in context: the end of the Late Bronze Age in the Eastern Mediterranean. *AJA* 120: 99–149.

Krauss, R. 1976. Untersuchungen zu König Amenmesse (1. Teil). *SAK* 4: 161–199.

Krauss, R. 1977. Untersuchungen zu König Amenmesse (2. Teil). *SAK* 5: 131–174.

Krauss, R. 2000. *Moïse le pharaon.* Paris: Éditions du Rocher.

Krauss, R. 2001. *Das Rätsel Moses: auf den Spuren einer biblischen Erfindung.* Munich: Ullstein.

Kubisch, S. 2018. The religious and political role of the high priests of Amun. In Kubisch, S., and Rummel, U. (eds.), *The Ramesside period in Egypt: studies into cultural and historical processes of the 19th and 20th Dynasties.* Berlin: De Gruyter, 189–203.

Kuhrt, A.L. 1995. *The ancient Near East, c. 3000–330 BC.* London and New York: Routledge.

Lakomy, K.C. 2016. *Der Löwe auf dem Schlachtfeld: das Grab KV 36 und die Bestattung des Maiherperi im Tal der Könige.* Wiesbaden: Reichert.

Langdon, S., and Gardiner, A.H. 1920. The treaty of alliance between Hattišili, king of the Hittites, and the pharaoh Ramesses II of Egypt. *JEA* 6: 179–205.

Leahy, A. (ed.) 1990. *Libya and Egypt, c 1300–750 BC.* London: School of Oriental and African Studies.

Leblanc, C. 1997. The tomb of Ramesses II and remains of his funerary treasure. *EA* 10: 11–13.

Leblanc, C. 2009. La tombe de Ramsès II (KV 7): de la fouille archéologique à l'identification du programme iconographique. *Memnonia* 20: 195–211.

Leblanc, C. 2016. Das Ramesseum. In Kehrer, N. (ed.), *Ramses: göttlicher Herrscher am Nil*. Petersberg: Imhof Verlag, 278–281.

Leblanc, C., Lecuyot, G., and Maher-Taha, M. 2003. Documentation, recherches et restauration au Ramesseum: bilan et perspectives. In Hawass, Z. (ed.), *Egyptology at the dawn of the twenty-first century: proceedings of the eighth international congress of Egyptologists, Cairo*. Cairo: American University in Cairo Press, 257–266.

Leitz, C. 1999. *Magical and medical papyri of the New Kingdom*. London: British Museum Press.

Leprohon, R.J. 2013. *The great name: ancient Egyptian royal titulary*. Atlanta, GA: Society of Biblical Literature.

Lesko, L.H. 1966. A little more evidence for the end of the Nineteenth Dynasty. *JARCE* 5: 29–32.

Lichtheim, M. 1976. *Ancient Egyptian literature, vol. II: the New Kingdom*. Berkeley: University of California Press.

Lichtheim, M. 2006. *Ancient Egyptian literature: a book of readings, vol. II: the New Kingdom*. Berkeley: University of California Press.

Lorand, D. 2011. Ramsès II "admirait" aussi Amenhotep III: à propos du groupe statuaire CG 555 du Musée Égyptien du Caire. *RdE* 62: 73–87.

Luiselli, M.M. 2014. Personal piety in ancient Egypt. *Religion Compass* 8: 105–116.

Lull, J., and Requena, Á. 2004. El mapa geológico-topográfico del museo egipcio de Turín (P. Turín 1879/1899/1969). *Boletín de la Asociación Española de Egiptología* 14: 189–222.

Magen, B. 2011. *Steinerne Palimpseste: zur Wiederverwendung von Statuen durch Ramses II. und seine Nachfolger*. Wiesbaden: Harrassowitz.

Manassa, C. 2003. *The great Karnak inscription of Merneptah: grand strategy in the 13th century BC*. New Haven, CT: Yale Egyptological Seminar.

Manassa Darnell, C. 2015. Transition 18th–19th Dynasty. In Wendrich, W. (ed.), *UCLA Encyclopedia of Egyptology*. Los Angeles: University of California, Los Angeles. Retrieved from https://escholarship.org/uc/item/0b9005fw (last accessed November 29, 2019).

Mandell, A. 2015. *Scribalism and diplomacy at the crossroads of cuneiform culture: the sociolinguistics of Canaano-Akkadian.* PhD thesis, University of California, Los Angeles. Retrieved from https://escholarship.org/uc/item/75498617 (last accessed November 29, 2020).

Martin, G.T., Eyre, C.J., Frazer, K.J., and van Dijk, J. 1989. *The Memphite tomb of Horemḥeb, commander-in-chief of Tutʿankhamūn, I: the reliefs, inscriptions, and commentary.* London: Egypt Exploration Society.

Maspero, G. 1871. Une enquête judiciaire à Thèbes au temps de la XXᵉ Dynastie: étude sur le Papyrus Abbott. Paris: Imprimerie nationale.

Maspero, G. 1882. Sur la cachette découverte à Dêr-el-Baharî en Juillet 1881. In Anonymous (ed.), *Verhandlungen des fünften internationalen Orientalisten-Congresses.* Berlin: Weidmann, 12–24.

Masquelier-Loorius, J. 2013. *Séthi Ier et le début de la XIXe dynastie.* Paris: Pygmalion.

McCarthy, H.L. 2008. Rules of decorum and expressions of gender fluidity in Tawosret's tomb. In Graves-Brown, C. (ed.), *Sex and gender in ancient Egypt: "Don your wig for a joyful hour."* Swansea: Classical Press of Wales, 83–113.

McClain, J.B. 2015. Continuing the Medinet Habu Fragment Project. *EA* 46: 14–16.

McClain, J.B., and Johnson, W.R. 2013. A fragment from the reign of Tausret reused at Medinet Habu. *JARCE* 49: 177–186.

Miller, W.K. 1986. The genealogy and chronology of the Ramesside period. *Dissertation Abstracts International A: the Humanities and Social Sciences* 47: 1448.

Mojsov, B. 2012. The monuments of Ramesses III. In Cline, E.H., and O'Connor, D. (eds.), *Ramesses III: the life and times of Egypt's last hero.* Ann Arbor: University of Michigan Press, 271–304.

Montet, J.P.M. 1947. *La nécropole royale de Tanis, I: les constructions et le tombeau d'Osorkon II à Tanis.* Paris: Jourde et Allard.

Montet, J.P.M. 1951. *La nécropole royale de Tanis, II: les constructions et le tombeau de Psousennès à Tanis.* Paris: Jourde et Allard.

Montet, J.P.M. 1960. *La nécropole royale de Tanis, III: les constructions et le tombeau de Chechanq III à Tanis.* Paris: Jourde et Allard.

Morenz, S. 1973. *Egyptian religion.* London: Methuen.

Morris, E. 2005. *The architecture of imperialism: military bases and the evolution of foreign policy in Egypt's New Kingdom.* Leiden: Brill.

Morris, E. 2018. *Ancient Egyptian imperialism*. Hoboken, NJ: Wiley-Blackwell.

Müller, M. 2004. Der Turiner Streikpapyrus (P. Turin 1880). In Wilhelm, G., and Janowski, B. (eds.), *Texte zum Rechts- und Wirtschaftsleben*. Gütersloh: Gütersloher Verlagshaus, 165–184.

Mumford, G. 2006. Egypt's New Kingdom Levantine empire and Serabit el-Khadim, including a newly attested votive offering of Horemheb. *Journal of the Society for the Study of Egyptian Antiquities* 33: 159–203.

Murnane, W.J. 1977. *Ancient Egyptian coregencies*. Chicago: The Oriental Institute of the University of Chicago.

Murnane, W.J. 1990. *The road to Kadesh: a historical interpretation of the battle reliefs of king Sety I at Karnak*. Chicago: The Oriental Institute of the University of Chicago.

Murnane, W.J. 1995. The kingship of the Nineteenth Dynasty: a study in the resilience of an institution. In O'Connor, D., and Silverman, D.P. (eds.), *Ancient Egyptian kingship*. Leiden: Brill, 185–217.

Nibbi, A. 1996. Some remarks on the Merenptah Stela and the so-called name of Israel. *Discussions in Egyptology* 36: 79–102.

Niwiński, A. 2007. The royal cache at Deir el-Bahri. In Mynárová, J., and Onderka, P. (eds.), *Thebes: city of gods and pharaohs*. Prague: National Museum, 172–175.

Niwiński, A. 2017. The mystery of the "high place" from the Abbott Papyrus revealed? The results of the works of the Polish cliff mission at Deir el-Bahari 1999–2014. In Guidotti, M.C., and Rosati, G. (eds.), *Proceedings of the XIth international congress of Egyptologists*. Oxford: Archaeopress, 457–461.

O'Connor, D. 2000. The Sea Peoples and the Egyptian sources. In Oren, E.D. (ed.), *The Sea Peoples and their world: a reassessment*. Philadelphia: University of Pennsylvania Museum of Archaeology and Anthropology, 85–102.

O'Connor, D. 2012. The mortuary temple of Ramesses III at Medinet Habu. In Cline, E.H., and O'Connor, D. (eds.), *Ramesses III: the life and times of Egypt's last hero*. Ann Arbor: University of Michigan Press, 209–270.

Ockinga, B.G. 1987. On the interpretation of the Kadesh record. *CdE* 62: 38–48.

Ockinga, B.G. 2012. Subversion oder Loyalität? Nochmal zur Frage der Beziehung zwischen den Hohepriestern Thebens und dem König in der späten Ramessidenzeit. In Beinlich, H. (ed.), *"Die Männer hinter dem König."* Wiesbaden: Harrassowitz, 87–101.

Peden, A.J. 1994. *The reign of Ramesses IV*. Warminster: Aris & Phillips.

Peden, A.J. 2001. *The graffiti of pharaonic Egypt: scope and roles of informal writings (c. 3100–332 BC)*. Leiden: Brill.

Peet, T.E. 1915a. The great tomb robberies of the Ramesside age. Papyri Mayer A and B, I: Papyrus Mayer A. *JEA* 2: 173–177.

Peet, T.E. 1915b. The great tomb robberies of the Ramesside age. Papyri Mayer A and B, II: Papyrus Mayer B. *JEA* 2: 204–206.

Peet, T.E. 1930. *The great tomb-robberies of the Twentieth Egyptian Dynasty, being a critical study with translations and commentaries of the papyri in which they are recorded*. Oxford: Clarendon Press.Phillips, A.K. 1977. Horemheb, founder of the 19th Dynasty? O. Cairo 25646 reconsidered. *Orientalia* 46: 116–121.

Polz, D. 1986. Die Särge des (Pa-)Ramessu. *MDAIK* 42: 145–167.

Porter, B., and Moss, R.L.B. 1937. *Topographical bibliography of ancient Egyptian hieroglyphic texts, reliefs, and paintings, V: Upper Egypt: Sites (Deir Rîfa to Aswân, excluding Thebes and the temples of Abydos, Dendera, Esna, Edfu, Kôm Ombo and Philae)*. Oxford: Clarendon Press.

Pusch, E.B. 1991. Recent work at northern Piramesse: results of excavations by the Pelizaeus-Museum, Hildesheim at Qantir. In Bleiberg, E., Freed, R., and Walker, A.K. (eds.), *Fragments of a shattered visage: the proceedings of the international symposium of Ramesses the Great*. Memphis, TN: Memphis State University, 199–220.

Pusch, E.B. 1999. Towards a map of Piramesse. *EA* 14: 13–15.

Raedler, C. 2006. Zur Struktur der Hofgesellschaft Ramses' II. In Gundlach, R., and Klug, A. (eds.), *Der ägyptische Hof des Neuen Reiches: seine Gesellschaft und Kultur im Spannungsfeld zwischen Innen- und Außenpolitik*. Wiesbaden: Harrassowitz, 39–87.

Raedler, C. 2009. Rank and favour at the early Ramesside court. In Gundlach, R., and Taylor, J.H. (eds.), *Egyptian royal residences*. Wiesbaden: Harrassowitz, 131–151.

Raedler, C. 2012. "Kopf der Schenut": politische Entscheidungsträger der Ära Ramses' II. In Beinlich, H. (ed.), *"Die Männer hinter dem König."* Wiesbaden: Harrassowitz, 123–150.

Raedler, C. 2016. Der Hofstaat unter Ramses II. In Kehrer, N. (ed.), *Ramses: göttlicher Herrscher am Nil*. Petersberg: Michael Imhof Verlag, 130–135.

Raven, M.J. 2017. Third Intermediate Period burials in Saqqara. In Amenta, A., and Guichard, H. (eds.), *Proceedings: first Vatican coffin conference.* Vatican City: Edizioni Musei Vaticani, 419–424.

Redford, D.B. 1984. *Akhenaten: the heretic king,* Princeton, NJ: Princeton University Press.

Redford, D.B. 1986. The Ashkelon relief at Karnak and the Israel stela. *IEJ* 36: 188–200.

Redford, D.B. 1992. *Egypt, Canaan and Israel in ancient times.* Princeton, NJ: Princeton University Press.

Redford, S. 2002. *The harem conspiracy: the murder of Ramesses III.* DeKalb: Northern Illinois University Press.

Reeves, N. 1990. *Valley of the Kings: the decline of a royal necropolis.* London and New York: Kegan Paul International.

Reeves, N. 2015. *The burial of Nefertiti?* Tucson, AZ: Amarna Royal Tombs Project.

Reeves, N. 2016. Tutankhamun's mask reconsidered. In Elleithy, H. (ed.), *Valley of the Kings since Howard Carter.* Cairo: Ministry of Antiquities, 117–134.

Revez, J., and Brand, P.J. 2015. The notion of prime space in the layout of the column decoration in the great Hypostyle Hall at Karnak. *Cahiers de Karnak* 15: 253–310.

Richter, B.A. 2008. The Amduat and its relationship to the architecture of early 18th Dynasty royal burial chambers. *JARCE* 44: 73–104.

Ridealgh, K. 2014. A tale of semantics and suppressions: reinterpreting Papyrus Mayer A and the so-called "war of the high priest" during the reign of Ramesses XI. *SAK* 43: 359–373.

Ritner, R. 1993. *The mechanics of ancient Egyptian magical practice.* Chicago: The Oriental Institute of the University of Chicago.

Roberson, J.A. 2012. *The ancient Egyptian Books of the Earth.* Atlanta, GA: Lockwood Press.

Roberson, J.A. 2013. *The awakening of Osiris and the transit of the solar barques: royal apotheosis in a most concise book of the underworld and sky.* Fribourg: Universitätsverlag; Göttingen: Vandenhoeck & Ruprecht.

Roberson, J.A. 2016. The royal funerary books: the subject matter of scenes and texts. In Weeks, K.R., and Wilkinson, R.H. (eds.), *The Oxford handbook of the Valley of the Kings.* Oxford: Oxford University Press, 316–332.

Robins, G. 1983. The god's wife of Amun in the 18th Dynasty in Egypt. In Cameron, A., and Kuhrt, A. (eds.), *Images of women in antiquity.* London: Duckworth, 65–78.

Roehrig, C.H. 2006. The building activities of Thutmose III in the Valley of the Kings. In Cline, E.H., and O'Connor, D. (eds.), *Thutmose III: a new biography.* Ann Arbor: University of Michigan Press, 238–259.

Roehrig, C.H. 2012. Forgotten treasures: Tausret as seen in her monuments. In Wilkinson, R.H. (ed.), *Tausret: forgotten queen and pharaoh of Egypt.* Oxford: Oxford University Press, 50–66.

Roehrig, C.H. 2016. Royal tombs of the Eighteenth Dynasty. In Wilkinson, R.H., and Weeks, K.R. (eds.), *The Oxford handbook of the Valley of the Kings.* Oxford: Oxford University Press, 183–199.

Romer, J. 1984. *Ancient lives: the story of the pharaoh's tombmakers.* London: Phoenix.

Roth, S. 2003. "Da wurden an diesem Tage die zwei großen Länder zu einem Lande": zum Verhältnis von Königsideologie und internationaler Heiratspolitik in der Zeit Ramses' II. In Gundlach, R., and Rößler-Köhler, U. (eds.), *Das Königtum der Ramessidenzeit: Voraussetzungen—Verwirklichung—Vermächtnis.* Wiesbaden: Harrassowitz, 175–195.

Roth, S. 2012. Harem. In Wendrich, W. (ed.), *UCLA Encyclopedia of Egyptology.* Los Angeles: University of California, Los Angeles. Retrieved from https://escholarship.org/uc/item/1k3663r3 (last accessed November 29, 2019).

Sadek, A.F. 1974. *Graffiti de la montagne Thébaine, IV/4: transcriptions et indices.* Cairo: Centre de Documentation et d'Études sur l'ancienne Égypte.

Schaden, O.J. 1993. Amenmesse project report. *Newsletter of the American Research Center in Egypt* 163: 1–9.

Schlögl, H.A. 2017. *Ramses der Große.* Berlin: Michael Haase.

Schneider, T. 2003. Siptah und Beja. *ZÄS* 130: 134–146.

Schneider, T. 2010a. Contributions to the chronology of the New Kingdom and the Third Intermediate Period. *ÄL* 20: 373–403.

Schneider, T. 2010b. Foreigners in Egypt: archaeological evidence and cultural context. In Wendrich, W. (ed.), *Egyptian archaeology.* Malden, MA: Wiley-Blackwell, 143–163.

Schneider, T. 2011. Conjectures about Amenmesse: historical, biographical, chronological. In Collier, M., and Snape, S. (eds.), *Ramesside studies in honour of K.A. Kitchen.* Bolton: Rutherford Press, 445–451.

Schulman, A.R. 1987. The great historical inscription of Merneptaḥ at Karnak: a partial reappraisal. *JARCE* 24: 21–34.

Shaw, I. 2011. Seeking the Ramesside royal harem: new fieldwork at Medinet el-Gurob. In Collier, M., and Snape, S. (eds.), *Ramesside studies in honour of K.A. Kitchen.* Bolton: Rutherford Press, 453–463.

Simon, C. 2016. Les campagnes militaires de Ramsès III à Médinet Habou: entre vérité et propagande. In Karlshausen, C., and Obsomer, C. (eds.), *De la Nubie à Qadech: la guerre dans l'Égypte ancienne.* Brussels: Safran, 171–194.

Smith, G.E. 1912. *Catalogue général des antiquités égyptiennes du Musée du Caire, nos. 61051–61100: the royal mummies.* Cairo: Institut français d'archéologie orientale.

Snape, S. 2003. New perspectives on distant horizons: aspects of Egyptian imperial administration in Marmarica in the Late Bronze Age. *Libyan Studies* 34: 1–8.

Snape, S. 2012. The legacy of Ramesses III and the Libyan ascendancy. In Cline, E.H., and O'Connor, D. (eds.), *Ramesses III: the life and times of Egypt's last hero.* Ann Arbor: University of Michigan Press, 404–441.

Snape, S., and Wilson, P. 2007. *Zawiyet Umm el-Rakham I: the temple and the chapels.* Bolton: Rutherford Press.

Sourouzian, H. 1988. Standing royal colossi of the Middle Kingdom reused by Ramesses II. *MDAIK* 44: 229–254.

Sourouzian, H. 1989. *Les monuments du roi Merenptah.* Mainz: Zabern.

Spalinger, A.J. 2002. *The transformation of an ancient Egyptian narrative: P. Sallier III and the battle of Kadesh.* Wiesbaden: Harrassowitz.

Spalinger, A.J. 2005. *War in ancient Egypt.* Malden, MA: Wiley-Blackwell.

Sternberg-El Hotabi, H. 2005. Aus den Annalen Thutmosis' III.: erster Feldzug gegen Megiddo. In Wilhelm, G., and Janowski, B. (eds.), *Staatsverträge, Herrscherinschriften und andere Dokumente zur politischen Geschichte.* Gütersloh: Gütersloher Verlagshaus, 212–220.

Sternberg-El Hotabi, H. 2012. *Der Kampf der Seevölker gegen Pharao Ramses III.* Rahden: Verlag Marie Leidorf.

Strudwick, N. 2013. Ancient robbery in Theban tombs. In Creasman, P.P. (ed.), *Archaeological research in the Valley of the Kings and ancient Thebes: papers presented in honor of Richard H. Wilkinson.* Tucson: University of Arizona Egyptian Expedition, 333–352.

Sweeney, D., and Yasur-Landau, A. 1999. Following the path of the Sea Persons: the women in the Medinet Habu reliefs. *Tel Aviv* 26: 116–145.

Szpakowska, K. 2010. Nightmares in ancient Egypt. In Mouton, A., and Husser, J.-M. (eds.), *Le cauchemar dans les sociétés antiques.* Paris: De Boccard, 21–39.

Szpakowska, K. 2011a. Demons in the dark: nightmares and other nocturnal enemies in ancient Egypt. In Kousoulis, P. (ed.), *Ancient Egyptian demonology: studies on the boundaries between the demonic and the divine in Egyptian magic.* Leuven: Peeters, 63–76.

Szpakowska, K. 2011b. Dream interpretation in the Ramesside age. In Collier, M., and Snape, S. (eds.), *Ramesside studies in honour of K.A. Kitchen.* Bolton: Rutherford Press, 509–517.

Taylor, J.H. 1999. The burial assemblage of Henutmehyt: inventory, date and provenance. In Davies, W.V. (ed.), *Studies in Egyptian antiquities: a tribute to T.G.H. James.* London: British Museum Press, 59–72.

Taylor, J.H., and Dorey, H. 2017. *Sir John Soane's greatest treasure: the sarcophagus of Seti I.* London: Pimpernel Press.

Teeter, E. 2012. Change and continuity in religion and religious practices in Ramesside Egypt. In Cline, E.H., and O'Connor, D. (eds.), *Ramesses III: the life and times of Egypt's last hero.* Ann Arbor: University of Michigan Press, 27–65.

Theis, C. 2011. Der Brief der Königin Dahamunzu an den hethitischen König Šuppiluliuma I. im Lichte von Reisegeschwindigkeit und Zeitabläufen. In Kämmerer, T.R. (ed.), *Identities and societies in the ancient East Mediterranean regions: comparative approaches: Henning Graf Reventlow memorial volume.* Münster: Ugarit-Verlag, 301–331.

Thijs, A. 1998. Two books for one lady: the mother of Herihor rediscovered. *GM* 163: 101–110.

Thijs, A. 2005. In search of king Herihor and the penultimate ruler of the 20th Dynasty. *ZÄS* 132: 73–91.

Thomas, S. 2000. Tell Abqa'in: a fortified settlement in the western delta: preliminary report of the 1997 season. *MDAIK* 56: 371–376.

Török, L. 2009. *Between two worlds: the frontier region between ancient Nubia and Egypt, 3700 BC–500 AD.* Leiden: Brill.

Tyldesley, J. 2000. *Ramesses: Egypt's greatest pharaoh.* London: Penguin.

Valbelle, D. 1985. *Les ouvriers de la tombe: Deir el-Médineh à l'époque Ramesside.* Cairo: Institut français d'archéologie orientale.

Van De Mieroop, M. 2007. *The Eastern Mediterranean in the age of Ramses II.* Malden, MA: Wiley-Blackwell.

Vandersleyen, C. 1995. La gloire de Ramsès III. *Cercle Lyonnais d'Égyptologie Victor Loret, Bulletin* 9: 45–51.

van Dijk, J. 2000. The Amarna period and the later New Kingdom (c. 1352–1069 BC). In Shaw, I. (ed.), *The Oxford history of ancient Egypt.* Oxford: Oxford University Press, 272–313.

van Pelt, W.P. 2013. Revising Egypto-Nubian relations in New Kingdom lower Nubia: from Egyptianization to cultural entanglement. *Cambridge Archaeological Journal* 23: 523–550.

Vernus, P. 1993. *Affairs and scandals in ancient Egypt.* Ithaca, NY: Cornell University Press.

Vinson, S. 2001. Ramses IV. In Redford, D.B. (ed.), *The Oxford encyclopedia of ancient Egypt.* Oxford: Oxford University Press, 120–121.

von Beckerath, J. 1962. Queen Twosre as guardian of Siptaḥ. *JEA* 48: 70–74.

von Beckerath, J. 1997. *Chronologie des pharaonischen Ägypten: die Zeitbestimmung der ägyptischen Geschichte von der Vorzeit bis 332 v. Chr.* Mainz: Zabern.

von Beckerath, J. 1999. *Handbuch der ägyptischen Königsnamen.* Mainz: Zabern.

Wachsmann, S. 2013. *The Gurob ship-cart model and its Mediterranean context.* College Station: Texas A&M University Press.

Waddell, W.G. 1940. *Manetho.* London: Heinemann.

Warburton, D. 2003a. Egypt and Mesopotamia in the Late Bronze and Iron Ages. In Matthews, R., and Roemer, C. (eds.), *Ancient perspectives on Egypt.* London: UCL Press, 101–104.

Warburton, D. 2003b. Love and war in the Late Bronze Age: Egypt and Hatti. In Matthews, R., and Roemer, C. (eds.), *Ancient perspectives on Egypt.* London: UCL Press, 75–100.

Weeks, K.R. 1995. Clearing KV 5: investigating the tomb of the sons of Ramesses II. *Minerva* 6: 20–24.

Weeks, K.R. (ed.) 2006. *KV 5: a preliminary report on the excavation of the tomb of the sons of Rameses II in the Valley of the Kings.* Cairo: American University in Cairo Press.

Weinstein, J.M. 1981. The Egyptian empire in Palestine: a reassessment. *BASOR* 241: 1–28.

Wente, E.F. 1990. *Letters from ancient Egypt.* Atlanta, GA: Society of Biblical Literature.

Wente, E.F., and Peden, A.J. 1996. Egyptian historical inscriptions of the Twentieth Dynasty. *JAOS* 116: 764.

Werning, D.A. 2011. *Das Höhlenbuch: Textkritische Edition und Textgrammatik.* Wiesbaden: Harrassowitz.

Wilkinson, R.H. 2000. *The complete temples of ancient Egypt.* London: Thames & Hudson.

Wilkinson, R.H. 2011. History of the temple. In Wilkinson, R.H., Denkowicz, S., Goodwin, A.D., Harwood, R.S., and Cirzan, A. (eds.), *The temple of Tausret: the University of Arizona Egyptian Expedition Tausret Temple Project, 2004–2011.* Tucson: University of Arizona Egyptian Expedition, 160–172.

Wilkinson, T. 2010. *The rise and fall of ancient Egypt: the history of a civilisation from 3000 BC to Cleopatra.* London: Bloomsbury.

Yurco, F.J. 1979. Amenmesse: six statues at Karnak. *Metropolitan Museum Journal* 14: 15–31.

28

Egypt's New Kingdom in Contact with the World

Pierre Grandet

28.1. The New Kingdom's neighbors and the long-distance route networks

The Egyptian New Kingdom broadly covers 480 years (1550–1069 BC),[1,2] during which time the country was ruled by the kings of the

---

1. The following bibliographical abbreviations are used in this chapter: EA = letter of the Amarna correspondence, as edited in Moran 1992 and Rainey 2014; KRI = Kitchen 1975–1990; Roberson 2018; with the companion volumes of translations (Kitchen 1993–2014; B.G. Davies 2013–2014) and notes (Kitchen 1993–1999); *Urk.* IV = Sethe 1906–1909; Helck 1955–1958. As there is a growing discrepancy between the sources for Egyptian history and the juggernaut of Egyptological bibliography, we will keep the latter on the light side. As those parts of this chapter concerning Western Asia are a revised and condensed version of Grandet 2008, we generally refer to it for the previous literature, providing otherwise only references to the most significant studies. More substantial references are provided for Nubia, as this was not covered in Grandet 2008. The chapter was language-edited by Karen Radner.

2. The dates follow von Beckerath 1997, but correcting Sethnakht's reign to four years (1185–1181 BC) because of a new stele found in Luxor in 2006 (published

Pierre Grandet, *Egypt's New Kingdom in Contact with the World* In: *The Oxford History of the Ancient Near East*. Edited by: Karen Radner, Nadine Moeller, and D. T. Potts, Oxford University Press. © Oxford University Press 2022. DOI: 10.1093/oso/9780190687601.003.0028

Eighteenth, Nineteenth, and Twentieth Dynasties. At this time, Egypt's foreign relations can be described as a combination of continuity and change. On one hand, the physical geography of its environment and the basic underpinnings of the relationship with its neighbors, whoever they were, remained constant, whatever political events affected Egypt. On the other hand, a change in attitude can be discerned from the textual and pictorial records documenting wars against newly emerging powers in the north and the east and an unprecedented effort to subjugate Nubia in the south (figure 28.1).

These wars in the east and the attempts to control Nubia were rooted in both domestic and international circumstances. The domestic context is rooted in Egypt's political makeup at the end of the Second Intermediate Period when the Hyksos ruled over Lower Egypt (chapter 23 in this volume) while the Nubian kingdom of Kush exercised control over the Nile valley between the First and Second Cataract (chapter 25). When these two powers tentatively cooperated, they tried to crush the kingdom established between their power spheres by the Thirteenth and Seventeenth Dynasties in Upper Egypt (chapter 24). The international context is fundamentally shaped by the emergence of new powers on Egypt's eastern and northern perimeter, before and during the establishment of the New Kingdom: the Mittani state (chapter 29) and later the kingdom of Assyria (chapter 32) in northern Mesopotamia; the Hittites in Anatolia (chapter 30); and the Mycenaeans in the Aegean (chapter 31), in whose wake came the famous Sea Peoples.

Rich textual, pictorial, and archaeological sources all contribute to the New Kingdom being one of the best-documented periods of

---

by Boraik 2007), which mentions Sethnakht's Year 4. Consequently, the reign of Rameses III is dated to 1181–1150 BC.

ancient Egyptian history. This abundance, however, is largely an illusion: the main compendia of written historical sources for the period offer us a grand total of about 7,500 printed pages of hieroglyphic text.[3] This certainly seems impressive, until we realize that divided by the 480 years of the New Kingdom, this drops to about 14–15 pages

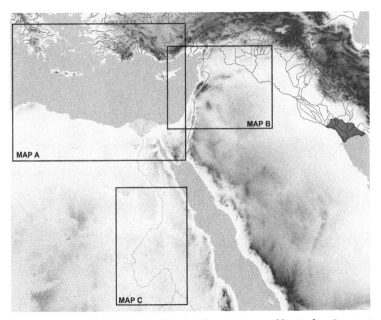

FIGURE 28.1A. Sites mentioned in this chapter. Prepared by Andrea Squitieri (LMU Munich).

3. Collected in KRI; *Urk.* IV; Helck 1983; 1995.

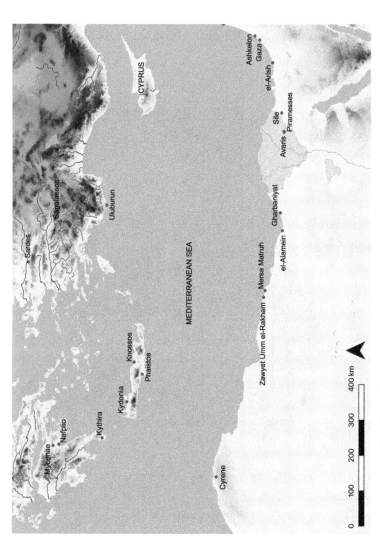

FIGURE 28.1B. Detail map A.

FIGURE 28.1C. Detail map B.

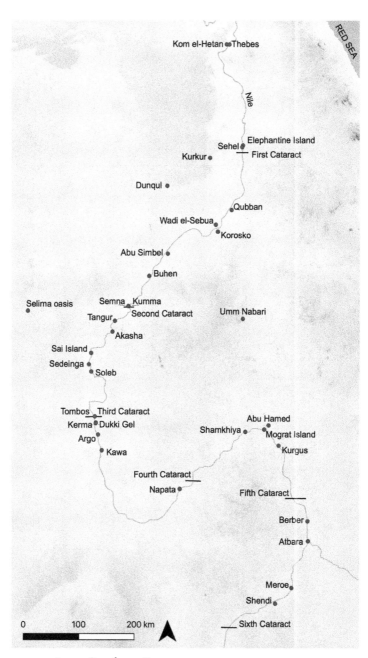

FIGURE 28.1D. Detail map C.

per year, which are moreover very unevenly distributed between the reigns of individual rulers: any present-day administration probably generates much more documentation per day than these five centuries worth of data. Furthermore, as far as historical events are concerned, the available material consists almost exclusively of narratives that commemorate the triumphs of various pharaohs according to ancient Egyptian mentality. History was then understood not as the factual knowledge of past events, but as the commemoration of victories in what was conceived as the metaphysical battle to restore *maat*, the perfect state of creation, fought by successive kings, acting as the gods' delegates on earth, against the forces of evil both at home and abroad. Reconstructing Egyptian political history according to our modern understanding of the term is therefore a difficult exercise. In our current practice, we prefer to use the few facts that we accept as certain in order to construct historical scenarios, while using explicative patterns to connect the dots. But this further complicates the matter, as these patterns are evidently guided by the modern historian's intellectual and cultural influences.

In the mid-second millennium BC, Egypt was surrounded by Nubians in the south, Libyans in the west, the Mediterranean Sea in the north and the northwest, and "Asiatics" in the east and the northeast, with various nomadic populations in between. Egypt had had interactions with all of these neighbors since prehistoric times (see chapter 2 in volume 1). Propelled by the dynamics of its unification in the late fourth millennium BC (see chapter 4 in volume 1), it began to project itself beyond its borders during the Old Kingdom period (see chapter 6 in volume 1). On the other hand, those of its neighbors who dwelled in the deserts tried to settle in its luxuriant countryside, thus creating the conditions for endemic conflicts.

Up to the period of the New Kingdom, with which we are concerned in this chapter, Egypt principally sought to extend its power beyond its traditional borders in order to control Nubia and its gold mines. The Libyans and various populations dwelling in the deserts were militarily always easily defeated and therefore considered more a nuisance than a threat. Along the eastern Mediterranean coast, Egypt established a permanent presence in southern Canaan already at the very beginning of the Early Dynastic period (see chapter 4), but eventually retreated, and afterward showed no particular interest in controlling the region, including during the heydays of the Middle Kingdom: what little Canaan had to offer to Egypt was easily acquired by trade. Further to the north, however, Egypt since prehistoric times carefully and constantly tended its relationship with the Lebanese coast, from where it acquired the timber necessary to build boats and construct large buildings and monuments.

Nubia's peculiar geography played a key role in this region's relationship with Egypt. First and foremost, while the Nile flows in Egypt without any obstacle down to the Mediterranean, it is repeatedly disrupted in Nubia by a series of rapids; the more important ones are known as "cataracts." Such obstacles make river navigation very difficult, but at the same time, they can easily assume the function of military buffer zones. Thus, the Twelfth Dynasty pharaohs of the Middle Kingdom had set their southern frontier south of the Second Cataract at Semna and Kumma (also known as Semna East). For about 150 km to the south, the barren and virtually uninhabited granite landscape today known as Batn el-Hagar ("Belly of Stone") formed a convenient natural barrier between their holdings and the kingdom of Kush (see chapter 20 in volume 2). Faced with such difficulties, it was often deemed more expedient to avoid navigating long sections of the Nubian Nile by using overland trails instead.[4] A long desert road connected Elephantine on the First Cataract with the island of Sai north of the Third Cataract via the oases of Kurkur, Dunqul, and Selima and thus conveniently bypassed the Second Cataract and the Batn el-Hagar.[5] South of the Third Cataract, where the Nile runs in a great double bend that is broadly shaped like the letter S rotated 90° counterclockwise (∽), another long desert road connected Kawa, situated at the double bend's northwestern point, with

---

4. For references, see Darnell and Haddad 2003: 73 n. 2–3; Roe 2005–2006.

5. Steles of Tutankhamun and Sety I demonstrate that Kurkur was the first station on this road; Darnell 2003; 2011.

the Berber-Shendi Reach of the Nile at its southeastern end via Napata, located at its geographical center.[6] There were two good additional reasons for wanting to avoid the lengthy detour necessitated by following the river: the almost complete lack of natural resources and population along the Nile banks between Kawa and the Berber-Shendi Reach (with the exception of the area of Napata),[7] and the fact that the river was almost impassable between Napata and Abu Hamed, at the top of the eastern bend.[8] A third important trail was the 350-km-long Korosko Road, which linked Korosko, on the eastern bank of the Nile 180 km south of Elephantine, with Abu Hamed via the Nubian Desert.[9] This trail was also accessible from Buhen at the northern end of the Second Cataract through a route that connected with the main branch of the Korosko Road near Umm Nabari, midway between Korosko and Abu Hamed.[10] This route system provided access to many gold deposits,[11] especially on a 50-km stretch west of Abu Hamed: this region likely corresponds to the gold-producing land of *Karoy* in Egyptian texts.[12] About 40 km further to the south, on an isolated quartz ridge on the eastern bank of the Nile near the village of Kurgus, known as Hagar el-Merwa ("Stone of Meroe") and situated in what the Egyptians called the land of

---

6. O'Connor 1987: 100–101; Lohwasser 2012.

7. As evidenced by the work of the Northern Dongola Reach Survey (Welsby 2001; 2012: 20) and of the Southern Dongola Reach Survey (Żurawski et al. 2017).

8. No pharaonic sites are known on its western part: Wolf and Nowotnick 2007; Emberling and Williams 2010.

9. Castiglioni and Castiglioni 2003; Davies 2014; Ruffieux and Bashir 2014.

10. Török 2009: 17 n. 58; Davies 2017: 96, fig. 36.

11. Klemm and Klemm 2013: 543–555; 2017.

12. *Urk.* IV 1654: 14–15; see Klemm and Klemm 2013: 341–342, 606–611, 642, maps 6.1, 7.4. Egyptian artifacts attest to New Kingdom gold-processing activity between Shamkhiya and Mograt Island on the top of the Abu Hamed bend, but none of these artifacts were found in situ and all had been reused at a later date; Klemm and Klemm 2013: 584–590.

Miu, the New Kingdom pharaohs Thutmose I and Thutmose III carved inscriptions that declared this spot to be their southern frontier.[13]

As far as ancient Egyptian history is concerned, the term "Libya" is used to designate more or less all of the lands west of the Nile as far as the border of the modern state by this name. This vast region can broadly be divided into two unequal parts. To the north, along the Mediterranean Sea, lies a strip of steppe with a width of ca. 100 km that the Egyptian sources call the land of *Tjehenu*, later called Marmarica by Greek geographers. This region forms a natural link between Egypt and Cyrenaica, the eastern coastal region of modern Libya. To the south lies the Western Desert, known in Egyptian sources as the land of *Tjemehu*, whose series of oases is connected with the parallel-running Nile valley and with each other by a relatively dense system of desert trails. The main route is the famous Darb el-Arbain ("Forty Days Trail"), which links Middle Egypt and western Sudan via the Kharga oasis.[14]

To the north of Egypt and Libya is the Mediterranean Sea, across whose expanses to the northwest lies the large island of Crete, the gate to the Aegean. By the beginning of the New Kingdom, the Aegean was still dominated by the Minoan kingdom of Crete, with which Egypt fostered a close relationship. By the middle of the Eighteenth Dynasty, however, Crete had been conquered by Mycenaeans coming from mainland Greece and thereafter became a base both for the long-distance maritime trade of Mycenaean goods with Egypt and for the raids of Mycenaean pirates in the Nile delta region.

We will now turn to the east, beginning with the Sinai. With the exception of scattered oases and strips of land on the coast, this peninsula is a desert, home to nomadic tribes. Despite the aridity, its northern parts played an important strategic role, as the so-called Ways of Horus led along the Mediterranean coast from Egypt to Canaan. Here, New Kingdom pharaohs built a series of forts that guarded crucial freshwater

---

13. Török 2009: 15–18. The most recent edition is Davies 2017: 67–87 (correcting previous translations).

14. Roe 2005–2006.

wells and ponds, thus serving as stations for the Egyptian armies going east.[15] This barren landscape, however, hides mineral treasures. Since the Early Dynastic period (see chapters 4 and 6 in volume 1), Egypt had exploited copper mines in the western part of the peninsula, supplemented in some places with turquoise deposits. Midway between Sile (modern Tell Hebwa) and Gaza, an overland route that starts in the region of modern el-Arish leads all the way down to the Gulf of Aqaba on the Red Sea. It was used by Egypt during the Nineteenth and Twentieth Dynasties to reach and exploit the rich copper deposit of Timna north of modern Eilat, which was second in importance only to Cyprus.

The rich agricultural lands of the so-called Fertile Crescent stretch from the Nile delta in the west to the Persian Gulf in the east, via the plains south of the Taurus mountains and west of the Zagros mountains.[16] Bordered in the west by the Mediterranean Sea and in the east by the Zagros mountains, the eastern part of the Fertile Crescent consists of the valleys of the Euphrates and Tigris, ancient Mesopotamia, while its western part is traditionally called the Levant, with Syria in the north, the coast of Lebanon and the Beqaa valley in the middle, and Canaan in the south. This region has the shape of a crescent, as the space between its branches is taken up by the northern reaches of the Arabian Desert. Except in its northernmost part, where it could be crossed via the oasis of Tadmor (Greek Palmyra), this desert formed a formidable barrier, so that someone traveling from, say, Babylon to Memphis (or the reverse) had to follow one of the horns of the crescent to the top of its arc in the north, and then down again on the other horn.

The lands of the Fertile Crescent were crisscrossed by an extensive network of roads, trails, and navigable waterways whose layout has not changed much since antiquity. The most important itineraries were the following: (1) Running roughly southeast to northwest, river routes followed the Tigris and Euphrates rivers and their tributaries. (2) Crossing east to west from the Zagros to the Mediterranean, a land route ran

---

15. Hoffmeier 2013; Mumford 2015.

16. Cf. Grandet 2008: 22–43.

through the plains south of the Taurus. (3) Running north to south from Syria to Egypt, a land road cut across the Syrian steppe, the Beqaa valley, and Canaan. As far as the relationship with Egypt is concerned, two cities formed crucial nodes in this network. The first was Carchemish (today Tell Jerablus, on the modern border between Turkey and Syria) at the foot of the Taurus mountains, situated on an important ford across the Euphrates where the river route (1) and the east-west land route (2) connected. The second was Aleppo in northern Syria, where the east-west land route (2) intersected with the north-south route (3). Secondary desert trails left the Euphrates at Mari (modern Tell Hariri near the modern border between Syria and Iraq), Emar (modern Tell Meskene on the great bend of the Euphrates, near the modern Assad Dam), and other nearby places, providing shortcuts through the desert via the oasis of Tadmor (Palmyra) to Qadesh (modern Tell Nebi Mend) or the Damascus region.

Once the routes from inland Syria reached the Mediterranean, they connected to maritime routes leading west to Cyprus and the Aegean. The physical geography of Syria, bordered in the west by a high coastal mountain range, allowed easy access to the sea only through two narrow corridors: in the south, the so-called Homs Gap between Qadesh on the Orontes and the Akkar coastal plain (ancient Amurru), where the strategic port of Simyra (modern Tell Kazel) was located; and in the north, the system of river valleys leading from the Orontes in the vicinity of modern Jisr al-Shughur to the famous port and city-state of Ugarit (modern Ras Shamra). The climatic and oceanographic conditions of the northeastern Mediterranean, in particular a series of currents running counterclockwise around Cyprus, coupled with the poor maneuvering possibilities of the square-sailed and keelless ancient ships, strongly suggest that these two ports served different functions: the southern port of Simyra being better suited for inbound traffic to Syria, and the northern port of Ugarit for outbound traffic leaving Syria.[17]

Of the various goods that traveled along these networks, the economically more significant ones were tin and copper, whose

---

17. Grandet 2008: 40–49.

alloy—bronze—was fundamental for most technologies used in the second millennium BC. But while copper is native to the Near East, tin is not. It had to be imported to the Mediterranean across about 3,000 km from the east, all the way from Central Asia, from what is today Afghanistan and its northern neighbor states, by routes that would later form part of the famous Silk Roads network. By land, the tin ingots were transported across the northern Iranian plateau and over the Zagros range, reaching northern Mesopotamia near Nineveh (modern Mosul), from where it continued its journey toward the Mediterranean on the route along the Taurus foothills. This route crossed on its way a fertile alluvial plain known as the Khabur Triangle, formed by the Khabur river and its tributaries that flow down from the Taurus range in the north. From its western tip, a road branched off from the main east-west route, and this road led to the northwest and served to transport tin and other materials across the mountains to central Anatolia (see chapter 17 in volume 2). But no less important than this land route was an alternate maritime and riverine route that was used to bring tin from Central Asia down the Indus to the Indian Ocean, then by sea to the Persian Gulf, from where it could be shipped to just about anywhere up the Tigris and Euphrates. Once the tin had reached the Levant, it continued its journey by sea to the west and the Aegean, or by land to the south. A famous late Eighteenth Dynasty shipwreck, found off Uluburun[18] on the Lycian coast of modern Turkey, with a cargo of tin and copper ingots in the precise proportion of 1:10 needed to make bronze, beautifully illustrates the tin's westward journey. The second route allowed the precious metal to reach Egypt through a series of intermediary cities and states.

Not only goods, but peoples, too, followed these routes.[19] The capital Waššukanni (probably Tell Fekheriye) of the kingdom of Mittani (chapter 29 in this volume) was situated in the Khabur Triangle at precisely the point where the overland route to Anatolia detached itself from the east-west route along the Taurus foothills. The kings of Mittani

---

18. Yalcin, Pulak, and Slotta 2005.

19. Grandet 2008: 52–66.

used names derived from a language related to Sanskrit and professed beliefs imbued by Vedic values. It is therefore possible, although not at all certain, that they originated in northern India, or the region where Indo-Iranian speakers diverged eastward and westward, and that they reached northern Mesopotamia following the movement of trade along the long-distance routes that connect India to the Middle East.[20] As befitted a traveling people, they employed a transport device—the chariot—that made use of the domesticated animal best suited to draw it: the horse, which was as yet unknown further west. The upper level of Mittani society was constituted by a chariot-fighting nobility whose members called themselves *márya* (from Sanskrit मर्य, "young man, young warrior"[21]). The use of the horse-drawn chariot, which combined a vehicle of prestige with a powerful weapon, became an instant rage among the political elites of the Middle East and Egypt, where the chariot fighters became known as *maryannu*, a Semitized and pluralized form of the Vedic Sanskrit term. Whatever their origin, the Mittani kings created a state in northern Mesopotamia with a population whose larger part consisted of people of a completely different ethnicity and language: the Hurrians, who are attested in the region already in textual sources of the mid-third millennium BC (see chapter 8 in volume 1). The Mittani rulers soon perceived themselves as Hurrian, retaining from their original cultural context most prominently some Vedic Sanskrit proper names. The kingdom of Mittani's territory was known to the Egyptians as Naharina, a Semitic term meaning "Land of the Rivers."

Meanwhile, the Hittites (see chapter 30 in the present volume) had established a state in central and eastern Anatolia, in the area where, at the beginning of the second millennium BC, traders from the city of Assur on the Tigris had established trading posts in Kaneš (modern Kültepe) and elsewhere (see chapter 17 in volume 2) through which they sold goods for a huge profit, including large quantities of copper and tin, used locally to produce bronze. The Hittites' need of bronze should

---

20. For a critical view on this, and also the assumed role in introducing the horse-drawn chariot in Mesopotamia, see chapter 29 in the present volume.

21. Monnier-Williams 1899: 791c.

have warned their neighbors about their taste for war. Around 1630 BC, their king Hattusili I, followed one generation later by his son Mursili I, reduced almost to nought the political importance of the northern Syrian city of Aleppo (see chapter 15 in volume 2). Then, around 1595 BC, Mursili I daringly conducted, down the Euphrates, a raid that contributed to the end of the kingdom of Babylon as forged by Hammurabi about a century and a half before (see chapter 18 in volume 2). Whatever its motivations, this raid brought the Hittites neither luck nor profit, as Mursili I returned back home only to be assassinated, inaugurating a cycle of civil struggles from which the Hittite kingdom emerged only more than two centuries later. But this had immense, if unintended, geopolitical consequences. No longer held in check, peoples from the periphery of the defunct Babylonian state came to occupy its former territories, thus creating the political setup of the Middle East as the New Kingdom pharaohs would come to know it. Around 1560 BC, the so-called Kassite Dynasty (see chapter 33 in the present volume) ruled over a new Babylonian state called Karduniaš in southern Mesopotamia, while in northern Mesopotamia, the Hurrians and the Mittani formed the kingdom of Mittani (see chapter 29 in the present volume).

28.2. Prologue to the New Kingdom

During the Second Intermediate Period, as we call the time between the Middle and the New Kingdom, the pharaohs of the Thirteenth and Seventeenth Dynasties ruled over a kingdom reduced to Upper Egypt (see chapter 24 in the present volume).[22] Meanwhile, kings of Asiatic descent, the Hyksos of the Fifteenth Dynasty, ruled the northern part of Egypt as well as the southern part of Canaan's coastal plain (see chapter 23 in the present volume), while the Nubian kingdom of Kush had seized what had once been the Middle Kingdom's Nubian possessions, as far as the First Cataract of the Nile (see chapter 25 in the present volume).

---

22. Grandet 2008: 60–66.

Against both adversaries, the last kings of the Seventeenth Dynasty, Seqenenra Taa and Kamose, began a war to reunify Egypt, while preventing them from forming a military alliance.[23] Kamose's death brought the Hyksos respite, as his successor Ahmose (1550–1525 BC; the first ruler of the Eighteenth Dynasty) was still a child. But when he came of age, he lost no time to bring to a close the wars of his predecessors. Between his Years 11 and 16, he took Avaris, the Hyksos kings' residence in the eastern delta, and then pursued them to southern Canaan, where he besieged their last stronghold of Sharuhen (modern Tell el-Ajjul) for three years, before they vanish from historical records. By right of conquest, the pharaohs inherited the Hyksos claim over their holdings in Canaan, so that Egypt gained a permanent foothold in Western Asia for the first time since the First Dynasty (see section 28.1).

By Year 20, Ahmose had turned south and to the reconquest of Lower Nubia, soon re-establishing Egypt's southern frontier at the Nile fortress of Semna, which the Twelfth Dynasty rulers of the Middle Kingdom had set as their border.[24] To its north, the town of Buhen was again established as the principal Egyptian administrative center of Nubia, as well as the seat of the Egyptian governor of all Nubian territories under the New Kingdom's control, who would, from the reign of Ahmose's successor Amenhotep I onward, bear the title of "King's Son of Kush."

This chapter is organized in a geographical rather than a purely chronological order. We shall begin with Nubia, as controlling this region was the Egyptians' primary concern until further developments made them shift their focus elsewhere. We then shall turn our attention in clockwise direction to Libya and the Aegean before addressing the broader issue of the New Kingdom's relationships with Canaan and Western Asia (table 28.1).

---

23. Helck 1975: 82–97. Also Davies 2003; Klotz 2010.

24. *Urk.* IV 5.4–6.15; 35.16–17.

Table 28.1. The relationship of New Kingdom Egypt with its neighbors: an overview

1550			1292	1185		1069
	XVIIIth dyn.			XIXth dyn.	XXth dyn.	
	1500	1415	1325	1259		
N. East	Peace (50 yrs)	Egypt/Mittani conflict (85 yrs)	Peace (90 yrs)	Egypt/Hatti conflict (66 yrs)	Peace (190 yrs)	
	1459			1210	1178	
Canaan	Peaceful rule (91 yrs)	Unrests and revolts (249 years)			Uneasy rule (32 yrs)	Disengagement Settling of Sea P. (109 yrs)
	1525	1432				
Nubia	Eg. conquest (118 yrs) [L. Nub. / Kush]	Egyptian rule (363 yrs)				
				1280	1171	
Libya	Endemic border unrest (270 yrs)			Clash with Egypt (109 yrs)	Border unrest Razzias (102 yrs)	
		1413	1280		1178	
The Sea	Relations with the Minoans (137 yrs)	Relations with the Mycenaeans (133 yrs)	Clash with the Sea Peoples (102 yrs)	Levantine piracy (109 yrs)		

Prepared by Pierre Grandet.

28.3. Egypt and Nubia

After Ahmose's victories, Egypt's relationship with Nubia went through two stages:[25]

(1) From Year 7 of Amenhotep I to Year 47 of Thutmose III (1502–1432 BC), Egypt conquered the kingdom of Kush in Upper Nubia and

---

25. Cf. O'Connor 1993; Redford 2004: 3–57; Spalinger 2006; Török 2009; Kahn 2013: 17–31; Morkot 2013; Spencer et al. 2017. On the relations between Egyptians and Nubians, see Smith 2013.

its capital Kerma before control was extended to the south as far as Napata on the Fourth Cataract and Kurgus, north of the Fifth Cataract.

(2) From Year 47 of Thutmose III to the end of the New Kingdom (1432–1069 BC), Nubia was submitted to Egypt's domination, although the frequency of "revolts" tends to relativize the extent of Egyptian control and implies a survival of a Kushite political entity further south, out of reach of the New Kingdom armies.

28.3.1. The New Kingdom conquest of Kush

The foreign policy of Ahmose's successor Amenhotep I (1525–1504 BC) was entirely focused on Nubia. He first completed the pacification of the regions north of the Second Cataract, then crossed the Batn el-Hagar in Years 7–8 (1532–1531 BC), and 200 km to the south, right on the border to enemy territory, he founded an urban center for a mixed Egyptian and Nubian population on Sai Island.[26]

His successor Thutmose I (1504–1492 BC) was a man of non-royal origins who became pharaoh after the death of Amenhotep I's sole heir and whose claim to the crown was secured by his marriage to his predecessor's daughter Ahmose. Although relatively brief, his reign was marked by such remarkable military achievement that we must conclude that he had been a senior army officer before assuming the crown. In Years 2–3 (1501–1500 BC), he led an army across Batn el-Hagar, commemorating its difficult crossing by boat at Tangur, Akasha, and possibly also Sai.[27] The Egyptian forces finally reached Tombos on the Third Cataract, only 15 km north of Kerma, the enemy's capital city, whose fate during this

---

26. *Urk.* IV 6.17–18.2; 36.1–2; 78.8–12; see Habachi 1959: 57–58. On the archaeology of Sai, see most recently Gabolde 2011; Budka and Doyen 2012/13; Budka 2015. On the very modest Egyptian presence in Batn el-Hagar, see Edwards and Mills 2013.

27. *Urk.* IV 8.4–9.6 (difficult crossing of the cataract: 8.4–10); 36.5–9; see most recently Davies 2017: 87–92. Return in Year 3: *Urk.* IV 89.4–9; see most recently Gasse and Rondot 2017: 128–130, 478.

campaign is unknown.[28] The most that can be said is that it was bypassed by the Egyptian expedition, as relevant inscriptions are only found further upstream at Kurgus, roughly 600 km to the south of Kerma.

As we have no evidence for the journey from Tombos to Kurgus, we cannot decide if the expedition traveled over land or along the Nile (or both). At first glance, the Nile seems the obvious choice, but we cannot completely exclude an overland journey, either partial or complete: if using the river, the Egyptian forces would first have had to cross, from beginning to end, a region that, with the exception of the area surrounding Napata, was almost uninhabited and without resources, and subsequently they would have had to negotiate against the current of the Nile at one of the river's worst navigable stretches. Whatever the route, the expedition eventually reached Abu Hamed and then stopped at Kurgus, where Thutmose I famously ordered a set of images and inscriptions to be engraved on Hagar el-Merwa (as later to be emulated by Thutmose III), which proclaimed this spot to be Egypt's southernmost border and warned would-be trespassers of dire reprisals. In the following year, Thutmose I would have had a parallel inscription engraved in Syria on the bank of the Euphrates, but nothing of this second monument remains.[29]

As no other traces of Thutmose I's presence have been found between Kerma and Kurgus, it seems obvious that the expedition of Years 2–3 was not intent on conquering the land in between, which, apart from the fertile river basin between Kerma and Kawa, was a desolate and largely uninhabited region. Hence, one must probably understand Thutmose's campaign as a raid of intimidation,[30] of the same kind as the one undertaken against the kingdom of Mittani that would reach the Euphrates

---

28. The excavations at Dokki Gel on the city's northern outskirts show that a group of Eighteenth Dynasty temples (and later Ramessides ones) was built there, but their founders cannot be identified. The reconstruction of the site's history through the interpretation of Egyptian inscriptions, as proposed by Bonnet and Valbelle 2018, is highly speculative. The style of the impressive surrounding fortifications is completely alien to Egyptian military architecture and they should therefore be indigenous.

29. *Urk.* IV 85.13–14.

30. *Urk.* IV 9.3–6.

a year later. The inscriptions left in both places could be compared to a warning sign not to cross a (unilaterally asserted) property line under penalty of retaliation. This probably implies that the spot at Kurgus, which could have been intermittently monitored from Lower Nubia via the Korosko Road (see section 28.1), did not represent, to the Egyptian mind, the border to a wasteland, crossed only by nomad tribes, but to the territories held by an enemy polity—and what better candidate is there than a surviving kingdom of Kush?

Indeed, the geography of the Nile's great double bend in Nubia (see section 28.1) makes it very likely that any indigenous power located at Kerma, apprehensive of an imminent Egyptian attack which it knew it could not stand against in conventional warfare, would be wise to retreat before such an attack, either along the Nile or, more probably, by the route linking Kawa, Napata, and Atbara. Having reached Tombos, one could imagine that Thutmose I intended to force this assumed Kushite power to retreat as far away as possible and that he marked Kurgus as his frontier to prevent its return. As he had his name engraved on the Nile bank south of Tombos in what looks like an actual border sign, we hesitate to think that he occupied Kerma, at least not permanently. The city might even have retained its position as the seat of an indigenous rump state: later, Thutmose II reports that by the end of his predecessor's reign, "Kush" had been divided into five "chieftaincies," whose geographical scope is unknown but one of which, at least, was in its "northern" part, i.e., in close contact with the Egyptians or even within nominally Egyptian territory.[31]

Back in Egypt in Year 3, Thutmose I began to implement the consolidation of the conquered territories by founding permanent settlements with Egyptian populations. Difficulties ensued due to this cohabitation and by the end of Thutmose's reign, the Nubian resentment resulted in

---

31. *Urk.* IV 138.12–139.7.

an uprising of the three northernmost Nubian chieftains, which were of Kushite royal descent. The Egyptian counterattack was underway when Thutmose died and probably concluded under Thutmose II (1492–1479 BC)[32] who, however, probably never set foot into Nubia in person. Egypt's eventual occupation of Kerma and the Kerma-Kawa region dates to the years following this revolt, as demonstrated by the founding of a settlement at Tabo on the Nile island of Argo just south of the city of Kerma.[33]

During her reign, Hatshepsut (1479–1458 BC) had only minor revolts to repress in Nubia.[34] But later, Thutmose III (1479–1425 BC) had to deal with a new "rebellion" in his Year 34 (1445 BC). The insurrection originated probably south of Kurgus, as four sons of the "Chief of *Irem*" (that is, the region of the Butana, later known as the "Island of Meroe") were among the prisoners subsequently sent to Egypt.[35] In his Year 47 at the latest, Thutmose moved the New Kingdom frontier forward from Kawa across the Nubian Desert to Napata, a city that he founded less than 15 km from the Fourth Cataract at the foot of Gebel Barkal.[36] This move makes a lot of sense if we assume that some kind of Kushite political establishment had previously retreated to this region, which would then be forced to flee once again to seek refuge in the future "Island of Meroe." Around his Year 50, Thutmose reached Kurgus and had a frontier inscription carved on Hagar el-Merwa, modeled after the one left by his grandfather Thutmose I.[37]

---

32. *Urk.* IV 137–141.

33. Jacquet-Gordon et al. 1969.

34. *Urk.* IV 1375; see Gasse and Rondot 2007: 135, 482; Davies 2008.

35. *Urk.* IV 708.9–709.3. We agree with O'Connor 1973: 128–130; 1998: 267–268 in equating *Irem* with the Butana; for alternative views, see Török 2009: 18, n. 61.

36. Date according to the Gebel Barkal Stele (Museum of Fine Arts, Boston: MFA 23.733): *Urk.* IV 1227–1243; Török 2009: 19.

37. Year 50 according to the inscription at Sehel: *Urk.* IV 814.10–815.2; see Gasse and Rondot 2007: 137–138, 483.

28.3.2. Egyptian rule over Kush

From the time of Thutmose III to the end of the New Kingdom, Nubia was firmly held in control by Egypt and saw an intense period of temple construction and exploitation of mineral resources, even as local insurrections never ceased to challenge Egyptian power. Indeed, despite their large military superiority, the pharaohs had evidently underestimated Kush's resilience, for these so-called rebellions, which took place on average once a decade, were most probably Kushite attempts to reassert independence and reclaim territory. This shows that their state had somehow been able to retain its structure and identity through successive retreats before the advancing Egyptian forces. The indigenous kingdoms of Napata, whose rulers would conquer Egypt during the early first millennium BC and constitute its Twenty-fifth Dynasty (see chapter 37 in volume 4), and of Meroe, which the Roman Empire would prove unable to conquer, would be its distant descendants.

By the time of Thutmose III, a functioning Egyptian administration had been gradually established in Nubia, which was headed by the "King's Son of Kush," a high-ranking official who held civil and military powers (often called viceroy of Kush in modern studies).[38] The territory he governed was divided into Lower Nubia and Upper Nubia or, in Egyptian terminology, *Wawat* and *Kush*, each directed by a lieutenant to the King's Son of Kush. Their seats of office varied throughout the period, as did the residence of the viceroy. At the local level, officials of Egyptian establishments exercised administrative power, while indigenous chieftaincies were retained to better control the native populations. As a region of frequent revolts and crucial economic interest for Egypt, Nubia was occupied by permanent Egyptian troops, garrisoned in a number of fortresses controlled by the chief of the troops of Kush, the King's Son of Kush's military second-in-command.

On an economic level, the most important Nubian contribution to Egypt's resources was undoubtedly its gold, mainly mined in the Nubian Desert in regions accessible through Wadi Allaqi and Wadi Gabgaba, but

---

38. Morkot 2013; Müller 2013.

also between the Second Cataract and Kerma. Nubia held the richest gold deposit of the Near East, still mined to this day. Besides the exploitation of mineral resources, the New Kingdom tried to develop agriculture in Nubia, even as it was facing difficult conditions. The Egyptian policy of building temples outside already existing settlements can be interpreted as the creation of agricultural colonies, as these institutions had to be given land, laborers, and management autonomy in order to fulfill their religious duties. The focus given in many of these temples to the cult of the pharaoh or the royal couple shows that they were also intended to promote Egypt's political system among the local populations. In addition to its gold mines and its agricultural potential, Nubia was also a large reservoir of mercenaries and workers for Egypt. Nubian soldiers had traditionally been held in high esteem. Now, these were mainly recruited from an ethnic group called the *Medjay*. As they were also employed as rural policing forces and desert rangers, their name ultimately became the usual designation for such personnel in the New Kingdom, now freed from any ethnic connotation. Nubia was also an important source of civilian labor. The repression of insurrections led to the reduction of the defeated enemies to slavery or serfdom, and if needed, the Egyptian governors simply raided the local population for forced labor. Finally, Nubia functioned as Egypt's "corridor to Africa"[39] by allowing passage of products from deeper within the continent to Egypt, most importantly wild animals and their products, such as panther pelts, ostrich eggs, and feathers or ivory. Economically, the destruction of the kingdom of Kush certainly freed Egypt from an onerous intermediary in this trade.

Year 8 (1389 BC) of Thutmose IV (1397–1388 BC) saw the biggest revolt against Egyptian rule since the days of Thutmose III.[40] Our only source tells us that Wawat (that is, Lower Nubia) was threatened by the approach of a Nubian leader and his forces. The Egyptian presence and the geographical obstacles between Abu Hamed and Lower Nubia would have made it impossible to realize such an advance through the

---

39. As aptly expressed in the title of Adams 1984.

40. *Urk.* IV 1545–1548.

Nile valley. We must therefore assume that the enemy had no other option than to use the Korosko Road and thus would have come from the region of Meroe, where we assume that the leadership of Kush resided in exile. In any case, the attack was easily foiled by an Egyptian counterattack led by the pharaoh in person.

Seven years later, in Year 5 (1382 BC) of Amenhotep III (1388–1350 BC), Nubia again saw a significant insurrection, led by another indigenous leader called Ikheny.[41] He was defeated by an Egyptian army that advanced past Kurgus toward Atbara as far as a place called the "Freshwaters (*qebehu*) of Horus," which we would identify with the Fifth Cataract,[42] thus striking deep into the heart of the surviving Kushite state. Some Egyptian gold-processing communities had probably already been established in the land of Karoy, west of Abu Hamed, as the expedition brought back from that region gold that was later used to decorate the Third Pylon of the temple of Karnak at Thebes.[43] The long reign of Amenhotep III allowed him to implement in Nubia an ambitious program of temple construction, with the King's and Queen's temples at Soleb and Sedeinga being the foremost examples. Around Year 30 (1358 BC), the viceroy Merymose furthermore led under unclear circumstances a raid against the land of Ibhat, situated on the eastern bank of the Nile in an unknown location.[44]

Nubia was the goal of the only military campaign of the reign of Akhenaten (1351–1334 BC). In Year 12 (1338 BC), the King's Son of Kush Thutmose had to repress a revolt of desert-dwellers in the land of *Akuyta* (probably situated in Wadi Allaqi) that obstructed Egyptian gold production.[45] During the reigns of Akhenaten's successors of the Eighteenth Dynasty, no notable unrests are reported for Nubia.

41. *Urk.* IV 1661–1666; 1734–1736 (?); 1758.15–17; 1959.10–19; see Topozada 1988: 157–163; O'Connor 1998: 264–269. Kozloff 2012: 70–81.

42. *Urk.* IV 1662. 7–12.

43. *Urk.* IV 1654.14–15; 1731.9–11.

44. Urk. IV 1659–1661; see Topozada 1988: 164; O'Connor 1987: 127–128; 1998: 269–270; Kozloff 2012: 166–181.

45. Török 2009: 18, n. 62.

The Ramesside Nineteenth Dynasty did not bring about any substantial changes to the Egyptian rule in Nubia. In his Year 8 or 9 (1276 or 1275 BC), Sety I (1290–1279 BC) had to counter a new revolt that included operations in the land of Irem, which shows that the Kushites had not renounced a claim to their former territories.[46] The future Rameses II had some unclear part in this campaign, as some of its episodes are depicted in his Nubian temple of Bet el-Wali.[47] Before he died, Sety I also implemented some organizational work in Nubia. He established a new fortified city at Amara West just south of Batn el-Hagar, to where the seat of the lieutenant of Kush was moved from his former residence on the island of Sai.[48] With the intention of providing water to the gold-miners of Wadi Allaqi, the king also began to excavate, near Qubban, a well that would be completed by his son Rameses II.[49]

Under Rameses II (1279–1213 BC), the situation in Nubia was generally calm, until ca. Year 20 (1259 BC), when a new attack from Irem had to be repelled.[50] In Year 44 (1235 BC), the King's Son of Kush Setau raided native people to gather a workforce in order to build the temple of Wadi el-Sebua. This sanctuary was one of a series of at least eight temples built during Rameses' reign, among which the famous pair of temples at Abu Simbel stands out most prominently. His raiding led Setau first to the land of Akuyta, deep in the Wadi Allaqi or on the Korosko Road, and then all the way to Kurgus, with a possible further incursion into Irem.[51]

Rameses II's successor Merenptah (1213–1203 BC) had to fight a campaign of some importance in Nubia in his Year 6 (1206 BC),[52] shortly

---

46. KRI I: 102–104; KRI VII: 8–11.

47. Ricke et al. 1967; KRI II: 195–200.

48. On this town and its development, see P. Spencer 1997–2013; N. Spencer et al. 2014.

49. KRI II: 353–360.

50. KRI II: 222.

51. KRI III: 91–94; Wente 1985; Davies 2017: 75, fig. 22, 80. For the location of Akuyta, see Török 2009: 18 n. 62.

52. KRI IV: 33–37.

after a victory in battle against the Libyans. It is not unlikely that the Nubians' move was more or less coordinated with the northern attack of the Libyan forces on Egypt and the general unrest of the Libyans in the Western Desert, as these peoples were well connected by its network of desert trails (see section 28.1). The unprecedented cruelty exhibited toward the prisoners seems to attest to Egypt's annoyance with these recurring and intertwined events: just like the Libyans who had survived the battle, the Nubians were publicly impaled south of Memphis. Possibly as a result of this policy, no further troubles are reported in Nubia during the late Nineteenth Dynasty.

During the Twentieth Dynasty, the record of Egyptian activities in Nubia is generally limited to rounds of inspection undertaken by administrative and military officials. Unless we miss some crucial bit of information, the situation appears to have been calmer than during the previous centuries. However, the very end of the New Kingdom saw the military forces hitherto stationed in Nubia deeply involved in the internal affairs of Egypt. In the early eleventh century BC during the reign of Rameses XI, the last king of the dynasty, severe civil unrest arose in Upper Egypt due to the complex interaction of various factors. When the local Theban authorities proved unable to cope with the situation, the pharaoh ordered, sometime before his Year 12 (1092 BC), that the King's Son of Kush Panehsy should rule Upper Egypt under martial law. This situation, however, resulted in open conflict with Amenhotep, the high priest of Amun of Thebes, who had de facto governed the region until then. Around Year 17 (1087 BC), Panehsy resolved the conflict by ousting Amenhotep from his post, who subsequently turned to the king for justice and protection. Panehsy then declared sedition and marched north to fight the royal army, but was pushed back to the south by a general of Libyan descent (either Piankh or Herihor; the chronological sequence of these two men is hotly debated) who re-established the king's rule in Thebes in Year 19 and inaugurated a local "Renaissance era." The victorious general then took for himself the combined military and religious powers previously held by Panehsy and Amenhotep, turning himself into a kind of Upper Egyptian viceroy (but crucially without adopting such a title), while Panehsy was pushed back to Nubia, where he seems to have succeeded in retaining political autonomy for some time.[53]

28.4. Egypt, the Libyans, and the Aegean

As there is a clear link between Libya and the Aegean during part of the New Kingdom period, we will discuss Egypt's relationship with both regions together. We may distinguish two phases in this relationship:

(1) From the beginning of the Eighteenth Dynasty to ca. Year 10 of Sety I (1280 BC), Egyptian sources record no actions against Libya, while Egypt's relations with the Aegean are characterized by peaceful commercial relationships with the Minoans of Crete and the Mycenaeans of mainland Greece until ca. Year 42 of Thutmose III (1413 BC), followed by commercial relations with the Mycenaeans until ca. Year 10 of Sety I (1280 BC); simultaneously, however, Egypt now had to repel raids of Aegean seafarers in the delta, either by Mycenaean groups or people culturally related to them: the so-called Sea Peoples.

(2) From Year 10 of Sety I (1280 BC) to Year 11 (1170 BC) of Rameses III, Egypt experienced clashes with the Libyans and the Sea Peoples, steadily growing in intensity. Against the northern Libyans, Egypt had to fight at least four battles on the western fringes of the delta, around Year 10 of Sety I (1280 BC), in Year 5 of Merenptah (1207 BC), and in Rameses III's Year 5 (1176 BC) and Year 11 (1170 BC). The Libyans received direct support by Mycenaean warriors in their conflict with Merenptah, while during Rameses III's second campaign in 1170 BC, they were equipped with Mycenaean weapons. In either Rameses III's Year 3 (1178 BC) or Year 8 (1173 BC), these same Sea Peoples attacked Egypt as part of the migrations marking the end of the Bronze Age. Meanwhile, the southern Libyans took to

---

53. Redford 2004: 54–57 provides a good survey. For in-depth discussions of these events and the debate concerning Piankh and Herihor, see in particular Jansen-Winkeln 1992; Kitchen 1996: xiv–xviii (§§A–N).

raid Middle Egypt from the beginning of the Nineteenth Dynasty on, resulting first in the establishment of a series of Egyptian military settlements on the western banks of the Nile and then in the implementation of a program of fortification around its cities and temples.

As a result of these conflicts, the Egyptian army was increasingly composed of former Libyan prisoners of war, who would later come to seize political power in the country (see chapter 35 in volume 4), whereas some of the Sea Peoples settled on the eastern Mediterranean coast, later taking part in the gradual expulsion of Egypt from its former possessions in that region.

28.4.1. From the early Eighteenth Dynasty to the reign of Sety I (1550–1278 BC)

By the time of the New Kingdom, there had long been a difficult relationship between Egypt and the northern Libyans from Marmarica (Egyptian *Tjehenu*), sustained by a structural factor: the attempts of the Libyans to settle in the lush western delta and the reluctance of the Egyptians to allow them to do so; whenever Egyptian control over the region in question was weakened, the Libyans infiltrated it. However, to the Egyptian state, the Libyan problem seems to never have amounted to more than a problem of regulating this immigration, which on the whole was allowed to proceed. Further to the south, the Libyans of the Western Desert (Egyptian *Tjemehu*) were probably always too few in numbers to represent a proper threat to Egypt, but since the Old Kingdom period, their movements had been monitored as Egypt exercised control over the oases. Whether from Marmarica or from the Western Desert, the Egyptians considered these people little more than a ragtag bunch, poorly organized and worse armed. In the almost three centuries between the beginning of the Eighteenth Dynasty and the reign of Sety I, Egyptian sources do not record any serious hostilities between Egypt and the Libyans. This does not necessarily imply that there were none, but whatever conflicts may have occurred were not deemed serious enough to be recorded.

Turning to the regions across the Mediterranean from Libya, at the beginning of the New Kingdom, Egypt had a peaceful relationship with the Aegean world,[54] especially with the Minoans of Crete. In addition to the depiction of gift-bearing Minoans in the tombs of several high-ranking officials at Thebes, the discovery of fragments of a large wall painting of Minoan craftsmanship in the remains of a palace of Thutmoside date, at the former Hyksos capital Avaris in the eastern Nile delta, bears eloquent testimony to these relations.[55] No less spectacular, a list of Aegean toponyms in Egyptian hieroglyphs is recorded on the base of one of the colossi that adorned the mortuary temple of Amenhotep III (1388–1350 BC) at Kom el-Hetan in Thebes West.[56] This list contains two sections: one is headed by the entry *Tinay* ("Danaia," a name for mainland Greece), and the other by the entry *Keftiu* ("Crete"). Each section lists places, probably according to a trade itinerary. From Greece, where, e.g., Mycenae and its harbor Nafplio are named, we cross via the island of Cythera to Crete, where we land at Kydonia; Knossos and its harbor Amnisos are listed here, as well as Phaistos, the most important harbor on Crete's southern coast, which faces Africa, and Egypt. The text was probably compiled about eighty years before the construction of Amenhotep's temple, sometimes before the Minoans' demise around 1450 BC.

Crete was conquered by the Mycenaeans ca. 1450 BC, bringing the Minoan civilization to an end (see chapter 31 in this volume). Egypt's relationship with the Aegean soon adjusted to accommodate these new partners, as shown by the substitution of Mycenaeans instead of Minoans in the gift-bearing scenes in some Theban tombs.[57] Sometime later, Thutmose III (1459–1425 BC) received a diplomatic gift from the

---

54. For a compendium of all available sources on Egypt's relationship with the Aegean, see Vivas Sainz 2013. See also chapter 31 in this volume.

55. Bietak et al. 2007; for a critical view regarding a supposed Minoan "ethnicity," see Matić 2014.

56. Base of Colossus E_n: Edel and Görg 2005: 161–213.

57. Wachsmann 1987; Hallmann 2006.

"prince" of *Tinay* in his Year 42 (1413 BC).[58] When the Mycenaeans began to expand into western Asia Minor around that time, the Hittites sources document a land of Ahhiyawa, likely a Hittite transcription of "Achaia," which in turn corresponds to *Tinay* in the Egyptian sources.[59] These toponyms are clear forerunners for the terms *Achaeans* (Ἀχαιοί) and *Danaans* (Δαναοί), two of the collective names for the Greeks in Homer's Iliad and Odyssey.

Although Egypt entertained a commercial relationship with the Mycenaeans, the delta region increasingly fell victim to Aegean raiders. A later memory of these times is preserved in a passage of the Odyssey (XIV, 229–272), where Ulysses, posing as a Cretan princeling, recalls the dispatching of a raiding party from Crete to plunder Egypt as his habitual way of turning a profit. While there are no explicit Eighteenth Dynasty sources about such pirate activity, Amenhotep III had the mouths of the Nile's branches placed under regular guard by soldiers and navy,[60] presumably to discourage such attacks.

As we shall further discuss later (section 28.4.2), these raiders were not Mycenaeans in the narrow sense (i.e., people from Tinay/Ahhiyawa and its dependencies), but also people whose material culture was Mycenaean, while their true ethnicity is a matter of conjecture. Nor were such raids limited to Egypt. Cyprus, for example, was affected too, as the king of Alašiya (Cyprus) complained in a cuneiform letter to Akhenaten (1351–1334 BC) of the sea-raiding activities of the *Lukka*, the people of the land on the southern coast of Turkey that is called Lycia in the classical sources.[61] From other letters of the Amarna correspondence,[62] we know that at that time, some Western Asian princes had incorporated into their guard mercenaries called *Širdanu*: a term that corresponds to

58. *Urk.* IV 733.4–7.

59. For a synthesis, see Kelder 2010; for the sources, see Beckman et al. 2011.

60. *Urk.* IV 1281.13–14.

61. EA 38 (for a translation, see Moran 1992: 111–112).

62. EA 81, 122 and 123 (for translations, see Moran 1992: 150–151, 201–202).

Shardana, as later attested as the Egyptian designation of one of the Sea Peoples.[63]

28.4.2. From Sety I to Year 11 of Rameses III (1289–1170 BC)

Tensions between Egypt and the Libyans, as well as Aegean raiding, took a turn for the worse during the Nineteenth Dynasty. Sometime in the second half of his reign, Sety I (1290–1279 BC) had to fight a proper battle, rather than a border skirmish, against an organized force of the northern Libyans from Marmarica (Egyptian *Tjehenu*).[64] On the Libyans' part, this shows a marked change in attitude and organization. As this more or less coincides with the beginning of the Sea Peoples' raids against Egypt, it is very likely that there is a connection. This assumption is further strengthened if we observe that the future Rameses II fought against both enemies during his father and predecessor's reign. In the reliefs of Sety I at Karnak, his name was added to the depiction of an Egyptian prince shown fighting the Libyans, while on a stele from Piramesses (modern Qantir), Rameses narrates how, at the time of his father, he victoriously fought the *Shardana*,[65] one of the Sea Peoples, some of whose members, after having been taken as prisoners of war, would later form the better part of his elite guard.

The link between the Sea Peoples and Libya is further corroborated by the presence of Mycenaean pottery at the site of Mersa Matruh on the Mediterranean shore of Marmarica.[66] Although there is clearly a connection between the Sea Peoples and Libya, we can but speculate regarding the practical details of this relationship. Geographical considerations prompt us to argue that there was an earlier maritime link established between Mycenaean Crete and Cyrenaica on the eastern

---

63. On the activities of the Sea Peoples, see Gilan 2013: 49–56.

64. KRI I: 20–24.

65. KRI II: 290.2–3.

66. White 2002; cf. also Schofield 2007: 110–111.

coast of modern Libya, as the distance from Crete to Africa is shortest between these regions.[67] From this western location, merchants and
pirates alike could easily access Egypt by land or along the coast, with
probably no other intermediate stop available than Mersa Matruh.[68]
Their tales of the Nile delta's luxuries could have further encouraged the
people of Cyrenaica, whose more sedentary lifestyle will have gone hand
in hand with a tighter social organization than the nomadic pastoralists
of Marmarica, to try to force entry into this paradise. In turn, tensions
in northern Libya could have easily contributed to the renewed unrest in
Nubia at the time, relayed via the desert routes by the southern Libyans,
who themselves began to habitually raid Middle and Upper Egypt.

There is no evidence of any direct confrontation with the northern
Libyans during Rameses II's long reign (1279–1213 BC). This period's
seeming peacefulness may well be due to the king's implementation of
a deliberate policy of containment and surveillance toward the Libyans.
He established some fortified settlements on the delta's western fringes,
while organizing a military road along the Mediterranean coast toward
Cyrenaica, modeled on the "Ways of Horus" leading to Canaan (see section 28.1).[69] There are three known forts along this road. Although only
a few stone blocks survive from the forts at Gharbaniyat and el-Alamein,
there are significant remains of the third at Zawyet Umm el-Rakham, 25
km west of Mersa Matruh.[70] Meanwhile, Rameses also tried to hold in
check the southern Libyans, who had begun a routine of raiding the Nile
valley from the Western Desert, by establishing a series of military colonies along the river's west bank, but the problem gradually worsened.

After more than 70 years of peace, the first of three serious attempts
of Libyans to force their entry into New Kingdom Egypt with methods
of conventional warfare took place in Year 5 (1207 BC) of Merenptah

67. Note also that the site of Cyrena was chosen to found a colony of Thera
(Santorini) in 630 BC.

68. White and White 1996; White 2002.

69. Snape 2013.

70. Snape and Wilson 2007.

(1213–1203 BC).[71] These attempts were not of a purely military character, but each time accompanied by the exodus of entire communities. During the reign of Merenptah, Egypt's principal opponents were the *Libu*, a designation that is attested for the first time in the Egyptian sources and of course connected to the name of Libya. The *Libu* were associated with the *Meshwesh* tribe (see section 28.6) and with warriors of a Mycenaean cultural affiliation.

Under the command of a chief of the *Libu* called Meryey, son of Ded, the invaders tried to reach the western Nile branch north of Memphis, from where the king left to meet them in battle. According to the available Egyptian sources, they were utterly defeated, with about 8,500 dead and 5,000 taken prisoners. A good third of the dead, about 2,500 individuals, were not Libyans but warriors that were collectively called "Foreigners of the Sea": the very expression that has been translated as "Sea Peoples" since the early pioneers of Egyptology (see section 28.6).

These "Foreigners of the Sea" consisted of five groups, whose name are best vocalized (according to the vocalization system based on the Egyptian syllabic orthography[72]) as *Aqaywasha*, *Turusha*, *Lukka*, *Shardana*, and *Shakalusha*; note that the consonantal forms *Ekwesh* (for *Aqaywasha*), *Teresh* (for *Turusha*), *Sherden* (for *Shardana*), and *Shekelesh* (for *Shakalusha*) are frequently used in the secondary literature. We have already encountered the *Shardana* and *Lukka*, whom we could attribute, broadly speaking, to the greater Aegean world (see section 28.4.1). If the name of the *Shakalusha* has indeed survived in the name of the city of Sagalassos in Pisidia, as has been convincingly argued, they would have been the *Lukka*'s northern neighbors. As for the *Aqaywasha*, they can be linked to the people from the land of *Ahhiyawa*, as attested in the Hittite sources (see section 28.4.1), which we understand to be Mycenaeans from mainland Greece. The origins of the *Shardana* are unknown, although a link with Sardes, the later capital of Lydia in western Asia Minor, is conceivable; some five centuries later, they would settle in the western

---

71. KRI IV: 1–24; 33–38; see Manassa 2003.

72. For the vocalization of the Egyptian syllabic orthography, see the overview by Hoch 1994: 506–512.

Mediterranean and give their name to the island of Sardinia. At roughly the same time, the descendants of the last group of "Foreigners of the Sea," the *Turusha*, would settle in Italy where they would be known as the Etruscans (Turush > (E)trusc). Herodotus (I, 94) says about their origins that they were a part of the Lydian people, sent away from their homeland because of a famine. Although the specifically Lydian origin of the Etruscans must be rejected (as the Lydian and Etruscan languages are very different), the tradition of their eastern origin has found corroboration especially in a proto-Etruscan inscription that was found on the northern Aegean island of Lemnos.[73] Although these peoples, and others who would later join them, probably did not share language and/ or ethnicity, they had in common, from the Egyptian point of view, their northern origins from beyond the sea, their seafaring and piratical way of life, and the common use of Mycenaean-style weaponry (see chapter 31 in this volume).

As the steppe lands of the Marmarica would not have been able to feed an apparently numerous population group such as the *Libu*, it seems obvious that they must have come from further west, all the way from Cyrenaica. It is from this very same location that Mycenaean traders and raiders probably made their way to the Nile delta, since their conquest of Crete and their reports of Egypt's riches may have encouraged the *Libu* attack. They certainly enabled the invasion not only by joining forces with them, but also by providing them with weapons. It is difficult to imagine how the *Libu*, with the limited resources of their land, could have manufactured the over 9,000 "Libyan swords" that Merenptah's texts list as part of his army's spoils and which twelfth-century reliefs of Rameses III (1181–1150 BC) at his mortuary temple at Medinet Habu would later show to be of Mycenaean craftsmanship.

As the subsequent Libyan attacks against Egypt are intimately associated with the activities of the Sea Peoples and the situation in the Levant, we shall address them in section 28.6.

---

73. Cf. De Simone 1996; Beekes 2003.

28.5. Egypt, Canaan, and the east

We discussed the establishment of the Egyptian control over Canaan during Ahmose's reign in section 28.2. The records of his successor Amenhotep I make no mention of any activity in Canaan or elsewhere in the east, and therefore we will resume our survey of the New Kingdom's relations with these regions with the reign of Thutmose I. These relations show a development over several stages:[74]

(1) From Year 3 of Thutmose I (1500 BC) to ca. Year 11 of Amenhotep II (1415 BC), Egypt fought a war against the northern Mesopotamian kingdom of Mittani. This gave way to a negotiated peace, which lasted from the reign of Thutmose IV (1397–1388 BC) to ca. Year 8 of Tutankhamun (1325 BC). Local troubles, however, repeatedly affected territories under nominal Egyptian control, including Canaan, Amurru, and Lebanon.

(2) From ca. Year 8 of Tutankhamun (1325 BC) to Year 21 of Rameses II (1259 BC), Egypt fought a new war, this time against the Hittite Empire. Eventually, a peace agreement was concluded, which between 1259–1069 BC gave respite to the New Kingdom, although there still were repeatedly revolts in Canaan. In the final century of the New Kingdom, the region saw Rameses III's campaign against the Sea Peoples (1178 or 1173 BC), followed at some point by their settling on the Canaanite coast, from where Egypt gradually withdrew.

During these two and a half centuries, New Kingdom armies would advance as far north as the city of Carchemish at the foot of the Taurus mountains on the western bank of the Euphrates, roam the Syrian hinterland, and conquer its cities in an unprecedented military effort, whose sheer magnitude calls for an explanation. While the New Kingdom's

---

74. Grandet 2008: 13–22; also Ahrens 2015. Cf. Müller 2011 for an interesting perspective that may, however, be too dependent on the *cordon sanitaire* model.

Table 28.2. War and peace in the Near East during
the New Kingdom

1550	1500		1415		1325	1259		1069
Peace (50 years)	Egypt-Mittani conflict (85 years)		Peace (90 years)		Egypt-Hatti conflict (66 years)	Peace (190 years)		
XVIIIth dynasty						XIXth dyn.		XXth dyn.
1550						1292	1185	1069

Prepared by Pierre Grandet.

motives and approach for moving against Nubia ("Take back the country and crush the opposition!") and against the Libyans and the Mycenaeans ("Get them before they get us!") were crystal clear, Egypt's eastern policy is not so easy to assess.

First, we must dissipate an illusion that is largely created by an uncritical approach of the available Egyptian sources. The inscriptions and reliefs covering the walls of the temples of the New Kingdom offer a ceaseless celebration of pharaohs' conquests and victories, but one needs to recognize their propagandistic purpose. Until today, they succeed in sustaining the idea that New Kingdom Egypt was an "empire of conquerors," whose main objective was unrelenting military conquests in Western Asia, for benefits that remain unclear. This interpretation, however, is false, as is easily demonstrated by using simple statistics. During the New Kingdom, the history of Egypt's relations with Western Asia is dominated by two major international conflicts: with the kingdom of Mittani during the Eighteenth Dynasty and with the Hittite Empire from the later part of the Eighteenth to the middle of the Nineteenth Dynasty. But within the 480 years of the New Kingdom, these two conflicts occupy only 85 and 66 years, respectively, or a total of 151 years, against more than twice the number of years being peaceful (329 years). Moreover, under the conditions of ancient warfare, these conflicts did not take the form of permanent fighting on a continuously maintained front, but rather manifested as a series of separate battles and campaigns that furthermore only took up a few months of the year (table 28.2).[75]

A CLOSER LOOK at our sources reveals that during these 151 years of conflict with the eastern powers, the New Kingdom only fought 24 military campaigns (Table 28.3): at the beginning of the period, the campaign to drive out the Hyksos; 15 campaigns during the conflict with Mittani (and of these, 10 were fought solely under Thutmose III); and 8 campaigns during the conflict with the Hittites.

In other words, even during these 151 years of conflict, 24 years of campaigning stand against 127 years without open warfare. For the whole duration of the New Kingdom, that amounts to 24 out of 480 years, corresponding to 5 percent of the total. In addition, there were often long gaps between individual operations, such as the more than four decades between the first and second campaigns of the conflict with Mittani.

We therefore reach the unavoidable conclusion that warfare was in fact an exceptional tool in the New Kingdom's relations with the East: diplomacy's bloody side, so to speak, given prominence only when negotiations failed. In addition, the scarcity of using warfare indicates that the goal was never as ambitious as destroying an enemy state, but only to circumscribe its power and/or to strengthen negotiations by territorial control. But even reduced to these far more modest proportions, the fact remains that the New Kingdom pharaohs routinely waged war against Western Asia, when their predecessors almost never had done so, and this raises the question of their motives. The sources themselves cannot help much in elucidating these, as their core message is that the pharaoh, with the gods' help, was Egypt's true and victorious defender against outside agents of chaos (see section 28.1). However, we can safely exclude that Egypt sought to create a "colonial empire": its population during the New Kingdom period is thought to have amounted to no

---

75. For the technical aspects of Egyptians armies and warfare, see Spalinger 2005; 2013.

Table 28.3. Key events in Egypt's interaction with the east

1	Expulsion of the Hyksos and the capture of Sharuhen by Ahmose (1535)
	The conflict between Egypt and Mittani
2	Thutmose I's raid to the Euphrates (1500)
3	Thutmose III's campaign against Megiddo (1458)
4	Thutmose III's campaign against Ullaza and Ardata (1453)
5	Thutmose III's campaign against Qadesh, Simyra and Ardata (1452)
6	Thutmose III's campaign against Ullaza (1451)
7	Thutmose III's campaign against Mittani and the crossing of the Euphrates (1450)
8	Thutmose III's campaign against Nuhašše (1449)
9	Thutmose III's campaign against Arana (1448)
10	Thutmose III's campaign against Nuhašše (1445)
11	Thutmose III's campaign against the Shasu (1444)
12	Thutmose III's campaign against Irqata and Tunip (1441)
13	Amenhotep II's campaign against Takhsy (1423)
14	Amenhotep II's campaign to the Orontes valley (1419)
15	Amenhotep II's campaign against Canaan (1417)
16	Amenhotep III's campaign against Abdi-Aširta of Amurru (1357)
	The conflict between Egypt and Hatti
17	Campaign under Tutankhamun against Qadesh and the Hittites (1325)
18	Sety I's campaign against Canaan and Lebanon (1290)
19	Sety I's campaign against Qadesh and Amurru (1285?)
20	Sety I's campaign against the Hittites (1284–1283?)
21	Rameses II's campaign against Canaan and Lebanon (1276)
22	Rameses II's campaign against Muwatalli and the battle of Qadesh (1275)
23	Rameses II's campaign against Canaan, Lebanon and Amurru (1272)
24	Rameses II's campaign against Lebanon? (1270)

Prepared by Pierre Grandet.

more than 4–5 million and therefore did not have the demographic surplus to establish colonies abroad (except for modest ones in Nubia); quite on the contrary, Egypt routinely had to import manpower.

On balance, it is most likely that the use of war and diplomacy in the East was intended to procure specific resources for Egypt. Of all the goods that Egypt imported from the Levant, there are only two that could have been important enough to warrant the exceptional use of the military: timber and tin. The first we can readily exclude from our reasoning, as the New Kingdom never had any difficulties to obtain timber, its trade being the principal source of wealth for the elites on the Lebanese coast. We therefore conclude that Egypt fought for guaranteeing its supply of tin, either in raw form or already incorporated into its alloy bronze.[76] This conclusion in turn leads to a new question. Tin is used to make bronze, and Egypt had used bronze for many centuries before, apparently without difficulties in obtaining it by peaceful commercial exchange. So why did the New Kingdom need to fight for it? As Egypt's archenemies in the East during this time were first the kingdom of Mittani and then the Hittite Empire (see chapters 29 and 30 in this volume), it seems reasonable to conclude that it was the emergence of these new states that had changed the situation.

Now, if we turn once again to the geography of Western Asia (see section 28.1), the reasons for these states' conflicts with Egypt in regard to tin are readily apparent. The kingdom of Mittani was positioned precisely where it could control the trade route linking the Zagros mountains with the Euphrates, as well as the route leading up this river from the Persian Gulf. Moreover, in the first flush of this state's existence, its influence stretched beyond the Euphrates deep into Syria and on to Cilicia in the north and the Beqaa valley and Canaan in the south, so that Mittani threatened to develop a monopoly of control over all

---

76. Although the importance of the tin trade is generally stressed, very little concrete evidence allows us to study it in any detail with regard to Egypt; this situation could change with just one lucky find, comparable to the Uluburun shipwreck (see section 28.1).

overland trade from the east. This put Egypt, and also the Hittite state, in danger of either being cut off from their supply of tin or else of having to pay any price Mittani would name. When the Hittites replaced Mittani as the principal power of Western Asia by conquering Syria and other former Mittani territories, they in turn took control of the main part of the trade routes for tin, to the disadvantage of Egypt.

We must therefore conclude that the New Kingdom's ultimate goal in the east was to ensure Egypt's sufficient supply of tin by the simultaneous means of war and diplomacy. The Egyptians certainly would have realized that the only means to achieve such a result was to enforce a binding agreement. To this end, they seem to have used two successive strategies. The first was to contain Mittani east of the Euphrates, and Thutmose I achieved this through a campaign to that river in 1500 BC. The second strategy underpinned all operations of his New Kingdom successors against Mittani and the Hittites. Presumably, its key objective was to control Amurru and specifically its harbor of Simyra, which was the main port of entry for Cyprus's copper on the Levantine coast (see section 28.1). If control over this vital part of the international trade network were achieved, Egypt would be in a position to regulate, or even block, copper imports to Western Asia and use this as leverage in securing adequate access to tin.

28.5.1. The war against Mittani (1500–1415 BC)[77]

As far as Egypt's foreign policy is concerned, Thutmose I's reign (1504–1492 BC) was a crucial one. Probably a senior general before ascending the throne, he conducted in his Year 3 (1501 BC), right after his Nubian campaign, a military raid to the northeast as far as Carchemish on the Euphrates, about 1,000 km from Egypt, where he defeated a Mittani army.[78] While there, he claimed the river as his kingdom's northern border by carving on its western bank, right across from Mittani territory, a frontier inscription paralleling the one carved at

---

77. Grandet 2008: 69–131.

78. *Urk.* IV 9.8–10.3; 36.9–11; 38.16–39.1.

Kurgus in Nubia.[79] While it is certain that this raid happened, only limited sources relating to it survive. We do not have any indication of which route the Egyptian forces took to reach the Euphrates, but the shortest connection—through the Beqaa valley, the Syrian steppe, and Aleppo—is the likeliest. As for the return route, however, the depiction, in Hatshepsut's mortuary temple at Deir el-Bahri, of elephant tusks brought back by Thutmose I from Niya in Syria implies that the army traveled on the way from Aleppo to Qadesh through this region and Shaizar.[80] We will return to this point when discussing Thutmose III's campaign to the Euphrates.

As no Egyptian garrison was established in Carchemish to enforce Thutmose I's border claim, it is obvious that it was not to be taken literally, but as a warning and a threat: as a warning to Mittani that claiming territory to the west of the Euphrates would be taken by Egypt as a *casus belli*; and as a threat to come back and chastise any transgressors, just like the inscription or Kurgus addressed to the Kushites. This warning and this threat were not to be taken lightly: in his ability to project so much power so far from its base, the New Kingdom army's campaign to the Euphrates would go unsurpassed until the peak of Assyrian power in the seventh century BC, when Esarhaddon (680–669 BC) marched his forces to the Nile.

There is no record of any Egyptian military activity in the East for the next forty-three years from 1492 to 1458 BC, the combined reigns of Thutmose II and Hatshepsut, which seems to show that Thutmose I's warning fulfilled its role. During this time, however, the kingdom of Mittani found a way to subvert its containment by using client states to expand its influence west of the Euphrates into Syria and Cilicia and southward all the way to Mount Carmel where the Egypt-controlled territories began.

Thutmose III's sole reign began after the death of Hatshepsut in his nominal Year 22 (1457 BC) and he was immediately faced with the

---

79. *Urk.* IV 697.3–5; see section 28.3.1.

80. Naville 1898: 80; *Urk.* IV 103–105 for a reconstruction of the preserved text.

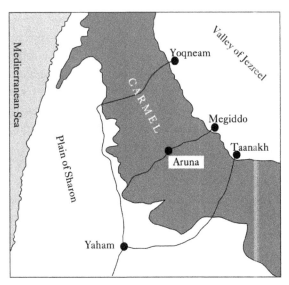

FIGURE 28.2. The roads to Megiddo across the Carmel. Prepared by Pierre Grandet.

necessity to cope with the threat posed by Mittani's influence, which had taken the form of an anti-Egyptian coalition of about 330 princes under the joint leadership of the rulers of Qadesh and Megiddo. These had assembled an army near Megiddo in the valley of Jezreel on the northern side of the Carmel range (figure 28.2). From Egypt via Gaza, the Egyptian forces rapidly advanced to its southern side, from where three passes allowed passage over it. Always keen to assign to the king a superhuman intellect, the Egyptian sources stress that Thutmose decided, against the advice of his officers, to use the Aruna Pass (today's Wadi Ara), the easiest and therefore main passage.[81] This choice allowed the Egyptians to exit in the Jezreel valley and regroup unopposed at Megiddo, while the enemy forces, convinced they would not use such

81. On the Aruna Pass and its alternatives, see Zertal 2011.

an obvious route, waited for them in vain at the exits of the other two passes.[82]

After two days of preparation, the two armies met in battle beneath the city walls of Megiddo. The allied forces proved no match for the Egyptian troops, as they disbanded at first contact and fled into the safety of Megiddo, leaving only eighty-five dead. Had they pursued them immediately, the Egyptians might have taken the city, but they instead looted the enemy camp, forcing Thutmose to put Megiddo under siege for seven months. In order to starve the powerfully fortified city atop its high settlement mound into surrendering, the Egyptians surrounded it by a circumvallation wall (the first written account of the use of such a device), while simultaneously devastating the surrounding countryside and living off it. Having exhausted its supplies, the besieged city finally surrendered, which allowed the Egyptians to stage a carefully managed, ritualized humiliation of the defeated enemy. After taking an oath to never oppose the pharaoh on penalty of death, the surviving leaders of the coalition, who had left their cities on magnificent horse-drawn war chariots, were sent back home astride humble donkeys.

This campaign allowed the Egyptians to annex the Jezreel valley, but this territorial gain had been a reaction to the threat of invasion of its existing Canaanite territories. From then onward, Thutmose III took the offensive, as made clear by his Karnak Annals, which cover his military activities until Year 42 (1441 BC).[83] The power backing the Megiddo coalition and the real enemy behind the scenes was of course Mittani. To take revenge, Thutmose III would have to attack this state in its own territory. However, the kingdom was separated by a considerable distance from the Egyptian zone of influence, mainly through hostile territories, and any attack had to be very thoroughly prepared.

This preparation would last no less than eight years and took the form of gradually occupying by conquest or by imposing some sort of control onto the lands between Egypt and Mittani. Above all, it required

---

82. *Urk.* IV 647–667; 757–763; 1246–1247; 1251–1275; see Grandet 2008: 81–94; 295–303; Vogel 2011.

83. *Urk.* IV 645–734.

defeating the two main vassal states that implemented Mittani's policy in the Levant: Qadesh and Tunip. Qadesh (modern Tell Nebi Mend) is located at the northern exit of the Beqaa valley at the highly strategic junction between the important north-south road connecting Syria to Egypt and the east-west route connecting inland Syria to the Mediterranean through the Homs Gap (see section 28.1). Tunip (modern Tell Asharneh) is situated on the route linking Aleppo to Amurru through the Masyaf Fault, which connects with the Homs Gap halfway between Qadesh and Amurru. Tunip's power extended to the northern part of the Lebanese coast, where it controlled the port of Ullaza (near modern Nahr el-Bared).

Unfortunately, Thutmose III's Annals do not record the king's second to fourth campaigns, but we can assume that these served to advance troops along the coast of Lebanon and to take control of the Beqaa valley, as the next offensives would take their departure from the northern parts of these regions. On his fifth campaign (Year 29; 1450 BC),[84] the king first took the port of Ullaza, which was garrisoned by Tunip's troops, and then the city of Ardata (modern Tell Arde, inland from the city of Tripoli), probably Amurru's seat of power. In the following year during his sixth campaign (Year 30; 1449 BC),[85] departing from the Beqaa valley, he once again attacked Ardata, but this time through the Homs Gap. He also besieged or took Simyra (modern Tell Kazel), Amurru's main harbor. Ullaza, once again occupied by soldiers of Tunip, had to be retaken in the seventh campaign (1447/1446 BC),[86] but then the Egyptian forces were ready to attack Mittani itself. It should be stressed that the idea that the Egyptians would have used maritime transport for their troops and equipment rests on a complete misunderstanding of the available sources.[87]

---

84. *Urk.* IV 685–688.

85. *Urk.* IV 689–690.

86. *Urk.* IV 690–696.

87. As discussed in Grandet 2008: 97–99.

At long last, in his eighth campaign (Year 33; 1450 BC),[88] about four decades after Thutmose I's raid to the Euphrates and after having defeated a Mittani force near Aleppo, Thutmose III reached Carchemish. To demonstrate the New Kingdom's continuing claim of the Euphrates as its border, he had another frontier inscription carved beside that of his grandfather on the cliffs above the river facing the territory of Mittani. Then Thutmose crossed into the enemy lands, using pine boats built in Lebanon and transported all the way from there on oxen carts. He chased the fleeing Mittani forces for a time, then returned to the Euphrates and concluded his victorious campaign by sailing down the river, possibly as far as Emar (modern Tell Meskene), 100 km to the south, while destroying settlements on both its banks.

While emerging unscathed from these battles, the return to Egypt almost cost Thutmose III his life. Heading from the Euphrates back to Aleppo, the army then did not directly turn southward but instead made a detour via Niya, situated at some distance north of Tunip at or near the site of later Apamea on the Orontes. This enterprise was in part designed to intimidate this city and ensure its compliance, but also to hunt a herd of 120 elephants. These animals were then still native to Western Asia and quite common in the Orontes's Ghab marshes, which the Egyptians called "Sea of Niya." This hunt was probably not mere sport but may primarily have served the purpose of procuring ivory, of which Egyptian craftsmanship had much use; it is very likely that Thutmose I had done the same when returning from the Euphrates (see earlier discussion, this section). Elephant-hunting was, however, a dangerous exercise, and Thutmose III was almost killed by a charging beast, saved only by the presence of mind of one of his officers.

From Niya, the Egyptians headed over the Orontes ford of Sendjar (modern Shaizar) southward to the city of Qadesh. Up to then, its hinterland (called *Takhsy* in the Egyptian sources) had been devastated whenever the Egyptian forces crossed it, but the city itself had not yet been taken. Now at last its time had come. This time, the Egyptians did not plan for a long siege: Qadesh was attacked and quickly entered by

---

88. *Urk.* IV 696–703; 889–897; 1231–1236; 1441–1445.

a breach in its fortification wall, while once again, its region was completely laid bare.

A single Egyptian victory could not instantly undermine decades of Mittani influence. Thutmose III's ninth and tenth campaigns (Year 33–34; 1426–1425 BC)[89] were devoted to the pacification of the country of Nuhašše, the Syrian steppe region north of Qadesh, followed by the crushing of a small Mittani-led coalition army somewhere to the northwest of Aleppo. Four years later, during his thirteenth campaign in Year 38 (1421 BC),[90] the king was back in Nuhašše in order to consolidate Egyptian power in the region. Thutmose agreed to let the local princes rule their polities as his vassals once they had taken an oath of allegiance, which also gave him the right to depose any of them if need arose. As the Annals attest, from Year 30 (1429 BC) onward, the local rulers' children were routinely taken as hostages, to be educated in Egypt at the pharaoh's court, a custom designed to stimulate their fathers' obedience and to raise loyal subjects as the future leaders of the vassal states.[91] Finally, in Year 42 (1417 BC), the last year to be recorded in the Annals,[92] Thutmose III's activities in the east were crowned by the successful attacks against Irqata (modern Tell Arqa) on the southern edge of the Amurru and Tunip, the city that had together with Qadesh acted as the champion of Mittani's political influence in Syria.

Egypt was now at the summit of its international influence. Even in an era of limited means of long-distance communication, Thutmose's crossing of the Euphrates apparently had a tremendous psychological impact on the contemporaries, and many states sent delegations to the pharaoh,[93] especially Mittani's fiercest enemies: the kingdom of Assyria, which had recently seceded from Mittani (see chapter 32 in this volume) in Years

---

89. *Urk.* IV 703–709; 709–714.

90. *Urk.* IV 716–721.

91. Grandet 2008: 97.

92. *Urk.* IV 729–734.

93. Grandet 2008: 103–109.

24 and 39, and then the Hittite Empire (see chapter 30 in this volume) in Years 33, 41, and possibly 42. The city-state of Alalakh (modern Tell Atchana in Turkey's Hatay province) on the Orontes, another former holding of Mittani, followed suite in Year 38. It is probably around this time that the New Kingdom and the Hittite Empire concluded a treaty concerning the deportation of the people of the (not localized) Hittite town of Kurustama to Egyptian territory,[94] which would later serve as a precedent for the peace treaty of Year 21 of Rameses II (1259 BC).[95] We have hypothesized that one of the tenets of the Egyptian eastern strategy was to control the import of copper into Syria through Amurru. As this ore was Cyprus's main resource, it is probably not by chance that we find no less than four or possibly five mentions of delegations from Alašiya, as the island was then known, to Egypt in the Annals of Thutmose III (Years 33, 34, 38, 39, and possibly 42). The last of these delegations in Year 42 is coupled with the mention of an envoy from *Tinay* (mainland Greece).

With Thutmose III's victories still fresh in everybody's mind, his son and successor Amenhotep II (1425–1397 BC) had little more to do to preserve the territorial gains than to demonstrate the Egyptian military presence in Syria in order to ensure the submission of the volatile local rulers.[96] His first campaign in Year 3 (1423 BC) was intended to ensure the safety of Egypt's lines of communication through the Beqaa valley by quelling the revolt of seven princes of the *Takhsy* region at its northern end. This inaugurated the use of widely publicized, extreme brutality to publicly punish rebel leaders, which served both as a means to frighten the local population into submission and to strengthen the Egyptians' confidence in their ruler. In this particular instance, Amenhotep II personally executed the rebel princes and took their bodies back to the Nile, where he had the corpses of six hung head down from Thebes's city

---

94. Singer 2004.

95. Breyer 2010.

96. Grandet 2008: 115–127.

walls, while the seventh was similarly displayed on the walls of Napata in Nubia.[97]

A few years later, in his Year 7 (1419 BC), Amenhotep II prominently displayed his military power in Syria in the form of a two-months-long campaign to the Orontes valley and to the Nuhašše region,[98] departing from the Beqaa valley via (probably) Aleppo and returning through Niya, as his predecessors had done. En route, the prince of Ugarit, who was faced with a local rebellion, asked Amenhotep for assistance. Although Ugarit was not one of his vassal states, the king obliged and took a detour of only ten days to resolve the problem. He then proceeded to Qadesh, whose prince's submission, as always, had to be enforced. To this end, the king staged a widely publicized display of his, and Egypt's, strength by shooting arrows at copper ingots used as targets. With the possible exception of the Ugaritic episode, this campaign was essentially a military propaganda tour for the Egyptian troops. Before it came to a close, however, an important event was to unfold: as Amenhotep rode homeward down the Sharon plain in the northern part of Canaan's coast, the pharaoh met an envoy of the king of Mittani, carrying a letter that was most probably an offer to open peace negotiations. The Egyptian sources record that before the end of Amenhotep's reign, diplomatic delegations arrived in Egypt not only from Babylonia and the Hittite Empire, but also of Mittani,[99] which implies that a peace treaty had been concluded by then.

Military and economic concerns must have ranked high among the reasons for Mittani's desire for peace with Egypt. From the Beqaa valley that was now under Egyptian control, the New Kingdom troops only had to cross Syria to reach the Euphrates, and this was easily achieved, as Amenhotep II had just demonstrated. Moreover, Thutmose III's conquest of Amurru, with the strategic port of Simyra, gave the New Kingdom the power to disrupt at will the greater part of Syro-Mesopotamia's copper

---

97. *Urk.* IV 1296–1298; see Grandet 2008: 305–306.

98. *Urk.* IV 1299–1305; see Grandet 2008: 306–309.

99. *Urk.* IV 1309: 13.

supply, therefore forcing Mittani to negotiate an agreement concerning the complementary tin trade; as discussed earlier (section 28.5), we assume this was the key agenda for Egypt's overall eastern strategy. In addition, Mittani found itself now surrounded by hostile countries, all of which had dispatched diplomatic missions to Egypt as soon as they had grasped its newfound power. Given these factors, it was clearly only a matter of time before Mittani submitted a peace offer, but its suddenness suggests a specific trigger. The most obvious options are the contemporaneous hostilities of the Hittite Empire against Mittani, whose military maneuvers toward Aleppo and diplomatic overtures to Egypt were probably deemed enough to tilt the balance. Much later, in the thirteenth century BC, it was the worrisome prospect of a war on two fronts that would prompt the Hittites to conclude their own peace treaty with Egypt under Rameses II, after the kingdom of Assyria in northern Mesopotamia had gained some muscle and had proven a serious opponent (see section 28.5.3).

One of the main consequences of the peace would have been the establishment of a mutually accepted boundary between the Egyptian and Mittani territories. Even as we lack direct information, circumstantial evidence suggests that this border followed a line from somewhere near Qadesh to the Mediterranean coast of Amurru through the Homs Gap; however, Qadesh would have kept its allegiance to Mittani and Simyra to Egypt, so that these cities were now enclaves within the other state's territory. With Simyra as the main entry port for copper into the Levant and Qadesh the main transit post for the tin trade toward Egypt, this makes a lot of sense because the control of these cities would allow each power to keep the other in check, under penalty of being cut from the much needed supply of copper and tin, respectively.

If all went well for Egypt on the international front, some acute social, economic, and political problems began to emerge in its Canaanite territories sometime after the beginning of the campaigns of Thutmose III (1458 BC). Until then, submission to Egypt had been the norm, but from then on, insurrections would take place on a recurrent basis. A high proportion of the region's settlements shows archaeological evidence for some kind of disruption, whose date has long been debated but is now generally assigned to the period of the New Kingdom's main military activity.[100] Not all evidence points to violent destruction, but also to the desertion of marginal sites in a general shift of the settlement pattern toward the coast.

Also social problems are on the record. So far, we have ignored the fourteenth campaign of Thutmose III in Year 39; 1420 BC), as it does not constitute part of the conflict with Mittani, but was meant to pacify the Shasu,[101] a nomadic people active in the Levant at the time.[102] The fact that the victorious king of Egypt had to lead a military campaign against the Shasu that was considered worth mentioning in his Annals highlights that they constituted a considerable danger behind the front lines. Furthermore, our sources also record the growing problem posed by another non-sedentary population group, the Apiru (also Hapiru). At the time, this term was not the name of an ethnic group (although it is much later linked to the origin of the term "Hebrew"[103]), but a general designation for people without a home, marginalized after having been deprived of their traditional sources of income (such as agriculture or craftsmanship), rejected from organized society, be that sedentary or nomadic, and ultimately forced into a life as day laborers, mercenaries, or bandits. In this last role, they greatly contributed to a chronic feeling of insecurity, while as mercenaries, they formed army contingents for hire that sold their services to the highest bidder, thus allowing ambitious local princes to acquire military power that outstripped their political importance.

That such groups existed in the first place makes it clear that by the time of Thutmose III, a substantial economic crisis had corroded the foundations of the traditional societies and institutions of Canaan. Given the historical context, the roots of this crisis must have been the New Kingdom's warfare in the region. The repeated crossing of huge

100. Grandet 2008: 112–114.

101. Urk. IV 721–723.

102. Cf. Hoffmeier, Davis, and Hummel 2016.

103. Cf. Na'aman 1986.

Egyptian armies alone, which had to be sustained by local food sources, could not have failed to seriously disrupt agriculture. This would have led to the abandonment of less productive farming regions and to the rise of a sizable population without regular employment and fixed home, who would no longer feel allegiance to the local rulers. One must assume that even those who were still part of the traditional societies would greatly resent the situation and the Egyptians who caused it, fostering a hunger for independence that would have put their princes into a difficult quandary: with whom should they side? With their people, but then they would face the pharaoh's wrath. With the pharaoh, but then their people would revolt. While the local rulers responded to the challenge according to the specific regional circumstances, one ground principle is clearly observable: the farther from pharaoh, the greater the independence aspirations. This principle was sometimes reinforced, sometimes contradicted by the princes' individual aspirations and regional power politics, so that an independence-seeking ruler could still solicit Egypt's help to dispose of a rival prince or that a hitherto loyal vassal might ally with an adversary to resist a third party that had the pharaoh's help. The Amarna Letters, a set of clay tablets inscribed in the cuneiform script found at Akhenaten's newly founded capital city of Akhetaten (modern Tell el-Amarna), provide ample evidence for the fact that the Egyptians quickly mastered the art of manipulating to their advantage the petty jealousies of the local rulers, sometimes in an apparently illogical way—helping their adversaries and wronging their allies—that shows an early implementation of the principle *divide et impera* ("divide and rule").

It is clear that for Egypt, Canaan was primarily a transit corridor to lands further north and east, to be protected and controlled by military posts, and secondarily a food-producing region. They had no real use for its hilly regions, including Judaea, Samaria, and the Carmel range, nor any stringent need to control these as long as their inhabitants did not interfere in the lowlands where the roads lay: the coastal plain, the Jezreel valley, and the Jordan valley. The hilly regions were therefore generally more focused on independence, as well a natural refuge for homeless and outlawed populations. In Amenhotep II's Year 9 (1417 BC), the Carmel range and parts of the Jezreel valley and Galilee rose up against Egyptian rule.[104] The New Kingdom of Egypt, which was then at the pinnacle of its power and had already made it clear that uprising would be dealt with brutally, beat down the insurrection in a merciless campaign. If we interpret the Egyptian sources correctly, some 40,000 prisoners of war were taken back to Egypt as a consequence of this war.[105] The total population of these regions could not have been very much larger, which implies that Amenhotep II organized the deportation of most of the survivors, following a practice commonly used by the great powers of the period, most notably the Hittites, to prevent future revolts in subject territories.

28.5.2. From peace with Mittani to conflict with the Hittites (1397–1325 BC)[106]

Thutmose IV (1397–1388 BC) seems to only have conducted two short campaigns, perhaps better seen as inspection tours, that brought him to Canaan, Lebanon, and the frontier with Mittani at the beginning of his reign in 1397–1398 BC.[107] But on the diplomatic front, his reign saw a very important event: the king's marriage to a Mittani princess, a daughter of Artatama I who is not known by name.[108] Such a dynastic union was a typical component when two powers conducted a peace treaty.

The long reign of Amenhotep III (1388–1350 BC) saw the New Kingdom reap the fruits of the peace with Mittani: in terms of its material culture, this period of Egyptian history is considered one of

---

104. *Urk.* IV 1305–1309; see Grandet 2008: 309–311.

105. Amenhotep II's sources give 90,000 as the grand total of prisoners brought back from his wars. Of these, we must exclude 15,070 people from Nuḫašše, which leaves us with 36,300 people from Canaan. To these, we add an estimate of 50 percent of the 3,600 Apiru and of the 15,200 Shasu quoted in the text, as these nomadic populations had a natural affinity for the regions in question, and arrive at a total of 40,000 prisoners in 1417 BC.

106. Grandet 2008: 127–144.

107. *Urk.* IV 1552–1556; see Grandet 2008: 127–131.

108. EA 29: 16–18 (for a translation of the letter, see Moran 1992: 92–99).

its highlights.[109] Around Year 10 (1378 BC), the alliance was renewed by Amenhotep's marriage to Kelu-Heba, a sister of the Mittani king Šuttarna II. But his reign was also marked by an increase in revolts in territories under Egyptian control in the Levant, and above all in his third decade as king, by Suppiluliuma I's accession to the Hittite throne, soon to emerge as Egypt's new archenemy.

Around this time begins the documentation of the Amarna Letters,[110] a collection of 350 clay tablets inscribed in the cuneiform script and mostly in the Akkadian language that form the principal remains of Egypt's diplomatic correspondence from ca. Year 30 of Amenhotep III (1358 BC) to the beginning of Tutankhamun's reign (1325 BC). These texts, however, cannot have represented the entirety of the state correspondence, as they include only 52 letters to or from the kings of Mittani, Hatti, Assyria, Babylonia, Cyprus, and Arzawa (a Hittite dependency in western Anatolia), whom the pharaoh considered his equals, while 307 letters were to and from princes from Syria and Canaan, whom he considered his vassals. This reduces the available international diplomatic correspondence to about two letters a year.

Nevertheless, the letters are one of the most important sources for this period's history,[111] and the only ones illuminating Egypt's administrative system of control over its Levantine holdings.[112] They show that on the local level, Egyptian power was founded on the personal allegiance of the local princes who were sworn to the pharaoh, which entailed rights and duties and were strengthened by the promise of rewards and the threat of punishment.

The Levantine territories were divided into three large districts, each under the jurisdiction of an Egyptian governor: Canaan with the

---

109. See Cline and O'Connor (eds.) 1998, in particular the papers by Weinstein 1998 and Kitchen 1998; Grandet 2008: 130–131; Kahn 2011; Kozloff 2012.

110. Most recent edition: Rainey 2014; for a widely used translation: Moran 1992. In addition to the letters, there are also 32 other compositions, mainly literary and school texts: Izre'el 1997.

111. Cf. Cohen and Westbrook 2002.

112. Mynářová 2014.

administrative center in Gaza; Upe (comprising the Beqaa valley and the Damascus oasis) with the administrative center in Kumidi (modern Kamid el-Loz in the Beqaa valley); Amurru and the Lebanese coast with the administrative center in Simyra. The Egyptian governors in Upe and Amurru also doubled as high commissioners seconded to the leading local rulers: the prince of Damascus and the prince of Ardata, respectively; but not in Canaan, which had no preeminent local ruler. The governors did not reside in Damascus and Ardata, but had their own seats in Egyptian settlements. They had Egyptian troops at their disposal, some of whom were provided to the local princes, nominally to protect them but clearly also to keep a close eye on them. Forts and strongholds completed the Egyptian occupation forces, with the most important one being Beth-Shean in Canaan at the crossroads between the Jezreel and Jordan valleys.[113]

During this period, the key event to shape the history of the entire eastern Mediterranean was the accession of Suppiluliuma I to the Hittite throne, a king who had the ambition and the means to make his kingdom the foremost power of the Near East.[114] Mittani, his nearest and most immediate rival, was fatally bound to be his first and prime target. However, although he was willing enough to strike at its political center in the Khabur Triangle as a means to weaken Mittani's military power, it was its Syrian territories that Suppiluliuma coveted. This shows that, just like Egypt and Mittani, Suppiluliuma's primary objective was to gain control over the tin trade.

A busy ruler, Suppiluliuma launched his first campaign against Mittani in the very year of his accession. Shortly before, Mittani's king Artaššumara, the successor of Šuttarna II, had been killed by a shadowy figure whose name is unknown. The king's younger brother Tušratta was suspected to have had a hand in the murder since he took the throne from his older brother Artatama II, who sought refuge at the Hittite court and thereby presented Suppiluliuma with an excellent pretext for

---

113. Mulins 2012.

114. Grandet 2008: 133–141.

an attack on Mittani: fighting for Artatama's lawful restoration. The plan succeeded, but only temporarily. The Hittite forces reached Nuhašše and even the Lebanon mountain range, but retreated soon after for causes unknown, which allowed Mittani to regain control over Syria. All the while, Egypt remained neutral, despite the peace treaty with Mittani. While this first campaign of Suppiluliuma was not successful, it served as a rehearsal for the next decisive one, undertaken seventeen years later (see section 28.5.3). This campaign had the same strategic concept of launching a two-pronged attack on two distant fronts in rapid succession: an assault against northern Mesopotamia in order to force Mittani to deploy its army to protect its capital, and then an onslaught against the Syrian territories, now empty of Mittani troops.

Due to the inherent vulnerability of their position, the princes along the Eastern Mediterranean coast had little choice but to accept to be the vassals of one of the great powers. All of them probably resented this condition to some extent, and a few had the will or opportunity to try to change it. But given that even the more ambitious local rulers were not powerful enough to achieve true independence, the best they could hope for was to expand their political base to the detriment of their neighbors, so they would have a better standing to negotiate changes to the terms of their allegiance if the opportunity arose.[115] Abdi-Aširta, prince of Amurru,[116] a vassal of Amenhotep III whose territory was, however, divided between Egypt and Mittani, apparently saw the newly revealed power of the Hittites as this kind of opportunity. With Suppiluliuma's first Syrian campaign indicating which way the wind was blowing, Abdi-Aširta began to expand his influence southward along the Lebanon coast. Several letters in the Amarna correspondence document the ensuing calls for help sent to the pharaoh by Rib-Hadda, prince of Byblos, who feared to be Abdi-Aširta's next victim. When the Hittites struck Mittani, Abdi-Aširta did not hesitate to claim the port of Simyra from the Egyptians. However, the time was not yet ripe for such a bold move: Mittani and

115. Grandet 2008: 133–141.

116. Cf. Benz 2016: 141–166.

Amenhotep III sent forces to retake Simyra, and Abdi-Aširta passed out of the limelight of history, his fate unknown. However, his son Aziru would be the ruler of Amurru during the reign of Amenhotep's successor Akhenaten and would resume his father's policy.

Further south, out of reach of Hittite influence, Canaan was home to chronic unrest as there was no preeminent prince, but some rulers were keen to rise to this position and willing to fight for it. Egypt's duplicitous policy was to encourage the candidates and to withdraw support at the critical moment.[117] In this way, these princes would police their region for Egypt, but were prevented from gaining enough power to truly represent a threat. In addition, there is the all-pervading and corrosive presence of the Apiru: here living a life of bandits, there hiring themselves to a prince short on military manpower (see section 28.5.1).

Among the Amarna correspondence, only thirteen letters (nine from the reign of Amenhotep III, four of Akhenaten) document the relationship between Egypt and Mittani, with half of these being devoted to the long negotiations regarding the marriage of Amenhotep III to a second Mittani princess: Tadu-Heba, daughter of Tušratta.[118] That provides us with only a tiny glimpse on the nature of the two countries' political bond during Amenhotep III's later years and until Akhenaten's Year 13 (1341 BC), when the correspondence stops.[119] All that can be said is that when Tušratta ascended the throne of Mittani around Amenhotep's Year 36 (1352 BC), he wrote to the pharaoh to renew the alliance, and that he did the same after Akhenaten's accession (1350 BC). Growing concerned by the Hittite threat to his realm, the letter to Akhenaten contains an especially long plea, which apparently elicited only minimal reassurance from the pharaoh. Akhenaten's (relative) unresponsiveness to this overture is quite understandable, without having to invoke his supposed pacifism or having to assume that he was entirely focused on his religious reforms (see chapter 26 in this volume). Even though he was tied to Tušratta by

---

117. Grandet 2008: 140–141; Finkelstein 2014.

118. These are the letters EA 19–25 (for translations, see Moran 1992: 43–84).

119. Grandet 2008: 145–153; Kahn 2011.

the bonds of a peace treaty, he was bound to the Hittite Empire in the same way, as Suppiluliuma reminded him shortly after the pharaoh's accession.[120] Akhenaten therefore had to remain neutral in the conflict between Mittani and the Hittites. It is only the knowledge of the consequences that allows us to consider—in retrospect—Akhenaten's stance as politically shortsighted.

In Akhenaten's Year 12 (1342 BC), his capital Akhetaten (modern Tell el-Amarna) served as the stage for a grand demonstration of Egypt's international standing and universal harmony when ambassadors of each state with which Egypt had an official relationship were invited to bring presents to the pharaoh, enthroned on a dais in the middle of a vast open space. Just one year later (1341 BC), Suppiluliuma attacked Mittani. During this campaign, which would be known as his "One-Year Campaign," the Hittite ruler used the same strategy as during his first foray into Syria in 1358 BC (see section 28.5.1): an attack on the northern part of Mittani's core territory, then a swift rerouting of his forces to invade and conquer Syria from the Euphrates to the Lebanon and from Aleppo to Qadesh. Of its Syrian holdings, despite some opposition on the part of the local princes, Mittani only retained Carchemish.

This defeat led to Tušratta of Mittani's murder at the hands of one of his own sons a few years later (ca. 1338 BC) and to the restoration of Artatama II, the Hittite-sponsored pretender (see section 28.5.1), to the throne of Mittani.[121] The eastern kingdom of Assyria, previously a vassal of Mittani, seized the opportunity to achieve full independence from its former overlord, and even Babylonia, from the south, tried to extend its territory at the expense of Mittani. While the rulers of both these countries initiated diplomatic contact with Egypt to verify its neutrality, Artatama II, the feeble king of Mittani, saw no other option than to use his treasures to literally buy peace from his enemies. Ironically, he who had started out as a Hittite puppet king, and his successors after him,

---

120. EA 41 (for a translation, see Moran 1992: 114–115).

121. EA 43; see Na'aman 1995.

would be the last defenders of Mittani's independence, while the descendants of Tušratta would become protégés of the Hittite Empire.

Shortly before Suppiluliuma's second Syrian campaign, Amurru's prince Aziru, son of Abdi-Aširta, whose rebellion against Egypt had been suppressed by Amenhotep III, resumed his father's separatist policies.[122] He rapidly expanded his power beyond Amurru to the Homs Gap and the Masyaf Fault as far as Tunip and southward along the Lebanese coast. This prompted Rib-Hadda, the prince of Byblos, to send letter after letter to Akhenaten in order to warn the pharaoh and to beg for his assistance, like he had previously done under Amenhotep III. This time, however, help never came, and Rib-Hadda had to flee for his life. It is clear that Akhenaten very deliberately chose not to intervene, for as long as Aziru fought north of the Egyptian border, the pharaoh had no real grounds to do so. Once Aziru had moved against Lebanon, however, Akhenaten's passivity is more difficult to explain, but we need to appreciate that he had no other means to evaluate the situation than the contradictory letters of the conflicting parties. Even when Aziru finally captured the port of Simyra, the seat of Egyptian authority, around 1338 BC and killed its governor, he was only summoned to Egypt to explain his deeds. Undeterred, he answered the pharaoh's summons and apparently gave satisfactory explanations, as he was allowed to return to Amurru unscathed.

Aziru's return to Amurru around 1336 BC coincided with a massive, if not total, uprising in Syria against Hittite rule.[123] The rebellion principally took place in inland Syria, whose rulers hoped and begged for Egyptian support, which did not come. However, the prominent cities Ugarit and Qadesh adopted a more realistic stance and sided with the Hittite Empire. As soon as he was safely back home from Egypt, Aziru of Amurru joined them and declared himself a vassal of Suppiluliuma.

The rebels were easily defeated, and in the wake of the rebellion's repression, Suppiluliuma made a first hostile move against Egypt. At his

122. Grandet 2008: 153–164.

123. Grandet 2008: 157–164.

instigation, Aitakama, prince of Qadesh, raided the Beqaa valley, assisted by some of his troops that kept to the background so that their participation could be denied. This suggests that the operation was conceived as a means to test Egypt's willingness to intervene in Syrian affairs and its military responsiveness, without overtly declaring war. The aggression prompted a flurry of activity of Akhenaten's messengers, who were sent across the Near East to prepare a military campaign. These measures alone were apparently sufficient to quench the Hittite threat, and there would be no open warfare between Egypt and the Hittite Empire until the reign of Tutankhamun (1333–1323 BC).

28.5.3. The war against the Hittites (1325–1259 BC)[124]

Until the Syrian revolt in 1336 BC, Akhenaten had maintained Egypt's neutrality in the conflict between Mittani and the Hittite Empire. But eleven years later, around Year 8 of Tutankhamun (1325 BC), a phase of open warfare between Egypt and the Hittites began, and it was Egypt that opened these hostilities, and moreover in cooperation with what remained of Mittani. This change of policy was evidently prompted by the realization of the Hittite Empire's growing power. The hostile move against the Beqaa valley at the end of the Syrian revolt suggested further ambitions to control the Levant, so that Egypt, once again, faced the threat of being cut from its sources of tin. A preemptive strike was therefore deemed necessary. The real power in Egypt, behind the boy-king Tutankhamun, was at that time the commander-in-chief of the army, Horemheb (who later became pharaoh), and this fact probably played a role in choosing the military option while a new revolt of the small Syrian states against Hittite control provided a good opportunity for launching the operation.

The Egyptian offensive inaugurated what Hittite sources call Suppiluliuma's "Six-Years War" (1325–1319 BC). It took the form of a coordinated offensive of Mittani against Syria westward from Carchemish

---

124. Grandet 2008: 165–262.

and of Egypt against Qadesh northward from the Beqaa valley.[125] But it soon appeared that the allies had grossly underestimated the Hittites. Even as Suppiluliuma had to fight on two fronts, he rapidly defeated both his adversaries, submitting them to a massive counteroffensive. While he forced the Mittani troops to retreat to Carchemish, to which he laid siege, he began to invade the Beqaa valley, thus crossing into Egyptian territories.

However, military operations came to a sudden standstill with the death of Tutankhamun (1323 BC), when his widow (who the "Deeds of Suppiluliuma" call Tahamunzu, a transcription of Egyptian *ta ham ensu*, "the king's wife") purportedly asked Suppiluliuma to send her any one of his sons as her new husband, with the promise that he would consequently ascend the Egyptian throne. Although skeptical at first, Suppiluliuma could not resist such an offer and sent his son Zannanza to Egypt. The prince, however, was assassinated en route by agents of the newly crowned Egyptian king Ay, who of course denied any involvement. Now, the offer sounds so definitely un-Egyptian that is difficult to believe that it is still taken at face value by modern scholars, without the shadow of a doubt.[126] We do not doubt that the offer was made, but its sincerity, so that we concur with the Hittites' own retrospective interpretation that it was a stratagem conceived by the Egyptian leadership to gain a respite from warfare. The ploy worked for a few months during which Suppiluliuma took Carchemish from Mittani and sent emissaries to Egypt to further inquire into the matter, but in the end it did not do much good to the Egyptians. After his son's death, Suppiluliuma resumed his offensive with a vengeance and ultimately drove the Egyptian forces out of the Beqaa valley.

The war raged throughout the brief reign of Ay (1323–1319 BC) and then, unexpectedly, stalled at the time of the accession of Horemheb (1319–1292 BC), when a murderous epidemic broke out in Anatolia,

---

125. Grandet 2008: 165–182.

126. Cf. Grandet 2018: 167–176; for the traditional view, see most recently Theis 2011. See also chapters 26 and 30 in this volume.

brought back from the Beqaa valley by Egyptian prisoners.[127] The disease killed Suppiluliuma and then his first successor and would ravage the Hittite Empire for a generation until the time of the coronation of Muwatalli II in 1295 BC. This put the hostilities between Egypt and the Hittites to rest until the accession of Sety I (1290–1279 BC), although Horemheb seems to have secretly subsidized the revolts of some Syrian princes against the Hittites. But this king's more important contribution to the conflict was that he anticipated its resumption. In preparation for future hostilities in the east, he established a powerful military base (the later Piramesses) on the site of ancient Avaris in the eastern Nile delta, and also selected as his successor the scion of a local family of senior and well-proven army officers: the future Rameses I, founder of the Nineteenth Dynasty.

Rameses I's reign was very short, so that it was during the reign of his son and successor Sety I that the second phase of the conflict between Egypt and the Hittites would unfold.[128] Both this king and his son and successor Rameses II (1279–1213 BC) followed the same basic strategy implemented by the Eighteenth Dynasty rulers against Mittani: namely to impose control over Amurru and thereby over the import of copper into Western Asia in order to force the enemy to negotiate over access to tin. A key element of this strategy was therefore to offer military assistance to the ruler of Amurru, who had probably expressed his willingness to again accept Egypt as his overlord. Only two itineraries would have allowed a sizable army to reach Amurru from Egypt, with a shared first leg: from Egypt to the north of the Sea of Galilee. From there, one could choose between two routes. The easier one, from a logistical point of view, led through the upper reaches of the Jordan to the Beqaa valley on to Qadesh and the Homs Gap, while the more difficult one ran through the mountainous Galilee and along the steep Lebanese coast. For an Egyptian army leader on his way to assist Amurru, the choice depended on the expected opposition he would meet en route, as there was no

---

127. Grandet 2008: 177–185.

128. Grandet 2008: 187–195.

point in reaching Amurru with already depleted forces. Therefore, as the Hittites held sway over the Beqaa valley since the reign of Tutankhamun, Sety had no choice but to take the route via the Galilee and Lebanon.

Sety I apparently intended to depart from Avaris in the eastern Nile delta, where he resided, immediately after his accession, with an army consisting of about 15,000–20,000 men. First, however, he had to secure his communications between Sile and Gaza, along the northern Sinai, by containing the nomads who routinely assaulted the fortified posts along the coastal road.[129] Second, he had to reconquer the strategic fortress of Beth-Shean in northern Canaan, which had been taken by the combined forces of some neighboring princes. These proved no match for the Egyptian army, which easily retook the city and then pacified the region,[130] for the time being at least: Sety I would have to come back later in his reign to subdue the belligerent tribes of Samaria and Transjordan as far as the Yarmuk valley.[131] Further south, around his Year 8 (1282 BC), he would also take control of the Timna mines, the second richest copper deposit of the Near East after Cyprus.

On his way north from Beth-Shean, Sety I also took the opportunity to discipline the ever rebellious town of Yenoam,[132] located southwest of the Sea of Galilee, which represented a constant danger to the Egyptian line of communications in Syria. He then crossed the Galilee to reach the Lebanese coast in the vicinity of Tyre.[133] At Byblos, he placed an order for pine logs with the local princes and then advanced to Ullaza on the border with Amurru.

Whether he succeeded in securing Amurru's allegiance to Egypt for good at the time is doubtful, as he returned again to the region in Year 5

---

129. KRI I: 6–16; KRI VII: 12. On this military road, see recently Hoffmeier 2013.

130. KRI I: 6–12; 15–16; 117; KRI VII: 12.

131. KRI I: 17.

132. On Yenoam in the epigraphic record of Karnak, see Raafat Abbas 2017.

133. The long-lost remains of a stele commemorating either Sety I's or Rameses II's passage to Adlun, north of Tyre (KRI II: 223.10–15), have recently been found again: Wimmer and Heindl 2018.

(1285 BC).[134] In this second campaign, however, he reached Amurru via the Beqaa valley and the Homs Gap, securing en route the submission of the city of Qadesh.[135] As the Hittite occupation of the Beqaa valley had prevented Sety from taking this route during his earlier campaign, one must conclude that, this time, the Hittite forces had now vacated the valley. We assume that this evacuation was prompted by the sudden occupation of Hanigalbat (the Assyrian designation for Mittani, now a Hittite protectorate) by Adad-nerari I of Assyria (see chapter 32 in this volume), and the necessity to redeploy troops on the Euphrates to cope with that problem.

As a result of this campaign, Sety I finally secured the allegiance of Amurru. However, before the end of his reign, the Hittites were able to take back Qadesh and to reclaim the Beqaa valley, or at least part of it (as the region of later Baalbek would seem to be under Egyptian control during the later campaign of Rameses II to Qadesh). However, they did not succeed in forcing back Amurru into their sphere of influence. Not that they did not try: already in his Year 4 (1276 BC), Sety's successor Rameses II had to rush to Amurru's aid via the Galilee and the Lebanese coast,[136] as the city was under attack from troops of Ugarit, a Hittite vassal state. It is probably due to the partially landlocked character of Amurru that the Hittites preferred this indirect course of action.[137] Due to the sustained aggression against Amurru, Rameses intended to return there in the following year (1275 BC). But the Hittites anticipated his plan and intended to deal his ambitions a fatal blow, by using their military power as well as a complex stratagem that would result in the famous battle of Qadesh.

---

134. Dated by the postulated synchronism with Adad-nerari I of Assyria's attack on Mittani/Hanigalbat; see Grandet 2008: 192.

135. KRI I: 24–25.

136. For the Adlun Stele, possibly a monument of Rameses II, see earlier discussion in the present section.

137. The so-called General's Letter from Ugarit (Izre'el and Singer 1990) can be dated to this time; see Grandet 2008: 199–200.

In 1275 BC, Rameses took the route through the Beqaa valley to reach Amurru, which seems significant, as his predecessor Sety I had indeed used the same way, but only after it had been abandoned by the enemy, in order to avoid reaching Amurru with depleted forces. It therefore stands to reason that Rameses II had intelligence that the Beqaa valley was empty of enemy troops. Now, when the Hittites had left the region during the reign of Sety I, they had had a compelling military reason to do so: the Assyrian conquest of Mittani. As far as we can see, they had no such reason in 1275 BC, and so we must assume that their evacuation of the Beqaa was a stratagem to lure Rameses to Qadesh at the northern end of the valley, where they plotted to destroy his army.

Much has been written about the battle of Qadesh, and the sequence of its events is generally accepted, although the evaluations of the battle's strategic importance differ. However, this famous event is exclusively documented by Egyptian sources whose purpose was not to compile a factual report, but to present Rameses II as a superhuman hero. While the Hittite sources do not mention the battle, they place the conflict in its proper historical context: "Muwatalli and the king of Egypt fought over the men of Amurru."[138] The Egyptian sources, on which the following discussion relies,[139] confirm the link between the battle of Qadesh and Amurru, and the intention of the Egyptian army to reach this country; they state that just before the battle, Rameses II had established a camp for the night to the northwest of Qadesh, which indicates that the plan for the following day was to move in the direction of the Homs Gap and Amurru. Indeed, Qadesh is situated at the center of a Y-shaped crossroads, whose southern stretch comes from the Beqaa valley, whereas the northwestern branch leads to the Homs Gap and the northeastern to distant Aleppo. The choice between these two itineraries must be made at or before Qadesh, as the routes separate immediately to the north of the city due to the marshes formed by the inner delta where the Orontes flows into the Homs Lake. Moreover,

---

138. Beckman 1996: 98–102, §5.

139. KRI II: 2–147; see Grandet 2008: 200–230; 313–335; Hasel 2011; Kenning 2014.

this body of water cannot be skirted around its western side due to the same marshy conditions.

Rameses II's forces were made up of four "divisions" of about 5,000 men each, bearing the names of the gods Amun, Ra, Ptah, and Seth. To those troops, we must add the royal guard of elite *Shardana* warriors (see section 28.4.2), so that the whole army numbered about 20,000–25,000 men, with each division a self-contained corps mixing infantry and chariotry. As Rameses had no inkling that he was led into a trap, when reaching Qadesh, his army was not battle-ready but spread out over a line of about 40 km, with each division at a good distance from the others. The Hittites had worked hard to achieve this. Not only had they evacuated the Beqaa valley to lure Rameses II into it, but in doing so, had succeeded to foil Egyptian intelligence about their true intentions, as Rameses would later reproach his officers. The next stage in the Hittite campaign of misinformation was to send to the king, on the morning of the battle, two Shasu nomads, who assured him that the Hittite king Muwatalli's forces were still at Aleppo, 150 km to the north. In fact, according to our sources, the Hittite army with 37,000 men and more than 3,500 chariots was lying in wait, hidden behind Qadesh's huge settlement mound (figure 28.3).

On the morning of the battle, Rameses II left his camp, located 20 km south of Qadesh at the northern threshold of the Beqaa valley, with the Amun Division and the Royal Guard. Around midday, he proceeded to ford the Orontes near a place called Shabtuna (probably near modern Ribla), where he encountered the two Shasu spies. Then, before evening fell, he reached the place where he intended to camp, northwest of Qadesh. There, his troops began to pitch the camp, unhitch the war chariots, and went off-duty. Meanwhile, the Ra Division was nearing the camp, while the Ptah Division was crossing the ford at Shabtuna and the Seth Division was still in the oasis of Labweh, deep inside the Beqaa valley. A further army contingent of elite troops (referred to, according to the time's fashion, by the Semitic term *na'arin*, "young men") was posted in operational readiness to protect the camp at some distance to its northwest, on the only side from where any danger was expected to materialize: the Homs Gap and Amurru.

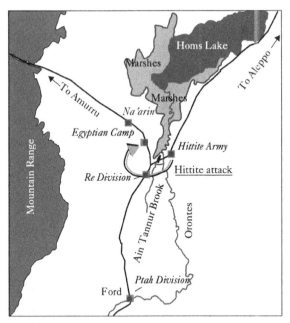

FIGURE 28.3. The setting of the Battle of Qadesh. Prepared by Pierre Grandet, after Grandet 2008: 211, fig. 10.

Suddenly, the Hittites launched south of Qadesh a charge of 2,500 chariots across the Orontes on the unsuspecting Ra Division, which disintegrated on impact. Forging ahead, the Hittite forces reached the Egyptian camp and breached into it. Just before this attack, however, Egyptian scouts had brought into the pharaoh's presence two of their Hittite counterparts, whom they had encountered and captured in the vicinity. After taking a beating, the captives revealed their army's presence and intentions, so that Rameses, after the first shock of realization, had had a crucial bit of time to at least partially put the Amun Division back under arms, marshal his guard, and summon the nearby *na'arin* contingent and Ptah Division for help.

The Egyptian sources make it perfectly clear that the Hittite attack was intended as a classic sickle-cut movement, pivoting clockwise around Qadesh, in such a manner that it would reach the Egyptian camp on its western side, pinning its troops between the Hittite forces and the Orontes marshes, with no other choice than to surrender or flee. An interesting detail is that the Hittite chariots were mounted by three men, an arrangement considered so unusual that the Egyptian sources keep mentioning it. In other instances, the Hittite chariots were mounted by only two men (driver and fighter), just like the Egyptian chariots, and the unusual arrangement cannot be explained by any technical reason; on the contrary, the additional weight of the third man would quickly exhaust the horses and make the chariots more difficult to steer. We therefore must interpret it as the attempt to quickly transport an additional 2,500 infantrymen on top of the 2,500 chariot-fighters for the intended attack on the Egyptian camp, so as to match the 5,000 strong Amun Division.

Owing to various factors, the ensuing fight did not meet the Hittite expectations. First, we know that the Hittite forces were a complex amalgam of contingents from various Hittite vassal states, and this kind of arrangement is known to make the troops' military value lesser than that of homogeneous armies. Second, it is likely that the urge to plunder the Egyptian camp, once they had reached it, distracted the Hittite attackers, succumbing to the same fatal lure as the Egyptian troops had done centuries before in 1475 BC at the battle of Megiddo. Third, we must consider that the Egyptian troops may have been in a less catastrophic state of unpreparedness than stated in the available sources, keen as they are to portray Rameses as a hero. Last, and by far the most important, the Hittites had not taken into account the *na'arin* contingent, posted at some distance west of the camp, so that while fighting on their front the king's forces in his camp, their rear was attacked by these elite forces. After a few Egyptian countercharges, the Hittite forces were progressively pushed back toward the Orontes marshes north of Qadesh, where their chariots broke and many of their troops drowned.

Reinforcements reached the Egyptian camp at sunset, and nightfall ended the fighting. On the following morning, after a half-hearted Hittite attack, it was Muwatalli, if we can believe the Egyptian sources, who offered an armistice, to which Rameses II readily agreed. But even if his well-devised plan had ultimately failed and had not succeeded in completely destroying the Egyptian army, the Hittite king still had reached his main goal of preventing Egypt from coming to Amurru's rescue. Rameses II, on his part, was able to return to Egypt with the largest part of his troops intact, having survived so mortal a danger that it was attributed to the miraculous intervention of the god Amun. In his footsteps, the Hittites re-occupied the Beqaa valley, and Amurru was now lost to Egypt for good.

Rameses II, however, would not let Amurru go without a fight.[140] In his Years 8 and 10 (1272 and 1270 BC), he twice reached the country on the route via the Galilee and the Lebanese coast. During the first campaign, he was able to take Irqata, another fortified city called Dapur that was held by a Hittite garrison but whose precise location is unknown, and a third city whose name may have been Hana. Nothing much is known about the second campaign, but the results were probably disappointing, as Rameses, from then on, would no longer lead an army to Syria.

During this time, unrest had become the usual state of things in Canaan. During the Syrian campaign of Year 8 (1272 BC), Rameses II had to pacify the Jezreel valley and the crossroads at Beth-Shean as well as the edge of the hilly regions bordering them: Mount Carmel, Samaria, and Galilee. Sometime later, at an unspecified date, the pharaoh even had to extend his interventions to Transjordan, just like his predecessor Sety I. This time, the goal was Moab, east of the Dead Sea, and Seir (later known as Edom), probably in order to ensure Egypt's control over the copper mines of Timna.

For the Hittites, the thirteen years between the battle of Qadesh and the peace treaty with Egypt were difficult times.[141] They definitely lost Mittani/Hanigalbat to Assyria (see chapter 32 in this volume), and experienced a bout of political unrest when the new Hittite king Mursili III was deposed by his uncle Hattusili III. In the same manner that the threat of the Hittites had in the past prompted the kingdom of Mittani to make peace with Egypt, the pressure that the Hittites now experienced

---

140. KRI II: 148–149; 153–158; 170–183; 213. Cf. Grandet 2008: 237–245.

141. Grandet 2008: 231–236; see chapter 30 in this volume.

from the Assyrians was key to the fact that they sought peace with Egypt, culminating in the conclusion of a peace treaty in Year 21 of Rameses II (1259 BC).

The complete text of this treaty is known by means of several surviving copies.[142] In its preamble, the document promotes the fiction of an era of peaceful relations between Egypt and Hatti until the reign of Muwatalli, thus rendering null and void all prior Hittite conquests. In its main part, it states the agreement between the two parties to end all belligerence and territorial conquest to each other's detriment, together with a pledge of mutual military assistance. Moreover, Rameses II also formally recognized Hattusili III and his line as the legitimate rulers of the Hittite Empire. Additionally, both kings agreed to the extradition of political opponents and illegal refugees, while guaranteeing physical integrity and the inviolability of their properties for them and their families. The acknowledgment of Hattusili III as king of Hatti, as well as this extradition clause, was in fact directed against Hattusili's predecessor Mursili III (now Prince Urhi-Teššub), whose rights to the Hittite throne were thereby declared forfeit.

From Rameses II's perspective, this agreement enshrined the success of the long-pursued Egyptian strategy. Undoing all Hittite territorial conquests after the time of Tutankhamun, the treaty re-established the border between the Egyptian and the Hittite zone of influence from Qadesh via the Homs Gap to Amurru, along the same line as previously between Egypt and Mittani, while additional evidence shows that also the system of mutual control through maintaining enclaves in each other's territory that monitored the traffic of copper and tin (Simyra for Egypt, Qadesh for the Hittites) was restored (see section 28.5.2).

A crisis resulting from the fate of the disposed Hittite king almost dealt a fatal blow to the treaty before it was ever put into practice.[143] Shortly after its conclusion, Prince Urhi-Teššub vanished from Nuhašše in Syria, where he had been confined after his deposition, and began

---

142. KRI II: 225–232; with the standard edition in Edel 1997. Cf. Grandet 2008: 244–255, 337–344.

143. Grandet 2008: 251–255.

FIGURE 28.4. Detail from the top of the Abu Simbel Marriage Stele: Hattusili III (right) sends his daughter (center) to Rameses II (left), who is shown seated between the gods Seth (to his left) and Tatenen (to his right). Drawing reproduced from Desroches-Noblecourt 1999: 254, with kind permission.

to travel the Near East, rallying support to regain his throne. As there were some difficulties in locating him, an angry Hattusili III suspected Rameses II of secretly helping his rival and even contemplated resuming hostilities with Egypt. The crisis sparked off a tense correspondence, in which Rameses II constantly denied all implications in the affair. His forces succeeded in locating the pretender first in Egyptian territory, then in a region under Hittite control where he had some success in raising support for his cause. When he was finally caught, Rameses proposed to Hattusili to allow Urhi-Teššub to retire to Egypt, and as he would reside there under the constant threat of the extradition clause of the peace treaty, the Hittite king agreed.

Once the crisis had passed, normal diplomatic relations could resume. In Years 34 (1245 BC) and 38 (1241 BC), Rameses II married two Hittites princesses, daughters of Hattusili III whose names are not known (figure 28.4).[144] Until Hattusili's death around 1340 BC, the two kings and various members of their courts exchanged letters[145] that, in addition

---

144. KRI II: 233–284.

145. Found in the Hittite capital Hattusa (modern Boğazköy) and edited by Edel 1994:

to polite protestations of friendship, discussed such subjects as sending Egyptian physicians to the Hittite court and planning a visit of Hattusili III to Egypt (which never took place).

Despite some periods of tension and although the relations between the two countries gradually became less close, the peace between Rameses II and Hattusili III held until the disintegration of the Hittite Empire, ca. 1180 BC.[146] Until the end of the New Kingdom (1069 BC), Egypt therefore enjoyed almost two centuries of peace with the neighboring powers, while the Hittites had to fight a bitter war against the kingdom of Assyria. However, in the eastern territories supposedly under Egyptian control, the situation was less peaceful. We have observed the progressive deterioration of Egypt's relations with Canaan since the time of Thutmose III. By the time of the reign of Rameses II's son and successor Merenptah (1213–1203 BC), there was no love left between them. Indeed, in Merenptah's Year 2 (1211 BC), the region saw a revolt of unprecedented extent and gravity, which included the cities of Ashkelon, Gezer, and Yenoam. If the third place, located in the northern reaches of Canaan, had long been adept at revolting against Egypt, the other two cities were situated in core Egyptian territory along the main route leading to Syria, with Ashkelon almost on Egypt's doorstep.[147] The ensuing war of repression saw the rebellious cities retaken and punished. In a famous passage in his victory stele from Thebes, Merenptah also claims to have defeated and exterminated, during the same campaign, the "people of Israel,"[148] one of the tribes from the hills, who until then had wisely refrained from taking part in anti-Egyptian actions but whose geographical position allowed them, from their probable home region of Samaria, to threaten the Egyptian lines of communications in the surrounding plains and valleys. The harshness of the repression probably explains that Canaan

---

146. Grandet 2008: 255–262.

147. KRI IV: 19.3–11; see Grandet 2008: 255–260. For the reliefs from Karnak that were formerly attributed to Rameses II, see KRI II: 164–167; with Yurco 1986. For a useful review of the evidence, see Brand 2011.

148. Cf., e.g., van der Veen, Theis, and Görg 2003.

remained at peace during the end of the Nineteenth Dynasty and the first decade of the Twentieth Dynasty.

28.6. The twilight of the New Kingdom

A generation after Merenptah's victories, Egypt again had to confront aggression from abroad: twice in the west by coalitions of Libyan tribes, and once in the east by a group of Sea Peoples.[149] In Rameses III's Year 5 (1176 BC), the *Libu* marched eastward on the same route as under Merenptah and with the same objective of attacking Memphis (see section 28.4.2), but they met a far worse fate than their ancestors, as they were almost annihilated, with 12,000 dead and 4,000 taken prisoner.[150] Five years later, in Year 11 (1170 BC), it was the turn of the *Meshwesh*, armed with Mycenaean swords (figure 28.5) and with the help of what remained of the *Libu* as well as of some other minor Libyan tribes, to try their hand at invading Egypt from the west, only to meet the same sticky end: 2,000 were left dead and 1,200 were taken captive.[151]

At roughly the same time (we will try to be more specific in the following), Rameses III had to counter an attack by a group of Sea Peoples[152] from the northeast on southern Canaan and on the coast of the Nile delta, whose names, according to the system of Egyptian syllabic orthography, should be realized as *Pulasti, Ṣikala, Shakalusha, Danuna,* and *Washasha* (instead of the forms in the basic unvocalized transcription by which they are generally quoted as *Peleset, Tjeker, Shekelesh, Denyen,* and *Weshesh*[153]). Apart from the *Shakalusha,* whom we already encountered

---

149. Grandet 2008: 284–292; Knapp and Manning 2016. Specifically on the Sea Peoples, see Grandet 2008: 260–262; 2017; Cline and O'Connor 2012: 188–189; Cline 2014; for a reappraisal of their historical role, see Gilan 2013: 57–66.

150. KRI V: 10–27; see Redford 2017: 1–20.

151. KRI V: 43–71; see Redford 2017: 42–71.

152. KRI V: 27–30; 32–43; see Redford 2017: 21–41.

153. According to Egyptian syllabic orthography and other phonetic considerations, Egyptian "tj" represents emphatic /ṣ/ and Egyptian "r" represents /l/. It must be stressed that the refusal of taking this into account in the names

FIGURE 28.5. Mesher son of Kaper, the defeated chief of the Libyan *Meshwesh*, is presented captive to Rameses III; behind him, tables with Mycenaean swords. As depicted in the first court (east wall, lower register) of the temple of Rameses III at Medinet Habu. Detail of Epigraphic Survey 1932: pl. 75.

of the Sea Peoples has important consequences: it turns the Ṣikala into the nonexistent people of the *Tjeker, thus blurring their identity with the Šikalayu of the documentation from Ugarit (see later discussion), the future Siculi of Sicily, while inducing scholars to equate the same Šikalayu with the Shakalusha, understood to be the future Siculi; cf., e.g., Cline and O'Connor 2012: 188–189; Cline 2014: 155–157, ignoring Edel 1984, who showed that the Shakalusha should be connected to Sagalassos in Pisidia, just north of Lycia.

in 1207 BC (see section 28.4.2), these peoples are here attested for the first time in historical records. But even if these groups were newcomers, the pictorial record of Rameses III's funerary temple at Medinet Habu (figure 28.6) shows that the *Šikala* and the *Pulasti* shared some of the same cultural traits as other Sea Peoples, notably the *Shardana* who are depicted fighting as mercenaries on the Egyptian side. They all wear the same typical Mycenaean-style outfit consisting of armor made of partially overlapping bronze plates sewn on a leather shirt, a metal helmet, a round shield, and a long, triangular sword. Only their helmets' shape differentiates them: the *Shardana* wear a kind of skullcap with a pair of horns, attached horizontally to resemble the lunar crescent, and with a

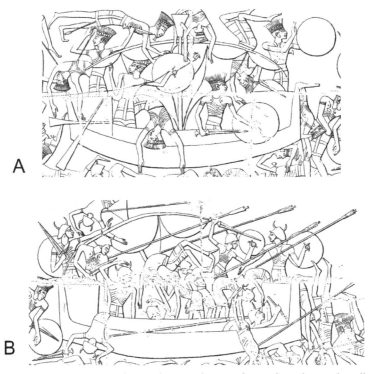

FIGURE 28.6. Sea Peoples on their warships, as depicted on the north wall of the temple of Rameses III at Medinet Habu: *Pulasti* (A) and *Šikala* (B). Reproduced from Epigraphic Survey 1930: pl. 39.

disc fixed on a stem on the middle; the *Ṣikala*, a horned helmet that covers the nape of the neck; the *Pulasti*, a close fitting helmet topped with a kind of mane; and the *Turusha*, a similar helmet but without a mane and instead with a frontal reinforcing band.

According to the Egyptian main textual witness, this constellation of Sea Peoples advanced against Egypt in two parties: one on sea and one on land. One can imagine that the seaborne party had the task of countering any opposition force by suddenly landing and attacking in its rear, while the land party advanced by land, accompanied by heavy ox-carts carrying women, children, and all belongings. After having destroyed the port of Ugarit on the northern coast of Syria, they regrouped in Amurru before advancing south. Egypt was forewarned of their coming by a flow of refugees, so that Rameses was able to deploy his troops to meet them in Canaan while blocking the Nile's mouths with warships. Probably in order to simplify the course of events, the Egyptian sources reduce the conflict to two great battles: one fought on land and one on the beaches, where the pictorial evidence shows a landing party being crushed between the Egyptian land troops and the Egyptian navy coming from the sea. No indication is given as to these battles' precise location, although the second is said to have taken place besides a "watchtower (*migdol*) of Rameses III," of which we know nothing else. However, as a favorite Egyptian tactic was to wait for the enemy instead of advancing to meet him, we can reasonably assume that the fighting would have taken place in the southern part of Canaan's coastal strip.

These events have been traditionally dated to Rameses III's Year 8 (1173 BC), midway between his two Libyan campaigns, as this is the date of composition of the main textual source relating to them in the mortuary temple of Medinet Habu. Recently, however, a fragment was identified of a royal stele at Amara West in Nubia, which contains the fragmentary name of the *[Pu]lasti* and possibly also of the *Ṣi[kala]* and therefore offers new data relating to this conflict.[154] From the much

---

154. Popko 2016, republishing a hieratic stele (Museum of Archaeology and Anthropology, University of Cambridge, accession number MAA 1939.552) that was previously known only from a faulty copy and incorrectly dated to Rameses IV (KRI VI: 63.11–64.4).

damaged text, we learn that the king sent troops to annihilate an enemy which had come by night, using ox-carts and ships. The concomitant use of these two vehicles is a characteristic feature of the Medinet Habu records,[155] and one feels inclined to recognize an allusion to the same events; however, the Amara West stele unequivocally dates them to Year 3 (1178 BC) instead of Year 8. The simplest way of resolving this discrepancy is to assume that the text composed for Medinet Habu in Year 8, which is stylistically characterized as the king addressing his dignitaries, deals with past events: the actual date of the attack of the Sea Peoples would therefore more likely be 1178 BC, Rameses III's Year 3.[156]

Whatever the exact chronology, it seems clear that the attempts of the Libyans and the Sea Peoples were, if not coordinated, at least interconnected as part of a much larger crisis that encompassed all of the eastern Mediterranean at the end of the Bronze Age. This crisis affected sites across the Aegean, Anatolia, the Levant, and Libya and included movements of populations that would contribute to the end of the Hittite Empire and its vassal states Ugarit and Amurru, dramatically bringing to an end the political organization of Western Asia. A great many factors would have contributed to this crisis, with a climatic change to a more arid condition likely to have disrupted the fragile balance between demography and agricultural resources in regions around the Mediterranean, which compelled parts of the population to try to find more prosperous new homes.[157]

As we have seen, almost all of the textual evidence relating to these events comes from Egyptian sources, with the exception of some letters from Ugarit exchanged, probably just before the time of Rameses III, between Ugarit's ruler and his Hittite overlord. These letters' main topic

---

155. Land battle (KRI V: 27–30) vs. sea battle (KRI V: 32–35); see also KRI V: 25.6.

156. Popko 2016 assumes two attacks, in Year 3 and Year 8, but we can easily dispense with the second of these. Popko points out that the campaign in Year 3 explains why the *Pulasti* are shown as mercenaries fighting on the Egyptian side in military campaigns predating Year 8, as depicted at Medinet Habu.

157. For a review of the probable causes, see Cline 2014: 139–180; Finkelstein et al. 2017a.

are the activities of sea-raiders called *Šikalayu* (the cuneiform transcription of *Ṣikala*) in and around Cyprus as well as on the Anatolian and Levantine coastlines.[158] Contrary to most of the previously discussed Sea Peoples, we know nothing of the *Ṣikala/Šikalayu*'s origins, nor of that of the *Pulasti* or the *Washasha*. As for the *Danuna* (whose name links them to the Δαναοί, a Homeric designation for the Greeks; see also section 28.4.2), there is some evidence that they were people of *Ahhiyawan* (Achaean) origin, who had settled in the kingdom of (A)danawa in Cilicia (in southeastern Anatolia) and had then taken the name of their adopted country.[159]

Although the combined efforts of the Nineteenth and Twentieth Dynasty pharaohs had prevented the Libyans and the Sea Peoples from invading Egypt, many nevertheless came to settle in the country as prisoners of war, with the physically stronger individuals being incorporated into the Egyptian army, as was then customary. Many were sent to Middle Egypt in order to populate military colonies on the western bank of the Nile. Here, former captives from all the wars of the New Kingdom could be found, including Libyans, *Shardana*, and Hittites. The purpose of these colonies was to contain the raids of the Libyans of the Western Desert that had plagued Egypt since at least the reign of Sety I (see section 28.4.2). Nevertheless, the raiding still increased, and Rameses III was forced to build strong defensive walls around the temples of Thinis, Abydos, Asyut, and Hermopolis and his own mortuary temple at Medinet Habu.[160]

As each new raid brought more prisoners, Libyans had become, by the end of the New Kingdom, the principal component of the Egyptian army. As such, they possessed a potential power that finally found its political translation at the end of the Twentieth Dynasty: from the Twenty-first Dynasty to the end of independent Egypt, all pharaohs who

---

158. Singer 2000.

159. Cf. Beckman et al. 2011: 263–266.

160. Cf. Grandet 1993.

were not foreign rulers would be of Libyan descent, both of *Libu* and *Meshwesh* stock.[161]

If Rameses III had prevented the Sea Peoples from invading Egypt, he could not prevent some of them from settling on the Levantine coast, notably in southern Canaan.[162] It is these newcomers that the Bible generically calls "Philistines" (Philistieim, from original *Pulasti*), even if not all of them were originally connected to this group. The "Account of Wenamun,"[163] an Egyptian literary text from the Twenty-first Dynasty, attests that the port of Dor, south of Mount Carmel, was a city controlled by a prince of the still sea-raiding *Šikala*. According to the Bible, it is the settling of the Sea Peoples in Canaan and the necessity to fight them that prompted the peoples of Judah and Israel to become a kingdom. The "Philistines," however, soon assimilated to the culture of their Semitic milieu, in the midst of which they formed a kind of confederacy, with commerce replacing piracy as their principal activity. As part of the Assyrian Empire from the ninth century BC onward, the southern coast of the Levant was called *Palastu* ("Philistia"),[164] a forerunner of the toponym Palestina that appears first in the works of Greek authors of the fifth century BC. Curiously, a post-Hittite Aramean kingdom in the region of Alalakh, which flourished briefly in northern Syria in the eleventh century BC, bore the name "Falastin," later shortened to "Patin" in the Assyrian records; if this name is really related to the *Pulasti* of the Sea Peoples, it would have only been a reminiscence of their temporary stay in the region during their migrations, for the local material culture shows no Mycenaean characteristics whatsoever.[165]

---

161. Snape 2012: 416–441.

162. For a survey, see Weinstein 2012. Among the immense bibliography see, e.g., Maeir et al. 2013; Finkelstein 2016; Finkelstein et al. 2017b; Bietak and Czerny (eds.) 2017.

163. Translation: Lichtheim 1976: 224–230.

164. Cf. Ben-Shlomo 2014.

165. Bryce 2012: 129–133; Gilan 2013: 63–66.

Only a portion of the Sea Peoples ever settled in the Levant but, in the eighth century BC, in the wake of the Phoenician expansion, many would settle in the western Mediterranean. We have already noted the *Turusha*'s likely connection with the Etruscans and that the *Shardana* gave their name to Sardinia (see section 28.4.2). In turn, the *Ṣikala* settled in Sicily, to which they lent their name, while the *Washasha* may have been the ancestors of the Osci of southern Italy.[166]

Just like in Nubia, these developments left no place for the Egyptians in the Levant, and the New Kingdom's formerly strong presence gradually dissolved between the reign of Rameses III and the end of the Twentieth Dynasty.[167]

REFERENCES

Adams, W.Y. 1984. *Nubia: corridor to Africa*. London: Allen Lane. 2nd rev. ed.

Ahrens, A. 2015. The early 18th Dynasty in the northern Levant: new finds and a reassessment of the sources. In Mynářova, J., Onderka, P., and Pavúk, P. (eds.), *There and back again: the crossroads, II*. Prague: Charles University, 353–372.

Beckman, G. 1996. *Hittite diplomatic texts*. Atlanta, GA: Scholars Press.

Beckman, G., Bryce, T.R., and Cline, E.H. 2011. *The Ahhiyawa texts*. Atlanta, GA: Society of Biblical Literature.

Beekes, R.S.P. 2003. *The origin of the Etruscans*. Amsterdam: Koninklijke Nederlandse Akademie van Wetenschappen.

Ben-Shlomo, D. 2014. Tell Jemmeh, Philistia and the Neo-Assyrian Empire during the Late Iron Age. *Levant* 46: 58–88.

Benz, B.C. 2016. *The land before the kingdom of Israel: a history of the southern Levant and the people who populated it*. Winona Lake, IN: Eisenbrauns.

Bietak, M., and Czerny, E. (eds.) 2007. *The synchronisation of civilizations in the Eastern Mediterranean in the second millennium BCE, III*. Vienna: Verlag der Österreichischen Akademie der Wissenschaften.

---

166. By the same consonantal evolution as in the name of the Etruscans: *Turush* > *Trusc* and *Wash(ash)* > *Wasc* > *Osc*.

167. Millek 2018.

Bonnet, C., and Valbelle, D. 2018. *Les temples égyptiens de Panébès, le Jujubier, à Doukki Gel (Soudan)*. Paris: Khéops.

Boraik, M. 2007. Stela of Bakenkhonsu, high-priest of Amun-Re. *Memnonia* 18: 119–126.

Brand, P.J. 2011. The date of the war scenes on the south wall of the Great Hypostyle Hall and the west wall of the Cour de la Cachette at Karnak and the history of the late Nineteenth Dynasty. In Collier, M., and Snape, S. (eds.), *Ramesside studies in honour of K.A. Kitchen*. Bolton: Rutherford Press, 51–84.

Breyer, F. 2010. Thutmosis III. und die Hethiter: Bemerkungen zum Kurustama-Vertrag sowie zu anatolischen Toponymen und einer hethitischen Lehnübersetzung in den Annalen Thutmosis' III. *SAK* 39: 67–83.

Bryce, T. 2012. *The world of the Neo-Hittites kingdoms: a political and military history*. Oxford: Oxford University Press.

Budka, J. 2015. The pharaonic town on Sai Island and its role in the urban landscape of New Kingdom Kush. *Sudan & Nubia* 19: 40–53.

Budka, J., and Doyen, F. 2012/13. Life in the New Kingdom towns in Upper Nubia: new evidence from recent excavations in Sai Island. *ÄL* 22/23: 167–208.

Castiglioni, An., and Castiglioni, Al. 2003. Pharaonic inscriptions along the Eastern Desert routes in Sudan. *Sudan & Nubia* 7: 47–51.

Cline, E.H. 1998. Amenhotep III, the Aegean, and Anatolia. In Cline, E.H., and O'Connor, D. (eds.) 1998: 236–249.

Cline, E.H. 2014. *1177 BC: the year civilization collapsed*. Princeton, NJ: Princeton University Press.

Cline, E.H., and O'Connor, D. (eds.) 1998. *Amenhotep III: perspectives on his reign*. Ann Arbor: University of Michigan Press.

Cline, E.H., and O'Connor, D. (eds.) 2006. *Thutmose III: a new biography*. Ann Arbor: University of Michigan Press.

Cline, E.H., and O'Connor, D. 2012a. The Sea Peoples. In Cline, E.H., and O'Connor, D. (eds.) 2012b: 180–208.

Cline, E.H., and O'Connor, D. (eds.) 2012b. *Ramesses III: the life and times of Egypt's last hero*. Ann Arbor: University of Michigan Press.

Cohen, R., and Westbrook, R. (eds.) 2002. *Amarna diplomacy: the beginnings of international relations*. Baltimore, MD: Johns Hopkins University Press.

Darnell, J.C. 2011. A stela of Seti I from the region of Kurkur Oasis. In Collier, M., and Snape, S. (eds.), *Ramesside studies in honour of K.A. Kitchen*. Bolton: Rutherford Press, 127–146.

Darnell, J.C., and Haddad, A. 2003. A stela of the reign of Tutankhamun from the region of Kurkur Oasis. *SAK* 31: 73–91.

Davies, B.G. 2013–2014. *Ramesside inscriptions, translated and annotated: notes and comments, vols. III–IV*. Malden, MA: Wiley-Blackwell.

Davies, W.V. 2003. Kush in Egypt: a new historical inscription. *Sudan & Nubia* 7: 52–54.

Davies, W.V. 2008. Tombos and the viceroy Inebny/Amenemnekhu. *BMSAES* 10: 39–63.

Davies, W.V. 2014. The Korosko Road Project: recording inscriptions in the Eastern Desert and elsewhere. *Sudan & Nubia* 18: 30–44.

Davies, W.V. 2017. The Egyptians at Kurgus. In Spencer, N., Stevens, A., and Binder, M. (eds.), *Nubia in the New Kingdom: lived experience, pharaonic control and indigenous traditions*. Leuven: Peeters, 65–106.

De Simone, C. 1996. *I tirreni a Lemnos: evidenza linguistica e tradizioni storiche*. Florence: L.S. Olschki.

Desroches-Noblecourt, C. 1999. *Le secret des temples de la Nubie*. Paris: Stock/Pernoud.

Dossin, G. 1970. La route de l'étain en Mésopotamie au temps de Zimri-Lim. *RA* 64: 97–106.

Edel, E. 1984. Sikeloi in den ägyptischen Seevolkertexten und in Keilschrifturkunden. *Biblische Notizen* 23: 7–8.

Edel, E. 1994. *Die ägyptisch-hethitische Korrespondenz aus Boghazköi in babylonischer und hethitischer Sprache*. Opladen: Westdeutscher Verlag.

Edel, E. 1997. *Der Vertrag zwischen Ramses II. von Ägypten und Ḫattušili III. von Hatti*. Berlin: Reimer.

Edel, E., and Görg, M. 2005. *Die Ortsnamenlisten im nördlichen Säulenhof des Totentempels Amenophis' III*. Wiesbaden: Harrassowitz.

Edwards, D.N., and Mills, A.J. 2013. Pharaonic sites in the Batn el-Hajjar: the "Archaeological Survey of Sudanese Nubia" revisited. *Sudan & Nubia* 17: 8–17.

Emberling, G., and Williams, B. 2010. The kingdom of Kush in the Fourth Cataract: archaeological salvage of the Oriental Institute Nubian Expedition 2007 season, part I: preliminary report on the sites of Hosh el-Guruf and El-Widay. *Gdánsk Archaeological Museum and Heritage Protection Fund: African Reports* 7: 17–66.

Finkelstein, I. 2014. The Shephelah and Jerusalem's western border in the Amarna period. *ÄL* 24: 265–274.

Finkelstein, I. 2016. To date or not to date: radiocarbon and the arrival of the Philistines. *ÄL* 26: 275–284.

Finkelstein, I., Arie, E., Martin, M.A.S., and Piasetzky, E. 2017. New evidence on the Late Bronze/Iron I transition at Megiddo: implications for the end of the Egyptian rule and the appearance of Philistine pottery. *ÄL* 27: 261–280.

Finkelstein, I., Langgut, D., Meiri, M., and Sapir-Hen, L. 2017. Egyptian imperial economy in Canaan: reaction to the climate crisis at the end of the Late Bronze Age. *ÄL* 27: 249–260.

Gabolde, L. 2011. Réexamen des jalons de la présence de la XVIIIe dynastie naissante à Saï. *CRIPEL* 29: 115–137.

Gasse, A., and Rondot, V. 2007. *Les inscriptions de Séhel*. Cairo: Institut français d'archéologie orientale.

Gilan, A. 2013. Pirates in the Mediterranean: a view from the Bronze Age. In Jaspert, N., and Kolditz, S. (eds.), *Seeraub im Mittelmeerraum: Piraterie, Korsarentum und maritime Gewalt von der Antike bis zur Neuzeit*. Paderborn: Ferdinand Schöningh, 49–66.

Gilboa, A. 2015. Dor and Egypt in the Early Iron Age: an archaeological perspective of (part of) the Wenamun Report. *ÄL* 25: 247–274.

Grandet, P. 1993. *Ramsès III: histoire d'un règne*. Paris: Pygmalion.

Grandet, P. 2008. *Les pharaons du Nouvel Empire (1550–1069 av. J.-C.): une pensée stratégique*. Paris: Éditions du Rocher.

Grandet, P. 2017. Les Peuples de la Mer. In De Souza, P., and Arnaud, P. (eds.), *The sea in history: the ancient world / La mer dans l'histoire: l'antiquité*. Woodbridge: Boydell Press, 175–186.

Habachi, L. 1959. The first two viceroys of Kush and their family. *Kush* 7: 45–62.

Hallmann, S. 2006. *Die Tributszenen des Neuen Reiches*. Wiesbaden: Harrassowitz.

Hasel, M.G. 2011. The Battle of Qadesh: identifying New Kingdom polities, places, and peoples in Canaan and Syria. In Bar, S., Kahn, D., and Shirley J.J. (eds.), *Egypt, Canaan and Israel: history, imperialism, ideology and literature*. Leiden: Brill, 65–86.

Helck, W. 1955–1958. *Urkunden der 18. Dynastie, Abteilung IV, Heft 17–22.* Berlin: Akademie Verlag.

Helck, W. 1983. *Historisch-biographische Texte der 2. Zwischenzeit und neue Texte der 18. Dynastie.* Wiesbaden: Harrassowitz. 2nd ed.

Helck, W. 1995. *Historisch-biographische Texte der 2. Zwischenzeit und neue Texte der 18. Dynastie: Nachträge.* Wiesbaden: Harrassowitz.

Hoch, J.E. 1994. *Semitic words in Egyptian texts of the New Kingdom and the Third Intermediate Period.* Princeton, NJ: Princeton University Press.

Hoffmeier, J.K. 2013. Reconstructing Egypt's eastern frontier defense network in the New Kingdom (Late Bronze Age). In Jesse, F., and Vogel, C. (eds.), *The power of walls: fortifications in ancient northeastern Africa.* Cologne: Heinrich-Barth-Institut, 163–194.

Hoffmeier, J.K., Davis, T., and Hummel, R. 2016. *New archaeological evidence for ancient Bedouin (Shasu) on Egypt's eastern frontier at Tell el-Borg. ÄL* 26: 285–311.

Izre'el, S. 1997. *The Amarna scholarly tablets.* Groningen: Styx.

Izre'el, S., and Singer, I. 1990. *The general's letter from Ugarit: a linguistic and historical reevaluation of RS 20.33 (Ugaritica V, no. 20).* Tel Aviv: Chaim Rosenberg School of Jewish Studies, Tel Aviv University.

Jacquet-Gordon, H., Bonnet, C., and Jacquet, J. 1969. Pnubs and the temple of Tabo on Argo Island. *JEA* 55: 103–111.

Kahn, D. 2011. One step forward, two steps backward: the relations between Amenhotep III, king of Egypt, and Tushratta, king of Mitanni. In Bar, S., Kahn, D., and Shirley, J.J. (eds.), *Egypt, Canaan and Israel: history, imperialism, ideology and literature.* Leiden: Brill, 137–154.

Kahn, D. 2012. A geo-political and historical perspective of Merenptah's policy in Canaan. In Galil, G., Gilboa, A., Maeir, A.M., and Kahn, D. (eds.), *The ancient Near East in the 12th–10th centuries BCE: culture and history.* Münster: Ugarit-Verlag, 255–268.

Kahn, D. 2013. The history of Kush: an outline. In Jesse, F., and Vogel, C. (eds.), *The power of walls: fortifications in ancient northeastern Africa.* Cologne: Heinrich-Barth-Institut, 17–31.

Kelder, J.M. 2010. *The kingdom of Mycenae: a great kingdom in the Late Bronze Age Aegean.* Bethesda, MA: CDL Press.

Kenning, J. 2014. *Der Feldzug nach Kadesch: das Ägypten des Neuen Reiches auf der Suche nach seiner Strategie.* Hildesheim: Olms.

Kitchen, K.A. 1975–1990. *Ramesside inscriptions: historical and biographical, vols. I–VIII.* Oxford: Blackwell.

Kitchen, K.A. 1993–1999. *Ramesside inscriptions, translated and annotated: notes and comments, vols.* I–II. Oxford: Blackwell.

Kitchen, K.A. 1993–2014. *Ramesside inscriptions, translated and annotated: translations, vols. I–VII.* Oxford: Blackwell.

Kitchen, K.A. 1996. *The Third Intermediate Period in Egypt.* Warminster: Aris & Phillips. 2nd rev. ed.

Kitchen, K.A. 1998. Amenhotep III and Mesopotamia. In Cline, E.H., and O'Connor, D. (eds.) 1998: 250–260.

Klemm, R., and Klemm, D. 2013. *Gold and gold mining in ancient Egypt and Nubia: geoarchaeology of the ancient gold mining sites in the Egyptian and Sudanese Eastern Deserts.* Berlin: Springer.

Klotz, D. 2010. Emhab versus the *tmhrtn*: monomachy and the expulsion of the Hyksos. *SAK* 39: 211–241.

Knapp, B., and Manning, S.W. 2016. The end of the Late Bronze Age in the Eastern Mediterranean. *AJA* 120: 99–149.

Kozloff, A.P. 2012. *Amenhotep III: Egypt's radiant pharaoh.* Cambridge: Cambridge University Press.

Lichtheim, M. 1976. *Ancient Egyptian literature, vol. II: the New Kingdom.* Berkeley and Los Angeles: University of California Press.

Lohwasser, A. 2012. A survey in the western Bayuda: the Wadi Abu Dom Itinerary Project (W.A.D.I.). *Sudan & Nubia* 16: 109–117.

Maeir, A.M., Hitchcock, L.A., and Kolska Horwitz, L. 2013. On the constitution and transformation of Philistine identity. *OJA* 32: 1–38.

Manassa, C. 2003. *The Great Karnak Inscription of Merneptah: grand strategy in the 13th century BC.* New Haven, CT: Yale Egyptological Seminar.

Matić, U. 2014. "Minoans," *kftjw* and the "Islands in the middle of *w3d wr*" beyond ethnicity. *ÄL* 24: 275–292.

Mazar, A. 2010. Tel Beth-Shean: history and archaeology. In Kratz, R.G., and Speckermann, L. (eds.), *One god—one cult—one nation: archaeological and biblical perspectives.* Berlin: De Gruyter, 239–271.

Mazar, A. 2011. The Egyptian garrison town at Beth-Shean. In Bar, S., Kahn, D., and Shirley J.J. (eds.), *Egypt, Canaan and Israel: history, imperialism, ideology and literature.* Leiden: Brill, 155–189.

Millek, J.M. 2018. Destruction and the fall of Egyptian hegemony over the southern Levant. *JAEI* 19: 1–21.

Monnier-Williams, M. 1899. *A Sanskrit-English dictionary*. Oxford: Clarendon Press. Retrieved from https://www.sanskrit-lexicon.uni-koeln.de (last accessed July 15, 2019).

Moran, W.M. 1992. *The Amarna letters*. Baltimore, MD: Johns Hopkins University Press.

Morkot, R. 2013. From conquered to conqueror: the organization of Nubia in the New Kingdom and the Kushite administration of Egypt. In Moreno García, J.C. (ed.), *Ancient Egyptian administration*. Leiden: Brill, 911–963.

Müller, I. 2013. *Die Verwaltung Nubiens im Neuen Reich*. Wiesbaden: Harrassowitz.

Müller, M. 2011. A view to a kill: Egypt's grand strategy in her northern empire. In Bar, S., Kahn, D., and Shirley, J.J. (eds.), *Egypt, Canaan and Israel: history, imperialism, ideology and literature*. Leiden: Brill, 236–257.

Mumford, G.D. 2015. The Sinai Peninsula and its environs: our changing perceptions of a pivotal land bridge between Egypt, the Levant, and Arabia. *JAEI* 7: 1–24.

Mynářová, J. 2014. Egyptian state correspondence of the New Kingdom: the letters of the Levantine client kings in the Amarna correspondence and contemporary evidence. In Radner, K. (ed.), *State correspondence in the ancient world: from New Kingdom Egypt to the Roman Empire*. Oxford: Oxford University Press, 10–31.

Na'aman, N. 1986. Ḫabiru and Hebrews: the transfer of a social term to the literary sphere. *JNES* 45: 271–288.

Na'aman, N. 1995. Tushratta's murder in Shuppiluliuma's letter to Akhenaten (EA 43). *Abr-Nahrain* 33: 116–118.

Naville, E. 1898. *Deir el-Bahari, vol. III*. London: Egypt Exploration Society.

O'Connor, D. 1987. The location of Irem. *JEA* 73: 99–136.

O'Connor, D. 1993. *Ancient Nubia, Egypt's rival in Africa*. Philadelphia: University of Pennsylvania Museum of Archaeology and Anthropology.

O'Connor, D. 1998. Amenhotep III and Nubia. In Cline, E.H., and O'Connor, D. (eds.) 1998: 261–270.

Popko, L. 2016. Die hieratische Stele MAA 1939.552 aus Amara West: ein neuer Feldzug gegen die Philister. *ZÄS* 143: 214–233.

Raafat Abbas, M. 2017. The town of Yenoam in the Ramesside war scenes and texts of Karnak. *Cahiers de Karnak* 16: 329–341.

Rainey, A.F. 2014. *The el-Amarna correspondence: a new edition of the cuneiform letters from the site of el-Amarna based on collations of all extant tablets*. Leiden: Brill.

Redford, D.B. 2004. *From slave to pharaoh: the black experience of ancient Egypt.* Baltimore, MD: Johns Hopkins University Press.

Redford, D.B. 2017. *The Medinet Habu records of the foreign wars of Ramesses III.* Leiden: Brill.

Ricke, H., Hughes, G.R., and Wente, E.F. 1967. *The Beit el-Wali temple of Ramesses II.* Chicago: The Oriental Institute of the University of Chicago.

Roberson, J.A. 2018. *Ramesside inscriptions: historical and biographical, vol. IX.* Wallasey: Abercromby Press.

Roe, A. 2005/06. The old "Darb al Arbein" caravan route and Kharga Oasis in antiquity. *JARCE* 42: 119–129.

Ruffieux, P., and Suliman Bashir, M. 2014. The Korosko Road Project: preliminary report on some New Kingdom amphorae from the Korosko Road. *Sudan & Nubia* 18: 44–46.

Schofield, L. 2007. *The Mycenaeans.* London: British Museum Press.

Sethe, K. 1906–1909. *Urkunden der 18. Dynastie, Abteilung IV, Heft 1–16.* Leipzig: Hinrichs.

Singer, I. 2000. New evidence on the end of the Hittite Empire. In Oren, E.D. (ed.), *The Sea Peoples and their world: a reassessment.* Philadelphia: University of Pennsylvania Museum of Archaeology and Anthropology, 21–33.

Singer, I. 2004. The Kuruštama Treaty revisited. In Groddek, D., and Rößle, S. (eds.), *Šarnikzel: Hethitologische Studien zum Gedenken an Emil Orgetorix Forrer.* Dresden: Verlag der Technischen Universität Dresden, 591–607.

Smith, S.T. 2013. Revenge of the Kushites: assimilation and resistance in Egypt's New Kingdom empire and Nubian ascendancy over Egypt. In Areshian, G. (ed.), *Empires and diversity: on the crossroads of archaeology, anthropology and history.* Los Angeles: Cotsen Institute of Archaeology, University of California, 84–107.

Snape, S. 2012. The legacy of Ramesses III and the Libyan ascendancy. In Cline, E.H., and O'Connor, D. (eds.) 2012b: 404–441.

Snape, S. 2013. A stroll along the corniche? Coastal routes between the Nile delta and Cyrenaica in the Late Bronze Age. In Förster, F., and Riemer, H. (eds.), *Desert road archaeology in ancient Egypt and beyond.* Cologne: Heinrich-Barth-Institut, 439–454.

Snape, S., and Wilson, P. 2007. *Zawiyet Umm el-Rakham, vol. I: the temple and chapels.* Bolton: Rutherford Press.

Spalinger, A.J. 2005. *War in ancient Egypt: the New Kingdom*. Malden, MA: Wiley-Blackwell.

Spalinger, A.J. 2006. Covetous eyes south: the background to Egypt's domination of Nubia by the reign of Thutmose III. In Cline, E.H., and O'Connor, D. (eds.) 2006: 344–369.

Spalinger, A.J. 2013. The organization of the pharaonic army (Old to New Kingdom). In Moreno García, J.C. (ed.), *Ancient Egyptian administration*. Leiden: Brill, 393–478.

Spencer, N., Stevens, A., and Binder, M. 2014. *Amara West: living in Egyptian Nubia*. London: British Museum Press.

Spencer, N., Stevens, A., and Binder, M. (eds.) 2017. *Nubia in the New Kingdom: lived experience, pharaonic control and indigenous traditions*. Leuven: Peeters.

Spencer, P. 1997–2013. *Amara West, vol. I–III*. London: Egypt Exploration Society.

Theis, C. 2011. Der Brief der Königin Daḫamunzu an den hethitischen König Šuppiluliuma I. im Lichte von Reisegeschwindigkeiten und Zeitabläufen. In Kämmerer, T.H. (ed.), *Identities and societies in the ancient East-Mediterranean regions: comparative approaches: Henning Graf Reventlow memorial volume*. Münster: Ugarit-Verlag, 301–331.

Topozada, Z. 1988. Les deux campagnes d'Amenhotep III en Nubie. *BIFAO* 88: 153–164.

Török, L. 2009. *Between two worlds: the frontier region between ancient Nubia and Egypt, 3700 BC–500 AD*. Leiden: Brill.

van der Veen, P., Theis, C., and Görg, M. 2003. Israel in Canaan (long) before pharaoh Merenptah? A fresh look at Berlin statue pedestal relief 21687. *JAEI* 2: 15–25.

Vivas Sainz, I. 2013. *Egipto y el egeo a comienzos de la XVIII dinastía: una visión de sus relaciones, antecedents e influencia iconográfica*. Oxford: British Archaeological Reports.

Vogel, C. 2011. Die Schlacht von Megiddo: Thutmosis III. im Kampf um Syrien und Palästina. *Isched* 1: 15–28.

von Beckerath, J. 1997. *Chronologie des pharaonischen Ägypten: die Zeitbestimmung der ägyptischen Geschichte von der Vorzeit bis 332 v. Chr.* Mainz: Zabern.

Wachsmann, S. 1987. *Aegeans in the Theban tombs*. Leuven: Peeters.

Weinstein, J.M. 1998. Egypt and the Levant in the reign of Amenhotep III. In Cline, E.H., and O'Connor, D. (eds.) 1998: 223–234.

Weinstein, J.M. 2012. Egypt and the Levant in the reign of Ramesses III. In Cline, E.H., and O'Connor, D. (eds.) 2012b: 160–180.

Welsby, D.A. 2001. *Life on the desert edge: 7000 years of settlement in the northern Dongola Reach, Sudan.* Oxford: Archaeopress.

Welsby, D.A. 2012. The Kerma *ancien* cemetery at site H 29 in the northern Dongola Reach. *Sudan & Nubia* 16: 20–28.

Wente, E.F. 1985. A new look at the viceroy Setau's autobiographical inscription. In Posener-Kriéger, P. (ed.), *Mélanges Gamal Eddin Mokhtar, vol. II.* Cairo: Institut français d'archéologie orientale, 347–359.

White, D., and White, A.P. 1996. Coastal sites of northeast Africa: the case against Bronze Age ports. *JARCE* 33: 11–30.

White, D. 2002. *Marsa Matruh: the University of Pennsylvania Museum of Archaeology and Anthropology's excavations on Bate's Island, Marsa Matruh, Egypt, 1985–1989.* Philadelphia, PA: Institute for Aegean Prehistory Academic Press.

Wimmer, S., and Heindl, P. 2018. Die zerstörte Felsstele von Adlun (Libanon) an der 'Enge von Sarepta' relokalisiert. *GM* 254: 127–137.

Wolf, P., and Nowotnick, U. 2007. The 4th season of the SARS Anglo-German expedition to the Fourth Nile Cataract. *Sudan & Nubia* 11: 26–34.

Yalcin, Ü., Pulak, C., and Slotta, R. (eds.) 2005. *Das Schiff von Uluburun: Welthandel vor 3000 Jahren.* Bochum: Deutsches Bergbaumuseum.

Yurco, F.J. 1986. Merenptah's Canaanite campaign. *JARCE* 23: 189–211.

Zertal, A. 2011. The Aruna Pass. In Bar, S., Kahn, D., and Shirley J.J. (eds.), *Egypt, Canaan and Israel: history, imperialism, ideology and literature.* Leiden: Brill, 342–356.

Żurawski, B., Cedro, A., Drzewiecki, M., and Łopaciuk, R. 2017. Fieldwork in 2015/2016 in the southern Dongola Reach and the Third Cataract Region. *Polish Archaeology in the Mediterranean* 26: 269–288.

29

Mittani and Its Empire

Eva von Dassow

29.1. Introduction

Mittani (figure 29.1) was a kingdom located in upper Mesopotamia that flourished during the first half of the Late Bronze Age, roughly the late sixteenth to mid-fourteenth century BC.[1] It was called by several names. The name Hanigalbat, which predated and outlasted Mittani, denoted the kingdom's heartland, centered on the upper Khabur River with its tributaries. Naharina (alternatively Nahrima), a West Semitic designation referring to the country's riverine location, was the denomination preferred

---

1. In this chapter, the following abbreviations are used for primary sources: AlT for cuneiform tablets from Alalakh, as catalogued in Wiseman 1953; CTH for cuneiform texts from Hatti according to the *Catalogue des Textes Hittites* of Laroche 1971, continued online by S. Košak and G.G.W. Müller at *Hethitologie Portal Mainz*: https://www.hethport.uni-wuerzburg.de/HPM/index.php (last accessed August 1, 2020); EA for cuneiform tablets found at Tell el-Amarna, as translated in Moran 1992; *Emar* for cuneiform texts edited in Arnaud 1985; RS for cuneiform tablets excavated at Ugarit (Ras Shamra); TB for cuneiform tablets excavated at Tell Brak; TQ for cuneiform tablets excavated at Terqa (Tell Ashara); TT for cuneiform tablets excavated at Qatna (Tell Mishrife); *Urk.* for Egyptian texts edited in Helck 1961. This chapter was written during a fellowship in 2019/20 with the Kolleg-Forschungsgruppe "Rethinking Oriental Despotism—Strategies of Governance and Modes of Participation in the Ancient Near East" (FOR 2615), funded by the Deutsche Forschungsgemeinschaft, at the Freie Universität Berlin.

Eva von Dassow, *Mittani and Its Empire* In: *The Oxford History of the Ancient Near East.* Edited by: Karen Radner, Nadine Moeller, and D. T. Potts, Oxford University Press. © Oxford University Press 2022.
DOI: 10.1093/oso/9780190687601.003.0029

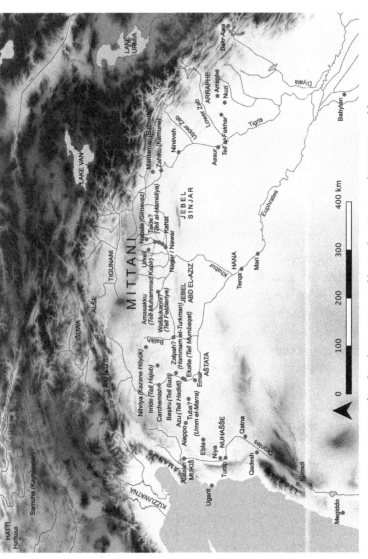

FIGURE 29.1. Sites mentioned in this chapter. Prepared by Andrea Squitieri (LMU Munich).

by Egypt and its Canaanite dependencies. The kingdom was also called the country of Hurri, and its ruler king of the Hurrians, in reference to its predominant population. It acquired the name Mittani by 1500 BC, and acquired an empire during the first century of its existence; from about 1400 BC onward it began losing territory to the Hittite kingdom. After suffering a dynastic fracture, Mittani met its demise as an independent state in conflicts with Hatti and Assyria during the late fourteenth century BC, thereafter surviving into the thirteenth century BC (under the name Hanigalbat) as a dependency of the Hittite Empire and then of Assyria. At its greatest extent, Mittani's empire embraced lands from Arraphe in the east, whose capital lies beneath present-day Kirkuk, to Kizzuwatna in the west, nestled between the Taurus Mountains and the Mediterranean Sea.

Hurrian was the principal language of Mittani, alongside Akkadian, which by this time was the language of writing shared by all who used the cuneiform script. Hurrian had been spoken in the region since at least the mid-third millennium BC, and perhaps much earlier, although it was seldom written before the mid-second millennium.[2] On present evidence, it did not long survive the transition to the first millennium. The only language known to be related to Hurrian is its ancient cousin Urartian, named for the land of Urartu (biblical Ararat) in the mountainous regions north of Mesopotamia, which is attested during the early first millennium BC. If the two languages have any living relatives, the relationship is too distant to be of any use in understanding them. Present knowledge of Hurrian depends heavily on bilingual texts, virtual bilinguals, and polyglot vocabularies produced in various places where the language was spoken or studied in antiquity. Hurrian therefore remains one of the more poorly understood languages of the ancient Near East, although ongoing research coupled with new discoveries has yielded substantial progress in recent years.

The name Mittani is a Hurrian formation based on the personal name Maitta, conjecturally the name of the dynasty's founder, although

---

2. In her grammar of Hurrian, Wegner 2007 surveys the sources, their temporal and spatial distribution, and the language's typology as well as (postulated) relationships. See also Giorgieri 2000; Campbell 2020.

no early ruler or ancestor by that name is known. Mittani would thus refer to the ruling family and its domain. This would account for its restricted use, alongside the continued use of the names Hanigalbat and Hurri, to refer to the kingdom. It must be emphasized that Mittani designates not a people but a state (or its ruling authority); accordingly, it cannot take a definite article in English. Note also the name's spelling (double t, single n), based on its linguistic analysis: Mitta (> Maitta) plus the Hurrian suffix -ni.[3]

29.2. Sources and sites

Mittani is known primarily from the archives of others. Archaeological excavations in its heartland have revealed Mittani-period occupations at many sites without, to date, striking upon substantial textual finds: no royal inscriptions, no family archives, only scraps of institutional archives, and no literature. Yet many such texts must have existed, in Hurrian as well as Akkadian, for several reasons. First, the surviving selection of the kingdom's correspondence with Egypt found at Akhetaten (modern Tell el-Amarna) includes, besides tablets written in Akkadian, one very long letter in Hurrian—dubbed the Mittani Letter (EA 24; figure 29.2)—which exhibits a phonologically precise system for spelling the Hurrian language in cuneiform. This must represent the standard Hurrian orthography of Mittani's court, and great numbers of tablets, including curricular ones, must have been written this way. Second, Hittite scribes recorded works of Hurrian literature using different orthographies and dialect(s), which they probably derived in part from Mittani, as well as other Hurrian-speaking lands Hatti conquered.[4] Third, documents issued directly from Mittani's court have turned up here and there: a royal letter at Nuzi, a certificate of status at Umm el-Marra, legal decisions at Alalakh, and so forth. Sparse as these

---

3. Wilhelm 1997: 290; 2004: 103.

4. On Hurrian in Anatolia, see de Martino 2017; on the writing of Hurrian in and beyond Anatolia, see Homan 2020 (especially chapter 3); on Hurrian dialectology, see Wilhelm 2017 and Campbell 2020.

FIGURE 29.2. The Mittani Letter (EA 24, obverse), with a cuneiform tablet from Baṣiru/Tell Bazi (Bz 51/23:21) for size comparison. Mittani Letter © Staatliche Museen zu Berlin—Vorderasiatisches Museum, photograph by Olaf M. Teßmer; Tell Bazi tablet photograph courtesy Berthold Einwag; composite created by Karen Radner.

finds are, they must represent regular practices of the imperial government. Mittani's scribes must have written many such tablets, and trained their successors to write them, too. But hardly any of their work has been found where it must have been done, in the principal cities of Mittani. It is almost as if we are confronted with dark matter—we cannot directly observe it, but we can detect its effects on other things—when seeking to investigate this kingdom.

The following enumeration sorts the textual sources pertaining to Mittani that are known to date according to provenience, starting from the kingdom's core territory and proceeding outward to the lands of its empire, then to lands beyond. The pertinent sources include texts referring to Naharina, to the land or king of Hurri or the Hurrians, and to Hanigalbat, the antecedent and successor of Mittani; thus, the sequence of enumeration concludes in reverse, for the latest sources are Assyrian texts referring to Hanigalbat as a province of Assyria.[5]

29.2.1. Textual sources from Mittani's core territory in the Khabur Triangle area

From the kingdom's central region:

- Taide (Tell al-Hamidiya):[6] Late in Mittani's history, when the kingdom was devolving into Hanigalbat, Taide became the royal residence; it was then destroyed and partly rebuilt by the Assyrian

---

5. Sources for Hanigalbat known up to the date of publication are collected in von Weiher 1975. For Mittani or the Hurrian king or country, see Wilhelm 1997; for Egyptian texts mentioning Mittani or Naharina, see Redford 1982. De Martino 2018 itemizes the principal sources in a recent study of Mittani's history and organization; Homan 2020: 40–56 enumerates tablets that (probably) originated from Mittani.

6. While Tell al-Hamidiya is confidently identified as the site of Taide/Taidu by the archaeologists who excavated it (Wäfler 2007; Kaelin 2013), this is not considered certain by all. For the alternative candidacy of Üçtepe on the Upper Tigris, see, e.g., Cancik-Kirschbaum and Hess 2017: 142–143.

king Adad-nerari I (1305–1274 BC). From the site's Mittanian (or Hanigalbatian) phases, excavations have yielded 51 inscribed tablets, dockets, and fragments, the remains of an early thirteenth-century-BC administrative file recording beer allocations, as well as six other administrative records.[7]

- Nawar or Nagar (Tell Brak), a major city in the district of Taide:[8] In various rooms of the Mittani-period palace, seven tablets or fragments were found: two legal documents bearing royal seals, one letter in Akkadian and a fragment of one in Hurrian, and three administrative records, as well as an uninscribed sealed docket.[9]

- Unprovenanced: Two letters in a private collection probably originated from a site within Mittani's core territory, based on the tablets' script and the names of the individuals involved. The sender of one letter, Waššu, bears the same uncommon name as Waššu of Mittani, who appears in the Akkadian letter found at Tell Brak.[10]

29.2.2. Textual sources from Mittani's empire

From the inner territories, between the Euphrates and Tigris:

- Baṣiru (Tell Bazi), a town on the eastern bank of the Euphrates, downstream from Carchemish: In the central building on the citadel were found two sealed tablets recording grants from kings of Mittani to the people of Baṣiru (figure 29.3).[11]

---

7. For the beer allocation file, excavated in 2007, see now Kessler 2020; as he notes, it includes numerous uninscribed sealed dockets as well. In the preliminary report, Kessler 2014 also describes six Mittani-period tablet fragments found in earlier excavation seasons.

8. Tell Brak was formerly identified as the site of Taide, until textual evidence for its identification as Nagar/Nawar was found; see Eidem 2001.

9. Eidem 1997 (with references).

10. George 2017: nos. 64 and 65; see commentary there and in Homan 2020: 55–56.

11. Sallaberger, Einwag, and Otto 2006.

FIGURE 29.3. One of the two cuneiform tablets from Baṣiru (Tell Bazi; Bz 51/ 23:21), sealed on the reverse by King Sauštatar, with his own seal (for a drawing, see figure 29.5). Photograph courtesy Berthold Einwag.

- Mardaman (Bassetki), a town just east of the Tigris, upstream from Nineveh (Mosul): Excavations have exposed three Mittani-period phases, in the latest of which were found one tablet (a memorandum) and a fragment.[12]
- Zahiku (Kemune): At this site on the eastern bank of the Tigris, situated just behind the modern Mosul Dam, excavations of a Mittani-period palatial building yielded ten tablets or fragments, one of which indicates that the town's name was Zahiku.[13]
- Zalpa (possibly Hammam et-Turkman), on the Balikh River: Within the bricks of the Late Bronze Age palace was found a sealed letter order addressed to one Šatuwatri from "the king," probably of Mittani, datable on archaeological grounds around 1500 BC.[14]

---

12. For the Mittani-period phases and tablets, see Pfälzner and Qasim 2018: 67–69; Pfälzner and Faist 2020: 351, 370–373.

13. On the excavations at Kemune, exposed when the water level of the Mosul Lake dropped in 2018, see Puljiz and Qasim 2019, with a contribution on the tablets by Betina Faist.

14. For the tablet and its archaeological context, see van Soldt 1995: 277–278; for the seal impression, see van Loon and Meijer 1987: 3 with fig. 13; and for the

From territories beyond the Euphrates and Tigris:

- Alalakh (Tell Atchana): This city ruled a kingdom called alternatively by the name of its capital or by the name Mukiš (Mugiš), after its core territory centered on the Amuq Plain. Alalakh was subject to Mittani during the late fifteenth and early fourteenth century BC, until its conquest by Hatti in the 1330s. Its subjection is attested by tablets found in the late fifteenth-century-BC level at Tell Atchana (Alalakh IV), as well as by the inscribed statue of the local king Idrimi.[15]
- Arraphe (Kirkuk) and Nuzi (Yorgan Tepe): The city of Arraphe—also called Al-ilani, "city of the gods"—was the capital of the kingdom of Arraphe lying northeast of Assyria. It was subject to Mittani until its conquest by Assyria in the mid-fourteenth century BC. Arraphe is known primarily from excavations at the town of Nuzi, which yielded family and institutional archives numbering about 5,000 tablets; numerous tablets also derive from Kirkuk (not archaeologically excavated) and from excavations at Tell al-Fakhar. In texts from Arraphe, the superordinate kingdom is referred to as Hanigalbat, not Mittani.[16]
- Azu (Tell Hadidi): At this site on the western bank of the Euphrates, upstream from Emar, fifteen tablets were found, eight of them in one jar. These include a sealed tablet recently identified as a letter-order between officials of Mittani, datable to the late fourteenth century BC.[17]

---

probable identification of Hammam et-Turkman as Zalpa, see Ziegler and Langlois 2016: 420–421.

15. On Alalakh under Mittani's rule, see von Dassow 2008; 2014. On the statue of Idrimi, see Lauinger 2019 and note Jake Lauinger's online edition: http://oracc.museum.upenn.edu/aemw/alalakh/idrimi/ (last accessed August 1, 2020).

16. For bibliography on Nuzi and Arraphe, see Maidman 2010, supplemented by von Dassow 2016. Tell al-Fakhar was previously thought to be the site of ancient Kurruhanni, an identification Koliński 2002 has shown to be incorrect. See also Postgate 2013: 343 n. 6.

17. Torrecilla and Cohen 2018. Most tablets found at Tell Hadidi remain unpublished, although an edition by Robert M. Whiting has long been announced.

- Emar (Tell Meskene), situated on the western bank of the great
  bend of the Euphrates: Among the several thousand tablets deriving
  from Emar and its vicinity are a few that attest the town's tributary
  relationship with the king of Hurrian country (Mittani) in the mid-
  fourteenth century BC, and hostilities ca. 1300 BC.[18]
- Qatna (Tell Mishrife), on a tributary of the upper Orontes: Recent
  excavations at the site yielded the remains of an archive that ended
  with the city's destruction in the 1330s. The archive includes records
  of troop mobilization, as well as five letters pertaining to an episode
  in Hatti's conquest of Mittani.[19]
- Terqa (Tell Ashara), on the middle Euphrates in the land of
  Hana: Among the tablets found in excavations at the site, about two
  dozen derive from the period of the Mittani empire, and some of
  these attest rulers of Mittani alongside local kings.[20]
- Umm el-Marra (possibly Tuba): One single tablet, a legal document
  sealed by the king of Mittani, was found at this site lying between
  Emar and Halab (Aleppo).[21]

29.2.3. Textual sources from other lands

From regions outside of Mittani's direct control:

- Ugarit: The kingdom of Ugarit, on the coast of present-day Syria, is
  not known to have been subject to Mittani at any time, but it may
  have corresponded with Mittani at some point. Thousands of tablets

18. On these documents, see von Dassow 2014: 17; Torrecilla and Cohen
    2018: 152–154.

19. These tablets are published in Richter and Lange 2012. Note that one of these
    (TT 62) duplicates a text found in the older excavations: Richter and Lange
    2012: 170–172.

20. On these tablets, which remain unpublished, see Podany 2014 (with references).

21. The tablet with its sealing is published in Cooper, Schwartz, and Westbrook
    2005. On Umm el-Marra, its Late Bronze Age occupation, and the arguments
    for identifying it as the site of Tuba, see most recently Schwartz 2018.

in several languages, including Hurrian, were found at Ras Shamra, site of the city of Ugarit. Among them is a fragmentary letter in Hurrian that speaks of entering (or invading) Carchemish. The likeliest historical context for someone to write to Ugarit in Hurrian, mentioning Carchemish, is the late fourteenth century BC, perhaps during the period when, after Hatti subjected Mittani, Hanigalbat briefly recovered its independence and hosted Ugaritians at Taide (Tell al-Hamidiya).[22]

- Hatti: The archives of the Hittite capital Hattusa include many texts pertaining to Mittani, especially its prehistory and its fall. Several compositions narrate conflicts between the kingdom of Hatti and Hurrian kingdoms during the seventeenth–sixteenth century BC.[23] Mittani's demise in the mid-to-late fourteenth century BC is illuminated by contemporaneous texts, above all the pair of treaties between Suppiluliuma I, king of Hatti, and Šattiwaza, king of Mittani (CTH 51, 52); the Deeds of Suppiluliuma (CTH 40); Mursili II's Plague Prayers; and the Aleppo Treaty (CTH 75), which refers to the kingdom alternately as Hanigalbat and Mittani.[24] Later texts from Hatti speak of Hanigalbat, the rump state that remained of Mittani after its conquest, or of the Hurrian country.[25] Foremost among non-historical compositions is the manual of horse training called the Kikkuli Text, after its incipit, "Thus (speaks) Kikkuli, horse

---

22. The tablet RS 11.853 is discussed by van Soldt 1991: 364, who considers it to have been sent from Carchemish and comments that its orthography resembles that of the Mittani Letter (EA 24); and by Singer 1999: 621, who considers it to have been sent from Mittani or Hanigalbat. For people from Ugarit at Taide, see section 29.4.4.

23. For the sources pertaining to the Old Hittite period, see Wilhelm 1997: 292; for their historical interpretation in conjunction with Babylonian (and other) sources, see van Koppen 2004: 19–23 and 2017: 71–72; also von Dassow 2008: 19–20.

24. For the treaties, see Beckman 1996 and Devecchi 2015. Selections from the Deeds of Suppiluliuma are given in Hoffner 1997; for a complete new edition, see del Monte 2009. For Mursili's Plague Prayers, see Singer 2002.

25. Harrak 1987 itemizes sources on Hanigalbat, including Hittite ones, from the period of its subjugation by Hatti and Assyria. See also chapter 30 in this volume.

trainer from the land of Mittani" (CTH 284).[26] Elsewhere in Hatti, one of the tablets found at Kayalıpınar, the site of Samuha, contains an account in Hurrian about an episode involving Mittani that must have transpired in the late fifteenth or early fourteenth century BC.[27]

• Egypt: We owe the earliest extant mention of Mittani to the tomb autobiography of Amenemhat, the astronomer and clockmaker who refers to a campaign that may have taken place as early as Ahmose's reign in the late sixteenth century BC.[28] Over the following century, Egyptian sources report repeated military conflicts with Mittani, which they usually called Naharina, or with its proxies. The two states resolved their hostilities with an alliance that began during the reign of Amenhotep II (late fifteenth century BC).[29] Thereafter the principal sources from or about Mittani are the tablets that survive from the pharaoh's correspondence left behind at Akhetaten (Tell el-Amarna), dating to the mid-fourteenth century BC. These include fourteen letters and other tablets sent by Tušratta, king of Mittani (EA 17–30). Numerous letters from Syro-Canaanite rulers also mention Mittani, sometimes by the name Hanigalbat or Nahrima.[30] From Egypt comes a very late mention of Mittani, too: an archaizing

---

26. On the Kikkuli Text, see Raulwing and Meyer 2004 (with references).

27. For the text and likely historical context of this tablet (Kayalıpınar 05/226), see Wilhelm 2006 and Rieken 2009. The text is now published by Wilhelm 2019 (as KpT 1.11). On the historical context, see also Wilhelm 2015: 73, and further discussion in section 29.4.3.

28. Brunner 1956. Older treatments of Amenemhat's inscription are now superseded by that of von Lieven 2016, whose study yields significant revisions to its interpretation. Among her results: the mention of Egypt's encounter with Mittani probably pertains to the introductory frame of the autobiography proper and thus to Amenemhat's father; the inscription says Mittani is called [. . .] (could Naharina be lost in the break?); and Amenemhat does not say he invented the water-clock, but a precisely calibrated timekeeping device that apparently combined the shadow-clock with the water-clock and featured moving figures. On this and other Eighteenth Dynasty sources pertaining to Mittani, see Kühne 1999: 212–215, and cf. chapter 28 in this volume.

29. *Urk.* §1326.

30. The Amarna correspondence is most readily accessible in the annotated English translation of Moran 1992. For Tušratta's Hurrian letter (EA 24), see Wilhelm

reference in Shoshenq I's inscription reporting his campaign in the Levant (ca. 925 BC).[31]

- Babylonia and Assyria: Here the kingdom of Mittani was called Hanigalbat. By this name, it is first mentioned in texts of the late Old Babylonian period (toward 1600 BC).[32] In the Amarna correspondence, one of the two letters from the Assyrian king to the pharaoh mentions Hanigalbat (EA 16), one of the pharaoh's letters to the Babylonian king quotes him using the gentilic Hanigalbatean (EA 1), and Tušratta also calls his own land Hanigalbat (EA 18, 20, 29). Assyrian royal inscriptions and other texts from the Middle Assyrian period record the conquest of Hanigalbat, its re-establishment as a subordinate kingdom, and finally its abolition in the early twelfth century BC.[33] The sole Assyrian attestation of the name Mittani is an archaizing reference in an inscription of Tiglath-pileser I from ca. 1100 BC.[34]

29.2.4. The missing sources from the capital

The site of Mittani's capital city Waššukanni is conspicuous by its absence from the preceding enumeration. Tell Fekheriye, at the headwaters of the Khabur near Ras al-'Ain, is almost certainly the site of Waššukanni— later Sikani—but excavations there have yet to yield any Mittani-period texts, never mind the archives one has reason to expect.[35]

2006a. On the corpus, its provenience, and its archaeological context, see Mynářová 2007. Rainey 2014 provides new transliterations and translations of all the letters.

31. See Kitchen 2016: 15. The name survived thereafter as a geographic designation, which appears in the works of Herodotus (Histories 1.72, etc.) and Strabo (Geography 11.14) in the form Matiēni.

32. For the earliest attestations, see van Koppen 2004: 21 with n. 65–66; 2017: 56 with n. 40, 69.

33. For citations of the texts, see Cancik-Kirschbaum and Hess 2016: 56; for discussion, see de Martino 2000: 98–101.

34. Cancik-Kirschbaum and Hess 2016: 96.

35. On Tell Fekheriye, the finds there, and the site's likely identification with Waššukanni, see Bonatz 2013; 2014. Its identification as Sikani is assured by later

While the dearth of textual sources from the kingdom's heartland frustrates a conventional approach to writing history, the wealth of archaeological remains excavated at sites large and small provides evidence of other kinds for the growth, territorial footprint, and structure of Mittani and its territories. Sites belonging to Mittani's realm, or occupation levels belonging to the period of its rule, may be identified based on elements of material culture, especially pottery and glyptic art.[36] Most recognizable among pottery types diagnostic of the Mittani period is the fine painted pottery called "Nuzi Ware," with its variant "Atchana Ware," after the sites in the easternmost and westernmost parts of Mittani where it was first discovered (figure 29.4). Nuzi Ware is found at every site where texts attest to Mittani's rule and therefore serves as an archaeological index of its extent.[37] Glyptic imagery was an equally distinctive element of Mittanian culture, but a mobile one; seals and sealed tablets traveled well beyond Mittani's frontiers. Major imperial centers (e.g., Tell Brak, Tell Fekheriye, Tell al-Hamidiya, and Kemune) feature monumental architecture and, when fortune preserves it, wall painting. Meanwhile, recent surveys and excavation of rural sites in Mittani's heartland indicate significant new settlement during the period of its rule.[38]

---

texts, above all the inscribed ninth-century-BC statue of Adad-it'i / Hadda-yis'i found there. If this is the same toponym as Sigan of the Ur III period, however, it remains to be explained how the Mittanian form of the name developed (de Martino 2000: 70).

36. Stein 1997 provides a general overview. Pottery types diagnostic of Mittani are described in a detailed survey of Late Bronze Age pottery found in the Jezirah by Pfälzner 2007. Recent excavations and surveys continue to add new material; see, e.g., Coppini 2018.

37. On this criterion, the site of Bakr Awa (in Iraqi Kurdistan), where no Nuzi Ware has turned up, would not appear to belong to Mittani: see Miglus 2016: especially 235; cf. Maidman 2016–2017: 23. No Nuzi Ware has yet been found at any site in Kizzuwatna (Cilicia) either, according to Novak and Rutishauser 2017: 141, which astonishes them because this land had been subject to Mittani during part of the fifteenth century BC.

38. Three such rural sites are the subject of Reiche 2014, who describes how they instantiate the change to a dispersed settlement pattern starting in this period.

FIGURE 29.4. Some examples of Nuzi Ware. Left: a beaker from Alalakh (British Museum, ME 125994; registration number 1938,108.7; excavation number ATP/37/2). Right top: a beaker from Nagar/Nawar (Tell Brak, registration number 85.19; Oates, Oates, and McDonald 1997: 192.193, fig. 196: no. 392); right bottom: a jar from Nagar/Nawar (Tell Brak, TB 8242, registration number 86.65; published in Oates, Oates, and McDonald 1997: 192–193, fig. 196: no. 402). Photograph courtesy Trustees of the British Museum; drawings courtesy the Tell Brak Project and the British Institute for the Study of Iraq; composite created by Karen Radner.

29.3. Kings and chronology

The origins of the lineage that ruled Mittani are a matter of conjecture, and the sequence of rulers is obscure at many points. Other than those who attained kingship, the only members of the royal family we know anything about are three princesses who were married to kings of Egypt (see section 29.3.1) and one queen, Yuni, wife of Tušratta (EA 26). Before it acquired the name Mittani and the eponymous dynasty, the kingdom or its antecedent existed under the name Hanigalbat, under rulers who were sometimes called kings of the Hurrians.

29.3.1. Working backward from downfall to origins

Given the gaps in the available evidence, it is simplest to start at the end of the line, with the ruler whose accession marked the kingdom's downfall, and work backward through the fixed points available. The kingdom's chronology is established by means of synchronisms between rulers of Mittani and rulers of other kingdoms (table 29.1), no method of dating being employed in the pertinent sources.[39]

After Tušratta, king of Mittani, was murdered by one of his sons, another of his sons, Keli-Teššub, sought refuge with Suppiluliuma, king of Hatti. The Hittite king then repudiated his treaty with Artatama II, rival king of the Hurrian country, and his son Šuttarna III, in favor of the fugitive prince. Keli-Teššub became king of Mittani under the throne name Šattiwaza, and under Hittite authority (ca. 1340 BC). Imperial Mittani was thus reduced to a subordinate state, which fought for its continued existence as the kingdom of Hanigalbat. It had, however, fractured already before the accession of Tušratta, son of Šuttarna II, who became king after the assassination of his brother Artaššumara; that was when the rival line of Artatama II split off. The reign of Tušratta, who sent his daughter Tadu-Heba to marry Amenhotep III, overlapped the last years of the latter's reign and the early years of Akhenaten's reign. Thus, the end of Mittani's royal line is fixed to Egyptian chronology. The extant Amarna correspondence includes eleven letters Tušratta addressed to Amenhotep III, Akhenaten, and the queen mother Tiye (EA 17–21, 23–24, 26–29); two lengthy inventories of gifts that accompanied his daughter to Egypt (EA 22, 25); and one sealed tablet the king of Mittani addressed to the kings of Canaan to assure safe passage to Egypt for his messenger Agiya (EA 30). The seal on this "passport" is presumably that of Tušratta.[40]

---

39. Maidman 2016–2017 collects most sources attesting the rulers of Mittani and seeks to establish their sequence and chronology. The reconstruction proposed by Mladjov 2019 distends the line and raises the chronology much too high.

40. For a drawing of the seal impression and previous literature, see Stein 1997: 297–298.

Table 29.1. The royal house of Mittani and the contemporary dynasties

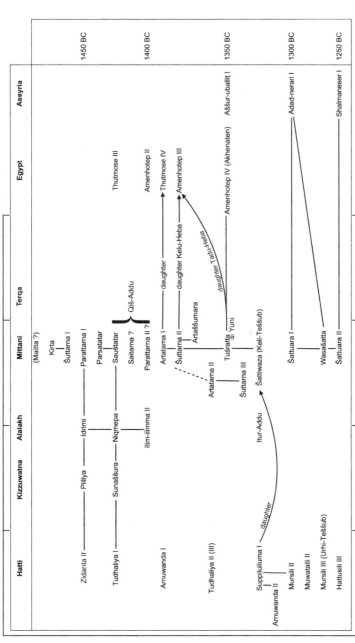

Horizontal and diagonal lines indicate explicitly attested contemporaneity, with Qiš-Addu of Terqa being the contemporary of three Mittani rulers. Vertical lines indicate filiations that are certain; the dashed line indicates an uncertain family relationship. Arrows represent dynastic marriages, pointing from the father of the bride to the groom. The table includes all known members of Mittani's royal house, and only those rulers of other realms whose interaction with rulers of Mittani is attested. Compiled by Eva von Dassow, drawn by Karen Radner.

FIGURE 29.5. Drawing of the impression of the seal of King Sauštatar. Courtesy of Diana Stein.

Almost all that is known of Artaššumara is that he reigned and was assassinated. Among the tablets found at Tell Brak, one is a deed concluded "before Artaššumara, king, son of Šuttarna, king," which he sealed with the seal of his forebear Sauštatar; another is a deed concluded before Tušratta, which he likewise sealed with Sauštatar's seal (figure 29.5). Their father, Šuttarna II, and grandfather, Artatama I, also used Sauštatar's seal, respectively, on the tablet found at Umm el-Marra, a deed written before Šuttarna, and on one of the two tablets found at Tell Bazi, a grant made by Artatama. Artatama and Šuttarna each sent a daughter to become a bride of the pharaoh, according to the letters of Tušratta. Šuttarna's daughter Kelu-Heba was married to Amenhotep III in the tenth year of his reign (1379 BC); Artatama's daughter, whose name is not mentioned, married Thutmose IV (early fourteenth century BC).[41] Whether it was Artatama or a predecessor who sent an embassy to Amenhotep II (see section 29.2.3) is unknown.

41. The sources are EA 17, 24, 29, and a commemorative scarab of Amenhotep III (*Urk.* §1738).

Who preceded Artatama on the throne is also unknown. His immediate predecessor was probably not Saustatar, whose seal he used. More
likely it was Parattarna II, who is attested as king by one tablet found at
Nuzi and several as yet unpublished tablets found at Terqa. The Nuzi tablet records the disbursement of garments, one of which was "burnt when
King Parattarna died."[42] Among the Terqa tablets are seven sealed documents recording transactions done under a local ruler of Hana together
with the superordinate king (of Mittani, though not so identified). The
same local potentate, Qiš-Addu, appears alongside three different kings,
Parattarna, Saitarna, and Sausadatra. The last-named is probably Saustatar
under a different spelling, and he probably reigned first of the three,
because Qiš-Addu was not yet king of Hana when he appeared alongside
him; Sausadatra would then have been succeeded by both Parattarna and
the otherwise unknown Saitarna.[43] In whichever order the latter two kings
ruled, and however briefly, their reigns must fall in the late fifteenth century BC. With their predecessor Saustatar we are on firmer ground, for he
can be synchronized with rulers of other realms and thus indirectly dated.

Saustatar, whose name is also spelled Saussatat(t)ar and Saussatar,
is the most prominent of Mittani's kings in later sources. Not only was
his seal used as a dynastic seal right down to the reign of Tušratta, he
is a point of reference for Šattiwaza in the historical prologue to his
treaty with Suppiluliuma (CTH 52). The legend on his seal identifies
him as "Saustatar, son of Parsatatar, king of Maitani," using the older
form of the kingdom's name. He is directly attested by sources from several different places, including the aforementioned tablets from Terqa
(assuming Sausadatra is another spelling of the same name). Two tablets found at Alalakh (AlT 13 and 14) record legal decisions Saustatar
issued for the local king Niqmepa, which he sealed with the seal of his

---

42. On the tablet (HSS 13 165), its context within the Nuzi archives, and the
 chronological implications of the attestation of Parattarna, see Wilhelm 1976;
 Stein 1989.

43. So according to Podany 2014, based on what is known of the text and sealings
 on these tablets. Mladjov 2019 observes that, whether or not Saitarna is an alternative form of Šuttarna, this king cannot be identical with any of the known
 Šuttarnas.

forebear Šuttarna I (discussed later in this section). Niqmepa's father, Idrimi, became king of Alalakh under the suzerainty of Sauštatar's predecessor Parattarna I, according to the inscription on Idrimi's statue. One tablet found at Tell Bazi is a grant Sauštatar made and sealed with his own seal (figure 29.3). It may also have been he who sent a letter to Ithiya (= Ithi-Teššub), king of Arraphe, which was found in the archives of Ithi-Teššub's grandson Šilwe-Teššub at Nuzi; this letter is called the "Sauštatar Letter" because it bears his seal, but it might have been sent and sealed by either Sauštatar or a successor.[44] Finally, Sauštatar's name may be restored in a passage recounting the deeds of Tudhaliya I, king of Hatti, in the fragmentary annals of Arnuwanda I (CTH 143).[45] These sources suffice to yield a concatenation of synchronisms, as follows.

Niqmepa, son of Idrimi, ruled at Alalakh under the suzerainty of Sauštatar, who issued a decision that the town of Alawari belonged to Niqmepa's kingdom rather than that of his northern neighbor Sunaššura, king of Kizzuwatna (AlT 14). Sunaššura repudiated his allegiance to Mittani in favor of allying with Hatti and concluded a treaty with Tudhaliya I (CTH 41).[46] Kizzuwatna had switched sides before: a predecessor of Sunaššura, Pilliya, made a treaty with Niqmepa's father, Idrimi, under the suzerainty of Parattarna (AlT 3); previously, however, Pilliya had also made a treaty with Zidanta (or Zidanza) II, king of Hatti (CTH 25).[47] On archival and archaeological grounds, Niqmepa's reign may be dated roughly around 1425 BC, and his father Idrimi's roughly around 1450; these dates carry over, with the requisite elasticity, to Sauštatar and Parattarna. Their elasticity accommodates the

---

44. On this letter, its archival context at Nuzi, and its chronological position, see Stein 1989 and Maidman 2016–2017. For the letter in translation, see von Dassow 2016.

45. See de Martino 2016: 101 (with references).

46. See Devecchi 2015: 73–91 for discussion and translation of this treaty, extant in both Akkadian and Hittite versions, and the identity of the parties.

47. For AlT 3, see von Dassow 2008: 34 and the present author's online translation at http://www.etana.org/node/576 (last accessed August 1, 2020); for CTH 25, see Devecchi 2015: 68–70. On relations among Kizzuwatna, Hatti, and Mittani, see also Miller 2020.

contemporaneity of Saustatar and Tudhaliya I indicated by the fragmentary annals; Tudhaliya's reign began in the late fifteenth century BC.

Parattarna's rule is attested both by the treaty between Pilliya and Idrimi and by the inscription on Idrimi's statue, where Parattarna is called king of the Hurrians. No source attests that Saustatar's father, Parsatatar, ruled as king; if he did, and followed Parattarna, his reign must have been brief. There do seem to be too many possible kings for the time available before Saustatar as well as after him, when a second Parattarna plus a Saitarna may have reigned before Artatama I, who was contemporary with Thutmose IV (early fourteenth century BC; see earlier in this section). The possibility should be considered that father-son succession may not have been the rule in Mittani (although it occurred in most cases that we know about). Rather, the fissioning seen toward the dynasty's end may have been the rule. If succession somehow proceeded through parallel lines of descent, that could account for the "extra" members of the royal lineage as well as for the tendency to fission.

Before Parattarna I, Mittani was ruled by Šuttarna I, whose seal Saustatar used. The seal legend reads "Šuttarna, son of Kirta, king of Maitani," and this is all that is known about him.[48] Šuttarna would have ruled in the early fifteenth century BC, perhaps preceded on the throne by his father, Kirta, who may in turn have been preceded by Maitta in the late sixteenth century BC, but by then the evidence has petered out into guesswork. The kings who previously ruled Hanigalbat or the Hurrians are at best faintly glimpsed in Hittite tales of war with them.

29.3.2. Names, their origins, and their significance

The names borne by Mittani's kings, at least as throne names, were Indo-Aryan.[49] Like the origin of the dynasty, the reason why its kings bore Indo-Aryan names remains obscure due to the lack of sources bearing on

---

48. On Šuttarna's seal, an ancient one made centuries earlier and recut, see Stein 1989: 40.

49. For the names with proposed Indo-Aryan analyses, see Parpola 2015: 88–89 (which, however, does not take into account the data from the Terqa tablets).

the formation of Mittani. No contemporaneous records are extant, nor is any historical or legendary retrospective. This informational vacuum has been filled by inference, speculation, and outright fantasy, ever since the early twentieth century AD, when scholars spotted Indic divine names in the treaty subjecting Mittani to Hatti. In 1910, Hugo Winckler misread the name Hurri in that text as Harri, and mistook it to mean "Aryan." He also proposed that the word *maryanni*, which he took to denote the retinue of the king of the supposed Aryans, derived from the Sanskrit word *márya*, "man," and that the group so denoted was therefore the Aryan ruling class.[50] The etymology is almost certainly correct, but the conclusion does not follow: the people designated by a word need not share the word's origin. In subsequent years, the horse-training instructions attributed to Kikkuli, the horse-trainer from Mittani, were also identified among the tablets found at Hattusa, and Indo-Aryan technical vocabulary was identified in these instructions.[51] No matter that the Indo-Aryan words appear in Hurrianized form, in a Hittite text written long after horses and chariots were introduced in the Near East; this discovery completed the false foundation of a myth that has been elaborated ever since. In this myth, Aryans rode horse-drawn chariots to supremacy over the Orient and founded Mittani, whose martial prowess and will to power were later transfused into Assyria.[52]

The evidence supports no such scenario. First, horses were introduced into southwestern Asia in the mid-third millennium BC, centuries before Mittani was founded, and the chariot, invented on the Eurasian steppe in the late third millennium, followed soon enough.[53] By 1500 BC,

---

50. Winckler 1910, citing F.C. Andreas for the Sanskrit etymology and meaning of *maryanni*.

51. Jensen 1919 is the earliest study of this vocabulary. Jensen, however, refrained from the ethno-historical inferences his contemporaries hastened to draw.

52. For dissection of this myth, with references to earlier literature, see von Dassow 2008: 77–90 and 2014: 12–13. See further Wiedemann 2017, who, rejecting the term "myth," examines the construction of "the Aryans" as a collective "character in historiographical narratives."

53. On horses in Mesopotamia during the mid-to-late third millennium, see Zarins 2014: 162–170. On the invention of horse-drawn chariots in the southern Urals

far from being the property of any one group, the techniques of chariot manufacture and chariot warfare were widely diffused. Second, rather than being an invading horde on the Mongol model, the class called *maryanni* was formed of the local nobility, within Mittani's territories and beyond.[54] Outside Mittani's royal family, Indo-Aryan personal names were lightly sprinkled into Near Eastern onomastica and were borne by men of all classes. Third, while a handful of Indo-Aryan words also entered Near Eastern lexica, not only is their number extremely small, they were already incorporated into the Hurrian language upon entry; for example, Indo-Aryan *márya* was provided with the Hurrian derivational suffix *-nni*. These words, then, do not represent a language anyone spoke in the region. Fourth, the quartet of Indic divine names— forms of Mithra, Varuna, Indra, and Nasatya—appears only in the treaty Suppiluliuma arranged with Šattiwaza; they moreover appear in long lists of gods of the Hittite and Hurrian kingdoms, and not first.[55] Had they been important in the kingdom, they should be attested before the moment of its fall. The only earlier attestation of an Indo-Aryan divine name is Agni's appearance in a Hittite tale of events predating Mittani, and Agni does not intervene on the Hurrian side (see section 29.4.1). Sources from Mittani itself show that the kingdom's principal deities were the Hurrian storm-god Teššub and his circle.

Nevertheless, it is true that horse-drawn chariotry was a significant factor in the transition to the Late Bronze Age, while linguistic evidence indicates that speakers of an Indo-Aryan language were instrumental

---

and their diffusion therefrom, see Parpola 2015: 56–68; for their introduction in Mesopotamia, see van Koppen 2017: especially 79.

54. The notion that the *maryanni* class was an Indo-Aryan group continues to be repeated even by those who, based on the scholarship they cite, should know better; e.g., Parpola 2015: 85. On the formation of this class, see section 29.5.1.

55. On the linguistic evidence, including onomastics and divine names, see von Dassow 2008: 84–89, with references there. Except for Indra, the divine names appear in plural forms: "Mithra-gods, Varuna-gods, Indra, Nasatya-gods"; this is noted by Lahe and Sazonov 2018, who interpret the first form as "gods of treaty" (rather than Mithra-gods). Varuna is now attested solo, as a recipient of beer, in a tablet from Taide (ca. 1300 BC); see Kessler 2020: 257–258 (ḪT 40), with comment on the divine name.

in its development and diffusion, and the names of Mittani's kings—some of which evoke chariotry—attest a role for Indo-Aryan-speakers in establishing their dynasty. The process and result have an intriguing parallel in the formation of the Kassite kingdom in Babylonia, as Frans van Koppen has argued.[56] His analysis identifies three phases of immigration, beginning in the late eighteenth century BC, by different groups of (predominantly) armed men, who variously fought Babylonian forces, were integrated into them, or collaborated with them, leading ultimately to the last group's political takeover and foundation of a new dynasty and kingdom under names belonging to an alien language that few spoke and no one wrote. In the case of both the Kassite kingdom and Mittani, which formed almost simultaneously, knowledge of how to use chariots in warfare (as distinct from using them for display or sport) played a role in the developments that led to their formation. In both cases, van Koppen proposes that "from among a linguistically heterogeneous migrant population . . . one individual group, whose language and especially names . . . became normative for their dynastic successors" rose to power, and the identity ascribed to this group is what we see today.[57] In the one case, the identity ascribed in antiquity was Kassite; in the other case, the modern identification of Mittani's rulers as (Indo-)Aryan, based on the language of their names, obscures our ignorance of how they identified themselves.

Extending the parallel further, in each case the new dynasty was superimposed on an existing political entity. In the case of Mittani, that was the land of the Hurrians that came to be called Hanigalbat. This name, first attested in the form Habingalbat, is neither Hurrian nor Semitic, nor is it Indo-Aryan nor yet Kassite, but it must have emerged from the heterogeneous influx through which elements of the latter two languages were introduced in southwestern Asia.[58] The land that got

---

56. van Koppen 2017.

57. van Koppen 2017: 81. He further postulates that Mittani's founder may have shared in the same cluster of group identities subsumed under Kassite.

58. The proposal of Valério 2011 to read the name as Hani-rabbat is invalidated by the form Habingalbat as well as by other evidence, including spellings with -n

the name Hanigalbat, the region of the Khabur Triangle, had long been inhabited by Hurrians, that is, people who spoke the Hurrian language, who had been forming kingdoms since the third millennium.[59] Like the people of Babylonia, they may now have become host to new immigrants and leaders, but the Hurrian people remained, thus their land and their kings were called the land and kings of the Hurrians. The multiplicity of names for the kingdom has sometimes suggested a multiplicity of referents. In his letters to the pharaoh, however, Tušratta calls his own land Hanigalbat, as well as the Hurrian land, and he calls himself the Hurrian king as well as king of Mittani, confirming that the names Hanigalbat, Hurrian land, and Mittani all had the same referent during the period his dynasty ruled it.

29.4. History and political organization
29.4.1. From proto-history to superpower

In the early second millennium, there were several Hurrian kingdoms along the upper reaches of the Tigris, the Euphrates, and their tributaries. The kingdom of Hatti bumped up against some of them in the seventeenth–sixteenth centuries when it expanded outward from central Anatolia under Hattusili I and Mursili I. The ensuing conflicts generated folk tales as well as entries in royal activity reports. One Hittite composition (CTH 13) features a Hurrian enemy capable of marching armies across Anatolia, but vulnerable to a god-sent plague that killed off its leaders; the king of the Hurrians himself, [. . . -]ruwa, died while overwintering in Arzawa, smitten by the god Agni.[60] Another Hittite tale

---

or -*m* preceding GAL (phonologically unlikely if GAL stood for *rab*) and spellings with KAL. Since the latter originate from different hands in different places (Nuzi, Hattusa, Egypt, and somewhere in Canaan), to explain them as convergent misspellings strains credulity (*pace* Valério 2011: 178).

59. On the antiquity of the Hurrian population in the region, see references in Buccellati 2013.

60. For CTH 13, its date, and references for Agni, the Indo-Aryan name of the god of fire, see de Martino 2003: 127–153; on the text's genre and attribution,

(CTH 17), which features encounters with an anthropophagous community, mentions plural kings of the Hurrians, and names them: Uwanta, Urutitta, Arka[-...], and Uwagazzana.[61] In the parodic tale of the Hittite siege of Uršu (CTH 7), the town's beleaguered ruler is a servant of the (deceased) "son of the Storm-god," apparently meaning the Hurrian king, whose sons are quarreling over kingship and whose troops he seeks to hire.[62] Turning from fictionalized history to fact, at least one Hurrian kingdom, Tigunanu (located somewhere in southeastern Anatolia), was drawn into the orbit of Hatti, as evidenced by the letter Hattusili wrote to its ruler Tuniya (hypocoristic of Tunip-Teššub).[63] In this letter the Hittite king dictates terms to his servant Tuniya, whose city and country he declares to be his own, while also offering to supply him silver and horses should he need them. Another kingdom, Hanigalbat, had meanwhile become synonymous with the Hurrian enemy, who invaded Hatti while Hattusili was campaigning in Arzawa, according to the report of his "Manly Deeds" (CTH 4): the "enemy from Hurri" in the Hittite version of this composition is the "enemy from Hanigalbat" in the Akkadian version.[64]

While in conflict with Hatti, Hanigalbat was in communication—through a translator—with Babylon, then under the rule of Ammi-ṣaduqa.[65] During the reign of Ammi-ṣaduqa's successor Samsu-ditana, Hattusili's grandson Mursili destroyed Halab (Aleppo), seat of a once-great kingdom; then he led his army downriver and attacked

---

see Gilan 2015: 243–248. Besides the king, the Hurrian enemy dead included three military leaders bearing what are probably Indo-Aryan names, Karawani, Parayuna, and Ayuktaeraya; see Kitazumi 2020.

61. On the "Cannibal Text" CTH 17, see Gilan 2015: 262–269 (with references).

62. For CTH 7, see Beckman 1995; Kühne 1999: 207; Gilan 2015: 278–295.

63. Published in Salvini 1994. More tablets from Tigunanu, which were found on the antiquities market, have been published since: George 2013: 101–128, 285–319.

64. See van Koppen 2004: 21 n. 67; Gilan 2015: 219 n. 796.

65. A "translator of the Hanigalbatian army" is mentioned in an unpublished tablet cited from I.J. Gelb in *CAD* T: 229.

Babylon, despoiling the city of its gods and terminating the dynasty of Hammurabi.[66] But the victor was not to enjoy the spoils, for Mursili was assassinated after he returned home to Hattusa. The Kassite dynasty took power in Babylon, and the Hurrian kingdom, presently ruled by the Mittani dynasty, took control of Halab and the other territories Hattusili and Mursili had won in Syria. Thus, the wars Hatti waged in Hurrian country led to a new political order dominated initially by Mittani. Probably the kingdom was already ruled from Waššukanni, since this city appears in a Hittite composition (CTH 12) that recounts Mursili I's attack on Babylon as well as the Hurrian invasion of Hatti.[67]

The earliest known reference to Mittani by that name comes from the tomb autobiography of Amenemhat the clockmaker. He mentions an Egyptian encounter with Mittani that may have taken place many years earlier than the campaign Thutmose I led as far as the Euphrates around 1500 BC (see section 29.2.3). This reference may testify equally to Egypt's reach and to Mittani's consolidation of power. Also from around 1500 BC comes the earliest direct testimony of a king of Mittani (unnamed), in the form of his sealed letter order found at Hammam et-Turkman (see section 29.2.2). By this time Mittani would have seized Halab (Aleppo), displaced its royal family, and acquired hegemony over the lands Halab once ruled, according to the inscription commemorating Idrimi of Alalakh, which was written a century or so later.[68] The inscription begins its story with a "misfortune" that happened in Halab, Idrimi's paternal house, causing his family to flee for refuge with his maternal kin in Emar. This misfortune may have been Mittani's seizure of Halab after the Hittites destroyed the city

---

66. On the course of events, reflected in both Hittite and Babylonian texts, see van Koppen 2017: 71–72. He compresses the chronology unduly, however, making Parattarna of Mittani contemporary with Samsu-ditana of Babylon, when the latter ruled in the sixteenth century BC and Parattarna in the fifteenth century BC.

67. For the fragmentary text of CTH 12, see de Martino 2003: 155–185; and recently Gilan 2015: 248–253.

68. Lauinger 2019 discusses the historical circumstances under which the statue is likely to have been inscribed for Idrimi.

and withdrew (alternatively, it may have been the Hittite destruction). The inscription then recounts how, in the following generation, Idrimi became king in Alalakh, but not before he negotiated peace and submission with Parattarna, "powerful king, king of the Hurrians," who had been hostile to him for seven years. The negotiation reportedly involved citing Idrimi's forefathers' service to the kings of the Hurrians, perhaps referring to cooperation between Halab and the Hurrians prior to Mursili's attack. If Halab's ruling house fled Mittani's takeover thereafter, that would explain why the misfortune that drove Idrimi's family from the city is unspecified.

Idrimi attained kingship, but as Parattarna's subject, and he became king not of Halab (the patrimony the inscription implicitly claims for him) but of its former dependency Alalakh. According to the inscription, he proceeded to undertake a military campaign in "Hatti," probably meaning the frontier of Kizzuwatna, a once and future Hittite ally immediately north of his kingdom. In the aftermath of war, he concluded a parity treaty with Pilliya, king of Kizzuwatna, under the aegis of Parattarna; this treaty (AlT 3) was preserved in the archives of Alalakh (see section 29.3.1). Halab, meanwhile, seems to have been left kingless, reduced to a province under a district governor, if one may extrapolate from later evidence (discussed in section 29.4.2).

By this point we have arrived at the mid-fifteenth century BC, when the expansion of Mittani's power clashed with that of Egypt under Thutmose III. The first Eighteenth Dynasty pharaohs had conquered Canaan and campaigned beyond; after the death of Hatshepsut, Thutmose III set out to enlarge the empire they created. The progress— and regress—of his campaigns can be followed from the annals he caused to be carved at Amun's shrine,[69] supplemented by other inscriptions. His first campaign culminated in the seven-month siege of Megiddo, chosen as a redoubt by the ruler of Qadesh and his allies under the suzerainty of Mittani (Naharina). Victory at Megiddo led to campaigns ever farther north, ultimately reaching the Euphrates, where Thutmose III

---

69. *Urk.* §§647–757.

reports placing a stela beside that of his grandfather, Thutmose I, in his eighth campaign.[70] He claims that his wretched foe, Mittani's ruler, fled before him rather than give battle, but in subsequent years his campaigns reached less and less far north. Evidently Mittani and its subjects did fight the Egyptians, and sometimes won.

During these campaigns Egypt's armies took captive both enemy troops and non-combatants, numbering in the hundreds and thousands. The report of the capture of Megiddo concludes with an exhaustive list of spoil and captives, including about 2,000 horses, 900 chariots, and dozens of the noblemen denoted *maryanni*. More than 700 captives from Naharina are reported for Thutmose III's eighth campaign. The pharaoh's troops, as well as the pharaoh himself, took captives and then showcased them in their own funerary monuments. Pictorial evidence from the reign of Hatshepsut onward illustrates captives from Mittani as a particular type, according to Ellen Morris: corpulent men, with unkempt limp dark or blond hair, a tuft at the front of the head, and a thin beard.[71] Absent comparable self-portraits, the Egyptian stereotype will have to do for visualizing Mittani's fearsome warriors.

Unfortunately, in keeping with Egyptian practice, Thutmose III's inscriptions never name enemy kings. One can only guess that it may have been Parattarna who first confronted this pharaoh, possibly followed by Parsatatar, whose son Sauštatar would then have won the victories that maintained Mittani's dominion and beat back Egypt's advance. That would account for Sauštatar's preeminence in Mittanian tradition. So would his conquest of Assyria, surmised from Šattiwaza's report a century later that Sauštatar despoiled Assyria of a door of silver and gold which he installed in his own palace at Waššukanni (CTH 52; see further discussion in section 29.4.3).

---

70. *Urk.* §§697–698 and §1232.

71. Morris 2014 characterizes this distinctive type based on imagery in about two dozen individuals' tombs near Thebes, dating to the fifteenth and early fourteenth centuries BC.

29.4.2. Organization and governance

Mittani seems to have reached its height in the mid-to-late fifteenth century BC. Scant as contemporaneous sources remain, they illuminate several parts of the realm, supplemented by later sources that fill in the contours somewhat. Mittani's territories now included different types of states or communities, and the sovereign's relations with the subjects varied commensurately. There were subordinate kingdoms such as Alalakh, Arraphe, and Assur; communities governed collectively, with or without a king, such as Baṣiru and Emar; provinces such as, apparently, Halab; and the sovereign kingdom, Hanigalbat. Other than native Hanigalbateans, members of each type of community now had two focuses of political orientation, first their own state and second the imperial kingdom. Few sources disclose the perspective of those who chose neither and sought to remain outside the state.

In the absence of sources pertaining to Hanigalbat itself, virtually nothing can be known about the sovereign kingdom's internal organization. Tablets found elsewhere, however, provide some information about the position of Hanigalbateans as well as the status of "Hanigalbatean" within the realm. Three of the very few extant legal documents issued by Mittani, one apiece from Alalakh, Umm el-Marra, and Tell Brak, concern *hanigalbatūtu*, "Hanigalbatean status."[72] At Alalakh, a man named Irip-Hazi sued the local ruler, Niqmepa, before the imperial king, Sauštatar, claiming that he had *hanigalbatūtu*, that is, he was a subject of Hanigalbat, not of Alalakh. Sauštatar decided against Irip-Hazi, who had to return to the service of Niqmepa. While Irip-Hazi lost his claim to *hanigalbatūtu*, the fact that he sued indicates that the possibility was real, and other such claims may have succeeded. The two documents from Umm el-Marra and Tell Brak each record a man's release of his dependents to *hanigalbatūtu*, an act done before and sealed by the king of Mittani, the authority in charge of granting this status. In each case the man must himself have possessed *hanigalbatūtu*, in order to confer it on his dependents. At Tell Brak, lying within Hanigalbat, one Yabbi

---

72. On these three tablets, see von Dassow 2014: 23–24.

had his son by a concubine elevated to his own status, and made him heir to his property. At Umm el-Marra, in the district of Halab, one Gubi obtained *hanigalbatūtu* for a woman, her children, and a man to whom he bequeathed property (unfortunately the scribe did not record their relationships). This family may have had to travel far to obtain an audience with the king and a tablet bearing his seal, authorizing their new status.

Taken together, these three documents show that the status of Hanigalbatean, or citizenship of Hanigalbat, was not available exclusively to native free-born residents of the sovereign kingdom but could be extended to residents of subject realms. They moreover indicate that Mittani's rule involved relations not only between sovereign and subordinate rulers but between sovereign and people.

The simplest relation of sovereign to subject state is a hierarchical dyad, with each party represented in the person of a king. For Mittani, this kind of relation is most clearly visible in the sources from Alalakh and Arraphe, which attest imperial regulation of the subject kingdom's affairs as well as the integration of the subject with the superordinate kingdom. The two corpora differ considerably: whereas the Alalakh tablets derive exclusively from the capital, and almost entirely from the state's own archives, the Arraphe tablets derive mostly from the subsidiary town of Nuzi, and mostly from family archives. Accordingly, the much smaller Alalakh corpus includes proportionally more documents issued by Mittani. They are concentrated in the reign of Niqmepa, son of Idrimi, and they reach into the kingdom's internal affairs while addressing its external relations, as follows.[73]

To start with, the kingdoms of Alalakh and Kizzuwatna had both become subjects of Mittani during the reign of Parattarna, under whose oversight Idrimi concluded a treaty with Pilliya (AlT 3). A dispute arose between the two kingdoms in the next generation, when Niqmepa sued his counterpart Sunaššura over the town of Alawari. The probable context is that Niqmepa was levying men of his kingdom for military service. His dispute with Kizzuwatna was arbitrated by Saustatar, who decided

---

73. See in more detail von Dassow 2008: 45–55; 2014: 15–16.

that Alawari fell under Niqmepa's jurisdiction (AlT 14); such setbacks as this may have provoked Sunaššura to switch allegiance to Hatti (see section 29.3.1). It was probably in the same context of a military levy that Irip-Hazi sued Niqmepa, claiming *hanigalbatūtu*, and lost (AlT 13), with the likely result that Irip-Hazi was conscripted for duty in Alalakh's army. Mittani's management of relations between Kizzuwatna and Alalakh may also be attested by a letter the king (perhaps Sauštatar) addressed to one Utti, ordering him to release Niqmepa's asses toll-free, a letter that ended up in Alalakh's archives (AlT 108). In this period, Mittani's scribes tended to be laconic in the extreme, sparing any information already known to the persons concerned, like their titles and the sovereign's name. Accordingly, the writer of this curt letter-order includes nothing to tell us who the addressee was. It is likely, however, that he was the same man as Utti, contemporary of Sunaššura, who features as proprietor of several villages in a later Hittite text detailing past grants in support of the cult of Išhara of Neriša, apparently on Kizzuwatna's mountainous eastern frontier (CTH 641.1).[74] Niqmepa's donkey caravan would have been arrested while traversing Utti's territory to get to Alalakh from the north. The two neighboring realms may have had many such grievances with each other.

Relations linking superior and subordinate kingdoms were supported by an administrative infrastructure, direct evidence of which is scant but clear in the Alalakh archives. Three letter-orders from the Mittanian official Tiriṣ-ra survive (AlT 110, 111, and 112): one instructs Niqmepa to seize certain men and send them along under guard, another regulates the disposition of a man's property, and a third orders Niqmepa to give a plaintiff, who has won his suit before the king (of Mittani), his women. A record of "men going to Mittani" (AlT 224), listing numbers of men from various towns or for various tasks, registers three for Tiriṣ-ra (his security detail?), suggesting that this official not only wrote

---

74. The text of CTH 641.1 is available via the *Hethitologie Portal Mainz*: http://www.hethport.uni-wuerzburg.de/hetkonk/hetkonk_abfrage.php?c=641 (last accessed August 1, 2020). For the most recent discussion, see Trameri 2020: 292–297.

to Alalakh but came to visit. The arrival of a visitor from Waššukanni named Haburu is reported in another tablet (AlT 90).[75]

Evidence for the empire's financial infrastructure is exiguous. One would assume that Mittani demanded tribute from kingdoms under its rule, but support for such an assumption is hard to find in the Alalakh tablets. A tablet listing amounts of silver from three regions of Alalakh's kingdom, totaling 2,394 shekels (AlT 395), has been interpreted as a record of tribute collected for Mittani, but more likely it records the kingdom's internal revenue collection.[76]

A much more elaborate document is the treaty Niqmepa concluded with Ir-Teššub, king of Tunip, upstream on the Orontes (AlT 2). Both treaty partners declared their allegiance to the "king of the Hurrians," i.e., Mittani. The treaty provides for restitution of spoils (including captives), rendition of fugitives, and regulation of traffic between the two kingdoms, among other issues. Its contents indicate that it was drawn up at the conclusion of a war, which both parties were free to fight, although they then had to treat with each other as Mittani's subjects. Perhaps the reason the king of the Hurrians is not named is that the treaty was meant to outlast any particular occupant of the throne, or perhaps the throne was vacant at the time, Sauštatar having died and a successor yet to be inaugurated. The treaty did not last, anyway: Alalakh renewed hostilities with Tunip during the reign of Niqmepa's successor Ilimilimma, according to the later treaty between Tunip and Hatti (CTH 135).[77]

Turning to Arraphe, among the thousands of tablets found in the kingdom, one tablet only originates from Mittani, that being the "Sauštatar Letter" (see section 29.3.1). In this letter, the imperial king informs the local king that he has reallocated towns between one Ukke and Amminaya, consort of the crown prince of Arraphe. Numerous records, however, disclose a close and multidimensional relationship

---

75. See Durand 2002: 61–62.

76. See von Dassow 2008: 55, with n. 129–131.

77. See von Dassow 2008: 51–54, 60–61, and for the text of AlT 2, http://www.etana.org/node/577 (last accessed March 6, 2020).

between the subordinate and the sovereign kingdom, which is always called Hanigalbat.[78] People and goods circulated between the two lands, Hanigalbateans took up residence in Arraphe, Arrapheans in Hanigalbat, and their judiciaries collaborated in handling legal affairs that involved each other's citizens. Arraphe hosted visiting dignitaries, troops, and entertainers from Hanigalbat, feeding them and if applicable their horses, putting chariots at their disposal if warranted. One imagines that Arrapheans on official business at the imperial court were supported likewise (or more lavishly). While extant texts do not attest payment of tribute, they do reveal the role of Hanigalbat in Arraphe's defense. Notably, Hanigalbatean troops and chariots were deployed to Arraphe in the mid-fourteenth century BC when both Mittani and Arraphe confronted Assyrian attacks—unsuccessfully; the result was the destruction of cities like Nuzi, preserving their archives for us to find and read.[79] These include the dossier of a Hanigalbatean officer named Ila-nišu, son of Hapira, who dwelt in Nuzi with part of his family, exemplifying the integration between the imperial kingdom and Arraphe. Ila-nišu's affairs are documented by tablets of his that were stowed, along with other people's, in the local temple of Ištar. Other tablets kept in the same place include a list of sixty *martiyanni*-men from Hanigalbat (*martiyanni* being effectively synonymous with *maryanni*; see section 29.5.1).[80] Moreover, a tablet that may originate from the capital, Arraphe, details work on the fortifications of Nuzi undertaken by men of Hanigalbat.[81]

---

78. Texts attesting Arraphe's relations with Hanigalbat were collected by Zaccagnini 1979. See also von Dassow 2014: 17; de Martino 2018: 42 (but note that the claim about tribute is not supported by the sources).

79. Babylonia is often credited with attacking Arraphe as well; see Maidman 2011: 87–98, with references therein. Maidman argues that only Assyria made war on Arraphe, an interpretation challenged by Zaccagnini 2020: 171–185. Nevertheless, Assyria was the ultimate victor.

80. For the dossier of Ila-nišu, son of Hapira, see Brigitte Lion in Lion and Stein 2016: 39–66; the list of *martiyanni* is text no. 56 in the same volume.

81. Lion 2010.

Not all the communities or states encompassed in Mittani's territories were organized as monarchies. While in the case of subject kingdoms Mittani's king dealt with the local king, he could deal directly with the people of a self-governing community. One of the two tablets found at Tell Bazi reads, "Sauštatar the king granted (the town) Baidali to the people of Baṣiru"; that is the entire text of the document, which Sauštatar sealed (figure 29.4). The other tablet records Artatama I's grant of another town to the people of Baṣiru, and its text is longer only because it describes the town's location. Albeit two texts form a slender basis for generalization, these two suggest that Baṣiru's communal polity survived and even thrived under Mittani's rule. This is one instance of a robust tradition of collective governance that flourished in the Middle Euphrates region, taking various forms; other instances include Ekalte (Tell Mumbaqat), Emar, and probably Azu. Where a corporate body such as a senate governed, it could vest authority in a king, who represented the community in its foreign affairs and thus became its liaison to imperial power. This model of collective governance is best documented by the sources from Emar and its vicinity.

Emar was governed by a senate, with a presiding king, in a polity that allowed citizens a significant role in their state's affairs. Indeed, more than once, citizens stepped in to help their community cope with imperial rule. The few documents from Emar that reflect its subjection to Mittani include the only extant sources that clearly attest the empire's exaction of tribute (Hurrian *arana*), and the amounts suggest it may have been imposed after the city resisted subjugation. In the early fourteenth century BC, when Ir'ib-Baʿal was king, the city of Emar sold property in order to raise the 30,000 shekels of silver and 700 shekels of gold demanded as tribute, and did so again to meet a subsequent tribute demand; one imagines the buyers were concerned citizens. Subsequently, when Ir'ib-Baʿal's son Li'mi-šarru was king, he presented his four daughters to the king of the Hurrians, along with 4,000 shekels silver and 400 shekels gold, but one Ir'ib-Baʿal, son of Lala, paid off the king of the Hurrians, so the local king got his daughters and the money back. The king and the city of Emar rewarded their benefactor Ir'ib-Baʿal with a priesthood in perpetuity. Several generations later the diviner

Mašrû-hamiṣ was likewise rewarded, after his divination apparently saved Emar when it was besieged by Hurrian troops.[82]

Other models of imperial rule appear to have been implemented in some places. In the land of Hana, a sort of dual kingship may be in evidence in the tablets from Terqa that record transactions done by (or under) both the local and the imperial king; the nature of this hegemonic relationship may become clearer with publication of the tablets (see section 29.2.2). Halab (Aleppo), formerly the seat of a great kingdom, may have been reduced to a province, as already mentioned, although the evidence is scant: a tablet from Alalakh records an extradition overseen by Arnuwar, *halṣoġli* of Halab, whose Hurro-Akkadian title means "district governor," and whose counterpart at Alalakh was the king, Niqmepa.[83] If Halab was governed by a *halṣoġli* after Mittani's conquest, the city apparently acquired a king again in time to ally with Tudhaliya I toward 1400 BC, only to betray its new Hittite ally by returning to Hanigalbat, according to the Aleppo Treaty (CTH 75, concluded a century later). The district (*halṣu*) of Halab surely included nearby Umm el-Marra, whose residents went directly to Šuttarna II to apply for Hanigalbatean citizenship, and it apparently extended north to the vicinity of Başiru, to whose people Artatama I granted a town in the district of Halab.

Finally, the form of dominion Mittani exercised over Assur is entirely obscure. Based on Šattiwaza's reference to Sauštatar's spoliation of Assur in the prologue of his treaty with Suppiluliuma (CTH 52), it is assumed that Assur was subject to Mittani from Sauštatar's reign until sometime in Tušratta's reign. Under Aššur-uballiṭ's rule, Assyria emerged from the Mittani Empire as from a chrysalis, becoming independent, then growing into a great power, and ultimately conquering its former overlord. Aššur-uballiṭ's predecessors, however, left scarce testimony about the period during which they would have ruled under Mittani's sovereignty. Each of them, going back to Puzur-Aššur III, ca. 1500 BC, reports restoring

82. For the sources, their interpretation, and date, see von Dassow 2014: 17–18 and Torrecilla and Cohen 2018: 152–154 (with references).

83. AlT 101; see von Dassow 2014: 20–21 with n. 27–30.

or adding to walls of Assur that Puzur-Aššur built.[84] This wall-building activity need not bespeak independence, for Mittani did not prohibit subject kingdoms like Alalakh and Arraphe from fortifying their cities (nor from pursuing war with their neighbors). But no extant source illuminates Assur's subjection to Mittani.

29.4.3. From hegemony to humiliation

While on campaign in the southern Levant, late in the fifteenth century BC, Amenhotep II captured a messenger of the ruler of Naharina who had a letter tied around his neck, according to an inscription of his at Memphis.[85] The inscription contains no word on what the letter said or to whom it was addressed. But soon enough, envoys of Mittani arrived at Amenhotep's court bearing gifts—a miracle effected by the will of Amun, declares his inscription at Karnak.[86] This miracle coincided with Hatti's resurgence during the reign of Tudhaliya I, who enlarged his kingdom through both military and diplomatic means. Mittani lost Kizzuwatna when Sunaššura took his kingdom into the Hittite fold, and temporarily lost Halab, which Tudhaliya then destroyed for its perfidy.[87] The citadel of Alalakh was also destroyed at about this time, an event often attributed to Tudhaliya, although it could have been the work of a closer enemy—such as Tunip, which had a *casus belli* according to the treaty it eventually made with Hatti.[88] In any case, Hittite aggression implicated the entire northern Levant.

Mittani's embassy to Egypt met a good reception. The former enemies made peace, began exchanging luxury goods as gifts, and secured their alliance with a series of marriages. First, Thutmose IV married a daughter

---

84. Grayson 1987: A.0.61.1–A.0.73.1. See also Lion 2011: 154–157.

85. *Urk.* §1304.

86. *Urk.* §1326.

87. CTH 41 (see section 29.3.1); CTH 75.

88. On the destruction of both castle and palace at Alalakh (Level IV), ca. 1400 BC, see Akar 2019 and von Dassow 2020. For Alalakh and Tunip, see section 29.4.2.

of Artatama I; then Amenhotep III married Šuttarna II's daughter Kelu-
Heba, and issued a commemorative scarab to celebrate the occasion, in
his tenth regnal year; perhaps two decades later, he also married Tušratta's
daughter Tadu-Heba (see section 29.3.1, and further discussion later in
the present section). Amenhotep III not only received two Mittanian
brides, he received two visits from the Hurrian goddess Šawuška, according to a letter of Tušratta (EA 23). Her cult image would have traveled
from Mittani to Egypt and back during the reign of Šuttarna II; when
Amenhotep requested that the goddess come again, Tušratta responded
favorably, rephrasing the request as the wish of Šawuška herself.

What was happening on Mittani's western front during the early
fourteenth century BC is obscure. Toward the middle of the century
Tudhaliya II (father of Suppiluliuma I) campaigned widely, including one campaign to Mount Nanni (Anti-Cassius), which would have
encroached further into territory Mittani held.[89] The sparse sources
have lately been augmented by the discovery at Kayalıpınar, the site
of Samuha, of a tablet fragment containing a historical narrative in
Hurrian.[90] Tudhaliya II resided for a time at Samuha, and the tablet's
palaeography fits the period of his reign. The text, partly composed in
the first person, narrates missions undertaken in and near Kizzuwatna
by two personages named Ehli-Tenu and Ili-Šarruma, both otherwise
unknown. What survives and can be understood of the text tells a dramatic tale: together, our two heroes traveled into the mountains and took
the way down to the sea; Ehli-Tenu ascended Mount Zallurbi, descended
to Mukiš (the territory of Alalakh), and proceeded to Mittani, while
Ili-Šarruma apparently went to Winuwanda (in eastern Kizzuwatna)
to do something else. After a passage in which the first-person narra-
tor relates an episode that involves a woman named Ammi-lu-šarra, the
storm-god Teššub, the entire pantheon, and a Hittite, the story returns

---

89. Tudhaliya II's campaign to Mount Nanni is reported in a fragment attributed
    (perhaps incorrectly) to the Deeds of Suppiluliuma; see del Monte 2009: 2, 5–7.

90. On this fragment from Kayalıpınar (published by Wilhelm 2019 as KpT 1.11)
    see section 29.2.3, and von Dassow 2020: 203. The interpretation of the text may
    change substantially with further progress in our knowledge of Hurrian.

to Winuwanda, now the focus of military action, in which Ehli-Tenu and Ili-Šarruma reappear and mention is made of the goddess Hebat (Heba) of Kizzuwatna. The fragment preserves no clear indication of the narrative's historical setting, and its genre is a mystery. Given that it was composed in Hurrian and relates events in Kizzuwatna, the story probably originated in Kizzuwatna; then the text was brought to or written at Samuha during Tudhaliya II's residence there. The likeliest context for the events narrated is the period when Kizzuwatna switched allegiance from Mittani to Hatti, during Tudhaliya I's reign.

Whatever was happening inside Mittani during this period, it eventuated in the fracture of the ruling dynasty. Sometime during the reign of Amenhotep III, Šuttarna II's son and successor Artaššumara was assassinated; sometime thereafter Tušratta, another son of Šuttarna, was enthroned. In the interim, a rival king took the throne under the name Artatama (II), and developed alliances with Hatti, newly independent Assyria, and the land of Alše to the northwest. But most of the action takes place off stage, from the perspective afforded us by the sources, so how all this came about can only be guessed.[91] The principal sources for Mittani in the mid-fourteenth century BC are as follows: the letters of Tušratta to Egypt, supplemented by occasional references elsewhere in the Amarna correspondence; the letters found at Qatna; the pair of treaties Suppiluliuma and Šattiwaza concluded in the 1330s, supplemented by treaties Hatti imposed on lands it wrested from Mittani; and certain passages in retrospective accounts written under Mursili II.

Suppiluliuma introduces his treaty with Šattiwaza (CTH 51) by referring to the treaty he made with Artatama (II), while Tušratta introduces himself to his "brother" (peer) Amenhotep III by referring to the assassination of Artaššumara that preceded his accession. Specifically, Tušratta writes, "When I sat on the throne of my father, I was young, and Pirhi, doing a bad deed to my country, had slain his lord" (EA 17). It

---

91. For a good guess, see Wilhelm 2015: 69–70 (details like the elderliness of Artatama II cannot be verified). His reconstruction of the course of events resulting in Hatti's conquest of Mittani is adopted here; see Wilhelm 2012 and 2015, with references to different views there.

must have been Artaššumara whom Pirhi slew, but who Pirhi was—and whether this is the correct reading of his name—no source discloses; he might have been the rival king before he took the throne name Artatama. In the treaties between Suppiluliuma and Šattiwaza, Artatama is titled "king of Hurri(-land)" while Tušratta is titled "king of Mittani," as he is in his own letters; the differentiation may have been specious, however, since Tušratta also refers to his country as the Hurrian land, and no evidence indicates how Artatama titled himself. Nor is it known where he resided. Artatama's son Šuttarna (III) evidently took over the palace at Waššukanni after the assassination of Tušratta (reported in CTH 51), for Šattiwaza opens his treaty with Suppiluliuma (CTH 52) by recounting how Šuttarna impoverished the palace that Tušratta built, exhausting its treasure by paying tribute to Assyria and Alše, returning the gold and silver door Sauštatar plundered from Waššukanni to Assyria, and committing further depredations against the Hurrian people.[92] These depredations include impaling noblemen at Taide, which must already have been a royal residence, but if Artatama ruled from there, he and Tušratta were very close neighbors.

In the letter quoted here, Tušratta concludes the passage about his troubled accession by assuring the pharaoh that "I slew the slayers of my brother Artaššumara, together with everything of theirs" (EA 17). Having thus cleared the way to reopen relations with Egypt, Tušratta gives a vague report of a Hittite attack that he repulsed—probably an encounter with the invading forces of Tudhaliya II—and presents a selection of the spoil he took from Hatti, besides other gifts for his "brother" the king of Egypt, as well as for his sister Kelu-Heba. Apparently, Amenhotep III accepted this demonstration of Tušratta's bona fides as king of Mittani, and he proceeded to request his daughter in marriage. Tušratta assented (EA 19). There follow several letters concerning Tušratta's preparation

---

92. Most translations of CTH 52 have Artatama doing his country wrong and exhausting the palace's treasure before his son Šuttarna did. These lines are read differently by Devecchi 2015: 254–255, with n. 1, who (following Wilhelm) understands the text to say, "Šuttarna, son of Artatama the king, changed the [...] of the land of Mittani, he did not act correctly with regard to Artatama, his father. He ruined the palace of the king. . . ."

and dispatch of his daughter Tadu-Heba, together with caravan-loads of gifts, and his reciprocal requests for gold, culminating with the long letter in Hurrian (EA 24; figure 29.2). He wants gold to decorate his grandfather's mausoleum, gold for the bride-price of his daughter, and a golden statue of his daughter. He effusively declares that his daughter's union with the king of Egypt will unite Hanigalbat and Egypt as one (EA 20; the Hurrian land and Egypt are conjoined more elaborately in EA 24: §15). His letters overdo the rhetoric of love and friendship, and the inventories of his gifts show that he invested considerable wealth in the relationship—chariots, horses, and their furnishings; weaponry, including iron weapons; shoes and clothes in many styles; accessories and jewelry, including iron jewelry; toiletries and perfume; ornate vessels and utensils of precious materials and fine craftsmanship—the lists go on and on.[93]

Egypt did not value the relationship equally. The pharaoh did send caravans to Hanigalbat, charging his vassals in Canaan to protect them, as attested by a letter from one such vassal (EA 255). But the gold that the pharaoh sent Tušratta was paltry, so paltry as to embarrass him before his whole court (EA 20), nothing like what he had sent his father. Nevertheless, Tušratta agreed to send the goddess Šawuška of Nineveh on a return visit to Egypt, urging his brother king to honor her ten times more than he had done in the time of his father, then send her back (EA 23). Evidently Šawuška did return home, where Tušratta could speak with her about that golden statue his brother was to make, which would be inscribed with these words: "This cast gold image is Tadu-Heba, daughter of Tušratta, lord of Mittani, whom he gave as wife to Immoriya, lord of Egypt. And Immoriya made a cast gold image and lovingly sent it to Tušratta" (EA 24: §25).[94] By honoring Tušratta with much

---

93. This summary is drawn from the inventories (EA 22, 25). Gifts also accompanied every letter.

94. Immoriya is a spelling of Amenhotep III's throne name, Neb-maat-Re, also spelled Nibmuareya and other ways in Tušratta's letters (kings of Egypt were normally called by their throne names in antiquity). The passage quoted (EA 24: iii 103–107) appears to give the wording of a text to be inscribed on the statue, as noted by Giorgieri 2000: 276–277, with n. 292.

gold, the king of Egypt would exalt him in the eyes of his fellow great kings. But the requested gifts, in the requested quantity, were not forthcoming. Someone has been speaking evil of Tušratta, some adversary has denounced him to his brother, who should not listen to these evil words (EA 24: §27).[95]

Things only got worse with the death of Amenhotep III and accession of Amenhotep IV, who soon transitioned to Akhenaten—and, fortunately for us, moved to his new city Akhetaten (modern Tell el-Amarna), where these letters were eventually left behind. Tušratta resorted to writing to Akhenaten's mother Tiye, pleading with her to inform her son of his father's promises (EA 26); in this letter he also puts his wife Yuni in touch with Tiye. There were to be two solid gold statues cast, one of Tušratta and one of his daughter, but Akhenaten has sent gilt wooden statues. Akhenaten should ask his mother Tiye about his father's promises (EA 27, 28). What does Tušratta have to do to get him to fulfill?—such a question is implicit in his verbose, plaintive letter offering a retrospective on the felicitous relations Egypt and Mittani had enjoyed during the reigns of his father and grandfather (EA 29). But the pharaoh must have assessed this king of Mittani, noted the existence of his rival Artatama II and the strength of his antagonist Suppiluliuma, and concluded that he should place his bets elsewhere.

What Tušratta's letters do not mention is Hatti's aggressive encroachment on his realm (or the share of it he still held), which escalated into a full-scale assault around the time Akhenaten and his family were settling into their new residence at Akhetaten. In the prologue to his treaty with Šattiwaza (CTH 51), Suppiluliuma represents this conflict as an altercation Tušratta started out of belligerence, compelling the Hittite king to invade the lands of Išuwa and Alše in the north, reaching even Waššukanni—whence, however, Tušratta fled, avoiding battle—then turning south to conquer Aleppo and neighboring kingdoms—Mukiš,

---

95. In this passage, some words are attributed to one Parattuiranna (EA 24: iv 12), otherwise unattested, whose name sounds Indo-Aryan. It is tempting to see Parattuiranna as a member of the rival branch of Mittani's royal family, who denounced Tušratta, but the text does not clearly support this interpretation.

Niya, Nuhašše, eventually Qatna, and even Kinza (Qadesh), which had not been his target (being in Egypt's territory) but whose king offered him battle—with the result that, "because of King Tušratta's hubris, in one year I took possession of all these lands and brought them to Hatti. I extended my territory from Mount Lebanon to the other bank of the Euphrates." Rib-Hadda, ruler of Byblos, the pharaoh's most voluble vassal, mentioned these developments to his lord, writing, "May the king be informed that the king of Hatti has seized all the lands (that were) subject to the king of Mittani, king of Nahrima, land of great kings" (EA 75: ll. 35–40).

The conquest of all those lands did not really take only a year.[96] Rather it required several years of warfare to secure the submission of kingdom after kingdom, as some fought Hittite subjugation, some sought Egypt's intervention, and some (re)turned to Mittani when the beleaguered realm endeavored to reassert itself. Tušratta, giving up at last on his alliance with Egypt, invaded the northernmost lands of its empire—which were the southernmost lands Hittite armies had yet reached—all the way to the coastal city of Ṣumur; so reports our informant Rib-Hadda (EA 85). The invasion was also reported to the pharaoh by the otherwise unknown Tehu-Teššub (EA 58). Ṣumur had been the seat of an Egyptian commissioner and became part of the kingdom of Amurru, which now, under its ruler Abdi-Aširta, became a tribute-paying subject of Mittani (EA 86, 90, 95, 101).[97] Thus Mursili II could later claim that his father, Suppiluliuma, took Amurru away from Mittani, not from Egypt.[98] But

---

96. For alternative reconstructions, each proceeding from the observation that the claim to have conquered them all "in one year" is rhetorical, see Cordani 2011 and Wilhelm 2012; 2015.

97. Rib-Hadda, again our main informant, suggests to the pharaoh that he may do the same, according to Rainey's reading of a fragmentary passage of EA 95 (Rainey 2014: 534–535). Cf. Singer 1991: 146–147, who at that time did not believe the sources claiming Amurru submitted to Mittani (and did believe the Egyptians executed Abdi-Aširta, an idea others refute; e.g., Wilhelm 2015: 75).

98. The initial join of fragments attesting to this claim by Mursili II was identified and published by Jared Miller (2007); see Miller 2017: 102 (with n. 17) for subsequent references. Miller has since identified further joins, showing that

Amurru's subjection to Mittani was provisional. Abdi-Aširta wrote to the king of Egypt urging him to send troops and complaining that his territory was threatened by kings subject to the king of the Hurrians (EA 60), even as he was (about to be) paying tribute to the latter. His son Aziru, still professing his loyalty to the pharaoh, threw his allegiance to Hatti.[99] Amurru's northern neighbor Qatna experienced similar contrary pressures, which its leaders managed less successfully. Qatna had been ruled by Addu-nirari for about half a century, apparently in relative peace.[100] Addu-nirari was succeeded by Idadda, son of Ula-šuda (perhaps from a different family), around the time of Mittani's intervention in the region. The city then came under intense pressure from the Hittites, as we read in the letters to Idadda that were found along with the remains of an administrative archive in Qatna's destroyed palace.

These five letters, like five stills from an action-packed movie, give us a glimpse of Hittite conquest from the standpoint of the conquered. They were sent by three different correspondents: Taguwe, ruler of nearby Niya, who had already submitted to Suppiluliuma; Hannutti, a general in the Hittite army; and Šarrupše, (one of the) ruler(s) of Nuhašše, who submitted alternately to the Hittite and Hurrian kings and fled the wrath of each in turn. All three correspondents employed scribes who liberally blended their spoken Hurrian into the Akkadian language of writing, which makes the letters difficult for us to understand, but what comes through clearly is that Idadda and the people of Qatna are

---

(following an insight of Itamar Singer's) the fragments belong to the Plague Prayer to the Assembly of the Gods (Jared Miller, personal communication, May 2017).

99. The sources for Aziru's career are assembled and interpreted in Singer 1991: 148–158.

100. So Bottéro (1949: 32) inferred from the series of temple inventories excavated at Qatna, according to which Addu-nirari reigned for at least forty-five years. Richter argues that Addu-nirari of Qatna, now attested also by a tablet found in the new excavations (TT 6), must be the same as Addu-nirari of Nuhašše (Richter and Lange 2012: 158, with n. 28); Wilhelm 2012: 239 n. 49 sees no basis for this identification. On Addu-nirari of Nuhašše, see later in this section.

being cajoled and threatened to submit to the Hittites.[101] Taguwe writes to Idadda as his "brother" (TT 1, 2), informing him of the disposition and movements of the Hittite king and his general Hannutti, as well as other matters, including dealings with the Suteans, whom Taguwe has urged, "Protect my brother Idadda until the army that is on the march reaches him" (TT 2: 15–17). He conveys his majesty the Hittite king's message that when it (? the army?) arrives in Qatna, "I shall not release you" (TT 1: 15–16), advises him to speak to the people of Qatna, warning that once the Hittite king seizes lands that vacillate (?) he will not let go, yet also tells him not to worry (TT 2: 43–55; also TT 1: 23–24: "Don't you worry your heart"). Taguwe and Hannutti jointly address a letter to Idadda and the nobility (*maryannina*), conveying the instruction of his majesty to fortify Qatna in advance of his arrival (which administrative records indicate was indeed done), and—Taguwe adds—not to worry, troops are en route to protect Qatna, but do read this tablet to the nobility (TT 3; see section 29.5.1). Hannutti separately addresses a long harangue to Idadda, telling him to assemble the nobility of Qatna and have them hear it:

> Thus [says] his majesty the king, my lord: "You are doing what Šarrupše did! Šarrupše spoke with the king of Hurri-land, then he came to me and he said, 'Save me!' I sent him help and Šaggapi saved him, and now I myself came and he opened the gate before me. When Šarrupše seized my hem, who plundered his fields?" (TT 4: 7–20)

There follows a recital of aggressions perpetrated by neighboring realms, consequent on either Šarrupše's submission to Suppiluliuma or his treachery, and a fresh admonition not to do likewise—because "you know that Mittani is gone" (TT 4: 34–35). Hannutti's harangue continues with a passage that refers to the fate of (now-subjugated) Aleppo,

---

101. TT 1–5; see Richter's *editio princeps* in Richter and Lange 2012: 44–75. My understanding of these texts differs at points from Richter's, and the summaries offered here are both somewhat loose and very uncertain.

Niya, and Mukiš, and closes with a warning about the prospect of nearby Kinza (Qadesh) attacking Qatna.

The two-faced Šarrupše, too, writes to Idadda, addressing him as his lord and father (TT 5). He covers many subjects—what happened in the town of Armatte (also mentioned by both Taguwe and Hannutti, TT 2: 39–42 and TT 3: 13–19), an incident involving the gods of Niya and the gods of "my father" (Idadda), Hannutti's entry into the land of Arazi, chariots and troops of Hatti, activities of the Suteans—then protests, "My lord, you say, 'Šarrupše does not speak truly to me!' But how could I not tell my lord the truth!" (TT 5: 55–59). In closing, Šarrupše assures Idadda that he is coming, and "my lord, you will see how the fortified positions of Hurri-land fight, indeed you, my lord, will see" (TT 5: 60–65).[102]

Idadda may have bowed to Hittite pressure, and to Suppiluliuma, to no avail. Akizzi replaced him as ruler of Qatna and restored the city to the Egyptian fold. He wrote several letters to Akhenaten, whom he—alone among vassal rulers—addressed by name.[103] Akizzi professes his and his city's eternal loyalty to Egypt (EA 52); in a fragmentary passage, he may also assure him of the loyalty of Addu-nirari, (another) ruler of Nuhašše (alongside Šarrupše).[104] Addu-nirari also wrote to the king of Egypt himself, avowing that he remained a faithful subject and refused the treaty offered by the king of Hatti (EA 51). Akizzi urges the pharaoh to send troops to secure the country against aggression perpetrated by Hatti and by neighboring realms, above all Qadeš, that were operating as Hittite proxies (EA 53, 55). He also passes on word that kings in the

---

102. The scribe has a habit of repeating in Hurrian something he has already written in Akkadian ("you will see"), not by way of glossing it, but for emphasis.

103. His throne name, that is. Akizzi's letters include EA 52–56, and perhaps EA 57. In EA 53 and 55, Akizzi addresses the king of Egypt as Namhurya (variant of Naphurureya, throne name of Amenhotep IV, as transcribed in cuneiform), "son of the sun."

104. The land of Nuhašše was ruled by a plurality of kings, according to some texts (e.g., CTH 45, 62). According to Rainey's reading, in EA 53: 24–29 Akizzi declares that Addu-nirari, king of Nuhašše, is hostile to Hatti and loyal to Egypt (Rainey 2014: 392, 1396).

land of Mittani were hostile to the king of Hatti.[105] So they were: besides Qatna, Mukiš, Niya, and Nuhašše sought to cast off the newly imposed Hittite yoke.[106] But if Akhenaten did send troops to save his beleaguered would-be subjects, they came too late.[107] Presently Qatna was destroyed and, as Hannutti had observed, Mittani was gone.

By then, Tušratta had been assassinated and Šuttarna III had taken over the royal residence at Waššukanni. Mittani had already lost Arraphe to Assyria, Šuttarna's ally. Suppiluliuma could proceed unhindered in subjugating Mittani's erstwhile subjects west of the Euphrates, confident that Šuttarna would preserve the treaty his father, Artatama, had made with Hatti. Meanwhile, according to Šattiwaza's retrospective account, Šuttarna set about eliminating internal opposition to his rule, targeting members of the nobility as well as Tušratta's branch of the royal family (CTH 52: §2). Agi-Teššub, presumably a scion of the latter, fled to Babylonia, whose king turned out to have no use for an extra prince of Mittani. Tušratta's son Keli-Teššub, the future puppet king Šattiwaza, fled to Hatti and had better luck. Most interpretations have Šattiwaza going to Babylonia, too, before fleeing for his life from either Agi-Teššub or the Babylonian king. This is not, however, what the text actually says. Elena Devecchi offers a more straightforward interpretation, reading CTH 52: §2 alongside CTH 51: §6, to wit: the story of Agi-Teššub's flight to Babylonia is inserted by way of contrast with that of Šattiwaza to Hatti; the latter never went to Babylonia and it was Šuttarna who—logically—sought to kill him.[108]

---

105. EA 56: ll. 36–42 (according to Moran 1992) or EA 54: ll. 38–43 (according to Rainey 2014, whose commentary neglects to explain this discrepancy).

106. Their rebellion, reported in various ways in CTH 45, 46, 47, 49, 51, and 53, would have followed Suppiluliuma's initially successful subjugation. See Wilhelm 2012: 237–241 for analysis of the narrative of CTH 51 in light of the other sources.

107. For the evidence that an Egyptian campaign was planned under Akhenaten, see Rainey 2014: 28–30.

108. One manuscript of CTH 51 has Šuttarna, where another erroneously has Šutatarra; see Devecchi 2015: 247 n. 3 and 256 n. 1 and 2 (with references).

Šattiwaza found Suppiluliuma at the Marassanta River, fell at his feet, and found grace. In his words,

> When I, Prince Šattiwaza, arrived in the presence of the Great King, I had [only] three chariots, two Hurrians and two servants who departed with me, plus the one set of clothes that I was wearing, and naught else. But the Great King took pity on me and gave me chariots plated with gold (CTH 52: §4 obv. 31–32)

and much else. Suppiluliuma could use a refugee with a valid claim to Mittani's throne. He proposed to adopt Šattiwaza as his son and place him on that throne, to which Šattiwaza responded by suggesting that he be appointed as successor of Artatama, in place of Šuttarna, who (he claimed) maltreated Mittani; that way the king of Hatti would not be displacing the line of Artatama (CTH 52: §3), to whom he was bound by treaty. This suggestion evidently suited Suppiluliuma, who proclaimed,

> When his son conspired with his servants he killed his father, King Tušratta. And when King Tušratta died, the Storm-god decided the case of Artatama, and his son restored the dead Artatama to life. All the land of Mittani went to ruin; Assyria and the land of Alše divided it between them. I, Great King, hero, king of Hatti, until now I did not cross to the other bank [of the Euphrates],

---

Following the conventional interpretation of CTH 52, Jankowska (1982) composes a novella about the sojourn of Agi-Teššub and Šattiwaza in Arraphe, drawing on administrative records from Nuzi, one of which bears the sealing of *Ša-ad-du-a-az-za* (for which see Stein 1989: 53). If Šattiwaza (= Keli-Teššub), son of Tušratta, did visit Nuzi—already bearing his future throne name—he had to have done so before the city was destroyed, which probably happened before his father's death (though not so early as argued by Maidman 2011). The Šattawazza who appears at Nuzi is surely not the prince, however, but another high-ranking Hanigalbatian; see Zaccagnini 2020: 196–198.

I did not take so much as straw or splinter from Mittani. (CTH 51: §6 obv. 48–52)[109]

The argument continues, turning reality inside out. Instead of taking advantage of his enemy's debility, Suppiluliuma was clement, saving Mittani from distress and its prince from Šuttarna's clutches. Accordingly:

> The Great King said thus: "The Storm-god has decided his case. Since I have taken Šattiwaza, son of King Tušratta, in my hand, I shall seat him on the throne of his father so that the great country of Mittani does not go to ruin." (CTH 51: §6 obv. 55–57)

To restore Mittani to life (as he puts it), Suppiluliuma gave Šattiwaza his daughter in marriage, set him alongside his son Piyassili at the head of his army, and dispatched the two princes to conquer Mittani. They started at Carchemish (CTH 52: §4), the defeat of which had given the Hittite forces considerable trouble, as related in the Deeds of Suppiluliuma (Tablet 7: A ii 1–A iii 42). From there they set out eastward against the city of Irride, did battle, and won the submission of Irride and its territory, as well as that of Harran on the Balikh River (CTH 52: §5). They then contended with Assyrian forces besieging Waššukanni, and pursued the Assyrians from there to Pakarripa to Nilapšini, without meeting them for battle (CTH 52: §6)—and the text becomes too fragmentary to follow their conquest to completion. Suppiluliuma appointed Keli-Teššub king of Mittani under the name Šattiwaza and appointed the daughter he gave him in marriage queen of Mittani (CTH 51: §7); meanwhile he appointed his son Piyassili king of Carchemish, under the name

---

109. The statement that "his son restored the dead Artatama to life" should not be taken literally, as if Artatama were mortally ill or politically defunct, yet still alive somewhere so that, after the defeat of Šuttarna, Šattiwaza had to enter into some sort of co-regency with him (cf., e.g., Jankowska 1982: 138; Wilhelm 2015: 70). It simply referred to the son as his father's living representative. Whose son he was (Artatama's or Tušratta's) the text leaves ambiguous (see Devecchi 2015: 247 n. 2).

Šarri-Kušuh (as he is called in the *Deeds of Suppiluliuma*), specifying by treaty (CTH 51) the territories allocated to him by right of conquest. Thus the Hittite king ensured that his own descendants would rule the kingdom of Mittani, much reduced in size and rank, as well as the lands of its former empire that he had won.

29.4.4. Coda

Suppose we had Šuttarna III's side of the story? We might then describe Tušratta as an illegitimate king, the beneficiary of treachery, unwitting architect of Mittani's dismemberment, who squandered Mittani's treasure in a vain effort to buy Egypt's friendship. The fact is that our histories accord Tušratta the role of Mittani's rightful king mainly because of the fortuitous discovery of the Amarna letters, in which he plays that role with increasing desperation until he disappears. Had we sources providing an external point of reference from which to evaluate his self-portrayal, alongside the self-serving narratives of Suppiluliuma and Šattiwaza, we might say that Tušratta's misrule ultimately precipitated Mittani's demotion from imperial power to Hittite vassal. Under Šattiwaza and his successors—Šattuara, Wasašatta (which is Šattiwaza in reverse), and Šattuara II—the once-great kingdom persisted for about a century, still carrying on the tradition of using Indo-Aryan throne names, although it soon lost the name Mittani. The erstwhile empire shrank to its core realm, Hanigalbat, and the royal residence moved from Waššukanni to Taide.

Having come to the throne as Suppiluliuma's protégé, after his patron's death Šattiwaza apparently sought to make his kingdom great again. Not only Suppiluliuma but his son and successor Arnuwanda II were reportedly struck down by an epidemic disease that Hittite troops and their Egyptian captives brought home from battle, and it was under these circumstances that Suppiluliuma's son Mursili II became king (chapter 30 in this volume). The epidemic is known mainly from Mursili's Plague Prayers, which give the impression that it devastated Hatti's population—even to the point of threatening the gods themselves, because their servants were all dying off. Of course Mursili had to emphasize the epidemic's severity, in order to persuade the gods to make it stop; the rhetoric of his prayers should not be mistaken for the reality of the epidemic's impact. Nevertheless, it must have seemed that the gods were punishing Hatti, encouraging recently subjected kingdoms to try to break free of Hittite rule. In this context Mittani (Hanigalbat), presumably still ruled by Šattiwaza, recovered its independence for a time. One of Mursili's prayers complains that Mittani, alongside Arzawa, is belligerent and has violated its sacred oath; Mursili accordingly asks the gods to turn the plague against Mittani and Arzawa, instead of Hatti.[110] Meanwhile, in his treaty with Niqmepa of Ugarit (CTH 66), Mursili included Hanigalbat among lands with which he might go to war, in which case Niqmepa is to mobilize troops in support of his sovereign; he is not to harbor fugitives from Hanigalbat, nor may he seek alliance with that kingdom. Later still, when Mursili's successor Muwatalli made a treaty with Alaksandu of Wilusa (CTH 76) around 1300, he listed the king of Hanigalbat among his peers, against whom Alaksandu should support him in case of war.

This is the historical context for the group of tablets recording allocations of beer that was excavated at Tell al-Hamidiya, the probable site of Taide. These tablets, found in debris from the palace where they had originally been stored, register deliveries of beer for (*inter alios*) men from Alašiya, Arraphe, Egypt, and Ugarit.[111] This implies that the kingdom of Hanigalbat was in a position to entertain foreign guests, not only from Mittani's former territories (Arraphe) and from overseas (Alašiya on Cyprus), but from Hatti's enemies (Egypt), and even from Hatti's subjects (Ugarit)—exactly what Mursili II stipulated against, in his treaty with Ugarit. The same dossier registers a delivery of beer for the charioteer of one Malizzi, a personage who also appears in a tablet found at Tell Brak, the site of Nawar (Nagar), a day's march away from Taide; the Tell

---

110. CTH 376A, §7; Singer 2002: no. 8. As Singer describes (2002: 49–50; 68 n. 6), while this prayer reuses material from an older one (CTH 376C, his no. 7), the complaint about belligerent neighbors has been updated—the older version spoke of the Hurrian land, Kizzuwatna, and Arzawa, Mursili's version speaks of Mittani and Arzawa—so it probably reflects the contemporary situation.

111. Kessler 2020: 260–261 (ḪT 43), 263–264 (ḪT 45).

Brak tablet (TB 8002) records "reeds, 10 (units), *heštirašše* from Nawar, in the district of Taide, they borrowed in the presence of Malizzi."[112] The destruction of the palace where this tablet was found, at Nawar, would have been contemporaneous with the destruction of the palace at Taide. The authors of destruction were troops of Adad-nerari I, king of Assyria (1305–1274 BC). According to inscriptions Adad-nerari commissioned for new construction at Taide,[113] first he made Šattuara, king of Hanigalbat, into a tribute-paying subject of Assyria, then Šattuara's son Wasašatta revolted from Assyria and sought support from Hatti, in vain (Hatti being occupied in war with Egypt). In response Adad-nerari sacked Taide and several other cities, including Waššukanni, plus he destroyed Irride, where he took captive Wasašatta's wife, sons and daughters, and personnel; not only did he conquer Irride and the towns of its district, he burned them, razed them, and sowed them with weeds. But he did not capture Wasašatta himself. Nor did he complete the constructions at Taide for which these inscriptions were written, as they were found at Assur. Adad-nerari's defeat of Hanigalbat was nevertheless decisive enough that Assyria displaced Hatti as the dominant power in the area Mittani once ruled. Correspondence between the two kingdoms ensued, the earliest extant scrap of which may be a fragmentary draft of a letter from Urhi-Teššub (Mursili III) to Adad-nerari (CTH 171). Herein the Hittite king, referring to a letter from his Assyrian counterpart highlighting what he has done in Hurrian country, acknowledges that his correspondent has prevailed in battle, but retorts that he's putting on airs:

> So now perhaps you've become Great King? And why do you
> keep on speaking of brotherhood and of visiting Mount Amanus?

---

112. See Eidem 1997: 43–44 for the text and the suggestion that bundles of arrows are meant by "reeds 10 *he-eš-ti-ra-še.*" The root of the Hurrian word *heštirašše,* an abstract formed from the agentive participle of *hešt-,* is understood to mean "block, lock, dam," thus reeds for making barrages may be meant, rather than arrows for equipping a garrison (cf. Richter 2012: 159). Malizzi appears in a text from Tell al-Hamidiya (ḤT 61); for the identification of Malizzi at Tell al-Hamidiya with Malizzi at Tell Brak, see Kessler 2020: 280–281.

113. Grayson 1987: A.0.76.3–6, 22.

What is this brotherhood, and what is this about visiting Mount Amanus? For what reason should I write to you of brotherhood? ... Are you and I born of the same mother? As my father and grandfather did not write to the king of Assur [of brotherhood], don't you keep writing about [visitin]g and of great kingship![114]

The relationship stabilized, with Hatti recognizing the Assyrian kingdom as a fellow great power, as indicated by a later letter that (probably) Hattusili III addressed to Adad-nerari (CTH 173; the address is broken). Among other matters, he raises the subject of a troublesome frontier town named Turira, whose people raid his land and accept fugitives therefrom, and which the king of Hanigalbat claims is his—but the king of Assyria claims it's not—so whose responsibility is it to punish Turira, mine or yours? asks the Hittite king, probably testing the boundaries of his new peer's power.[115]

Hittite and Assyrian forces had the opportunity to do battle with each other in the following decades. Shalmaneser I (1273–1244 BC) repeated his father's conquest of Hanigalbat, or at least repeated part of his father's report of conquest, after Šattuara II enlisted the support of Hatti and the Ahlamû to strengthen his position. This composite army successfully defended Hanigalbat against Assyrian attack, as Shalmaneser almost acknowledges before claiming to have defeated his opponents, slaughtered them, and pursued Šattuara at arrow-point all day long.[116] But he did not vanquish Šattuara and his country—yet. Šattuara would have been the king of Hanigalbat who wrote to his "father" the king of Hatti to plead his case under the circumstances of being practically the servant of two masters, pressed by both Assyria and Hatti as he was (CTH 179); he does not address his "father" by name, however, and it

---

114. CTH 171: 4–19; my translation is based on that of Mora and Giorgieri 2004: 184–194, no. 20, who also discuss who might be writing whom.

115. See Beckman 1999, no. 24b; also Mora and Giorgieri 2004, no. 1, whose translation differs from Beckman's on certain points.

116. Grayson 1987: A.0.77.1.

is not clear when, in relation to the campaign Shalmaneser's inscription reports, he made this appeal.[117] During Shalmaneser's reign, in any case, Hanigalbat was subsumed under Assyrian control as a subordinate kingdom, ruled by a secondary line of Assyrian kings (see chapter 32 in this volume). Mittani's epigone ended in absorption by Assyria.

29.5. Society and culture

Assyria probably absorbed much of Mittani's form and content well before annexing Hanigalbat, although just what elements it inherited is difficult to specify, given inadequate sources from the earlier imperial state. With regard to territorial organization, continuity may be discerned in the settlement pattern, featuring extensive broadly distributed rural occupation in which the type of fortified rural compound called *dimtu* in Mittani's eastern territories (notably Arraphe) became the *dunnu* of the Middle Assyrian period. Certain Assyrian legal and administrative usages may have originated in Hanigalbat, for example, the use of the Akkadian word *pūhu* to mean "loan, debit" rather than "exchange, substitute."[118] On a broader sociopolitical scale, Assyria may have inherited from Mittani a distinction between local and imperial citizenship. What it meant to be "Assyrian" developed, over time, to the point that membership in the Assyrian imperial community came to be conceptualized as a status superseding local identities or allegiances; this idea might be traced back to the concept of Hanigalbatean status as distinct from membership in subordinate communities (see section 29.4.2).

To describe the society or culture of Mittani requires distinguishing what pertains to this kingdom from what pertains to its Hurrian background. The diffusion of the Hurrian language across the Near East was

---

117. Opinions have been divided over whether his addressee was Hattusili III or Tudhaliya IV, and whether his Assyrian oppressor was Shalmaneser I or Tukulti-Ninurta I. For the latest discussion, see Bilgin 2018: 47, with literature therein.

118. This usage is found in administrative records from fifteenth-century-BC Alalakh as well as fourteenth-century-BC Tell Brak and Emar; see Niedorf 2008: 347. For Middle Assyrian usage, see Postgate 2013: especially 123–125.

boosted by Mittani's expansion, but it had begun centuries earlier, and the like is true for the diffusion of cultural content carried along with language—poetry, rituals, deities and their cults, as well as intangible culture that leaves little trace in texts or material remains. The political phenomenon of Mittani's hegemony has sometimes been conflated with the cultural phenomenon of Hurrianization. There is, moreover, a tendency to extrapolate to Mittani observations about parts of its empire, given the unbalanced distribution of the surviving sources. Thus, Alalakh and Nuzi in particular have served as surrogates for describing Mittani, because they have each yielded lots of legible evidence; considering how dissimilar the two corpora are, however, this procedure is valid only when both provide comparable material. Meanwhile, changes that took place in tandem with the formation of Mittani are sometimes erroneously attributed to it: for example, the reconfiguration of society consequent on the use of chariotry has been imputed to Mittani, or even to an invading population identified therewith (see section 29.3.2). People do move, sometimes in groups, but words, things, and ideas are portable, too. The spread of Hurrian language can be accounted for without positing an influx of Hurrians, by whatever criteria people might be identified as such. So much less need any "Mittanian" population be posited; it bears emphasizing that "Hanigalbatean" was a political status. The developments that are diagnostic of Mittani's presence or influence may be explained primarily by its exercise of political power.

29.5.1. The formation of classes

One such development can be discerned in the formation of social classes. Throughout the Near East—not only in the Mittani Empire— the adoption of chariotry as a standard component of military forces promoted formalizing the distinction between noble and commoner. There had always been status differences, but now they could be enhanced by new and costly measures, whether the costs of horse and chariot were borne by the fighting men themselves or by the political power they fought for. The new Hurrian word for the newly defined nobility was *maryanni*, correctly translated "nobleman" by Hugo Winckler when he discussed its meaning and etymology in 1910 (see section 29.3.2), and mistranslated as "charioteer" or "chariot warrior" by almost everyone since; the connotation "chariot warrior" developed secondarily. This word first appears as the designation of a social class in the fifteenth century BC (a judgment that remains unimpaired by the single earlier attestation reported to date).[119] Men so designated were those whose status entitled them to ride into battle on horse-drawn chariots—driven by a charioteer—while regular troops fought on foot. Thutmose III's military scribes took special note of *maryanni* captives in recording troops captured during his campaigns (see section 29.3.2), supplying our earliest extant evidence for this class. The word and its referent then entered Egypt, and remained in use throughout the New Kingdom, supplying the writer of Papyrus Anastasi I with his comic image of the *maryanni* towing his horses and carrying his chariot through Levantine terrain too rough to ride in.[120]

The differentiation of chariot-riding nobility from the main body of the citizenry became a structuring principle of Late Bronze Age society, from Babylon to Mycenae. This bipartite class division overlaid existing criteria of differentiation, above all between free and unfree, membership in a given community versus non-membership, ruler and ruled, and any locally salient status distinctions. In the Levant, while the new noble class was generally called by the Hurrianized loanword *maryanni* (Hurrian plural *maryannina*, Semitic plural *maryannū(ma)*), the class of commoners was generally called *hupšu*, a Common Semitic word that originally referred to men subject to conscription and that ultimately

---

119. According to Eidem 2014: 142, with n. 16, the word *maryanni* appears in a tablet found at Tell Leilan, two centuries older than any other extant attestation. This would mean that sustained contact between speakers of Hurrian and speakers of an Indo-Aryan language took place long before the foundation of Mittani (in accord with van Koppen 2017: 79–80). As long as it remains an isolated (and unpublished) instance, however, it contributes no information about social organization or, for that matter, the use of chariotry.

120. For Papyrus Anastasi I in English translation, see Allen 2003: 9–14, who gives the composition's original date as the early reign of Rameses II.

generated the Hebrew word meaning "free."[121] These two main classes are widely attested, typically in different contexts, but occasionally together. The Qatna tablets include a series of records reflecting the organization of *maryanni* and *hupšu* men into groups, under overseers, apparently in order to work on fortifying the town—as they had been enjoined to do by the Hittite king.[122] This injunction was addressed to the *maryannina* by the general Hannutti (TT 3: 9–11), who also addressed them in a hortatory message (TT 4), evidently treating the nobility of Qatna as a collective body who had power to determine the city's policy (see section 29.4.3). In the Amarna correspondence and in Hittite treaty prologues, the *maryanni* class appears as the elite surrounding the ruler (e.g., EA 24), as chariot warriors (e.g., EA 107), and as collective historical actors (e.g., CTH 51, 52). The *hupšu* class, too, exercised political agency, for instance at Emar when they conspired with peers of the king to perpetrate a coup.[123] More typically this class or its individual members appear as the peasantry, the infantry, or in general the population of free subjects on whose arms, labor, and allegiance every state depended.

Within the Mittani Empire, two additional classes were differentiated. One was a class of impoverished subjects, the other a class of occupational specialists. The resulting quadripartite class division is so far attested only in the kingdoms of Alalakh and Arraphe, where census lists or rosters of troops have been found that categorize men enlisted or eligible for conscription by class. At Alalakh, the process of creating the four classes can even be traced through successive sets of census lists and troop rosters drawn up over the course of a generation (or less) during the late fifteenth century BC. The evidence from Arraphe is poorer: clandestine

---

121. On the usage and meaning of *hupšu*, see in brief von Dassow 2011: 213–214, and in more detail von Dassow 2015 (with an overview of sources); 2018.

122. These tablets are TT 19–25, 27, and 29. Richter infers that they record the allocation of bricks, because TT 29 records "[t]otal 40,000 bricks, of the *hupšu* men," although the other tablets give numbers without indicating the object numbered; he also infers fortification as the purpose, and refers to the Hittite king's injunction to fortify Qatna (Richter 2012: 99–100).

123. The coup, which failed, is reported in *Emar* 17, on which see von Dassow 2018: 671.

finds at the capital, Al-ilani (Kirkuk), include rosters that record men mustered out of service during the defensive war against Assyria in the mid-fourteenth century BC. These tablets, which must derive from a much larger file, are complemented by others from the archives of Nuzi and Arraphe that likewise categorize men by class.[124] The terminology used in Arraphe differs from that of Alalakh, but in each case the words share the same denotation and referent, and together form the same quadripartite series. Because the sources mostly pertain to census and conscription, they yield little information about women's class status, and only the Alalakh tablets provide quantitative data adequate to establish the relative proportions of the four classes. Here is an outline description of each class and the words that denoted them in each kingdom:

- Regular free subjects, who bore the duty of military and labor service: The service obligation is expressed by the Akkadian term used to denote this class in Arraphe, *ālik ilki*, "doer of *ilku*-duty," *ilku* being the general term for the service that free men owed the state of which they were citizens. One of the terms used for this class at Alalakh, the Hurrian word *unuššoǧoli*, "duty-man," effectively translates *ālik ilki*. More often, the scribes of Alalakh called this class either by the Common Semitic word *ḫupšu*, "commoner," or by the Akkadian phrase *ṣābū namê*, "people of the countryside," i.e., "peasantry." This class comprised the majority of the free citizenry—about 75 percent, according to the census lists of Alalakh—and as such it was distinguished by no special characteristics. Members of the common, "duty-owing" class held property within the realm where they owed service, property rights being the basis for assessment of that duty. Some accumulated wealth, some practiced trades, some worked for other men or institutions, and some held office.
- Elite subjects, or nobles, who did their military service in the chariotry: The latter feature is expressed by the Akkadian term used to

---

124. For a comprehensive treatment of the rosters and census lists from Alalakh IV, see von Dassow 2008, especially chapter 3, and on the classes themselves, chapter 4; for those from Arraphe (including Nuzi), von Dassow 2009.

denote this class in Arraphe, *rākib narkabti*, "chariot rider." The former feature, "nobility," is expressed by the term *maryanni*, used everywhere else. This elite was not a caste, its members did not belong to a specific ethnic group, and they did not originate outside the Near East. The chariot-riding nobility was everywhere formed of local high-status families. But one did not have to be born into it: the archives of Alalakh and Ugarit include royal grants conferring *maryanni* status and documents securing this status for the offspring of marriage. The members of this elite can truly be understood to constitute a ruling class, inasmuch as they collectively exercised political authority alongside their kings (whom they might depose), participating in government whether or not they held office (as some did). They were distinguished by social proximity to royalty, but not residential proximity; practically every village or hamlet included members of the nobility. Few noblemen practiced a trade, although some engaged in commerce. Some possessed substantial wealth, but there was no property qualification for noble status, beyond that necessary for assessment of the service obligation.[125] Moreover, administrative records from Alalakh and Arraphe indicate that chariots and horses required for military service were provided by the state, not necessarily by the noblemen themselves. While the nobility may normally have been exempt from labor service, the tablets from Qatna demonstrate that they did labor, when circumstances required, along with commoners. No relationship between Hanigalbatean status and nobility is evident.

- Occupational specialists: The terms used to denote this class are derivatives of words meaning "release" or "rescue, save." At Alalakh, the term used was *eġelli* (plural *eġellina*) in Hurrian, or *šūzubu* in Akkadian, both meaning "saved." In Arraphe, the class was designated by the Hurrian adjective *nakkošše* (plural *nakkoššena*), "released."

---

125. The tablet found at Tell Brak that records a man's elevation to *hanigalbatūtu* (TB 8001; see von Dassow 2014: 23–24) includes the bequest of "lands of a *maryanni*." This is part of the grantee's father's property, enabling his heir to maintain his status.

Members of this class were typically practitioners of specialized trades, employees in the service of a patron, or both; some were functionaries in the service of the palace or state. Occasionally, the Alalakh tablets identify an individual as "*eǵelli* of" someone else, sometimes the king, suggesting that the individual's patron was also his "savior." Taken together, the positions of the class members and the semantics of the class designations suggest that redemption from bondage (for debt or other delicts) was the mechanism for constituting this class, at least initially, and that occupational specialization was the qualification for membership in it; additional members could then have been recruited without redemption. Notably, a considerable number of *eǵellina* are identified as cartwrights, chariot drivers, specialists in the care of horses, or makers of weaponry—skills in high demand by states and noblemen alike in this period. It is also possible that the designation "released" refers to exempting this class from labor service so as to devote its members to their specialized labor. They were not, in any case, exempt from military service, for both the Alalakh and Arraphe tablets attest their enlistment for it. Cadastral records from Alalakh confirm that members of this class held property in land, the normal basis for assessment of the service obligation.

- Impoverished free subjects: This class, which is treated as a subset of the "commoner" class at Alalakh, appears to have been constituted of subjects who had lost property rights. The term used for it in Arraphe was the Akkadian word *aššābu*, literally "resident," which denoted tenants on land held by others. A special word was coined to denote this class at Alalakh: *haniahhe*, a Hurrian adjective formed from West Semitic ʿ*aniy-*, "poor," for which the scribes used the Akkadian word *ekû*, "poor," as an equivalent. The Alalakh tablets occasionally record lack of property for members of this class—the man has no ox, no arable land, or nothing whatsoever—not necessarily implying that the others did have property.[126] Nonetheless, the "poor" were eligible for enlistment, suggesting that their property-less condition was considered to be provisional. Alternatively, perhaps they did labor

---

126. For details, see von Dassow 2008: 337.

and military service on behalf of the landlords to whom they had forfeited title to their property; the archives of Nuzi are full of documents recording forfeiture of property rights by people who continued to live on their former property and bear the duty of service assessed on it. It might be objected that this class ought then to have been far larger. Nevertheless, it is noteworthy that such a class as "the poor" was distinguished at all.

The appearance of essentially identical systems of class differentiation at opposite extremities of the Mittani Empire is not simply an instance of similar conditions yielding similar outcomes. It must reflect a deliberate imperial policy of sorting people into socioeconomic categories, not according to ethnos, clan affiliation, mode of subsistence, occupation, or something else. Mittani's government apparently developed the idea of categorizing citizens on the criteria of differences in the social and economic basis for their relation to the state, and communicated this policy to constituent states of its empire. Hence the same system was implemented in both Alalakh and Arraphe. It was not, however, implemented in the same language: the concepts, not the vocabulary, were its essential elements. The scribes of Alalakh created a composite Hurrian and West Semitic terminology, with Akkadian equivalents, to designate the new census classes, while the scribes of Arraphe chose mostly Akkadian words. Presumably the same classes were differentiated in Hanigalbat, perhaps under yet other terms.

One tablet from Nuzi that lists men of Hanigalbat identifies them as *martiyanni*, a Hurrianized Indo-Aryan word of exactly the same formation and practically the same meaning as *maryanni*.[127] The word *martiyanni* is attested nowhere else, as yet, but it could have been current in Hanigalbat. Its isolated appearance at Nuzi, alongside the differing terminologies of different kingdoms, should serve as a caution against attaching decisive importance to lexemes rather than to their referents.

---

127. The text is Lion and Stein 2016: no. 56 (HSS 15 32). In the one case, Indo-Aryan *mártiya-*, "man, warrior," and in the other case, *márya-*, "man, warrior," is provided with the Hurrian derivational suffix *-nni*.

With luck, archives may yet be found in other parts of Mittani's empire that confirm or refute the foregoing hypotheses about class formation under its rule.

29.5.2. Arts and letters

Virtually no room has been found in this chapter for spiritual and material culture, or for the arts. This is not for lack of material, although another chapter by another author would be required to handle it properly. As noted earlier, in many domains of culture it is not clear what is Mittanian as distinct from Hurrian, but in pottery and glyptic art it is (see section 29.2.4). Dozens of sites have yielded Mittanian pottery types, and thousands of Mittani-style seals have surfaced, some as far afield as the Peloponnese.[128] Glass production may well have been invented in the land of Hanigalbat, where some of the earliest extant glass vessels and glazed pottery have been found at Tell Brak (figure 29.6).[129] Mittanian relief sculpture may even be recovered from the stone palimpsest of recycled orthostats found at Tell Halaf (Guzana), near neighbor of Tell Fekheriye (probable site of Waššukanni), according to the analysis of Aslı Özyar.[130] Texts such as the inventories of gifts that accompanied the princess Tadu-Heba to Egypt reveal that haute couture in Mittani featured various styles of clothing and footwear, as well as jewelry and other accessories (see section 29.4.3).

The most attractive pottery of Mittani, Nuzi Ware apparently developed from the earlier painted pottery of the Khabur area, with external input. Although Aegean pottery seldom made it as far east as

---

128. Mittani-style seals fall into two categories, "Common Style" and "Elaborate Style"; see Porada and Collon 2016: 87–120, with pls. 49–54. See Salje 1990: 168–195 for a catalogue and pl. XXIX for a map illustrating the distribution of Mittani "Common Style" seals, including quite a few found in Greece. A collection of imported seals found at Boeotian Thebes that includes eight Mittanian seals has been restudied by Kopanias 2008.

129. Oates et al. 1997: 72–73, 81–100; Pfälzner 2007: 244.

130. Özyar 2008.

FIGURE 29.6. A core-molded bottle of opaque turquoise glass, decorated with combed strands of opaque white and yellow glass, from Nagar/Nawar (Tell Brak; TB 7023). Published in Oates, Oates, and McDonald 1997: 3 fig. 11, 82 fig. 119 (individual fragments), 236–237 fig. 218: no. 1 (drawing), frontispiece (color photograph). Photograph courtesy the Tell Brak Project and the British Institute for the Study of Iraq.

Hanigalbat, Aegean influence has been seen in Nuzi Ware ever since its western variant was first identified at Tell Atchana.[131] While it is an index of the Mittani Empire's extent, Nuzi Ware is not an index of imperial control, rather of fashion. It is found in villages as well as cities, ordinary

---

131. See Pecorella 2000: especially 357, 360 and Soldi 2006 (with references). One lone Mycenaean vessel was found at Tell Brak (Oates et al. 1997: 79), while Mycenaean and other Aegean pottery is found in plenty at sites near the Mediterranean like Tell Atchana. For the relation between Khabur Ware and Nuzi Ware, see Soldi 2006.

households as well as palaces and elite residences, and mineralogical analysis of samples from three sites shows that it was locally made.[132] This pottery came in gracefully shaped vessels painted variously with floral and geometric motifs, sprigs of foliage blooming across the body, birds or sometimes quadrupeds flocking about the shoulder. Other flora and fauna populate seal designs.[133] Along with ordinary animals, humans, and well-known deities with their usual attributes, Mittanian glyptic exhibits a veritable menagerie of monsters composed of diverse selections of wings, tails, limbs, bodies, and heads (sometimes more than one head), arrayed in static or dynamic compositions filled with foliage, stars, guilloches, or severed heads. A favorite motif appearing in many variations is the palmette tree or sacred tree, often flanked by creatures of this world or another, surmounted by a winged sun-disk, sometimes distilled into a foliate standard flaring into a winged sunburst.

Among written sources, the only composition that identifies itself as Mittanian in origin is the instruction manual ostensibly dictated by Kikkuli, the horse-trainer from Mittani (see section 29.2.3). It was, however, written down by Hittite scribes, who also preserved a considerable amount of Hurrian literature, both in the original language and in Hittite translation. Much of this literature predates the formation of Mittani; for example, the Song of Liberation was composed in Hurrian in the time of Hattusili I (or soon after) and recorded in a bilingual edition in the time of Tudhaliya I, two centuries later.[134] It will become possible to tell which Hurrian works to attribute to Mittani, should literary texts be found within Hanigalbat. But whether or not it took textual form, poetry and myth must have flourished in the land of the Hurrians, to judge by the material transmitted in Hatti.

---

132. Erb-Satullo et al. 2011: especially 1188–1189. For rural sites with Nuzi Ware, see Reiche 2014.

133. Salje 1990 is a thorough study of Mittanian "Common Style" seals. A handy reference guide to a large segment of Mittanian glyptic from Nuzi is the analysis of the seal impressions in the Šilwe-Teššub archive by Stein 1993.

134. See von Dassow 2013; de Martino 2019.

We may imagine the verbal and musical arts of Mittani to have been alive with fantasy, corresponding to the phantasmagoria portrayed in glyptic art, where otherworldly creatures crowd into inscrutable scenes. The evidence of material culture complemented by that of texts gives us reason to envision Mittani's people clad in brightly colored garments, flowers and birds decorating their dishes, their walls enlivened with brilliant paint and their textiles with hallucinatory motifs, and an occasional shard of glass glinting from their trash.

REFERENCES

Akar, M. 2019. Excavation results. In Yener, K.A., Akar, M., and Horowitz, M.T. (eds.), *Tell Atchana, Alalakh, vol. 2: the Late Bronze II city—2006–2010 excavation seasons*. Istanbul: Koç University Press, 11–75.

Allen, J.P. 2003. New Kingdom model letters. In Hallo, W.W., and Younger, K.L. (eds.), *The context of scripture, vol. 3: archival documents from the biblical world*. Leiden: Brill, 9–17.

Arnaud, D. 1985. *Recherches au pays d'Aštata (Emar VI/1–4): textes sumériens et accadiens*. Paris: Éditions Recherche sur les Civilisations.

Beckman, G. 1995. The Siege of Uršu text (CTH 7) and Old Hittite historiography. *JCS* 47: 23–33.

Beckman, G. 1999. *Hittite diplomatic texts*. Atlanta, GA: Scholars Press. 2nd rev. ed.

Bilgin, T. 2018. *Officials and administration in the Hittite world*. Berlin: De Gruyter.

Bonatz, D. 2013. Tell Fekheriye: renewed excavations at the "Head of the Spring." In Bonatz, D., and Martin, L. (eds.), *100 Jahre archäologische Feldforschungen in Nordost-Syrien: eine Bilanz*. Wiesbaden: Harrassowitz, 209–234.

Bonatz, D. 2014. Tell Fekheriye in the Late Bronze Age: archaeological investigations into the structures of political governance in the Upper Mesopotamian piedmont. In Bonatz, D. (ed.), *The archaeology of political space: the Upper Mesopotamian piedmont in the second millennium BCE*. Berlin: De Gruyter, 61–84.

Bottéro, J. 1949. Les inventaires de Qatna. *RA* 43: 1–40.

Brunner, H. 1956. Mitanni in einem ägyptischen Text vor oder um 1500. *MIO* 4: 323–327.

Buccellati, G. 2013. When were the Hurrians Hurrian? The persistence of ethnicity in Urkesh. In Aruz, J., et al. (ed.), *Cultures in contact: from Mesopotamia to the Mediterranean in the second millennium BC*. New York: Metropolitan Museum of Art, 84–95.

Campbell, D.R.M. 2020. Hurrian. In Hasselbach-Andee, R. (ed.), *A companion to ancient Near Eastern languages*. Hoboken, NJ: Wiley-Blackwell, 203–219.

Cancik-Kirschbaum, E., and Hess, C. 2017. *Toponyme der mittelassyrischen Texte: der Westen des mittelassyrischen Reiches*. Paris: Société pour l'étude du Proche-Orient ancien.

Cooper, J., Schwartz, G., and Westbrook, R. 2005. A Mittani-era tablet from Umm el-Marra. In Owen, D.I., and Wilhelm, G. (eds.), *General studies and excavations at Nuzi 11/1*. Winona Lake, IN: Eisenbrauns, 41–56.

Coppini, C. 2018. The Land of Nineveh Archaeological Project: preliminary results from the analysis of the second millennium BC pottery. In Salisbury, R.B., Höflmayer, F., and Bürge, T. (eds.), *Proceedings of the 10th international congress on the archaeology of the ancient Near East, vol. 2*. Wiesbaden: Harrassowitz, 65–82.

Cordani, V. 2011. One-year or five-year war? A reappraisal of Suppiluliuma's first Syrian campaign. *AoF* 38: 240–253.

del Monte, G.F. 2009. *L'opera storiografica di Mursili II re di Hattusa, vol. I: le gesta di Suppiluliuma*. Pisa: Edizioni Plus Pisa University Press.

de Martino, S. 2000. Il regno hurrita di Mittani: profilo storico politico. In André-Salvini, B., de Martino, S., Giorgieri, M., Parmegiani, N., Pecorella, P.E., Salvini, M., and Trémouille, M.-C., *La civiltà dei Hurriti*. Naples: Macchiaroli, 68–102.

de Martino, S. 2003. *Annali e res gestae antico ittiti*. Pavia: Italian University Press.

de Martino, S. 2016. Išuwa and Ḫatti during the early Hittite Empire (Tutḫaliya I—Šuppiluliuma I). In Velhartická, Š. (ed.), *Audias fabulas veteres: Anatolian studies in honor of Jana Součková-Siegelová*. Leiden: Brill, 98–110.

de Martino, S. 2017. The Hurrian language in Anatolia in the Late Bronze Age. In Mouton, A. (ed.), *Hittitology today: studies on Hittite and Neo-Hittite Anatolia in honor of Emmanuel Laroche's 100th birthday*. Istanbul: Institut Français d'Études Anatoliennes-Georges Dumézil, 151–162.

de Martino, S. 2018. Political and cultural relations between the kingdom of Mittani and its subordinated polities in Syria and southeast Anatolia. In Gianto, A., and Dubovský, P. (eds.), *Changing faces of kingship in Syria-Palestine 1500–500 BCE*. Münster: Ugarit-Verlag, 37–50.

de Martino, S. 2019. The Hurrian Song of Release and the fall of Ebla. *Studia Eblaitica* 5: 123–155.

Devecchi, E. 2015. *Trattati internazionali ittiti*. Brescia: Paideia.

Durand, J.-M. 2002. *Le culte d'Addu d'Alep et l'affaire d'Alahtum*. Paris: SEPOA.

Eidem, J. 1997. The inscriptions. In Oates, D., et al. (eds.) 1997: 39–46.

Eidem, J. 2001. Nagar. *RlA* 9: 75–77.

Eidem, J. 2014. The kingdom of Shamshi-Adad and its legacies. In Cancik-Kirschbaum, E., Brisch, N., and Eidem, J. (eds.), *Constituent, confederate, and conquered space: the case of the Mitanni transition*. Berlin: De Gruyter, 137–146.

Erb-Satullo, N.L., Shortland, A.J., and Eremin, K. 2011. Chemical and mineralogical approaches to the organization of Late Bronze Age Nuzi Ware production. *Archaeometry* 53: 1171–1192.

George, A.R. 2013. *Babylonian divinatory texts chiefly in the Schøyen Collection*. Bethesda, MD: CDL Press.

George, A.R. 2017. Babylonian documents from North Mesopotamia. In George, A.R., Hertel, T., LLop, J., Radner, K., and van Soldt, W.H., *Assyrian archival texts in the Schøyen Collection and other documents from North Mesopotamia and Syria*. Bethesda, MD: CDL Press, 95–108.

Gilan, A. 2015. *Formen und Inhalte althethitischer historischer Literatur*. Heidelberg: Winter.

Giorgieri, M. 2000. Schizzo grammaticale della lingua hurrica. In André-Salvini, B., de Martino, S., Giorgieri, M., Parmegiani, N., Pecorella, P.E., Salvini, M., and Trémouille, M.-C., *La civiltà dei Hurriti*. Naples: Macchiaroli, 171–277.

Grayson, A.K. 1987. *Assyrian rulers of the third and second millennia BC (to 1115 BC)*. Toronto: University of Toronto Press.

Harrak, A. 1987. *Assyria and Hanigalbat*. Hildesheim: Olms.

Helck, W. 1961. *Urkunden der 18. Dynastie: Übersetzung zu den Heften 5–22*. Berlin: Akademie-Verlag.

Hoffner, H.A. 1997. Deeds of Suppiluliuma. In Hallo, W.W. (ed.), *The context of scripture, vol. 1: canonical compositions from the biblical world*. Leiden: Brill, 185–191.

Homan, Z.S. 2020. *Mittani palaeography*. Leiden: Brill.

Jankowska, N.B. 1982. The Mitannian Šattiwasa in Arrapḫe. In Dandamayev, M.A., Gershevitch, I., Klengel, H., Komoróczy, G., Larsen, M.T., and Postgate, J.N. (eds.), *Societies and languages of the ancient Near East: studies in honour of I.M. Diakonoff*. Warminster: Aris & Phillips, 138–149.

Jensen, P. 1919. Indische Zahlwörter in keilschrifthittitischen Texten. *Sitzungsberichte der Preußischen Akademie der Wissenschaften* 1919: 367–372.

Kaelin, O. 2013. Tell al-Hamidiyah/Ta'idu? Residenzstadt des Mitanni-Reiches. In Bonatz, D., and Martin, L. (eds.), *100 Jahre archäologische Feldforschungen in Nordost-Syrien: eine Bilanz*. Wiesbaden: Harrassowitz, 181–192.

Kessler, K. 2014. Neue Tontafelfunde aus dem mitannizeitlichen Taidu: ein Vorbericht. In Bonatz, D. (ed.), *The archaeology of political space: the Upper Mesopotamian piedmont in the second millennium BCE*. Berlin: De Gruyter, 35–42.

Kessler, K. 2020. Das maittanische Keilschriftarchiv. In Wäfler, M. (ed.), *Tall al-Ḥamīdīya 5: Bericht 2002–2011*. Berlin: OpenScienceTechnology, 251–295.

Kitazumi, T. 2020. Drei indo-arische Personennamen und der Gott Akni in CTH 13. In Fritz, M., Kitazumi, T., and Veksina, M. (eds.), *Maiores philologiae pontes: Festschrift für Michael Meier-Brügger*. Ann Arbor, MI: Beech Stave Press, 90–98.

Kitchen, K.A. 2016. The Levant campaign of Shoshenq I (945–924 BCE). In Younger, K.L. (ed.), *The context of scripture, vol. 4: supplements*. Leiden: Brill, 14–18.

Koliński, R. 2002. Tell al-Fakhar: a *dimtu*-settlement or the city of Kurruḫanni? In Owen, D.I., and Wilhelm, G. (eds.), *General studies and excavations at Nuzi* 10/3. Bethesda, MD: CDL Press, 3–39.

Kopanias, K. 2008. The Late Bronze Age Near Eastern cylinder seals from Thebes (Greece) and their historical implications. *Mitteilungen des Deutschen Archäologischen Instituts, Athenische Abteilung* 123: 39–96.

Kühne, C. 1999. Imperial Mittani: an attempt at historical reconstruction. In Owen, D.I., and Wilhelm, G. (eds.), *Nuzi at seventy-five*. Bethesda MD: CDL Press, 203–221.

Lahe, J., and Sazonov, V. 2018. Some notes on the first mention of Mitra in CTH 51. *NABU* 2018: 22–25 (no. 17).

Laroche, E. 1971. *Catalogue des textes hittites*. Paris: Klincksieck.

Lauinger, J. 2019. Discourse and meta-discourse in the statue of Idrimi and its inscription. *Maarav* 23: 19–38.

Lion, B. 2010. Les fortifications de Nuzi d'après une tablette du Louvre. In Fincke, J.C. (ed.), *Festschrift für Gernot Wilhelm anläßlich seines 65. Geburtstages*. Dresden: ISLET, 203–216.

Lion, B. 2011. Assur unter der Mittaniherrschaft. In Renger, J. (ed.), Assur: Gott, Stadt und Land. Wiesbaden: Harrassowitz, 149–167.

Lion, B., and Stein, D. 2016. *The tablets from the temple precinct at Nuzi*. Bethesda MD: CDL Press.

Maidman, M.P. 2010. *Nuzi texts and their uses as historical evidence*. Atlanta, GA: Society of Biblical Literature.

Maidman, M.P. 2011. Nuzi, the club of the great powers, and the chronology of the fourteenth century. *KASKAL: Rivista di storia, ambienti e culture del Vicino Oriente Antico* 8: 77–139.

Maidman, M.P. 2016–2017. Mittanni royalty and empire: how far back? *JCSMS* 11/12: 15–28.

Miglus, P.A. 2016. About Bakr Awa. In Kopanias, K., and MacGinnis, J. (eds.), *The archaeology of the Kurdistan region of Iraq and adjacent regions*. Oxford: Archaeopress, 229–239.

Miller, J.L. 2007. Amarna age chronology and the identity of Niphururiya in the light of a newly reconstructed Hittite text. *AoF* 34: 252–293.

Miller, J.L. 2017. Political interactions between Kassite Babylonia and Assyria, Egypt and Hatti during the Amarna Age. In Bartelmus, A., and Sternitzke, K. (eds.), *Karduniaš: Babylonia under the Kassites*. Berlin: De Gruyter, 95–111.

Miller, J. 2020. Two notes on Kizzuwatna's status as a Hittite vassal in the Middle Hittite period. In Cammarosano, M., Devecchi, E., and Viano, M. (eds.), *Talugaeš witteš: ancient Near Eastern studies presented to Stefano de Martino on the occasion of his 65th birthday*. Münster: Zaphon, 345–350.

Mladjov, I. 2019. The kings of Mittani in light of the new evidence from Terqa. *NABU* 2019: 33–36 (no. 22).

Mora, C., and Giorgieri, M. 2004. *Le lettere tra i re ittiti e i re assiri ritrovate a Ḫattuša*. Padua: Sargon.

Morris, E. 2014. Mitanni enslaved: prisoners of war, pride, and productivity in a new imperial regime. In Galán, J.M., et al. (eds.), *Creativity and*

innovation in the reign of Hatshepsut. Chicago: The Oriental Institute of
the University of Chicago, 361–379.

Mynářová, J. 2007. *Language of Amarna—language of diplomacy: perspectives
on the Amarna Letters.* Prague: Charles University.

Niedorf, C. 2008. *Die mittelbabylonischen Rechtsurkunden aus Alalaḫ (Schicht
IV).* Münster: Ugarit.

Novak, M., and Rutishauser, S. 2017. Kizzuwatna: archaeology. In Weeden, M.,
and Ullmann, L.Z. (eds.), *Hittite landscape and geography.* Leiden: Brill,
134–145.

Oates, D., Oates, J., and McDonald, H. (eds.) 1997. *Excavations at Tell Brak,
vol. 1: the Mitanni and Old Babylonian periods.* London: British School of
Archaeology in Iraq.

Özyar, A. 2008. Untersuchungen zu den kleinen Orthostaten aus Tell
Halaf: späthethitische Kunst, aramäische Bildwerke oder hurritisches
Erbe? In Wilhelm, G. (ed.), *Ḫattuša-Boğazköy: das Hethiterreich im
Spannungsfeld des Alten Orients.* Wiesbaden: Harrassowitz, 397–420.

Parpola, A. 2015. *The roots of Hinduism: the early Aryans and the Indus civilization.* Oxford: Oxford University Press.

Pecorella, P.E. 2000. Note sulla produzione artistica hurrita e mitannica.
In André-Salvini, B., de Martino, S., Giorgieri, M., Parmegiani, N.,
Pecorella, P.E., Salvini, M., and Trémouille, M.-C., *La civiltà dei Hurriti.*
Naples: Macchiaroli, 349–365.

Pfälzner, P. 2007. The Late Bronze Age ceramic traditions of the Syrian Jazirah.
In al-Maqdissi, M., Matoïan, V., and Nicolle, C. (eds.), *Céramique de l'âge
du bronze en Syrie 2: l'Euphrate et la région de Jézireh.* Beirut: Institut français du proche-orient, 231–313.

Pfälzner, P., and Faist, B. 2020. Eine Geschichte der Stadt Mardama(n). In
Baldwin, J., and Matuszak, J. (eds.), *Altorientalistische Studien zu Ehren
von Konrad Volk: mu-zu an-za₃-še₃ kur-ur₂-še₃ ḫe₂-ĝal₂.* Münster: Zaphon,
347–389.

Pfälzner, P., and Qasim, H.A. 2018. Urban developments in northeastern
Mesopotamia from the Ninevite V to the Neo-Assyrian periods: excavations at Bassetki in 2017. *ZOrA* 11: 42–87.

Podany, A. 2014. Hana and the Low Chronology. *JNES* 73: 49–71.

Porada, E., and Collon, D. 2016. *Catalogue of the Western Asiatic seals in the
British Museum—cylinder seals, IV: the second millennium BC beyond
Babylon.* London: The British Museum.

Postgate, J.N. 2013. *Bronze age bureaucracy: writing and the practice of government in Assyria.* Cambridge: Cambridge University Press.

Puljiz, I., and Qasim, H.A. 2019. A new Mittani centre on the middle Tigris (Kurdistan region): report on the 2018 excavations at Kemune. *ZOrA* 12: 10–43.

Rainey, A.F. 2014. *The el-Amarna correspondence: a new edition of the cuneiform letters from the site of el-Amarna based on collations of all extant tablets.* Leiden: Brill.

Raulwing, P., and Meyer, H. 2004. Der Kikkuli-Text: hippologische und methodenkritische Überlegungen zum Training von Streitwagenpferden im Alten Orient. In Burmeister, S., and Fansa, M. (eds.), *Rad und Wagen, der Ursprung einer Innovation: Wagen im Vorderen Orient und Europa.* Mainz: Zabern, 491–506.

Redford, D.B. 1982. Mitanni. In Helck, W., and Westendorf, W. (eds.), *Lexikon der Ägyptologie, vol. 4.* Wiesbaden: Harrassowitz, 149–152.

Reiche, A. 2014. Tell Abu Hafur "East," Tell Arbid (northeastern Syria), and Nemrik (northern Iraq) as examples of small-scale rural settlements in Upper Mesopotamia in the Mittani period. In Bonatz, D. (ed.), *The archaeology of political space: the Upper Mesopotamian piedmont in the second millennium BCE.* Berlin: De Gruyter, 43–59.

Richter, T., and Lange, S. 2012. *Das Archiv des Idadda: die Keilschrifttexte aus den deutsch-syrischen Ausgrabungen 2001–2003 im Königspalast von Qaṭna.* Wiesbaden: Harrassowitz.

Rieken, E. 2009. Die Tontafelfunde aus Kayalıpınar (mit einem Beitrag von Gernot Wilhelm). In Pecchioli Daddi, F., et al. (eds.), *Central-North Anatolia in the Hittite period: new perspectives in light of recent research.* Rome: Herder, 119–143.

Salje, B. 1990. *Der "Common Style" der Mitanni-Glyptik und die Glyptik der Levante und Zyperns in der späten Bronzezeit.* Mainz: Zabern.

Sallaberger, W., Einwag, B., and Otto, A. 2006. Schenkungen von Mittani-Königen an die Einwohner von Baṣīru: die zwei Urkunden aus Tall Bazi am Mittleren Euphrat. *ZA* 96: 69–104.

Salvini, M. 1994. Una lettera di Ḫattušili I relative alla spedizione contro Ḫaḫḫum. *SMEA* 34: 61–80.

Schwartz, G. 2018. Late Bronze Age chronology at Umm el-Marra: problems and possibilities. In Otto, A. (ed.), *From pottery to chronology: the Middle Euphrates region in Late Bronze Age Syria.* Gladbeck: PeWe-Verlag, 19–46.

Singer, I. 1991. A concise history of Amurru. In Izre'el, S., *Amurru Akkadian: a linguistic study, vol. II.* Atlanta, GA: Scholars Press, 135–195.

Singer, I. 1999. A political history of Ugarit. In Watson, W.G.E., and Wyatt, N. (eds.), *Handbook of Ugaritic studies.* Leiden: Brill, 603–733.

Singer, I. 2002. *Hittite prayers.* Atlanta, GA: Society of Biblical Literature.

Soldi, S. 2006. La ceramica dipinta nella Siria e Mesopotamia settentrionali tra Bronzo Medio e Bronzo Tardo: considerazioni sull'origine e lo sviluppo della ceramica di Nuzi. *Agōgē* 3: 81–97.

Stein, D. 1989. A reappraisal of the "Sauštatar Letter" from Nuzi. *ZA* 79: 36–60.

Stein, D. 1993. *Das Archiv des Šilwa-teššup, vol. 8–9: the seal impressions.* Wiesbaden: Harrassowitz.

Stein, D. 1997. Mittan(n)i, B: Bildkunst und Architektur. *RlA* 8: 296–299.

Torrecilla, E., and Cohen, Y. 2018. A Mittani letter order from Azu (Had 8). *RA* 112: 149–158.

Trameri, A. 2020. *The land of Kizzuwatna: history of Cilicia in the second millennium BCE until the Hittite conquest (ca. 2000–1350).* PhD thesis, New York University.

Valério, M. 2011. Hani-Rabbat as the Semitic name of Mitanni. *Journal of Language Relationship* 6: 173–183.

van Koppen, F. 2004. The geography of the slave trade and northern Mesopotamia in the late Old Babylonian period. In Hunger, H., and Pruzsinszky, R. (eds.), *Mesopotamian dark age revisited.* Vienna: Verlag der Österreichischen Akademie der Wissenschaften, 9–33.

van Koppen, F. 2017. The early Kassite period. In Bartelmus, A., and Sternitzke, K. (eds.), *Karduniaš: Babylonia under the Kassites.* Berlin: De Gruyter, 45–92.

van Soldt, W. H. 1991. *Studies in the Akkadian of Ugarit: dating and grammar.* Kevelaer: Butzon und Bercker.

van Soldt, W. H. 1995. Three tablets from Tell Hammām et-Turkman. In van den Hout, T.P.J., and de Roos, J. (eds.), *Studia historiae ardens: ancient Near Eastern studies presented to Philo H.J. Houwink ten Cate.* Istanbul: Nederlands Historisch-Archaeologisch Instituut, 275–291.

von Dassow, E. 2008. *State and society in the Late Bronze Age: Alalaḫ under the Mittani Empire.* Bethesda, MD: CDL Press.

von Dassow, E. 2009. Sealed troop rosters from the city of Arraphe. In Wilhelm, G. (ed.), *General studies and excavations at Nuzi 11/2*. Winona Lake, IN: Eisenbrauns, 605–636.

von Dassow, E. 2011. Freedom in ancient Near Eastern societies. In Radner, K., and Robson, E. (eds.), *The Oxford handbook of cuneiform culture*. Oxford: Oxford University Press, 205–224.

von Dassow, E. 2013. Piecing together the Song of Release. *JCS* 65: 127–162.

von Dassow, E. 2014. Levantine polities under Mittanian hegemony. In Cancik-Kirschbaum, E., et al. (eds.), *Constituent, confederate, and conquered space: the emergence of the Mittani state*. Berlin: De Gruyter, 11–32.

von Dassow, E. 2015. Hupshu. In Bagnall, R., et al. (eds.), *The encyclopedia of ancient history*. Malden, MA: Wiley-Blackwell. Retrieved from https://doi.org/10.1002/9781444338386.wbeah26146 (last accessed March 6, 2020).

von Dassow, E. 2016. Texts from Nuzi. In Younger, K.L. (ed.), *The context of scripture, vol. 4: supplements*. Leiden: Brill, 119–129.

von Dassow, E. 2018. Liberty, bondage and liberation in the second millennium BCE. *History of European Ideas* 44: 658–684.

von Dassow, E. 2020. Alalaḫ between Mittani and Ḫatti. *Asia Anteriore Antica: Journal of Ancient Near Eastern Cultures* 1: 193–226.

von Lieven, A. 2016. The movement of time: news from the "clockmaker" Amenemhet. In Landgráfová, R., and Mynářová, J. (eds.), *Rich and great: studies in honor of Anthony J. Spalinger on the occasion of his 70th Feast of Thoth*. Prague: Charles University, 207–231.

von Weiher, E. 1975. Ḫanigalbat. *RlA* 4: 105–107.

Wäfler, M. 2003. *Tall al-Ḥamīdīya 4: Vorbericht 1988–2001*. Fribourg: Academic Press.

Wäfler, M. 2007. Tall al-Ḥamīdīya: Ta'idu. *Hefte des Archäologischen Seminars der Universität Bern* 20: 33–58.

Wegner, I. 2007. *Hurritisch: eine Einführung*. Wiesbaden: Harrassowitz. 2nd rev. ed.

Wiedemann, F. 2017. The Aryans: ideology and historiographical narrative types in the nineteenth and early twentieth centuries. In Roche, H., and Demetriou, K.N. (eds.), *Brill's companion to the classics, fascist Italy and Nazi Germany*. Leiden: Brill, 31–59.

Wilhelm, G. 1976. Parattarna, Sauštatar und die absolute Datierung der Nuzi-Tafeln. *Acta Antiqua Academiae Scientiarum Hungaricae* 24: 149–161.

Wilhelm, G. 1997. Mittan(n)i, Mitanni, Maitani. A. Historisch. *RlA* 8: 286–296.

Wilhelm, G. 2004. Hurrian. In Woodard, R.D. (ed.), *Cambridge encyclopedia of the world's ancient languages*. Cambridge: Cambridge University Press, 95–118.

Wilhelm, G. 2006a. Der Brief Tušrattas von Mittani an Amenophis III. in hurritischer Sprache (EA 24). In Janowski, B., and Wilhelm, G. (eds.), *Texte aus der Umwelt des Alten Testaments, Neue Folge* 3: *Briefe*. Gütersloh: Gütersloher Verlagshaus, 180–190.

Wilhelm, G. 2006b. Die hurritischsprachige Tafel Kp 05/226. *MDOG* 138: 233–236.

Wilhelm, G. 2012. Šuppiluliuma I. und die Chronologie der Amarna-Zeit. In Hachmann, R. (ed.), *Kāmid el-Lōz* 20: *die Keilschriftbriefe und der Horizont von El-Amarna*. Bonn: Habelt, 225–257.

Wilhelm, G. 2015. Suppiluliuma and the decline of the Mittanian kingdom. In Pfälzner, P., and al-Maqdissi, M. (ed.), *Qaṭna and the networks of Bronze Age globalism*. Wiesbaden: Harrassowitz, 69–79.

Wilhelm, G. 2017. Synchronic variety and diachronic change in Hurrian. *Mesopotamia* 52: 75–84.

Wilhelm, G. 2019. Die hurritischen Texte aus Šamuha. In Rieken, E. (ed.), *Keilschrifttafeln aus Kayalıpınar 1: Textfunde aus den Jahren 1999–2017*. Wiesbaden: Harrassowitz, 197–209.

Winckler, H. 1910. Die Arier in den Urkunden aus Boghaz-köi. *OLZ* 13: 289–302.

Wiseman, D.J. 1953. *The Alalakh tablets*. London: British Institute of Archaeology at Ankara.

Zaccagnini, C. 1979. Les rapports entre Nuzi et Hanigalbat. *Assur: Monographic Journal of the Near East* 2/1: 1–26.

Zaccagnini, C. 2020. Pomp and circumstance at Nuzi, on the eve of the end. *KASKAL: Rivista di storia, ambienti e culture del Vicino Oriente Antico* 17: 141–210.

Zarins, J. 2014. *The domestication of equidae in third-millennium BCE Mesopotamia*. Bethesda, MD: CDL Press.

Ziegler, N., and Langlois, A.-I. 2016. *Les toponymes paleo-babyloniens de la Haute-Mésopotamie*. Paris: Société pour l'étude du Proche-Orient ancien.

30

The Hittite Empire

Mark Weeden

30.1. Introduction

When writing histories of the ancient world it is frequently prudent to define our terms of reference, as not doing so can lead to assumptions being made that nomenclatures applied to population groups in the ancient world are comparable to those used in the ideology of the modern nation-state, where bordered territories are allegedly populated by communities of people who speak unified languages.[1] "Hittite" should be understood as a political rather than an ethnic term, even if the boundaries between the two can be fluid: it is the people who were directly loyal to the political power at Hattusa (modern Boğazköy) and belonged to its immediate

---

[1]. This chapter was completed during a research semester at the DFG-funded Kolleg-Forschungsgruppe "Re-thinking Oriental Despotism—Strategies of Governance and Modes of Participation in the Ancient Near East" (FOR 2615) at the Free University of Berlin in January and February 2019. Hittite chronology is still very uncertain, and absolute dates are thus used sparingly. For the regnal dates of Egyptian rulers, we follow von Beckerath 1997, but correct Sethnakht's reign to four years (1185–1181 BC) because of a stele found in Luxor in 2006 (published by Boraik 2007), which mentions this king's Year 4. Consequently, the reign of Rameses III is dated to 1181–1150 BC. For the regnal dates of Assyrian rulers, the longer chronology that allots 46 years (instead of 36 years) to Aššur-dan I is used, hence assigning him the dates 1178–1133 BC; for this, see chapter 32 in this volume. The chapter was language-edited by Denise Bolton.

Mark Weeden, *The Hittite Empire* In: *The Oxford History of the Ancient Near East*. Edited by: Karen Radner, Nadine Moeller, and D. T. Potts, Oxford University Press. © Oxford University Press 2022.
DOI: 10.1093/oso/9780190687601.003.0030

sphere of influence as a settlement on the central Anatolian plateau.[2] They were the people who participated in the Hittite pattern of administration and government that spread, however unevenly, from its base in Hattusa across large parts of Anatolia (figure 30.1), a definition that can be understood culturally as well as politically. It is not a term that necessarily has anything to do with a particular spoken language, and the evidence associating the speakers of that language with some kind of Indo-European-tongued immigration movement is so tenuous as to be unsusceptible to historical evaluation.[3] In their written documentation, they referred to themselves as the "men/women of Hattusa" (Hittite *Hattusumenes*), using a geographical term inherited from speakers of an earlier prestige language of central Anatolia, Hattian, from which a number of key Hittite religious and mythological concepts were derived.[4] Their own language they called *Nesumnili*, "in the language of the people of (the city) Nesa," using the name of a town otherwise known as Kaneš (in Hattian and Akkadian), located at the site of Kültepe.[5] We call them the Hittites, and the language of most of their documents the same, due to the fact that the modern world's first encounter with "Hittites," or at least what turned out to be the later inheritors of their southern powerbases, was through the Hebrew Bible and then through the annals of Assyrian and Egyptian kings, where they were referred to by a name approaching the same sound as this.[6]

---

2. Klinger 1996: 85–87; Starke 1996: 180 n. 162; 1998: 185–186; Gilan 2007: 309–310; 2008: 108; 2015: 195–201.

3. Gilan 2008: 108. For the negative evidence of genetic analysis for immigration into Turkey that might be related to people speaking Hittite, see De Barros Damgaard et al. 2018.

4. For early Hattian bilingualism with Anatolian dialects in central Anatolia, see Singer 1981; Tischler 1998; Soysal 2004: 142–155; 2008; Goedegebuure 2008a; 2008b (particularly for Luwian, rather than Hittite, as coexisting with Hattian).

5. Barjamovic 2011; Larsen 2015.

6. This chapter does not use the common distinction made by Hittitologists between the land "Hatti" and the city "Hattusa." *Hatti* is a writing for Hattusa that was borrowed from Akkadian, but did not exist as a Hittite term in its own right. It was the land of Hattusa, the city of Hattusa, and the people of Hattusa; see Kryszeń 2017; Gerçek 2018: 5–7. However, the step toward calling them the Hattusans rather than the Hittites is currently an innovation too far, as renaming an entire discipline of historical research would be likely to cause confusion, despite the increased accuracy.

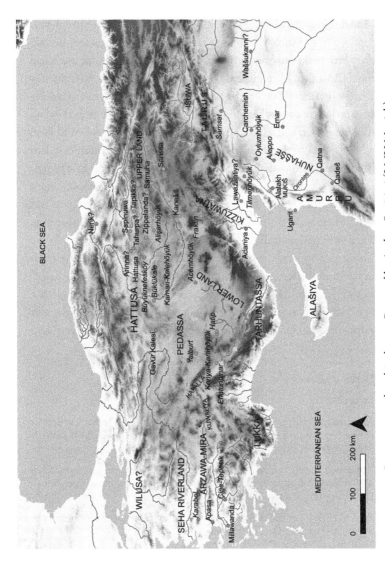

BLACK SEA

WILUSA?

Nerik?

HATTUSA

Arinna?
Sapinuwa
Tahurpa? Tapikka?
Hattusa
Büyüknefesköy
Alişarhöyük
Kaman-Kalehöyük Kaneš

Zippalanda? Samuha

UPPER LAND

Sarissa

TAURUS

Išuwa

Šamšat

Waššukanni?

Carchemish

Oylumhöyük
Aleppo

Emar

NUHASSE

Qatna

Gâvur Kalesi

Acemhöyük

Frakdin

LOWER LAND

Lawazantiya?
Tilmenhöyük

Alalakh

Orontes

A M U R R U

SEHA RIVERLAND

Karabel

PEDASSA

Yalburt

Adaniya

KIZZUWATNA

Ugarit

Qadeš

MUKIŠ

Apasa

ARZAWA-MIRA

Çiğe-Tepesik

HAPALLA

KUNASSA

Koriya-Karahöyük Hatip

ARHUNTASSA

ALAŠIYA

Millawanda

Eflatunpınar

LUKKA

MEDITERRANEAN SEA

0   100   200 km

FIGURE 30.1. Sites mentioned in this chapter. Prepared by Andrea Squitieri (LMU Munich).

The Hittite state was not known to the classical historians who largely set the blueprint for modern European and Anglophone historiography at the end of the nineteenth and through most of the twentieth centuries AD. The first identifications of "Hittite remains" were given to hieroglyphic inscriptions from Hama, which in fact dated to the ninth century BC and had very little to do with the Hittite state apart from using a script that it had invented (Anatolian Hieroglyphs) as well as the language that was primarily associated with that script—today known as Luwian.[7] The leap was quickly made to include under the Hittite moniker ruins still visible at Boğazköy and Gavur Kalesi in Central Anatolia, as well as the hieroglyphic relief at Karabel between the Cayster and Hermos valleys of the western coastline (modern Küçükmenderes and Gediz).[8] All of these in fact belonged to the Late Bronze Age and were, to varying degrees, related to the Hittite Empire. Excavations conducted by the German Orient-Society began at Boğazköy in 1906 and have continued under the leadership of the German Archaeological Institute with few interruptions until the present day (figure 30.2).[9]

Some 30,000 cuneiform tablets and fragments thereof have been excavated at this site, the vast majority of which have been published.[10] Other sites are bringing more tablets to light, all inscribed with a recognizably homogeneous type of Hittite cuneiform, in particular the site of Ortaköy (ancient Sapinuwa).[11] Cuneiform tablets and

---

7. Wright 1874; Sayce 1876.

8. Sayce 1882.

9. Alaura 2006; Seeher 2008; Schachner 2011; 2017a; Schachner, Seeher, and Seeher-Baykal 2012; for the annual publications of excavation results, see the periodicals *Mitteilungen der Deutschen Orient-Gesellschaft* and *Archäologischer Anzeiger*.

10. Publication details can be found in S. Košak's *Konkordanz der hethitischen Keilschrifttafeln* at www.hethiter.net, the basic research tool of the discipline of Hittitology (last accessed December 9, 2019).

11. Typical Hittite cuneiform tablets have thus far been found in Anatolia at Boğazköy (Hattusa), Ortaköy (Sapinuwa), Maşathöyük (Tapikka), Kayalıpınar (Samuha), Oymaağaç (Nerik?), Alacahöyük (Arinna?), Eskiyapar (Tahurpa?), Kuşaklı Höyük (Sarissa), Uşaklı Höyük (Zippalanda?), Büyüknefesköy-Yassıhöyük, and Büklükale; and south of the Taurus at Tell Atchana (Alalakh), Tell Afis, Carchemish, Oylumhöyük, and Ugarit. The progress of those excavations based in Turkey can be followed in the Turkish Ministry of Culture and Tourism's annual publication series *Kazı Sonuçları Toplantısı*.

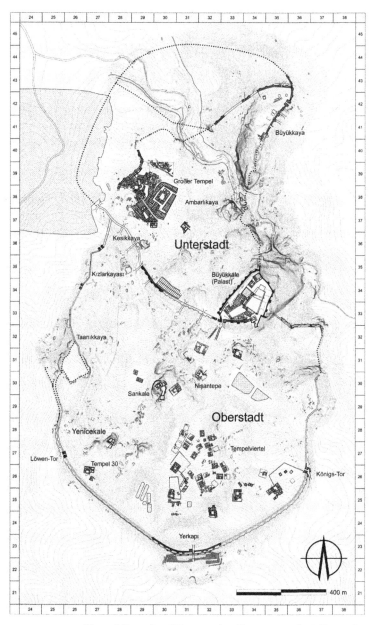

FIGURE 30.2. Plan of Boğazköy/Hattusa, the Hittite capital. © Deutsches Archäologisches Institut (2010).

their contents provide the first foundation for a narrative of Hittite history, although they need to be used with caution. Like any written document, they were produced under certain concrete circumstances, with particular readerships, agendas, and genre-conditioned expectations that circumscribe the kind of information that can be reasonably gleaned from them.[12] In earlier phases of research the narratives reconstructed from these documents, such as the destruction of Hattusa by fire in the early fourteenth century BC, also found their way into the periodization of archaeological excavations.[13] Nowadays the results of archaeological research are evaluated for their historical import on their own terms as far as possible, and then compared with the results from the analyses of textual sources to obtain a more nuanced view.[14] Data from archaeology must also be regarded with some caution when writing a history, not least because excavations tend to focus on monumental buildings, while ground survey work tends to offer data that are too patchy and incomplete to provide sufficient resolution.[15] There are still considerable obstacles to writing a history of this period "from below," as our sources are skewed to the perspective of the extended ruling family. But already, tracing the story of Hittite power reveals the persistent difficulty the royal house had in exercising control at all.

30.2. The earliest period

Starting in the period of Assyrian traders at Kaneš (modern Kültepe), from the nineteenth to the eighteenth centuries BC, we catch glimpses of local people speaking an Anatolian language in the mainly

---

12. Klinger 2001; 2008; Gilan 2015: 56–63.

13. Schoop 2008: 35.

14. See the contributions to Mielke, Schoop, and Seeher 2006 and Schoop 2008.

15. For significant attempts to integrate the results of survey work into the reconstruction of Hittite history, see Glatz 2009; Matessi 2017.

Assyrian-language tablets that were left behind there (cf. chapter 17 in volume 2). However, that language now appears slightly different from the Hittite known later from Hattusa.[16] And there appears to have been a variety of governmental structures, most frequently characterized by the presence of a king and a queen, distributed across a fragmented political landscape.[17] The governmental reach of a city barely extended further than its local area, which was typically bordered by physical landscape features.[18] The process that resulted in the development of this fragmented political landscape into a territorial formation can be illustrated by looking at the kinds of settlements where the elements of a central Anatolian culture associated with the Hittite state, the instruments of Hittite state control, and its administration developed through the seventeenth and sixteenth centuries BC and beyond. The monumental defensive walls from the Early to Middle Bronze Age (ca. 2000–1600 BC) at the site of Büklükale on the western bank of the Kızılırmak river, for example, point to the east, against Hattusa in the center of the bend of the Kızılırmak river.[19] When the Hittite state extended its control to the west of the river, this site must have been incorporated, its earlier massive walls now misplaced and irrelevant. However, the question arises repeatedly, throughout Hittite history: how stable and permanent were such incorporations? In effect, to what level had a uniform process of state formation been achieved throughout the area claimed by the Hittites in the texts they left behind?[20] The relationship between the varied pictures painted by the different text-genres and the material data on the ground as assessed by archaeology must be constantly tested and recalibrated.

---

16. Kloekhorst 2019.

17. Larsen 2015: 138–141.

18. Matessi 2017: 26; Palmisano 2018: 5–8.

19. Matsumura and Weeden 2017: 111; Matsumura 2018: 13.

20. Matessi 2017.

It can be presumptuous to equate the development of writing with nascent state formation on the assumption that writing and the state always go together, but it is a possibility that one should not neglect.[21] In the case of the indigenous Anatolian Hieroglyphic script, the development of the symbolic repertoire that eventually became an identifiable writing system, at least by the fifteenth century BC, was a lengthy process. Furthermore, state formation is usually reflected in manifold power-shifts other than movements in style. And yet the site of Konya-Karahöyük on the western side of the Konya plain provides a *terminus post quem* for the appearance of certain uniform developments in glyptic designs, some of which were later to form part of the codification and standardization of symbols into a hieroglyphic writing system.[22] Konya-Karahöyük has to be dated to after the end of Kültepe Level Ib in the first quarter of the seventeenth century BC.[23] One cannot yet speak of any development of a notation system that could be described as writing on the many seal impressions found on clay at Konya-Karahöyük; this changes in the early sixteenth century BC at the latest, when similar symbolic elements are used in a way that resembled a script at sites including Büklükale, Eskiyapar, and Boğazköy (ancient Hattusa).[24] By then, it is clear the use of these symbols had evolved beyond the heraldic-style use of motifs of the earlier period (e.g., Konya-Karahöyük and Kültepe), which was suited to communicate and affirm local loyalties and addressed only those who already understood the symbols' meaning; there is no evidence yet that the system would have worked in the more abstract way necessary for using a writing system to communicate also across distances. It would be some time before the hieroglyphic script developed by the Hittites

---

21. For a study comparing the legibility required by writing systems and the "legibility" required by state structures and institutions, see Wang 2014.

22. Alp 1968.

23. Boehmer 1996; Weeden 2018: 56–57.

24. Weeden 2018: 55.

was used in the regularized and standardized format on seals that one can associate with a self-branding state.[25] In fact, it was not until the early to mid-fourteenth century BC,[26] so possibly these uses of proto- or pseudo-writing on seals pointed backward to earlier formations of power as much as they announced a new cultural or political development (figure 30.3).

Therefore, we can expect the Hittite state (i.e., an attempt to coordinate central Anatolian polities using power structures and prestige media that left their strongest impression on the city of Hattusa) emerged at some point after the date of the material from Konya-Karahöyük, and this was likely to have been contemporary with Kültepe Level Ia (perhaps dating to the mid-seventeenth century BC). Archaeologically speaking, however, little can be connected to this transitional period. We begin to see large-scale building projects at Hattusa (modern Boğazköy) only in the sixteenth century BC, notably with the installation of massive grain-silos connected to the postern wall of the capital city's citadel of Büyükkale, which have been radiocarbon-dated to that time.[27] The grain silos also date the postern wall to this period and thus provide a date for the beginning of the construction of the Upper City at Hattusa.[28] Such a time lag is not surprising—any period of primary accumulation through state expansion based on force is likely to show its material consequences in the form of wealth laid down in architecture and urban planning only some time after that wealth has been grabbed.[29] For this reason, it is quite

---

25. For the concept of (commodity) "branding" in association with the use of seals and the expansion of states in Early Bronze Age Mesopotamia, see Wengrow 2008: 13.

26. Around the time of Suppiluliuma I (ca. 1350 BC), seal styles become symmetrically standardized, with names spelled in a central column and titles arranged antithetically; see Herbordt 2006. However, it seems that this style of arrangement had already developed somewhat before this time.

27. Schoop and Seeher 2006: 59; Schachner 2009.

28. For the discussion concerning the dating of the Upper City, see Seeher 2008.

29. Compare, e.g., the building boom of the Umayyad caliphate, some thirty to forty years after the Arab conquests.

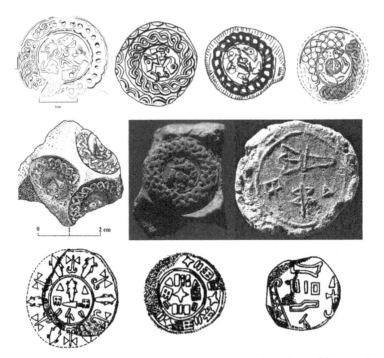

FIGURE 30.3. Seal styles from the sixteenth through to the mid-fourteenth century BC. Row 1: sixteenth century (left to right): Büklükale (Weeden 2016); Eskiyapar (Dinçol and Dinçol 1988); Hattusa (Güterbock 1942; Boehmer and Güterbock 1987). Row 2: fifteenth century from Sarissa (modern Kuşaklı): Müller-Karpe 1995; 2001. Row 3: fourteenth century from Hattusa: Herbordt 2006. Reproduced with kind permission of the authors.

likely that the traditional historical narrative, whereby Hattusili I established himself in Hattusa as king, reflects a reality that corresponds to the second half of the seventeenth century BC, i.e., the time before the wealth his immediate predecessors and successors somewhat fitfully accumulated was converted into visible monumental capital.

As far as evidence for the time before Hattusili is concerned, there is the *Anitta Text*, a narrative composition found on a cuneiform tablet at Hattusa. On the basis of its paleography, the oldest tablet of the

Anitta Text controversially dates to sometime in the early fifteenth or late sixteenth century BC, although it contains traces of more archaic orthography. It narrates the conquest of Nesa/Kaneš (modern Kültepe) by Anitta and his father, Pithana, the king of Kussara.[30] This Kussara is referred to in later inscriptions as the seat of Hattusili I, who also died there according to his *Testament*, and its location is still unknown.[31] Anitta himself is attested in Old Assyrian documents from Kültepe and Ališarhöyük, along with his father Pithana, as well as on a spearhead that was found on the citadel mound at Kültepe Level Ib.[32] The *Anitta Text* has been construed as an attempt to collect information concerning this king from up to three different inscriptional sources, although the narrative can also be understood in a more unified fashion than this analytical approach might imply.[33] Most strangely for its posterity, the *Anitta Text* pronounces a curse on any future king who would resettle the city of Hattusa after Anitta had destroyed it during a campaign against the northern city of Zalpuwa (also Zalpa), whose king had previously purloined "our god."[34]

That such a document should be found at Hattusa, where some king after Anitta had clearly resettled the "cursed" city, may be disquieting for modern tastes. However, much Hittite historiography is motivated by the desire to gather the information needed to identify past guilt (in the form of broken oaths, for example) that might explain present crises. It may indeed be the curse itself that inspired the inclusion of this narrative in the Hittite archives at Hattusa, as well as its subsequent reworking in the later Empire period on a collective tablet along with other narrative texts from the Old Kingdom.

---

30. Neu 1974; Carruba 2003; Beckman in Beckman et al. 2006: 216–219.

31. *Hattusili's Testament*, colophon 1–3; see Gilan 2015: 83.

32. For the documents, see Kryszat 2008: 161–165; for the spearhead, see Wilhelmi 2016: 231, fig. 1.

33. Steiner 1984; Wilhelmi 2016: 230–231. The insightful analyses of Starke 1979: 70 and Singer 1995 may require a more unitary textual structure, even if it is one that has arisen from a compilation of older sources.

34. *Anitta Text*, ll. 49–52; see Neu 1974: 12–13; Singer 1995.

Despite a consensus that the *Anitta Text* is a very ancient narrative that has been preserved in the Hittite archives, one should also not dismiss the possibility that the text is itself a reworking, or compilation, from the early fifteenth century BC, to which the earliest manuscript might be dated (although it could also be of much earlier date), and that it represents an attempt to account for current territorial or religious issues by referencing historical ones.[35] This can only remain speculation until we have a clearer idea of the (likely chaotic) geopolitics of the earlier fifteenth century (or alternatively, of the period during which the text was composed or compiled). Certainly the Hittite kings were assassinated at a fairly speedy rate, as we shall see later, even if archaeology might suggest that this period was the capital's heyday.[36]

A similarly contemporary motivation may lie behind the preservation of a further composition relating to Zalpa, also preserved in one manuscript likely to be from the fifteenth century, as well as a later one.[37] The composition consists of two parts. The first part is set in mythical time, when the Queen of Kaneš had thirty sons and exposed them all by putting them in the river in baskets until they floated out to sea, where they were rescued by the gods, who then raised them. Later they return and we understand that they may be about to unwittingly marry their thirty sisters, with the possible exception of one brother, but at this point the text breaks off. When it resumes on the other side of the tablet, the narrative is set in historical time: the period of the king's grandfather, his father, the king himself (probably Hattusili I), and the "old king."[38] At the end of the narrative, the king breaks his siege on the city of Zalpa,

---

35. The *Anitta Text* has also been supposed to be an Old Hittite period composition memorializing earlier events in support of contemporary dynastic claims against the line represented by Hattusili I; see Forlanini 2010: 130.

36. For the beginnings of an imperial-style "symmetrical" architecture in the early fifteenth or late sixteenth century BC, see Schachner 2015; 2017a: 299. For an overview of assassinations and conspiracies at the Hittite court, see Giorgieri 2008.

37. Otten 1973; Holland and Zorman 2007; Gilan 2015.

38. For possible historical scenarios, see Beal 2003; Gilan 2007: 316–317; 2015: 207–210; Forlanini 2010.

where his enemies are hiding out, and returns to Hattusa to worship the gods. While he is away performing his pious task, the "old king" goes to Zalpa with his troops and "takes" it. There the narrative ends. It is possible that the text was meant to exculpate the king from some kind of mishap or crime.[39] Rituals relating to Zalpa have also been preserved but are very fragmentary, so it is unclear what their function would have been.[40] Zalpa has been equated with the site of İkiztepe in northern Turkey on the Black Sea, but it is unclear whether chronologically relevant archaeological layers have been excavated there thus far.[41]

The king in the Zalpa text is likely to be Hattusili I.[42] The grandfather of the king has been identified with a Huzziya, whose name occurs in one (or possibly two) late manuscripts of offering lists to previous royal figures, as well as occupying the position of the first king on the "cruciform seal" from Hattusa (figure 30.4).[43] This document is a seal in the shape of a Maltese cross that has been reconstructed from seal impressions connected with a door in a temple.[44] On one side it lists the immediate predecessors of the late-fourteenth-century BC king Mursili II. On the other side it contains the kings of the early dynasty, starting on

---

39. Gilan 2007 takes a sophisticated view of the text's function in the context of the perpetual Hittite problem of throne succession; see also Gilan 2015: 204–207. For the view that the text is a foundation myth for Anatolian kingship, see Taracha 2016: 366 n. 5 (with further literature).

40. Corti 2010 sees a connection between a king's death and the recovery of previously lost northern territories in the thirteenth century BC; see further Taracha 2016: 369–371.

41. Corti 2017: 226; Glatz 2017: 80.

42. Beal 2003: 22–23.

43. A list of offerings of the House of the Cooks (Offering List C: i 1′–5′; Otten 1951: 64–66 contains the statement (unique in these lists) that "the musician [. . .] the name of Huz[ziya]"; cf. Offering List A: obv.? 1′. For assessment of the social, historical, and intellectual context of the offering lists and of their subsequent value as historical sources, see Archi 2007: 50–51; Gilan 2014. For attempts to identify Huzziya, see Dinçol et al. 1993; Beal 2003: 31 (remote ancestor of Hattusili I); Forlanini 2010: 116 (grandfather of Hattusili I).

44. Dinçol et al. 1993.

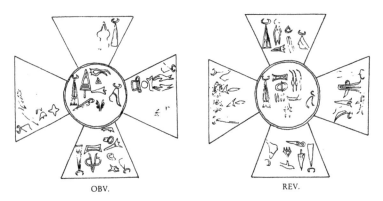

OBV.   REV.

FIGURE 30.4. The so-called cruciform seal from Hattusa. Reproduced from Dinçol et al. 1993: 88 figs. 1–2, with kind permission.

the left wing and proceeding clockwise from a name that is difficult to read (but is probably Huzziya), along with his queen (whose name is illegible apart from the final sign). This was the king that the Hittite historians behind the offering lists and the cruciform seal thought had started it all.[45]

Huzziya is not mentioned in the document that is usually employed as the primary source for the outline of early Hittite history: the *Telipinu Edict*.[46] Preserved in later copies in both Hittite and Akkadian, its peculiar marriage of historical narrative, administrative regulation, and prescriptive instrument is unique among historical sources. King Telipinu narrates a potted version of the history of the bloodshed that had preceded his reign in order to propose a fixed order of succession that favored the oldest son, apparently a novel concept. In addition, the text serves to regulate the use of the royal storage depots (the so-called seal houses) to exclude future mismanagement by local officials,[47] and also pronounces some rules concerning witchcraft.

---

45. Beal 2003: 31; Gilan 2014.

46. Hoffmann 1984; Goedegebuure 2006; Gilan 2015: 137–177.

47. Singer 1984.

From the *Telipinu Edict* we learn that during the reign of the kings Labarna and Hattusili the land was united, and that it was only after this that things started to go wrong.[48] This is clearly a whitewash to serve Telipinu's own propaganda purposes. Hattusili himself, in his own documents, is peculiarly reticent about his own lineage, calling himself the son of the brother of Tawananna in his bilingual *Annals*, which are preserved both in Hittite and Akkadian on much later tablets.[49] In his bilingual *Testament* we learn that his predecessor Labarna had been chosen as king in Sanahuitta by Hattusili's grandfather.[50] However, the nobles had rejected this and installed one Papahdilmah instead.[51] "The households of the high noblemen, where are they, haven't they perished?" asks Hattusili.[52] This does not sound like the idyll of unity that the *Telipinu Edict* describes for us. Hattusili himself took the name Labarna when he became king and is referred to in documents as such, which led to some modern scholars identifying the two separate kings as one person. Hattusili also wanted to install yet another Labarna ("the Younger") as his successor, who may have been his "sister's child." This did not go according to plan, as the young man showed himself to be "cold" and "heartless," which seems to have been sufficient grounds to justify removing him from the succession, although he was recompensed with an estate.[53] Labarna

---

48. *Telipinu Edict*, §7; see Gilan 2015: 140.

49. *Huttusili's Annals*, §1; see De Martino 2003: 30 (Hittite version); Devecchi 2005: 34–35 (Akkadian version); Beckman in Beckman et al. 2006: 219–222.

50. *Hattusili's Testament*, §20; see Gilan 2015: 79; Goedegebuure in Beckman et al. 2006: 224.

51. Many assume that Papahdilmah is Hattusili's father (cf. Beal 2003: 25–26). The evidence consists mainly of a broken passage in an offering list and is not entirely convincing (Gilan 2014: 88), although later Hittite kings were not averse to reference their father's deeds as an example of how not to behave. See section 30.4 on Tudhaliya IV and the example of Masturi, a vassal favored by his own father, Hattusili III.

52. *Hattusili's Testament*, §20; see Gilan 2015: 80; Goedegebuure in Beckman et al. 2006: 226.

53. *Hattusili's Testament*, §1; see Gilan 2015: 68; Goedegebuure in Beckman et al. 2006: 224.

the Younger was also accused of obeying his mother ("the Snake") rather than Hattusili, which implies he was Hattusili's nephew. In place of Labarna the Younger, Hattusili's son or grandson Mursili was installed on the throne at what appears to have been a very young age.[54] Thus succession problems and internal strife are well attested during the reigns of Labarna I and Hattusili I, and indeed form the backdrop to Hittite history more generally.

The *Telipinu Edict* tells us that Labarna established control over seven Central Anatolian towns, and sent his sons out to govern them.[55] A similar pattern of familial delegation is repeated under Hattusili I, according to the *Edict*. This solution to territorial administration is prone to promoting splits and secessions due to diverging interests and competing claims for the throne.[56] Other documents, like the so-called Palace Chronicles—a series of didactic stories about officials told in the context of a banquet—suggest that this form of governance was limited, and that representatives could be moved around the territory. It is also not always clear precisely to what degree these officials could be said to be "governing" the areas to which they were assigned.[57] The example of Nunnu is a case in point: he was the man from Hurma in the east who was located in Arzawa in the west, although the text does not tell us that he actually fulfilled an administrative role there. Rather, he was accused

---

54. Steiner 1996.

55. *Telipinu Edict*, §4; see Gilan 2015: 138–139; van den Hout 1997: 194. The towns are Hupisna (classical Kybistra near Ereğli), Tuwanuwa (classical Tyana), Nenassa, Landa, Zallara, Parsuhanta, and Lusna (classical Lystra). Some proposed localizations for Nenassa, Landa, and Parsuhanta fall outside of the south-central Anatolian ambit. If Parsuhanta is identical with Old Assyrian Purušḫattum, then it could conceivably be located quite far to the west, beyond Konya (following the reconstruction of Barjamovic 2011). Other reconstructions locate this town at Acemhöyük, to the southeast of the Great Salt Lake. The matter is highly significant for any assessment of the military capabilities of the early Hittite state.

56. Gilan 2007: 314. The Abbasid Caliphate had just such a system that depended largely on provincial governance delegated to members of the Caliphal dynasty, which directly resulted in the disastrous civil wars of 809–813 AD; see Kennedy 2004: 7–8.

57. Dardano 1997; Gilan 2015: 115–135.

of not delivering silver and gold (to Hattusa) and of keeping whatever he finds in his house.[58] He gave another man, Sarmassu, written instructions to take his place, but this person did not take up his post and, in the end, the father of the king, who is the main protagonist in all of these tales, was forced to send a Golden Spear Man. Similarly, we learn from the same text that another man from Hurma, Sanda, was in Hassuwa in northern Syria, but he was afraid of the Hurrians and left his post, for which he was punished. After that, a man called Hani "held Hassuwa," before he too was found guilty of an indiscretion and punished.[59] The theme here is superficially the king's power to punish his incompetent officials, but the underlying assumption is that Hittite representation is needed in these places. It is unclear whether these men were anything more than local trading representatives in more distant areas (Arzawa and Hassuwa) who were able to call on Hittite military assistance if necessary, rather like the representatives of the East India Company (so-called factors) in the early days of the British Empire.

Strangely, Telipinu does not mention Hattusili's adventures beyond Anatolia, about which we receive ample information in that ruler's bilingual *Annals*. Hattusili's initial activities appear to have been focused on the North, with Sahuitta (= Sanahuitta) and Zalpa coming quickly under fire.[60] If the varying names refer to the same place, he returned to Sanahuitta later in his reign to conduct a six-month siege, indicating that this was a settlement that provided a significant counterweight to Hattusa's claims on the central territories.[61] In the meantime he conducted

---

58. *Palace Chronicles*, §3; see Gilan 2015: 117–118.

59. *Palace Chronicles*, §§5–6; see Gilan 2015: 118–119.

60. *Huttusili's Annals*, Akkadian version: obv. 2, see Devecchi 2005: 34–35; Hittite version: obv. i 4; see De Martino 2003: 30–31; Beckman et al. 2006: 219. Sanahuitta (Old Assyrian Šinahuttum) is usually located somewhere in the Çekerek and Yozgat regions (Alparslan 2017: 210–211). Labarna I had been named successor by Hattusili's grandfather there (*Hattusili's Testament*, §20; see Gilan 2015: 79–80), and during the time of the texts of Kültepe Level Ib it had probably been the site of a conflict with Hattusa (Larsen 1972: 100–101).

61. *Hattusili's Annals*, Akkadian version: obv. 23; see Devecchi 2005: 42–43; Hittite version: §7, obv. i 46; see De Martino 2003: 44–45; Beckman et al. 2006: 220.

expeditions to northern Syria. If the city Alhalha, that was destroyed during his second campaign, can indeed be identified with Alalakh (modern Tell Atchana), then this important synchronism could help to integrate the Hittite expansion with established Syro-Mesopotamian chronologies.[62] However, while not excluding the possibility that the destruction of Alalakh level VII is identical with Hattusili's early campaigns, the most recent assessment of the evidence from the earlier Alalakh texts stresses their ambivalence in this regard.[63] We can date neither the end of Alalakh level VII, nor the start of Hattusili's campaigning in northern Syria on the basis of this synchrony.[64] However, Alhalha (even if it is Alalakh) is not the main narrative focus of the bilingual *Annals*, and the same year saw visits to Ikakali and Tišhiniya in Syria and the destruction of Uršu/Waršuwa on the way back.[65]

By venturing beyond the Taurus mountains, Hattusili was encroaching on the territories that were later to come under the control of the Mittani state (see chapter 29 in this volume), whose official language was Hurrian. He was unable to return to northern Syria for a number

62. *Hattusili's Annals*, Akkadian version: obv. 6: see Devecchi 2005: 36–37; Hittite version: §4, obv. i 15 (as Alalha): see De Martino 2003: 34–35; Beckman et al. 2006: 220; for some justified doubts about the equation with Alalakh, see Ünal 2015: 29.

63. Lauinger 2015: 206.

64. A person called Zukrasi appears in a late document from Alalakh VII, whose name also appears in a narrative about military activities in northern Syria on a later Hittite tablet, the so-called *Zukrasi Text* (obv. ii 14; see De Martino 2003: 112–113). Whether this was the same person or not depends to an extent on the reading of his title on the Alalakh document, which is disputed (Lauinger 2015: 206 with n. 16). On the Hittite tablet, see Klinger 2006: 10–11; Gilan 2015: 14. A further possible synchronism is the diviner Kuzzi who may be attested at Alalakh Level VII and in the archives of Tigunanu (contemporary with Hattusili I); see George 2013: 104–105.

65. *Hattusili's Annals*, Akkadian version: obv. i 6–10; see Devecchi 2005: 36–37; Hittite version: §4, obv. i 16–17; see De Martino 2003: 32–35. This siege of Uršu may also be the subject of a literary text dating to the reign of Hattusili I (Beckman 1995), although it has also been dated to the reign of Labarna I (Forlanini 2010). The location of Uršu is debated (Cohen 2017b: 297), but it was clearly within easy range of Kizzuwatna, Carchemish, and Aleppo.

of years, because no sooner had he departed to campaign in western Anatolian Arzawa than a Hurrian invasion from the East seems to have sparked a widespread rebellion in Central Anatolia.[66] If Amir Gilan has correctly interpreted a fragmentary text, Mursili I narrates the course of the invasion against his adopted father Hattusili I, which seems to have reached far into (central) western Anatolia and may have involved collaboration with local city-elites such as the man of Purushanda.[67] This disrupted any gains that had been made in Central Anatolia and meant that Hattusili had to attend to matters there, rather than looking for further expansion elsewhere. The central Anatolian town of Nenassa seems to have surrendered to him, while it became necessary to destroy Ullumma/Ulma, and in the following year there was the lengthy siege at Sanahuitta.[68] This pattern of expansion and retraction following internal rebellions that broke out the moment the Hittites' back was turned was repeated a number of times throughout Hittite history. This pattern ended in the later fourteenth century BC when Suppiluliuma I finally set up a vice-regency in Carchemish on the Euphrates which directed Hittite affairs in Syria, and his successor Mursili II sectioned up West Anatolian Arzawa into four separate principalities, thus rendering it less of a threat.

Once Hattusili was able to return to his Syrian adventures, the towns of Haššu/Haššuwa and Hahha (possibly Samsat or the adjacent Lidarhöyük on the Euphrates) became his primary goal. Hahhu(m)/ Hahha had been an important node on the Old Assyrian trader's route into Anatolia (see chapter 17 in volume 2), and Haššu(m) would seem to have also been a significant trading center, possibly on a Babylonian trading route, and an early conduit for Hurrian culture into Anatolia during

---

66. "Enemy (of/from) Hanigalbat:" *Hattusili's Annals*, Akkadian version: obv. 10–13; see Devecchi 2005: 36–39; "Hurrian enemy:" Hittite version: §5, obv. i 24; see De Martino 2003: 36–37. According to Gander 2017a: 264; 2017b, the Old Hittite Arzawa would have not included the Aegean region as in later years, but would have spread over a more central western area.

67. Gilan 2015: 243–248.

68. For localizations, see De Martino 2017: 255; Alparslan 2017: 210–211.

the same period.[69] After facing resistance supported by former regional power Aleppo, Hattusili was able to defeat the forces of Haššu at Mount Adalur (possibly the southern Kurt Dağ or somewhere on the Amanus range) and then crossed the river Puran (either the Ceyhan/Pyramos or the Afrin) as well as the Euphrates to take the city of Hahha (i.e., earlier Hahhum), comparing himself to the great Mesopotamian king Sargon of Akkad in the process.[70] A vivid letter that Labarna/Hattusili wrote to King Tunip-Teššub of Tigunanu, on the other side of the Euphrates, is preserved in Akkadian. In it he exhorts Tunip-Teššub to eat up the Hahhaean's grain ration "like a dog," take his oxen and sheep, and together with Labarna/Hattusili to surround him on one side and the other "like iron and the lion."[71] With this the Hittites had arrived on the international scene, and Hattusili used comparisons fitting such status to underscore his achievement, which had likely sewn up the two main trade routes leading into Anatolia. The kings of Haššu and Hahha were yoked to Hattusili's chariot, and a long list of booty for transport back to Hattusa was presented.[72] Neither of these cities had any significance in the following period. This was clearly the crown of the Syrian campaigns as far as Hattusili was concerned, but it by no means rounded off Hittite intervention in the area.

When his adopted son Mursili I took the throne at a very young age, he may have been under the tutelage of a family member (either brother or uncle) called Pimpira (or Pimpirit), who was designated as a "son of"

---

69. Wilhelm 2008. Tilmenhöyük in the Islahiye valley is one candidate for identification of Haššu (or more likely Zalwar); see Marchetti 2011: 110–111 for a Babylonian seal discovered there. Another candidate is Oylumhöyük, a site further east in the Upper Queiq valley; see Ünal 2015: 27–32. See also Cohen 2017a: 297–298.

70. *Hattusili's Annals*, Akkadian version: obv. 32–rev. 21; see Devecchi 2005: 44–47; Hittite version: §§10, 16, 18; see De Martino 2003: 51–75. For discussion of these place names, see Cohen 2017a: 297–298 (with further literature).

71. Salvini 1994: 61–65; Miller 2001; for alternative translations, see Durand 2006: 220–221; Hoffner 2009: 75–80; Cohen 2017b: 542.

72. *Hattusili's Annals*, Akkadian version: rev. 4–25; see Devecchi 2005: 52–57; Hittite version: §§16–19; see De Martino 2003: 66–77.

the city Nenassa, which had previously submitted to Hattusili after participating in the Hurrian-inspired uprising.[73] Giving Pimpira a post so close to the young king was perhaps a slightly risky means of securing the support of a potential enemy. The *Telipinu Edict*, in its abbreviated narrative style, mentions Mursili's destruction and the plundering of Aleppo and Babylon before he was murdered by his cupbearer and brother-in-law, Hantili, who was in league with one Zidanta (or Zidanza).[74] Mursili's raid on Babylon is thought to have brought an end to the First Dynasty of Babylon (chapter 18 in volume 2) and is given the date of 1595 BC (according to the Middle Chronology; see chapter 11 in volume 2), although the imprint it left on Babylonian historiography and collective memory was rather weak.[75] On the other hand, one fragmentary Old Hittite text (preserved on a later tablet) seems to have taken a negative view of Mursili's assault on Babylon, apparently because of the looting (as Amir Gilan argues), and it may even have been part of the justification for his murder.[76] As was so frequently the case, Hittite historiography sought in historical events the origin of the assumed guilt and consequent divine wrath that was the cause of present ills. By contrast, a later Hittite prayer to the sun-goddess of Arinna contains a commemoration of the event as a past glory to which the author wishes the Hittites could return with the help of the deity.[77] There was clearly not a unified, state-sanctioned view of the past at Hattusa.

---

73. For the edict concerning Pimpira, see Cammarosano 2006.

74. *Telipinu Edict*, §§9–11; see Gilan 2015: 141.

75. A later Babylonian chronicle remarks that "At the time of Samsu-ditana, the Hittite went to Akkad" (Grayson 1975: 45, 152: Chronicle 20: B rev. 11; Glassner 2004: 272–273). There is also the Agum-Kakrime inscription, known from later copies, that claims the statues of Marduk and his consort Ṣarpanitum were returned from the land of Hana on the Middle Euphrates, and the so-called Prophecy of Marduk known from a Neo-Assyrian tablet from Nineveh, according to which the statue of the god spent twenty-four years in Hatti (Borger 1971: 3–24; Paulus 2018: 131–134).

76. Hoffner 1975: 56–58; Gilan 2014: 203, who sees the text as a morality tale on the behavior of the whole land.

77. Mursili II's prayer to the sun-goddess of Arinna, §8; see Singer 2002: 53.

This synchronism with the fall of the First Dynasty of Babylon (see chapters 11 and 18 in volume 2) provides one of the key points in Old Hittite chronology. It is unclear how long after his return Mursili was murdered; it may have been some time. Our main source for the following period is still the abbreviated narrative of the *Telipinu Edict*, which is arranged around the provocation of divine vengeance through the murderous behavior of Hittite kings and grandees. From this we learn that Hantili lived to a great age, despite having had a kind of epiphany in Tagarama (modern Elbistan or plain of Malatya) about his misdeeds in the meantime.[78] His reign was dogged by further Hurrian invasions, which he seems to have repulsed, at least according to the Akkadian version of the *Telipinu Edict*, as well as more internal schisms, including the murder of the queen of Sukziya and her children.[79] According to the most cogent interpretation of the fragmentary Akkadian text of the bilingual *Telipinu Edict*, this occurred during the repulse of the Hurrian invasion; it may even have occurred in reaction to the death of Hantili's queen Harapseli in that city.[80] Any unity that was achieved within central Anatolia under Hattusili or Mursili seems to have been extremely fragile—local city rivalries remained primary—and it appears that Sukziya's loyalty could have been further conflicted, as Hurrian forces may have wintered there during a previous invasion.[81] Even while Hantili was dying, his son Piseni and his family were murdered by one Zidanta, presumably a different person than Hantili's co-conspirator in

---

78. *Telipinu Edict*, §§12–19; see Gilan 2015: 142–144.

79. Hoffmann 1984: 60.

80. Soysal 1990; cf. Gilan 2015: 176, who identifies the wife of Hantili as the queen of Sukziya.

81. Whether it was a previous invasion rather than the same one depends on whether one dates the Hurrian invasion referred to in the text CTH 13 to the time of Hattusili I (Kempinski and Košak 1982: 96–99; Gilan 2015: 243–248, narrated by Mursili I), of Mursili I (Heinhold-Krahmer 1977: 23–27; Soysal 1989: 136–138; de Martino 1992: 24–28); or of Hantili I (Forlanini 2010: 125–126; 2017: 243). Sukziya has not been identified, but must have been located near Hurma.

the murder of Mursili.[82] Zidanta himself was then murdered by his own son, Ammuna, as the gods sought vengeance for the "blood of Piseni."[83] By this time we are presumably in the second half of the sixteenth century BC.

Telipinu presents Ammuna's reign as a complete disaster, blighted by droughts and famine, rebellions, and invasions, but the reality is likely to have been quite different.[84] The lands became enemies to the Hittite king from Arzawa to the west of Adaniya in the region of Kizzuwatna (modern Adana), which may have been partially visited with violence from Hattusili I, if not annexed in the strictest sense.[85] Ammuna's own annals, which are preserved on a later collective tablet along with a copy of the *Anitta Text*, present a very different picture.[86] Ammuna was campaigning in the northeast at Tipiya, a location not mentioned in Telipinu's version of the same events, although admittedly we do not know where all the places he names are located.[87] He also seems to have campaigned at Hahha, presumably the same one attacked by Hattusili, and he made "the sea a border."[88] It even seems possible that Telipinu's version of the same events directly inverted one of Ammuna's phrases, although the text is damaged.[89] This would cast considerable doubt, once again, on the

82. Most accounts assume that the two are identical, which is perfectly possible; see Bryce 2005: 102; Gilan 2015: 159.

83. *Telipinu Edict*, §19; see Gilan 2015: 144.

84. For an assessment of the evidence, see Shelestin 2014.

85. Ataniya (modern Adana), Arusna, and Kummani are mentioned, with Arusna being destroyed according to a fragment that may be attributed to Hattusili I (KUB 48: no. 81); see de Martino 2003: 127, 150–151; Hawkins and Weeden 2017: 286.

86. Hoffner 1980: 305–306; Shelestin 2014: 805–814; Gilan 2015: 160 n. 572.

87. Parduwata, which has not been identified, occurs in both texts: *Telipinu Edict*, §21 (see Gilan 2015: 145); and KUB 21: no. 71: rev. iv 8′ (see Shelestin 2014: 810).

88. Shelestin 2014: 810 (KUB 21: no. 71: rev. iv 14′).

89. *Telipinu Edict*, §20: "Grain, vines, cattle and sheep not . . ." (see Gilan 2015: 145); KUB 21: no. 71: rev. iv 7′: "[They] distribut[ed grain] and vine cattle and sheep" (see Shelestin 2014: 811).

value of Telipinu's narrative for establishing a sequence of events here, or
as a source for anything beyond its own perspective.

Quite what that perspective was is a matter for debate.[90] The *Telipinu
Edict* is clear about the need to reform the succession and end the bloodshed, but it is unclear whether Telipinu himself participated in this. After
Ammuna's natural death, a further bloodbath ensued. Once more, two
people, presumably sons of Ammuna, were murdered, together with their
children, and a Huzziya took the throne. Telipinu was married to his
eldest sister, despite apparently being the son of Ammuna.[91] Presumably
this was a diplomatic arrangement. Huzziya would have killed the two
of them, but the plot was revealed and Telipinu was able to chase off his
attackers, according to his account. Instead of killing Huzziya and his
five brothers, Telipinu gave them a house to live in and turned the other
cheek: "They have done me wrong, but I will not do them wrong."[92]
Only later do they end up being murdered, but allegedly this occurred
without the king's knowledge. This seems rather thin as an explanation.[93]
The murders seem to have happened while Telipinu was away, attempting to reassert a successful Hittite foreign policy. He attacked Haššuwa
in northern Syria as Hattusili I and perhaps also Mursili I had done, but
he suffered a defeat at Zizlippa (location unknown) before being confronted by a rebellion at Lawazantiya (either in Kizzuwatna/Cilicia or
in the Elbistan area, as Old Assyrian Luhuzattiya).[94] Thus, this was not

---

90. For a recent detailed discussion, see Gilan 2015: 137–177.

91. Cf. *Telipinu Edict*, §24: "When I sat on the throne of my father," if this can be
taken literally; see Gilan 2015: 146.

92. *Telipinu Edict*, §23; see Gilan 2015: 146.

93. Hoffner 1975: 51.

94. *Telipinu Edict*, §§24–25; see Gilan 2015: 146–147. For Lawazantiya, see Hawkins
and Weeden 2017: 284–287; Novák and Rutishauser 2017: 138. For Luhuzattiya,
see Barjamovic 2011: 133–143. Whether Telipinu was successful in quelling
this rebellion is unclear from the damaged text, even though most translations
assume that he was: *Telipinu Edict*, §25, ms A: (21) *n=an* [. . .] (22) *kissari=mi
dāir* could read "and they [. . .] took it (Lawazantiya) from my power." It is usually understood differently: "Doch die [Götter] gaben ihn in meine Hand" (so
Gilan 2015: 147); "the gods put him at my mercy" (thus van den Hout 1997: 196).

a campaign full of victories, despite some initial success. Possibly these uneven results caused a feeling that the anger of the gods still needed to be appeased, and the subsequent murders (of which Telipinu was allegedly unaware) may have been a consequence. Whatever actually happened, the *Telipinu Edict* was designed to put the past behind him for the sake of the population of Hattusa and to end the bloodshed.

And yet this did not happen. However, before we proceed further, we should briefly review what other evidence we have for the period of the sixteenth century, most of which was in turmoil, according to Telipinu. A number of texts from the period contain moralizing maxims about correct and incorrect behavior, such as the so-called Palace Chronicles mentioned earlier, which collected tales of incompetent officials that were suited to a banqueting scene, as most of them had to do with eating and drinking.[95] The participants in the banquet are listed at the end of the text, and present what Michele Cammarosano has called an "organizational chart of the family."[96] To a certain extent, one could also see in this table arrangement a microcosm of the Hittite state established by Hattusili I, with his sons and lords from various areas gathered around him. Additional texts, such as the *Decree of Pimpira*, also contain behavioral maxims, based around the "words of the father of the king" (who was presumably Hattusili I). These maxims were directed toward preventing the exploitation of the poor by the rich and encouraged feeding the hungry.[97] It is possible that collections such as the Hittite Laws, the earliest manuscript of which is likely to be dated to around the time of Telipinu, grew during this period out of texts similar to these types.[98] Even if the idea for a collection of behavioral norms that illustrated the king's capacity to rule originated in Mesopotamia, the content of the Laws, including the anecdotal character of a number of examples,

95. *Palace Chronicles*, §§35–40; see Gilan 2015: 125–127; Pecchioli Daddi 1995: 321–332; Dardano 1997: 113.

96. Cammarosano 2006: 50 ("organigramma familiare").

97. Cammarosano 2006.

98. Hoffner 1997.

was largely Anatolian, and gives us a good deal of insight into society at the time. This is true even if these, or the Mesopotamian collections, were very unlikely to have had any status as laws as we might understand them, being discursive explorations of groups of concepts rather than prescriptive rules.

It is during this period that building works began in Hattusa and other cities, which may indicate the formation of a coordinated state, although much research remains to be done on how well embedded these structures were into local communities or whether they remained superficial, and to what extent they paralleled each other chronologically. Over the sixteenth century BC, the Upper City at Hattusa was gradually transformed from a largely agricultural area to one that contained at least three temples, with many more to come, as well as large ponds for water management.[99] Large grain silos capable of feeding far more mouths than can have resided in the individual cities are found at Hattusa (early sixteenth century), Sarissa (late sixteenth century), Kaman-Kalehöyük (fifteenth century), and Alacahöyük.[100] These silos preserved grain by creating an airtight enclosure, using straw as an insulation layer; the microorganisms within used up all the oxygen, making it impossible for pests to survive. However, such silos could only be opened once, and then their contents needed to be used up completely.[101] Therefore, they were of value only in times of famine or when an army was visiting. It is tempting to see these installations in various towns of the older period as a centrally managed system of storage depots that carried a typically Hittite urban blueprint across Central Anatolia,[102] but much research needs still to be done on their chronology to establish if they were actually contemporary with

---

99. Hüser 2007; Schachner 2009; Schachner and Wittenberg 2012.

100. For the silos in Hattusa (modern Boğazköy), see Seeher 2006; Schoop and Seeher 2006: 59–60; Schachner 2009: 12; in Sarissa (modern Kuşaklı), see Müller-Karpe 2002: 182; 2017b: 64; Hüser 2007: 117, 119; in Kaman-Kalehöyük, see Omura 2002; Fairbairn and Omura 2005; in Alacahöyük, see Çınaroğlu and Genç 2002: 428–429.

101. Müller-Karpe 2017a: 82.

102. Schachner 2009.

each other, or not. Furthermore, with the advent of a state, in the second half of the fourteenth century BC, that branded itself much more clearly as a homogeneous political entity through the use of a standardized iconographic repertoire on seals and sealings, for example, and claimed to hold power over much larger territories, such massive storage installations seem to become either smaller or to have gone out of use.[103] This is a paradox between the material evidence and the picture that the texts paint of a powerful and efficient, integrated political and economic structure, or at least with our own construction of that picture according to our preconceptions of what a well-organized state should look like.

According to radiocarbon data taken from tree rings at Sarissa (modern Kuşaklı), the earliest buildings in that city were founded around 1530 BC, thus approaching the time of Telipinu himself, although we do not have specific dates for his reign. The clearly structured, grid layout of the city, which radiated outward from the orientation of the building interpreted as a temple of the storm-god (Building C), is evidence for a remarkably organized approach to city foundation and town planning.[104] This layout appears to have even had consequences for the parceling of the agricultural land around the city. This was a city newly founded and planned at the drawing board, rather than a city that grew out of a pre-existing settlement.[105] Surrounding settlements from the earlier period seem to have been deserted around this time, which suggests population management and large-scale social control.[106] The new city may have been founded in this spot because an increase in temperature had changed the regional ecology, causing the pine coverage to retreat to higher altitudes. This made the site appropriate for agricultural exploitation despite its

---

103. At Kaman-Kalehöyük, smaller, round structures in a far less monumental style replace the older stone-lined structure; see Omura 2002: 19; Fairbairn and Omura 2005: 18.

104. The Hittites used a standard measure for their mud bricks wherever they built; see Seeher 2017; Schachner 2015; Müller-Karpe 2017a: 113.

105. Müller-Karpe 2017a: 16–20.

106. Müller-Karpe 2017a: 20–21.

high elevation.[107] But the key impetus was certainly internal colonialism. Sarissa was the city which most clearly demonstrated the typical early Hittite blueprint, consisting of grain silos that collected from the surrounding areas and complex water-management systems in the form of reservoirs outside the city walls.[108]

This period at the end of the sixteenth century BC, at Hattusa and further abroad, thus seems to have been a time of urban transformation and planned landscapes, with Telipinu's reign singled out by modern scholars as a possible catalyst for a great many of these changes.[109] There is much to be said for this view, but one must be careful not to fall for Telipinu's own propaganda by thinking that the period prior to his rule was one of chaos, in which no such building work might have been possible. In the field of artistic representation, too, it has been argued that the end of the sixteenth century saw developments in iconography that began to pull away from the styles of the previous periods, especially of the Middle Bronze Age, toward a more unified regional style exemplified not only by works at Hattusa itself, but Gavur Kalesi in the central western area, as well as İnandıktepe and Hüseyindede in the central northern area.[110] The adoption of the cuneiform script to write Hittite rather than Akkadian and the creation of official archival collections of cuneiform tablets are now also thought to have happened around this time, and with them the development of instruments of state that used the script and the archives to manage its products, although this remains debatable.[111] In particular the land-donation deed started to take shape as a genre, usually written in Akkadian with some Hittite phrases, on distinctive pillow-shaped tablets and stamped with a cuneiform seal of the king. At first these were anonymous kings (using so-called Tabarna seals), but prosopographical study of the officials mentioned on various

---

107. Hüser 2007: 24; Müller-Karpe 2017a: 27–31.

108. Hüser 2007.

109. Schachner 2009: 26; Müller-Karpe 2017a: 26.

110. Schachner 2012.

111. van den Hout 2012a: 76–80; 2012b.

land-donation documents has been able to show that the earliest tablets of this type must date to around the reign of Telipinu, or possibly shortly before.[112] These land-donation documents provide invaluable data on the arrangement, distribution, and population of arable land, fields, and vineyards and are thus a fascinating source for social history, documenting the Hittite state's attempt to standardize and parcel out the Anatolian landscape. Often they list the people who belonged to the land by name, which on the one hand indicates claimed property rights over individuals, but on the other hand shows that these people needed to be named as individuals—simple numbers would not do.

The land-donation tablets are also among the only sources we have for the political history of the Hittite state for the first half of the fifteenth century BC. On the basis of these, as well as later offering lists to deceased members of the royal family, it has been possible to reconstruct a series of rulers: Alluwamna; succeeded by his son Hantili II; succeeded by either Tahurwaili and then Zidanta (II), or Zidanta (II) and then Tahurwaili; succeeded by Huzziya, who was murdered by Muwatalli I.[113] Land donations appear to have been used particularly during this period to shore up property relations in contested areas in favor of Hittite emissaries. Thus Hantili II made a land donation to the official Hillariz ("Chief of the Deaf") in Kammama, a city which was often on the front line in disputes with the "Kaska" people to the northeast, a term used by the Hittites to refer to non-Hittite agro-pastoralist population groups in northern and northeastern Anatolia.[114] Another land donation was made by Zidanta II to an official, Nakkiliya, and mentions (in addition to other places in different areas around central Anatolia) the area of Hupisna (classical Kybistra or nearby) in southern Cappadocia on the way to Cilicia.[115]

---

112. Wilhelm 2005; Rüster and Wilhelm 2012.

113. Klengel 1999: 84–103; Bryce 2005: 111–120; Freu and Mazoyer 2007: 153–184; Rüster and Wilhelm 2012: 49–57.

114. Land donation tablet 28; see Rüster and Wilhelm 2012: 158–159. For the Kaska, see Gerçek 2021.

115. Land donation tablet 39; see Rüster and Wilhelm 2012: 178–179.

This is of interest with regards to the other main type of documentation we have for this period. Starting with Telipinu, we have a series of treaties with the area of Kizzuwatna, which was of great strategic importance to Hattusa.[116] The exact extent of the area of Kizzuwatna is unclear, but there is a general consensus that the core area consisted of the region around Adana between the Amanus and the Taurus mountains.[117] Doubt remains only as to whether it extended further into the region of the Upper Seyhan and Zamantı Su rivers, near where the Fraktin rock relief depicts the thirteenth-century Hittite king Hattusili III and his wife Pudu-Heba (see section 30.4), who is given the epithet "daughter of Kizzuwatna" on the relief, possibly thus indicating a border or other feature that would make such a description significant.[118] The series of treaties with this region that belong to the fifteenth century chart Hattusa's changing relationships not only with Kizzuwatna, but also with the powers that had influence in northern Syria beyond the Amanus mountains, especially the Mittani state (for which, see chapter 29 in this volume).[119] The treaties regulated such matters as the return of refugees, fugitive artisans, or other populations, and the fortification of settlements and borders. Typically, Hittite treaties are graded by modern scholars according to the power relationships that existed between the parties, from those where Hattusa seemed to be treating another power more or less equally (parity treaty), to those where there was a clear power imbalance, or even a supposed vassal or client relationship (subjugation treaty). The Kizzuwatna treaties can be assessed at various points along these scales, with those between Telipinu and Isputaḫsu, Zidanta II and Pilliya, Tahurwaili and Eheya, and that of an unnamed Hittite king (probably Huzziya

116. Beckman 1996: 11–22; Wilhelm 2011; 2014a–c; Devecchi 2015: 63–92.

117. Trémouille 2001; Novák and Rutishäuser 2017; Hawkins and Weeden 2017.

118. For the Fraktin rock relief, see Kohlmeyer 1983: 71–72, figs. 24–25; Ehringhaus 2005: 59–65; Glatz and Plourde 2011: 47, fig. 6.

119. For the often sharply differing views of the history of Kizzuwatna, compare, e.g., the accounts of Börker-Klähn 1996; Freu 2001; Novák 2010; Ünal 2014; and Yağcı 2015.

II) and Paddatiššu of Kizzuwatna classed as parity treaties, where the stipulations are reciprocally shared between Hattusa and Kizzuwatna. However, the stakes appear to be changing. The treaty between Pilliya and Zidanta II seems to have emerged from a somewhat changed situation, which may also be reflected in the fact that Zidanta is giving land donations to Hittite officials near the border to Kizzuwatna (as earlier at Hupisna): in the fragmentary treaty-text, Pilliya pledged not to fortify certain fortified cities, whereas "My Majesty," the Hittite king, agrees not to do something to deserted cities (presumably re-fortify them). More typical of a subjugation treaty, however, was the one-sided clause indicating that Pilliya would be "transgressing the oath" if he does this.[120]

The treaty between Zidanta II and Pilliya also offers a further synchronism with the chronology of Alalakh, as Pilliya of Kizzuwatna also had an agreement with Idrimi of Alalakh, the document of which was excavated at Alalakh (Tell Atchana, Level IV). The treaty dealt solely with the reciprocal restitution of fugitives and has been dated to after Idrimi's campaign against "Hatti," which he mentions in his statue inscription also found at the site.[121] This would imply that Hatti also included Kizzuwatna from Idrimi's perspective, even if the treaty with the Hittite Zidanta II would seem to have left Pilliya quite independent, although less so than prior kings. Parattarna, the king of Mittani, is supposed to have presided over the treaty-signing between Idrimi and Pilliya, which has repercussions for our understanding of the power relations between the trio of Kizzuwatna–Alalakh–Mittani, but in fact he is only mentioned in a clause which talks about the date from which the (agreement concerning) return of fugitives will be valid—namely since

---

120. Wilhelm 2014a: §2, l. 13; Devecchi 2015: 22–23, 68–69.

121. von Dassow 2008: 38. The archaeological correlate for this event is also a matter of dispute, and relates either to the transition from Alalakh Level Va to Vb, or to that from Level V to level IV (the latter if we agree with von Dassow that Idrimi is responsible for building the Level IV palace usually associated with his son Niqmepa). For Idrimi's statue inscription, see Jacob Lauinger's online edition (http://oracc.museum.upenn.edu/aemw/alalakh/idrimi/; last accessed December 22, 2018).

Idrimi and Parattarna swore an oath.[122] Thus Idrimi's Alalakh was subject to Parattarna of Mittani, while Pilliya's Kizzuwatna was beginning to be overshadowed by the kingdom of Hattusa to the north. It was also presumably around this time that a specific wave of ritual texts originating from Kizzuwatna and associated with Pilliya began to make their way to Hattusa, where they were curated in the royal archives and are preserved in later copies.[123] Such movement of cultural knowledge is a sign that the Hittite eye was firmly set on a particular area in a political sense as much as anything else. In concrete terms, this might mean that Hittite officials or scribes had access to Kizzuwatnian archives. By the time we reach the Hittite king Tudhaliya I in the later fifteenth century, Kizzuwatna was more decisively subjugated, but it seems there had been some disturbance in the meantime:

At the time of my grandfather the land of Kizzuwatna started to belong to the Land of Hatti, but later the land of Kizzuwatna released (itself) from the land of Hatti and turned around to the land of Hurri.[124]

Tudhaliya I's grandfather was probably Huzziya II, who may also have been responsible for a treaty with a king of Kizzuwatna called Paddatiššu.[125]

---

122. Wiseman 1953: no. 3 rev. 40–43; von Dassow 2008: 23–39. However, the presence of the seal of Parattarna on the document only has relevance for Idrimi's authorization to conclude the treaty (contra von Dassow 2008: 38; Bryce 2005: 422, among others). It does not necessarily mean that Kizzuwatna was subject to Mittani at this time.

123. Ritual of Pa/illiya; see Beckman 2013.

124. Beckman 1996: 14 §2 (Šunaššura Treaty); Wilhelm 2014b §2; Devecchi 2015: 78 (with n. 4 linking this to the time of the agreement between Pilliya and Idrimi). For an overview of the complex history of the drafts, including the best preserved version between Šunaššura and Tudhaliya I, see Wilhelm 2011; Devecchi 2015: 73–76.

125. Beckman 1996: 11–13; Wilhelm 2014c; Devecchi 2015: 70–73 (with an overview of other proposals for Paddatiššu's Hittite treaty partner); de Martino 2010: 189.

However, before Tudhaliya I could take the throne, there occurred considerable confusion and internecine carnage. The king who followed Zidanta II was either Tahurwaili (unless he preceded him) about whom we know very little aside from his treaty with Eheya of Kizzuwatna, or Tahurwaili was followed as king by Huzziya II, presumably legitimately as the son of either Tahurwaili or of Zidanta II. We know little more about Huzziya II than that he was murdered by a Muwatalli.[126] This was reported in a slightly later instructional oath text for princes, lords, and military officers, which most likely dated to the reign of Tudhaliya I, where it served as an exemplar of how servants should not kill their lords.[127] Nevertheless, we now know from a seal impression from Hattusa that Tudhaliya's father was called Kantuzzili.[128] There seems to have been a number of officials called Kantuzzili around at the same time,[129] but this one was likely to have been the one of the Himuili and Kantuzzili who were responsible for the murder of Muwatalli I. We know about this murder from the fragmentary testimony in a series of oath-texts dealing with securing the dynastic succession of Tudhaliya I and then later of Tudhaliya II, both of whom took the throne under difficult circumstances.[130] In this sense, the documents have a similar function as the *Telipinu*

---

126. Klengel 1999: 97–100; Bryce 2005: 114–115; Freu and Mazoyer 2007: 167–174. For the treaty with Eheya of Kizzuwatna, see Devecchi 2015: 65–68.

127. Miller 2013: 179, no. 12 §34. Miller considers that the text could alternatively be dated to the reign of Arnuwanda I, immediately after that of Tudhaliya I (Miller 2013: 168 with further literature). The context is too fragmentary to be certain, but that Tudhaliya I should have wanted to ensure that his courtiers and relatives would not murder him was possibly even more urgent than one might normally expect, given the circumstances under which he took the throne, or at least was put on the throne by his likely regicidal father.

128. Otten 2000: 375–376; Freu 2004.

129. Soysal 2003; de Martino 2010: 186–188; Herbordt et al. 2011: 87–89; Soysal 2011.

130. Miller 2013: 158–159, §2 (ms A$_2$, ll. 9′–10′). Differently, Freu and Mazoyer 2007b: 36, 43.

Edict, which also followed, and attempted to put an end to, a period of bloodshed.[131] It remains a guess that Kantuzzili's father was the Huzziya II who had been murdered by Muwatalli, although it is likely that by disposing of Muwatalli I the original dynastic line had in some way been re-established.[132] Muwatalli I does not seem to have made it into the offering lists for dead kings, but he does appear to have tried, in time-honored fashion, to cement his authority by means of land donations to nobles, with the witnesses possibly including those who eventually murdered him.[133] Among the places mentioned in these is Zipishuna, later known to have been on the outskirts of Maşathöyük (ancient Tapikka), which seems to have been considered a border region between the northeast and the uncontrolled Kaska populations there, despite being located not terribly far from Hattusa.[134] It is usually assumed that he did not remain on the throne for a long period, but his reign and the bloodshed that accompanied it set the stage for the following period of attempted Hittite expansion, which, like the similar period under Telipinu, was preceded by an allegedly chaotic time that had resulted in the recalibration of loyalties, a reorganization of the administration, and a temporary expansion by military means in the following reign. However, he must have reigned long enough for the land of Kizzuwatna to exploit the power vacuum and turn away from Hattusa to Mittani, although this view depends on one's dating and interpretation of the Kizzuwatna treaties, especially the agreement between Idrimi of Alalakh and Pilliya of Kizzuwatna.

30.3. The Early Empire Period

Tudhaliya I's reign, even though not marked by durable successes, is often thought to signal a change in Hittite strategy, imperial constitution,

---

131. Miller 2013: 155 (with further literature).

132. Klengel 1999: 110; Bryce 2005: 114.

133. Rüster and Wilhelm 2012: 198 (no. 46), 202–203 (no. 47).

134. Rüster and Wilhelm 2012: 202–203 (no. 47).

military objectives, and cultural focus. It is unclear whether actual strategy and military objectives had changed since Hattusili I; rather it is thought that the capacity of the Central Anatolian state to affect them had shifted. The "Provinces" of the Lower and Upper Lands are thought to have been set up at this time.[135] Tudhaliya introduced a new tradition of queens with Hurrian names with his queen Nikkal-mati, and it is also from his reign onward (or at least that of his successor) that a more intensive engagement with Hurrian (religious) culture in the royal archives is thought to be dated.[136] Mesopotamian and Hurrian goddesses such as Išhara or the "deity of the night" are "split" from their homes and temples in Kizzuwatna and transferred to more definitely Hittite territory—in particular to Samuha (now identified securely with modern Kayalıpınar on the Eastern bend of the Kızılırmak).[137] He was also the first king to write his name in Anatolian hieroglyphs on his seal.

Tudhaliya I's treaty with Sunaššura (Šunaššura) of Kizzuwatna laid down a border between the two areas, and guaranteed Kizzuwatna a degree of autonomy, as long as it did not turn back to supporting Mittani (cf. chapter 29 in this volume)—in fact the treaty clearly stated that while the Hurrian had treated Sunaššura like a slave, the Hittite treaty would make him a king.[138] The main version of the treaty was mostly based on reciprocal parity, but there is the question of Sunaššura being called into the presence of "My Majesty," even if he was allowed to send one of his sons instead, while there was no allowance for such a summons to work the other way around.[139] The same paragraph informs us that Sunaššura did not have to pay tribute, presumably because that is what would usually be expected on the occasion of such visits to the

---

135. Matessi 2017: 26.

136. Campbell 2016.

137. Miller 2004: 350–356.

138. Second treaty with Sunaššura of Kizzuwatna, §9; see Beckman 1996: 15; Wilhelm 2014b; Devecchi 2015: 80.

139. Second treaty with Sunaššura of Kizzuwatna, §10.

Hittite king. The historical introduction to the main (second) version of the treaty mentions a conflict with the "Man of Hurri" over Išuwa (in the modern-day region of Elazığ) which stretched back into the time of the Hurrian's grandfather, when entire communities had moved from that area into the territory of Mittani.[140] Not only had the Hurrian refused to send them back, he also seems to have used their presence in his territory as a pretext to raid Išuwa behind the Hittite king's back while he was trying to put down a rebellion there. The whole Išuwa narrative was presumably introduced as a backdrop to what was then happening with Kizzuwatna: in the past, at least (according to the treaty with Paddatiššu), the transfer of entire towns or communities from one side of a border to another had also been an issue. Indeed the Paddatiššu treaty was careful to point out that the whole town must be moved, with not a single person left behind.[141] Presumably if anyone was left behind, then cross-border rights to property could be claimed; the Hurrian may have been enforcing such a claim by means of his army in the case of Išuwa.

Like some of the other Kizzuwatna treaties, the Sunaššura treaties are embedded into synchronisms that at least help us to orient ourselves with regard to relative chronologies known from northern Syria and further afield. At Alalakh Level IV there is a legal document of an adjudication regarding a dispute over a town called Alawari. The disputants were Sunaššura and Niqmepa of Alalakh, who was the son of the same Idrimi who previously had an agreement with Pilliya of Kizzuwatna.[142] The adjudication was ratified by the Mittanian king Sauštatar (or Saussatar), but sealed with the "dynastic" seal of Šuttarna son of Kirta.[143] Thus one gains several synchronicities (table 30.1).

---

140. Second treaty with Sunaššura of Kizzuwatna, §§3–6.

141. Paddatiššu treaty, §6; see Beckman 1996: 13; Devecchi 2015: 72.

142. Wiseman 1953: no. 14; von Dassow 2008: 48 (with further literature).

143. Wilhelm 1989: 28, 114 fig. 14; von Dassow 2008: 46.

Table 30.1. Synchronisms between the kingdoms of Hattusa, Kizzuwatna, Alalakh, and Mittani.

Kingdom of	Hattusa	Kizzuwatna	Alalakh	Mittani
(1)	Zidanta II	Pilliya	Idrimi	Parattarna
(2)	Tudhaliya I	Sunaššura	Niqmepa	Sauštatar

These synchronisms are not as neat as one would like them to be.[144] Tudhaliya I, as we saw earlier, spoke of the time of his grandfather when Kizzuwatna was becoming "of Hatti." We do not know who that grandfather was, whether Huzziya II or Zidanta II. On the other hand, Niqmepa was the son of Idrimi. Clearly, the generations are not parallel and some people are blessed with long lives, whereas others may have only been on the scene for a short time. All that we can securely conclude is that these entities were interlinked closely over time and that their interests collided, particularly those of Hattusa and Mittani.

Tudhaliya I likely dates to the second half of the fifteenth century BC. Fragmentary annals of this king and his successor Arnuwanda I were preserved in the archives at Hattusa, albeit mostly on later copies, which obscured for some time whether their attribution was to this Tudhaliya or a later one.[145] The broken text picks up on the king's return from a campaign against Arzawa in the West, including references to areas known from elsewhere to belong to that region, such as the Seha River Lands, the land of Hapalla, and the land of Wallarima.[146] However, he

---

144. There is no need to interpolate an additional Kizzuwatnean king Talzu before Sunaššura on the basis of the text regulating property and provisions of the temple of the goddess Išhara in Kizzuwatna (Chrzanowska 2017: §2), as the assumption that Talzu was a king is based on a modern restoration of this title, which is not found in the text itself. Even if he were a king, given that he is setting up a temple and disposing of lands, there is no indication that he ruled at this time rather than in the distant past.

145. Carruba 1977.

146. Carruba 1977: KUB 23: no. 11: obv. ii 2′–12′.

was forced to turn around by a revolt of several lands that came together under the banner of the land of Assuwa. Although difficult to locate and frequently confused by modern scholars with Arzawa, Assuwa seems to have been centered in north central-western Anatolia, with an important city at a place called Aldanna, but its alliances reached as far as Wilusa and Taruisa, which are famously and controversially located by many modern scholars in the northwestern coastal region.[147] At any rate, Tudhaliya's Assuwa campaign was so successful that, on the one hand, Assuwa ceased to have any geopolitical significance in the region,[148] and on the other, its name was significant enough to be remembered in later documents (even as far as Egypt)[149] and its defeat was celebrated by Tudhaliya himself on a sword inscribed in the prestige language of Akkadian; coincidentally, this sword was found near modern-day Boğazkale during road works.[150]

As so frequently happened in Hittite history, once the Hittite king's back was turned to deal with the uprising in Assuwa, he faced incursions from another part of the territory, namely from the Kaska in the north(east), whom he pursued back into Kaska territory and defeated in a forest at a place called Tiwara.[151] Next it was Išuwa and the Hurrian king who caused difficulties for Tudhaliya, where the account in the annals appears to overlap with the historical introduction to the second treaty of Tudhaliya I with Sunaššura of Kizzuwatna mentioned earlier. A later historical introduction to a deed ratified with the king of Aleppo

147. On Assuwa, see Gander 2015. On Wilus(iy)a, see Heinhold-Krahmer 1977: 157–178; 2013; Hawkins 1995.

148. If this is the same as Assuwa (?) of the annals of Thutmose III (1479–1425 BC), then the last delivery of gifts to the pharaoh from this land happened in his thirty-ninth year, so Tudhaliya's Assuwa campaign presumably took place after this. See Redford 2003: 250–251; Gander 2015: 446 n. 12.

149. It is quite possible that Assuwa is the land referred to as the homeland of foreign captives on an inscription of Amenhotep III (1388–1350 BC) at Kom el-Hetan, which is from some fifty years after Tudhaliya's destruction of Assuwa; Gander (2015: 452) supposes that the pharaoh's scribes may have been compiling his inscription from out-of-date lists.

150. Ünal 1992; 1993.

151. Carruba 1977.

(Halab) by his cousin, the Hittite king Mursili II, looks back on the destruction of that city by a Hittite king Tudhaliya, after Aleppo had sided with the king of Hanigalbat/Mittani (the text uses both terms).[152] This is very likely to have been Tudhaliya I, who extended his campaigning into Syria in order to counter Mittanian activities in that region after Hurrian support for the insurrection in Išuwa. A fragmentary treaty is also preserved that likely dates to his reign; it regulated relations between Tunip on the middle Orontes and Alalakh. This indicates that Tudhaliya must have been pursuing a relatively wide regional strategy for a number of years, and possibly exploited the effects of Egyptian interference in the area (if a chronological overlap between the two can be found).[153]

However, once again local problems in Anatolia seem to have curtailed Hittite ambitions in Syria. Although the sequence of events has not been precisely established, Tudhaliya seems to have had unfinished business in Arzawa. The so-called *Indictment of Madduwatta* details problems that clearly stretched over a number of years and the reigns of at least two Hittite kings (Tudhaliya I and Arnuwanda I), including a likely co-regency between the two, and are all bound up with the activities of the local central western Anatolian potentate after whom the text is named today.[154] Madduwatta starts with his being saved by the "Father of My Majesty" from Attarissiya, the man of Ahhiya, and

---

152. Beckman 1999: 93–95; Devecchi 2010; 2015: 233–237.

153. Devecchi 2015: 185. Presumably this treaty came about after or between the various encounters between Thutmose III (1479–1425 BC) and the city of Tunip and its representatives: Years 29, 31 (at Ullaza), 42 (Breasted 1906: 196, 199, 215; Redford 2003: 239). Klinger (1995: 246) speaks of a "Hittite intermezzo" ("hethitisches Intermezzo") in Syria between Years 31 and 42. Singer 2004: 636 dates the Kurustama Treaty with Egypt (likely Tudhaliya I) to the time of Amenhotep II (1425–1397 BC), which allows a more appropriate time frame to fit three Hittite kings until Suppiluliuma I around 1350 BC. However, the lower of three Egyptian chronologies proposed by Gautschy 2014 also allows a reduced duration for this period, and thus for the Kurustama Treaty to have been concluded between Tudhaliya and Thutmose III. A complex reconstruction of events with various further Hittite kings can be found in Freu and Mazoyer 2007b: 53–56.

154. Beckman 1996: 144–151; Bryce 2005: 129–138; Freu and Mazoyer 2007b: 106–116; Beckman et al. 2011: 69–100.

he was initially given a mountain region to occupy that was relatively close to Hattusa ("mountain land of Hariyati"), but he refused this and was then given another mountain region to occupy (Zippasla). He swore the usual kind of loyalty oath that is known from subjugation treaties, also agreeing not to expand beyond the confines of the area he had been given to settle. But Madduwatta continuously interfered in other regions of western Anatolia, particularly in areas roughly corresponding, but not confined, to classical Lycia (later known as the Lukka Lands), and occupied further territories, including at one point "all Arzawa."[155] He even led a Hittite general to his death through deceitful collaboration with local forces and laughed about it. He also seems to have been active around Cyprus (ancient Alašiya). In total, this text does not cohere with the image of successful campaigning in the Arzawa area that we are given by the annals of Tudhaliya I, even if fragmentary. In fact, the Hittites appear in the *Indictment of Madduwatta* as "wannabe" imperialists, out of their depth and bogged down in a region that they attempt to claim control over while the locals point fingers and make fun of them.

The *Indictment of Madduwatta* thus gives a view of a persistent problem with western Anatolia that will be reflected in later texts as well, including proxy conflicts with a ruler of Ahhiya/Ahhiyawa (presumably transmarine Greece or the islands off the Anatolian coast; see chapter 31 in this volume), and an inability to exercise control in the region over at least two reigns, even if Tudhaliya I was able to gain a decisive victory over Assuwa, which appears to be further north and more central than Arzawa.

Despite Tudhaliya I's and Arnuwanda I's efforts to emphasize the level of their administrative control, there is evidence of governmental instability in the so-called *Instruction Texts*, which outline the officials' duties and often require an oath of them.[156] There are a good number of these texts from the reigns of these two kings, especially Arnuwanda I. However, rather as the *Telipinu Edict* and possibly the written form

---

155. *Indictment of Madduwatta*, §19; see Beckman 1996: 149.

156. Miller 2013.

of the Hittite Laws (often attributed to his reign) can be seen as reactions to a period of instability and internecine strife, so too can the many instruction texts from the later fifteenth century BC, coming as they do after another period of serial dynastic murder. And while these instruction texts can certainly be seen as a concerted attempt to consolidate the Hittite state, one can question just how successful they were as instruments of social or territorial control. Despite undisputed victories in Assuwa and later in Syria, even for the reign of Tudhaliya I the *Indictment of Madduwatta* shows signs of the acceleration of the process of territorial disintegration (rooted in the difficulty of asserting state or military control over a fragmented geographical landscape) that was to last another eighty years, at least until the mid-fourteenth century BC.[157]

One further expression of this territorial insecurity can be found in the many treaties with the agro-pastoralist "Kaska" groups from northern and northeastern Anatolia, a number of which most likely date to the reign of Arnuwanda I.[158] It had not been necessary to draw up treaties with such groups before, although there may be a precursor in the form of an Old Hittite "loyalty oath" with a similar group referred to as Hapiru (employing a term for loose bands of nomads that was common in northern Syria; cf. chapter 28 in this volume).[159]

Arnuwanda I is usually referred to in texts and on seals as the son of Tudhaliya I, and in turn mentions the latter as "the father of My Majesty" in the *Indictment of Madduwatta*. Nevertheless there are seal impressions of his queen Asmu-Nikkal, which call her the "daughter of great queen Nikkal-mati," i.e., of the wife of Tudhaliya I.[160] So it is possible that he was a son-in-law of Tudhaliya I who had been adopted as a son.[161] Arnuwanda and Asmu-Nikkal had a number of sons, of whom one became King Tudhaliya II (previously often referred to as

---

157. Stavi 2015: 64 dates the beginning of the process to the end of Arnuwanda's reign.

158. Devecchi 2015: 110–124; Gerçek 2021.

159. Giorgieri 2005: 323–325.

160. Güterbock 1940: no. 60, 77; Herbordt et al. 2011: 85, 109, no. 3.

161. Beal 1983: 115–119; Miller 2004: 356 n. 504; Herbordt et al. 2011: 66, 85.

Tudhaliya III).[162] Tudhaliya II had two wives, one attested on hieroglyphic seal impressions from Tapikka (modern Maşathöyük) and the other on a hieroglyphic mold from Sapinuwa (modern Ortaköy), and both are attested in fragmentary cuneiform texts from Hattusa. Both had Hurrian names: Satandu-Heba and Tadu-Heba.[163] Extensive purification rites (Hurrian *itkalzi* ritual) in association with a wedding ceremony between Tudhaliya (under the name of Tašmi-Šarri: a Hurrian alternative name, such as Hittite kings from this period onward often began to take) and his queen Tadu-Heba are preserved on tablets both from Hattusa and from Sapinuwa.[164] The ceremony was supposed to have taken place in the unidentified northern town of Zithara, but seems to have been of great significance for the archives both at Hattusa and at Sapinuwa, with copies of some of the tablets from Hattusa kept in Sapinuwa, according to their colophons. And indeed Sapinuwa was where Tudhaliya II resided for much of his reign, and a wealth of cuneiform tablets dating to this period, including international correspondence and ritual content in Hittite, Hurrian, Hattic, and Akkadian, is preserved from there.[165] The correspondence particularly illustrates the difficulties experienced by the Hittites in achieving territorial integrity in Central Anatolia during this period, illuminating the reach and coordination of those within Anatolia and without who opposed their interests, but also the wide-ranging network of contacts that the Hittite royal

---

162. Whether a king Hattusili II should be inserted here or shortly before is a matter for debate hinging on the interpretation of one text: the historical preamble to the *Aleppo Treaty*, which is susceptible to text-internal reinterpretation, including that the Hattusili mentioned there is Hattusili I: Herbordt et al. 2011: 86–89. Because this debate has not been decided, this chapter refers to the contemporary of Rameses II (1279–1213 BC) in the traditional way as Hattusili III.

163. Tapikka (modern Maşathöyük): Alp 1980: 54, pl. 1–2; Sapinuwa (modern Ortaköy): M. Süel 2008: 476; Herbordt et al. 2011: 85–86, 89 (with the contention based on difficult-to-read signs on the "Cruciform Seal"—see earlier in this section—that Tašmi-Šarri is in fact Suppiluliuma I); De Martino 2010b.

164. De Martino, Murat, and Süel 2013; De Martino and Süel 2017.

165. Süel and Süel 2017.

family were able to draw on, even during such a period of weakness, which extended at least as far as Ugarit in northern Syria.[166] Indeed, a Hurrian-language text excavated at Samuha (modern Kayalıpınar) may suggest a campaign conducted, most likely by Tudhaliya II based on the use of Hurrian, against Mittanian holdings in Mukiš (the Amuq region) via Kizzuwatna.[167] This may tally with a reference to Tudhaliya II campaigning around Mount Nanni (the Anti-Cassius) in an otherwise difficult to place fragment of the *Deeds of Suppiluliuma* (son of Tudhaliya II) as narrated by his own son, Mursili II.[168]

On the basis of a narrative found in a later text, from the reign of Hattusili III (mid-thirteenth century BC), which purports to sum up the events of this period, it is frequently referred to as the time of the concentric invasions, because enemies were thought to be invading from all compass directions, and the city of Hattusa itself is thought to have been burned to the ground.[169] There is no archaeological evidence for a destruction of the city taking place at this time in Hattusa.[170] In this text, which is actually a decree exempting a particular institution known as the Hekur of Pirwa from the payment of taxes, Hattusili III, who himself came to power by usurping his nephew's throne, attempted to present himself as a savior of the realm, much like his grandfather, Suppiluliuma I, who brought an end to the concentric invasions. So it is part of this document's rhetorical strategy to present this period in time as a complete catastrophe. However, even if Hattusa was not certifiably burned down during this period, Tudhaliya II does not seem to have resided there for much of his reign. He moved his capital first to Sapinuwa (modern Ortaköy), which

166. For letters mentioning Tarhun(d)aradu and other names typical of Arzawan royalty, as well as refugees and contacts between anti-Hittite powers to the west and to the east, see A. Süel 2014; regarding contacts with Syria in letters found at Sapinuwa (modern Ortaköy), see A. Süel 2017.

167. Wilhelm *apud* Rieken 2009: 130–133; Wilhelm 2012: 231–233.

168. del Monte 2008: 6–7.

169. Stavi 2015: 38–43.

170. Klengel 1999: 152 n. 52.

was definitely burned down, and then to Samuha (modern Kayalıpınar). Other cities in the Hittite heartland (Maşathöyük = ancient Tapikka; Kuşaklı = ancient Sarissa) also suffered temporary destruction around this time. So there is a kernel of truth in Hattusili's historical summary, but we should not assume that this was something that happened over a short period. It is likely that the "concentric invasions" lasted a long time, capitalizing on territorial fractures already apparent in the reigns of Tudhaliya I and Arnuwanda I and even including long-term hostile occupations from north, west, and east at certain sites located dangerously close to the Hittite capital.[171] Hattusili's account is telescoped for dramatic effect. Indeed it also seems that long-range campaigning activity also may have occurred during Tudhaliya II's reign, as seen earlier, so the situation was not completely out of control.[172]

However, at some point during the later stages of this period, the central authority at Hattusa was so weakened that Arzawa in western Anatolia took over from Hattusa as the main contact point for the Egyptians in Anatolia, and correspondence in Hittite between Amenhotep III (1388–1350 BC) and one Tarhundaradu, with whom a dynastic marriage was being arranged, was preserved at Akhetaten (modern Tell el-Amarna) in Egypt (see also chapter 28 in this volume).[173] That the language of communication was Hittite, and that the Arzawan scribe asked his Egyptian counterpart to please use that language, shows that Hittite had assumed a similar status in Anatolia to that of Akkadian at the same time throughout the Levant and in Egypt, namely that of the main language of international written communication. That the letter from the pharoah reported that "the land of Hattusa has been frozen" and asked Tarhundaradu in the west of Anatolia to send him Kaska

---

171. For apparent diplomatic texts found at Büklükale on the western bend of the Kızılırmak and possible implications, see Weeden 2017.

172. Stavi 2015: 77.

173. EA 31–32; for a convenient English translation, see Moran 1992: 101–103. Moran 1992: xxxiv argues that the Amarna archive must have started around Amenhotep III's Year 30 (= 1359 BC), so these letters should not be earlier. See Stavi 2015: 65.

people (i.e., from the northeast!) indicates that Hattusa territory had been seriously infringed.[174]

Another important corpus of primary source material, probably mostly from the reign of Tudhaliya II, are the letters from Tapikka (modern Maşathöyük, Level III), which was burned down in the first half of the fourteenth century.[175] Approximately half of these are either to or from the king.[176] These letters frequently concern the threat posed by "the enemy," which may have included the neighboring Kaska people, who appear to have lived in the mountains and came down to cause problems in the area of the Maşat plain, or alternately to find employment as laborers.[177] Given the relatively short distance of 116 km between Maşathöyük (Tapikka) and Boğazköy (Hattusa), this again provides the modern reader the disturbing impression of a state whose territorial integrity was porous, and partially inhabited by significant population groups that could both be useful economically or turn suddenly hostile and destructive. The non-epistolary documents from Maşathöyük's Level III give insight into the local, palace-based economy, as well as into the range and effectiveness of local government.[178] One document seems to record low crop yields.[179] This tablet may have been preserved because it was exceptional, but it may also provide a glimpse into the kind of environment in which disaffection with Hittite authority could grow.

30.4. The Empire Period

Tudhaliya II was eventually succeeded by his son, Suppiluliuma I, although not without interruption, as we learn from later texts (see later

---

174. Moran 1992: 101, no. 31, 22–27; Stavi 2015: 57–58.

175. For a seal of Suppiluliuma I from Maşathöyük Level II, see Özgüç 1982: 78. Radiocarbon dates on tree rings recovered from Maşathöyük have provided some support, albeit ambiguous and dubious; see Yakar 2011: 81.

176. Alp 1991. On the dating debate, see Klinger 1995b; van den Hout 2007.

177. Alp 1991: no. 10; 23; 66.

178. del Monte 1995.

179. Marazzi 2008: 77–79; Süel and Weeden 2017: 204–205.

discussion in this section). We know that Suppiluliuma was the son of Tudhaliya from seal impressions found at Hattusa and at Maşathöyük Level II.[180] For Suppiluliuma's reign, the main ancient source is the account of his *Deeds* (Hittite *pesnatar*, literally "Manliness") made by his son Mursili II, the narrative of which begins with Tudhaliya II, who is ill and residing in Samuha (modern Kayalıpınar on the eastern bend of the Kızılırmak).[181] He dispatched his son Suppiluliuma from Samuha to the central areas around Hattusa in order to deal with the Kaska and to the east in order to counter the Hayasans, resulting in their "tribal troops" and booty being brought back to Samuha. Evacuated villages were repopulated and provided with watchtowers. Suppiluliuma also conducted a successful campaign against Arzawa; as also attested by the summary in the text of Hattusili III concerning Hekur of Pirwa, Arzawa had established control over the region of Tuwanuwa (classical Tyanitis, the region around modern Niğde), from where attacks had been mounted against outposts in the Upper Land (i.e., the area of Samuha and further east).[182] Later, Tudhaliya himself recovered and was able to advance from the Upper Land to deal with further groups of Kaska beyond the western bend of the Kızılırmak (Masa and Kammala), before returning to face the Hayasans in the northeast at Kummahi.[183] In all these instances of warfare, the Hittite king and his son Suppiluliuma were able to cover huge distances with their troops while fighting enemies on all sides.

The details of Suppiluliuma's ascent to the throne are unclear due to a gap in the *Deeds*, but it would appear from his son Mursili II's *Plague Prayers* that a crime was committed against Tudhaliya "the younger"

---

180. Alp 1980: 56; Otten 1993: 10.

181. *Deeds of Suppiluliuma*, fragment 10; see del Monte 2008: 12–13, 25–29; Hoffner 1997b: 186.

182. *Deeds of Suppiluliuma*, fragment 14–17; see del Monte 2008: 30–37 (putting Suppiluliuma's action against the Arzawan presence in Tuwanuwa before Tudhaliya's recovery, in contrast to Hoffner 1997b: 187, following Güterbock 1956).

183. *Deeds of Suppiluliuma*, fragment 13; see del Monte 2008: 42–43 (with a different order of the fragments and thus of the action to Hoffner 1997b: 187).

(thus Tudhaliya III),[184] which an oracle question posed by Mursili II established as a possible cause for a plague that had been ravaging Hattusa for the last twenty years.[185] With this passage in mind, it is easy to suspect that Suppiluliuma murdered his brother in order to take the throne. When the narrative picks up again in the *Deeds*, Suppiluliuma's activities in the northeast are cut short by further disruption in the west, where three local princes from Arzawa and Mira had invaded the area bordering the central Hittite territory (Mahuirasa and Pedassa). Suppiluliuma initially sent a general (Himuili, the "Chief of Wine"), who was defeated, and then himself intervened, winning a victory and re-fortifying several cities (including the key strategic city of Sallapa). He then proceeded back to northeastern Hakpis to continue fighting on that front. In the beginning of the following year, he dispatched Hannutti, the "Chief of the Charioteers," to deal (successfully) with the western area of Hapalla, where the rebels had fled, as the king himself was preoccupied by the long and complex festival of the spring crocus.[186]

There is no further information about the west in the *Deeds of Suppiluliuma* as narrated by his son Mursili; but other, later texts, including Mursili II's own annals, as well as treaties between the Hittite kings and the western states, give us glimpses of further-reaching contacts— such as the fact that King Kukunni of Wilusa was loyal to Suppiluliuma during his Arzawa campaigns,[187] that good relations had been upheld with the king of the Seha River Lands during this time,[188] that there may have been a treaty with Uhhaziti of Arzawa,[189] and that Suppiluliuma

---

184. Tudhaliya "the Younger" = Tudhaliya III: tentatively Klengel 1999: 148 n. 27; Miller 2004: 8–9. That this Tudhaliya was also king is suggested by Mursili II's *First Plague Prayer*, §2; see Singer 2002: 61.

185. *First Plague Prayer*, §§2–4; see Singer 2002: 61–62.

186. del Monte 2008: 65; Matessi 2017: 135.

187. Alaksandu treaty (Muwatalli II), §3; see Beckman 1996: 82; Devecchi 2015: 153.

188. Manapa-Tarhunda treaty (Mursili II), §11; see Wilhelm and Fuscagni 2014; Devecchi 2015: 136.

189. Manapa-Tarhunda treaty (Mursili II), §4; see Wilhelm and Fuscagni 2014; Beckman 1996: 78; Heinhold-Krahmer 1977: 73–74; Devecchi 2015: 134–135.

had received Mashuiluwa, a refugee prince expelled from Arzawa, and given him his own daughter in marriage.[190] These diplomatic relations established during Suppiluliuma's reign set the template for Hittite alliances in the west during the reign of his son, Mursili II, who could even be said to have found a partial solution to Hittite problems there. Thus Suppiluliuma's western campaigns combined long-term geopolitical diplomatic strategy with outright military force, but it is only the latter we hear about in the annalistic narrative.

A similar pattern was repeated in northern Syria south of the Taurus mountains, where Suppiluliuma's return to Hittite expansion in the region required him to deal with situations that encroached on the interests of international forces in the balance of power in the eastern Mediterranean: Egypt in the south and the state of Mittani to the northeast. The sources for Hittite activity in this region during this period include the *Deeds of Suppiluliuma*, as noted earlier, complemented by letters found at Amarna in Egypt (documenting the correspondence of the Mittanian king Tušratta, as well as of Suppiluliuma himself and of local Levantine rulers with Egyptian pharaohs),[191] local correspondence excavated from sites in Syria (particularly Qatna, modern Tell Mishrife),[192] but most importantly the historical narrative in a treaty that Suppiluliuma made with Šattiwazza, son of Tušratta and exiled heir to the Mittanian throne after the murder of Tušratta by his relatives.[193]

Like Tudhaliya I, it was the situation in Išuwa that initially attracted Suppiluliuma's attention, with the large-scale movement of Hittite subjects and other population groups both into and out of that land.[194]

---

190. Treaty between Mursili II and Kupanta-Kuruntiya, §2; see Beckman 1996: 69; Devecchi 2015: 140; Heinhold-Krahmer 1977: 73–74; Klengel 1999: 151; Mursili's *Extensive Annals*, Year 12; see Goetze 1933: 140–147.

191. Moran 1992.

192. Richter and Lange 2012.

193. *Mittani Treaty*; see Wilhelm 2016; Beckman 1996: 38–44; Devecchi 2015: 242–253.

194. *Mittani Treaty*, §§1–2; see Wilhelm 2016: 18–40; Beckman 1996: 38–39; Devecchi 2015: 243–244; further Wilhelm 2012: 235; Cordani 2011: 242.

Suppiluliuma returned everyone to their places and crossed the Euphrates to advance east as far as Waššukanni (likely Tell Fekheriye), the Mittanian capital, where Tušratta avoided confronting him on the battlefield, according to the accounts in both the *Mittani Treaty* and the *Deeds*.[195] Allegedly, this motivated Suppiluliuma to employ a combination of diplomacy and military force against areas loyal to Mittani west of the Euphrates: Aleppo, Mukiš (Alalakh), Niya, Qatna, Nuhašše, Kinza (= Qadesh, modern Tell Nebi Mend), Apzuya, and Abina (Damascus).[196] The central narrative found in the Mittani Treaty is frequently referred to by modern historians as the "One-Year Campaign," due to the fact that Suppiluliuma explicitly recapitulated his account with the words:

> Because of the arrogance of Tušratta, I took possession of all these countries in one year, and brought them into the land of Hatti. From this side, I made Mount Niblani (= Lebanon?), from that side, the Euphrates into my border.[197]

However, a source-critical analysis by Gernot Wilhelm suggests that the retrospectively associative narrative style that the text uses means that the account included events that happened much later.[198] This interpretation is supported by evidence from contemporary local documents. One example from Qatna names different main protagonists than those found in the "one-year" summary, or in other accounts in the *Deeds of*

---

195. *Mittani Treaty*, §3; see Wilhelm 2016: 47–49; Beckman 1996: 39; Devecchi 2015: 245.

196. *Mittani Treaty*, §§4–5, 50–65; see Wilhelm 2016; Beckman 1996: 39–40; Devecchi 2015: 245–247; *Deeds of Suppiluliuma*, fragment 26; see del Monte 2008: 78–79; Hoffner 1997b: 189.

197. *Mittani Treaty*, §5, 83–85; see Wilhelm 2016; Beckman 1996: 40; Devecchi 2015: 246–247.

198. Wilhelm 2012: 233–240; cf. Cordani 2013: 44. Cordani 2011 argues on the basis of stylistic comparison with the *Ten-Year Annals* of Mursili II that the number of times Suppiluliuma says he took booty back to Hattusa should correspond to the number of years that he was engaged in this campaign, namely five.

Suppiluliuma.[199] The Amarna letters and other local treaties preserved at Hattusa (such as with Tette of Nuhašše) also demonstrate a very different relationship to the people mentioned in the "One-Year Campaign" to the one presented in the Suppiluliuma-Šattiwazza Treaty, one that must have pertained later, after resistance to Hittite domination in the area had crystallized.[200] In fact, the narrative goals of Suppiluliuma's summary can perhaps be reduced to two essential features: the need to blame the attack on Mittanian territory on Tušratta's arrogance; and the desire to make clear that Suppiluliuma had no intention whatsoever of attacking Egypt or encroaching on Egyptian territory.[201] Of course it had been the aggressive behavior of the rulers of Kinza/Qadesh (modern Tell Nebi Mend near Homs), Apzuya, and Abina (Damascus) that forced him to sack and loot these towns, although he omitted to mention that they had close relations with Egypt.[202]

The importance of Suppiluliuma I's activities in northern Syria to the history of Western Asia cannot be underestimated. The Mittani state ruled by Tušratta was clearly already riven by internal discord (see chapter 29 in this volume), while the Hittites and Assyrians supported proxy parties from both sides (see chapter 32 in this volume); it collapsed shortly after Tušratta's murder, and only a rump state, known as Hanigalbat, continued to survive into the thirteenth century BC in the east. Suppiluliuma, who had previously supported the anti-Tušratta faction in Mittani, was able, toward the end of his reign, to save the life of and install Šattiwazza (a grateful son of Tušratta) as a friendly head of state in Waššukanni. This signaled the end of Mittani's domination of the northern part of the area west of the Euphrates, thus aiding the rise of Assyrian power to the east, which would have severe consequences for the Hittite state later in its history. It also brought Hittite forces into contact, and eventually conflict, with Egyptian interests in the Levant.

199. Richter and Lange 2012.

200. Wilhelm 2012: 239–240.

201. Wilhelm 2012: 233.

202. *Mittani Treaty*, §§5, 72–82.

Before returning to Syria after the "One-Year Campaign," at least according to the remains of the narrative in the *Deeds*, Suppiluliuma conducted successful campaigns in northern Anatolia along with his generals Himuili and Hannutti.[203] After an incompletely preserved passage in the *Deeds*, we find that victories had been won in Syria that persuaded all regional powers to make peace with the Hittite king, with one exception: the city of Carchemish, an important, and to Hittite eyes Hurrian-leaning, center on the west bank of the Euphrates, today situated right on the Turkish-Syrian border.[204] That Suppiluliuma had not mentioned Carchemish suggests that earlier reports of his victories during the "One-Year Campaign" were exaggerated. However, the narrative of the siege of Carchemish plays second fiddle to the overarching theme of this section of the *Deeds*: the brewing conflict with Egypt, which seems to have taken root when Suppiluliuma attacked and looted Kinza/Qadesh without actually having planned to do so, according to his own statement in the Mittani treaty with Šattiwazza (see earlier discussion). According to the *Deeds of Suppiluliuma*, when the king was provoked by "Hurrian" activities in the region of Murmurik to abandon the performance of his religious duties on the Anatolian plateau, he besieged Carchemish and sent two deputies to attack Amka (i.e., the Beqaa valley to the south of Qadesh, modern Tell Nebi Mend), which caused consternation among the Egyptians. Subsequently, he received a letter from Tahamunzu ("the king's wife" in Egyptian), the widow of the Egyptian pharaoh, who wrote that the pharaoh had died childless and that she was worried about the "shame" of marrying one of her subjects: could she therefore marry one of Suppiluliuma's sons? Surprised by this approach from the opposing side, Suppiluliuma sent first a representative and finally a son (Zannanza, quite possibly from Egyptian "the king's son") to Egypt. This son died under suspicious circumstances

---

203. *Deeds of Suppiluliuma*, fragment 28; see del Monte 2008: 100–105; Hoffner 1997b: 189.

204. Recent Turkish-Italian excavations at Carchemish have brought forth numerous sealings of officials with Hurrian names from the period of Hittite domination; see Peker 2017.

while there.[205] A raging letter of accusation in Hittite concerning the death of a son is preserved in a copy at Hattusa, which may have been a draft of a missive from Suppiluliuma to the (next) pharaoh.[206] Which pharaohs and their widows are meant here remains unclear (Akhenaten, Tutankhamun, Smenkhkara, and Ay are all candidates for the dead pharaoh), and while this matter is of great importance for ancient Near Eastern chronology, such details do not touch the essence of the narrative.[207] Most likely, Mursili II assembled these stories about his father together as a form of contextualization for his own repeated search for the causes of the plague in his own time. This search is also attested in his prayers, where we read other versions of this same episode.[208] While clearly accepting that blame was attached to his father, he repeatedly took pains to exculpate him and demonstrate his piety.

It is in this sense that we should understand Mursili II's insistence that Suppiluliuma ended the siege of Carchemish swiftly, within eight days, and that he did not defile the sanctuaries of the gods on the citadel, but only looted the lower city.[209] Indeed, recent excavations at Carchemish led by Nicolò Marchetti have uncovered what appears to be a considerable and widespread layer of burning at the end of the Late Bronze Age I period in the lower-lying Inner Town, which could be the result of Suppiluliuma's siege.[210] A key event for all future Hittite engagement with the region south of the Anti-Taurus mountains was the installation of Suppiluliuma's son Piyassili (whose Hurrian name was Šarri-Kušuh) as king of Carchemish, equipped with a special status within the Hittite state hierarchy,[211] and the parallel appointment of his

---

205. *Deeds of Suppiluliuma*, fragments 28–31; see del Monte 2008: 104–127; Hoffner 1997b: 189–191; cf. Freu 2004.

206. van den Hout 1994.

207. Miller 2007; Wilhelm 2009.

208. Mursili's *Second Plague Prayer*, §4; see Singer 1992: 58.

209. del Monte 2008; Hoffner 1997b: 190.

210. Marchetti 2015: 20; Zaina et al. 2019: 357.

211. del Monte 2008: 118–119, ms. 1E$_3$ 18: "He made him a king separately."

brother "Telipinu the Priest" as the head of the temple of the storm-god at Aleppo. This famous shrine was likely a center of worship for most of the regional powers. Four generations of kings of Carchemish descended from Piyassili, until the end of the Hittite Empire, paralleling the four generations of Hittite kings at Hattusa from Mursili II to Suppiluliuma II. There is even evidence that the kings of Carchemish survived the end of the central Hittite authority in Anatolia.[212] At Aleppo, too, "Telipinu the Priest" was also succeeded by his own line. The danger of installing family members as local kings (the equivalent of provincial governors) is well attested by empires throughout history, but this does not seem to have been a problem for Hittite succession south of the Taurus.

Having a base on the other side of the Taurus/Anti-Taurus mountains made a huge difference to Hittite policy in the area. Now that a permanent presence had been established, local conflicts could be managed more easily before they got out of hand, and a Hittite king at Carchemish was a visible and approachable entity for smaller polities seeking guidance, although the king at Hattusa often seems to have remained the final arbiter.[213] Finally, the vicious cycle that saw the repeated loss of any gains made across the Taurus, because the troops had to immediately rush back to control the unrest in Anatolia that had erupted in their absence, had ended. However, the fires in Anatolia were difficult to stifle, and Suppiluliuma found that he needed to conduct another large-scale campaign in the north. Additionally, the Hittite presence in Syria associated with the fatally fumbled attempts at marital diplomacy now pitted them against a much bigger enemy: Egypt (see chapter 28 in this volume). However, this would not become acute for some time.

Again from the soul-searching prayers of Mursili II, we learn that the plague which decimated the Hittite kingdom was thought to have been brought back to Hattusa by soldiers returning from engagements with the Egyptians around Amka.[214] Despite having carefully researched

---

212. Weeden 2013: 6–10.

213. For an example, see Miller 2007b.

214. Mursili's *Second Plague Prayer*, §4; see Singer 2002: 59.

the history of diplomatic relations between Egypt and Hattusa by consulting the tablet of the so-called Kurustama Treaty, Suppiluliuma had apparently broken a treaty-oath and died himself of this plague. His son Arnuwanda II, who played a prominent role in the fighting around Murmurik and Carchemish, alongside Suppiluliuma's brother Zida, assumed the throne for a brief time; impressions of some of his seals are attested from Hattusa, where he appears together with his father's last queen, the Babylonian princess Tawananna.[215] However, he became ill and died, and was succeeded by his brother Mursili II, who was still very young according to the account in his own annals.[216]

Not only was Mursili II responsible for producing a third-person, annalistic-style account of his father's reign, he also produced two annalistic histories of his own, using first-person narrative.[217] Here, the year-by-year style of documentation reached its apogee in a literary form that may well have inspired neighboring cultures, such as the Assyrians, to create similar histories. The young Mursili was faced with a comprehensive rebellion, echoing the ones that had occurred during his father's reign. Despite his repeated insistence in the *Deeds of Suppiluliuma* that his father had piously celebrated the festivals of the gods, Mursili pointed out that Suppiluliuma did actually neglect the festival of the sun-goddess of Arinna while he was held up fighting in Mittani.[218] So this was the first thing Mursili atoned for, even while the insults of his neighboring enemy lands rang in his ears, and the sun-goddess of Arinna became his personal deity.

---

215. Herbordt et al. 2011: 71.

216. The precise date of Mursili's accession is tied to discussion of a solar phenomenon (eclipse?) which was allegedly seen (in Hattusa?) while he was campaigning in Azzi in his tenth regnal year. If this can be linked to an actual eclipse, then one possibility is the solar eclipse of June 24, 1312 BC (so Wilhelm 2009: 115 n. 34). Gautschy 2014: 149–150; 2017 presents arguments for the "less spectacular" eclipse of April 13, 1308 BC.

217. *Ten-Year Annals*; see Goetze 1933; Grélois 1988. *Extensive Annals*; see Goetze 1933.

218. *Ten-Year Annals*, §5; see Grélois 1988: 55.

Mursili's fields of military enterprise were very similar to those of his father: first he dealt with Kaska uprisings to the immediate east, then with Arzawa in the west, then the repeating pendulum of action between the north (from east to west) and Syria across the Taurus mountains began to swing. However, he may only have visited Syria twice, preferring (and being able) to delegate effectively. Once again, astute navigation of the diplomatic landscape through a combination of brute force and the forging of treaties was the apparent key to success; it seems that whenever Hittite kings found themselves unable to forcefully exact tribute, agreeing to a treaty with the polity in question was the usual alternative.[219] Mursili explained his motivation for attacking the west in a letter to his Arzawan enemy, Uhhaziti: insults against his competence, and the failure to return "deportees" from the land of Hattusa.[220] Although fragmentary, certain details of the account suggest that also the king of Ahhiyawa (i.e., Greece or the Aegean islands; see chapter 31 in this volume), in some way, supported an anti-Hittite faction in Arzawa.[221] Mursili's accounts of the Arzawa campaign (Years 3–4 of Mursili's reign), from both his ten-year and comprehensive annals, give us a vivid description of his march toward the west, including the sighting of a celestial phenomenon of some kind (a meteorite?) that struck down his enemy, the Arzawan Uhhaziti, with illness. Joined by troops led by his brother, the king of Carchemish (Šarri-Kušuh/Piyassili), at the key western invasion muster-point of Sallapa, he was met at Aura by the same Mashuiluwa who had married Mursili's sister.[222] Even if we are not completely sure of

---

219. Mursili's hymn and prayer to the sun goddess of Arinna makes an interesting distinction between lands that are *kuriwanas* (variously translated as "autonomous": Rieken et al. 2016: §6: 94; "protectorates": Singer 2002: 52, §7; "juridically equal": Pallavidini 2017a) and those that are "lands of the land of Hattusa alone." The latter pay tribute, the former do not.

220. The *Extensive Annals* (Year 3) mention "my servants, the deportees" from Hu(wa)rsanassa, Attarimma, and Suruda at a later stage in the narrative (Goetze 1933: 58–59), which are all likely to be in the southwestern coastal regions.

221. *Ten-Year Annals*, §25; see Grélois 1988: 64, 82.

222. *Extensive Annals*, Year 3; see Goetze 1933: 46–49.

the geography, it appears that Mashuiluwa, a key Hittite ally, was operating in the central western region, at least bordering the area of Mira,
which makes one wonder how blameless the Hittites were in the genesis
of this conflict.

After defeating Uhhaziti's son and crossing into Mira (part of Arzawa),
Mursili progressed swiftly to Uhhaziti's capital city, Apasa, which must
have been somewhere near the sea (perhaps Ephesus), because Uhhaziti
escaped by boat (along with a significant part of the population) "into
the sea," where he later died.[223] Mursili was only able to dispatch some
of the remaining population of Apasa, who had been hiding on a mountain, before he moved into his winter quarters. But he returned the next
year to smoke out the rest from the fortress-city of Puranda, in addition
to winning another victory against a further son of Uhhaziti's.[224] Having
set his course for the Seha River Lands to the north, which seems to
have switched allegiance from Hattusa to Apasa, Mursili was met by the
mother of its ruler Manapa-Tarhunda, as well as the old men and women
of the region, who pleaded for his life. This was duly granted.[225] After
Mursili returned to Mira, Arzawa was carved into three principalities.
Despite having betrayed Hittite trust, Manapa-Tarhunda was rewarded
with a subjugation treaty giving him control of the Seha River Lands.
Mashuiluwa, an old ally of Mursili's father, was given Mira and Kuwaliya,
and the land of Hapalla was given to Targasnalli. Copies of these treaties
were preserved at Hattusa, except for Mashuiluwa's, which was replaced
by a treaty with his son (Kupanta-Kuruntiya) after the father had been
removed from power.[226] During the reign of Muwatalli II, a treaty was

---

223. *Ten-Year Annals*, §18; see Grélois 1988: 61, 79.

224. *Ten-Year Annals*, §§20–23; see Grélois 1988: 62–64, 80–82.

225. *Ten-Year Annals*, §26; see Grélois 1988: 65, 82–83.

226. Treaty with Manapa-Tarhunda: Beckman 1999: 82–86, Devecchi 2015: 132–
139; Wilhelm and Fuscagni 2014; treaty with Targasnalli: Friedrich
1926: 52–94; Beckman 1999: 69–73; Devecchi 2015: 126–132; treaty with
Kupanta-Kuruntiya: Friedrich 1926: 95–179; Beckman 1999: 74–82; Devecchi
2015: 139–151.

also made with Alaksandu of Wilusa which, in combination with the others, essentially placed western Anatolia under (at least nominal) sub-jugation to Hattusa.[227] After this we hear no more of Arzawa, but only of these four principalities of the west (although there is a reference to Arzawa in one other text with a disputed dating, see later discussion in the present section). We do hear of Mashuiluwa again in Mursili's annals, when he was replaced in Year 12 for having broken his oath by fomenting insurrection in Pitassa, an episode that is also related in the treaty with his son Kupanta-Kuruntiya.[228]

Further campaigning stretched through the first decade of Mursili's reign in the north (particularly Tipiya) and in Syria (particularly Nuhašše), where a proxy war with Egypt seems to have been fought and the Hittite king once more enjoyed the support of his brother, the king of Carchemish.[229] While in Kizzuwatna celebrating the goddess Hebat of Kummani during Year 9 of his reign, Mursili was joined by his brother Šarri-Kušuh/Piyassili from Carchemish, who died there unexpectedly.[230] As so often happened, various elements in the population used a per-ceived disruption in the chain of authority as an opportunity to rebel. In this case it was Hayasa in the northeast of Central Anatolia and Nuhašše and Qadesh/Kinza in Syria. Mursili sent one general, Nuwanza, to deal with the Hayasans and another to deal with Nuhašše and Qadesh, dur-ing which Nuhašše was "destroyed," and Qadesh, where the local king had been murdered by his son, was accepted into vassal-status.[231] Mursili managed to install Sahurunuwa, the son of Šarri-Kušuh, (also known by the name of [. . .]-Šarruma, according to a fragmentary passage in

---

227. Alaksandu treaty; see Beckman 1999: 87–93; Devecchi 2015: 151–159.

228. *Extensive Annals*, Year 12; see Goetze 1933: 140–147.

229. If the Egyptian Arma'a in Year 9 of the *Extensive Annals* (as reconstructed by Miller 2007a) is identified with the future pharaoh Horemheb (Greek Armais), this attestation would provide key information for the reconstruction of the chronology of the period; cf. Wilhelm 2009.

230. *Extensive Annals*, Year 9; see Goetze 1933: 108–109.

231. *Extensive Annals*, Year 9; see Goetze 1933: 114–121.

the *Annals*) on the throne in Carchemish. He also managed to place Talmi-Šarruma, son of "Telipinu the Priest" (known from a hieroglyphic inscription found bricked into the wall of a mosque in that city), on the throne at Aleppo.[232] Despite claims to the contrary in many history books, there is no evidence in the sources for an Assyrian conquest of, or attack on, Carchemish at this time, although it is clear that the contemporary Assyrian assault on Mittani was the source of some consternation as early as the first year of Mursili's reign.[233]

The situation in Anatolia, particularly in the north, was to occupy Mursili II for the rest of his reign, however long that actually may have been; estimates based on assessments of the length of the *Extensive Annals* range from twenty-five to thirty-one years.[234] He fought first against Azzi and Hayasa in the northeast, with whom a treaty may have been made, much like in the time of his father, and then against diverse Kaska-groups ranging from east (Kummesmaha river = Kelkit Irmağı?) to central west (Tummana and Pala).[235] In doing so, Mursili seems to have largely repeated and expanded on his father's victories. This was a clear theme within the narrative agenda in the annals, which begin with Mursili being derided as an incapable child by "all the lands." Indeed his narration of the events in Syria during his Year 9 seems to demand a direct comparison with what must have been thought of as his father's greatest achievement: the conquest of Carchemish.[236] And indeed, in contrast to the situation in Anatolia, where Hittite forces continually fought largely defensive battles against neighbors that they simply could not control, Hittite control over Syria seems to have been largely successful and stable, with the exception of the coming clash with Egypt.

232. Goetze 1933: 124–125; for the Talmi-Šarruma inscription, see Meriggi 1975: 330 no. 306.

233. Miller 2010.

234. Gautschy 2014: 146.

235. Goetze 1933: 130–197.

236. Miller 2010.

All practical matters of governance had been delegated from the Hittite power base in Anatolia to Carchemish, and the mechanics of Hittite control are particularly apparent in documents excavated at Ugarit and Emar, which provide a (sometimes very detailed) view of the Hittite state authorities' navigation of local disputes over several generations.[237]

The Hittite archaeological imprint from this end of the fourteenth/ beginning of the thirteenth century period, and more certainly from the first half or more of the thirteenth century BC, becomes difficult to quantify, not only across Anatolia generally, but also specifically in the capital Hattusa. Whereas previous archaeological opinion, largely following the picture painted by the texts, had posited that much of the city should have been built during this period, recent observations based on more secure stratigraphic dating methods show that the city's heyday was well past, and monumental architectural features, as well as occupation at the site, were considerably reduced.[238] It appears that the Upper City was largely deserted for most of the thirteenth century, or at least its temples had been shut down and had fallen into disrepair and the area had largely turned into an industrial quarter.[239] Precisely when these changes began to set in is unclear. It is quite possible that even the Hittite capital had never really recovered from the period of extended "concentric invasions."[240] We would have no inkling of this material change if we had based our history entirely on the narratives found in the cuneiform texts, which continued to glorify Hittite achievements, even if any critical reading of these same texts makes it glaringly obvious that Hittite

---

237. For Ugarit, see Singer 1999; Lackenbacher 2002; Lackenbacher and Malbran-Labat 2016. For Emar, see Beckman 1995b; Heltzer 2001; d'Alfonso 2005; Cohen 2011.

238. Schachner 2011: 9–95.

239. Schachner 2011: 276.

240. The desertion of the Upper City is associated with the move of the Hittite capital to Tarhuntassa during the reign of Muwatalli II; see Schachner 2011: 94. For the move as a symptom of a more profound geopolitical development, whereby the Lower Land had essentially become the nodal point and main area of contestation for the Hittite Empire after the reign of Suppiluliuma I, see Matessi 2017.

power-mongers were only holding on to their more immediate domains by their fingernails.

In addition to fighting all over Anatolia and in Syria, Mursili was confronted with a devastating plague in the central territories, which he had inherited from his father, along with a number of court intrigues involving the Babylonian princess Tawananna, the last wife of his father, whom he also inherited as the surviving high priestess ("God Mother") and Great Queen.[241] Mursili blamed her for the death of his own queen Gassulawiya, as we learn from prayers and later documents, as well as for his speech defect, which required significant ritual treatment.[242] Later in his reign, Mursili seems to have married Tanu-Heba, who would also become controversial.[243] It is unclear which of these was the mother of the next king, Muwatalli II/Šarri-Teššub, although it seems unlikely that it would have been Tanu-Heba, who may have been the mother of Muwatalli's initial heir, Urhi-Teššub/Mursili III.

Muwatalli's reign is marked by two events, neither of which is particularly well documented in the Hittite archives: his victory against Egyptian forces under Rameses II (1279–1213 BC) at Qadesh in Year 5 of the latter's reign, and his relocation of the capital, specifically the (statues of the) gods and the ghosts (of the ancestors), to Tarhuntassa.[244] This city has not yet been located, but it must have lain somewhere further south and nearer to the access points to northern Syria, although also possibly not too far away from the constant sources of unrest that were found in southwestern Anatolia. Modern scholars assume that the lack of Muwatalli-period documentation from Hattusa can be explained by the removal of his archives to this new capital, which means that anything found at Hattusa dating to his reign must come from the earlier part of it.[245] We

---

241. *Plague Prayers*; see Singer 2002: 47–68. Prayers concerning Gassulawiya and Tawananna; see Singer 2002: 70–77. For all prayers, see Rieken et al. 2016.

242. Lebrun 1985; Görke 2015.

243. Cammarosano 2010.

244. On Tarhuntassa, see d'Alfonso 2014.

245. Giorgieri and Mora 1996: 13; Klengel 1999: 202.

have only later reports about the battle of Qadesh from Hattusa, so presumably Rameses II's Year 5 occurred quite late in the reign of Muwatalli II. Extensive Egyptian sources, including an epic poetic composition, claim a dramatic victory for the pharaoh,[246] but the ensuing geopolitical arrangements, especially regarding the political orientation of Amurru (roughly the northern part of modern Lebanon), whose allegiance had turned from Egypt to Hattusa during the reign of Suppiluliuma I, rather suggest that the more matter-of-fact Hittite reports about the victory have slightly more historical substance to them.[247]

Presumably, political, military, diplomatic, and economic concerns played a role in the move to Tarhuntassa, although religious/ideological developments are also thought to have been important, particularly considering Muwatalli's devotion to the Storm-god of Lightning, as expressed in a prayer to the assembly of gods using this deity as his intercessor.[248] However, the relocation was short-lived, and it certainly did not last long enough to have been the cause of the elite desertion of the Upper City at Hattusa, a trend that may have prevailed for most of the thirteenth century BC and which may have had longer term political and economic trends at its root, possibly including those that also brought about the establishment of a "province" of the Lower Land.[249] Muwatalli's son and heir, Urhi-Teššub/Mursili III, moved the capital back to Hattusa. It is unclear how long this took, but the vacancy in the north had left space for Muwatalli's brother, Hattusili, to be established as "king" in that region, allegedly taking the crown in the town of Hakpis, while looking after what he himself refers to as the ruined cities and repelling Kaskan attacks. The main source for all this is Hattusili's own so-called *Apology*, in which he tells us at great length how he was

---

246. Maderna-Sieben 2018: 4 (with further literature).

247. On Amurru, see Singer 1991.

248. Singer 1996: 191–193; Klengel 1999: 255–256; Matessi 2017.

249. According to Matessi 2017, the establishment of the Lower Land province accompanied a shift in the center of the Hittite Empire, but this argument remains to be assessed in detail.

compelled to dislodge his nephew from the throne in an armed campaign.[250] The text itself takes the form of a dedication of various building complexes and cult institutions to the goddess Ištar of Samuha, and the detailed historical narrative serves the function of demonstrating how events had shown that Hattusili enjoyed her patronage, and that his son and heir Tudhaliya would also continue in her service. Looking beyond Hattusili's own narrative, it is likely that Urhi-Teššub's act of moving the capital back to Hattusa from Tarhuntassa encroached upon his uncle's domain over the northern regions and forced the latter to act to get rid of him.[251] Hattusili pursued Urhi-Teššub to Samuha, where a large portion of the wooden section of the wall construction collapsed during the siege, rendering Hattusili victorious. Urhi-Teššub fled, trying and failing to claim asylum in Babylon. He was heard of in Syria (Amurru) and may have turned up later in Egypt, or at least that was the accusation of the Hittite king and queen in their correspondence with their nominal allies.[252]

Much of the documentation from Hattusili's reign is preoccupied with the maneuvers and decrees most likely to win political factions to his side after he took the throne from its rightful occupant. In particular, Hattusili needed to appease the other son of Muwatalli, Kuruntiya, who had allegedly been entrusted to his care as a child and whom he had brought up himself like a son.[253] He gave Kuruntiya the kingdom of Tarhuntassa and closed a treaty with him under the Hurrian name of Ulmi-Teššub, which contained a long description of the border.[254] Hattusili's son and heir Tudhaliya IV also concluded a treaty with Kuruntiya (this time under his Anatolian name), which is preserved on a bronze tablet excavated at Hattusa, also with a long description of

---

250. Otten 1984; van den Hout 1997; Pallavidini 2017b.

251. Cf. Pallavidini 2017b.

252. Singer 2006.

253. According to the text of the bronze tablet (§2), see Otten 1988: 10–11.

254. Ulmi-Teššub treaty; see van den Hout 1995. In the past, it was debated whether Ulmi-Teššub and Kuruntiya were different people.

the border, although in the meantime it seems to have expanded considerably in favor of Tarhuntassa at the expense of the Hittite state.[255] It has traditionally been assumed that the establishment of a kingdom of Tarhuntassa involved a split in the empire and a territorial rupture from which the Hittite state did not recover, thus leading directly to its demise.[256] While some degree of credence might be given to this version of events, we must remember that throughout its history the Hittite state depended on negotiating federal relationships of different kinds, usually expressed in the form of treaties, with its neighbors in Anatolia. This was not really very different from what had gone before, even if we do have two documents, a seal impression from Hattusa and a hieroglyphic rock inscription from Hatıp near Konya, where Kuruntiya calls himself "Great King."[257] It would be a different matter if Kuruntiya was given the title "Great King of Hattusa," or if this title appeared in the cuneiform documentation from Hattusa.

Even before his reign began, one of Hattusili's military achievements was his victory over the town of Nerik, which had been lost to the Hittites since the reign of Hantili (I or II?), according to Hattusili.[258] As the king of Hakpis, he was particularly well positioned to achieve this victory; Hapkis was probably located just around the Tavşan Mountains from the likely location of Nerik.[259] Excavations, which included tablet finds, strongly suggest that the site of Nerik was identical to the mound at Oymaağaç in the Vezirköprü region, which seems to have shown an initial occupation level with central Anatolian connections, followed by a change in pottery style that appears to have been more local, and then a central Anatolian re-occupation toward the end of the Hittite Empire.[260]

255. For the bronze tablet, see Otten 1988.

256. E.g., Matessi 2017: 36–37.

257. Herbordt et al. 2011: 100.

258. *Hattusili's Apology*, §10b; see van den Hout 1997: 202.

259. Alparslan 2010.

260. Czichon et al. 2016.

Fragmentary tablets of the annals of Hattusili III are also preserved, which document the military exploits of this king toward the west.[261] These may be complemented by an intriguing document known to modern scholarship as the Tawagalawa Letter (figure 30.5), which attempts to persuade a "Great King" king of Ahhiyawa, presumably located in the Greek islands (Rhodes?) or possibly even mainland Greece (Mycenae?), to hand over a man called Piyamaradu, probably a dislodged member of the Arzawan royal house that had been deposed during the time of Mursili II.[262] At any rate, this name had already appeared in association with troublemaking along the western coast, including Lazpa (= Lesbos?). This troublemaking may have involved obstructing the passage of tributaries as documented in a letter sent by Manapa-Tarhunda of the Seha River Lands to a Hittite king, probably Muwatalli II.[263] Piyamaradu's activities therefore stretched across a long period of time, and thus illustrate the perennial difficulties that the Hittites experienced in maintaining control over the western areas. This was similar to the example of Madduwatta in the previous century, although in that case the Ahhiyawan was attacking the Hittite renegade while during the reign of Hattusili the Ahhiyawan king protected Piyamaradu. However, Hattusili had a solid ally in Masturi, king of the Seha River Lands, who had supported him during the transition from Urhi-Teššub/Mursili III's rule to his own. Masturi's brother had married Muwatalli's sister after he had, according to a well-established pattern, been expelled by relatives.[264]

In terms of Syrian foreign policy, Hattusili's reign was significant for a number of reasons, not least including the peace treaty with Rameses II in Year 21 of the pharaoh's reign (see chapters 27 and 28 in this volume). This treaty was concluded in the wake of the battle at Qadesh, which had been fought in Rameses' Year 5. Politically speaking, the treaty may have

---

261. Gurney 1997.

262. Beckman et al. 2011: 101–122; Heinhold-Krahmer and Rieken (eds.) 2020.

263. Beckman et al. 2011: 140–144.

264. Note the negative evaluation of this loyalty by Hattusili's own son Tudhaliya IV in the Šaušga-muwa treaty, §8; see Kühne and Otten 1971: 10; Beckman et al. 2011: 50–68; Devecchi 2015: 225–232.

FIGURE 30.5. The so-called Tawagalawa Letter. VAT 6692, Vorderasiatisches Museum Berlin. © Staatliche Museen zu Berlin–Vorderasiatisches Museum, photograph by Olaf M. Teßmer.

been intended to form a defensive alliance against Assyria, but this never actually materialized. The treaty is preserved in two languages: Egyptian, found in the Ramesseum and on a stele at Karnak, which is a translation of the Hittite version of the treaty; and Akkadian, preserved on two tablets from Hattusa, a translation of the Egyptian version.[265] Unusually the treaty does not contain the usual historical review of relations between the two countries, perhaps to avoid embarrassment on either side, even though a letter from Rameses found at Hattusa was very explicit about his version of events, making clear just how fragile the diplomatic situation was.[266] An extensive correspondence was carried on between the two courts in Akkadian, which is preserved mainly on tablets at Hattusa. From this we learn of the diplomatic exchanges that led to the completion of the treaty text on a silver tablet (not preserved).[267] The tomb of one of the key Egyptian diplomats, Parihnawa, has been discovered at the burial site on the cliff at Saqqara in Egypt, where one of his titles is translated as "ambassador."[268] Further exchanges concern advice on construction projects and medical matters. A cuneiform tablet, along with other artifacts with allegedly Anatolian or North Syrian connections, has also been found at Rameses' capital Piramesses (modern Qantir), and may belong to a later stage of this correspondence.[269]

The documentation from both Hattusili's time and that of his son, Tudhaliya IV, contains extensive references to Pudu-Heba, his wife, who was the daughter of the priest of the storm-god of Kummani in Kizzuwatna. They had married in Lawazantiya on his way back from Muwatalli's Syrian campaign against Egypt, before the beginning of his

---

265. Treaty between Rameses II and Hattusili III; see Edel 1997; Beckman et al. 2006: 244–248; Devecchi 2015: 265–270.

266. Edel 1994: 58–65.

267. Edel 1994.

268. Zivie 2006: 69.

269. Zivie 2006: 70 n. 17 also refers to the alleged attestations of the name Pirikhnawa at Piramesses, according to information from Piramesses's excavator Edgar Pusch.

reign.[270] Pudu-Heba corresponded with Rameses II, instigated a long and complex court case concerning pilfering and mismanagement by officials, and left behind a number of dream oracle texts. She was well represented on seals and sealings, either together with her husband or alone.[271] She was also associated with an effort to collect ritual texts, particularly those associated with her home area of Kizzuwatna. This activity was documented in the colophons to their tablets. At the beginning of Tudhaliya's reign she appears to have issued documents in collaboration with him, particularly related to the land donations connected to the children of the official Sahurunuwa, which included properties in geographically quite disparate places.[272]

There is a qualitative change in our sources during the reign of Hattusili's son, Tudhaliya IV. Annalistic accounts are no longer available, and we are reliant on the letters written, and treaties made by this king, with their historical reviews. Additionally, we have hieroglyphic building inscriptions with annalistic narratives, if that is how they are to be understood, which seem to take up where the annalistic literature leaves off in supplying accounts of the Hittite state's military activities.[273] The reign of Tudhaliya also saw a great deal of omen literature.[274] This distribution of sources should not be seen as a reflection of this king's preoccupations, but rather as a reflection of the fact that we are nearing the end of the Hittite archives. More ephemeral documents, that would usually have been thrown away, have been preserved than in previous generations of scribal activity. Here we should also mention the large numbers of cult inventories, listing the contents of temples, which have been taken as a sign that Tudhaliya initiated a major cultic reorganization throughout

---

270. *Hattusili's Apology*, §9; see van den Hout 1997: 202.

271. de Roos 2006.

272. Imparati 1974.

273. Bolatti Guzzo and Marazzi 2003.

274. van den Hout 1998.

Anatolia.[275] Again, this is possibly an archival mirage, and it is likely that such documents existed also in previous reigns but were not preserved.

It was Tudhaliya who was badly defeated at the battle of Nihriya, somewhere in southeastern Anatolia, by an Assyrian king (see chapter 32 in this volume). This king may have been Tukulti-Ninurta I at the beginning of his reign (1243–1207 BC), based on two of his later royal inscriptions which claim to have taken 28,800 "Hittites from across the Euphrates" captive, or it may have been Shalmaneser I (1273–1244 BC), late in his reign.[276] However, the dating of the relevant document from Hattusa, a long text that mentions Nihriya as part of an example of a person who had not behaved correctly, is still under dispute as to whether it should be assigned to Tudhaliya IV or to one of his children, Arnuwanda III, or the last Hittite king, Suppiluliuma II.[277] It has similarities to documents from both the reigns of Suppiluliuma II and Tudhaliya IV. An Assyrian letter found at Ugarit that refers to the battle and the victory over Tudhaliya in an open effort to sway Ugarit from its allegiance to Hattusa is also disputed as to whether it should be dated to Tukulti-Ninurta I or Shalmaneser I, with the latter being more likely due to the albeit paltry remains of the addressee's name on the tablet.[278] If both documents refer to the same Nihriya, then dating the battle to early in the reign of Tudhaliya and before the accession of Tukulti-Ninurta I seems likely. Despite having clearly been a serious defeat for Hittite forces, it does not seem that the Assyrian side pressed home its advantage, or at least not for very long, and peaceful relations are evidenced by letters sent from Tudhaliya at the beginning of Tukulti-Ninurta's reign.[279] Rather, a more hands-off strategy of waiting and watching seems to have

---

275. Cammarosano 2012; 2018.

276. Grayson 1987: 272–275: A.0.78.23, ll. 27–30; A.0.78.24, ll. 23–25. This event is not mentioned at all in the earlier inscriptions of Tukulti-Ninurta I, and thus seems rather suspect: Yamada 2011: 203.

277. Suppiluliuma II: Bemporad 2002; Fuscagni 2014. Tudhaliya IV: Singer 1985.

278. Lackenbacher 1976.

279. Mora and Giorgieri 2004: 155–174; Hoffner 2009: 324–326.

been preferred by the Assyrian side, right up until the end of the Hittite Empire itself, which was especially sensible given the internal problems they faced at home.

Nevertheless, it would appear that the Hittite strategy of maintaining alliances with Egypt and Babylon in an attempt to hold back Assyrian expansion had reached its limits. A number of letters from Hattusa, as well as administrative documents from the Assyrian sites of Dur-Katlimmu (modern Tell Sheikh Hamad), Harbe (modern Tell Chuera), and Tell Sabi Abyad, indicate that much of Tukulti-Ninurta's reign was spent in peace with the Hittites (see chapter 32 in this volume). Yet an intriguing letter from Hattusa indicates a "first" peace treaty made at Kummahi, which the author accuses the recipient of having broken, as well as undermining his relationship with his vassals, particularly on the bend of the Euphrates.[280] If this document refers to Tukulti-Ninurta and Tudhaliya (rather than their predecessors Shalmaneser I and Hattusili), it is possible that the relationship was fractious. Despite his marriage to a Babylonian princess, as had been the custom of Hittite rulers since Suppiluliuma I, Tudhaliya backed Assyria, at least by the time that Tukulti-Ninurta's assault on Babylonia started in the late 1230s BC.[281] Egypt, too, might have noted an opportunity to interfere in Hittite affairs, as a letter from the pharaoh Merenptah (1213–1203 BC) preserved at Ugarit indicates: the pharaoh had donated a statue of the god Ba'al to his temple in Ugarit, but seemed reluctant to also donate a statue of himself. It seems that he was ambivalent about making an outright statement against Hittite governance in the area.[282]

It is likely that Tudhaliya also faced some sort of trouble in the west, as most Hittite kings did, even after Mursili II's Arzawa settlement. However, the main document that attests to this is the so-called "Sins of the Seha River Lands Text", whose dating is in dispute. Some

---

280. Miller 2008: 121–124, no. 35; Alexandrov and Sideltsev 2009; Yamada 2011.

281. Singer 2008; Alexandrov and Sideltsev 2009: 74. Differently, Yamada 2011: 208–209. See also chapter 32 in this volume.

282. Morris 2015.

FIGURE 30.6. Part of Tudhaliya IV's YALBURT inscription. Reproduced from Ehringhaus 2005: fig. 69, with kind permission of Mirko Novák, University of Bern.

scholars hold that it is a late reworking of a much older document that shares some personnel with a tablet from Sapinuwa (modern Ortaköy) from the time of Tudhaliya II in the earlier part of the fourteenth century BC.[283] Otherwise, the so-called Milawata Letter demonstrates that Tudhaliya had inherited problems with groups of hostages/captives from his father's time and that the area of Millawanda (Miletos; see chapter 31 in this volume) still needed a border beyond which Hittite authority did not extend, even nominally.[284] However, a building containing Hittite imperial seal impressions at Çine-Tepecik shows that Hittite outposts in the area were at least sustainable, even if one cannot speak of anything approaching an occupation.[285] The hieroglyphic inscription from Yalburt (figure 30.6) in northwestern Konya details his campaigns in the west, including place names that might have been associated with the

283. Süel 2005; Soysal 2012b: 174–177, no. 5.

284. Beckman et al. 2011: 123–133.

285. Günel 2017: 126.

area of classical Lycia and associated population groups.[286] Dam-building works such as at Eflatun Pınar may also hint at both environmental/agricultural and military/defensive engagement in the region. An invasion of Cyprus (ancient Alašiya), reported by his son, Suppiluliuma II, probably aimed at undercutting support for enemies that used the coasts and seas from Madduwatta to Piyamaradu as a refuge.[287]

There is considerably less documentation for the last two kings at Hattusa, Arnuwanda III and Suppiluliuma II, in comparison to that of Tudhaliya IV, not only in terms of cuneiform texts, but also in the number of sealed objects they left behind.[288] Arnuwanda died childless, presumably after only a short time, and from Suppiluliuma's reign we have oath-texts from officials, a largely broken collective tablet with inscriptions detailing the exploits of himself and of his father, and a text concerning his dedication of a statue of his father in an "eternal (rock) sanctuary," which may be the extra-mural compound at Yazılıkaya.[289] If the Südburg hieroglyphic inscription is to be assigned to his reign, rather than to that of his ancestor Suppiluliuma I, then it is clear that Suppiluliuma II was plagued by all of the same problems that his predecessors at Hattusa were forced to deal with—uprisings by western population groups (Lukka and Masa), and likely problems in northern Anatolia as well.[290] Texts have been found dating to his reign at Oymaağaç (most probably ancient Nerik) in the north. That he definitely conducted some rebuilding work in the Upper City is shown by his large inscription on Nişantepe, near where an imperial archive of land donations and sealings was found, as well as a monumental structure above the inscription.[291] The Nişantaş inscription is long and poorly understood due to weathering, but the progress made in reading it tends to indicate that its contents are similar

286. Poetto 1993.

287. Hoffner 1997c.

288. Herbordt et al. 2011: 21–23.

289. Klinger 2015.

290. Hawkins 1995; cf. Klinger 2015.

291. Neve 2018.

to the Südburg inscription, which was found not far away.[292] A letter from Suppiluliuma found at Ugarit warns of people called *Šikilayu*, who "live on boats."[293] These have been associated by modern historians with the so-called Sea Peoples (an early translation of a term used once in one inscription of the Egyptian pharaoh Merenptah; 1213–1203 BC) and the widespread destruction of cities along the Levantine coast at the end of the Late Bronze Age, including Ugarit and Tell Kazel (in ancient Amurru, likely ancient Simyra).[294] However, the paradigm of a dramatic end to the Late Bronze Age at the hands of mass hordes of migrants from across land and sea has little to recommend it, even if modern historiography has found it difficult to shake off.[295]

30.5. Collapse and aftermath

Precisely why the Hittite Empire did collapse is unclear. Doubtless it was the result of a number of interwoven factors, including economic decline, climate, natural disasters, over-investment abroad, internal faction, and the difficulties of maintaining territorial political control within Anatolia—all stressors that the Hittite state had managed to endure before. The older historiographical narrative that a famine had occurred in the central area, the so-called hunger years, is not supported by more recent interpretations of the texts.[296] The capital city of the Hittite Empire was evacuated before it was partially burned, which indicates that reports in the inscriptions of Egyptian pharaoh Rameses III (Year 5 = 1176 BC, and Year 8 = 1173 BC) concerning the destruction of

---

292. Hawkins *apud* Neve 2018; Hawkins 1995.

293. Dietrich and Loretz 1978.

294. "Sea Peoples" is a term derived from the designation as coming from "foreign lands of the sea" in Merenptah's Great Karnak Inscription, l. 52 (Manassa 2003: 163). All other applications of this term are extrapolated from this one context.

295. Weeden 2013: 1–4; cf. Altaweel and Squitieri 2018: 25.

296. Klengel 1974; Miller 2020.

"Hatti" and Carchemish at the hands of seaborne enemies are not to be trusted.[297] Indeed, at Carchemish it appears that a Hittite dynasty continued into the Iron Age, an impression won from sealings showing a king of Carchemish who was the son of the last-known imperial Hittite king of the same. The evidence of the sealings is now also supported by archaeological evidence.[298]

In contrast, and with some significant exceptions, on the Anatolian plateau we have very few signs of continuity: an almost total collapse is registered archaeologically in the central area within the bend of the Kızılırmak. The grounds for this surely lie in the very weak political and administrative, let alone military, imprint that the Hittites seem to have made in their own heartland. Despite notable achievements in political landscape and settlement planning, especially during a heyday that seems to have stretched over the late sixteenth and fifteenth centuries BC when one considers the archaeological evidence, it appears likely that local structures of governance and regulation, even very close to the Hittite center, were far more resilient than anything the overarching imperial framework was able to impose, or the unified symbolic culture it tried to create across its territory. Time and again, the central Hittite power was forced to confront the same population groups in the same areas, with the situation occasionally growing so volatile that the capital city or king's residence had to be moved back and forth. In northeastern Syria, trade-based wealth was probably more easily generated and trade routes to the southeast less liable to geographical disruptions. The collapse, which may have taken a very long time, did not occur to the same extent there. When we resume the history of the area in the Iron Age, we can no longer speak of Hittites in Central Anatolia, because the capital at Hattusa, from which they derived their political self-designation, had ceased to be relevant. But the symbolic culture that had its origins in that city had a long and influential history yet to come.

---

297. Seeher 1998; Weeden 2013: 4.

298. Hawkins 1988; Pizzimenti and Scazzosi 2017: 170.

The Hittites had achieved the remarkable feat of establishing a state in a geographically difficult area where no other territorial state capital had existed before or after, until Ankara became the capital of the Turkish Republic in 1923.[299] It had many of the features that can be used as markers of ancient state activity: attempted territorial parcelization, population control, large-scale storage and control of consumables, standardization in representation, exchange, administrative instruments, grand landscape planning and urban foundation projects, reasonably effective communication networks, the delegation and professional separation of functions,[300] as well as varying degrees of military reach and extensive external diplomacy. Possibly this achievement was made possible by a break in the pace of the ongoing climate change that made life in the Central Anatolian highlands temporarily more bearable (see section 30.2 on Kuşaklı), but it would not have been possible without a conjunction of other factors, such as the location of Hattusa in the center of a trade network connecting cities that had likely been wealthy due to mineral exploitation and trade since the Early Bronze Age, and an efficient and pragmatic approach to planning and logistics combined with an interaction with a difficult landscape that effectively maximized its advantages over its disadvantages. However, the difficulties with which the Hittite state had to struggle in its immediate area were simply too great for it to function cohesively over long periods, given that the landscape itself had been largely parcelized by its own natural topography, which tended to encourage the formation of resilient local political structures and quite possibly even identities, even if these last are difficult to ascertain.

The history of the Hittite project in Anatolia is one of fragile territoriality experiencing near-continual resistance, compounded by internal faction. The federal nature of the Hittite state, its dependence on the complex balance of internal and external loyalty relationships, was forced on it due to its circumstances, but it managed to turn this into

---

299. Schachner 2011.

300. Bilgin 2018.

a significant virtue, an operational system that may have influenced its neighboring cultures in the Middle East, particularly in the Levant and Assyria. The Hittites did not invent the format of politics by treaty/ oath, but they certainly practiced it on a grand scale. That a replica of the main tablet from Hattusa of the treaty between Rameses II (1279– 1213 BC) and Hattusili III is kept in the United Nations headquarters at New York, having been gifted by the Turkish Republic in 1970, is a testimony to this legacy.

REFERENCES

Alaura, S. 2006. *"Nach Boghasköy!" Zur Vorgeschichte der Ausgrabungen in Boğazköy und zu den archäologischen Forschungen bis zum ersten Weltkrieg. Darstellung und Dokumente.* Wiesbaden: Harrassowitz.

Alexandrov, B., and Sideltsev, A.V. 2009. Hittite *āššweni*. *RA* 103: 59–84.

Alp, S. 1968. *Zylinder- und Stempelsiegel aus Karahöyük bei Konya.* Ankara: Türk Tarih Kurumu.

Alp, S. 1980. Die hethitischen Tontafelentdeckungen auf dem Maşat-Höyük: Vorläufiger Bericht. *Belleten* 44: 25–59.

Alp, S. 1991. *Hethitische Briefe aus Maşat-Höyük.* Ankara: Türk Tarih Kurumu.

Alparslan, M. 2010. Das Land Hakmiš: Geschichte, Lokalisation und politische Bedeutung einer hethitischen Metropole. In Hazırlayan, Y., and Süel, A. (eds.), *Acts of the VIIth international congress of hittitology / VII Uluslararası Hititoloji Kongresi Bildirileri.* Ankara: T.C. Çorum Valiligi, 29–44.

Alparslan, M. 2017. The East: Upper Land, Išuwa-Malitiya, Azzi-Hayaša: philology. In Weeden, M., and Ullmann, L.Z. (eds.) 2017, 209–218.

Altaweel, M., and Squitieri, A. 2018. *Revolutionizing a world: from small states to universalism in the Pre-Islamic Near East.* London: UCL Press.

Archi, A. 2007. The cult of the royal ancestors at Hattusa and the Syrian practices. In Alparslan, M., Doğan-Alparslan, M., and Peker, H. (eds.), *VITA: Festschrift in honor of Belkıs Dinçol and Ali Dinçol.* Istanbul: Ege, 49–55.

Barjamovic, G. 2011. *A historical geography of Anatolia in the Old Assyrian colony period.* Copenhagen: Museum Tusculanum Press.

Beal, R.H. 1983. Studies in Hittite history. *JCS* 35: 115–126.

Beal, R.H. 2003. The predecessors of Ḫattusili I. In Beckman, G., Beal, R.H., and McMahon, G. (eds.), *Hittite studies in honor of Harry A. Hoffner Jr.* Winona Lake, IN: Eisenbrauns, 13–35.

Beckman, G. 1995a. The Siege of Uršu text (CTH 7) and Old Hittite historiography. *JCS* 47: 23–34.

Beckman, G. 1995b. Hittite provincial administration in Anatolia and Syria: the view from Maşat and Emar. In Onofrio Carruba, O., Giorgieri, M., and Mora, C. (eds.), *Atti del II Congresso Internazionale di Hittitologia.* Pavia: Gianni Iuculano, 19–37.

Beckman, G. 2013. The ritual of Palliya of Kizzuwatna (CTH 475). *JANER* 13: 113–145.

Beckman, G., Bryce, T.R., and Cline, E.H. 2011. *The Ahhiyawa texts.* Atlanta, GA: Society of Biblical Literature.

Beckman, G., Goedegebuure, P., Hazenbos, J., and Cohen, Y. 2006. Hittite historical texts, I. In Chavalas, M.W. (ed.), *The ancient Near East: historical sources in translation.* Malden, MA: Wiley-Blackwell, 215–256.

Bemporad, A. 2002. Per una riattribuzione di KBo 4.14 a Šuppiluliuma II. In de Martino, S., and Pecchioli Daddi, F. (eds.), *Anatolia antica: studi in memoria di Fiorella Imparati.* Florence: LoGisma, 71–86.

Bilgin, T. 2018. *Officials and administration in the Hittite world.* Berlin: De Gruyter.

Boehmer, R.M. 1996. Nochmals zur Datierung der Glyptik von Karahöyük Schicht I. *IstMit* 46: 17–22.

Boehmer, R.M., and Güterbock, H.G. 1987. *Glyptik aus dem Stadtgebiet von Boğazköy: Grabungskampagnen 1931–1939, 1952–1978.* Berlin: Mann.

Bolatti Guzzo, N., and Marazzi, M. 2004. Storiografia hittita e geroglifico anatolico: per una revisione di KBo 12.38. In Groddek, D., and Rößle, S. (eds.), *Šarnikzel: hethitologische Studien zum Gedenken an Emil Orgetorix Forrer.* Dresden: Verlag der Technischen Universität Dresden, 155–185.

Boraik, M. 2007. Stela of Bakenkhonsu, high-priest of Amun-Re. *Memnonia* 18: 119–126.

Borger, R. 1971. Gott Marduk und Gott-König Šulgi als Propheten: zwei prophetische Texte. *BiOr* 28: 3–24.

Börker-Klähn, J. 1996. Grenzfälle: Šunaššura und Sirkeli oder die Geschichte Kizzuwatnas. *UF* 28: 37–104.

Breasted, J.H. 1906. *Ancient records of Egypt: historical documents from the earliest times to the Persian conquest, vol. II: the Eighteenth Dynasty.* Chicago: University of Chicago Press.

Bryce, T. 2005. *The kingdom of the Hittites.* Oxford: Oxford University Press. 2nd rev. ed.

Cammarosano, M. 2006. *Il decreto antico-ittita di Pimpira.* Florence: LoGisma.

Cammarosano, M. 2010. Tanuḫepa, a Hittite queen in troubled times. *Mesopotamia* 45: 47–64.

Cammarosano, M. 2012. Hittite cult inventories, part 2: the dating of the texts and the alleged "cult reorganization" of Tudḫaliya IV. *AoF* 39: 3–37.

Cammarosano, M. 2018: *Hittite local cults.* Atlanta, GA: Society of Biblical Literature.

Campbell, D.R.M. 2016. The introduction of Hurrian religion into the Hittite Empire. *Religion Compass* 10: 295–306.

Carruba, O. 1977. Beiträge zur mittelhethitischen Geschichte, I: die Tuthalijas und die Arnuwandas, II: die sogenannten "Protocoles de succession dynastique." *SMEA* 18: 137–195.

Carruba, O. 2003. *Anittae Res Gestae.* Pavia: Italian University Press.

Chrzanowska, A. 2017. *Einrichtung und Organisation eines Isḫara-Kultes im Land Kizzuwatna (CTH 641.1).* Retrieved from www.hethiter.net (last accessed February 21, 2019).

Çınaroğlu, A., and Genç, E. 2002. Alaca Höyük 1999–2000 Yılı Kazı Çalışmaları. *Kazı Sonuçları Toplantısı* 23: 427–434.

Cohen, Y. 2011. The administration of cult in Hittite Emar. *AoF* 38: 145–157.

Cohen, Y. 2017a. The historical geography of Hittite Syria: philology. In Weeden, M., and Ullmann, L.Z. (eds.) 2017: 295–310.

Cohen, Y. 2017b. Heads or tails? The transmutations and peregrinations of a sapiential theme. In Baruchi-Unna, A., Forti, T., Ahituv, S., Eph'al, I., and Tigay, J.H. (eds.), *"Now it happened in those days": studies in Biblical, Assyrian and ancient Near Eastern historiography presented to Mordechai Cogan.* Winona Lake, IN: Eisenbrauns, 539–552.

Cordani, V. 2011. One-year or five-year war? A reappraisal of Suppiluliuma's first Syrian campaign. *AoF* 38: 240–253.

Cordani, V. 2013. Suppiluliuma in Syria after the first Syrian War: the (non-)evidence of the Amarna Letters. In de Martino, S., and Miller, J.L. (eds.), *New results and new questions on the reign of Suppiluliuma I.* Florence: LoGisma, 43–64.

Corti, C. 2010. "Because for a long time (the gods of Zalpa) have been ignored . . . hence these offerings in this way do we donate": new celebrations in the Zalpuwa Land. *JANER* 10: 92–102.

Corti, C. 2017. The north: Hanhana, Hattena, Ištahara, Hakpiš, Nerik, Zalpuwa, Tummana, Pala and the Hulana River Land. In Weeden, M., and Ullmann, L.Z. (eds.) 2017: 219–236.

Czichon, R.M., et al. 2016. Archäologische Forschungen am Oymaağaç Höyük/Nerik, 2011–2015. *MDOG* 148: 5–141.

d'Alfonso, L. 2005. Free, servant and servant of the king: conflict and change in the social organisation at Emar after the Hittite conquest. In Prechel, D. (ed.), *Motivation und Mechanismen des Kulturkontaktes in der späten Bronzezeit*. Florence: LoGisma, 19–38.

d'Alfonso, L. 2014. The kingdom of Tarhuntassa: a reassessment of its timeline and political significance. In Taracha, P. (ed.), *Proceedings of the 8th international congress of hittitology*. Warsaw: Agade, 216–235.

Dardano, P. 1997. *L'aneddoto e il racconto in età antico-hittita: la cosiddetta "Cronaca di Palazzo."* Rome: Il Calamo.

de Barros Damgaard, P., et al. 2018. The first horse herders and the impact of Early Bronze Age steppe expansions into Asia. *Science* 360, no. 6396. Retrieved from https://doi.org/10.1126/science.aar7711 (last accessed February 21, 2019).

del Monte, G.F. 1995. I testi amministrativi da Maşat Höyük/Tapika. *Oriens Antiqui Miscellanea* 2: 89–138.

del Monte, G.F. 2008. *Le gesta di Suppiluliuma: traslitterazione, traduzione e commento*. Pisa: Plus–Pisa University Press.

de Martino, S. 1992. I rapporti tra ittiti e hurriti durante il regno di Muršili I. *Hethitica* 11: 19–37.

de Martino, S. 2003. *Annali e Res Gestae anticó ittiti*. Pavia: Italian University Press.

de Martino, S. 2010a. Some questions on the political history and chronology of the early Hittite Empire. *AoF* 37: 186–197.

de Martino, S. 2010b. The Hittite queen Šata(n)duḫepa. In Fincke, J. (ed.), *Festschrift für Gernot Wilhelm anläßlich seines 65. Geburtstages*. Dresden: ISLET, 91–98.

de Martino, S. 2017. Central west: philology. In Weeden, M., and Ullmann, L.Z. (eds.) 2017: 253–261.

de Martino, S., Murat, L., and Süel A. 2013. The eleventh tablet of the *itkalzi* ritual from Šapinuwa. *KASKAL: Rivista di storia, ambienti e culture del Vicino Oriente Antico* 10: 131–148.

de Martino, S., and Süel, A. 2017. The *"Great itkalzi Ritual"*: the Sapinuwa *tablet or 90/1473 and its duplicate ChS I/1 5*. Florence: LoGisma.

de Roos, J. 2006. Materials for a biography: the correspondence of Puduḫepa with Egypt and Ugarit. In van den Hout, T.P.J. (ed.), *The life and times of Ḫattušili III and Tutḫaliya IV*. Leiden: NINO, 17–26.

Devecchi, E. 2005. *Gli annali di Ḫattušili I nella versione accadica*. Pavia: Italian University Press.

Devecchi, E. 2010. "We are all descendants of Šuppiluliuma, Great King": the Aleppo Treaty reconsidered. *WdO* 40: 1–27.

Devecchi, E. 2015. *Trattati internazionali ittiti*. Brescia: Paideia.

Dietrich, W., and Loretz, O. 1978. Das "seefahrende Volk" von Šikila. *UF* 10: 53–56.

Dinçol, A., and Dinçol, B. 1988. Hieroglyphische Siegel und Siegelabdrücke aus Eskiyapar. In Neu, E., and Rüster, C. (eds.), *Documentum Asiae Minoris: Festschrift für Heinrich Otten zum 75. Geburtstag*. Wiesbaden: Harrassowitz, 87–97.

Dinçol, A.M., Dinçol, B., Hawkins, J.D., and Wilhelm, G. 1993. The "Cruciform Seal" from Boğazköy-Hattusa. *IstMit* 43: 87–116.

Durand, J.-M. 2006. La lettre de Labarna au roi de Tigunânum: un réexamen. In del Olmo Lete, G., Feliu, L., and Millet Albà, A. (eds.), *Šapal tibnim mû illakū: studies presented to Joaquín Sanmartín*. Sabadell: Editorial AUSA, 219–227.

Edel, E. 1994. *Die ägyptisch-hethitische Korrespondenz aus Boghazköi in baby-lonischer und hethitischer Sprache*. Opladen: Westdeutscher Verlag.

Edel, E. 1997. *Der Vertrag zwischen Ramses II. von Ägypten und Hattušili III. von Hatti*. Berlin: Mann.

Ehringhaus, H. 2005. *Götter, Herrscher, Inschriften: die Felsreliefs der hethi-tischen Grossreichszeit in der Türkei*. Mainz: Zabern.

Fairbairn, A., and Omura, S. 2005. Archaeological identification and signifi-cance of ÉSAG (agricultural storage pits) at Kaman-Kalehöyük, Central Anatolia. *AnSt* 55: 15–23.

Forlanini, M. 2010. An attempt at reconstructing the branches of the Hittite royal family of the early kingdom period. In Cohen, Y., Gilan, A., and Miller, J.L. (eds.), *Pax Hethitica: studies on the Hittites and their neighbours in honour of Itamar Singer.* Wiesbaden: Harrassowitz, 115–135.

Forlanini, M. 2017: South central: the lower land and Tarḫuntašša. In Weeden, M., and Ullmann, L.Z. (eds.) 2017: 239–252.

Freu, J. 2001. De l'indépendance à l'annexion: le Kizzuwatna et le Hatti aux XVIᵉ et XVᵉ siècles avant notre ère. In Jean, É., Dinçol, A.M., and Durugönül, S. (eds.), *La Cilicie: espaces et pouvoirs locaux (2ᵉ millénaire av. J.-C.–4ᵉ siècle ap. J.-C.).* Istanbul: Institut Français d'Études Anatoliennes-Georges Dumézil, 13–36.

Freu, J. 2004a. Le Grand Roi Tutḫaliya, fils de Kantuzzili. In Mazoyer, M., and Casabonne, O. (eds.), *Antiquus Oriens: mélanges offerts au Professeur René Lebrun.* Paris: L'Harmattan, 271–304.

Freu, J. 2004b. *Šuppiluliuma et la veuve du Pharaon: histoire d'un mariage manqué: Essai sur les relations égypto-hittites.* Paris: L'Harmattan.

Freu, J., and Mazoyer, M. 2007a. *Des origines à la fin de l'ancien royaume Hittite.* Paris: L'Harmattan.

Freu, J., and Mazoyer, M. 2007b. *Les débuts du nouvel empire Hittite: les Hittites et leur histoire.* Paris: L'Harmattan.

Friedrich, J. 1926. *Staatsverträge des Ḫatti-Reiches in hethitischer Sprache, vol. I: die Verträge Muršiliš II. mit Duppi-Tešup von Amurru, Targašnalliš von Ḫapalla.* Leipzig: Hinrich.

Fuscagni, F. 2014. *Vertrag mit einem unbekannten Herrscher (CTH 123).* Retrieved from www.hethiter.net (last accessed February 21, 2019).

Gander, M. 2015. Asia, Ionia, Maeonia und Luwiya? Bemerkungen zu den neuen Toponymen aus Kom el-Hettan (Theben-West) mit Exkursen zu Westkleinasien in der Spätbronzezeit. *Klio* 97: 443–502.

Gander, M. 2017a. The west: philology. In Weeden, M., and Ullmann, L.Z. (eds.) 2017: 262–281.

Gander, M. 2017b. An alternative view on the location of Arzawa. In Mouton, A. (ed.), *Hittitology today: studies on Hittite and Neo-Hittite Anatolia in honor of Emmanuel Laroche's 100th birthday.* Istanbul: Ege, 163–190.

Gautschy, R. 2014. A reassessment of the absolute chronology of the Egyptian New Kingdom and its "brotherly" countries. *ÄL* 24: 141–158.

Gautschy, R. 2017. Remarks concerning the alleged solar eclipse of Muršili II. *AoF* 44: 23–29.

George, A.R. 2013. *Babylonian divinatory texts chiefly in the Schøyen Collection.* Bethesda, MD: CDL Press.

Gerçek, İ. 2018. Hittite geographers: geographical perceptions and practices in Hittite Anatolia. *JANEH* 4: 39–60.

Gerçek, İ. 2021. *The Kaska and the northern frontier of Hatti*. Berlin: De Gruyter.

Gilan, A. 2007. How many princes can the land bear? Some thoughts on the Zalpa text (CTH 3). In Archi, A., and Francia, R. (eds.), *VI Congresso Internazionale di Ittitologia, vol. I.* Rome: Istituto di Studi sulle Civiltà dell'Egeo e del Vicino Oriente, 305–318.

Gilan, A. 2008. Hittite ethnicity? Constructions of identity in Hittite literature. In Collins, B.J., Bachvarova, M., and Rutherford, I.C. (eds.), *Anatolian interfaces: Hittites, Greeks and their neighbours*. Oxford: Oxbow, 107–115.

Gilan, A. 2014. The Hittite "Offering Lists" of deceased kings and related texts (CTH 610–611) as historical sources. *KASKAL: Rivista di storia, ambienti e culture del Vicino Oriente Antico* 11: 85–102.

Gilan, A. 2015. *Formen und Inhalte althethitischer historischer Literatur*. Heidelberg: Winter.

Giorgieri, M. 2005. Zu den Treueiden mittelhethitischer Zeit. *AoF* 32: 322–346.

Giorgieri, M. 2008. Verschwörungen und Intrigen am hethitischen Hof: zu den Konflikten innerhalb der hethitischen Elite anhand der historisch-juristischen Quellen. In Wilhelm, G. (ed.), *Ḫattuša—Boğazköy: das Hethiterreich im Spannungsfeld des Alten Orients*. Wiesbaden: Harrassowitz, 351–375.

Giorgieri, M., and Mora, C. 1996. *Aspetti della regalità ittita nel XIII secolo a.C.* Como: Edizioni New Press.

Glassner, J.-J. 2004. *Chroniques mésopotamiennes*. Atlanta, GA: Society of Biblical Literature.

Glatz, C. 2009. Empire as network: spheres of material interaction in Late Bronze Age Anatolia. *Journal of Anthropological Archaeology* 28: 127–141.

Glatz, C. 2017. The north: archaeology. In Weeden, M., and Ullmann, L.Z. (eds.) 2017: 75–88.

Glatz, C., and Plourde, A.M. 2011. Landscape monuments and political competition in Late Bronze Age Anatolia: an investigation of costly signaling theory. *BASOR* 361: 33–66.

Goedegebuure, P. 2006. The proclamation of Telipinu. In Chavalas, M. (ed.), *The ancient Near East: historical sources in translation*. Malden, MA: Wiley-Blackwell, 228–235.

Goedegebuure, P. 2008a. Hattian origins of Hittite religious concepts: the syntax of "to drink (to) a deity" (again) and other phrases. *JANER* 8: 67–73.

Goedegebuure, P. 2008b. Central Anatolian languages and language communities in the colony period: a Luwian-Hattian symbiosis and the independent Hittites. In Dercksen, J. (ed.), *Anatolia and the Jazira during the Old Assyrian period*. Leiden: NINO, 137–180.

Goetze, A. 1933. *Die Annalen des Muršiliš*. Leipzig: Hinrich.

Görke, S. 2015. *Muršilis Sprachlähmung (CTH 486)*. Retrieved from www.hethiter.net (last accessed February 21, 2019).

Grayson, A.K. 1975. *Assyrian and Babylonian chronicles*. Locust Valley, NY: Augustin.

Grayson, A.K. 1987. *Assyrian rulers of the third and second millennia BC (to 1115 BC)*. Toronto: University of Toronto Press.

Grélois, J.-P. 1988. Les annales décennales de Mursili II (CTH 61, 1). *Hethitica* 9: 17–145.

Günel, S. 2017. The west: archaeology. In Weeden, M., and Ullmann, L.Z. (eds.) 2017: 119–133.

Gurney, O.R. 1997. The annals of Hattusilis III. *AnSt* 47: 127–139.

Güterbock, H.G. 1940. *Siegel aus Boğazköy, vol. I: die Königssiegel der Grabungen bis 1938*. Berlin: Selbstverlag E.F. Weidner.

Güterbock, H.G. 1942. *Siegel aus Boğazköy, vol. II: die Königssiegel von 1939 und die übrigen Hieroglyphensiegel*. Berlin: Selbstverlag E.F. Weidner.

Güterbock, H.G. 1956. The deeds of Suppiluliuma as told by his son, Mursili II. *JCS* 10: 41–68, 75–98, 107–130.

Hawkins, J.D. 1988. Kuzi-Tešub and the "Great Kings" of Karkamiš. *AnSt* 38: 99–108.

Hawkins, J.D. 1995a. Tarkasnawa king of Mira "Tarkondemos": Boğazköy sealings and Karabel. *AnSt* 48: 1–31.

Hawkins, J.D. 1995b. *The Hieroglyphic inscription of the sacred pool complex at Hattusa*. Wiesbaden: Harrassowitz.

Hawkins, J.D., and Weeden, M. 2017. Kizzuwatna and the Euphrates states: Kummaha, Elbistan, Malatya: philology. In Weeden, M., and Ullmann, L.Z. (eds.) 2017: 281–294.

Heinhold-Krahmer, S. 1977. *Arzawa: Untersuchungen zu seiner Geschichte nach den hethitischen Quellen*. Heidelberg: Winter.

Heinhold-Krahmer, S. 2013. Zur Lage des hethitischen Vasallenstaates Wiluša im Südwesten Kleinasiens. In Mazoyer, M., and Aufrère, S.H. (eds.), *De Hattuša à Memphis: Jacques Freu in honorem*. Paris: L'Harmattan, 59–74.

Heinhold-Krahmer, S., and Rieken, E. (eds.) 2020. *Der Tawagalawa-Brief: Beschwerden über Piyamaradu: eine Neuedition*. Berlin: De Gruyter.

Heltzer, M. 2001. The political institutions of ancient Emar as compared with contemporary Ugarit (13th–beginning of the 12th century BCE). *UF* 33: 219–236.

Herbordt, S. 2006. Hittite glyptic: a reassessment in the light of recent discoveries. In Mielke, D.P., Schoop, U., and Seeher, J. (eds.), *Strukturierung und Datierung in der hethitischen Archäologie: Voraussetzungen, Probleme, neue Ansätze*. Istanbul: Ege, 95–108.

Herbordt, S., Bawanypeck, D., and Hawkins, J.D. 2011. *Die Siegel der Großkönige und Großköniginnen auf Tonbullen aus dem Nişantepe-Archiv in Hattusa*. Mainz: Zabern.

Hoffmann, I. 1984. *Der Erlaß Telipinus*. Heidelberg: Winter.

Hoffner, H.A. 1975. Propaganda and political justification in Hittite historiography. In Goedicke, H., and Roberts, J.J.M. (eds.), *Unity and diversity: essays in the history, literature, and religion of the ancient Near East*. Baltimore, MD: Johns Hopkins University Press, 49–62.

Hoffner, H.A. 1997a. *The laws of the Hittites: a critical edition*. Leiden: Brill.

Hoffner, H.A. 1997b. Deeds of Suppiluliuma. In Hallo, W.W. (ed.), *The context of scripture, vol. 1: canonical compositions from the biblical world*. Leiden: Brill, 185–192.

Hoffner, H.A. 1997c. The Hittite conquest of Cyprus: two inscriptions of Suppiluliuma II. In Hallo, W.W. (ed.), *The context of scripture, vol. 1: canonical compositions from the biblical world*. Leiden: Brill, 192–193.

Hoffner, H.A. 1980. Histories and historians of the ancient Near East: the Hittites. *Orientalia* 49: 283–332.

Hoffner, H.A. 2009. *Letters from the Hittite kingdom*. Atlanta, GA: Society of Biblical Literature.

Holland, G., and Zorman, M. 2007. *The Tale of Zalpa: myth, morality and coherence in a Hittite narrative*. Pavia: Italian University Press.

Hüser, A. 2007. *Hethitische Anlagen zur Wasserversorgung und Entsorgung* (Kuşaklı-Sarissa 3). Rahden: Verlag Marie Leidorf.

Imparati, F. 1974. *Una concessione di terre da parte di Tudhaliya IV*. Paris: Klincksieck.

Kempinski, A., and Košak, S. 1982. CTH 13: the extensive annals of Hattušili I (?). *Tel Aviv* 9: 87–116.

Kennedy, H. 2004. The decline and fall of the first Muslim empire. *Der Islam* 81: 3–30.

Klengel, H. 1974. "Hungerjahre" in Ḫatti. *AoF* 1: 165–174.

Klengel, H. 1999. *Geschichte des hethitischen Reiches*. Leiden: Brill.

Klinger, J. 1995a. Synchronismen in der Epoche vor Šuppiluliuma I: einige Anmerkungen zur Chronologie der mittelhethitischen Geschichte. In Onofrio Carruba, O., Giorgieri, M., and Mora, C. (eds.), *Atti del II Congresso Internazionale di Hittitologia*. Pavia: Gianni Iuculano, 235–248.

Klinger, J. 1995b. Das Corpus der Maşat-Briefe und seine Beziehungen zu den Texten aus Ḫattuša. *ZA* 85: 67–78.

Klinger, J. 1996. *Untersuchungen zur Rekonstruktion der hattischen Kultschicht*. Wiesbaden: Harrassowitz.

Klinger, J. 2001. Historiographie als Paradigma: die Quellen zur hethitischen Geschichte und ihre Deutung. In Wilhelm, G. (ed.), *Akten des IV. Internationalen Kongress für Hethitologie*. Wiesbaden: Harrassowitz, 272–291.

Klinger, J. 2006. Der Beitrag der Textfunde zur Archäologiegeschichte der hethitischen Hauptstadt. In Mielke, D.P., Schoop, U., and Seeher, J. (eds.), *Strukturierung und Datierung in der hethitischen Archäologie: Voraussetzungen, Probleme, neue Ansätze*. Istanbul: Ege, 5–17.

Klinger, J. 2008. Geschichte oder Geschichten: zum literarischen Charakter der hethitischen Historiographie. In Adam, K.-P. (ed.), *Historiographie in der Antike*. Berlin: De Gruyter, 27–47.

Klinger, J. 2015. Šuppiluliuma II. und die Spätphase der hethitischen Archive. In Müller-Karpe, A., Rieken, E., and Sommerfeld, W. (eds.), *Saeculum: Gedenkschrift für Heinrich Otten anlässlich seines 100. Geburtstags*. Wiesbaden: Harrassowitz, 87–112.

Kloekhorst, A. 2019. *Kanisite Hittite: the earliest attested record of Indo-European*. Leiden: Brill.

Kohlmeyer, K. 1983. Felsbilder der hethitischen Großreichszeit. *APA* 15: 7–154.

Kryszat, G. 2008. Herrscher, Kult und Kulttradition in Anatolien nach den Quellen aus den altassyrischen Handelskolonien, Teil 3/1: Grundlagen für eine neue Rekonstruktion der Geschichte Anatoliens und der altassyrischen Handelskolonien in spätaltassyrischer Zeit. *AoF* 35: 165–189.

Kryszeń, A. 2017. Ḫatti and Ḫattuša. *AoF* 44: 212–220.

Kühne, C., and Otten, H. 1971. *Der Šauşgamuwa-Vertrag: eine Untersuchung zu Sprache und Graphik*. Wiesbaden: Harrassowitz.

Lackenbacher, S. 1976. Nouveaux documents d'Ugarit, I: une lettre royale. *RA* 76: 141–156.

Lackenbacher, S. 2002. *Textes Akkadiens d'Ugarit: textes provenant des vingt-cinq premières campagnes.* Paris: Les éditions du Cerf.

Lackenbacher, S., and Malbran-Labat, F. 2016. *Lettres en Akkadien de la "Maison d'Urtenu": fouilles de 1994.* Leuven: Peeters.

Larsen, M.T. 1972. A revolt against Hattuša. *JCS* 24: 100–101.

Larsen, M.T. 2015. *Ancient Kanesh: a merchant colony in Bronze Age Anatolia.* Cambridge: Cambridge University Press.

Lauinger, J. 2015. *Following the Man of Yamhad: settlement and territory at Old Babylonian Alalah.* Leiden: Brill.

Lebrun, R. 1985. L'aphasie de Mursili II: CTH 486. *Hethitica* 6: 103–137.

Maderna-Sieben, C. 2018. *Königseulogien der frühen Ramessidenzeit: politische Propaganda im Dienst der Legitimierung einer neuen Dynastie.* Heidelberg: Propylaeum.

Manassa, C. 2003. *The Great Karnak Inscription of Merneptah: grand strategy in the 13th century BC.* New Haven, CT: Yale Egyptological Seminar.

Marazzi, M. 2008. Messa a coltura e procedure di gestione e controllo dei campi nell'Anatolia hittita: caratteristiche della documentazione e stato della ricerca. In Perna, M., and Pomponio, F. (eds.), *The management of agricultural land and the production of textiles in the Mycenaean and Near Eastern economies.* Paris: De Boccard, 63–88.

Marchetti, N. (ed.) 2011. *KINKU: sigilli dell'età del bronzo dalla regione di Gaziantep in Turchia.* Bologna: AnteQuem.

Marchetti, N. 2015. Karkemish: new discoveries in the last Hittite capital. *Current World Archaeology* 70: 18–25.

Matessi, A. 2017. The making of Hittite imperial landscapes: territoriality and balance of power in South-Central Anatolia during the Late Bronze Age. *JANEH* 3: 117–162.

Matsumura, K. 2018. The glass bottle and pendant from Büklükale and their dating. *Anatolian Archaeological Studies* 21: 11–29.

Matsumura, K., and Weeden, M. 2017. Central west: archaeology. In Weeden, M., and Ullmann, L.Z. (eds.) 2017: 106–118.

Meriggi, P. 1975. *Manuale di eteo geroglifico, parte II: testi—2a e 3a serie.* Rome: Edizioni dell'Ateneo.

Mielke, D.P., Schoop, U., and Seeher, J. (eds.) 2006. *Strukturierung und Datierung in der hethitischen Archäologie: Voraussetzungen, Probleme, neue Ansätze.* Istanbul: Ege.

Miller, J.L. 2001. Hattušili I's expansion into northern Syria in light of the Tikunani Letter. In Wilhelm G. (ed.), *Akten des IV. Internationalen Kongresses für Hethitologie*. Wiesbaden: Harrassowitz, 410–429.

Miller, J.L. 2004. *Studies in the origins, development and interpretation of the Kizzuwatna rituals*. Wiesbaden: Harrassowitz.

Miller, J.L. 2007a. Amarna Age chronology and the identity of Nibhururiya in the light of a newly reconstructed Hittite text. *AoF* 54: 252–293.

Miller, J.L. 2007b. Mursili II's dictate to Tuppi-Teššub's Syrian antagonists. *KASKAL: Rivista di storia, ambienti e culture del Vicino Oriente Antico* 4: 121–152.

Miller, J.L. 2008. Joins and duplicates among the Boğazköy Tablets (31–45). *ZA* 98: 117–137.

Miller, J.L. 2010. Revisiting the conquest of Karkamiš of Mursili's 9th year: Assyrian aggression or Mursili in the long shadow of his father? In Fincke J. (ed.), *Festschrift für Gernot Wilhelm anläßlich seines 65. Geburtstages*. Dresden: ISLET, 235–239.

Miller, J.L. 2013. *Royal Hittite instructions and related administrative texts*. Atlanta, GA: Society of Biblical Literature.

Miller, J.L. 2020. Are there signs of a decline of the Late Hittite state in textual documentation from Hattuša? In de Martino, S., and Devecchi, E. (eds.), *Anatolia between the 13th and 12th century BCE*. Florence: LoGismo, 237–255.

Mora, C., and Giorgieri, M. 2004. *Le lettere tra i re Ittiti e i re Assiri ritrovate a Ḫattuša*. Padua: Sargon.

Moran, W.L. 1992. *The Amarna letters*. Baltimore, MD: Johns Hopkins University Press.

Morris, E. 2015. Egypt, Ugarit, the god Baʿal, and the puzzle of a royal rebuff. In Mynářová, J., Onderka, P., and Pavúk, P. (eds.), *There and back again: the crossroads, II*. Prague: Charles University, 315–351.

Müller-Karpe, A. 1995. Untersuchungen in Kuşaklı 1992–94. *MDOG* 127: 5–36.

Müller-Karpe, A. 2001. Untersuchungen in Kuşaklı 2000. *MDOG* 133: 176–189.

Müller-Karpe, A. 2002. Kuşaklı-Sarissa: Kultort im Oberen Land. In Kunst- und Ausstellungshalle der Bundesrepublik Deutschland (ed.), *Die Hethiter und ihr Reich: das Volk der 1000 Götter*. Stuttgart: Theiss, 176–189.

Müller-Karpe, A. 2017a. *Sarissa: die Wiederentdeckung einer hethitischen Königsstadt*. Mainz: Zabern.

Müller-Karpe, A. 2017b. The east: the Upper Land, Azzi-Hayaša, Išuwa: archaeology. In Weeden, M., and Ullmann, L.Z. (eds.) 2017: 58–74.

Neu, E. 1974. *Der Anitta-Text.* Wiesbaden: Harrassowitz.

Neve, P. 2019. *Die Oberstadt von Hattuša: die Bauwerke, III: die Bebauung im südlichen Vorfeld von Büyükkale: Nişantepe – Südburg – Ostplateau (Grabungen 1988–1993).* Berlin: De Gruyter.

Novák, M. 2010. Kizzuwatna – Ḫiyawa – Quwe: ein Abriss der Kulturgeschichte des Ebenen Kilikien. In Becker, J., Hempelmann, R., and Rehm, E. (eds.), *Kulturlandschaft Syrien: Zentrum und Peripherie. Festschrift für Jan-Waalke Meyer.* Münster: Ugarit, 379–425.

Novák, M., and Rutishäuser, S. 2017. Kizzuwatna: archaeology. In Weeden, M., and Ullmann, L.Z. (eds.) 2017: 134–144.

Omura, S. 2002. Preliminary report on the 16th excavation at Kaman-Kalehöyük (2001). *Anatolian Archaeological Studies* 11: 1–43.

Otten, H. 1951. Die hethitischen "Königslisten" und die altorientalische Chronologie. *MDOG* 83: 47–71.

Otten, H. 1973. *Eine althethitische Erzählung um die Stadt Zalpa.* Wiesbaden: Harrassowitz.

Otten, H. 1988. *Die Bronzetafel aus Boğazköy: ein Staatsvertrag Tuthaliyas IV.* Wiesbaden: Harrassowitz.

Otten, H. 1993. *Zu einigen Neufunden hethitischer Königssiegel.* Stuttgart: Franz Steiner.

Otten, H. 2000. Ein Siegelabdruck Dutḫaliyaš I? *ArchAnz* 2000: 375–376.

Pallavidini, M. 2017a. The Hittite word *kuri/ewana, kui/erwana-*: a new assessment. *Journal of Ancient Civilizations* 32: 1–11.

Pallavidini, M. 2017b. Ḫakpiš, la prima "Sekundogenitur" di Ḫatti? Considerazioni sul rapporto giuridico di Ḫattušili con Muwatalli e Urḫi-Teššup/Muršili III sulla base di CTH 81. *Res Antiquae* 17: 205–220.

Palmisano, A. 2018. *The geography of trade: landscapes of competition and long-distance contacts in Mesopotamia and Anatolia in the Old Assyrian colony period.* Oxford: Archaeopress.

Paulus, S. 2018. Fraud, forgery and fiction: is there still hope for Agum-Kakrime? *JCS* 70: 115–166.

Pecchioli Daddi, R. 1995. Le cosi dette "Cronache di Palazzo." In Onofrio Carruba, O., Giorgieri, M., and Mora, C. (eds.), *Atti del II Congresso Internazionale di Hittitologia.* Pavia: Gianni Iuculano, 321–332.

Peker, H. 2017. Some remarks on the imperial Hittite sealings from the 2017 excavations at Karkemish. *NABU* 2017: 178–179 (no. 101).

Pizzimenti, S., and Scazzosi, G. 2017. The urban structure of Karkemish in the Late Bronze Age and the settlements of the Middle Euphrates Valley. *Anatolica* 43: 157–172.

Poetto, M. 1993. *L'iscrizione luvio-geroglifica di Yalburt: nuove acquisizioni relative alla geografia dell'Anatolia sud-occidentale.* Pavia: Gianni Iuculano.

Redford, D.B. 2003. *The wars in Syria and Palestine of Thutmose III.* Leiden: Brill.

Richter, T., and Lange, S. 2012. *Das Archiv des Idadda: die Keilschrifttexte aus den deutsch-syrischen Ausgrabungen 2001–2003 im Königspalast von Qaṭna.* Wiesbaden: Harrassowitz.

Rieken, E. 2009. Die Tontafelfunde aus Kayalıpınar. In Pecchioli Daddi, F., Torri, G., and Corti, C. (eds.), *Central-north Anatolia in the Hittite period: new perspectives in light of recent research.* Rome: Herder, 119–143.

Rieken, E., Lorenz, J., and Daues, A. 2016. *Hymnen und Gebete an die Sonnengöttin von Arinna (CTH 376.1).* Retrieved from www.hethiter.net/txhet_gebet (last accessed February 21, 2019).

Rüster, C., and Wilhelm, G. 2012. *Landschenkungsurkunden hethitischer Könige.* Wiesbaden: Harrassowitz.

Salvini, M. 1994. Una lettera di Ḫattušili I relative alla spedizione contro Ḫaḫḫum. *SMEA* 34: 61–80.

Sayce, A.H. 1876. The Hamathite inscriptions (read 2nd May 1876). *Transactions of the Society of Biblical Archaeology* 5: 22–32.

Sayce, A.H. 1882. The monuments of the Hittites (read 6th July 1880). *Transactions of the Society of Biblical Archaeology* 7: 248–293.

Schachner, A. 2009. Das 16. Jahrhundert v. Chr.: eine Zeitenwende im hethitischen Zentralanatolien. *IstMit* 59: 9–34.

Schachner, A. 2011. *Hattuscha: auf der Suche nach dem sagenhaften Großreich der Hethiter.* Munich: Beck.

Schachner, A. 2012. Gedanken zur Datierung, Entwicklung und Funktion der hethitischen Kunst. *AoF* 39: 130–166.

Schachner, A. 2015. Zu Hause beim GAL MEŠEDI in Ḫattuša. In Müller-Karpe, A., Rieken, E., and Sommerfeld, W. (eds.), *Saeculum: Gedenkschrift für Heinrich Otten anlässlich seines 100. Geburtstags.* Wiesbaden: Harrassowitz, 189–209.

Schachner, A. 2017a. The first period of scientific excavations at Boğazköy-Hattuša (1906–1912). In Alparslan, M., Doğan-Alparslan, M., and Schachner, A. (eds.), *The discovery of an Anatolian empire: the 100th anniversary of the decipherment of Hittite language*. Istanbul: Türk Eskiçağ Bilimleri Enstitüsü Yayinlari, 42–68.

Schachner, A. 2017b. *Ausgrabungen und Forschungen in der westlichen Oberstadt von Ḫattuša, II: Ausgrabungen auf dem Mittleren Plateau zwischen Sarıkale und Yenicekale (2006–2009)*. Berlin: De Gruyter.

Schachner, A., Seeher, J., and Seeher-Baykal, A. 2012. *Hattuşa'da 106 yıl: Hitit kazılarının fotoğraflarla öyküsü / 106 Years in Hattusha: photographs tell the story of the excavations in the Hittite capital*. Istanbul: Yapi Kredi Yayinlari.

Schachner, A., and Wittenberg, H. 2012. Zu den Wasserspeichern in Boğazköy/ Hattuša und der Frage Ihrer Befüllung. In Klimscha, F., Eichmann, R., Schuler, C., and Fahlbusch, H. (eds.), *Wasserwirtschaftliche Innovationen im archäologischen Kontext: von den prähistorischen Anfängen bis zu den Metropolen der Antike*. Rahden: Verlag Marie Leidorf, 245–256.

Schoop, U. 2008. Wo steht die Archäologie in der Erforschung der hethitischen Kultur? Schritte zu einem Paradigmenwechsel. In Wilhelm, G. (ed.), *Ḫattuša—Boğazköy: das Hethiterreich im Spannungsfeld des Alten Orients*. Wiesbaden: Harrassowitz, 35–60.

Schoop, U., and Seeher, J. 2006. Absolute Chronologie in Boğazköy-Ḫattuša: das Potential der Radiokarbondaten. In Seeher, J. (ed.), *Ergebnisse der Grabungen an den Ostteichen und am mittleren Büyükkale-Nordwesthang in den Jahren 1996–2000*. Mainz: Zabern, 53–75.

Seeher, J. 1998. Neue Befunde zur Endzeit von Hattuša: Ausgrabungen auf Büyükkaya in Boğazköy. In Alp, S., and Süel, A. (eds.), *III. Uluslararası Hititoloji Kongresi bildirileri /Acts of the IIIrd International Congress of Hittitology*. Ankara: Uyum Ajans, 515–523.

Seeher, J. 2006. Der althethitische Getreidesilokomplex. In Seeher, J. (ed.), *Ergebnisse der Grabungen an den Ostteichen und am mittleren Büyükkale-Nordwesthang in den Jahren 1996–2000*. Mainz: Zabern, 45–84.

Seeher, J. 2007. *Die Lehmziegel-Stadtmauer von Hattuša: Bericht über eine Rekonstruktion*. Istanbul: Ege.

Seeher, J. 2008. Abschied von Gewußtem: die Ausgrabungen in Ḫattuša am Beginn des 21. Jahrhunderts. In Wilhelm, G. (ed.), *Ḫattuša—Boğazköy: das Hethiterreich im Spannungsfeld des Alten Orients*. Wiesbaden: Harrassowitz, 1–13.

Shelestin, V. 2014. The foreign policy of the late Old Hittite kingdom: the case of Ammuna. In Taracha, P. (ed.), *Proceedings of the 8th International Congress of Hittitology*. Warsaw: Agade, 800–826.

Singer, I. 1981. Hittites and Hattians in Anatolia at the beginning of the second millennium BC. *Journal of Indo-European Studies* 9: 119–134.

Singer, I. 1984. The AGRIG in the Hittite texts. *AnSt* 34: 97–127.

Singer, I. 1985. The battle of Niḫriya and the end of the Hittite Empire. *ZA* 75: 100–123.

Singer, I. 1991. A concise history of Amurru. In Izreʾel, S., *Amurru Akkadian: a linguistic study*. Atlanta, GA: Scholars Press, 134–195.

Singer, I. 1995. "Our god" and "their god" in the Anitta Text. In Onofrio Carruba, O., Giorgieri, M., and Mora, C. (eds.), *Atti del II Congresso Internazionale di Hittitologia*. Pavia: Gianni Iuculano, 343–349.

Singer, I. 1996. *Muwatalli's prayer to the assembly of gods through the storm-god of lightning (CTH 381)*. Atlanta, GA: Scholars Press.

Singer, I. 1999. A political history of Ugarit. In Watson, W.G.E., and Wyatt, N. (eds.), *Handbook of Ugaritic studies*. Leiden: Brill. 603–733.

Singer, I. 2002. *Hittite prayers*. Leiden: Brill.

Singer, I. 2004. The Kuruštama Treaty revisited. In Groddek, D., and Rößle, S. (eds.), *Šarnikzel: hethitologische Studien zum Gedenken an Emil Orgetorix Forrer*. Dresden: Verlag der Technischen Universität Dresden, 591–607.

Singer, I. 2006. The Urḫi-Teššub affair in the Hittite-Egyptian correspondence. In van den Hout, T.P.J. (ed.), *The life and times of Ḫattušili III and Tutḫaliya IV*. Leiden: NINO, 27–38.

Singer, I. 2008. KBo 28.61–64 and the struggle over the throne of Babylon at the turn of the 13th century BCE. In Wilhelm, G. (ed.), *Ḫattuša—Boğazköy: das Hethiterreich im Spannungsfeld des Alten Orients*. Wiesbaden: Harrassowitz, 223–245.

Soysal, O. 1989. *Mursili I.: eine historische Studie*. PhD thesis, University of Würzburg.

Soysal, O. 1990. Noch einmal zur Šukziya-Episode im Erlass Telipinus. *Orientalia* 59: 271–279.

Soysal, O. 2003. Kantuzzili in Siegelinschriften. *BiOr* 60: 41–56.

Soysal, O. 2004. *Hattischer Wortschatz in hethitischer Textüberlieferung*. Leiden: Brill.

Soysal, O. 2008. Philological contributions to Hattian-Hittite religion (I). *JANER* 8: 45–66.

Soysal, O. 2012a. Neues zu den Kantuzzili- und älteren Tutḫaliya-Siegeln. *NABU* 2011: 65–70 (no. 62).

Soysal, O. 2012b. Joins, duplicates, and more from the unpublished BO 9000 fragments. *Anatolica* 38: 169–190.

Starke, F. 1979. Ḫalmašuit im Anitta-Text und die hethitische Ideologie vom Königtum. *ZA* 69: 47–120.

Starke, F. 1998. Hattusa. In Cancik, H., and Schneider, H. (eds.), *Der Neue Pauly* 5. Stuttgart: Metzler, 186–198.

Stavi, B. 2015. *The reign of Tudhaliya II and Šuppiluliuma I: the contribution of the Hittite documentation to a reconstruction of the Amarna Age.* Heidelberg: Winter.

Steiner, G. 1984. Struktur und Bedeutung des sogenannten Anitta-Textes. *Orientalia* 23: 54–73.

Steiner, G. 1996. Muršili I: Sohn oder Enkel Labarna-Hattušilis I? *UF* 28: 561–618.

Süel, A. 2001. Ortaköy tabletleri ışığında Batı Anadolu ile ilgili bazı konular üzerine. In Wilhelm, G. (ed.), *Akten des IV. Internationalen Kongress für Hethitologie.* Wiesbaden: Harrassowitz, 670–678.

Süel, A. 2014. Tarhunnaradu/Tarhundaradu in the Ortaköy texts. In Taracha, P. (ed.), *Proceedings of the 8th International Congress of Hittitology.* Warsaw: Agade, 932–942.

Süel, A. 2017. The Anatolian-Syrian relationship in the light of the Ortaköy-Šapinuwa tablets. In Maner Ç., Horowitz, M.T., and Gilbert, A.S. (ed.), *Overturning certainties in Near Eastern archaeology: a Festschrift in honor of K. Aslıhan Yener.* Leiden: Brill, 634–644.

Süel, A., and Süel, M. 2017. The discovery of a Hittite city: developments in Hittite geography based on the identification of Ortaköy-Šapinuwa. Weeden, M., and Ullmann, L.Z. (eds.) 2017: 28–36.

Süel, A., and Weeden, M. 2017. Central east: philology. In Weeden, M., and Ullmann, L.Z. (eds.) 2017: 200–208.

Süel, M. 2008. Ortaköy-Şapinuva'da bulunan bir grup kalıp. In Tarhan, T., Tibet, A., and Konya, E. (ed.), *Muhibbe Darga Armağanı.* Istanbul: Sadberk Hanım Müzesi, 475–484.

Taracha, P. 2016. On Anatolian traditions of the Old Hittite kingship. In Velharticka, Š. (ed.), *Audias fabulas veteres: Anatolian studies in honor of Jana Součková-Siegelová.* Leiden: Brill, 365–373.

Trémouille, M.-C. 2001. Kizzuwatna, terre de frontière. In Jean, É., Dinçol, A.M., and Durugönül, S. (eds.), *La Cilicie: espaces et pouvoirs locaux (2ᵉ millénaire av. J.-C.–4ᵉ siècle ap. J.-C.)*. Istanbul: Institut Français d'Études Anatoliennes-Georges Dumézil, 57–78.

Ünal, A. 1992. Ein hethitisches Schwert mit akkadischer Inschrift aus Boğazköy. *Antike Welt* 23: 256–257.

Ünal, A. 1993. Boğazköy kılıcının üzerindeki akadca adak yazısı hakkında yeni gözlemler. In Mellink, M.J., Porada, E., and Özgüç, T. (eds.), *Aspects of art and iconography: Anatolia and its neighbors. Studies in honor of Nimet Özgüç*. Ankara: Türk Tarih Kurumu, 727–730.

Ünal, A. 2014. Fraudulent premises of Anatolian historiography and early Hittite involvement in and direct control of Cilicia-Kizzuwatna. In Çınardalı-Karaaslan, N., et al. (eds.), *Compiled in honor of Armağan Erkanal: some observations on Anatolian cultures / Armağan Erkanal'a Armağan: Anadolu kültürlerine bir bakış*. Ankara: Hacettepe Üniversitesi Yayınları, 469–500.

Ünal, A. 2015. A Hittite treaty tablet from Oylum Höyük in southeastern Turkey and the location of Ḫaššu(wa). *AnSt* 65: 19–34.

van den Hout, T.P.J. 1994. Der Falke und das Küken: der neue Pharao und der hethitische Prinz? *ZA* 84: 60–88.

van den Hout, T.P.J. 1995. *Der Ulmitešub-Vertrag: eine prosopographische Untersuchung*. Wiesbaden: Harrassowitz.

van den Hout, T.P.J. 1997. Apology of Ḫattušili III. In Hallo, W.W. (ed.), *The context of scripture, vol. 1: canonical compositions from the biblical world*. Leiden: Brill, 199–204.

van den Hout, T.P.J. 1998. *The purity of kingship: an edition of CTH 569 and related Hittite oracle inquiries of Tuthaliya IV*. Leiden: Brill.

van den Hout, T.P.J. 2007. Some observations on the tablet collection from Maşat Höyük. In Archi, A., and Francia, R. (eds.), *VI Congresso Internazionale di Ittitologia, vol. I*. Rome: Istituto di Studi Sulle Civiltá Dell'Egeo e del Vicino Oriente, 387–398.

van den Hout, T.P.J. 2012a. Die Rolle der Schrift in einer Geschichte der frühen hethitischen Staatsverwaltung. In Wilhelm, G. (ed.), *Organization, Representation and symbols of power in the ancient Near East*. Winona Lake, IN: Eisenbrauns, 73–84.

van den Hout, T.P.J. 2012b. Administration and writing in Hittite society. In Balza, M.E., Giorgieri, M., and Mora, C. (eds.), *Archivi, depositi, magazzini presso gli Ittiti: nuovi materiali e nuove ricerche*. Genoa: Italian University Press, 48–58.

von Beckerath, J. 1997. *Chronologie des pharaonischen Ägypten: die Zeitbestimmung der ägyptischen Geschichte von der Vorzeit bis 332 v. Chr.* Mainz: Zabern.

von Dassow, E. 2008. *State and society in the Late Bronze Age: Alalaḫ under the Mittani Empire.* Bethesda, MD: CDL Press.

Wang, H. 2014. *Writing and the ancient state: early China in comparative perspective.* Cambridge: Cambridge University Press.

Weeden, M. 2013. After the Hittites: the kingdoms of Karkamish and Palistin in northern Syria. *Bulletin of the Institute of Classical Studies* 56: 1–20.

Weeden, M. 2016. Hittite epigraphic finds from Büklükale 2010–14. *Anatolian Archaeological Studies* 19: 81–104.

Weeden, M. 2017. A cuneiform fragment from the 2016 season at Büklükale, BKT 3: part of a diplomatic text? *Anatolian Archaeological Studies* 20: 17–21.

Weeden, M. 2018. Hieroglyphic writing on Old Hittite seals and sealings? Towards a material basis for further research. In Ferrara, S., and Valerio, M. (eds.), *Paths into script formation in the ancient Mediterranean.* Rome: Edizioni Quasar, 51–74.

Weeden, M., and Ullmann, L.Z. (eds.) 2017. *Hittite landscape and geography.* Leiden: Brill.

Wilhelm, G. 2005. Zur Datierung der älteren hethitischen Landschenkungsurkunden. *AoF* 32: 272–279.

Wilhelm, G. 2008. Hurrians in the Kültepe texts. In Dercksen, J. (ed.), *Anatolia and the Jazira during the Old Assyrian period.* Leiden: NINO, 181–194.

Wilhelm, G. 2009. Muršilis II. Konflikt mit Ägypten und Haremhabs Thronbesteigung. *WdO* 39: 108–116.

Wilhelm, G. 2011. *Vertrag Tutḫaliyas I. mit Šunaššura von Kizzuwatna (1. akk. Fassung; CTH 41.I.1).* Retrieved from www.hethiter.net (last accessed February 21, 2019).

Wilhelm, G. 2012. Šuppiluliuma I. und die Chronologie der Amarna-Zeit. In Hachmann, R. (ed.), *Die Keilschriftbriefe und der Horizont von El-Amarna* (Kamid el-Loz 20). Bonn: Habelt, 225–257.

Wilhelm, G. 2014a. *Vertrag Zidanzas II. (?) mit Pillija von Kizzuwatna (CTH 25).* Retrieved from www.hethiter.net (last accessed February 21, 2019).

Wilhelm, G. 2014b. *Vertrag Tutḫaliyas I. mit Šunaššura von Kizzuwatna (2. akk. Fassung; CTH 41.I.2).* Retrieved from www.hethiter.net (last accessed February 21, 2019).

Wilhelm, G. 2014c. *Der Vertrag eines Hethiterkönigs mit Paddatiššu von Kizzuwatna (CTH 26)*. Retrieved from www.hethiter.net (last accessed February 21, 2019).

Wilhelm, G. 2016. *Der Vertrag Šuppiluliumas I. von Ḫatti mit Šattiwazza von Mittani (CTH 51.I)*. Retrieved from www.hethiter.net (last accessed February 21, 2019).

Wilhelm, G., and Fuscagni, F. 2014. *Der Vertrag zwischen Muršili II. und Manapa-Tarḫunta vom Šeḫa-Fluss-Land (CTH 69)*. Retrieved from www.hethiter.net (last accessed February 21, 2019).

Wilhelmi, L. 2016. Materiality and presence of the Anitta Text in primary and secondary context: considerations on the original nature of the Proclamation of Anitta (CTH 1) and its transmission as part of Hittite traditional literature. In Balke, T.E., and Tsouparopoulou, C. (eds.), *Materiality of writing in early Mesopotamia*. Berlin: De Gruyter, 264–269.

Wiseman, D.J. 1953. *The Alalakh tablets*. London: British Institute of Archaeology at Ankara.

Wright, W. 1874. The Hamah inscriptions: Hittite remains. *British and Foreign Evangelical Review* 23: 90–98.

Yağcı, R. 2015. Kizzuwatna in the Bronze Age and in later periods: continuity and/or discontinuity? In Stampolidis, N.C., Maner, Ç., and Kopanias, K. (eds.), *NOSTOI: indigenous culture, migration and integration in the Aegean Islands and Western Anatolia during the Late Bronze and Early Iron Age*. Istanbul: Koç University Press, 499–516.

Yakar, J. 2011. Anatolian chronology and terminology. In Steadman, S., and McMahon, G. (eds.), *The Oxford handbook of ancient Anatolia*: 10,000–323 BCE. Oxford: Oxford University Press, 56–93.

Yamada, M. 2011. The second military conflict between "Assyria" and "Ḫatti" in the reign of Tukulti-Ninurta I. *RA* 105: 199–220.

Zaina, F. (ed.) 2019. *Excavations at Karkemish, I: the stratigraphic sequence of Area G in the Inner Town*. Bologna: AnteQuem.

Zivie, A. 2006. Le messager royal égyptien Pirikhnawa. *BMSAES* 6: 68–78.

31

The Aegean in the Context of the Eastern Mediterranean World

Dimitri Nakassis

31.1. Introduction

In the Late Bronze Age, the Aegean (figure 31.1) witnessed the emergence
of an intensely connected network of town centers with monumental
architecture, palaces, wealthy burials, and writing.[1] It is often understood in terms of "Minoans" and "Mycenaeans," the two cultural-historical labels used to describe the archaeological cultures of Crete and
the Greek mainland, respectively. It would be a mistake, however, to
understand these labels as anything but archaeological shorthand since
there is no evidence that the communities living on Crete or the mainland understood themselves to be well-bounded entities that self-identi-
fied in this way.[2] Consequently, in this chapter I use the terms "Minoan"

---

1. I thank Manfred Bietak, Eric Cline, Mary Dabney, Dan Davis, Oliver Dickinson,
   Marian Feldman, Kevin Fisher, Sarah James, Priscilla Keswani, Carl Knappett,
   Naoíse Mac Sweeney, Jana Mokrišová, Magda Nakassis, Sarah Parcak, Peter
   Pavúk, Shari Stocker, Salvatore Vitale, Constance von Rüden, and not least the
   librarians at the University of Colorado Boulder for their assistance. I have tried
   to keep references to a minimum, focusing on recent publications.

2. Broodbank 2004: 50–54.

Dimitri Nakassis, *The Aegean in the Context of the Eastern Mediterranean World* In: *The Oxford History of
the Ancient Near East.* Edited by: Karen Radner, Nadine Moeller, and D. T. Potts, Oxford University Press.
© Oxford University Press 2022. DOI: 10.1093/oso/9780190687601.003.0031

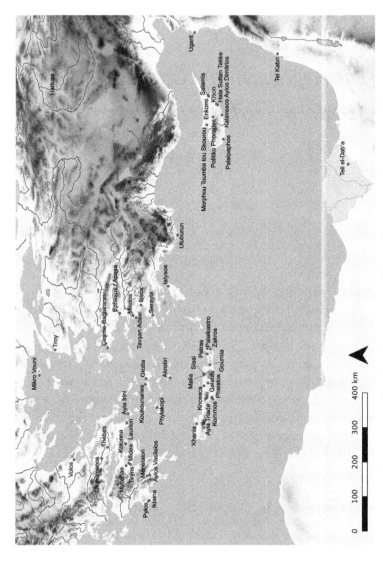

FIGURE 31.1. Sites mentioned in this chapter. Prepared by Andrea Squitieri (LMU Munich).

and "Mycenaean" to describe archaeological assemblages and practices, but never individuals or groups. Much ink has been spilled in the construction of traditional cultural historical narratives in which change is understood as an outcome of the interaction between these cultures, such as the establishment of Minoan colonies in the Aegean islands, or the Mycenaean invasion and occupation of Minoan Crete. Recent work has avoided such essentializing premises, with productive results. Indeed, the past generation has seen a rapid proliferation of scholarship that has significantly changed our image of the Late Bronze Age Aegean.[3]

This period in the Aegean and on Cyprus is effectively prehistoric. Contemporary writing systems are either undeciphered (Linear A in Crete, Cypro-Minoan in Cyprus) or, in the case of the one deciphered script (Linear B), used almost exclusively to document economic transactions.[4] The only contemporary texts that can be used to construct traditional historical narratives come from the Near East, but those relevant to the Aegean are few in number and do not correspond neatly to the archaeological evidence. Some scholars continue to find value in later (first millennium BC) traditions that purport to describe the Bronze Age despite manifold historiographical problems in doing so, but most Aegean prehistorians now view these sources as impediments, rather than aids, to understanding. This chapter therefore draws heavily on the material and archaeological evidence, since it constitutes the vast majority of what is known about the Aegean Bronze Age.

31.2. Chronology

The southern Aegean is traditionally divided into three sub-regions: the island of Crete, the Cycladic islands, and the Greek mainland, which are referred to as Minoan, Cycladic, and Helladic, respectively; the island of Cyprus is referred to as Cypriot. The relative chronological frameworks of Aegean prehistory correspond to these regions, such

3. For recent assessments, see Tartaron 2008; Driessen and Langohr 2014.

4. Palaima 2010; Tomas 2010.

that archaeologists will identify the beginning of the Late Bronze Age regionally as Late Minoan (LM) I, Late Helladic (LH) I, Late Cycladic (LC) I, or Late Cypriot (LC) I (figure 31.2). This system is doubly tripartite, in that it is structured by Early, Middle, and Late Bronze Ages, with each phase further subdivided into I, II, and III. Further ceramic subdivisions may be indicated by A, B, and C, and still further 1 and 2 (e.g., LH IIIA2). Although southern Aegean chronologies are generally synchronized, total congruence does not exist across regions; for example, the production of LH IIA pottery on the Greek mainland is contemporary with the use of LM IA on Crete and LC I pottery in the

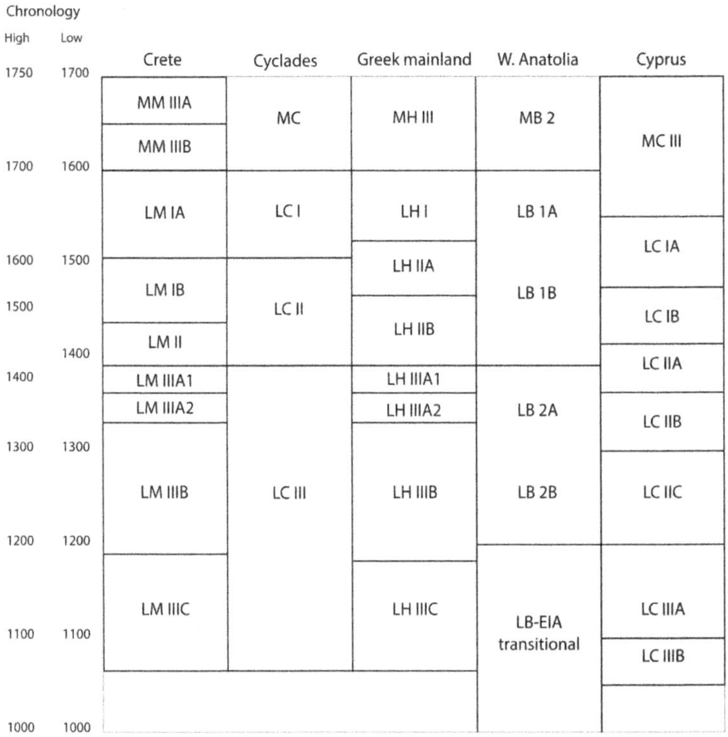

Chronology						
High	Low	Crete	Cyclades	Greek mainland	W. Anatolia	Cyprus
1750	1700	MM IIIA	MC	MH III	MB 2	MC III
1700	1600	MM IIIB				
1600	1500	LM IA	LC I	LH I	LB 1A	LC IA
1500		LM IB	LC II	LH IIA	LB 1B	LC IB
	1400	LM II		LH IIB		LC IIA
1400		LM IIIA1		LH IIIA1		
		LM IIIA2		LH IIIA2	LB 2A	LC IIB
1300	1300	LM IIIB	LC III	LH IIIB	LB 2B	LC IIC
1200	1200					
1100	1100	LM IIIC		LH IIIC	LB-EIA transitional	LC IIIA
						LC IIIB
1000	1000					

FIGURE 31.2. Simplified relative and absolute chronology of the Late Bronze Age Aegean and Cyprus. Knapp 2013a; Manning 2010a; Pavúk 2015; Warren 2010.

Cyclades. Western Anatolia does not have a comparable system but relies on site-specific sequences. Non-local chronological terms may be used where imported ceramics can provide more precision (e.g., Troy VI Late is LH IIIA in the mainland sequence).

This chronological picture is complicated by at least two issues. First, the absolute chronology is controversial, especially at the beginning of the period.[5] The Low Chronology, based on archaeological synchronisms with the eastern Mediterranean and especially Egypt, differs by a century or so from the High Chronology, based on scientific dating methods. Particularly at issue is the date of the eruption of the volcano on the island of Thera (Santorini), which occurred toward the end of the LM IA ceramic period. The Traditional (Low) Chronology suggests a date in the last quarter of the sixteenth century BC, but calibrated radiocarbon dates are about one century earlier, in the late seventeenth century BC. A recent radiocarbon study incorporating calendar-dated tree rings suggests that a recalibration of the radiocarbon curve is required. This would move the absolute date of the Theran eruption to the mid-sixteenth century BC.[6]

Second, ceramic phases can be problematic, both because there may be significant disagreement about terminology, and because historical developments do not always neatly correspond to ceramic phases. Consequently, many scholars have preferred alternative periodizations based on non-ceramic criteria. On Crete, these are the Neopalatial, Final Palatial, and Postpalatial periods; on the Greek mainland, Early Mycenaean (or Prepalatial), Palatial, and Postpalatial; for Cyprus, Knapp has proposed Protohistoric Bronze Age 1, 2, and 3.[7] These alternative schemes can be useful, although they may also create a false sense of harmony and suppress regional and chronological variation. They may also reinforce particular narratives: on the Greek mainland, for instance, the use of palaces as the basis for the chronological scheme ignores the

---

5. Wiener 2009; Manning 2010a; 2010b; Warren 2010.

6. Pearson et al. 2018.

7. Knapp 2008; 2013a.

fact that not all regions were palatial, making the palatial system the high point of the period and marginalizing other developments.

31.3. The late Middle Bronze Age to the early Late Bronze Age

This period is contemporary with the Neopalatial period on Crete: MM IIIA–LM IB in ceramic terms, which corresponds to 1750/1700–1470/1450 BC (figure 31.2). In all regions discussed here, important changes began before the end of the Middle Bronze Age and continued into the early Late Bronze Age. This period witnessed increasing material complexity, associated especially with new forms of elite display and an increasingly dense network of (especially maritime) connections. Crete was a leader in this period, as demonstrated by the palpable influence of Cretan material culture on the islands, along the western Anatolian coast, and on the Greek mainland. It would be wrong to understand this period purely from a Cretan perspective, however, since non-Cretan communities were active contributors to the dynamics of the period.

31.3.1. Neopalatial Crete

The term "Neopalatial" (the New Palace period) should not be interpreted literally to mean that a new set of palaces simply replaced the old palaces at Knossos, Phaistos, and Malia, which were badly damaged by fire in MM IIB. Local histories of destruction and rebuilding were complex. The term is justified by the construction of some new palaces in this period, such as Galatas and Zakros (built in MM IIIA and LM IA, respectively),[8] yet this period is better understood as an extension and acceleration of earlier trends rather than something entirely new. It was characterized by a proliferation of monumental elite architecture, the high quality of craft and artistic production, and the spread of Minoan influence beyond Cretan shores. The period ended in widespread

---

8. Platon 2010; Rethemiotakis and Christakis 2013.

FIGURE 31.3. Plan of the palace at Knossos. Drawing by Dan Davis.

destructions, of unknown cause, toward the end of the LM IB period, ca. 1450 BC.

The definition and functions of Cretan palaces are hotly debated. Although they are traditionally considered the primary residences of a political authority whose economic base was redistributive, recent work suggests that they are better understood as communal monuments involved in large-scale religious rituals.[9] The circulation pattern in a Cretan palace did not culminate in a throne room, but instead drew visitors into a large central court (figure 31.3). Although the functions

9. Day and Relaki 2002; Driessen 2002.

of these courts are uncertain, they have a long history in Crete that goes back to the Prepalatial Early Bronze Age and seem designed for large-scale gatherings.[10] Identifying a ruling elite is complicated by the apparent absence of an iconography of rulership and of royal tombs; indeed, there are very few tombs of any kind in Neopalatial Crete. Consequently, a number of scholars have advocated, largely unsuccessfully, for the abandonment of the term "palace" on the grounds that it carries unhelpful baggage and for the adoption of a more neutral term such as "court-centered building."[11]

The criteria most often employed to define a Neopalatial palace are architectural, the most characteristic element being a rectangular, central court. The largest of these were over 1,000 m^2, with the long, north-south axis being roughly twice the length of the shorter, east-west axis. These central courts were flanked by elaborate façades, beyond which lay suites of rooms. These structures typically included blocks of narrow storage rooms, elegant staircases leading to large reception or banqueting halls, and elaborate residential quarters.[12] Several palaces also have western courts with imposing eastern façades, stone pavements criss-crossed by raised walkways, and stepped "theatral areas" (figure 31.3). They employed an elaborate elite architectural style characterized by extensive use of massive wood beams, coursed ashlar masonry, orthostats, and a dizzying array of complex architectural forms.[13] These building techniques and forms are not confined to palaces, however, but are widespread across Neopalatial Crete. A strict architectural definition of "palace" includes the buildings at Knossos, Phaistos, Malia, Galatas, and Zakros, but excludes a growing number of other structures that display elite architectural styles and served important functions, including administration.[14]

---

10. Tomkins and Schoep 2010.

11. Driessen 2002; Schoep 2002; Tsipopoulou 2002.

12. McEnroe 2010; Shaw 2015.

13. Shaw 2015.

14. Schoep 2002.

Two syllabic scripts, Cretan Hieroglyphic and Linear A, emerged at the beginning of the Middle Bronze Age.[15] The use of the former script, which is unrelated to Egyptian Hieroglyphic, was abandoned by the beginning of the Late Bronze Age, whereas Linear A continued in use through LM IB. Although these writing systems are undeciphered, it is clear that they were used for administrative purposes. Records were typically inscribed on clay tablets and sealings, but Linear A is also attested on other media in religious contexts, especially metal and stone. Indirect evidence of writing on small parchment sheets, carefully folded and affixed to flat-based clay nodules, also exists.[16] Because the deciphered Linear B script (sections 31.4.1 and 31.4.3) was derived from Linear A, many commodities attested in the latter can be securely identified. This suggests that written administrative activity was concerned with woolen textiles, agricultural goods (especially grain, figs, olive oil, olives, wine, and livestock), and personnel. The combination of a literate administration concerned with agricultural products and the significant storage capacities of palatial and non-palatial centers alike suggests a complex administrative operation that probably involved the collection of staples for the support of personnel and large-scale feasting.[17] Written administration is attested at a number of sites, including palaces, but also at places not fitting the architectural definition of a palace but that nevertheless functioned as administrative centers.[18]

It has been widely assumed that each palace was the administrative center of a hierarchically organized territorial state. Many scholars also believe that Knossos became the center of a larger, supra-regional state that exerted broad influence or control. Its territory has been hypothesized to comprise central Crete; additionally, it might have included portions of coastal eastern Crete, the rest of the island, or even colonies

---

15. Tomas 2010.

16. Tomas 2010: 348–349.

17. Christakis 2011.

18. Schoep 2002; La Rosa 2010a; cf. Andreadaki-Vlazaki 2010.

off-island.[19] The Neopalatial palaces at Galatas and Zakros have been interpreted as Knossian foundations, the former to secure territorial control over an elevated plain to the southeast of Knossos, the latter as an eastern port.[20] The empirical evidence for the hypothesis of Knossian domination includes the relatively large size of the settlement and the palace,[21] the concentration of elite buildings at Knossos, the presence of architectural forms and other elite styles (such as figural wall painting) that are associated with Knossos,[22] and transformations in settlement in LM I.[23] While the administrative texts furnish no evidence for a Knossian super-administration, Knossian "replica rings" might.[24] Multiple gold rings were used to impress clay sealings, many of which are flat-based nodules, found at five or six sites in Crete (in LM IB) and on the island of Thera (in LM IA), which certainly indicates communication and perhaps the involvement of a central Knossian administration.[25]

While these are plausible interpretations of the evidence, they are not without their problems.[26] The hypothesis that Cretan palaces were centers of hierarchically organized territorial states relies on analogical evidence from contemporary states in the eastern Mediterranean and Aegean polities on Crete and the Greek mainland that date to the end of the Late Bronze Age (see sections 31.4.1 and 31.4.3). It is not at all clear, however, that Neopalatial political systems were comparably organized. Some scholars have suggested that Neopalatial sociopolitical structures were non-hierarchical. Yannis Hamilakis argued that the proliferation of elite buildings conducive to large social gatherings, often located in

---

19. Warren 2004; 2012; Wiener 2007; 2013.

20. Platon 2010; Rethemiotakis and Christakis 2013.

21. Whitelaw 2004; 2018.

22. Betancourt 2002; Warren 2002; 2004; Blakolmer 2010.

23. Cunningham and Driessen 2004.

24. Schoep 1999.

25. Adams 2017: 172–180; Karnava 2018.

26. Adams 2017: 231–234; Whitelaw 2018.

close proximity to each other, and subject to cycles of destruction and rebuilding, suggests that Neopalatial sociopolitical structures were characterized by factions.[27] Similarly, Jan Driessen convincingly proposed that residential corporate groups were the most important social units in prehistoric Crete.[28] These corporate groups or "houses" were internally ranked and presumably ranged from high-ranking to low-ranking "houses." While large elite buildings can be interpreted as high-ranking Minoan "houses," the palaces might represent "monumental communal structures" designed for large-scale gatherings that reflect multiple "houses" working together.[29]

Palaces are only a small part of a complex settlement system with a long history. The Neopalatial town of Knossos reached some 100 hectares in size with a population of 22,000–25,000, making it far and away the largest urban center on the island.[30] The largest towns on Crete are internally complex, and contain a number of large, architecturally elaborate houses displaying the same elite architectural styles as the palaces.[31] Most Neopalatial towns are in the 4–10 hectare range, and often include central elite buildings, either small palaces or structures anachronistically known as "villas." The region of Knossos is particularly dense with such settlements, suggesting that Knossos inhabited a complex settlement system. Although most larger settlements possess some kind of central building, this is not always the case. For example, although the town of Palaikastro in eastern Crete covers an estimated 30 hectares, over a century of archaeological work has failed to reveal a central building within the well-organized settlement, which consists of large, elaborate houses.[32]

---

27. Hamilakis 2002; cf. Schoep 2002.

28. Driessen 2010; 2018.

29. Driessen 2018: 306.

30. Whitelaw 2004; 2017.

31. McEnroe 2010: 94–100.

32. Cunningham 2007a.

A wide variety of evidence suggests that Crete was in regular contact with off-island communities.[33] Texts from mid-eighteenth century Mari in Syria refer to Cretans and Cretan vessels, weapons, clothing, and boats.[34] A papyrus dated to the reign of Amenhotep II (1425–1397 BC) mentions ships described as *Keftiu*, i.e., Cretan.[35] The faint textual traces of Cretan interaction with Egypt and the Near East are corroborated by two types of wall paintings. The earliest Egyptian representations of Cretans consist of emissaries bearing gifts in tomb paintings at Thebes beginning in the reign of Thutmose III (1479–1425 BC), contemporary with the Neopalatial period.[36] In addition, wall paintings showing significant Cretan influence, both stylistic and technical, have been found in the Levant at Tell Atchana (Alalakh) and Tel Kabri, and in Egypt at Tell el-Dab'a (Avaris).[37] The most striking composition, at Tell el-Dab'a, is a large (over 4 m long, 0.89 m high) frieze showing bulls and bull-leapers (figure 31.4). These wall paintings are best understood not as simple Cretan products, but as the results of complex artistic hybridization through extended processes of collaboration involving Aegean artisans.[38]

Cretan material culture exerted significant influence across the Aegean, a phenomenon commonly referred to as "Minoanization." Traditionally, this influence has been interpreted as evidence for a maritime empire centered on Knossos, the memory of which was preserved by later Greek traditions about the thalassocracy of King Minos.[39] Most scholars now understand Cretan influence in terms of acculturation and

---

33. Cline 1994; Phillips 2010; Yasur-Landau 2010a.

34. Foster 2018.

35. Bietak 2010. For a recent study of the text (Papyrus BM 10056), which confirms its dating to the reign of Amenhotep II (rather than Thutmose III), see Gundacker 2017.

36. Panagiotopoulos 2001; Phillips 2010.

37. Niemeier and Niemeier 2000; Bietak et al. 2007; Cline et al. 2011. The wall paintings at Qatna are probably later in date: von Rüden 2011; but see Pfälzner 2013.

38. Pfälzner 2013; von Rüden 2014.

39. Wiener 2013.

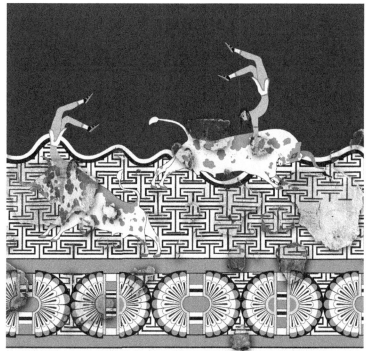

(c) Manfred Bietak, Nanno Marinatos, and Clairy Palyvou, computer reconstruction by C. Palyvou and Marian Negrete-Martinez

FIGURE 31.4. Section of Taureador fresco from Tell el-Dab'a (Avaris). © Manfred Bietak, Nanno Marinatos, and Clairy Palyvou, computer reconstruction by Clairy Palyvou and Marian Negrete-Martinez.

hybridization.[40] No matter how "Minoanization" is explained, however, it is clear that its effects were highly variable across the Aegean and even between neighboring communities (see sections 31.3.2–4).

The Neopalatial period was a time of rapid change, the dynamics of which varied widely across Crete. For example, the Knossos palace underwent multiple phases of remodeling, while in the surrounding town, a number of large, architecturally impressive houses were

40. Knappett 2016.

constructed.[41] Elite architectural structures are also found at a number of sites in the vicinity of Knossos.[42] Other sites and regions experienced episodic growth, however. At Phaistos, the palace was apparently abandoned for over a century, from the end of MM IIIA until the beginning of LM IB, when a new palace was built, only to be destroyed some fifty years later.[43] Monumental elite buildings were in use at nearby Kommos in MM IIIA–LM IA,[44] and at nearby Ayia Triada in MM IIIB–LM IB.[45] In east Crete, the small palace at Petras was rebuilt in MM III but experienced setbacks in LM IB,[46] whereas the palace at Gournia displays evidence of continuous building and rebuilding throughout the Neopalatial period.[47] On the other hand, some new palatial foundations were fairly short-lived. The palace at Galatas, built in MM IIIA, gradually lost its importance beginning in MM IIIB and was destroyed in mature LM IA, whereas the court-centered building at Sissi was only in use from MM IIIA to early LM IA. These changes have been explained variously as the result of factional competition, the machinations of Knossian power politics, or as a broader destabilization of the island in the wake of the Theran volcanic eruption.

The massive volcanic eruption of the island of Thera—the largest such eruption in the past 10,000 years—discharged up to 100 km³ of material.[48] It deposited ash on Crete and generated multiple tsunamis; it was, moreover, accompanied by earthquakes, and its 40 km-high plume would have produced a cooling of the climate. Although the absolute

41. Macdonald 2005: 80–194; McEnroe 2010: 93–100.

42. Adams 2017: 109–117.

43. La Rosa 2010b.

44. Shaw and Shaw 2010.

45. La Rosa 2010a.

46. Tsipopoulou 2002.

47. Buell and McEnroe 2017.

48. McCoy 2009.

date remains debated (see section 31.2), in ceramic terms the eruption occurred in late LM IA. How Crete was affected by the eruption, materially and otherwise, is unclear. Jan Driessen and Colin Macdonald argue that the Theran eruption engendered, both through direct damage and secondary effects, a period of political fragmentation and economic disruption on Crete that contributed to the widespread destructions in LM IB.[49] One critical effect of the eruption was the destruction of an important maritime node (Thera), which in turn may have introduced instability into the Aegean exchange network.[50] Yet theses such as these have been met with dissent by scholars who characterize LM IB as a period of prosperity rather than crisis.[51]

Widespread destructions in LM IB brought an end to the Neopalatial period. The nature of these destructions has been the subject of intense study and debate. On the one hand, some have argued that LM IB was a relatively long period, with destructions occurring at different times in different places;[52] others have suggested that the destructions were effectively simultaneous within a short period.[53] The proximal causes of the destructions have been explained in natural terms, typically earthquakes,[54] or in human terms, either internal conflicts or an invasion from the Greek mainland.[55] Although there is little agreement about the appropriate historical context of these destructions, there is no doubt that they precipitated significant and wide-ranging changes on Crete and around the Aegean in the advanced Late Bronze Age (see section 31.4).

---

49. Driessen and Macdonald 1997; Driessen 2019.

50. Knappett et al. 2011.

51. E. Hallager 2010; McEnroe 2010; Warren 2012.

52. Rutter 2011.

53. Warren 2012.

54. Warren 2012.

55. Driessen and Macdonald 1997; Cunningham 2007b; Wiener 2015.

31.3.2. Cyclades

The early Late Bronze Age in the Cyclades is associated with the development of sophisticated coastal towns, the largest and most elaborate of which is Akrotiri on the island of Thera. This period also represents the apogee of Cretan influence in the Cyclades, and a great deal of attention has been paid to understanding the nature of Cretan-Cycladic interaction.[56] As mentioned earlier (section 31.3.1), later traditions of a Minoan thalassocracy, in which the mythical King Minos of Crete colonized the Cycladic islands and controlled the Aegean through naval power, have suggested to some scholars that the evidence reflects Cretan colonization and imperialism. The archaeological record, however, suggests that Cretan influence, or "Minoanization," was a far more complex and subtle process in which Cycladic communities actively participated.[57]

The Cycladic Middle Bronze Age is poorly understood, due in large part to later building and the history of archaeological exploration.[58] Although the houses of this period were fairly simple structures, towns were well planned: Phylakopi on Melos, the best-understood settlement of this period, is composed of house blocks tightly packed around a grid-like network of streets, and was probably fortified, like Ayia Irini on Kea.[59] The settlements of LC I–II are better understood, especially at Akrotiri on Thera, where the volcanic pumice and ash created excellent conditions for archaeological preservation. While Ayia Irini and Phylakopi were ca. 1 and 2 hectares in size, respectively, Akrotiri seems to have been ca. 10 hectares or more.[60] The town was organized around large, stone-paved streets, some of which opened onto public spaces.

No palatial structures comparable to those on Crete have been discovered in the Cyclades. As on Crete, few burials are known, none

---

56. Davis 2008; Berg 2019: 171–213.

57. Broodbank 2004.

58. Sotirakopoulou 2010.

59. Schofield 1998; Whitelaw 2005.

60. Palyvou 2005: 26–29.

of which is "royal." However, many Late Bronze Age Cycladic towns have large, architecturally elaborate houses. The "typical" houses of Akrotiri were well-appointed structures with multiple stories, ashlar masonry, figural wall paintings, and lavatory installations connected to a communal drainage system.[61] Exceptional buildings at Akrotiri, at Ayia Irini, and Phylakopi,[62] characterized by elite Cretan architectural forms and more extensive wall painting, may have had public and ritual functions.[63] In addition, a small temple was excavated at Ayia Irini. This free-standing, five-room structure was located just inside the town's gate and contained the remains of over fifty large female terracotta figures.[64]

Although administrative centers have not been identified, locally produced Linear A texts have been found at Ayia Irini, Phylakopi, and Akrotiri,[65] demonstrating the adoption of Cretan administrative practices. The paucity of sealings, which were critical to Neopalatial administration, and the distinctiveness of the few locally produced seals, suggest important differences, however.[66] In fact, the largest deposit of sealings, at least sixty-seven, was found at Akrotiri but the sealings were Cretan in origin and execution. Most were flat-based nodules that sealed small folded leather documents.[67] These remarkable finds indicate direct written communication, probably economic in nature, between Crete and Thera,[68] reflecting one dimension of a complex phenomenon: Cretan influence on the Cyclades. This influence normally took the form of Cretan ceramic imports and the local production of Cretan-style

---

61. Palyvou 2005: 46–53.

62. Davis 2008: 195–197.

63. Palyvou 2005: 54–61; Vlachopoulos 2010.

64. Davis 2008: 196.

65. Berg 2019: 190–191.

66. Karnava 2008: 385; 2018.

67. Karnava 2018.

68. Karnava 2018: 237.

ceramics, as well as the use of Cretan elite architectural forms, wall paintings, weaving equipment, and administrative tools. The processes whereby Cretan influence was exerted, normally lumped together under the umbrella term "Minoanization," have been the subject of an immense and varied literature.[69] Until recently, the debate had largely been framed by models of Cretan colonization on the one hand and acculturation on the other.[70] These explanations, which still exert influence, have been criticized for being overly schematic: the archaeological evidence suggests that Cretan influences manifested themselves in very different ways across space and time.

For example, beginning at the start of the Neopalatial period (MM IIIA), ca. 10 percent of the Akrotiri ceramic assemblage was imported Cretan material. Although Cretan types were also manufactured locally, their production was highly restricted, as was the use of the potter's wheel, which was introduced from Crete.[71] By LC I, the influence of Cretan ceramic types, decorative motifs, and the use of the wheel had expanded significantly. Nevertheless, local production was not simply imitative of Cretan prototypes, nor was the production of local ceramic types eclipsed.[72] Similarly, the adoption of the potter's wheel and Cretan-inflected ceramic types was not uniform across the Cyclades. Whereas the wheel was adopted rapidly at the end of the Middle Bronze Age at Akrotiri and Ayia Irini, it was gradually adopted at Phylakopi, where it was used almost exclusively to produce careful imitations of Cretan vessels.[73] In contrast, Cretan architectural forms and wall painting are not attested at Akrotiri until LC I. Although both involved specialized technical skills that must be attributed to mobile artisans, there is considerable evidence of local variation. Thus, LC I architecture at Akrotiri was

69. Gorogianni et al. 2016.

70. Broodbank 2004; Berg 2019: 206–213.

71. Knappett and Nikolakopoulou 2008.

72. Nikolakopoulou 2009.

73. Berg 2007; Gorogianni et al. 2016.

thoroughly rooted in Cretan traditions, whereas wall painting exhibited features belonging to a distinctively Cycladic style.[74]

It may be that the high levels of Cretan influence seen on Thera, Melos, and Kea reflect a highly trafficked maritime trade route known as the "Western String."[75] Certainly the rich metal sources of Laurion in southeastern Attica, opposite the island of Kea, must have been a significant attraction to merchants. On the other hand, the evidence for exchange with other Cycladic islands such as Naxos is suggestive of dense networks throughout the southern Aegean, in which the various communities of Crete (rather than Crete as a monolithic whole) played an important, but hardly exclusive, role.[76] For example, the system of weights used in this period has been normally understood as Cretan, but is probably better viewed as Aegean, for most of the weights have been found in the Cyclades.[77] Instead of focusing on particular Cretan, Cycladic, and Helladic (i.e., of the Greek mainland) practices, it is more productive to consider "Minoanization" as the result of the formation of an Aegean identity sparked by a new environment of intense interaction and competition across the southern Aegean.[78] As we shall see, this interaction zone extended well beyond the Cyclades.

31.3.3. The Greek mainland

This period on the Greek mainland (MH III–LH IIA) is referred to as the "Shaft Grave Period," referring to the famous tombs at Mycenae whose excavation by Heinrich Schliemann in 1876 virtually inaugurated the field of Aegean prehistory. It may also be referred to as Early

---

74. Davis 1990; Palyvou 2005: 179–188; Nikolakopoulou and Knappett 2016; cf. Vlachopoulos 2015; Morgan 2018.

75. Davis and Gorogianni 2008: 345; Berg 2019: 208–209.

76. Vlachopoulos 2016.

77. Berg 2019: 187–189.

78. Davis and Gorogianni 2008. Cf. Broodbank 2004; Vlachopoulos 2015; Knappett 2016.

Mycenaean or Prepalatial.[79] Strictly speaking, Mycenaean refers to a Late Bronze Age archaeological culture that begins in LH I with the production of fine, Minoanizing pottery with lustrous paint. LH I pottery represents only a small percentage of the assemblage, however, such that it can be difficult to distinguish between MH III and LH I phases chronologically; the two are thus generally treated as a unit. The most significant transformations of this period are the emergence of wealthy burials in new and monumental tomb forms, settlement growth, and dynamic contacts with the islands, including Crete.[80] This phenomenon is effectively limited to southern and central Greece, however, while northern Greece witnessed its own distinctive developments.[81] In broad terms these appear as a sudden transformation of the village culture of the earlier Middle Bronze Age, which is often characterized as stagnant, isolated, and simple. Yet recent work demonstrates that the dynamics of the early Late Bronze Age have deep historical roots extending into the beginning of the Middle Bronze Age and beyond.[82]

The offshore islands of Cythera and Aegina played important roles in these developments. Located between the Peloponnese and western Crete, Cythera was effectively Cretan in this period. The earliest Minoanizing pottery there dates to the Early Bronze Age, and local ceramic production exactly paralleled developments on Crete from the start of the Middle Bronze Age through the end of the Neopalatial period.[83] During the Middle Bronze Age the site of Kolonna on Aegina, located further to the north, was a flourishing town whose material culture was oriented toward the Greek mainland, while at the same time displaying important influences from the Cyclades and Crete.[84] Aegina

---

79. Wright 2008.

80. Wright 2008; Voutsaki 2010.

81. Andreou 2010; 2020.

82. Wright 2008; Dickinson 2010a; Voutsaki 2010.

83. Lindblom et al. 2015: 225–228.

84. Gauß 2010.

was a major center of ceramic manufacture and its distinctive products were exported widely across southern and central Greece.[85] Kolonna was protected by impressive fortifications paralleled in this period only at Troy; within the town, a large building complex may have functioned as the center of political authority.[86] Outside the walls, a built tomb contained the body of a young man, multiple bronze weapons, obsidian arrowheads, a helmet of boars' tusks, a gold diadem, and imported Cretan and Cycladic pottery.[87]

The Aeginetan burial was a precursor to massive changes in mortuary practices. MH I–II tombs, while hardly simple, generally had rare or modest offerings. The end of the Middle Bronze Age witnessed not only the emergence of very wealthy burials, but also increased effort expended upon the physical form of the tomb, the practice of multiple interments, greater elaboration in the treatment of the dead, and the widespread use of extramural cemeteries.[88] At Mycenae, this was expressed by the construction of two grave circles, in use from MH III to LH II. The graves dug into these grave circles, most of which were deeply excavated shaft graves, contained ceramic and metal vessels, bronze weaponry, gold jewelry and ornaments, and other precious and finely crafted goods. The wealthiest of these burials date to the end of the period.[89] In the southwest Peloponnese, rock-cut chamber tombs and stone-built circular tombs known as *tholoi* first appeared in MH III.[90] *Tholoi* were rapidly monumentalized and their entrances elaborated with ashlar masonry or dressed conglomerate.[91] Elsewhere in the Peloponnese the form was

---

85. Gauß et al. 2015.

86. Gauß et al. 2011.

87. Kilian-Dirlmeier 1997.

88. Voutsaki 2010; Boyd 2015.

89. Voutsaki 2012.

90. Mee 2010.

91. Wright 2006: 16–18.

adopted for high-status burials, especially at Mycenae, where at least six *tholos* tombs were constructed during the LH II period.[92]

The complexity of the mortuary sphere is difficult to parallel in settlement and residential architecture. The results of archaeological surveys suggest an overall increase in the numbers of sites and in the size of major centers, suggesting population growth.[93] The internal constitution of the largest towns is not well known, although many settlements were apparently reorganized and consolidated, in some cases with encircling fortification walls.[94] There are precious few signs of the well-built, large houses that characterize many island towns. Some sites, including Mycenae and Pylos, have indications of monumental structures in LH I–II.[95] Various forms were adopted: the Pylian remains suggest Cretan-style constructions with pseudo-ashlar masonry and orthostat slabs, while at the Menelaion, an LH II "mansion" of rubble masonry consisted of a central residential unit flanked by suites of rooms accessed by long corridors.[96]

These changes were clearly significant, even if they remain poorly understood. Nor were they smooth, uniform processes. It seems clear that the austere villages of the Middle Bronze Age were radically transformed into communities that included highly competitive elite groups. The presence of multiple elite burial groups, for instance at Mycenae, suggests the existence of factions, perhaps organized around lineages. These elite groups displayed their status in the mortuary sphere through competitive and emulative display involving the inhumation of opulent, exotic objects. The emphasis in elite male burials was on implements of warfare, hunting, and the feast.[97]

Neopalatial Crete and the southern Aegean were certainly critical to these developments. Not only was mainland decorated pottery

---

92. For developments in central Greece, see Burns and Burke 2019.

93. Wright 2008: 233–242.

94. Wiersma 2014: 245–246.

95. Wright 2008: 245–249.

96. Wright 2006; Catling et al. 2009; Nelson 2017: 353–357.

97. Wright 2008.

influenced by Cretan ceramics, but many high-value goods found in mainland tombs were either imports from Crete or local products that were strongly influenced by Cretan forms and styles.[98] The use of ashlar masonry, too, seems to owe much to Cretan practices.[99] Much of this influence may have been transmitted to the mainland by island communities. Imports from further afield are also known, such as the Anatolian silver stag rhyton at Mycenae, Baltic amber, and objects from central-eastern Europe.[100] Such exotica were valuable objects in the competitive displays of mainland elites.

31.3.4. The eastern Aegean

There is a great deal of variation across the islands of the eastern Aegean and the mainland of western Anatolia with respect to local production and exchange networks. Coastal communities in the southeastern Aegean show much greater exposure to, and interaction with, Crete and the southern Aegean. The heterogeneity of the eastern Aegean and the fact that it has been less well studied than the rest of the Aegean have prevented the production of regional archaeological syntheses.[101] A few Old Kingdom Hittite texts suggest that at least some parts of this area were within the Hittite sphere of influence in this early period. Arzawa, located in western Anatolia, was attacked by Hattusili I in the late seventeenth century BC.[102] A single line of Luwian poetry dated linguistically to the sixteenth century BC—"When they came from steep Wilusa"—also points to knowledge of Troy, which is identified as the central community of the region of Wilusa.[103] This meager documentary evidence attests to Hittite awareness of, and interest in, these western

98. Blakolmer 2015; Davis and Stocker 2016.

99. Nelson 2017: 351–352.

100. Koehl 1995; Maran 2013; Maran and Van de Moortel 2014.

101. Pavúk 2015; Mokrišová 2016: 48.

102. Bryce 2011; Gander 2017: 263–264. See also chapter 30 in this volume.

103. Watkins 1995: 144–151.

communities, and implies that they were significant enough to warrant such interest.

Indeed, the coastal centers of the eastern Aegean were substantial, on a par with their contemporaries in the Cyclades. In the north, Troy was an important regional center, growing into a large town with monumental fortifications surrounding the citadel and an elaborate defensive ditch protecting the lower town.[104] The presence of wealthy burials is suggestive of the emergence of an elite, perhaps paralleled by the construction of large, well-built, free-standing residences on the citadel.[105] What buildings may have stood on the heights of the Trojan citadel will never be known because of later leveling, yet if other centers in western Anatolia are any guide, we might not expect a palace. Comparable coastal centers were well-organized towns like Çeşme-Bağlararası, which preserves a dense layout of residential blocks and narrow streets, with evidence for wine production and metallurgy.[106]

Similar settlements have been excavated on the islands of the northern Aegean. Unlike their counterparts on the mainland, however, these provide more evidence of contact with the southern Aegean, out of which a new hybrid island culture, distinct from the cultures of the Anatolian mainland, developed.[107] Evidence of Cretan influence, including administrative documents, has been found at Mikro Vouni on Samothrace.[108] The influence of the southern Aegean on Troy was, by contrast, limited. Initially, Trojan ceramics emulated the shapes of central Greece in local Anatolian Gray Ware. Later, however, these shapes were abandoned, and ceramics were imported from nearby islands.[109] Further south, the coastal town at Çeşme-Bağlararası provides more

---

104. Rose 2014: 19–25.

105. Pavúk and Pieniążek 2016.

106. Şahoğlu 2015.

107. Girella and Pavúk 2015; 2016.

108. Girella and Pavúk 2015: 394–395.

109. Girella and Pavúk 2015: 399–400.

evidence of exchange and interaction with Cretan and Cretan-inflected ceramics.[110]

A different pattern entirely appears in the southeastern Aegean. Miletos on the Anatolian mainland and Ialysos on the island of Rhodes, in particular, seem to have been active participants in the "Minoanization" of the southern Aegean, comparable perhaps to sites like Akrotiri. Middle Bronze Age Ialysos was a densely occupied town with relatively simple houses, some of which had finely plastered walls and floors.[111] A large building, richly decorated with non-figural wall paintings, was architecturally sophisticated, incorporating ashlar masonry and elaborate Cretan forms.[112] Workshop areas attest to the skilled production of Aegean jewelry.[113] These remarkably early associations with Crete appear in an overwhelmingly local, eastern Aegean, and Anatolian context. Late Bronze Age Ialysos was a substantial town (ca. 18 hectares) with large houses that were decorated with wall paintings, and incorporated ashlar masonry and elite Cretan architectural features.[114] The pottery found there is largely local but heavily influenced by Cretan ceramic production, with some imports from east Crete and Kos, while the mortuary evidence finds its closest parallels in Anatolian cemeteries.[115]

Recent excavations at Miletos have revealed a similar pattern. The early Middle Bronze Age material there is characteristic of the Anatolian coast, with some Cretan imports.[116] Later levels show extensive evidence of influence from Crete and the southern Aegean. Nearly all the domestic pottery, which was produced locally or elsewhere in the southeastern Aegean, conforms to Cretan and southern Aegean types. Decorated

---

110. Şahoğlu 2015.

111. Marketou 2010a.

112. Marketou 2014: 182–186; 2018: 261–266.

113. Marketou 2014: 189–190.

114. Marketou 2010a: 781.

115. Girella 2005: 130–131.

116. Raymond 2009.

wares were mostly imported from Crete, but also from the Greek mainland, the Cyclades, and Cyprus.[117] The use of Linear A, loom weights, the
potter's wheel, and wall paintings all show skilled knowledge of Cretan
technologies.[118] The ongoing presence of Anatolian material culture is,
however, also discernible.[119] Excavations revealed a sanctuary centered
on a courtyard, with evidence of sacrificial meals and Cretan cult para-
phernalia.[120] While no domestic or workshop contexts have been identified at Miletos, recent excavations at the nearby site of Tavşan Adası have
revealed a settlement of south Aegean character.[121]

Other sites in the southeastern Aegean present a somewhat different
picture. Iasos was a substantial coastal Anatolian town, but shows few
links to the southern Aegean world. Ceramics imported from its immediate vicinity include shapes produced in both Aegean and Anatolian
traditions on Miletos, Rhodes, and Kos.[122] The large, well-organized
town of Serayia on the island of Kos was a significant ceramic production center in which a vibrant local tradition was blended with Cretan
and Aegean elements. These ceramics were exported to sites across the
southern Aegean.[123]

The networks that bound the communities of the eastern Aegean
were complex. Despite the fragmentary nature of the evidence, it seems
clear that there was a significant difference between the dynamics of the
northeastern Aegean (i.e., north of Miletos) and those of the southeastern Aegean. The latter region was enmeshed in the dense networks
of the southern Aegean.[124] These networks were largely a maritime

---

117. Niemeier 2005: 4–10; Kaiser 2009.

118. Del Freo et al. 2015.

119. Kaiser and Zurbach 2015; Raymond et al. 2016.

120. Niemeier 2005: 6–8.

121. Bertemes 2013.

122. Momigliano 2012: 164–170.

123. Marketou 2010b: 762–766; Vitale 2016.

124. Davis and Gorogianni 2008.

phenomenon. Major centers were located in coastal locations with good harbors, and Aegean influence did not penetrate to inland Anatolian centers.[125] Nevertheless, the nature of Aegean influence was varied. The centers displaying the most Cretan influence have been described as an "Eastern String," perhaps reflecting a highly traveled maritime trade route by means of which Cretan traders acquired Anatolian metals and other goods. Yet it seems clear that a great deal of exchange occurred independently of Crete, and the variations observed in the archaeological record suggest that eastern Aegean communities played active roles.

31.3.5. Cyprus

The beginning of the Late Bronze Age (LC I) on Cyprus is closely connected to the end of the Middle Bronze Age (MC III). Bernard Knapp combined these chronological periods under the rubric Protohistoric Bronze Age (ProBA).[126] This period witnessed significant changes that accelerated into the later Late Bronze Age. These included the emergence of towns (especially on the coasts), status differentiation, and increased interregional exchange. For some scholars, this period marks a quantum leap from the relatively simple villages of the Middle Bronze Age, a revolution in sociopolitical complexity associated with the emergence of an early state at Enkomi.[127] Others suggest that these changes, while significant, were an intensification of dynamic processes that began at least by MC II.[128] In any case, the large-scale abandonment of settlements, destructions, and the construction of fortifications in many parts of the island suggest that this transition was not entirely smooth.[129]

The earliest texts that refer to Cyprus (assuming that Alašiya is correctly identified as Cyprus or part of it) are slightly earlier than the

---

125. Greaves 2010: 882.

126. Knapp 2013a; see also Crewe 2017: 149.

127. Knapp 2013b.

128. Crewe 2017; Keswani 2018.

129. Knapp 2013a: 434; Steel 2014: 580.

beginning of the period under consideration here.[130] An inscription from the reign of the Middle Kingdom pharaoh Amenemhat II (ca. 1900 BC) may record an Egyptian military raid on Cyprus, although the reading of the place name has recently been contested.[131] Later, texts from Mari and Babylon consistently associate Cyprus with copper or bronze, while texts from Alalakh record rations allocated to individuals from Alašiya, and perhaps silver received from Alašiya.[132] This emphasis on copper is hardly surprising, for a significant factor in the changes that Cyprus underwent must have been the increasing exploitation of the extensive copper sources in the Troodos foothills. This development is attested archaeologically. Excavations at Politiko Phorades have revealed an LC I industrial site in the metal-bearing foothills that was a seasonal workshop for the primary stages of copper processing.[133] This rural workshop is contemporary with the evidence for fully developed metallurgical production in the earliest levels of the monumental "fortress" at Enkomi.[134]

The establishment of new towns in coastal locations and the presence of imported Canaanite jars at these sites has led to the suggestion that these settlements were oriented toward maritime exchange, with copper being a major export.[135] These towns differed substantially from their predecessors: large domestic complexes were loosely spaced within the settlement, with open areas within and between the units used for intramural burial, breaking a long tradition of extramural cemeteries.[136] Some have suggested that Enkomi achieved state-like status at the start

---

130. Knapp 2013a: 432–447.

131. Kitchen 2009: 2–3. For arguments against the identification with Cyprus, see Marcus 2007: 146–148. See also chapter 21 in volume 2.

132. The texts are collected in Knapp 1996: 17–20, 30, and discussed in Knapp 2008: 307–308.

133. Knapp and Kassianidou 2008.

134. Kassianidou 2012.

135. Crewe 2007: 155–156, 158–160.

136. Fisher 2014: 187–190. Extramural cemeteries remained in use outside of major towns; see Keswani 2004: 86–88.

of the Late Bronze Age through its exploitation of inland copper sources, access to which was protected by a series of fortifications established at this time.[137] Certainly Enkomi was an important site in this period that furnishes evidence of copper production, monumental architecture, writing, imported goods from the Levant and Egypt, and glyptic production. Yet a close study of the fortifications of this era suggests that they served a wide variety of purposes, and cannot simply be explained as a protective network for the movement of copper.[138] Lindy Crewe's study of early Enkomi, furthermore, concluded that the site was probably not an "early capital of Cyprus" controlling the extraction and export of copper.[139] Although Enkomi is, archaeologically, the best-known site in this transitional period, it was certainly not alone. Other coastal towns, like Morphou (*Toumba tou Skourou*), Palaipaphos, and Hala Sultan Tekke, provide evidence for an active elite with access to a variety of imported luxury goods.[140] Pottery and imported goods attest to increased traffic between Cyprus and Egypt, the Levant, and the Aegean.[141] Cypriot elite groups apparently made creative use of both imports and local products to craft distinctive identities, including a Levantine-inflected warrior status.[142]

Another sign of the eclectic adoption of non-local features is the emergence of the Cypro-Minoan script.[143] As its name implies, this writing system shows clear influence from Cretan Linear A (see section 31.3.1), yet of the three Cypro-Minoan texts that can be dated to this early period, the first is an unusual clay tablet whose closest morphological similarities are found in the Aegean; the second is probably a clay label

---

137. Peltenburg 1996; see also Webb 1999; Knapp 2013a: 432–438.

138. Monahan and Spigelman 2018.

139. Crewe 2007: 158–160.

140. Keswani 2004: 121–129; Crewe and Georgiou 2018.

141. Crewe 2012; Knapp 2013a: 416–427.

142. Keswani 2004: 121–129.

143. Hirschfeld 2010.

with parallels on Crete; and the third is a steatite cylinder seal, a non-Aegean type common in the Near East.[144] The script's development and use thus point to the creative fusion of Aegean and Levantine influences that are visible elsewhere in the archaeological record.

31.4. The advanced Late Bronze Age

Following the eruption of the Theran volcano and the subsequent destructions at the end of the Neopalatial period, Cretan influence in the Aegean waned, and concurrently the influence of mainland Mycenaean centers grew, especially during the fourteenth–thirteenth centuries BC (LH IIIA–B), commonly known at the Palatial period on the mainland. In simple terms, it seems that a period of "Minoanization" was followed by one of "Mycenaeanization." Aegean connections with the eastern Mediterranean and the Near East continued to be strong, and indeed expanded to include the central Mediterranean. The palatial system came crashing down in the decades after 1200 BC. Palaces were destroyed and not rebuilt. The causes of this collapse are poorly understood, but seem to have been part of a broader horizon of disruption and transformation in the eastern Mediterranean. An increase in aridity after the collapse was surely a significant factor during the final century of the Late Bronze Age,[145] a transitional and turbulent period in which existing traditions persisted while cultural novelties and new opportunities appeared that anticipated developments in the Iron Age.

31.4.1. Final Palatial and Postpalatial Crete

The chronological framework for Crete from the end of the Neopalatial period (ca. 1450 BC) to the end of the Bronze Age (ca. 1100 BC) is much discussed and controversial.[146] The most significant debate concerns the date of the final destruction of the palace of Knossos, but the site's

---

144. Steele 2018: 4–44.

145. Finné et al. 2011.

146. Preston 2008; E. Hallager 2010; E. Hallager and B. Hallager 2015; see the papers collected in Langhor 2017a.

complexity and the nature of its excavation have rendered it impossible to answer important questions with confidence.[147] The palace certainly suffered a major destruction within the LM IIIA2 period, which most scholars identify as the end of its life as an administrative center.[148] Yet there are some grounds for arguing that Knossos maintained this status after LM IIIA2, perhaps much reduced in its authority, into LM IIIB.[149]

Almost as controversial is the way that this 350-year period has been subdivided. One common solution is to use the term "Final Palatial" for as long as there is clear evidence for palatial administration on the island, and "Postpalatial" thereafter.[150] The latest certain evidence for Cretan Palatial administration, at the site of Khania, dates to LM IIIB1 and so formally the Final Palatial period would correspond in ceramic terms to LM II to LM IIIB1, and Postpalatial to LM IIIB2 to LM IIIC. This neat picture is confounded, however, by the fact that the destruction of Knossos in LM IIIA2 seems to have precipitated major changes across much of the island.[151] Outside of western Crete, therefore, the Postpalatial period began during LM IIIA2.

Cretan administration underwent radical transformation as a result of destructions at the end of the Neopalatial period. Linear A, the administrative script of the Neopalatial palaces, was abruptly abandoned and from it a new script, Linear B, was developed. Whereas Linear A was painted and inscribed on a variety of media, including folded leather, Linear B was almost exclusively written on clay.[152] Linear B administrators also abandoned many of the clay sealing types of the

---

147. Hatzaki 2017.

148. Langohr 2009: 21–36. Because it has proved impossible to distinguish between pre- and post-destruction ceramics of LM IIIA2 date (Hatzaki 2017), the absolute and relative dates of the destruction within the LM IIIA2 period are uncertain.

149. Driessen 2008.

150. Rehak and Younger 2001: 384; cf. Dickinson 2006: 10; E. Hallager 2010.

151. Langohr 2009: 13–14.

152. Tomas 2010; Palaima 2010; 2011.

Neopalatial period.[153] The decipherment of Linear B by Michael Ventris in 1952 showed that this new script was used to write an early form of the Greek language. This fact, along with the introduction of features with mainland associations, has led to the characterization of this period as "Mycenaean" Crete. Many scholars believe that these developments reflect a takeover of Knossos in this period by a Greek-speaking, mainland elite.[154] Others suggest that these changes are better understood as the responses of local groups to a dynamic sociopolitical landscape on Crete and in the southern Aegean more broadly.[155]

After the destructions that ended the Neopalatial period, the Knossian palace was substantially renovated. This included a new program of figural wall paintings.[156] Rebuilding was also widespread in the surrounding town. The vitality of Knossos in this period is also visible in the construction of tombs that experimented with new symbolic forms and ostentatious behavior. Both the tomb types and their contents have clear mainland antecedents.[157] Knossos thus retained its preeminence after the Neopalatial destructions, when it seems to be the only remaining palatial site. Not only was the palatial building reoccupied, but evidence of significant administrative activity abounds. Driessen has argued convincingly that the Linear B tablets from the Room of the Chariot Tablets date to early LM IIIA1 (ca. 1400 BC).[158] In contrast to this immediate, post-destruction recovery at Knossos, the rest of the island experienced a brief decline in LM II, followed by growth in LM IIIA, especially at coastal sites.[159]

---

153. Weingarten 2010: 325.

154. E. Hallager 2010; Wiener 2015.

155. Driessen and Langohr 2007; Preston 2008; Langohr 2009; Dickinson 2019a: 37–38.

156. McEnroe 2010: 117–132.

157. Preston 2008.

158. Driessen 2008: 70–72; but see E. Hallager 2010: 154.

159. Langohr 2009: 192–195, 199–212.

The decipherment of Linear B has enabled the reconstruction of palatial operations at Knossos in LM IIIA2, the period to which most of the Linear B tablets and tablet fragments from Knossos are thought to date.[160] The toponyms in the texts indicate an administrative reach extending from Khania in western Crete to east-central Crete, stretching from the northern to the southern coast, but excluding east Crete.[161] This would suggest a polity of some 4,500 square kilometers, although it seems unlikely that this entire territory was under direct Knossian oversight. The texts seem to reflect a somewhat patchy network of economic control. The Knossian state had a monarch whose title was *wanax* (Linear B *wa-na-ka*), although the extent of his powers is uncertain.[162] A number of other officials are attested, but many of the most important agents of the state are known only by name. These were presumably members of a broad elite group who undertook various administrative duties for the state.[163] The scribes are themselves anonymous, but have been identified through palaeography.[164] They must have been members of an administrative elite, since writing was effectively limited to this class.

The preserved texts concern landholding, animal husbandry, the organization of labor, the provisioning of religious festivals, the payment of taxes, and the production of a wide variety of goods (textiles, weapons, chariots, perfumed oil, furniture, metal objects, etc.).[165] Although the palace's socioeconomic reach was once considered total and absolute, it is now clear that palatial activities were highly selective and dependent on extra- or para-palatial actors and institutions.[166] Land, for example, appears to have been largely in the hands of local agricultural institutions

---

160. Driessen 2008: 70–72; but see E. Hallager and B. Hallager 2015.

161. Bennet 2011: 148–151.

162. Shelmerdine 2008: 127–129.

163. Nakassis 2013.

164. Palaima 2011.

165. Del Freo and Perna 2016.

166. Galaty et al. 2011.

known as *dāmoi* (sing. *dāmos*, Linear B *da-mo*), although the interest shown in some estates suggests that the palace was entitled to some surplus.[167] Although palatial accounts record some 80,000 sheep from which wool was delivered to the center, it seems clear that these flocks were not self-sustaining. The palatial system was predicated upon the existence of large, "private" flocks belonging to named individuals who are listed against the "palatial" flocks in the texts.[168] The palatial economy was thus much more complex than is usually thought. Rather than being simply redistributive, palatial extraction involved multiple types of transactions.[169]

Cretan rulers appear in contemporary Egyptian inscriptions and tomb paintings.[170] Yet understanding how this kingdom operated locally from the archaeological record of Crete alone is not straightforward. Ceramic production in LM II–IIIA was fairly homogeneous across the island (outside of east Crete), with Knossian production setting the standard. This might reflect political centralization, but detailed studies of individual communities suggest a great deal of local variation.[171] Architectural evidence beyond Knossos is difficult to identify and is hampered by uncertain chronology.[172]

The collapse of the Knossian state seems to have led to increased prosperity at a number of centers across Crete.[173] Khania emerged as a major administrative center by LM IIIB1. Excavations there have revealed a flourishing town with a distinctive pottery workshop and literate administration (Linear B tablets).[174] West Crete was also a major source of

---

167. Killen 2008.

168. Halstead 2001: 41–44.

169. Parkinson et al. 2013; Bennet and Halstead 2014; Nakassis et al. 2016.

170. Rehak 1998; Kelder et al. 2018.

171. Langohr 2009: 200–204; Hatzaki 2018.

172. D'Agata 2005.

173. Langohr 2017a.

174. Andreadaki-Vlazaki 2010; 2015.

stirrup jars, a transport and storage vessel that was widely distributed in the Aegean and beyond.[175] Imported goods, especially at coastal sites like Khania and Kommos, show that Crete continued to play an important role in Aegean and Mediterranean trade and mobility.[176] This is confirmed by the "Aegean list" at the mortuary temple of Amenhotep III (1388–1350 BC), which mentions a number of Cretan sites.[177]

These indications, as well as the dense occupation of the island in this period, are suggestive of general prosperity, but there are also signs of significant transformations.[178] The demotion of Knossos in size and power had significant effects because the site was a major center of prestigious artistic production (wall paintings, seals, and elaborate metal objects) until, but not apparently after, LM IIIA2.[179] After the end of Knossian hegemony, material culture displayed much greater regionalism.[180] Religious practices also exhibited marked changes, including a new form of shrine and new types of terracotta figurines and figures.[181] Moreover, toward the end of LM IIIB, significant disruptions occurred. Many, though not all, major sites were abandoned, especially on the coasts, while a number of new sites, many in defensible locations, were founded. Even major towns like Knossos experienced significant shifts in settlement.[182]

This disruption to the Postpalatial system on Crete was surely affected by the widespread crisis in the Aegean and indeed the entire eastern Mediterranean ca. 1200 BC.[183] Although this crisis in the Aegean is most often associated with the collapse of palatial systems on the Greek

---

175. Haskell et al. 2011; Pratt 2016.

176. Langohr 2009: 230; Shaw and Shaw 2010; B. Hallager 2017.

177. Cline and Stannish 2011.

178. Langohr 2009: 219–233.

179. Rehak and Younger 2001: 445–451. On post-destruction Knossos, see Hatzaki 2005; 2017.

180. McEnroe 2010: 139–145; Langohr 2017b.

181. Gaignerot-Driessen 2014.

182. Hatzaki 2005; Wallace 2010: 68–71.

183. Dickinson 2006: 24–57; 2010b; Cline 2014.

mainland (see section 31.4.3), such systems were, in all likelihood, already defunct on Crete by the end of the thirteenth century BC. Yet for all that, the transformation in Cretan society was significant, far-reaching, and permanent.[184] It is possible that the turmoil that attended the collapse led to an increased concern for security, and that these new priorities resulted in a move away from the coasts and other easily raided locations.[185] Many new settlements were founded in conspicuous positions along major terrestrial routes, close to the resources required for a mixed agro-pastoral economy.[186] Crete and much of the Aegean probably experienced an episode of increasing aridity at this time, which may have made these uplands attractive.[187] The resulting settlement pattern, while considerably transformed from earlier periods, was remarkably resilient and successful, lasting well into the Iron Age.[188]

31.4.2. Cyclades

Evidence from the Cyclades in this period is scant: there are no texts and only a handful of archaeological sites. Much of the scholarly discussion concerns the relationship between the Cyclades and other parts of the Aegean. Whereas the Cyclades in the earlier Late Bronze Age are thought to have been "Minoanized," "Mycenaeanization" has been invoked as a trait of the later Late Bronze Age.[189] Scholars are divided on how to understand this phenomenon. Some suggest a military-political takeover by mainland forces, while others propose selective acculturation and cultural influence.[190]

---

184. Wallace 2010; Gaignerot-Driessen 2016.

185. Nowicki 2011.

186. Gaignerot-Driessen 2016.

187. Moody 2005; Finné et al. 2011.

188. Wallace 2010; Gaignerot-Driessen 2016.

189. Berg 2019: 278–305.

190. Barber 1999; Mountjoy 2008; Gorogianni et al. 2016.

As indicated by the shifting quantities of imported pottery, influence from the Greek mainland was increasing in the Cyclades at the expense of Crete even before the end of the Neopalatial period. At Phylakopi and Ayia Irini, most of the imported pottery has a mainland provenance. This includes pottery that had been identified as Cretan on stylistic grounds, but was actually produced in Attica.[191] These interactions accelerated in the fourteenth and thirteenth centuries BC, contemporary with the complex palatial societies on the Greek mainland (LH IIIA–B; see section 31.4.3). Mainland influence manifested itself in highly variable ways across different island communities, however. It also seems to have differed from earlier "Minoanization." In particular, mainland Mycenaean fine-ware ceramics, which were imported in large quantities, did not transform local pottery production in the way that Cretan shapes and techniques did. Local ceramics, which still dominated Cycladic assemblages quantitatively, were largely utilitarian types.[192]

At Phylakopi, a number of constructions were initiated in LH IIIA–B, including a fortification wall. A large building (the "Megaron") was built in LH IIIA1 on top of the ruins of an LC I–II predecessor. In plan, it resembles structures on the mainland such as the LH II "mansion" at the Menelaion (see section 31.3.3), and on this basis it has been identified as a mainland imposition.[193] It has also been tentatively identified as a "central administrative building" or even a "palace," but its size is unremarkable, and our ignorance about its contents makes such labels little better than guesses.[194] A small, free-standing shrine, first built in LH IIIA2 and expanded in LH IIIB, has parallels with similar buildings on the Greek mainland in both form and contents.[195] Yet influences

---

191. Mountjoy 2008: 470.

192. Gorogianni 2016: 147.

193. Barber 1999; but cf. Earle 2016: 103–104.

194. Berg 2019: 285. The "Megaron" is ca. 365 m² in size, comparable to large houses known from the mainland but much smaller than mainland palaces; cf. Darcque 2005: 315–340.

195. Renfrew 1985.

and imports were not limited to the mainland, but included Levantine ritual objects and perhaps practices.[196] Mainland influence has also been observed in funerary practices. Mainland-style *tholos* tombs, containing rich grave goods, were built on Mykonos and Tinos.[197]

Significant transformations occurred in the Cyclades toward the end of the Late Bronze Age. Remarkably little LH IIIB2 mainland pottery has been found, perhaps suggesting a disruption in trade in the second half of the thirteenth century BC. The twelfth century brought more changes. Fortified sites were established in new locations, perhaps reflecting the unsettled conditions of the LH IIIC period. These differ in date and style, however, and do not seem to have resulted from a single process.[198] While several major settlements, including Phylakopi, were destroyed over the course of this period, others thrived.[199] Grotta on the island of Naxos, for example, was rebuilt and fortified early in LH IIIC. The associated cemeteries of chamber tombs were furnished with rich grave goods and, together with a thriving ceramic workshop on the island, this suggests that the twelfth century was a period of prosperity on Naxos.[200] Likewise a richly furnished mansion, protected by a fortification wall, was built on the low hill of Koukounaries on Paros, located immediately above an enclosed bay.[201] The evidence for various influences and contacts in these settlements suggests that the Cyclades continued to play an important role in Aegean connectivity. The transition to the Early Iron Age at the end of the Late Bronze Age is poorly understood, but a number of important sites were abandoned, suggesting discontinuity.[202]

---

196. Maran 2011.

197. Mountjoy 2008: 473; see also Vlachopoulos 2016: 127.

198. Vlachopoulos 2008: 490.

199. Mountjoy 2008: 475.

200. Vlachopoulos 2008; 2016.

201. Schilardi 2016.

202. Vlachopoulos and Charalambidou 2020: 1013–1014.

31.4.3. The Greek mainland

The mainland underwent rapid change in the LH III period. Especially striking was the emergence of palatial systems in central and southern Greece in LH IIIA–B (ca. 1400–1200 BC) and concurrent growth in the scale and extent of settlement and the dominance of Mycenaean material culture in the southern Aegean. Our understanding is primarily based on archaeological evidence, supplemented by Linear B texts from various palatial centers and possible references to mainlanders in contemporary Near Eastern texts.

The processes whereby mainland states were formed are still not well understood. The creation of a new Knossian state in LM II–IIIA1, the administrative institutions of which made use of the new Linear B script and the Greek language (see section 31.4.1), must have been important to developments on the mainland, where Linear B is attested as early as LH IIIA2.[203] Yet the material forms of the early mainland palaces were eclectic and cannot be explained in terms of simple influence.[204] Rather, local dynamics must have driven the particular configurations of these developments.[205] Although no single pattern is associated with the rise of mainland palaces, it seems clear that palatial centers grew in size and concentrated wealth, often at the expense of their neighbors and potential competitors. These were, however, relatively small polities. The largest settlements were on the order of 15–30 hectares with populations in the thousands and, where political territories can be reasonably estimated, they were not much larger than 2,000 square kilometers.[206]

Mycenaean palaces were monumental in size, architecturally elaborate, and elegantly decorated with wall paintings.[207] They served as royal residences and administrative centers as well as loci of economic and

---

203. Driessen 2008.

204. Wright 2006.

205. Maran and Wright 2020: 106–112.

206. Bennet 2013: 244–246.

207. Brecoulaki et al. 2015.

ritual activity. In their final phases, the palaces whose architecture is best understood were organized around an axial "megaron" unit comprising a porch, vestibule, and a main room (the megaron), in the center of which was a circular hearth flanked by four columns.[208] An emplacement for the royal throne is preserved at Pylos and Tiryns. The central megaron unit, typically accessed via a monumental gate and open courtyard, was flanked by corridors that opened onto suites of rooms (figure 31.5). Although this architectural complex is generally considered the standard layout of the mainland palaces, in fact there is a great deal of variation, especially in the LH IIIA period. The palace at Ayios Vasileios (LH IIIA2) and the early palace at Pylos (LH IIIA) resemble Cretan palatial complexes in that they seem to be centered on an open central court.[209] Even in the LH IIIB period, the standard "megaron"-style palace is only attested at Tiryns, Mycenae, and Pylos.[210]

Large-scale, monumental construction is a hallmark of this period on the mainland. Massive tombs, terraces, gates, and fortifications all required significant labor and organization as well as skilled craftspeople. The widespread use of "Cyclopean" masonry, a specifically mainland construction style that made use of massive stones for inner and outer wall faces, between which was set an earth and rubble fill, is typical of this period. This was used in the construction of impressive fortification walls as well as terraces, bridges, culverts, polders, and dams. There is significant evidence for large-scale engineering projects across the mainland in this period, from an artificial harbor in the vicinity of Pylos to the drainage of Lake Kopais in the region of Orchomenos.[211] The latter was a massive undertaking that involved the building of canals (constructed of ca. 2 million m^3 of earth and 250,000 m^3 of stone) to divert water into sinkholes and the construction of fortified centers to administer and defend the new agricultural system.

---

208. Darcque 2005: 367–386.

209. Nelson 2017; Vasilogamvrou 2018.

210. Darcque 2005: 336–339.

211. Hope Simpson and Hagel 2006.

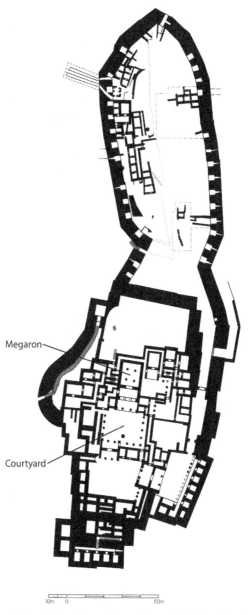

Megaron

Courtyard

10m 0   50m

FIGURE 31.5. Plan of the palace at Tiryns. Drawing by Dan Davis.

Textual evidence provides a vivid snapshot of palatial administration. Linear B tablets (figure 31.6) or inscribed sealings have been found at Volos, Thebes, Mycenae, Tiryns, Midea, Ayios Vasileios, Iklaina, and Pylos on the mainland, and Khania and Knossos on Crete (see section 31.4.1). Because all these texts are administrative, they do not refer to historical events, but they do shed light on administrative, social, economic, and religious systems from a palatial perspective. Together, the Linear B tablets and the archaeological evidence suggest that palatial administrations concentrated on a limited array of economic interests, e.g., the production of textiles, metal products, and perfumed oil, that represent only a small fraction of total economic activity and were highly dependent on a large and active extra-palatial sector.[212] Recent studies of the administrative and social structure of palatial communities have shown that they were complex and dynamic. Communal and religious institutions were quasi-autonomous and commanded substantial resources.[213] The most important administrative roles in the texts were filled not by titled officials, but by named individuals, possibly entrepreneurial elites with substantial "private" interests.[214] Thus, communities in palatial polities were not rigid hierarchies that simply reflected the state's bureaucratic structure, but complex networks of individuals and institutions. Linear B texts also reveal details about religion, specifically ritual practices that included ceremonial feasting, as well the names of deities, many of which were worshipped in later Greek religion, such as Zeus, Hera, Hermes, and Dionysus.[215]

The conventional view that mainland palatial centers were independent polities has been recently challenged by several scholars who posit the existence of a single political entity centered on Mycenae that

212. Nakassis 2020.

213. Lupack 2011.

214. Nakassis 2013.

215. Lupack 2010.

FIGURE 31.6. Linear B tablet, Pylos Aq 64. Dimensions: 23.2, 14.6 cm. Courtesy of the Department of Classics, University of Cincinnati.

controlled central and southern Greece as well as most of Crete.[216] This model is based on two bodies of evidence: (1) the homogeneity of Mycenaean material culture in the Aegean and (2) Hittite references to the kingdom of Ahhiya/Ahhiyawa, which should be located in the Aegean.[217] Most scholars do not feel that such a monolithic view accurately reflects the archaeological and textual records of the Aegean, which are better understood as the products of intense interactions between "a mosaic of principalities large and small."[218] Some scholars have therefore hypothesized that Ahhiyawa represented confederations or contingent coalitions of independent Aegean polities.[219] On the other hand, this view fits awkwardly with the high political status accorded to the king of Ahhiyawa, who is sometimes addressed as "my brother" and a "Great King" in letters from the Hittite king (although this status may have been withdrawn by the end of the thirteenth century BC).[220] Ahhiyawa does not appear in any other texts from the eastern Mediterranean, although it seems abundantly clear that the Greek mainland was well known in Egypt.[221] The Egyptian term *Tj-na-jj* (*Tanaja* or *Tanaju*) likely refers to some part of mainland Greece. A prince (*wer*) of *Tanaja* is recorded as giving metal vessels in the Annals of Thutmose III (1479–1425 BC).[222]

The Hittite texts that refer to Ahhiyawa date from the late fifteenth to late thirteenth centuries BC (in ceramic terms, LH II–IIIB) and indicate that political relations between the kingdoms were unstable. Although there were periods of apparently friendly relations, the king of Ahhiyawa

---

216. Eder and Jung 2015; Kelder and Waal 2019a.

217. Gander 2017: 275–278.

218. Dickinson 2019a: 42.

219. Beckman et al. 2011: 4–6.

220. Waal 2019. It may be that this political status is more rhetorical than real; see Bryce 2003 and Weeden 2018 and cf. Beckman et al. 2011: 122. On the withdrawal of the status of "Great King," see Beckman et al. 2011 (text: AhT 2 = CTH 105 = KUB 23: no. 1).

221. But see Jung 2017: 24.

222. Cline 1994: 114–116.

occasionally seems to have encouraged rebellious Hittite vassals and to have supported renegade agents in western Anatolia, from Wilusa in the north to Arzawa in the south.[223] In contrast to the lively picture presented by the texts, artifactual evidence for contact between the Hittites and the Greek mainland is scant.[224]

Archaeological evidence suggests somewhat different contacts than those revealed by texts. Mycenaean pottery was exported in large quantities to the eastern and central Mediterranean. What began as a small trickle at the beginning of the Late Bronze Age became a flood in LH IIIA2–B1. Exported pottery included both well-made, mass-produced fine-ware and closed shapes that contained scented oils and unguents. Open fine-ware shapes, used primarily for the consumption of wine, were apparently highly valued. The prevalence of certain shapes in the eastern Mediterranean, especially in Cyprus, Egypt, and Syria-Palestine, strongly suggests that some ceramic manufacture by mainland producers was oriented to export markets by merchants.[225] As the flow of mainland pottery diminished at the end of the thirteenth century (LH IIIB2), production centers in Cyprus and Syria-Palestine began turning out local imitations. Shipwrecks confirm close connections between Cyprus/Syria-Palestine and the Aegean, and reveal yet another dimension of this commerce, namely the extent to which raw materials and especially metals were traded.[226]

At the end of LH IIIB2, the mainland palatial system suffered a catastrophic collapse ca. 1200 BC or shortly thereafter. Many sites, including palatial centers, were destroyed and burned. While rebuilding took place at some sites, many were abandoned. The palaces themselves were not rebuilt, and the administrative and economic systems that supported them crumpled permanently. Despite the scholarly attention that the collapse has received, there is little consensus on the immediate causes of

223. For Ahhiya/Ahhiyawa in the Hittite sources, see chapter 30 in this volume.

224. Beckman et al. 2011: 268–269; cf. Blackwell 2014; Murray 2017: 251–253.

225. Dabney 2007; Papadimitriou 2012.

226. Bass 2010; Pulak 2010.

these destructions, which may have occurred over several decades, or the long-term processes that laid the foundations for collapse.[227] Nor is it clear to what extent the events on the Greek mainland should be connected to roughly contemporary destructions in the eastern Mediterranean, some of which have been blamed on "Sea Peoples," a modern term for a heterogeneous group that attacked Egypt and were defeated by Rameses III in the first half of the twelfth century BC.[228] In general, mono-causal explanations, whether military, economic, or environmental, of systems collapse have not found favor among Aegean prehistorians.[229]

LH IIIC, the period following the collapse, roughly the twelfth century BC, was turbulent.[230] Certainly it was a time of radical transformation for much of the Greek mainland. The palaces and the practices associated with them were swept away (writing, large-scale engineering projects, etc.) or steeply curtailed (representational arts), and the coherence of Mycenaean palatial culture gave way to significant regional variation.[231] There seems to have been a significant demographic decline, as well as an increase in population mobility, producing in some cases radically transformed settlement networks.[232] Some regions suffered more than others. Whereas Pylos and its hinterland seem to have been virtually abandoned, other communities showed signs of vitality. The fortifications at Tiryns were repaired and the settlement grew to ca. 25 hectares.[233] Indeed, Tiryns remained a cosmopolitan port town during the first half of LH IIIC, with evidence of Cypriots resident at the site.[234]

---

227. Deger-Jalkotzy 2008; Dickinson 2010b; Middleton 2017: 129–154; Murray 2017; Wiener 2017.

228. Cline 2014: 1–11, 154–160; Fischer and Bürge 2017; see also chapter 28 in this volume.

229. Dickinson 2010b; Cline 2014: 139–170; Knapp and Manning 2016.

230. Dickinson 2006: 58–78; Deger-Jalkotzy 2008.

231. Eder and Lemos 2020: 135–143.

232. Murray 2017: 210–246; 2018.

233. Maran 2010; Maran and Papadimitriou 2020: 702–704.

234. Vetters 2011; cf. Cohen et al. 2010.

In other cases, coastal regions that were apparently outside of (or at the margins of) palatial control in the fourteenth–thirteenth centuries BC, such as the Euboean gulf and the northwestern Peloponnese, were dynamic and prosperous in the Postpalatial period.[235]

The sociopolitical organization of these communities is poorly understood. The fact that the Mycenaean word *g^w asileus*, used in Linear B to describe local leaders, became the later Greek word for king (*basileus*) may indicate that in the political reorganizations after the collapse, these individuals became leaders of small-scale political units.[236] Although the material culture of this period is simpler than that of earlier periods, there is clear archaeological evidence of differentiation in domestic and mortuary contexts, suggesting the continued existence of wealthy elite groups. The presence of warrior burials in many cemeteries and representations of warriors on painted pottery also suggests that military prowess was central to claims of legitimacy.[237]

Contact with the outside world diminished but hardly ended in the LH IIIC period. Imports and influence from the central and eastern Mediterranean are attested.[238] Trade with the Adriatic and the influence of Adriatic forms, especially in the communities located along the western coast of the mainland, seem to have intensified. Although mobility and interaction are generally acknowledged, hypothesized large-scale migrations from the Greek mainland to Cyprus and Syria-Palestine remain controversial,[239] while the invasion of central and southern Greece by Dorians, once considered a historical fact, has been laid to rest on both archaeological and historiographical grounds.[240]

---

235. Eder and Lemos 2020: 137–138.

236. Crielaard 2011.

237. Deger-Jalkotzy 2008: 403–404.

238. Murray 2017: 254–259.

239. Yasur-Landau 2010b; Manolova 2020: 1196–1198. For Cyprus, see section 31.4.5.

240. Kotsonas and Mokrišová 2020: 221–222.

The end of LH IIIC was marked by transformation and decline. Although it is impossible to discern a clear break between the Late Bronze Age and the Early Iron Age, the progressive abandonment of sites and cemeteries suggests a significant reorganization of the landscape and a substantial decrease in population.[241] Although some threads of continuity can be sketched, in language, economy, and religion, the cumulative effect of the changes affecting the Greek mainland, beginning in the thirteenth century BC, resulted in a breakdown of Late Bronze Age traditions and their transformation into something different in the Early Iron Age.[242]

31.4.4. The eastern Aegean

The dynamics that characterized the eastern Aegean in the early Late Bronze Age (see section 31.3.4) continued into the later Late Bronze Age. Hittite texts inform us of the expansion of Hittite political power, albeit with some difficulty, into western Anatolia during the fourteenth century BC. These sources imply that the region consisted of a number of independent kingdoms that occasionally confederated. From north to south, the principal Aegean polities were Wilusa, around Troy; the Seha River Lands, in the watersheds of the Kaikos (Bakırçay) and/or Hermos (Gediz) rivers; Arzawa "Minor," whose capital Apasa is identified with ancient Ephesus; and Millawanda (Miletos).[243] Further south in southwestern Anatolia, the Lukka lands did not apparently constitute a political unit. These political configurations were dynamic. For example, the kingdom of Arzawa "Minor" was defeated and broken up by Mursili II toward the end of the fourteenth century BC (on the Arzawa campaign conducted in Mursili's Years 3–4, see chapter 30 in this volume), after

---

241. Murray 2017: 210–246.

242. Dickinson 2006: 76–77; Eder and Lemos 2020. On the issue of continuity, see Papadopoulos 2014; Murray 2017: 16–18; Nakassis 2020.

243. Hawkins 2015; Gander 2017.

which the inland kingdom of Mira may have expanded westward to the Aegean coast.[244]

The archaeological record provides little evidence of Hittite influence, however. Many communities in western Anatolia retained distinctive local traditions. Exchange and influence were primarily oriented toward the southern Aegean and the Greek mainland in particular.[245] As in earlier periods, there were significant differences between the northern and southeastern Aegean. Not only was the latter region more receptive to influences from the rest of the Aegean, but this regional division also reflected differences in local ceramic production.[246] Penelope Mountjoy identified the eastern Aegean north of Miletos and the Maeander river as the "Upper and Central Interface," in which Mycenaean pottery, both genuine and local imitations, comprised a very small percentage of the total ceramic assemblage.[247] Luca Girella and Peter Pavúk have convincingly argued that Aegeanizing pottery, jewelry, seals, and metal objects were selectively chosen for consumption by communities in the northeastern Aegean because these objects complemented local material culture, but did not transform it.[248]

Troy remained the largest site in northwestern Anatolia in this period, reaching a size of 30 hectares in the fourteenth century BC (Troy VI Late, LH IIIA in the mainland ceramic sequence). Following an earthquake, the city was reoccupied without a break in material culture (Troy VIIa, LH IIIB), although some significant changes can be identified. New structures, the ground floors of which were outfitted with storage jars set into the floor, were built in previously open spaces within the citadel. The citadel fortifications were enhanced and a new ditch extended the defenses of the lower town.[249] These changes may have been a response

---

244. Bryce 2011: 365–367; Beal 2011: 589.

245. Glatz 2011.

246. Pavúk 2015.

247. Mountjoy 1998.

248. Girella and Pavúk 2016: 31–35.

249. Rose 2014: 30.

to disruptions known from Hittite texts, specifically the probable seizure of Wilusa by Piyamaradu, an obscure actor who attempted to establish a kingdom in western Anatolia during the early thirteenth century BC.[250] Toward the end of the century, the king of Wilusa was deposed against the wishes of the Hittite king Tudhaliya IV.[251] The destruction of the city by fire at the beginning of the twelfth century BC brought about changes to the site. Initially these were minor, such as the retreat of settlement to the citadel and changes in the ceramic repertoire. Later a significant reorientation of the material culture occurred showing influences from the north, especially Thrace and the Balkans, thus marking a shift to the Early Iron Age pattern.[252]

Further south, in the "Lower Interface," influence from the Greek mainland was strong, especially in coastal communities.[253] This "Mycenaeanization" appears to have been a continuation and transformation of earlier "Minoanization" (see section 31.3.4). There is considerable debate about whether this process is best understood in terms of economic exchange, cultural influence, and small-scale mobilities, or of large-scale migration and colonization. Recent studies tend to favor the former explanation.[254] Indeed, much of the "Mycenaean" pottery consumed in the southeastern Aegean was produced locally or imported from nearby production centers like Miletos and Rhodes, and was found in association with local pottery.[255] While these communities adopted Mycenaean tomb types, mortuary practices were generally heterogeneous, combining Mycenaean elements with local traditions.[256]

---

250. Bryce 2005: 224–227, 290–293.

251. Bryce 2005: 306–308.

252. Aslan and Hnila 2015; Rose 2014: 38–40.

253. Pavúk 2015: 97–101.

254. Mariaud 2020: 968–971; cf. Kotsonas and Mokrišová 2020.

255. Mokrišová 2016: 50–52.

256. Georgiadis 2020: 985–987.

An exception may be the important site of Miletos, generally identified with Hittite Milawata or Millawanda, which had a pronounced "Mycenaean" character. Beginning in the fourteenth century BC, locally made, Aegeanizing vessels dominated ceramic assemblages. At the start of this period (Miletos V, corresponding to LH IIIA), local Anatolian-style pottery was found in limited quantities (10–15 percent of the assemblage).[257] Anatolian and Aegeanizing wares were found in the same archaeological contexts, suggesting a local mix of traditions. Miletos was violently destroyed at the end of the fourteenth century BC, after which the site's material culture exhibited even stronger affiliations with the Greek mainland, including tomb types, although its fortification wall, built in the thirteenth century BC, has casemates and regularly spaced, rectangular bastions in Hittite style.[258] The textual sources indicate that Millawanda was a Hittite vassal state prior to its destruction by Mursili II in the late fourteenth century BC, an event which seems to correspond to the archaeologically attested destruction. Despite the fact that this military action was prompted by Millawanda's alliance with the king of Ahhiyawa, the town was apparently still subject to the king of Ahhiyawa in the mid-thirteenth century and Hittite political control was only reestablished at the end of that century.[259] It is possible to harmonize the textual and archaeological records and suggest that Miletos's subservient status to Ahhiyawa is reflected in the Mycenaean material culture of the settlement, which is furthermore interpreted as evidence for the presence of inhabitants from the Greek mainland.[260] However, such an interpretation conflates material culture, identity, and political affiliation.[261] Large coastal centers like Miletos were probably heterogeneous

---

257. Kaiser and Zurbach 2015.

258. Niemeier 2005: 12–13, 20.

259. Bryce 2005: 289–293; Niemeier 2005: 16–20.

260. Bryce 2011: 370–371.

261. Dickinson 2019b; cf. Pavúk 2015: 103.

communities in which material production and political status varied independently of each other.[262]

Offshore island communities in the southeastern Aegean displayed similar patterns. Chamber tomb cemeteries are attested on a number of islands in the Dodecanese, chiefly Rhodes and Kos, suggesting the presence of somewhat wealthy and flourishing communities, although not on a scale implying that they constituted the powerful kingdom of Ahhiyawa.[263] Although the burials in these cemeteries generally conform to contemporary mortuary practices on the Greek mainland, subtle differences can be observed.[264] Mycenaean pottery was both imported and produced locally. Chemical analyses indicate that significant quantities of fine-ware pottery were imported to Rhodes from the Argolid, including vessels that seem to have been produced especially for export to the Dodecanese.[265] Nevertheless, the persistence of workshops that maintained local ceramic traditions has been noted on both Rhodes and Kos.[266] While local Mycenaean pottery production differed from local traditions, some workshops were clearly influenced by Cretan and Anatolian ceramics in both form and decoration.[267]

The lack of good archaeological evidence, especially from settlements, makes it difficult to generalize about how the southeastern Aegean was affected by the disturbances ca. 1200 BC, but there are few signs of violent destruction, and in general the region displayed continuity into the twelfth century BC (LH IIIC in the mainland ceramic sequence).[268] The Dodecanese experienced settlement nucleation and an increase in the

---

262. Mountjoy 1998; Mee 2008: 373.

263. Mee 2008: 368–369; Marketou 2010a; 2010b.

264. Mountjoy 1998: 37; Georgiadis 2003: 106–110.

265. Mee 2008: 369; Georgiadis 2020: 989.

266. Karantzali 2009; Vitale and Trecarichi 2015.

267. Mountjoy 1998: 37–45; Marketou 2010a: 787.

268. Benzi 2013.

number of tombs and associated wealth.[269] Although modest in absolute terms, such changes suggest that the collapse of the palatial system allowed these communities to take advantage of their strategic locations along major trade routes.[270] Rhodes in particular seems to have been an important center of maritime exchange and distribution to the eastern Mediterranean,[271] while Kos displayed connections to Europe.[272] By the end of the twelfth century, widespread abandonment of chamber tomb cemeteries and settlements marked a fundamental shift to the configurations of the Iron Age.[273]

31.4.5. Cyprus

In LC II–IIIA (ca. 1450–1100 BC), Cyprus experienced a growth of urban, coastal settlements with monumental architecture and a filling-in of the landscape with sites of diverse types, including villages engaged in the exploitation of the island's copper sources. Cyprus also became an important node in the increasingly dense maritime trading networks of the eastern Mediterranean. The natural resources of the island and its role as a hub of exchange brought Cyprus into the orbit of contemporary power politics in the ancient Near East. The king of Alašiya is attested in royal correspondence involving Akhenaten (fourteenth century BC), the king of Ugarit (thirteenth century BC), and the Hittite king (thirteenth century BC).[274]

As in the earlier Bronze Age, much of the textual evidence from this period concerns Cypriot copper, which was sent to Egypt, Ugarit, Emar

---

269. Georgiadis 2020: 990.

270. Voutsaki 2001: 209–211.

271. Marketou 2010a: 788.

272. Benzi 2013: 523–525.

273. Georgiadis 2020: 991–993.

274. The texts are collected in Knapp 1996: 21–58 and discussed in Knapp 2008: 298–341; see also Mantzourani et al. 2019 and chapters 28 and 30 in the present volume.

(located in Syria on the western bank of the Euphrates), and the Hittite capital Hattusa.[275] Other Cypriot exports included timber, furniture, textiles, sweet oil, and high-value luxuries.[276] These commodities appear in royal diplomatic correspondence, indicating that Cyprus was counted among the political players in the eastern Mediterranean. Cypriot merchants and messengers circulated in Egypt and Ugarit, and Cypriots appeared in the administrative texts of Alalakh and Ugarit. The personal name Kuprios appears in the Linear B texts from Pylos and Knossos, and the name Alas(s)ios at Knossos. While these individuals need not have been actual Cypriots (however defined), their presence does suggest significant contact between the Aegean and Cyprus.

A great deal of ink has been spilled over what these texts reveal about Cyprus' international standing and internal organization.[277] Hittite texts suggest that Alašiya was a vassal state (cf. chapter 30 in this volume). A late fifteenth-century letter reveals that an unruly vassal had raided Alašiya, despite it being a Hittite possession.[278] Hittite exiles were sent to Alašiya in the reign of Mursili II.[279] A generation after his father Tudhaliya IV had conquered Alašiya, Suppiluliuma II claimed that he reconquered it following a series of battles on both land and sea.[280] The mid-fourteenth-century Amarna Letters, on the other hand, indicate an independent Cyprus, with a close but not subordinate relationship to Egypt. In letters from the king of Ugarit dated to the late thirteenth century BC, the king of Alašiya is addressed as "my father," indicating Ugarit's subordinate position. This may also be reflected in the presence of Cypro-Minoan administrative texts at Ugarit.[281] An Ugaritic scribe is

---

275. Knapp 2008: 309–312.

276. Knapp 2008: 312–314.

277. Mantzourani et al. 2019.

278. Knapp 1996: 31 (KUB 14: no. 1).

279. Knapp 1996: 31–32 (KUB 14: no. 14; KUB 1: no. 1).

280. Knapp 1996: 32–33 (KBo 12: no. 38). The treaty between Alašiya and Tudhaliya IV may be fragmentarily preserved; see Knapp 1996: 32 (KBo 12: no. 39).

281. Kitchen 2009: 4; *contra* Yon 2007: 18; Ferrara 2012: 132–145.

attested at the Cypriot court.[282] Alašiya had a king (Kušmešuša) as well as high officials (Ešuwara, Šinama, and Šangiwa).[283] Regardless of how one interprets these texts, Cyprus appears to have been an important player, in close communication with the great powers at this time.

The image of Cyprus's sociopolitical structure that emerges from the textual evidence is a poor match for the archaeological record, which indicates that Cypriot political authority was distributed among numerous small, largely coastal polities. No single site stands out as a political capital. Excavations have revealed no palatial buildings, nor is a coherent iconography of rulership readily visible. It is unclear how to resolve these discrepancies. Edgar Peltenburg suggested that standard models of kingship and statehood do not apply on Cyprus. Rather than a unified, hierarchical state ruled by an autocrat, Alašiya was "a decentralised polity comprising a patchwork of variably autonomous territories, loosely affiliated to the state."[284] Bernard Knapp proffered a more hierarchical model, arguing that only a powerful centralized authority would have been able to control the resources implied by the high-value, large-scale exchanges attested in the written sources, and he interpreted the homogeneity of material culture as an expression of this central authority and its ruling ideology.[285] The concentration of Cypro-Minoan inscriptions and cylinder seals at Enkomi might suggest that it was the seat of such a central authority.[286] Unfortunately, the undeciphered Cypro-Minoan script is of little help in clarifying the internal workings of Cypriot sovereignty. These texts are both few in number and, for the most part, extremely short.[287] Indeed, the economic archives that one might expect based on Aegean and Near Eastern parallels are absent on Cyprus.

---

282. *RS* 94.2177+2491, discussed by Yon 2007: 20.

283. Yon 2007.

284. Peltenburg 2012: 351; see also Mantzourani et al. 2019.

285. Knapp 2008: 324–341; 2013a: 438–447. Cf. Webb 1999: 305–308.

286. Georgiou and Iacovou 2020: 1141–1142.

287. Ferrara 2012: 35. There are only 216 texts and ca. 3,150 extant signs of Cypro-Minoan.

One of the most striking developments in this period was the expansion and transformation of settlement. The number of sites increased markedly, while major centers continued to flourish on the south coast of the island.[288] One notable fact about these centers is their comparatively small size. The largest centers are estimated at 25 hectares, but many are considerably smaller. Kalavasos *Ayios Dhimitrios*, for instance, covers only 11.5 hectares.[289] What distinguished primary centers was therefore not their size, but the presence of high-value and high-status features and artifacts, such as ashlar masonry, luxury goods, imports, inscriptions, and seals. Some settlements show signs of urban planning, culminating in Enkomi's organized grid of twenty blocks, surrounded by a fortification wall. In contrast to earlier towns, most of the space in these centers was taken up by buildings and planned streets.[290]

These sites, while sharing a common architectural vocabulary and material culture, were nevertheless highly varied. While some seem to have been hierarchically organized, others were not.[291] Enkomi, for instance, possessed multiple ashlar buildings located in different neighborhoods across the 11-hectare urban center, none of which appears to have been a central place or palace. Extensive, impressive structures like the Ashlar Building were residential complexes organized around large rooms and courtyards in which "public-inclusive" receptions and ceremonies (such as feasting) took place.[292] Other sites were dominated by a single monumental structure. Building X at Kalavasos *Ayios Dhimitrios*, an imposing ashlar building, was located in the site's administrative quarter. Organized around a central court, it was probably used for feasting ceremonies, but it also included large-scale storage facilities for ca. 50,000 liters of olive oil.[293] Such extensive storage implies an elaborate

---

288. Steel 2009; Georgiou and Iacovou 2020.

289. South 2014.

290. Fisher 2014.

291. Keswani 1996.

292. Fisher 2009. On the "sanctuaries" in the Ashlar Building, see Webb 1999: 91–101.

293. Keswani 2018.

administrative structure and large estates, suggesting that the production of olive oil and aromatic oils was an important aspect of elite economic strategies.[294]

The most archaeologically visible products of Cyprus are, however, copper and pottery, both of which were present in significant quantities on the late fourteenth-century Uluburun shipwreck.[295] Copper was mined and processed into ingots on a massive scale. Fine Cypriot pottery has been found extensively in Levantine and Egyptian contexts, while smaller quantities are attested on Crete, Sardinia, and in Italy.[296] As mentioned earlier (section 31.4.3), fine-ware pottery produced on the Greek mainland specifically for Cypriot consumers was especially common in the late fourteenth–early thirteenth century BC. Cypriot marks on Aegean pottery found in the Levant suggest, moreover, that merchants based in Cyprus handled much of the Aegean pottery that was imported to Cyprus and the Levantine coast.[297]

Cyprus did not escape the widespread political collapse of the eastern Mediterranean ca. 1200 BC. The textual evidence implies significant disruption. According to an inscription in the funerary temple of Rameses III at Medinet Habu, Cyprus was devastated by the "Sea Peoples"; Ugarit was also attacked around the same time.[298] There are signs of widespread destruction and abandonment on Cyprus, both on the coast and in the interior. Nevertheless, the island seems to have weathered the storm relatively successfully, certainly in comparison to communities in the Aegean.[299] There is substantial evidence of Cyprus's economic prosperity over the course of the twelfth century BC. This is indicated by the increasing production of finished goods in bronze and

---

294. Bunimovitz and Lederman 2016.

295. Pulak 2010.

296. Sherratt 2003.

297. Hirschfeld 2010.

298. Singer 1999: 719–731; Knapp 2013a: 447–451. See also chapter 28 in this volume.

299. Knapp 2013a: 447–470; Georgiou 2017.

iron and the mass production of fine, wheel-made ceramics.[300] Cypriot merchants, already an important force prior to the collapse of the palatial states, continued to flourish in the twelfth century BC.[301] The island's prosperity is best attested at the large coastal towns of Enkomi, Kition, and Palaipaphos, which emerged as leading centers.[302] The construction of monumental cult buildings at these sites in the LC IIIA period, and of new fortifications at Kition, suggest the presence of well-organized political elites.

These transformations have been variously explained. One line of argumentation focuses on new populations from the Aegean who may have settled the island. Vassos Karageorghis argued that a number of innovations represent material evidence of the arrival of Aegean settlers in early LC IIIA. These include locally made Mycenaean-style ceramics, the use of a central hearth, baths and bathtubs, megalithic fortifications, and religious iconography.[303] Linguistic evidence is also suggestive, for the Greek dialect used in first-millennium BC Cyprus is closely related to Linear B Greek.[304] A *terminus ante quem* for the use of the Greek language on Cyprus is probably provided by an iron spit dating to ca. 1000 BC, on which the Greek name *Opheltās* is inscribed in Cypro-Minoan script.[305] While Aegeanizing influences are undeniable, they did not appear in discrete packages, but were absorbed into local practices displaying strong continuity from earlier periods. Moreover, several elements identified as intrusive are probably better understood as local developments.[306] Knapp argued that Cypriot material culture in this

---

300. Georgiou 2017: 220–222.

301. Sherratt 2003.

302. Iacovou 2013.

303. Karageorghis 2002: 71–113.

304. Morpurgo Davies and Olivier 2012.

305. Steele 2018: 56–58.

306. Iacovou 2008; 2013.

period should be understood as a complex—but ultimately Cypriot—blend of local, Aegean, and Levantine elements.[307]

The succeeding LC IIIB period (perhaps ca. 1100–1050 BC) represents a break from Late Bronze Age Cypriot traditions, and is generally understood as the beginning of the Cypriot Iron Age.[308] A new settlement pattern emerged that persisted into the Iron Age. This is illustrated by the gradual abandonment of the long-lived Bronze Age urban city of Enkomi and the foundation in the eleventh century BC of a new city, Salamis, three kilometers to the northeast.[309]

31.5. Epilogue

The Late Bronze Age in the Aegean and Cyprus is distinctive for the dynamism and intensity of its regional and interregional contacts across the Aegean sea and beyond. A truly Aegean culture emerged, initially under the influence of Crete and later of the Greek mainland. Whereas it was once usual to understand these influences in terms of large-scale population movements and political domination, recent work has demonstrated that these complex developments should be understood as long-term, reciprocal interactions between heterogeneous communities. These processes did not stop at the end of the period, which was characterized by turbulence and regionalization. In fact, the new systems of the Iron Age Aegean and Cyprus were influenced by developments in the final two centuries of the Late Bronze Age. The palatial societies (and periods of palatial rule) of the Aegean were once considered static and centralized, and their collapse ca. 1200 BC has been regarded as the decisive moment ending the Late Bronze Age. This view, however, is mistaken. The communities of these periods were just as dynamic as any other. Certainly the collapse of palatial systems ca. 1200 BC played a role

---

307. Knapp 2013a: 451–470.

308. Georgiou and Iacovou 2020: 1147–1150.

309. Iacovou 2013. On the linguistic dimension, see Steele 2018: 155–162.

in developing and perhaps accelerating certain transformations, but collapse did not bring an end to the Late Bronze Age, chronologically or culturally. The final century of the period was a critical transitional phase that both harkened back to the Bronze Age past and looked forward to the eventual establishment of a new Iron Age order.

REFERENCES

Adams, E. 2017. *Cultural identity in Minoan Crete: social dynamics in the Neopalatial period.* Cambridge: Cambridge University Press.

Andreadaki-Vlazaki, M. 2010. Khania (Kydonia). In Cline, E.H. (ed.), *The Oxford handbook of the Bronze Age Aegean (ca. 3000–1000 BC).* Oxford: Oxford University Press, 518–528.

Andreadaki-Vlasaki, M. 2015. Sacrifices in LM IIIB: early Kydonia palatial centre. *Pasiphae* 9: 27–42.

Andreou, S. 2010. Northern Aegean. In Cline, E.H. (ed.), *The Oxford handbook of the Bronze Age Aegean (ca. 3000–1000 BC).* Oxford: Oxford University Press, 643–659.

Andreou, S. 2020. The Thermaic gulf. In Lemos, I.S., and Kotsonas, A. (eds.), *A companion to the archaeology of early Greece and the Mediterranean.* Hoboken, NJ: Wiley-Blackwell, 913–938.

Aslan, C.C., and Hnila, P. 2015. Migration and integration at Troy from the end of the Late Bronze Age to the Iron Age. In Stampolidis, N.C., Maner, Ç., and Kopanias, K. (eds.), *NOSTOI: indigenous culture, migration and integration in the Aegean islands and western Anatolia during the Late Bronze Age and Early Iron Age.* Istanbul: Koç University Press, 185–209.

Barber, R.L.N. 1999. Hostile Mycenaeans in the Cyclades? In Laffineur, R. (ed.), *Polemos: le contexte guerrier en Égée à l'âge du Bronze.* Liège: Université de Liège, 133–139.

Bass, G.F. 2010. Cape Gelidonya shipwreck. In Cline, E.H. (ed.), *The Oxford handbook of the Bronze Age Aegean (ca. 3000–1000 BC).* Oxford: Oxford University Press, 797–803.

Beal, R.H. 2011. Hittite Anatolia: a political history. In Steadman, S.R., and McMahon, G. (eds.), *The Oxford handbook of ancient Anatolia, 10,000–323 BCE.* Oxford: Oxford University Press, 579–603.

Beckman, G., Bryce, T., and Cline, E.H. 2011. *The Ahhiyawa texts.* Atlanta, GA: Society of Biblical Literature.

Bennet, J. 2011. The geography of the Mycenaean kingdoms. In Duhoux, Y., and Morpurgo Davies, A. (eds.), *A companion to Linear B: Mycenaean Greek texts and their world, vol. 2*. Leuven: Peeters, 137–168.

Bennet, J. 2013. Bronze Age Greece. In Bang, P.F., and Scheidel, W. (eds.), *The Oxford handbook of the state in the ancient Near East and Mediterranean*. Oxford: Oxford University Press, 235–258.

Bennet, J., and Halstead, P. 2014. O-no! Writing and righting redistribution. In Nakassis, D., Gulizio, J., and James, S.A. (eds.), *KE-RA-ME-JA: studies presented to Cynthia W. Shelmerdine*. Philadelphia, PA: Institute for Aegean Prehistory Academic Press, 271–282.

Benzi, M. 2013. The southeast Aegean in the age of the Sea Peoples. In Killebrew, A.E., and Lehmann, G. (eds.), *The Philistines and other "Sea Peoples" in text and archaeology*. Atlanta, GA: Society of Biblical Literature, 509–542.

Berg, I. 2007. *Negotiating island identities: the active use of pottery in the Middle and Late Bronze Age Cyclades*. Piscataway, NJ: Gorgias Press.

Berg, I. 2019. *The Cycladic and Aegean islands in prehistory*. London and New York: Routledge.

Bertemes, F. 2013. Tavşan Adası: das Thera-Event und seine Auswirkung auf das minoische Kommunikationsnetzwerk. In Meller, H., Bertemes, F., Bork, H.R., and Risch, R. (eds.), *1600: kultureller Umbruch im Schatten des Thera-Ausbruchs?* Halle (Saale): Landesmuseum für Vorgeschichte, 191–210.

Betancourt, P. 2002. Who was in charge of the palaces? In Driessen, J., Schoep, I., and Laffineur, R. (eds.), *Monuments of Minos: rethinking the Minoan palaces*. Liège: Université de Liège, 207–211.

Bietak, M. 2010. Minoan presence in the Pharaonic naval base of "Perunefer." In Krzyszkowska, O. (ed.), *Cretan offerings: studies in honor of Peter Warren*. London: British School at Athens, 11–24.

Bietak, M., Marinatos, N., and Palivou, C. 2007. *Taureador scenes in Tell el-Dab'a (Avaris) and Knossos*. Vienna: Verlag der Österreichischen Akademie der Wissenschaften.

Blackwell, N.G. 2014. Making the Lion Gate relief at Mycenae: tool marks and foreign influence. *AJA* 118: 451–488.

Blakolmer, F. 2010. La peinture murale dans le monde Minoen et Mycénien: distribution, fonctions des espaces, déclinaison du répertoire iconographique. In Boehm, I., and Müller-Celka, S. (eds.), *Espace civil, espace religieux en Égée durant la période Mycénienne*. Lyon: Maison de l'Orient et de la Méditerranée, 147–171.

Blakolmer, F. 2015. Was there a "Mycenaean art"? Or: tradition without inno-
vation? Some examples of relief art. In Weilhartner, J., and Ruppenstein,
F. (eds.), *Tradition and innovation in the Mycenaean palatial polities.*
Vienna: Verlag der Österreichischen Akademie der Wissenschaften, 87–112.

Boyd, M.J. 2015. Explaining the mortuary sequence at Mycenae. In Schallin,
A.-L., and Tournavitou, I. (eds.), *Mycenaeans up to date: the archaeol-
ogy of the north-eastern Peloponnese—current concepts and new directions.*
Stockholm: Swedish Institute at Athens, 433–447.

Brecoulaki, H., Davis, J.L., and Stocker, S.R. (eds.) 2015. *Mycenaean wall painting in context: new discoveries, old finds reconsidered.* Athens: National
Hellenic Research Foundation.

Broodbank, C. 2004. Minoanisation. *Proceedings of the Cambridge Philo-
sophical Society* 50: 46–91.

Bryce, T. 2003. Relations between Hatti and Ahhiyawa in the last decades
of the Bronze Age. In Beckman, G., Beal, R., and McMahon, G. (eds.),
*Hittite studies in honor of Harry A. Hoffner Jr. on the occasion of his 65th
birthday.* Winona Lake, IN: Eisenbrauns, 59–72.

Bryce, T. 2005. *The kingdom of the Hittites.* Oxford: Oxford University Press.

Bryce, T. 2011. The Late Bronze Age in the West and the Aegean. In Steadman,
S.R., and McMahon, G. (eds.), *The Oxford handbook of ancient Anatolia,
10,000–323 BCE.* Oxford: Oxford University Press, 363–375.

Buell, D.M., and McEnroe, J.C. 2017. Community building/building community at Gournia. In Letesson, Q., and Knappett, C. (eds.), *Minoan architecture and urbanism: new perspectives on an ancient built environment.*
Oxford: Oxford University Press, 204–227.

Bunimovitz, S., and Lederman, Z. 2016. Opium or oil? Late Bronze Age Cypriot
base ring juglets and international trade revisited. *Antiquity* 90: 1552–1561.

Burns, B.E., and Burke, B. 2019. Memorializing the first Mycenaeans at Eleon.
In Borgna, E., Caloi, I., Cirinci, F.M., and Laffineur, R. (eds.), *MNHMH/
MNEME: past and memory in the Aegean Bronze Age.* Leuven: Peeters, 269–276.

Catling, H.W., Hughes-Brock, H., Brodie, N., Jones, G., Jones, R.E., and
Tomlinson, J.E. 2009. *Sparta: Menelaion I: the Bronze Age.* London: British
School at Athens.

Christakis, K.S. 2011. Redistribution and political economies in Bronze Age
Crete. *AJA* 115: 197–205.

Cline, E.H. 1994. *Sailing the wine-dark sea: international trade and the Late
Bronze Age Aegean.* Oxford: BAR.

Cline, E.H. 2014. *1177 BC: the year civilization collapsed*. Princeton, NJ: Princeton University Press.

Cline, E.H., and Stannish, S.M. 2011. Sailing the great green sea? Amenhotep III's "Aegean list" from Kom el-Hetan, once more. *JAEI* 3: 6–16.

Cline, E.H., Yasur-Landau, A., and Goshen, N. 2011. New fragments of Aegean-style painted plaster from Tel Kabri, Israel. *AJA* 115: 245–261.

Cohen, C., Maran, J., and Vetters, M. 2010. An ivory rod with a cuneiform inscription, most probably Ugaritic, from a Final Palatial workshop in the lower citadel of Tiryns. *ArchAnz* 2010/2: 1–22.

Crewe, L. 2007. *Early Enkomi: regionalism, trade and society at the beginning of the Late Bronze Age on Cyprus*. Oxford: Archaeopress.

Crewe, L. 2012. Beyond copper: commodities and values in Middle Bronze Cypro-Levantine exchanges. *OJA* 31: 225–243.

Crewe, L. 2017. Interpreting settlement function and scale during MC III-LC IA using old excavations and new: western Cyprus and Kisonerga (Kissonerga) Skalia in context. In Pilides, D., and Mina, M. (eds.), *Four decades of hiatus in archaeological research in Cyprus: towards restoring the balance*. Vienna: Holzhausen, 140–152.

Crewe, L., and Georgiou, A. 2018. Settlement nucleation at the beginning of the Late Bronze Age in Cyprus: the evidence from Palaepaphos. In Hulin, L., Crewe, L., and Webb, J.M. (eds.), *Structures of inequality on Bronze Age Cyprus: studies in honour of Alison K. South*. Nicosia: Astrom Editions, 53–70.

Crielaard, J.P. 2011. The "wanax to basileus model" reconsidered: authority and ideology after the collapse of the Mycenaean palaces. In Mazarakis Ainian, A. (ed.), *The "Dark Ages" revisited*. Volos: University of Thessaly Press, 83–111.

Cunningham, T. 2007a. In the shadows of Kastri: an examination of domestic and civic space at Palaikastro (Crete). In Westgate, R., Fisher, N., and Whitley, J. (eds.), *Building communities: house, settlement and society in the Aegean and beyond*. London: British School at Athens, 99–109.

Cunningham, T. 2007b. Havoc: the destruction of power and the power of destruction in Minoan Crete. In Bretschneider, J., Driessen, J., and Van Lerberghe, K. (eds.), *Power and architecture: monumental public architecture in the Bronze Age Near East and Aegean*. Leuven: Peeters, 23–43.

Cunningham, T., and Driessen, J. 2004. Site by site: combining survey and excavation data to chart patterns of socio-political change in Bronze Age

Crete. In Alcock, S.E., and Cherry, J.F. (eds.), *Side-by-side survey: comparative regional studies in the Mediterranean world*. Oxford: Oxbow Books, 101–113.

Dabney, M.K. 2007. Marketing Mycenaean pottery in the Levant. In Betancourt, P.P., Nelson, M.C., and Williams, H. (eds.), *Krinoi kai limenes: studies in honor of Joseph and Maria Shaw*. Philadelphia, PA: Institute for Aegean Prehistory Academic Press, 191–197.

D'Agata, A.L. 2005. Central southern Crete and its relations with the Greek mainland in the Postpalatial period. In D'Agata, A.L., and Moody, J. (eds.), *Ariadne's threads: connections between Crete and the Greek mainland in Late Minoan III (LM IIIA2 to LM IIIC)*. Athens: Scuola Archeologica Italiana di Atene, 109–143.

Darcque, P. 2005. *L'habitat Mycénien: formes et fonctions de l'espace bâti en Grèce continentale à la fin du IIe millénaire avant J.-C.* Athens: École française d'Athènes.

Davis, E.N. 1990. The Cycladic style of the Thera frescoes. In Hardy, D.A., Doumas, C.G., Sakellarakis, J.A., and Warren, P.M. (eds.), *Thera and the Aegean World III, vol. 1: archaeology*. London: Thera Foundation, 214–228.

Davis, J.L. 2008. Minoan Crete and the Aegean islands. In Shelmerdine, C.W. (ed.), *The Cambridge companion to the Aegean Bronze Age*. Cambridge: Cambridge University Press, 186–208.

Davis, J.L., and Gorogianni, E. 2008. Potsherds from the edge: the construction of identities and the limits of Minoanized areas of the Aegean. In Brodie, N., Doole, J., Gavalas, G., and Renfrew, C. (eds.), *Horizon: a colloquium on the prehistory of the Cyclades*. Cambridge: McDonald Institute for Archaeological Research, 339–348.

Davis, J.L., and Stocker, S.R. 2016. The lord of the gold rings: the Griffin Warrior of Pylos. *Hesperia* 85: 627–655.

Day, P., and Relaki, M. 2002. Past factions and present fictions: palaces in the study of Minoan Crete. In Driessen, J., Schoep, I., and Laffineur, R. (eds.), *Monuments of Minos: rethinking the Minoan palaces*. Liège: Université de Liège, 217–234.

Deger-Jalkotzy, S. 2008. Decline, destruction, aftermath. In Shelmerdine, C.W. (ed.), *The Cambridge companion to the Aegean Bronze Age*. Cambridge: Cambridge University Press, 387–415.

Del Freo, M., Niemeier, W.-D., and Zurbach, J. 2015. Neue Inschriften und Zeichen der Linear A-Schrift aus Milet. *Kadmos* 54: 1–22.

Del Freo, M., and Perna, M. (eds.) 2016. *Manuale di epigrafia micenea: introduzione allo studio dei testi in lineare B*. Padua: libreriauniversitaria.it Edizioni.

Dickinson, O.T.P.K. 2006. *The Aegean from Bronze Age to Iron Age: continuity and change between the twelfth and eight centuries BC*. London and New York: Routledge.

Dickinson, O.T.P.K. 2010a. The "third world" of the Aegean? Middle Helladic Greece revisited. In Philippa-Touchais, A., Touchais, G., Voutsaki, S., and Wright, J.C. (eds.), *Mesohelladika: la Grèce continentale au Bronze Moyen*. Athens: École française d'Athènes, 13–27.

Dickinson, O.T.P.K. 2010b. The collapse at the end of the Bronze Age. In Cline, E.H. (ed.), *The Oxford handbook of the Bronze Age Aegean (ca. 3000–1000 BC)*. Oxford: Oxford University Press, 483–490.

Dickinson, O.T.P.K. 2019a. What conclusions might be drawn from the archaeology of Mycenaean civilisation about political structure in the Aegean? In Kelder, J.M., and Waal, W.J.I. (eds.), *From "LUGAL.GAL" to "wanax": kingship and political organisation in the Late Bronze Age Aegean*. Leiden: Sidestone, 31–48.

Dickinson, O. 2019b. The use and misuse of the Ahhiyawa texts. *SMEA Nuova Serie* 5: 7–22.

Driessen, J. 2002. "The king must die": some observations on the use of Minoan court compounds. In Driessen, J., Schoep, I., and Laffineur, R. (eds.), *Monuments of Minos: rethinking the Minoan palaces*. Liège: Université de Liège, 1–14.

Driessen, J. 2008. Chronology of the Linear B texts. In Duhoux, Y., and Morpurgo Davies, A. (eds.), *A companion to Linear B: Mycenaean Greek texts and their world, vol. 1*. Leuven: Peeters, 69–79.

Driessen, J. 2010. Spirit of place: Minoan houses as major actors. In Pullen, D.J. (ed.), *Political economies of the Aegean Bronze Age*. Oxford: Oxbow Books, 35–65.

Driessen, J. 2018. Beyond the collective . . . The Minoan palace in action. In Relaki, M., and Papadatos, Y. (eds.), *From the foundations to the legacy of Minoan archaeology: studies in honour of Professor Keith Branigan*. Oxford: Oxbow, 291–313.

Driessen, J. 2019. The Santorini eruption: an archaeological investigation of its distal impacts on Minoan Crete. *Quaternary International* 499: 195–204.

Driessen, J., and Langohr, C. 2007. Rallying 'round a "Minoan" past: the legitimation of power at Knossos during the Late Bronze Age. In Galaty, M.L., and Parkinson, W.A. (eds.), *Rethinking Mycenaean palaces II*. Berkeley and Los Angeles: University of California Press, 178–189.

Driessen, J., and Langohr, C. 2014. Recent developments in the archaeology of Minoan Crete. *Pharos* 20: 75–115.

Driessen, J., and Macdonald, C.F. 1997. *The troubled island: Minoan Crete before and after the Santorini eruption*. Liège: Université de Liège.

Earle, J.W. 2016. Melos in the middle: Minoanisation and Mycenaeanisation at Late Bronze Age Phylakopi. In Gorogianni, E., Pavúk, P., and Girella, L. (eds.), *Beyond thalassocracies: understanding processes of Minoanisation and Mycenaeanisation in the Aegean*. Oxford: Oxbow, 94–115.

Eder, B., and Jung, R. 2015. "Unus pro omnibus, omnes pro uno": the Mycenaean palace system. In Weilhartner, J., and Ruppenstein, F. (eds.), *Tradition and innovation in the Mycenaean palatial polities*. Vienna: Verlag der Österreichischen Akademie der Wissenschaften, 113–140.

Eder, B., and Lemos, I.S. 2020. From the collapse of the Mycenaean palaces to the emergence of Early Iron Age communities. In Lemos, I.S., and Kotosonas, A. (eds.), *A companion to the archaeology of early Greece and the Mediterranean*. Hoboken, NJ: Wiley-Blackwell, 133–160.

Ferrara, S. 2012. *Cypro-Minoan inscriptions, vol. 1: analysis*. Oxford: Oxford University Press.

Finné, M., Holmgren, K., Sundqvist, H.S., Weiberg, E., and Lindblom, M. 2011. Climate in the eastern Mediterranean, and adjacent regions, during the past 6000 years: a review. *Journal of Archaeological Science* 38: 3153–3173.

Fisher, K.D. 2009. Elite place-making and social interaction in the Late Cypriot Bronze Age. *JMA* 22: 183–209.

Fisher, K.D. 2014. Making the first cities on Cyprus: urbanism and social change in the Late Bronze Age. In Creekmore, A.T., III, and Fisher, K.D. (eds.), *Making ancient cities: space and place in early urban societies*. Cambridge: Cambridge University Press, 181–219.

Fischer, P.M., and Bürge, T. (eds.) 2017. *"Sea Peoples" up-to-date: new research on transformations in the eastern Mediterranean in the 13th–11th centuries BCE*. Vienna: Verlag der Österreichischen Akademie der Wissenschaften.

Foster, K.P. 2018. Mari and the Minoans. *Groniek* 217: 343–362.

Gaignerot-Driessen, F. 2014. Goddesses refusing to appear? Reconsidering the Late Minoan III figures with upraised arms. *AJA* 118: 489–520.

Gaignerot-Driessen, F. 2016. *De l'occupation postpalatiale à la cité-état grecque: le cas du Mirambello (Crète).* Leuven: Peeters.

Galaty, M.L., Nakassis, D., and Parkinson, W.A. (eds.) 2011. Forum: redistribution in Aegean palatial societies. *AJA* 115: 175–244.

Gander, M. 2017. The West: philology. In Weeden, M., and Ullmann, L.Z. (eds.), *Hittite landscape and geography.* Leiden: Brill, 262–280.

Gauß, W. 2010. Aegina Kolonna. In Cline, E.H. (ed.), *The Oxford handbook of the Bronze Age Aegean (ca. 3000–1000 BC).* Oxford: Oxford University Press, 737–751.

Gauß, W., Klebinder-Gauss, G., Kiriatzi, E., Pentedeka, A., and Georgakopoulou, M. 2015. Aegina: an important centre of production of cooking pottery from the prehistoric to the historic era. In Spataro, M., and Villing, A. (eds.), *Ceramics, cuisine and culture: the archaeology and science of kitchen pottery in the ancient Mediterranean world.* Oxford: Oxbow, 65–74.

Gauß, W., Lindblom, M., and Smetana, R. 2011. The Middle Helladic large building complex at Kolonna: a preliminary view. In Gauß, W., Lindblom, M., Smith, R.A.K., and Wright, J.C. (eds.), *Our cups are full: pottery and society in the Aegean Bronze Age: papers presented to Jeremy B. Rutter.* Oxford: Archaeopress, 76–87.

Georgiadis, M. 2003. *The south-eastern Aegean in the Mycenaean period: islands, landscape, death and ancestors.* Oxford: Archaeopress.

Georgiadis, M. 2020. The southeastern Aegean. In Lemos, I.S., and Kotosonas, A. (eds.), *A companion to the archaeology of early Greece and the Mediterranean.* Hoboken, NJ: Wiley-Blackwell, 985–1005.

Georgiou, A. 2017. Flourishing amidst a "crisis": the regional history of the Paphos polity at the transition from the 13th to the 12th centuries BCE. In Fischer, P.M., and Bürge, T. (eds.), *"Sea Peoples" up-to-date: new research on transformations in the eastern Mediterranean in the 13th–11th centuries BCE.* Vienna: Verlag der Österreichischen Akademie der Wissenschaften, 207–227.

Georgiou, A., and Iacovou, M. 2020. Cyprus. In Lemos, I.S., and Kotosonas, A. (eds.), *A companion to the archaeology of early Greece and the Mediterranean.* Hoboken, NJ: Wiley-Blackwell, 1133–1162.

Girella, L. 2005. Ialysos: foreign relations in the Late Bronze Age: a funerary perspective. In Laffineur, R., and Greco, E. (eds.), *Emporia: Aegeans in the central and eastern Mediterranean*. Liège: Université de Liège, 129–139.

Girella, L., and Pavúk, P. 2015. Minoanisation, acculturation, hybridization: the evidence of the Minoan presence in the north east Aegean between the Middle and Late Bronze Age. In Stampolidis, N.C., Maner, Ç., and Kopanias, K. (eds.), *NOSTOI: indigenous culture, migration and integration in the Aegean islands and western Anatolia during the Late Bronze Age and Early Iron Age*. Istanbul: Koç University Press, 387–420.

Girella, L., and Pavúk, P. 2016. The nature of Minoan and Mycenaean involvement in the northeastern Aegean. In Gorogianni, E., Pavúk, P., and Girella, L. (eds.), *Beyond thalassocracies: understanding processes of Minoanisation and Mycenaeanisation in the Aegean*. Oxford: Oxbow, 15–42.

Glatz, C. 2011. The Hittite state and empire from archaeological evidence. In Steadman, S.R., and McMahon, G. (eds.), *The Oxford handbook of ancient Anatolia, 10,000–323 BCE*. Oxford: Oxford University Press, 877–899.

Gorogianni, E. 2016. Keian, Kei-noanised, Kei-cenaeanised? Interregional contact and identity in Ayia Irini, Kea. In Gorogianni, E., Pavúk, P., and Girella, L. (eds.), *Beyond thalassocracies: understanding processes of Minoanisation and Mycenaeanisation in the Aegean*. Oxford: Oxbow, 136–154.

Gorogianni, E., Pavúk, P., and Girella, L. (eds.) 2016. *Beyond thalassocracies: understanding processes of Minoanisation and Mycenaeanisation in the Aegean*. Oxford: Oxbow.

Greaves, A.M. 2010. Western Anatolia. In Cline, E.H. (ed.), *The Oxford handbook of the Bronze Age Aegean (ca. 3000–1000 BC)*. Oxford: Oxford University Press, 877–889.

Gundacker, R. 2017. Papyrus British Museum 10056: Ergebnisse einer Neukollationierung und Anmerkungen zur inhaltlichen Auswertung im Rahmen der militärischen Ausbildung Amenophis' II. *ÄL* 27: 281–334.

Hallager, B. 2017. The LM IIIB settlements at Khania, west Crete. In Langohr, C. (ed.), *How long is a century? Late Minoan IIIB pottery: relative chronology and regional differences*. Louvain-la-Neuve: Presses universitaires de Louvain, 37–52.

Hallager, E. 2010. Late Bronze Age: Crete. In Cline, E.H. (ed.), *The Oxford handbook of the Bronze Age Aegean (ca. 3000–1000 BC)*. Oxford: Oxford University Press, 149–159.

Hallager, E., and Hallager, B. 2015. When the saints go marching in. In Kaiser, I., Kouka, O., and Panagiotopoulos, D. (eds.), *Ein Minoer im Exil: Festschrift zum 65. Geburtstag von Wolf-Dietrich Niemeier*. Bonn: Habelt, 99–124.

Halstead, P. 2001. Mycenaean wheat, flax and sheep: palatial intervention in farming and its implications for rural society. In Voutsaki, S., and Killen, J. (eds.), *Economy and politics in the Mycenaean palace states*. Cambridge: Cambridge Philological Society, 38–50.

Hamilakis, Y. 2002. Too many chiefs? Factional competition in Neopalatial Crete. In Driessen, J., Schoep, I., and Laffineur, R. (eds.), *Monuments of Minos: rethinking the Minoan palaces*. Liège: Université de Liège, 179–199.

Haskell, H.W., Jones, R.E., Day, P.M., and Killen, J.T. 2011. *Transport stirrup jars of the Bronze Age Aegean and east Mediterranean*. Philadelphia, PA: Institute for Aegean Prehistory Academic Press.

Hatzaki, E. 2005. Postpalatial Knossos: town and cemeteries from LM IIIA2 to LM IIIC. In D'Agata, A.L., and Moody, J. (eds.), *Ariadne's threads: connections between Crete and the Greek mainland in Late Minoan III (LM IIIA2 to LM IIIC)*. Athens: Scuola Archeologica Italiana di Atene, 65–108.

Hatzaki, E. 2017. To be or not to be in LM IIIB Knossos. In Langohr, C. (ed.), *How long is a century? Late Minoan IIIB pottery: relative chronology and regional differences*. Louvain-la-Neuve: Presses universitaires de Louvain, 53–77.

Hatzaki, E. 2018. Visible and invisible death: shifting patterns in the burial customs of Bronze Age Crete. In Relaki, M., and Papadatos, Y. (eds.), *From the foundations to the legacy of Minoan archaeology: studies in honour of Professor Keith Branigan*. Oxford: Oxbow, 190–209.

Hawkins, J.D. 2015. The political geography of Arzawa (western Anatolia). In Stampolidis, N.C., Maner, Ç., and Kopanias, K. (eds.), *NOSTOI: indigenous culture, migration and integration in the Aegean islands and western Anatolia during the Late Bronze Age and Early Iron Age*. Istanbul: Koç University Press, 15–35.

Hirschfeld, N. 2010. Cypro-Minoan. In Cline, E.H. (ed.), *The Oxford handbook of the Bronze Age Aegean (ca. 3000–1000 BC)*. Oxford: Oxford University Press, 373–384.

Hope Simpson, R., and Hagel, D.K. 2006. *Mycenaean fortifications, highways, dams and canals*. Gothenburg: Paul Åströms.

Iacovou, M. 2008. Cultural and political configurations in Iron Age Cyprus: the sequel to a protohistoric episode. *AJA* 112: 625–657.

Iacovou, M. 2013. Historically elusive and internally fragile island polities: the intricacies of Cyprus's political geography in the Iron Age. *BASOR* 370: 15–47.

Jung, R. 2017. The Sea Peoples after three millennia: possibilities and limitations of historical reconstruction. In Fischer, P.M., and Bürge, T. (eds.), *"Sea Peoples" up-to-date: new research on transformations in the eastern Mediterranean in the 13th–11th centuries BCE.* Vienna: Verlag der Österreichischen Akademie der Wissenschaften, 23–42.

Kaiser, I. 2009. Miletus IV: the locally produced coarse wares. In Macdonald, C.F., Hallager, E., and Niemeier, W.-D. (eds.), *The Minoans in the central, eastern and northern Aegean: new evidence.* Athens: Danish Institute at Athens, 159–165.

Kaiser, I., and Zurbach, J. 2015. Late Bronze Age Miletus: the Anatolian face. In Stampolidis, N.C., Maner, Ç., and Kopanias, K. (eds.), *NOSTOI: indigenous culture, migration and integration in the Aegean islands and western Anatolia during the Late Bronze Age and Early Iron Age.* Istanbul: Koç University Press, 557–579.

Karageorghis, V. 2002. *Early Cyprus: crossroads of the Mediterranean.* Los Angeles, CA: J. Paul Getty Museum.

Karantzali, E. 2009. Local and imported Late Bronze Age III pottery from Ialysos, Rhodes: tradition and innovations. In Danielidou, D. (ed.), *Δώρον: Τιμητικός Τόμος για τον Καθηγητή Σπύρο Ιακωβίδη.* Athens: Academy of Athens, 355–382.

Karnava, A. 2008. Written and stamped records in the Late Bronze Age Cyclades: the sea journeys of an administration. In Brodie, N., Doole, J., Gavalas, G., and Renfrew, C. (eds.), *Horizon: a colloquium on the prehistory of the Cyclades.* Cambridge: McDonald Institute for Archaeological Research, 377–386.

Karnava, A. 2018. *Seals, sealings and seal impressions from Akrotiri in Thera.* Heidelberg: Propylaeum.

Kassianidou, V. 2012. Metallurgy and metalwork in Enkomi: the early phases. In Kassianidou, V., and Papsavvas, G. (eds.), *Eastern Mediterranean metallurgy and metalwork in the second millennium BC.* Oxford: Oxbow, 94–106.

Kelder, J.M., Cole, S.E., and Cline, E.H. 2018. Memphis, Minos, and Mycenae: Bronze Age contact between Egypt and the Aegean. In Spier,

J., Potts, T., and Cole, S.E. (eds.), *Beyond the Nile: Egypt and the classical world*. Los Angeles, CA: J. Paul Getty Museum, 9–17.

Kelder, J.M., and Waal, W.J.I. (eds.) 2019. *From "LUGAL.GAL" to "wanax": kingship and political organization in the Late Bronze Age Aegean*. Leiden: Sidestone.

Keswani, P. 1996. Hierarchies, heterarchies, and urbanization processes: the view from Bronze Age Cyprus. *JMA* 9: 211–250.

Keswani, P. 2004. *Mortuary ritual and society in Bronze Age Cyprus*. London: Equinox.

Keswani, P. 2018. On the relationship between modes of agricultural production and social inequality in Bronze Age Kalavasos: a theoretical essay. In Hulin, L., Crewe, L., and Webb, J.M. (eds.), *Structures of inequality on Bronze Age Cyprus: studies in honour of Alison K. South*. Nicosia: Astrom Editions, 139–154.

Kilian-Dirlmeier, I. 1997. *Das mittelbronzezeitliche Schachtgrab von Ägina*. Mainz: Zabern.

Killen, J.T. 2008. Mycenaean economy. In Duhoux, Y., and Morpurgo Davies, A. (eds.), *A companion to Linear B: Mycenaean Greek texts and their world, vol. 1*. Leuven: Peeters, 1159–1200.

Kitchen, K.A. 2009. Alas(h)i(y)a (Irs) and Asiya (Isy) in ancient Egyptian sources. In Michaelides, D., Kassianidou, V., and Merrilles, R.S. (eds.), *Egypt and Cyprus in antiquity*. Oxford: Oxbow, 2–8.

Knapp, A.B. (ed.) 1996. *Near Eastern and Aegean texts from the third to the first millennia BC: sources for the history of Cyprus, vol. II*. Altamont, NY: Greece and Cyprus Research Center.

Knapp, A.B. 2008. *Prehistoric and protohistoric Cyprus: identity, insularity and connectivity*. Oxford: Oxford University Press.

Knapp, A.B. 2013a. *The archaeology of Cyprus: from earliest prehistory through the Bronze Age*. Cambridge: Cambridge University Press.

Knapp, A.B. 2013b. Revolution within evolution: the emergence of a "secondary state" on protohistoric Bronze Age Cyprus. *Levant* 45: 19–44.

Knapp, A.B., and Kassianidou, V. 2008. The archaeology of Late Bronze Age copper production: Politiko Phorades on Cyprus. *Anatolian Metal* 4: 135–147.

Knapp, A.B., and Manning, S.W. 2016. Crisis in context: the end of the Late Bronze Age in the eastern Mediterranean. *AJA* 120: 99–149.

Knappett, C. 2016. Minoanisation and Mycenaeanisation: a commentary. In Gorogianni, E., Pavúk, P., and Girella, L. (eds.), *Beyond thalassocracies: understanding processes of Minoanisation and Mycenaeanisation in the Aegean.* Oxford: Oxbow, 202–206.

Knappett, C., and Nikolakopoulou, I. 2008. Colonialism without colonies? A Bronze Age case study from Akrotiri, Thera. *Hesperia* 77: 1–42.

Knappett, C., Rivers, R., and Evans, T. 2011. The Theran eruption and Minoan palatial collapse: new interpretations gained from modelling the maritime network. *Antiquity* 85: 1008–1023.

Koehl, R. 1995. The silver stag BIBRU from Mycenae. In Carter, J., and Morris, S.P. (eds.), *The ages of Homer: a tribute to Emily Townsend Vermeule.* Austin: University of Texas Press, 61–66.

Kotsonas, A., and Mokrišová, J. 2020. Mobility, migration, and colonization. In Lemos, I.S., and Kotosonas, A. (eds.), *A companion to the archaeology of early Greece and the Mediterranean.* Hoboken, NJ: Wiley-Blackwell, 217–246.

Langohr, C. 2009. *Περιφέρεια: étude régionale de la Crète aux Minoen Récent II–IIIB (1450–1200 av. J.-C.), vol. 1: la Crète centrale et occidentale.* Louvain-la-Neuve: Presses universitaires de Louvain.

Langhor, C. (ed.) 2017a. *How long is a century? Late Minoan IIIB pottery: relative chronology and regional differences.* Louvain-la-Neuve: Presses universitaires de Louvain.

Langohr, C. 2017b. The Late Minoan IIIB phases on Crete: the state of play and future perspectives. In Langohr, C. (ed.), *How long is a century? Late Minoan IIIB pottery: relative chronology and regional differences.* Louvain-la-Neuve: Presses universitaires de Louvain, 11–35.

La Rosa, V. 2010a. Ayia Triada. In Cline, E.H. (ed.), *The Oxford handbook of the Bronze Age Aegean (ca. 3000–1000 BC).* Oxford: Oxford University Press, 495–508.

La Rosa, V. 2010b. Phaistos. In Cline, E.H. (ed.), *The Oxford handbook of the Bronze Age Aegean (ca. 3000–1000 BC).* Oxford: Oxford University Press, 582–595.

Lindblom, M., Gauß, W., and Kiriatzi, E. 2015. Some reflections on ceramic technology transfer at Bronze Age Kastri on Kythera, Kolonna on Aegina, and Lerna in the Argolid. In Gauß, W., Klebinder-Gauß, G., and von Rüden, C. (eds.), *The transmission of technical knowledge in the production of ancient Mediterranean pottery.* Vienna: Österreichisches Archäologisches Institut, 225–237.

Lupack, S. 2010. Mycenaean religion. In Cline, E.H. (ed.), *The Oxford handbook of the Bronze Age Aegean (ca. 3000–1000 BC).* Oxford: Oxford University Press, 263–276.

Lupack, S. 2011. A view from outside the palace: the sanctuary and the *damos* in Mycenaean economy and society. *AJA* 115: 207–217.

Macdonald, C. 2005. *Knossos.* London: Folio Society.

Manning, S.W. 2010a. Chronology and terminology. In Cline, E.H. (ed.), *The Oxford handbook of the Bronze Age Aegean (ca. 3000–1000 BC).* Oxford: Oxford University Press, 11–28.

Manning, S.W. 2010b. Eruption of Thera/Santorini. In Cline, E.H. (ed.), *The Oxford handbook of the Bronze Age Aegean (ca. 3000–1000 BC).* Oxford: Oxford University Press, 457–474.

Manolova, T. 2020. The Levant. In Lemos, I.S., and Kotosonas, A. (eds.), *A companion to the archaeology of early Greece and the Mediterranean.* Hoboken, NJ: Wiley-Blackwell, 1185–1214.

Mantzourani, E., Kopanias, K., and Voskos, I. 2019. A great king on Alashia? The archaeological and textual evidence. In Kelder, J.M., and Waal, W.J.I. (eds.), *From "LUGAL.GAL" to "wanax": kingship and political organisation in the Late Bronze Age Aegean.* Leiden: Sidestone, 95–130.

Maran, J. 2010. Tiryns. In Cline, E.H. (ed.), *The Oxford handbook of the Bronze Age Aegean (ca. 3000–1000 BC).* Oxford: Oxford University Press, 722–734.

Maran, J. 2011. Evidence for Levantine religious practice in the Late Bronze Age sanctuary of Phylakopi on Melos? *Eretz-Israel* 30: 65–73.

Maran, J. 2013. Bright as the sun: the appropriation of amber objects in Mycenaean Greece. In Hahn, H.P., and Weiss, H. (eds.), *Mobility, meaning and transformations of things: shifting contents of material culture through time and space.* Oxford: Oxbow, 147–169.

Maran, J., and Papadimitriou, A. 2020. Mycenae and the Argolid. In Lemos, I.S., and Kotosonas, A. (eds.), *A companion to the archaeology of early Greece and the Mediterranean.* Hoboken, NJ: Wiley-Blackwell, 693–718.

Maran, J., and Van de Moortel, A. 2014. A horse-bridle piece with Carpatho-Danubian connections from Late Helladic I Mitrou and the emergence of a warlike elite in Greece during the Shaft Grave period. *AJA* 118: 529–548.

Maran, J., and Wright, J.C. 2020. The rise of the Mycenaean culture, palatial administration and its collapse. In Lemos, I.S., and Kotosonas, A. (eds.), *A companion to the archaeology of early Greece and the Mediterranean*. Hoboken, NJ: Wiley-Blackwell, 99–132.

Marcus, E.S. 2007. Amenemhet II and the sea: maritime aspects of the Mit Rahina (Memphis) inscription. *ÄL* 17: 137–190.

Mariaud, O. 2020. Ionia. In Lemos, I.S., and Kotosonas, A. (eds.), *A companion to the archaeology of early Greece and the Mediterranean*. Hoboken, NJ: Wiley-Blackwell, 961–983.

Marketou, T. 2010a. Rhodes. In Cline, E.H. (ed.), *The Oxford handbook of the Bronze Age Aegean (ca. 3000–1000 BC)*. Oxford: Oxford University Press, 775–793.

Marketou, T. 2010b. Dodecanese. In Cline, E.H. (ed.), *The Oxford handbook of the Bronze Age Aegean (ca. 3000–1000 BC)*. Oxford: Oxford University Press, 762–774.

Marketou, T. 2014. Time and space in the Middle Bronze Age Aegean world: Ialysos (Rhodes), a gateway to the eastern Mediterranean. In Souvatzi, S., and Hadji, A. (eds.), *Space and time in Mediterranean prehistory*. London and New York: Routledge, 176–195.

Marketou, T. 2018. The art of wall-painting at Ialysos on Rhodes: from the early second millennium BC to the eruption of the Thera volcano. In Vlahopoulos, A.G. (ed.), *Paintbrushes: wall-painting and vase-painting of the second millennium BC in dialogue*. Athens: University of Ioannina, 261–275.

McCoy, F.W. 2009. The eruption within the debate about the date. In Warburton, D.A. (ed.), *Time's up! Dating the Minoan eruption of Santorini*. Aarhus: Aarhus University Press, 73–90.

McEnroe, J. 2010. *Architecture of Minoan Crete: constructing identity in the Aegean Bronze Age*. Austin: University of Texas Press.

Mee, C. 2008. Mycenaean Greece, the Aegean and beyond. In Shelmerdine, C.W. (ed.), *The Cambridge companion to the Aegean Bronze Age*. Cambridge: Cambridge University Press, 362–386.

Mee, C. 2010. Death and burial. In Cline, E.H. (ed.), *The Oxford handbook of the Bronze Age Aegean (ca. 3000–1000 BC)*. Oxford: Oxford University Press, 277–290.

Middleton, G.D. 2017. *Understanding collapse: ancient history and modern myths*. Cambridge: Cambridge University Press.

Mokrišová, J. 2016. Minoanisation, Mycenaeanisation, and mobility: a view from southwest Anatolia. In Gorogianni, E., Pavúk, P., and Girella, L. (eds.), *Beyond thalassocracies: understanding processes of Minoanisation and Mycenaeanisation in the Aegean*. Oxford: Oxbow, 43–57.

Momigliano, N. 2012. *Bronze Age Carian Iasos: structures and finds from the area of the Roman Agora (c. 3000–1500 BC)*. Rome: Bretschneider.

Monahan, E., and Spigelman, M. 2018. Negotiating a new landscape: Middle Bronze Age fortresses as a component of the Cypriot political assemblage. In Kearns, C., and Manning, S.W. (eds.), *New directions in Cypriot archaeology*. Ithaca, NY: Cornell University Press, 133–159.

Moody, J. 2005. Unravelling the threads: climate changes in the Late Bronze III Aegean. In D'Agata, A.L., and Moody, J. (eds.), *Ariadne's threads: connections between Crete and the Greek mainland in Late Minoan III (LM IIIA2 to LM IIIC)*. Athens: Scuola Archeologica Italiana di Atene, 443–474.

Morgan, L. 2018. Inspiration and innovation: the creation of wall-paintings in the absence of a pictorial pottery tradition at Ayia Irini, Kea. In Vlahopoulos, A.G. (ed.), *Paintbrushes: wall-painting and vase-painting of the second millennium BC in dialogue*. Athens: University of Ioannina, 277–291.

Morpurgo Davies, A., and Olivier, J.-P. 2012. Syllabic scripts and languages in the second and first millennia BC. In Cadogan, G., Iacovou, M., Kopaka, K., and Whitley, J. (eds.), *Parallel lives: ancient island societies in Crete and Cyprus*. London: British School at Athens, 105–118.

Mountjoy, P.A. 1998. The East Aegean-West Anatolian interface in the Late Bronze Age: Mycenaeans and the kingdom of Ahhiyawa. *AnSt* 48: 33–67.

Mountjoy, P.A. 2008. The Cyclades during the Mycenaean period. In Brodie, N., Doole, J., Gavalas, G., and Renfrew, C. (eds.), *Horizon: a colloquium on the prehistory of the Cyclades*. Cambridge: McDonald Institute for Archaeological Research, 467–477.

Murray, S.C. 2017. *The collapse of the Mycenaean economy: imports, trade and institutions 1300–700 BCE*. Cambridge: Cambridge University Press.

Murray, S.C. 2018. Imported exotica and mortuary ritual at Perati in Late Helladic IIIC east Attica. *AJA* 122: 33–64.

Nakassis, D. 2013. *Individuals and society in Mycenaean Pylos*. Leiden: Brill.

Nakassis, D. 2020. The economy. In Lemos, I.S., and Kotsonas, A. (eds.), *A companion to the archaeology of early Greece and the Mediterranean*. Hoboken, NJ: Wiley-Blackwell, 271–291.

Nakassis, D., Galaty, M., and Parkinson, W. (eds.) 2016. Discussion and debate: Reciprocity in Aegean palatial societies: Gifts, debt, and the foundations of economic exchange. *JMA* 29: 61–132.

Nelson, M.C. 2017. The architecture of the Palace of Nestor. In Cooper, F.A., and Fortenberry, D. (eds.), *The Minnesota Pylos Project, 1990–98*. Oxford: BAR, 283–383.

Niemeier, B., and Niemeier, W.-D. 2000. Aegean frescoes in Syria-Palestine: Alalakh and Tel Kabri. In Sherratt, S. (eds.), *The wall paintings of Thera*. Athens: Thera Foundation, 763–802.

Niemeier, W.-D. 2005. Minoans, Mycenaeans, Hittites and Ionians in western Asia Minor: new excavations in Bronze Age Miletus-Millawanda. In Villing, A. (ed.), *The Greeks in the East*. London: British Museum Press, 1–36.

Nikolakopoulou, I. 2009. "Beware Cretans bearing gifts": tracing the origins of Minoan influence at Akrotiri, Thera. In Macdonald, C.F., Hallager, E., and Niemeier, W.-D. (eds.), *The Minoans in the central, eastern and northern Aegean: new evidence*. Athens: Danish Institute at Athens, 31–39.

Nikolakopoulou, I., and Knappett, C. 2016. Mobilities in the Neopalatial southern Aegean: the case of Minoanisation. In Kiriatzi, E., and Knappett, C. (eds.), *Human mobility and technological transfer in the prehistoric Mediterranean*. Cambridge: Cambridge University Press, 102–115.

Nowicki, K. 2011. Settlement in crisis: the end of the LM/LH IIIB and early IIIC in Crete and other south Aegean islands. In Mazarakis Ainian, A. (ed.), *The "Dark Ages" revisited: acts of an international symposium in memory of William D.E. Coulson*. Volos: University of Thessaly Press, 435–450.

Palaima, T.G. 2010. Linear B. In Cline, E.H. (ed.), *The Oxford handbook of the Bronze Age Aegean (ca. 3000–1000 BC)*. Oxford: Oxford University Press, 356–372.

Palaima, T.G. 2011. Scribes, scribal hands and palaeography. In Duhoux, Y., and Morpurgo Davies, A. (eds.), *A companion to Linear B: Mycenaean Greek texts and their world, vol. 2*. Leuven: Peeters, 33–136.

Palyvou, C. 2005. *Akrotiri Thera: an architecture of affluence 3,500 years old*. Philadelphia, PA: Institute for Aegean Prehistory Academic Press.

Panagiotopoulos, D. 2001. Keftiu in context: Theban tomb-paintings as a historical source. *OJA* 20: 263–283.

Papadimitriou, N. 2012. Regional or "international" networks? A comparative examination of Aegean and Cypriot imported pottery in the Eastern Mediterranean. *Talanta* 44: 92–136.

Papadopoulos, J. 2014. Greece in the Early Iron Age: mobility, commodities, polities, and literacy. In Knapp, A.B, and van Dommelen, P. (eds.), *The Cambridge prehistory of the Bronze and Iron Age Mediterranean.* Cambridge: Cambridge University Press, 178–195.

Parkinson, W., Nakassis, D., and Galaty, M. (eds.) 2013. Forum: crafts, specialists, and markets in Mycenaean Greece. *AJA* 117: 413–459.

Pavúk, P. 2015. Between the Aegeans and the Hittites: western Anatolia in the 2nd millennium BC. In Stampolidis, N.C., Maner, Ç., and Kopanias, K. (eds.), *NOSTOI: indigenous culture, migration and integration in the Aegean islands and western Anatolia during the Late Bronze Age and Early Iron Age.* Istanbul: Koç University Press, 81–114.

Pavúk, P., and Pieniążek, M. 2016. Towards understanding the socio-political structures and social inequalities in western Anatolia during the Late Bronze Age. In Meller, H., Hahn, H.P., Jung, R., and Risch, R. (eds.), *Arm und Reich: zur Ressourcenverteilung in prähistorischen Gesellschaften.* Halle (Saale): Landesmuseum für Vorgeschichte, 531–551.

Pearson, C.L., Brewer, P.W., Brown, D., Heaton, T.J., Hodgins, G.W.L., Jull, A.J.T., Lange, T., and Salzer, M.W. 2018. Annual radiocarbon record indicates 16th century BCE date for the Thera eruption. *Science Advances* 4/8: eaar8241. Retrieved from DOI: 10.1126/sciadv.aar8241 (last accessed September 11, 2020).

Peltenburg, E. 1996. From isolation to state formation in Cyprus, c. 3500–1500 B.C. In Karageorghis, V., and Michaelides, D. (eds.), *The development of the Cypriot economy: from the prehistoric period to the present day.* Nicosia: University of Cyprus and Bank of Cyprus, 17–44.

Peltenburg, E. 2012. King Kušmešuša and the decentralised political structure of Late Bronze Age Cyprus. In Cadogan, G., Iacovou, M., Kopaka, K., and Whitley, J. (eds.), *Parallel lives: ancient island societies in Crete and Cyprus.* London: British School at Athens, 345–351.

Pfälzner, P. 2013. The Qatna wall paintings and the formation of Aegeo-Syrian art. In Aruz, J., Graff, S.B., and Rakic, Y. (eds.), *Cultures in contact: from Mesopotamia to the Mediterranean in the second millennium BC.* New York: Metropolitan Museum of Art, 200–213.

Phillips, J. 2010. Egypt. In Cline, E.H. (ed.), *The Oxford handbook of the Bronze Age Aegean (ca. 3000–1000 BC)*. Oxford: Oxford University Press, 820–831.

Platon, L. 2010. Kato Zakros. In Cline, E.H. (ed.), *The Oxford handbook of the Bronze Age Aegean (ca. 3000–1000 BC)*. Oxford: Oxford University Press, 509–517.

Pratt, C.E. 2016. The rise and fall of the transport stirrup jar in the Late Bronze Age Aegean. *AJA* 120: 27–66.

Preston, L. 2008. Late Minoan II to IIIB Crete. In Shelmerdine, C.W. (ed.), *The Cambridge companion to the Aegean Bronze Age*. Cambridge: Cambridge University Press, 310–326.

Pulak, C. 2010. Uluburun shipwreck. In Cline, E.H. (ed.), *The Oxford handbook of the Bronze Age Aegean (ca. 3000–1000 BC)*. Oxford: Oxford University Press, 862–876.

Raymond, A.E. 2009. Miletus in the Middle Bronze Age: an overview of the characteristic features and ceramics. In Macdonald, C.F., Hallager, E., and Niemeier, W.-D. (eds.), *The Minoans in the central, eastern and northern Aegean: new evidence*. Athens: Danish Institute at Athens, 143–156.

Raymond, A.E., Kaiser, I., Rizzotto, L.-C., and Zurbach, J. 2016. Discerning acculturation at Miletus: Minoanisation and Mycenaeanisation. In Gorogianni, E., Pavúk, P., and Girella, L. (eds.), *Beyond thalassocracies: understanding processes of Minoanisation and Mycenaeanisation in the Aegean*. Oxford: Oxbow, 58–73.

Rehak, R. 1998. Aegean natives in the Theban tomb paintings: the Keftiu revisited. In Cline, E.H., and Harris-Cline, D. (eds.), *The Aegean and the Orient in the second millennium*. Liège: Université de Liège, 39–51.

Rehak, P., and Younger, J.G. 2001. Neopalatial, Final Palatial, and Postpalatial Crete. In Cullen, T. (ed.), *Aegean prehistory: a review*. Boston: Archaeological Institute of America, 383–465.

Renfrew, C. 1985. *The archaeology of cult: the sanctuary at Phylakopi*. London: Thames & Hudson.

Rethemiotakis, G., and Christakis, K. 2013. The Middle Minoan III period at Galatas: pottery and historical implications. In Macdonald, C.F., and Knappett, C. (eds.), *Intermezzo: intermediacy and regeneration in Middle Minoan III Palatial Crete*. London: British School at Athens, 93–105.

Rose, B. 2014. *The archaeology of Greek and Roman Troy*. Cambridge: Cambridge University Press.

Rutter, J. 2011. Late Minoan IB at Kommos: a sequence of at least three distinct stages. In Brogan, T.M., and Hallager, E. (eds.), *LM IB pottery: relative chronology and regional differences*. Athens: Danish Institute at Athens, 307–343.

Şahoğlu, V. 2015. Çeşme-Bağlararası: a western Anatolian harbour settlement at the beginning of the Late Bronze Age. In Stampolidis, N.C., Maner, Ç., and Kopanias, K. (eds.), *NOSTOI: indigenous culture, migration and integration in the Aegean islands and western Anatolia during the Late Bronze Age and Early Iron Age*. Istanbul: Koç University Press, 593–608.

Schilardi, D.-U. 2016. *Koukounaries, Paros: the excavations and history of a most ancient Aegean acropolis*. Athens: Paros Excavations.

Schoep, I. 1999. Tables and territories? Reconstructing Late Minoan IB political geography through undeciphered documents. *AJA* 103: 201–221.

Schoep, I. 2002. The state of the Minoan palaces or the Minoan palace-state? In Driessen, J., Schoep, I., and Laffineur, R. (eds.), *Monuments of Minos: rethinking the Minoan palaces*. Liège: Université de Liège, 15–33.

Schofield, E. 1998. Town planning at Ayia Irini, Kea. In Mendoni, L.G., and Mazarakis Ainian, A. (eds.), *Kea-Kythnos: history and archaeology*. Athens: National Hellenic Research Foundation, 117–122.

Shaw, J. 2015. *Elite Minoan architecture: its development at Knossos, Phaistos, and Malia*. Philadelphia, PA: Institute for Aegean Prehistory Academic Press.

Shaw, J., and Shaw, M. 2010. Kommos. In Cline, E.H. (ed.), *The Oxford handbook of the Bronze Age Aegean (ca. 3000–1000 BC)*. Oxford: Oxford University Press, 543–555.

Shelmerdine, C.W. 2008. Mycenaean society. In Duhoux, Y., and Morpurgo Davies, A. (eds.), *A companion to Linear B: Mycenaean Greek texts and their world, vol. 1*. Leuven: Peeters, 115–158.

Sherratt, S. 2003. The Mediterranean economy: "globalization" at the end of the second millennium BCE. In Dever, W.G., and Gitin, S. (eds.), *Symbiosis, symbolism and power of the past: Canaan, ancient Israel and their neighbors from the Late Bronze Age through Roman Palaestina*. Winona Lake, IN: Eisenbrauns, 37–62.

Singer, I. 1999. A political history of Ugarit. In Watson, W.G.E., and Wyatt, N. (eds.), *Handbook of Ugaritic studies*. Leiden: Brill, 603–733.

Sotirakopoulou, P. 2010. The Cycladic Middle Bronze Age: a "Dark Age" in Aegean prehistory or a dark spot in archaeological research? In Philippa-Touchais, A., Touchais, G., Voutsaki, S., and Wright, J.C. (eds.),

Mesohelladika: la Grèce continentale au Bronze Moyen. Athens: École française d'Athènes, 825–839.

South, A. 2014. From pots to people: estimating population for Late Bronze Age Kalavasos. In Webb, J.M. (ed.), *Structure, measurement and meaning: studies on prehistoric Cyprus in honour of David Frankel.* Uppsala: Åströms Förlag, 69–77.

Steel, L. 2009. Exploring regional settlement on Cyprus in the Late Bronze Age: the rural hinterland. In Hein, I. (ed.), *The formation of Cyprus in the 2nd millennium BC: studies of regionalism during the Middle and Late Bronze Ages.* Vienna: Verlag der Österreichischen Akademie der Wissenschaften, 135–145.

Steel, L. 2014. Cyprus during the Late Bronze Age. In Killebrew, A.E., and Steiner, M. (eds.), *The Oxford handbook of the archaeology of the Levant: c. 8000–332 BCE.* Oxford: Oxford University Press, 577–591.

Steele, P.M. 2018. *Writing and society in ancient Cyprus.* Cambridge: Cambridge University Press.

Tartaron, T.F. 2008. Aegean prehistory as world archaeology: recent trends in the archaeology of Bronze Age Greece. *Journal of Archaeological Research* 16: 83–161.

Tomas, H. 2010. Cretan Hieroglyphic and Linear A. In Cline, E.H. (ed.), *The Oxford handbook of the Bronze Age Aegean (ca. 3000–1000 BC).* Oxford: Oxford University Press, 340–355.

Tomkins, P., and Schoep, I. 2010. Early Bronze Age: Crete. In Cline, E.H. (ed.), *The Oxford handbook of the Bronze Age Aegean (ca. 3000–1000 BC).* Oxford: Oxford University Press, 66–82.

Tsipopoulou 2002. Petras, Siteia: The palace, the town, the hinterland and the Protopalatial background. In Driessen, J., Schoep, I., and Laffineur, R. (eds.), *Monuments of Minos: rethinking the Minoan palaces.* Liège: Université de Liège, 133–144.

Vasilogamvrou, A. 2018. Ἀνασκαφή στον Ἅγιο Βασίλειο Λακωνίας. *Praktika tes en Athenais Archaiologikes Etaireias* 171: 131–184.

Vetters, M. 2011. A clay ball with a Cypro-Minoan inscription from Tiryns. *ArchAnz* 2011/2: 1–49.

Vitale, S. 2016. Cultural entanglements on Kos during the Late Bronze Age: a comparative analysis of "Minoanisation" and "Mycenaeanisation" at the "Serraglio," Eleona, and Langada. In Gorogianni, E., Pavúk, P., and Girella,

L. (eds.), *Beyond thalassocracies: understanding processes of Minoanisation and Mycenaeanisation in the Aegean.* Oxford: Oxbow, 75–93.

Vitale, S., and Trecarichi, A. 2015. The Koan tradition during the Mycenaean Age: a contextual and functional analysis of local ceramics from the "Serraglio," Eleona, and Langada. In Stampolidis, N.C., Maner, Ç., and Kopanias, K. (eds.), *NOSTOI: indigenous culture, migration and integration in the Aegean islands and western Anatolia during the Late Bronze Age and Early Iron Age.* Istanbul: Koç University Press, 311–335.

Vlachopoulos, A. 2008. A Late Mycenaean journey from Thera to Naxos: the Cyclades in the twelfth century BC. In Brodie, N., Doole, J., Gavalas, G., and Renfrew, C. (eds.), *Horizon: a colloquium on the prehistory of the Cyclades.* Cambridge: McDonald Institute for Archaeological Research, 479–491.

Vlachopoulos, A. 2010. L'espace rituel revisité: architecture et iconographie dans la Xestè 3 d'Akrotiri, Théra. In Boehm, I., and Müller-Celka, S. (eds.), *Espace civil, espace religieux en Égée durant la période mycénienne.* Lyon: Maison de l'Orient et de la Méditerranée, 173–198.

Vlachopoulos, A. 2015. Detecting "Mycenaean" elements in the "Minoan" wall paintings of a "Cycladic" settlement: the wall paintings at Akrotiri, Thera within their iconographic koine. In Brecoulaki, H., Davis, J.L., and Stocker, S.R. (eds.), *Mycenaean wall painting in context: new discoveries, old finds reconsidered.* Athens: National Hellenic Research Foundation, 36–65.

Vlachopoulos, A. 2016. Neither far from Knossos nor close to Mycenae: Naxos in the Middle and Late Bronze Age Aegean. In Gorogianni, E., Pavúk, P., and Girella, L. (eds.), *Beyond thalassocracies: understanding processes of Minoanisation and Mycenaeanisation in the Aegean.* Oxford: Oxbow, 116–135.

Vlachopoulos, A., and Charalambidou, X. 2020. Naxos and the Cyclades. In Lemos, I.S., and Kotsonas, A. (eds.), *A companion to the archaeology of early Greece and the Mediterranean.* Hoboken, NJ: Wiley-Blackwell, 1007–1027.

von Rüden, C. 2011. *Die Wandmalereien aus Tall Mišrife/Qatna im Kontext überregionaler Kommunikation.* Wiesbaden: Harrassowitz.

von Rüden, C. 2014. Beyond the East-West dichotomy in Syrian and Levantine wall paintings. In Brown, B.A., and Feldman, M.H. (eds.), *Critical approaches to ancient Near Eastern art.* Berlin: De Gruyter, 55–78.

Voutsaki, S. 2001. Economic control, power and prestige in the Mycenaean world: the archaeological evidence. In Voutsaki, S., and Killen, J. (eds.), *Economy and politics in the Mycenaean palace states*. Cambridge: Cambridge Philological Society, 195–213.

Voutsaki, S. 2010. Middle Bronze Age: Mainland Greece. In Cline, E.H. (ed.), *The Oxford handbook of the Bronze Age Aegean (ca. 3000–1000 BC)*. Oxford: Oxford University Press, 99–112.

Voutsaki, S. 2012. From value to meaning, from things to persons: the grave circles of Mycenae reconsidered. In Papadopoulos, J.K., and Urton, G. (eds.), *The construction of value in the ancient world*. Los Angeles: Cotsen Institute of Archaeology, University of California, 160–185.

Waal, W.J.I. 2019. "My brother, a great king, my peer": evidence for a Mycenaean kingdom from Hittite texts. In Kelder, J.M., and Waal, W.J.I. (eds.), *From "LUGAL.GAL" to "wanax": kingship and political organisation in the Late Bronze Age Aegean*. Leiden: Sidestone, 9–29.

Wallace, S. 2010. *Ancient Crete: from successful collapse to democracy's alternatives, twelfth to fifth centuries BC*. Cambridge: Cambridge University Press.

Warren, P. 2002. Political structure in Neopalatial Crete. In Driessen, J., Schoep, I., and Laffineur, R. (eds.), *Monuments of Minos: rethinking the Minoan palaces*. Liège: Université de Liège, 201–205.

Warren, P. 2004. Terra cognita? The territory and boundaries of the early Neopalatial Knossian state. In Cadogan, G., Hatzaki, E., and Vasilakis, A. (eds.), *Knossos: palace, city, state*. London: British School at Athens, 159–168.

Warren, P. 2010. The absolute chronology of the Aegean, circa 2000 BC–1400 BC: a summary. In Müller, W. (ed.), *Die Bedeutung der minoischen und mykenischen Glyptik*. Mainz: Zabern, 383–394.

Warren, P. 2012. The apogee of Minoan civilization: the final Neopalatial period. In Mantzourani, E., and Betancourt, P.P. (eds.), *Philistor: studies in honor of Costis Davaras*. Philadelphia, PA: Institute for Aegean Prehistory Academic Press, 255–272.

Watkins, C. 1995. *How to kill a dragon*. Oxford: Oxford University Press.

Webb, J.M. 1999. *Ritual architecture, iconography and practice in the Late Cypriot Bronze Age*. Jonsered: Åströms Förlag.

Weeden, M. 2018. Hittite-Ahhiyawan politics as seen from the tablets: a reaction to Trevor Bryce's article from a Hittitological perspective. *SMEA: Nova Series* 4: 217–227.

Weingarten, J. 2010. Minoan seals and sealings. In Cline, E.H. (ed.), *The Oxford handbook of the Bronze Age Aegean (ca. 3000–1000 BC)*. Oxford: Oxford University Press, 317–328.

Whitelaw, T. 2004. Estimating the population of Neopalatial Knossos. In Cadogan, G., Hatzaki, E., and Vasilakis, A. (eds.), *Knossos: palace, city, state*. London: British School at Athens, 147–158.

Whitelaw, T. 2005. A tale of three cities: chronology and Minoanisation at Phylakopi in Melos. In Dakouri-Hild, A., and Sherratt, S. (eds.), *Autochthon: papers presented to O.T.P.K. Dickinson*. Oxford: Archaeopress, 37–69.

Whitelaw, T. 2017. The development and character of urban communities in prehistoric Crete in their regional context: a preliminary study. In Letesson, Q., and Knappett, C. (eds.), *Minoan architecture and urbanism: new perspectives on an ancient built environment*. Oxford: Oxford University Press, 114–180.

Whitelaw, T. 2018. Recognising polities in prehistoric Crete. In Relaki, M., and Papadatos, Y. (eds.), *From the foundations to the legacy of Minoan archaeology: studies in honour of Professor Keith Branigan*. Oxford: Oxbow, 210–255.

Wiener, M.H. 2007. Neopalatial Knossos: rule and role. In Betancourt, P.P., Nelson, M.C., and Williams, H. (eds.), *Krinoi kai limenes: studies in honor of Joseph and Maria Shaw*. Philadelphia, PA: Institute for Aegean Prehistory Academic Press, 231–242.

Wiener, M.H. 2009. The state of the debate about the date of the Theran eruption. In Warburton, D.A. (ed.), *Time's up! Dating the Minoan eruption of Santorini*. Aarhus: Aarhus University Press, 197–206.

Wiener, M.H. 2013. Realities of power: the Minoan thalassocracy in historical perspective. In Koehl, R.B. (ed.), *Amilla, the quest for excellence: studies presented to Guenter Kopcke in celebration of his 75th birthday*. Philadelphia, PA: Institute for Aegean Prehistory Academic Press, 149–173.

Wiener, M.H. 2015. The Mycenaean conquest of Minoan Crete. In Macdonald, C.F., Hatzaki, E., and Andreou, S. (eds.), *The great islands: studies of Crete and Cyprus presented to Gerald Cadogan*. Athens: Kapon Editions, 131–142.

Wiener, M.H. 2017. Causes of complex systems collapse at the end of the Bronze Age. In Fischer, P.M., and Bürge, T. (eds.), *"Sea Peoples" up-to-date: new research on transformations in the eastern Mediterranean in the*

13th–11th centuries BCE. Vienna: Verlag der Österreichischen Akademie der Wissenschaften, 43–74.

Wiersma, C. 2014. *Building the Bronze Age: architectural and social change on the Greek mainland during Early Helladic III, Middle Helladic and Late Helladic I*. Oxford: Archaeopress.

Wright, J.C. 2006. The formation of the Mycenaean palace. In Deger-Jalkotzy, S., and Lemos, I.S. (eds.), *Ancient Greece: from the Mycenaean palaces to the age of Homer*. Edinburgh: Edinburgh University Press, 7–52.

Wright, J.C. 2008. Early Mycenaean Greece. In Shelmerdine, C.W. (ed.), *The Cambridge companion to the Aegean Bronze Age*. Cambridge: Cambridge University Press, 230–257.

Yasur-Landau, A. 2010a. Levant. In Cline, E.H. (ed.), *The Oxford handbook of the Bronze Age Aegean (ca. 3000–1000 BC)*. Oxford: Oxford University Press, 832–848.

Yasur-Landau, A. 2010b. *The Philistines and Aegean migration at the end of the Late Bronze Age*. Cambridge: Cambridge University Press.

Yon, M. 2007. "Au roi d'Alasia, mon père. . . ." *Cahier du Centre d'Études Chypriotes* 37: 15–39.

32

Assyria in the Late Bronze Age

Hervé Reculeau

32.1. Introduction

The history of Assyria (figure 32.1) during the Late Bronze Age (fifteenth–twelfth centuries BC) roughly corresponds to what is usually termed the Middle Assyrian period, although its roots lie in the preceding centuries and its most salient features extend well into the early Iron Age (eleventh–early tenth centuries).[1] Due to these uncertainties, even the chronological boundaries of the period are debated: while its beginning is often set in the fourteenth century, with Aššur-uballiṭ I (1363–1328 BC),[2] some would have it start as early as the fifteenth century,[3] or even the sixteenth century.[4] Similarly, the transition between the Middle Assyrian period and the following Neo-Assyrian period can be set at the time of the reign of Tiglath-pileser I (1114–1076 BC), or at the accession

---

1. For the regnal dates of Assyrian kings, see the discussion on chronology in section 32.2. The abbreviation CTH refers for *Catalogue des Textes Hittites* (available online at https://www.hethport.uni-wuerzburg.de/HPM/index.php; last accessed September 10, 2020).

2. Most recently, Jakob 2017a.

3. Miglus 2011; Tenu 2017.

4. Fales 2015.

Hervé Reculeau, *Assyria in the Late Bronze Age* In: *The Oxford History of the Ancient Near East*. Edited by: Karen Radner, Nadine Moeller, and D. T. Potts, Oxford University Press. © Oxford University Press 2022.
DOI: 10.1093/oso/9780190687601.003.0032

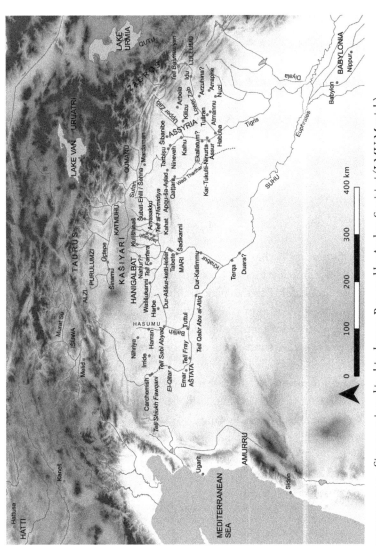

FIGURE 32.1. Sites mentioned in this chapter. Prepared by Andrea Squitieri (LMU Munich).

to the throne of Aššur-dan II (934–912 BC), which marks the end of over a century for which almost no historical sources are available.[5]

This period is primarily defined by the rise of the city-state of Assur (Qal'at Sherqat)[6] to regional dominance over Upper Mesopotamia, ruling at its maximal extent over a vast area bordered, to the north and east, by the highlands of the Anatolian plateau and Zagros mountain range, to the south by Babylonia, and to the west by the Euphrates river. For the first time in history, the "land of Assur" (*māt Aššur*)— or Assyria—had become a prominent actor in the geopolitics of the Middle East, laying the foundations for the imperial realizations of the Iron Age.

32.2. *Matters of chronology*

There is still considerable disagreement among scholars in regard to the absolute chronology of the second millennium BC, which needs to be reconstructed from a variety of written sources (more often than not poorly preserved and contradictory), a handful of radiocarbon and dendrochronological dates, and the rare mention of astronomical events in cuneiform records. This vexing problem has been the object of scholarly debate for over a century, and proposed dates for the fall of Babylon at the hands of the Hittite king Mursili I still vary in current scholarship by ca. 150 years, depending on which of the various chronologies is followed, and based on the chronology adopted by the respective authors, historical reconstructions of the formative years of the kingdom of Assyria also vary substantially and, crucially, the assessment of its relationships with neighboring polities. According to the Middle Chronology, which current radiocarbon evidence suggests to be the most likely reconstruction, Samsi-Addu ascended the throne of Ekallatum around 1833 BC, conquered Assur in 1808 BC, and died in 1776 BC (see chapter 11 in volume 2).

---

5. Frahm 2017a. For this period, see chapter 37 in volume 4.

6. For a survey of the archaeological evidence, see Tenu 2009: 57–75.

Another set of chronological difficulties is linked to assumptions
made by scholars when reconstructing the regnal years of Middle
Assyrian kings. The basis for these reconstructions is the Assyrian King
List, an official document compiled at different periods by royal scribes
of the Assyrian court, which is preserved in five fragmentary manuscripts from the Neo-Assyrian period, beginning in the reign of Tiglath-
pileser II (966–935 BC).[7] Breaks in the manuscripts and inconsistencies
between them, and with a different tradition represented by one single
manuscript from Aššur,[8] have led to diverging reconstructions of Middle
Assyrian chronology, most of which amend the extant manuscripts of
the King List for Aššur-dan I's rule from 46 to 36 years, hence assigning him the dates 1168–1133 BC.[9] This has recently been contested, and
the 46-year count (as suggested by two manuscripts of the King List)
has regained popularity among specialists[10]—but this, in turn, has been
criticized, and no consensus has been reached.[11]

A further assumption is that the Assyrian official year, which was
named after an eponym (*limmu*) who changed every year, followed
the solar cycle, whereas the administrative calendar followed the lunar
cycle. Since a year of twelve lunar months contains roughly 354 days and
a solar year just over 365, there is a difference of slightly under 11 days
between the two computational systems.[12] In effect, this implies that
eponyms were appointed during different months of the lunar calendar
each year, hence that the official start of the year was disconnected from
the succession of months.[13] This theory has been challenged by scholars for whom the lunar calendar was tied to the solar year by the use of

---

7. Grayson 1983: 101–115; S. Yamada 1994.

8. Grayson 1983: 115–116.

9. Boese and Wilhelm 1979.

10. Bloch 2010a: 64–78; Salah 2014; Jeffers 2017.

11. Janssen 2012: 16.

12. Jeffers 2017: 151.

13. Reade 2001: 2.

"invisible" intercalation—that is, the unmarked repetition of a month in the lunar calendar when required to adjust it to the solar year.[14] Under both hypotheses, one can more or less securely tie the reigns of Assyrian kings with dates in the Julian or Gregorian calendars (which rely on the solar year), because the ancient lists of eponyms were the basis for the counts of regnal years in the Assyrian King List. This would not be the case, however, if the Middle Assyrian calendar was purely lunar and did not become luni-solar until the reign of Tiglath-pileser I (1114–1076 BC) or Aššur-bel-kala (1073–1056 BC).[15] This latter hypothesis would mean that, for the entire period under consideration here, the beginning of each Assyrian regnal year would have slowly drifted when expressed in the Julian[16] or proleptic Gregorian[17] calendar, and that the standard dates are well off the mark.

These uncertainties raise critical issues for the general chronology of the Late Bronze Age, given the central role played by the Assyrian royal sequence for the assessment of synchronisms between the various kingdoms of the time, especially at a moment when other key chronologies (Egypt, Hatti, Babylonia) are also undergoing critical re-evaluations.[18] Frustrating as it is, these ongoing developments still need to be assessed holistically and integrated into a broad, overarching chronology. For these reasons, and even if the hypothesis of a purely lunar calendar appears the most plausible at this point, I shall refrain from using the dates associated with it until a consensus has been reached. Absolute dates are given here only as a tool for readers to roughly place the sequence of events in the general time frame of the period, using lower

---

14. Cancik-Kirschbaum and Johnson 2011–2012; Jeffers 2017: 153 n. 8; Mahieu 2018. This hypothesis is not supported by the available evidence (Gauthier 2016: 725–739; Jeffers 2017).

15. Bloch 2012; Jeffers 2017; *contra* Mahieu 2018.

16. Bloch 2012: 43–48.

17. Jeffers 2017: 189.

18. Cf. Pruzsinszky 2009: 213–215; Giorgieri 2011: 187–189; Wilhelm 2004; Bryce 2005: 375–382; Bloch 2010b; Janssen 2012; 2013 (with widely diverging conclusions).

Middle Chronology and a forty-six-year-long reign for Aššur-dan I.[19] It must be stressed, however, that the only certainty at this point is that they are, to a greater or a lesser extent, wrong.

A final chronological difficulty lies in the previously mentioned fact that Assyrians named their years after an eponymous official (*limmu*). While official lists compiled by the Assyrian chancery in order to keep their accounts in order must have existed—and indeed, such lists are known for both the preceding Old Assyrian and following Neo-Assyrian periods—these have not been recovered for the Middle Assyrian period, which means that eponyms need to be assigned to—and, when possible, ordered within—the different reigns through a tedious process of reconstruction. Such efforts have produced a general sequence of eponyms between the fifteenth and twelfth centuries, but there is still a considerable amount of disagreement between scholars.[20]

32.3. *The slow birth of Assyria in the fifteenth and early fourteenth centuries* BC

For the entire Middle Bronze Age, there existed no such thing as Assyria, and Assur was only one among many petty kingdoms, independent at first and then integrated into the short-lived eighteenth-century territorial kingdom of Samsi-Addu, centered on Šubat-Enlil/Šehna (Tell Leilan) (see chapter 15 in volume 2). While Samsi-Addu's heritage was contested shortly after his death,[21] he and his son Išme-Dagan came to be seen as "kings of Assyria" by later Assyrian scribes, kings, and officials—explicitly in one inscription of Aššur-uballiṭ I that depicts Samsi-Addu as "a king of Assyria, a king who preceded me"[22] and implicitly attested

---

19. Specifically, the dates follow the ones offered in Frahm 2017b, corrected to account for a forty-six-year-long reign for Aššur-dan I (for which see Jeffers 2017: 162 n. 34).

20. Saporetti 1979a; Freydank 1991; 2016; Bloch 2008; 2010c; Llop 2013; Jakob 2013; Salah 2014: 57–62; Maul 2017: 97–98.

21. S. Yamada 2017: 109–113.

22. Grayson 1987: 116, A.0.73.1001: ll. 5′–7′.

by the fact that they kept him and his genealogy in the Assyrian King List,[23] and that subsequent rulers used royal names like Šamši-Adad (the "Akkadized" version of Samsi-Addu's Amorite name) and Išme-Dagan.[24] This, however, was a secondary reworking of the historical narrative that projected the notion of Assyria back into times when it did not yet exist. Therefore, when modern scholars talk about an "Old Assyrian kingdom" of "Šamši-Adad I," they fall prey to that ideologically motivated rewriting of history.

32.3.1. Puzur-Aššur III and the affirmation of a territorial kingdom (early fifteenth century BC)

The notion of a territorial kingdom centered on Assur and bearing its name was a slow process that evolved over a relatively long period of time, at the end of which the conception of power was drastically altered. During the so-called Old Assyrian period (twentieth–sixteenth centuries BC, leaving aside the Samsi-Addu parenthesis), the ruler of the city-state appears to have been content with limited powers and ambitions. The king was *primus inter pares* (*rubāʾum*, "the great one"), the voice of the city assembly (*ālum*), the legal and judicial enforcer of its decisions in his quality of "overseer" (*waklum*), and the privileged intermediary between his subjects and the gods—especially the tutelary deity Aššur who was the namesake of the city and represented the divinized form of the rocky outcrop on which it perched. This appears most explicitly in the title used in royal inscriptions and on the royal seal, where the ruler is called "vice-regent (ensi/*iššiakum*) of the god Aššur."[25]

While he is mentioned as his subjects' lord (*bēlum*), reflecting a patrimonial conception of power common throughout the second millennium in Syria and Mesopotamia,[26] the ruler never appears as king

---

23. S. Yamada 1994.

24. Frahm 2017b: 614.

25. Veenhof 2017: 70–71.

26. Reculeau 2016.

(*šarrum*) in this "theocratic" ideology, which distinguished him quite clearly from most of his contemporaries (with the documented exceptions of Ešnunna—a much more powerful state at the time—for the "theocratic" aspects, and Sippar—another major trading center—for the city assembly).[27] The king's power appears to have been balanced by the traditional prerogatives of the city assembly and those of the elite urban families who competed for the privilege of being named eponym for the year, which has led to the depiction of its constitution as a mix between "monocratic," "aristocratic," and "democratic" power.[28]

Things changed in the Late Bronze Age, even if the old traditional powers never entirely disappeared until the end of Assyria itself.[29] We know very little about Assur's history after the death of Samsi-Addu: the privileged relations between Išme-Dagan and the First Dynasty of Babylon (see chapter 18 in volume 2), as well as the apparent continuity in the local dynasty, suggest that the city avoided the fate of many Upper Mesopotamian cities destroyed by the Babylonian armies of Hammurabi (1792–1750 BC) and Samsu-iluna (1749–1712 BC),[30] but textual evidence for the late eighteenth to the late sixteenth centuries is limited to a handful of inscriptions, celebrating construction works in Assur, from Šamši-Adad III and Aššur-nerari I in the late sixteenth century.[31]

Some of the latter's inscriptions suggest that the times might not have been entirely peaceful, and that Assur had at this point entered a more bellicose phase of interaction with its neighbors, as they mention repairs on the city wall.[32] While the preserved inscriptions of his son and successor Puzur-Aššur (first quarter of the fifteenth century BC) only celebrate

---

27. Charpin 2004: 64–65, 91–94.

28. Liverani 2011: 263.

29. Liverani 2011: 259–263; Radner 2014: 107–109.

30. Charpin 2004: 327–330, 349–351; 2011; S. Yamada 2017: 113.

31. Šamši-Adad III: Grayson 1987: 79–82: A.o.59.2–1003; Aššur-nerari I: Grayson 1987: 83–87: A.o.60.1–6.

32. Grayson 1987: 86–87: A.o.60.5–6.

civilian works,[33] we know from a later inscription by his descendant Aššur-bel-nišešu (end of the fifteenth century BC) that this king had expanded the city's fortifications to enclose the "new city" (*ālu eššu*) that had developed to the south of Assur (see table 32.1 for a genealogical chart of the Assyrian royal house).[34] His foundational role in the evolution of Assyrian kingship can be inferred from the fact that, more than a century later, his remote descendent Aššur-uballiṭ I mentioned him as the earliest of his ancestors in an unusually long list of antecedents.[35]

Though not the first mentioned in the manuscript (which erroneously starts with Aššur-bel-nišešu, who ruled some seventy-five years after him), Puzur-Aššur is the earliest king[36] mentioned in a first-millennium chronicle known as the *Synchronistic History*, which reflects the biased history of Assyro-Babylonian relationships from an Assyrian perspective.[37] The same applies to its Babylonian counterpart, known as *Chronicle P* (the names of the kings are lost, but parallels with the *Synchronistic History* suggest that the passage referred to the establishment of the border between Puzur-Aššur III and Burna-Buriaš I).[38] This does not mean that first-millennium scholars perceived Puzur-Aššur as inaugurating a new era of Assyrian history in and by itself, but it is telling that with his reign, one of the most fundamental geopolitical and cultural patterns in the history of Assyria until its demise began, namely the complex set of relationships and frequent confrontations with its southern neighbor to establish their common border.

The treaty between Puzur-Aššur and Burna-Buriaš shows that at this point Assur no longer was a city-state *stricto sensu*, and that it considered the region southward along the Tigris as its dominion. Archaeology confirms Assyrian expansion east of the Tigris and

33. Grayson 1987: 90–93: A.0.61.1–5.

34. Grayson 1987: 99–100: A.0.69.1; Tenu 2009: 60–65.

35. Grayson 1987: 109–114: A.0.73.1–2; [4]; 5.

36. Grayson 1975: 158–159: Chronicle 21: i 5'–7'.

37. Grayson 1975: 50–56.

38. Grayson 1975: 171: Chronicle 22: 2–4; see also chapter 33 in this volume.

Table 32.1. The genealogy of the Assyrian royal house and the synchronisms with contemporary rulers.

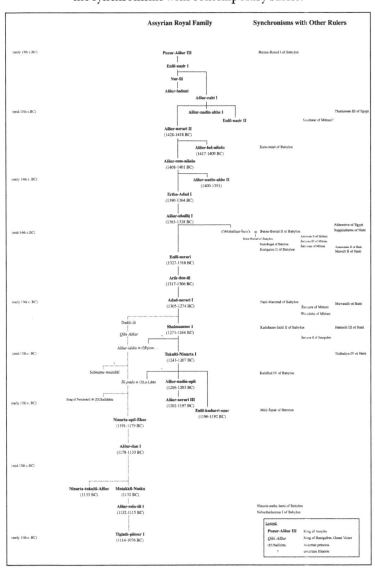

toward the Lower Zab around that period, and even the foundation of the new city of Habuba (modern Tell Farha) by Puzur-Aššur III.[39] The balance of power had shifted in the former merchant city-state: its ruler now mirrored other Mesopotamian kings in political ambitions and he had acquired the means to achieve them through war—even if, for the time being, he still depicted himself as "vice-regent of Aššur," not as "king" (*šarru*). This must have been correlated with an increase in military capacities and organization, but the few details that we have about the Middle Assyrian army come from the better-documented thirteenth century.[40]

For all these reasons, Puzur-Aššur III can be considered the first king to inaugurate a new era: the moment when "Assur" (the city-state) gave way to "Assyria" (the territorial kingdom)[41]—even if the explicit expression "land of Assur" (*māt Aššur*) only appears in the extent sources about one hundred years later.

32.3.2. Assur under Mittani rule: mid-fifteenth to mid-fourteenth century BC

One key issue, about which frustratingly little is known, is how this shift in Assyrian politics relates to the rise, at the turn of the sixteenth and fifteenth centuries, of the kingdom of Mittani. In the early fifteenth century, around the time when Puzur-Aššur III ruled over Assur, Mittani was ruled by Šuttarna I and included at least the Khabur triangle and the Upper Tigris around Diyarbakır (see chapter 29 in this volume). It was flanked by the kingdom's two main royal cities: Waššukanni (modern Tell Fekheriye) in the west,[42] and Taide in the east. Because two cities bore that name, the location of this Mittanian royal city is debated: some

39. Miglus 2011.

40. Jakob 2003: 191–222; 2017b: 152–153.

41. Tenu 2017: 530–532.

42. Cancik-Kirschbaum and Hess 2016: 19–20.

place it along the banks of the Jaghjagh, the Khabur's main tributary,[43] while others seek it on the Upper Tigris, possibly at Üçtepe.[44] Both sites are located to the northwest of Assur, at a distance of ca. 350 km and 240 km, respectively, across the Jezirah (and the Tur Abdin range for Üçtepe), while Waššukanni lies ca. 320 km to the west of Assur.

While Mittani expanded west of the Euphrates in the early fifteenth century BC, it seems that for some time Assur maintained its political independence. Not only did Puzur-Aššur act as an independent king, but Egyptian texts from the time of Thutmose III (1479–1425 BC) record gifts by (an) unnamed Assyrian king(s) in this pharaoh's twenty-fourth (1455 BC), thirty-third (1446 BC), and fortieth (1439 BC) regnal years.[45] This correlates with a later statement by Aššur-uballiṭ I that his forefather Aššur-nadin-ahhe I (who ruled in the mid-fifteenth century) had received gold from Egypt.[46]

Such diplomatic activity would not have been tolerated had Mittani been Assyria's overlord at this point, but it is possible that it was perceived as a threat by the Mittanian kings, who would have feared dual, hostile fronts with Egypt in the west and Assyria in the east. This correlates well with the only direct mention of a Mittanian conquest of Assur, in the historical preambles of two treaties drawn up in the mid-fourteenth century BC by the Hittite king Suppiluliuma with the (by that time) much weakened king of Mittani, Šattiwaza.[47] According to them, the Mittanian king Sauštatar (a contemporary of Amenhotep II in the last quarter of

---

43. Possibly to be identified with Tell al-Hamidiya (Cancik-Kirschbaum and Hess 2016: 142–143) or Tell Farfara (Heather Baker in Bryce 2009: 687); see also chapter 29 in this volume.

44. Radner and Shachner 2001.

45. Lion 2011: 159–160.

46. Rainey 2015: 130–133: EA 16: ll. 19–21; Llop 2011: 601; Radner 2015a: 64–67. The hypothesis that this Aššur-nadin-ahhe was the second king of that name, who ruled some thirty years before Aššur-uballiṭ I and was his uncle, is less probable, because in his first letter to the Egyptian pharaoh (Rainey 2015: 128–129: EA 15: ll. 9–10), Aššur-uballiṭ clearly states that his (direct) forefathers had not written to Egypt.

47. Beckman 1999: 41–54, no. 6; see also chapter 29 and chapter 30 in this volume.

the fifteenth century BC) had conquered and plundered Assur and taken to his capital Waššukanni its gold and silver door. This could have triggered a coup orchestrated in Assur by Enlil-naṣir II who, according to the Assyrian King List, usurped the throne of his brother Aššur-nadin-ahhe around 1420 BC,[48] but this remains quite speculative.

This episode is usually considered the starting point of Assur's vassalage to Mittani, which according to the same treaty lasted until the time of Tušratta (mid-fourteenth century). Recent studies have, however, pointed out that direct evidence of the suzerainty of Mittani over Assyria remains elusive at best,[49] and some scholars go so far as to call it into question.[50] An argument supporting the integration of Assyria into the Mittanian dominion around 1420 BC is the fact that Arraphe, which bordered Assyria east of the Tigris, along the Lower Zab, was a vassal of Mittani at least during the period of the archives of Nuzi (modern Yorgan Tepe), between ca. 1430 and 1330 BC.[51] Around the same time, Mittanian overlordship was recognized to the west of Assur by a Middle Euphratean dynasty that ruled over an area roughly encompassing the borders of the eighteenth century kingdom of Mari and had taken over the ancient title of "King of the Hana-Land" (lit., "of the nomads)" (*šar māt Hanâ*).[52] Archives from Terqa (modern Tell Ashara) show that these kings were vassals of at least three Mittanian kings around the last quarter of the fifteenth century.[53]

---

48. Grayson 1983: 108: §§35–36.

49. Lion 2011.

50. Llop 2015: 244; Tenu 2017: 540–541.

51. Lion 2011 (with previous literature); S. Yamada 2017: 114–115; *contra* Tenu 2017: 540–541.

52. In its original use, the term *hanûm*, "tent-dweller" (Durand 1998: 417–420), of which *Hanâ* is derived, represents the semi-nomadic pastoralists over whom the kings of eighteenth-century Mari claimed power. By the Late Bronze Age, the term acquired a more strictly topographic use that applied to various regions (Cancik-Kirschbaum 2009; H. Kühne 2018).

53. Both the sequencing and the absolute chronology of the Mittani and Terqa rulers are highly disputed (Rouault 2004; S. Yamada 2011; Podany 2014; Mladjov 2019). See also chapter 29 in this volume.

If Assyria was indeed a vassal of Mittani from the late fifteenth to the mid-fourteenth century, this seems to have hardly had any effect on its kings' capacity to act as sovereigns, except perhaps for the tribute they had to pay annually (as can be inferred from Šattiwaza's complaint that they had ceased doing so after Tušratta's murder). Not only were the Assyrian kings Aššur-nerari II (1424–1418 BC),[54] Aššur-bel-nišešu (1417–1409 BC),[55] and Aššur-rem-nišešu (1408–1401 BC)[56] able to grant land or other royal possessions to their subjects without any reference to their putative overlords,[57] but the former had regular economic and diplomatic relationships with Arraphe.[58] Some cities formerly under Assyrian control, like Habuba, had been lost to Arraphe, so the extension of Assyria in this area was more limited than under Puzur-Aššur III.[59]

Aššur-bel-nišešu was nevertheless able to act in a way that echoes the feats of his forefather: he reinforced and expanded the fortification wall he had built around the new city of Assur,[60] and signed a new peace treaty with the Kassite king Kara-indaš (certainly after a renewed episode of hostilities) to fix the southern border with Babylon.[61] This may have been done with the support (or even at the instigation) of his Mittanian overlord—a fact that the *Synchronistic History* would never acknowledge, given its pro-Assyrian bias—but it clearly attests to some military agency of Assyria toward the end of the fifteenth century BC.

54. Ebeling 1927: no. 177; Saporetti 1982: 106 (a field).

55. Ebeling 1927: no. 162; Saporetti 1982: 47 (a farmstead with land and equipment); Saporetti 1979b: 60 (a "palace share").

56. Freydank 1976: no. 41; Saporetti 1982: 110 (a "palace share").

57. Lion 2011: 157; Maidman 2011: 87.

58. Lion 2011: 163.

59. Miglus 2011: 227–229.

60. Grayson 1987: 99–100: A.0.69.1.

61. Grayson 1975: 158: Chronicle 21: i 1′–4′.

32.4. The affirmation of Assyria as a great power (mid- to late fourteenth century BC)

The mid- to late fourteenth century marks the emergence of Assyria from the shadows, both in terms of documentation and of political might. Archaeological remains from the period are limited, mostly because the buildings recovered by the German excavations at Assur were later rebuilt, erasing most traces of the earlier phases known almost exclusively from royal inscriptions.[62] From this period also date the earliest steles with the king's or eponym's name, although it is probable that the tradition goes back to earlier periods.[63] For the first time, cuneiform archives recovered in private houses shed some light on the life of the urban elites under Aššur-bel-nišesu, Aššur-rem-nišešu, Eriba-Adad I, and Aššur-uballiṭ I (i.e., the time from 1417 to 1328 BC).[64] Finally, eleventh-century copies preserve fourteenth-century laws covering various legal matters, grouped by subject on fourteen tablets. Most are poorly preserved, and what remains pertains to the status of women (Tablet A), landed property (Tablet B), and movable property (Tablet C+G).[65] Another compilation preserves palace decrees regulating life at the Assyrian court, most prominently that of the women of the royal harem (hence their common qualification as "harem edicts"), but also that of other courtiers and palace employees.[66]

32.4.1. Eriba-Adad I and the emancipation of Assyria (1390–1364 BC)

Aššur-uballiṭ I is often credited with the emancipation of Assyria from Mittani and the elaboration of a new conception of royal power in

---

62. Tenu 2009: 57–75; Düring 2020: 50–52.

63. Tenu 2009: 69–72; Düring 2020: 52–54.

64. Archive M 9 = Pedersén 1985: 89–99; Saporetti 1979b; 1982; Maul 2016.

65. Roth 1997: 153–194; Lafont 2003: 521.

66. Roth 1997: 195–209, especially 196–197 (Aššur-uballiṭ I) and 197–198 (Enlil-nerari); Lafont 2003: 521; Jakob 2017b: 148.

© Staatliche Museen zu Berlin - Vorderasiatisches Museum, Foto: Sandra Steiß

FIGURE 32.2. Cuneiform tablet (4.3 × 4.4 cm) bearing the impression of the royal seal of Eriba-Adad I of Assyria (1390–1364 BC). Vorderasiatisches Museum Berlin (accession number VAT 90009). © Staatliche Museen zu Berlin— Vorderasiatisches Museum, photograph by Sandra Steiß.

Assur.[67] Some elements, however, suggest that the process began under his father Eriba-Adad I (figure 32.2). While only two inscriptions are known for this ruler,[68] one of them bears the epithet "appointee of (the god) Enlil" (*šakin Enlil*),[69] a title that had not been used in Assur since the time of Samsi-Addu, which points to a theoretical claim of universal kingship, since the god Enlil in Nippur was the one who conferred

---

67. Harrak 1987: 7–60; S. Yamada 2017: 115; Jakob 2017a: 117–118; Düring 2020: 43.

68. Grayson 1987: 107–108: A.0.72.1–2.

69. Grayson 1987: 108: A.0.72.2: 2.

the desirable title of "king of Sumer and Akkad," symbol of supremacy over Mesopotamia.[70] Whereas it is clear that Eriba-Adad did not control Nippur (which was securely in Babylonian territory) any more than Samsi-Addu had in his time, use of this title reflects a long-term strategy by Assyrian kings to elevate their own capital Assur as the northern equivalent of Nippur—and their own national god Aššur as the equivalent of Enlil.[71] This led to the temple of the god Aššur being renamed "House of the Land" (É.KUR)—like Enlil's temple in Nippur—and the god himself placed at the head of the Mesopotamian pantheon, his sanctuary becoming the "House of Entirety" (É.ŠARA) housing the chapels of other gods. In the meantime, the city of Assur and its cultic center took over Nippur's designation as the "Heart of the (primeval) City" (URU–ŠÀ–URU/*Āl-Libbi-Āle*),[72] and was depicted by Eriba-Adad's successor Aššur-uballiṭ I as "seat of the dynasty" (*šubat palê*) and "seat of kingship" (*šubat šarrūte*).[73]

The extant documentation does not confirm that all these elements were indeed promoted under Eriba-Adad I, and it is probable that they gained popularity over time as Assyria grew stronger. However, the reaffirmation of an ideology anchored in the memory of Samsi-Addu's dominion over the entire Jezirah signals Assyria's increased ambitions at a time when Mittani was weakened by internal divisions and pressure from Suppiluliuma I of Hatti (see chapters 29 and 31 in this volume). Eriba-Adad was probably the first to depict himself not only as "vice-regent of Aššur" (as was traditional), but as king (*šarrum*) in the full sense of the term, and more specifically as "king of the land of Assur"

---

70. The epithet is noted by both Cifola 1995: 19–20 and Sazonov 2016: 38, but curiously enough, its political significance is only acknowledged when used by Aššur-uballiṭ I (Cifola 1995: 20). This can only be attributed to the a priori opinion that any significant change only occurred under the latter's reign, but the importance of Eriba-Adad's change in titles was already pointed out by Garelli 1990: 98.

71. Maul 1998: 191–192.

72. Cancik-Kirschbaum 2014: 302–304.

73. Cancik-Kirschbaum 2011: 74; for the archaeological remains of the temple, see Tenu 2009: 60–61.

(*šar māt Aššur*), our "Assyria."[74] There is, however, only indirect proof of this: none of the instances where he bears that title is contemporary with his reign, and he did not use it in his two extant inscriptions. However, even his successors who clearly bore the title "king of Assyria" used it only sparingly: Aššur-uballiṭ (who is often credited with this major change in the Assyrian conception of power) used it on his cylinder seal,[75] and in the two letters he sent to the Egyptian pharaoh,[76] but not in the five inscriptions dedicating buildings to the gods, where he stuck to the traditional title "vice-regent of Aššur" and, like his father before him, "appointee of Enlil."[77] Enlil-nerari did not use the new title in his only preserved inscription,[78] and Arik-den-ili used it in only three out of six inscriptions.[79]

The title "king of Assyria" is attributed to Eriba-Adad both by his great-grandson Arik-den-ili,[80] and by his distant descendent Ninurta-apil-Ekur (1191–1179 BC).[81] While it remains possible that in both cases it was applied retrospectively, this could also suggest that our perception is biased by the available documentation, and that he indeed was the first to picture himself as "king of Assyria." This is further suggested by a legal document from his reign in which his son Aššur-uballiṭ was designated "crown prince"—literally "son of the king" (*mār šarre*).[82] A stele attributed to Eriba-Adad I bears the title "king of the universe" (*šar kiššate*), but its date is debated and some scholars have suggested dating it to Eriba-Adad II (1055–1054 BC)—mostly because of the reluctance to give the title "king" to his fourteenth-century namesake, and despite the fact

74. Tenu 2017: 535–536.

75. Grayson 1987: 115: A.0.73.6: 3.

76. Rainey 2015: 128: EA 15: 3; 130: EA 16: 3.

77. Grayson 1987: 109–114: A.0.73.1–5.

78. Grayson 1987: 118–119: A.0.74.1.

79. Grayson 1987: 120–125: A.0.75.1–2; 7.

80. Grayson 1987: 121: A.0.75.1: 46–47.

81. Freydank 1976: no. 53: 7; Jakob 2003a: 514.

82. Ebeling 1927: no. 160: 14; Saporetti 1979b: 91.

that this disrupts the apparent chronological order of the steles' alignment.[83] Finally, it is remarkable that, after his usurpation of the Assyrian throne, the twelfth-century king Ninurta-apil-Ekur (and later Assyrian historiography, in the form of the Assyrian King List) used the epithet "son/offspring of Eriba-Adad (I)"[84]—not of Aššur-uballiṭ, let alone of Adad-nerari I, his closest ancestor to have ruled Assyria.[85] All of this suggests that Assyria had started to shrug off the Mittanian yoke, or at least expressed strong tendencies toward independence, as early as the reign of Eriba-Adad I, and that he was the king considered the founder of the Middle Assyrian kingdom by later Assyrians.

32.4.2. The first "great king" of Assyria: Aššur-uballiṭ I (1363–1328 BC)

Aššur-uballiṭ I added substance to his father's ambitions and established Assyria as one of the major players on the Late Bronze Age stage. While his inscriptions only refer to civilian works in both the "old" and "new" parts of Assur (i.e., the traditional center of the Old Assyrian period and the southern extension enclosed under Puzur-Aššur III), his letters to Egypt (see chapter 28 in this volume) depict him as a newcomer eager to join the "Great Powers' Club"—the select group of powerful kings who acknowledged one another with the title of "great king" (*šarru rabû*) and maintained parity relationships through correspondence, gift exchanges, and dynastic marriages.[86]

Two letters to Akhenaten show the progressive affirmation of Assyria under Aššur-uballiṭ. The first letter (figure 32.3),[87] simply addressed to "the king of Egypt" by "the king of Assyria," initiated contact between

83. Tenu 2009: 70.

84. Freydank 1976: no. 53: 7; Grayson 1983: 111: Assyrian King List, §50; Jakob 2003a: 514.

85. Cancik-Kirschbaum 1999.

86. Liverani 2000.

87. Faist 2001: 80–81; Rainey 2015: 128–129: EA 15: ll. 9–10.

FIGURE 32.3. Cuneiform tablet (5.5 × 7.7 cm) inscribed with a letter from Aššur-uballiṭ I of Assyria (1363–1328 BC) to pharaoh Akhenaten of Egypt, found in Akhetaten (modern Tell el-Amarna) in Egypt (EA 15). Metropolitan Museum of Art, New York (accession number 24.2.11). Photograph courtesy Metropolitan Museum of Art. CC0 1.0 Universal (CC0 1.0) Public Domain Dedication.

the two courts (the Assyrian king stressed that his ancestors did not have diplomatic ties with Egypt) by sending envoys and greeting gifts, all the while hoping for a prompt response. The gifts (a chariot, two horses, and lapis lazuli) were standard prestige goods, in part imported from the Zagros highlands (horses) and Babylonia (lapis lazuli), the main trading partners of Assyria after Hatti and its Syrian dominion.[88] Babylon had long been a key player in the international game, and the influence of Babylonian scribal traditions is clear under Aššur-uballiṭ, who even employed a high-profile Babylonian scholar, Marduk-nadin-ahhi, as his royal scribe.[89]

This cautious tone was largely abandoned when, a few years later, the second letter was sent, attesting to the fact that Egypt looked favorably upon the Assyrian request for partnership.[90] This time, Aššur-uballiṭ addressed Akhenaten by his throne name, Neferkheperura (or rather, what an Assyrian scribe made of it: Naphuriya),[91] and he used the language of brotherhood (a sign that he considered himself pharaoh's equal), even calling himself a "great king." The letter employs all the tricks and codes of egalitarian diplomatic relationships of the Amarna Age, showing that at this point Assyria had fully mastered the rules of the game.[92] Not only did Aššur-uballiṭ delay beyond what was necessary his partner's emissaries (and made no apology for it), all the while requesting that his own envoys should not be delayed, but he also complained about the treatment received by his ambassadors at the Egyptian court, and taunted Akhenaten for not sending him the gold he had requested, recalling the generosity of pharaoh's ancestors' toward Aššur-nadin-ahhe I and toward his former overlord Mittani, whose equal he now claimed to be.

---

88. Faist 2001: 53–76.

89. Radner 2015a: 83–86; Pongratz-Leisten 2015: 9.

90. Faist 2001: 11–17; Rainey 2015: 130–133: EA 16: ll. 19–21.

91. Miller 2007.

92. Liverani 2000.

Assyria's ascent displeased Burna-Buriaš II of Babylon (see chapter 33 in this volume), who vehemently opposed the establishment of diplomatic relations between Egypt and a kingdom he considered his vassal.[93] While the reality of Babylonian suzerainty over Assyria in this period cannot be demonstrated, it reflects a shift of power in Mesopotamia, as Assyria assumed the role formerly enjoyed by Mittani as the main regional power in Upper Mesopotamia, directly opposing Babylonia in the south. Relations between the two powers were not always bad, though: Aššur-uballiṭ married his daughter Muballiṭat-Šerua to Burna-Buriaš, and their son Kara-Hardaš succeeded his father on the throne of Babylon (in 1333 BC). His assassination in a coup caused Aššur-uballiṭ to invade Babylonia and restore the dynasty.[94]

For the most part, though, Aššur-uballiṭ targeted areas that were formerly under Mittanian control. By then, Assyria had expanded into the Jezirah to the west, at least as far as Qaṭṭara (modern Tell al-Rimah)[95] and the area of the Wadi Tharthar (known in Assyrian as Šiššar), where Assyrian elites owned tracts of land.[96] Mittani had become a weak state, deprived of its possessions west of the Euphrates by Suppiluliuma I of Hatti, who also played the role of king-maker in the troubled succession over the Mittanian throne (see chapters 29 and 30 in this volume). The king of Mittani and ally of Egypt, Tušratta, who had ascended the throne after his brother's murder, was facing a competitor kingdom ("of the Hurrians") established by his brother Artatama (II), a Hittite protégé. After he had been murdered and his son Šattiwaza (who seems to have been party to the coup) exiled, Artatama ascended the throne and was soon succeeded by his son Šuttarna III.[97] According to the treaty between Suppiluliuma and Šattiwaza, however, Artatama, faced with a

---

93. Rainey 2015: 92–95: EA 9. See also chapter 33 in this volume.

94. Grayson 1975: 159: Chronicle 21: i 8′–17′; 171–172: Chronicle 22: i 5–14. See also chapter 33 in this volume.

95. Llop 2011: 600.

96. Bagg 2000: 84–86; Reculeau 2011: 76–78.

97. Koliński 2015: 9–10.

coalition between Aššur-uballiṭ's Assyria to the south and Alzi (Alše) to the north,[98] chose to submit and pay tribute. His son followed suit, returning to Assur the door that Sauštatar had taken as booty a century earlier and delivering the Mittanian supporters of Šattiwaza to Aššur-uballiṭ, who had them impaled in the royal city of Taide,[99] thereby initiating a tradition of severe and graphic punishment for the enemies of Assyria deemed guilty of rebellion and perjury that would define Assyrian propaganda until the end.[100]

This episode prompted Suppiluliuma to switch alliances and favor Šattiwaza, who reconquered Mittani (now reduced to the Khabur triangle) with the help of Piyassili (Šarri-Kušuh), the Hittite viceroy of Carchemish. While direct confrontation between Hatti and Assyria was avoided, a new balance of power was established in Upper Mesopotamia and northern Syria, with the Hittites in direct control of the right bank of the Euphrates (from Carchemish down to Aštata with the capital city of Emar) and westward, Assyria in control of the eastern Jezirah, and the rump state of Mittani (or Hanigalbat, as it was called by the Assyrians) acting as a buffer-state.

East of the Tigris, the former Mittani vassal of Arraphe suffered a series of violent destructions and conquests around 1330 BC. While some have suggested that the kingdom was also attacked from the south by the Babylonians (possibly acting as allies of Assyria following the dynastic marriage between the two courts),[101] others maintain that Assyria alone was involved in the war against Arraphe.[102] In any case, it is now clear that the final blow was struck by the Assyrians, after what seems to have been a series of campaigns by Aššur-uballiṭ's armies against the

---

98. For this kingdom, located in the Elazığ region of present-day Turkey, east of the Euphrates and south of the Murat Su, see Cancik-Kirschbaum and Hess 2016: 10–11.

99. Beckman 1999: 49, no. 6B §2.

100. The practice was used only for the most prominent enemy leaders; see Radner 2015b.

101. Müller 1994: 4; Lion 1995; C. Kühne 1999: 218–219; Lion 2011: 166.

102. Maidman 2011: 93–98.

king of Arraphe and his Mitannian overlord, most probably Tušratta.[103] Ultimately, both Nuzi and the eponymous capital Arraphe (modern Kirkuk) were destroyed, and a unique document in "Nuzi-style" but dated by an Assyrian eponym suggests that Assyrian control was established over the former Mittani dominion, at least for a short period of time.[104] This may have occurred very early in Aššur-uballiṭ's reign, even before the establishment of alliances with Egypt and Babylon, and possibly as early as his second regnal year.[105] This would be all the more plausible if, as suggested earlier, the emancipation of Assyria from Mittanian overlordship occurred in the reign of Eriba-Adad I, rather than in the very first year of Aššur-uballiṭ.[106]

Aššur-uballiṭ is also credited by his great-grandson Adad-nerari I with having expanded the borders of Assyria to the northeast, toward Muṣru and Šubar(t)u,[107] i.e., the region between the Upper Zab river, Lake Urmia, and Lake Van, at the present-day intersection of Iran, Turkey, and Iraqi Kurdistan.[108] While it is highly improbable that the Assyrian army really conquered these distant mountain lands, it suggests skirmishes with the local people in an attempt to expand Assyrian control beyond what would become, until the end of the empire in 612 BC, the heart of Assyria: the Assur-Nineveh-Arbela triangle, which came under Assyrian control for the first time under Aššur-uballiṭ—at least for Nineveh (modern Mosul), Arbela (modern Erbil) being only securely attested as an Assyrian center under Shalmaneser I in the early thirteenth

---

103. Maidman 2011: 98–102.

104. Maidman 2014.

105. Maidman 2011: 115–126.

106. Maidman 2011: 124–125.

107. Grayson 1987: 132: A.0.76.1: ll. 31–32.

108. Bryce 2009: 484–485, 663–665; Cancik-Kirschbaum and Hess 2016: 135–138.

century BC, although earlier control is probable.[109] The areas east of the Tigris offered more fertile lands than the traditional hinterland of Assur and, more importantly for an increasingly expansionist kingdom, allowed control of routes emanating in all four directions. While both Assur and Nineveh controlled fords on the Tigris, Assur was the easternmost station of the steppe route to the west (that ultimately led to the Khabur and Middle Euphrates),[110] Nineveh was on the overland route that connected the Zagros to the Mediterranean via the foothills of the Taurus range, and Arbela controlled routes that crossed the Zagros to reach Iran and all points east. Moreover, Nineveh had been, since the third millennium, the center of a highly prestigious cult of the goddess Ištar, and its control conferred tremendous prestige on the Assyrian kings.[111]

Suppiluliuma's death triggered a new episode in the brewing conflict between Hatti and Assyria. Egypt-backed rebellions had plagued the Hittite dominions in Syria for several years, and after Arnuwanda II's short reign, the new king Mursili II was busy fighting in Anatolia (see chapter 31 in this volume). According to Mursili's Annals for the second year of his reign, the Assyrians had become a threat to the kingdom of Carchemish, which had to be defended by a Hittite general dispatched from Anatolia. The maneuver was enough to deter the Assyrian king,[112] who remained unnamed and is usually identified with Aššur-uballiṭ,[113] based on the assumption that Suppiluliuma died in 1322 BC,[114] and Aššur-uballiṭ in 1318. However, given the uncertainties affecting both the Assyrian and Hittite chronologies, it could also have been his successor, Enlil-nerari.

---

109. Tenu 2004; Llop 2011: 600.

110. H. Kühne 2013: 477.

111. Radner 2011: 321–323.

112. CTH 61.II.2.A: i 9–19; Miller 2010; see also chapter 30 in this volume.

113. Klengel 1992: 115, 122; Cancik-Kirschbaum 2008b: 207.

114. Bryce 2005.

32.4.3. Precarious consolidation: Enlil-nerari (1327–1318 BC) and Arik-den-ili (1317–1306 BC)

First-millennium Assyrian chronicles mention a victory of Enlil-nerari over the Kassite king Kurigalzu II, the very king who had been installed on the Babylonian throne by Aššur-uballiṭ I,[115] but the Babylonian *Chronicle P* describes the event as a victory for Kurigalzu (while erroneously identifying the king as Adad-nerari I).[116] That the former sources are probably closer to the truth is suggested by a badly preserved inscription of Enlil-nerari himself,[117] and by two Assyrian sources closer in time to the events, if no less biased: his grandson Adad-nerari I's claim that he had defeated the Kassites,[118] and the Tukulti-Ninurta Epic.[119] Nevertheless, the fact that the decisive battle occurred at Sugaga, a day's journey south of Assur on the Tigris,[120] shows that the Babylonians were the invaders, and that Assyria had to defend the very heart of its kingdom. This is also true of another episode, preserved in a fragmentary Assyrian chronicle,[121] that mentions a Babylonian attack on Kilizu (modern Qasr Shamamok), 28 km west of Arbela and well within the Assyrian heartland.[122] While the location of the border is not precisely defined, the mention of the city of Ša-Sila suggests that Babylonia extended as far north as the Lower Zab,[123] hence that it had incorporated most of the

---

115. Grayson 1975: 159–160: Chronicle 21: i 18′–23′; 185: Assyrian Chronicle Fragment 1.

116. Grayson 1975: 175: Chronicle 22: iii 20–22; see also chapter 33 in this volume.

117. Grayson 1987: 119: A.0.74.1001; see also chapter 33 in this volume. This king's only other extent inscription (Grayson 1987: 118–119: A.0.74.1) celebrates his renovation of the city wall, without adding any relevant historical details.

118. Grayson 1987: 132: A.0.76.1: ll. 25–26.

119. Machinist 1978: 78: A ii 29–30.

120. Nashef 1982: 235; Jakob 2017a: 118–119.

121. Grayson 1975: 185: Assyrian Chronicle Fragment 1.

122. Bryce 2009: 385.

123. Bryce 2009: 635.

former kingdom of Arraphe once conquered by Aššur-uballiṭ I. These Babylonian attacks were still remembered a century later in the Tukulti-Ninurta Epic, where the breaching of the peace treaty established in the time of Aššur-uballiṭ epitomizes the depravity and treachery of Babylonian rulers, a literary and propagandistic motif that would endure well into the imperial age.[124]

There is little evidence of Enlil-nerari's military activities toward the west and the Hittite dominion. Although Hittite annals from the time of Suppiluliuma I and Mursili II, whose reigns were coeval with those of Assyrian kings from Aššur-uballiṭ I to Adad-nerari I,[125] regularly mention "the Assyrian enemy" and the ongoing possibility of war between the two powers, direct confrontations are not attested.[126] Even the long-assumed conquest of the Hittite vice-kingdom of Carchemish by Assyria in Mursili's ninth regnal year has proven to be but a modern construct.[127]

Enlil-nerari's son and successor Arik-den-ili is credited by his own son Adad-nerari I with having conquered Nigimhu and other lands (Turukku, Qutu) in the Zagros piedmont and the mountains to the east.[128] This is echoed by a fragmentary inscription with chronicle-like features of Arik-den-ili himself, which recounts his attack on the kingdom of Nigimhu, followed by retaliation against Assyria by its king Esini, and another Assyrian expedition during which Esini was besieged in his city of Arnuna and defeated.[129] Adad-nerari also mentions his father's expeditions toward Katmuhu in the north (in the northeastern part of the Tur Abdin range),[130] which are said to have received the support of tribal groups (the Ahlamû, Sutû, and Ya'uri).

---

124. Jakob 2017a: 119.

125. Giorgieri 2011: 187.

126. Giorgieri 2011: 179.

127. Miller 2010; see chapter 30 in this volume.

128. Bryce 2009: 506 (Nigimhu); 586 (Qutu); 721–722 (Turukku).

129. Grayson 1987: 126: A.0.75.8: ll. 9′–17′.

130. Cancik-Kirschbaum and Hess 2016: 77–80.

Despite the aggrandizing rhetoric of Assyrian propaganda, it is clear that these regions were not incorporated into Assyria at this point, and Arik-den-ili's reign might in fact have been a time of respite for Assyria's ambitions. Not only does Katmuhu still appear as a distant foreign land in documents from the time of Shalmaneser I,[131] but another section of Arik-den-ili's inscription mentions cities in the immediate vicinity of Nineveh (including Tarbiṣu, modern Sherif Khan, about 5 km to the northwest),[132] which could hint at rebellions within the Assur-Nineveh-Arbela triangle.

The situation seems to have been difficult along the southern border as well, with recurring fights against a Kassite king (probably Kurigalzu II) mentioned in a fragmentary Epic of Adad-nerari I.[133] Arik-den-ili's reputation may have suffered from his inability to contain his southern neighbor, if he was deliberately omitted from the (very biased) "history" of Assyro-Kassite relationships presented in the prologue of the Tukulti-Ninurta Epic to justify Tukulti-Ninurta's attack on Babylonia.[134]

32.5. Assyria's short-lived apex in the thirteenth century BC

If Assyria appears on the defensive at the end of the fourteenth century, the thirteenth century qualifies as a golden age preceding the imperial era of the first millennium, one often referred to by early Neo-Assyrian kings to justify military conquests as a return to a previous order. The three long reigns of Adad-nerari I (1305–1274 BC), Shalmaneser I (1273–1244 BC), and Tukulti-Ninurta I (1243–1207 BC) represent a period of political stability, territorial expansion, administrative cohesiveness, and economic development, even if the latter ended in chaos and the seeds of troubled times were already sprouting.

---

131. Llop 2015: 260.

132. Grayson 1987: 126–127: A.0.75.8: 18′–26′.

133. Weidner 1963: 113–115; Frazer 2013: 194–195; Llop 2015: 245.

134. Machinist 1978: 235, 241–242.

Excavations at sites located in the provinces conquered during the thirteenth century,[135] especially on the Lower Khabur (at Dur-Aššur-ketta-lešir, modern Tell Bderi,[136] and Dur-Katlimmu, modern Tell Sheikh Hamad),[137] offer a finer stratigraphy and better assessment of material assemblages than the early twentieth-century excavations at Assur, which yielded most of the extant early Middle Assyrian material. This includes a better ceramic chronology, beginning with the reigns of Shalmaneser I and Tukulti-Ninurta I.[138] Comparable ceramics have been recorded in a number of field surveys in various parts of the kingdom.[139] This evidence, in turn, can be combined with texts to offer an enhanced perspective on the Assyrian expansion and settlement patterns throughout the century.[140]

This is also a period in which the textual documentation becomes richer. Palace decrees are known for all three kings,[141] and royal inscriptions are more numerous and longer, incorporating narratives of the reign's events. A number of archives (dated primarily to Shalmaneser I and Tukulti-Ninurta I) were recovered at Assur, Kar-Tukulti-Ninurta, and the provinces. At Assur, official archives were produced by several institutions that catered to the royal court and/or the religious sanctuaries of the city. Administrative letters and documents from the reigns of Shalmaneser I and his son were recovered in a discarded archive from the Aššur temple courtyard[142] and in a series of buildings along the western city wall, initially identified as attack gates but which were more likely

---

135. Tenu 2009: 94–147; H. Kühne 2013: 474–479.

136. Cancik-Kirschbaum and Hess 2016: 46.

137. Cancik-Kirschbaum and Hess 2016: 46–48.

138. Pfälzner 1995: 235–236; Tenu 2009: 45–47.

139. Düring 2020: 64–91.

140. Tenu 2009; Brown 2014; Düring 2020: 64–94.

141. Roth 1997: 198 (Adad-nerari I); 198–199 (Shalmaneser I); and 199–201 (Tukulti-Ninurta I).

142. Archive M 5, see Pedersén 1985: 53–56.

the royal magazines and silos (*karmū*).[143] Some thirteenth-century documents also form the earliest texts of archives which are better documented for later periods, such as the archive of the House of Offerings to the god Aššur,[144] that of the chief steward (*abarakku rabiʾu*)—an office responsible for provisioning the court with raw materials and for finished goods belonging to the palace—and related texts from the office of the chief feltmaker (*rāb sāpiʾe*).[145] From the reign of Tukulti-Ninurta I, official archives have also been recovered in his new, eponymous city, Kar-Tukulti-Ninurta (modern Tulul al-ʿAqar),[146] as well as in various provincial centers. From the core area comes the archive of Aššur-kašid and his son Sin-apla-eriš, who successively acted as governor (*ḫassiḫlu*) of Šibanibe (modern Tell Billa), and whose archive shows them acting both in a public and private capacity.[147] Archives from the governor of Mardaman were recently recovered at Bassetki and are currently being studied.[148] Small archives were also recovered in the Lower Zab region at Tell Basmusiyan (ancient name unknown)[149] and Atmannu (modern Tell Ali), a small administrative center where herding activities took place under Shalmaneser.[150] Finally, important administrative archives were recovered in the west, at Dur-Katlimmu (modern Tell Sheikh Hamad), the capital of the western part of the kingdom and seat of the grand vizier (*sukkallu rabiʾu*) Aššur-iddin;[151] in the former Mittani capital of

---

143. Archive M 8, see Pedersén 1985: 82–89; Llop 2005.

144. Archive M 4, see Pedersén 1985: 43–53; Postgate 2013: 89–146; Gauthier 2016.

145. Archive M 7, see Pedersén 1985: 68–81; Frahm 2002: 85; Postgate 2013: 147–176; Maul 2017: 91–93.

146. Pedersén 1998: 88–90.

147. Finkelstein 1953; Postgate 2013: 268–278.

148. Pfälzner and Qasim 2018.

149. Læssøe 1959. His proposal to identify the site with Alaia is dubious; see Tenu 2009: 171.

150. Ismail and Postgate 2008; Postgate 2013: 294–298.

151. Cancik-Kirschbaum 1996; Röllig 2008; H. Kühne 2013: 474–476; Postgate 2013: 298–326; Salah 2014.

Waššukanni (modern Tell Fekheriye);[152] as well as in the governor's palace at Harbe (modern Tell Chuera).[153] Additionally, a handful of texts from the antiquities market can be linked to the city of Kulišhinaš (modern Tell Amuda). These include both private/legal[154] and official/administrative documents[155] from the last decade of Shalmaneser and the very first years of his son, possibly linked to a governor's archive.[156] A letter and some other cuneiform tablets were recovered at Kahat (modern Tell Barri).[157] Their dating is uncertain and their content rather generic,[158] but an inscribed stone bowl belonging to a cook (*kakardinnu*) attests to the presence there of a palace of Adad-nerari I.[159] The same can be deduced from an inscribed brick of Shalmaneser I at Tell al-Hamidiya (possibly ancient Taide).[160]

Outside of official buildings, archives have been found in the houses of several upper-class Assyrians, all engaged in public activities on behalf of the king in one way or another. It is therefore not uncommon to find texts related to "public" activities in what are predominantly "private" archives—even though the use of these two terms is divisive among specialists, and evidence suggests that, even if both activities were conceptually distinct, they were conducted from the same places and by the same individuals.[161] In the capital Assur, the archives of some of the most prominent Assyrians were recovered, such as the family of Meli-sah,

---

152. Güterbock 1958; Pedersén 1998: 96–98. Additional tablets from the local palace were discovered in 2009 and 2010; see Bartl and Bonatz 2013.

153. Jakob 2009.

154. Aynard and Durand 1980.

155. Machinist 1982.

156. Tenu 2009: 104–106.

157. Cancik-Kirschbaum and Hess 2016: 73.

158. Salvini 1998; 2004; 2005; 2008a; 2008b.

159. Salvini 1998: 147; 2008b: 78–81.

160. Eichler and Wäfler 1989–1990; Tenu 2009: 103–104.

161. Postgate 2010; 2013: 79–85.

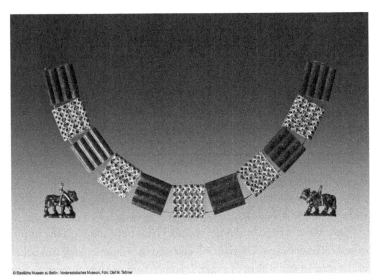

FIGURE 32.4. A gold and lapis lazuli necklace (Length: 27.5 cm), excavated in Assur as part of the burial goods of Grave 45, which is associated with the family of the vizier Babu-aha-iddina (second half of the thirteenth century BC). Vorderasiatisches Museum Berlin (accession number VA Ass 1008). © Staatliche Museen zu Berlin—Vorderasiatisches Museum, photograph by Olaf M. Teßmer.

governor of Nahur (possibly Tell Aylun)[162] in the Khabur triangle under Shalmaneser, and whose archives (rather, those of his son Urad-Šeru'a) were recovered in the family's house in the capital.[163] More prominent still was Babu-aha-iddina, who played an important role at court late in Shalmaneser's reign and early in Tukulti-Ninurta's reign, may have held the title of vizier (*sukkallu*), and whose house (including lavish burials assumed to be his and his wife's; see figure 32.4) was recovered less than 100 m from Meli-sah's.[164] Both archives primarily document the

162. Cancik-Kirschbaum and Hess 2016: 98–99; Ziegler and Langlois 2016: 243–245.

163. Archive M 10; see Pedersén 1985: 99–106; Postgate 2013: 237–259.

164. Archive M 11; see Pedersén 1985: 106–113; Postgate 2013: 201–236.

management of the magnates' households, although a handful of tablets appear to reflect their official activities as well.

Smaller archives include that of Uṣur-bel-šarra, who was promoted from the role of herdsman (*nāqidu*) to that of district governor (*bēl pāhete*) of Abilate, a city near Kalhu (modern Nimrud).[165] Another lot comprises the archive of Ṣilli-Aššur the coppersmith (*nappāhu ša erê*) and that of the millers (*alahhinū*) Atanah-ili and Hazi, both groups apparently working under the command of the palace.[166] Finally, one house contained the archives of Adad-zera-iqiša, a shepherd who managed flocks on his own account and on behalf of the palace.[167]

In the provinces, the family of Athi-nada and six generations of his descendants operated from Qaṭṭara (modern Tell al-Rimah) in the western Jezirah,[168] where they might have been settled even before the Assyrian conquest of Hanigalbat, in the late fourteenth–early thirteenth century BC. Here the family engaged in a mixture of business and financial activities, both for their own profit and on behalf of the royal administration.[169] At Tell Sabi Abyad (ancient name unknown) in the Balikh valley, excavators exposed a fortified farmstead (*dunnu*) that served as a seat of Assyrian administration, a garrison station, customs post, and private rural estate catering to the needs of three successive grand viziers: Aššur-iddin, Salmanu-mušabši, and Ili-pada (see table 32.1). The first two were contemporaries of Tukulti-Ninurta, while the last ruled over the western part of the kingdom under his three immediate successors. Thirty-five out of the 400 tablets date from the late thirteenth century, when the farmstead was managed by a steward named Mannu-ki-Adad on behalf of the first two owners.[170] Only a few of these,

165. Archive M 12; see Pedersén 1985: 113–117; Jakob 2003a: 111; Llop 2012a: 89.

166. Archive M 13; see Pedersén 1985: 118–120; Maul 2017: 93–98.

167. Archive M 14; see Pedersén 1985: 120–125.

168. Cancik-Kirschbaum and Hess 2016: 113–114.

169. Postgate 2002; 2013: 260–268.

170. Akkermans and Wiggermann 2015.

pertaining to agriculture[171] and pottery,[172] have been published. A small archive with Middle Assyrian features is said to have been recovered in fourteenth- to thirteenth-century layers at Tell Fray (possibly Yahariša, or Šaparu/Šipri),[173] but the only text published so far was discovered on the surface of the site and is in the local scribal tradition.[174] The city, whose ancient name is debated, was under Hittite control at least until the reign of Hattusili III (a contemporary of Shalmaneser I),[175] and it has been suggested that the archive could have belonged to Assyrian merchants living within a local community, in the fashion of the Old Assyrian *karum* in Kaneš, rather than a city under direct Assyrian control;[176] a final assessment must await the publication of the material. Finally, a private document with Middle Assyrian traits, tentatively dated to the thirteenth century, was discovered at el-Qitar, on the right bank of the Euphrates in northern Syria, but Assyrian occupation there is doubtful.[177]

32.5.1. The expansion of Assyria under Adad-nerari I (1305–1274 BC)

By the early thirteenth century BC, what had once been the powerful state of Mittani was but a rump state known as Hanigalbat. Extending from the Khabur triangle to the bend of the Euphrates, Hanigalbat was situated politically between two powerful neighbors: the Hittites to the north and west, and the Assyrians to the south and east. The situation preceding the Assyrian intervention is unclear. In his inscriptions, Adad-nerari I (figure 32.5) justified his attack on Hanigalbat by depicting

---

171. Wiggermann 2000.

172. Wiggermann 2008.

173. Bounni 1988.

174. Wilhelm 2018.

175. Giorgieri 2011: 177. The traditionally assumed synchronism between Hattusili III and Adad-nerari I is dubious.

176. Tenu 2009: 208–209.

177. Snell 1983–84; Llop 2012b: 213; McClellan 2019.

FIGURE 32.5. Sickle sword (length: 54.3 cm) inscribed with the name of
Adad-nerari I of Assyria (1305–1274 BC), with an engraving of a resting ante-
lope. Metropolitan Museum of Art, New York (accession number 11.166.1).
Photograph courtesy Metropolitan Museum of Art. CC0 1.0 Universal (CC0
1.0) Public Domain Dedication.

its king Šattuara as a rebellious vassal,[178] but at the same time the kingdom was still considered one of the "great powers" by the Hittites.[179]
Archaeological evidence suggests that many of the kingdom's cities had
fallen into disrepair or had been abandoned even prior to the Assyrian
attack,[180] which could suggest that its weakness made it an attractive
prey for Adad-nerari's ambitions. Based on the extant eponyms from his

178. Grayson 1987: 135–158: A.0.76.3–6; 22.

179. Beckman 1999: 87–93, no. 13.

180. Kertai 2008–09: 29.

reign, the conquest of Hanigalbat occurred at least seven years before Adad-nerari's death.[181]

Adad-nerari reinstalled Šattuara on the throne of Hanigalbat after having captured him and brought him to Assur, which suggests that he had been independent until then, and that the conquest reduced him to an Assyrian vassal. The situation displeased Šattuara's son Wasašatta, who rebelled and sought Hittite help—in vain. This prompted a military campaign during which Adad-nerari's armies conquered the main cities of the kingdom, including the two royal cities of Taide and Waššukanni in the Khabur triangle, localities in the Kašiyari mountains (Tur Abdin) to the north, Harran[182] and Irride (possibly Tell Hajeb)[183] in the Balikh valley, all the way to the Euphrates.[184] Booty brought back to Assur included cedar pillars plundered in Nahur[185] and alabaster vases from Taide and Irride.[186] This time, the rebellion was perceived by the Assyrians as a breach of the oath formerly sworn to the king and, more importantly, to the god Aššur, and the punishment was far more drastic: even if Wasašatta himself escaped, the king's family was deported to Assur, corvée work duties were imposed on former Hanigalbatian subjects, and Irride and its dependent settlements were destroyed and sown with salty plants.[187] There are indications, however, that Adad-nerari had plans to rebuild Taide,[188] with an administrative center (palace),[189] but it is doubtful that this ever happened since the inscriptions commemorating the deed were recovered at Assur, not in Taide, where

---

181. Alexandrov 2014: 53 n. 14.

182. Cancik-Kirschbaum and Hess 2016: 59–60.

183. Cancik-Kirschbaum and Hess 2016: 70–71.

184. Grayson 1987: 136; A.0.76.3: ll. 15–30; Harrak 1987: 161–185; Koliński 2015: 10.

185. Grayson 1987: 159–160: A.0.76.25.

186. Grayson 1987: 160–161: A.0.76.26.

187. Grayson 1987: 13–137: A.0.76.3: ll. 31–51.

188. Grayson 1987: 137: A.0.76.4: ll. 37–41.

189. Grayson 1987: 158: A.0.76.22: ll. 55–60.

they should have been used as foundation deposits; in fact, one text even had the name of the building left blank, to be completed later.[190] In any case, there is a thirteenth-century Middle Assyrian occupation at Tell al-Hamidiya, if this indeed was the site of the former Mitanni capital.[191]

Conspicuously absent from Adad-nerari's inscriptions are mentions of any campaign toward the Lower Khabur and Euphrates valley, which were then controlled by small, independent kingdoms. One of these was the kingdom of Hana, whose kings had been vassals of Mittani in the fifteenth century BC. Since then, they had gained their independence and ceased referring to Mitanni in their internal documents. Unfortunately, the chronology of this kingdom is still extremely unclear, with divergent reconstructions and dating of its kings' reigns.[192] The territory of the kingdom of Hana roughly corresponded to that of the eighteenth-century kingdom of Mari (see chapter 15 in volume 2), with its heartland on the Middle Euphrates around Terqa (modern Tell Ashara), where most Hanaean documents have been recovered and which might have been the capital.[193] It also extended over the Lower Khabur, reaching at some point in the fourteenth century as far upstream as Ṭabete (modern Tell Ṭaban), where a document dated by Ahuni, king of Hana, was recovered.[194] This area might have been perceived as their "traditional" domain, since it covered the territory of the antecedent kingdom that had flourished in the area after Hammurabi's destruction of Mari in 1761 BC.[195] By the mid- to late fourteenth century, however, the area had been lost and another kingdom, with Ṭabete as its capital, took over the name "Land of Mari" (*māt Māri*)." Although the third known king, Adad-bel-gabbe I, bore a very "Assyrian" name, both his father and grandfather, who ruled before him, bore Hurrian names. While the earlier kings may have used

---

190. Grayson 1987: 137–138: A.0.76.4: l. 38.

191. Pfälzner 1995: 187; Tenu 2009: 103–104.

192. Rouault 2004; S. Yamada 2011; Podany 2014; Mladjov 2019.

193. Charpin 2002.

194. S. Yamada 2011.

195. Charpin 2002: 68.

Hurrian onomastics as an homage to the kings of Mittani/Hanigalbat (or simply identified as Hurrians), the adoption of an Assyrian throne-name by Adad-bel-gabbe clearly reflected the recognition, by the local ruler, of his new Assyrian sovereign. Whereas Adad-bel-gabbe's reign is not securely dated, his (direct?) successor Aššur-ketta-lešir I is attested for over four decades, from the eighth year of Shalmaneser I (eponym year of Aššur-nadin-šume = 1256 BC) to the middle of Tukulti-Ninurta I's reign (eponym year of Ber-išmanni, ca. 1215–1210 BC).[196] This shows that the Lower Khabur became an Assyrian dominion under Adad-nerari, not under Shalmaneser as is commonly assumed.[197] The alliance was secured by inter-dynastic marriages with the royal house of Assur, at least for his two successors, Aššur-ketta-lešir I and Adad-bel-gabbe II.[198]

This chronology is confirmed by the foundation of the provincial administrative center (Building P) at Dur-Katlimmu (modern Tell Sheikh Hamad). This city (once a fortress of the kingdom of Hana called Dur-Iggid-Lim) was conquered and renamed by the Assyrians, who turned it into the capital of their western dominion. The earliest text there dates from the eponym year of Šerriya, corresponding to the third year of Shalmaneser I (1271 BC),[199] but it was discovered in the second occupation phase of the building. The previous phase, when Building P was erected, was destroyed by an earthquake early in the reign of Shalmaneser. The existence of a reduced kingdom of Hana under Shalmaneser is still a matter of debate,[200] but it is most probable that, unlike his northern neighbor in Ṭabete, the local king did not submit voluntarily and his kingdom was conquered by force and integrated into Assyria. From the start, then, Assyria exercised both direct and indirect rule in its western dominion.

---

196. Shibata 2011a; 2011b.

197. H. Kühne 2016.

198. Shibata 2015.

199. H. Kühne 2016: 194–195 (re-dated after Salah 2014).

200. H. Kühne 2018; *contra* S. Yamada 2011; Podany 2014.

Troubles were also brewing along the southern border. The *Synchronistic History*,[201] *Chronicle P*,[202] and Adad-nerari's inscriptions[203] recall the war that brought him into conflict with Nazi-Maruttaš of Babylon (see chapter 33 in this volume). Mentions of the strategic cities of Lubdu (in the former kingdom of Arraphe)[204] and Rapiqu (modern Tell Anbar, on the Euphrates)[205] may suggest that Assyria instigated the war with the aim of establishing hegemony over Mesopotamia as a whole,[206] but it could also simply be a metonymic description of Babylonia by the easternmost and westernmost strongholds of its northern border. In any case, the decisive battle occurred close to the Assyrian homeland,[207] and the new border between Assyria and Babylonia was established some 75 km south of the Lower Zab and the border established under Enlil-nerari,[208] up to the mountains of Lullumu (near modern Sulaymaniyah, in Iraqi Kurdistan).[209] While this can be seen as an Assyrian victory, the Babylonian domain still extended very close to the heart of Assyria. Forays further to the east in the Zagros mountains may be alluded to in Adad-nerari's claim of having defeated, in addition to the Kassites and "Šubareans" (i.e., Hanigalbateans),[210] the people of Qutu (the region south of Lake Urmia, in present-day Iran)[211] and Lullumu,[212] but details

201. Grayson 1975: 160–161: Chronicle 21: i 24ʹ–31ʹ.

202. Grayson 1975: 175: Chronicle 22: iii 23–24.

203. Grayson 1987: 156–157: A.0.76.21: ll. 5ʹ–14ʹ.

204. Bryce 2009: 423.

205. Bryce 2009: 590–591.

206. Jakob 2017a: 120–121.

207. The site of the decisive battle has been altered by the text's transmission but it is probably to be located at Kar-Ištar on the Tigris; see Grayson 1975: 160.

208. Jakob 2011: 193.

209. Bryce 2009: 424–425.

210. Cancik-Kirschbaum and Hess 2016: 138.

211. Bryce 2009: 586.

212. Grayson 1987: 131: A.0.76.1: ll. 3–4.

remain unknown. It has been suggested that two very fragmentary texts recovered in a secondary context at Assur may represent a treaty between Adad-nerari and Nazi-Maruttaš's successor, Kadašman-Turgu,[213] but this remains highly speculative.

Assyria's renewed expansionism did not go unnoticed in Hattusa, but for a while the two courts seem to have maintained diplomatic relations.[214] However, chronological imprecisions and the fact that letters more often than not name kings only by their title makes it difficult to link events to any given reign. Most scholars think that Adad-nerari sought recognition from the Hittite king (either Muwatalli or Urhi-Teššub) after his victory over Wasašatta, claiming for himself the status of "great king" and "brother" formerly held by Mittani within the "Great Powers' club," but that the Hittite king refused to acknowledge brotherhood, even if he had to acknowledge his opponent's power.[215] However, like most of the diplomatic letters found in Hattusa, the document on which this narrative is based is badly preserved,[216] represents either a model or a summary of an actual letter (it is written in Hittite, while a proper letter to Assyria would have been written in Akkadian), may never have been sent, or at least not in this form, and may not even belong to the corpus of Assyro-Hittite correspondence or to the time of Adad-nerari (the mention of Wasašatta in a broken context, especially, is doubtful).[217] This text might actually be an example of a letter between the Hittite great king and one of his vassals—possibly Šattuara II of Mittani, dating either to the very end of Adad-nerari's reign, or the beginning of the reign of his son and successor, Shalmaneser.[218]

---

213. Frahm 2009: 127–128, no. 65 (VAT 14400 and VAT 15420); both texts are from the discarded archive M5; see Pedersén 1985: 53–56.

214. Hagenbuchner 1989; Mora and Giorgieri 2004.

215. Bryce 2005: 258–259; Kertai 2008–2009: 28–29; Tenu 2017: 548; see also chapter 29 in this volume.

216. Mora and Giorgieri 2004: 184–197, no. 20 (CTH 171).

217. Mora and Giorgieri 2004: 184–187; Giorgieri 2011: 180.

218. Faist 2008: 424.

32.5.2. The consolidation of Assyrian control under Shalmaneser I (1273–1244 BC)

Shalmaneser I was a contemporary of both Hattusili III and Tudhaliya IV of Hatti, Šattuara II of Hanigalbat and Kadašman-Enlil II of Babylon.[219] According to his own inscriptions, his military activities started in his first regnal year with a campaign against the land of Uruatri, in the region of Lake Van.[220] Whereas, in the Iron Age, this name designated Assyria's northern archenemy (Urartu), at this point the region was divided into small, independent kingdoms, which Shalmaneser paints as rebels. More probably, though, the area was outside of Assyrian control and the raid was aimed at acquiring plunder and tribute, the "rebellious" nature of the local rulers being a thinly veiled justification for Assyrian aggression.[221]

Shalmaneser's main military accomplishment was the final annexation of Mittani into Assyria, which occurred no later than his seventh year (1266 BC).[222] The event is commemorated in Shalmaneser's inscriptions, which state that Šattuara had rebelled against him, seeking support from the Hittites and the Ahlamû tribal groups, but that the Assyrian was victorious (even if he could not capture his enemy, who managed to flee after having been "chased at arrow-point until sunset") and deported some 14,400 Hanigalbateans to Assyria.[223]

It is usually assumed that, following Adad-nerari's victory over Hanigalbat, the Assyrians maintained it as a vassal state, with Wasašatta's son Šattuara II at its head, and that he remained faithful until rebelling early in the reign of Shalmaneser I.[224] However, Assyrian sources are silent on that kingdom until Shalmaneser's (re)conquest, and Hittite sources may point to a more complex scenario. One badly broken letter

219. Giorgieri 2011: 188.

220. Bryce 2009: 747.

221. Tenu 2017: 550–551.

222. Alexandrov 2014: 65.

223. Grayson 1987: 183–184: A.0.77.1: ll. 56–80; see chapter 29 in this volume.

224. Koliński 2015: 10.

with Assyrian features,[225] found in Hattusa and addressed to dignitaries at the Hittite court, recalls Adad-nerari's conquest of Hanigalbat and suggests that, afterward, a "Subarean king" (i.e., of Hurrian origin) allied to the Hittites had regained control of the country.[226] Later, that king rebelled against the Hittites, and the author of the letter suggests that the Hittites should want Hanigalbat destroyed. The situation has been interpreted in many different ways, but the most probable scenario is that this refers to the "king of Hanigalbat" residing in Šinamu (modern Pornak near Diyarbakır);[227] this ruler is known as the author of another letter to the Hittite king, in which he defends himself against accusations by two other Hittite vassals (the kings of Aleppo and Išuwe) that he was now favoring Assyria, to which he replies that he is Assyria's enemy, as befits a Hittite vassal.[228] This letter and its protagonists have also been dated to different periods in the thirteenth century,[229] but the most plausible is the period of Hanigalbat's independence prior to Shalmaneser's conquest of Šattuara's kingdom. The unnamed vassal is also probably mentioned in a letter from a Hittite king to his Assyrian counterpart.[230] Traditionally assigned to the royal correspondence between Hattusili III and Adad-nerari I, it may instead date to the early days of Tudhaliya IV and Shalmaneser I.[231] The letter mentions raids on Hittite territories in Upper Syria launched from the city of Turira (somewhere to the east and/or north of Carchemish).[232] From

225. Mora and Giorgieri 2004: 76–84, no. 2 (CTH 208.1). In spite of its "Assyrian" (rather: Upper Mesopotamian) features, it seems hardly plausible that this letter came from Assyria proper, given that its author recognizes Hittite sovereignty, which Assyria never did.

226. Alexandrov 2014: 67–68.

227. Bryce 2009: 643; Cancik-Kirschbaum and Hess 2016: 133–134.

228. Hagenbuchner 1989: 313–315, no. 213 (CTH 179.1).

229. Alexandrov 2014: 56–65; Bilgin 2018: 47; see chapter 29 in this volume.

230. Mora and Giorgieri 2004: 57–75, no. 1 (CTH 173).

231. Mora and Giorgieri 2004: 58–60.

232. Bryce 2009: 720.

the Hittite perspective, the Assyrians were the ones who should settle the problem.

It thus seems that an otherwise poorly attested king of Hurrian origin took over Hanigalbat as a Hittite vassal, then turned to Assyria before being replaced by a member of the dynasty of Wasašatta, surely at the instigation of the Hittites, which finally triggered the Assyrian invasion and the final demise of Hanigalbat as an independent entity.[233] These complex games of influence between Hittites and Assyrians explain why the land Shalmaneser claims to have conquered is an almost exact duplicate of the one Adad-nerari had claimed after his war against Wasašatta, which has led some scholars to doubt the veracity of the claim.[234] The most probable scenario is that Šattuara had received the entire territory once held by his father, and that Shalmaneser's conquest brought it in its entirety under Assyrian control.[235]

As was the case in Adad-nerari's time, relations with Hatti ebbed and flowed, characterized both by attempts at diplomacy (primarily on the Hittite side) and general defiance. Hattusili III sought Assyrian support after his controversial accession to the throne, only to be rejected in a less than friendly way: the Assyrian king refused to send the traditional gifts as acknowledgment of his accession and called him "the substitute for a great king" (*pūhšu ša šarri rabî*). The snub, which Rameses II reminded his newfound Hittite ally of with apparent delight,[236] is sometimes attributed to Adad-nerari,[237] but the synchronism between the two kings is doubtful,[238] and Shalmaneser is a better candidate.[239] Later, Tudhaliya IV would remind Tukulti-Ninurta that their fathers did not

---

233. Alexandrov 2014: 63–70.

234. Heinhold-Krahmer 1988: 80.

235. Faist 2008: 420.

236. Edel 1994: I 25, no. A 4 (CTH 216).

237. E.g., Bryce 2995: 276.

238. Giorgieri 2011: 177.

239. Edel 1994: II 41; Jakob 2017a: 121.

write to one another.[240] Having succeeded Hattusili, Tudhaliya IV tried to develop better relations with Shalmaneser, calling him a great king and a brother—only to complain that the Assyrian had failed to send him the customary greetings upon his accession to the throne.[241] He also mentions a former "controversy" between them, and dwells extensively on Shalmaneser's unfriendly behavior and military operations toward the west, especially in the area of Melid (modern Arslantepe). Even so, the two superpowers appear to have tried to avoid direct confrontation, with the Assyrian king asking for a Hittite envoy to inspect the situation.[242] The Hittites, however, did not trust him, as is reflected in an oracular query regarding his entry into the city.[243] Shalmaneser's aggression against Hittite dominions even extended west of the Euphrates, with a raid against Amurru recorded in 1241 BC (eponym year of Ekaltayu).[244]

Shalmaneser invested massively in (re)building programs, documented at great length in his inscriptions. Most concern religious buildings at Assur: the temple of the god Aššur, which had been destroyed by fire;[245] the stepped temple tower (ziqqurat);[246] the temples of the Assyrian[247] and Ninevite[248] Ištar; and the shrines of Šeru'a (Aššur's consort) and Dagan.[249] Like his father before him, Shalmaneser renovated

---

240. Mora and Giorgieri 2004: 159–167, no. 17.1 (CTH 178).

241. Hagenbuchner 1989: 327–328, no. 223; Mora and Giorgieri 2004: 159–167, no. 18 (CTH 177/2).

242. Hagenbuchner 1989: 242–243, no. 188; Mora and Giorgieri 2004: 87–98, no. 4 (CTH 187).

243. CTH 577: iii 12. Cancik-Kirschbaum 2009: 216–217; Giorgieri 2011: 175; De Martino 2012: 376.

244. Postgate 1988; Jakob 2017a: 122.

245. Grayson 1987: 180–194: A.0.77.1–5; 209–211: A.0.77.20–22.

246. Grayson 1987: 204–205: A.0.77.16; 211–212: A.0.77.23; Tenu 2009: 61–62; Düring 2020: 48–52.

247. Grayson 1987: 194–196: A.0.77.6; Tenu 2009: 62–64; Düring 2020: 48–52.

248. Grayson 1987: 196: A.0.77.7.

249. Grayson 1987: 197: A.0.77.8.

the royal palace that dated back to Aššur-nadin-ahhe who had, in turn, built it upon the ruins of the one erected by Samsi-Addu.[250] Shalmaneser also had a palace built for his son, the crown-prince Tukulti-Ninurta,[251] and renovated an older palace with unclear functions,[252] possibly related to the role of the king as high priest of Aššur.[253]

Shalmaneser also provided the impetus for the rise of Nineveh, a prestigious and ancient cultic center of Ištar, to become the second most important city in the kingdom.[254] Not only did he rebuild the goddess's temple and *ziqqurat*, which had been destroyed by the previously mentioned earthquake (section 32.5.1),[255] but he also erected the first Assyrian royal palace in the city.[256] Finally, Shalmaneser erected the temple of Salmanu at Dur-Katlimmu, the primary cult center of this god to whom he was particularly devoted.[257]

The integration of Hanigalbat into Assyria led to the systematic organization of the kingdom into a provincial system that would become the "backbone of [its] administrative organisation."[258] The creation of this system is often attributed to Aššur-uballiṭ I,[259] due to the already mentioned trope of seeing this king as the "founder" of the Middle Assyrian state and all that would become, over the years, its distinctive traits. However, the terminology used to describe "provinces" (*pāhutu*)

250. "Old Palace": Grayson 1987: 199–200: A.0.77.10–11; 215–216: A.0.77.28; Preusser 1955: 6–27; Pedde and Lundholm 2008; Tenu 2009: 66–68; Düring 2020: 48–52.

251. Grayson 1987: 201: A.0.77.12; Preusser 1955: Tenu 2009: 62–64.

252. "Palace of the Priest-King": Preusser 1955: 28–29; Tenu 2009: 68–69; Düring 2020: 48–52.

253. Jakob 2017b: 144–145.

254. Tenu 2004.

255. Grayson 1987: 205–209: A.0.77.17–19; 212–213: A.0.77.24; 216–217: A.0.77.29.

256. Grayson 1987: 217: A.0.77.30; Grayson 1991: 57–59: A.0.87.12.

257. Radner 1998; H. Kühne 2013.

258. Faist 2010: 18.

259. E.g., Cancik-Kirschbaum 1996; 2014; Jakob 2003a; Faist 2010.

or "districts" (*halṣu*) and their officials-in-charge (the *bēl pāhete* and *halṣuhlu/hassihlu*, respectively, to which would be added the "prefect," *šaknu*)[260] does not appear in texts before the reign of Adad-nerari I and, more systematically, Shalmaneser I.[261]

The first provinces appeared in the heartland under Adad-nerari I, with Šibanibe (modern Tell Billa) being the earliest attested district (*halṣu*).[262] The entire Assur-Nineveh-Arbela triangle must have been organized into provinces at that time, even if other examples are only attested at a later date. The capital and its hinterland had a specific administrator, known as the "prefect of the land" (*šakin māte*), first attested under Adad-nerari or Shalmaneser with Aššur-šumu-lešir, whose family retained this office until the reign of Tiglath-pileser I.[263]

East and south of Assur, harvest reports from the cities of Tušran (modern Tell Mahuz), Sira, and Tarbašhe, as well as the archives from Tell Basmusiyan and Tell Ali, suggest direct Assyrian control of the Lower Zab area under Shalmaneser. While the area might have been integrated into the provincial system as early as Adad-nerari's reign,[264] the regional center Idu (modern Satu Qala) is only securely attested as a provincial seat under Shalmaneser's successor, Tukulti-Ninurta I.[265]

Thanks to the integration of Mittani into Assyria, the number of provinces drastically expanded in the west under Shalmaneser. New provincial centers include the former Mitannian royal cities Waššukanni and Taide, and cities along the Lower Khabur, including Dur-Katlimmu (modern Tell Sheikh Hamad).[266] There, provinces under direct Assyrian

---

260. Jakob 2003a: 111–147.

261. Llop 2011; 2012a.

262. Jakob 2003a: 141; Llop 2012a: 102.

263. Llop 2012a: 88–89.

264. van Soldt et al. 2013.

265. Llop 2012a: 104–105; Pappi 2018.

266. Llop 2012a: 92.

rule coexisted with the vassal kingdom of Mari. The nearby city of Šadikanni (modern Tell Ajaja),[267] where a local dynasty is attested in the eleventh century, was the seat of a governor in the late thirteenth and twelfth centuries BC.[268]

Whether the Upper Tigris became integrated as a province at this point or functioned as a march (border zone) depends on whether one places the Mittanian royal city of Taide at Üçtepe or Tell al-Hamidiya. In any case, the northern frontier of Assyria was established along the Upper Tigris, with Šinamu and Taide as strongholds according to a later inscription by Ashurnasirpal II (883–859 BC),[269] and archaeological evidence of an Assyrian presence amidst the local population.[270]

Another innovation of Shalmaneser I was the creation of the office of grand vizier (*sukkallu rabi'u*). The first certain holder of this office was Qibi-Aššur, a grandson of Adad-nerari I and therefore a cousin of the king (see table 32.1).[271] The position appears to have been mostly hereditary. Qibi-Aššur was succeeded by his son Aššur-iddin (the main protagonist of the Dur-Katlimmu archive)[272] toward the end of Shalmaneser's reign, and received (presumably from his royal cousin) the site of Tell Sabi Abyad as his personal estate and as a stronghold on the western fringes of the Assyrian domain.[273] He in turn was succeeded by his son Ili-pada, a few years after the office had been held by one Salmanu-mušabši, whose filiation is obscure.[274] The fact that some northwestern provinces were collectively known as the province (*pāhutu*) of, respectively, Aššur-iddin

---

267. Cancik-Kirschbaum and Hess 2016: 128–129.

268. Cancik-Kirschbaum 2008a; 2014; *contra* H. Kühne 2018: 144.

269. Grayson 1991: 99–100: A.0.89.7: iii 14; Radner and Schachner 2001: 757–758.

270. Radner and Schachner 2001; D'Agostino 2015.

271. Cancik-Kirschbaum 1999; Jakob 2003a: 59; Radner 2015a: 41–44. Whether Qibi-Aššur's father Ibašši-ili held the title of grand vizier is still debated, but rather dubious.

272. Cancik-Kirschbaum 1996: 19–32; Jakob 2003a: 59–62.

273. Akkermans and Wiggermann 2015: 91–97, 117–118.

274. Jakob 2003a: 62–63.

in the reign of Tukulti-Ninurta and Ili-pada in that of Enlil-kudurri-uṣur,[275] attests to an unprecedented degree of personalization of power. The role of grand vizier appears to have grown out of that of vizier (*sukkallu*). Various holders of this office are known throughout the kingdom, starting with Babu-aha-iddina under Shalmaneser.[276] The office combined diplomatic, military, civil, and judicial functions,[277] and in the east seems to have been second only to the king. In the west, local viziers (possibly including Sin-mudammeq, the principal actor in the Harbe archive, whose seat was at Waššukanni)[278] were subordinated to the grand vizier,[279] who also held the title "King of Hanigalbat" (*šar māt Hanigalbat*), an obvious reference to the newly conquered kingdom. The meaning of this title is debated. It has been described as strictly religious, as a way to appease local populations, or even simply as an honorary title for its holder.[280] Others picture the situation in the west as somewhat comparable to that of Carchemish vis-à-vis Hatti,[281] or even as a dual kingdom split between east and west.[282] In fact, kingship over Hanigalbat mirrors—albeit at a much higher level—the situation

275. Llop 2012a: 96; Cancik-Kirschbaum 2014: 298; Cancik-Kirschbaum and Hess 2016: 106. The last two references attribute the "provinces (*pāhātu*) of Ibašši-ili" to the father of Qibi-Aššur and putative grand vizier in the early days of Shalmaneser. This, however, must be rejected, as the list of offerings (Freydank and Feller 2005: no. 21) that mentions them dates from the time of Ninurta-apil-Ekur and refers to a much later homonym, also attested as governor of Kilizu. Similar cases are known under Tiglath-pileser I, with the provinces of Salmanu-ašared and Šuzub-Adad (Gauthier 2016: 159).

276. Jakob 2003a: 55–59; 2017b: 147.

277. Lafont 2003: 523; Jakob 2003a: 59–63; 2017b: 147.

278. Jakob 2003a: 60–61; 2009: 4.

279. As is most clearly expressed, in the early twelfth century, by grand vizier Ili-pada vis-à-vis Sin-mudammeq; see Wiggermann 2006; Jakob 2009: 6–7.

280. Fales 2011: 53.

281. Fales 2011.

282. Wiggermann 2000: 171.

already known for the kings of Mari: the holders of the title were kings at home, and officials of the Assyrian state.[283]

As with other vassals, the relationship between the kings of Assur and their distant cousins in Hanigalbat was strengthened through dynastic marriages, with Assyrian princesses married to both Aššur-iddin (Epirat- . . .) and his son Ili-pada (La-libbi, who lived in Assur with her children).[284] Unlike those on the periphery, vassal kingdoms in the western Jezirah were fully integrated within the Assyrian kingdom, and the central authority kept an eye on the affairs of the "king of Hanigalbat" through local governors and viziers. As in the east, the king's command (*abat šarre*) and decrees (*riksū*) had full legal authority, and emissaries known as "representatives of the king" (*qēpūtu ša šarre*) controlled activities of direct interest to the crown, such as agrarian production.[285] Similar representatives worked for wealthy Assyrians, e.g. the vizier Babu-aha-iddina, helping manage his estates scattered through the provinces while he was in office at Assur. These and the king's representatives supervised stocks and personnel, and acted as messengers for the local officials in charge.[286] The entire kingdom was the king's royal household, inside of which the households of vassal kings and courtiers were "nested," while having their own legal and practical autonomy.[287]

32.5.3. The golden age of the Middle Assyrian kingdom: Tukulti-Ninurta I (1243–1207 BC)

The reign of Tukulti-Ninurta I (1243–1207 BC; figure 32.6) is by far the best documented of that of all Middle Assyrian kings, and can be considered the apex of the kingdom's military, political, and cultural influence, even if it ended in disarray. The sequence of eponyms can be reconstructed

---

283. Reculeau 2016.

284. Shibata 2015: 239–240.

285. Röllig 2008.

286. Jakob 2003a: 282–286; 2017b: 146.

287. Reculeau 2016: 205–207.

FIGURE 32.6. Carved stone pedestal (58 × 57.5 × 23.5 cm) with a dedicatory inscription to the god Nusku, picturing Tukulti-Ninurta I of Assyria (1243–1207 BC) praying in front of a similar pedestal but bearing the attributes to the god Nabû: a clay tablet and writing stylus. Vorderasiatisches Museum Berlin (accession number VAT 8146). © Staatliche Museen zu Berlin—Vorderasiatisches Museum, photograph by Olaf M. Teßmer.

fairly securely until his fourteenth regnal year (1230 BC, eponym year of Uṣur-namkur-šarre), after which date it becomes hotly debated.[288]

The early days of Tukulti-Ninurta's reign are documented by Hittite documents recording, on a single tablet, three letters to Assyria: one to the young king himself; one to the highest-ranking official in Assur, the vizier Babu-aha-iddina; and one to (an) unidentified Assyrian official(s).[289] Assyrian envoys to the Hittite court had broken the news of Shalmaneser's death and Tukulti-Ninurta's accession to the throne, stressing the young king's desire to gain fame through military prowess. In his letter to the vizier, Tudhaliya IV assumes the senior role of guide and counselor for his novice Assyrian counterpart, but he also warns him against antagonizing too strong an enemy—meaning, rather clearly, Hatti itself. He was concerned about Assyrian plans to conquer the land of Pap(an)hu, southwest of Lake Van on the Upper Tigris,[290] which the Hittites considered as within their own sphere of influence.

Tudhaliya's fears were justified, and Tukulti-Ninurta's own inscriptions recall a vast (series of) campaign(s) in the mountainous regions to the north and east of Assyria in the first years of his reign. The initial target was the land of the Qutu to the east, near Lake Urmia,[291] the local kings of which were constantly rebelling against Assyrian attempts at overlordship since the days of Arik-den-ili. Shalmaneser I had faced one such revolt and, in spite of his boasting of having deported its people and subdued the land,[292] his son had to fight again in the region in the very year of his accession.[293] On his way there, Tukulti-Ninurta captured

---

288. Saporetti 1969a; Freydank 1992; 2016; Bloch 2010c; Jakob 2013; Llop 2013; Salah 2014: 58–62.

289. Beckman 1999: 149–150, no. 24C; Mora and Giorgieri 2004: 159–174, no. 17 (CTH 178).

290. Bryce 2009: 526; Cancik-Kirschbaum and Hess 2016: 107–108.

291. Bryce 2009: 586.

292. Grayson 1987: 185: A.0.77.1: ll. 88–106; 205–207: A.0.77.17–18.

293. Grayson 1987: 234–235: A.0.78.1: ii 14–iii–20 (and *passim* in this king's royal title); Bloch and Peri 2016–17.

the borderlands of (U)qumanu (to the north and east of the Alqosh plain),[294] whose king was seized but returned to his throne as an Assyrian vassal, as well as the otherwise poorly attested Šarnida,[295] and Mehru,[296] where he cut timber with the help of defeated Qutean troops.

Another early target was the region of Katmuhu in the northeastern parts of the Kašiyari mountains (modern Tur Abdin), with which a peace treaty had existed at least since the reign of Shalmaneser I, but which was annexed and turned into a province when it became hostile.[297] Further expeditions targeted Šubar(t)u (the Hurrian-speaking kingdoms of the region),[298] which had rebelled against Shalmaneser, and reached as far as Alzi. In his early inscriptions, the king depicts his zone of control as extending from the area southeast of the Lower Zab and into the Zagros (Lullumu and Qutu), to the borders of Nairi around Lake Van in the north,[299] and to the Euphrates in the west.[300] At this point, Nairi was clearly beyond Assyria's reach, and the defeated king of Alzi even managed to find refuge there, but in later inscriptions Tukulti-Ninurta claims to have received tribute from "the forty kings of Nairi."[301] Although these mountainous regions were not incorporated into Assyria, their kings seem to have at least for a while recognized Tukulti-Ninurta's suzerainty, paying tribute and sending royal hostages to the Assyrian court.[302]

---

294. Bryce 2009: 584–585.

295. Bryce 2009: 635.

296. Bryce 2009: 466–467.

297. Grayson 1987: 235–236: A.0.78.1: iii 21–29; Cancik-Kirschbaum and Hess 2016: 77–80.

298. Cancik-Kirschbaum and Hess 2016: 135–138.

299. Bryce 2009: 495–496.

300. Grayson 1987: 236–237: A.0.78.1: iv 24–36 (and *passim*). For the metaphorical use of Makkan in Assyrian inscriptions as a designation for the Egyptian possessions in Western Syria, see Heimpel 1990: 196.

301. Grayson 1987: 244: A.0.78.5: ll. 38–47 (and *passim*).

302. Grayson 1987: 236: A.0.78.1: iii 30–iv 23; Llop 2015: 250–253.

As is obvious from the tone of Tudhaliya's letter, Tukulti-Ninurta's activity in Anatolia displeased the Hittites, but the issue of direct confrontation in the early years of his reign is hotly debated. Two late inscriptions mention that he campaigned "across the Euphrates" and deported some 28,800 "Hittites" (i.e., subjects from the vassal kingdoms of Hatti in northwestern Syria),[303] but no specific kingdom is named. This feat is entirely absent from his early inscriptions (the ones supposedly contemporaneous with the campaign), and no Hittite deportees are ever mentioned in Assyrian administrative records from the period, which has led some scholars to posit that this victory was a fabrication concocted by doubling the number of deportees that Shalmaneser claimed to have taken from Hanigalbat.[304]

Assyrian control of the Middle Euphrates in this period is debated.[305] Most archaeological evidence of Assyrian presence in the Euphrates bend dates to the late twelfth–early eleventh century BC,[306] but some thirteenth-century ceramics were found at the small fortress of Tell Qabr Abu al-Atiq, on the eastern bank of the Khanuqa gorge,[307] and more controversially, perhaps at Tell Shiukh Fawqani (ancient Marina),[308] upstream toward the Syrian-Turkish border.[309] Texts (but not archaeological evidence) attest to Assyrian control of Tuttul (modern Tell Biʿa) at the Balikh-Euphrates junction,[310] and possibly of the

303. Grayson 1987: 272: A.0.78.23: ll. 27–30; 275: A.0.78.23: ll. 23–25; Deller et al. 1994: 464–465 (IM 76787: ll. 24–26); Talon 2005: 126: ll. 24–26.

304. Galter 1988; Giorgieri 2011: 182; Llop 2015: 255; *contra* M. Yamada 2011: 203; Postgate 2013: 17.

305. Harrak 1987; Tenu 2009: 247–249; Fales 2011; Montero Fenollós 2015: 15–24; *contra* Cancik-Kirschbaum 1996; 2009; Pfälzner 1997: 340: Llop 2012b; H. Kühne 2013.

306. Tenu 2009: 182–190; Montero Fenollós 2015: 15–24; Düring 2020: 80–83.

307. Montero Fenollós 2015.

308. Cancik-Kirschbaum and Hess 2016: 92–93.

309. Capet 2005; Tenu 2009: 201–202; Montero Fenollòs 2015: 12; Düring 2020: 80.

310. Llop 2012b: 212; Cancik-Kirschbaum and Hess 2016: 150.

west bank of the Euphrates in what had been the kingdom of Hana, if the Terqa where the Assyrians harvested grain is the one located at Tell Ashara.[311] This could, however, be a homonym in the Balikh area.[312] The former identification would be reinforced if Duara, where the Assyrian administration of Dur-Katlimmu held land, is to be identified with what later became Dura Europos (modern Qal'at es-Salihiye)—but this, too, remains hypothetical.[313]

Hittites and Assyrians clashed in the region of present-day Urfa and Diyarbakır at Nihriya (perhaps Kazane Höyük),[314] but chronological uncertainties plague historical reconstructions: the episode has been attributed alternately to the end of Shalmaneser's rule,[315] to the early years of Tukulti-Ninurta, in conjunction with his campaigns across the Tur Abdin,[316] or even later, at the time of his Babylonian conquests.[317] The second option is the most plausible, and is consistent with the mention of Assyrian troops at Nihriya in the second year of Tukulti-Ninurta (1242 BC, eponym year of Qibi-Aššur).[318] The Assyrians were victorious. Not only did Tukulti-Ninurta boast of his victory to Ibiranu of Ugarit (Hatti's main vassal in the northern Levant),[319] but many years later Tudhaliya IV still scolded his vassal Ehli-šarri (possibly the king of

---

311. Cancik-Kirschbaum 1996: 94–196, no. 2: ll. 25–26; DeZ 2508 (unpublished).

312. Cancik-Kirschbaum and Hess 2016: 146–147.

313. Frahm 2020.

314. Cancik-Kirschbaum and Hess 2016: 103.

315. Harrak 1987; Dietrich 2003; 2004; Jakob 2017a: 122.

316. Singer 1985 (with a problematic identification of Nihriya with Nairi); M. Yamada 2011: 202–203.

317. Bányai 2011.

318. Wiseman 1968: pl. lviii (TR 3005); Cancik-Kirschbaum 2008b: 213; M. Yamada 2011: 203.

319. Lackenbacher 1991: 90–100 (RSO 7 46); Dietrich 2003; 2004; M. Yamada 2011: 202–203.

Išuwe)[320] for having let him down (and perhaps even switched sides)[321] and having forced him to flee the battlefield.[322] The war caused the severing of diplomatic ties between Hatti and Assyria for three years, and Hittite vassal treaties like the one with Šaušga-muwa of Amurru explicitly forbade Hittite vassals in western Syria from trading with the Assyrian enemy.[323] This state of affairs did not last long, though, and a few years later the Hittite king sent back an Assyrian messenger he had held hostage, together with his own emissary, to restore peaceful relations.[324]

This event is recounted to his own king by a Babylonian envoy to Assur—a clear sign that, at this point, relations between Assyria and its southern neighbor were still amicable. In the following years, however, the situation descended into open warfare, as documented by the later chronicles, albeit in unclear ways that have led to much speculation.[325] The Babylonian wars are recorded in various administrative letters and documents, while contemporary and later traditions attest to the symbolic importance of Tukulti-Ninurta's conquest of Babylon, a feat that he celebrated not only in his inscriptions,[326] but also in a composition known as the *Tukulti-Ninurta Epic*.[327] This is by far the best preserved Middle Assyrian royal epic (roughly half of the original text is extant). Manuscripts were recovered both at Assur and Nineveh, where a Middle

---

320. *Contra* Singer 1985, this king is for chronological reasons to be distinguished from the homonymous king of Išuwe mentioned in CTH 179.1. He could have been one of his successors (M. Yamada 2011: 202, n. 23).

321. Dietrich 2004.

322. CTH 123.

323. Beckman 1999: 103–107, no. 17; Faist 2001: 218–224.

324. M. Yamada 2011 proposes that another Assyro-Hittite conflict erupted afterwards, in the late 1220s BC, but this remains hypothetical and predicated on synchronisms with the Hittite vassal state of Emar, on the Middle Euphrates, that are highly debated; see the alternate chronologies by Cohen and D'Alfonso 2008; Démare-Lafont and Fleming 2015.

325. S. Yamada 2003.

326. Grayson 1987: 244–245: A.0.78.5: ll. 23–47 (and *passim* in later inscriptions).

327. Machinist 1978.

Assyrian manuscript was still preserved in the seventh century BC alongside Neo-Assyrian copies. The *Epic* is not as unique as was once thought. This celebratory genre is attested in Upper Mesopotamia at least since the Middle Bronze Age,[328] and fragments of an epic about Adad-nerari I's own victory over Babylon show that the *Epic* had antecedents in Assyria at least two generations earlier.[329] There also exist traces of a second epic of Tukulti-Ninurta, again dealing with the Babylonian conquest,[330] and it is quite possible that fragments of similar compositions for other kings still await identification.

While Assyrian inscriptions customarily depict enemies as treacherous and rebellious, the lack of any such indication in Tukulti-Ninurta's account of the episode is striking,[331] and has generally led to the conclusion that the Assyrian attack on Babylon was unprovoked, or even defensive. The *Tukulti-Ninurta Epic*, however, offers a more straightforward justification for the war. Its portrayal of the Babylonian king Kaštiliaš IV as treacherous, impious, and murderous situates Tukulti-Ninurta's enemy at the end of a long line of perfidious Kassite kings, dating back to the days of Enlil-nerari and Kurigalzu II, who kept breaching their sacred oaths. Therefore, the Assyrian conquest was but a form of divine judgment rendered by the god of justice himself, the sun god Šamaš, for what was perceived (from the Assyrian perspective) as the illegal occupation by Babylonians of territories in the eastern Tigris region that had once been Assyrian (if only briefly).[332]

There were two attacks on Babylon and the hostilities lasted over several years, but details remain obscure due to uncertainties in the order of eponyms for these crucial years and the difficulty of pinpointing events and actors in letters and documents that are often elusive. The same documents have been used to reconstruct widely divergent narratives

---

328. Guichard 2014.

329. Weidner 1963.

330. Jakob 2017c.

331. Grayson 1987: 244–245: A.0.78.5: ll. 48–69 (and *passim*).

332. Jakob 2017a: 123.

that cannot be reconciled, nor discussed in detail here.[333] The campaign probably started in the Diyala region east of the Tigris,[334] and a first victorious attack on Babylonia was launched in 1231 BC (eponym year of Etel-pi-Aššur); the main body of the Assyrian army returned home under the direction of the king's herald with significant booty and many deportees; nevertheless, the return trip proved difficult, and the Assyrian soldiers and their prisoners were starving by the time they reached Assyria.[335] Meanwhile, the king led the remainder of the army upstream the Euphrates, in a campaign against Suhu.[336] This could have been in response to an attack against Assyria's vassal the "Land of Mari" by the Babylonian "prefect" (*š/sakinnu*) of Suhu, as mentioned in a letter from Emar, but the dating of Emar documents is an especially thorny issue[337] and the reading of the relevant passage is debated.[338] The presence of deported Suheans at Harbe (modern Tell Chuera)[339] may relate to this event,[340] while that of Elamite bowmen and their families[341] might indicate that the Babylonians were supported by Elam—if the

333. Cancik-Kirschbaum 1996: 9–18; S. Yamada 2003; Bloch 2012; Llop 2010; Bányai 2011; Jakob 2013; 2017a: 122–126.

334. Jakob 2017a; see chapter 33 in this volume.

335. Freydank 1976: no. 1; Jakob 2013; 2017a: 124.

336. Llop 2010; Jakob 2013: 515–516; 2017a: 124.

337. Cohen and d'Alfonso 2008; Démare-Lafont and Fleming 2015.

338. Emar 263, with Durand and Marti 2005 for the reading "Land of Mari," and Bányai 2011, who sticks to the original reading Qaṭni, identified with Middle Assyrian Qaṭṭun in the vicinity of Dur-Katlimmu (possibly Tell Fadghami; Cancik-Kirschbaum and Hess 2016: 114–115). This letter is undated, and the correlation with the Babylonian war is only hypothetical. The suggestion that another document (Emar 536) relates to this episode must be abandoned, as it is contemporary with the king of Emar Yaṣi-Dagan, who ruled in the second half of the fourteenth century.

339. Cancik-Kirschbaum and Hess 2016: 57–58.

340. Jakob 2009: 94, no. 66 (undated).

341. Jakob 2009: 97–103, nos. 69–72 (the first text dated to Enlil-nadin-apli).

eponym Enlil-nadin-apli is to be placed before Aššur-bel-ilane and thus represents the year 1229 BC.[342]

At some point, the Babylonian king Kaštiliaš IV was seized by the Assyrians, but when this crucial event occurred remains debated. A capture of Kaštiliaš in the eponym year of Aššur-bel-ilane (perhaps 1228 BC)[343] would be consistent with several documents that attest to Assyrian control over Babylon in the following year (eponym year of Aššur-zera-iddina), with the mention of booty (including grain, carried upstream by boat),[344] Babylonian deportees in Assyria,[345] and the presence of Tukulti-Ninurta in the city, where he performed religious rites.[346] However, this could also have happened while the Babylonian king still held his last stronghold around Dur-Kurigalzu,[347] or upon the accession of his third successor Adad-šuma-iddina.[348] In any case, a dated royal inscription shows that, by the beginning of the eponym year of Ina-Aššur-šumi-aṣbat (perhaps 1226 BC) at the latest, Kaštiliaš IV had fallen into the hands of the Assyrian army.[349] Just a few months later, an unnamed "Kassite king" (šarru kašši'u), his wife, and their retinue toured the western provinces together with the Assyrian king and his court, with a documented stop at Dur-Katlimmu.[350] This must have been Kaštiliaš, now living in a

342. Salah 2014: 59 and 250; different in Jakob 2013: 518. Elam is known to have intervened at least twice to replace pro-Assyrian kings in Babylon, but the details depend on the dating of Kaštiliaš' capture; for the most widely accepted reconstruction of these events, see chapter 33 in this volume, and for an alternative scenario, see Jakob 2013; 2017a.

343. As suggested by Bányai 2011, who, however, assigns this eponym to the year 1229 BC.

344. Ebeling 1927: no. 106, dated to the first month of Aššur-zera-iddina.

345. Ebeling 1927: no. 103, dated to the fifth month of Aššur-zera-iddina.

346. Freydank and Feller 2007: no. 7.

347. Bloch 2010b: 47–50; see also chapter 33 in this volume.

348. Jakob 2013: 517–518.

349. Grayson 1987: 246–247: A.0.78.6.

350. Cancik-Kirschbaum 1996: 147–153, no. 10.

gilded cage in Assyria, where he seems to have been treated with honors in spite of the tone adopted by his captor in both his inscriptions and the *Tukulti-Ninurta Epic*. One or two years later,[351] Kaštiliaš even received the supreme honor of having the year named after him. Such treatment of a defeated king and his family is not unique, as the archives of Kar-Tukulti-Ninurta record the presence, as hostages or deportees, of the king of Bušše (in the western part of the Tur Abdin[352]) and his sons.[353]

Assyria's troubles with Babylonia were not over yet: that same year, the king scolded his grand vizier (*sukkallu rabi'u*) for his complacency toward Karduniaš, while the Assyrians began maneuvers aimed at occupying the Babylonians' eastern flank. They attacked Lubdu, a Babylonian possession south of the Lower Zab, in the former kingdom of Arraphe.[354] It is doubtful whether the Babylonians later reconquered the area, and five or six years later the region was securely in Assyrian hands.[355] Tukulti-Ninurta exacted terrible vengeance on Babylon and its inhabitants, razing the city's walls, slaughtering the population, plundering the main temple of the city (the Esagil), and bringing to Assyria the statue of its main god, Marduk. He is said to have ruled over the city for seven years,[356] but Tukulti-Ninurta's name is absent from later Babylonian king lists. Depending on the reconstruction of events one chooses, this period would either correspond to the reigns of the Babylonian kings

---

351. Eponym year of Kaštiliaš = 1225 BC (according to Jakob 2013) or 1224 BC (following Salah 2014: 60).

352. Cancik-Kirschbaum and Hess 2016: 37.

353. Llop 2015: 252–252.

354. Cancik-Kirschbaum 1996: 140–161, nos. 9–12; Jakob 2013: 519. Bloch 2010b and Bányai 2011 propose that the letter mentions a Babylonian attack against the city, rather than the other way around.

355. Freydank 1982: no. 17+, dated to the eponym year of Abi-ili son of Katiri (with Jakob 2013: 521); Grayson 1987: 273: A.0.78.23: l. 79, among a list of mostly obscure places in the eastern Tigris/Zagros area that Tukulti-Ninurta claims to rule.

356. Grayson 1975: 175–176: Chronicle 22: iv 1–13; 161: Chronicle 21: ii 1*–2; Walker 1982: 400: Chronicle 25: ll. 1–2.

Enlil-nadin-šumi and Adad-šuma-iddina, ruling as Assyrian vassals,[357] or to a period of personal rule that came after these kings.[358] In any case, Tukulti-Ninurta assumed traditional Babylonian titles like "king of Karduniaš," "king of Sippar and Babylon," "king of Sumer and Akkad," and "king of Dilmun and Meluhha,"[359] and presented himself as ruling (directly or indirectly) over an area that extended from the Middle Euphrates to the Zagros mountains,[360] and "from the Upper to the Lower Sea,"[361] that is, from Lake Van (the Mediterranean being out of reach) to the Persian Gulf.

Tukulti-Ninurta's conquest of Babylon resonated among the powers of the day. A series of letter-orders dated to the eponym year of Ninu'ayu[362] were issued by the grand vizier to stations located along the northern route across the Jezirah, in order to assure the provisioning of foreign ambassadors. Emissaries from (at least) Hatti, Sidon, and Amurru visited Assur (*Āl-libbi-Āle*), presumably on the occasion of Tukulti-Ninurta's triumph.[363] A Sidonian envoy acted as proxy for the city's Egyptian overlord, and it is probable that the highest dignitary of the Hittite embassy, Tili-šarruma, was the son of the former king of

---

357. See chapter 33 in this volume. Another king, Enlil-nadin-šumi, who ruled for a little over a year between the two, was placed on the throne by the Elamites and would presumably not have been counted as part of Tukulti-Ninurta's reign.

358. Jakob 2013 and 2017a (capture of Kaštiliaš in the year of Etel-pi-Aššur, second conquest of Babylon in the year of Ber-nadin-apli) would start this personal rule over Babylon around 1222 BC, while Bloch 2010b: 62–67 (capture of Kaštiliaš in the year of Ina-Aššur-šumi-aṣbat) prefers a date around 1215 BC, after the ca. nine years covered by the three successors of Kaštiliaš IV.

359. S. Yamada 2003: 168–72; Sazonov 2016: 89–94.

360. Grayson 1987: 273: A.0.78.23: ll. 69–84.

361. Grayson 1987: 275: A.0.78.24: l. 16.

362. Possibly 1225 BC (so Salah 2014) or 1221 BC (so Jakob 2013), *contra* Freydank 2016: 10–14.

363. Jakob 2009: 59–69 nos. 22–28; see Jakob 2003b; 2017: 129–130.

Carchemish, Ini-Teššub.[364] At this point, the two northern powers were on good terms, collaborating economically and militarily on several occasions,[365] although possibly after some additional tensions.[366]

Babylonia's situation was dire for at least a couple of years: documents dated to the eponym year of Abi-ili, son of Katiri,[367] attest to the construction of river boats to carry grain upstream to Assyria,[368] matching a pattern of long-distance transport of bulk cereals that also followed the conquest of Zamban in the Diyala, an event that is difficult to date.[369] According to later traditions, Tukulti-Ninurta's rule over Babylon came to an end through a coup restoring Adad-šuma-uṣur, the legitimate heir, to the throne, although the actual legitimacy of this king has also been questioned.[370] This may have been the occasion when a unique letter, recovered in Hattusa, was written in which Tukulti-Ninurta bitterly complained about the situation in Babylon and Suhu, lamenting Suppiluliuma II's lack of support and looking gloomily at his own future.[371]

Troubles were also brewing in the north and west for most of Tukulti-Ninurta's reign. A document from Dur-Katlimmu confirms the presence

364. C. Kühne 1995.

365. Cancik-Kirschbaum 1996: 117–128; Singer 2008; Jakob 2017a: 131 (*contra* Bányai 2011).

366. M. Yamada 2011.

367. Placed either one year (so Jakob 2013) or two years after the year of Ninu'ayu (so Llop 2013; Salah 2014). The suggestion to place it two years before Ninu'ayu (so Freydank 1991: 62; 2016: 10–14) would be more problematic, if the ambassadors mentioned in Harbe indeed are correlated with the conquest of Babylon.

368. Freydank 2001: no. 34; Jakob 2013: 521; 2015: 184.

369. Freydank 1976: no. 9; Jakob 2015: 184. Jakob 2013: 520 sees this event, dated to the year of Qarrad-Aššur, as a prelude to the Babylonian war, but most scholars would place this eponym much later in Tukulti-Ninurta's reign.

370. Grayson 1975: 176: Chronicle 22: iv 7–9, and Walker 1982: 400: Chronicle 25: 2–10; Singer 2008; see also chapter 33 in this volume.

371. Mora and Giorgieri 2004: 113–127: no. 8 (KBo 28.61–64). Singer 2008, re-dated with Jakob 2013: 522.

768 OXFORD HISTORY OF THE ANCIENT NEAR EAST

of an enemy in the countryside that prevented the completion of the harvest and the sowing of barley on the Lower Khabur, resulting in two years of grain shortage in the eponym years of both Etel-pi-Aššur (1231 BC) and Uṣur-namkur-šarre (1230 BC).[372] Assuming the date of 1229 BC for the year of Enlil-nadin-apli,[373] the episode can be correlated with an attack on the city of Šaluša, south of the Hasumu range (modern Tektek Dağları), hence with troubles coming from the northwest.[374] While the cereal cultivation around Dur-Katlimmu could be partly restored (but with poor results) in the eponym year of Aššur-bel-ilane (perhaps 1228 BC),[375] the city of Duara (which commonly appears alongside Dur-Katlimmu in harvest records) had fallen into enemy hands.[376] Things were even worse with respect to summer crops like sesame and legumes, the cultivation of which coincided with the military campaign season, and which were not harvested for up to four years in a row (perhaps 1231–1228 BC).[377] In the eponym year of Ina-Aššur-šumi-aṣbat (perhaps 1226 BC), at the time of the second campaign against Babylon, the grand vizier still had to battle "Hurrian" enemies launching raids from the mountains of Hasumu against the Upper Balikh (Nihriya, Panua) and the steppe between Balikh and Khabur (including Harbe and the "Upper Hana" district),[378] while others attacked to the east, between Alem Daği and the Tigris, along the Subnat (modern Sufan Çay/Sufandere)[379] and Sarua rivers.[380] The situation was all the more critical in that the region

---

372. Röllig 2008: 151, no. 79; Reculeau 2011: 256–257.

373. Salah 2014: 62; *contra* Llop 2012b: 213.

374. Cancik-Kirschbaum 2009: 140–141; Cancik-Kirschbaum and Hess 2016: 130.

375. Reculeau 2011: 175.

376. Röllig 2008: 152–152, no. 80; Reculeau 2011: 257.

377. Röllig 2008: 184, no. 106.

378. Cancik-Kirschbaum 2009b: 123–128; H. Kühne 2018: 145.

379. Cancik-Kirschbaum and Hess 2016: 120.

380. Cancik-Kirschbaum 1996: 106–139, nos. 3–4 and 6–8; Jakob 2015: 181.

was already suffering from locust infestations,[381] and the conjunction of both calamities meant the destruction of harvests and thus brought about grain shortages in major cities including Waššukanni and Harbe. A military campaign led by the king against a city in Hanigalbat—the western part of the kingdom, theoretically under the control of the grand vizier—in the eponym year of Abi-ili (1223 BC) suggests the need to reconquer cities that had fallen into enemy hands.[382]

Tukulti-Ninurta's reign was not just one of sweeping military conquests and backlashes, but also a time of massive investments in the Assyrian heartland through construction programs that can be traced both in inscriptions and in the archaeological record.[383] Like his predecessors, the king invested heavily at Assur, where he had a new palace built,[384] a moat (re-)dug[385] and several temples restored and embellished.[386] Moreover, he created a new city on the eastern bank of the Tigris, opposite Assur, which he named after himself, Kar-Tukulti-Ninurta ("Tukulti-Ninurta's Harbor," modern Tulul al-ʿAqar).[387] The foundation of the city is celebrated in foundation deposits[388] and stamped bricks[389] from its buildings, while archives attest to the existence of a palace and royal administration. Inscriptions celebrate the

---

381. Cancik-Kirschbaum 1996: 94–114, nos. 2 and 4; Jakob 2009: 41, no. 1; 48–50, nos. 9–10; Jakob 2015: 181–182; see also Radner 2004: 13–15.

382. Freydank 1982: no. 17; Jakob 2013: 521–5212; 2015: 184.

383. Baffi 1997.

384. Grayson 1987: 231–253: A.0.78.1–10; 282: A.0.78.30; Preusser 1955: 30–31; Tenu 2009: 68.

385. Grayson 1987: 266–267: A.0.78.19.

386. Grayson 1987: 253–263: A.0.78.11–16 (temple of the Assyrian Ištar); 264–265: A.0.78.17 (temple of the Lady of Nineveh); 265–266: A.0.78.18 (temple of the gods Sin and Šamaš); 278–279: A.0.78.26 (temple of Aššur).

387. For a survey of the site's archaeology, see Tenu 2009: 75–80; Düring 2020: 57–58.

388. Grayson 1987: 269–278: A.0.78.22–25; Deller et al. 1994 (IM 57821 and IM 76787).

389. Grayson 1987: 285–289: A.0.78.35–38.

founding of the city alongside the victory over Babylon, making it his second-most important achievement in the king's own eyes. However, the project was central to Tukulti-Ninurta's ambitions early in his reign, and construction had started even before the first campaign against Kaštiliaš IV.[390] Often described as a new capital (although this is a projection into the Middle Assyrian political landscape of the practices of later Neo-Assyrian kings), Kar-Tukulti-Ninurta's foundation echoes similar feats in the Assyrian heartland, starting with Kalhu (modern Nimrud) under Shalmaneser, and followed by Apqu-ša-Adad (modern Tell Abu Maryam) under Aššur-reša-iši (1132–1115 BC). Kar-Tukulti-Ninurta was but one among many district capitals within the kingdom, albeit a very prestigious one, and the only one featuring an extension of the Aššur temple beyond the capital itself, possibly linked with processions and joint festivals.[391] The capital and the new royal residence were linked not only by geography and royal patronage, but also by a cadre of high-ranking courtiers who exercised their functions at both Assur and Kar-Tukulti-Ninurta, the highest among them being the eunuch (*ša rēši*) Uṣur-namkur-šarre, who gave his name to the year 1230 BC, acted as representative of the king (*qēpu ša šarre*), and exercised the crucial functions of palace administrator (*mašennu*) at Assur and governor (*bēl pāhete*) at Kar-Tukulti-Ninurta.[392]

The foundation of Kar-Tukulti-Ninurta fits into a broader picture of differential development of the kingdom, documented by archaeological surveys, excavations, and texts. Some regions were prioritized over others for economic development and administrative integration: in areas that were traditionally densely populated and heavily cultivated, like the Khabur triangle that had constituted the Mittani core, Assyrian control mostly reflected the continuation of older practices.[393] Other areas experienced massive investments in irrigation and the settlement of deportees

---

390. Gilibert 2008: 177–180.

391. Miglus 1993; Gilibert 2008: 181–182; *contra* Pongratz-Leisten 2015: 1.

392. Gilibert 2008: 182; Jakob 2003a: 96–108, 114, 120, 268, 276–279.

393. Düring 2020: 70–75.

to develop agrarian production, especially in the Assyrian core[394] and along the Lower Khabur.[395] Other areas, like the Balikh valley, may have experienced a decline of local agrarian settlements reflecting the concentration of labor and resources in the hands of absentee Assyrian landlords, as with the fortified farmstead (*dunnu*) of Tell Sabi Abyad.[396]

For all his achievements, Tukulti-Ninurta's reign ended in chaos, even if the events of the last decades of his thirty-seven-year long reign are poorly documented. The two major thirteenth-century archives from the western part of the kingdom, Harbe and Dur-Katlimmu, end in the late 1220s BC, both associated with violent conflagrations. By the end of Tukulti-Ninurta's reign, the fortress at Tell Sabi Abyad had fallen into disrepair. However, it was rebuilt soon afterward,[397] and Assyrian occupation is attested for at least several decades at Harbe, Dur-Katlimmu, and other cities in the Syrian Jezirah.[398] Meanwhile, troubles were also brewing in the Assyrian core. *Chronicle P* mentions that Tukulti-Ninurta was murdered in a coup instigated by his son and successor, Aššur-nadin-apli (misidentified as Aššur-naṣir-apli), and some Assyrian courtiers,[399] and the event is recalled in a letter from Tell Sabi Abyad that mentions the mourning ceremonies for the deceased and the enthronement of his successor. Its author, Ili-pada (see table 32.1), had by then taken over the position of grand vizier and king of Hanigalbat that his father Aššur-iddin once held. This change in the upper echelons of the kingdom might also be correlated with the internecine war that accompanied Tukulti-Ninurta's demise.[400]

---

394. Freydank 2009; Reculeau 2011: 78–79, 99–100; Düring 2020: 65–70.

395. Reculeau 2010; H. Kühne 2018: 148–150; Düring 2020: 75–80.

396. Lyon 2000; Düring 2020: 86–91.

397. Akkermans and Wiggermann 2015: 97, 117–118.

398. Jakob 2009: 6–7; 2015: 184–185; Akkermans and Wiggermann 2015: 120.

399. Grayson 1975: 176: Chronicle 22: iv 8–11; see Jakob 2017a: 132.

400. Wiggermann 2006.

32.6. *Assyria in the twelfth century BC: a time of confusion, decline, and renewal*

The century between the death of Tukulti-Ninurta I (1206 BC) and the accession of Tiglath-pileser I (1114 BC) is poorly documented, both archaeologically and textually. This period is represented at Tell Sheikh Hamad, and corresponds to Phase II of the Middle Assyrian ceramic typology, subdivided into Phase IIa (last years of Tukulti-Ninurta I down to Aššur-nerari III); Phase IIb (Enlil-kudurri-uṣur and Ninurta-apil-Ekur); and Phase IIc (Aššur-dan I and Ninurta-tukulti-Aššur). Missing at Tell Sheikh Hamad but present at Tell Bderi, Phase III began at the end of the period or during the reign of Tiglath-pileser I.[401]

Of the eight kings who ruled Assyria between 1206 BC and the accession of Aššur-reša-iši in 1132 BC, only one royal inscription of importance is known. This belongs to Tukulti-Ninurta's immediate successor, Aššur-nadin-apli, and celebrates hydraulic works along the Tigris and the erection of a shrine on its banks.[402] A handful of stamped bricks from his palace attest to his presence in Assur, but little else.[403] After him, only two inscriptions are known for Ninurta-apil-Ekur[404] and one for Aššur-dan I (1178–1133 BC),[405] none of which contains any information on military operations or construction work. Only with the reign of Aššur-reša-iši (1132–1115 BC) do we see a renewal of this celebratory genre, with at least fourteen much more detailed inscriptions.[406]

---

401. Pfälzner 1995: 235–236; Tenu 2009: 45–47.

402. Grayson 1987: 300–301: A.0.79.1; Bagg 2000: 45–48.

403. Grayson 1987: 301–302: A.0.79.2–3.

404. Grayson 1987: 303–304: A.0.82.1–2.

405. Grayson 1987: 305: A.0.83.2.

406. Grayson 1987: 309–322: A.0.86.1–14 (and additional possible and/or fragmentary inscriptions: Grayson 1987: 322–329).

Although palace decrees of three kings of this period are known,[407] archival records are few and far between. Within the Assyrian heartland, the documentation of the archive of the House of Offerings becomes denser in the reigns of Ninurta-apil-Ekur and his successor Aššur-dan I, only to become sparse again until the reigns of Aššur-reša-iši I and his successor Tiglath-pileser I, to which the bulk of the evidence can be assigned.[408] Most tablets from the Stewards' archive are contemporary with the latter part of this period.[409] To only one single year in the reign of Aššur-dan I—during the regency of his son and short-lived successor Ninurta-tukulti-Aššur—dates the small archive of Mutta the animal fattener (*ša kurulti'e*), an official attached to the Assur palace who received animals as audience gifts to the king by various members of the Assyrian elites, both in Assur and in the provinces, and who oversaw their redistribution to members of the court and for the king's meals.[410] The archival situation is even worse in the provinces, where most archives come to an end by the end of the thirteenth century. An exception is Tell Sabi Abyad, where Level 5 attests to massive repairs of the fortress associated with Ili-pada, who remained in office until the reign of Enlil-kudurri-uṣur (1196–1192 BC). The building was destroyed and the archives came to an end under Ninurta-apil-Ekur (1191–1179 BC), possibly as the result of internecine wars within the Assyrian royal family.[411] With the exception of a few documents concerning the management of land,[412] the production of pots,[413] and the previously

---

407. Roth 1997: 201–203 (Ninurta-apil-Ekur); 203–204 (Aššur-dan I); 204–205 (Aššur-reša-iši I).

408. Archive M 4; see Pedersén 1985: 43–53; Postgate 2013: 89–146; Gauthier 2016: 7–9.

409. Archive M 7; see Pedersén 1985: 68–81; Frahm 2002: 85; Postgate 2013: 147–176; Maul 2017: 91–93.

410. Archive M 6; see Pedersén 1985: 56–68; Postgate 2013: 177–200.

411. Wiggermann 2006; Akkermans and Wiggermann 2015: 101.

412. Wiggermann 2000.

413. Wiggermann 2008.

mentioned letter by Ili-pada,[414] the archive remains largely unpublished. Finally, two badly preserved private contracts from the time of Aššur-dan I were recovered in a secondary context at the Middle Assyrian fort of Haradu (modern Khirbet ed-Diniye) on the Middle Euphrates.[415] To complicate matters even more, the sequence of eponyms for the entire period remains largely conjectural.[416]

32.6.1. The last descendants of Shalmaneser I: Aššur-nadin-apli (1206–1203 BC), Aššur-nerari III (1202–1197 BC), and Enlil-kudurri-uṣur (1196–1192 BC)

Almost nothing is known of the ca. fifteen years that followed Tukulti-Ninurta's assassination, which, according to the Assyrian King List, correspond to the reigns of his son Aššur-nadin-apli, his grandson Aššur-nerari III, and another of his sons, Enlil-kudurri-uṣur.[417] These kings seem to have wielded little power, while their distant cousin Ili-pada, the king of Hanigalbat, expanded his sphere of influence, acting as de facto sovereign in what was still formally the western part of the Assyrian dominion. He married his daughter Uballiṭittu to the king of Purulumzi[418] (a northern vassal state located between the Tur Abdin and the Murat Su),[419] at the same time as he himself was bound to the royal house of Assur through his marriage with La-libbi.[420] He entertained a friendly and fruitful relationship with the Hittite king of Carchemish, even leading a support army to assist him in a war against

---

414. Wiggermann 2006.

415. Clancier 2012.

416. Freydank 2016.

417. Grayson 1983: 110–111: §§47–49.

418. Llop 2015: 252.

419. Cancik-Kirschbaum and Hess 2016: 112.

420. Shibata 2015: 239–240.

Emar around the time of Aššur-nerari III's accession (ca. 1200 BC).[421] He also concluded a bilateral agreement with the Sutean nomads without any reference to the Assyrian king, going so far as to name the Assyrians as potential enemies of both parties.[422] Ili-pada's newfound importance is best illustrated by a Middle Babylonian literary letter attributed to Adad-šuma-uṣur of Babylon which, in spite of its fictive and heavily propagandistic nature, reflects elements of the geopolitical situation of Assyria and Babylonia in the early twelfth century BC.[423] While the accusations of drunkenness, impiety, and general inability to rule should be taken with a dose of skepticism, it is telling that the letter was addressed to both Ili-pada and Aššur-nerari as "kings of Assyria"—either reflecting the independence of the former western part of the kingdom, or mocking the inability of the Assyrian king to constrain his vassal.

The relationship between the two branches of the royal family soured rapidly: after the death of Ili-pada around 1193 BC,[424] his son and putative successor Ninurta-apil-Ekur appears to have antagonized the new Assyrian king, Enlil-kudurri-uṣur. His estate at Tell Sabi Abyad was violently destroyed after several years of troubles,[425] and later traditions picture him as an exile in Babylonia, where he received the support of Adad-šuma-uṣur. The Babylonian king went to war with Enlil-kudurri-uṣur, was victorious in battle, and the Assyrian may even have been delivered by his own subjects into the hands of his Babylonian opponent.[426] His protégé conquered Assur, ensuring the de facto reunification of the

421. Akkermans and Wiggermann 2015: 120 (re-dated according to the chronology used here); Llop 2015: 256–257.

422. Wiggermann 2010; Llop 2015: 252.

423. Grayson 1972: 137–138: §§889–891 (ABL 924); Llop and George 2001–02: 9–11; Llop 2015: 256–257; see also chapter 33 in this volume.

424. Akkermans and Wiggermann 2015: 120 (re-dated according to the chronology used in the present chapter).

425. Akkermans and Wiggermann 2015: 101; 118–120.

426. Llop and George 2001–02: 17; Llop 2015: 257.

eastern and western parts of the kingdom.[427] Parts of the estate at Tell Sabi Abyad were rebuilt, but the fortress never regained its former glory, and only a few texts survive in the west from the following period.[428] While the title "King of Hanigalbat" seems to disappear at this time,[429] that of "grand vizier" survived at least until the reign of Tiglath-pileser I, although it does not seem to have carried the same geopolitical connotations, or the family ties with the ruling dynasty, that it previously had.[430]

32.6.2. The difficult establishment of a new royal lineage: from Ninurta-apil-Ekur (1191–1179 BC) to Aššur-reša-iši I (1132–1115 BC)

With Ninurta-apil-Ekur started a new line of rulers that claim legitimacy by virtue of their descent from Adad-nerari I (see table 32.1),[431] even if, tellingly, both he and later traditions preferred to tie him to an earlier ancestor, Eriba-Adad I, the founder of the Middle Assyrian kingdom.[432] The foundational nature of Ninurta-apil-Ekur's own reign is best illustrated by the genealogy of his great-great-grandson, Tiglath-pileser I, who named him as the oldest among his ancestors and depicted his reign as one when the god Aššur favored the king, who in turn rightfully

---

427. Assyrian sources: Grayson 1983, 111: Assyrian King List, §50; Grayson 1975: 161–162: Chronicle 21: ii 3–8; Babylonian sources: Walker 1982: 400: Chronicle 25: ll. 3–10; Llop and George 2001–02: 11–12 (literary letter of a Kassite king to Mutakkil-Nusku: A$_2$ rev. 6′–8′, 12); see S. Yamada 2003: 156–159; Jakob 2017a: 132; and chapter 33 in this volume.

428. Akkermans and Wiggermann 2015: 101–103, 118; Llop 2012b.

429. Reculeau 2016: 206–207.

430. Jakob 2003a: 55–56: grand viziers Eru-apla-iddina (Aššur-dan I), Ibašši-ili (Aššur-bel-kala?), Ninurta-nadin-apli (Aššur-reša-iši I), and the unnamed son of the former (Tiglath-pileser I).

431. Cancik-Kirschbaum 1999.

432. Freydank 1976: no. 53: 7; Jakob 2003a: 514; Grayson 1983: 111: Assyrian King List, §50.

protected his people.[433] Contemporary evidence, however, offers a more nuanced perspective. On the one hand, a text from the Stewards' archive shows that Ninurta-apil-Ekur maintained peaceful relations with Adad-šuma-uṣur's successor Meli-Šipak of Babylon, who sent him rugs and horses as gifts.[434] He is also credited with nine palace decrees (as many as all his predecessors combined and almost twice as many as all his successors until Tiglath-pileser I), regulating the interactions of courtiers with the women of the harem (*Palace Decrees*, §9) and the women's behavior, especially when quarrelling or cursing the name of the god(s) or that of the king and his family (*Palace Decrees*, §§10–17).[435]

Not everything was peaceful during Ninurta-apil-Ekur's tenure, though. His troubled accession to power and the civil war that accompanied it caused massive disruptions in the Assyrian economy, as reflected in the documents from the House of Offerings from the early years of his reign.[436] Even more dramatic was the crisis that broke out during his eighth year (1184 BC; eponym year of Salmanu-zera-iqiša) and that was not fully resolved until the first year of his son and successor, Aššur-dan I (1179 BC). Some important provinces, starting with Katmuhu in the northeastern parts of the Tur Abdin, defaulted on their tax payments, and the crisis hit very close to home, moving southwestward to the Upper Khabur (Šudu,[437] Taide, Amasakku = modern Tell Muhammad Kabir,[438] and the "Upper Province"[439]) and even reaching the core provinces of Assur and Kulišhinaš. Much later, Tiglath-pileser I (1114–1076 BC) would state that the territories between the Euphrates, the Murat Su and the Tur Abdin range (Alzi and Purulumzi) had fallen into the hands

---

433. Grayson 1991: 28, A.0.87.1: vii 55–59.

434. Frahm 2002: 75 (Ass.2001.D–2217); Llop 2015: 257.

435. Roth 1997: 201–203 (*Palace Decrees*, §§9–17); Lafont 2003: 521.

436. Gauthier 2016: 507–515 ("accession crisis").

437. Cancik-Kirschbaum and Hess 2016: 138–139.

438. Cancik-Kirschbaum and Hess 2016: 12–13.

439. Cancik-Kirschbaum and Hess 2016: 105.

of the Mušku "fifty years" (a mere approximation) before he was able to reconquer them.[440] While a direct connection between the two episodes can only be surmised, it is tempting to link the provisioning crisis to the progressive loss of the areas north of the Tur Abdin mountain range that had been integrated under Tukulti-Ninurta I.[441]

Aššur-dan I's forty-six-year reign (1178–1133 BC) is the longest in all of Assyrian history, but very little is known about it. If anything, it seems that Aššur-dan profited from a period of Babylonian weakness (due to pressure from Elam) to attack its possessions on the Diyala (Ugar-ṣallu, Irreya, and Zamban,[442] the latter having been lost to Babylonia at some point following its conquest by Tukulti-Ninurta I), and to levy tribute.[443] He also seems to have started the policy of establishing fortresses along the Middle Euphrates that would become a hallmark of Tiglath-pileser's conquest of the region, if the two tablets dated from his reign reflect the construction of the fort at Haradu (modern Khirbet ed-Diniye).[444]

Aššur-dan I's building works are known only from references made to them by his successors, who state that he had torn down the dilapidated temple of Anu and Adad in Assur, but failed to rebuild it,[445] an episode that was possibly linked to the earthquake that ruined several buildings at Nineveh during his reign.[446] Aššur-dan also rebuilt (?) a structure that may have been the temple of the Assyrian Ištar,[447] and re-dug a canal that had dried up.[448]

---

440. Grayson 1991: 14: A.0.87.1: i 62–88. See chapter 37 in volume 4.

441. Gauthier 2016: 516–531 ("Liptānu crisis"), with Llop 2015: 258–261 for the loss of Katmuhu at the latest in the second half of Aššur-dan's reign (different ordering of eponyms in Freydank 2016: 29–32).

442. Bryce 2009: 783.

443. Grayson 1975: 162: Chronicle 21: ii 9–12; see also chapter 33 in this volume.

444. Clancier 2012; Tenu and Clancier 2012:

445. Grayson 1991: 28: A.0.87.1: vii 60–70 (Tiglath-pileser I).

446. Ištar temple: Grayson 1987: 311: A.0.86.1: ll. 8–10; 313: A.0.86.2: ll. 3–7; armory: Grayson 1987: 314: A.0.86.4: ll. 4–6 (Aššur-reša-iši I).

447. Grayson 1991: 75–78: A.0.87.1007–1010 (Tiglath-pileser I).

448. Grayson 1991: 105: A.0.89.7: v 20–31 (Aššur-bel-kala); Bagg 2000: 53–55.

From the archive of Mutta the animal fattener, one can gain an impression of the territories that were still under Assyrian control at the very end of Aššur-dan's reign, by considering the origins of the people who brought audience gifts (*namurtu*) to court.[449] These came from the formerly threatened Kulišhinaš and Amasakku in the Khabur triangle, Arraphe and Arzuhina (or Narzuhina) east of the Tigris, and even the land of Suhu on the Middle Euphrates. As had been the case for centuries, the kings of the Land of Mari on the Lower Khabur remained on friendly terms with Assyria, but their emissaries were treated as foreign delegates, which may suggest that they enjoyed a greater degree of autonomy.[450]

The archives from the House of Offerings in Assur attest to another crisis in Assyria around the middle of Aššur-dan's reign. The sequence of eponyms is very hypothetical, but the evidence suggests kingdom-wide shortages of agricultural commodities, primarily non-grain commodities regularly sent as offerings to the god (sesame, fruits, honey), for almost fifteen years, with at least two major episodes separated by a few years of relative plenty. The widespread and selective nature of the shortages suggest climatic rather than military facts were at work.[451]

Aššur-dan's succession was chaotic: according to the Assyrian King List[452] and a Babylonian literary letter addressed to Mutakkil-Nusku that casts a very derogatory light on relations between Assyria and Babylonia at the time,[453] Aššur-dan was succeeded by his son Ninurta-tukulti-Aššur (1133 BC), who reigned only for the duration of "his tablet" (*tuppišu*)— that is, his accession year when he acted as eponym—only to face a revolt by his brother Mutakkil-Nusku (1132 BC), who forced him into exile in

449. Archive M 6 = Pedersén 1985: 56–68; Postgate 2013: 177–200.

450. Llop and George 2001–02: 13–16; Jakob 2017a: 133.

451. Gauthier 2016: 531–549 ("Da"ānī-Ninurta crisis").

452. Grayson 1983: 111–113: §§52–53.

453. Llop and George 2001–02.

Šišil, east of the Tigris and south of the Diyala (a former Assyrian possession then under Babylonian control). Mutakkil-Nusku did not profit from this for long, as he died in his own accession year.[454] Some elements suggest that the cult statue of Marduk, which had been taken to Assyria by Tukulti-Ninurta, was returned to Babylon under Ninurta-tukulti-Aššur—an episode attributed by *Chronicle P* to an otherwise unknown Tukulti-Aššur, presumably an erroneous rendering of this royal name.[455] The letter also refers to a meeting between the kings of Assyria and Babylonia, which was supposed to take place in the city of Zaqqa, an Assyrian fortress alongside the frontier, by the Lower Zab. If the fictional letter is to be trusted, Mutakkil-Nusku failed to show up, triggering the scornful reply from his opponent.[456]

By comparison, the reign of Aššur-resa-iši I (1132–1115 BC) marked a renewal of Assyrian prosperity and regional power, especially vis-à-vis its southern neighbor. For the first time in almost a century, we have a significant number of royal inscriptions commemorating the rebuilding of the Ištar temple[457] and the armory[458] of Nineveh that had been destroyed by an earthquake in the time of Aššur-dan I; the rebuilding of the temples of Anu and Adad,[459] Ištar,[460] and Aššur[461] at Assur; and the erection of palaces at Assur,[462] Nineveh,[463] and Apqu-ša-Adad (modern Tell Abu Maryam),[464]

---

454. Llop and George 2001–02: 16–18; Jakob 2017a: 133.

455. Grayson 1975: 176: Chronicle 22: iv 12–13; Llop and George 2001–02: 12; see also chapter 33 in this volume.

456. Llop and George 2001–02: 8–9.

457. Grayson 1987: 311: A.o.86.1: ll. 8–10; 313: A.o.86.2: ll. 3–7.

458. Grayson 1987: 314: A.o.86.4: ll. 4–6.

459. Grayson 1987: 317–318: A.o.86.7–8.

460. Grayson 1987: 318: A.o.86.9.

461. Grayson 1987: 319–320: A.o.86.11–12.

462. Grayson 1987: 321–322: A.o.86.14.

463. Grayson 1987: 315: A.o.86.5.

464. Grayson 1987: 319: A.o.86.10.

the latter two left for his successors to finish.[465] His royal title also reflects a time of confidence, with epithets such as "avenger of Assyria" (*mutēr gimil māt Aššur*) and claims of victories both in the northeast (Lullumu, Qutu) and in the west, against the Ahlamû nomads.[466] Relations between the two Mesopotamian powers once again soured, however, and later chronicles mention Aššur-resa-iši's victories over both Ninurta-nadin-šumi[467] and Nebuchadnezzar I, who tried twice to seize border towns along the Lower Zab (the aforementioned Zaqqa/Zanqi, and Idu), only to be routed twice, forced first to burn his siege engines and then to witness his field marshal and chariots captured by the enemy.[468]

The comparative weakness of Assyria in the twelfth century BC, compared to the days of Shalmaneser and Tukulti-Ninurta, is often described as the beginning of a dark age, only sparsely illuminated by short-lived moments of renewed glory (first and foremost under Tiglath-pileser I).[469] While traditional narratives associated these changes of fortune with the more or less energetic nature of rulers or with the devastating influence of unruly nomads,[470] more recent scholarship has shifted the perspective toward environmental degradation and climate change. This explanatory model was initially developed for the eleventh- and tenth-century "eclipse of Assyria,"[471] but the archaeological and paleo-climatic data used then is largely outdated.[472] Nevertheless, the hypothesis has been revived in recent years and expanded back in time to the aftermath of

---

465. Nineveh: Grayson 1991: 54: A.0.87.10: ll. 63–70 (Tiglath-pileser I); Apqu-ša-Adad: Grayson 1991: 105: A.0.89.7: v 32–37 (Aššur-bel-kala).

466. Grayson 1987: 310–311: A.0.86.1: ll. 1–8.

467. Grayson 1975: 188: Assyrian Chronicle Fragment 3: iv 1–21; Llop 2015: 262; see also chapter 33 in this volume.

468. Grayson 1975: 163–164: Chronicle 21: ii 1′–13′; van Soldt 2008: 73; Llop 2015: 262; Jakob 2017a: 133–134; see also chapter 33 in this volume.

469. Jakob 2017a: 132–139; Düring 2020: 46–47.

470. Cline 2014.

471. Neumann and Parpola 1987.

472. Reculeau 2011.

Tukulti-Ninurta's murder, based on low-resolution paleo-climatic data from various parts of the Middle East which have been tied to an abrupt episode of climate change (the so-called 3.2 kiloyear event) that would have precipitated the end of the Late Bronze Age.[473] Assyria's "crisis years"[474] would thus be a delayed response to a broader systemic crisis,[475] which could have been at least partly climate-induced.[476] Leaving aside the broader issue of the end of the Late Bronze Age, it should be noted that Assyria's weakening was comparatively limited, which allowed it soon after to emerge as the unchallenged military superpower of early Iron Age Upper Mesopotamia.[477] While it is not to be doubted that Assyria suffered setbacks in territories it had once conquered, this really happened only in the eleventh and tenth centuries BC (see chapter 37 in volume 4), and the twelfth century BC is marked by elements of continuity rather than disruption. Ninurta-apil-Ekur and Aššur-dan had to face recurring incursions by northern people, but so did Tukulti-Ninurta.

Recently published, high-resolution paleo-climatic data helps to clarify the assumed correlation between climate change and social disruption. While Assyria does appear to have enjoyed comparatively wetter conditions starting around the mid-fourteenth century BC compared to the previous two hundred years,[478] this lasted until the very last years of the twelfth century BC. Significantly increased aridity only began during Tiglath-pileser's rule, and even this needs to be qualified, since the century and a half that followed remained much wetter, for example, than conditions in the region since the early nineteenth century AD, not to mention the 1950s and the acceleration of anthropogenic climate change,

---

473. Kirleis and Herles 2007: 19–29.

474. Klengel 2000; Fales 2011: 47.

475. Liverani 1988; Fales 2011: 31.

476. Kirleis and Herles 2007; Jakob 2015: 185; for a more nuanced opinion, see Düring 2020: 133–137.

477. Radner 2015a: 4–5.

478. *Contra* Reculeau 2011: 68–69.

by far the driest period in recorded history for the region.[479] There is no apparent correlation between the climatic situation of Assyria and the troubles it faced at the end of the thirteenth century and during most of the twelfth century BC. It is true that even in years when the fields could be harvested, the productivity of grain crops was generally poor, including in areas where massive investments in agriculture and irrigation are attested.[480] The reasons for this poor productivity remain obscure, but coupled with the previously mentioned military incursions, crop destructions and locusts invasions, the extraordinary demands occasioned by the construction of Kar-Tukulti-Ninurta and the associated resettlement of deportees help explain why vast quantities of grain needed to be brought at great cost to the king's new city, both from conquered territories in the south and from various other parts of the kingdom.[481] Similarly, ebbs and flows during the reigns of Tukulti-Ninurta's successors can be attributed to a multitude of causes, from internal and external wars to decade-long, adverse climatic conditions (a normal feature of the climate in the region), and even in the latter case the primary staple of the kingdom (barley) seems to have been less affected than fruit-bearing trees and other delicacies.

32.7. In conclusion: Assyria's "middle period" in context

The history of Assyria is often seen as an ascent from city-state to empire, ending in a sudden and brutal demise.[482] In this rather linear narrative, the Middle Assyrian period is the time when the former merchant city-state with limited political and military ambitions metamorphosed into an aggressive player on the international scene. The fourteenth and thirteenth centuries BC, especially, are seen as the blueprint for the imperial

---

479. Sinha et al. 2019: Supplementary Materials, Table 1.

480. Freydank 2009; Reculeau 2011.

481. Llop 2010; Jakob 2015: 183–185.

482. Liverani 2011.

realizations of the Neo-Assyrian period—a prelude to empire, or even an early stage of imperialism.[483] Debates focus on the nature of Middle Assyrian dominion in the Syrian Jezirah: either as a "network empire" of interconnected Assyrian strongholds embedded in a local "Hurrian" native population;[484] a "territorial empire" with complete control of the land through a hierarchy of provinces;[485] or a "patchwork empire" marked by diverse trajectories through space and time.[486] In many respects, though, the idea of "proto-imperialism" appears anachronistic, and the consolidation of Assyria's direct rule was often the accidental result of its failure to control conquered areas through proxies.[487]

Late Bronze Age Assyria built upon long-standing traditions in Upper Mesopotamia: those of its former overlord Mittani (from which it borrowed part of its administrative and military organization and terminology),[488] but also those of the local kingdoms it subdued and incorporated, such as the kingdom of Hana on the lower Khabur, whose infrastructure provided the backbone for the administrative and economic development centered on Dur-Katlimmu.[489] These, in turn, find their place in practices that go back to the Middle Bronze Age and the time of the Mari archives: the way that the Assyrian king chose to delegate power to a high-ranking family member in the western part of his dominion might have been influenced by contemporary Hittite practice in northern Syria, but it was also the heir to a long Upper Mesopotamian tradition that privileged man-to-man relations of power over territorial control.[490] The same applies to the relationship of Assyrian subjects to

---

483. Postgate 1992; Liverani 2017; Düring 2020.

484. Liverani 1988.

485. H. Kühne 1995; Cancik-Kirschbaum 2008c; Fales 2011.

486. Düring 2020: 91–94.

487. Cf. Jakob 2015: 177–178 ("the reluctant annexation of Hanigalbat").

488. Postgate 2011: 90–92.

489. Reculeau 2010; H. Kühne 2018.

490. Reculeau 2016.

their king through service to the crown (*ilku*), a practice that is generally understood through the militaristic lens of the right of conquest and theoretical ownership of the king over the entire land.[491] It is, however, better understood as part of a contractual relationship, in which service is contributed in exchange for land and/or provisions, that goes back to the eighteenth century BC at least.

Administrative structures provide a case in point: while the early terminology for provinces and their administrators (*halzu, halzuhlu/hassihlu*) directly reflect Mittanian ones (*halṣu* and *halṣoġli*),[492] these terms are in turn borrowings from Middle Bronze Age Akkadian terminology and practice.[493] At the lowest echelon of cities, towns, and villages, the royal administration was served by the *hazi'ānu* (poorly translated as "mayor") who, contrary to what the etymology of the term might suggest, did not represent local interests to the king, but the other way around.[494] He was in charge of agricultural production on crown land, the organization of labor, and the supply of rations.[495] This, again, mirrors practices known in Middle Bronze Age Upper Mesopotamia as well as on the contemporary Middle Euphrates under Hittite influence.[496]

Far from being a prelude to an empire-to-be or a simple successor state of Mittani, Late Bronze Age Assyria was a highly idiosyncratic synthesis of long-standing Upper Mesopotamian practices and innovations which, coupled with its unique status as a city (later kingdom) coterminous with a god, and increasing Babylonian influences,[497] came to redefine what it meant to be a (super-)power in a time of troubles. This explains why kings of the Neo-Assyrian era would later look back at

---

491. Postgate 1982; Lafont 2003: 524–525.

492. See chapter 29 in this volume.

493. Fleming 2000: 133–139.

494. Marti 2010.

495. Jakob 2003a: 151–160; 2017b: 151.

496. Marti 2010.

497. Postgate 2011: 92.

the golden days of the thirteenth century BC to invent and justify their imperialistic policies.[498]

REFERENCES

Akkermans, P.M.M.G., and Wiggermann, F. 2015. West of Aššur: the life and times of the Middle Assyrian *dunnu* at Tell Sabi Ayad, Syria. In Düring, B.S. (ed.), *Understanding hegemonic practices of the early Assyrian Empire.* Leiden: NINO, 89–123.

Alexandrov, B. 2014. The letters from Hanigalbat in the Boğazköy archives. In Taracha, P. (ed.), *Proceedings of the eighth international congress of hittitology.* Warsaw: Agade, 52–76.

Aynard, M.-J., and Durand, J.-M. 1980. Documents d'époque médio-assyrienne. *Assur* 3/1: 1–63.

Baffi, F. 1997. Tukulti-Ninurta I, re costruttore. In Matthiae, P. (ed.), *Contributi e materiali di archeologia orientale VII.* Rome: Università degli studi di Roma "La Sapienza," 7–26.

Bagg, A.M. 2000. *Assyrische Wasserbauten.* Mainz: Zabern.

Bányai, M. 2011. Die Niḫrīya-Schlacht: vorher und danach. *Anatolica* 37: 207–237.

Bartl, P., and Bonatz, D. 2013. Across Assyria's northern frontier: Tell Fekheriye at the end of the Late Bronze Age. In Yener, A. (ed.), *Across the border: Late Bronze-Iron Age relations between Syria and Anatolia.* Leuven: Peeters, 263–292.

Beckman, G. 1999. *Hittite diplomatic texts.* Atlanta, GA: Scholars Press. 2nd rev. ed.

Bilgin, T. 2018. *Officials and administration in the Hittite world.* Berlin: De Gruyter.

Bloch, Y. 2008. The order of eponyms in the reign of Shalmaneser I. *UF* 40: 143–178.

Bloch, Y. 2010a. Solving the problems of the Assyrian King List: toward a precise reconstruction of Middle Assyrian chronology, part I and part II. *Journal of Ancient Civilizations* 25: 21–87.

---

498. Radner 2014.

Bloch, Y. 2010b. Setting the dates: re-evaluation of the chronology of Babylonia in the 14th–11th centuries BCE and its implications for the reigns of Ramesses II and Ḫattušili III. *UF* 42: 41–95.

Bloch, Y. 2010c. The order of eponyms in the reign of Tukultī-Ninurta I. *Orientalia* 79: 1–35.

Bloch, Y. 2012. Middle Assyrian lunar calendar and chronology. In Ben-Dov, J., Horowitz, W., and Steele, J. (eds.), *Living the lunar calendar*. Oxford: Oxbow, 19–61.

Bloch, Y., and Peri, L. 2016–2017. "I placed my name there": the great inscription of Tukulti-Ninurta I, king of Assyria, from the collection of David and Cindy Sofer, London. *Israel Museum Studies in Archaeology* 8: 2–55.

Boese, J., and Wilhelm, G. 1979. Aššur-dān I, Ninurta-apil-Ekur und die mittelassyrische Chronologie. *Wiener Zeitschrift für die Kunde des Morgenlandes* 71: 19–38.

Bounni, A. 1988. Découvertes archéologiques récentes en Syrie. *Comptes rendus des séances de l'Académie des Inscriptions et Belles-Lettres* 132: 361–380.

Brown, B. 2014. Settlement patterns of the Middle Assyrian state: notes toward an investigation of state apparatuses. In Bonatz, D. (ed.), *The archaeology of political spaces: the Upper Mesopotamian piedmont in the second millennium BC*. Berlin: De Gruyter, 85–106.

Bryce, T. 2005. *The kingdom of the Hittites*. Oxford: Oxford University Press.

Bryce, T. 2009. *The Routledge handbook of the people and places of Western Asia*. London and New York: Routledge.

Cancik-Kirschbaum, E. 1996. *Die mittelassyrischen Briefe aus Tall Šēḫ Ḥamad*. Berlin: Reimer.

Cancik-Kirschbaum, E. 1999. Nebenlinien des assyrischen Königshaus in der 2. Hälfte des 2. Jts. v. Chr. *AoF* 26: 210–222.

Cancik-Kirschbaum, E. 2008a. Šadikanni. *RlA* 11: 485–486.

Cancik-Kirschbaum, E. 2008b. Assur und Hatti: zwischen Allianz und Konflikt. In Wilhelm, G. (ed.), *Ḫattuša—Boğazköy: das Hethiterreich im Spannungsfeld des Alten Orients*. Wiesbaden: Harrassowitz, 205–222.

Cancik-Kirschbaum, E. 2008c. Emar aus der Perspektive Assurs im 13. Jh. v. Chr. In D'Alfonso, L., Cohen, Y., and Sürenhagen, D. (eds.), *The city of Emar among the Late Bronze Age empires*. Münster: Ugarit-Verlag, 91–99.

Cancik-Kirschbaum, E. 2009. Ortsnamenreihungen als Quellen zur historischen Geographie: der Westen des mittelassyrischen Reiches unter

Tukultī-Ninurta I. In Cancik-Kirschbaum, E., and Ziegler, N. (eds.), *Entre les fleuves, I*. Gladbeck: PeWe-Verlag, 121–150.

Cancik-Kirschbaum, E. 2011. Ashur: the making of an imperial capital in the 15th and 14th century BC. *Mesopotamia* 46: 71–78.

Cancik-Kirschbaum, E. 2014. ^{URU}ŠÀ.URU, *māt* ^{d}*Aššur* und die Binnenstruktur des mittelassyrischen Reiches. In Cancik-Kirschbaum, E., and Ziegler, N. (eds.), *Entre les fleuves, II*. Gladbeck: PeWe-Verlag, 291–314.

Cancik-Kirschbaum, E., and Hess, C. 2016. *Toponyme der mittelassyrischen Texte: der Westen des mittelassyrischen Reiches*. Paris: Société pour l'étude du Proche-Orient ancien.

Cancik-Kirschbaum, E., and Johnson, J.C. 2011–2012. Middle Assyrian calendrics. *SAAB* 19: 87–152.

Capet, E. 2005. Les installations de la fin du Bronze Récent et du début du Fer. In Bachelot, L., and Fales, F.M. (eds.), *Tell Shiukh Fawqani 1994–1998*. Padua: Sargon, 379–407.

Charpin, D. 2002. Chroniques du Moyen-Euphrate, 1: le "royaume de Hana," textes et histoire. *RA* 95: 61–92.

Charpin, D. 2004. Histoire politique du Proche-Orient amorrite. In Charpin, D., Edzard, D.O., and Stol, M., *Mesopotamien: die altbabylonische Zeit*. Fribourg: Academic Press; Göttingen: Vandenhoeck & Ruprecht, 25–480.

Charpin, D. 2011. Le "pays de Mari et des Bédouins" à l'époque de Samsu-iluna de Babylone. *RA* 105: 41–59.

Cifola, B. 1995. *Analysis of variants in the Assyrian royal titulary from the origins to Tiglath-pileser III*. Naples: Istituto Universitario Orientale.

Clancier, P. 2012. Les deux tablettes médio-assyriennes. In Kepinski, C. (ed.), *Haradum III*. Paris: De Boccard, 241–246.

Cline, E.H. 2014. *1177 BC: the year civilization collapsed*. Princeton, NJ: Princeton University Press.

Cohen, Y., and d'Alfonso, L. 2008. The duration of the Emar archives and the relative and absolute chronology of the city. In D'Alfonso, L., Cohen, Y., and Sürenhagen, D. (eds.), *The city of Emar among the Late Bronze Age empires*. Münster: Ugarit-Verlag, 3–25.

D'Agostino, A. 2015. The rise and consolidation of Assyrian control on the northwestern territories. In Düring, B.S. (ed.), *Understanding hegemonic practices of the early Assyrian Empire*. Leiden: NINO, 33–43.

Deller, K., Fadhil, A., and Kozad, M.A. 1994. Two new royal inscriptions dealing with construction work in Kar-Tukulti-Ninurta. *BaM* 25: 459–472.

Démare-Lafont, S., and Fleming, D.E. 2015. Emar chronology and scribal streams: cosmopolitanism and legal diversity. *RA* 109: 45–77.

De Martino, S. 2012. Malatya and Išuwa in Hittite texts: new elements of discussion. *Origini* 34: 375–383.

Dietrich, M. 2003. Salmanassar I. von Assyrien, Ibirānu (VI.) von Ugarit und Tudḫalija IV. von Ḫatti. *UF* 35: 103–139.

Dietrich, M. 2004. Salmanassar I. von Assyrien, Ibirānu (VI.) von Ugarit und Tudḫalija IV. von Ḫatti: ein Korrekturnachtrag. *UF* 36: 41–42.

Durand, J.-M. 1998. *Documents épistolaires du palais de Mari, vol. 2*. Paris: Les éditions du Cerf.

Durand, J.-M., and Marti, L. 2005. Chroniques du Moyen-Euphrate, 5: une attaque de Qatna par le Suhum et la question du "pays de Mari." *RA* 99: 123–132.

Düring, B. 2020. *The imperialisation of Assyria: an archaeological approach.* Cambridge: Cambridge University Press.

Ebeling, E. 1927. *Keilschrifttexte aus Assur juristischen Inhalts.* Leipzig: Hinrichs.

Edel, E. 1994. *Die ägyptisch-hethitische Korrespondenz aus Boghazköi in babylonischer und hethitischer Sprache.* Opladen: Westdeutscher Verlag.

Eichler, S., and Wäfler, M. 1989–1990. Tall al-Hamîdîya. *AfO* 36–37: 249–251.

Faist, B. 2001. *Der Fernhandel des assyrischen Reiches zwischen dem 14. und 11. Jh. v. Chr.* Münster: Ugarit-Verlag.

Faist, B. 2008. Review of Mora and Giorgieri 2004. *Orientalia* 77: 418–424.

Faist, B. 2010. Kingship and institutional development in the Middle Assyrian period. In Lanfranchi, G.B., and Rollinger, R. (eds.), *Concepts of kingship in antiquity.* Padua: Sargon, 15–24.

Fales, F.M. 2011. Transition: the Assyrians at the Euphrates between the 13th and the 12th century BC. In Strobel, K. (ed.), *Empires after the empire: Anatolia, Syria and Assyria after Suppiluliuma II (ca. 1200–800/700 BC).* Florence: LoGisma, 9–59.

Fales, F.M. 2015. Il caso dell'Assiria: l'ascesa storica verso uno *status* elezionista. In Politi, G. (ed.), *Popoli eletti: storia di un viaggio oltre la storia.* Milan: Unicopli, 35–48.

Finkelstein, J.J. 1953. Cuneiform texts from Tell Billa. *JCS* 7: 111–176.

Fleming, D.E. 2000. *Democracy's ancient ancestors: Mari and early collective governance.* Cambridge: Cambridge University Press.

Frahm, E. 2002. Assur 2001: die Schriftfunde. *MDOG* 134: 47–86.

Frahm, E. 2009. *Historische und historisch-literarische Texte* (Keilschrifttexte aus Assur literarischen Inhalts 3). Wiesbaden: Harrassowitz.

Frahm, E. 2017a. The Neo-Assyrian period (ca. 1000–609 BCE). In Frahm, E. (ed.), *A companion to Assyria*. Malden, MA: Wiley-Blackwell, 161–208.

Frahm, E. 2017b. List of Assyrian kings. In Frahm, E. (ed.), *A Companion to Assyria*. Malden, MA: Wiley-Blackwell, 613–616.

Frahm, E. 2020. Dūr-Katlimmu, an alleged Neo-Assyrian library text, Ḫana, and the early history of Dura-Europos. *NABU* 2020: 37–41 (no. 17).

Frazer, M. 2013. Nazi-Maruttaš in later Mesopotamian tradition. *KASKAL: Rivista di storia, ambienti e culture del Vicino Oriente Antico* 10: 187–220.

Freydank, H. 1976. *Mittelassyrische Rechtsurkunden und Verwaltungstexte*. Berlin: Akademie-Verlag.

Freydank, H. 1982. *Mittelassyrische Rechtsurkunden und Verwaltungstexte, vol. II*. Berlin: Akademie-Verlag.

Freydank, H. 1991. *Beiträge zur mittelassyrischen Chronologie und Geschichte*. Berlin: Akademie-Verlag.

Freydank, H. 2001. *Mittelassyrische Rechtsurkunden und Verwaltungstexte, vol. IV: Tafeln aus Kar-Tukulti-Ninurta*. Saarbrücken: Saarbrücker Druckerei und Verlag.

Freydank, H. 2009. Kar-Tukulti-Ninurta als Agrarprovinz. *AoF* 36: 16–84.

Freydank, H. 2016. *Assyrische Jahresbeamte des 12. Jh. v. Chr.* Münster: Ugarit-Verlag.

Freydank, H., and Feller, B. 2005. *Mittelassyrische Rechtsurkunden und Verwaltungstexte, vol. VI*. Saarbrücken: Saarbrücker Druckerei und Verlag.

Freydank, H., and Feller, B. 2007. *Mittelassyrische Rechtsurkunden und Verwaltungstexte, vol. VIII*. Wiesbaden: Harrassowitz.

Galter, H.D. 1988. 28.800 Hethiter. *JCS* 40: 217–235.

Garelli, P. 1990. L'influence de Samsî-Addu sur les titulatures royales assyriennes. In Tunca, O. (ed.), *De la Babylonie à la Syrie en passant par Mari*. Liège: Université de Liège, 97–102.

Gauthier, P. 2016. *Managing risk for the gods: the Middle Assyrian* gināu *agency*. PhD thesis, University of Chicago. Retrieved from https://knowledge.uchicago.edu/record/550 (last accessed September 10, 2020).

Gilibert, A. 2008. On Kār-Tukultī-Ninurta: chronology and politics of a Middle Assyrian ville neuve. In Bonatz, D., Czichon, R.M., and Kreppner, F.J. (eds.), *Fundstellen: gesammelte Schriften zur Archäologie und Geschichte*

Altvorderasiens ad honorem Hartmut Kühne. Wiesbaden: Harrassowitz, 177–188.

Giorgieri, M. 2011. Das Verhältnis Assyriens zum Hethiterreich. In Renger, J. (ed.), *Assur: Gott, Stadt und Land*. Wiesbaden: Harrassowitz, 169–190.

Grayson, A.K. 1972. *Assyrian royal inscriptions, 1*. Wiesbaden: Harrassowitz.

Grayson, A.K. 1975. *Assyrian and Babylonian chronicles*. Locust Valley, NY: Augustin.

Grayson, A.K. 1983. Königslisten und Chroniken. B. Akkadisch. *RlA* 6: 86–135.

Grayson, A.K. 1987. *Assyrian rulers of the third and second millennia BC (to 1115 BC)*. Toronto: University of Toronto Press.

Grayson, A.K. 1991. *Assyrian rulers of the early first millennium BC, I (1114–859 BC)*. Toronto: University of Toronto Press.

Guichard, M. 2014. *L'Épopée de Zimrī-Lîm*. Paris: Société pour l'étude du Proche-Orient ancien.

Güterbock, H.G. 1958. The cuneiform tablets. In McEwan, C., Braidwood, L.S., Frankfort, H., Güterbock, H.G., Haines, R.C., Kantor, H.J., and Kraeling, C.H., *Soundings at Tell Fakhariyah*. Chicago: The Oriental Institute of the University of Chicago, 86–90.

Hagenbuchner, A. 1989. *Die Korrespondenz der Hethiter*. Heidelberg: Winter.

Harrak, A. 1987. *Assyria and Hanigalbat*. Hildesheim: Olms.

Heimpel, W. 1990. Magan. *RlA* 7: 195–199.

Heinhold-Krahmer, S. 1988. Zu Salmanassars I. Eroberungen im Hurritergebiet. *AfO* 35: 79–104.

Ismail, B.K., and Postgate, J.N. 2008. A Middle Assyrian flock-master's archive from Tell Ali. *Iraq* 70: 147–178.

Jakob, S. 2003a. *Mittelassyrische Verwaltung und Sozialstruktur: Untersuchungen*. Leiden: Brill.

Jakob, S. 2003b. Diplomaten in Assur: Alltag oder Anzeichen für eine internationale Krise? *Isimu* 6: 103–114.

Jakob, S. 2009. *Die mittelassyrischen Texte aus Tell Chuēra in Nordost-Syrien*. Wiesbaden: Harrassowitz.

Jakob, S. 2011. Das Osttigrisgebiet im strategischen Konzept mittelassyrischer Könige zwischen 1350 und 1056 v. Chr. In Miglus, P.A., and Mühl, S. (eds.), *Between the cultures: the central Tigris region from the 3rd to the 1st millennium BC*. Heidelberg: Heidelberger Orientverlag, 191–208.

Jakob, S. 2013. Sag mir quando, sag mir wann. In Feliu, L., Llop, J., Millet Albà, A., and Sanmartín, J. (eds.), *Time and history in the ancient Near East*. Winona Lake, IN: Eisenbrauns, 509–523.

Jakob, S. 2015. Daily life in the Wild West of Assyria. In Düring, B.S. (ed.), *Understanding hegemonic practices of the early Assyrian Empire*. Leiden: NINO, 177–187.

Jakob, S. 2017a. The Middle Assyrian period (14th to 11th c. BCE). In Frahm, E. (ed.), *A companion to Assyria*. Malden, MA: Wiley-Blackwell, 117–142.

Jakob, S. 2017b. Economy, society and daily life in the Middle Assyrian period. In Frahm, E. (ed.), *A companion to Assyria*. Malden, MA: Wiley-Blackwell, 143–160.

Jakob, S. 2017c. "One epic or many?" Das Tukultī-Ninurta-Epos zum Ersten, zum Zweiten und zum . . . ? In Drewnowska, O., and Sandowicz, M. (eds.), *Fortune and misfortune in the ancient Near East*. Winona Lake, IN: Eisenbrauns, 259–268.

Janssen, T. 2012. Zur Klärung der assyrischen Distanzangaben: Bemerkungen und Alternativvorschläge zu einem Kapitel in R. Pruzsinszkys *Mesopotamian Chronology* (*CChEM* 22). *Akkadica* 133: 1–20.

Janssen, T. 2013. Weitere Überlegungen zur mesopotamischen und ägyptischen Chronologie (14.–12. Jahrhundert v. Chr.). *Akkadica* 134: 135–157.

Jeffers, J. 2017. The nonintercalated lunar calendar of the Middle Assyrian period. *JCS* 69: 151–191.

Kertai, D. 2008–2009. The history of the Middle Assyrian Empire. *Talanta* 40/41: 25–51.

Klengel, H. 1992. *Syria, 3000 to 300 BC: a handbook of political history*. Berlin: Akademie-Verlag.

Klengel, H. 2000. The "crisis years" and the new political system in Early Iron Age Syria: some introductory remarks. In Bunnens, G. (ed.), *Essays on Syria in the Iron Age*. Leuven: Peeters, 21–30.

Koliński, R. 2015. Making Mittani Assyrian. In Düring, B.S. (ed.), *Understanding hegemonic practices of the early Assyrian Empire*. Leiden: NINO, 9–32.

Kühne, C. 1995. Ein mittelassyrisches Verwaltungsarchiv und andere Keilschrifttexte. In Orthmann, W. (ed.), *Ausgrabungen in Tell Chuēra in Nordost-Syrien, 1: Vorbericht über die Grabungskampagnen 1986 bis 1992*. Wiesbaden: Harrassowitz, 203–225.

Kühne, C. 1999. Imperial Mittani: an attempt at historical reconstruction. In Owen, D.I., and Wilhelm, G. (eds.), *Nuzi at seventy-five*. Bethesda, MD: CDL Press, 203–221.

Kühne, H. 1995. The Assyrians on the Middle Euphrates and the Hābūr. In Liverani, M. (ed.), *Neo-Assyrian geography*. Rome: Università degli studi di Roma "La Sapienza," 69–85.

Kühne, H. 2013. State and empire of Assyria in northeast Syria. In Orthmann, W., Matthiae, P., and al-Maqdissi, M. (eds.), *Archéologie et histoire de la Syrie, vol. I*. Wiesbaden: Harrassowitz, 473–498.

Kühne, H. 2016. The impact of earthquakes on Middle Assyrian Tell Sheikh Hamad (ancient Dur-Katlimmu). In MacGinnis, J., Wicke, D., and Greenfield, T. (eds.), *The provincial archaeology of the Assyrian Empire*. Cambridge: McDonald Institute for Archaeological Research, 189–198.

Kühne, H. 2018. Politics and water management at the Lower Ḫābūr (Syria) in the Middle Assyrian period and beyond: a new appraisal. In Kühne, H. (ed.), *Water for Assyria*. Wiesbaden: Harrassowitz, 137–194.

Lackenbacher, S. 1991. Lettres et fragments. In Bordreuil, P. (ed.), *Une bibliothèque au sud de la ville*. Paris: Éditions Recherche sur les Civilisations, 83–104.

Læssøe, J. 1959. The Basmuzian tablets. *Sumer* 15: 15–18.

Lafont, S. 2003. Middle Assyrian period. In Westbrook, R. (ed.), *A history of ancient Near Eastern law*. Leiden: Brill, 522–563.

Lion, B. 1995. La fin du site de Nuzi et la distribution chronologique des archives. *RA* 89: 77–88.

Lion, B. 2011. Assur unter der Mittaniherrschaft. In Renger, J. (ed.), *Assur: Gott, Stadt und Land*. Wiesbaden: Harrassowitz, 149–167.

Liverani, M. 1988. The growth of the Assyrian Empire in the Habur/Middle Euphrates area: a new paradigm. *SAAB* 2: 81–98.

Liverani, M. 2000. The great powers' club. In Cohen, R., and Westbrook, R. (eds.), *Amarna diplomacy: the beginnings of international relations*. Baltimore, MD: Johns Hopkins University Press, 15–27.

Liverani, M. 2011. From city-state to empire: the case of Assyria. In Arnason, J.P., and Raaflaub, K.A. (eds.), *The Roman Empire in context*. Malden, MA: Wiley-Blackwell, 251–269.

Liverani, M. 2017. *Assyria: the imperial mission*. Winona Lake, IN: Eisenbrauns.

Llop, J. 2005. Die königlichen "großen Speicher" (*karmū rabi'ūtu*) der Stadt Assur in der Regierungszeit Salmanassars I. und Tukultī-Ninurtas I. *MDOG* 137: 41–55.

Llop, J. 2010. Barley from Alu-ša-Sîn-rabi: chronological reflections on an expedition in the time of Tukultī-Ninurta I (1233–1197 BC). In Vidal, J. (ed.), *Studies on war in the ancient Near East: collected essays on military history*. Münster: Ugarit-Verlag, 105–116.

Llop, J. 2011. The creation of the Middle Assyrian provinces. *JAOS* 131: 591–603.

Llop, J. 2012a. The development of the Middle Assyrian provinces. *AoF* 39: 87–111.

Llop, J. 2012b. Did the Assyrians occupy the Euphrates-elbow in the Middle Assyrian period (Late Bronze Age)? In Borrell, F., Bouso, M., Gómez A., Tornero C., and Vicente O. (eds.), *Broadening horizons, vol. 3*. Bellaterra: Universitat Autònoma de Barcelona, 203–225.

Llop, J. 2013. The eponym Bēr-nādin-apli and the documents referring to the expeditions to the city of Tille in the reign of Tukultī-Ninurta I (1233–1197 BCE). In Feliu, L, Llop, J., Millet-Albà, A., and Sanmartín, J. (eds.), *Time and history in the ancient Near East*. Winona Lake, IN: Eisenbrauns, 549–559.

Llop, J. 2015. Foreign kings in the Middle Assyrian archival documentation. In Düring, B.S. (ed.), *Understanding hegemonic practices of the early Assyrian Empire*. Leiden: NINO, 243–275.

Llop, J., and George, A. 2001–02. Die babylonisch-assyrischen Beziehungen und die innere Lage Assyriens in der Zeit der Auseinandersetzung zwischen Ninurta-tukulti-Aššur und Mutakkil-Nusku nach neuen keilschriftlichen Quellen. *AfO* 48–49: 1–23.

Lyon, J.D. 2000. Middle Assyrian expansion and settlement development in the Syrian Jezira: the view from the Balikh valley. In Jas, R.M. (ed.), *Rainfall and agriculture in northern Mesopotamia*. Leiden: NINO, 89–126.

Machinist, P. 1978. *The epic of Tukultī-Ninurta I: a study in Middle Assyrian literature*. PhD thesis, Yale University.

Machinist, P. 1982. Provincial governance in Middle Assyria and some new texts from Yale. *Assur* 3/2: 1–137.

Mahieu, B. 2018. The Old and Middle Assyrian calendars, and the adoption of the Babylonian calendar by Tiglath-Pileser I. *SAAB* 24: 63–85.

Maidman, M.P. 2011. Nuzi, the club of the great powers, and the chronology of the fourteenth century. *KASKAL: Rivista di storia, ambienti e culture del Vicino Oriente Antico* 8: 77–139.

Maidman, M.P. 2014. An important new early Middle Assyrian letter. *Cuneiform Digital Library Bulletin* 2014: 2. Retrieved from http://cdli. ucla.edu/pubs/cdlb/2014/cdlb2014_002.html (last accessed September 10, 2020).

Marti, L. 2010. Le *ḫazannu* à Mari et sur le Moyen-Euphrate. *Babel und Bibel* 5: 153–170.

Maul, S. 1998. Marduk, Nabû und der assyrische Enlil: die Geschichte eines sumerischen Šu'ilas. In Maul, S.M. (ed.), *tikip santakki mala bašmu: Festschrift für Rykle Borger*. Groningen: Styx, 159–197.

Maul, S. 2016. Ein assyrisches Familienarchiv aus dem 14. Jh. v. Chr. und die über 100jährige Geschichte seiner Erforschung. *Zeitschrift für altorientalische und biblische Rechtsgeschichte* 22: 29–45.

Maul, S. 2017. Mittelassyrische Rechtsurkunden und Verwaltungstexte aus dem Besitz der Staatlichen Museen zu Istanbul. *ZA* 107: 89–104.

McClellan, T.L. 2019. *El-Qitar: a Bronze Age fortress on the Euphrates*. Turnhout: Brepols.

Miglus, P.A. 1993. Architektur der Festhäuser in Assur und Uruk sowie des Aššurtempels in Kār-Tukultī-Ninurta. *BaM* 24: 195–215.

Miglus, P.A. 2011. Middle Assyrian settlement in the South. In Miglus, P.A., and Mühl, S. (eds.), *Between the cultures: the central Tigris region from the 3rd to the 1st millennium BC*. Heidelberg: Heidelberger Orientverlag, 221–229.

Miller, J.L. 2007. Amarna Age chronology and the identity of Nibḫururiya in the light of a newly reconstructed Hittite text. *AoF* 34: 252–293.

Miller, J.L. 2010. Revisiting the conquest of Karkamiš of Mursili's 9th year: Assyrian aggression or Mursili in the long shadow of his father? In Fincke, J. (ed.), *Festschrift für Gernot Wilhelm anläßlich seines 65. Geburtstages*. Dresden: ISLET, 235–239.

Mladjov, I. 2019. The kings of Mittani in light of the new evidence from Terqa. *NABU* 2019: 33–36 (no. 22).

Montero Fenollòs, J.-L. 2015. *Asirios en el Medio Éufrates*. Ferrol: PAMES-UDC/Sociedade Luso-Galega de Estudos Mesopotámicos.

Mora, C., and Giorgieri, M. 2004. *Le lettere tra i re ittiti e i re assiri ritrovate a Ḫattuša*. Padua: Sargon.

Müller, G.G.W. 1994. *Studien zur Siedlungsgeographie und der Bevölkerung des mittleren Osttigrisgebietes*. Heidelberg: Heidelberger Orientverlag.

Neumann, J., and Parpola, S. 1987. Climate change and the eleventh-tenth-century eclipse of Assyria and Babylonia. *JNES* 46: 161–182.

Pappi, C. 2018. The land of Idu: city, province, or kingdom? *SAAB* 24: 97–123.

Pedde, F., and Lundstrom, S. 2008. *Der Alte Palast in Assur: Architektur und Baugeschichte*. Wiesbaden: Harrassowitz.

Pedersén, O. 1985. *Archives and libraries in the city of Assur: a survey of the material from the German excavations, part I*. Uppsala: Almqvist & Wiksell.

Pedersén, O. 1998. *Archives and libraries of the ancient Near East, 1500–300 B.C.* Bethesda, MD: CDL Press.

Pfälzner, P. 1995. *Mittanische und mittelassyrische Keramik: eine chronologische, funktionale und produktionsökonomische Analyse*. Berlin: Reimer.

Pfälzner, P., and Qasim, H.A. 2018. Urban developments in northeastern Mesopotamia from the Ninevite V to the Neo-Assyrian periods: excavations at Bassetki in 2017. *ZOrA* 11: 42–87.

Podany, A. 2014. Hana and the Low Chronology. *JNES* 73: 51–73.

Pongratz-Leisten, B. 2015. *Religion and ideology in Assyria*. Berlin: De Gruyter.

Postgate, J.N. 1982. *Ilku* and land tenure in the Middle Assyrian kingdom: a second attempt. In Dandamayev, M.A., Postgate, J.N., and Larsen, M.T. (eds.), *Societies and languages of the ancient Near East: studies in honour of I.M. Diakonoff*. Warminster: Aris & Phillips, 304–313.

Postgate, J.N. 1988. *The archive of Urad-Šerū'a and his family*. Rome: Roberto Denicola.

Postgate, J.N. 1992. The land of Assur and the yoke of Assur. *World Archaeology* 23: 247–263.

Postgate, J.N. 2002. Business and government at Middle Assyrian Rimah. In Al-Guilani Werr, L., Curtis, J., Martin, H., McMahon, A., Oates, J., and Reade, J. (eds.), *Of pots and plans: papers on the archaeology and history of Mesopotamia and Syria presented to David Oates*. London: NABU Publications, 297–308.

Postgate, J.N. 2010. The debris of government: reconstructing the Middle Assyrian state apparatus from tablets and potsherds. *Iraq* 72: 19–37.

Postgate, J.N. 2011. Die Stadt Assur und das Land Assur. In Renger, J. (ed.), *Assur: Gott, Stadt und Land*. Wiesbaden: Harrassowitz, 87–94.

Postgate, J.N. 2013. *Bronze Age bureaucracy*. Cambridge: Cambridge University Press.

Preusser, C. 1955. *Die Paläste in Assur*. Berlin: Mann.

Pruzsinszky, R. 2009. *Mesopotamian chronology of the 2nd millennium BC: an introduction to the textual evidence and related chronological issues*. Vienna: Verlag der Österreichischen Akademie der Wissenschaften.

Radner, K. 1998. Der Gott Salmānu ("Šulmānu") und seine Beziehung zur Stadt Dūr-Katlimmu. *WdO* 29: 33–51.

Radner, K. 2004. Fressen und gefressen werden: Heuschrecken als Katastrophe und Delikatesse im Alten Orient. *WdO* 34: 7–22.

Radner, K. 2011. The Assur-Nineveh-Arbela triangle. In Miglus, P.A., and Mühl, S. (eds.), *Between the cultures: the central Tigris region from the 3rd to the 1st millennium BC.* Heidelberg: Heidelberger Orientverlag, 321–329.

Radner, K. 2014. The Neo-Assyrian Empire. In Gehler, M., and Rollinger, R. (eds.), *Imperien und Reiche der Weltgeschichte.* Wiesbaden: Harrassowitz, 101–118.

Radner, K. 2015a. *Assyria: a very short introduction.* Oxford: Oxford University Press.

Radner, K. 2015b. High visibility punishment and deterrent: impalement in Assyrian warfare and legal practice. *Zeitschrift für altorientalische und biblische Rechtsgeschichte* 21: 103–128.

Radner, K., and Schachner, A. 2001. From Tushhan to Amedi: topographical questions concerning the Upper Tigris region in the Assyrian period. In Tuna, N., Öztürk, J., and Velibeyoğlu, J. (eds.), *Salvage project of the archaeological heritage of the Ilisu and Carchemish dam reservoirs: activities in 1999.* Ankara: METU, 752–776.

Rainey, A.F. 2015. *The El-Amarna correspondence.* Leiden: Brill.

Reade, J.E. 2001. Assyrian king-lists, the royal tombs of Ur, and Indus origins. *JNES* 60: 1–29.

Reculeau, H. 2010. The Lower Ḫābūr before the Assyrians: settlement and land use in the first half of the second millennium BCE. In Kühne, H. (ed.), *Dūr-Katlimmu 2008 and beyond.* Wiesbaden: Harrassowitz, 187–215.

Reculeau, H. 2011. *Climate, environment and agriculture in Assyria in the 2nd half of the 2nd millennium BCE.* Wiesbaden: Harrassowitz.

Reculeau, H. 2016. Claiming land and people: conceptions of power in Syria and Upper Mesopotamia during the 2nd millennium BCE. In Schmidt-Hofner, S., Ambos, C., and Eich, P. (eds.), *Raum-Ordnung: Raum und soziopolitische Ordnungen im Altertum.* Heidelberg: Winter, 175–214.

Roth, M.T. 1997. *Law collections from Mesopotamia and Asia Minor.* Atlanta, GA: Scholars Press. 2nd rev. ed.

Rouault, O. 2004. Chronological problems concerning the Middle Euphrates during the Bronze Age. In Hunger, H., and Pruzsinszky, R. (eds.),

Mesopotamian Dark Age revisited. Vienna: Verlag der Österreichischen Akademie der Wissenschaften, 51–60.

Salah, S. 2014. *Die mittelassyrischen Personen- und Rationenlisten aus Tall Šēḫ Ḥamad / Dūr-Katlimmu.* Wiesbaden: Harrassowitz.

Salvini, M. 1998. I testi cuneiformi delle campagne 1989 e 1993 a Tell Barri/ Kahat. In Pecorella, P.E. (ed.), *Tell Barri/Kahat, 2.* Florence: Florence University Press, 187–198.

Salvini, M. 2004. I documenti cuneiformi della campagna del 2001. In Pecorella, P.E., and Pierobon Benoit, R. (eds.), *Tell Barri/Kahat: la campagna del 2001, relazione preliminare.* Florence: Florence University Press, 146–151.

Salvini, M. 2005. I documenti cuneiformi della campagna del 2002 a Tell Barri. In Pecorella, P.E., and Pierobon Benoit, R. (eds.), *Tell Barri/Kahat: la campagna del 2002, relazione preliminare.* Florence: Florence University Press, 143–153.

Salvini, M. 2008a. Lista di cavalli e carri. In Pecorella, P.E., and Pierobon Benoit, R. (eds.), *Tell Barri/Kahat: la campagna del 2004, relazione preliminare.* Florence: Florence University Press, 111–114.

Salvini, M. 2008b. Spigolature dai documenti cuneiformi di Tell Barri. *La Parola di Passato* 63: 76–101.

Saporetti, C. 1979a. *Gli eponimi medio-assiri.* Malibu, CA: Undena.

Saporetti, C. 1979b. *Assur 14446: La famiglia A.* Malibu, CA: Undena.

Saporetti, C. 1982. *Assur 14446: Le altre famiglie.* Malibu, CA: Undena.

Sazonov, V. 2016. *Die assyrischen Königstitel und -epitheta vom Anfang bis Tukulti-Ninurta I. und seinen Nachfolgern.* Helsinki: The Neo-Assyrian Text Corpus Project.

Shibata, D. 2011a. The toponyms "the land of Māri" in the late second millennium BC. *RA* 105: 95–108.

Shibata, D. 2011b. The origins of the dynasty of the land of Māri and the city-god of Ṭābetu. *RA* 105: 165–180.

Shibata, D. 2015. Dynastic marriages in Assyria during the late second millennium BC. In Düring, B.S. (ed.), *Understanding hegemonic practices of the early Assyrian Empire.* Leiden: NINO, 235–242.

Singer, I. 1985. The battle of Niḫriya and the end of the Hittite Empire. *ZA* 75: 100–123.

Singer, I. 2008. KBo 28.61–4 and the struggle over the throne of Babylon at the turn of the 13th century BCE. In Wilhelm, H. (ed.), *Ḫattuša-Bogazköy.* Wiesbaden: Harrassowitz, 223–245.

Sinha, A., Kathayat, G., Weiss, H., Li, H., Cheng, H., Reuter, J., Schneider, A.W., Berkelhammer, M., Adalı, S.F., Stott, L.D., and Edwards, R.L. 2019. Role of climate in the rise and fall of the Neo-Assyrian Empire. *Science Advances* 5/11: eaax6656. Retrieved from DOI: 10.1126/sciadv.aax6656 (last accessed September 10, 2020).

Snell, D.C. 1983–1984. The cuneiform tablet from el-Qitar. *Abr-Naḫrain* 22: 159–170.

Talon, P. 2005. Une nouvelle inscription de Tukulti-Ninurta I. In Talon, P. and Van der Stede, V. (eds.), *Si un homme... Textes offerts en hommage à André Finet*. Turnhout: Brepols, 125–134.

Tenu, A. 2004. Ninive et Aššur à l'époque médio-assyrienne. *Iraq* 66: 27–33.

Tenu, A. 2009. *L'expansion médio-assyrienne: approche archéologique*. Oxford: Archaeopress.

Tenu, A. 2017. Naissance de l'Assyrie. In Lafont, B., Tenu, A., Joannès, F., and Clancier P., *La Mésopotamie: de Gilgamesh à Artaban, 3300–120 av. J.-C.* Paris: Belin, 529–583.

Tenu, A., and Clancier, P. 2012. Haradu dans l'empire assyrien XIIe–VIIIe siècles. In Kepinski, C. (ed.), *Haradum III*. Paris: De Boccard, 247–261.

van Soldt, W.H. 2008. The location of Idu. *NABU* 2008: 72–74 (no. 55).

van Soldt, W.H., Pappi, C., Wossink, A., Hess, C.W., and Ahmed, K.M. 2013. Satu Qala: a preliminary report on the seasons 2010–2011. *Anatolica* 39: 197–239.

Veenhof, K. 2017. The Old Assyrian period (20th–18th century BCE). In Frahm, E. (ed.), *A companion to Assyria*. Malden, MA: Wiley-Blackwell, 57–79.

Walker, C.B.F. 1982. Babylonian Chronicle 25: a chronicle of the Kassite and Isin II dynasties. In van Driel, G., Krispijn, T.J.H., Stol, M., and Veenhof, K.R. (eds.), *Zikir šumim: Assyriological studies presented to F.R. Kraus*. Leiden: Brill, 398–417.

Weidner, E. 1963. Assyrische Epen über die Kassiten-Kämpfe. *AfO* 20: 113–116.

Wiggermann, F. 2000. Agriculture in the northern Balikh valley: the case of Middle Assyrian Tell Sabi Abyad. In Jas, R.M. (ed.), *Rainfall and agriculture in northern Mesopotamia*. Leiden: NINO, 171–231.

Wiggermann, F. 2006. The seal of Ilī-padâ, grand vizier of the middle Assyrian Empire. In Taylor, P. (ed.), *The iconography of cylinder seals*. London: University of London Press, 92–99.

Wiggermann, F. 2008. Cuneiform texts from Tell Sabi Abyad related to pottery. In Duistermaat, K., *The pots and potters of Assyria*. Turnhout: Brepols, 377–382.

Wiggermann, F. 2010. Wein, Weib und Gesang in een Midden-Assyrische ned-
erzetting aan de Balikh. *Phoenix* 56: 17–60.

Wilhelm, G. 2004. Generation count in Hittite chronology. In Hunger, H., and
Pruzsinszky, R. (eds.), *Mesopotamian Dark Age revisited*. Vienna: Verlag
der Österreichischen Akademie der Wissenschaften, 71–77.

Wilhelm, G. 2018. Ein Testament aus Tell Fray. In Kleber, K., Neumann, G.,
and Paulus, S. (eds.), *Grenzüberschreitungen: Studien zur Kulturgeschichte
des Alten Orients*. Münster: Zaphon, 791–796.

Wiseman, D. 1968. The Tell al Rimah tablets, 1966. *Iraq* 30: 175–205.

Yamada, M. 2011. The second military conflict between "Assyria" and "Ḫatti"
in the reign of Tukulti-Ninurta I. *RA* 105: 199–220.

Yamada, S. 1994. The editorial history of the Assyrian King List. *ZA* 84: 11–37.

Yamada, S. 2003. Tukulti-Ninurta I's rule over Babylonia and its aftermath: a
historical reconstruction. *Orient* 38: 153–177.

Yamada, S. 2011. An adoption contract from Tell Taban, the kings of the land
of Hana, and the Hana-style scribal tradition. *RA* 105: 61–84.

Yamada, S. 2017. The transition period (17th to 15th century BCE). In Frahm,
E. (ed.), *A companion to Assyria*. Malden, MA: Wiley-Blackwell, 108–116.

Ziegler, N., and Langlois, A.-I. 2016. *Les toponymes paléo-babyloniens de la
Haute-Mésopotamie*. Paris: Société pour l'étude du Proche-Orient ancien.

33

Kassite Babylonia

Susanne Paulus

33.1. Sources and matters of chronology

Sketching an overview of the history of Kassite Babylonia (figure 33.1) makes it necessary to address what is meant by this designation.[1] In modern research, the time between the fall of the First Dynasty of Babylon (chapter 18 in volume 2) and 1155 BC is commonly described as the "Kassite period" or the "Middle Babylonian period." The latter designation is based on the modern term for the dialect of the Akkadian language as recorded during this period and includes also the rule of the Second Dynasty of Isin over Babylonia (for the latter period, see chapter 41 in volume 4).[2] Note that the term "Kassite dynasty" is only attested in post-Kassite sources of the first millennium BC.[3]

This chapter will present an overview of the history of Babylonia under the rule of the Kassite dynasty. As elsewhere in *The Oxford History*

---

1. I thank Jane Gordon for correcting my English and helpful suggestions. Furthermore, I am grateful to my colleagues Antoine Cavigneaux, Tim Clayden, Elena Devecchi, and Helen Malko for giving me access to their research prior to publication.

2. Brinkman 2017: 30–31.

3. Shelley 2017: 200.

Susanne Paulus, *Kassite Babylonia* In: *The Oxford History of the Ancient Near East.* Edited by: Karen Radner, Nadine Moeller, and D. T. Potts, Oxford University Press. © Oxford University Press 2022. DOI: 10.1093/oso/9780190687601.003.0033

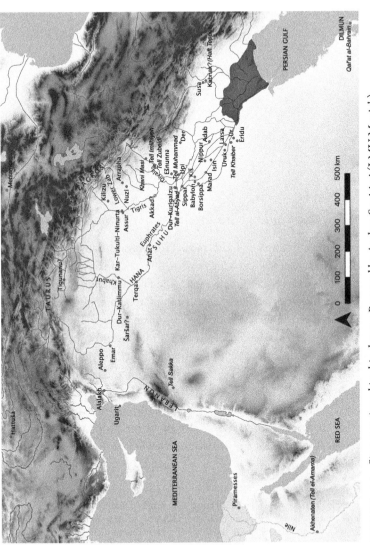

FIGURE 33.1. Sites mentioned in this chapter. Prepared by Andrea Squitieri (LMU Munich).

of the Ancient Near East, the term "Babylonia" is used as a geographical designation, as it was only introduced many centuries after the Kassite period.[4] The Kassite kings referred to their land most commonly by the historical terms "land of Sumer and Akkad" and "land [of the city of] Babylon." They also introduced the new, likely Kassite, term "Karduniaš" for the entity later known as Babylonia.[5]

The term "Kassite" merits explanation. This gentilic adjective is derived from the Akkadian word *kaššû*, which may be an adaptation of a word in the Kassite language (*g/kalž-*).[6] The word "Kassite" was used by Babylonian scribes from the later Old Babylonian period onward as a label of identity for a possibly ethnically distinctive population group with its own language and religion.[7] Only traces elucidating these aspects of Kassite identity survive in the extant cuneiform documentation,[8] which was written in Akkadian and Sumerian but not in the Kassite language. While the rulers of the dynasty rarely called themselves "Kassite,"[9] many bore Kassite-language names.[10]

There is a wide array of sources at our disposal for writing on the history of Kassite Babylonia.[11] This includes contemporary textual sources written during the Kassite period, as well as later texts that formed part of the Babylonian literary and historiographical tradition. Contemporary sources are royal inscriptions, international and administrative correspondence, legal and economic texts from different archives, inscriptions on *kudurru* stones (figure 33.2) and seals, and scholarly and literary

---

4. Beaulieu 2018: 25.

5. Paulus 2015.

6. Zadok 2013; Shelley 2017: 197–198; cf. van Koppen 2017: 47, who notes that the lexical equivalence is late.

7. Brinkman 2004: 284; Shelley 2017; Malko 2020.

8. For the still most comprehensive overview of the Kassite language, see Balkan 1954; on Kassite religion, see Bartelmus 2017 and Malko 2020.

9. Shelley 2017: 200.

10. Brinkman 1980: 467; Sassmannshausen 2014.

11. For the most comprehensive if slightly outdated overview, see Brinkman 1976.

texts composed during the rule of the Kassite dynasty. Most Kassite royal inscriptions are short texts in the Akkadian or Sumerian language and can be classified as building, votive, or possessive inscriptions.[12] Only a few of these texts ever refer to historical events beyond religiously motivated building projects and donations. Royal inscriptions are attested in the original for most Kassite rulers starting with Kara-indaš (see section 33.2) while the inscriptions of earlier Kassite kings, as well as also some later rulers, survive only in later copies, created for scholarly or educational purposes. As the authenticity of some of those inscriptions has been contested, their historic value needs to be carefully evaluated on an individual basis.[13]

The practice of assigning to each year a name that commemorates an important event, as was common in earlier periods of Mesopotamian history (see e.g. chapter 14 in volume 2), was abandoned under Burna-Buriaš II (1359–1333 BC) in favor of a continuous count of regnal years, and this change deprives the modern historian of an important source of information.[14]

Royal correspondence is an important source for diplomatic relations and moreover frequently provides synchronisms between Kassite kings and their Egyptian, Assyrian, Hittite, and Elamite counterparts.[15] Letters sent to and from members of the Kassite royal family have been found in the core of their realm (Dur-Kurigalzu), but also abroad, namely in Egypt at the royal residence cities of Akhetaten (modern Tell el-Amarna) and Piramesses, in Ugarit on the Syrian coast, and in the Hittite capital of Hattusa (modern Boğazköy).[16]

---

12. There is presently no comprehensive edition of all Kassite royal inscriptions. For the inscriptions in Akkadian language, see Stein 2000, while Niek Veldhuis and Alexa Bartelmus maintain the online *Corpus of Kassite Sumerian Texts* (http://oracc.museum.upenn.edu/ckst/; last accessed August 17, 2020). For the structural typology of the inscriptions, see Brinkman 1976: 49–73.

13. Paulus 2018.

14. Brinkman 1976: 402–404. Note that Brinkman 2020: 240-241 discusses potential year names of Šagarakti-Šuriaš.

15. Paulus 2013; Devecchi 2017; Frahm 2017: 289–291; Jacob 2017a; Miller 2017; Roaf 2017.

16. Miller 2017: 93–94 (with references, to which add Gurney 1949: no. 12 for a letter found in Dur-Kurigalzu).

Also non-royal votive and seal inscriptions[17] can be useful for historical reconstruction. The monuments typically called *kudurru* are stone steles that were created to protect real estate property rights (figure 33.2), an important body of sources for Kassite Babylonia. The practice of creating such monuments continued into the subsequent periods of Babylonian history. The inscriptions incised on these artifacts provide information about historical events, provincial organization and administration, and the Kassite royal court. While *kudurru*s have been found throughout Babylonia, most of the Kassite pieces were found in the Elamite city of Susa, where they had been taken as booty by the kings of Elam as a result of their raids on Babylonia at the end of the Kassite period.[18]

In addition to these textual sources, excavations have yielded over 15,000 archival documents of economic and legal content, including letters and memos, dating to the Kassite period.[19] Written by the scribes of palatial, temple, and provincial administrations, such documents have been found primarily in Nippur, but also in the northern royal residence city of Dur-Kurigalzu, in Dur-Enlile (an unidentified site that was possibly located near Nippur),[20] and at Qal'at al-Bahrain on the island of Dilmun (modern Bahrain).[21] These texts from institutional contexts give valuable information about the provincial administration, taxation, agriculture, craft production, and trade. They are complemented by private archives from Babylon, Nippur, Ur, Tell Imlihiye, and Tell Muhammad, as well as a further archive of unknown provenance (known after the first editor as the "Peiser Archive").[22] Legal and economic sources from both administrative and private archives are chronologically and geographically unevenly distributed. Most texts come from the site of Nippur and

17. Matthews 1992; Stiehler-Alegria Delgado 1996; Porada and Collon 2016: 55–85.

18. Paulus 2014b: 17–27.

19. Brinkman 1976; Pedersén 1998: 103–119; Sassmannshausen 2001b: 3–6.

20. Devecchi 2020b; van Soldt 2015. Cf. Murai 2020 for identifying Dur-Enlile as the likely origin of other texts from the antiquity trade.

21. The texts will be published by Antoine Cavigneaux and Béatrice André-Salvini.

22. Pedersén 1998: 103–119; Sassmannshausen 2001b: 3–6; for Babylon, see Pedersén 2005: 69–108.

FIGURE 33.2. *Kudurru* stone decorated with divine symbols and an inscription documenting the donation of King Meli-Šipak to his son, the future king Marduk-apla-iddina I. Louvre, Paris (accession number Sb 22). Photograph © RMN-Grand Palais (musée du Louvre)/Daniel Arnaudet/Jean Schormans 2007 RMN/René-Gabriel Ojéda.

from the period of 1360–1223 BC, some date to the Late Kassite period (1222–1155 BC; see section 33.5), and a very few to the Early Kassite period (before 1375 BC; see section 33.2).[23]

Scholarly compositions and school texts are well attested during the Kassite period and have recently received renewed scholarly attention, but they can contribute less to our reconstruction of the history of Kassite Babylonia.[24] More relevant are some learned texts which were compiled after the fall of the Kassite dynasty, especially historiographic texts like king lists and chronicles, but also some other literary compositions. Careful source criticism is necessary for all these texts in order to access their value for historical reconstruction. The so-called chronicles, compiled both in Babylonia and Assyria, cover historical events pertaining to the Kassite dynasty. The earliest chronicles mentioning Kassite rulers are Assyrian compositions, which mostly concern military encounters between Assyria and the southern neighbor state.[25] The most detailed of these chronicle texts is the *Synchronistic Chronicle*, discovered as a late copy in the seventh-century library of Ashurbanipal of Assyria (668–631 BC).[26] This chronicle covers encounters between both kingdoms from the time of the early Kassite king Kara-indaš (late fifteenth century BC) to the penultimate ruler of the Kassite dynasty, Zababa-šuma-iddina (1159 BC). Important information about the earliest Kassite kings prior to the reign of Kara-indaš is included in a fragment of the *Chronicle of Ancient Kings*, also known from a copy in Ashurbanipal's library.[27] Comparable chronicles were likely in use in Babylonia also in later times, which indicates a continued interest in the

---

23. Brinkman 2017: 33–34.

24. Sassmannshausen 2008a; Veldhuis 2014: 226–269; Bartelmus 2016; Heeßel 2017; Zomer 2018.

25. Frahm 2009: 114–115. Middle Assyrian chronicle fragments include the *Chronicle of Enlil-nerari* (Glassner 2004: 184–185, no. 11) and the *Chronicle of Tukulti-Ninurta I* (Glassner 2004: 186–187, no. 13).

26. Glassner 2004: 176–183, no. 10.

27. Glassner 2004: 272–275, no. 41.

times of the Kassite dynasty.[28] The *Chronicle of the Kassite Kings* (also known as *Chronicle P*)[29] and the *Chronicle of the Last Kassite Kings and Kings of Isin* are part of this later tradition.[30]

The Kassite kings, and certain events of their reigns, were also popular in the later literary tradition,[31] ranging from the simple mentions of the Kassite kings in colophons of learned texts to the composition of elaborate literary letters and various other narratives including an epic, a prophecy, and a poem.[32] Some of these compositions contain narratives of the fall of the First Dynasty of Babylon that preceded Kassite rule and of the conquest of Babylonia by the Elamites at the end of the Kassite dynasty.[33]

King lists are our most important source for reconstructing the sequence of Kassite rulers and the length of their reigns. King List A states in the summary that the Kassite dynasty consisted of thirty-six kings who ruled together 576 years. However, the section concerning the Kassite monarchs is severely damaged. Part of the missing information can be restored with the help of the fragmentarily preserved Assyrian composition known as the Synchronistic King List, which covers both Assyrian and Babylonian rulers. Due to the fragmentary condition of both of these sources, and because of contradictions between them as well as between the information gained from the king lists and other historic documents, the names and sequence of the Kassite kings and the lengths of their reigns are still subject to discussion.[34] Whenever relevant, ongoing controversies are highlighted in the following.

---

28. Waerzeggers 2012.

29. Glassner 2004: 278–281, no. 45.

30. Glassner 2004: 282–285, no. 46.

31. Bartelmus and Taylor 2014; Frazer 2013: 205–206; 2015; Paulus 2018.

32. Frazer 2013; Brinkman 2017: 33.

33. Foster 2005: 367–391; Richardson 2016.

34. Brinkman 1976: 6–34, 424–439; 2017; Sassmannshausen 2014.

One major point of controversy is the absolute chronology of the Kassite period. From the contemporary sources and the already mentioned king lists, the absolute chronology of Kassite rule can be reconstructed with confidence only from Kurigalzu I (?–1375 BC) onward, likely the seventeenth ruler of the dynasty.[35] Due to synchronisms with Egyptian, Hittite, and Assyrian history, the chronology of Babylonia can generally be aligned with other local chronologies of the late second and early first millennium BC.[36] However, for the earliest Kassite kings, the lengths of their reigns are not preserved in the available king lists, and the sequence of the rulers itself is unclear.

To make matters even more complicated, while it is certain that some of the early Kassite rulers mentioned in the king lists were contemporaries of the First Dynasty of Babylon, no secure synchronism between the two dynasties is presently known. Furthermore, cuneiform tablets with year names or regnal years, which could help to fill this gap in our knowledge, are almost completely absent for the Early Kassite period. The period of unknown length between the end of the First Dynasty of Babylon and the Kassite period can therefore be described as a "dark age." This chronological problem is not unique to Babylonia, but affects also the neighboring regions. Different strategies have been employed to achieve a solution, including analysis of later records pertaining to astronomical events in early second millennium Babylonian history and the mention of chronological intervals between stages of building work undertaken by various rulers on important temples, as recorded in Assyrian royal inscriptions (the so-called *Distanzangaben*).[37] Those strategies have led to a multitude of chronologies being proposed for the period, but so far no consensus has been reached and no secure chronology could be established; doing so may be out of reach without the discovery of new sources.[38]

---

35. Brinkman 1976: 6–34, 424–439; 2017: 36; Sassmannshausen 2004a.

36. Devecchi 2017; Miller 2017.

37. For a comprehensive overview of the sources and the strategies used to establish a sound chronology, see Pruzsinszky 2009.

38. Brinkman 2017: 29–30.

For matters of convenience, this chapter uses the so-called Middle Chronology and J.A. Brinkman's reconstructed sequence of the Kassite rulers.[39] Furthermore, this chapter employs the commonly used tripartite periodization into

(1) the Early Kassite period until the mid-fifteenth century, when primary sources from Babylonia become more abundant (section 33.2);
(2) the Middle Kassite Period until the Babylonian conquest of Tukulti-Ninurta I of Assyria in the 1220s BC (section 33.3); and
(3) the Late Kassite period until the fall of the Kassite dynasty (1155 BC) (section 33.5).[40]

33.2. The Early Kassite period

In this section, we cover the first emergence of the Kassites as foreigners in Babylonia during the late Old Babylonian period; the possible evidence for Kassite leaders controlling parts of Mesopotamia during the late Old Babylonian period; and the reigns of the first Kassite rulers after the fall of Babylon until the Kassite conquest of Babylonia was completed with the integration of the Sealand. The period after the fall of Babylon is characterized by a paucity of primary sources from Babylonia, both archival texts and royal inscriptions.

The dissolution of Hammurabi's kingdom of Babylon began already under his successor Samsu-iluna (1749–1712 BC), who lost control over the south, which then came under the influence of the First Dynasty of the Sealand.[41] The name of Samsu-iluna's ninth regnal year mentions that he "ripped out the foundation of the Kassite army," and this is the first historically secure mention of the Kassites.[42] Other year names record

---

39. Brinkman 2017: 36.

40. Brinkman 2017. This periodization is based not only on historical events and source distribution but also the clearly discernible internal policies.

41. Charpin 2004: 335–336; Boivin 2018: 86–125; see chapter 18 in volume 2.

42. Brinkman 2017: 3–4.

similar hostilities, and a year name of Rim-Sin II of Larsa, a contemporary of Samsu-iluna, describes the Kassites in a stereotypical manner as uncivilized mountain people.[43]

Kassite groups arrived in Babylonia as a result of a larger migration event.[44] The geographic origin of the people(s) involved is unknown, but an immigration route to Mesopotamia via the Zagros mountains and a possible origin on the Iranian plateau have been suggested.[45] From the reign of Samsu-iluna onward, the presence of a Kassite population is traceable in Babylonia. Frans van Koppen has suggested that the immigration happened in waves, each receiving its own gentilic label by the Babylonian scribes, designating them with the terms Kaššû, Bimatû, and Samharû. According to his reconstruction, the Kaššû ("Kassites") arrived prior to Samsu-iluna, and being not very numerous, they were mostly conscripted into the Babylonian army. The second wave consisted of the Bimatû, who were settled in military colonies at the periphery of the Babylonian state. The third wave consisted of the Samharû who, together with the Bimatû, were responsible for disruptive events under Ammi-ṣaduqa and Samsu-ditana.[46]

Old Babylonian texts show a clear military specialization on the part of the Kassite immigrants, including as charioteers. While little is known about the Kassite language, many of the preserved Kassite words concern horses and their breeding, suggesting that the Kassites played an important role in introducing those animals and the connected chariot technology to Babylonia.[47] Discussions of Kassite tribal organization have focused mainly on the mention of Kassite "houses" (Akkadian

---

43. "Year: Ninmah raised Rim-Sin to kingship over all countries in the Keš temple, the temenos of heaven and earth, and the enemy, the evil Kassites from the barbarous country, who could not be driven back to the mountains [?] . . . "; see Stol 1976: 54.

44. Heinz 1995; van Koppen 2017.

45. Potts 2006: 113; Fuchs 2017: 127–141.

46. van Koppen 2017.

47. Balkan 1954: 11–40; Fuchs 2017: 160; van Koppen 2017: 79–80.

bītu), but these likely reflect common Babylonian household structures rather than a native form of Kassite organization.[48] Typical for the latter seems to be a grouping around "animal pens" (Akkadian *tarbaṣu*), perhaps reflecting a former (semi)nomadic lifestyle.[49] The Kassites settling in Babylonia were integrated into local society as army and work units, received land provisions, adopted Babylonian names, and participated in economic and legal life.[50] At that time, Kassites, labeled with the gentilic adjective *kaššû*, are also attested in Alalakh near the Syrian coast, while in Upper Mesopotamia, people with Kassite personal names are attested as far as Tigunanu in the Upper Tigris area.[51]

While newer studies have shed more light on the arrival of Kassites during the late Old Babylonian period, very little is still known about the earliest Kassite kings, as listed in King List A and the Synchronistic King List. Those kings are Gandaš, Agum (I), Kaštiliaš (I), Abi-rattaš, Kaštiliaš (II),[52] and Urzigurumaš.[53] In an inscription known only from later copies, Agum (II), who ruled in Babylon shortly after the fall of the First Dynasty of Babylon, names Agum (I), Kaštiliaš (I), Abi-rattaš, and Urzigurumaš as his ancestors,[54] which would indicate that those rulers were contemporary with the late Old Babylonian kings; but there is no further evidence to support this assumption. There is a fragmentary royal inscription for Gandaš, the founder of the Kassite dynasty according to the king lists, but it is known only from a manuscript dating to the Neo-Babylonian period (sixth century BC), or later. Therein, Gandaš is introduced with the titles "king of the four corners of the world, king of

---

48. Paulus 2014b: 179–185; van Koppen 2017: 49–51, cf. Brinkman 1980: 465.

49. van Koppen 2017: 51–52, cf. Sassmannshausen 2004b.

50. de Smet 1990; Van Lerberghe 1995; De Graef 1999: 5–15; Sassmannshausen 2001a; 2004b; van Koppen 2017.

51. Brinkman 2017: 4–5.

52. Kaštiliaš is not listed in King List A and is omitted from the genealogy of Agum II, which Sassmannshausen 2014: 172 argued might be by mistake.

53. Brinkman 1976: 9–11.

54. Paulus 2018: 124–126.

Sumer and Akkad" and "king of Babylon," and a temple building project after the conquest of Babylon is mentioned. Based on stylistic and
historical analysis, this text is likely a later composition rather than an
authentic inscription of Gandaš, possibly created with the intention to
flesh out the story of the otherwise unknown founder of the dynasty.[55]

Of special interest for the reconstruction of early Kassite history are
the texts from Terqa, the likely capital of the kingdom of Hana in the
Middle Euphrates region (see chapter 15 in volume 2). Several texts mention a king called Kaštiliaš, who ruled during the late Old Babylonian
period.[56] Attempts to connect this Kaštiliaš attested at Terqa with one or
the other of the two early Kassite rulers called Kaštiliaš in the Babylonian
king lists are inconclusive.[57] Instead, it has been proposed that he was
a local ruler, independent from the Kassite kings.[58] This Kaštiliaš, the
only ruler in the Terqa texts with a Kassite name, pursued local projects
with a focus on Terqa and the Khabur river and defeated the Suteans (a
nomadic population group active in the Syrian desert), as his year names
document.[59] It is likely that this Kaštiliaš was also the author of a letter
discovered at Tell Sakka near Damascus, which is addressed to a certain
Zimri-Lim, apparently the local ruler.[60]

It remains of course possible that some of the early Kassite rulers
included in the king lists did not actually rule over central Babylonia,
which was then still under the control of the First Dynasty of Babylon,
but over smaller territories in its periphery. This scenario is very likely
for the two kings listed after Urzigurumaš as the seventh and eighth rulers of the Kassite dynasty according to the king lists. While the readings
of their names are uncertain in the king lists, it has been convincingly

55. Paulus 2018: 150–151.

56. Podany 2002: 43–51.

57. Podany 2002: 46–51 thinks he was a contemporary of Samsu-iluna, while
Charpin 2002: 71 proposes a later date under Abi-ešuh.

58. Podany 2019: 133 (with further references).

59. Podany 2019: 133.

60. Abdallah and Durand 2014: 234–237; Podany 2019: 133.

proposed to interpret them as Hurbah and Šipta-ulzi, two kings who are also attested in the texts from Tell Muhammad, a site close to modern Baghdad.[61] These texts are written in the language typical of the late Old Babylonian period,[62] but use the year names of these two rulers instead of the kings of the First Dynasty of Babylon. Hurbah's year names suggest that he controlled the Diyala region, including Ešnunna.[63] Of particular importance and interest are the year names of Šipta-ulzi, as he combines these with an era designation of "Year x in which they settled Babylon." This has been interpreted as counting the years since the fall of Babylon,[64] and this would therefore indicate that the rule of the First Dynasty of Babylon ended during, or shortly before, the reign of Šipta-ulzi.

The fall of Babylon is generally attributed to the raid of Hittite king Mursili I and the Hurrians, as recounted in Hittite sources (see chapter 30 in this volume). However, according to a recently published text known as the *Epic of Gulkišar*, this king of the Sealand stated that he strove to defeat Samsu-ditana, suggesting the active participation of the Sealand in the conquest of Babylon.[65] Later sources mention several other enemies, including the Elamites, the Hanaens (i.e., the inhabitants of the kingdom of Terqa; see earlier discussion in this section), the Kassites, and the Samharû (another label for Kassites; see earlier in this section),[66] which suggests the possibility that the Kassites too played an active role in the end of the First Dynasty of Babylon. However, sources that can be connected to the Kassites rarely allude to the conquest of Babylon, with the sole exceptions being the previously mentioned year

---

61. As first elaborated in detail by Boese 2008; for further references, see van Koppen 2017: 59 n. 53, cf. Brinkman 2014; 2017: 5 n. 29.

62. Alubaid 1983.

63. van Koppen 2017: 59–60.

64. Gasche et al. 1998: 83–87, but note van Koppen 2010: 462; 2017: 59–61, who prefers an earlier date for those events.

65. Boivin 2018: 117–121. See also chapter 18 in volume 2.

66. Richardson 2016.

names in texts from Tell Muhammad and a *kudurru* inscription that was likely first composed under King Kadašman-Harbe I, but which only survives as a later copy. This text mentions that borders were changed at the end of the "Amorite dynasty" (i.e., the First Dynasty of Babylon) due to an "assault of the Hanaens" and "the army of the Kassites."[67]

Important information about the political situation in Babylonia during that time comes from an inscription of Agum II.[68] As the text survives only in later copies, its authenticity has long been contested; however, detailed analysis and new evidence support its authenticity.[69] The inscription recounts the restoration and embellishment of the temple and the statues of the god Marduk and his spouse Ṣarpanitu.[70] Agum describes how the gods ordered him to return the statue of Marduk from the land of the Hanaens. The common interpretation of this passage is that the Hittites had stolen the statue of Marduk during their raid of Babylon and had left it in Terqa, or that for political reasons, the toponym Hana is used in this text instead of Hatti, the Hittite kingdom.[71] The absence of Marduk from Babylon is also mentioned in the *Marduk Prophecy*, a later literary source of limited historic value, which describes how Marduk left Babylon of his own will and stayed in Hatti for twenty-four years.[72]

The inscription of Agum II also mentions resettling the land of Ešnunna, which was already under Kassite control during the time of Hurbah and Šipta-ulzi. Agum's kingdom now extended further into the Zagros mountains, as his titles "king of the land of Padan and (H)alman" illustrate. From that time onward, those regions were a core part of

---

67. Paulus 2014b: 296–297; see also Brinkman 2015 (for the identification as a later copy); 2019: 143 (for an important correction).

68. This inscription is commonly referred to as the *Agum-kakrime Text*, after the epithet of the ruler that is attested only in this inscription's first line.

69. Paulus 2018.

70. Foster 2005: 360–364.

71. van Koppen 2017: 74.

72. Paulus 2018: 131–134.

Kassite Babylonia,[73] and the recent excavations at Khani Masi in the upper valley of the Diyala have revealed strong Babylonian influence on the site's material culture dating to the fifteenth or possibly even early sixteenth century BC.[74] Frans van Koppen has recently proposed that Agum II might have seized control of the Diyala region, including Ešnunna, from Šipta-ulzi, pointing out that Šipta-ulzi and his predecessor Hurbah are absent from the genealogy of Agum II, as given in this inscription.[75] He also proposed that Agum II is to be identified with that Agum who is attested with the title *bukāšu* in a letter dating to the time of Samsu-ditana of Babylon.[76] If this identification is correct, it would mean that, before the fall of Babylon, Agum II was a military leader in the nineteenth year of Samsu-ditana and hosted ambassadors from Aleppo,[77] and this would indicate a very short transition between the reign of Samsu-ditana and of Agum II. Future research will hopefully further clarify the matter.

While the events during and after the conquest of Babylon and its holdings remain uncertain, the inscription of Agum II gives us important information about the extent of the Kassite kingdom after the fall of Babylon.[78] Agum describes himself as the "king of the Kassites and Akkadians," and "the king of the wide land of Babylon," indicating this Kassite ruler's control over the northern Babylonian area, while the absence of Sumer in these titles suggests that southern Babylonia was still under the control of the Sealand dynasty (see chapter 18 in volume 2).

Thanks to new texts originating from illicit diggings at an unidentified site, as well as from recent archaeological excavations at Tell Khaiber, the reigns of the Sealand kings Pešgaldarameš and Ayadaragalama (likely

---

73. Fuchs 2011: 235–238; 2017.

74. Glatz et al. 2019.

75. van Koppen 2017: 66; see also Fuchs 2011: 235–238.

76. This letter was formerly attributed to Samsu-iluna.

77. van Koppen 2017: 65–70.

78. Astour 1986: 329 (with summary of previous literature); van Koppen 2017: 74–77; Paulus 2018: 126–130.

contemporaries of the early Kassite kings) are now much better attested.[79] These texts highlight that the internal organization of the Sealand kingdom centered around palaces and document offerings made to the local sanctuaries as well as diplomatic contacts with Kassite leaders.[80] The geographical extent of the Sealand kingdom is still uncertain, but it undoubtedly had access to the Persian Gulf and likely covered large portions of southern Babylonia, perhaps including cities like Uruk, Larsa, and Ur.[81] It is possible that the Sealand kings even controlled Nippur, as a hymn of Ayadaragalama to the gods of Nippur demonstrates the importance of those deities for the Sealand kingdom.[82] Taken together with the conspicuous absence of the toponyms Sumer and Nippur in Agum's inscription, this supports the view that large parts of southern Babylonia were not yet controlled by Agum II, or by his immediate successor Burna-Buriaš I.

However, Agum's position in the sequence of Kassite rulers is still not certain. The genealogy in a dedicatory inscription of Kaštiliaš III (preserved only as a later copy) names Agum II as the father of his father Burna-Buriaš I, and Agum II would fit perfectly in the ninth position of sequence of Kassite rulers, after Šipta-ulzi and before his son Burna-Buriaš I.[83] However, this section of the sequence is poorly preserved in the king lists, and the attempt to match the remaining traces in the Synchronistic King List with the name of Agum II have been disputed.[84]

Little is known about Agum's son Burna-Buriaš I, as no contemporary sources survive from his reign. The *Synchronistic Chronicle* mentions that he swore an oath together with the Assyrian king Puzur-Aššur III, likely

79. Dalley 2009; Campbell et al. 2017; Boivin 2018.

80. Boivin 2018.

81. Boivin 2018: 61–69.

82. Gabbay and Boivin 2018, with a discussion of the evidence for the Sealand exercising control over Nippur.

83. Abraham and Gabbay 2013: 187–189; Paulus 2018: 124–126.

84. Brinkman 1976: 11; Astour 1986; Oshima 2012: 227–229.

as part of a treaty concerning the Babylonian border with Assyria.[85] This treaty is thought to have been made before the city-state of Assur came under the dominion of Mittani (see chapter 29 in this volume).[86] The relationship between the Kassites and the rising power Mittani remains unclear. An episode in the annals of the Egyptian pharaoh Thutmose III (1479–1425 BC) mentions that he received tribute from Babylonia after he campaigned through the territories of Mittani.[87] Several generations of Kassite families, likely dating back to the fifteenth century BC, are attested in the texts from Nuzi which, as part of the kingdom of Arraphe, later came under the control of Mittani.[88]

The sequence of Kassite kings following Burna-Buriaš I is very uncertain. The Synchronistic King List is broken in several places, and with the exception of the twelfth position in the sequence of rulers, which likely names Kaštiliaš III, nothing is preserved until the twenty-fourth position. The fifteenth position is usually assigned to Kara-indaš, whom we will discuss as the first king of the Middle Kassite period (see section 33.3.1). Modern research typically reconstructs the names of three to four kings in the preceding gap, including Ulam-Buriaš, Kaštiliaš III, and Agum III.[89]

During the time of those kings, the attention of the Kassite dynasty shifted southward, concentrating on the conquest of the Sealand territories. A fragment of the *Chronicle of Ancient Kings* mentions that Ulam-Buriaš, the brother of Kaštiliaš III, conquered and governed the Sealand after its last king had fled to Elam, and that Agum III, son of Kaštiliaš III, marched again against the Sealand and conquered the city

85. Glassner 2004: 176–177: *Synchronistic Chronicle*: i 5′–7′. The episode is not listed in its correct chronological position.

86. Lion 2011: 160–161.

87. Brinkman 2017: 7; van Koppen 2017: 77.

88. Brinkman 2017: 7–8 (with further references).

89. Brinkman 1976: 11–15; Sassmannshausen 2014: 175–178.

FIGURE 33.3. Mace head with an inscription of Ulam-Buriaš, king of the Sealand. Vorderasiatisches Museum, Berlin (accession number VA Bab 645). © Staatliche Museen zu Berlin—Vorderasiatisches Museum, photograph by Olaf M. Teßmer.

of Dur-Enlile.[90] The information from this chronicle can be fleshed out by further evidence relating to those three kings.

Two original inscriptions of Ulam-Buriaš are known. One is on a mace head that was excavated at Babylon (figure 33.3), and the other a weight in the shape of a frog, found in a later burial at Metsamor, an archaeological site in Armenia (located in the Caucasus southwest of Yerevan). In both texts, Ulam-Buriaš is called the son of Burna-Buriaš I, while the mace head from Babylon names him additionally as king of the Sealand, supporting the idea that the conquest of the Sealand took place during his lifetime.[91]

---

90. Glassner 2004: 272–273: *Chronicle of Ancient Kings*: rev. 12′–17′; see also Boivin 2018: 84–85.

91. Stein 2000: 129–130; Brinkman 2017: 11. Note that in other contemporary sources and in later sources, Ulam-Buriaš is never called "king of Babylon" (or by a similar title), although this may be coincidental.

The previously mentioned dedicatory inscription of Kaštiliaš III, the brother of Ulam-Buriaš, is preserved in a later copy. The text states that the god Enlil handed the land of Yamutbal (an Amorite term for the region around Larsa, south of Nippur and possibly including the Sealand territory) and its army over to Kaštiliaš III.[92] The inscription also features Nippur and its god Enlil prominently, making it very likely that this important religious center was now under Kassite control. Indeed, Kaštiliaš III bears the title "governor of Enlil" as the first Kassite king, and he is said to have built the Sumundar canal, which transported water to Nippur.[93]

So far, no inscription of Kaštiliaš' son Agum III is known. Administrative texts found at Qal'at al-Bahrain on the island of Dilmun (modern Bahrain) in the Persian Gulf are dated according to the regnal years of this king.[94] The texts also mention other, possibly Kassite kings, including a certain Ur[…]iaš (possibly a variant for Ulam-Buriaš, or Burna-Buriaš) and Kadašman-Sah, who is otherwise not attested in the available sources.[95] Importantly, King Ea-gamil of the Sealand is also attested in the Qal'at al-Bahrain archive, making it very likely that the Kassites took over control of Bahrain directly from the Sealand dynasty.[96] It is possible that the governorship of Dilmun, a prestigious position in the state administration, was established around this time.[97]

With the conquest of the Sealand, the Kassite kings had complete control over what is traditionally considered Babylonia, reaching from an unknown border in northern Mesopotamia to the ancient cities of Babylon and Nippur and on to the shores of the Persian Gulf, and even

92. Abraham and Gabbay 2013.

93. Abraham and Gabbay 2013: 184–185, 189–191.

94. André-Salvini and Lombard 1997: 167–168; Potts 2006: 115–116; Sassmannshausen 2008b: 320.

95. Personal communication, Antoine Cavigneaux and Béatrice André-Salvini, whose edition of these texts is in preparation.

96. Boivin 2018: 84–85.

97. Brinkman 1993; 2017: 8 n. 57.

including the island of Bahrain. In the east, the control of the Kassite dynasty extended to the Diyala region and into the western reaches of the Zagros mountain range.

33.3. The Middle Kassite period

The Middle Kassite period can be divided into two different phases. The first phase extends from Kara-indaš to Burna-Buriaš II and can be described as a phase of stabilization after the years of conquest, marked by significant building activity and the resumption of international relations, for which there is now ample evidence. There are, however, few extant archival sources available for this phase, whereas archival texts constitute the most numerous source material for the second phase of the Middle Kassite period, spanning the time from Kurigalzu II to Kaštiliaš IV.

33.3.1. From Kara-indaš to Burna-Buriaš II

The Kassite rulers of the first phase followed up the completion of the conquest of Babylonia with an extensive building program that targeted the traditional temples and cities of the region, but also profoundly altered the political landscape by constructing the northern royal residence city of Dur-Kurigalzu. The kings' building and dedicatory inscriptions were mostly composed in Sumerian; this was likely a result of the integration of the former Sealand territory, the heartland of ancient Sumer (see chapter 18 in volume 2). The earliest known archival documents from Nippur and the first *kudurru* stones date to this phase. While internally the rulers' attention focused on rebuilding Babylonia, their foreign relations were shaped by the forging of a series of strategic alliances that were cemented by dynastic marriages with the great powers of the time: Egypt (see chapter 28 in this volume), Hatti (chapter 30), Assyria (chapter 32), and Elam (chapter 34).

The first ruler of the first phase of the Middle Kassite period is Kara-indaš, possibly the fifteenth Kassite king (although both king lists are broken at this point in the sequence; see section 33.1). His building

FIGURE 33.4. Façade of the temple dedicated to the goddess Inana (Akkadian Ištar) in Uruk, built by King Kara-indaš. Vorderasiatisches Museum, Berlin (accession number VA 10983). Photograph © Staatliche Museen zu Berlin— Vorderasiatisches Museum, photograph by Olaf M. Teßmer.

inscriptions were discovered in Uruk, where Kara-indaš built a temple in the Eanna complex for the goddess Inana (Akkadian Ištar) (figure 33.4).[98] Little is known about this ruler's other activities. The *Synchronistic History* records that he and the Assyrian king Aššur-bel-nišešu swore an oath together concerning the border between Babylonia and Assyria,[99] and this treaty may have been meant to secure the Babylonian trade and

98. Brinkman 1976: 169–170.

99. Glassner 2004: 176–177: *Synchronistic History*: i 1'–4'. During this period, Assyria was likely under the political domination of Mittani, but the chronicle, which is focused on Assyria, does not mention Mittani involvement; see Lion 2011: 161; Jakob 2017a.

communication routes toward the west.[100] This would fit the later testimony of the Amarna correspondence, according to which the Kassite diplomatic contacts with Egypt started under Kara-indaš.[101]

Kadašman-Harbe I, likely Kara-indaš's immediate successor, also pursued interests in the west. According to an episode in the *Chronicle of the Kassite Kings*, he annihilated the Suteans from the east to the west and strengthened the fortification of the citadel of Šaršar (possibly located in Jebel Bishri in central Syria), digging wells and settling people there.[102] While the scribes of the chronicle confused Kadašman-Harbe I, son of Kara-indaš, with the late fourteenth-century ruler Kara-Hardaš, the episode can be attributed with certainty to Kadašman-Harbe I, as the defeat of the Suteans is also attested in a *kudurru* inscription of this king.[103] In the east, Kadašman-Harbe I built a canal for Diniktum, a city on the Diyala,[104] as recorded in a year name found in one of the earliest Kassite archival texts from Nippur.[105] Texts found at the Elamite city of Haft Tappeh (probably ancient Kabnak) show that diplomatic contacts between Babylonia and Elam were already well established during this time. The possible mention of Kadašman-Harbe I's expulsion in a year name of Haft Tappeh has fueled discussion whether this king may have been defeated by Tepti-ahar of Elam. However, the orthography of the royal name and the fact that most year names from Haft Tappeh typically refer to messengers, and not kings, render this potential synchronism uncertain.[106]

While textual sources are still sparse for the time of Kara-indaš and Kadašman-Harbe I, the situation changes dramatically for the better

---

100. Fuchs 2011: 240–241.

101. Rainey 2015: 95–97: EA 10: obv. 8–9.

102. Glassner 2004: 278–279: *Chronicle of the Kassite Kings*: i 5′–9′.

103. Paulus 2014b: 297, 301 (*KH I* 1: i 32–41).

104. For a discussion of the contested localization of Diniktum, see Gentili 2006.

105. Brinkman 1976: 146–147.

106. Paulus 2013: 444–446; Roaf 2017: 168–169; see also chapter 34 in this volume.

with the reign of Kurigalzu I (?–1375 BC). However, if the ruler's father is not named, it is difficult to distinguish clearly between texts dated to Kurigalzu I, son of Kadašman-Harbe I, and those dated to the later king Kurigalzu II, son of Burna-Buriaš II.[107] Kurigalzu I conducted a massive building program all over Babylonia that was on a scale that far exceeded the activities of all other Kassite kings and that included work at the cities of Adab, Der, Dur-Kurigalzu, Isin, Kiš, Nippur, Sippar, Ur, and Uruk, and likely also Akkad, Borsippa, and Eridu.[108] While many of Kurigalzu's building inscriptions are short and standardized, there are also some unique compositions, like the lengthy Sumerian statue inscriptions found at Dur-Kurigalzu,[109] as well as an account of a donation of a large estate to the goddess Ištar for the purpose of providing regular temple offerings.[110]

Significant changes to the political landscape of Babylonia resulted from the new foundation of a royal residence at Dur-Kurigalzu (Akkadian "Fortress of Kurigalzu") at a site with earlier occupation levels (figure 33.5). This city was strategically located near the confluence of the Tigris and Diyala rivers, in the area of modern Baghdad where the Euphrates comes closest to the Tigris; it may have served as a stronghold against Mittani and Assyria.[111] Together with Babylon, it served the Kassite kings as a royal residence, while Nippur remained the realm's most important religious center.[112]

Through a series of diplomatic marriages with Egypt and Elam, Kurigalzu I strengthened Babylonia's international standing. One of his daughters married the Egyptian king Amenhotep III (1388–1350 BC), who later also married one of Kurigalzu's granddaughters.[113] It

---

107. Brinkman 1976: 205–207; Bartelmus 2010: 154–157.

108. Clayden 1996; Bartelmus 2010; 2017: 280–281.

109. Veldhuis 2008.

110. Paulus 2014b: 308–313.

111. Clayden 2017; Malko 2017.

112. Novák 2014: 316–320; Clayden 2017: 453–454.

113. Rainey 2015: 58–65; EA 1.

FIGURE 33.5. The stepped temple tower (*ziqqurat*) of Dur-Kurigalzu (modern Aqar Quf) in March 2010. US Army photo by Specialist David Robbins, via Wikimedia Commons (https:// commons.wikimedia.org/w/index. php?curid=26813043), Creative Commons CC0 1.0 Universal Public Domain Dedication.

seems that Kurigalzu's realm was well-known in Egypt, as both Babylon and Dur-Kurigalzu were mentioned in the geographic lists included in the inscriptions of Amenhotep III's funerary temple at Thebes.[114] Maintaining a good relationship with Egypt was clearly important for Kurigalzu I: when the Canaanites sought an alliance with him against Egypt, he did not support them, but remained loyal to the pharaoh.[115] As a result of that good relationship, much gold was sent from Egypt to Babylonia.[116]

A carnelian cylinder seal that was found, like the already mentioned frog weight bearing the inscription of Ulam-Buriaš, in a later burial at

---

114. Edel and Görg 2005: 131–133, 141–143; Clayden 2017: 450.

115. Rainey 2015: 92–95: EA 9: ll. 19–30; also Clayden 2017.

116. Rainey 2015: 104–105: EA 11: ll. 19–23.

Metsamor in Armenia (see section 33.2) carries an inscription in Egyptian hieroglyphs with Kurigalzu's name and the title of "great overseer of Babylonia."[117] While it is uncertain when and how these objects arrived in the Caucasus, it is extremely unlikely that their presence reflects an extension of Babylonian influence as far as Armenia.

There is good evidence of close contacts with Elam, Babylonia's direct neighbor in the east. Two daughters of Kurigalzu I married the Middle Elamite kings Pahir-iššan and Humban-numena, as recorded in the so-called *Berlin Letter*, either a later school copy of an authentic letter sent by an Elamite king to his Babylonian counterpart during the Late Kassite period or else a later composition (a so-called literary letter).[118] It was either Kurigalzu I or II who conducted a successful campaign against Elam and conquered the city of Susa; in the present chapter, the relevant sources for that event are attributed to Kurigalzu II (see section 33.3.2).

Kurigalzu I was certainly considered to have been one of the most important kings of the Kassite dynasty, as later Kassite and even Elamite rulers traced their ancestry back to him.[119] Many activities attested during his reign continued under his successors Kadašman-Enlil I (1374–1360 BC)[120] and Burna-Buriaš II (1359–1333 BC), including building activities and diplomatic marriages with Elam and Egypt. Kadašman-Enlil I continued existing building projects in Nippur and Isin, but also undertook new work in Larsa.[121]

Under the Kassite rulers from Kadašman-Harbe I to Burna-Buriaš II, the first *kudurru* stones are attested. Their inscriptions document how officials received large estates as donations from the king. As part

---

117. Brinkman 2017: 11.

118. *Berlin Letter*: obv. 6′–8′; see Paulus 2013: 430–439; Roaf 2017: 182–195. For a more sceptical view on the *Berlin Letter*'s value for the reconstruction of Elamite history, see chapter 34 in this volume.

119. Brinkman 1976: 242; Paulus 2013: 435–437.

120. Note that it is difficult to distinguish between the sources referring to Kadašman-Enlil I and to the later king Kadašman-Enlil II; see Brinkman 1976: 130.

121. Bartelmus 2017: 281–282; Brinkman 2017: 23.

of these land donations, the beneficiaries were also rewarded with tax
exemptions so that these estates would benefit from funds and work that
would otherwise have been due to the state. Most of the early land donations were associated with temple personnel,[122] and these royal gifts may
therefore be an aspect of the traditional royal sponsorship of Babylonian
temples.

During this period, the information available on international
relations derives from letters found in the Egyptian royal residence
Akhetaten (modern Tell el-Amarna). According to this material,
Kadašman-Enlil I corresponded with Amenhotep III of Egypt (1388–
1350 BC), mostly about the planned marriage of his daughter to the pharaoh. Other topics include the Kassite ruler's building projects and his
need of Egyptian gold in order to complete them.[123] Kassite Babylonia
was a well-established partner in an international system of diplomatic
relationships linking it to Egypt, Mittani, and Hatti. These relations
were based on regular messenger contacts, dynastic marriages, and an
economically mutually advantageous gift exchange.[124] The Kassite kings
mostly received gold from Egypt and in return presented horses and
lapis lazuli. For procuring these goods, the Zagros region that connected Babylonia with the trade routes of western Iran and its horse-
breeding places was especially important.[125]

Under Burna-Buriaš II (1359–1333 BC), likely the son of Kadašman-
Enlil I, many of the activities pursued during his father's reign continued. Burna-Buriaš built temples for the gods Enlil and Ninlil in Nippur
and for the sun-god Šamaš in Larsa. At this time, we see an increase in
dedicatory inscriptions that commemorate the king's gifts to the gods.[126]
Most noteworthy is the dedication of a chariot for Enlil, as mentioned
in a bilingual Sumerian and Akkadian inscription that is known from

---

122. Paulus 2017: 233–236.

123. Rainey 2015: 58–75: *EA* 1–4.

124. Cohen and Westbrook 2000; Podany 2010: 191–304.

125. Fuchs 2017: 155–157.

126. Bartelmus 2017: 282–290.

later copies.[127] It is during the reign of Burna-Buriaš II that the archival records in Nippur are available in great numbers,[128] and many legal and economic texts connected to the activities of the *šandabakku* (so the traditional title of the governor of Nippur) have been preserved.[129] To that same period date the earliest documents known from Dur-Enlile, an as yet unlocated town in the vicinity of Nippur.[130]

On the international scene, Burna-Buriaš II forged new connections between his family and the important courts of the time and engineered diplomatic marriages with Elam, Egypt, and likely also the Hittites and the emerging power of Assyria. The marriage between a daughter of Burna-Buriaš II and the Middle Elamite king Untaš-Napiriša is listed in the previously mentioned *Berlin Letter*.[131] From the Amarna correspondence, we know about another dynastic marriage between a daughter of Burna-Buriaš II and pharaoh Amenhotep IV (better known as Akhenaten; 1350–1334 BC).[132] Burna-Buriaš' letters exchanged with his Egyptian counterpart show tensions in relations between the two kingdoms, as the Kassite king complained about the decreasing quantity and quality of the gold received from Egypt, about the robbing and killing of Babylonian merchants and messengers, and about the establishment of diplomatic relationships between Egypt and Babylonia's northern neighbor and rival, Assyria.[133]

The relations between Egypt, Hatti, Assyria, and Babylonia were complicated due to the political and military weakness of Mittani, which

---

127. Bartelmus 2016: 489–532.

128. Note that only very few documents from Nippur date to an earlier time.

129. Brinkman 1976: 111–116; Pedersén 1998: 113–116.

130. Devecchi 2020b.

131. *Berlin Letter*: obv. 10′–11′ (see earlier discussion in this section); for the potential identification of the princess with the Elamite queen Napirasu, see Radner 2020: 68–70.

132. Rainey 2015: 100–105, 108–127 for EA 11, and the possibly corresponding dowry lists EA 13–14; see Radner 2020: 70–71.

133. Rainey 2015: 80–105: EA 6–12.

was exploited by both the Hittites and the Assyrians. Aššur-uballiṭ I of Assyria had used the momentum of his success against Mittani to establish direct relations with Egypt, presenting himself as one of the great kings on the international stage, and also forged an alliance with the land of Alše (also known as Alzi), northwest of Mittani.[134] The Kassite reaction to these new developments with Babylonia's northern neighbor seems to have been to strengthen its alliance with Hatti, as the Hittite king Suppiluliuma I married another Babylonian princess, possibly a daughter of Burna-Buriaš II.[135]

This is the context for Burna-Buriaš's complaint about direct contacts between the old ally Egypt and the rising power Assyria (see chapter 32 in this volume), as the Kassite ruler stated in a letter to the pharaoh that the Assyrian king was a Babylonian vassal who should not be received at the Egyptian court.[136] But while Burna-Buriaš clearly tried to prevent the rise of Assyria, the sources demonstrate that Aššur-uballiṭ I of Assyria, too, likely married a Babylonian princess.[137] This marriage was a crucial factor in a succession crisis of the Kassite crown, as recorded in the *Synchronistic Chronicle* and the *Chronicle of the Kassite Kings*,[138] although the value of the latter account is sadly reduced by a series of misunderstandings. According to these chronicles, Kassite troops rebelled against their king Kara-Hardaš,[139] a son of Aššur-uballiṭ's daughter, Muballiṭat-Šerua.[140] Neither chronicle mentions whether this

---

134. Rainey 2015: 128–133: EA 15–16; see Fuchs 2011: 242–244; Jakob 2017a: 117–119.

135. Miller 2017: 99; for the potential identification of the princess with Malnigal, see Radner 2020: 71–73.

136. Rainey 2015: 94–95: EA 9: 31–35.

137. Fuchs 2011: 312–314.

138. Glassner 2004: 178–179: *Synchronistic Chronicle*: i 8′–17′; 278–279: *Chronicle of the Kassite Kings*: i 9′–14′.

139. Later in the *Synchronistic Chronicle*, this man is called Kara-indaš, whereas the *Chronicle of the Kassite Kings* by mistake names the earlier Kassite king Kadašman-Harbe I son of Kara-indaš.

140. See Radner 2020: 74.

king, likely the successor of Burna-Buriaš II, was also his son. After the rebels had killed Kara-Hardaš they raised to the throne one Nazi-Bugaš, a Kassite of non-royal descent.[141] To avenge his grandson, Aššur-uballiṭ I of Assyria campaigned against Babylonia, killed the usurper, and gave the crown to Kurigalzu II, son of Burna-Buriaš II. While there is no contemporary information about either Kara-Hardaš or Nazi-Bugaš, and even the readings of their names are uncertain,[142] the episode is important, as it marks the transition to the second phase of the Middle Kassite period.

33.3.2. From Kurigalzu II to Kaštiliaš IV

The second phase of the Middle Kassite period is defined by a sharp increase in the available archival documentation: most documents from Nippur were written during this time; the archives from Dur-Kurigalzu start with texts from the reign of Nazi-Maruttaš;[143] those of Babylon with texts from the reign of Kurigalzu II;[144] the archive from Ur with Kadašman-Turgu's reign;[145] and both the archive excavated at Tell Imlihiye and the so-called Peiser Archive with the reign of Kadašman-Enlil II.[146]

Politically speaking, there is no break between the first and second phases of the Middle Kassite period, as Kurigalzu II (1332–1308 BC) was a son of Burna-Buriaš II. So far, no building activities can be attributed to this king.[147] However, many short votive inscriptions from his reign

---

141. The *Chronicle of the Kassite Kings* has Šuzigaš instead.

142. Brinkman 1976: 166–168, 260–261; Sassmannshausen 2014: 182.

143. Clayden 2017: 478.

144. Pedersén 2005: 70–106.

145. Pedersén 1998: 118.

146. Brinkman 1976: 46; Pedersén 1998: 119.

147. This may be partially due to a tendency to assign most building projects to his synonymous predecessor; for Kurigalzu I, see section 33.3.1.

have survived.[148] Two conflicts played major roles during his reign: in the north, the battle against the steadily rising power of Assyria, and in the southeast, hostilities with Elam.

While Aššur-uballiṭ of Assyria had successfully campaigned against Kassite Babylonia, the locations of the subsequent battles reported in the available sources make it likely that the Babylonians were the aggressors and that they threatened the very existence of Assyria. Beyond extinguishing the Assyrian ambition, another motivation for the Kassite aggression was likely the desire to incorporate the territories of Arraphe (with Nuzi) into the Babylonian kingdom.[149] According to the *Synchronistic Chronicle*, Kurigalzu II fought Enlil-nerari of Assyria at Sugaga on the Tigris but was defeated by him.[150] A battle resulting in an Assyrian victory is mentioned in connection with the city of Kilizu in the Assyrian *Chronicle of Enlil-nerari* as well as in several Assyrian royal inscriptions.[151] From these battle locations, it is clear that the Babylonians ventured deep into Assyrian territory: Sugaga (a hitherto unidentified site) is said to be located only a day's march south of the capital city of Assur,[152] while Kilizu is situated right in the middle of the Assyrian heartland at modern Qasr Shamamok.[153] While these battles ended favorably for the Assyrian defenders, the *Chronicle of the Kassite Kings* reports a Babylonian victory over Assyria,[154] and a *kudurru* monument from the time of Kaštiliaš IV records a land donation in favor of

148. Bartelmus 2017: 284–285.

149. Fuchs 2011: 247–248. Secure evidence that Nuzi was temporarily part of the Kassite kingdom is only available for the Late Kassite period.

150. Glassner 2004: 178–179: *Synchronistic Chronicle*: i 18'–23'.

151. Glassner 2004: 184–185: *Chronicle of Enlil-nerari*. See also Grayson 1987: 118–119: A.074.1001, and the later inscriptions of Adad-nerari I, which mention a victory of Enlil-nerari.

152. Brinkman 1970: 309, 313–314; Fuchs 2011: 246–247; Jakob 2017a: 118–119.

153. Rouault 2016.

154. Glassner 2004: 280–281: *Chronicle of the Kassite Kings*: iii 20–22.

an official who was thus rewarded for his success in fighting the Assyrian forces.[155] Despite such temporary successes, the Assyrian victories meant that the border between the two realms remained as before.[156]

The other major conflict of this time was with Elam, although as already stated, it remains uncertain whether some of the events described here ought to be better attributed to Kurigalzu I. Evidence for hostilities mostly comes from the *Chronicle of the Kassite Kings*, which records in a fragmentary context an episode concerning Kurigalzu's victory over an unknown enemy and his rich booty, which included horses and other precious goods.[157] This episode is reminiscent of the tribute list in the literary *Kurigalzu Letter* (known only from a much later, first millennium manuscript), which mentions large amounts of tribute received from Hatti, Egypt, Meluhha (traditionally, the term for the Indus region), and Parsu (a first millennium toponym for a region in Iran), as well as from the Kaššû ("Kassites").[158] The *Chronicle of the Kassite Kings* continues with a battle of Kurigalzu against an otherwise unknown Elamite king called Hurbatela at Dur-Šulgi (an unidentified place likely situated west of Halman in the Zagros mountains).[159]

Further information derives from a votive inscription of Kurigalzu II that is known from later copies and that commemorates the dedication of two swords to the god of Nippur, offered in gratitude for punishing an unnamed enemy.[160] The text reports an invasion by "a son of a nobody" coming down from the mountains, who mobilized an army, mustered

---

155. Paulus 2014b: 360 (*Ka IV* 2: i 3–8).

156. Glassner 2004: 178–179: *Synchronistic Chronicle*: i 18′–23′.

157. Glassner 2004: 278–281: *Chronicle of the Kassite Kings*: ii 1′–iii 9.

158. Al-Rawi and George 1994: 135 n. 2; Wiseman 1967. As the text is a Neo-Babylonian source, it remains unclear who is labeled as Kaššû in this context; likely this refers to people living outside of Babylonia.

159. Glassner 2004: 278–281: *Chronicle of the Kassite Kings*: iii 10–19; see Fuchs 2011: 241–242; Paulus 2013: 441–442; Roaf 2017: 179–180; and chapter 34 in this volume.

160. George 2011: 117–118; Paulus 2018: 153–154.

support troops at the city of Der, and proceeded to slaughter the inhabitants of Nippur in the courtyard of a temple named Esagdingirene. While the enemy remains unnamed, the fact that his forces came down from the mountains and allied with troops from Der, situated east of the Tigris in the Zagros piedmont, makes it likely that this episode alludes to the battle with Elam that is also mentioned in the *Chronicle of the Kassite Kings.*

Evidence for a conflict with Elam can also be found in two contemporary inscriptions of Kurigalzu and in the *Berlin Letter.* The first inscription is written on a statue fragment found in Susa and mentions that Kurigalzu struck Susa and Elam, while the seizing of the palace of Susa in Elam is recorded in the second inscription, an agate stone tablet found at Nippur.[161] The deterioration of relations between Babylonia and Elam is also obvious from the *Berlin Letter,* according to which the Elamite king Kidin-Hutran did not marry a Babylonian princess, but simply a Babylonian woman.[162] This information may also be recorded in a fragmentarily preserved literary text known as the *Epic of Kurigalzu II,* which mentions not only fighting against the Elamites, but also a daughter of Enlil-kidinni, the latter possibly the governor of Nippur of that name.[163] While the epic is of a later date and only fragmentarily preserved, this daughter of a high-ranking official may have been the "daughter of Babylonia" who was married to the Elamite king.

Furthermore, a literary text known as *The Dream of Kurigalzu* is concerned with his wife's barrenness;[164] but this may be only a fictional episode, as Kurigalzu II's son Nazi-Maruttaš succeeded him on the throne. According to King List A, Nazi-Maruttaš (1307–1282 BC) ruled for

---

161. Paulus 2013: 442–444; Roaf 2017: 169–170.

162. *Berlin Letter*: obv. 10′–11′; for a discussion of the passage, see Paulus 2013: 432–433; for alternative reconstructions, see Roaf 2017: 182–195 and cf. chapter 34 in this volume.

163. Grayson 1975: 47–55.

164. Finkel 1983.

twenty-six years.[165] For his reign, there is evidence of renewed building activity and important, religiously motivated land donations, while in the north, hostilities with Assyria continued.

Bricks inscribed with the name of Nazi-Maruttaš have been found at Larsa and Tell al-Abyad, a site near Dur-Kurigalzu. Later sources also mention that this king built a temple for the goddess Nanaya in Uruk.[166] Most votive inscriptions of Nazi-Maruttaš come from Nippur and record dedications to the gods Enlil, Ninurta, and Nusku.[167] Following an oracular decision of Enlil, the king gave twelve cities, perhaps located in the Zagros province Namri, to the god Enlil and his priest.[168] While Enlil was certainly the dominant deity of that time, a *kudurru* monument records a large land donation for Marduk in the immediate vicinity of Babylon,[169] and based on the administrative records from Nippur, Jonathan Tenney observed that the god Marduk gained more prominence during the Middle Kassite period, around the reign of Nazi-Maruttaš.[170] Beyond land donations to temples, Nazi-Maruttaš also gave endowments to specific officials and priests. The lands allocated with these endowments were located on the western and eastern banks of the Tigris, as far north as Dur-Kurigalzu, and in the lower Diyala region formerly centered on Ešnunna.[171] These land allocations were part of a strategy to secure the border with Assyria, which remained a major conflict zone during the reign of Nazi-Maruttaš. The *Synchronistic Chronicle* and the *Chronicle of the Kassite Kings*, as well as several Assyrian royal inscriptions, record that Nazi-Maruttaš fought Adad-nerari I of Assyria at Kar-Ištar in Ugar-sallu, south of Assur, and that he was severely defeated

---

165. Brinkman 1976: 262; 2001a.

166. Bartelmus 2017: 283.

167. Clayden 2011; Bartelmus 2017: 284, 287–288.

168. Frazer 2013: 202–203, 206–212.

169. Paulus 2014b: 325–334 (*NM 2*).

170. Tenney 2016.

171. Paulus 2014b: 185–198.

by Assyrian forces.[172] Consequently, the border was fixed as extending from Ugar-ṣallu on the Tigris to the Lower Zab as far as Lullumu in the Zagros mountains.[173]

Beyond the contemporary evidence, Nazi-Maruttaš is also well-known from the later literary tradition. He is mentioned by name in the literary compositions *Poem of the Righteous Sufferer* and *In Praise of the Just*, in a literary letter, and in the *Assyrian Name Book*,[174] and the colophon of a hemerology states that during his time, scholars copied (and compiled) tablets from the cities Sippar, Nippur, Babylon, Ur, Uruk, and Eridu.[175]

According to most modern scholars, Kadašman-Turgu (1281–1264 BC) followed his father Nazi-Maruttaš on the throne and ruled for eighteen years.[176] However, some have suggested switching around the sequence of Kadašman-Turgu and his successor Kadašman-Enlil II, or even introducing a third king of this name, based on a text that has the reign of Kadašman-Turgu follow that of Kadašman-Enlil; but as this is likely an ancient forgery, the conventional sequence of rulers is preferred here.[177]

Kadašman-Turgu's reign is well-attested in legal and economic documents, but little is known of his political achievements. He enlarged a temple of the god Lugal-Marada, likely situated in the vicinity of Nippur, and established offerings for this deity.[178] Otherwise, only some votive inscriptions from Nippur survive.[179]

---

172. For the so-called Epic of Adad-nerari I, see Frazer 2013: 194–195; Devecchi 2017: 113; with Grayson 1987: 128–132: A.076.1; 156–157: A.076.21. See also chapter 32 in this volume.

173. Glassner 2004: 178–179: *Synchronistic Chronicle*: i 24′–31′; 280–281: *Chronicle of the Kassite Kings*: iii 23–24 (fragmentarily). For the locations of the toponyms, see Parpola and Porter 2001: 11, 28; Fuchs 2011: 246–247.

174. Frazer 2013.

175. Heeßel 2011.

176. Brinkman 1976: 153.

177. Boese 2009; Brinkman 1983; 2016; Sassmannshausen 2014: 184–185.

178. Beckman 1987: 1–2; Bartelmus 2017: 283.

179. Clayden 2011; Bartelmus 2017: 284, 287–288. The excavators of Nippur reported bricks from the stepped temple tower (*ziqqurat*) of Enlil at Nippur;

In regard to Babylonian foreign relations, the border conflict with Assyria seems to have been temporarily settled, while the Hittites appear as an important political partner. Two text fragments from Assur have been tentatively labeled as a treaty between Kadašman-Turgu and Adad-nerari I of Assyria, although it is possible that they are part of an epic, or of narrative texts;[180] mention is also made of how Adad-nerari I cleared someone's son, possibly that of Kadašman-Turgu, from his sins.

In his need to balance Assyrian power, Kadašman-Turgu understandably entertained contacts with the strong Hittite realm. This is demonstrated by a letter of Kadašman-Turgu concerning an incantation priest, which was discovered at the Hittite capital of Hattusa (modern Boğazköy).[181] Another letter, sent to Kadašman-Turgu's successor Kadašman-Enlil II from the Hittite king Hattusili III, reports that friendly diplomatic relations were established under the latter's predecessor, Muwatalli II, and the language of the letter suggests that these were strengthened by a treaty between both countries.[182] This letter also alludes to the growing conflict between Egypt and Hatti, which culminated in the battle of Qadesh (see chapters 28 and 30 in this volume). Kadašman-Turgu promised to support the Hittite king with infantry and chariotry but refused to extradite an unnamed enemy of Hattusili III, likely his dethroned predecessor Mursili III/Urhi-Teššub, who had attempted to flee to Babylonia before traveling to Amurru and later Egypt.[183] Thus, the diplomatic relationship between the two countries markedly deteriorated between the death of Kadašman-Turgu and the early years of his successor Kadašman-Enlil II.

---

see Brinkman 1976: 164. However, they likely confused Kadašman-Turgu and Kadašman-Enlil; see Schneider 2020.

180. Frahm 2009: 128–129; Devecchi 2017: 113.

181. Hagenbuchner 1989: 106.

182. Hattusili III's letter to Kadašman-Enlil II: §4; see Beckman 1999: 139; Devecchi 2017: 115–116.

183. Hattusili III's letter to Kadašman-Enlil II: §7; see Beckman 1999: 141; Devecchi 2017: 115; also chapter 30 in this volume.

The previously mentioned letter of Hattusili III is the most detailed source of information at our disposal for the reign of Kadašman-Enlil II (1263–1255 BC), who ruled for only nine years.[184] The letter mentions that he ascended the throne as a child and was under the influence of a certain Itti-Marduk-balaṭu. The Hittite king Hattusili III claimed that Itti-Marduk-balaṭu was "evil," and that he himself supported Kadašman-Enlil.[185] Nevertheless, relations between the two countries were troubled, as the Assyrians and the Ahlamû (a term later used for the Arameans) prevented messengers from traveling between them.[186] The Hittite king stressed that the Babylonian army was superior to the Assyrian one, and taunted Kadašman-Enlil as someone who "sits around," avoiding war.[187] While this might have been pure rhetoric, no military encounters with Assyria are attested during Kadašman-Enlil's reign.[188] In the later part of his reign, relations with Hatti must have improved, as Babylonian specialists were again sent to the capital Hattusa and the Hittite king asked for gifts, including horses and lapis lazuli.[189] A diplomatic letter found at Dur-Kurigalzu is addressed to Kadašman-Enlil and possibly forms part of this correspondence.[190]

From all this evidence, Kadašman-Enlil II emerges as a relatively weak king, and the scarce evidence from Babylonia does not contradict this assessment. Consequently, most building activities of a "Kadašman-Enlil" are usually attributed to Kadašman-Enlil I rather than the second ruler of this name, and only a few votive inscriptions are attested from

184. Brinkman 2017: 25–26.

185. Hattusili III's letter to Kadašman-Enlil II: §§4–5; see Beckman 1999: 141–142.

186. Hattusili III's letter to Kadašman-Enlil II: §§5–7; see Beckman 1999: 142–143.

187. Hattusili III's letter to Kadašman-Enlil II: §14; see Beckman 1999: 143.

188. Devecchi 2017: 113.

189. Hattusili III's letter to Kadašman-Enlil II: §17; see Beckman 1999: 142–143; Devecchi 2017: 115–116.

190. Gurney 1949: 149 n. 12. The letter is sent from a king of equal status. Devecchi 2017: 115 n. 13 speculates that this might be a Hittite king; Brinkman 2017: 15 n. 116 prefers an Elamite king.

his reign.[191] In the only known *kudurru* inscription from this time, he confirms an endowment made by Kadašman-Turgu.[192]

Kadašman-Enlil II was succeeded by Kudur-Enlil (1254–1246 BC), who also only reigned for nine years.[193] According to King List A, he was a son of his predecessor, but this is unlikely, mainly because of the young age of Kadašman-Enlil II at the time of his accession to the throne and his subsequent short reign. Johannes Boese speculated that Kadašman-Enlil II might have been a son of Kadašman-Turgu, and therefore brother of his predecessor.[194] This king's building activities and votive inscriptions are attested in Nippur, where Kudur-Enlil built a temple for the goddess Ištar and at the Ekur temple of Enlil.[195] A *kudurru* stone from Larsa documents a large land donation to an official closely connected with the Ebabbar temple in Larsa; the land was mainly located in the Sealand province and in Bit-Sin-magir, south of Dur-Kurigalzu on the eastern bank of the Tigris.[196]

At the time, the border with Assyria seemed to have been stable and was located further to the north, not far away from the bank of the Lower Zab.[197] No military interactions with Assyria are recorded, possibly because the Assyrian king Shalmaneser I concentrated his campaigns toward the north and northwest of his realm rather than the south.[198] A letter found at Dur-Kurigalzu proves that the Babylonians closely followed the diplomatic and military actions of the Assyrians.[199]

---

191. Brinkman 1976: 130; 2017: 25–26; Bartelmus 2017: 284–288.

192. Paulus 2014b: 238–239 (*KaE II* 1).

193. Brinkman 1976: 190.

194. Boese 2009: 93–95.

195. Brinkman 1976: 190–191; Bartelmus 2017: 282, 284, 287; Schneider 2020.

196. Paulus 2014b: 340–348 (*KuE* 1).

197. Llop 2011: 210–211.

198. Baker 2008; Devecchi 2017: 115; see also chapter 32 in this volume.

199. For the letter from Zikir-ilišu about Assyrian messengers and military operations, see Gurney 1949: no. 10; Devecchi 2017: 113–114 n. 116.

A series of diplomatic marriages may have strengthened the position of Kassite Babylonia, although at least Rameses II of Egypt doubted that its king still counted among the "great kings."[200] Rameses II had married a Babylonian princess, but the Hittite queen Pudu-Heba complained in a letter addressed to him that he did not treat the Babylonian messenger with due respect,[201] mentioning in the same letter that she had a Babylonian daughter-in-law and that the Babylonian king himself had married a Hittite princess.[202] Those marriages took place either late in the reign of Kudur-Enlil, or late in the reign of his predecessor Kadašman-Enlil II.[203]

Open questions surround the descent and indeed the legitimacy of the two rulers succeeding Kudur-Enlil: Šagarakti-Šuriaš and Kaštiliaš IV. According to King List A and an inscription of Nabonidus of Babylon (556–539 BC), Šagarakti-Šuriaš was the son of Kudur-Enlil,[204] and succeeded by his son Kaštiliaš IV.[205] While Johannes Boese proposed that Šagarakti-Šuriaš was yet another son of Kadašman-Turgu,[206] it has been argued that one of the kings, either Šagarakti-Šuriaš or Kaštiliaš IV, may have been a usurper. J.A. Brinkman stressed that both rulers had long accession years, meaning that they ascended to the throne around the New Year festival, which is traditionally the time of renewal of kingship and therefore could indicate that their reigns had an irregular start; in addition, an unprovenanced document refers to Kudur-Enlil as king at

---

200. Letter from the Hittite queen Pudu-Heba to Rameses II: obv. 56′; see Hoffner 2009: 287.

201. Pudu-Heba's letter: obv. 53′–56′, rev. 7–9; see Hoffner 2009: 286–288.

202. Pudu-Heba's letter: obv. 47′–56′; see Hoffner 2009: 286–287.

203. Devecchi 2017: 116–117.

204. Brinkman 2008.

205. A contemporary inscription likely included his filiation, but the passage is no longer readable; see Brinkman 2017: 26 n. 231.

206. Boese 2009: 94–95.

a time while Šagarakti-Šuriaš was already on the throne.[207] The strongest argument for irregularities in the royal succession at the time comes from the letter of an Assyrian ruler to the Hittite king, which mentions Šagarakti-Šuriaš several times in broken context, but also a "non-son of Kudur-Enlil" and a "servant of Suhu";[208] this "non-son of Kudur-Enlil" might be either Šagarakti-Šuriaš or Kaštiliaš IV.[209] New evidence is needed to solve the open questions surrounding these kings.

In any case, according to the extant sources, Šagarakti-Šuriaš (1245–1233 BC) ruled for thirteen years. The available records document building projects and a decree, while evidence for foreign relations remains meager. Šagarakti-Šuriaš's inscriptions are preserved in the form of later copies and concern building works at the Eulmaš temple of the goddess Ištar in Sippar-Annunitu and at the Ebabbar temple of the sun-god Šamaš in Sippar.[210] According to an unpublished legal text, Šagarakti-Šuriaš issued a decree freeing the enslaved women of Nippur,[211] and the inscription on a fragmentary *kudurru* stone may also refer to some action

---

207. Brinkman 2017: 26 n. 232.

208. For the letter of an Assyrian king to a Hittite king, see Mora and Giorgieri 2004: 113–127; Devecchi 2017: 120–122. The author of the letter is commonly identified as Tukulti-Ninurta I and the addressee with Suppiluliuma II; see Devecchi 2017: 120.

209. Brinkman 2017: 26 n. 232, who tentatively suggests Šagarakti-Šuriaš. Durand and Marti 2005: 127–128 suggested Kaštiliaš, proposing that he had served as a governor of Suhu before taking the Babylonian throne. As we have discussed earlier in section 33.2 for the kingdom of Hana, the name Kaštiliaš is also otherwise linked to the Middle Euphrates region. Other proposals link the terms "non-son of Kudur-Enlil" and "servant of Suhu" to later kings who ruled in Babylon after the invasion of Tukulti-Ninurta I of Assyria: Singer 2008 proposed Adad-šuma-uṣur (see section 33.5), while Bányai 2011: 226–230 suggested Nabû-apla-iddina, otherwise only known from the *Berlin Letter* as offspring of a daughter of Hattusili III and a Babylonian king. Most recently, Devecchi 2017: 120–122 discussed those opinions and argued the case for identifying Kadašman-Harbe II as the "non-son of Kudur-Enlil" and Adad-šuma-uṣur as the "servant of Suhu."

210. Schaudig 2001: nos. 2.12 and 2.14; Bartelmus and Taylor 2014; Bartelmus 2017: 283.

211. Brinkman 2008; 2017: 16.

of the king's for the benefit of the inhabitants of Nippur and Babylon;[212] this same text also mentions the city of Assur. Otherwise, however, relatively little is known about the foreign relations of Babylonia during this time. An administrative text lists many foreigners, some of them labeled as captives,[213] which hints at involvement in hostilities and war. A letter written by Ini-Teššub, the Hittite viceroy of Carchemish, to Šagarakti-Šuriaš, but discovered at Ugarit on the Syrian coast, discusses security problems on the roads linking Babylonia and Hatti,[214] possibly caused by the Assyrian military campaigns into Syria. Šagarakti-Šuriaš's votive inscriptions not only were found in Nippur, but also were brought as loot to Assyria and Elam,[215] which is surely linked to the fact that troubled times started for Babylonia with the reign of his successor Kaštiliaš IV.

The reign of Kaštiliaš IV (1232–1225 BC) who, as discussed, is of uncertain descent, represents the end of the Middle Kassite period, and is marked by the conquest of Babylonia by Tukulti-Ninurta I of Assyria (see chapter 32 in this volume). Little is known about Kaštiliaš IV's activities within his realm, as only a few votive inscriptions and two *kudurrus* survive from his reign.[216] According to the inscription of the first *kudurru*, Kaštiliaš IV confirmed an earlier donation by Kurigalzu II, and according to the other, he granted land to a refugee leatherworker from Hanigalbat (Mittani).[217]

The events leading to the Assyrian conquest can be reconstructed in some detail using Babylonian and Assyrian sources, although the exact chronology remains uncertain.[218] It is still debated who provoked the war between the two countries. In the Assyrian *Epic of Tukulti-Ninurta*, Kaštiliaš IV is described as an aggressive oath-breaker who plundered

---

212. Paulus 2014b: 353–356 (*ŠŠ* 1).

213. Brinkman 2017: 25.

214. Singer 1999: 652.

215. Bartelmus 2017: 284, 286–288.

216. Bartelmus 2017: 285, 287–288.

217. Paulus 2014b: 357–359 (*Ka IV* 1); 360–363 (*Ka IV* 2).

218. For reconstructions, see Yamada 2003; Bloch 2010; Fuchs 2011: 249–254; Llop 2011; Jakob 2017a: 122–132, and chapter 32 in this volume.

Assyrian lands.[219] On the other hand, before the conflict escalated, Tukulti-Ninurta I actively tried to annex Babylonian territories in the eastern Tigris region.[220] The Kassite archive from Tell Imlihiye ends already in the sixth regnal year of Kaštiliaš IV, which is presumably connected to this regional Assyrian aggression and indicates how Kaštiliaš first lost control over the Diyala region.[221] The conflict dragged on for several years. Kaštiliaš lost control over Nippur and Ur likely in the second half of his seventh year, while the last text from Dur-Kurigalzu is dated to the fifth month of his eighth year,[222] so this royal city was likely the last stronghold of the Kassite king.[223]

In his inscriptions, Tukulti-Ninurta I of Assyria states that he captured Kaštiliaš IV,[224] and the *Chronicle of the Kassite Kings* adds that the Kassite ruler was led to Assyria in iron chains, and that Tukulti-Ninurta battered the walls of Babylon and took away rich booty from the Esagil temple, including the statue of the god Marduk.[225] The *Epic of Tukulti-Ninurta* mentions treasures, prisoners, and scholarly texts as part of the Babylonian booty,[226] while Assyrian administrative texts list several thousands of Babylonian prisoners of war at Kar-Tukulti-Ninurta and Assur.[227]

The fate of Kaštiliaš IV remains unclear, and there is some evidence that he may have survived these events. A letter found at the Assyrian city

219. Foster 2005: 298–317; Machinist 2016; Jakob 2017b.

220. Jakob 2017a: 122–123.

221. Pedersén 1998: 119. Note that at Dur-Enlile, the last attested year of Kaštiliaš is his fifth regnal year; see van Soldt 2015: nos. 59, 268, 335, and 421.

222. For Nippur and Ur, see Brinkman 1976: nos. O.2.7.151–152; Bloch 2010: 62–63; for Dur-Kurigalzu, see Brinkman 1976: no. O.2.7.154.

223. Bloch 2010: 48–49.

224. Grayson 1987: A.o.78.6: ll. 23–24; A.o.78.23: ll. 56–68 (in more detail). For more attestations of Kaštiliaš in the Assyrian sources, see Llop 2015: 23 n. 42.

225. Glassner 2004: 280–281: *Chronicle of the Kassite Kings*: iv 1–6.

226. Foster 2005: 314–317.

227. Bloch 2010: 46–48; Jakob 2017a: 124–126.

of Dur-Katlimmu in the Khabur valley mentions an unnamed Kassite king, his wife, and his magnates traveling in the Assyrian royal entourage, suggesting that Kaštiliaš was likely kept alive and enjoyed a certain importance as a high-value hostage.[228] Later in the reign of Tukulti-Ninurta I, a dignitary named Kaštiliaš, possibly the dethroned Kassite monarch, had the honor of serving as the Assyrian year eponym.[229]

In Babylonia, the continuity in the dynastic line of the Kassite kings was emphasized, as Adad-šuma-uṣur called himself the son of Kaštiliaš IV.[230] However, Tukulti-Ninurta's conquest caused much disruption, as evidenced by a break in the archival records: the rich text archives from Nippur especially dried up in the years following the Assyrian conquest.

33.4. On the political organization and economy of Kassite Babylonia

The political organization of Kassite Babylonia can be reconstructed using documents from the Middle and Late Kassite periods, although precious little is revealed about the administration of the kingdom.

Legitimized by the gods, the king was the ultimate earthly authority in Babylonia. He served as the highest judge and as the most important provider for the gods, as made visible in a multitude of building projects and donations.[231] The king traveled regularly throughout his realm and had several royal residences, including in Babylon and the newly founded residence city Dur-Kurigalzu (see section 33.3.1). The southern city of Nippur, as the seat of the god Enlil, was of great religious and also economic importance, as were Akkad and Ešnunna in the north.[232]

---

228. Cancik-Kirschbaum 1996: no. 10; Bloch 2010: 47.

229. Llop 2015: 254. See chapter 32 in this volume.

230. Dossin 1962: 151, pl. XIII.

231. Sassmannshausen 2001b: 7–14; Paulus 2007; Bartelmus 2017.

232. Brinkman 2004: 387 n. 4; 2017: 13–15; Tenney 2011: 140–144; Novák 2014: 313–314, 316–318; Paulus 2014a.

Based on the witness lists of the *kudurru* inscriptions, it is possible to identify several key members of the royal court beyond the royal family: these include the *sukkalmahhu* (the highest-ranking official in the state administration, whose title is often translated as "vizier"), the herald of the land, the *sakrumaš* (the highest-ranking chariot warrior of the realm), various officials with the title *sukkallu* (high state officials, possibly to be understood as secretaries of state), and various royal courtiers with the title *ša rēši*.[233]

As an innovation of the Kassite period, the territories of the kingdom were organized into provinces.[234] These administrative units were under the control of a governor (*šakin māti*)[235] and often were created around an established city as its center, including the provinces of Babylon, Dur-Kurigalzu, Isin, Larsa, Nippur, Upi (Opis), and Ur; other provinces include multiple cities. The extreme south of the realm was divided into the provinces of Sealand in the southwest and Malgû in the southeast. In the east, entirely new administrative structures seem to have been created, including the provinces of Apsû-Ištar, Bagdada, Bit-Sin-ašared, Bit-Sin-šeme, and Dur-Papsukkal; east of the Tigris, the province of Bit-Sin-magir; and in the western reaches of the Zagros range, the provinces of Halman, Namar, Padan, and Tupliaš.[236] In the north, the provinces of Bit-Per'i-Amurru and Irreya marked the border with Assyria.

In addition, Babylonia may have exercised some level of control over the strategically important areas further up the Euphrates, including Suhu.[237] There is also evidence that Babylonia controlled the island of Dilmun (modern Bahrain) in the Persian Gulf, at least until the Middle

---

233. Paulus 2014b: 105–115.

234. Sassmannshausen 2001b: 22–23; Paulus 2014b: 185–198.

235. Only at Nippur, the corresponding title was *šandabakku*; see Brinkman 2004: 286–287.

236. Fuchs 2011: 229–235; 2017.

237. Sassmannshausen 2001b: 23.

Kassite period. Found at Nippur, the so-called Dilmun Letters mention temple construction and mercantile activities there.[238]

Babylonia was poor in natural resources like wood, stone, and metals, and international trade was therefore important.[239] Also for this reason, Babylonia entertained relationships with its direct neighbors Assyria, Elam, and Mittani, as well as other important powers of the time, including the Hittites, some Levantine cities, and Egypt.[240] Positive diplomatic relations habitually included treaties secured by dynastic marriages, and the exchange of gifts and specialists. As we have already seen in the previous sections, most of the available evidence comes from correspondence and other documentation found outside of Babylonia, as well as later chronicles.

The domestic economy of Kassite Babylonia can mainly be reconstructed on the basis of the documents from the Nippur province. As in previous times, Babylonia remained an agricultural economy dependent on artificial irrigation. While the king initiated canal-building projects, the provincial administration was responsible for the maintenance and repair of the canal system.[241] Furthermore, the provincial administration managed the agricultural production, administered large herds of sheep, goats, and cattle, and collected the dues from dependent villages, taxing principally the agricultural production, especially grain, sesame, dates, and livestock (figure 33.6).[242] The inhabitants of the villages owed the provincial administration also additional duties called *ilku* and *tupšikku*,

238. Brinkman 1993; Potts 2006: 115–116; Sassmannshausen 2008b.

239. While there is information on long-distance trade, especially from the archives from Nippur, Babylon, and Dur-Kurigalzu, this evidence has not yet been studied in detail. For now, see Brinkman 2017: 17–18, 27–28; for trade with contemporary Assyria, see Faist 2001.

240. For the diplomatic relations of the Late Bronze Age, see Cohen and Westbrook 2000; Podany 2010. For the relationship with Assyria, see Devecchi 2017; Frahm 2017; with Elam, see Roaf 2017; with the Hittites and Egypt, see Devecchi 2017; Miller 2017; with Mittani, see chapter 29 in this volume.

241. van Soldt 1988; Sassmannshausen 2001b: 37–40, 229–231.

242. deJong Ellis 1976: 109–132; Sassmannshausen 2001b: 229–231; Devecchi 2020a; Paulus 2020.

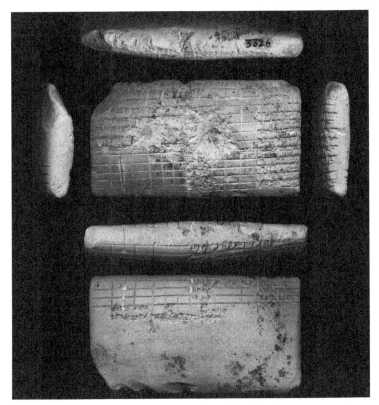

FIGURE 33.6. A large tablet with a tax ledger, from the administrative archives found at Nippur. University of Pennsylvania, Museum of Archaeology and Anthropology, Philadelphia (accession number CBS 3326). Photo courtesy The Cuneiform Digital Library Initiative (https://cdli.ucla.edu/P259700).

which consisted of public work and military service.[243] At Nippur, the provincial administration invested its income to provide for a large dependent labor force working in food and craft production, administration, herding and gardening, and other services.[244] Some of those

---

243. Paulus 2014b: 163–169.

244. Tenney 2011; 2017.

workers were foreigners, and included Assyrians, Elamites, Hittites, Hurrians, and West Semites, likely including prisoners of war.[245]

Perhaps also in order to balance the power of the provincial administrations, but certainly in order to provide an income for members of the royal family and of the royal court, as well as to strengthen control in the Babylonian border regions, villages in these areas were given in the form of land grants to certain state officials and holders of priestly offices. According to a system that is widely attested in the *kudurru* inscriptions, the crown exempted these villages from taxes and duties to the benefit of the new landowners who received this revenue instead.[246] Other royal grants favored specific population groups and could exempt the inhabitants of certain cities from taxes, or could free debt slaves.[247]

33.5. The Late Kassite period

For the first phase of the Late Kassite period, following the defeat of Kaštiliaš IV by Tukulti-Ninurta I of Assyria and with Babylonia possibly under the rule of Assyrian overlords, there are relatively few sources at our disposal. More abundant textual sources are available beginning with the reign of Adad-šuma-uṣur. Whereas the Assyrians lost control over Babylonia during the period of weakness following the death of Tukulti-Ninurta I (see chapter 32 in this volume), the rising pressure from Elam is a defining element during the Late Kassite period, and this ultimately caused the end of the Kassite dynasty. The *kudurru* stones (most of them looted from Babylonia in Elamite raids and brought to Susa, where they were excavated) become an important source of information, while royal inscriptions are increasingly rare. Private archives from Babylon and Ur document economic activity and continuity, while administrative texts are rare as the abundant archives from Nippur have dried up.

245. Sassmannshausen 2001b: 130–136; Brinkman 2004: 284–286; Tenney 2011: 121–129.

246. Paulus 2017: 233–238.

247. Brinkman 2017: 16.

n=1

33.5.1. After the Assyrian conquest of Babylonia

After his conquest of Babylonia, Tukulti-Ninurta I of Assyria took several traditional Babylonian titles that emphasized his control over Babylonia, including "king of Karduniaš," "king of Sippar and Babylon," "king of Sumer and Akkad," and "king of Dilmun and Meluhha (i.e., the Indus region)."[248] At least one economic text from Nippur is dated to the accession year of Tukulti-Ninurta as king of Babylon, namely its twelfth month.[249] However, he is not mentioned as a Babylonian king in King List A, this being a Babylonian composition. According to the *Chronicle of the Kassite Kings*, Tukulti-Ninurta installed governors in Babylonia and dominated it for seven years,[250] and modern research traditionally assigns this period to the kings Enlil-nadin-šumi, Kadašman-Harbe II, and Adad-šuma-iddina, ruling either as Assyrian vassals or usurpers.[251]

Enlil-nadin-šumi (perhaps 1224 BC) is mentioned in King List A as the twenty-ninth king of the Kassite dynasty, ruling for one year and six months. Nothing is known about his origins and ancestry. A text from Tell Zubeidi in the Diyala region, in the vicinity of Tell Imlihiye, is dated to this king, although the year is not preserved.[252]

---

248. Yamada 2003: 168–172; Sazonov 2016: 89–94.

249. Brinkman 1976: 315, no. W.2.4. Note that Bloch 2010: 65–67 inserts the reign of Tukulti-Ninurta after the dethronement of Adad-šuma-iddina. This is unlikely, as the archives from Nippur cease with the reign of Kadašman-Harbe II and as no texts dating to Adad-šuma-iddina have been found there.

250. Glassner 2004: 280–281: *Chronicle of the Kassite Kings*: iv 6–8. This is perhaps also mentioned in the *Chronicle of the Last Kassite Kings and Kings of Isin* (= *Walker Chronicle*): ll. 1–2 (Glassner 2004: 282–283), although the passage may equally refer to Adad-šuma-uṣur; see Reade 2000 and section 33.5.2.

251. Brinkman 1976: 313–317 for a summary of sources; see also Yamada 2003; Streck 2016: 177.

252. Kessler 1985: 77, no. 719. Excavation records from Babylon erroneously mention a tablet dated to the reign of Enlil-nadin-šumi; see Brinkman 1976: 125, no. G.2.1. However, this tablet is correctly dated to the reign of Enlil-nadin-ahi, which matches the other texts from the same archive; see Pedersén 2005: 83–85.

Enlil-nadin-šumi's short reign was terminated by a raid of the Elamite king Kidin-Hutran, son of Pahir-iššan.[253] The *Chronicle of the Kassite Kings* records that the Elamite attacked Nippur and Der, destroyed the Edimgalkalama temple of the god Ištaran at Der, deported people, and drove king Enlil-nadin-šumi from power.[254] It has been suggested that Enlil-nadin-šumi may have been an Assyrian vassal, while his successor Kadašman-Harbe II was supported by the Elamites.[255]

According to King List A, Kadašman-Harbe II (perhaps 1223 BC) succeeded as the thirtieth king of the Kassite dynasty and ruled only for a year and a half.[256] He is so far not mentioned in any extant chronicle texts, and no historical information survives for his reign, although he is attested in several economic texts from Nippur, Ur, and Babylon.[257]

Kadašman-Harbe II was succeeded by Adad-šuma-iddina (1222–1217 BC), the thirty-first king of the Kassite dynasty, who ruled for six years.[258] This king is attested in economic texts from Ur and in one text from the unidentified site of Dur-Enlile.[259] There are no further texts from the archives at Nippur, but the inscription of a *kudurru* stone from the time of Meli-Šipak mentions legal decisions of this king, as well as his predecessors Adad-šuma-iddina and Adad-šuma-uṣur, concerning property in Nippur, showing that there was a certain continuity in those troubled times.[260] Kidin-Hutran of Elam attacked Babylonia for the second time

---

253. Roaf 2017: 180–181.

254. Glassner 2004: 280–281: *Chronicle of the Kassite Kings*: iv 14–16.

255. Brinkman 1976; Yamada 2003: 167; Bloch 2010: 64.

256. Brinkman 1976: 146.

257. Brinkman 1976: 148; Pedersén 2005: 98, no. M8: 18 (with commentary of Brinkman 2016); Bloch 2010: 63–64.

258. Brinkman 1976: 87.

259. Brinkman 1976: 87; van Soldt 2015: no. 256 (dating to the fourth year of this king).

260. Paulus 2014b: 403–404 (*MŠ* 4: i 1–38).

in the reign of Adad-šuma-iddina. The *Chronicle of the Kassite Kings* states that the Elamite king attacked Isin and then crossed the Tigris to attack Marad, where he inflicted a severe defeat to the Babylonian forces.[261]

33.5.2.   From Adad-šuma-uṣur to Marduk-apla-iddina I

Adad-šuma-iddina's successor was Adad-šuma-uṣur (1216–1187 BC), the thirty-second king of the Kassite dynasty, who ruled for thirty-two years according to King List A, although the latest year attested in the extant archival sources is his twenty-sixth regnal year.[262] However, assessing the attested dates is complicated by a novel year-counting system that was first introduced under Adad-šuma-uṣur and continued in use under his successors Meli-Šipak and Marduk-apla-iddina I. This system consists of a double ordinal counting, e.g., "second second year." As the meaning of this is unclear,[263] such dates cannot currently be sorted in the traditional sequence of regnal years.

As mentioned in the *Chronicle of the Kassite Kings* and the *Berlin Letter*, Adad-šuma-uṣur was placed on the Babylonian throne by the Babylonian magnates.[264] According to his own inscription on a bronze dagger,[265] he was the son of Kaštiliaš IV (who had been defeated and captured by Tukulti-Ninurta I; see section 33.3.2), and he thus claimed descent from the old Kassite dynasty. However, the *Berlin Letter*

---

261. Glassner 2004: 280–281: *Chronicle of the Kassite Kings*: iv 17–22.

262. van Soldt 2015: no. 256.

263. Brinkman 1976: 410–411 proposed that these year dates may be understood either literally (i.e., second second year would be the fourth year) or in ten-year cycles (i.e., second second year would be the twelfth year). However, Rowton 1966: 255–256 suggested that these year dates refer to a co-regency between two kings, while Sassmannshausen 2006: 169 proposed that the double-counting is caused by substitute king rituals.

264. Glassner 2004: 280–281: *Chronicle of the Kassite Kings*: iv 8; Paulus 2013: 434 (*Berlin Letter*, rev. 3–4).

265. Dossin 1962: 151, pl. XIII.

challenged this ancestry, calling Adad-šuma-uṣur "a son of Dunna-Sah from the bank of the Euphrates."[266]

During Adad-šuma-uṣur's reign, Babylonia gained its independence from Assyria, and there is again richer documentation, including inscriptions and economic documents. The *Chronicle of the Last Kassite Kings and Kings of Isin* (also known as the *Walker Chronicle*) possibly refers to the events at the beginning of his reign.[267] If so, he gained power over Babylon and Sippar and restored the walls of Nippur.[268] Contemporary inscriptions attest to his building activity at Nippur and Isin,[269] while a later copy preserves an inscription that he deposited at an unlocated gate of Marduk, possibly situated in Babylon.[270] It is likely that the statue of Marduk was returned to Babylon at the beginning of Adad-šuma-uṣur's reign.[271] The inscriptions on two *kudurru* stones document that the king judged a legal dispute in Nippur that had begun under his predecessor, and that he issued a land grant in the eastern Tigris region, hinting that Adad-šuma-uṣur started to regain control over this strategically important region.[272] Furthermore, there is an increase in the available archival documentation from Ur and Babylon, while the evidence for the late Kassite kings in (unidentified) Dur-Enlile remains meager.

---

266. *Berlin Letter*, rev. 3–5; see Paulus 2013: 434–435.

267. Reade 2000.

268. Glassner 2004: 282–283: *Chronicle of the Late Kassite Kings*: 1–2; see also Reade 2000. This reconstruction challenges others who argue that Adad-šuma-uṣur gained power over Babylon only later in his reign. See also Pedersén 2005: 98, no. M8: 16 and Brinkman 2017: 27 n. 236.

269. Brinkman 1976: 90; Bartelmus 2017: 282.

270. Paulus 2018: 156–157 (with collations and further references).

271. The *Chronicle of the Kassite Kings*: iv 12–13 states that the statue was returned after 6 (?) years under a certain Tukulti-Aššur. There have been attempts to equate this king with Ninurta-tukulti-Aššur; see Glassner 2004: 280–281; Llop and George 2001–02: 12. However, this is problematic, as he would be a contemporary of the kings of the Second Dynasty of Isin and the statue was stolen again by the Elamites at the end of the Kassite period; see later discussion in this chapter and Bloch 2010: 60; Brinkman 2017: 28 n. 248; Nielsen 2018: 170.

272. Paulus 2014b: 403–406 (*MŠ* 4: i 39–iv 10); 366–368 (*AŠU* 1).

Most of the historical evidence for Adad-šuma-uṣur's reign concerns Babylonia's relationship with Assyria, whose king Tukulti-Ninurta I had been killed in an internal revolt, likely led by the prince Aššur-nadin-apli, who followed his father on the throne (1206–1203 BC),[273] and he was succeeded after a short reign by his brother Aššur-nerari III (1202–1197 BC). In a literary letter, Adad-šuma-uṣur accuses Aššur-nerari III and his influential relative Ili-pada (the viceroy of Hanigalbat; see chapter 32 in this volume) of drunkenness that would render them unable to make decisions;[274] whatever the circumstances, this clearly indicates Assyrian weakness from a Babylonian point of view. Aššur-nerari III's short reign was followed by that of a third brother, Enlil-kudurri-uṣur (1196–1192),[275] but he lost the throne to Ninurta-apil-Ekur (1191–1179 BC), son of Ili-pada. According to the *Chronicle of the Late Kassite Kings*, the *Synchronistic Chronicle*, and another literary letter attributed to a king of the Second Dynasty of Isin (which succeeded the Kassite Dynasty; see chapter 41 in volume 4), Adad-šuma-uṣur attacked and defeated Enlil-kudurri-uṣur of Assyria and enabled Ninurta-apil-Ekur, who was at the time in Babylonia, to return to Assur to seize the Assyrian throne.[276] Thus, power relations between the two neighbors Babylonia and Assyria had shifted again, and this included a redrawing of the border in Babylonia's favor, as emerges from the documentation available for the Kassite kings Meli-Šipak and Marduk-apla-iddina I.[277]

In regard to the Babylonian relationship with Elam, the *Berlin Letter* mentioned that Adad-šuma-uṣur defeated the unidentified Elamite king who authored this letter, and that this defeat was followed by a dynastic

---

273. The *Chronicle of the Kassite Kings*: iv 9–11 has Aššur-naṣir-apli (Ashurnasirpal) by mistake; see Glassner 2004: 280–281; Jakob 2017a: 132.

274. Llop and George 2001–02: 9–11 (*ABL* 924 from Nineveh); Jakob 2017a: 132.

275. Jakob 2017a: 132.

276. Glassner 2004: 282–283: *Chronicle of the Last Kassite Kings*: ll. 3–10; 178–179: *Synchronistic Chronicle*: ii 3'–8'; Llop and George 2001–02: 8, 11–12 (literary letter), see also Jakob 2017a: 132.

277. Glassner 2004: 280–281: *Chronicle of the Kassite Kings*: iv 12–13.

marriage between him and the eldest daughter of Meli-Šipak, Adad-šuma-uṣur's son and successor,[278] thus giving the Elamite royal house a claim to the Babylonian throne via the maternal line.

Meli-Šipak (1186–1172 BC) was the thirty-third king of the Kassite dynasty and ruled for fifteen years.[279] He called himself a descendant of Kurigalzu, thereby linking the last Kassite kings to this successful king of the Middle Kassite period (see section 33.3.1).[280] Meli-Šipak conducted building works in Isin, Nippur, and possibly also Sippar.[281] A fragmentary stele of this king was found in Susa, taken there by Elamite raiders.[282] The private archives from Ur and Babylon continue during the reign of Meli-Šipak, as well as his successor Marduk-apla-iddina I, and there is also one text from Dur-Enlile.[283] Another text was found at Emar on the Middle Euphrates and likely was written in Anat, perhaps indicating that the Kassite kings exercised control over the Suhu region on the Middle Euphrates.[284]

While the chronicles do not list any military encounters of Meli-Šipak or of his son Marduk-apla-iddina I, many *kudurru* stones of these two kings have been found at Susa, having been stolen during the Elamite raids that happened shortly after the end of Marduk-apla-iddina's reign. Notably, two of Meli-Šipak's land grants favored his children, namely

---

278. *Berlin Letter*, obv. 13′–14′, rev. 3–5, 10–13. The author of the letter has often been identified as Šutruk-Nahhunte of Elam, whereas the present author prefers Kidin-Hutran, as the argument centers around the perceived illegitimacy of Adad-šuma-uṣur and a marriage with a daughter of Meli-Šipak, while no later events are mentioned; see Paulus 2013: 435–437; for critical recent discussion, see Roaf 2017: 182–194.

279. Brinkman 1976: 253: King List A. An alternative reading of the royal name Meli-Šipak is Meli-Šihu; see Sassmannshausen 2014: 190.

280. Brinkman 1976: 254–255, no. S.2.3; Paulus 2013: 435.

281. Brinkman 1976: 253–255; Bartelmus 2017: 282, 285.

282. Paulus 2014b: 421–422 (with discussion).

283. van Soldt 2015: no. 250.

284. Arnaud 1986: 36–37; see Brinkman 2017: 28.

his daughter Hunnubat-Nanaya, who held a role connected to the cult of the goddess Nanaya in Uruk, and his son and eventual successor Marduk-apla-iddina I (figure 33.2).[285]

The parcels of land granted by Meli-Šipak and Marduk-apla-iddina I to various recipients were clustered in Babylonia's northeastern holdings, including the provinces of Bit-Per'i-Amurru and Irreya on the border to Assyria, as well as the cities Nuzi and Halman in the western piedmont regions of the Zagros mountains.[286] The Kassite crown's aim was certainly to re-establish and strengthen control over these strategic border regions. The geographical distribution of the land also shows that the Assyrian conquest under Tukulti-Ninurta I did not result in any long-term territorial gains for the Assyrian state.[287]

Marduk-apla-iddina I (1171–1159 BC) succeeded his father Meli-Šipak and reigned for thirteen years as thirty-fourth king of the Kassite dynasty.[288] According to an inscription that survives as a later copy, he built for the god Marduk at the Ezida temple in Borsippa.[289] His restoration of the Ezida temple and of the stepped temple tower (*ziqqurat*) in Borsippa are also mentioned in the inscription of a *kudurru* in connection with a land grant.[290] The inscription of another *kudurru* of Marduk-apla-iddina I mentions that Habhu people (a designation used for the mountainous regions in the Zagros range) crossed the Lower Zab and raided Irreya, the Babylonian province on the border to Assyria. The governor of Irreya, who was the beneficiary of the land grant recorded in this monument, successfully fought back the invasion and piled up the heads of the killed enemies in the city of Akkad.[291] Finally, there are

---

285. Paulus 2014b: 369–383 (*MŠ* 1); 390–401 (*MŠ* 3).

286. Paulus 2014b: 185–198, 282–284; see Bit-Per'i-Amurru in the texts *MŠ* 1, *MŠ* 2, *MŠ* 5, *MAI I* 5, Tigris and Diyala in *MAI I* 6, Irreya in *MŠ* 7 and *MAI I* 9.

287. Fuchs 2011: 253–254; Jakob 2017a: 125; for Nuzi see *MAI I* 9: i 11.

288. Brinkman 1976: 247: King List A.

289. Bartelmus 2017: 282; Paulus 2018: 157.

290. Paulus 2014b: 441–448 (*MAI I* 2).

291. Paulus 2014b: 480–483 (*MAI I* 9: i 6–15).

a few administrative texts from Dur-Kurigalzu that date to the reign of Marduk-apla-iddina I and concern textile production and trade.[292]

33.5.3. The end of the Kassite dynasty

The last two kings of the Kassite dynasty are Zababa-šuma-iddina (1158 BC) and his successor Enlil-nadin-ahi, whose ancestry is unclear.[293] A tablet from Babylon dated to the accession year of Zababa-šuma-iddina is the only contemporary document known so far for this ruler.[294] According to the *Synchronistic Chronicle*, the Assyrian king Aššur-dan I (1178–1133 BC) attacked the border provinces of Ugar-ṣallu, Irreya, and Zabban (Zamban) and took massive booty to Assyria during his reign.[295]

In addition to the Assyrian aggression, there is evidence for an Elamite invasion at the same time. In Elam, the so-called Igihalkid dynasty (Middle Elamite II period) ended and power fell to the so-called Šutrukid dynasty (Middle Elamite III period; see chapter 34 in this volume),[296] and this may have been a reason for the renewed hostilities toward Babylonia. A fragmentary literary text from Nineveh (known today as *The Failed War with Elam*) reports the military encounters between the Elamite and the late Kassite kings as a prelude to the reconquest of Babylonia by Nebuchadnezzar I (1125–1104 BC; see chapter 41 in volume 4). According to this text, a king whose name is not preserved attacked Zababa-šuma-iddina and thus ended his reign.[297] This king is usually identified as Šutruk-Nahhunte of Elam.[298] According to his own

---

292. Brinkman 2001b; Clayden 2017: 472, 478.

293. Brinkman 1976: 321; 2018.

294. Pedersén 2005: no. M8: 20.

295. Glassner 2004: 178–179: *Synchronistic Chronicle*: ii 9′–12′. For the reasons for assigning to Aššur-dan I the regnal dates 1178–1133 BC (rather than 1168–1133 BC), see chapter 32 in this volume.

296. Potts 2016: 224–225.

297. Frame 2002: 19: B.2.4.6: ll. 2′–3′; Brinkman 2018; Nielsen 2018: 29.

298. Roaf 2017: 181–182.

inscriptions, Šutruk-Nahhunte looted several Babylonian cities, including Akkad, Dur-Kurigalzu, Sippar, Upi (Opis), as well as Ešnunna,[299] and *The Failed War with Elam* suggests that the Elamite king installed his son Kutir-Nahhunte in an official position in Babylonia.[300]

According to King List A, Zababa-šuma-iddina was succeeded by Enlil-nadin-ahi (1157–1155 BC), the thirty-sixth and last Kassite king who ruled for three years before the final Elamite strike ended the dynasty's long reign over Babylonia.[301] Initially, Zababa-šuma-iddina must still have exercised some control over his kingdom, as there are documents dated to this king's reign from Babylon and Ur, as well as one *kudurru* monument with his inscription.[302] *The Failed War of Elam* records that an Elamite king, often identified as Kutir-Nahhunte, plotted against Babylonia and went on to overwhelm its people, taking away rich booty including the Marduk statue and thus putting an end to the reign of Enlil-nadin-ahi.[303] Kutir-Nahhunte is also attested in the so-called "Kedor-Laomer Texts", a series of literary letters that are preserved in manuscripts from the Achaemenid period and were composed as an exchange between the two Kassite and Elamite kings.[304] In these texts, Kutir-Nahhunte states that he sees himself as a descendant of the Kassite kings and a legitimate candidate for the Babylonian throne, thus justifying his conquest of Babylonia, including the destruction of Nippur and Borsippa.

Although events surrounding the end of the Kassite dynasty are recorded in chronicles, literary letters, and other compositions, many details are unknown or unclear. But it is certain that the long reign of the Kassite dynasty over Babylonia ended with the Elamite conquest.

---

299. Potts 2016: 225–226; Roaf 2017: 177–178.

300. Potts 2016: 229.

301. Brinkman 1976: 122.

302. Brinkman 1976: 122; Pedersén 2005: nos. M5:1, M5:7, M8:47, and likely M8:68; Paulus 2014b: 485–486 (*ENAh 1*).

303. Frame 2002: 20.

304. Foster 2005: 369–375; Nielsen 2018: 33–34.

33.6. *Conclusions*

No other Babylonian dynasty reigned longer than the Kassite Dynasty, and this was facilitated by their smart policies. The Kassite ruling elite were foreigners with their own traditions and language, but they adapted well to the Babylonian social and political environment and catered to the local elites by following traditional conventions of kingship, such as commissioning royal inscriptions and providing continuous worship for the Babylonian gods. At the same time, the early Kassite rulers seem to have been militarily successful, as the inclusion of individual Kassite groups in the Babylonian armies during the later Old Babylonian period was followed by their conquest of Babylonia, the Zagros regions, and the Sealand.

However, the Kassite kings never mentioned their military success or their campaigns prominently in their inscriptions. It is therefore mainly through later sources, such as chronicles, that it is apparent that the Kassites matched the military powers of their western and northern neighbors and tried to expand their zone of influence further at their expense. Those efforts were combined with innovations in the geopolitical sphere. In particular, a new residence was founded in the north (Dur-Kurigalzu), and Babylonia was divided into provinces—a novel administrative system that helped to overcome the power structures of the old cities. The provincial administration controlled artificial irrigation and agricultural production, and collected taxes from villages to finance craft production and a large labor force. The network of diplomatic relations that connected Babylonia with its neighbors included dynastic marriages, gift exchange, and trade with the entire Middle East. Babylonians ventured to Assyria, Elam, and into the Persian Gulf, and as far away as Egypt and Anatolia. From what we know, literature, science, and education flourished, and Babylonian scholars were valued as experts all over the Middle East.

While Elamite raids finally ended the rule of the Kassite dynasty, many innovations of Kassite Babylonia survived. The term "Karduniaš" became a standard designation for Babylonia, and Kassite names can still be found in the first millennium BC, while the system of land donations and the connected *kudurru* inscriptions survived until the end of the seventh century

BC. First-millennium-BC student-scribes copied Kassite inscriptions and learned about those kings, while many scholars traced their ancestors back to the Kassite period. The transmission of compositions such as chronicles, literary royal letters, and literary accounts show that Babylonian scholars were interested in the Kassite dynasty until the Hellenistic period.

The study of the Kassite period is limited by the fact that the sources are unevenly distributed over time, and that moreover some of the most significant sources (including the archives from Babylon and many texts from Nippur) are still unpublished. However, the recent discovery and publication of texts pertaining to the Sealand dynasty and the renewed interest in the study of the evidence for the early Kassite period have shown how quickly and profoundly our picture of the Kassite period can change. As we have seen, the publication of a single new royal inscription (like the dedicatory inscription of Kaštiliaš III) or a new archive (like the texts presumed to come from Dur-Enlile) can have a major impact on our reconstruction of Kassite history.

REFERENCES

Abdallah, F., and Durand, J.-M. 2014. Deux documents cunéiformes retrouvés au Tell Sakka. In Ziegler, N., and Cancik-Kirschbaum, E. (eds.), *Entre les fleuves, II: d'Aššur à Mari et au-dèla.* Gladbeck: PeWe-Verlag, 233–248.

Abraham, K., and Gabbay, U. 2013. Kaštiliašu and the Sumundar canal: a new Middle Babylonian royal inscription. *ZA* 103: 183–195.

Al-Rawi, F.N.H., and George, A.R. 1994. Tablets from the Sippar Library, III: two royal counterfeits. *Iraq* 56: 135–148.

Alubaid, I.J. 1983. *Unpublished cuneiform texts from Old Babylonian period Diyala region: Tell Muhammad.* MA thesis, College of Arts, University of Baghdad.

André-Salvini, B., and Lombard, P. 1997. La découverte épigraphique de 1995 à Qal'at al-Bahrein: un jalon pour la chronologie de la phase Dilmoun Moyen dans le Golfe Arabe. *Proceedings of the Seminar for Arabian Studies* 27: 165–170.

Arnaud, D. 1986. *Recherches au pays d'Aštata: textes sumériens et accadiens.* Paris: Éditions Recherche sur les Civilisations.

Astour, M.C. 1986. The name of the ninth Kassite ruler. *JAOS* 106: 327–331.

Baker, H. 2008. Salmanassar I. *RlA* 11: 579–580.

Balkan, K. 1954. *Kassitenstudien 1: die Sprache der Kassiten*. New Haven, CT: American Oriental Society.

Bányai, M. 2011. Die Niḫrīya-Schlacht—vorher und danach. *Anatolica* 37: 207–237.

Bartelmus, A. 2010. Restoring the past: a historical analysis of the royal temple building inscriptions from the Kassite period. *KASKAL: Rivista di storia, ambienti e culture del Vicino Oriente Antico* 7: 143–171.

Bartelmus, A. 2016. *Fragmente einer großen Sprache: Sumerisch im Kontext der Schreiberausbildung des kassitenzeitlichen Babylonien*. Berlin: De Gruyter.

Bartelmus, A. 2017. Die Götter der Kassitenzeit: eine Analyse ihres Vorkommens in zeitgenössischen Textquellen. In Bartelmus, A., and Sternitzke, K. (eds.), *Karduniaš: Babylonia under the Kassites*. Berlin: De Gruyter, 245–312.

Bartelmus, A., and Taylor, J. 2014. Collecting and connecting history: Nabonidus and the Kassite rebuilding of the E(ul)maš of (Ištar)-Annunītu in Sippar-Annunītu. *JCS* 66: 113–128.

Beaulieu, P.-A. 2018. *A history of Babylon: 2200 BC–AD 75*. Malden, MA: Wiley-Blackwell.

Beckman, G. 1987. Three bricks from Yale. *Annual Review of the Royal Inscriptions of Mesopotamia Project* 5: 1–3.

Beckman, G. 1999. *Hittite diplomatic texts*. Atlanta, GA: Society of Biblical Literature.

Bloch, Y. 2010. Setting the dates: re-evaluation of the chronology of Babylonia in the 14th–11th centuries BCE and its implications for the reigns of Ramesses II and Ḫattušili III. *UF* 42: 41–95.

Boese, J. 2008. "Ḫarbašipak," "Tiptakzi" und die Chronologie der älteren Kassitenzeit. *ZA* 98: 201–210.

Boese, J. 2009. Kadašman-Enlil, Kadašman-Turgu und die kassitische Chronologie des 14. und 13. Jahrhunderts v. Chr. *AoF* 36: 85–96.

Boivin, O. 2018. *The First Dynasty of the Sealand in Mesopotamia*. Berlin: De Gruyter.

Brinkman, J.A. 1970. Notes on Mesopotamian history in the thirteenth century BC. *BiOr* 72: 301–314.

Brinkman, J.A. 1976. *Materials and studies for Kassite history, vol. 1: a catalogue of cuneiform sources pertaining to specific monarchs of the Kassite dynasty.* Chicago: The Oriental Institute of the University of Chicago.

Brinkman, J.A. 1980. Kassiten. *RlA* 5: 464–473.

Brinkman, J.A. 1983. Istanbul A. 1998, Middle Babylonian chronology, and the statistics of the Nippur archives. *ZA* 73: 67–74.

Brinkman, J.A. 1993. A Kassite seal mentioning a Babylonian governor of Dilmun. *NABU* 1993: 89–91 (no. 106).

Brinkman, J.A. 2001a. Nazi-Maruttaš. *RlA* 9: 190–191.

Brinkman, J.A. 2001b. Assyrian merchants at Dūr-Kurigalzu. *NABU* 2001: 70–71 (no. 73).

Brinkman, J.A. 2004. Administration and society in Kassite Babylonia. *JAOS* 124: 283–304.

Brinkman, J.A. 2008. Šagarakti-Šuriaš. *RlA* 11: 515.

Brinkman, J.A. 2014. The seventh and eighth kings of the Kassite dynasty. *NABU* 2014: 31–32 (no. 20).

Brinkman, J.A. 2015. Dating YBC 2242, the Kadašman-Ḫarbe I Stone. *NABU* 2015: 19–20 (no. 18).

Brinkman, J.A. 2016. The green tiger, revisited. *NABU* 2016: 75–76 (no. 45).

Brinkman, J.A. 2017. Babylonia under the Kassites: some aspects for consideration. In Bartelmus, A., and Sternitzke, K. (eds.), *Karduniaš: Babylonia under the Kassites.* Berlin: De Gruyter, 1–44.

Brinkman, J.A. 2018. Zababa-šuma-iddina. *RlA* 15: 169–170.

Brinkman, J.A. 2019. Review of S. Paulus, Die babylonischen Kudurru-Inschriften von der kassitischen bis zur frühneubablylonischen Zeit: Untersucht unter besonderer Berücksichtigung gesellschafts- und rechtshistorischer Fragestellungen. *JNES* 78: 141–144.

Brinkman, J.A. 2020. Two little-known governors of Nippur under the Kassite Dynasty: Bēlānu and Ninurta-apla-iddina. *NABU* 2020: 238–242 (no. 115).

Campbell, S., Moon, J., Killick, R., Calderbank, D., Robson, E., Shepperson, M., and Slater, F. 2017. Tell Khaiber: an administrative centre of the Sealand period. *Iraq* 79: 21–46.

Cancik-Kirschbaum, E. 1996. *Die mittelassyrischen Briefe aus Tall Šēḫ Ḥamad.* Berlin: Reimer.

Charpin, D. 2002. Chroniques du Moyen-Euphrate, 1: le "royaume de Hana": textes et histoire. *RA* 96: 61–92.

Charpin, D. 2004. Histoire politique du Proche-Orient amorrite (2002–1595). In Charpin, D., Edzard, D.O., and Stol, M., *Mesopotamien: die altbabylonische Zeit*. Fribourg: Academic Press; Göttingen: Vandenhoeck & Ruprecht, 25–480.

Clayden, T. 1996. Kurigalzu I and the restoration of Babylonia. *Iraq* 58: 109–121.

Clayden, T. 2011. The Nippur "hoard." *Al-Rāfidān* 32: 1–56.

Clayden, T. 2017. Dūr-Kurigalzu: new perspectives. In Bartelmus, A., and Sternitzke, K. (eds.), *Karduniaš: Babylonia under the Kassites*. Berlin: De Gruyter, 437–478.

Cohen, R., and Westbrook, R. (eds.) 2000. *Amarna diplomacy: the beginning of international relations*. Baltimore, MD: Johns Hopkins University Press.

Dalley, S. 2009. *Babylonian tablets from the First Sealand dynasty in the Schøyen Collection*. Bethesda, MD: CDL Press.

De Graef, K. 1999. Les étrangers dans les textes paléobabyloniens tardifs de Sippar (première partie). *Akkadica* 111: 1–48.

deJong Ellis, M. 1976. *Agriculture and the state in ancient Mesopotamia*. Philadelphia: University of Pennsylvania Museum of Archaeology and Anthropology.

de Smet, W.A.J. 1990. "Kashshû" in Old-Babylonian documents. *Akkadica* 68: 1–19.

Devecchi, E. 2017. On kings, princesses, and messengers: Babylonia's international relations during the 13th century BC. In Bartelmus, A., and Sternitzke, K. (eds.), *Karduniaš: Babylonia under the Kassites*. Berlin: De Gruyter, 112–122.

Devecchi, E. 2020a. Managing the harvest in Kassite Babylonia: the evidence for *tēlītu*. In Paulus, S., and Clayden, T. (eds.), *Babylonia under the Sealand and Kassite dynasties*. Berlin: De Gruyter, 205–227.

Devecchi, E. 2020b. *Middle Babylonian texts in the Cornell University Collections, II: the earlier kings*. Bethesda, MD: CDL Press.

Dossin, G. 1962. Bronzes inscrits du Luristan de la Collection Foroughi. *IrAnt* 2: 149–164.

Durand, J.-M., and Marti, L. 2005. Chroniques du Moyen-Euphrate, 5: une attaque de Qaṭna par le Sûhum et la question du "Pays de Mari." *RA* 99: 123–132.

Edel, E., and Görg, M. 2005. *Die Ortsnamenlisten im nördlichen Säulenhof des Totentempels Amenophis' III*. Wiesbaden: Harrassowitz.

Faist, B. 2001. *Der Fernhandel des assyrischen Reiches zwischen dem 14. und 11. Jh. v. Chr*. Münster: Ugarit-Verlag.

Finkel, I. J. 1983. The dream of Kurigalzu and the tablet of sins. *AnSt* 33: 75–80.

Foster, B.R. 2005. *Before the muses: an anthology of Akkadian literature.* Bethesda, MD: CDL Press.

Frahm, E. 2009. *Historische und historisch-literarische Texte* (Keilschrifttexte aus Assur literarischen Inhalts 3). Wiesbaden: Harrassowitz.

Frahm, E. 2017. Assyria and the south: Babylonia. In Frahm, E. (ed.), *A companion to Assyria.* Malden, MA: Wiley-Blackwell, 286–298.

Frame, G. 2002. *Rulers of Babylonia from the Second Dynasty of Isin to the end of Assyrian domination (1157–612 BC).* Toronto: University of Toronto Press.

Frazer, M. 2013. Nazi-Maruttaš in later Mesopotamian tradition. *KASKAL: Rivista di storia, ambienti e culture del Vicino Oriente Antico* 10: 187–220.

Frazer, M. 2015. *Akkadian royal letters in later Mesopotamian tradition.* PhD thesis, Yale University.

Fuchs, A. 2011. Das Osttigrisgebiet von Agum II bis Darius I. In Miglus, P.A., and Mühl, S. (eds.), *Between the cultures: the central Tigris region from the 3rd to the 1st millennium BC.* Heidelberg: Heidelberger Orientverlag, 229–320.

Fuchs, A. 2017. Die Kassiten, das mittelbabylonische Reich und der Zagros. In Bartelmus, A., and Sternitzke, K. (eds.), *Karduniaš: Babylonia under the Kassites.* Berlin: De Gruyter, 123–165.

Gabbay, U., and Boivin, O. 2018. A hymn of Ayadaragalama, king of the First Sealand dynasty, to the gods of Nippur: the fate of Nippur and its cult during the First Sealand dynasty. *ZA* 108: 22–42.

Gasche, H., Armstrong, J.A., Cole, S.W., and Gurzadyan, V.G. 1998. *Dating the fall of Babylon: a reappraisal of second-millennium chronology.* Ghent: University of Ghent; Chicago: The Oriental Institute of the University of Chicago.

Gentili, P. 2006. Where is Diniktum? Remarks on the situation and a supposition. *Rivista di Studi Orientali* 79: 231–238.

George, A.R. 2011. *Cuneiform royal inscriptions and related texts in the Schøyen Collection.* Bethesda, MD: CDL Press.

Glassner, J.-J. 2004. *Mesopotamian chronicles.* Atlanta, GA: Society of Biblical Literature.

Glatz, C., Casana, J., Bendrey, R., Baysal, E., Calderbank, D., Chelazzi, F., Del Bravo, F., Erskine, N., Hald, M.M., Lauinger, J., Jensen, E., and Perruchini,

E. 2019. Babylonian encounters in the Upper Diyala valley: contextualizing the results of regional survey and the 2016–2017 excavations at Khani Masi. *AJA* 123: 439–471.

Grayson, A.K. 1975. *Babylonian historical-literary texts.* Toronto: University of Toronto Press.

Grayson, A.K. 1987. *Assyrian rulers of the third and second millennia BC.* Toronto: University of Toronto Press.

Gurney, O.R. 1949. Texts from Dur-Kurigalzu. *Iraq* 11: 131–149.

Hagenbuchner, A. 1989. *Die Korrespondenz der Hethiter, 2. Teil: Briefe mit Transkription, Übersetzung und Kommentar.* Heidelberg: Winter.

Heeßel, N. 2011. "Sieben Tafeln aus sieben Städten": Überlegungen zum Prozess der Serialisierung von Texten in Babylonien in der zweiten Hälfte des zweiten Jahrtausends v. Chr. In Cancik-Kirschbaum, E., van Ess, M., and Marzahn, J. (eds.), *Babylon: Wissenskultur in Orient und Okzident.* Berlin: De Gruyter, 171–195.

Heeßel, N. 2017. Zur Standardisierung und Spezialisierung von Texten während der Kassitenzeit am Beispiel der Opferschau-Omina. In Bartelmus, A., and Sternitzke, K. (eds.), *Karduniaš: Babylonia under the Kassites.* Berlin: De Gruyter, 219–228.

Heinz, M. 1995. Migration und Assimilation im 2. Jt. v. Chr.: die Kassiten. In Bartl, K., Bernbeck, R., and Heinz, M. (eds.), *Zwischen Euphrat und Indus: aktuelle Forschungsprobleme in der vorderasiatischen Archäologie.* Hildesheim: Olms, 165–174.

Hoffner, H.A. 2009. *Letters from the Hittite kingdom.* Atlanta, GA: Society of Biblical Literature.

Jakob, S. 2017a. The Middle Assyrian period (14th to 11th century BCE). In Frahm, E. (ed.), *A companion to Assyria.* Malden, MA: Wiley-Blackwell, 117–142.

Jakob, S. 2017b. "One epic or many?" Das Tukultī-Ninurta-Epos zum Ersten, Zweiten und zum . . . ? In Drewnowska, O., and Sandowicz, M. (eds.), *Fortune and misfortune in the ancient Near East.* Winona Lake, IN: Eisenbrauns, 259–268.

Kessler, K. 1985. Die Tontafeln. In Boehmer, R.M., and Dämmer, H.-W. (eds.), *Tell Imlihiye; Tell Zubeidi; Tell Abbas.* Mainz: Zabern, 74–79.

Lion, B. 2011. Assur unter der Mittaniherrschaft. In Renger, J. (ed.), *Assur: Gott, Stadt und Land.* Wiesbaden: Harrassowitz, 149–167.

Llop, J. 2011. The boundary between Assyria and Babylonia in the east Tigris region during the reign of Tukultī-Ninurta I (1233–1197 BC). In Miglus, P.A., and Mühl, S. (eds.), *Between the cultures: the central Tigris region from the 3rd to the 1st millennium BC*. Heidelberg: Heidelberger Orientverlag, 209–215.

Llop, J. 2015. Foreign kings in the Middle Assyrian archival documentation. In Düring, B.S. (ed.), *Understanding hegemonic practices of the early Assyrian Empire: essays dedicated to Frans Wiggermann*. Leiden: NINO, 243–273.

Llop, J., and George, A.R. 2001–02. Die babylonisch-assyrischen Beziehungen und die innere Lage Assyriens in der Zeit der Auseinandersetzung zwischen Ninurta-tukulti-Aššur und Mutakkil-Nusku nach neuen keilschriftlichen Quellen. *AfO* 48/49: 1–23.

Machinist, P. 2016. Tukultī-Ninurta-Epos. *RlA* 14: 180–181.

Malko, H. 2017. Dūr-Kurigalzu: insights from unpublished Iraqi excavation reports. In Bartelmus, A., and Sternitzke, K. (eds.), *Karduniaš: Babylonia under the Kassites*. Berlin: De Gruyter, 479–491.

Malko, H. 2020. The Kassites of Babylonia: a re-examination of an ethnic identity. In Paulus, S., and Clayden, T. (eds.), *Babylonia under the Sealand and Kassite dynasties*. Berlin: De Gruyter, 177–189.

Matthews, D.M. 1992. *The Kassite glyptic of Nippur*. Fribourg: Academic Press; Göttingen: Vandenhoeck & Ruprecht.

Miller, J.L. 2017. Political interactions between Kassite Babylonia and Assyria, Egypt and Ḫatti during the Amarna Age. In Bartelmus, A., and Sternitzke, K. (eds.), *Karduniaš: Babylonia under the Kassites*. Berlin: De Gruyter, 93–111.

Mora, C., and Giorgieri, M. 2004. *Le lettere tra i re ittiti e i re assiri ritovate a Ḫattuša*. Padua: Sargon.

Murai, N. 2020. Sealing practices in Middle Babylonian administrative transactions. *Mesopotamia* 55: 97–112.

Nielsen, J.P. 2018. *The reign of Nebuchadnezzar I in history and historical memory*. London and New York: Routledge.

Novák, M. 2014. The phenomenon of residential cities and city foundations in the ancient Near East: common idea or individual case. In Osborne, J. (ed.), *Approaching monumentality in archaeology*. Albany: State University of New York Press, 311–332.

Oshima, T. 2012. Another attempt at two Kassite royal inscriptions: the Agum-Kakrime inscription and the inscription of Kurigalzu the son of Kadeshmanharbe. *Babel and Bibel* 6: 225–268.

Parpola, S., and Porter, M. 2001. *The Helsinki atlas of the Near East in the Neo-Assyrian period.* Helsinki: The Neo-Assyrian Text Corpus Project.

Paulus, S. 2007. "Ein Richter wie Šamaš": zur Rechtsprechung der Kassitenkönige. *Zeitschrift für altorientalische und biblische Rechtsgeschichte* 13: 1–22.

Paulus, S. 2013. Beziehungen zweier Großmächte—Elam und Babylonien in der 2. Hälfte des 2. Jt. v. Chr.: ein Beitrag zur internen Chronologie. In De Graef, K., and Tavernier, J. (eds.), *Susa and Elam: archaeological, philological, historical and geographical perspectives.* Leiden: Brill, 429–449.

Paulus, S. 2014a. Akkade in mittelbabylonischer Zeit. In Ziegler, N., and Cancik-Kirschbaum, E. (eds.), *Entre les fleuves, II: d'Aššur à Mari et au-delà.* Gladbeck: PeWe-Verlag, 199–206.

Paulus, S. 2014b. *Die babylonischen Kudurru-Inschriften von der kassitischen bis zur frühneubabylonischen Zeit.* Münster: Ugarit-Verlag.

Paulus, S. 2015. Karduniash. In Bagnall, R., Brodersen, K., Champion, C., Erskine, A., and Huebner, S. (eds.), *The encyclopedia of ancient history.* Malden, MA: Wiley-Blackwell. Retrieved from https://onlinelibrary. wiley.com/doi/full/10.1002/9781444338386.wbeah26282 (last accessed August 19, 2020).

Paulus, S. 2017. The Babylonian *kudurru* inscriptions and their legal and sociohistorical implications. In Bartelmus, A., and Sternitzke, K. (eds.), *Karduniaš: Babylonia under the Kassites.* Berlin: De Gruyter, 229–244.

Paulus, S. 2018. Fraud, forgery, and fiction: is there still hope for Agum-Kakrime? *JCS* 70: 115–166.

Paulus, S. 2020. Taxation and management of resources in Kassite Babylonia: remarks on *šibšu* and *miksu.* In Mynářová, J., and Alivernini, S. (eds.), *Economic complexity in the ancient Near East: management of resources and taxation (third–second millennium BC).* Prague: Charles University: 299–326.

Pedersén, O. 1998. *Archives and libraries in the ancient Near East 1500–300 BC.* Bethesda, MD: CDL Press.

Pedersén, O. 2005. *Archive und Bibliotheken in Babylon: die Tontafeln der Grabung Robert Koldeweys 1899–1917.* Saarbrücken: Saarländische Druckerei und Verlag.

Podany, A.H. 2002. *The land of Hana: kings, chronology, and scribal tradition.* Bethesda, MD: CDL Press.

Podany, A.H. 2010. *Brotherhood of kings: how international relations shaped the ancient Near East.* Oxford: Oxford University Press.

Podany, A.H. 2019. Family members, neighbors, and a local shrine in Terqa, Syria, in the late Old Babylonian period. In Abrahami, P., and Battini, L. (eds.), *Ina ᵈmarri u qan ṭuppi = par la bêche et le stylet! Cultures et sociétés syro-mésopotamiennes: mélanges offerts à Olivier Rouault.* Oxford: Archaeopress, 125–134.

Porada, E., and Collon, D. 2016. *The second millennium BC: beyond Babylon.* London: British Museum Press.

Potts, D.T. 2006. Elamites and Kassites in the Persian Gulf. *JNES* 65: 111–119.

Potts, D.T. 2016. *The archaeology of Elam: formation and transformation of an ancient Iranian state.* Cambridge: Cambridge University Press. 2nd rev. ed.

Pruzsinszky, R. 2009. *Mesopotamian chronology of the 2nd millennium BC.* Vienna: Österreichische Akademie der Wissenschaften.

Radner, K. 2020. *A short history of Babylon.* London: Bloomsbury.

Rainey, A.F. 2015. *The el-Amarna correspondence: a new edition of the cuneiform letters from the site of el-Amarna based on collations of all extant tablets* Leiden: Brill.

Reade, J.E. 2000. The reign of Adad-šuma-uṣur. *NABU* 2000: 87 (no. 76).

Richardson, S. 2016. The many falls of Babylon and the shape of forgetting. In Nadali, D. (ed.), *How memory shaped ancient Near Eastern societies.* London: Bloomsbury, 101–142.

Roaf, M. 2017. Kassite and Elamite kings. In Bartelmus, A., and Sternitzke, K. (eds.), *Karduniaš: Babylonia under the Kassites.* Berlin: De Gruyter, 166–195.

Rouault, O. 2016. Qasr Shemamok (ancient Kilizu), a provincial capital east of the Tigris: recent excavations and new perspectives. In MacGinnis, J., Wicke, D., and Greenfield, T. (eds.), *The provincial archaeology of the Assyrian Empire.* Oxford: Oxbow, 151–163.

Rowton, M.B. 1966. The material from Western Asia and the chronology of the Nineteenth Dynasty. *JNES* 25: 240–258.

Sassmannshausen, L. 2001a. The adaptation of the Kassites to the Babylonian civilization. In Van Lerberghe, K., and Voet, G. (eds.), *Languages and cultures in contact: at the crossroads of civilizations in the Syro-Mesopotamian realm.* Leuven: Peeters, 409–424.

Sassmannshausen, L. 2001b. *Beiträge zur Verwaltung und Gesellschaft Babyloniens in der Kassitenzeit.* Mainz: Zabern.

Sassmannshausen, L. 2004a. Babylonian chronology of the 2nd half of the 2nd millennium BC. In Hunger, H., and Pruzsinszky, R. (eds.), *Mesopotamian Dark Age revisited.* Vienna: Verlag der Österreichischen Akademie der Wissenschaften, 61–70.

Sassmannshausen, L. 2004b. Kassite nomads: fact or fiction? In Nicolle, C. (ed.), *Nomades et sédentaires dans le Proche-Orient ancien.* Paris: Éditions Recherche sur les Civilisation, 287–306.

Sassmannshausen, L. 2006. Zur mesopotamischen Chronologie des 2. Jahrtausends. *BaM* 37: 157–177.

Sassmannshausen, L. 2008a. Babylonische Schriftkultur des 2. Jahrtausends v. Chr. in den Nachbarländern und im östlichen Mittelmeerraum. *Aula Orientalis* 26: 263–293.

Sassmannshausen, L. 2008b. Dilmun/Bahrein und Babylonien im 15.–14. Jahrhundert v. Chr. aus assyriologischer Sicht. In Olijdam, E., and Spoors, R.H. (eds.), *Intercultural relations between South and Southwest Asia: studies in commemoration of E.C.L. During Caspers (1934–1996).* Oxford: Archaeopress, 316–328.

Sassmannshausen, L. 2014. Die kassitischen Herrscher und ihre Namen. In Sassmannshausen, L. (ed.), *He has opened Nisaba's house of learning: studies in honor of Åke Waldemar Sjöberg.* Leiden: Brill, 165–199.

Sazonov, V. 2016. *Die assyrischen Königstitel und -epitheta: vom Anfang bis Tukulti-Ninurta I. und seinen Nachfolgern.* Helsinki: The Neo-Assyrian Text Corpus Project.

Schaudig, H. 2001. *Die Inschriften Nabonids von Babylon und Kyros' des Großen samt den in ihrem Umfeld entstandenen Tendenzschriften.* Münster: Ugarit-Verlag.

Schneider, B. 2020. Studies concerning the Kassite period Ekur of Nippur: construction history and finds. In Clayden, T., and Paulus, S. (eds.), *Babylonia under the Sealand and Kassite dynasties.* Berlin: De Gruyter, 146–164.

Shelley, N. 2017. Kaššû: cultural labels and identity in ancient Mesopotamia. In Bartelmus, A., and Sternitzke, K. (eds.), *Karduniaš: Babylonia under the Kassites.* Berlin: De Gruyter, 196–208.

Singer, I. 1999. A political history of Ugarit. In Watson, W.G.E., and Wyatt, N. (eds.), *Handbook of Ugaritic studies.* Leiden: Brill, 603–733.

Singer, I. 2008. A Hittite-Assyrian diplomatic exchange in the late 13th century BCE. *SMEA* 50: 713–720.

Stein, P. 2000. *Die mittel- und neubabylonischen Königsinschriften bis zum Ende der Assyrerherrschaft: grammatische Untersuchungen*. Wiesbaden: Harrassowitz.

Stiehler-Alegria Delgado, G. 1996. *Die kassitische Glyptik*. Munich: Profil-Verlag.

Stol, M. 1976. *Studies in Old Babylonian history*. Istanbul: Leiden: NINO.

Streck, M.P. 2016. Tukultī-Ninurta I. *RlA* 14: 176–178.

Tenney, J.S. 2011. *Life at the bottom of Babylonian society: servile laborers at Nippur in the 14th and 13th centuries BC*. Leiden: Brill.

Tenney, J.S. 2016. The elevation of Marduk revisited: festivals and sacrifices at Nippur during the high Kassite period. *JCS* 68: 153–180.

Tenney, J.S. 2017. Babylonian populations, servility, and cuneiform records. *Journal of the Economic and Social History of the Orient* 60: 715–787.

van Koppen, F. 2010. The Old to Middle Babylonian transition: history and chronology of the Mesopotamian Dark Age. *ÄL* 20: 453–463.

van Koppen, F. 2017. The early Kassite period. In Bartelmus, A., and Sternitzke, K. (eds.), *Karduniaš: Babylonia under the Kassites*. Berlin: De Gruyter, 45–92.

Van Lerberghe, K. 1995. Kassites and Old Babylonian society. In Van Lerberghe, K., and Schoors, A. (eds.), *Immigration and emigration within the ancient Near East: Festschrift E. Lipinski*. Leuven: Peeters, 379–393.

van Soldt, W. H. 1988. Irrigation in Kassite Babylonia. *Bulletin of Sumerian Agriculture* 3: 105–120.

van Soldt, W. H. 2015. *Middle Babylonian texts in the Cornell University Collections, I: the later kings*. Bethesda, MD: CDL Press.

Veldhuis, N. 2008. Kurigalzu's statue inscription. *JCS* 60: 25–51.

Veldhuis, N. 2014. *History of cuneiform lexical tradition*. Münster: Ugarit-Verlag.

Waerzeggers, C. 2012. The Babylonian chronicles: classification and provenance. *JNES* 71: 285–298.

Wiseman, D.J. 1967. A Late Babylonian tribute list? *Bulletin of the School of Oriental and African Studies* 30: 495–504.

Yamada, S. 2003. Tukulti-Ninurta I's rule over Babylonia and its aftermath: a historical reconstruction. *Orient* 38: 153–177.

Zadok, R. 2013. Kassite. *Encyclopedia Iranica* 16: 113–118.

Zomer, E. 2018. *Corpus of Middle Babylonian and Middle Assyrian incantations*. Wiesbaden: Harrassowitz.

34

Elam in the Late Bronze Age

Behzad Mofidi-Nasrabadi

34.1. Introduction

The political dominance of Mesopotamia over Elam (figure 34.1) in the
Ur III period (cf. chapter 13 in volume 2) resulted in strong and lasting
cultural influences at the beginning of the second millennium BC, which
are attested over several centuries during the so-called *Sukkalmah* period
(cf. chapter 16 in volume 2).[1] Most prominently, the Akkadian language
and writing system of Mesopotamia became the official language and
script for Elamite royal and administrative texts, in which rulers used the
Mesopotamian term *sukkalmah* (in its original Sumerian context conventionally translated as "great vizier") as their primary royal title, which
in the Elamite context may be understood to mean "supreme regent."

Around the middle of the second millennium BC, Elam underwent
changes that resulted in the rise of local political and economic powers,
as well as the strengthening of local traditions. The ancient title "king of
Susa and Anšan"—first used by the Šimaškian king Ebarat (see chapter 16
in volume 2)—appeared again in royal inscriptions.[2] While the Susiana
plain with its capital city of Susa, situated in the modern Iranian province

---

1. This chapter was language-edited by D.T. Potts and Karen Radner.

2. Vallat 1997.

Behzad Mofidi-Nasrabadi, *Elam in the Late Bronze Age* In: *The Oxford History of the Ancient Near East.*
Edited by: Karen Radner, Nadine Moeller, and D. T. Potts, Oxford University Press. © Oxford University Press
2022. DOI: 10.1093/oso/9780190687601.003.0034

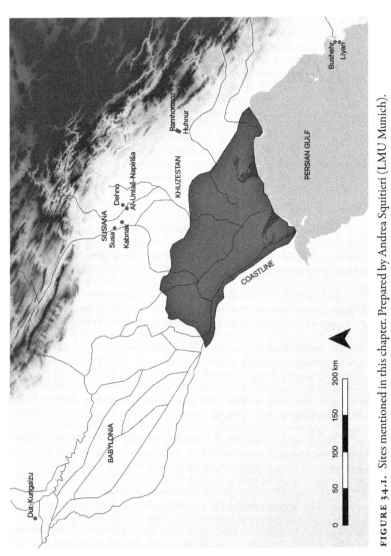

FIGURE 34.1. Sites mentioned in this chapter. Prepared by Andrea Squitieri (LMU Munich).

of Khuzestan, was called Elam, the ancient city of Anšan (modern Tell-e Malyan in the Iranian province of Fars) was the most important city of the eastern Elamite regions formerly known as Šimaški.[3] Scholars consider the renewed use of the old Anšanite royal title an indication of the beginning of a new era in Elamite history, today designated the Middle Elamite (ME) period. This was marked by the decline of Mesopotamian influence and the strengthening of eastern Elamite traditions.

This chapter will first survey the periodization of the Middle Elamite period before discussing the chronologically and geographically (very unevenly distributed) textual sources. We then focus on the power structures that held the kingdom of Elam together, specifically the king, the royal family, the centralized administration, and the temples and cults. The chapter closes with a consideration of residential architecture, funerary practices, and material culture.

34.2. The periodization of the Middle Elamite period

The title "king of Susa and Anšan" was used continuously until the reign of Šilhak-Inšušinak in the twelfth century BC, after which it went out of use for several centuries. The end of the Middle Elamite period is today generally taken to be the fall of Šilhak-Inšušinak's successor, Hutelutuš-Inšušinak, ca. 1100 BC (but see section 34.2.3, for a possible later king).

The Middle Elamite period corresponds broadly to the Late Bronze Age elsewhere in the Near East. Its modern division into further chronological sub-units is the result of a combination of different approaches that take into account archaeological and/or philological evidence, but there is currently no complete agreement among modern scholars on whether the Middle Elamite period should be divided into two, three, or even more sub-phases.[4] The most widely accepted periodization scheme,

---

3. Mofidi-Nasrabadi 2010a.

4. Mofidi-Nasrabadi 2018a: Table 12.1.

which we will follow in this chapter, dates the Middle Elamite period from 1500 to 1100 BC and divides it into three phases (ME I–III), each correlated with a sequence of rulers or dynasty.

34.2.1. Middle Elamite I (ME I)

The first group of Middle Elamite kings includes Kidinu, Tan-Ruhuratir II, Tepti-ahar, Inšušinak-šar-ili, and Šalla, although the last ruler is not known to have used the title "king of Susa and Anšan." These rulers are sometimes referred to as the "Kidinuid dynasty" because they were once considered the descendants of Kidinu, who was, in turn, assumed to be the first ruler of the Middle Elamite period.[5] Kidinu is attested only in an inscription on his cylinder seal. This was found at Susa and calls him "king of Susa and Anšan" and son of Adad-šarru-rabu, an otherwise unknown individual.[6] Although the term "Kidinuid dynasty" implies that Kidinu was the founder of a dynasty, this is entirely speculative since no family ties have been confirmed with and between the other previously mentioned rulers. Therefore, the term is better abandoned.

Furthermore, a recent discovery has brought to light a ruler who probably preceded Kidinu. An inscribed brick, located in the storage rooms of a museum in Tehran and published in 2015, mentions the rule of one Igi-hatet over Susa and Anšan.[7] Later, it was recognized that several bricks with the same inscription had previously been discovered at Dehno, located about 33 km southeast of Susa. However, because the last part of the name was damaged on all these bricks, the royal name on them had been incorrectly restored as Igi-halki, the ancestor of the ME II Elamite rulers (see section 34.2.2).[8] The philological analysis of the text suggests that it dates to the very early Middle Elamite period,

---

5. Steve et al. 1980: 78; Vallat 1994: 13.

6. Steve et al. 1980: 92–93; Amiet 1980: 139, no. 11; Mofidi-Nasrabadi 2009: 50, no. 41; Potts 2016: 179.

7. Daneshmand and Abdoli 2015.

8. Steve et al. 1980: 100; Steve 1987: 11–13; Mofidi-Nasrabadi 2013a: 93–97.

shortly after the *Sukkalmah* period.[9] This being the case, we can identify at least six ME I rulers. Although their chronological sequence remains uncertain, its reconstruction is informed by new evidence, especially the finds from Haft Tappeh (probably ancient Kabnak), situated about 15 km southeast of Susa. First, the assumption that Tepti-ahar reigned before Inšušinak-šar-ili is based on the recovery of seal impressions from Haft Tappeh, as the sealings from Tepti-ahar's reign were found in earlier archaeological contexts than those of Inšušinak-šar-ili.[10] Second, this sequence is confirmed by prosopographic data in purchase contracts from Tappeh Bormi (ancient Huhnur), near modern Ramhormoz, which further suggests the chronological sequence Tepti-ahar–Inšušinak-šar-ili–Šalla.[11] While Šalla is not attested with the title "king of Susa and Anšan" (as mentioned earlier), his name appears in an oath formula attested in a legal text from Susa[12] and in the purchase contracts known as the "Malamir tablets."[13] These are so similar to a formula used for Tepti-ahar[14] that one can assume Šalla also ruled over Elam. This suggests the following provisional sequence of six rulers during the ME I period:

- Igi-hatet
- Kidinu
- Tan-Ruhuratir II
- Tepti-ahar
- Inšušinak-šar-ili
- Šalla

---

9. Daneshmand and Abdoli 2015; Mofidi-Nasrabadi 2018a: 233.

10. Mofidi-Nasrabadi 2017: 140–142.

11. Mofidi-Nasrabadi 2018c.

12. Scheil 1932: no. 327.

13. For a discussion of the provenience of the "Malamir texts," see Mofidi-Nasrabadi 2018c; cf. also section 34.3.

14. Scheil 1930: nos. 52, 71, 72–75, 81, 132, 154, 162 (Šalla); 1930: no. 76 (Tepti-ahar).

The absolute dating of these rulers' reigns is uncertain. The only clue currently available to us is provided by a date formula from the reign of Tepti-ahar, which is attested in texts from Haft Tappeh and mentions "the year when the king expelled Kadašman-DINGIR.KUR.GAL."[15] Since the divine name constituting the final component of this personal name is written with a logographic spelling derived from Mesopotamian writing practices and its realization in an Elamite context is uncertain, there is currently no agreement among scholars concerning the identity of Kadašman-DINGIR.KUR.GAL. Pablo Herrero, the first commentator on this text, assumed that he was the Kassite king Kadašman-Enlil I (1374–1360 BC; cf. chapter 33 in this volume).[16] Later, however, Steven Cole and Leon De Meyer argued that Kadašman-DINGIR.KUR.GAL may have been Kadašman-Harbe I of Babylon (late fifteenth century BC).[17] While this identification was accepted by François Vallat,[18] Jean-Jacques Glassner and Jeremy Goldberg both rejected it categorically.[19]

From an archaeological point of view, Haft Tappeh provides the most important evidence for the ME I phase. The site was first excavated by Ezatollah Negahban from 1965 to 1978, and in 2005 the present author resumed excavations that continue until now. Based on stratigraphy, four Elamite building levels have been identified at Haft Tappeh: the earliest of these (I) dates to the *Sukkalmah* period, while the next three (II–IV) date to the ME I period.[20] The ceramic assemblage changes partly throughout the three building levels of the ME I phase.[21]

Building Level II, which includes monumental complexes from the reigns of Tepti-ahar and Inšušinak-šar-ili, ended when at least one of the

---

15. Herrero 1976: 102.

16. Herrero 1976: 102.

17. Cole and De Meyer 1999.

18. Vallat 2000.

19. Glassner 2000; Goldberg 2004.

20. Mofidi-Nasrabadi 2014b: 102–106; 2016: 97–98.

21. Mofidi-Nasrabadi 2016: 98–104.

buildings was destroyed by fire. Thereafter, attempts were made to rebuild the monumental structures in the northern part of the city, but this work was never completed. Only the lower parts of the buildings' walls were reconstructed (Building Level III). Most probably, these buildings were eventually abandoned. Afterward, new dwellings were built within these monumental ruins (Building Level IV). This occupation was likely terminated by some devastation, an inference based on the discovery of a mass grave with several hundred skeletons, lying in haphazard positions on top of each other, in a street behind the northeastern wall of Building Complex C, which was used as a domestic dwelling in the late ME I period (figure 34.2: top).

The chronology of these ME I building levels is based on radiocarbon dates spanning the period from ca. 1525 to 1395 calBC (table 34.1), although it is possible that all building levels should be dated several decades later.[22] A series of botanical samples from Building Level II, assigned to the reigns of Tepti-ahar and Inšušinak-šar-ili, were radiocarbon-dated to 1525–1435 BC, suggesting that both rulers reigned prior to the Babylonian kings Kadašman-Enlil I and Kadašman-Harbe I. If this is correct, then the Kadašman-DINGIR.KUR.GAL mentioned in the previously quoted date formula from Haft Tappeh was an otherwise unknown individual, a possibility already recognized by Marie-Joseph Steve, Hermann Gasche, and Leon De Meyer.[23] However, it must be remembered that radiocarbon dates offer a range of probability, especially when derived from charcoal samples, which can easily cause discrepancies on the order of 50–100 years vis-à-vis historical dates.[24] If this is taken into account, then the reigns of Tepti-ahar and Inšušinak-šar-ili (Building Level II) may still date to ca. 1450–1350 BC, placing the destruction of the latest building level at Haft Tappeh (IV) in the late fourteenth century BC.

---

22. For the raw data and interpretation of the dates, see Mofidi-Nasrabadi 2015a.

23. Steve et al. 1980: 97 n. 57.

24. Taylor et al. 2010; Zerbst and van der Veen 2015.

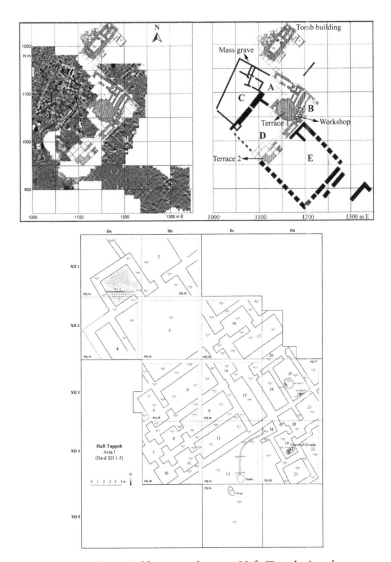

FIGURE 34.2. Top: Building complexes at Haft Tappeh, based on geophysical prospection. Bottom: Administrative building in the southern part of Haft Teppeh. Top: Reproduced from Mofidi-Nasrabadi 2017: fig. 1. Bottom: Reproduced from Mofidi-Nasrabadi 2014b: pl. 2.

Table 34.1. Radiocarbon dating of different building levels
at Haft Tappeh

Building Levels	Radiocarbon Dating
Building Level I (*Sukkalmah* era)	2030–1980 cal BC (2-sigma, 95% probability)
Building Level II (ME I)	1525–1435 cal BC (2-sigma, 95% probability)
Building Level III (ME I)	—
Building Level IV (ME I)	1435–1395 cal BC (2-sigma, 95% probability)

A Mesopotamian composition known as the *Chronicle of the Kassite Kings* mentions Elam's conquest by a King Kurigalzu of Babylon, who is said to have defeated an otherwise unknown Elamite king called Hurbatela.[25] Two other Mesopotamian texts also mention that Kurigalzu conquered Susa and Elam.[26] Two rulers of Babylon bore this name: the rule of the first is thought to have ended in 1375 BC, while the second is conventionally dated to 1332–1308 BC (cf. chapter 33 in this volume). It is currently unclear which Kurigalzu conducted the campaign against Susa and Elam. Either the destruction by fire, marking the end of Building Level II, or the massacre of the city's inhabitants at the end of Building Level IV may be connected to this military campaign. If we assume that the radiocarbon dates deviate by an average of about seventy years from the historical dates, then the end of Building Level IV, when the massacre took place at Haft Tappeh, dates to ca. 1325 BC and therefore to the time of Kurigalzu II of Babylon. According to this scenario, the Elamite ruler Hurbatela named in the *Chronicle of the Kassite Kings* could have been the last king of the ME I phase.

34.2.2. Middle Elamite II (ME II): the Igihalkid dynasty

This phase corresponds to the reigns of a group of rulers descended from Igi-halki (table 34.2). Hence it is also called the Igihalkid period. Igi-halki was previously considered the founder of the dynasty. However, not one

---

25. Glassner 2004: 278–281, no. 45.

26. Stein 2000: no. 9; Radner 2005: 184–186.

878   OXFORD HISTORY OF THE ANCIENT NEAR EAST

Table 34.2.   The Igihalkid rulers in the inscription of Šilhak-Inšušinak
and in the "Berlin Letter" in comparison

Inscription of Šilhak-Inšušinak	"Berlin Letter"
Pahir-iššan son of Igi-halki	Pahir-iššan?
Attar-kittah son of Igi-halki	Humban-numena
Untaš-Napiriša son of	Untaš-Napiriša son of
Humban-numena	Humban-numena
Unpahaš-Napiriša son of Pahir-iššan	Kidin-Hutran son of Untaš-Napiriša
Kidin-Hutran son of Pahir-iššan	Napiriša-untaš son of Kidin-Hutran

text refers to Igi-halki as king, since a brick inscription from Dehno (see
section 34.2.1), once attributed to him, has now been assigned to Igi-hatet
instead.[27] Igi-halki is only attested in an inscription of Šilhak-Inšušinak
(twelfth century BC) as the father of two kings, namely the brothers
Pahir-iššan and Attar-kittah,[28] who rebuilt the temple of Inšušinak at
Susa. Other kings mentioned in the same text who performed the same
service include Untaš-Napiriša son of Humban-numena, Unpahaš-
Napiriša son of Pahir-iššan, and Kidin-Hutran son of Pahir-iššan.[29] As
Pahir-iššan's name appears as the earliest Igihalkid ruler in this text and
in an inscription of Šutruk-Nahhunte (twelfth century BC),[30] it is commonly assumed that he was the eldest son of Igi-halki.

---

27. Despite this new evidence, Michael Roaf (2017: 186) recently assumed Igi-halki
    to be the king who restored the temple of Manzat at Dehno.

28. König 1965: no. 48b.

29. Not all persons mentioned in the inscription of Šilhak-Inšušinak (König
    1965: no. 48) were inevitably king: For example, Lankuku was certainly no
    ruler and is cited only as the father of Kuk-Kirmaš, while Atta-hušu (König's
    Attapakšu) was only a high official. Moreover, the rulers are not all mentioned
    in the historically correct sequence: e.g., Širuktuh and Siwepalarhupak reigned
    some generations after Kuk-Kirmaš, and not before him, while Atta-hušu lived
    some decades before these three rulers, and not after them. For a discussion of
    the chronology of Elam in the second millennium BC, see Mofidi-Nasrabadi
    2009: 3–34.

30. König 1965: 81.

A Neo-Babylonian copy of an original text probably written in the twelfth century BC, known as the "Berlin Letter" because it is kept in the Vorderasiatisches Museum in Berlin, lists the following Elamite rulers who married the daughters of Babylonian kings:

> Pihiranu-DINGIR.U [married] ... of the mighty king Kurigalzu, Humban-immeni [married] his daughter; this one bore [him] Hundaša-Napiriša. Hunda[ša-Napiriša] married the daughter of Burna-Buriaš; this one bore [him] Kidin-[hud]uru[di]š. Kidin-[hudurudiš] marr[ied] the daughter of ... -duniaš; this one bore [him] Nap[iriša-h]und[aš]. I, the [daughter's] son, married the eldest daughter of Meli-Šipak.[31]

As Pihiranu-DINGIR.U is generally believed to be Pahir-iššan,[32] the following sequence of Elamite kings married to Babylonian princesses can be reconstructed: Pahir-iššan–Humban-immeni/Humban-numena–Hundaša-Napiriša/Untaš-Napiriša–Kidin-hudurudiš/Kidin-Hutran–Napiriša-hundaš/Napiriša-untaš. In contrast to the aforementioned inscription of Šilhak-Inšušinak, Kidin-Hutran is not mentioned as the son of Pahir-iššan, but of Untaš-Napiriša. Because of this discrepancy, some scholars have assumed that there were two different Elamite kings called Kidin-Hutran, the first being the son of Pahir-iššan and the other the son of Untaš-Napiriša, who would have reigned several decades after the first Kidin-Hutran.[33] Goldberg supposed that the passage "Pihiranu-DINGIR.U [married] ... of the mighty king Kurigalzu, Humban-immeni [married] his daughter" in the Berlin Letter indicates that Humban-numena, known from his own inscriptions as the son of Attar-kittah, married the daughter of his uncle Pahir-iššan.[34] In this case, the descendants of Humban-numena

---

31. van Dijk 1986.

32. Vallat 1987.

33. Steve and Vallat 1989: 226; Vallat 2006; Potts 2016: 198, Table 7.5; see also chapter 33 in this volume.

34. Goldberg 2004.

were descendants of Attar-kittah through the paternal line and of Pahir-iššan through the maternal line. If this is correct, then Kidin-Hutran son of Untaš-Napiriša son of Humban-numena could be considered also a descendant of Pahir-iššan, as mentioned in the inscription of Šilhak-Inšušinak.

Another problem raised by the Berlin Letter is the fact that the spouses of Humban-numena and Untaš-Napiriša were arguably Elamite, not Babylonian. According to his inscription, Humban-numena restored a temple at Liyan and dedicated it to the god Napiriša and the goddess Kiririša, for his own life and for the lives of Mišimruh and Rishap-La.[35] As such formulae traditionally mention the spouse and other members of the royal family, Mišimruh was probably Humban-numena's wife. In the case of Untaš-Napiriša, his wife Napirasu is well known from the inscription on her life-sized statue from Susa (cf. section 34.5.3).[36] Moreover, Mišimruh and Napirasu are Elamite names, and unless one assumes that the princesses received new names upon marriage into the Elamite royal family, which is certainly possible,[37] then these women are unlikely to have been the Babylonian royal daughters mentioned in the Berlin Letter.

Because of discrepancies between the different available textual sources, the sequence of the ME II rulers and the dates of their reigns cannot be exactly determined. According to the inscriptions currently available, the following five kings ruled in this period:

- Pahir-iššan
- Attar-kittah
- Humban-numena (Berlin Letter: Humban-immeni)
- Untaš-Napiriša (Berlin Letter: Hundaša-Napiriša)
- Kidin-Hutran (Berlin Letter: Kidin-hudurudiš).

---

35. Malbran-Labat 1995: no. 21.

36. König 1965: no. 16.

37. Thus Radner 2020: 68–70.

At the end of the Igihalkid period, synchronisms attested in Mesopotamian textual sources provide further evidence for Elamite chronology, most importantly the invasions of Babylonia by Kidin-Hutran of Elam during the brief reign of Enlil-nadin-šumi of Babylon (1224 BC) and again during the reign of Adad-šuma-iddina of Babylon (1222–1217 BC).[38]

34.2.3. Middle Elamite III (ME III): the Šutrukid dynasty

Textual sources do not allow us to determine the length of Kidin-Hutran's reign or whether he was the final king of the Igihalkid dynasty. That a transition of power from the Igihalkids to a new royal house took place at the beginning of the twelfth century BC seems likely because there is no discernible, direct link between Šutruk-Nahhunte, the ruler next attested, and the Igihalkids. Several hundred bricks with inscriptions of Šutruk-Nahhunte are attested from the sanctuaries that he had built or renovated at different sites.[39] As his father Hallutuš-Inšušinak is not referred to as a king in these texts, Šutruk-Nahhunte is generally considered the founder of a new dynasty, which modern scholars have labeled the Šutrukid dynasty and which represents the third phase of the Middle Elamite period (ME III).

Šutruk-Nahhunte undertook military campaigns against Zababa-šuma-iddina of Babylon (1158 BC) and successfully invaded Babylonia, from which he returned with a large quantity of booty to Elam. This included, e.g., the monumental steles of Naram-Sin of Akkad (see figure 10.5 in volume 1) and Hammurabi of Babylon ("Codex Hammurabi"; see figure 18.4 in volume 2), which were probably placed as votive offerings in the temple of Inšušinak at Susa.[40] Naram-Sin's stele was labeled with Šutruk-Nahhunte's own inscription. In addition to

---

38. Glassner 2004: no. 45: iv 14′–22′.

39. König 1965: nos. 17–19; Steve 1987: 20–26, 29; Malbran-Labat 1995: nos. 33–34.

40. Potts 2016: 226, Table 7.9.

collecting Mesopotamian monuments, Šutruk-Nahhunte also brought valuable objects from various Elamite sites to Susa.[41]

Šutruk-Nahhunte has sometimes been identified with the unnamed author of the Berlin Letter (cf. section 34.2.2), who was married to the daughter of the Babylonian king Meli-Šipak and claimed the crown of Babylon on the basis of his maternal lineage.[42] However, it should be noted that Šilhak-Inšušinak, son of Šutruk-Nahhunte, identified his mother by the name Beyak,[43] and unless she took this as her new name upon marriage it is unlikely that she was this Babylonian princess. Šutruk-Nahhunte's sons could, of course, have had different mothers, as he probably had several wives like many other Late Bronze Age rulers.

Šutruk-Nahhunte was followed by his son Kutir-Nahhunte, who continued to exert military pressure on Babylonia in an attempt to exercise control. Enlil-nadin-ahi of Babylon (1157–1155 BC), who was probably appointed as his client ruler over Babylonia, later revolted against the Elamite sovereignty, albeit unsuccessfully. This prompted Kutir-Nahhunte to invade Babylonia again and abducted the statue of the god Marduk.[44] For unknown reasons, Kutir-Nahhunte was succeeded not by a son, but by his brother Šilhak-Inšušinak, who continued the pattern of Elamite military aggression against Babylonia, as attested in an inscription found near Dezful that mentions the conquest of various places.[45] Compared to his brother and father, Šilhak-Inšušinak undertook much more building activity, particularly the construction of sanctuaries in different Elamite cities, during his reign,[46] suggesting that it was characterized by both stability and prosperity.

---

41. König 1965: nos. 20, 21, 28.

42. Steve and Vallat 1989: 228; Goldberg 2004.

43. König 1965: no. 54, §2.

44. Frame 1995: no. B.2.4.6.

45. Ganjavi 1976: 35–36.

46. König 1965: nos. 32–59; Malbran-Labat 1995: nos. 38–50.

Šilhak-Inšušinak was succeeded by Hutelutuš-Inšušinak, who called himself "prince of Elam and Susa" rather than "king of Susa and Anšan."[47] In his inscriptions, Hutelutuš-Inšušinak mentions both Kutir-Nahhunte and Šilhak-Inšušinak as his fathers, and in some cases, he called himself the son of Šutruk-Nahhunte, Kutir-Nahhunte, and Šilhak-Inšušinak (see section 34.4.2). Hutelutuš-Inšušinak is attested in texts from both Susa and Anšan (modern Tell-e Malyan), where he had a temple built.[48] The invasion of Elam by Nebuchadnezzar I of Babylon, a ruler of the Second Dynasty of Isin (1125–1104 BC), resulted in the defeat of Hutelutuš-Inšušinak and the recovery of the statue of Marduk of Babylon from Susa,[49] leaving Elam in turmoil. This marked the end of the Šutrukid dynasty and, with it, the Middle Elamite period. However, the possibility that this was likely not an entirely clear-cut process is suggested by a Neo-Elamite inscription of the early first millennium BC, according to which Hutelutuš-Inšušinak was succeeded as ruler of Elam by his younger brother Šilhina-hamru-Lagamar.[50] He is not attested in contemporary sources, however, and the absence of any written sources for several centuries is indicative of Elam's decline at this time.

We close with the sequence of the rulers of the Šutrukid dynasty:

- Šutruk-Nahhunte
- Kutir-Nahhunte
- Šilhak-Inšušinak
- Hutelutuš-Inšušinak
- Šilhina-hamru-Lagamar.

---

47. König 1965: nos. 60–63; Malbran-Labat 1995: nos. 51–53.

48. Lambert 1972: 66.

49. Foster 1993: 298.

50. König 1965: no. 72; cf. Vallat 1996: 79.

34.3. *The textual sources*

As was the case during the *Sukkalmah* period, ME I Elam witnessed the use of Mesopotamian cuneiform writing and the Akkadian language. The brick inscription of Igi-hatet from Dehno, commemorating the construction of a temple for the goddess Manzat (see section 34.2.1), can be considered the first royally commissioned text of this period (table 34.3). Brick inscriptions from Susa of the subsequent rulers, Tepti-ahar and Inšušinak-šar-ili, refer to the reconstruction of the temple of Inšušinak.[51] As both rulers were also very active at nearby Haft Tappeh (probably ancient Kabnak), it is remarkable that no inscribed bricks of theirs have been recovered there. This renders Erica Reiner's assumption that the inscribed bricks of Tepti-ahar from Susa may actually have been brought from Haft Tappeh highly unlikely.[52] Florence Malbran-Labat's publication of all of Tepti-ahar's inscribed bricks has now demonstrated beyond doubt that Susa was indeed their original findspot.[53]

But while excavations at Haft Tappeh did not yield any inscribed bricks from this period, they revealed rich archives of clay tablets inscribed in Akkadian cuneiform. Near a workshop, a large archive of several hundred tablets was found. Most of these are administrative texts documenting deliveries of gold, silver, bronze, and other objects, and sometimes mentioning the recipients of these items.[54] School texts, omens, and letters have been recovered as well.[55] Recent excavations have brought to light more than 600 tablets and tablet fragments. Most of these were found in an administrative building used for managing and storing valuable commodities in the southern part of the site.[56]

---

51. Malbran-Labat 1995: nos. 19–20.

52. Reiner 1973a: 95.

53. Malbran-Labat 1995: 244, no. 20. Cf. Potts 2016: 185.

54. Mofidi-Nasrabadi 2016: 72–77.

55. Herrero 1976; Negahban 1991: 103–106; Herrero and Glassner 1990; 1991; 1993; 1996; Daneshmand 2004; Prechel 2010.

56. Mofidi-Nasrabadi 2010b: 19–23; 2012a: 56–58; 2012b; 2014b: 69–72.

Table 34.3. Textual evidence from the ME I phase

Reign	Textual Sources
Igi-hatet	• Akkadian brick inscription (originally from Dehno) about the restoration of the temple for the goddess Manzat (Daneshmand and Abdoli 2015)
Kidinu	• Seal inscription from Susa on the tablet TS.XII.13 in Akkadian: "Kidinu, king of Susa and Anšan, Son of Adad-šarru-rabu (^{d}IM.SAR.GAL), servant of his god Kirwašir" (Amiet 1980: 139; Steve, Gasche, and De Meyer 1980: 92–93)
Tan-Ruhuratir II	• Seal inscription from Collection Koenitzer in Akkadian: "To give health, to create life, to protect . . . , protect the weak, to save the life, to hear prayers (all) is in your power. . . . -ili, . . . of Tan-ruhuratir, the king of Susa and Anšan" (Porada 1971: 32; Amiet 1973: pl. XIII, Z; Steve, Gasche, and De Meyer 1980: 83, 95–96; Mofidi-Nasrabadi 2009: 50)
Tepti-ahar	• Akkadian brick inscription from Susa (Malbran-Labat 1995: no. 20): Description relating the building of a temple for Inšušinak by Tepti-ahar • Administrative texts from Haft Tappeh in Akkadian, mentioning Tepti-ahar (Herrero and Glassner 1990: no. 17; 1991: no. 153?; 1993: nos. 203 and 206) • Two stele fragments from Haft Tappeh with Akkadian inscription (Reiner 1973a: 89; Negahban 1991: 123–124): listing the sacrifices for different festivities, among them a sheep sacrificed before the chariot of the king Tepti-ahar

(continued)

Table 34.3. Continued

Reign	Textual Sources
	• Seal inscription of Tepti-ahar from Haft Tappeh in Akkadian (Herrero 1976: nos. 7 and 9; Herrero and Glassner 1990: nos. 12, 18; 1991: nos. 71, 87, 88, 95, 97; Mofidi-Nasrabadi 2011a: no. 11): "Tepti-ahar, king of Susa and Anšan, servant of the gods Kirwašir and Inšušinak. So long as he is alive, may they heartily recognize him."
	• Seal inscription of Athibu from Haft Tappeh in Akkadian (Herrero 1976: no. 6; Herrero and Glassner 1993: no. 134; Mofidi-Nasrabadi 2011a: no. 13): "Athibu, the great governor of Kabnak, administrator and confidante of Tepti-ahar, the king of Susa, servant of the god Adad."
	• Legal texts ("Malamir tablets") from Tappeh Bormi in Akkadian, citing Tepti-ahar in oath formula (Scheil 1902: no. 15 = 1930: no. 76)
	• Legal text from Susa in Akkadian, mentioning Tepti-ahar in an oath formula (Scheil 1932: no. 248)
Inšušinak-šar-ili	• Akkadian brick inscription from Susa (Malbran-Labat 1995: no. 19), describing the reconstruction of the temple of Inšušinak by Inšušinak-šar-ili.
	• Seal inscriptions from Haft Tappeh in Akkadian (Herrero and Glassner 1990: no. 2; Mofidi-Nasrabadi 2011a: nos. 7 and 196; 2011b; 2017: nos. 14, 21, 22, 23?, 24)
	• Legal texts from Tappeh Bormi in Akkadian, citing Inšušinak-šar-ili in oath formula (Mofidi-Nasrabadi 2018c)
Šalla	• Legal texts ("Malamir tablets") from Tappeh Bormi in Akkadian, mentioning Šalla in oath formula (Scheil 1902: 169–194 = 1930: nos. 52, 71, 72–75, 81, 132, 154, 162)
	• Legal text from Susa in Akkadian, mentioning Šalla in oath formula (Scheil 1932: no. 327)

Moreover, excavations at Haft Tappeh in the 1970s uncovered three fragmentary stone inscriptions in the courtyard of a tomb building (Fragments 1–2) and in the courtyard in front of the aforementioned workshop (Fragment 3).[57] Despite their different findspots, both their content and script suggest that Fragments 1 and 3 are parts of the same stele.[58] The notion that this stele originally belonged to Tepti-ahar's tomb is, however, unfounded.[59] Rather, it must have been placed close to Terrace 1, where Fragment 3 was found. The stele inscription, which is damaged, documents stipulations concerning the maintenance of the temple in question and food offerings for various rituals and festivities in honor of several different deities. Specifically, the fragmentary text mentions deliveries of flour, beer, and sheep to six guards for sacrifices during festivals in the months Abu (V) and Tašritu (VII); offerings for the god Kirwašir, (probably) for the god Padi, before the chariot of the god Inšušinak and before the chariot of King Tepti-ahar; regular sacrifices for the deceased (see also section 34.5.2); sacrifices for further rituals involving a priestess and the *ippu* priest of Susa; and the duties of six guards and twelve women concerned with the maintenance of the temple. The ceremonies involving chariots must have taken place while Tepti-ahar was still alive, as the text refers to him as king. The use of chariots as well as the numbers of people involved suggests that the ritual activities either took place in a very large building complex or outdoors.

While these texts provide insights into the central administration and religious life of the temple, they shed very little light on the daily life of ordinary people. Moreover, archives from private houses and private legal texts are rare in the ME I phase. Other than a purchase contract from Susa dating to the reign of Tepti-ahar,[60] the only private texts are a group of legal texts known as the "Malamir Tablets," the provenance of

57. Negahban 1991: 102–103, 123–125, pl. 52.

58. Herrero and Glassner 1990: 3; Erica Reiner in Negahban 1991: 125.

59. *Contra* Carter and Stolper 1984: 158; Negahban 1991: 7–9, 12–15; Harper et al. 1992: 9.

60. Scheil 1932: no. 248.

which was long unclear. They were named thus as they were purchased in Paris at the beginning of the twentieth century AD from a man from the Iranian city of Izeh (also known as Malamir), but it was soon recognized that Malamir was not their place of origin, which must instead be sought somewhere in Susiana.[61] A connection with the city of Huhnur (modern Tappeh Bormi, near Ramhormoz) was thought possible, both because the texts mention Ruhuratir, the main deity of Huhnur, and because of their prosopography.[62] The discovery in 2014 of some cuneiform tablets at Tappeh Bormi reignited the discussion of the Malamir Tablets,[63] as the Tappeh Bormi texts are legal documents from the reign of Inšušinak-šarili incorporating oaths sworn by the gods Inšušinak and Ruhuratir and share compositional and grammatical features with the Malamir Tablets. These facts support the hypothesis that the Malamir Tablets came from Tappeh Bormi (ancient Huhnur).[64]

During the ME II phase, Elamite rulers increasingly began to use the Elamite language for their royal inscriptions. Humban-numena was the first to commission inscriptions in Elamite in addition to Akkadian, seemingly in contrast to his father Attar-kittah, whose sole extant inscription was written in Akkadian (table 34.4). During the reign of Humban-numena's son and successor Untaš-Napiriša, most royal inscriptions were composed in Elamite. These commemorate the construction of various temples and have been discovered at several sites. Most importantly, Untaš-Napiriša's new foundation, Al-Untaš-Napiriša (modern Chogha Zanbil, about 45 km southeast of Susa), has produced many different inscribed bricks concerning the monumental stepped temple tower (*ziqqurat*) and various sanctuaries situated in the sacred precinct (*siankuk*) of the city. Curiously, examples of nearly all of these bricks have also been discovered at Susa.[65] Walther Hinz and Heidemarie Koch assumed

---

61. Cf. Reiner 1963: 170; Steve et al. 1980: 96–97; Stolper 1990: 279–280.

62. Hinz 1963: 19; Glassner 1991: 115–118.

63. Mofidi-Nasrabadi 2005.

64. Mofidi-Nasrabadi 2018c.

65. Scheil 1901.

Table 34.4. Textual sources from the ME II phase

Ruler/Queen	Textual Sources
Attar-kittah	• Two property inscriptions on mace heads from Chogha Zanbil in Akkadian (Steve 1967: 112–113, VI)
Humban-numena	• Votive inscription in Akkadian dedicated to Išmeqarab from Susa (Steve 1987: 13)
	• Votive inscription in Akkadian dedicated to Ishtar, unknown provenance (Steve 1987: 14)
	• Brick inscription in Elamite from Liyan, near modern Bushehr (Vallat 1984)
	• Brick inscription in Elamite from Susa about the reconstruction of a temple for Napiriša and Kiririša at Liyan (Pézard 1914: 42–65; Malbran-Labat 1995: no. 21)
Untaš-Napiriša	• Brick inscriptions in Elamite and Akkadian from Chogha Zanbil and Susa about the construction of temples and sacral structures for different divinities (Steve 1967; Malbran-Labat 1995: nos. 22–32; Basello 2013; Badamchi 2015)
	• Brick inscriptions from the "acropolis" of Susa (Steve, Gasche, and De Meyer 1980: 85; Steve and Gasche 1971: 197–198)
	• Brick inscription in Elamite from Gotvand about construction of a temple for Upurkupak (Steve 1987: 15–17).
	• Brick inscriptions in Elamite from Chogha Pahan East (Stolper and Wright 1990)
	• Brick inscriptions in Elamite, unknown provenance (Steve 1987: 17–18)
	• Elamite inscription on a stele from Susa (Vallet 1981)
	• Elamite inscription on a statue from Susa (Vallat 1988)
	• Akkadian inscription on a statue originally from *siankuk* at Chogha Zanbil (Scheil 1908: 85–86)
Napirasu	• Elamite inscription on a bronze statue from Susa, which mentions her as the wife of the king Untaš-Napiriša (König 1965: 69–71, no. 16)

that the bricks from Susa were originally brought there from Chogha Zanbil.[66] Alternatively, it is possible that prototype bricks were originally written at Susa, as models for the production of bricks at Chogha Zanbil, and that some of these models remained at Susa. This is indeed likely, as such a practice is also attested in the case of the inscribed bricks relating to the reconstruction of a temple for the god Napiriša and the goddess Kiririša at Liyan, near modern Bushehr, under King Humban-numena, Untaš-Napiriša's father, examples of which bricks have also been found at Susa.[67] It is therefore likely that the building activities of the Igihalkid rulers throughout their realm were organized at the capital Susa, where the inscriptions composed for these buildings were created in close consultation with the king.

While various royal inscriptions dating to ME II are known, no other text genres are currently attested. Perhaps the switch to the Elamite language went hand in hand with changes in the materiality of writing, and organic and hence perishable writing materials were preferred to clay tablets? Similarly, only royal inscriptions are attested in ME III (Šutrukid Dynasty), nearly all of which were composed in the Elamite language. Most describe the construction of temples or the fashioning of cult objects (table 34.5). As noted earlier, Šutruk-Nahhunte was an avid collector of monuments, especially statues (cf. section 34.2.3). Artifacts from conquered Mesopotamian cities as well as from various Elamite centers, including Anšan (modern Tell-e Malyan), Al-Untaš-Napiriša (modern Chogha Zanbil), and Tikni (location unknown), were brought to Susa, where Šutruk-Nahhunte had his own inscriptions added to many of them.

34.4. Power structures

The Middle Elamite period can be seen as an era of increasing power, as the Elamite kingdom was not only able to establish supremacy over

---

66. Hinz and Koch 1987: 1329: UntN; Mofidi-Nasrabadi 2013b: 62–66.

67. Malbran-Labat 1995: no. 21.

Table 34.5. Textual sources from the ME III phase

Ruler	Textual Evidence
Šutruk-Nahhunte I	• Elamite inscription on a stele (Scheil 1904: 8–9; König 1965: no. 20) • Elamite inscription on a statue (Pézard and Pottier 1926: 191–192; Harper et al. 1992: no. 111) • Elamite inscription on a statue (Scheil 1905: 12–13) • Elamite inscriptions on stone vessels from Susa (König 1965: nos. 26–27) • Elamite inscription on a stone tablet from Susa (König 1965: no. 28) • Elamite inscription on a stele of Untaš-Napiriša (Scheil 1901: 43; König 1965: no. 21) • Three inscriptions in Elamite on three statues of Maništušu of Akkad (König 1965: no. 24) • Elamite inscription on the stele of Naram-Sin of Akkad (Scheil 1901: 40–42; König 1965: no. 22) • Elamite inscription on a stele of Meli-Šipak of Babylon (Scheil 1902: 163–165; König 1965: no. 23) • Brick inscriptions in Elamite from Susa about the reconstruction of temples (Scheil 1901: 44–46; König 1965: nos. 17–18; Malbran-Labat 1995: 79–83) • Brick inscriptions in Elamite from the "acropolis" of Susa (Steve, Gasche, and De Meyer 1980: 85, 120; Steve and Gasche 1971: 197–198) • Brick inscriptions in Elamite from Dehno about the reconstruction of the temple of Manzat and NIN.DAR.A (Steve 1987: 20–29; Mofidi-Nasrabadi 2013a: 97) • Brick inscription in Elamite from Liyan (near modern Bushehr) about the reconstruction of the temple for Kiririša (Pézard 1914: 66–72; König 1965: no. 19) • Brick inscription in Elamite, unknown provenance (Steve 1987: 19–20)

(continued)

Table 34.5. Continued

Ruler	Textual Evidence
Kutir-Nahhunte	• Brick inscriptions in Elamite from Susa about the reconstruction of temples (Scheil 1901: 47–49; König 1965: nos. 29–30; Steve 1987: 38–40; Malbran-Labat 1995: 83–87) • Brick inscriptions in Elamite from the "acropolis" of Susa (Steve, Gasche, and De Meyer 1980: 85, 120) • Brick inscription in Elamite from Susa about the reconstruction of a sacral structure for Lagamal (Steve 1987: 30) • Brick inscription in Elamite from Liyan (near modern Bushehr) about the reconstruction of the temple for Kiririša (Pézard 1914: 73–75; König 1965: no. 31) • Brick inscription in Elamite from Dehno about the reconstruction of the temple for Manzat and NIN.DAR.A (Steve 1987: 31)
Šilhak-Inšušinak	• Brick inscriptions in Elamite from Susa about the reconstruction of temples (König 1965: nos. 32–43; Steve 1987: 32–34; Malbran-Labat 1995: 88–117) • Brick inscriptions in Elamite from the "acropolis" of Susa (Steve, Gasche, and De Meyer 1980: 85, 120) • Brick inscription in Akkadian and Elamite from Susa about the reconstruction of a sacral structure for Inšušinak (Steve 1987: 35–37) • Elamite inscription on glazed wall plaques (König 1965: no. 44) • Elamite inscription on brick façade from Susa about the construction of a sacral structure for Inšušinak (Malbran Labat 1995: 103–106) • Elamite inscription on a stele from Susa about the restoration of different temples in twenty different cities (König 1965: nos. 47–48)

Table 34.5. Continued

Ruler	Textual Evidence
	• Elamite inscriptions on different stelae from Susa (König 1965: nos. 46, 49–55)
	• Elamite inscription on a bronze beam from Susa (König 1965: no. 45)
	• Elamite inscription on a bronze model from Susa concerning the sunrise ritual (*ṣit šamši*; König 1965: no. 56)
	• Elamite inscription on a stone bead about a dedication to Šilhak-Inšušinak's daughter, Bar-uli (Sollberger 1965)
	• Elamite inscription on stone door sockets from Susa (König 1965: no. 48a–b)
	• Brick inscriptions in Elamite from Liyan (near modern Bushehr) about the reconstruction of the temple for Napiriša and Kiririša (Pézard 1914: 76–87; König 1965: nos. 57–59)
	• Brick inscription in Elamite from Tol-e Sepid invoking Kilahšupir (König 1965: no. 41A)
	• Brick inscription in Elamite from Chogha Pahan West about the reconstruction of a sacral structure (Stolper 1978: 89–91; Steve 1987: 32)
Hutelutuš-Inšušinak	• Brick inscriptions in Elamite from Susa about the reconstruction of temples (König 1965: nos. 60–64; Steve 1987: 41–45; Malbran-Labat 1995: 117–122)
	• Brick inscription in Elamite from the "acropolis" of Susa (Steve, Gasche, and De Meyer 1980: 120)
	• Brick inscription in Elamite from Tall-e Malyan about the construction of temples (Reiner 1973b; Lamber 1972: 65–66; Steve 1987: 46–47)
	• Elamite inscription on stone door socket from Susa (König 1965: no. 65)

different regions in Iran, but also to conquer and at times control Mesopotamian territories. This was undoubtedly related to improved economic circumstances which provided Elam with prosperity and surplus resources. This section analyzes the power structures that held the realm together. We will discuss the king; the royal family; the centralized administration; and the temples and cults.

34.4.1. The king

The Middle Elamite period is clearly characterized by the concentration of power in the person of the king. As discussed earlier, the ME rulers adopted a new royal titulary and referred to themselves as "king of Susa and Anšan" instead of using the traditional title of *sukkalmah* (see section 34.1). This change in titulary reflects changes in the structure of power. At the head of the Elamite state of the *Sukkalmah* period stood a triumvirate consisting of the *sukkalmah* as the supreme ruler of the realm, the *sukkal* (regent) of Susiana, and the *sukkal* (regent) of Susa. In the ME period this tripartite power structure was replaced by a unitary one, in which supreme power was vested in a single person, the king.[68] Whereas oath formulae in legal documents of the *Sukkalmah* period typically invoke two or all three of these political authorities, oaths in the ME period invoked the king's name only, as attested by documents from the reigns of the ME I rulers Tepti-ahar, Inšušinak-šar-ili, and Šalla (see section 34.2.1).

In addition to wielding secular power, Elamite kings also fulfilled certain religious functions. The clearest indication for this appears in the inscription on the fragmentary ME I stone stele from Haft Tappeh (discussed in section 34.3), which describes Tepti-ahar's participation in religious festivities, during which sacrificial sheep were offered before his chariot and before the chariot of the god Inšušinak. The king was personally involved in the state administration and directly controlled the realm's economic transactions. He even kept records of these, as one

---

68. Mofidi-Nasrabadi 2009: 22–37.

text, sealed by Athibu, the governor of Kabnak, explicitly states.[69] This indicates that while Athibu held administrative responsibility for the transaction, it was the king who oversaw and recorded it.

The monumental building activities of Tepti-ahar and Inšušinak-šar-ili (ME I) at Haft Tappeh imply a strong economy capable of supporting a large number of workers. The same is true of Untaš-Napiriša's construction of his new foundation Al-Untaš-Napiriša ("City of Untaš-Napiriša," modern Chogha Zanbil) in ME II. Such massive construction projects give us some idea of the surplus financial resources available to the state, even if the economic situation during the ME period is otherwise obscure. These projects consolidated royal power across the Elamite kingdom and encouraged ME rulers to seek to expand the territories under their control. Kidin-Hutran's conquest at the end of ME II established a pattern of Elamite interest in and periodic control over Babylonia that continued to grow under the Šutrukid dynasty (ME III).

34.4.2. The royal family

Several royal inscriptions emphasize the importance of strong family ties and express the king's great affection for his family members. Thus, the ME I king Tepti-ahar had statues made of himself and his "beloved wife" to be placed in the temple of Inšušinak at Susa.[70] This seems to have been a relatively common royal practice. A bronze statue of Napirasu, wife of the ME II king Untaš-Napiriša, was placed in the temple of the goddess Ninhursag at Susa, while this ruler had himself depicted on a stele, standing before the enthroned god Inšušinak, along with Napirasu and another woman named Utik.[71] The ME III king Šilhak-Inšušinak was pictured on the molded brick façade of the Inšušinak temple at Susa together with a female, most likely his wife Nahhunte-utu.[72] This ME practice stands in the tradition of the

---

69. Beckman 1991.

70. Malbran-Labat 1995: no. 20.

71. Harper et al. 1992: 80, fig. 42.

72. Harper et al. 1992: 11, fig. 13.

eastern Elamite regions,[73] where such depictions of the ruler alongside his queen have long been attested, e.g., in the case of Ebarat, the first documented king of Šimaški, at the beginning of the second millennium BC.[74]

The important social and political role of the Elamite queen is particularly apparent in the ME II and III phases. Queen Nahhunte-utu was one of the most important individuals in the royal court during the Šutrukid era (ME III). She was first married to Kutir-Nahhunte and, after his death, to his brother Šilhak-Inšušinak, serving as the queen throughout the reigns of both rulers.[75] Several royal inscriptions refer to the dedication of various temples for the life of Nahhunte-utu and her offspring.[76] She gave birth to at least nine children, who are listed in the inscriptions of her second husband Šilhak-Inšušinak, either in order of their age or according to their gender, which allows us to reconstruct the sequence in table 34.6.

All of Nahhunte-utu's children enjoyed the status of prince or princess. The first six children seem to have been fathered by her first husband Kutir-Nahhunte and were later adopted by her second husband Šilhak-Inšušinak. The last three children listed, Temti-turkataš, Lili-irtaš, and Bar-uli, must have been the offspring of Šilhak-Inšušinak himself because an inscription mentioning the first of these, Temti-turkataš, explicitly states that Šilhak-Inšušinak and Nahhunte-utu had produced a descendant.[77]

The eldest son of Nahhunte-utu is the later king Hutelutuš-Inšušinak, who called himself the son of Kutir-Nahhunte as well as the son of Šilhak-Inšušinak. An inscription that calls him "beloved son of

---

73. Mofidi-Nasrabadi 2009: 80–81.

74. Lambert 1979: no. 42; 1992; Steve 1989: 14–18.

75. It has been suggested that Nahhunte-utu was the sister of both rulers, and some early scholars even assumed that Nahhunte-utu may also have had a sexual relationship with her father Šutruk-Nahhunte, and later with her son Hutelutuš-Inšušinak. However, such assumptions are not directly supported by the available sources; for references and a critical assessment, see Stolper 2001b; Potts 2018.

76. König 1965: nos. 31, 34–36, 38, 40, 41, 44–47, 52, 54, 58, 59, 65; 1971: 226.

77. König 1965: no. 40.

Table 34.6. The children of Nahhunte-utu classified according to their gender and order of birth

Sons of Nahhunte-utu:	Daughters of Nahhunte-utu:
Hutelutuš-Inšušinak	
	Išniqarab-huhun (Išmeqarab-huhun)
	Urutuk-Elhalahu
Šilhina-hamru-Lagamar	
Kutir-Huban	
	Utu-ehihhi-Pinigir
Temti-turkataš	
Lili-irtaš	
	Bar-uli

Šutruk-Nahhunte, Kutir-Nahhunte and Šilhak-Inšušinak, beloved brother of Išniqarab-huhun" describes his restoration of the temple of Inšušinak in gratitude for his life and for the lives of his brothers and sisters.[78] Another inscription mentions Hutelutuš-Inšušinak as the "beloved brother of Melir-Nahhunte."[79] Since she is not listed anywhere as one of Nahhunte-utu's children, Melir-Nahhunte may have been the daughter of a concubine and thus only a half-sister of Hutelutuš-Inšušinak's. This finds some support in the fact that, on an inscribed brick from Anšan (modern Tell-e Malyan),[80] Hutelutuš-Inšušinak listed her after his other eight brothers and sisters, possibly indicating her lower social status. According to the same inscribed brick from Tell-e Malyan, Hutelutuš-Inšušinak had at least two children, a daughter named Utuk-Hutekasan and a son named Temti-pitet.

---

78. Malbran-Labat 1995: no. 52.

79. König 1965: no. 63.

80. Lambert 1972: 65; Reiner 1973b: 59.

Hutelutuš-Inšušinak was in power when Nebuchadnezzar I of Babylon invaded Elam and was probably the last ruler of his dynasty, although a later source names Šilhina-hamru-Lagamar as his successor (as discussed in section 34.2.3).

34.4.3. A centralized administration

A study of the cylinder seals and sealings from Haft Tappeh shows that the ME I king Tepti-ahar's seal was used more often than that of any other individual,[81] indicating his direct involvement in a range of transactions as head of the centralized administration.

The king seems to have directly supervised transactions involving precious materials. In one text, gold and lapis lazuli objects were delivered under the supervision of the king,[82] while another, sealed by Tepti-ahar, documents a delivery of silver to the goldsmith Tab-adaru for the production of bracelets.[83] Moreover, a centrally controlled system of record-keeping of the state's economic activities is suggested by a text explicitly mentioning that Tepti-ahar had such transactions recorded (see also section 34.4.1):

> 46 oxen of Išepiltirra, 30 oxen of Tašritu—total: 76 oxen, administrative responsibility of Atta-Napir, which the king investigates and adds to the royal cumulative record [literally, "big tablet of the king"].[84]

Although the administrator in charge of the specific transaction was Atta-Napir, the tablet was sealed and the process authorized by Athibu, governor of Kabnak, while Tepti-ahar oversaw this and apparently other transactions like it, having them registered in centrally compiled records.

---

81. Mofidi-Nasrabadi 2011a: 27–28, 287–288.

82. Herrero and Glassner 1990: no. 14.

83. Herrero and Glassner 1990: no. 18.

84. Beckman 1991.

Thus, this transaction involved three separate levels of the administrative hierarchy. In another case, Tepti-ahar himself authorized the activities of an administrator called Šamaš-iriba by sealing the document.[85]

In some cases, however, transactions were overseen by Athibu without the explicit involvement of the king. For example, the governor sealed a document recording deliveries of silver and gold to Dadar and silver to Tašritu by an official called Tamišak,[86] who is also attested in connection with the delivery of precious materials in other texts.[87] While Tamišak, the previously mentioned Atta-Napir, and various other officials seem to have had a key role in distributing commodities,[88] such transactions were overseen either by the king or his governor. No governor is attested in the texts from Haft Tappeh during the reign of Tepti-ahar's successor Inšušinak-šar-ili, presumably due to the chances of preservation and recovery, but Adad-ereš, identified as an "official supervisor" (UGULA.KUŠ$_7$.MEŠ), appears in connection with the delivery of precious commodities.[89]

"Archivists" (Elamite *puhu-teppu*), who were responsible for the registration of the transfer and storage of valuable goods, played a key role in the centralized administration. The rich burial of Ginadu, *puhu-teppu* to Inšušinak-šar-ili, was recently identified close to an administrative building in the southern part of Haft Tappeh (figure 34.2: bottom)[90] that contained two of his cylinder seals (figure 34.3: E–F),[91] In the northern part of this building, a scribal workroom or *scriptorium* (no. 1), paved with mud brick, was identified. A small channel carried the water used for making clay tablets out of the room. In the southern part of the building were three long, parallel storage rooms (nos. 6, 9, 12) that were difficult

---

85. Herrero and Glassner 1991: no. 71.

86. Herrero and Glassner 1990: no. 6.

87. Mofidi-Nasrabadi 2016: 46.

88. Mofidi-Nasrabadi 2016: 67–68.

89. Mofidi-Nasrabadi 2016: 66.

90. Mofidi-Nasrabadi 2010b: 19–23; 2012b; 2016: 2; 2017: 130–133.

91. Mofidi-Nasrabadi 2011b.

FIGURE 34.3. A: Clay heads from Haft Tappeh; B: clay mask from Haft Tappeh; C: nude female terracotta figurine from Haft Tappeh; D: terracotta bed model from Haft Tappeh; E: cylinder seal of Ginadu, made from lapis lazuli with golden caps; F: cylinder seal of Ginadu. Prepared by the author.

to access because of a series of anterooms (nos. 4, 7, 10 and nos. 5, 8, 11). Several hundred clay tablets were discovered mainly in the *scriptorium* (no. 1) as well as in Rooms 5 and 12. According to some of these texts,[92] military equipment such as arrows, quivers, harnesses, and other horse tack were stored in this building. The archivist Ginadu may well have been in charge of this facility.

92. Prechel 2010.

Excavations at Tell-e Malyan (ancient Anšan) brought to light parts of another administrative building dating to the late second millennium BC [93] which yielded cuneiform tablets documenting transactions involving various metals and manufactured products.[94] Although the structure was not completely excavated, it features a central, rectangular courtyard surrounded by several rooms which may have been for storage, as in the administrative building at Haft Tappeh.[95] In any case, as the cuneiform archives confirm, both the Haft Tappeh and Tell-e Malyan buildings are examples of administrative structures used in the centralized management of valuable commodities in Elam.

As noted in the following section (34.4.4), some of the temples at Haft Tappeh and Chogha Zanbil had associated workshops. These sanctuaries were likely part of the same centralized system of resource management. The inscription on the Haft Tappeh stele (see section 34.3) lists the offerings required for various religious ceremonies and the duties of certain temple attendants, pointing to the existence of a well-organized administrative system for the running of the temples and the cults, and the evidence strongly suggests that, ultimately, the king would have been in charge.

34.4.4. Deities, temples, and cult

Most ME royal inscriptions on brick or stone commemorate the numerous temple-building projects that took place during this period in different locales and emphasize the piety of the ME kings and their respect for the gods. Often, large numbers of deities are attested in these sources. Some divine names are written with logograms commonly used in the Mesopotamian scribal tradition, including those for the storm-god Adad and the moon-god Sin. It is impossible to decide with certainty whether these Mesopotamian deities were actually worshipped in Elam or whether these logograms stood for the names of conceptually similar Elamite

---

93. Carter 1996.

94. Stolper 1984.

95. Mofidi-Nasrabadi 2018b: 515–517.

gods. In the case of the sun-god, whose name is usually written with the logogram [(d)]UTU, this spelling definitely stands for Nahhunte (and not Šamaš, the Mesopotamian deity), as this god is attested as an element of the name Kutir-Nahhunte (I) in both syllabic and logographic spellings.[96]

The god Inšušinak (a name of Sumerian origin meaning "Lord of Susa") was the principal god of the capital city of Susa and the main deity worshipped in Elam. For reasons that are obscure, several ME I kings seem to have held the god Kirwašir in special regard, in addition to Inšušinak. Thus, Kidinu identified himself in his seal inscription as the servant of the god Kirwašir,[97] while Tepti-ahar's seal inscription called him the servant of the gods Kirwašir and Inšušinak.[98] According to the Haft Tappeh stele inscription, both of these deities received offerings during the reign of Tepti-ahar (see section 34.3).[99]

However, while royal inscriptions clearly allow us to discern which deities were favored by the ME kings, this does not mean that the same gods were those most popular in Elamite society at large. Indeed, an analysis of theophoric personal names demonstrates that the most commonly attested deities were not necessarily the recipients of royal patronage, and this is confirmed by a study of the gods invoked as personal protectors in ME I seal inscriptions.[100] Despite the indications of royal favor mentioned earlier, neither god seems to have played a major role in the personal worship of the wider population at Haft Tappeh. The private seal inscriptions found there mention the sun-god Nahhunte, the god Šimut,[101] and the

96. Syllabic spellings of the divine element: Scheil 1905: pl. 7 ([d]Na-ah-hu-un-di); 1930: no. 157 (Na-hu-un-di); 1932: no. 201 ([d]Na-hu-un-di), no. 202 ([d]Na-ah-un-di); 1933: no. 347 (Na-hu-ti), no. 368 (Na-ah-hu-di), no. 376 ([d]Na-ah-hu-un-di), no. 382bis (Na-hu-di), no. 392 (Na-ah-hu-di); 1939: no. 7 (Na-ah-hu-un-di). Logographic spellings: Scheil 1932: no. 203; 1933: nos. 375 and 377. For the god Nahhunte, see Stolper 2001a.

97. Amiet 1980: 139, no. 11.

98. Herrero 1976: no. 7.

99. Reiner 1973a: ll. 25–26, 29.

100. Mofidi-Nasrabadi 2011a: 302–303, Table 17.

101. Henkelman 2011.

storm-god Adad (who possibly had another Elamite designation), but never Kirwašir and Inšušinak.[102] Šimut, Adad, and Nahhunte are also the most commonly attested gods in theophoric personal names at Haft Tappeh, where Šimut features in twenty-two names; Adad in thirteen names; and Nahhunte in eight names. In addition, Inšušinak, Šubur, and Enlil each appear in five names; Ruhuratir and Sin, in four names; Humban and Napiriša, in three names; Manzat, Amurru, Išmeqarab, and Šubula, in two names; and Ea, Išhara, Ištar, Ištaran, Kirmeš, Kirmešir (= Kirwašir), Lagamal, Ninšubur, and Tan-azinua, in one name.[103] It seems, therefore, that the deities in whose honor large-scale festivities took place in the city, according to the testimony of the Haft Tappeh stele, enjoyed only limited popularity in the population at large. While Susa's supreme deity Inšušinak is attested a handful of times in personal names at Haft Tappeh, the god Kirwašir/Kirmešir only appears in a single name, whereas Padi, the third deity mentioned in the Haft Tappeh stele, does not appear as a theophoric element in personal names there at all.

Moreover, considerable regional variation can be observed across Elam in theophoric personal names. Inšušinak, the main deity of the capital Susa, appears relatively often in names there, but much less frequently at nearby Haft Tappeh and hardly at all at Huhnur (modern Tappeh Bormi in Khuzestan), where Nahhunte and Humban were seemingly preferred— although the limited numbers of texts and names known from Susa and Tappeh Bormi makes it of course difficult to generalize. At Huhnur the gods Nahhunte and Humban are attested in three and two theophoric names, respectively, while Šimut, Adad, Hili, Narunde, Išhara, and Manzit/ Manzat each feature only once.[104] Although Ruhuratir, the city god of Huhnur, was routinely invoked alongside Nahhunte in the oath formulae

---

102. Mofidi-Nasrabadi 2011a: 302–303, Table 17.

103. For the attestations, see Mofidi-Nasrabadi 2016: 77–83.

104. Nahhunte: Scheil 1930: no. 73; Mofidi-Nasrabadi 2018c: Tappeh Bormi 1. Humban: Scheil 1930: no. 71, no. 163 (here as Humbaba). Šimut: Mofidi-Nasrabadi 2018c: Tappeh Bormi 1. Adad: Scheil 1930: no. 71. Hili: Scheil 1930: no. 72. Narunde: Scheil 1930: no. 52. Išhara: Scheil 1930: no. 72. Manzit (= Manzat): Scheil 1930: no. 76.

of the legal documents from this site, it is a remarkable fact that this god is not attested at all in the personal names attested at Huhnur. At Susa, only two legal documents of ME I date are known, one dating to the reign of Tepti-ahar and the other to the reign of Šalla.[105] Among the eighteen names mentioned in these texts, seven are theophoric. Inšušinak and Sin are each attested in two names, while Šimut, Humma (= Humban?), and Adad each appear once.

With respect to temples (Elamite *sian*, also written with the sumerograms É "house" or É.DÙ.A "built house," the latter only attested in the ME I period)[106] and other architectural evidence, Haft Tappeh provides the best ME I material. During the earliest excavations at Haft Tappeh two large mud-brick terraces (Terraces 1 and 2) with several adjacent buildings were unearthed and attributed to the ME I period.[107] More recently, geophysical prospection undertaken in the same area has revealed how these structures fit into a building ensemble consisting of several monumental structures (figure 34.2: top: Buildings A–D).[108] In light of the roughly contemporary architecture at Dur-Kurigalzu (modern Aqar Quf) in Babylonia,[109] we may speculate that these terraces served as platforms on which temples stood. But as the buildings at Haft Tappeh were generally constructed of sun-dried mud brick and are therefore badly eroded, no evidence survives that could reveal more about the nature of these potential sanctuaries. However, the Haft Tappeh texts mention two temples that were surrounded by a mud-brick wall and a palace (É.GAL). One of the temples was dedicated to the god Padi, while the other was called a "great building" (É.DÙ.A GAL) and É.KUR, a frequently attested temple name which denotes a

105. Scheil 1932: nos. 248 and 327.

106. E.g., the temple of Inšušinak: Malbran-Labat 1995: nos. 19 and 20; or the temple of Padi: Erica Reiner in Negahban 1991: 125–126; Herrero and Glassner 1990: no. 1.

107. Negahban 1991: 9–11, 15–19.

108. Mofidi-Nasrabadi 2003–2004.

109. Heinrich 1982: 224–225.

"mountain-like" sanctuary (Sumerian KUR), and was erected on a terrace, all of which suggests a monumental appearance.[110] It is therefore tempting to identify the structures revealed at Haft Tappeh by excavation and magnetometer survey with these buildings. Additionally, the geophysical survey has indicated the presence of a monumental square building with a wide courtyard to the south of the mud-brick platforms (figure 34.2, top: Building E), and the layout of this building resembles that of the Middle Elamite palaces at Chogha Zanbil (figure 34.4: A–B), although its dimensions are considerably larger. On the other hand, close to Terrace 1, a workshop was excavated (briefly discussed in section 34.3 in the context of the clay tablets found in its vicinity). The workshop is situated in Building Complex B and integrated within the terrace of Building Complex A, indicating that it was connected to the hypothesized sanctuary. Several of the cuneiform texts recovered from a nearby room record the receipt of gold, silver, and bronze, and the delivery of manufactured products.[111] Such activities could well be connected to the workings of a temple workshop.

The ME II king Untaš-Napiriša chose Chogha Zanbil, about 45 km southeast of Susa, as the site for his new city, which he named Al-Untaš-Napiriša, "City of Untaš-Napiriša," abbreviated in later sources as Dur-Untaš, "Fortress of Untaš" (figure 34.5). The sanctuaries of Al-Untaš-Napiriša and attested in the associated brick inscriptions can be taken to represent the official Elamite pantheon, as championed by Untaš-Napiriša.

The cylinder seal inscriptions of the ME II and III periods were increasingly standardized and came to feature an almost identical text. Those of Chogha Zanbil mention three deities whose names are all written logographically,[112] only one of which ($^{(d)}$UTU = Nahhunte) can be identified with an Elamite name (see earlier discussion in this section). In addition, according to some inscribed bricks found

---

110. Herrero 1976: 108–111; cf. Mofidi-Nasrabadi 2003–2004: 236–237.

111. Mofidi-Nasrabadi 2016: 70, 72–73.

112. Erica Reiner in Porada 1970: 133–137.

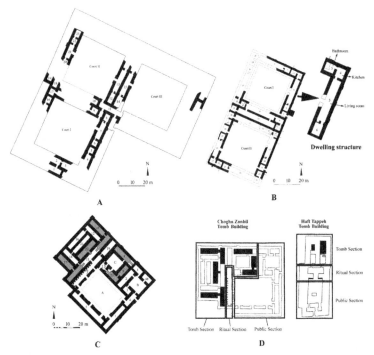

FIGURE 34.4. A: Plan of Palace 2 at Al-Untaš-Napiriša (modern Chogha Zanbil); B: plan of Palace 3 at Chogha Zanbil; C: plan of the tomb building ("Palace Hypogeum") at Chogha Zanbil; D: the spatial order of the tomb buildings at Haft Tappeh and Chogha Zanbil. Prepared by the author.

at Chogha Zanbil, a temple dedicated to Nahhunte was planned in this city.[113] While the monumental stepped temple tower in the city's center seems, initially, to have been intended for the god Inšušinak, it was later dedicated jointly to both Inšušinak and Napiriša, indicating Untaš-Napiriša's particular affinity for the latter god whose name also features as a divine element in his own name. This stepped tower played the most important role in the planning of the new city. In order to render it visible from afar, it was constructed on a plateau ca. 40 m

113. Steve 1967: no. 27.

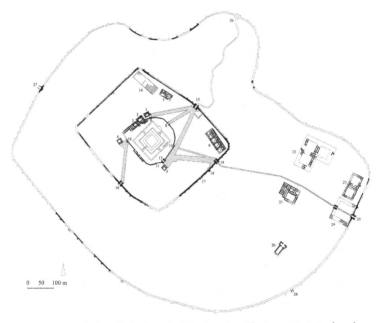

FIGURE 34.5. Plan of the Middle Elamite city Al-Untaš-Napiriša (modern Chogha Zanbil). 1: Temple of Napiriša. 2: Temple of Išmeqarab. 3: Temple of Kiririša. 4–5: Square temples. 6: Eastern temple complex. 7: Temple of Hišmitik and Ruhuratir. 8–10 and 12–13: Gates of the inner wall (8 = northeastern gate; 9 = northern gate; 10 = western gate; 12 = southeastern gate; 13 = eastern gate). 11: Drainage canal of the inner wall. 14: Storage area for building material. 15–17 and 19: Gates of the middle wall (15 = northeastern gate; 16 = southwestern gate; 17 = small gate; 19 = southeastern gate). 20: So-called temple of Nusku. 21: Tomb building. 22: Palace 2. 23: Palace 3. 24: Gate building. 25–26: Gates of the outer wall (25 = southeastern gate; 26 = assumed northeastern gate). 27–28: Drainage canals of the outer wall. Reproduced from Mofidi-Nasrabadi 2018a: fig. 12.4.

high above the river plain to the south of the river Dez. This prominent position underlined the tower's importance and advertised the magnificence of the king's accomplishment. The tower was used as the point of reference for the construction of the entire sacred precinct of Al-Untaš-Napiriša. At a distance of twice the stepped tower's length, measured from the midpoint of its southeastern side in the direction where the sun rose on New Year's day, a tower was constructed that was designated in the brick inscriptions with the Akkadian term *nur kibrat* ("Light of the World"),[114] and alongside this structure and parallel to the stepped tower, the enclosing wall that surrounded the holy precinct was erected (figure 34.6: A). Indeed, the identification of the sun's exact position at sunrise on New Year's day must have been the very first step in planning the city's architecture, as the location of the "Light of the World" tower had to be chosen in such a way that it enabled the correct performance of the annual New Year's ritual at sunrise (designated with the Akkadian term *sit šamši*).

The performance of this ritual is depicted on a bronze model discovered at Susa that bears an inscription of the ME III ruler Šilhak-Inšušinak.[115] It shows two nude male figures, presumably priests, performing ritual purification, with two rectangular basins, two podiums, a platform, a storage vessel, and the fragmentary remains of trees arranged around them. The ritual takes place in front of a three-stepped structure resembling a stepped temple tower. The two rows of four conical pedestals on the stepped structure's side are similar to the two rows of small pedestals in front of the Chogha Zanbil temple tower's central, southeastern entrance (which faces the rising sun), where a large storage vessel was found beneath the paved floor, perfectly positioned for the performance of a purification ritual.[116] On the bronze model, a tower-like element stands opposite the three-stepped structure and likely represents the "Light of the World" tower. We may assume that the sunrise ritual was performed annually in the other Elamite cities as well, with stepped temple towers and "Light of the World" towers together serving as the essential architectural elements of the ceremony.

As the main architectural element of the sacred precinct (Elamite *sian-kuk*) and the city, the stepped temple tower determined where all other buildings were positioned and therefore must have been

---

114. Steve 1967: no. 21.

115. Harper et al. 1992: 137–141.

116. Mofidi-Nasrabadi 2013b: 263–267.

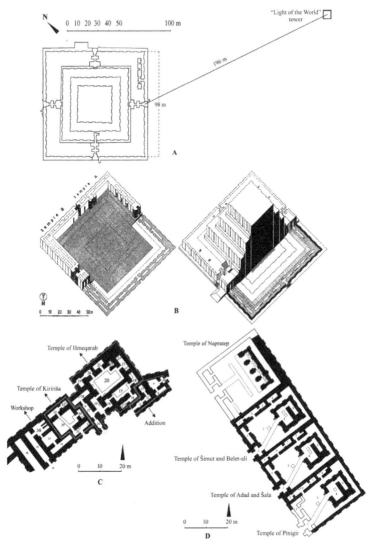

FIGURE 34.6. A: The "Light of the World" tower as an indicator for the position of the enclosing wall of the sacred precinct of Chogha Zanbil; B: the two building phases of the stepped temple tower at Chogha Zanbil; C: the temples of the god Išmeqarab and the goddess Kiririša at Chogha Zanbil; D: the temples in the eastern corner of Chogha Zanbil's sacred precinct. B reproduced from Ghirshman 1966: figs. 27 and 29, otherwise prepared by the author.

constructed first. At Chogha Zanbil, Roman Ghirshman identified two building stages for the stepped tower (figure 34.6: B).[117] During the first stage, a large square construction with a central courtyard was built. Two temples for Inšušinak were situated on its southeastern side, one accessible from inside the courtyard (Temple A) and the other from outside (Temple B). Storerooms were constructed on the other sides of the complex, all accessible from the courtyard. The terraces of the temple tower were built during the second building stage by filling the central courtyard with mud brick. Thus, the entrance to Temple A was blocked. The entrances to the storerooms were also blocked, but they continued to be accessible through new entrances that were now opened in the rooms' ceiling and that enabled entry via a stairway from the surface of the first terrace of the temple tower. Finally, all terraces were provided with a socle and a baked-brick mantle. The brickworks of the different terraces were not joined to each other, and Ghirshman was able to distinguish gaps between them, thus identifying four terraces with a high temple on top. The first and second terraces were still partly preserved, and while Ghirshman was able to calculate the extent of the other terraces based on the position of the gaps,[118] he could not identify any apparent logic to their dimensions. However, new research has demonstrated that, contrary to Ghirshman's assumption, no specific measure of length was used to calculate the buildings' size.[119] Instead, the size of the mud brick itself served to determine the extent of different public buildings in the city. A mud brick together with the surrounding mortar measured approximately 43 cm in length.[120] The number of mud bricks in the core in all terraces was based on a sexagesimal system, which results in a specific sequence (table 34.7).

This sequence shows a disconnect between the first and second terraces because logic would lead one to expect 5 × 6 × 6 (resulting in 180

117. Ghirshman 1966: 38–45.

118. Ghirshman 1966: 36–38, 58–61.

119. Ghirshman 1966: 59. See Mofidi-Nasrabadi 2013b: 81–82.

120. Mofidi-Nasrabadi 2013b: 98–108; 2015b: 37–42.

Table 34.7. The numerical order of mud bricks in the different terraces of the stepped tower at Chogha Zanbil

Terrace 1	216 mud bricks	(36×6) or $(6 \times 6 \times 6)$
Terrace 2	144 mud bricks	(24×6) or $(4 \times 6 \times 6)$
Terrace 3	108 mud bricks	(18×6) or $(3 \times 6 \times 6)$
Terrace 4	72 mud bricks	(12×6) or $(2 \times 6 \times 6)$
High Temple	36 mud bricks	(6×6) or $(1 \times 6 \times 6)$

bricks) to follow $6 \times 6 \times 6$. Why did the architects not use this number? One must take into account that the numbers $6 \times 6 \times 6$ (for the whole stepped tower) and 6×6 (for the high temple, Akkadian *kukunnum*) could not be varied, as they had a highly symbolic meaning: both are multiples of six, on which the mathematical system was based, and represent the concepts of entirety, completeness, and holiness. If we accept that the numbers $6 \times 6 \times 6$ and 6×6 are significant, two options can be considered for planning the building. The first option was to build five terraces instead of four, and the second was to avoid the number $5 \times 6 \times 6$. This was the option chosen, one which accommodates the functional aspects of various parts of the building that separated the lower part from the sacred upper section.

The stepped temple tower was surrounded by a 2.4-m-thick wall (figure 34.5). Taken as a whole, the complex consists of three separate parts with different functions. The first consists of the first terrace with its storerooms and was accessible from all four sides by stairways, allowing for easy and apparently unrestricted access. The second section was the sacred area of the complex and consisted of the upper part of the temple tower, including the high temple. This section of the structure could only be entered from the southwestern side via a stairway that led directly from the ground to the level of the second terrace. In order to reach the third terrace from there, it was necessary to go to the southeastern side where the stairway was located. In order to advance to the fourth terrace, one had to traverse the building again to reach its northeastern side and the stairs there. Finally, one had to go to the building's northwestern side in order to enter the high temple.[121] The discovery of a door on the well-preserved stairway of the second terrace indicates that access to this terrace, and presumably also the higher stairways leading to the upper terraces, was restricted. Thus, in contrast to the easily accessible first terrace, access to the upper terraces was increasingly more limited on every level. This is consistent with the interpretation of the upper levels, and in particular the high temple, as sacred areas, unlike the easily accessible first terrace with its storerooms. If we therefore bear in mind the fact that the lower and upper parts of the building were characterized by very different levels of accessibility and sanctity, then this could explain why the architects, by omitting number $5 \times 6 \times 6$, implemented a break in the numerical sequence of bricks between the accessible, profane first terrace and the second terrace, the gateway to the protected, sacred upper part of the complex. The jump in size between these two terraces also had the advantage of increasing the size of the patio covering the first terrace, which allowed for better access to its storerooms.

In addition to these two sections, the third part of the building complex consists of Temple B, dedicated to the god Inšušinak and located in the southeastern wing of the stepped tower. Although this temple was embedded within the first terrace, it was directly accessible from outside the complex and therefore completely separate from the other two building parts. It is probable that Temple B was used for cult activities allowing large outside audiences to observe the ritual action taking place inside the complex. For example, a pedestal constructed in the vestibule directly in front of the shrine's entrance would have made it possible to place a statue of the deity there, so that it would be visible to people outside the complex.[122] Temple B's entrance was equipped with a heavy door, the large stone door-sockets of which have been discovered. These doors played an important role in protecting the sacred space and all of the valuable objects within. Another door, which could only be locked from the inside, was installed in the ante-cella.[123] This means that in

---

121. Mofidi-Nasrabadi 2015b: 47–51.

122. Mofidi-Nasrabadi 2013b: 121–126.

123. Ghirshman 1966: 28–36.

order to lock the door, someone would have had to remain inside the cella. According to an inscription concerning the Inšušinak temple at Susa, the ME I Tepti-ahar commanded that four women were to sleep inside the shrine in order to guard it, and their garments were to be fastened with laces to prevent the possibility of hiding any pieces of gold.[124] Tepti-ahar's inscription demonstrates the high level of protection given to Elamite temples, and such safety concerns may explain why the interior door of the Inšušinak temple at Chogha Zanbil could only be locked from the inside.

Two temples dedicated to the goddess Kiririša and the god Išmeqarab, respectively, were situated outside the thick wall surrounding the stepped tower to the northwest of the complex but could still be accessed from the sacred area encircled by the wall (figure 34.6: C).[125] The temple of Išmeqarab consists of three sections, connected to each other through a main vestibule (no. 19) that was directly accessible from the sacred precinct. The cella (no. 17) is located in the first section and contains a pedestal coated with gypsum plaster that presumably served as a base for the statue of a deity. The nearby kitchen (no. 18) probably served in the preparation of offerings. In order to reach the cella, one passed through a vestibule (no. 14), a courtyard (no. 15), and an ante-cella (no. 16). The arrangement of doors and rooms did not permit a direct view into the cella from other parts of the building.

The second section of the temple of Išmeqarab consists of a courtyard (no. 20) and the rooms around it, one of which was a kitchen with four ovens (no. 21), while another may have been a storeroom (no. 23). The stairway to the temple's roof was situated in Room 22, while a back door leading through Rooms 24 and 25 offered direct access from the outside to this section (cf. figure 34.5). With its large kitchen, this section seems to have been a supply area, used for preparing and delivering food for the priests and other temple personnel, accessible directly from the outside without disturbing the sacred area encircled by the inner wall.

124. Malbran-Labat 1995: no. 20.

125. Ghirshman 1966: 85–104.

The third section of the temple of Išmeqarab consisted of three rooms that form a T-shape (nos. 26–28). Via Room 26, this section had a separate entrance from the sacred precinct but was nevertheless connected to the central vestibule (no. 19) which provided the main access from the sacred precinct. Opposite the entrance leading into Room 28 was a pedestal constructed against the wall. As all doorways in this section were positioned along the same axis, it was possible to see this pedestal from outside the temple. Like Temple B of Inšušinak, this part of Išmeqarab's temple was probably a chapel used for festivities during which the statue of the god was meant to be visible to viewers standing outside the shrine.

The temple of the goddess Kiririša was situated right next to the Išmeqarab shrine (figure 34.6: C). It included a vestibule (no. 31) that provided access from the sacred precinct, a courtyard (no. 29), a kitchen (no. 30) with an oven and a well, an ante-cella (no. 33), and the cella (no. 32). As in the temple of Išmeqarab, the cella of this temple and the pedestal for the cult statue were relatively isolated and protected from view. A second pedestal, coated with gypsum plaster, was situated in the vestibule (no. 31) on the wall directly opposite the gateway leading into the room from the sacred precinct. Again, we may assume that whatever was placed on that base was meant to be visible to outside onlookers during certain festivities.[126]

Further temples were situated beyond the wall enclosing the sacred precinct in an area that was in turn encircled by a second wall about 5 m wide (figure 34.5). In this way, the temple area was kept strictly separate from the residential quarters, and even the royal palaces were constructed outside this holy district. The entire city was surrounded by a third outer wall that was about 4.6 m thick and 4 km long. The strict separation between sacred precinct and profane residential areas is unlikely to have grown out of public desire, but was presumably in the interest of the king and his architects, who understood close control over access to the divine as a royal prerogative. However, after the reign of Untaš-Napiriša, this control gradually faded. In the centuries following his death, the people

---

126. Mofidi-Nasrabadi 2013b: 135–147.

of the city began to build houses in close proximity to the sanctuaries within the holy precinct, as recent excavations have demonstrated.[127]

Within the sacred area between the first and second wall stood the temple of Napiriša, which was located next to the sanctuaries of Išmeqarab and Kiririša. Relatively near the inner wall sit two square buildings (figure 34.5: nos. 4 and 5), one at the western gate and the other at the southeastern gate. Based on their ground plans, these have been identified as sanctuaries.[128] The other known temples were constructed at a greater distance from the stepped tower. The temple dedicated to the gods Hišmitik and Ruhuratir was located about 100 m northeast of the inner wall, close to the second wall.[129] A complex of four parallel shrines stood close to the eastern corner of this wall (figure 34.6: D). The first of these was dedicated to the goddess Pinigir/Pinengir,[130] the middle one to the storm-god Adad and his consort Šala, and the third to Šimut and his consort Belet-ali. The ground plans of these three shrines are identical.[131] The fourth sanctuary was dedicated to a group of four pairs of deities called collectively the Napratep and consequently had four chapels, each with two pedestals for statues.

Furthermore, Ghirshman identified a building in the southeastern part of the city, outside the holy area demarcated by the second wall and at a distance of about 500 m from the precinct of the stepped temple tower, as the temple of Nusku because he found bricks with an inscription dedicated to Nusku in the adjacent rubble.[132] However, examples of the same type of inscribed brick have been discovered in the holy area between the first and second wall.[133] Therefore, the identification of this structure as a temple is not certain.

127. Mofidi-Nasrabadi 2007: 40–42, 90–92.

128. Ghirshman 1966: 105–107.

129. Ghirshman 1968: 25–34.

130. Koch 2005.

131. Ghirshman 1968: 9–21.

132. Steve 1967: nos. 23–24; Ghirshman 1968: 84–87.

133. Steve 1967: no. 43.

Generally speaking, Elamite temples housed sacred spaces in which the cult statues of deities were placed, typically seated on a throne, and these were certainly not intended for public observation. Statues depicting members of the royal family, in an attitude of worship, could be placed nearby in a respectful standing pose, with the arms crossed in front of the body, as illustrated by the statue of Queen Napirasu (see section 34.2.2) and inscriptions of the ME I ruler Tepti-ahar and the ME III king Šilhak-Inšušinak.[134]

The temples of Chogha Zanbil can be divided into two categories based on their spatial order and degree of accessibility. The first group includes the temples of Išmeqarab, Kiririša, and Napiriša, which are all situated in, or directly connected to, the sacred precinct, inside the inner wall around the stepped temple tower. They must have been constructed together with the stepped tower as part of the earliest building phase of the city. In these shrines, the cella, the innermost sanctum of the deity, was designed to be difficult to access and was situated beyond an ante-cella, to be reached only after passing through several other rooms. With the inner sanctum so strongly protected from the outside, these temples have an introverted character.

The second group of temples includes the complex of shrines near the eastern corner of the second wall (figure 34.6: D), which exhibit completely different concepts of accessibility and room connectivity. One might assume that these sanctuaries were constructed sometime after those built close to the temple tower.[135] The entrance to the vestibule (no. 1) and the gateway opposite the courtyard (no. 2) were notably large and placed on the same axis, offering the possibility of viewing the interior from the outside. The cella (no. 8) was built in the middle of the courtyard and had no ante-cella. The pedestals for the divine statues were placed directly opposite of the entrance in the middle of the cella, so that they were well visible from the exterior.

It seems that the "introverted" type of temple, with its particularly isolated and protected cella, gave way over time to an "extroverted" type with an easily accessible chapel in the center. How long this process may

---

134. Malbran-Labat 1995: no. 29; König 1965: no. 46, §11, and no. 47, §13.

135. Cf. Mofidi-Nasrabadi 2013b: 209–217.

have taken is unclear, but it may have been connected to shifts in the way the sanctuaries were used. Untaš-Napiriša's monumental building activities and his creation of a new city with its sacred precinct may have piqued the interest of the people, engendering a social dynamic calling for a new form of sanctuary that offered greater possibilities for participation in and communication with the cult, which led to a reconsideration of accessibility to sacred space and the inner sanctum. However, based on the later testimony of the royal inscriptions of Ashurbanipal of Assyria (668–631 BC), the new temple type attested at Chogha Zanbil may never have been more widely enjoyed throughout Elam since, according to Ashurbanipal's report on the conquest of Susa, the temple of the god Inšušinak was a hidden holy space that was not accessible to the public.[136]

According to inscribed bricks from Chogha Zanbil, there were temples dedicated to at least the following twenty-four deities: Adad, Belili, Dumuzi, Hišmitik, Humban, Inana, Inšušinak, Išmeqarab, Kilahšupir, Kiririša, Kirwašir, Manzat, Nabû, Nahhunte, Napiriša, Napratep, NIN.É.GAL (Elamite name unknown), Nusku, Pinigir, Ruhuratir, Šala, Siašum, Šimut, and Sunkir-rišara.[137] Most of these deities also had temples at Susa.[138] Sometimes deities are mentioned with a title, e.g., the goddess Manzat as Belet-ali, "Lady of the City," who was worshipped together with her husband Šimut in a sanctuary in the eastern corner of the holy area of Chogha Zanbil. As the inscriptions of the ME III king Šutruk-Nahhunte attest, the divine couple Šimut and Manzat also shared a temple at Susa.[139] In addition to divine couples like Šimut and Manzat or Adad and Šala, divine siblings such as Dumuzi and Belili also shared the same temple.[140]

---

136. Novotny and Jeffers 2018: no. 9, v 21–23; no. 11, vi 30–32: "Inšušinak, the god of their secret lore who lives in seclusion and whose divine acts have never been seen by anyone."

137. Steve 1967; Potts 2010: 60–64.

138. Potts 2010.

139. König 1965: nos. 47 and 65.

140. König 1965: no. 10B; Steve 1967: no. 50.

As emphasized earlier, temples and sacred precincts were not easily accessed and public participation in cult and religious rituals must have been limited. The general populace was probably only involved in ceremonies that took place during the most important annual festivals, but written sources provide very little evidence about religious practices per se. According to the Haft Tappeh stele (see section 34.3), important, multi-day festivals took place in the months Abu (V) and Tašritu (VII). These included processions in which both the king and the cult statue of Inšušinak were conveyed on a chariot. While such ceremonies must have taken place in public spaces, other rites were likely to have been performed without a large audience in the presence of only a few priests, perhaps like the sunrise ceremony on New Year's day depicted on the bronze model from Susa, discussed earlier.

Although our knowledge of the religious practices of the ordinary population is limited, the widespread attestation of nude terracotta female figurines with their hands clasped beneath their breasts (figure 34.3: C) suggests the popularity of a fertility goddess, as do clay models of beds showing nude couples engaged in the sexual act (figure 34.3: D). Although goddesses such as Pinigir, Kiririša, and Manzat are attested textually, none can be related convincingly to specific female figurines or otherwise linked to the known Elamite pantheon. This is yet another indication, along with personal names and seal inscriptions, that the religious beliefs and practices of ordinary people did not necessarily coincide with royally sponsored cult. Moreover, while the cylinder seals of elite individuals typically depict only the worshipper in front of a deity, without any additional motifs (figure 34.3: E–F), the seals of ordinary people are filled out with nude female figures and various apotropaic motifs.[141]

Thus, Elamite religious practice seems to have taken two relatively separate forms: on the one hand, the official, royal-sponsored state cult practiced at a large number of temples across the realm with complex sacred rituals conducted by priests in the presence of only a small elite, and on the other hand, the beliefs and practices of the wider population,

---

141. Mofidi-Nasrabadi 2011a: 61.

which seem to have been characterized by apotropaic symbols and simple, repetitive practices.

34.5. *Society*

In closing this chapter, we offer some further perspectives on society in the ME period. Although a lack of concrete information in the written sources makes it difficult to construct a comprehensive picture, archaeological evidence provides some insights, at least into the lifestyles of Elam's urban population.

34.5.1. Perspectives from residential architecture

During the *Sukkalmah* period, a characteristic type of residential building developed, the main feature of which was a large, easily accessible hall with adjoining rooms, situated close to a central courtyard.[142] Later, an intimate private room was added at the rear side of the hall. Excavations at Susa have shown that several small houses were removed to make room for the construction of such larger and more imposing buildings, indicating a growing concentration of economic power in the hands of the elite.

In the ME period, however, the opposite can be observed, whereby small houses again began to fill the space formerly occupied by such grand residences.[143] Perhaps this is an indication that the concentration of absolute power in the hands of the king (see section 34.4.1) reduced the financial resources available to private households.

Despite such potential social and economic changes, the architectural template of the *Sukkalmah* period continued to be used for residential architecture with little variation throughout the ME period, as the combination of a large hall backed by a more intimate private section constituted the typical architectural form. A simplified version of this structural scheme combined the large hall and the private room into

---

142. Mofidi-Nasrabadi 2018b: 507–511.

143. Steve, Gasche, and De Meyer 1980: A XII and A XI (figs. 6 and 8).

a single space: a wide living room with two lateral chambers accessible from the courtyard. In the first millennium BC, this Elamite building template is widely attested in Babylonian domestic architecture,[144] and as it had no local antecedents,[145] its adoption in Babylonia may reflect Elamite influence.

At Chogha Zanbil, these architectural schemes were also used in the two "palaces" excavated by Ghirshman in the eastern corner of the city. Both constructions included two or three similar sections with central, rectangular courtyards.[146] Suites of three or more rooms were situated around the courtyards, each provided with a wide, central hall and adjoining small rooms. Neither of these buildings possessed features typically associated with a royal palace, such as a throne hall, large-scale storage areas, or administrative facilities. Although very sizable, they are on a much smaller scale and of a less imposing character than other Near Eastern palaces. Perhaps these buildings served as temporary accommodation for members of the royal family when they stayed at Al-Untaš-Napiriša, assuming that their primary royal palaces were at Susa. The overall structure of the two buildings is largely identical, but a few details allow us to tease out their distinct functions.

In the larger building ("Palace 2"; figure 34.4: A), three rectangular sections were connected to each other, allowing contact between the inhabitants of every section. Thus, the construction seems to have been planned for an extended family that consisted of three sub-units occupying the suites of rooms arranged around the courtyards of the three sections.

In contrast to this, the smaller building ("Palace 3"; figure 34.5: B) had only two sections, which were not interconnected but separately accessible from the outside. Importantly, the entrances to both sections were constructed in a manner that prevented visual access from the outside,

---

144. Miglus 1999: 188–193.

145. Miglus 1999: 98.

146. For the structure of both constructions and their reconstruction, see Mofidi-Nasrabadi 2013b: 217–235; 2018b: 511–514.

offering great privacy to the residents. Situated between the two sections was a suite of five rooms, including a large central hall (no. 9) with kitchen and bathroom on one side (nos. 8 and 12) and the more intimate living room (no. 11) and its small side chamber (no. 31) placed at the back. The other seven suites of the building were identical, each consisting of a large central hall, a kitchen and bathroom on one side, and a small side chamber on the other side. Their matching ground plans imply that they were occupied by people of equal social standing who were not closely related to each other, while the larger central suite housed a higher-status occupant. One possible interpretation could be that the seven identical suites served as residences for the king's concubines, with the larger suite reserved for the favorite.

Even the simpler dwellings at Chogha Zanbil were in some cases provided with a bathroom. A section of the courtyard was usually equipped with an oven used for cooking.[147] The many spindles recovered in residential spaces at Haft Tappeh and Chogha Zanbil show that spinning and presumably other aspects of textile production took place in these homes.[148] Most likely, such work was performed by women, as a stone relief from Susa indicates.[149] At least some women could also own property, including fields and gardens, as attested by legal documents from Huhnur (modern Tappeh Bormi) that mention women as buyers and sellers of real estate and witnesses in legal proceedings, indicating that their legal status was equal to that of men.[150]

34.5.2. Perspectives from funerary practices

Due to a lack of relevant written sources, our knowledge of funerary practices in the Middle Elamite period is mainly based on archaeological

---

147. Mofidi-Nasrabadi 2007: 52.

148. Mofidi-Nasrabadi 2007: 44–45, 53, 59, 67, 79, 88–89; 2014b: 82–83.

149. Harper et al. 1992: 200, no. 141.

150. Scheil 1930: nos. 52, 71, 72–76, 81, 132, 154, 162; Mofidi-Nasrabadi 2018c.

evidence. Several graves excavated recently at Haft Tappeh provide important information about the location and contents of graves.[151]

Generally speaking, a ceramic goblet and/or bowl were placed next to the skeleton at the time of burial, presumably to provide the dead with nourishment. After the burial, regular offerings (*kispu*) were made in yearly ceremonies meant to nourish and support the deceased, as well as the deities of the underworld.[152] Otherwise, ordinary graves identified at Haft Tappeh and Chogha Zanbil contained few grave goods, mainly personal jewelry such as earrings and bracelets. While the early excavations at Susa attributed clay human heads to some graves,[153] such items have not been found at Haft Tappeh, Chogha Zanbil, or elsewhere in Elam, and their attribution to graves should be viewed with considerable caution due to the poor excavation and registration practices of the time.

Different types of burials were in use simultaneously as the deceased were buried either simply in the soil or else put into large pottery vessels or covered with large pieces of pottery, with terracotta coffins used for certain high-status individuals such as Ginadu,[154] the "archivist" (*puhu-teppu*) of the ME I king Inšušinak-šar-ili (see section 34.4.3). Ginadu's sarcophagus was found on the floor of a room (no. 19) in a building adjoining an administrative complex (figure 34.2: bottom),[155] while two pit graves were excavated underneath the floor of another room (no. 25).[156] It is unclear whether these three interments occurred while the building was still in use or after it had been abandoned. Otherwise, graves at Haft Tappeh were typically located in ruined areas near inhabited zones or in open spaces within the settlement. Graves were never placed in temple areas, even after the shrines had fallen into ruin. Thus,

---

151. Mofidi-Nasrabadi 2010b: 45–48; 2012a: 91–94; 2014b: 99–102.

152. Tsukimoto 1985; Mofidi-Nasrabadi 1999: 62–66.

153. Cf. Álvarez-Mon 2005; Gasche and Cole 2018: 752.

154. Mofidi-Nasrabadi 2011b.

155. Mofidi-Nasrabadi 2011b: 152.

156. Mofidi-Nasrabadi 2014b: 70–71, 99.

the extensive excavations of Building Complex D, which should be identified as a sanctuary because of its monumental terraces, yielded no burials at all, while many graves came to light in the neighboring administration area of Building Complex C (figure 34.2: top). Similarly, all known burials at Al-Untaš-Napiriša (modern Chogha Zanbil) lay inside the city,[157] but none was found in the sacred area demarcated by the second inner wall where all of the temples were situated (see section 34.4.4).[158]

The abandoned administrative complex in the southern part of Haft Tappeh (figure 34.2: bottom) provides a good example of a ruined building that served as a cemetery. The building's last phase of use dates to the reign of Inšušinak-šar-ili when, judging from a thick layer of ash on the floor of several rooms as well as fragments of burned roof beams, the structure was destroyed by fire.[159] Thereafter, the ruins were used as a burial ground. Graves were dug into the debris within the building, and the burials often reached the original floors. Several different types of burial are attested inside this ruin.[160] The northern part (Room 2) contained a terracotta coffin holding a female and jar graves used for children and in one case a woman (each consisting of two large pottery vessels placed upon each other), while the southern part (Rooms 11 and 13) featured simple pit graves, with the dead individuals (adult males and females and a child about seven years old) placed in a flexed position directly in the ground. Pit graves included a limited range of objects, typically a ceramic goblet or bowl, while the dead in the jar graves were provided with many and more valuable grave goods, such as bronze objects, and the terracotta coffin contained a golden earring. The distribution of jar and coffin burials on the one hand, and pit graves on the other hand, as well as associated grave goods, seems to reflect differences in the deceaseds' social status.

157. Ghirshman 1968: 88–89, 101; Mofidi-Nasrabadi 2013b: 256–259.

158. Mofidi-Nasrabadi 2012c: 261–263.

159. Mofidi-Nasrabadi 2012b.

160. Foruzanfar 2012; Mofidi-Nasrabadi 2012a: 95–96.

At both Haft Tappeh and Chogha Zanbil, large funerary buildings that must have belonged to wealthy and important families have
been found. Three vaulted subterranean tombs made of mud brick
were located in the vicinity of the house (not inside them) at Chogha
Zanbil.[161] The tomb interiors had two or three platforms, on which the
deceased were placed next to the walls. Based on the position of the skeletons, these tombs were used for several successive burials, presumably
members of an extended family who were buried over the course of time.
One tomb contained as many as nine individuals. A much larger funerary building was situated in the eastern residential area of the city (figure
34.4: C), relatively close to two palaces.[162] This building consisted of five
large, vaulted chambers, constructed of baked bricks and mortar made
from gypsum and bitumen. The walls of the tomb chambers were plastered with gypsum and painted with broad, ribbon-like designs in brown
pigment. In the above-ground parts of the building, several functional
sections could be distinguished.[163] A small courtyard (B) that was surrounded by a kitchen (no. 4) and three more rooms were accessible from
the entrance (no. 6). This part of the building may have been occupied by
the caretaker of the tombs and his family, while the larger courtyard (A),
also accessible from the entrance, with long halls along two of its sides
(nos. 1 and 5), likely served for the public part of the funerary practices.

The inner part of the building was accessible from Courtyard A and
consisted of two parts: from Room 7, one reached the back of the building with a suite of rooms from which three underground tombs were
accessible, and from Room 13, one entered a third courtyard (C) and the
rooms around it, which provided access to another two tombs. Room
7 was a long hall with fifteen altars, most likely used for ritual offerings,
and connected to Courtyard A through three, evenly spaced entrances.
Near the western entrance, a large jar and goblet were found that may
have been connected to a purification ritual performed before entering

161. Ghirshman 1968: 101–107; Mofidi-Nasrabadi 2013b: 254–258.

162. Ghirshman 1968: 47–58.

163. Mofidi-Nasrabadi 2012c; 2013b: 236–254.

the section with the underground tombs. The entrance room (no. 13) to the tombs around Courtyard C was also equipped with such a jar and goblet. The arrangement of the altars in Room 7 seems to indicate the course of the ritual action, suggesting that one entered through the western door and exited through the eastern one. The funerary rituals carried out in this tomb building consisted most importantly of regular food offerings for the dead (Akkadian *kispu*).[164] We may assume that these rituals took place in those rooms whose intermediate position between the public part of the building and the section with the tombs were well suited to connecting the living with their deceased ancestors.

The two areas with subterranean tombs housed tombs of one or two chambers. The area accessible from the long hall (no. 7) seems to have been reserved for the more important dead. Here, two tombs, each consisting of two chambers arranged in an L-shape, flanked a central tomb with only one chamber that was, however, considerably larger than all comparable structures. Its dimensions and central position in this part of the building, as well as the platform in the center of the chamber and the valuable grave goods found therein, suggest that this tomb was the most important feature of the entire building. The second burial area around Courtyard C housed a tomb with two chambers and another with a single one. These tombs were smaller than those found in the other part; perhaps this wing was used to bury a secondary branch of the larger family.

The same spatial order as in the tomb building at Chogha Zanbil can be observed in a similar building at Haft Tappeh of earlier date, although this structure was less complex (figure 34.4: D). It consisted of a large courtyard (no. 2) that was connected via a wide room (no. 4) with a rear area (nos. 5–6). Two socles, most likely for ritual use, stood on either side of the entrance to Room 4, which occupied an intermediate position between the accessible and public area of the courtyard and the tomb section. The Haft Tappeh building contained two tombs, which varied in size, means of access, and construction technique.[165] A rectangular cavity

---

164. Tsukimoto 1985; Mofidi-Nasrabadi 1999: 62–66.

165. Mofidi-Nasrabadi 2012c: 263–266.

in Room 5 served as the entrance to a large, vaulted, semi-subterranean tomb, the roof of which stood about 1.3–1.5 m higher than the pavement of Room 5. The tomb chamber was only partially subterranean as it was built over some earlier ruins, which had not been completely removed. The entrance to this tomb was blocked off with a stone, which could be removed to allow access to the tomb chamber for further burials. The chamber had a platform divided into three parts by small walls, thus allocating specific spaces for different groups, probably sub-units of an extended family.[166] A total of 21–22 individuals were buried in this tomb over the course of time.

The second, much smaller tomb was situated behind Room 6, parallel to the first tomb.[167] It seems to have been added during a later construction phase in the eroded northern part of the building and was constructed in a rather careless manner from baked bricks. The open area around the tomb chamber was filled with mud brick and rubble. The chamber does not have an entrance, as its southeastern wall was blocked up following a single burial of twenty-three individuals. Because of limited space, the deceased were packed into the chamber side by side, and on top of each other. The lack of care in the construction of this tomb and the simultaneous burial of twenty-three people raise questions,[168] as does the recent discovery of several hundred skeletons in the street next to the tomb building and along the northern wall of the Building Complex C (figure 34.2: top). The deceased may have been the victims of a massacre which, according to stratigraphic evidence, must have occurred at the end of the ME occupation of Haft Tappeh.[169] The mass burial in the adjacent tomb may have taken place at the same time. The tomb may have been constructed quickly in the eroded part of the older tomb building in order to house the bodies of high-status individuals, while the rest of the dead were simply heaped

---

166. Mofidi-Nasrabadi 2003–2004: 231–232.

167. Negahban 1991: 15.

168. Cf. Negahban 1991: 22.

169. Mofidi-Nasrabadi 2014b: 72–75, 105–106.

up nearby and only covered by earth. On the other hand, the deposition of ceramic artifacts like goblets and food offerings such as dates among the bodies indicates that some attempt was made to offer funerary sacrifices for the deceased.

In conclusion, we must address the idea that the Haft Tappeh tomb building may have been a "funerary temple";[170] that this is unjustified has already been stressed by D.T. Potts.[171] The suggestion resulted from the discovery of an inscribed stele fragment in the tomb building's courtyard that mentions offerings before the chariots of the god Inšušinak and the king Tepti-ahar, as well as other sacrifices (discussed in section 34.3). However, several arguments invalidate this idea. Generally speaking, Elamite temples were considered the "house" (É or É.DÙ.A) of a deity. Also, the plan of the Haft Tappeh tomb building is completely different from that of securely identified Elamite temples (cf. section 34.4.4). Most importantly, as stressed previously, ME temples were never used for burials, as the strict separation between temple areas and spaces used for burials at Haft Tappeh and Chogha Zanbil clearly demonstrates. Finally, the rites to be conducted according to the stele inscription demand much more space than is available in the Haft Tappeh tomb building (see section 34.3).

The idea of a "funerary temple" is also contradicted by the findspot of the second fragment of the stele. The original excavator Ezatollah Negahban did not consider the stratigraphic relationship between the different construction phases, and Wolfram Kleiss, who prepared the excavation plans, did not record the elevations of the different levels.[172] This initially led to the false deduction that all of the buildings at Haft Tappeh were contemporary. In fact, the tomb building must be younger than Terrace 1 and the adjacent structures, where another fragment of the inscribed stele (Fragment 3) was discovered in a courtyard, as the elevation of the tomb building was ca. 1.5–2 m higher than this fragment's

---

170. Thus Carter and Stolper 1984: 158; Negahban 1991; Harper et al. 1992: 9.

171. Potts 2016: 184–186.

172. Neghaban 1991: xxix.

findspot (figure 34.2: top).[173] Therefore, it is most likely that the stele originally stood in the courtyard near Terrace 1. After its destruction, one of its fragments eventually made its way into the courtyard of the tomb building. The notion that the Haft Tappeh tomb building was a "funerary temple" must therefore be abandoned for good. The building served exclusively as the final resting place for the members of an elite, extended family.

34.5.3. Perspectives from material culture

Archaeological evidence of ME I date comes mainly from Haft Tappeh, where a large number of terracotta figurines, bronze objects, sealings, and pottery have been excavated. Nude female figurines with hands cupping both breasts were very common (figure 34.3: C). Similar looking figures often appear on the cylinder seals of this period, generally as a minor motif within an adoration scene (cf. section 34.4.4), occasionally also as the primary motif.[174]

The adoration scene was the most common image on ME I cylinder seals and was used particularly by high-status individuals, including the king and his officials. The seal impressions of Tepti-ahar and Athibu, the governor of Kabnak, illustrate two variants of the adoration scene. The first can be described as "direct adoration" of a deity, showing the worshipper in the typical Elamite gesture of prayer, with both arms bent and raised in front of the enthroned deity. The second can be categorized as "indirect adoration," as the actual worshipper is not shown and the seal instead depicts a goddess who intervenes with the deity on his behalf.[175] Ginadu, the "archivist" of Inšušinak-šar-ili, possessed two cylinder seals, one of the first category and one of the second (figure 34.3: E–F).[176] The first seal, made of lapis lazuli, shows carving

---

173. Mofidi-Nasrabadi 2012a: 86–88, 98–99; 2012c: 263–266; 2014b: 89–93.

174. Mofidi-Nasrabadi 2011a: 48–49, 58.

175. Mofidi-Nasrabadi 2011a: 43, 54–61.

176. Mofidi-Nasrabadi 2011b: 155–158; 2017: 63–65, nos. 21–22.

of extremely high quality and ends fitted with caps of hammered gold foil. A second cylinder seal of lapis lazuli was discovered in the courtyard of the Building Complex B, directly in front of the entrance of the workshop there (figure 34.2: top),[177] and these may have been produced locally.

The diversity of finds encountered in this workshop shows that various activities were conducted there, including the manufacture of ivory and bone figures, mosaic fragments, decorative bitumen elements, jewelry, bronze weapons, and ceramics, some of which had not yet been finished,[178] while an elephant tusk presumably served as raw material.[179] The bronze objects reflect highly advanced manufacturing techniques, including lead-soldering and silver-plating.[180] Two life-sized human heads of very different style and manufacturing technique suggest that multiple craftsmen worked here together (figure 34.3: A–B).

As already discussed (section 34.4.3), the central administration oversaw the raw materials needed for the manufacture of precious objects commissioned for the cult or as gifts for high-status individuals.[181] Contemporary texts record the receipt of raw materials by goldsmiths, silversmiths, and other metalworkers. In one case, Ina-bubla received half a mina of silver to produce four bracelets,[182] while another text mentions him as receiving gold to make chariot parts.[183] Since he was also given bronze, he was presumably a master metalsmith who worked on a wide range of projects.[184] Ina-bubla's work was even commemorated

177. Mofidi-Nasrabadi 2017: 76–78, no. 35.

178. Negahban 1994.

179. Negahban 1991: 10.

180. Rafiei-Alavi 2012; 2015; Pakgohar et al. 2013.

181. Mofidi-Nasrabadi 2016: 76–77.

182. Herrero and Glassner 1990: no. 15.

183. Herrero and Glassner 1990: no. 8.

184. Herrero and Glassner 1990: no. 65.

in a year formula: "the year when the king installed the cone of Ina-bubla,"[185] presumably referring to the dedication of the cone in a temple. A second year formula reads: "the year when Habil-banutu received the order of the king for the construction of the *arattu* (an unknown type of object)."[186] Another text mentions Habil-banutu as the recipient of gold.[187] Ina-bubla and Habil-banutu were both active during the reign of Tepti-ahar,[188] as was Tab-adaru, who received gold and silver to manufacture jewelry.[189]

At Chogha Zanbil, the new ME II foundation, diverse and often innovative objects were manufactured. New methods for creating faience, in particular architectural elements such as wall knobs, seem to have been developed in Elam at this time.[190] Statues of the king and members of the royal family showcase the use of sophisticated production methods. The most important artifact to highlight the great technical and artistic ability of Elamite craftsmen is the almost life-sized bronze statue of Napirasu (see section 34.4.2), which was produced using lost-wax hollow casting.[191] Its surviving parts weigh 1,750 kg and consist of a bronze core with 11 percent tin, and a copper shell containing only 1 percent tin. The alloy used for the shell has a high melting point, making it very difficult to maintain in a molten state, as it can quickly solidify, causing bubbles. The bronze core, with its lower melting point, was subsequently poured into the sculpture. Because of the extraordinary weight of the molten bronze, a lifting mechanism or system of pulleys must have been used in the casting process.

---

185. Beckman 1991: 82–83; Mofidi-Nasrabadi 2016: 91, no. 3.

186. Herrero and Glassner 1990: no. 18; 1991: no. 82; Mofidi-Nasrabadi 2016: 91, no. 2.

187. Herrero and Glassner 1990: no. 44.

188. Mofidi-Nasrabadi 2016: 53–58.

189. Mofidi-Nasrabadi 2016: 49.

190. Caubet 2007: 123; Tourtet 2013: 182.

191. Lampre 1905; Harper et al. 1992: 132–135, no. 83; Meyers 2000.

Equally famous today is a relief panel from Susa, made of colorfully glazed molded bricks depicting the king and the queen as well as mythological figures. An inscription dates this to the reign of the ME III king Šilhak-Inšušinak and identifies it as part of the façade of the Inšušinak temple.[192] Other artifacts from this period at Susa, including stone steles, bronze statues, and glazed architectural elements, indicate that manufacturing techniques for stone, metal, and glazed objects were being further developed, while the glazed wall knobs of Anšan (modern Tell-e Malyan) demonstrate that a mastery of such advanced techniques was not limited to the capital Susa.[193]

The aforementioned ME I workshop at Haft Tappeh also served for the production of pottery. A large ceramic kiln was found in the building's courtyard.[194] Later at Chogha Zanbil, during the ME II phase, pottery production in temple workshops is well attested. One of these had two large pottery kilns inside the sacred precinct enclosed by the inner wall, close to the southwestern side of the Kiririša temple (figure 34.5: no. 3).[195] A diverse range of finds from the workshop's different rooms, including bronze objects, ivory fragments, shell and faience beads, stone and bitumen inlays, and a faience vessel, indicates that, like the workshop at Haft Tappeh, this facility was used for manufacturing a wide variety of items.[196] The temple of Hišmitik and Ruhuratir also had a kiln in the rear part of its courtyard, most likely used to fire ceramics.[197]

The pottery repertoire of the ME period is rich in variation, and most vessel types were mass-produced. Beakers with a button-shaped base were particularly common. Initially, these were produced individually; eventually, faster mass production was introduced, resulting in lower-quality

---

192. Malbran-Labat 1995: no. 41; cf. Harper et al. 1992: 11, 141–144, 281–282.

193. Carter 1996: 32–33, figs. 30–31.

194. Rafiei-Alavi 2015: 323–326.

195. Ghirshman 1966: 95–99; Mofidi-Nasrabadi 2013b: 150–155.

196. Mofidi-Nasrabadi 2013b: Table 38.

197. Ghirshman 1968: 30, fig. 11.

products with simpler shapes.[198] If these vessels were used as containers
to hand out rations of drink (possibly beer), then the trend toward mass
production may have been driven by the monumental building activities
at Haft Tappeh and Chogha Zanbil, which increased the demand for
particular vessel types needed to provide for the construction workers.

34.6. Conclusions

The Middle Elamite period was characterized by the rise of the political
and economic power of the institution of Elamite kingship. At this time,
Elam developed into one of the most significant political players in the
Near East. Elamite rulers laid claim to a vast empire and began to use
again the ancient, traditional title "king of Susa and Anšan" instead of
the Mesopotamian designation *sukkalmah* which had been usual in the
previous period. This demonstrative turn to Elamite identity mirrors a
kind of cultural self-confidence and independence.

Elamite specialists generally divide this new era in three phases: ME
I–III. Currently, six rulers—Igi-hatet, Kidinu, Tan-Ruhuratir II, Tepti-
ahar, Inšušinak-šar-ili, and Šalla—are known to have reigned in the first
phase, although their sequence and dates are still uncertain. Most of the
available information on ME I rulers comes from the reigns of Tepti-
ahar and Inšušinak-šar-ili. Apart from the capital city, Susa, these kings
were also active at Haft Tappeh (ancient Kabnak), situated about 15 km
southeast of Susa, where excavations and geophysical prospection have
documented monumental building activities by both rulers. Several
building complexes with large courtyards were constructed of mud brick
around at least two massive terraces, which were most likely temple
platforms. Wall painting fragments were found on the gypsum plaster
in some rooms. A workshop was integrated into the building complex,
close to one of the terraces, in which raw materials as well as finished
objects of bronze, bitumen, gold, carnelian, frit, bone, and clay were
found. Recent excavations and radiocarbon dating have documented at
least four building levels (I–IV) at Haft Tappeh, the last three of which

---

198. Mofidi-Nasrabadi 2014a.

(II–IV) belong to the ME I period. Cuneiform documents confirm that the monumental constructions of Level II date to the reigns of Tepti-ahar and Inšušinak-šar-ili. Cuneiform tablets found close to the previously mentioned workshop and in an administrative building in the southern part of the site bear witness to a well-organized, centralized administration at this time. The end of Level II was marked by devastation, clearly evident in the destruction of the administrative building by fire. Thereafter, in Level III, the rebuilding of some of the constructions in the northern part of the city was begun but never completed. Very soon thereafter the inhabitants of the site built simple dwellings within the ruins of older buildings (Level IV). This last phase of occupation seems to have ended in a violent disaster, since several hundred skeletons, lying in a disorderly fashion on top of each other, were discovered in a street behind the outer wall of a large building. However, an epidemic cannot be entirely excluded. Thereafter, Haft Tappeh lost its importance and was abandoned in the late fourteenth century BC.

It did not take long before a new dynasty was established in Elam (ME II). This period is known as Igihalkid era, named after Igi-halki, an ancestor of its later rulers. It is, however, unclear whether or not Igi-halki himself was also a king. Due to a paucity of written sources, the chronological sequence and dates of the Igihalkid kings are uncertain. Nevertheless, five rulers—Pahir-iššan, Attar-kittah, Humban-numena, Untaš-Napiriša, and Kidin-Hutran—can be definitely assigned to this period. The Igihalkid dynasty reached its peak of political power under Untaš-Napiriša, who erected a new foundation about 45 km southeast of Susa, called Al-Untaš-Napiriša ("City of Untaš-Napiriša") and now known as Chogha Zanbil. This site is well known in the specialist literature thanks to its monumental, stepped temple tower (*ziqqurat*) dedicated to the main Elamite deities Inšušinak and Napiriša. The city area was divided into different sections by three walls. The outer wall, which surrounded the entire city, was about 4 km long. In the middle of the city, an area of ca. 16 hectares was enclosed by an even slightly larger wall as a sacred precinct (Elamite *sian-kuk*) containing multiple sanctuaries. The stepped temple tower lay in the middle of this area and was also enclosed by a wall. With the foundation of this city, Untaš-Napiriša clearly demonstrated his religious affinity for the Elamite pantheon and exhibited his power through the monumentality of the architecture erected at Al-Untaš-Napiriša. Elsewhere, hundreds of inscribed bricks bearing dedicatory inscriptions of Untaš-Napiriša indicate his systematic building activity at sites across Elam.

We have very little information about the successors of Untaš-Napiriša and the end of the Igihalkid period. In the twelfth century BC, textual sources provide evidence of a new dynasty (ME III) known as the Šutrukids, after its first king Šutruk-Nahhunte. Under Šutruk-Nahhunte, Elam developed into one of the most powerful political centers in the region. In 1158 BC, Šutruk-Nahhunte conquered Babylonia and brought rich booty, e.g., the steles of Naram-Sin of Akkad and of Hammurabi of Babylon, back to his capital city, Susa. His son and successor, Kutir-Nahhunte, continued the military policies of his father, undertaking further campaigns in Mesopotamia. After a Babylonian revolt, Kutir-Nahhunte conquered Babylonia again and brought the statue of Marduk, the main Babylonian god, to Elam. Some of his brick inscriptions attest to his building activities in different Elamite towns. Even more building inscriptions date to the reign of his brother and successor, Šilhak-Inšušinak, who built or reconstructed numerous temples in different parts of the country. Šilhak-Inšušinak was succeeded by Hutelutuš-Inšušinak, who, according to Mesopotamian sources, was defeated by Nebuchadnezzar I of the Second Dynasty of Isin. After Hutelutuš-Inšušinak, the Elamite sources fell silent for several centuries. According to a Neo-Elamite inscription, written some centuries later, Hutelutuš-Inšušinak was succeeded by his brother Šilhina-hamru-Lagamar, who, however, is not attested in other sources.

To conclude, the rise of Elam as a political power in the Middle Elamite period should undoubtedly be connected with the economic development of the country. Large-scale building activities were conducted in different cities and new foundations were created. The last Igihalkid and, especially, the Šutrukid rulers were powerful enough to pursue an expansionary military policy that led to Elamite supremacy in Babylonia for some decades. The increase of political power in Elam had an impact on different cultural domains and intensified traditional Elamite features, a phenomenon reflected by the use of the Elamite language for recording historical events. Whereas in the ME I phase, all inscriptions were written in Akkadian, the ME II era saw a marked preference for Elamite. This tendency grew even more marked by the end of the Šutrukid period, when Elamite became the exclusive language of written inscriptions.

REFERENCES

Álvarez-Mon, J. 2005. Elamite funerary clay heads. *NEA* 68: 131–180.

Amiet, P. 1980. La glyptique du second millénaire en provenance des chantiers A et B de la Ville Royale de Suse. *IrAnt* 15: 133–147.

Beckman, G. 1991. A stray tablet from Haft Tépé. *IrAnt* 26: 81–83.

Carter, E. 1996. *Excavations at Anshan (Tal-e Malyan): the Middle Elamite period*. Philadelphia: University of Pennsylvania Museum of Archaeology and Anthropology.

Carter, E., and Stolper, M. 1984. *Elam: surveys of political history and archaeology*. Berkeley and Los Angeles: University of California Press.

Caubet, A. (ed.) 2007. *Faïences et matières vitreuses de l'Orient ancien: étude physico-chimique et catalogue des oeuvres du département des antiquités orientales*. Ghent: Snoeck.

Cole, S. W., and De Meyer, L. 1999. Tepti-ahar, king of Susa, and Kadašman-ᵈKUR.GAL. *Akkadica* 112: 44–45.

Daneshmand, P. 2004. An extispicy text from Haft-Tappe. *JCS* 56: 13–17.

Daneshmand, P., and Abdoli, M. 2015. A new king of Susa and Anshan. *CDLB* 2015: 1. Retrieved from http://cdli.ucla.edu/pubs/cdlb/2015/cdlb2015_001.html (last accessed May 15, 2019).

Foruzanfar, F. 2012. Anthropological report related to the findings from Haft Tappeh. *Elamica* 2: 183–198 (in Farsi).

Foster, B.R. 1993. *Before the muses: an anthology of Akkadian literature*. Bethesda, MD: CDL Press.

Frame, G. 1995. *Rulers of Babylonia: from the Second Dynasty of Isin to the end of Assyrian domination (1157–612 BC)*. Toronto: University of Toronto Press.

Ganjavi, S. 1976. Survey in Xuzestān, 1975. In Bagherzadeh, F. (ed.), *Proceedings of the IVth annual symposium on archaeological research in Iran*. Tehran: Iranian Centre for Archaeological Research, 34–39.

Gasche, H., and Cole, S.W. 2018. Elamite funerary practices. In Álvarez-Mon, J., Basello, G.P., and Wicks, Y. (eds.), *The Elamite world*. London and New York: Routledge, 741–762.

Ghirshman, R. 1966. *Tchoga Zanbil (Dur Untash), vol. I: la ziggurat.* Paris: Geuthner.

Ghirshman, R. 1968. *Tchoga Zanbil (Dur Untash), vol. II: temenos, temples, palais, tombes.* Paris: Geuthner.

Glassner, J.-J. 1991. Les textes de Haft Tépé, la Susiane et l'Elam au 2ème millénaire. In De Meyer, L., and Gasche H. (eds.), *Mésopotamie et Elam.* Ghent: University of Ghent, 109–126.

Glassner, J.-J. 2000. ᵈKUR.GAL à Suse et Haft-Tépé. *NABU* 2000: 40 (no. 36).

Glassner, J.-J. 2004. *Mesopotamian chronicles.* Atlanta, GA: Society of Biblical Literature.

Goldberg, J. 2004. The Berlin Letter, Middle Elamite chronology and Šutruk-Nahhunte I's genealogy. *IrAnt* 39: 33–42.

Harper, P.O., Aruz, J., and Tallon, F. 1992. *The royal city of Susa: ancient Near Eastern treasures in the Louvre.* New York: Metropolitan Museum of Art.

Heinrich, E. 1982. *Die Tempel und Heiligtümer im Alten Mesopotamien: Typologie, Morphologie und Geschichte.* Berlin: De Gruyter.

Henkelman, W.F.M. 2011. Šimut. *RlA* 12: 511–512.

Herrero, P. 1976. Tablettes administratives de Haft-Tépé. *DAFI* 6: 93–116.

Herrero, P., and Glassner, J.-J. 1990. Haft-Tépé: choix de textes, I. *IrAnt* 25: 1–45.

Herrero, P., and Glassner, J.-J. 1991. Haft- Tépé: choix de textes, II. *IrAnt* 26: 39–80.

Herrero, P., and Glassner, J.-J. 1993. Haft- Tépé: choix de textes, III. *IrAnt* 28: 97–135.

Herrero, P., and Glassner, J.-J. 1996. Haft-Tépé: choix de textes, IV. *IrAnt* 31: 51–82.

Hinz, W. 1963. Elamica. *Orientalia* 32: 1–20.

Hinz, W., and Koch, H. 1987. *Elamisches Wörterbuch, I-II.* Berlin: Reimer.

Koch, H. 2005. Pinengir. *RlA* 10: 568–569.

König, F.W. 1965. *Die elamischen Königsinschriften.* Graz: Selbstverlag E.F. Weidner.

König, F.W. 1971. Geschwisterehe in Elam. *RlA* 3: 224–231.

Lambert, M. 1972. Hutélutush-Inshushinak et le pays d'Anzan. *RA* 66: 61–76.

Lambert, W.G. 1979. Near Eastern seals in the Gulbenkian Museum of Oriental Art, University of Durham. *Iraq* 41: 1–46.

Lampre, G. 1905. Statue de la reine Napir-Asou. In de Morgan, J., Jequier, G., Gautier, J.-E., and Lampre, G., *Délégation en Perse: mémoires de la mission archéologique de Perse. vol. 8: recherches archéologiques, troisième série.* Paris: E. Leroux, 245–250.

Malbran-Labat, F. 1995. *Les inscriptions royales de Suse: briques de l'époque paléo-élamite à l'empire néo-élamite.* Paris: Éditions de la Réunion des musées nationaux.

Meyers, P. 2000. The casting process of the statue of queen Napir-Asu in the Louvre. In Mattusch, C., Brauer, A., and Knudsen, S.E. (ed.), *From the parts to the whole: acta of the 13th international bronze congress.* Portsmouth, RI: Journal of Roman Archaeology, 11–18.

Miglus, P. 1999. *Städtische Wohnarchitektur in Babylonien und Assyrien.* Mainz: Zabern.

Mofidi-Nasrabadi, B. 1999. *Untersuchungen zu den Bestattungssitten in Mesopotamien in der ersten Hälfte des ersten Jahrtausends v. Chr.* Mainz: Zabern.

Mofidi-Nasrabadi, B. 2003–2004. Archäologische Untersuchungen in Haft Tape (Iran). *AMIT* 35–36: 225–239.

Mofidi-Nasrabadi, B. 2005. Eine Steininschrift des Amar-Suena aus Tape Bormi (Iran). *ZA* 95: 161–171.

Mofidi-Nasrabadi, B. 2007. *Archäologische Ausgrabungen und Untersuchungen in Čoğā Zanbil.* Münster: Agenda.

Mofidi-Nasrabadi, B. 2009. *Aspekte der Herrschaft und Herrscherdarstellungen in Elam im 2. Jt. v. Chr.* Münster: Ugarit-Verlag.

Mofidi-Nasrabadi, B. 2010a. Herrschaftstitulatur der Könige von Susa und Anšan. *Akkadica* 131: 109–119.

Mofidi-Nasrabadi, B. 2010b. *Vorbericht der archäologischen Ausgrabungen der Kampagnen 2005–2007 in Haft Tappeh (Iran).* Münster: Agenda.

Mofidi-Nasrabadi, B. 2011a. Die Glyptik aus Haft Tappeh: interkulturelle Aspekte zur Herstellung und Benutzung von Siegeln in der Anfangsphase der mittelelamischen Zeit. *Elamica* 1: 1–355.

Mofidi-Nasrabadi, B. 2011b. The grave of a *puhu-teppu* from Haft Tappeh. *Akkadica* 132: 151–161.

Mofidi-Nasrabadi, B. 2012a. Vorbericht der archäologischen Ausgrabungen der Kampagnen 2008–2010 in Haft Tappeh (Iran). *Elamica* 2: 55–159.

Mofidi-Nasrabadi, B. 2012b. Arbeitszimmer eines Schreibers aus der mittel-elamischen Zeit. In Wilhelm, G. (ed.), *Organisation, representation, and symbols of power in the ancient Near East.* Winona Lake, IN: Eisenbrauns, 747–756.

Mofidi-Nasrabadi, B. 2012c. The spatial order in the tomb buildings of the Middle Elamite period. In Pfälzner, P., Niehr, H., Pernicka, E., and Wissing, A. (eds.), *(Re-)constructing funerary rituals in the ancient Near East*. Wiesbaden: Harrassowitz, 261–270.

Mofidi-Nasrabadi, B. 2013a. Neue archäologische Untersuchungen in Dehno, Khuzestan (April–Mai 2012). *Elamica* 3: 89–132.

Mofidi-Nasrabadi, B. 2013b. *Planungsaspekte und die Struktur der altorientalischen neugegründeten Stadt in Chogha Zanbil*. Aachen: Shaker.

Mofidi-Nasrabadi, B. 2014a. Qualitative Veränderungen in der serienmäßigen Herstellung des Knopfbechers in der Spätbronzezeit Elams. In Luciani, M., and Hausleiter, A. (eds.), *Recent trends in the study of Late Bronze Age ceramics in Syro-Mesopotamia and neighbouring regions*. Rahden: Verlag Marie Leidorf, 385–398.

Mofidi-Nasrabadi, B. 2014b. Vorbericht der archäologischen Ausgrabungen der Kampagnen 2012–2013 in Haft Tappeh (Iran). *Elamica* 4: 67–167.

Mofidi-Nasrabadi, B. 2015a. Ergebnisse der C14-Datierung der Proben aus Haft Tappeh. *Elamica* 5: 7–36.

Mofidi-Nasrabadi, B. 2015b. Reconstruction of the *ziqqurrat* of Chogha Zanbil. *Elamica* 5: 37–51.

Mofidi-Nasrabadi, B. 2016. Archaeological and historical evidence from Haft Tappeh. *Elamica* 6: 1–226.

Mofidi-Nasrabadi, B. 2017. Die Siegelungen aus den Ausgrabungen in Haft Tappeh zwischen 2005–2012. *Elamica* 7: 41–144.

Mofidi-Nasrabadi, B. 2018a. Elam in the Middle Elamite period. In Álvarez-Mon, J., Basello, G.P., and Wicks, Y. (ed.), *The Elamite world*. London and New York: Routledge, 232–248.

Mofidi-Nasrabadi, B. 2018b. Elamite architecture. In Álvarez-Mon, J., Basello, G.P., and Wicks, Y. (ed.), *The Elamite world*. London and New York: Routledge, 507–530.

Mofidi-Nasrabadi, B. 2018c. Who was ᵈMÙŠ.EREN.EŠŠANA.DINGIR. MEŠ? *Elamica* 8: 113–126.

Negahban, E. 1991. *Excavations at Haft Tepe, Iran*. Philadelphia: University of Pennsylvania Museum of Archaeology and Anthropology.

Negahban, E. 1994. The artist's workshop of Haft Tepe. In Gasche, H., Tanret, M., Janssen, C., and Degraeve, A. (eds.), *Cinquante-deux réflexions sur le proche-orient ancien: offertes en hommage à Léon De Meyer*. Leuven: Peeters, 31–41.

Novotny, J., and Jeffers, J. 2018. *The royal inscriptions of Ashurbanipal (668–631 BC), Aššur-etel-ilāni (630–627 BC) and Sîn-šarra-iškun (626–612 BC), kings of Assyria, part 1.* University Park, PA: Eisenbrauns.

Pakgohar, S., Bahrololumi, F., and Ghasemi, M. 2013. Metallographic and SEM-EDX analysis of the Middle Elamite bronze buttons from Haft Tappeh. *Elamica* 3: 171–183.

Pézard, M. 1914. *Mission à Bender-Bouchir: documents archéologiques et épigraphiques.* Paris: E. Leroux.

Pézard, M. 1916. Reconstitution d'une stele d'Untaš [NAP]GAL. *RA* 13: 119–124.

Pézard, M., and Pottier, E. 1926. *Catalogue des antiquités de la Susiane (Mission J. De Morgan).* Paris: Musées Nationaux.

Porada, E. 1970. *Tchoga Zanbil (Dur Untash), vol. IV: la glyptique.* Paris: Geuthner.

Porada, E. 1971. Aspects of Elamite art and archaeology. *Expedition* 13: 28–34.

Potts, D.T. 2010. Elamite temple building. In Boda, M.J., and Novotny, J. (eds.), *From the foundations to the crenellations: essays on temple building in the ancient Near East and Hebrew Bible.* Münster: Ugarit-Verlag, 49–70, 479–509.

Potts, D.T. 2016. *The archaeology of Elam: formation and transformation of an ancient Iranian state.* Cambridge: Cambridge University Press. 2nd rev. ed.

Potts, D.T. 2018. The epithet "sister's son" in ancient Elam: aspects of the avunculate in cross-cultural perspective. In Kleber, K., Neumann, G., and Paulus, S. (eds.), *Grenzüberschreitungen: Studien zur Kulturgeschichte des Alten Orients. Festschrift für Hans Neumann.* Münster: Zaphon, 523–555.

Prechel, D. 2010. Die Tontafeln aus Haft Tappeh, 2005–2007. In Mofidi-Nasrabadi, B., *Vorbericht der archäologischen Ausgrabungen der Kampagnen 2005–2007 in Haft Tappeh (Iran).* Münster: Agenda, 51–57.

Radner, K. 2005. *Die Macht des Namens: altorientalische Strategien zur Selbsterhaltung.* Wiesbaden: Harrassowitz.

Radner, K. 2020. *A short history of Babylon.* London: Bloomsbury.

Rafiei-Alavi, B. 2012. Ein Hinweis auf die Herstellungsmethode eines Dolchtyps aus Haft Tappeh. *Elamica* 2: 169–175.

Rafiei-Alavi, B. 2015. *Archäologische Untersuchungen der Metallartefakte aus Haft Tappeh.* PhD thesis, Johann Wolfgang Goethe-Universität Frankfurt.

Reiner, E. 1963. Mâlamir. *RA* 57: 169–174.

Reiner, E. 1973a. Inscription from a royal Elamite tomb. *AfO* 24: 87–102.

Reiner, E. 1973b. The location of Anšan. *RA* 67: 57–62.

Roaf, M. 2017. Kassite and Elamite kings. In Bartelmus, A., and Sternitzke, K. (ed.), *Karduniaš: Babylonia under the Kassites*. Berlin: De Gruyter, 166–195.

Scheil, V. 1901. *Textes élamites-anzanites, premiére série*. Paris: E. Leroux.

Scheil, V. 1902. *Textes élamites-sémitiques, deuxième série*. Paris: E. Leroux.

Scheil, V. 1904. *Textes élamites-anzanites, deuxième série*. Paris: E. Leroux.

Scheil, V. 1905. *Textes élamites-sémitiques, troisième série*. Paris: E. Leroux.

Scheil, V. 1908. *Textes élamites-sémitiques, quatrième série*. Paris: E. Leroux.

Scheil, V. 1930. *Actes juridiques Susiens*. Paris: E. Leroux.

Scheil, V. 1932. *Actes juridiques Susiens, suite: no. 166 à no. 327*. Paris: E. Leroux.

Scheil, V. 1933. *Actes juridiques Susiens, suite: no. 328 à no. 395: inscriptions des Achéménides*. Paris: E. Leroux.

Scheil, V. 1939. *Mélanges épigraphiques*. Paris: E. Leroux.

Sollberger, E. 1965. A new inscription of Šilhak-inšušinak. *JCS* 19: 31–32.

Stein, P. 2000. *Die mittel- und neubabylonischen Königsinschriften bis zum Ende der Assyrerherrschaft*. Wiesbaden: Harrassowitz.

Steve, M.-J. 1967. *Tchoga Zanbil (Dur-Untash), vol. III: textes élamites et accadiens de Tchoga Zanbil*. Paris: Geuthner.

Steve, M.-J. 1987. *Nouveaux mélanges épigraphiques: inscriptions royales de Suse et de la Susiane*. Nice: Éditions Serre.

Steve, M.-J. 1989. Des sceaux-cylindres de Simaški? *RA* 83: 13–26.

Steve, M.-J., and Gasche, H. 1971. *L'Acropole de Suse*. Paris: Geuthner.

Steve, M.-J., Gasche, H., and De Meyer, L. 1980. La Susiane du deuxième millénaire: à propos d'une interprétation des fouilles de Suse. *IrAnt* 15: 49–154.

Steve, M.-J., and Vallat, F. 1989. La dynastie des Igihalkides: nouvelles interprétations. In De Meyer, L., and Haerinck, E. (eds.), *Archaeologia iranica et orientalis: miscellanea in honorem Louis Vanden Berghe*. Leuven: Peeters, 223–238.

Stolper, M.W. 1978. Inscribed fragments from Khuzestan. *DAFI* 8: 89–91.

Stolper, M.W. 1984. *Texts from Tall-i Malyan, I: Elamite administrative texts (1972–1974)*. Philadelphia: University of Pennsylvania Museum of Archaeology and Anthropology.

Stolper, M.W. 1990. Malamir: B. Philologisch. *RlA* 7: 276–281.

Stolper, M.W. 2001a. Nahhunte. *RlA* 9: 82–84.

Stolper, M.W. 2001b. Nahhunte-utu. *RlA* 9: 84–86.

Taylor, R.E., Beaumont, W.C., Southon, J., Stronach, D., and Pickworth, D. 2010. Alternative explanations for anomalous 14C ages on human skeletons associated with the 612 BCE destruction of Nineveh. *Radiocarbon* 52: 372–382.

Tourtet, F. 2013. Distribution, materials and functions of the "wall knobs" in the Near Eastern Late Bronze Age: from south-western Iran to the Middle Euphrates. In De Graef, K., and Tavernier, J. (eds.), *Susa and Elam: archaeological, philological, historical and geographical perspectives.* Leiden: Brill, 173–190.

Tsukimoto, A. 1985. *Untersuchungen zur Totenpflege (kispum) im Alten Mesopotamien.* Münster: Ugarit-Verlag.

Vallat, F. 1981. L'inscription de la stele d'Untash-Napirisha. *IrAnt* 16: 27–33.

Vallat, F. 1984. Une inscription cunéiforme de Bouchir. *Dédalo* 23: 255–260.

Vallat, F. 1987. ^{d}U = élamite *usan/iššan*. *NABU* 1987: 48 (no. 89).

Vallat, F. 1988. Légendes élamites de fragments de statues d'Untaš-Napiriša et Tchogha Zanbil. *IrAnt* 23: 169–177.

Vallat, F. 1994. Succession royale en Elam au IIème millénaire. In Gasche, H., Tanret, M., Janssen, C., and Degraeve, A. (eds.), *Cinquante-deux réflexions sur le proche-orient ancien: offertes en hommage à Léon De Meyer.* Leuven: Peeters, 1–14.

Vallat, F. 1996. Le retour de Hutelutuš-Insušnak à Suse. *NABU* 1996: 78–89 (no. 88).

Vallat, F. 1997. La politesse élamite à l'époque des Igihalkides. *NABU* 1997: 73 (no. 74).

Vallat, F. 2000. L'Elam du IIe millénaire et la chronologie courte. *Akkadica* 119–120: 7–17.

Vallat, F. 2006. La chronologie méso-élamite et la letter de Berlin. *Akkadica* 127: 123–136.

van Dijk, J. 1986. Die dynastischen Heiraten zwischen Kassiten und Elamern: eine verhängnisvolle Politik. *Orientalia* 55: 159–170.

Zerbst, U., and van der Veen, P. 2015. Does radiocarbon provide the answer? In James, P., and van der Veen, P.G. (eds.), *Solomon and Shishak: current perspectives from archaeology, epigraphy, history and chronology.* Oxford: Oxbow, 199–224.

Index